The Libby Family In America, 1602-1881

Your Kinsman,

Chas T. Libby.

THE

LIBBY FAMILY

IN

AMERICA.

1602-1881.

PREPARED AND PUBLISHED BY

CHARLES T. LIBBY.

PORTLAND, ME.:
PRINTED BY B. THURSTON & CO.
1882.

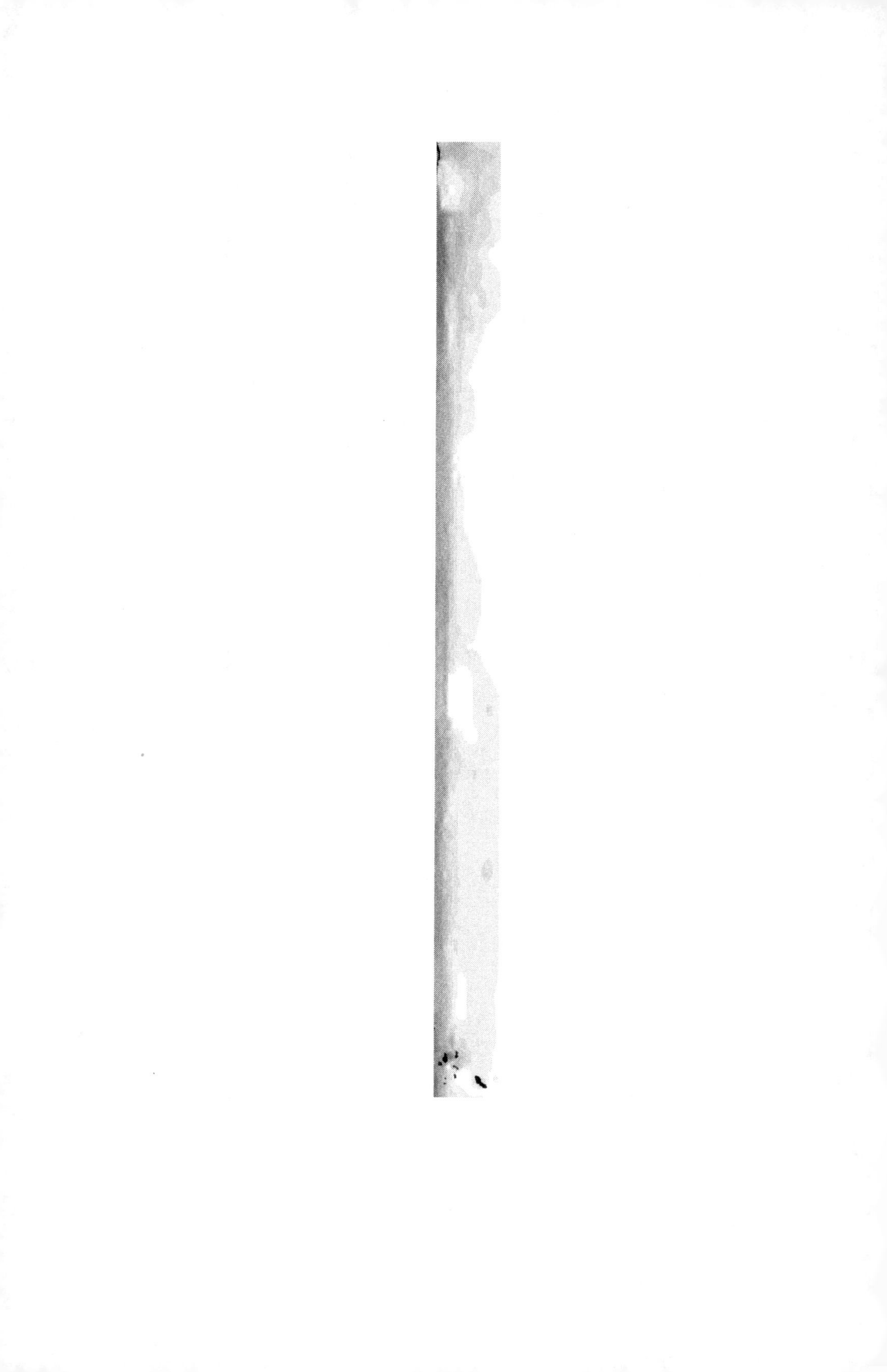

Cordially Yours.

TO

CHARLES F. LIBBY, ESQ.,

OF

PORTLAND, MAINE,

IN RECOGNITION OF THE
IMPORTANT PART WHICH HIS
CHEERFUL ASSISTANCE AND HEARTY SUPPORT
HAVE PLAYED IN ITS BEGINNING AND END;
AND
IN THE HOPE
THAT HE MAY HEREIN FIND
SOME MEASURE OF SATISFACTION,

THIS VOLUME IS

RESPECTFULLY DEDICATED

BY THE COMPILER.

PREFACE.

GENEALOGY is so generally called useless, that the producers of genealogical books most always feel called upon to defend themselves. I wish to state here simply my own opinions in the matter. I fully believe that carelessness of the past almost always accompanies carelessness of the future, and an interest in the past, thoughtfulness for the future. To see the truth most plainly, compare the extremes of society. On the one hand, the great body of criminals, who indulge in present pleasures without a thought of the consequences to themselves or others—what do or can they care for the memory of father and grandfather? On the other hand—those whose aim it is to lead useful and noble lives, who are ready to give up present pleasure for future advantage, who conduct their daily actions with a view to future results—how can such fail to have an interest in the causes which have preceded present results? Only those who live for the present alone, and are careless of the inheritance they leave their offspring, can consistently be indifferent to the lives of the ancestors from whom they inherited their own characters.

To the question so often asked, "What good will it do?" I say, when I speak plainly, "Make it personal." And when it is then asked, "What good will it do *me?*" I reply, "If you take no more interest in it than you do now, it will do you *no* good. Like everything else, no benefit can be derived from it until it is appropriated. If you scoff at it, as some others scoff at the sciences, music, and painting, you will gain no more benefit from the one than they do from the other. But if you cultivate the spirit of the antiquary, and study cause and effect in the past, with a view to imitating the good and avoiding the bad, you will possess yourself of one of the most ennobling influences that exists outside of religion."

This volume I do not offer as a *subject*, but only as a *means*, of genealogical study, chiefly for the benefit of those members of future generations who may wish to take lessons from the past, who might be unable, had not this work been done now, even to learn who their forefathers were. To those who wish to reap the true benefits of genealogy, this book will be (like a dictionary in other studies) but an aid to their search into the *inner* lives of their forefathers.

My own interest in genealogy, although I am naturally inclined to such things, did not become very manifest until the winter of 1878–9. In a record book which my great-grandfather, Samuel Tompson, kept of his doings as trial justice, was recorded an account of his descent, through a long line of Harvard graduates and "Orthodox" clergymen, from the original Tompson immigrant, the first minister of Braintree, Mass. This book came into my hands at the time mentioned, and I conceived the idea of tracing all my ancestors back to their immigration. I had heard of family trees, and thought to reverse it so as to hold all my ancestors, who, of course, doubled in number each generation that I traced back. However, I found that the tree would not answer the purpose very well, and finally conceived the "cartwheel," a number of concentric circles of which the inner was intended for my own name; the next outer divided into two parts, for my parents; the next into four, for my grandparents, and so on. I have since found that this contrivance has been in use many years. In my own chart, when made, I filled in the single pedigree then in my possession, and at once went to work, with the zeal that such a pastime always creates, to fill it out. My mother's ancestorage had been thoroughly worked out by one of her brothers, my father's mother was a daughter of Samuel Tompson, Esq., mentioned above, and the only quarter of my chart in which my research was original, was that belonging to the ancestors of my lineal grandfather, Storer Libby. I traced his pedigree to his great-grandfather, Lieut. Andrew Libby, and then came to a standstill. I despaired of ever learning his parentage, and began to trace the generations of his descendants, being all of the Libby family that I knew to be related to me. I had not proceeded far, however, when I learned from a source unknown before, that Lieut. Andrew Libby was a son of Matthew Libby, who was a son of John Libby, the first of the name in this country, and from whom I supposed all of the name descended. So I began to collect records of the whole family, with the thought that I might some day publish them. In July, 1879, shortly after my graduation from the High School, I called at the law office of Charles F. Libby, Esq., of my own city, at that time a stranger to me, and proposed that he should pay my expenses in visiting the towns of Alfred, Me., and Exeter, N. H., where are deposited the probate records, records of deeds, and court records, for the towns in which the early generations of the family had resided; and that I should take special pains to trace his pedigree. Much to my satisfaction, and somewhat to my surprise, (I was then not eighteen years old), Mr. Libby accepted my proposition, and at his expense I spent several weeks in the places named, and in visiting various aged members of the family. The result of this search was the strong conviction that a few years would make it impossible to trace the genealogy of the family, and the thought of the family's becoming a great number of individuals, impossible to connect with their early ancestors and with each other, first suggested the idea of staying from college a year, and devoting my time to collecting the records of the family. I trace thus fully the origin of the book for the satisfaction of the curious.

The lack of records in the early generations, which is very obvious when compared with genealogies of Massachusetts families, is a common defect in Maine genealogies. No record of the birth or death of any member of the family was made, so far as is now known, until after the rise of the eighteenth century. No deaths, and only four births, occurring in the seventeenth century, are found recorded.

A large portion of the family has been inclined to ask the question alluded to above, "What good will it do?" and almost all of the errors and omissions in the later generations are due to the carelessness or negligence of those immediately concerned. I hope the offspring of those persons, when, in future years, they are vexed at these defects, will look twice at this last sentence before attributing them to me.

Yet I by no means wish to complain of a lack of support. All members of the family have given me what information they could when called upon by me in person, and a large portion has replied, with more or less promptness and care, to my inquiries by mail. I used an original version of Abraham Lincoln's boyhood ballad, "If at first you don't succeed, write, write again," and very few have persisted in refusing my appeals. In a financial point of view, my support has been still better. The family is so numerous, and so many of its members have subscribed for the book, that there is the prospect of an anomaly—that of a family history, thoroughly prepared, paying not only its cost, but fair compensation for the compiler's time. Those who have contributed or subscribed twenty-five dollars and upward, are the following:

Mr. Arthur A. Libby of Chicago, Ill.,	$150.00
Charles F. Libby, Esq., of Portland, Me.,	50.00
Mr. H. J. Libby of Portland, Me.,	50.00
Dr. H. W. Libbey of Boston, Mass.,	50.00
Mr. William P. Libby of Brooklyn, N. Y.,	50.00
Mr. William H. Libby of Augusta, Me., and brothers,	50.00
Hon. Artemas Libbey of Augusta, Me.,	25.00
Mr. Joseph Libbey of Georgetown, D. C.,	25.00
Mr. James B. Libby of Portland, Me.,	25.00
Mr. Augustus F. Libby of New York, N. Y.,	25.00
Mr. John Henry Smith of Salt Lake City, Utah,	25.00

The spelling of the name has been a matter of constant vexation to me. Starting with the intention of following the usual plan of spelling the name of each individual as he himself spelt it, I was met at the outset by the fact that many of the early generations left nothing to show how they spelled their own names, and that many, in different documents, spelled their names in different ways with seeming indifference. Also in the later generations, and especially in the present day, the most unwarranted freedom has been used in adopting whatever spelling strikes the individual fancy. Many are so careless as not to adopt any particular spelling, and use one one year, and another the next, while frequently, in writing to me, persons have spelled their name in two ways in one letter. To have carried out my original plan would have demanded an almost endless amount of search and inquiry, and the result, to a great extent, must have consisted of guess-work. I have, therefore, used the true spelling of the name throughout the book, giving in the introduction such an account as I can of the general drift of the spelling in the different families and localities.

The method of numbering grew out of my manner of arranging the records during the compilation. The same method may have been used by others, but not to my knowledge. I am aware that in introducing an unusual method I lay myself open to criticism, and I fear that I shall be most severely criticised by those who take the least trouble to master the plan. To myself its only disadvantage is that a special number cannot be found quite so readily as in some other methods, but it affords many satisfactions which they do not. I believe that all who make themselves familiar with it will find it equally satisfactory. It has the further advantage of saving fully one-tenth part of the space, which, in a book of this sort, is an important feature.

The system of indexing the christian names of the family, giving the place of residence, and the blank form for family records, have never been used before so far as I know. My purpose in forming the index was to make it possible for the most casual acquaintance to find readily any one of the family, at the same time preserving economy of space. By this method, all, or nearly all the family are so distinguished in the index that anyone can readily recognize in the index itself the name he is in search of. It is recommended that in keeping the family records in the blank forms, the system of numbering be continued, and that greater pains be taken in the future than has been in the past, to keep an absolutely complete record of all births, marriages, and deaths.

The gratitude of all that derive any satisfaction from this book is due to Charles F. Libby, Esq.,* of this city. It was he that gave me my first encouragement; it was he that paid my expenses during my first extended searches; it was to him that I first mentioned my project of a book, and he first suggested a method of raising funds; it was from him and from others at his personal solicitation that the funds were obtained to pay for the researches in England; and, finally, it was he that lent me his name in the contract with the printers, when I, being a minor under guardianship, would have been put to some trouble to per-

*At this last moment, I have the pleasure of adding to Mr. Libby's record his nomination by the Republicans for Mayor of Portland. It is conceded by his opponents that he will be elected.

fect the contract otherwise. Throughout the work his large influence has been cast in my favor, and has done much to render the work a financial success. Without his encouragement I should never have undertaken it. But while Mr. Libby is so intimately connected with the history of the book, it is due him to say that he has had nothing whatever to do with the compilation, arranging, and printing, and that all mistakes of judgment and execution in those particulars are chargeable to myself alone. His action in the matter merits a faultless production, which I can only regret this falls so far short of being.

I have to acknowledge the assistance of Mrs. Mary B. L. Dowst of Epsom, N. H., Mr. P. Rand Libby of Gilford, N. H., Mr. Henry A. Libbey of Machiasport, Me., Mr. Alonzo S. Libbey of Berlin, Vt., Mr. Charles Libby of Berwick, Me., Mr. Henry F. Libby of Pittsfield, Me., Mr. Wm. P. Libby of Brooklyn, N. Y., Mrs. Jane S. Osgood, and others to a greater number than I can mention, for special assistance in their own branches, and in some cases in other branches of the family. My work in Rye, N. H., was materially lightened by research made while in college by Mr. Jonas M. Libbey of New York. The persons who have furnished me the most valuable traditional lore are Mrs. Laura McKenney of Gorham, Rev. Peter Libby of Buxton, and the Misses Eunice and Lois Libby of Scarborough. I was much aided by a quite complete genealogy of the families in Kittery, now Eliot, prepared by Mr. William Fogg, and now in possession of Dr. John S. H. Fogg of South Boston, who kindly furnished me a copy of it. William M. Sargent, Esq., and Mr. S. M. Watson, Librarian of the Public Library, kindly allowed me the use of their copies of the Scarborough records; the former first called my attention to the petition given on page 24, and the latter gave me valuable assistance in his position as librarian. I have gained assistance from the collections of the Hon. Joseph Dow of Hampton, N. H., the Hon. Thomas Moulton of Porter, Me., Mr. Thomas J. Parsons of Rye, N. H., and the Rev. A. H. Quint of Dover, N. H., and have copied freely from all published matter. It is a pleasure to me to testify to the almost universal courtesy I have received at the hands of the custodians of records, both public and private, to which I have had need to refer.

The portraits have nearly all been furnished at my personal solicitation, and in most cases the expense has been borne wholly by those most nearly interested.

In closing I must express my indebtedness to the printers, Messrs. B. Thurston & Co. Besides the mechanical execution of the work, which will speak for itself, they have corrected a great many defects in the copy, resulting from my inexperience and other causes, and have responded nobly to the unusual call made upon them in printing a work for so poorly qualified a writer.

CHARLES T. LIBBY.

PORTLAND, ME., Nov. 26, 1881.

NOTICE.

MUCH interesting matter has been left out for want of room; many persons are but very briefly mentioned for lack of information; many records are defective. It is hoped that at some future day a much more full and complete history of the family will be published.

Therefore, send in the correction of every mistake you discover: send in every date of birth, marriage, or death, that you can find out from time to time; send every additional fact that would be interesting if the history should fill three or four volumes.

The new history will not be published for many years, but now is the time, while our aged people are yet with us, to perfect our history and records. Remember that even *one date* is worth sending. Let this notice stay here, so that all that read the book may know where to send more facts. Address

CHARLES T. LIBBY,

Scarborough, Maine.

TABLE OF CONTENTS.

LIST OF PORTRAITS.

EXPLANATIONS.

The NUMBERS *used here take the place of what is usually given in words in two lines for each head of a family; it follows that no intelligent use of this book can be made without first mastering the system of numbering.*

The method may be simply stated as follows:

1 The immigrant has no number.

2 The number of each child of the immigrant is the figure which represents his position in the family.—*First child*, 1; *second child*, 2, *etc.*

3 The number of each member of the following generations is formed by adding to his father's number the number representing his own position among his father's children. *The immigrant's oldest child's oldest child is* 1-1; *and his second child*, 1-2. *The immigrant's fifth child's oldest child is* 5-1; *and his second*, 5-2, *etc.* The numbers of the later generations are formed in the same way.

To illustrate by the compiler's own pedigree: On page 25 it will be seen that Matthew Libby was the immigrant's eleventh son. Turning over to the second generation, there will be found in large figures in the middle of the page, the number 11, and under that number will be found an account of Matthew Libby, and a list of his children. It will be seen that his seventh child was Andrew Libby, and his number must be 11-7. Turning to the third generation, there will be found on page 52 the number 11-7, in the middle of the page as before, and under it an account of Andrew Libby, and a list of *his* children. The second child was Joshua Libby, and, in the fourth generation, his name will be found, on page 90, under the number 11-7-2. An account of Joshua Libby's fourth son, Matthias, with a list of *his* children, will be found in the fifth generation, under his proper number, 11-7-2-4, on page 192. Matthias Libby's eighth child, Storer Libby, the compiler's grandfather, will be found in the next generation, on page 412, under his number, 11-7-2-4-8, and in that place will be found an account of all his children and grandchildren except the family of the eldest son, who, having grandchildren of his own, is carried forward to the next generation. And so with the other branches of the family. Any member of the family who does not know his pedigree, will have first to find his own name, by means of the index, and then, having learned his number, can trace his line either backward, or, as above, downward. Beside this use of tracing backward and forward, which is all that numbers are usually used for, the numbers in this case afford other information, as follows:

First. Each number shows the generation of the person to which it belongs. The number of numbers in the number of each individual is one less than the number of his generation. Thus Matthew Libby, 11, is of the second generation; Andrew Libby, 11-7, is of the third generation; Joshua Libby, 11-7-2, is of the fourth generation, and so on.

Second. The number of any individual shows the number of each one of his ancestors. Thus, from the number of Storer Libby, 11-7-2-4-8, it is evident that his father was 11-7-2-4; his grandfather, 11-7-2; his great-grandfather, 11-7; his great-great-grandfather, 11; and his great-great-great-grandfather, the immigrant. So, knowing the number of any individual, it is possible to turn directly to his ancestor in any generation.

Third. The number of each individual shows his relation, either to the persons whose records precede or follow, or to any other person whose kinship it is desired to trace. For instance, where two members of the family intermarry, the relationship between them can be at once learned from their numbers. The following table will illustrate.

Storer Libby,	11-7-2-4-8.	brothers.
Edward Libby,	11-7-2-4-6.	cousins.
Joshua Libby,	11-7-2-6-2.	second-cousins.
Andrew Libby,	11-7-8-2-6.	third-cousins.
Amzi Libby,	11-9-5-3-1.	fourth-cousins.
Elias Libby,	5-7-8-1-1.	uncle and nephew.
Isaac H. Libby,	5-7-8-1-9-8.	grand-nephew and great-uncle.
Moses Libby,	5-7-8-2.	cousin-uncle and cousin-nephew.
Luther Libby,	5-7-11-3-1.	second-cousin-grand-nephew, and second-cousin-great-uncle.
Joshua Libby,	11-7-2.	

Fourth. Each branch of the family is distinguished from the others by the numbers. Thus the numbers of all the offspring of Henry Libby of Scarborough begin with 5. All the numbers of the offspring of his son, Lieut. Samuel Libby, begin with 5-2. All the descendants of the first Nathaniel Libby of Berwick begin their numbers with 11-9. All the offspring of Dea. Joshua Libby of Scarborough begin their numbers with 11-7-2. And so of each branch of the family.

INTRODUCTION.

IN ENGLAND.

THE Libby family is unquestionably of humble origin. The earliest mention of the name that has been found is in the herald's visitation of Oxfordshire for 1574. It there appears that, "Richard Libbe of Taston, in Coun. Devon, Gent., marryed Bridgett daughter and one of the heirs of ——— Justice of Readinge in County Berk., Gent., and by her had yssue Richard, Mary, married to Robert Fitche of Hasley in Coun. Warv. and Elizabeth married to Ninian Coxon, Cittizen of London." The son Richard married Joane, daughter of John Corker of Checkenden in Oxfordshire, and settled in that place. He was a young man when the visitation of 1574 was made. This family was afterward "long settled at Whitechurch in Oxfordshire, where they were lords of the manor of Hardwick." Its pedigree has been worked out very thoroughly by Col. Joseph L. Chester, LL.D., D.C.L., and it is certain that the American family did not spring from that source. The family is mentioned for the reason that it was the *only* one that belonged to the landed gentry in early times, and the pre-eminence of *this* family seems to have dated only from the marriage of the first Richard Libbe with the daughter of a justice. Had the grandfather of Richard Libbe of Checkenden been of the same social rank as himself, he would not have begun his pedigree with his own father.

The name seems to have belonged either in Cornwall or Devon. The Oxfordshire family, the earliest, as has been said, of which mention is found, evidently sprang from the latter county. According to Col. Chester, the only wills of the name, deposited at London, beside those of the Oxfordshire family, are those of William Libbye and Henry Libby, proved in 1653 and 1655, and both of these men belonged in Cornwall, where the name still abounds. The simple circumstances of the emigration of the originator of the American family make it supposable that he came from the neighborhood of Devon or Cornwall. The tradition among his descendants is also that he was from the West of England. These, with other less important circumstances, render it reasonably certain that the family belonged either in East Cornwall or West Devon. Whether it is of Saxon or Welch origin, or whether (as is not likely) it springs from some French immigrant that crossed over to engage in tin mining or the fisheries, will probably never be more than a matter of conjecture.

CHARACTERISTICS.

"Of the people" from the start, the family has retained in a very remarkable degree, the position which it held when it first emerged from the mists of early times. With scarcely any exception, its members have been strikingly devoid of ambition for power, place, and wealth. Contented with the enjoyment of present happiness, they have willingly obeyed the instruction, "be not anxious for the morrow;" and have been firm believers in the doctrine that "sufficient unto the day is the evil thereof." Avoiding the responsibilities, rather than seeking the honor of public office, they have been satisfied with the happiness of their own homes, and with but few exceptions each person has been known only in his own locality. Inclining to manual, rather than mental labor, they have seldom gained more than the rudiments of education, so that even now our colleges show but few graduates of the name, and most of those in late years. As will be seen, the story of almost every individual of the family is but one of quiet effort to make for himself a home. The daily wants supplied, nothing further is desired. It is indeed remarkable that in so numerous a family there is no person of national fame, no one who has figured largely in history, no one who has won renown in letters, nor in the arts.

Yet, as a family, they have been largely respected by their neighbors as men of sterling worth, and uprightness and honesty of character. They have generally belonged to that law-abiding class which forms the bone and muscle of a nation, content to render the wise efforts of others effective by its hearty support, and willing to concede all the glory to the leader. The family numbers its Revolutionary soldiers by scores, and many hundreds risked their lives for their country in the late war. In Maine alone there were two hundred and fifty-six enlistments. They are, as a family, very devout, and have figured much more largely in the religious than in the civil institutions of the communities in which they have lived. The family has abounded in Christian ministers, elders, and deacons, while generation after generation has died in the faith. There are of course black sheep in every flock, and in this as others, but so few have been the criminals, and so generally have the helpless ones been supported by their own relatives, that even in Maine, where the family is so numerous as to rank with the Smiths and Browns, it has been remarked by many to the compiler of this volume, that they *never knew of a criminal nor a pauper named Libby*.

SPELLING OF THE NAME.

As written by strangers, the manners of spelling the name have been almost endless; but the methods that have been used by the members themselves of the American family are thought to be only the following:

Libby	Libbie	Lebbey
Libbey	Libbe	Lebbee
Libbee	Lebby	Lebbe

Those which exist to-day are:

Libby	Libbee	Lebby
Libbey	Libbie	

The immigrant has left no original signature, and it cannot be known for certainty how he spelled his own name. Probably the best authority is John Winter, who came from the same part of England as himself. He spelled it *Libby*, which spelling was early in use in England, and now is, and has long been, the only form used. Of the other forms that have been used in this country, the only one ever used in England is *Libbe*. Hence, of the spellings now in use, the only one that has continental precedence is *Libby*.

Of the immigrant's eight sons, two left no signatures; three, reared in the midst of Indian wars, never learned to write; and, of the other three, John spelled his name *Libby*, and Henry and Anthony used *Libbe*.

Among the grandsons the spelling assumed more varieties than it has ever had since. Up to 1750, the family was chiefly confined to Scarborough, Falmouth, Kittery, (now Eliot), and Berwick, Me.; and to Portsmouth, Rye, Epsom, and Dover, N. H. On either side of the Piscataqua River, including Portsmouth, Kittery, Berwick and Dover, the ending *ey*, came early into use. For a long time the vowels *i* and *e* were almost indiscriminately used in the first syllable, but, by 1750, the spelling Libbey became the standard one. Isaac Libby, who was reared in Portsmouth, but lived afterward in Rochester, used *Lebby*. In Scarborough and Falmouth, the most general spelling used by the best educated members of the family, was *Libbee*. The final *y*, however, was always used by those who went from Portsmouth to Scarborough, and it was generally spelled by them *Libby*, but sometimes *Libbey*. In Rye, on the other side of the "Libbey" towns, and in Epsom, which was settled by Rye families, the standard spelling was *Libbee*, although *Libbe* occurred occasionally at first. The following table gives a substantially correct account of the various spelling:

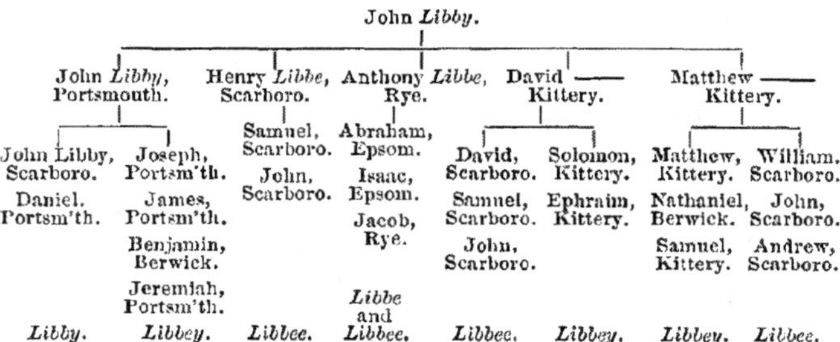

In Scarborough, more than a hundred years ago, the spelling *Libby* was universally adopted, and has continued since. From Scarborough that spelling has spread almost everywhere, and is now used by nearly the whole family.

The only families that left Scarborough before the adoption of the spelling *Libby* were those that settled in Machias, and spread from that place into neighboring towns. In those towns the spelling *Libbee* was continued until the present century, and then *Libby* was generally adopted, although some of that family now use *Libbey*. As a rule it may be said that all the Maine Libbys use the spelling *Libby*. In Portsmouth and Dover, and the families springing from those places, the spelling *Libbey* has, for the most part, continued.

The spelling *Libbey* has been generally continued in Eliot, (formerly Kittery), and Berwick, but some individuals use *Libby*. The Sanford, Lebanon, and Milton branches of the Berwick family generally adhere to the former spelling, while the Tuftonborough family uses *Libby*. The Saco branch of the Eliot family generally uses *Libby*, but in the branch of the Saco family that settled in Limington *Libbey* occurs. The branches of the Berwick and Eliot families that settled in Newfield, Limerick, and Shapleigh, use *Libby*. The Durham and Rochester branches of the Eliot family use *Libbey*.

In Rye, and the towns in which the Rye family settled, the spelling *Libbee* was used almost exclusively until the present century. In Epsom, Candia, Chester, New Durham, Wolfborough, Chichester, Canterbury, N. H., Strafford, Vt., and most all places in New Hampshire and Vermont, the spelling *Libbey* has gradually been adopted; but in some cases the spelling *Libbee* has been retained, which in one case has been varied to *Libbie*. The branch of the Rye family that settled in Gilford, N. H., and the many families that settled in the state of Maine, all adopted *Libby*. The New Brunswick branch of the family uses sometimes *Libby* and sometimes *Libbey*.

While these facts cover the general drift which the spelling has taken, yet many individuals have changed from one mode to another for no reason but their own fancy. While it is a questionable step to depart from the mode of spelling used by one's immediate ancestors, yet it is gratifying to notice that most of the changes now made are changes not *from*, but *to* the true spelling. Doubtless fifty names would now include all who spell their names other than *Libby* and *Libbey*, and the latter is used by probably not more than one-tenth part of the family.

INTER-MARRIAGE.

A notable feature of the family has been the frequency of inter-marriage. Ten of the immigrant's grandchildren married their own blood, and the same tendency has continued ever since. There is now but a small portion of the family that has only one descent from the immigrant. The following pedigree of one family is rather remarkable. It will be observed that the persons have *eleven* descents from the patriarch.

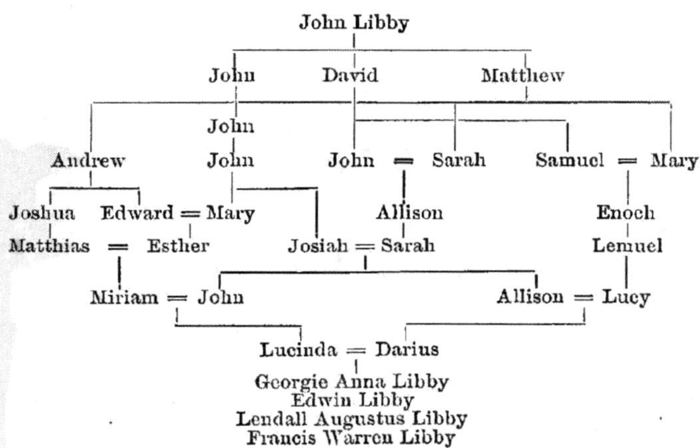

PROLIFACY.

So far as discovered,—

		Generation
The immigrant's sons numbered	8	*sons.*
Their sons numbered	25	*grandsons.*
Their sons numbered	105	*gt.-grandsons.*
Their sons numbered	288	*gt.-gt.-grandsons.*
Their sons numbered	772	*gt.-gt.-gt.-grandsons.*

The number of descendants of the immigrant, in the male lines, and of each of his sons and grandsons, as mentioned in this volume, may be seen in the following table:

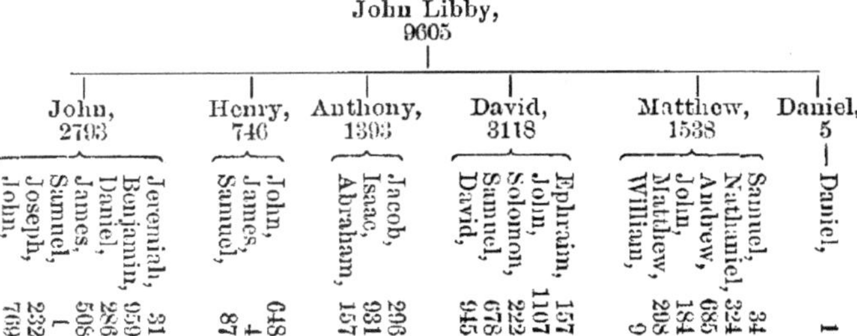

If, as it is natural to suppose, the daughters in all the generations, on an average, have had as numerous progeny as the sons, the whole number of the immigrant's descendants cannot be less than 300,000.

A TABLE of the males in the first four generations, who have lineal descendants in the year 1881—giving name, and place of death.

First Generation	Second Generation	Third Generation	Fourth Generation
John Libby. Scarborough. 1602-1682	John. Portsmouth, N. H. 1636–1720	John.—Scarborough.	James.—Scarborough.
			John.—Scarborough.
			Jonathan.—Scarborough.
			Josiah.—Scarborough.
		Joseph.—Portsmouth.	Benjamin.—Dover, N. H.
			Joshua.—Portsmouth.
		James.—Portsmouth.	James.—Scarborough.
			Isaac.—Rochester, N. H.
			John.—Portsmouth.
		Daniel.—Portsmouth.	William.—Falmouth, Me.
		Benjamin.—Berwick, Me.	Joseph.—Berwick.
			Daniel.—Berwick.
			Charles.—Berwick.
		Jeremiah.—Portsmouth.	Theodore.—Portsmouth.
	Henry. Scarborough. 1647–1732	Samuel.—Scarborough.	Ebenezer.—Scarborough.
			Nehemiah.—Scarborough.
		John.—Scarborough.	Stephen.—Limington, Me.
			Jesse.—Hampden, Me.
			Philemon.—Limington.
			Seth.—Scarborough.
			Nathan.—Scarborough.
	Anthony. Hampton, now Rye, N. H. 1649–1718	Abraham.—Epsom, N. H.	Joseph.-NewDurham,N.H.
		Isaac.—Epsom, N. H.	John.—Porter, Me.
			Isaac.—Epsom, N. H.
			Arthur.—Candia, N. H.
			Reuben.—Albany, Me.
		Jacob.—Rye, N. H.	Samuel.—St. Stephen, N. B.
			Abraham.—Chester, N. H.
	David. Kittery, now Eliot, Me. 1657–1736	David.—Scarborough.	Josiah.—Machias, Me.
			Timothy.—Machias.
			David.—(Scarborough ?)
			Thomas.—Scarborough.
		Samuel.—Scarborough.	Samuel.—Scarborough.
			Enoch.—Scarborough.
		Solomon —Eliot.	Joseph.—Saco, Me.
			Reuben.—Eliot.
			Nathan.—Eliot.
		John.—Scarborough.	Elisha.—Scarborough.
			Matthew.—Webster, Me.
			Mark.—Scarborough.
			Allison.—Scarborough.
			Nathaniel.—Scarborough.
			Luke.—Scarborough.
		Ephraim.—Eliot.	Ephraim.—Eliot.
	Matthew. Kittery, now Eliot, Me. 1663–1741	Matthew.—Eliot.	Matthew.—Eliot.
			Zebulon.—Newfield, Me.
			Azariah.—Limerick, Me.
			William.—Newfield.
		John.—Scarborough.	Peter.—Scarborough.
			Thomas.—Scarborough.
		Andrew.—Scarborough.	Andrew.—Gray, Me.
			Joshua.—Scarborough.
			Daniel.—Scarborough
			Edward.—Scarborough.
			Simon.—Scarborough.
		Nathaniel.—Berwick.	Nathaniel.—Berwick.
			Stephen.—Shapleigh, Me.
			Zebulon.—Berwick.
		Samuel.—Eliot.	Seth.—Eliot.

THE LIBBY FAMILY

IN AMERICA.

THE IMMIGRANT.

Maine was settled chiefly through speculative enterprises of English merchants. They sent yearly many vessels to fish on her coast, and established trading houses at convenient points to supply the wants of their fishermen and to obtain furs from the Indians. One of those stations was located on Richmond's Island, a small island on the coast of Cumberland county, distant about one mile from the coast of Cape Elizabeth. There had been one Walter Bagnall there, trading with the Indians; but he had dealt unjustly with them and they had murdered him. In 1631 Robert Trelawny and Moses Goodyeare, of Plymouth, Devonshire County, England, procured a patent which included that island, and soon after established a trading post, with John Winter as their agent. In John Winter's employ first appears he, the generations of whose descendants this volume records.

John Libby was born in England about the year 1602. In July, 1677, he stated that, "the good and pieous report that was spread abroad, into our Native Land of this country, caused your Petitioner to come for this Land 47 yeares agoe, where he hath ever since Continued." According to this, the year of his immigration was 1630; but "47 yeares" was probably a slight exaggeration. The "good and pieous report" was doubtless set afloat by Trelawny in his efforts to obtain men to carry on his fisheries, and there can be little doubt that John Libby was sent over by him.

In Winter's report to Trelawny of his management of the station for the year ending 15 July 1639, occurs the following account:*

Jno Libby Debitor							
for aquauite	...	.4	.6				
for wine	...	13	..				
for Monie disburst by Mr Trelawny to Mr Jno Sharpe for him	..3	..	..	ꝑ Contra Creditor for his yeares seruice	..5	..	..
pd him in in beaur att 8s for ye ballance	..1	.2	.6				

*This and the following accounts were copied from the MS. of the "Trelawny Papers," about to be published by the Maine Historical Society, through the courtesy of Hon. J. W. Bradbury, Chairman of the Standing Committee, and Gen. John Marshall Brown, Chairman of the Publishing Committee of that society.

In Winter's next report, the following — evidently a back account — occurs:

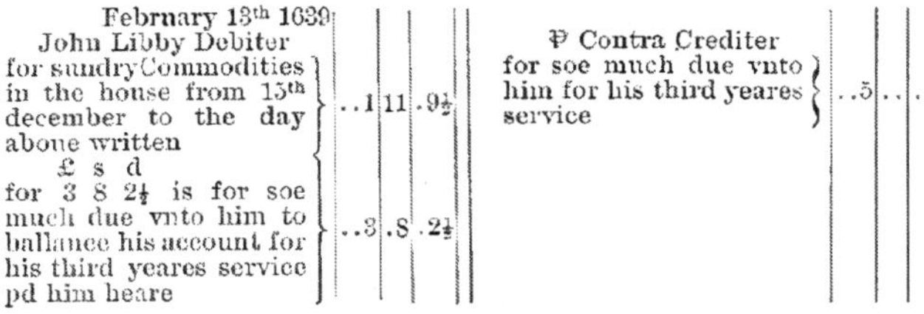

February 13th 1639 John Libby Debiter	£	s	d	℔ Contra Crediter	£	s	d
for sundry Commodities in the house from 15th december to the day aboue written	..1	11	.9½	for soe much due vnto him for his third yeares service	..5	..	..
£ s d for 3 8 2½ is for soe much due vnto him to ballance his account for his third yeares service pd him heare	..3	.8	.2½				

In the reports for the two following years, his name does not appear; but in an "act. of Disbursements for the use of the Plantation at Richmon," between June 1642 and June 1643, is the following item:

for money pd John Lebby for 6 weekes worke at 6s ℔ weeke	..1	16	..

From this we gather that John Libby was in the employ of Trelawny four years,— from the summer of 1635 until the summer of 1639, — and that during that time a large part of his earnings was paid for him in England. This was doubtless for the support of the wife whom he had left behind him; and probably in 1640 he sent for her, and took up his permanent abode on the neighboring main land, on the possessions of Thomas Cammock, the patentee of Black Point.

A few miles west of Richmond's Island, formed by the little river now called Nonesuch, on the west, and a still smaller stream, since dignified by the name Libby River, on the southeast, was a low neck of land. Broad acres of salt marsh — ready hay-fields — reached away to the southwest, to where the two streams united with each other and with a third, forming a sheltered bay, and then flowing out over a sand-bar into the ocean. On that neck, close to the marsh of the stream that bears his name, in what is now the town of Scarborough, John Libby built his house. The land which he selected was afterward laid out to him by Henry Jocelyn, (who had come into possession of the Cammock patent), and for many years he doubtless occupied it as his tenant. During those years much of his time was probably devoted to fishing, but as his land gradually became more productive, he doubtless depended less upon the sea, and applied himself exclusively to the tilling of the soil.

1 Jan. 1663, by a document in which he was described as a "planter," he received from Jocelyn, "a certain tract of land bounded as followeth, vise. the Marsh to begine at the next cricke to ye Eastward of the sayd Libby's coman landing place, and from thence to his dwelling house, according as his fence goeth, & was formerly bounded by mee, [Jocelyn], from thence Westward & North Westward to a tree marked by me formerly & from thence

to goe over upon a viswall lyne upon the dwelling house of Mr. Hene: Watts at Bleu poynt, [across the mouth of Nonesuch River,] So far as the flatts Also the Marsh halfe of that Necke his dwelling house stands upon, according to the bounds formerly be mee layd out & further all the Marsh to yᵉ Eastward of the Bridg [over Libby River] on that side the cricke to the Upland so far as the Mayn Cricke called the pine Cricke & over against Godfrey Shelldens house & soe far up the sayd Cricke until it comes close up unto the upland & also fivety acres of upland adjoining to the sayd Marsh & and to go into the land according to the marked trees formerly laid out unto him, one hundred and sixty pooles to every acer Sixteen foote & an a halfe to every poole, also to have free comage, with lyberty of fishing & fowling & cutting for ordinary uses in any Swamp or Elsewhere, unbounded forth to others, in such lands as is or shall be unfenced"; in consideration of him his heirs, administrators, and assigns, "Yielding & paying unto the sayd Henery Jocelyn his heyres & Assignes for every fivety acers of Upland & Meddow annually three days worke forever, that is to say two days worke in harvest, or foode tyme, & one day in cutting of wood, against the feast of Christ tyde, if it bee lawfully demanded."

From the time of his six weeks work for Winter, between June 1642 and June 1643, until the above transfer, his name occurs only once in existing records. 14 April 1661, he was one of the appraisers of the estate of Andrew Heffers.

John Libby was (to use the words of the History of Scarborough) "for many years one of the town's principal planters"; but he took no part in the affairs of the province, and little, so far as is known,* in the management of the town. It incidentally appears, however, that he was constable in 1664, and his name stands first of the four selectmen in a town grant bearing date 1669. His name, except as constable, does not appear at all in the provincial court records, and that at a period when quarrels and litigations were the order of the day, and indictments were issued for the most trivial offences, and on most questionable testimony. That in point of morality he took a stand far above his class, is very evident from a comparison between his accounts while on Richmond's Island and those of his fellow fishermen. Whereas most of them spent their entire wages for spirits and tobacco, he used no tobacco and very little intoxicating drink of any sort; while nearly all of what he did use was wine. He seems to have practiced that quiet, correct, peaceful mode of life which has always characterized his descendants.

In Philip's war, in which were devastated all the more exposed settlements of Maine, John Libby suffered in common with the other inhabitants. He lost everything he had except his plantation. In the late summer of 1675, hostile Indians began to appear at Black Point, shooting cattle, etc. Those of the inhabitants

*The existing town records of Scarborough date back so as to include only the declining years of his life.

who lived at any distance from the garrison (and among them John Libby) were compelled to leave their habitations for the safer abode. Their crops had to be gathered under the protection of soldiers who went from Boston. The burning of John Libby's house was recorded in the diary of Capt. Joshua Scottow, who had charge of the Boston soldiers, as follows: "Sept. 7th, 1675. Being Lord's day . . . . . .* the enemy . . . . . before of their designs early in the morning burnt those houses and barnes our Capne saved the day before—they burnt also 8 or 9 deserted houses belonging to Libby and children."

In October, 1676, Black Point garrison was deserted, and most of the inhabitants fled to Boston. The able-bodied men returned soon after and again took possession of the garrison, which the Indians, contrary to their custom, had left unburnt. Probably the women and children did not return until the close of the war; at any rate, John Libby with his wife and younger children were in Boston 10 July 1677, and on that date petitioned the Governor and Council there assembled, that his sons Henry and Anthony, on whom he stated he was dependent for support, might be discharged from the Black Point garrison. The petition was granted the same day.†

He returned to Black Point probably very soon after. There was no serious trouble there subsequent to June 1677, and 12 Apr. 1678 terms of peace were finally ratified. In a short time Black Point had regained something of its former prosperity and in the few remaining years of his life, John Libby acquired a comfortable property. He died at about eighty years of age. In his will, dated 9 Feb. 1682, he gave "unto my [his] Children five Shillings

---

*Original defective.

†The petition, doubtless written by an attorney, was as follows:

To ye Honoured Governor and Counsell
Now, Assembled at Bostone

The Humble Petition of John Liby sinr Late of Scarbrow Humbly Sheweth That the good and pieous report that was spread abroad, into our Native Land of this Country) caused your Petitioner to come for this Land 47 yeares agoe, where he hath Ever since Continued (but now by the Incursion of ye Barbarions Enimys,) had his houses burned; and his Catle and Corne destroyed, Soe that yor poore Petitionr is in a very Low Condition, being about, ye age of 75 years Therefore not any way Capable to procure A Livlihood neither hath he been noe ways Chargable to ye Country hitherto) but yor poore Petitionr and his wife with 8 Smale Children was mentained from perrishing; By 4 Sonns of yor Petitioner whereof one is Latly Kild at Black point and two were sickened at Black point of which two) one) was brought here to Boston about Tenn dayes agoe and died Last night And the other two Sonns are at Black point, and hath been there this 9 months

Therefore yor poore Petitioner Intreats yor worships seriously to Consider of yor petitioner helplesse Condition by ordreing that his two Sonns be dischargd from ye Garrison at Black point) May it please yor Worships first to Consider of your petitionr age 2d That hee haueing 9 in family which hath there dependence vpon the Labours of yor petitionrs two Sonns, namly Henry Liby and Anthony Liby) 3d That yor petitionr Beseeches yor Worships to Consider that 9 months is a goe time to Continue in Garrison And that few or non ever Continued soe Long in Garrison

Soe yor petitionr hops that these Considerations beeing but Seriously Considered off; will move yor worships to Grant yor petitionr an order for ye Discharging of yor Petitionr two Sonns) which wilbe a meance to preserue yor petitionr & family from perishing) Soe yor Subplicant with his wife and Children shall haue great cause to pray for yor health and Happynese and Subscribe himselfe yor poore Distresed Subplicant

JOHN LIBY

July ye 10th
1677

This Request is
Granted 10 July 77
E. R S.

Apeece, to every one of them, & to my [his] two younger sonns namely Mathew & Daniell, fivety Shillings out of ye Estate when they come [should come] to age"; and willed that "my [his] wife shall [should] have it all to her disposeing to Mantayn the children." 5 May 1683, William Burrine and Andrew Brown made oath before Capt. Scottow to the truth of the following inventory:

Impr^s^ To 4 Cows at	12	00	00
Two Heffers at	04	00	00
to foure steares at	12	00	00
to five yearelings at	08	00	00
to one calfe at tenn shillg^s^	00	10	00
Two sheeps at	00	16	00
eleven swine at 40	02	00	00
one horse at 20 shillings	01	00	00
to weareing apparell & to household Goods all at	8	00	00
house & Lands* at	70	00	00
	£118	06	00

That John Libby had two wives is certain. Of the first, nothing is known but that she was the mother of all his sons except Matthew and Daniel, and probably *all* his daughters. Of the second there is nothing known but her christian name, which appears from the mention in bounding a town grant, 1 May 1686, of "Mary Libby's marshes." How long Mary Libby outlived her husband is uncertain; but she probably lived to be again driven from her home by the Indians, as no attempt was made to settle her estate. 6 Apr. 1720, a warrant was issued to Captain John Libby, 1-1, to administer upon his *grandfather's* estate; the will being either forgotten or set aside. The inventory mentioned only the real estate at Black Point—100 acres of upland, 9 acres of fresh meadow, and 100 acres of salt marsh.

The children† of John Libby, probably all born in this country except the eldest, were:

1 John, b. 1636; m. Agnes ——.
2 James. } These both lost their lives in Philip's war; unmarried.
3 Samuel. } One was killed at Black Point in the spring of 1677; the other was taken sick in the garrison, carried to Boston, and there died 9 July 1677.
4 Joanna, m. Thomas Bickford of Black Point. His father lived at Dover, N. H., and in the second Indian war his family removed from Scarborough to that place.
5 Henry, b. 1647; m. Honor Hinkson of Scarborough.
6 Anthony, b. about 1649; m. Sarah Drake of Hampton, N. H.
7 Rebecca, married Joshua Brown of Scarborough.
8 Sarah, b. 1653; m. Robert Tidy of Scarborough.
9 Hannah, married Daniel Fogg of Scarborough.
10 David, b. 1657; m. Eleanor ——.
11 Matthew, b. 1663; m. Elizabeth Brown of Scarborough.
12 Daniel, m. Mary Ashton of Scarborough.

*Thirty-seven years later these lands alone were apprized at £130½.

†From the fact that a number of his children, or their heirs, quitclaimed to other parties one-thirteenth part of his property each, it seems that he left twelve children—probably two more daughters whose names do not appear. The four whose names are given were discovered, not by direct search, but casually; in the same way the others may some day come to light.

SECOND GENERATION.

1

JOHN LIBBY, born probably in England, in the year 1636; married AGNES ———.

He was reared in Scarborough. In August 1668, which was probably soon after his marriage, he bought fifty acres of land adjoining his father's plantation. This was no doubt his residence while he lived at Black Point, although he afterward received several grants from the town. He took quite an active part in the public matters of the town, and served as selectman in the years 1670, 1674, 1683, and 1687.

The settlement at Black Point was still in rather poor condition, when the Indians, instigated by the French, again began to disturb the quiet of the settlers all along the coast of Maine, and became more and more aggressive until May 1690, when Fort Loyal, on Casco Neck, a few miles north of Black Point, was attacked by a large body of Indians with their French allies. After a siege of five days, the fort was surrendered, and the inhabitants of Scarborough, without waiting to be attacked themselves, immediately deserted their homes and fled to safer localities.

John Libby with his whole family fled to Portsmouth, N. H. His youngest son, Jeremiah, was then ten months old. In Portsmouth, where he lived until his death, he followed the calling of miller, and during the earlier years of his residence there, was frequently chosen to fill the minor town offices. He lived to very old age; how old, is not known, but as late as 1719–20 he made a deposition about early Scarborough matters. He probably died soon after. His wife* was living in March 1717, but probably died before her husband.

Their children† were all born in Scarborough.

---

*She was probably not a Scarborough woman. In a joint deposition of herself and husband, taken 15 Mar. 1717, her husband testified that one Joseph Winnock had lived at Black Point *between sixty and seventy* years before, but she limited her testimony to *fifty* years. It would seem that her recollection of Winnock reached back only to the time of her marriage.

†No list of John Libby's children appears. He disposed of his property before his death, deeding his real estate to his sons John and Daniel. That the others were his sons, there is no *positive* proof; but there are many circumstances which might be said to prove it to all practical purposes, and there is *nothing* which would tend in the least degree to disprove it. All but Benjamin first appeared in Portsmouth, and among the descendants

Children:

1 John, married Eleanor Kirke.
2 Joseph, married Rebecca ——.
3 Samuel, married Sarah Wells.
4 James, married Mary Hanson.
5 Daniel, married Elizabeth Kirke.
6 Benjamin, b. 4 June 1682; m. Sarah Stone.
7 Jeremiah, b. 1689; married Lydia Badger.

5

HENRY LIBBY, born in Scarborough, in the year 1647; married HONOR HINKSON, daughter of Peter Hinkson,* whose plantation joined his father's.

He was selectman of Scarborough in 1686. In 1690 he fled, with his father-in-law, to Lynn, Mass. He was one of the company which first attempted to re-settle their possessions. Tradition says that they came from Lynn in a sloop, and built a garrison on Prout's Neck, which they successfully defended from a force of five hundred French and Indians.

Henry Libby and his sons were all present at the first town meeting, in 1720. With one John Boden, he was chosen to go and show the old highways to the selectmen. In September, 1728, at the age of 81, he became a member of the Congregational church at Black Point, which had just been organized under the pastoral charge of the Rev. William Tompson.

His house stood on the lot which was recently added to the south side of the Black Point burying-ground, and was afterward occupied by his eldest son. He died 21 Oct. 1732. His wife died 24 Aug. 1724, aged sixty.

Children:

1 Mary, m. 13 Jan. 1715, at Marblehead, Mass., Richard Webber.
2 Samuel, b. 6 July 1689; m. Abigail Meserve and Mary Jones.
3 Sarah, died in Scarborough, 1 Mar. 1723.
4 James, married 16 Mar. 1738, Abigail Larrabee. His name scarcely appears except in deeding away what property he inherited from his father and mother. The baptisms of the following children occur:

---

of Benjamin the tradition is that he went to Berwick (where the records first show him) from Portsmouth. 14 June 1712, Capt. John Libby, 1-1, bought from the widow of his brother Daniel, and of Samuel Libby's widow, the rights of their husbands in the town commons. James and Jeremiah were both at Scarborough at the first town-meeting after the re-settlement of the town, in 1720, and both received town grants as their rights. Jeremiah's name occurs several times as a witness to documents executed by John, 1, and John, 1-1. Benjamin had a son Joseph, and Joseph had a son Benjamin. Benjamin had also Agnes, Daniel, and Jeremiah. John had a son James; and James, a son John. Daniel had a son Samuel, and Samuel, it is thought, a son Daniel. Jeremiah had a son John. Altogether, in the absence of *positive* proof, more convincing evidence that these seven were John Libby's sons could hardly be expected. What daughters he had will probably never be known.

*Philip and Peter Hinkson, probably brothers, were from Hobberton, (or Heberton), Devonshire County, England. Philip emigrated first, and settled at Saco. His widow, Margaret, married George Taylor of Black Point. She had two children by her first husband, Sarah and Meribah, both under age in 1662. In that year, Peter, who had not then left England, received a power of attorney to let a tenement in Heberton, which had fallen by inheritance to Philip. Within a year or two Peter came to Black Point, where he was one of the principal inhabitants until the second Indian war, when he removed to Lynn, Mass. He had children, Peter, Simon, Honor, and perhaps others.

1 Joanna, bap. 27 May 1744. It may have been she, that married Isaac Myrick, 4 June 1764.
2 Hannah, } twins, bap.
3 Susannah, } 3 May 1847.
4 Priscilla, bap. 19 May 1751.

5 Hannah, m. 15 Dec. 1720, in Marblehead, John Pollow,* and died at an early age, leaving only:
1 Hannah (Pollow). It seems that she lived with her grandfather Libby and her uncle Samuel. She married Joshua Brown, 7-1-6, and died 21 Aug. 1810.

6 Elizabeth, m. 16 Mar. 1727, Sampson Plummer. Children:
1 Elizabeth (Plummer), b. 27 Feb. 1728.
2 James (Plummer), b. 29 Sept. 1730.
3 Jeremiah (Plummer), b. 16 June 1733.
4 Joseph (Plummer), b. 8 Feb. 1735.
5 John (Plummer), bap. Mar. 1737; died young.
6 Jonathan (Plummer), b. 20 Oct. 1739.
7 Samuel (Plummer), b. 16 Sept. 1742; m. Sarah Bragdon.
8 Phebe (Plummer), b. 29 Sept. 1744; m. Benj. Small. [See the footnote under David, 10.]
9 Hannah (Plummer), b. 15 June 1747; m. Thomas Libby, 11-6-5.

7 John, married Mary Goodwin, and Anna Fogg, 9-5-2.

6

Anthony Libby, born in Scarborough, about 1649; married Sarah Drake, born 20 Aug. 1656, daughter of Abraham and Jane Drake, of Hampton, N. H.

Anthony Libby was a carpenter. He lived in his native town until some years after Philip's war. In May, 1681, he was one of a committee chosen to purchase timber for building a "fort", Scottow's garrison. In November following, he was taxed for 50 acres of land, 6 acres of marsh, 1 cow, 2 hogs, and 1 mare. In the first part of 1682, he moved to Falmouth. There he found his wife, who was a sister of the wife of Anthony Brackett of that place. In 1685, he removed to her native town of Hampton, and settled in the northeast part of that town, subsequently set off to Rye. His wife died 12 June 1716. He married second, 6 Jan. 1717-18, Jane Rackley of Portsmouth, and lived only a few weeks.

His will was as follows:

In the name of God Amen. The twentieth day of February 1717 [1718] Anthony Lebe of Hampton in the Province of New Hampshire in New England farmer being very sick and week in body but of perfect mind & memory thanks be given unto God therfore calling unto mind ye mortality of my body & knowing it is appointed for all men once to Dye do make & ordain this my last will & Testament That is to say Principally & first of all I give & Recomend to ye earth to be buried in decent Christian buriall at ye Descretion of my Executor nothing doubting but at ye Generall Resurection I shall receive ye same again by ye mighty power of God and as touching such worldly Estate wherewith it hath pleased God to bless me in this life I give Devise & Dispose of ye same in ye following manner & form

*He afterward removed to Falmouth, where he married a second wife, Susannah ——, and had: 1 Sarah, b. 13 Dec. 1731; m. Joshua Lawrence. 2 Mary, b. 5 Dec. 1735. 3 Joseph, b. 9 Jan. 1738; died a young man, without issue.

Imprimis. I Give to Jean my dearly beloved wife my orchard those trees that are mine my pasture as far as y[e] barn & my great Bason one Cow & y[e] white faced heifer & Thirty pounds in money & my great Pat & a piece of surge in y[e] chest four sheep and pasturing the west end of my house all during her widowhood & no longer

2[d]ly I Give to my well beloved son Abraham Lebe a calf & his son Joseph one sheep

3[d]ly I give to my well beloved son Isaac Lebe two sheep & one half of my cove of marsh

4[th]ly I give to my well beloved Daughter Sarah six pounds money,

5[th]ly I give to my well beloved Daughter Mary Six pounds money

6[th]ly I give to my well beloved Daughter Hannah twenty shillings money

7[th]ly I give my well beloved Daughter Jane my brass Kettle & y[e] red mantle & two sheep & a cow on marriage day

8[th]ly I give to my well beloved son Jacob Lebe whom I likewise constitute make ordain my sole Executor to this my last will & testament all & singular of my houses edifices

[Original defective]

Lands mesuages both reall and personall Except what is above disposed of in the order as it is to be performed by him and after my Decease to be by him freely possess[d] and Injoyed and I do hereby desallow revoke and disannull all and every other former testament will legaces and by me in any ways before named will[d] and bequeathed Ratifying and Confirming this and no other to be my last Will and Testament in Witness whereof I have hereunto set my hand and seall the day and year above written

Signed sealed published pronounced and Declared by the s[d] Anthony Lebe as his last Will and Testament in the Presents of us the subscribers.

Thomas Ward
Robert Drake
Sam[ll] Chapman

mark
Anthony | | ! Lebe
his

It was proved 5 Mar. 1718. The inventory of his estate was as follows:

A true and just inventory of the estate both reall and personal of Anthony Lebe late Dec[d]

	£	s.	d.
to Buildings	40	—	—
To Meadow	10	—	—
To land	70	—	—
To Cattell	24	—	—
To Sheep	04	10	—
To 2 horse kind	07	—	—
To Implements	03	10	—
To part mill	01	10	—
To beds and Bed Cloaths	30	—	—
To Brass	02	18	—
To Iron	03	—	—
To barrells and tubs	01	—	—
To putter and Books	01	5	—
To wooden moveables in house	01	15	—
To Boots and shoes	01	—	—
To Hats and wareing cloathes	08	15	—
To a Gun	—	10	—
To Provision and swine	07	—	—
To money	06	—	—
To Sarge and a Mantle	01	5	—
To 6 pound wooll	—	6	—

Apraised by Jabez Dow and Richard Jennis

The children of Anthony Libby were:

1 Sarah, m. 18 June 1701, Israel Smith of Hampton.
2 Mary, m. 7 Mar. 1709, John Lane of Hampton.
3 Abraham, m. Sabina Philbrick.
4 Isaac, m. Mary ——.
5 Hannah.
6 Jacob, b. 25 May 1695; m. Sarah Marston.
7 Jane, b. 5 Aug. 1700; m. 9 May 1720, Deacon Abraham Moulton of Hampton, afterward of Kensington.

7

REBECCA LIBBY, born in Scarborough, about 1651; married JOSHUA BROWN, a son of Andrew Brown, one of the earliest and most prominent settlers of Black Point. She was a widow in Portsmouth in 1721, and was living as late as 1732.

Children:

1 Andrew (Brown), m. Susannah ——.
2 Sarah (Brown), m. William Libby, 11-1.
3 Charles (Brown).
4 Samuel (Brown).
5 Hannah (Brown).
6 Mary (Brown).
7 Ephraim (Brown).

8

SARAH LIBBY, born in Scarborough, in the year 1653; married ROBERT TIDY. He was the first, and perhaps the only person of his surname that settled in Maine or New Hampshire. He first appeared as one of the Black Point garrison in 1676. His family afterward lived at Kittery, where his widow married second, —— Rogers, and third, Christopher Bampfield. She was living in Kittery, a widow, in January, 1729.

Children:

1 John (Tidy), m. Hannah, dau. of John Morrell of Kittery; died 10 Jan. 1706. Children:
  1 Sarah (Tidy), b. 17 Jan. 1714; m. —— Stacey.
  2 Edah (Tidy), b. 22 Jan. 1716; m. —— Emery.
  3 Hannah (Tidy), b. 6 July 1718; d. about 1799; unm. With her the name became extinct.
  4 Robert (Tidy), b. 12 Oct. 1720; m. Hannah ——. They were both dead in May 1790. No children.
  5 Meribah (Tidy), b. 12 Sept. 1722; died without issue.
  6 John (Tidy), b. 29 June 1724; d. 1749; unm.
2 Elizabeth (Tidy), m. 8 Jan. 1708, John Witham of York.
3 Hannah (Tidy), m. Daniel Witham of Kittery.
4 Mary (Tidy), m. —— Brown.

9

HANNAH LIBBY, born in Scarborough, about 1655; married DANIEL FOGG. He was a son of Samuel Fogg, of Hampton, N. H., supposed to have come from Wales.

Daniel Fogg learned the blacksmith's trade, and settled at

Black Point as early as 1681. At the breaking up of the settlement in 1690, he removed to Portsmouth, and about ten years later to Kittery, now Eliot, Me. There he died, in 1755, having outlived his wife many years.

Children:

1 Hannah (Fogg), m. 21 May 1704, John Rogers.
2 Mary (Fogg), m. 11 Aug. 1709, Wm. Brooks.
3 Rebecca (Fogg), m. 1726, Joseph Pilsbury.
4 Sarah (Fogg), m. 1 Jan. 1815, Thomas Hanscom.
5 Daniel (Fogg), b. 12 Apr. 1694; m. Anna Hanscom.
6 John (Fogg), m. Mary Hanscom.
7 Joseph (Fogg), m. 1st, 13 Jan. 1725, Sarah Hill; 2d, Eleanor Libby, 1-1-4. He settled on a farm in Scarborough. Having no children, he took to live with him Josiah Libby, 1-1-6-4. He died some time before his wife, whose death took place 3 Jan. 1790, at the age of 95.
8 Seth (Fogg), b. Dec. 1701, in Eliot; m. Mary Pickernale.
9 James (Fogg), b. 17 Mar. 1704; m. Elizabeth Fernald.

10

DAVID LIBBY, born in Scarborough, in the year 1657; married ELEANOR ———.

From the town records it appears that, 11 Feb. 1681, he and four others were chosen to renew the bounds between Casco (afterward Falmouth, and now Cape Elizabeth) and Scarborough, and that he received several town grants.

When the town was deserted in 1690, he went to Portsmouth, where he lived about ten years. In December, 1699, he, his brother Matthew, his brother-in-law Daniel Fogg, Joseph Hammond and Stephen Tobey, the first three being then of Portsmouth and the others of Kittery, bought what was known as the Knowles purchase. It was in that part of Kittery which is now Eliot. It fronted on the Piscataqua river, at the "Long Reach," about three-fourths of a mile, and stretched back into the town a long distance. The following spring they divided it lengthwise, so that each had a fronting on the river. Hammond had the northwest portion, Fogg the next, Matthew Libby the next, David Libby the next, and Tobey the southeast lot.

The division line between the portions of David Libby and his brother passed over a piece of rising ground since known as Libby Hill. On this hill, within a few rods of each other, they built their houses. They laid out a lane between their lands, reaching way from the river to their northeast boundary; portions of this lane are still open. David Libby built his house, a two-storied one, on the site of the present residence of Moses Libby, 10-7-1-3-8. It remained until after the death, in 1807, of his great-grandson, Joel Libby, the father of Moses. In that house David Libby lived the rest of his life, a well-to-do farmer.

In his will, dated 6 May 1725, he provided for his wife, and left his homestead to his son Ephraim. To David he gave twenty acres of land on the northeast of, and adjoining, the county road; to Solomon he gave a two-acre house lot on the southwest side of the road; to John he had already given, by deed, his Scarborough lands. He probably died in 1736, for in December of that year his will was proved. The amount of the inventory was £1329, 5s. He was buried on his own farm, and with him now lie five generations of his descendants.

His children were:

1 David, m. Esther Hanscom.
2 Samuel, m. Mary Libby, 11-3.
3 Mary, m. 12 April 1722, Joseph Small.*
4 Solomon, m. Martha Hanscom.
5 John, m. Sarah Libby, 11-8.
6 Elizabeth, m. Sept. 1738, Edward Cloudman, of Biddeford. She was probably also a party in the following marriage, recorded in the Biddeford town records: Abraham Townsend and Elizabeth Libbe, both of Biddeford, married 17 Nov. 1743.
7 Ephraim, b. 2 Feb. 1702, in Kittery; m. Mary Ambler.
8 Eleanor, b. 21 June 1705, in Kittery; m. 1st, Zebulon Trickey; 2d, Lt. Andrew Libby, 11-7.
9 Abigail, b. 29 Sept. 1707; m. Nov. 1725, Richard Nason.

11

Matthew Libby, born in Scarborough, in the year 1663; married Elizabeth Brown, daughter of Andrew Brown, one of the principal inhabitants of Black Point.

As has been already told, he went to Portsmouth in 1690, and

---

*Francis Smale seems to have been the ancestor of a great portion of the Smalls, and Smalleys, of New England. He was born 1627. It is probable that he was a son of "Mr." Edward Smale, who was of Kittery as early as 1640, and in 1645 had commission as magistrate: of whose family nothing appears. Francis Smale first appeared at Dover, 1648; was of Falmouth 1657 and 1663; of Kittery 1668, where he spent the chief part of his life; in old age removed to Truro, Cape Cod, where he died about 1714 He was an Indian-trader, and had a trading house "back of Wells," on land which he afterward bought of Capt. Sandy, the Indian, twenty miles square, afterward known as the "five Ossipee townships" His wife was Elizabeth ——, probably that servant of Capt. Francis Champernoune mentioned in his will. She was born 1634, and lived to old age. They had the following children:

1 Edward, died before his father.
2 Francis, died before his father.
+3 Samuel, b. 1666; settled on the homestead in Kittery.
4 Benjamin, settled in Connecticut.
5 Daniel, a carpenter, lived first at Truro, then at Provincetown. Had children: 1 Isaac; 2 Daniel; 3 John; 4 Edward; 5 Elisha; 6 Benjamin; 7 Anna, (m. —— Dyer); and perhaps others.
6 Elizabeth (probably), m. John Pugsley, of Kittery.

3 Samuel Small married Elizabeth, widow of James Chadbourne, and daughter of Ensign James Heard. Children:

1 Elizabeth, b. 9 Nov. 1695; m. 10 Feb. 1714, Benjamin March.
+2 Samuel, b. 17 Apr. 1700; m. Anna Hatch.
3 Joseph, b. 3 Dec. 1702; m. Mary Libby, 10-3.

3-2 Deacon Samuel Small settled in Scarborough. Children:

+1 Samuel, b. 26 May 1718; m. Dorothy Hubbard.
2 Anna, b. 10 Sept. 1720; m. Josiah Libby, 1-1-6.
3 John, b. 30 Jan. 1722-3; m. 1st, Sarah Atkins; 2d, Mary McKenney.
4 Joshua, b. 26 Feb. 1725-6; m. Susannah Kennard of Kittery.
5 Elizabeth, b. 3 Feb. 1727-8; m. James Harmon.
6 Sarah, b. 26 Aug. 1729.
7 Benjamin, b. 27 June 1732.
8 James, b. 14 July 1736.
9 Mary, b. 13 Jan. 1739.

3-2-1 Dea. Samuel Small always lived in Scarborough. Children:

thence to Kittery, in the winter of 1699-1700. He built his house close by the one now occupied by Thomas Adlington. It was built with hewn timber, and the upper story projected over the lower one for protection against the Indians. In that house he lived until his death. It was taken down in the early part of this century, and the present one built.

Some time before the second organization of the town of Scarborough, he, with Roger Deering, John Libby, 1–1, and Roger Hunnewell, went down to Black Point and built a sawmill on Nonesuch River, a short distance above the present Congregational church. His interest in that mill he afterward gave to his three sons, William, John and Andrew, and it is doubtful if he ran the mill himself longer than a very short time. He died in March, 1740–1, leaving his homestead to his son Samuel. His widow died two or three years later. In the family burying-ground lie Matthew Libby and his wife and five generations of their descendants, with nothing but rough stones to mark their graves.

Their children—the first six born in Scarborough and Portsmouth, and the rest in Kittery—were:

1 William, m. Sarah Brown, 7–2.
2 Matthew, m. Mary Nason.
3 Mary, m. Samuel Libby, 10–2.
4 Rebecca, m. 21 Jan. 1723, Thomas Musset.
5 Hannah, m. Jan. 1722. Samuel Hanscom.
6 John, b. 1698; m. Keziah Hubbard.
7 Andrew, b. 1 Dec. 1700; m. Esther Furber; 2d, Eleanor (Libby) Trickey, 10–8.
8 Sarah, b. 7 Sept. 1702; m. John Libby, 10–5.
9 Nathaniel, b. 2 Nov. 1704; m. Miriam Knight.
10 Dorcas, b. 2 Feb. 1706; m. 24 June 1729, James Staples.
11 Samuel, b. 5 June 1709; m. Margaret Rogers.
12 Mehitable, b. 14 March 1711; m. 2 Aug. 1733, Daniel Knight.
13 Lydia, b. 27 April 1713; m. 17 Oct. 1730, Benj. Stacy.
14 Elizabeth, m. 26 Nov. 1734, John Smith, jr., of Berwick.

12

DANIEL LIBBY, born in Scarborough, about 1665; married, 23

---

1 Abigail, b. 7 Oct. 1742; m. John Meserve. [See page 37.]
2 Benjamin, b. 11 Aug. 1744; m. Phebe Plummer, 5-6-8.
3 Sarah, b. 25 Aug. 1746; m. Timothy Waterhouse, 10-2-2-4.
4 Samuel, b. 23 Oct. 1748; d. at sea; a young man; unm.
5 Francis, b. 17 Aug. 1751.
6 Martha, b. 28 Nov. 1752; m. Philemon Libby, 5-7-12.
7 Dorothy, b. 22 Apr. 1754; died young.
+8 James, b. 26 Apr. 1757; m. Mary Fogg, 9-3-4-7.
9 William, b. 8 June 1759; m. Mary and Sarah March, 11-6-1-6 and 12.
10 Anna, b. 24 Mar. 1760; m. Charles Fogg, 9-5-4-10.
11 Dorothy, b. 14 Jan. 1762; m. Dominicus Libby, 10-2-4-3.

3-2-1-8 CAPT. JAMES SMALL lived and died in Scarborough. Children:

1 Dorothea, b. 29 Sept. 1783; m. James, son of James Marr, 1-5-3-2-2.
2 David, b. 27 Mar. 1785; m. Elizabeth Jordan.
3 Margaret, b. 4 Dec. 1787; died unmarried, aged about 55.
4 Samuel, b. 13 June 1789; m. Mary Libby, 10-2-4-2-10.
5 James, b. 29 Dec. 1790; m. Catherine Fogg, 9-6-6-4-3.
6 Mary, b. 30 Apr. 1793; m. Joshua Libby, 11-7-2-6-2.
7 Sarah, b. 5 July 1795; m. Benjamin Switcher.
8 John Hubbard, b. 5 July 1797.
9 Reuben, b. 30 Mar. 1799; d. a young man; unm.
10 Benjamin, b. 13 Oct. 1801.

Feb. 1687, MARY ASHTON, dau. of John and Susannah (Foxwell) Ashton, then living at Black Point. (Susannah Foxwell's mother was a daughter of Richard Bonython, the original patentee of Saco.)

At the second depopulation of the town he went with his wife's father to Marblehead, Mass. There he was a carter. He was living there as late as 1735, and his wife as late as June 1737.

Children:

1 Daniel,* m. in Marblehead, 22 Jan. 1714, Abigail Martin. Nothing further appears of him except that he had a daughter:
  1 Mary, b. 11 Nov. 1715; m.* 24 July 1730, Wm. Fabens.
2 Sarah,* m. in Marblehead, 28 Oct. 1721, Chas. Dennis.
3 Hepsibah, bap. 23 Jan. 1703. in Marblehead.
4 Beulah, bap. same day; m. 22 May 1727, John Williams.

*In all probability.

THIRD GENERATION.

1-1

CAPT. JOHN LIBBY, born in Scarborough, probably as early as 1665; married 29 Dec. 1690, ELEANOR KIRKE, dau. of Henry and Ruth (Glanfield) Kirke, of Portsmouth.

He accompanied his father to Portsmouth in 1690. He was a mechanic, and we find him mentioned at different times as housewright, millwright, and wheelwright. He, with his uncle Matthew Libby and others, went down to Scarborough and built a sawmill some years before 1720, and in the winter of 1729-30 he transferred his residence thither, and settled on the original homestead of his grandfather. He was part owner in, and probably the builder of, the gristmill on Libby River, a little below the bridge, afterward known as Fogg's mill. He acquired the title Captain in New Hampshire, and always retained it.

The time of his death is unknown, but it was between August, 1746, and December, 1751. The last time that his wife's name appears in any records is in January, 1734.

Their children* were:

1 Elizabeth, m. Seth Ring of Newington, N. H.
2 James, b. 1700; m. Mary Furber of Newington.
3 John, m. Mary Miller of Portsmouth.
4 Eleanor, b. 1704; m. Joseph Fogg, 9-7.
5 Jonathan, b. 1706; m. Martha Hasty of Scarborough.
6 Josiah, b. 1715; m. Anna Small of Scarborough.

1-2

JOSEPH LIBBY, born in Scarborough, probably as early as 1670; m. REBECCA ——.

His name first appears in the following deposition:

The Deposition of Joshua Peirce aged about twenty six years, who testificing saith

That yesterday being ye twenty fifth day of this Instant Novem^r^ I being in company with Coll Packer going up to his farme wee met with Tho:

*Capt. John Libby, like his father, disposed of his property in his lifetime. No full list of his children appears. He probably had a number of daughters whose names cannot be learned.

Perkins and two of Capt Pickren^{s} servants namely Tho: Pumery and Joseph Leby a driveing away a certain parcel of neat cattle of from ye land of ye s^{d} Coll Packer; ye cattle being reputed his owne namely Coll Packers; he required them to forbear driving away his cattle; and he turned ye cattle back through ye woods homeward afterward ye same day I being helping of m^{r} Packer to drive ye same parcel of cattle down to his own house att ye banke was met by Capt Pickren him selfe and Tho: Perkins att ye further end of Sherbuns Lane who forcibly took from us ye cattle, ye s^{d} Pickren did also say y^{t} he would detain ye cattle and did also abuse ye s^{d} Coll Packer in word^{s} and threatnd to strike him of his horse and to breake his bones farther sayth not:

I farther testifie y^{t} ye cattle above mentioned I saw y^{m} in ye pound and knew them to be cattle belonging to ye s^{d} Coll Packers farme

this 26 Novem^{r} 1696

Sworne in open Court Decemb^{r} 2^{d} 1696

attest Wm Redford Cer.

He lived in Portsmouth thirty-five years or more, but whether he died there, or moved away, does not appear.

Children, doubtless all born in Portsmouth:

1 Benjamin, b. 1693; m. Elizabeth Ham.

2 Joseph, m. 29 Dec. 1726, Elizabeth Meserve, of Dover. About 1731 he settled on a farm in Rochester, but after two or three years returned to Portsmouth, where the chief part of his life was spent as a sailor and fisherman. Nothing appears of him nor his wife after Nov. 1739, when they were both living in Portsmouth. Children:
   1 Daniel, bap. in Dover, 25 Feb. 1728.
   2 Rebecca, bap. 1729, in Greenland.

3 Joshua, m. Elizabeth ——.

4 Sarah.

5 Nathaniel (probably), m. Deborah ——, apparently a relative of John Beard and Josiah Ladd, of Exeter. In 1742 or 3 he removed from Portsmouth to Exeter, where he followed his calling of potter, and also kept a store in which he kept his wares for sale, and also a small quantity of staple merchandise. January, 1752, administration of his estate was granted to Josiah Thing. No children appear.

1-3

Samuel Libby, born in Scarborough, about 1674; married Sarah Wells, daughter of John Wells of Wells. He died a young man. He lived in Portsmouth, where his widow afterward married Samuel Waterhouse.

Children:*

1 Daniel, b. 1697; m. Martha Trickey 6 Nov. 1722, in Berwick, where he ever afterward lived. Little is known of him other than what appears from the following deposition:

The Deposition of Daniel Libby of Berwick in the County of York in the Seventy Sixth year of his age Testifieth and saith that he with Capt Humphry Chadbourn, Capt Ichabod Goodwin John Key Josiah Black Nicholas Sewall and sundry others to the Number of fourty four some time in the year 1722 or thereabouts went out from Berwick on Scout after the Indians thro the Country so far as Great Ossabe River & Pond and in

*No list of his children appears; there can be little doubt, however, that Daniel was his son, and quite likely he may have had daughters also.

their March on the southerly side of s[d] River the s[d] Chadbourn & Black who were then Elderly Men and as they sayd had been there before sayd to the Company they were near the place where one Franc[s] Small an Indian Trader formerly dwelt upon which in searching they soon found mark'd Trees which lead to a piece of ground which appeared to have been improv[d] by Planting as the Corn Hills appeared and a cellar in which he Enter'd wth Cap[t] Goodwin & others. There was also a Well and the s[d] Chadbourn & Black say'd that was Smalls Settlement and it lay near Great Ossobe Pond, the Depon[t] adds that he knows of none of the s[d] Company now Living save himself, Cap[t] Jon[a] Bane, Cap[t] Ichabod Goodwin & John Key Sep'. 6, 1773. DANIEL LIBBEY.

1-4

JAMES LIBBY, born in Scarborough, probably about 1676; married 9 June 1698, MARY HANSON, daughter of Isaac and Mary Hanson, of Portsmouth.

He grew up, and always lived in Portsmouth, where he followed the calling of house-carpenter. Among the New Hampshire state papers is preserved an order about *agreeing with James Libby, carpenter*, for finishing a line of fortifications near Portsmouth. He was at the first town meeting of Scarborough, and received large grants of land, which he afterward gave to his son James. Up to 1747 he lived on a farm, but in that year he sold to Col. Nath'l Meserve, and bought a house and garden-spot, where he died in 1754. He was a member of the Church of Christ. In 1712 he was constable "for the Bank," (Strawberry Bank), and afterward filled many town offices, from selectman, down.

The last mention of his wife Mary, who seems to have been the mother of all his children, was in Aug., 1718, and in 1736 he had married a second wife, whose name was Elizabeth. She outlived him ten years or more.

His children were:

1 James, b. 23 Nov. 1700; m. Elizabeth Meserve.*

---

*CLEMENT MESERVE came from New Hampshire to Scarborough soon after the second settlement. He was a carpenter. He died about 1740, leaving the following children:

1 Elizabeth, m. James Libby, 1-4-1.
2 Clement, m. Sarah ——.
3 Nathaniel, the celebrated New Hampshire colonel.
4 George.
+5 Daniel, m. Mehitable Bragdon.
6 Joseph.
+7 John, b. 21 Mar. 1708; m. Jemima Hubbard.

5 DEACON DANIEL MESERVE, lived and died in Scarborough. Children:

1 Daniel, b. 5 May 1739; m. Susannah ——.
2 Elisha, b. 19 Jan. 1741; m. Hannah Fogg, 9-8-6.
3 Solomon, b. 9 July 1743; m. Isabella Jordan.
4 Sarah, b. 27 June 1745; m. Joseph Libby, 11-7-6.
5 Nathaniel, b. 20 Apr. 1747; m. Anna Hunnewell, 7-1-2-7.
6 Gideon, b. 31 Jan. 1749; m. Elizabeth Fogg, 9-5-4-6.
7 Elizabeth, b. 5 Jan. 1754; m. Samuel Smith, of Arundel.
8 Abigail, b. 1756; m. David Fogg, 9-5-4-4.

7 JOHN MESERVE died in Scarborough, 9 Mar. 1763. His wife died 8 Dec. 176[illegible]. Their children were:

2 Mary, b. 14 Feb. 1703.
3 Sarah, b. 10 June 1705; died before 1751, leaving children.
4 Isaac, b. 3 Dec. 1707; m. Sarah Waldron of Dover.
5 John, m. 1st, Mary ——; 2d, Margaret Crussy.
6 Hanson, was a carpenter. His name last appears in his father's will, 1751.
7 Ichabod, m. Mary Jackson.
8 Shuah, } mentioned in their father's will, 1751.
9 Elizabeth, }

1-5

Daniel Libby, born in Scarborough, probably about 1678; married Elizabeth Kirke, a sister of his brother John's wife. He was a carpenter in Portsmouth, and died a young man, shortly before June 1712. His widow married 10 Nov. 1724, Daniel Meder, "a friend," and died before Oct. 1735.

Children:

1 Daniel, m. Eleanor ——. He was a miller. He died in Biddeford, where he had lived many years, in about the year 1740. His inventory mentioned five yokes of oxen and 46.442 feet of pine boards. His widow married Daniel Brooks. In the settlement of the estate, mention is made of *children*, but nothing further of them appears.
2 William, m. Elizabeth Goodwin.
3 Abigail, m. 2 May 1728, in Durham. Joseph Hill. Children:
  1 Abigail (Hill), m. 7 Nov. 1751, James Foss.
  2 Lydia (Hill), m. 1 Jan. 1752, James Marr. Children:

---

1 Dorothy, b. 13 Oct. 1733; m. Roger Libby. 1-1-2-3.
2 Abigail, b. 21 Feb. 1735; m. Elisha Libby, 10-5-1.
+3 John, b. 7 Dec. 1738; m. Abigail Small. [See page 33.]
4 George, b. 21 Dec. 1740; m Susanna Staples.
5 Mary, b. 19 Nov 1742; m. Nathaniel Libby. 10-5-5.
+6 William, b. 26 Oct 1744; m. Margery Deering.
7 Clement, b. 6 July 1746; m. Mary Jose.
8 Joseph, b. 1 Nov. 1748; m. Elizabeth Haines.
9 Thomas, b. 17 Oct. 1751; m. —— ——.

7-3 John Meserve died in Scarborough, 4 May 1804. His widow died 8 Feb. 1830. Their children were:

1 Joseph, b. 26 Oct. 1763; m. Mary Stone.
2 Dorothy, b. 4 Apr. 1765; m. Mark Marr, of Limington.
3 Abigail, died aged 2 or 3 years.
4 John, died young.
5 Benjamin, m. Hannah McKenney.
6 Samuel Small, b. 3 Dec. 1772; m. Elizabeth McDaniel.
+7 John, b. 26 Sept. 1779; m. Anna, dau. of Philip and Sally (Smith) Larrabee. [See under 5-2.]
8 Anna, b. 29 Sept. 1783; d. 5 May 1849; unm.

7-6 William Meserve died 24 Feb. 1827, in Scarborough His widow died 13 Mar. 1837. Their children were:

1 John, b. 7 Aug. 1767; m. Hannah Libby, 11-7-2-8.
2 Jane, b. 2 May 1770; m. Jacob Larrabee.
3 Dorothy, b. 7 Mar. 1773; m. Isaac Libby, 10-5-6-5.
4 Keziah, b. 17 Nov. 1776; m. Humphrey Libby, 10-5-6-8.
5 William, died aged 2 years.

7-3-7 John Meserve died 18 Jan. 1866. His wife died 28 Mar. 1860. Their children were:

1 Abigail, b. 21 Nov. 1803; m. Woodbury Libby, 11-7-2-6-8.
2 Sally, b. 21 Aug. 1805.
3 Joseph, b. 4 Oct. 1808; d. 8 Apr. 1877; unm.
4 Horace, b. 20 June 1811; m. Esther Libby, 11-7-2-6-13.
5 Mary, b. 14 Mar. 1814.
6 Nancy, m. Converse Libby, 10-2-4-3-1-4.

1 John (Marr), bap. 1752; m. Sarah Jordan.
2 James (Marr), bap. 1754; m. Lydia Libby, 11-7-2-5.
3 Mercy (Marr), m. Reuben Libby, 10-5-2-3.
4 William (Marr), probably died young.
5 Lydia (Marr), m. George Fogg, 9-5-4-9.
6 Catherine (Marr), unmarried in 1804.
7 Abigail (Marr), m. 29 Dec. 1797, Jos. Calef.
8 Daniel (Marr), m. Elizabeth Sawyer.
9 Rufus (Marr), m. Lucy March, 11-6-1-14.

3 Susannah (Hill), m. 15 July 1755, Nathl. Jordan.
4 Elizabeth (Hill), m. Thomas Millett, of Falmouth.
5 Daniel (Hill), of Scarborough in 1762.
6 Mary (Hill), of Scarborough, unmarried in 1762.

4 Samuel, b. about 1707; died 1734; unm. He lived in Scarborough and Falmouth, and acquired considerable real estate in each town.

1-6

DEACON BENJAMIN LIBBY, born in Scarborough, 4 June 1682; married 20 Dec. 1707, SARAH STONE, daughter of Daniel and Patience (Goodwin) Stone, of Kittery.

He was carried by his father to Portsmouth in 1690, and afterward went to Berwick and "lived and served his time" seven years with Col. John Plaisted. He never left Berwick, but settled near what is now South Berwick Junction, on the "Witchtrot" road, and there lived until his death.

Deacon Libby was for many years one of the principal inhabitants of the town; frequently placed on the most important town committees, often presiding over the meetings of the town, and from 1719 to 1736, selectman. He was one of the original proprietors of Lebanon and took a prominent part in the early management of that township. 16 Sept. 1725, he was chosen deacon of the Congregational church, of which he and his wife had been members from 7 Oct. 1716, and filled that position until 25 June 1761. There is a record of special thanks voted him for his services. He died 9 Nov. 1768. Whether his wife died before or after is unknown, but she was living as late as February, 1764.

Their children were:

1 Agnes, b. 24 May 1709; m. ——— Clark.
2 Joseph, } twins, born } m. Anna ———, and Mrs. Eliz. Shorey.
3 Benjamin, } 5 Apr. 1711; } m. Sarah ———; died 1734. Probably it was his widow that was of Boston in 1754, and was put under guardianship as being *non compos mentis*. The children of Benjamin Libby were:

1 Paul, bap. 1733; m. 31 Dec. 1758, Meribah Lord. He was a farmer in the North Parish of Berwick as late as 1784. No children appear.
2 Anna, bap. 9 Feb. 1734-5; m. 1755, Joshua Brackett.

The widow Libby bore to Benjamin Chadbourne a child:
a Mary, bap. Dec. 1741.

4 Sarah, b. 8 Feb. 1713; m. ——— Lord.
5 Daniel, b. 21 Feb. 1715; m. Abigail ———, and Lois (Jones) Wentworth.
6 Mary, b. 8 May 1717; m. ——— Hodgdon.
7 Jeremiah, b. 9 Jan. 1719; } died without issue; probably unmarried.
8 Anna, b. 1 Mar. 1720; }
9 Charles, b. 29 Dec. 1721; m. Abigail Hilton.
10 Elisha, bap. 24 May 1724; died young.

1-7

JEREMIAH LIBBY, born in Scarborough in 1689; married 28 April 1715, LYDIA BADGER, daughter of John and Hannah (Swett) Badger, of Portsmouth.

He was ten months old when his father was driven from his home in Scarborough, and fled to Portsmouth. In Portsmouth he ever afterward lived, and practiced successfully the calling of house-carpenter. He took no active part in town affairs, but that he had the confidence and esteem of his townsmen is evident from his being several times on important committees, and that he was at times chosen moderator of the town meetings. He and his wife were both members of the Church of Christ. She died before him by a number of years. He died in the spring of 1766, having outlived six of his eight children.

They were:

1 Jeremiah, b. 21 Feb. 1717; m. 1st, Mary Symmes; 2d, Sarah Newmarch.
2 George, b. 20 Jan. 1719; m. Elizabeth ——.
3 John, b. 2 Nov. 1720; probably died without issue, as he was not mentioned in his father's will.
4 Lydia, b. 18 Oct. 1722; m. —— Brown. She lived to a great age, and died with her nephew, Jeremiah Libby, Esq., 1-7-1-2.
5 Sarah, died in infancy.
6 Theodore, b. 10 Dec. 1726; m. —— ——.
7 Sarah, b. 21 Oct. 1728; probably married an Ayres, as her father, in his will, mentioned his grand-daughter, Hannah Ayres.
8 Abigail, m. —— Pike.

5-2

LIEUT. SAMUEL LIBBY, born in Scarborough, 6 July 1689; married first, 29 Feb. 1727, ABIGAIL MESERVE; (died 10 Nov. 1734); second, 17 Jan. 1739, MARY JONES, daughter of John and Joanna (Cotton*) Jones,* of Scarborough. She died in June, 1754.

In the flight from Scarborough in 1690, he was carried to Lynn, Mass., and there he must have received his education, which was much superior to that of most of the second settlers of Scarborough. He was present at the first town meeting, and was chosen clerk. From that time on he took a leading part in the affairs of both town and church. In February, 1726, it was voted by the town that divine services should be held "one Sabbath day at the house of Col. Westbrook at Dunstan, and another at the house of Samuel Libby on Black Point," that is, alternately. In May, 1728, he was on the committee chosen to oversee the building of the meeting-house. It was built a few rods north of his house, and the land between became the burying-ground, into which, a few years since, the site of his house was taken. He filled nearly all the offices in the gift of the town. He was clerk during the first six years of the town's organization; selectman from 1721 to 1742,

*Both natives of Portsmouth, N. H.

except the year 1727; and frequently moderator, and placed on the most important committees.

He was a skilled land-surveyor, and probably surveyed more during the thirty years that succeeded the re-organization of the town in 1720, than any other man in that region. He was lot-layer for the proprietors, and was also proprietors' clerk from 1727 until old age. In his latter days he became very feeble, and during the last fifteen years of his life his townsmen had to look to others for the many services which they had been accustomed to receive from him. He died 1 Jan. 1770.

His children by his first wife, were:

1 Asa, b. 6 Sept. 1731. } doubtless died young.
2 Amy, b. 10 Aug. 1733, }

By his second wife:

3 Ebenezer, b. 9 Nov. 1740; m. Miriam Larrabee.*

---

*WILLIAM LARRABEE, tradition says, was a Frenchman. He married, Nov. 1655, in Malden, Mass., Elizabeth, dau. of George and Elizabeth (Wilkinson) Felt. George Felt was the most prominent of the early settlers of North Yarmouth, Me., and thither his son-in-law, Larrabee, removed. He bought land of an Indian named Warromby. It was probably during Philip's war that he returned to Malden, where he died. His will was probated 24 Oct. 1692. His children were:

1 Stephen, m. Isabel ——; lived in Malden.
2 William, b. 1658; m. Catherine ——; lived in Wells, Me.
+3 Thomas, m. Elizabeth ——.
4 John (probably), returned "beyond the sea."
5 Isaac b. 1664; lived in Lynn, Mass.
6 Benjamin, b. 1666; m. Deborah Ingersol; lived in Falmouth, Me.
7 Samuel, died before 1727.

3 THOMAS LARRABEE, settled in Scarborough; fled to Kittery, 1790; returned at the second settlement of Scarborough; was killed by the Indians, with his son Anthony, 19 Apr. 1723. He lived, was killed, and was buried, on the "ten acre home lot," on the west side of Black Point road, which now forms part of the Storer Libby (11-7-2-4-8) homestead. Children:

+1 Thomas, m. Abigail Pitman, May, 1815.
2 Eleanor, m. 1 Dec. 1715, Christopher Mitchell.
3 Anthony, was killed with his father, 19 Apr. 1723.
+4 Benjamin, b. 1700; m. Sarah Johnson.
+5 John, m. Mary Ingersol.
6 Hannah, m. 28 Feb. 1737, Benjamin Richards.
7 Jane.

3-1 THOMAS LARRABEE, lived in Kittery, Portsmouth, and Scarborough. No list of his children appears, but they were probably as follows:

1 Abigail, m. James Libby, 5-4.
2 Samuel, m. Sarah Brown.
3 Thomas, m. Mary ——.
4 Isaac, m. Deborah Larrabee, 3-5-2; settled in Machias.
5 Ezekiel, bap. 10 June 1733; died young.
6 Joseph, bap. 8 Jan. 1737.
7 Ezekiel, bap. 23 Apr. 1738.
8 Olive, bap. 12 June 1743; m. 12 Nov. 1760, Joseph Drisco.

3-4 BENJAMIN LARRABEE, born 1700; lived on Pleasant Hill, in Scarborough; died 17 Dec. 1763. His widow died 26 Dec. 1789. Children:

1 William, b. 2 May 1727; m. Mary Burns, Lydia Mitchell, Lucy Stone, and Abigail Dyer.
2 Sarah, b. 28 June 1729; m. 19 Oct. 1755, John Adams.
3 Hannah, } twins, b. 18 May 1732; { m. Deacon Joshua Libby, 11-7-2.
4 Elizabeth, } { m. 1st, John Watson; 2d, Robert Hasty. [See under 1-1-5.]
5 Lydia, b. 6 Apr. 1736; m. Moses Fogg, 9-6-6.
6 Benjamin, b. 23 Mar. 1740; m. Hannah (Hasty) Skillings. [See under 1-1-5.] He was a captain in the Revolution, colonel in the militia, representative to the General Court of Massachusetts, etc. Children:

4 Lemuel, b. 1 March 1743; died young.
5 Abigail, b. 7 Jan. 1745; m. 5 Feb. 1771, John Warren of Scarborough, afterward of New Gloucester.
6 Ezekiel, b. 13 Feb. 1747; m. 17 Mar. 1779, Sarah, daughter of Wm. Larrabee. [See page 41.] He was drowned shortly after at Machias, and his widow married, 27 Oct. 1782, Josiah Milliken. No children.
7 Nehemiah, b. 14 May 1749; m. Abigail Hunnewell, 7-1-2-8.

5-7

Capt. John Libby, born probably soon after the year 1700; married first, 15 June 1728, Mary Goodwin, daughter of Wm. and Deliverance (Taylor) Goodwin, of Berwick; (died after a few years); second, 24 Aug. 1738, Anna Fogg, 9-5-2.

He accompanied his father from Lynn to Scarborough, and settled on a farm. His house was on Oak Hill, on the north side of what afterward became the post-road between Portland and Saco, a little west of the road leading to Gorham Corner.

He was a man of unusual energy and ability, and filled repeatedly the most important positions in the town. We find him chosen "to locate Black Point school," and "to inspect the law relative to the killing of deer." He was also a land surveyor and succeeded in a measure to the position which his brother had filled. He was lieutenant in Capt. George Berry's company in 1745, and after the death of Capt. John Libby, 1-1, became known as Captain, and retained that epithet until his death, which was the result of an accident. He was on a fishing trip, with two others, and the small boat in which they were was upset near the mouth of Nonesuch River, and although an expert swimmer, he never rose. The two others escaped, and there were suspicions of foul play at the time of his death.

His children, by his first wife, were:

1 Henry, b. 6 Oct. 1729; doubtless died young.
2 Hannah, b. 4 Mar. 1731; m. John Fogg, 9-6-2.
3 Lucy, bap. June 1735; died in infancy.
4 Edward, b. 21 June 1736; doubtless died young.

---

1 Hannah, b. 8 June 1779; died unm., aged 28.
2 Benjamin, b. 24 June 1781; m. Susannah Libby, 5-7-14-3.
3 Joseph, b. 22 Feb. 1788; m. Phebe Libby, 5-7-14-6.
7 Miriam, b. 24 Feb. 1744; m. Ebenezer Libby, 5-2-3.

3-5 John Larrabee, lived and died in Scarborough. Children:

1 John, died in infancy.
2 Deborah, b. 24 July 1728; m. Isaac Larrabee, 3-1-4.
3 Solomon, b. 7 Oct. 1731; m. Elizabeth Winter; died 6 Aug. 1759. Only child:
 1 Phebe, m. 18 Aug. 1774, Joseph Gilkey of Gorham.
4 Mary, b. 29 Apr. 1736; m. Thomas Libby, 10-1-8.
5 Stephen, b. 3 Nov. 1738; m. Hannah McKenney. [See under 5-2-3.]
6 Phebe, b. 26 Aug. 1740.
7 Eunice, b. 24 Nov. 1741; m. Moses McKenney. [See under 5-2-3.]
8 Philip, b. 3 Mar. 1744; m. Sally Smith.
9 John, b. 23 Apr. 1746.
10 Jonathan, b. 16 Apr. 1748; m. Alice Davis.

By his second wife:

5 Rhoda, } twins, born { probably died young.
6 Abner, } 4 July 1739; { m. 29 Nov. 1762, Lucy Hunnewell, 7-1-2-6. He "went off and never was heard from." It was probably his widow that married, 1 Dec. 1767, George Berry of Georgetown.
7 Olive, b. 6 Feb. 1741; probably died young.
8 Stephen, b. 13 Jan. 1743; m. Margaret Miller.
9 Moses, } twins, born { died young.
10 Aaron, } 18 Mar. 1745; { m. Elizabeth Weeman.
11 Jesse, bap. March 1747; m. Keziah March, 11-6-1-1.
12 Philemon, b. 29 May 1749; m. Martha Small.
13 Eunice, b. 22 Oct. 1752; m. Major Josiah Libby, 1-1-6-4.
14 Seth, b. 1 May 1755; m. Lydia Jordan.

By Lydia (Skillings), widow of Mark Libby, 10-5-3:

15 Nathan,* b. 16 Aug. 1766; m. Abigail Davis, 11-1-8-1.

6-3

ABRAHAM LIBBY, born in Hampton, N. H., about 1688; married 14 Jan. 1713, SABINA PHILBRICK, daughter of Joseph and Tryphene Philbrick, of Hampton.

He was a farmer. He lived in Hampton until 1718 or 19, and then moved to Portsmouth, onto a farm which he had purchased. There he abode until the spring of 1757, when he moved to North Hampton. Within a year he moved to Exeter, where he lived two or three years, near the "old pickpocket mill." Thence he moved to Epsom, where he died in the spring of 1767. His wife died probably before he left Portsmouth.

Their children were:

1 Betty, b. 6 Oct. 1713; m. 19 July, 1733, Ephraim Holmes, of Barrington.
2 Joseph, b. 15 Aug. 1715; m. Margaret Abbot.
3 Sarah, b. 4 Nov. 1717; m. 17 Jan. 1744, Penuel Chapman.
4 Phebe, b. 15 April 1720; }
5 Abraham, b. 2 May 1722; } probably died young.
6 Anthony, b. 13 Dec. 1724; }
7 Ephraim, bap. 1734; }

6-4

ISAAC LIBBY, born about 1690, in Hampton, N. H.; married MARY ———.

He was a farmer, and spent the chief part of his life in Rye. He took an active part in the settlement of Epsom, and for a number of years he doubtless divided his time between those two places. That he was a man of good ability is evident from the positions to which he was chosen by his townsmen. He was chairman of the committee which built the first meeting-house in Epsom, 1663. He probably died there in Epsom about ten years later.

---

*He was brought up by his mother, and really derived his surname from her; but rather than give him the broken number, 1-5-3-a, which he must have had, it seems preferable to the compiler to place him in his true descent.

Children:

1 John, b. 1 Aug. 1720; m. Eleanor Berry.
2 Mary, b. 4 Nov. 1722; m.* 11 Oct. 1744, James Knowles.
3 Elizabeth, } twins, b. } m.* 11 Oct. 1744, Amos Knowles.
4 Isaac, } 28 Feb. 1725; } m. 1st, Ann Symmes; 2d, Margaret Kalderwood.
5 Arthur, b. 5 April 1728; m. Deborah Smith.
6 Ruth, b. 5 Sept. 1730; m.,† perhaps, 27 Sept. 1753, Jos. Edmunds.
7 Jane, b. 11 Sept. 1733.
8 Reuben, b. 11 Aug. 1734; m. 1st, Sarah Goss; 2d, Sarah Tucker.
9 Joanna, b. 16 Oct. 1737; m. 2 Nov. 1761, Amos Blazo, of Chichester; moved to North Parsonsfield, Me., 1778; died there 30 Aug. 1810.

6-6

JACOB LIBBY, born in Hampton, 25 May 1695; married, 29 Oct. 1719, SARAH MARSTON, born 29 May 1699, daughter of Samuel and Sarah Marston, of Hampton.

He had his father's homestead, and it is thought he always lived on it. His son Abraham lived at home, and he probably died with him, soon after 1765.

Their children were:

1 Samuel, b. 9 Feb. 1720; m. 1st, Abigail Symmes; 2d, Penelope (Huntingdon) Barber.
2 Anthony, b. 7 Jan. 1722; d. young.
3 Sarah, b. 2 Feb. 1724-5; m. 24 Nov. 1743, Samuel Blake.
4 Ruth, b. 21 Jan. 1727; m., perhaps, 27 Sept. 1753, Jos. Edmunds.
5 Jacob, b. 25 July 1729; d. young.
6 Hannah, b. June 1731; m.* Benjamin Jenness, 16 Mar. 1752.
7 Job, b. 15 Jan. 1734-5; died young.
8 Joseph, } twins, b. } m. Mary ——.
9 Benjamin, } 25 Feb. 1737; } m. 1st, Jane ——; 2d, Abigail Haines.
10 Abraham, b. 29 Dec. 1739; m. 1st, Abigail Page; 2d, Mary Tarlton.
11 Hepsibah, bap. Aug. 1742; probably died young.

7-1

ANDREW BROWN, born probably in Scarborough; married SUSANNAH ———. He removed from Portsmouth to Scarborough after the second settlement, and continued there until his death.

Children:

1 Rebecca (Brown), m. 16 Nov. 1730, Josiah Hunnewell. Children: 1 Mary (Hunnewell); 2 John; 3 Andrew; 4 Abigail; 5 Jonathan; 6 Zerubbabel; 7 Benjamin; 8 Leah; 9 Sarah; 10 Sarah.
2 Hannah (Brown), m. 1731, Richard Hunnewell.‖

*Probably.
†Joseph Edmunds married Ruth Libby, either 6-6-4, or 6-4-6.

‖ROGER HUNNEWELL settled in Saco and died in 1654. He had at least two sons:

1 John, settled in Wethersfield, Conn. He married Elizabeth, daughter of Daniel Harris of Middletown.
+2 Richard, settled in Scarborough.

2 LT. RICHARD HUNNEWELL was one of the leading inhabitants of Scarborough.

3 Abigail (Brown).
4 Susannah (Brown).
5 Sarah (Brown), m., as second wife, Richard Hunnewell.
6 Joshua (Brown), m. Hannah Pollow, 5-5-1.

9-5

CAPT. DANIEL FOGG, born probably in Portsmouth, 12 April 1694; m. 30 July 1715, ANNA HANSCOM, daughter of Thomas and Alice Hanscom, of Kittery.

He lived in Kittery until 1727, and then moved to Scarborough, and settled on Libby River, opposite the original Libby homestead. He was for many years one of the principal men in the town, and died 1 Dec. 1782. His wife died 15 April 1775.

Their children, born in Kittery, were:

1 Samuel (Fogg), b. 1 June 1716; m. Rachel Marmer.
2 Anna (Fogg), b. 16 Feb. 1718; m. John Libby, 5-7.
3 Hannah (Fogg), b. 12 Nov. 1719; m. 8 Sept. 1743, Wm. Hasty.
4 Reuben (Fogg), b. 1 June 1722; m. Margaret Elder.
5 Mary (Fogg), b. 28 July 1724; m. 13 Nov. 1746, Geo. Hanscom.
6 Keturah (Fogg), b. 5 Feb. 1727, probably in Kittery; m. Elisha Hanscom.

Born in Scarborough:

7 Esther (Fogg), b. 13 Oct. 1729; m. Elisha Libby, 10-5-1.
8 Rhoda (Fogg), b. 15 Mar. 1733; probably died young.
9 Daniel (Fogg), b. 5 Dec. 1735; m. Sarah Scott.* He became one of the first settlers of Machias, and died there 7 Feb. 1766. To use the words of the record made by his niece, Anna (Fogg) Roberts, 9-5-1-7, "He was killed by the fall of a limb, which unhappily fell from the tree on which he was cutting."

9-6

JOHN FOGG, born probably in Portsmouth, about 1696; married 30 Sept. 1725, MARY HANSCOM. He removed to Scarborough, and settled on the farm now occupied by William and John Fogg, 9-6-6-4-4-1 and 3. There he died, in the year 1749.

Children, all born in Scarborough:

1 Mary (Fogg), b. 30 June 1727; d. young.
2 John (Fogg), b. 12 Oct. 1729; m. Hannah Libby, 5-7-2.
3 Sarah (Fogg), b. 10 Feb. 1732; d. young.

His wife was a daughter of Richard Moore. He was a noted killer of Indians, and finally lost his life at their hands. Child:

1 Roger, married Mary ——.

2-1 ROGER HUNNEWELL returned to Scarborough at the second settlement of the town, and died 13 June 1720, aged 45. His widow out-lived him many years. Children:

1 Josiah. See above.
2 Richard. See above.
3 Elizabeth, m. Robert Gilmore, of Londonderry, N. H.
4 Zerubbabel, b. 15 Apr. 1716. He settled in Windham, and had sons Nathaniel, Zerubbabel, William, and Elijah.
5 Roger, b. 28 Dec. 1719; m. 7 Nov. 1750, Lydia Ervine; d. 27 Dec. 1810. His widow died 14 Dec. 1811. Children: Jane, b. 24 May 1752; Jesse, b. 1754, died young; Richard, b. 26 Feb. 1756; Roger, b. 14 July 1758; Lydia, b 21 Jan. 1761; Martha, b. 8 Dec. 1763, m. 6 Aug. 1789, James Robinson; Mary, b. 21 Mar. 1767; John, b. 4 Jan. 1770.

4 Hannah (Fogg), b. 27 April 1734: d. young.
5 Abigail (Fogg), b. 20 July 1736; m. George Hanscom.
6 Moses (Fogg), b. 14 Oct. 1738; m. Lydia Larrabee, and Catherine Libby, 1-1-5-5.
7 Jonathan (Fogg), b. 13 Feb. 1741; m. Anna Maxwell.
8 Joseph (Fogg), b. 29 June 1743; m. Mercy Berry.
9 Mary (Fogg), b. 18 Nov. 1746.

9-8

SETH FOGG, born in Kittery, now Eliot, Dec. 1701; married 28 Nov. 1727, MARY PICKERNALE, daughter of John Pickernale of Kittery. He settled in Scarborough, on Scottow's hill, and there died in the fall of 1748.

His children were:

1 Seth (Fogg), b. probably in Kittery; m. Ruth Waterhouse, 10-2-2-1.
2 Timothy (Fogg), b. 19 June 1732; m. 15 April 1760, Abigail Hanscom. Children: 1 Benning; 2 Simon; 3 Timothy; 4 Eunice. In 1773 he moved to Gray.
3 Lydia (Fogg), b. 5 April 1734; m. 18 July 1754, Isaiah Foster.
4 James (Fogg), b. 8 April 1736; m. 9 June 1757, Molly Scammon. Children: 1 John Scammon (Fogg); 2 Nelson; 3 Hannah; 4 James; 5 Welmot; 6 Isaac; 7 Scammon; 8 Silas.
5 Mary (Fogg), b. 11 Oct. 1738; m. 17 Nov. 1757, Ezekiel Foster.
6 Hannah (Fogg), b. 24 May 1741; m. 17 Nov. 1757, Elisha Meserve.
7 Benning (Fogg), b. 27 June 1744; d. young.

9-9

JAMES FOGG, born in Eliot, 17 Mar. 1704; married 23 Oct. 1728, ELIZABETH FERNALD, daughter of Dea. James and Mary Fernald, of Kittery.

He lived and died on the farm where he was born. His death occurred 24 Dec. 1787. His wife died about 1766.

Their children were:

1 James (Fogg), b. 23 June 1731; m. 1st, Anne Remmick; (died Apr. 1783); 2d, about 1800, Mary Twambly. He died in Wolfborough, N. H., on a visit to his daughter, in 1805. Children:
  1 Mark (Fogg), b. 15 July 1757; m. 1st, Eunice Fernald; 2d, Mary Keay: settled in Wolfborough.
  2 Anne (Fogg), b. 28 Jan. 1761; m. 19 Dec. 1781, Stephen Randall.
  3 James (Fogg), b. 12 Sept. 1763; m. Sarah Keay.
  4 Elizabeth (Fogg), b. 26 Apr. 1765; d. 1778.
  5 Joseph (Fogg), b. 8 Feb. 1767; m. 1st, Mary Hammond; 2d, Lydia Keay. He settled first in Wolfborough and then in eastern Maine.
  6 John (Fogg), b. 7 Mar. 1769; was drowned in Union River in 1781.
  7 Susannah (Fogg) b. 29 Apr. 1771; m. 25 July 1793, Aaron Chick.
  8 Mary (Fogg), b. 12 Oct. 1773; m. Love Keay.
  9 Simon (Fogg), b. 8 Feb. 1777; m. Lydia Felch.
  10 Elizabeth (Fogg), b. 27 May 1779; m. James Brackett.
  11 Levi (Fogg), b. 2 Mar. 1783; m. Mary Perkins; settled in Brunswick, Me.
2 Mary (Fogg), b. 21 Feb. 1734; m. 4 July 1752, James Emery of Eliot.
3 Elizabeth (Fogg), b. 2 Sept. 1737; m. Nathaniel Libby, 11-9-5.

4 Anne (Fogg), b. 2 Mar. 1739; m. 1767, John Toby of Eliot.
5 Hannah (Fogg), b. 24 July 1741; d. 10 Dec. 1819; unm.
6 Eunice (Fogg), b. 12 Nov. 1743; m. Capt. Josiah Staples.
7 Joseph (Fogg), b. 12 Feb. 1745; m. Mary Littlefield. He settled in Berwick, where he died 30 Sept. 1807. Children:
   1 Joseph (Fogg), b. 9 Feb. 1772; m. Phebe Hayes.
   2 Daniel (Fogg), b. 29 Aug. 177 ; m. Peggy Hodgdon.
   3 Jane (Fogg), b. 10 May 1776; m. David Hodgdon.
   4 James (Fogg), b. 10 Aug. 1781; m. Olive Hodgdon.
   5 Isaac (Fogg), b. 13 Nov. 1783; m. Susannah Hayes.
8 Abigail (Fogg), b. about 1747; d. aged 2 or 3 years.
9 John (Fogg), b. 17 Sept. 1750; m. Abigail Leighton.
10 Daniel (Fogg), b. 24 Sept. 1752; died young.

10-1

David Libby, born probably in Scarborough before his parents were driven away in 1690; married Esther Hanscom, daughter of Thomas and Alice Hanscom, of Kittery.

He lived on a part of his father's homestead, in Kittery, now Eliot, until about 1731. During a portion of that time he was a licensed retailer. From Kittery he moved to Scarborough, and settled on a farm on Scottow's Hill. His house was a garrison, and stood about two rods southeast of the late residence of Leonard Libby, 10-2-4-8-6. There it was that Nathaniel Dresser was killed by the Indians. David Libby shot the Indian that did the deed, and wounded him so severely that he died soon after. David Libby died in February, 1765, and was buried on the 6th of that month. His wife died in March, 1761. They were doubtless both buried a few rods northeast of the house of Lemuel Libby, mentioned above. This spot was for many years the principal burying-ground of the inhabitants of that locality, and it is said that more than a hundred interments were made there; but it is now covered by a dense growth of shrubs and underbrush, and not more than three or four graves are discernible.

The children of David and Esther Libby were:

1 Alice, b. 28 Nov. 1714; m. 2 Sept. 1736, Solomon Stone.
2 Josiah, b. 25 Oct. 1716; m. Mary Stone.
3 George, b. 18 Jan. 1719; d. 15 Jan. 1790; unm. He was one of the original settlers of Machias, 1763, and from that year until his death divided his time between that place and Scarborough. He gave to the town of Machias the lot on which the town hall now stands. "On a part of this lot 'sleep the rude forefathers of the hamlet.' It has also been the site successively of two churches. In 1850, the old meeting-house standing on this lot, though not occupied for some years as a place of worship, was taken down by the town, which erected upon the same spot a large and handsome edifice, containing convenient and spacious rooms for two high schools and a commodious town hall. To this building the town voted should be given the name of Libby Hall, in honor of George Libby, and in remembrance of his generous gift of the land to the people of Machias."* He died with his nephew, Thomas Libby, 10-1-8-1, to whom he had given the farm which became his homestead.

*Letter of Peter Thatcher, Esq., to the author of the History of Scarborough.

4 Esther, b. 7 Apr. 1721; m. 9 June 1740, William Harmon.
5 Timothy, married Sarah Stone.
6 David, married Dorcas Means, and Joanna (Jose) Page.
7 Eleanor, bap. in Scarborough, Aug. 1731; died young.
8 Thomas, b. 16 Nov. 1833; m. Mary Larrabee.

10-2

Samuel Libby, born about 1690; married 31 May 1713, Mary Libby, 11-3.

He was reared in that part of Kittery which is now Eliot, and became a carpenter. He built him a house on a portion of the homestead of his father-in-law, his uncle Matthew Libby, and there lived until about 1731. He then removed to Scarborough and settled on the farm now occupied by Samuel Manson Libby, 10-2-4-9-3. He was a thrifty, enterprising man, and accumulated a large property for those times. His inventory mentions his homestead, (valued at £280), 322 acres of land beside, half a sawmill, a negro man, (his name was Nimrod), eight oxen, eight cows, four steers, four heifers, one horse, one bull, thirty sheep, four swine, a clock, (this was in 1754), one-eighth of a sloop, one-sixth and one-sixteenth of a schooner, and a pew in the meeting-house. He was buried 15 May 1754. His wife outlived him twenty years, and died in January, 1774.

Their children were:

1 Samuel, b. 7 July 1714; m. Elizabeth Hubbard.
2 Mary, b. 12 Apr. 1716 or 17; m. Joseph Waterhouse.
3 Olive, m. 21 Feb. 1739. Theophilus Smith of Saco.
4 Enock, m. Elizabeth Plummer.
5 Abigail, b. 2 Mar. 1733; m. 9 Jan. 1752, Josiah Graffam.

10-4

Solomon Libby, born probably in Portsmouth, about 1695; married, 4 Mar. 1725, Martha Hanscom, daughter of Thomas and Tamsen Hanscom, a half-sister of his brother David's wife.

He was a carpenter, and at first built him a house on his father's land, southwest of the road. He afterward came into possession of the twenty acres on the northeast side of the road, on which his brother David lived until his removal to Scarborough, and there lived until the time of his death, which occurred in the spring of 1756. He had acquired considerable real estate, and settled each of his sons on a farm. His homestead he gave to Nathan. His widow died in February, 1789, having outlived her husband thirty-three years.

Their children were:

1 Joseph, b. 14 Dec. 1725; m. Shuah Staples.
2 Gideon, b. 20 July 1728; was dumb; died at an early age.
3 Reuben, b. 29 Aug. 1731; m. Catherine Staples.
4 Anna, b. 20 Dec. 1733; m. David Staples.
5 Martha, bap. Nov. 1738; was deaf and dumb; lived to an advanced age; unm.
6 Nathan, bap. Sept. 1740; m. Jemima (Littlefield) Shapleigh.
7 Simon, bap. May 1745; d. 1776; unm. He was a housewright.
8 Eunice, died without issue, probably in childhood.

10-5

JOHN LIBBY, born probably in Portsmouth, about 1697; married, 14 Nov. 1724, SARAH LIBBY, 11-8.

He received from his father by deed of gift bearing date March, 1719, all his lands in Scarborough, and doubtless moved at once to his father's old home, as he was present at the first town meeting. His farm, on which he lived and died, included the present Robinson homestead and the land on both sides of the road between that and the *old* Fogg farm. (The present Fogg farm includes part of the Libby homestead.) Three of his sons, Matthew, Nathaniel, and Luke, he settled on parts of his homestead, and to Elisha and Allison, he gave lands in the interior of the town. He had an extra finger on each hand, below the little finger, and from this was called, to distinguish him from the other John Libbys in Scarborough at that time, Five Fingered John Libby.* After the death of his wife Sarah, he married, 9 Jan. 1755, Deborah Dunnivan of Falmouth, who probably died before him. He died 1 July 1764.

Children, all born in Scarborough:

1 Elisha, b. 1725; m. Esther Fogg, 9-5-7, and Abigail Meserve.
2 Matthew, b. 25 Feb. 1729; m. Sarah Hanscom and Hannah Hasty.
3 Mark, b. 8 June 1731; m. Lydia Skillings.
4 Allison, b. 12 Sept. 1733; m. Sarah Skillings, and Mary Libby, 1-1-3-10.
5 Nathaniel, b. 5 Sept. 1735; m. Mary Meserve.
6 Luke, b. 15 Aug. 1738; m. Dorothy McKenney.
7 John, b. 15 Sept. 1744; never married. He was a mental imbecile. His father, at his death, provided for his support. He died in middle age.

10-7

EPHRAIM LIBBY, born in Kittery, now Eliot, 2 Feb. 1702; married, 1728, MARY AMBLER, daughter of John and Elizabeth (Trickey) Ambler of Dover, N. H.

He received from his father by will the home lot of the homestead farm, and lived and died on the spot on which he was born. His death occurred in the winter of 1776-7. His wife outlived him.

Their children were:

1 Ephraim, b. 22 Mar. 1732; m. Sarah Morrill and Anne Spinney.
2 Eleanor, b. 26 Nov. 1734; m. 20 Jan. 1759, Thomas Langley of Durham, N. H.
3 John, b. 2 May 1737; was impressed in the French war; marched 3 Sept. 1755, and never returned. He died in the service.
4 Mary, m. 1763, William Spinney.
5 Abigail, m. Thomas Allison.

*The other John Libbys were called respectively: John Libby, 1-1. *Captain John*; his son John, *Blue John*; John Libby, 5-7, *Black John*, and later, *Captain John*: John Libby, 1-1-2-1, *Little John*. There was also John Libby, 11-6, living at the same time, but his nickname, if he had any, is unknown. These names seldom appear in the records, but the places were supplied either by numbers, second, third, etc., or by stating the father's name. In the latter method occur frequent illustrations of the original formation of the patronymic class of surnames. John Libby, John's son; John Libby, Henry's son; and John Libby, David's son, were frequently written John Libby Johnson, John Libby Henryson, and John Libby Davidson: so that to a casual reader, *Johnson*, *Henryson* and *Davidson* would seem to be the surnames of the men, and *Libby* only a *middle* name.

10-8

Eleanor Libby, born in Kittery, Me., 21 June 1705; married, 1727, Zebulon Trickey. They moved at once to Scarborough, and settled at Black Point, but a few years after removed to that part of Falmouth which is now Cape Elizabeth. There he died, and she married second, 1757, Lieut. Andrew Libby, 11-7.

Children of Zebulon and Eleanor Trickey:

1 Eleanor (Trickey), b. 13 Oct. 1728, in Scarborough.
2 Rebecca (Trickey), b. 13 Mar. 1731, in Scarborough.
3 Mary (Trickey), b. 2 Aug. 1733, in Scarborough.
They probably all died young, as nothing more appears of them.
4 Zebulon (Trickey), b. 20 July 1736, in Falmouth; m. Rebecca Skillings. Children:
  1 Zebulon (Trickey), m. Lucy Skillin.
  2 John (Trickey), m. —— White, of Windham.
  3 Rebecca (Trickey), m. Robert Libby, 10-1-6-4.
  4 Susannah (Trickey), m. Edward Skillin.
  5 Eleanor (Trickey), m. 6 June 1782, John Johnson.
  6 Lucy (Trickey), m. John Tyler.
  7 Mary (Trickey), m. Wm. Major Tate, 7 Dec. 1797.
5 Thomas (Trickey), bap. 1740; probably died young.
6 David (Trickey). His children were:
  1 Eunice (Trickey), m. Richard Johnson.
  2 Mary (Trickey), m. Zebulon Wescott.
  3 Daniel (Trickey).
  4 David (Trickey), m. Sylvia Barbour of Gray; settled in North Yarmouth.
  5 Enock (Trickey).
  6 Eleanor (Trickey).
  7 William (Trickey).
  8 Statira (Trickey).

11-1

William Libby, born probably in Scarborough, before the desertion of the town in 1690; married, 11 Nov. 1722, Sarah Brown, 7-2.

He removed to Scarborough in 1719 or 1720. He was chosen constable at the first town meeting. He seems to have been a man whom his townsmen respected. He served at different times as selectman, and in other minor offices. His chief activity, however, was in religious matters; he served on nearly or quite all the committees which the town chose which related to the church.

He settled on a farm in the interior of the town, and both he and his wife lived to advanced age.

Their children were:

1 William, b. about 1723; died young.
2 Noah, b. about 1725; died unm. The last appearance of his name is as private in Capt. George Berry's company in 1745.
3 Mary, b. about 1727; died in girlhood.
4 Hezekiah, b. 5 April 1729; was a bachelor. He always lived on his father's homestead. He and his sister Elizabeth kept house together. They took their sister Sarah's children to bring up, and, in old age, gave their property to Nathan Libby, 5-7-15, who married Abigail, to support them until death. Hezekiah died 27 Oct. 1798.

5 Susannah, b. about 1731; died young.
6 Elizabeth, b. 9 May 1733; d. 31 Dec. 1818; unm. She always lived in her father's house; first with Hezekiah, and then with Nathan Libby.
7 Mehitable, b. 17 Nov. 1735; died young.
8 Sarah, b. 10 May 1737; m. 31 July 1766, Michael Davis, from Canterbury, Mass. She died early in life, and Davis married again and lived in Lewiston. Children:
  1 Abigail (Davis), b. about 1767; m. Nathan Libby, 5-7-15.
  2 Sarah Libby (Davis), b. about 1769; died unmarried.
  3 Mary (Davis), d. 3 Sept. 1810; unm.
9 William, b. 12 Nov. 1740; d. in middle age; unm.

11-2

Matthew Libby, born probably during his father's stay in Portsmouth, 1690–1700; married 3 Sept. 1730, Mary Nason.

He was a farmer. He moved down to Scarborough after the second settlement, but, after a few years, returned to Kittery, and settled on part of his father's homestead. He lived on the 24-acre lot on the northeast side of the road, now owned by Albert W. Libby, 10-7-1-4-6-3. He died in the winter of 1760–1, having outlived his wife.

Their children were:

1 Jerusha, b. 3 Mar. 1731; m. 30 Nov. 1762, Benj. Staples; died early, leaving no children.
2 Matthew, b. 2 Feb. 1733; m. Lydia Libby, 11-11-2.
3 Zebulon, b. Nov. 1737; m. Sarah Milliken.
4 Azariah, b. 1740; m. Elizabeth Paul.
5 William, b. 30 Jan. 1749; m. Elizabeth Clark.

11-6

John Libby, born doubtless in Portsmouth, in the year 1698; married 1 Jan. 1734, in Scarborough, Keziah Hubbard, daughter of John and Sarah (Collensby) Hubbard, of Kingston, N. H., a native of Salisbury, Mass. She was a sister of the wife of the Rev. William Tompson.

He removed to Scarborough soon after the second settlement. His house was on the site of that recently occupied by Abraham Plummer, near the present Congregational church. He died of a severe cold, (caught while working with an adz in the hold of a vessel), 7 Oct. 1756. He took no part in public affairs, but was an enterprising man, and left a good property. His widow died 29 June 1788.*

Their children were:

1 Anna, b. 17 Nov. 1734; m. Col. Samuel March.
2 Peter, b. 8 March 1736; m. Ruth Libby, 1-1-5-3, and Anna Lazzel.
3 Keziah, b. 14 Sept. 1738; m. 20 Dec. 1759, Jonathan Mitchell.
4 Richard, b. 28 May 1741; m. three wives.
5 Thomas, b. 23 March 1743; m. Hannah Plummer and Dorcas (Fogg) Ring, both of Libby blood.
6 Jane, b. 25 June 1746; died 13 June 1766; unm.

*They had a negro slave whose name was Sambo—called Sambo Libby. It is still told how he used to cross the Nonesuch River. He would lower himself into the river on one side, and in two or three minutes, having crawled across on the bottom of the river, would appear climbing up the opposite bank.

11-7

LIEUT. ANDREW LIBBY, born in Kittery, now Eliot, Me., 1 Dec. 1700; married ESTHER FURBER, daughter of Jethro Furber, of Newington, N. H.

He returned to Scarborough, and settled on the farm afterward occupied by his son Simon. His house stood in the orchard opposite the present residence of John Adams Libby, 11-7-11-8-6. He became one of the largest farmers in the town, but took no part in town business. We find him, however, in 1743, one of a committee of three, chosen "to get a schoolmaster." It is not known that he was in actual service in the French war, but from 1745 until his death, he was known as Lieut. Andrew Libby. He died 5 Jan. 1773, leaving a good property. He and his wife were both members of the Congregational church. She died 1 Oct. 1756, and during the next year he married Eleanor (Libby) Trickey, 10-8. She outlived him, and died 27 Sept. 1781.

The children of Lieut. Andrew and Esther Libby were:

1 Andrew, b. 13 Feb. 1732; m. Miriam Burns.
2 Joshua, b. 17 Mar. 1734; m. Hannah Larrabee.
3 Elizabeth, b. 28 Apr. 1736; m. Samuel Plaisted.
4 Henry, b. 1737; died in infancy.
5 Abigail, b. 5 Nov. 1738; m. 1st, John Dam; 2d, Thomas Jackson.
6 Joseph, b. 6 Jan. 1740; m. Sarah Meserve.
7 Daniel, b. 22 Dec. 1742; m. Dorothy Hasty.
8 Edward, b. 10 Apr. 1743; m. Mary Libby, 1-1-3-10.
9 Sarah, b. 1746; died in infancy.
10 Esther, b. 16 Dec. 1750; died young.
11 Simon, b. 7 June, 1752; m. Elizabeth Thompson.

11-9

NATHANIEL LIBBY, born in Kittery, Me., 2 Nov. 1704; married, 11 Oct. 1730, MIRIAM KNIGHT.

In 1735 or 6, he removed to the adjoining town of Berwick, and settled at Blackberry Hill. This was at that time a frontier wilderness. It was much exposed to the Indians, and they had frequently to seek the shelter of the garrison. On one occasion, it is told, when Mr. Libby was away from home, the house was surrounded by savages, but his wife scared them away by deceiving them into the belief that there were men there. In that spot Nathaniel Libby cleared for himself a farm, which he occupied until his death.

After the death of his first wife, the mother of his children, he married, 16 Nov. 1757, the widow Hannah Staples, of Kittery. After his death in the spring of 1761, she returned to Kittery. He was the father of thirteen children, but only four survived him. It is said that he lost six of the thirteen, in one week, by a throat distemper.

His children were:

1 Nathaniel, b. about 1731; died young.
2 Susannah, b. about 1733; died young.

3 Miriam, b. about 1735; m. 24 Jan. 1779, Ephraim Goodwin.
4 Stephen, b. about 1736; died young.
5 Nathaniel, b. about 1738; m. Elizabeth Fogg, 9-9-3, and Eleanor Johnson.
6 ——, b. about 1740; died young.
7 Stephen, b. about 1741; m. Alice Guptil and Hannah Young.
8 Zebulon, b. about 1742; m. Sarah Brackett.
9 John, b. about 1744;
10 Susannah, b. about 1747;
11 Reuben, b. about 1749; } all died young.
12 Mary, b. about 1751;
13 Hannah, b. about 1752;

11-11

Samuel Libby, born in Kittery, now Eliot, Me., 5 June 1709; married 12 Jan. 1736, Margaret Rogers. He was a farmer, and spent all his days in the house in which he was born. He died in 1788 or '9. His wife was alive in 1782, but how much longer she lived is unknown.

Their children were:

1 Samuel, b. about 1736; died young.
2 Lydia, b. about 1737; m. Matthew Libby, 11-2-2.
3 Elizabeth, b. about 1739; m. 30 July 1761, Jonathan Hanscom.
4 Hannah, b. about 1741; m. 6 Mar. 1796, Benj. Staples.
5 Samuel, b. 13 Jan. 1743; m. Mary Staples.
6 Seth, b. 15 Feb. 1745; m. Mary Jenkins.
7 Anne, b. 6 Feb. 1747; died young.
8 Sarah, b. 19 June 1750; m.,* as second wife, 11 June 1780, Elisha Hammond.
9 Mary,* m. 24 June 1776, Elisha Hammond, before mentioned.

*No knowledge of these daughters is retained in the family. The only authority for the statements made is the records of marriage, and the fact that Samuel Libby mentioned in his will his *son-in-law, Elisha Hammond.*

FOURTH GENERATION.

1-1-2

James Libby, born in Portsmouth, N. H., in the year 1700, married Mary Furber, dau. of Jethro Furber of Newington, N. H.

He removed to Scarborough a few years before his father did, and at his father's death came into possession of the original Libby homestead. He took little part in town business, but his occasionally serving on committees of importance shows that he did not lack the confidence of his townsmen. That he was a charitable man appears from the following narrative: His son Eliakim, returning home from the Revolutionary war with nothing but his discharge to compensate him for his services, was taken sick and obliged to ask assistance of a stranger. On talking with the man to whom he applied, it appeared that many years before, while journeying penniless through Scarborough he had been taken in and cared for by Eliakim's parents and sent on his way with money to reach home. The man cared for him until he had sufficiently recovered, and then gave him money to last him home, just as he himself had been treated long before by Eliakim's parents.

James Libby died 18 Feb. 1776, and his widow, 29 Mar. 1777.

Their children were:

1 John, b. 18 July 1724; m. 13 Mar. 1749, Anna Libby, 1-4-1-2. He and his brother Jethro bought a tract of wild land in the interior of the town, on the banks of the Nonesuch, and divided it between them and settled on it. He had no children, and gave his farm to his brother's son Charles for the support of himself and wife. He sold it and removed to another on Beach Ridge. There John Libby died, 13 Dec. 1808; and his widow, 1 Nov. 1819.

2 Jethro, b. about 1726; m. Mary Libby, 1-1-5-1, and Hannah (Woodbury) Moody.

3 Roger, b. 14 Aug. 1729; m. 28 May 1752, Dorothy Meserve. [See page 37.] He was a farmer and settled on wild land in the northwest part of his native town. He had no children, and gave his farm to Jonathan McKenney, whose grandson, Granville McKenney, now occupies it. He was known as Captain. He died 1 Feb. 1825. After his first wife's death, he married, 1 Jan. 1805, Hannah (Manny) Watson, widow of Jonathan Watson. The records say that she died 13 Dec. 1828, "after losing four husbands, Seavey, Chandler, Watson, and Libby."

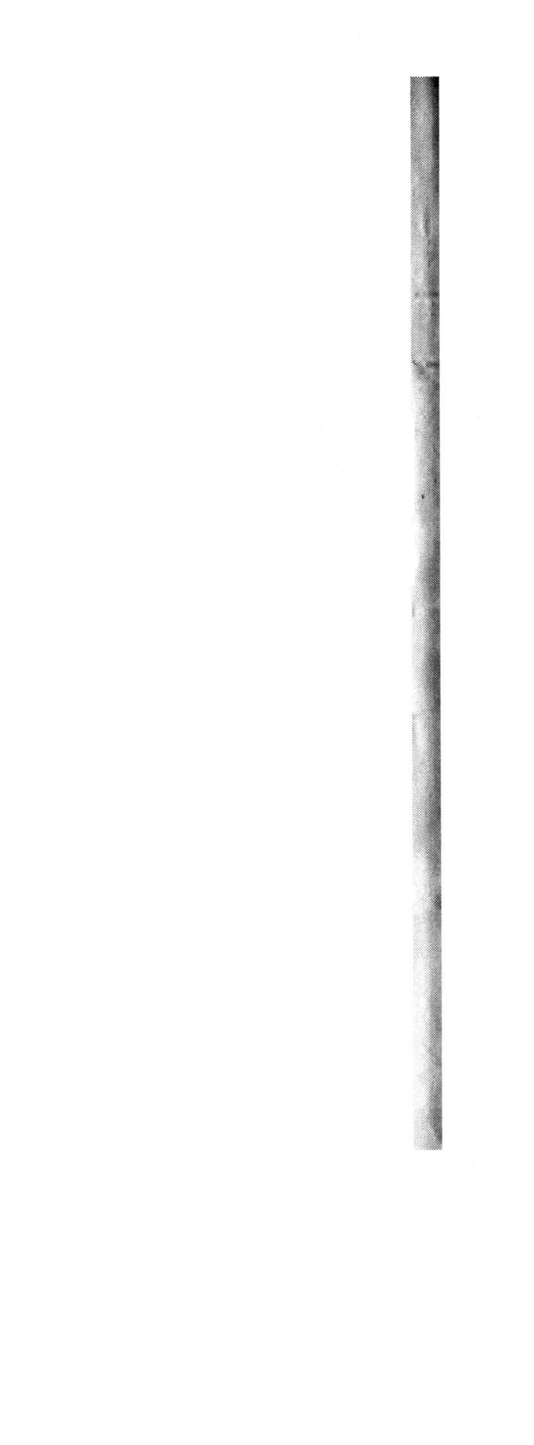

4 Leah, b. 4 Mar. 1732; died young.
5 Abigail, b. 17 Apr. 1734; m. 12 Nov. 1753, Elisha Douglass of Falmouth.
6 Hatevil, b. 28 Nov. 1736; m. Jane Watson.
7 Anthony, b. 1738; m. 19 July 1767, Lucy Libby, 10-2-4-1. He followed coasting many years, owning his own vessel, and acquiring the title of Captain. He settled on his father's farm which was the original Libby homestead, and there died, 1 May 1809. He had no children. The old house was a large two-storied one, and stood southwest of the road, opposite the sharp bend a few rods from the bridge over Libby River. His widow occupied this house until her death, which occurred in her 95th year, 6 Mar. 1842, and it was then taken down. The Libby homestead went into the possession of Israel Perry, who had married the widow's niece, Elizabeth Libby, 10-2-4-2-4, and their son, Oakes Perry, now owns the farm from which emanated the whole race of Libbys.
8 Leah, b. 1741; died young.
9 Eliakim, b. 20 Apr. 1745; m. 3 July 1766, Mehitable, dau. of Thos. Cummings of Standish. He was a farmer and settled where William Jose now lives. He served eight months in the Continental army. He was a very active christian. He died in December, 1836, aged 91. His wife died 17 Mar. 1822. Their only child was:
1 Mary Furber, b. 1 Apr. 1774; m. 2 Sept. 1795, Daniel Moulton, 3d.

1-1-3

JOHN LIBBY, born in Portsmouth, N. H., probably in the year 1702; married, 10 Nov. 1726, MARY MILLER, dau. of Benjamin and Lydia (Fernald) Miller of Portsmouth.

He removed to Scarborough with his brother James. He was a carpenter, but his chief occupation was farming. He lived on the western slope of Oak Hill, and died probably in the spring of 1767. His widow died 23 Oct. 1780.

Their children were:

1 Phebe, b. 12 May 1728; m.* 12 Oct. 1747, Joseph Martin.
2 Benjamin, b. 28 July 1730; died 1759; unm.
3 Eleanor, b. 20 Aug. 1732; m. 1st, Benj. Sallis; 2d, John Milliken.
4 Jonathan, b. 5 Feb. 1735; m. Hannah Hunnewell, 7-1-2-2.
5 Jotham, b. 5 Apr. 1737; m. Catherine Skillings.
6 Abigail, b. 18 Dec. 1739; m. 15 June 1758, John Haskell of Falmouth.
7 Lydia, b. 5 June 1743; m.* 10 Jan. 1760, Jos. Knight of Falmouth.
8 Joab, } twins, b. } m. Susannah Lombard.
9 Josiah, } 13 Sept. 1745; } m. Sarah Libby, 10-5-4-4.
10 Mary, b. 4 June 1749; m. 1st, Edward Libby, 11-7-8; 2d, Allison Libby, 10-5-4.

1-1-5

DEACON JONATHAN LIBBY, born in Portsmouth, N. H., in 1706; married, 27 Nov. 1735, MARTHA HASTY,† born in Ireland about 1710.

---

*Probably.

†DANIEL HASTY, the first of the name in Maine and New Hampshire, and thought to be the first in New England, came from Ireland, with his wife, and, so far as is known, four children. He appeared first at Portsmouth, N. H., and in Dec. 1731, bought land in Scarborough, and shortly after took up his residence there. He died 3 Aug. 1756. His widow died 8 Feb. 1758. Their children were:

He accompanied his father to Scarborough in the winter of 1729-30. He settled west of Oak Hill, and became a successful farmer. He was an ensign in the French war, 1745. 12 April 1749, he was chosen a deacon of the Congregational church, and held that office until his death, which took place 28 Oct. 1759. His widow died 27 Nov. 1791.

Their children were:

1 Mary, b. 27 Apr. 1736; m. Jethro Libby, 1-1-2-2.
2 Elizabeth, b. 15 Feb. 1738; d. in old age; unm.
3 Ruth, b. 22 Apr. 1740; m. Peter Libby, 11-6-2.
4 Lydia, b. 1742; died young.
5 Catherine, b. 1743; m. Moses Fogg, 9-6-6.
6 Rhoda, b. 1746; m. 2 Sept. 1770, Charles Morris, a Welchman.
7 Jonathan, b. 1748; died young.
8 Lydia, b. 1750; m. 15 Oct. 1770, Aaron Plummer.
9 Jonathan, b. 1752; m. Abigail Libby, 10-2-4-7.
10 Daniel, b. 1756; m. 26 Aug. 1778, Elizabeth Harmon. He was a mariner, and went master of a vessel which was lost at sea with all on board. His family occupied part of his father's house until his widow's marriage, 4 Oct. 1787, to Josiah Moses, when they moved to Standish. Children:
   1 Anna, b. 7 Jan. 1779; m. 27 Mar. 1800, Dea. Wm. Cummings; died 10 Sept. 1811.
   2 William, bap. May 1781; } both followed the sea, and both
   3 Jonathan, bap. July 1782; } died in early manhood; unm.

---

1 Martha, b. 1711; m. Dea. Jonathan Libby, 1-1-5.
+2 William, b 1718; lived in Scarborough.
+3 Robert, settled in Limington.
4 Mary, m. 2 Dec. 1742, John Harmon.

2 William Hasty m. 1st, Hannah Fogg, 9-5-3; 2d, Agnes McCartney. She died 8 Jan. 1787. He died 11 Oct. 1787. Children, by first wife:

1 Anna, b. 7 June 1744; m. John Hoyt of Durham.

By second wife:

2 Hannah, b. 13 May 1747; m. 1st, Capt. John Skillin; 2d, Col. Benjamin Larrabee. [See page 41.]
3 Daniel, b. 18 Mar. 1749; m. Martha McLaughlin; settled in Standish.
4 James, b. 2 Mar. 1751; m. —— Dean; settled in Standish.
+5 William, b. 19 Aug. 1753; lived in Scarborough.
+6 Robert, b. 11 Jan. 1757; lived in Scarborough.
7 Joseph, b. 16 Nov. 1760; d. at sea, 1784, unm.
8 Mary, b. 19 Aug. 1765; m. Capt. John Watson.

3 Robert Hasty m. 1st, Hannah Jordan; 2d, Elizabeth (Larrabee) Watson. [See page 41.] She died in Limington, 24 Jan. 1810. Children, by first wife:

1 Nathaniel, b. 1746; m. Sally Weeman.
2 Dorothy, b. 1748; m. Daniel Libby, 11-7-7.
3 Hannah, b. 1752; m. Matthew Libby, 10-5-2.

By second wife:

4 Benjamin.
5 David, m. Susannah Jordan.
6 Robert.
7 Mary, m. Dominicus McKenney. [See under 5-2-3.]
8 Lydia, m. —— Brackett.

2-5 Judge William Hasty m. Anna Clark. He died on the 22d, and she on the 28th, of December, 1831. Children:

+1 John, b. 2 Nov. 1782: m. Lydia Libby, 5-7-14-4.
2 Child died in infancy.

2-6 Robert Hasty m. Margaret Patterson. She died 23 Oct. 1813. He died 19 Dec. 1821. Children:

1 William, b. 19 Dec. 1779; d. 2 May 1799.
2 Agnes, b. 10 Sept. 1781; m. Capt. Stephen Libby, 5-7-8-3.
3 Joseph, b. 19 July 1783; m. Hannah Ring. [See next page.]

1-1-6

JOSIAH LIBBY, born in Portsmouth, N. H., 1715; married, 23 Mar. 1737, ANNA SMALL. [See page 32.]

He was but a boy when his father carried him to Scarborough. He grew up on the original Libby homestead, and then settled on Oak Hill. His house stood in what is now the southeast corner of the cross roads, and his farm extended to the south. He was a trumpeter in the French wars, and was known as *Trumpeter 'Siah*. He died at the age of thirty-five, 2 Feb. 1751, leaving a good property. His widow married, 10 Jan. 1755, Nathaniel Milliken, by whom she also had children, and died 12 Jan. 1784. The following narrative, of her telling, is remembered still.

It was during an Indian trouble, when, in their exposed position on Oak Hill, it was not safe to pass the night in their own home, and they were accustomed every day, at nightfall, to seek the protection of the garrison. One day her husband, the trumpeter, was away from home. He was expected back, but did not return at the appointed time. Darkness came on, the calls of the Indians were heard in the surrounding woods, but the husband did not appear. Nothing had been seen of the Indians for a few days previous, and he had allowed himself to be delayed, little knowing the danger his family was in. The wife and mother, not daring to have a light, sat trembling with her children in the darkness. At last her husband approached his home, and he too heard the calls of the Indians. Stealthily he made his way to his house, and in whispers prepared for their departure. With the cries of the Indians on all sides of them, they crept through the Flaggy Meadow, and by their good fortune, reached the garrison in safety. The next day they found their house pillaged. In such dangers, the days of this generation were passed.

The children of Josiah and Anna Libby were:

1 Lucy, b. 25 Nov. 1739; m. 19 Dec. 1760, Thomas Milliken.
2 Jane, b. 1742; m. 26 Nov. 1761, Elisha Berry.
3 Joel, b. 1744; d. 19 Sept. 1760.
4 Josiah, b. 16 Feb. 1746; m. Eunice Libby, 5-7-13, Elizabeth (Parcher) Foss, and Mary (Chase) Jones.
5 Phineas, b. 22 July 1749; m. Sarah Libby, 10-2-4-4.
6 Anna, b. 4 Sept. 1751; m. Jeremiah Libby, 10-2-1-1.

---

4 Jane, b. 1785; m. Moses Thomes.
5 Robert, b. 23 Nov. 1786; m. 1st, —— Dyer; 2d, Esther (Libby) Meserve, 11-7-7-10.
6 Paul, b. 3 Oct. 1788; d. 9 Oct. 1788.
7 Margaret, b. 13 Oct. 1789; d. unmarried.
8 Polly, b. 17 Mar. 1792; d. 24 Aug. 1797.
9 Anna Clark, b. 20 Apr. 1794; m. Robert Libby, 10-1-6-5- .
10 Hannah, b. 11 Aug. 1796; m. —— Cressy.
11 Luther, b. 5 Mar. 1798; d. 14 Mar. 1798.
12 William, b. 6 June 1799; d. in Gorham.
13 Edward, b. 20 Feb. 1802; m. Mary Ann Wilson.
14 Thomas Jefferson, b. 6 Aug. 1804.

2-5-1 JOHN HASTY lived in Scarborough. Children:

1 William, b. 18 July 1805; m. Elizabeth Ann Tompson.
2 Daniel, m. —— Smith.
3 Seth L., m. Catherine, dau. of Hannah (Fogg) Tompson, 9-6-6-9.
4 John. 5 Cyrus, m. —— Hunt. 6 James.

1-2-1

Benjamin Libby, born in Portsmouth, N. H., in the year 1693; married Elizabeth Ham, daughter of Joseph and Tamson (Meserve) Ham of Dover. He was a cordwainer. He lived in Dover, where he died 3 Aug. 1781. His widow died 17 Aug. 1788.

Their children were:

1 Ham, m. Esther Drew, and Sarah Wentworth.
2 Benjamin, m. Abigail Titcomb.
3 James, b. 27 July 1739; m. Lydia, widow of Joseph Runnals.
4 Joseph, m. Elizabeth ———. He was a farmer. He lived many years in the parish of Madbury in Dover, and then settled in Barrington, where he died, 1811. His widow died about 1821. They had no children, and took his nephew, Joshua Libby, 1-2-1-3-3, to live with them.

1-2-3

Joshua Libby, born in Portsmouth, N. H., about 1700; married Elizabeth ———. He was a mariner, and owned no real estate except his house lot. He died about 1736. His wife outlived him.

Their children were:

1 Joshua, bap. 28 Sept. 1729; m. —— ———.
2 Elizabeth, bap. 13 June 1731.
3 Love, bap. 20 July 1734.

1-4-1

James Libby, born in Portsmouth, N. H., 23 Nov. 1700; married 23 Dec. 1725, Elizabeth Meserve, daughter of Clement Meserve. [See page 37.]

He was a carpenter by trade, but receiving from his father all his lands and rights in Scarborough, he took up his residence there about 1729, and became a farmer. He lived to the east of Oak Hill, and died about 1770. His widow lived to an advanced age, and died about 1790.

Their children were:

1 Clement, b. 23 Oct. 1729; died young.
2 Anna, b. 2 Feb. 1732; m. John Libby, 1-1-2-1.
3 Arthur, b. 19 Aug. 1734; died young.
4 Asa, b. 1737; m. Abigail Coolbroth.
5 James, b. 1740; was a bachelor; died in middle age. He and his sister Elizabeth kept house together on a farm which he settled in the north part of the town. The spot on which the buildings stood is now owned by Charles Parker. One day he fell asleep on the tongue of the ox-team he was driving, tumbled off, and was run over and killed.
6 Ichabod, b. 1742; m. Mary Fickett.
7 Elizabeth, b. 1746; never married. She lived first with her brother James, then with Ichabod, and still later with his son James. She died about 1820.

1-4-4

ISAAC LIBBY, born in Portsmouth, N. H., 3 Dec. 1707; married, 22 Dec. 1730, SARAH WALDRON, dau. of Col. John, and Mary (Ham) Waldron of Dover.

After his marriage he lived in Dover. He was a saddler by trade, and built himself a house, barn, and workshop in Dover, which he sold to Joseph Hanson, jr., after his removal to Rochester in 1745 or 6. He settled on a farm in Rochester which he occupied until his death. Beside his trade and farming, he engaged in retailing West India goods and liquor. His old account books are still preserved. He took an important part in the management of the town, and was selectman and town clerk many years. He died 5 Feb. 1776.

His children were:

1 Anna, b. 25 Feb. 1732; d. 29 Jan. 1735.
2 Isaac, b. 26 Feb. 1733; d. 31 Dec. 1736.
3 Paul, b. 7 Sept. 1736; m. Hannah Tibbetts and Mary Tibbetts.
4 Isaac, b. 11 Feb. 1738; m. Sarah Coleman.
5 Mary, b. 31 July 1741; died young.
6 Sarah, b. 20 April 1744; m. —— Burnham of Rochester.
7 Betsey, b. 20 Apr. 1747; married, probably, 5 Dec. 1784, William Palmer. She moved into the interior of New Hampshire.
8 Mary, b. 9 June 1749; m. Nathaniel Horn, jr., of Dover.

1-4-5

JOHN LIBBY, born in Portsmouth, N. H., about the year 1710; married first, MARY ——; second,* 9 Sept. 1761, MARGARET CRUSSY. He was a mast-hewer in Portsmouth.

Children, by wife Mary:

1 James, bap. May 1747; m. Sarah Gibbs.
2 Mary, bap. Mar. 1740.

By second wife:

3 Joseph,* b. about 1762; m. Mary Cole, and Mehitable Leavitt.

1-4-7

CAPT. ICHABOD LIBBY, born in Portsmouth, N. H., about 1715; married MARY JACKSON, a daughter of Thomas Jackson, of New Castle. He was a shoemaker by trade, but adopted the calling of mariner, and became a master. He died before 1794.

Children:

1 Sally, m. 25 July 1777, John Mills.
2 Molly, m. Stephen Emery.
3 Ann, married Nehemiah Eliot.
4 Mehitable, m., (probably), 15 Sept. 1794, Joshua Elliot.

*This Joseph Libby was certainly a son of John and Margaret (Crussy) Libby, who were married 9 Sept. 1761. That John Libby who married Margaret Crussy, and John Libby, 1-4-5, were the same person, there is no *positive* proof, but there can, in reason, be no doubt that they are identical.

1-5-2

WILLIAM LIBBY, born in Portsmouth, N. H., about 1702; married, 29 Oct. 1725, ELIZABETH GOODWIN, daughter of William and Deliverance (Taylor) Goodwin, of Berwick.

In 1727 or 8, he removed from Berwick to Scarborough, and thence, about seven years later, to Falmouth, where he settled on the Presumpscot River. He died in 1752. His widow outlived him.

Children:

1 Lydia, married, 1754, John Motley of Falmouth. After his death in 1764, she married John Blake.* She died in June, 1824, at a very advanced age.
2 Abigail, b. 14 November 1729, in Scarborough; m. 1 Aug. 1754, William Wiswall.
3 Joseph, b. 24 Mar. 1732, in Scarborough; m. Mary Huston and Hannah Hanson.
4 Samuel, b. 1 Feb. 1737, in Falmouth; m. Mary Frost and Jemima Leighton.
5 Daniel, b. 1742; m. Sarah Doughty.

1-6-2

JOSEPH LIBBY, born 5 Apr. 1711; married first, ANNA ———; second the widow ELIZABETH SHOREY. He was a farmer and lived on that part of his father's homestead which is now owned by Geo. W. Thompson. Administration on the estate was granted 21 May 1787; his death occurred probably very shortly before. His widow married, 20 Dec. 1787, Daniel Furbish.

Children, by first wife:

1 Benjamin, bap. Aug. 1735; m. Elizabeth Smith.
2 Sarah, bap. Mar. 1737.
3 Anna, bap. Jan. 1740; died young.
4 Joseph, bap. Mar. 1744; m. Lydia Shorey.
5 Margaret, bap. Oct. 1748.
6 Dorcas, bap. 1751.
7 Nathan, m. Ruth Shorey.
8 Elisha, bap. 1755; went to sea and was lost.
9 Patience, bap. 1759.
10 Ichabod, bap. Nov. 1759; died in infancy.

By second wife:

11 Ann, bap. 1762; m. a Furbish of, it is thought, Milton, N. H.

One of the daughters married a Low of York, and one a Twambly of Milton.

1-6-5

DANIEL LIBBY, born in Berwick, Me., 21 Feb. 1715; married first, ABIGAIL ———; (born 16 Sept. 1722; died 28 Feb. 1771); second, 31 Oct. 1771, LOIS (JONES) WENTWORTH, widow of Saml. Wentworth of Berwick. She died 1813.

He settled in his native town, on the south side of the road leading from Blackberry Hill to Beaver Dam Brook, and became a well-to-do farmer. He was much in town business; selectman thirteen years, town treasurer twenty successive years, and frequently moderator of the town meetings. He was on the Committee of Correspondence and Safety all through the Revolution. He died 31 July 1804, leaving his homestead to his son James. It is now all grown up to woods except a mound, containing about one-half an acre, on which the house stood. The old orchard, a few rods northeast of the site, still remains.

Children, by his first wife:

1 Abigail, born 2 June 1745; m. 1762, John Stone.
2 Daniel, b. 28 Mar. 1746; m. Lucy Chadbourne.
3 Jeremiah, b. 28 Dec. 1747; m. Elizabeth Guptil.
4 Elizabeth, b. 8 Dec. 1749; m. 1 Dec. 1768, Humphrey Chadbourne.
5 John, b. 20 Nov. 1751; m. Sarah Woodsum.
6 Martha, b. 28 July 1753; m. 29 Nov. 1781, Samuel Butler, jr.
7 Sarah, } twins, born } m. 5 June 1783, Stephen Pray.
8 Mary, } 24 Nov. 1755; } m. 27 Oct. 1774, Hugh Ross, jr.
9 Benjamin, b. 18 Jan. 1758; m. Polly Heard.
10 Samuel, b. 24 Aug. 1760; m. Betsey Hardison.
11 Anna, b. 26 Aug. 1763; m. Hanson Libby, 1-6-2-1-1.
12 Lydia, b. 11 Sept. 1765; m. 24 Feb. 1789, Ephraim Butler.
13 Keziah, b. 22 Feb. 1768; m. 3 Feb. 1791, Ephraim Varney.

By second wife:

14 Eunice, } twins, born } m. John Lord of Limington.
15 James, } 31 Jan. 1774; } m. Sarah Johnson.

1-6-9

Charles Libby, born in Berwick, Me., 29 Dec. 1721; married, 27 Dec. 1744, Abigail Hilton. He was a farmer, and lived and died on his father's homestead. His death occurred 8 Sept. 1772. His wife outlived him.

Their children were:

1 Hannah, b. 18 Sept. 1745; m. 8 Sept. 1763, Samuel Shorey.
2 Mary, b. 19 Oct. 1746; m. 21 Mar. 1765, Joseph Pray.
3 Ebenezer, b. 8 Feb. 1748; m. Elizabeth Quint.
4 Charles, b. 16 Dec. 1749; m. Sarah Pray.
5 Mehitable, b. 27 Oct. 1751; m. first, 1 May 1771, Nathaniel Pray; second, —— Hayes of Farmington, N. H.
6 Abigail, b. 30 Mar. 1753; m. William Quint.
7 Jeremiah, b. 6 Feb. 1755; went out in an American privateer during the Revolution, and never returned. He was unmarried.
8 Benjamin, b. 4 Nov. 1756; m. Mary Hamilton.
9 John, b. 4 Oct. 1758; d. 20 Mar. 1761.
10 James, b. 18 Aug. 1760; m. Hannah Woodsum.
11 Sarah, b. 23 Sept. 1763; m. 26 Aug. 1781, John Gowen.
12 John, b. 2 Jan. 1768; m. Mary Gowen.

1-7-1

Jeremiah Libby, born in Portsmouth, N. H., 21 Feb. 1717; married first, Mary* Symmes, daughter of John and Hannah

*My authority for stating that she was a daughter of John Symmes is as follows: 1st, Joseph Symmes was appointed guardian of her two sons, after their father's death; 2d, in July 1771, Jeremiah, her only surviving child, quitclaimed to the same person, his right in the estate of John and Hannah Symmes.

Symmes of Portsmouth. She died 11 July 1750, and he married second, Sarah, apparently daughter of Thomas Newmarch.

It cannot be learned what occupation he followed, for in all legal documents he was described as *a gentleman.* His inventory mentions no real estate, except his house lot and garden. He was selectman in 1754. He and his first wife were members of the "Church of Christ." He died shortly before May 1757. His widow seems to have married as second husband, —— Newmarch.

His children, by his first wife, were:

1 John, b. 6 Oct. 1746; d. 25 May 1770; probably unmarried.
2 Jeremiah, [Esq.], b. 14 Aug. 1748; married, 23 June 1772, Elizabeth, dau. of Daniel and Margaret Lunt of Portsmouth. He was a "shop-keeper" probably before he was of age, and became a successful merchant on Market street. He was for many years one of Portsmouth's leading inhabitants, closely connected with every advance. He was an intimate friend, and enjoyed the high esteem, of Gov. Belknap. He was clerk of a company of volunteers in the Revolution, held repeatedly the highest town offices, and was for many years postmaster. In 1801, 1802, and 1805, he was candidate for the state legislature, and went ahead of his ticket, but, with the rest of his party, was defeated. It is told of him that he "wore a very large wig, and was one of the committee that received Washington in 1790." He died 4 Sept. 1824, and his widow, 20 Jan. 1826. He had no children. His house, located at the foot of Vaughan street, is now known as the White Hart Hotel.

By second wife:

3 Nathaniel, bap. 29 July 1753; died young.
4 Benjamin, bap. 15 Dec. 1754; died young.

1-7-2

George Libby, born in Portsmouth, 20 Jan. 1719; married Elizabeth, apparently a daughter of Thomas and Ann Harvey of Portsmouth.

He was a sea-captain. 25 Feb. 1744, it was voted by the General Assembly of New Hampshire, "that Mr. George Libby be Commissary to go with the forces that go from this Province on ye Expedition ag^st^ Louisburg * * * & have four pound ten shilling pr month for his wages." It appears that he refused to go "for the allowance made him by the Genl Assembly." He was auditor of Portsmouth 1748. He was a member of the "Church of Christ." He died between Oct. 1759, and Dec. 1760. His wife outlived him.

Their children were:

1 George, bap. May 1747; m. 9 Oct. 1776, Mary Lunt, sister of his cousin Jeremiah's wife. He was a merchant in Portsmouth and an inn-holder in Greenland. He died Oct. 1796, leaving a good property, but no children. His widow married, 27 Jan. 1799, Benjamin Brown, Esq., of Chester.
2 William, bap. 25 Dec. 1748; died young.
3 Elizabeth, bap. 11 Feb. 1749-50; died young.
4 Jane, m. John Fisk Osgood of Boston.

1-7-6

THEODORE LIBBY, born in Portsmouth, 10 Dec. 1726. Nothing is known of him except that, 11 March 1757, he was chosen clerk of "Lt. Young's company." He was not living when his father made his will, Dec. 1760. It is probable he died in the service.

His children were:

1 Paul, bap. 17 June 1750; died young.
2 Mary, bap. 8 Mar. 1752.
3 John, m. Hannah Varrill.

5-2-3

EBENEZER LIBBY, born in Scarborough, 9 Nov. 1740; married 19 Mar. 1767, MIRIAM LARRABEE. [See page 41.]

In 1765 he became one of the early settlers of Machias, but returned soon after and settled on Pleasant Hill. Like his father he was a land surveyor, and was clerk of the proprietors of the town from 1776 until his death. He engaged largely in ship-building, and in trade with the West Indies. He accumulated a large property, and became probably the most wealthy man in Black Point parish. He died 4 Feb. 1817, and his widow, 20 Sept. 1833.

Their children were:

1 Samuel, b. 12 April 1768; m. Lydia Fogg, 9-6-6-3.
2 Sarah, b. 18 June 1770; m. first, 30 May 1790, Jacob Fogg, 9-5-4-2-1; second, 1810, James Randall.
3 Benjamin, b. 11 July 1773; d. 24 Oct. 1780.
4 Mary, b. 30 Jan. 1776; d. 23 Oct. 1780.
5 Luther, b. 21 April 1778; d. 10 Oct. 1780.
6 Lydia, b. 6 July 1780; m. 11 Nov. 1798, Christopher Dyer.
7 Mary, b. 31 Oct. 1783; m. 9 May 1805, Nathaniel Blake.
8 Luther, b. 1 July 1786; m. Lydia McKenney.*

---

*JOHN MCKENNEY is said to have been an Irishman. He was a planter. He had a house at Black Point as early as August 1668. It is not known that he had any other children than the following:

1 ROBERT MCKENNEY. He returned at the second settlement, and died in July, 1725. He is the ancestor of very nearly, if not quite, all of the name in Maine. His children were:

+1 John, lived in Scarborough.
+2 Robert, lived in Scarborough.
+3 Isaac, lived in Scarborough.
+4 Henry, lived in Cape Elizabeth.
5 Rebecca, m. Daniel Burnham of Scarborough.
6 Hannah, m. William Grover of Damariscotta.

1-1 JOHN MCKENNEY married Margaret ——. They lived and died in Scarborough, and had children:

1 Rebecca, b. 23 Dec. 1732.
2 John, b. 4 April 1734; died young.
+3 John, b. 9 Feb. 1737.
4 Elizabeth, b. 16 May 1739.
5 James, b. 21 Mar. 1742.
6 Samuel, b. 4 Oct. 1744.
7 Abigail, b. 28 May 1747; m. Gideon Davis.
8 Thomas Wright, b. 3 Oct. 1749.
9 Abner, b. 3 July 1754.

1-2 ROBERT MCKENNEY married Margaret ——. He settled in the Second Parish. He died Feb. 1758. His children were:

1 Robert, b. 28 Feb. 1729; m. Jane Holmes.

5-2-7

NEHEMIAH LIBBY, born in Scarborough 14 May 1749; married 1 Mar. 1770, ABIGAIL HUNNEWELL, 7-1-2-8.

He settled on Beech Ridge, in Scarborough, and cleared the farm now occupied by George Pilsbury. He built a one-storied house a few rods south of the one now on the farm. In 1800 he tore this down and built a brick house with bricks of his own manufacture, on the site of the house now standing. It was among the first brick houses in Scarborough. He engaged largely in apple raising and vinegar making. It was from this circumstance that the road now known as the Vinegar road derived its name. He was chiefly instrumental in obtaining this road, and someone who had opposed it, vexed with his defeat, called it the *vinegar* road.

His wife, Abigail, the mother of his children, died 21 April 1809, and 29 Mar. 1810, he married Mary, widow of David Fogg, 9-6-7-3. He died 9 March 1827, leaving a good property. His widow died with her daughter, Sarah Mitchell.

Children:

1 Lemuel, b. 8 Nov. 1770; m. Patience Whitmore.
2 Lucy, b. 18 May 1773; m. 30 July 1794, John Roberts of Westbrook.
3 Mary, b. 16 Feb. 1776; m. 10 Oct. 1799, Joseph Berry, son of Jane (Libby) Berry, 1-1-6-2.

---

2 William, b. 24 May 1730.
3 Mary, b. 1733; m. John Hodgdon.
4 Jane, b. 1736; died unmarried.
5 Hannah, b. 1739; m. Robert McLaughlin.
6 Rebecca, b. 1742; m. James Holmes.

1-3 ISAAC MCKENNEY married, 1 Apr. 1731, Elizabeth Drisco. They lived in Scarborough. Children:

1 Jacob, settled in Greene.
+2 Moses.
3 Hannah, m. Stephen Larrabee. [See page 41.]
4 Dorothy, m. Luke Libby, 10-5-6.
5 Isaac, m. Hannah Jordan; settled in Danville.
6 Priscilla Getchell.
7 William, m. Miriam Jordan; settled in Danville.
8 Lydia.
9 Joseph, died in Greene.

1-4 HENRY MCKENNEY married Sarah Hanscom. They removed to Cape Elizabeth. They had among other children:

1 Humphrey, m. Elizabeth, dau. of Joshua Small, [see page 32], and had among others:
  1 Dominicus, m. Mary Hasty. [See page 55.]

1-1-3 JOHN MCKENNEY married Mary Rand. Children:

1 Jonathan, m. Lillis Watson; 2 Jeremy; 3 John; 4 Sarah; 5 Thomas; 6 Abner; 7 Molly.

1-3-2 MOSES MCKENNEY married 1st, Eunice Larrabee. [See page 41.] 2d, Lucy Plummer. Children, by first wife:

1 Mary, m. Philip Libby, 10-1-8-4.
2 Dorothy, m. Dominicus Libby, 10-5-6-2.
3 Hannah, m. William Libby, 10-5-6-7.
4 Betsey, m. Dennis Libby, 1-4-1-6-3.
5 Eunice, m. Ebenezer Casely.
6 Moses, m. Salome Libby, 11-7-2-9.
7 Lydia, died at the age of 74, unmarried.

By second wife:

8 Sally, m. James Thurston of Danville.
9 Aaron.
10 Isaac.

4 Abigail, b. 23 Jan. 1779; m. 1 Nov. 1801, Daniel Waterhouse, a son of Samuel Waterhouse, 10-2-2-6.
5 Nehemiah, b. 14 Feb. 1783; m. Parmela Harmon.
6 Elizabeth, b. 18 Sept. 1785; m. 13 Mar. 1814, Thomas Varney of Windham.
7 Anna, b. 6 Aug. 1788; died 5 Jan. 1814; unmarried.

5-7-8

Stephen Libby, born in Scarborough, 13 Jan. 1743; married 17 Oct. 1765, Margaret Miller, born 1744, daughter of Moses Miller of Portsmouth, N. H.

He was a farmer and settled on Oak Hill, on a portion of his father's homestead. His house was where that occupied by Dr. J. Sturdevant now stands. His wife died 31 Dec. 1794. About 1814 he accompanied his son, John A., to Limington, and died there 24 Aug. 1820.

His children were:

1 Abner, b. 27 Dec. 1766; m. Anna Harding.
2 Moses, b. 27 March 1769; m. Elizabeth Libby, 1-1-6-5-1.
3 Stephen, b. 4 Nov. 1771; m. Agnes Hasty.
4 Henry, b. 14 April 1774; m. Margaret Meserve.
5 Elias, bap. 30 June 1776; d. 31 Aug. 1776.
6 Mary, b. 30 Sept. 1777; m. 15 July 1797, Moses Waterhouse, a son of Samuel Waterhouse, 10-2-2-6.
7 Margaret, b. about 1779; m. 15 Dec. 1803, Rufus Fogg, 9-8-1-12.
8 Nicholas, b. 8 Oct. 1780; died 11 Mar. 1805, in the West Indies; unmarried.
9 George Washington, } triplets, b. 19 March 1790; died at sea, age 21.
10 John Adams, } triplets, b. 19 March 1790; m. Abigail Sawyer.
11 Benjamin Franklin, } triplets, b. 19 March 1790; died at the age of six.

5-7-10

Aaron Libby, born in Scarborough, 18 Mar. 1745; married 29 May 1766, Elizabeth Weeman, daughter of Valentine Weeman of Cape Elizabeth.

Aaron Libby was a shoemaker by trade. He lived at first on Oak Hill in Scarborough, and then settled on a large farm in Limington. The latter years of his life he ran a country store. It is said that he was the first man that ever kept shop in Limington.

He was a very athletic man. One of his feats was to stand on his head on the ridge-pole of a barn, and drink from a bottle.

In 1798 the whole family was stricken down by fever. March 19th of that year the mother died.* Her husband was recovering at the time of her burial, but in attending her funeral, brought on a relapse, from which he did not recover. He died in May, 1798.

His children, born in Scarborough, were:

1 Mary, b. 9 Mar. 1767; m. 29 Feb. 1788, Walter Higgins of Limington.

*Her daughter Elizabeth, now living, at the age of almost one hundred years, states this date with the greatest positiveness.

2 John, b. 3 Jan. 1769; m. 21 Mar. 1793, Phebe, dau. of Dominicus Jordan of Cape Elizabeth. He died in 1801 or 1802, and his widow married Wm. Hazeltine of Buxton. Only child:
    1 Dorcas, b. 5 May 1794; m. 3 May, 1813, Frank Maxwell of Cape Elizabeth.
3 Hannah Jordan, b. 28 May 1773; m. 24 Jan. 1793, Jonathan Sparrow.
4 Seth, bap. 1 Mar. 1778; died about 1800; unm.

Born in Limington:

5 Eunice, b. 29 Aug. 1780; m. 1801, Wentworth Lombard of Wales, Me.; died 29 April 1874, aged nearly ninety-four.
6 Elizabeth, b. 28 Feb. 1783; m. Major Moses Moody; is still living.
7 Annie, died in Limington, in May 1798, the day following her father's burial; unm.

5-7-11

Jesse Libby, born in Scarborough, 1747; married, 6 Dec. 1769, Keziah March, 11-6-1-1.

12 June 1776, he was living in Limington on a hundred-acre lot which he on that day received by deed of gift from his father-in-law. He was a farmer in Limington, but also kept public house. He was the first collector chosen after the incorporation of the town in 1792. In 1797 he sold his farm and probably removed at once to Hampden, where he was located in Jan. 1800. He kept the tavern at Hampden many years. Soon after the war of 1812 closed, he sold his place at Hampden Corner, built a vessel, and went in her to Philadelphia, Penn. Shortly after he removed to New York city. His wife died there and he returned to Hampden. He bought a small place about two miles from the village, and there died about 1822.

Children:

1 Jesse, b. in Scarborough; m. Mary Myrick.
2 David, b. 16 Dec. 1772; m. Hannah Knight.
3 Samuel March, b. 11 Mar. 1775; m. Eliza Myrick.
4 Anna, b. 14 Sept. 1781, in Limington; m. William Reed.
5 Jane, b. 14 Nov. 1784; m. Stephen Dolbeer.
6 Richard, b. 29 Oct. 1790; m. Hannah Holbrook.
7 John, b. 26 Aug. 1793; never married. He was a sailor, and went on a voyage from which he never returned.

5-7-12

Philemon Libby, born in Scarborough, 29 May 1749; married 8 May 1771, Martha Small. [See Small, page 32.]

He received from his wife's grandfather, Deacon Samuel Small, a grandson of Francis Small who purchased the five Ossipee townships, one hundred acres of land in what is now Limington, and became one of the first settlers of that town. His house was at Limington Corner, on the site of the present residence of William McArthur, Esq. He was for many years a licensed innholder. He died 22 Dec. 1811. After his death, his widow went with her son Abner to Limerick, and died 27 Aug. 1837.

Their children, born in Scarborough, were:

1 Rufus, b. 4 May 1773; m. Dorcas Strout.
2 Philemon, b. 7 July 1775; m. Liberty Norris.
3 Eunice, b. 2 Sept. 1776; d. 23 Oct. 1782.

Born in Limington:

4 James, b. 11 Jan. 1779; m. Emma Chase.
5 Abner, b. 29 May, 1781; m. Olive Gray Chase.
6 Martha, b. 28 Aug. 1783; m. 26 Nov. 1801, Isaac Mitchell, Esq., of Limington.
7 Eunice, b. 13 April 1786; d. 9 Jan. 1787.
8 Anna Small, b. 29 Jan. 1788; m. 28 Nov. 1805, David Otis.
9 Dorothy, b. 28 June 1791; m. 29 Nov. 1810, Francis Small.
10 Eunice, b. 4 July 1795; m. Benjamin Tyler.

5-7-14

Seth Libby, born on Oak Hill, Scarborough, 1 May 1755; married 12 May 1779, Lydia Jordan, born 22 Mar. 1760, daughter of Dominicus Jordan of Cape Elizabeth, the same known as "Old Stuff."

He lived and died on the spot where he was born. His house was on the post-road between Portland and Boston, and in addition to carrying on his farm, he kept a tavern. He died 9 Dec. 1836. His widow lived to the age of ninety-two, and died 17 Oct. 1852.

Their children were:

1 Aaron, b. 1780; d. 27 July 1791.
2 Lois, b. 2 Oct. 1782; m. Capt. Cyrus Libby, 1-1-6-4-6.
3 Susannah, b. 16 Nov. 1784; m. 11 Oct. 1804, Benjamin Larrabee. [See page 41.]
4 Lydia, b. 8 Oct. 1786; m. 22 Nov. 1804, John Hasty.
5 Anna, b. 5 Aug. 1788; m. 15 Mar. 1808, Joseph Watson.
6 Phebe, b. 28 Oct. 1790; m. 17 Jan. 1816, Joseph Larrabee.
7 Rhoda, b. 13 June 1792; m. 23 Sept. 1819, Capt. William Tompson.
8 Hannah, b. 22 Oct. 1795; d. 10 June 1801.
9 Jordan, b. 20 Nov. 1796; m. Sarah Libby, 5-2-3-1-2.
10 Aaron, b. 10 May 1799; m. 1st, Rachel McKenney; 2d, Ruth Hazeltine.
11 Hannah, b. 7 July 1801; m. 28 Aug. 1825, Geo. F. Randall of Portland.
12 Eunice, b. 28 Jan. 1803; m. 28 Feb. 1828, Jonathan M. Coolbroth.
13 John, b. 17 Oct. 1807; m. Jane Milliken.

5-7-15

Nathan Libby, born in Scarborough, 16 Aug. 1766; married, 24 Jan. 1790, Abigail Davis, 11-1-8-1. His wife was the only grandchild of William Libby, 11-1, that ever married, and he came into possession of her grandfather's homestead farm. He died 11 Feb. 1829. His widow died 6 Mar. 1848.

Children, by his wife Abigail, born in Scarborough:

1 Elmira, b. 22 Oct. 1790; m. 17 May 1807, Enock Skillings.
2 William, b. 11 Aug. 1792; was drowned at the causeway bridge, between schools, 6 Jan. 1802.
3 Amos, b. 28 July 1794; m. Eunice Skillings.

4 Gardner, b. 13, died 19, Aug. 1797.
5 Lydia, b. 26 Jan. 1800; m. Enos Libby, 10-2-1-5-8.
6 Sally, m. 22 Feb. 1818, Josiah Skillings.
7 Emily, m. 1st, 5 July 1824, Floran Berry; 2d, —— Davis.
8 Statira, m. 21 Dec. 1823, Thomas O. Skillings.

By a repetition of his father's sin, he became the father of another child:

9 Nathan (Libby), m. 15 Aug. 1852, Mary E. Morrill of Portland. He was brought up by Joshua Plummer. He was a stevedore in Portland awhile, and later an engineer on the Grand Trunk Railway. He was afterward a sailor many years, and died in the Homeopathic Hospital, in New York, 19 July 1881. His wife was divorced from him, and removed to Charlestown, Mass., where she married again. Children, born in Portland:
1 Georgianna, m. —— Thompson of Charlestown.
2 Ida, m. —— —— of Charlestown.
3 Charles, b. about 1860; is a sailor.

6-3-2

Joseph Libby, born in that part of Hampton, N. H., which is now Rye, 15 Aug. 1715; married, 23 Feb. 1741, Margaret Abbot.

He was a farmer. He moved from Rye to Portsmouth, where he lived some years, and, probably in 1758, removed thence to Barrington. From Barrington he became the second settler of New Durham, N. H., which was probably in 1767. He settled on New Durham Ridge, on the farm now owned, in two farms, by Charles Brackett and James Berry. There he lived until his death, which took place in the middle of July, 1778. His widow was living as late as April 1794.

Children:

1 Reuben, bap. 13 Mar. 1743; m. 1st, Sarah Fullerton; 2d, Abigail (Pinkham) Smith.
2 Mary, bap. 2 Sept. 1744; m. Joseph Glidden of Eppingham.
3 Jane, bap. 11 Jan. 1747; m. —— Rowe.
4 Abraham, bap. 17 July 1748; died young.
5 Abraham, bap. 26 Aug. 1750; m. Hannah Copp. He had half his father's homestead on New Durham Ridge, but after a few years sold it to Durrell Stevens and settled on the farm in Alton, now owned by Oliver Gilman. He was a volunteer in the Revolution and was at the battle of Bunker Hill. He was afterward on a committee for hiring soldiers. He died in Alton 4 Mar. 1829, and his wife a few years later. They had no children, but adopted a child (said to have been his own):
a Hannah (Libby) m. 8 June 1797, Thomas C. Edgerly.
6 Joseph, bap. 5 Nov. 1752; unm. He was a blacksmith, and was killed in the assault on Quebec.
7 Moses, bap. 29 Nov. 1754; died young.
8 Ephraim, bap. 30 Nov. 1755; m. Judith Page.
9 Olley, bap. 30 April 1758; was mentioned in her father's will, 1771, but probably died unmarried.
10 Anthony, m. Lydia Ayers.
11 Benjamin, b. 12 June 1761; m. Sarah Mason.
12 Margaret, died in New Durham at an advanced age; unm.

6-4-1

John Libby, born in Rye, N. H., 1 Aug. 1720; married 26 June 1743, Eleanor Berry, said to have been a French woman.

Not long after his marriage, he removed to Epsom, where he and his cousin Samuel had bought land some years before. He there served two years as selectman, and filled other town offices. About 1762 he moved to Chester, and thence, probably in 1765, to Chichester. In 1779 he removed to Parsonsfield, Me., and then, in the year 1781 it is said, he and his sons Meshack and Stephen became the first settlers of what is now Porter, Me. For this service they received each a hundred-acre lot of land. That which John Libby received is now owned by Wm. T. Taylor. He died about the year 1804, and his wife about the same time. They were buried a few rods westerly from their house.

Their children were:

1 Keziah, bap. 20 May 1744; m. 21 Mar. 1769, Daniel Sargent.
2 Meshack, bap. 5 May 1745; m. Deborah Ely.
3 John, bap. 29 Mar. 1747; died in middle age; unm. He was of remarkable memory, but otherwise of weak intellect. He was prone to wander from place to place, but his chief abode was Parsonsfield, where he died.
4 Mary, bap. 25 Sept. 1748; m. Daniel Knowles.
5 Jonathan, bap. 14 April 1751; m. Hannah McCoy.
6 Enoch, bap. 18 April 1755; m. Mary Newbegin.
7 Josiah, died a young man, unm., in the Revolution.
8 Simeon, married Hannah Knowles.
9 Stephen, b. 26 April 1763; m. Mary Knowles, and Nancy and Sally Matthews.

6-4-4

Isaac Libby, born in Rye, N. H., 28 Feb. 1725; married first, 5 Feb. 1748, Ann Symmes; second, 20 Sept. 1766, Margaret Kalderwood.

He removed to Epsom a few years after his marriage, and settled near what is now Epsom Center, in the locality which became known as *New Rye*. In addition to his farming, he owned and ran a gristmill, built on his own farm, on the little Suncook River; also a lathe, in which he turned out the old-fashioned wooden dishes. He served two years as selectman and filled many minor town offices. He died 28 Aug. 1810. His second wife died 29 July 1807.

His children by his first wife were:

1 Mary, bap. Sept. 1748; m. 22 Oct. 1765, Abner Evans of Chichester; lived in Barre, Vt.
2 Isaac, bap. April 1750; m. Abigail ———.
3 Elizabeth, bap. Jan. 1752; m. 27 Feb. 1772, Aaron Burbank, and settled in Strafford, Vt.
4 Arthur Bennick, (corrupted to Bennet), b. Jan. 1754; m. Eleanor Haynes.
5 Abigail, married Jethro Libby, 6-4-8-3.
6 Job, b. 14 Feb. 1759; m. 24 Mar. 1785, Rebecca Pearson.
7 Susannah, m. 28 Jan. 1786, Theophilus Cass.

By his second wife:

8 Nathan, b. 20 July 1767; m. Abigail Fowler.
9 Lucy, b. 17 April 1769; m. 24 May 1787, Capt. John Ham.
10 Abraham, b. 15 Aug. 1773; m. Abigail Pearson.

11 Margaret, b. 10 Aug. 1776; m. 12 Feb. 1795, William Sherborne of Epsom, afterward of Stanstead, Que.
12 Joshua, b. 7 Aug. 1778; m. Sally Grant.

6-4-5

ARTHUR LIBBY, born in Rye, N. H., 5 April 1728; married 23 April 1852, DEBORAH SMITH. He was a farmer. He lived in Rye until his removal to Candia. 17 May 1777, he bought an eighty-acre lot in that town, the original right of Jonathan Kimball, and probably removed to his purchase at once. The farm was in the southern part of Candia, and is now owned by Edmund E. Smith. He died 21 July 1798, and his widow 23 Sept. 1824. Her age was 93 years.

Their children, all born in Rye, were:

1 Deborah Smith, b. 27 May 1754; d. 3 Aug. 1828; unm.
2 James, b. 14 May 1757. He was a captain in the Revolution, and was afterward drowned. He was never married.
3 Jonathan, b. 29 Jan. 1759; d. 18 Jan. 1831; unm. He was a farmer and always lived on the homestead.
4 Daniel, b. 12 Jan. 1762. He was a Revolutionary soldier. He died a young man; unm.
5 Meribah Smith, b. 9 Nov. 1765; d. 11 May 1827; unm.
6 Abraham, b. 5 April 1767; m. Ruth Palmer.
7 Isaac, b. 9 Jan. 1771; m. Ann Seavey.
8 Jacob, b. 20 Mar. 1774; m. Polly King.

6-4-8

REUBEN LIBBY, born in Rye, N. H., 11 Aug. 1734; married, first, 1 July 1754, SARAH GOSS of Rye; second, 31 Mar. 1773, in Portsmouth, N. H., SARAH TUCKER.*

He was a farmer. In 1764 he was of Epsom; and in 1767 of North Hampton; but he doubtless returned to Rye soon after. Upon his second marriage he removed to Gorham, Me., and from that place served a year in the Continental army. He reared his second family in Gorham, but died in Albany, where he was living with his son Benjamin, about 1820. His second wife died in Gray where Benjamin was then living, about 1815.

Children, by his first wife:

1 Olive, bap. 2 Feb. 1755; m. 30 Sept. 1797, Jabez Hayris, an Englishman.
2 Samuel, b. July 1757; m. Mehitable Seavey.
3 Jethro, bap. 9 Dec. 1759; m. Abigail Libby, 6-4-4-5.
4 Richard, b. 1762; m. Sarah Ross.
5 Reuben, b. 1763; m. Abigail Irish.
6 Sarah, bap. 30 Aug. 1767; m. —— Bagley, of Warren, Me.
7 Isaac, bap. 3 Mar. 1769; died young.

By second wife:

8 Abigail, m. Isaac Allen of Pownal.
9 Isaac, b. 27 June 1776; m. Rebecca Crockett.
10 Mary, b. 30 July 1779; m. Wallis Foss of Pownal.

*One grand-daughter says her name was *Abigail Foss.*

11 Elizabeth, b. 15 Oct. 1781; probably died young.
12 John, b. 22 Jan. 1784; m. Joanna Baker.
13 Benjamin, b. 4 May 1786; m. Priscilla Clay.
14 William, went into the eastern woods, a young man, and was never heard from.
15 Jacob, a bachelor; died 8 April 1864. He was a farmer, and lived for the most part with his sister Abigail, in Pownal.
16 Rachel, m. Charles E. Paine of Bethel.

6-6-1

SAMUEL LIBBY, born in Rye, N. H., 9 Feb. 1720; married first, 4 Dec. 1744, in Rye, ABIGAIL SYMMES; second, before 1759, PENELOPE (HUNTINGDON) BARBER. The first husband of the last wife had been carried off by the Indians, and was supposed to be dead, but after seven years he returned home and found his wife married. The two husbands gave the wife her choice: she chose her second husband, and Barber went off.

Upon his marriage, Samuel Libby probably settled in Epsom, where he already owned land. In Epsom he took an important part in the management of the town, serving repeatedly as selectman, town clerk, and in other offices. The last mention of his name in the Epsom town records is as selectman in 1763, and he doubtless left town immediately. He appeared in Machias, Me., in 1768, and lived there until after the Revolution. He then lived a short time at a place called Carleton's Streams, and finally went with his sons to St. Stephen, N. B., where he died of small pox some time after 27 Sept. 1791.

Children, probably all born in Epsom; by first wife:

1 Sarah, bap. 1745; probably died young.
2 Jacob, bap. 1747; m. Unity Parker of Annapolis, N. S.
3 Hannah, bap. 1751; probably died young.
4 ———, bap. 3 June 1754; probably died young.

By second wife:

5 Eben, b. about 1760; m. Lydia Young.

6-6-8

JOSEPH LIBBY, born in Rye, N. H., 25 Feb. 1737; married MARY ———. In 1763 he bought Paul Randall's inn, near Rye Center, and after running it about a year, [illegible]d. In 1765 or 6 his widow married Reuben Dearborn, jr., of North Hampton.

Joseph Libby's only child was:

1 Molly, bap. March 1763; m. Nathaniel Batchelder of Deerfield.

6-6-9

BENJAMIN LIBBY, born in Rye, N. H., 25 Feb. 1737; married first, JANE ———; second, 3 Oct. 1765, ABIGAIL HAINES, daughter of Matthias and Abigail Haines of Greenland, N. H.

He was a farmer. He lived in his native town until 1778, and then removed to a farm which he had purchased in Chester, N. H. In 1795 he sold that, and settled in Candia, close by the Chester line. When his grand-daughter, Nabby Hill, was married, he went to live with her, in Alexandria, and there died, at an advanced age. His wife outlived him several years.

Children, by first wife:

1 Sarah, bap. 17 Aug. 1760; m. —— Lane of Candia. It is probable that she first married, in 1779, in Chester, Israel Clifford.

By second wife:

2 Jane, b. about 1766; m. 1st, Samuel Worthen; 2d, —— Colley of Bridgewater.
3 Abigail, bap. June 1768; m. 3 March 1802, John Webster of Peeling, now Woodstock, N. H.
4 Mary, bap. 30 Sept. 1770; m. Henry Hill. Children:
  1 Sally (Hill), b. 9 March 1792; m. Jonathan Dearborn. She lives in Manchester, N. H.
  2 Nabby (Hill), b. 25 March 1794; m. Timothy Simonds.
  3 Mary (Hill), b. 1796; lives in Broom, Que.
  4 Henry (Hill), died aged 6 years.
5 Josiah, bap. 15 Sept. 1776; died young.

6-6-10

Abraham Libby, born in Rye, N. H., 29 Dec. 1739; married first, 24 Feb. 1763, Abigail Page; (died 2 June 1764); second, Mary Tarlton of Portsmouth.

He was a farmer in Rye until the death of his brother Joseph, when he administered upon his estate, and from that time run the tavern himself. It stood on the north side of the road from Rye Center to Breakfast Hill. It was burnt down one night and he did not rebuild it, but, in 1789, which was probably immediately afterward, removed to Chester, where he died 3 Aug. 1799. He was a sergeant in Capt. Joseph Parson's company of state troops in the Revolution, and later was on the town committee to hire men for the Continental army. After his death, his widow lived with her son Joseph, in Gilford, until 1833 or 4, when she went to live with her daughter Fogg, in North Sandwich, N. H., and there died, 3 June 1836, aged nearly 93.

Children, all born in Rye, by first wife:

1 Abigail, b. 13 Nov. 1763; m. John Morrison.

By second wife:

2 Joseph, b. 10 Nov. 1765; m. Deborah Rand.
3 Job, b. 18 June 1767. It is thought that he followed the sea, and died early in life, unmarried.
4 Mary, b. 28 Aug. 1768; m. 1794, Benjamin Gross.
5 Jacob, b. 19 Dec. 1770; m. Mary Brickett.
6 Elias Tarlton, b. 6 Sept. 1773; m. Phebe Dennett.
7 Abraham, b. 10 Feb. 1777; m. Betsey Hill, Susan Moore, and Betsey Whittier.
8 Sarah, b. 20 June 1779; m. 1st, Stephen Norris; 2d, Isaiah Fogg.
9 Benjamin, b. 20 June 1782; m. Rhoda Wilkinson.

7-1-2

HANNAH BROWN, married in 1731, RICHARD HUNNEWELL. She died 15 Dec. 1760.

Their children were:

1 Susannah (Hunnewell), b. 13 March 1734; d. 15 May 1754.
2 Hannah (Hunnewell), b. 30 Oct. 1735; m. Jonathan Libby, 1-1-3-4.
3 Elizabeth (Hunnewell), b. 17 Jan. 1738; d. 23 May 1754.
4 Lydia (Hunnewell), b. 6 Dec. 1741; d. 11 April 1754.
5 Richard (Hunnewell), b. 22 Feb. 1743; d. 6 May 1754.
6 Lucy (Hunnewell), b. 28 July 1746; m. Abner Libby, 5-7-6.
7 Anna (Hunnewell), b. 27 June 1750; m. 25 Feb. 1773, Nathaniel Meserve.
8 Abigail (Hunnewell), b. 12 Aug. 1752; m. Nehemiah Libby, 5-2-7.

7-1-5

SARAH BROWN, married, 30 April 1761, her deceased sister's husband, RICHARD HUNNEWELL. She died in 1817, at a very advanced age.

Their children were:

1 Elizabeth (Hunnewell), b. 27 Aug. 1763; m. Benjamin Libby, 1-1-2-2-3.
2 Richard (Hunnewell), b. 28 Feb. 1765; m. 19 Dec. 1786, Anna Wescott of Cape Elizabeth. They had the following children:
 1 Lucy (Hunnewell), b. 13 Sept. 1787.
 2 Joseph (Hunnewell), b. 1 July 1789.
 3 Anna (Hunnewell), b 9 April 1791.
 4 Richard (Hunnewell), b. 4 Aug. 1792.
 5 Theodosia (Hunnewell), b. 9 June 1795.
 6 Hannah (Hunnewell), b. 4 July 1798.
 7 Polly (Hunnewell), b. 16 Nov. 1800.
3 John (Hunnewell), b. 13 Jan. 1767; m. 23 May 1802, Mary Wescott. They had, among other children, the following:
 1 Narcissa (Hunnewell).
 2 Sarah (Hunnewell).
 3 William H. (Hunnewell), m. Sarah Ann Blossom.
 4 John (Hunnewell), m. Hannah Libby, 1-1-2-2-11-1.
 5 Richard (Hunnewell), lived a bachelor.
4 Sarah (Hunnewell), b. 29 Nov. 1769; m. Amos Libby, 10-5-3-5.
5 Phebe (Hunnewell), b. 13 April 1771; m. 7 Sept. 1800, Simeon Jones.

7-1-6

JOSHUA BROWN, m. 12 Nov. 1741, HANNAH POLLOW, 5-5-1. They lived in Scarborough.

Their children were:

1 Andrew (Brown), b. 7 Sept. 1742; died young.
2 John (Brown), b. 27 Dec. 1745; died young.
3 Joshua (Brown), b. 26 Aug. 1747; m. 16 July 1778, Esther Dam, 11-7-5-1, and settled in Raymond.
4 Hannah (Brown), b. 1749.
5 Andrew (Brown), b. 1752; m. 20 Nov. 1777, Rachel Small; settled in Gray, Me.
6 Abigail (Brown), b. 1755.
7 Susannah (Brown), b. 1758.
8 Joseph (Brown), b. 1761.
9 John (Brown), b. 1763.
10 Sarah (Brown), b. 1767.

9-5-1

SAMUEL FOGG, born in Kittery, Me., 1 June 1716; married 27 Jan. 1743, RACHEL MARINER of Falmouth, born 19 Aug. 1723.

He was carried to Scarborough by his father, and lived there until about 1775, when he moved to New Gloucester. He was a tailor by trade. In his younger days he was a school teacher. In 1741, for teaching school in Black Point meeting-house, he received "32 pounds in lumber."

His wife Rachel, the mother of his children, died 24 Mar. 1768, and he married second, 12 Nov. 1770, the widow Elizabeth Moody. She died 17 Mar. 1774, aged about fifty-eight. He died 30 Oct. 1798.

His children were:

1 Jeremiah (Fogg), b. 11 June 1744; m. Mary Warren.
2 Enoch (Fogg), b. 28 Mar. 1746; settled in New Gloucester.
3 Edmund (Fogg), b 28 Mar. 1748; settled in Parsonsfield.
4 Esther (Fogg), b. 29 Mar. 1750; d. 1 Jan. 1768.
5 Sarah (Fogg), b. 6 Aug. 1752; d. 4 July 1767.
6 —— (Fogg), b. 2 July 1754; d. next day.
7 Anna (Fogg), b. 29 Nov. 1755; m. Joseph Roberts.
8 Samuel (Fogg), b. 26 April 1760; settled in New Gloucester.
9 Rhoda (Fogg), b. 26 April 1762.
10 Rachel (Fogg), b. 12 Sept. 1764.

9-5-4

COL. REUBEN FOGG, born in Kittery, (now Eliot), Me., 1 June 1722; married 15 May 1744, MARGARET ELDER of Falmouth.

He accompanied his father to Scarborough, and had his homestead after his death. The old house stood on the site of the house now occupied by Joseph Larrabee. The farm included both his farm and the farm of Jordan L. Larrabee.

Col. Reuben Fogg was one of the chief inhabitants of the town of Scarborough. He was possessed of a fine estate, and filled nearly all the offices in the control of his townsmen. He was a colonel in the Revolutionary army. He died 25 Oct. 1797, having been for more than forty-five years a member of the Congregational church. His widow died 8 Jan. 1804.

Their children were:

1 Hannah (Fogg), b. 4 Mar. 1745.
2 Reuben (Fogg), b. 9 Dec. 1746; m. Rhoda Moody.
3 William (Fogg), b. 16 Dec. 1748; m. Mary Jordan.
4 David (Fogg), b. 18 April 1751; m. 5 Oct. 1775, Abigail Meserve.
5 Susannah (Fogg), b. 10 July 1753; m. 4 March 1773, Joseph Davis.
6 Betty (Fogg), b. 22 April 1755; m. Gideon Meserve.
7 Mary (Fogg), b. 24 Nov. 1757; m. 10 Dec. 1782, Capt. James Small. [See page 32.]
8 Jane (Fogg), bap. 23 Feb. 1760; died young.
9 George (Fogg), b. 16 Dec. 1760; m. 1 Aug. 1785, Lydia Marr, 1-5-3-2-5.
10 Charles (Fogg), b. 6 June 1763; m. 14 Oct. 1788, Anna Small of Scarborough.
11 Daniel (Fogg), b. 10 Nov. 1766; m. 6 Sept. 1789, Eunice March, 11-6-1-10.

9-5-6

KETURAH FOGG, born 5 Feb. 1727; married 3 Dec. 1753, ELISHA HANSCOM. They lived in Scarborough. He died 25 Feb. 1776. She outlived him.

Their children were:

1 Humphrey (Hanscom), b. 28 Jan. 1754; m. 20 Sept. 1781, Esther Libby, 11-7-2-2. Children:
 1 Joshua (Hanscom), b. 1782; m. Abigail Libby, 11-7-11-6.
 2 Keturah (Hanscom), b. 1784; m. William Libby, 1-1-2-2-11.
 3 Hannah (Hanscom), b. 1787; m. John Bradbury.
 4 John (Hanscom), m. 1st, Fannie Riggs; 2d, the widow Sloan.
2 Mary (Hanscom), b. 26 April 1756; died in old age; unmarried.
3 Daniel (Hanscom), b. 9 Sept. 1758; m. 10 Dec. 1789, Mary Dam, 11-7-5-7. They settled in Limington.
4 Esther (Hanscom), b. 9 June 1761; m. Richard Hunnewell Libby, 1-1-3-4-1.
5 Anna (Hanscom), b. 22 Nov. 1763; m. 15 Nov. 1787, Nelson Fogg, 9-8-4-2.
6 Elisha (Hanscom), b. 2 March 1766.
7 Hannah (Hanscom), bap. 1769; m. 27 Dec. 1804, Ebenezer Carle of Dunstan, Scarborough.

9-6-6

MOSES FOGG, born in Scarborough, 14 Oct. 1738; married 12 Feb. 1760, LYDIA LARRABEE. [See Larrabee, page 41.] She died soon after, and he married second, 15 Dec. 1763, Catherine Libby, 1-1-5-5.

He was a farmer, and settled on the homestead. He died 30 March 1812. His second wife outlived him, and died 12 Oct. 1822.

His children, by first wife, were:

1 Mary (Fogg), b. 25 Oct. 1760; m. William Libby, 11-7-1-4.
2 Moses (Fogg), b. 2 July 1762; m. Hannah Libby, 11-7-7-1.

By second wife:

3 Lydia (Fogg), b. 31 Jan. 1765; m. Samuel Libby, 5-2-3-1.
4 Abner (Fogg), b. 20 Nov. 1766; m. Anna Plummer.
5 Jonathan (Fogg), b. 3 Aug. 1769.
6 Benjamin (Fogg), b. 22 June 1771; m. Jane Fogg, daughter of William Fogg, 9-5-4-3; settled in Wales, Me.
7 Daniel (Fogg), b. 14 April 1773; m. Hannah Hanscom of Kittery; settled in Gorham, Me.
8 Ephraim (Fogg), b. 4 May 1775; m. Mary Gold of Kittery; settled in Wales, Me.
9 Hannah (Fogg), b. 5 May 1777; m. Samuel Tompson, Esq.*

*Samuel Tompson, Esq., born in Standish, Me., 11 Oct. 1773; was a son of Rev. John Tompson, afterward pastor of the Congregational church at South Berwick. His grandfather was the Rev. Wm. Tompson, mentioned on page 27. His mother was Sarah (Small) Tompson, dau. of Joshua Small, Esq. (See page 32.) His first wife was Mary, dau. of Rev. Thomas and Lydia (Jones) Lancaster. She died 11 Feb. 1813, and he married, second, 13 Oct. 1814, Hannah Fogg, as above. His children by his first wife were:

1 Sarah, b. 6 Dec. 1795; d. 9 Dec. 1876; unm.
2 William, b. 20 Nov. 1796; m. Rhoda Libby, 5-7-14-7.
3 Lydia Jones, b. 27 April 1798; m. William Maynard.
4 John Adams, b. 19 Sept. 1800; d. 16 Feb. 1825; unm.
5 Mary Lancaster, b. 12 Mar. 1802.

[OVER.]

10 Abigail (Fogg), b. 2 July 1779; m. 13 June 1833, Isaac Harmon.
11 John (Fogg), b. 13 Sept. 1781; lived a bachelor. He was a carpenter by trade, a major in the militia, and an exemplary christian. He died 12 Nov. 1854.
12 Elizabeth (Fogg), b. 13 Sept. 1783; died 23 Aug. 1804; unmarried.
13 Sarah (Fogg), b. 1 Jan. 1786; died at the age of seventy; unm.

9-8-1

SETH FOGG, born about 1730; married 25 July 1754, RUTH WATERHOUSE, 10-2-2-1. He was a shoemaker by trade, and lived on Scottow's Hill in Scarborough.

His children were:

1 Seth (Fogg), b. 22 Mar. 1755; m. 12 Dec. 1776, Leah Blake.
2 Mary (Fogg), b. 10 Oct. 1757.
3 Olive (Fogg), b. 13 Nov. 1759.
4 Ruth (Fogg), b. 8 Nov. 1761.
5 Elias (Fogg), b. 17 Aug. 1763.
6 Lydia (Fogg), b. 20 Mar. 1765.
7 Keziah (Fogg), b. 7 Dec. 1767.
8 Enoch (Fogg), b. 21 June 1769.
9 Dorothy (Fogg), b. 30 Oct. 1770.
10 Paulina (Fogg), b. 18 June 1772.
11 Dominicus (Fogg), b. 16 Mar. 1774; m. Lydia Ann Chute.
12 Rufus (Fogg), b. 22 Mar. 1776; m. 15 Dec. 1803, Margaret Libby, 5-7-8-7.
13 Joseph (Fogg), b. 19 Oct. 1779.

9-9-9

JOHN FOGG, born 17 Sept. 1750; married 17 Oct. 1776, ABIGAIL LEIGHTON, daughter of Dea. William Leighton.

He had his father's homestead and occupied the same house. He died 8 April 1827. His widow died 27 Sept. 1840.

Children:

1 Abigail (Fogg), b. 22 Dec. 1777; d. 22 Mar. 1825; unm.
2 Elizabeth (Fogg), b. 27 Feb. 1780; m. 28 Nov. 1799, Nathaniel Hammond.
3 John (Fogg), b. 8 Feb. 1783; m. Mary Staples.
4 Mary (Fogg), b. 23 Aug. 1785; m. 17 Mar. 1814, Samuel Kennard.
5 James (Fogg), b. 21 July 1788; d. 25 Oct. 1798.
6 William (Fogg), b. 3 Nov. 1790; m. 1st, Betsey D. Hill; 2d, Mehitable P. Moody.
7 Joseph (Fogg), b. 3 Mar. 1793.
8 Nancy (Fogg), b. 29 March 1795.
9 Miriam (Fogg), b. 5 Oct. 1797; m. Nathaniel Kennard.

---

6 Samuel, b. 31 Aug. 1804; died in infancy.
7 Dorothy Lancaster, b. 24 Sept. 1805; m. Storer Libby, 11-7-2-4-8.
8 Elizabeth Ann, b. 27 July 1807; m. Capt. Wm. Hasty. [See page 55.]
9 Samuel, b. 25 Oct. 1809; d. 15 Jan. 1827.
10 Hannah, b. 3 Nov. 1812.

By second wife, Hannah, 9-6-6-9:

11 Edward, b. 16 Nov. 1815; m. 5 Dec. 1844, Hannah, dau. of Susannah (Libby), Larrabee, 5-7-14-3. She died 7 Sept. 1875.
12 Catherine Fogg, b. 21 June 1818; m. Capt. Seth L. Hasty. [See Hasty, p. 55.]

10-1-2

JOSIAH LIBBY, born in Kittery, (now Eliot), Me., 25 Oct. 1716; married 22 June 1742, MARY STONE of Scarborough.

He left Kittery with his father and became a farmer. He lived on, or near, Scottow's Hill for about ten years succeeding his marriage, and then moved to Machias. He was probably among the first settlers in 1763. He lived at what is now Machias Village, and died shortly before April, 1786. His wife outlived him.

Their children were:

1 Eleanor, bap. 13 Nov. 1743; m. Stephen Fogg of Machias.
2 Reuben, bap. 3 Mar. 1745; m. Rebecca Weston.
3 Joseph, bap. 15 Mar. 1747; m. Jane Cole.
4 Elijah, bap. 11 Dec. 1748; m. 1st, Mary Dresser; 2d, Mindwell Dresser.
5 Hannah, bap. 7 Oct. 1750; m. Peter Coolbroth of what is now Machiasport.
6 Josiah, b. 17 Feb. 1758; m. Sarah Holmes.
7 Nathan, bap. 19 Aug. 1759; m. Polly Larrabee.

10-1-5

TIMOTHY LIBBY, born about 1724, in that part of Kittery, Me., which is now Eliot; married 9 Oct. 1746, SARAH STONE of Scarborough.

He was carried by his father to Scarborough when a child. He grew up and settled on a farm near Scottow's Hill, where all his children were born. In 1763 he became one of the first settlers of Machias. The following narrative of the cause of the settlement of Machias is given by Henry A. Libby of Machiasport, 10-1-5-5-3-3. It differs from published accounts, yet, although it may be incorrect in some of its details, it is probably a substantially correct account of the discovery of Machias by those Scarborough people who formed the first permanent settlement there.

Speaking of his grandfather, he says: He told me one day when I was at work with him (I was quite small) how his father came to settle in Machias. When he lived in Scarborough it was his practice in the winter to go east in a small vessel on a sealing voyage. It was on a return voyage, some hundred and fifteen or twenty years ago, that he encountered a gale and storm and tried to make what is now called Cutler Harbor. He made a mistake in the headland, ran ashore in a small cove, and lost his vessel and cargo. Then he had to get home in his small boat. In following along the coast, as was necessary for him to do, he rowed into Machias River. Struck with its beauty, he followed it to its head. Here he found the natural facilities so good that he determined to make it his future home. He returned to Scarborough, ... and the next spring, taking his own family, and getting some eight or ten families more, they moved to their new abode.

He received, as one of the original settlers, a seven-acre lot, where the village of Machias now stands. Here he made his residence, and a few years later, (previous to June 1766), died. His widow improved this land until near the close of her life, and then all but her dower was sold to John Underwood. She was living as late as Nov. 1787.

The children of Timothy Libby were:

1 Sarah, bap. 27 Dec. 1747; m. 30 Sept. 1767, John Berry of Machias.
2 Esther, bap. 4 June 1749; m. Jonathan Pine of Machias.
3 Timothy, bap. 6 Jan. 1751; m. Martha Holmes. He was a farmer, and lived on the southern side of Pleasant Point. He died in 1785. His widow married —— Richardson, and moved west. Only child:
   1 Sarah, b. 1781; either died in childhood or went west with her mother.
4 Mary, bap. 22 April 1753; m. Amos Boynton of Machias.
5 David, b. 31 Aug. 1755; m. Abigail Fitts.
6 Obadiah, bap. 15 Jan. 1758; m. Mary Hill.
7 Daniel, bap. 21 Aug. 1763; m. Hannah Eastman.

10-1-6

Capt. David Libby, born in Kittery, now Eliot, Me., about 1727; married first, 13 Dec. 1750, Dorcas Means; she died, and he married second, in April, 1766, the widow Joanna (Jose) Page, daughter of Martin and Mercy Jose of Scarborough.

David Libby early adopted the following of the sea, and became captain of a coaster. During the French war he was engaged in transporting supplies to the garrison at Black Point. He bought a lot at Blue Point, and built him a house there. He sold this property in December, 1762, and was one of the company who formed the first settlement at Machias, in 1763. He did not stay there long. In June, 1768, he sold his seven-acre home lot to Samuel Libby, 6-6-1, and soon after removed to Providence, R. I., where he resided during the Revolution, and some years after. In his old age he and his wife returned to Maine. She died near the home of her childhood. After her death, her husband led an unsettled, homeless life, stopping here and there in the neighborhood of Scarborough. The time and place of his death are unknown.

His children, by his first wife, were:

1 Jane, bap. 16 Feb. 1752; m. Benjamin Rice of Scarborough Corner.
2 George, bap. 30 Sept. 1753; probably died young.
3 Joseph, bap. 8 Feb. 1756; probably died young.
4 Robert, bap. 13 Aug. 1757; m. 1st, Hannah Prout; 2d, Rebecca Trickey, 10-8-4-3.
5 Isaac, bap. 12 Oct. 1760; m. Sarah Waterhouse.
6 Dorcas, bap. 19 June 1763; lived with her sister, Mrs. Rice, in the early part of her life, and then became housekeeper for Jordan Prout, a bachelor, with whom she lived more than forty years. She died 17 March 1849.

By second wife:

7 David, b. 1770; m. Elizabeth McKenney.
8 Hannah,* married in Providence.
9 Nancy,* married in Providence.
10 Lucy,* married in Providence. It was probably she that married James Franklin in Providence, 6 May 1804.

*Tradition.

10-1-8

THOMAS LIBBY, born in Scarborough 16 Nov. 1733; married, 15 Nov. 1753, MARY LARRABEE. [See Larrabee, page 41.]

He was a farmer, and had his father's homestead. For a short time after his marriage he lived in the old garrison-house, and then built a house about two rods northeast of the old burying ground. In 1775 he bought a large tract of land, part of the Bonython patent, then partly in Saco and partly in Scarborough, but now all in Saco, and shortly after moved onto it. He built his house about twenty-five rods west of the present "Heath" meeting-house, and there ended his days 6 Jan. 1821, aged 87. His wife died 6 Sept. 1818, aged 83.

He was on the Committee of Correspondence and Safety, during the Revolution, and served a number of years as selectman, and as town clerk.

His children were:

1 Thomas, b. 12 Nov. 1754; m. Mary Libby, 10-2-1-4, and three other wives.
2 Zebulon, bap. 10 April 1757; m. Lydia Andrews.
3 Solomon, bap. 26 Aug. 1759; m. Sarah Seavey.
4 Philip, b. 16 May 1762; m. Mary McKenney.
5 John, b. 24 March 1764; m. Drusilla Graffam.
6 Mary, bap. Sept. 1766; m. 1783, James Rice.
7 Rebecca, bap. 18 Nov. 1770; probably died young.
8 Eunice, bap. 10 Sept. 1775; m. Stephen Seavey.
9 Jennie, bap. 10 Sept. 1775; died 13 Sept. 1777.

10-2-1

SAMUEL LIBBY, born 7 July 1714, in Kittery, Me.; married 25 Dec. 1745, in Scarborough, ELIZABETH HUBBARD, daughter of Richard Hubbard of Kingston, N. H., and niece of the wife of John Libby, 11-6, with whom she was living. She was an aunt of John Hubbard, Governor of Maine 1850, 1851, and 1852.

Samuel Libby went with his father to Scarborough, and when he was married settled on Scottow's Hill, then thickly covered with oaks, and cleared him a farm. He was industrious and accumulated sufficient real estate to give to each of his four sons large farms. He died of starvation, caused by the palsy, which prevented his swallowing. His death occurred 12 May 1787. His widow died in 1796.

Their children were:

1 Jeremiah, b. 5 Nov. 1746; m. Anna Libby, 1-1-6-6.
2 Theophilus, b. 15 April 1749; m. Hannah Berry.
3 Ruth, bap. 24 Dec. 1754; buried 15 Oct. 1756.
4 Mary, b. 27 May 1756; m. Thomas Libby, 10-1-8-1.
5 Samuel, b. 17 Dec. 1759; m. Abigail Graffam.
6 Richard Hubbard, b. 27 Oct. 1763; m. Anne Berry, dau. of Jane (Libby) Berry, 1-1-6-2.

10-2-2

MARY LIBBY, born 12 April 1716 or 1717, in Kittery, Me.: married, 12 June 1735, JOSEPH WATERHOUSE; died 21 Nov. 1756.

Joseph Waterhouse was born in Portsmouth, N. H., 11 April 1711. His father was Timothy Waterhouse, and his grandfather Richard Waterhouse, whose wife was a daughter of Reinald Fernald, the first surgeon that emigrated to New Hampshire.

About 1733 Joseph Waterhouse moved to Scarborough, where he married and settled near Scottow's Hill. He was by trade both a tanner and shoemaker, and these trades, in connection with his farming, enabled him to gain a good property.

After his first wife's death, he married the widow Rachel (Norman) Smith, by whom he had Betsey, married Richard Berry; Susannah, married Timothy Berry; and Sarah, married Isaac Libby, 10-1-6-5. He died 6 July 1796.

The children of Joseph and Mary Waterhouse were:

1 Ruth (Waterhouse), b. 21 June 1736; m. Seth Fogg, 9-8-1..
2 Joseph (Waterhouse), b. 12 Feb. 1738; died at the age of 16
3 Olive (Waterhouse), b. 14 Sept. 1739; m. 30 July 1761, William Harmon.
4 Timothy (Waterhouse), b. 18 July 1741; m. Sarah Small.
5 Molly (Waterhouse), b. 31 May 1743; m. 25 April 1763, Ephraim Carter.
6 Samuel (Waterhouse), b. 21 Dec. 1744; settled in Scarborough.
7 Enoch (Waterhouse), b. 23 Nov. 1746; settled in Machias.
8 John (Waterhouse), b. 21 March 1748; m. Betsey Banks.
9 George (Waterhouse), b. 21 Jan. 1750; m. 28 Oct. 1775, Dorcas Libby, 1-5-2-3-1.
10 Theophilus (Waterhouse), b. 17 Dec. 1751; m. Hannah Goodwin.
11 Joseph (Waterhouse), b. 12 Feb. 1754; m. Lydia Harmon.
12 Nathaniel (Waterhouse), b. 6 Feb. 1756; m. Elizabeth Cane of Wells.

10-2-4

Enoch Libby, born about 1724, in Kittery; married 5 March 1746, Elizabeth Plummer, daughter of Aaron Plummer.

Enoch Libby, it is said, was seven years old when his father removed to Scarborough. He grew up and settled on his father's homestead. He was a prosperous farmer, and gave each of his sons a farm of his own. He died 1794. His widow died about 1807.

Their children were:

1 Lucy, b. 1747; m. Capt. Anthony Libby, 1-1-2-7.
2 Lemuel, bap. Sept. 1749; m. Mehitable Bragdon.
3 Dominicus, b. 27 Dec. 1751; m. Dorothy Small.
4 Sarah, bap. May, 1754; m. Phineas Libby, 1-1-6-5.
5 Olive, bap. July, 1757; m. Solomon Bragdon.
6 Elizabeth, bap. Sept., 1759; m. Joseph Pilsbury.
7 Abigail, bap. Jan., 1762; m. Lieut. Jonathan Libby, 1-1-5-9.
8 Enoch, m. 1st, Rebecca Harmon; 2d, Abigail Libby, 10-5-4-1-6.
9 Samuel, m. Nell Patrick.

10-4-1

Joseph Libby, born in Kittery, 14 Dec. 1725; married Shuah Staples, daughter of Enoch Staples of Kittery.

Soon after his marriage he settled in Saco, on land which he had received from his father, the same now owned by Silas W. Milliken. There he lived and died.

Although he always lived on a farm, he was an excellent millwright, and built many mills in the region about him. He was a number of years one of the selectmen of Saco. His death occurred 26 July 1802. His widow died 22 Mar. 1826, aged 94.

Their children were:

1 Joseph, b. 16 June 1750, in Kittery; m. Priscilla Carl.
2 Anne, b. 3 April 1753, in Saco; died 10 Jan. 1801; unm.
3 Martha, b. 27 Oct. 1755; died young.
4 Eunice, b. 14 Feb. 1760; m. John Cleaves.
5 Shuah, b. 2 Oct. 1762; m. Samuel Tarbox.
6 David, b. 25 Mar. 1765; m. Elizabeth Cleaves.
7 Gideon, b. 9 Oct. 1767; was a seaman; lived until middle age, and then was numbered among the missing.
8 Daniel, b. 28 Mar. 1772; m. Mary Tarbox.

10-4-3

Reuben Libby, born 29 Aug. 1731, in Kittery; married Catherine Staples.

Shortly after his marriage he settled at "Pudding-hole," on land which his father gave him. The house he then built is still standing, occupied by the widow of his grandson, Asa Libby. Here he died 24 Sept. 1804. His widow died 2 Nov. 1818.

Their children were:

1 Olive, b. 27 Dec. 1758; m. 31 July 1786, Capt. Samuel Langdon of York.
2 George, b. 21 Jan. 1760, the first child born in the new house; m. Mary Bartlett.
3 Anna, b. 14 April 1762; m. 3 Feb. 1785, Capt. Samuel Paul.
4 Nathan, b. 24 April 1768; died young.
5 Eunice, b. 23 Aug. 1770; m. 17 Mar. 1796, Dea. John Hill.
6 Nathan, b. 17 June, 1776; died young.

10-4-6

Nathan Libby, born about 1740; married 26 Sept. 1771, the widow of Tobias Shapleigh, whose maiden name was Jemima Littlefield of Wells.

He was a farmer and settled on his father's homestead, where he died 23 Dec. 1816. His widow died about 1835.

Children:

1 Gideon, b. 2 Sept. 1772; m. Anna Hammond.
2 Anna, b. 1775; m. 15 May 1799, Capt. Elisha Goodwin.
3 Solomon, b. 31 July 1777; m. Elizabeth Hammond.
4 Jane, m. 1st, James Libby, 10-7-1-4-1; 2d, Capt. Caleb Frost.
5 Nathan, b. 1782; died a young man; unm.
6 Simon, b. 1784, m. 25 Oct. 1807, Isabella Shapleigh. He received his father's homestead, and always lived on it. He gave, off his farm, the lot on which stood the Congregational church, which was burned in 1880. He died suddenly, 20 Sept. 1840, having outlived his wife only a few weeks. He had no children and left his property to Ira Paul.

10-5-1

Elisha Libby, born in 1725; married first, 9 Feb. 1748, Esther Fogg, 9-5-7; second, 28 Nov. 1753, Abigail Meserve, daughter of John and Jemima (Hubbard) Meserve of Scarborough.

He grew up in Scarborough and settled on land given him by his father. He cleared up the farm now owned by Osgood Libby, 10-5-1-10-6. His house stood on the site of the main part of the present one. He died 18 Mar. 1791. His widow died 5 June 1817.

His children, all by wife Abigail, were:

1 Elisha, b. 28 July 1754; m. Eunice Jones.
2 Moses, b. 13 May 1756; m. Anna Libby, 11-7-1-2.
3 Esther, b. 29 Sept. 1758; m. 2 Mar. 1784, James Jones.
4 Benjamin, b. 17 Feb. 1760; m. Phebe Rackliff.
5 Abigail, b. 20 June 1763; m. 16 Feb. 1802, Jos. Stevens of Unity, Me.
6 Dorothy, b. 25 March 1765; d. 9 Oct. 1805; unmarried.
7 Anna, b. 24 April 1767; m. Mark Libby, 10-5-4-7.
8 Jane, b. 1 May 1769; m. 2 Oct. 1791, Benjamin Irish of Gorham.
9 Lucy, b. 13 Aug. 1772; m. 1st, 14 March 1803, John Rackliff; 2d, John McDaniel.
10 Rufus, b. 23 April 1777; m. 1st, Charlotte Plummer; 2d, Esther Libby, 11-7-11-5; 3d, Ann (Bickford) Lord.
11 Martha, b. 13 May, 1780; m. 25 April 1802, Abraham Plummer.

10-5-2

Matthew Libby, born 25 April 1729; married first, 5 June 1750, Sarah Hanscom; second, 10 Feb. 1774, Hannah Hasty. [See page 55.]

He settled on part of his father's homestead. He was a shoemaker by trade, and served many years as sealer of leather. His house stood a short distance to the east of the present residence of Charles Robinson. He lived there until March, 1800, and then, with his second wife and family, and his son-in-law Moody, moved onto a farm which he had purchased, in what was then the town of Litchfield, but now Webster. There he died three or four years later. His widow died about 1818.

Children, by first wife:

1 Mark, b. 2 March 1751; m. Relief Berry.
2 Sarah, b. 16 June 1752; m. 4 Nov. 1773, Benjamin Mitchell of Windham.
3 Reuben, b. 3 March 1755; m. Mercy Marr, 1-5-3-2-3.
4 Eleanor, b. 22 April 1756; probably died young.
5 Joanna, m. 11 June 1786, Isaac Fly of Gorham.
6 Margery, m. 30 March 1796, William Ingalls of Baldwin.
7 Martha, m. 27 Nov. 1788, John Burnal of Gorham.

By second wife:

8 Letis, b. 23 Sept. 1778; m. 31 Feb. 1799, Elias Moody.
9 Samuel Small, b. 2 May 1781; m. Rebecca (Ross) Borden.
10 Hannah, m. John Given of Wales.
11 Rufus King, b. 30 Sept. 1788; m. Roxanna and Betsey Jones.

10-5-3

MARK LIBBY, born 8 June 1731, in Scarborough; married 22 Nov. 1753, LYDIA SKILLINGS.

He was a farmer, and settled about two miles north of Oak Hill. His house is still standing, though unoccupied. He died a young man, in 1763 or 4. His widow married, 9 Aug. 1774, Samuel Lowell, and died 12 Oct. 1812.

Children of Mark and Lydia Libby:*

1 Dorcas, b. 28 Nov. 1755; m. 11 Nov. 1776, William Jose.
2 Betty, bap. 7 May 1758; died young.
3 Lois, b. 15 Nov. 1759; died 15 Feb. 1832; unmarried.
4 John Skillings, b. 23 Nov. 1761; m. Rhoda Cummings.
5 Amos, b. 1 Dec. 1763; m. Sarah Hunnewell, 7-1-5-4.

10-5-4

ALLISON LIBBY, born 12 Sept. 1733; married first, 24 Oct. 1754, SARAH SKILLINGS; second, 12 Sept. 1775, MARY LIBBY, 1-1-3-10, widow of Edward Libby, 11-7-8.

He was by trade a shoemaker, but farming was his chief occupation. He settled in the interior of the town, on the farm now occupied by Demas Libby, 10-5-4-16-4. He died 8 April 1813, leaving a good property. His widow died 8 Dec. 1818.

His children, by his first wife, were:

1 Simeon, b. 3 Sept. 1755; m. Abigail Smith.
2 Allison, b. 6 April 1757; m. Sarah Dam, 11-7-5-3.
3 Edward, b. 10 Feb. 1759; m. Elizabeth Libby, 11-7-7-2.
4 Sarah, b. 3 Jan. 1761; m. Josiah Libby, 1-1-3-9.
5 Joseph, bap. 5 June 1763; died young.
6 Solomon, died young.
7 Mark, b. 15 Feb. 1765; m. Anna Libby, 10-5-1-7.
8 Betsey, b. 8 Feb. 1767; m. 15 Aug. 1791, Paul Lombard.
9 Hannah, b. 2 Nov. 1769; m. 12 April 1787, William Jones.
10 Josiah S., b. 21 Oct. 1773; m. 1st, Sarah Libby, 11-7-11-2; 2d, Lydia (Harmon) Davis.
11 Alexander, bap. 18 Dec. 1774; died young.

By second wife:

12 Simon, bap. 28 Oct. 1777; died young.
13 Morris, b. 7 Sept. 1780; m. Mary Ann Swain.
14 Charlotte, b. 18 Jan. 1783; m. 5 Jan. 1800, Joseph Bryant.
15 Solomon, b. 22 March 1785; m. Fanny Sylvester.
16 Demas, b. 4 May 1787; m. Mary Berry.
17 Naomi, b. 11 Sept. 1789; died 1 May 1808; unmarried.

10-5-5

NATHANIEL LIBBY, born 5 Sept. 1735; married 19 Dec. 1759, MARY MESERVE. [See page 37.]

He was a farmer and lived at first on part of his father's homestead. Later he sold this, and bought land of the Prout

*Nathan Libby, 5-7-15, was brought up in this family, and really derived his surname from his mother, but he and his descendants will be found under his father, Capt. John Libby, 5-7.

estate, on which he lived until his death, 18 Oct. 1798. His widow died 13 May 1832.

Their children were:

1 Robert, b. 20 Oct. 1761; m. Elizabeth March, 11-6-1-5.
2 Harvey, b. 18 Dec. 1763; m. Sarah Small.
3 Polly, m. 13 Sept. 1786, Andrew Plaisted, 11-7-3-6.
4 Sally, m. 20 June 1790, Benjamin Weeks of Durham.
5 Jemima, m. 2 April 1790, George Meserve of Limington.
6 Betsey, m. 20 Nov. 1790; Joseph Dearborn of Buxton.
7 Joseph, died 10 March 1802, in the West Indies; unm.
8 Lydia, m. 4 Oct. 1797, Stephen Meserve of Hollis.
9 Nathaniel, m. 1st, Lucy Weston; 2d, Lorana Moses.
10 Luke, b. 2 Feb. 1780; m. Susannah Matthews.
11 Simon, died on shipboard, a young man, unmarried.
12 Dorothy, b. Sept. 1787; m. Capt. Reuben Libby, 10-5-2-1-1.

10-5-6

Luke Libby, born in Scarborough 15 Aug. 1738; married 21 Aug. 1760, Dorothy McKenney. [See page 63].

He received from his father by will part of his homestead farm. This he sold in 1771 to Col. Benjamin Larrabee, and bought a part of the Prout estate, on which he lived until his death. In 1789 his widow and children sold this to Reuben Fogg, jr., (it now forms part of the pasture of Jordan L. Larrabee, and is known as the *Luke field*), and removed to Danville, now Auburn. There she died about 1836.

Children:

1 Reuben, m. 6 Feb. 1782, Elizabeth Burnham.
2 Dominicus, b. 13 June 1763; m. Dorothy McKenney.
3 Eunice, died in Scarborough, 10 April 1850; unm.
4 Luke, b. 1767; m. Betsey Mitchell.
5 Isaac, b. 1768; m. Dorothy Meserve.
6 Hannah, m. John Vosmus of Durham.
7 William, b. 1 Jan. 1772; m. Hannah McKenney.
8 Humphrey, m. 3 Jan. 1799, Keziah Meserve. [See page 37.] He was a farmer in Danville until the war of 1812. He died of fever at Saggett's Harbor. His widow lived to old age and died with her daughter Jane. Children:
    1 Emily, m. Israel Jones, son of Hannah (Libby) Jones, 10-5-4-9.
    2 Jane, m. Sewall Blanchard of Cumberland.
    3 Margaret, m. Levi Prince of Pittsfield.
    4 Mary, b. 7 Mar. 1807; m. Isaiah Knight of Colebrook, N. H.; lives in Boston.
    5 Martha, m. Enoch Howes of Boston.
    6 Hannah, m. as 2d wife, John Jones, a brother of Israel.
    7 Keziah, m. Stebben Andros of Oswego, N. Y.

10-7-1

Ephraim Libby, born 22 March 1732, in Eliot, then Kittery, Me.; married first, 31 March 1757, Sarah Morrell; she died 29 Oct. 1760, and he married second, 24 June 1762, Anne Spinney, daughter of Andrew Spinney.

He was a farmer, and lived and died in the house where he was born. His death took place 11 April 1783. His widow died 16 March 1818, aged 77.

Children, by first wife:

1 Elizabeth, b. 10 Jan. 1758; d. 15 June 1760.
2 John, b. 29 Jan. 1760; m. Sarah Leathers.

By second wife:

3 Joel, b. 13 May 1762; m. 1st. Betty Staples; 2d, Sarah Hanscom.
4 David, b. 15 May 1764; m. Abigail Tobey.
5 Abel, b. 2 Aug. 1767; d. 6 Aug. 1767.
6 Clement, b. 4 Sept. 1768; m. Phebe Tibbetts.
7 Ezra, b. 20 Dec. 1770; m. 1st, Mary Remmick; 2d, Elizabeth Tobey.
8 Sarah, b. 27 April 1774; m. 2 Sept. 1804, Eli Cole.
9 Anne, b. 1776; m. 3 Jan. 1805, Andrew Spinney.
10 Elinor, b. 1778; d. 24 Feb. 1815; unmarried.

11-2-2

MATTHEW LIBBY, born in Kittery, now Eliot, Me., 2 Feb. 1733; married, 1 Sept. 1754, LYDIA LIBBY, 11-11-2.

He died within five or six years after his marriage. His widow died between April, 1780, and March, 1782.

They had a son:

1 Matthew, married, 5 April 1781, Lois Hanscom.

11-2-3

ZEBULON LIBBY, born Nov. 1737, in Eliot, then Kittery; married 11 May 1769, SARAH MILLIKEN of Scarborough.

His father had lived in Scarborough a short time, and had received a grant of land on Scottow's Hill. A portion of this Zebulon received from his father by will, and soon after moved onto it. He was by trade a cordwainer, but seems to have given his chief attention to agriculture. He married in Scarborough, and lived there until about the time of the breaking out of the Revolution. He had been in the French war, and looked forward to further war service with aversion. It was his determination to avoid this that led him to settle in the remote wilds of what afterward became Washington Plantation, and is now Newfield. It is said that he and Paul McDonald were the first settlers. He cleared the farm in the northeast corner of the town, now owned by John M. Thompson, and there died 21 Sept. 1804. His widow died in the winter of 1733-4.

Their children were:

1 Robert, b. 24 Aug. 1769; m. Lydia Bean.
2 Jerusha, b. 2 April 1771; m. 1796, Stephen Moulton.
3 Zebulon, b. 29 March 1773; m. Jemima Smith.
4 Mary, said to have been the first child born in Newfield, born 9 Jan. 1776; m. 1st, 9 Oct. 1803, Isaac Milliken of Scarborough; 2d, Robert Hasty of Limington; died 3 Jan. 1876, being within six days of 100 years old.
5 Abigail, b. 30 Nov. 1778; m. 18 Aug. 1805, Charles Dorman.

6 Matthew, died at the age of 12 years.
7 Stephen, b. 1783; died 2 Dec. 1897; unmarried. His death was caused by eating poisonous wild plums.
8 Sally, b. 1787; d. 12 Jan. 1805.
9 Lucy, b. Oct. 1788; d. 12 Oct. 1805.

11-2-4

AZARIAH LIBBY, born 1740, in Kittery, now Eliot; married 16 Dec. 1762, ELIZABETH PAUL.

He had his father's homestead, and lived on it till after his daughter Anne was married, and soon after sold his farm to David Libby, 10-7-1-4, and followed his son Nathaniel to Limerick. He bought a farm about one-fourth of a mile west of the present Limerick village, and there lived until his death, 5 May 1820. His widow died 29 Dec. 1829.

Their children, beside three who died in Kittery, all in one week of a throat distemper, were:

1 Nathaniel, b. 22 Feb. 1763; m. Miriam Gilpatrick.
2 Anne, m. 6 Aug. 1788, George Spinney of Kittery.
3 Joseph, b. 13 May 1767; m. Sarah Staples.
4 Azariah, b. 20 Feb. 1770; m. Jane Staples.
5 Elizabeth, m. Joseph Dixon of Eliot.
6 James, m. 19 Feb. 1801, Sarah Sands of Buxton. He was a farmer. He emigrated to New York about 1815, and when last heard from lived at Willow Creek. When he left Maine he had children:
  1 Luke.
  2 Betsey, } twins.
  3 Polly, }
  4 Sands.
7 Abigail, died Nov. 1865, in Limerick; unm.
8 Lucy, died in Limerick, aged 22; unm.

11-2-5

WILLIAM LIBBY, born in what is now Eliot, Me., 30 Jan. 1749; married 10 Aug. 1780, ELIZABETH CLARK, daughter of Edward and Dorothy (Mendum) Clark.

Left an orphan when but a boy, he was brought up by his sister, Mrs. Staples. He served seven years in the Continental army, and after the war settled in Newfield, near his brother Zebulon. His wife died 10 Dec. 1830. He died 5 Jan. 1835. His farm was divided by his sons, Edward and Joshua S.

He introduced the first wagon into Newfield.

His children were:

1 Benjamin, b. 5 May 1781; m. Clarissa Dorman.
2 Edward, b. 22 Mar. 1783; m. 1 June 1824, Mrs. Susannah (Barker) Drown. He lived on his father's homestead until 1836, and then sold it and settled in Thorndike, Me. There his wife died, about 1852, and he, about 1866. Only child:
  1 Betsey Jewett, b. 11 Aug. 1825; m. —— Haseltine of Thorndike.
3 Dorothy, b. 1 Mar. 1785; d. 19 April 1803.
4 Joshua Small, b. 9 July 1787, m. Eliza Libby, 11-2-4-1-2.
5 Eleanor, b. 8 Nov. 1789; m. 1807, John Dunnell.
6 Betsey, b. 2 Sept. 1794; d. 31 April 1810; unm.

11-6-1

Anna Libby, born in Scarborough, 17 Nov. 1734; married 27 Jan. 1752, Col. Samuel March of Scarborough, a son of Benjamin and Elizabeth (Small) March of Kittery. [See page 32.]

Col. Samuel March came to Scarborough where his uncle, Dea. Samuel Small was living, and continued his residence there until his death. He was by trade a cordwainer, but early dropped that occupation. He kept the tavern east of Oak Hill, since known as the "Sweetsir place." He was for many years one of the leading men of the town. He repeatedly filled the most important town offices; was for many years a deputy sheriff for Cumberland County; and was a lieut.-colonel in the Revolution. He died 30 Oct. 1804. His widow died 13 Nov. 1815.

Their children were:

1 Keziah (March), b. 26 May 1752; m. Jesse Libby, 5-7-11.
2 Benjamin (March), b. 12 Feb. 1754; died young.
3 John (March), b. 18 July 1755.
4 Anna (March), b. 27 Feb. 1757; m. 26 Nov. 1797, Major Nathaniel Wilson of Westbrook.
5 Elizabeth (March), b. 16 Jan. 1759; m. Robert Libby, 10-5-5-1.
6 Mary (March), b. 27 Aug. 1761; m. 7 Jan. 1782, William Small of Limington.
7 Benjamin (March), } twins, born 20 May 1763;
8 Samuel (March), } m. 13 Dec. 1788, Lydia Chapman.
9 Jane (March), b. 20 July 1765; m. 22 June 1784, Joseph Tyler.
10 Eunice (March), b. 30 May 1767; m. Daniel Fogg, 9-5-4-11.
11 James (March), b. 9 Feb. 1769; m. Sally Jose.
12 Sarah (March), b. 22 Jan. 1771; m., as second wife, William Small, her deceased sister's husband.
13 Nathaniel (March).
14 Lucy (March), m. Rufus Marr, 1-5-3-2-9.

11-6-2

Peter Libby, born in Scarborough, 8 March 1736; married 5 Aug. 1760, Ruth Libby, 1-1-5-3; she died, and was buried 7 Aug. 1771. He married second, Anna Lazzel, of Kennebunk.

Peter Libby, when he was first married, lived on the farm on Pleasant Hill, which afterward became the homestead of Daniel Libby, 11-7-7. There his oldest son was born. He afterward lived on the farm now occupied by Charles Robinson, and moved thence to Beech Ridge, where he settled on the farm now owned by Mr. Clough. There he died 7 Nov. 1822. He was a man of firm, decisive character. He was in town business considerably; was selectman 1774, 5, 6, 1781, and from 1791 to 1799.

His widow died in Gardiner about 1830. Her sons all died of excessive bleeding. Old people still shake their heads solemnly and say, "They were under a curse." The dim tradition is that some man, on shipboard, the subject of some grevious injury at the hands of a Lazzel, in his last moments called down a curse upon him, that all his male descendants for a number of generations, should bleed to death. And the old people add, "It certainly came true in *this* family."

The children of Peter Libby, by his first wife, were:

1 Francis, b. 17 March 1761; m. 1st, Lucy Moulton; 2d, Dorcas (Plummer) Higgins.
2 Pelatiah, b. 1 Sept. 1762; died in the Revolution, in an American privateer, of a wound.
3 Isaac, b. 13 Aug. 1764; m. Abigail Jose.
4 Elias, b. 30 Oct. 1768; died young.
5 Ruth, b. 28 July 1771; m. 19 Jan. 1800, Nathaniel Rice.

By second wife:

6 Charles, died young, and was buried 18 March 1778.
7 Anne, died in infancy.
8 Jane, b. 28 Sept. 1778; m. Allison Milliken.
9 Elias, b. 9 Oct. 1780; died in boyhood.
10 Pelatiah, b. 22 Sept. 1782; was at first a school-teacher; afterward kept a country store above Coal-Kiln Corner, in partnership with James H. Morris; died 28 Dec. 1810; unmarried.
11 Dennis, b. 13 Feb. 1785; d. young.
12 Thaddeus, b. 2 April 1787; d. young.
13 William, died young.

11-6-4

RICHARD LIBBY, born 28 May 1741; married first, SARAH STAPLES, daughter of Joseph and Sarah Staples of Kittery; she died 21 Aug. 1797, and he married as second wife, 1 March 1798, Mary (Jordan) Simonton, widow of Capt. Matthew Simonton of Cape Elizabeth; she died ten or twelve years later, and he married his third wife, the widow Sarah Warren, 3 Dec. 1813, and died in about a year. His widow returned to Saco.

Before he was married he settled on Beech Ridge, in the second parish of Scarborough. There he built a house, and cleared a farm, and thither, later, he took his wife. He afterward built the house now standing, about two rods west of the old one. There he lived until his death. He was an enrolling officer during the Revolution, and was for many years a deputy sheriff for Cumberland County. He was of an accumulative turn, and amassed a considerable property. He had no children, and made an heir of his sister's son, Richard Mitchell, whose grandson, Wm. H. Mitchell, now occupies the homestead.

The following story shows something of his character: He and his two brothers were all powerful wrestlers, but Peter was the smartest. One day at a raising, Peter had "cleared the ring." No one appearing to give him further trial, he called out to his brother, "Come, brother Dick, don't you want to take a fall?" Richard accepted the challenge, and, by a lucky movement, threw his brother. From that day forth he never wearied of saying, "I threw Peter, the last time we wrestled," but he could never be persuaded to give his brother an opportunity to regain his leadership.

11-6-5

THOMAS LIBBY, born 23 March 1743; married, 2 June 1767, HANNAH PLUMMER, 5-6-9. She died 23 Sept. 1789, aged 42, and he married second, 26 April 1790, Dorcas (Fogg) Ring, widow of Joseph Ring, and daughter of John and Hannah (Libby) Fogg, 9-6-2 and 5-7-2. She died 1 Sept. 1799.

He was a farmer, and lived and died on his father's homestead. His death occurred 14 April 1824.

His children, by wife Hannah, were:

1 John, b. 5 Dec. 1771; was lame; lived many years with his brother Thomas, and died with him, 30 April 1841.
2 Silas, b. 8 Dec. 1777; died at sea, 11 May 1801; unm.
3 Keziah, b. 20 Jan. 1780; d. 14 June 1821; unm.
4 Richard, b. 8 Jan. 1782; m. Elizabeth Mills.
5 Thomas, b. 11 Dec. 1784; m. Mary Plummer.
6 Peter, b. 5 Dec. 1786; m. Tamsen Quinby.

By second wife:

7 Joseph, b. 15 Dec. 1790; m. 2 Nov. 1821, Amelia Lowell of Portland. He was lame, and in his younger days used to teach penmanship, in which he was proficient. He afterward moved to Portland, and was a member of the firm of Lunt & Libby, grocers. He died 12 Aug. 1822, and his widow married second, 17 June 1825, Simeon Hall of Portland. No children.
8 Zenas, b. 25 July 1792; m. Miriam Fogg, 9-5-4-2-1-2.
9 Dorcas, b. 4 May 1795; died 22 Aug. 1822; unm.
10 Jane, b. 30 May 1798; d. 22 Aug. 1799.

11-7-1

Andrew Libby, born in Scarborough, 13 Feb. 1732; married 16 Nov. 1755, Miriam Burns, who was born on the passage of her parents from Ireland to this country.

He settled first in the interior of the town on land adjoining his brother Joshua. There he lived until 1789, when, with his four youngest sons, who were all that then remained in his family, he moved to Gray "to settle his boys," and settled on Dutton Hill. There he died 21 Feb. 1801. His widow died at the age of 90, 13 Mar. 1827.

Their children were:

1 Elizabeth, b. 17 October 1757; m. 15 March 1781, William Davis. They accompanied her father to Gray, and settled near by.
2 Anna, b. 23 Aug. 1759; m. Moses Libby, 10-5-1-2.
3 Esther, b. 1 Sept. 1760; m. 9 March 1784, Isaac Plummer.
4 William, b. 16 May 1763; m. Mary Fogg, 9-6-6-1.
5 Jane, b. 6 Jan. 1765; m. Edward Libby, 11-7-8-2.
6 Rebecca, b. 12 Jan. 1767; m. 11 Oct. 1785, Christopher Plummer.
7 Mary, b. 17 March 1769; m. Samuel Waterhouse of Cape Elizabeth.
8 Andrew, b. 27 May 1771; m. Sarah Cummings.
9 Joseph, b. 14 May 1773; m. Mary Doughty. When he was married he settled on land now owned by David Libby, 11-7-1-11-3; after a few years he moved onto the farm now owned by William Libby, 11-7-1-11-11; shortly before his wife's death he sold this and bought a farm in the Ramsdell neighborhood. Here his wife died, 24 Dec. 1838, aged 63, and himself, 1 May 1843. They had no children.
10 David, b. 18 March 1776; m. Mary Cobb.
11 Simon, b. 19 Dec. 1778; m. Elizabeth Small.

11-7-2

DEACON JOSHUA LIBBY, born in Scarborough, 17 March 1734; married 2 Nov. 1755, HANNAH LARRABEE. [See page 41.]

He was by trade a cordwainer, but never followed that occupation. He settled on the Nonesuch River, about three miles north of Oak Hill, and became a successful farmer. His first house, the cellar of which is still visible, he built in the "old house field." He afterward built a larger house, about fifty rods north of his first residence, and moved the old house onto another part of his farm, for his son Matthias. It is still standing, the property of Randolph McKenney.

In addition to his extensive farming, he engaged in ship-building and the West India trade, and became one of the richest and most influential men in the town. He was chairman of selectmen 1792, 3, and 4, and town treasurer from 1800 until his death. 9 Feb. 1783, he and his wife became members of the Congregational church, and 1 July 1792, he was chosen deacon, and filled this position at the time of his death, which occurred 13 Jan. 1813. His widow died 13 Dec. 1818.

Their children were:

1 ——, born and died in June, 1756, aged 15 days.
2 Esther, b. 7 Sept. 1757; m. Humphrey Hanscom, 9-5-6-1.
3 Sarah, b. 5 May 1760; m. 25 Dec. 1783, Joshua Hutchins.
4 Matthias, b. 5 Jan. 1762; m. Esther Libby, 11-7-8-1.
5 Lydia, b. 2 March 1765; m. James Marr, 1-5-3-2-2.
6 Joshua, b. 31 Aug. 1768; m. Ruth Libby, 11-7-11-1.
7 Theodore, b. 18 July 1773; m. Sarah Harmon.
8 Hannah, b. 1 Sept. 1775; m. John Meserve. [See page 37.]
9 Salome, b. 15 Oct. 1778; m. 11 June 1799, Moses McKenney.

11-7-3

ELIZABETH LIBBY, born in Scarborough, 28 April 1736; m. 22 Feb. 1753, SAMUEL PLAISTED of Scarborough.

Samuel Plaisted was a son of Elisha Plaisted, Esq., of Berwick, who was one of the original proprietors of Scarborough, and acquired large landed possessions there; and from him he received a farm on Winnock's neck. There he spent the chief part of his life, and there his wife died. He afterward went to Limington, and died with his daughter Elizabeth.

Children:

1 Hannah (Plaisted), b. 20 June 1754; m. 17 Feb. 1779, Joseph Dam of Kittery.
2 Elisha (Plaisted), b. 20 Nov. 1755; probably died young.
3 Esther (Plaisted), b. 9 Sept. 1757; probably died young.
4 John (Plaisted), bap. 1 July 1759; m. Lydia Moulton, and settled in Standish.
5 Samuel (Plaisted), bap. 24 May 1762; m. Hannah Cilley of Saco, and settled in Gorham.
6 Andrew (Plaisted) b. 1 June 1763; m. 13 Sept. 1786, Molly Libby, 10-5-5-3. He settled in Gorham. Children:
1 Betsey (Plaisted), b. 20 Dec. 1787; m. Stephen Cram.

2 Sally Libby (Plaisted), b. 1 July 1788; m. as 1st wife, William Thomes.
3 Joseph (Plaisted), b. 9 May 1790; m. Eunice Thomes. Lived in Harrison.
4 Andrew (Plaisted), b. 18 Sept. 1792; m. Abigail True.
5 Mary (Plaisted), b. 30 Oct. 1795; m. 1st, John Phinney; 2d, Oliver Arthurton.
6 Major (Plaisted), b. 17 Mar. 1798; married Mary Gage Libby, 10-5-4-2-4-7. He lives on his father's homestead in Gorham. Children:
   1 John Milton (Plaisted), b. 14 July 1850; unm. He is a shoe-dealer in Manchester, N. H.
   2 Helen Aitchison (Plaisted), b. 11 Sept. 1852; m. Herman S. Whitney.
   3 Louisa Mary (Plaisted), b. 27 Aug. 1854; m. J. Granville Clement.
   4 George Preble (Plaisted), b. 25 April 1857.
   5 Edward Wentworth (Plaisted), b. 22 May 1860.
   6 Alice Belle (Plaisted), b. 30 May 1870.
7 Hannah (Plaisted), b. 10 April 1803; m. as 2d wife, William Thomes.
8 Harriet (Plaisted), died aged 4 years.

7 Elizabeth (Plaisted), m. 10 July 1783, Joseph Moody of Limington.
8 Simon (Plaisted), m. Hannah Small, and settled in Limington.
9 William (Plaisted), settled in Portland; m. 2 May 1805, Hannah Dyer.
10 Abigail (Plaisted), m. Simon Moulton of Standish.
11 Sarah (Plaisted), died unmarried.
12 Mary (Plaisted), m. 1st, Ebenezer Moulton of Waterford; 2d, Josiah Willard of the same place.

11-7-5

Abigail Libby, born in Scarborough, 6 Nov. 1736; married 24 Jan. 1757, John Dam, probably from Kittery. He died 23 Oct. 1776, and she married second, 2 Nov. 1780, Thomas Jackson of Cape Elizabeth, and died about 1814.

Her children, by John Dam, were:

1 Esther (Dam), b. 23 June 1757; m. Joshua Brown, 7-1-6-3.
2 Elizabeth (Dam), b. 23 Nov. 1758; m. 16 July 1778, Henry Small.
3 Sarah (Dam), b. 1760; m. Allison Libby, 10-5-4-2.
4 Abigail (Dam), b. 1763; m. 4 Dec. 1783, Reuben Wescott.
5 Eleanor (Dam), b. 1765; m. 18 Dec. 1783, Ephraim Nason.
6 John (Dam), b. 1767; m. Polly Webb of Gorham; settled in Pownal.
7 Mary (Dam), b. 1770; m. Daniel Hanscom, 9-5-6-3.
8 Olive (Dam), b. 1773.
9 Andrew (Dam), b. 1774.
10 Joseph (Dam), b. 1776; lived to old age, a bachelor.

11-7-6

Deacon Joseph Libby, born in Scarborough, 6 Jan. 1740; married, 31 Oct. 1765, Sarah Meserve. [See page 37.]

He removed to Machias in 1765, soon after the first settlement, and was for many years one of the leading inhabitants. He was on the Committee of Safety during the Revolution and, after the organization of the town, was several years selectman. He and his wife were both original members of the first church, and he was chosen the first deacon. Afterward he was continually called upon to perform funeral services, and in that capacity and many other kindnesses, to which his earnest christian spirit prompted him, he won the love of all about him. He died in the spring of 1816, and his widow six years later. His homestead, which is now owned by Ellery Munson, was left to his adopted son, whose surname was Getchell.

Adopted son:

a Francis (Libby), married Sally Burnham.

11-7-7

DANIEL LIBBY, born 22 Dec. 1742; married 14 March 1765, DOROTHY HASTY. [See page 55.]

He was a farmer, and settled on Pleasant Hill, on the land next north of the Larrabee place. His wife, Dorothy, died 28 Aug. 1805. At the age of eighty, 24 Nov. 1820, he married Sarah (Eldrich) Plummer, widow of Jeremiah Plummer. He died 31 Aug. 1828. His widow returned to her children, and died 28 Mar. 1842.

The children of Daniel Libby were:

1 Hannah, b. 3 Nov. 1767; m. Moses Fogg, 9-6-6-2.
2 Elizabeth, b. 8 Feb. 1769; m. Edward Libby, 10-5-4-3.
3 Daniel, b. 9 April 1772; m. Polly Hoyt.
4 Eleanor, b. 3 Aug. 1774; m. 1st, 14 April 1804, Capt. Edward Gee; 2d, 16 April 1822, Deacon Matthew Duran.
5 Walter, b. 13 Nov. 1776; m. Elizabeth Jordan.
6 Sewall, b. 6 March 1779; m. Sarah Libby, 1-1-6-5-2.
7 Joseph, b. 9 Oct. 1781; m. 27 Sept. 1810, Charlotte Jordan. He was humpbacked, and for that reason learned the shoemaker's trade. He, however, settled on a farm, the old Brown place, adjoining his father's farm on the north, and carried it on successfully. He died 22 Sept. 1855. His widow died 15 May 1876, with her brother, Clement Jordan of Cape Elizabeth. No children.
8 Andrew, b. 27 Dec. 1783; m. 1st, Abigail Tappan; 2d, Margaret Todd.
9 Dorothy, b. 12 Dec. 1785; m. 20 Dec. 1808, Israel Jordan of Cape Elizabeth.
10 Esther, b. 4 April 1788; m. 1st, 25 June 1809, Robert Meserve; 2d, 30 Nov. 1814, Robert Hasty.

11-7-8

EDWARD LIBBY, born in Scarborough, 10 April 1745; married, 12 Feb. 1767, MARY LIBBY, 1-1-3-10.

He grew up a farmer, and settled on part of the homestead of his wife's father. One day in September, 1773, he and other young men had been down to the seashore on horseback, and on the return, near the house of Major Josiah Libby, 1-1-6-4, he was thrown from his horse, and dislocated his neck. He was taken into Josiah Libby's house, and a physician called, who, as it proved, did not know enough to set it. The unfortunate man lived a number of days in great agony, and died 11 Sept. 1773, of strangulation.

The regular physician of the place, Doctor Deguio, (who used to say, "My father was one French gentleman, and my mother was one Indian squaw"), was away at the time of the accident, but returned almost immediately after death had taken place. He was in a towering passion at the ignorance which had caused the loss of a promising young man. "Look here," he said, and in a second the dislocated neck was replaced. He then dislocated and replaced it again and again, as fast as he could move his hands, raging all the while, until he had exhausted his indignation. Probably not one of the witnesses ever forgot that lesson.

The widow married, 12 Sept. 1775, Allison Libby, 10-5-4, and took her children into his family.

They were:

1 Esther, b. 2 Nov. 1767; m. 1st, Matthias Libby, 11-7-2-4; 2d, Rev. Thomas Lancaster.
2 Edward, b. 7 Nov. 1770; m. Jane Libby, 11-7-1-5.
3 Joseph, b. 6 March 1772; m. Anna Plummer.

11-7-11

Simon Libby, born in Scarborough, 7 June 1752; married, 1 Dec. 1772, Elizabeth Thompson, daughter of George and Ruth Thompson of Scarborough, from old York.

He always lived on his father's homestead, a well-to-do farmer. His wife died 10 Jan. 1825. He died 12 Oct. 1826.

Their children were:

1 Ruth, b. 16 Oct. 1773; m. Joshua Libby, 11-7-2-6.
2 Sarah, b. 12 April 1775; m. Josiah Libby, 10-5-4-10.
3 Elizabeth, b. 23 April 1777; m. Major Josiah Libby, 1-1-6-4-4.
4 Frances, b. 8 April 1779; d. 3 Sept. 1797.
5 Esther, b. 9 July 1781; m. Rufus Libby, 10-5-1-10.
6 Abigail, b. 24 March 1783; m. Joshua Hanscom, 9-5-6-1-1.
7 Simon, b. 5 Sept. 1785; m. Hannah Berry.
8 George, b. 4 Feb. 1791; m. Lydia Libby, 10-5-1-10-4.

11-9-5

Nathaniel Libby, born in Berwick, Me., about 1738; married first, 1763, Elizabeth Fogg, 9-9-3. She died 17 Jan. 1787. He married second, 1789, Eleanor Johnson of Kittery.

He was a farmer, and always lived on his father's homestead. He was active in church matters, and was often chosen delegate. He died 11 Mar. 1798. His widow married second, a Randall, but died on the Libby homestead 17 April 1826.

Children, by first wife:

1 Nathaniel, b. 23 Jan. 1765; d. 8 June 1786; unm.
2 James, b. 8 Jan. 1766; died in infancy.
3 James, b. 18 Aug. 1767; m. Polly Ayers.
4 Elizabeth, b. 12 Mar. 1769; m. 14 May 1789, Aaron Ricker.

5 Mark, b. 28 May 1771; m. Olive Lord.
6 Anna, b. 28 Dec. 1772; d. 2 Aug. 1825; unm.
7 Susannah, b. 6 May 1774; d. 2 Mar. 1822; unm.
8 John, b. 5 Mar. 1776; died young.
9 Joseph, bap. 1777; died young.

By second wife:

10 Johnson, } twins, } died in infancy.
11 Nathaniel, } bap. 1792; }
12 Lydia, b. 1793; was crazy; died about 1865; unm.

11-9-7

STEPHEN LIBBY, born in Berwick, about 1741; married first, 22 April 1761, ALICE GUPTIL; second, 21 July 1773, HANNAH YOUNG.

When he was married he settled in what is now North Berwick, on the Beech Ridge road, close by Spencer brook. On this brook he owned and ran a grist-mill. In 1777 he bought one hundred acres of land, about a mile from the headline of Lebanon, in what afterward became Shapleigh, and is now Acton. He cleared the farm about a mile north of Acton Corner, now owned by Ephraim Wentworth, and there died 8 May 1793. 10 June 1797, his widow married Jacob Hersom, and they continued to reside on the Libby farm, and are both buried there. She died about 1829.

Stephen Libby's children, by his first wife, were:

1 Miriam, m. 22 Oct. 1778, Miles Thompson.
2 Stephen, b. 12 April 1764; m. Sally Butler.
3 Samuel, m. Anna Cook.
4 Alice, b. about 1770; died young.

By second wife:

5 Alice, b. 15 April 1774; m. April, 1792, John Hersom.
6 Abigail, b. 31 Mar. 1778; m. 23 Nov. 1815, Thos. Thurston of Acton.
7 Zebulon, b. 15 May 1780; m. Dorcas Holmes.
8 Peter, b. 3 July 1781; m. Sarah Bean.
9 Hannah, b. 25 May 1788; m. 17 Sept. 1806, Benjamin Tibbetts.
10 John, b. 5 Feb. 1790; m. Betsey Bean.
11 Lydia, b. 27 March 1792; m. 1st, 20 Jan. 1804, Jacob Lord; 2d, Miles Thompson.

11-9-8

ZEBULON LIBBY, born in Berwick, about 1742; married, 1763, SARAH BRACKETT.

About the time of his marriage, he settled on Beech Ridge, in what is now North Berwick, and cleared a farm there, on which he resided until his death. His chief livelihood was farming, yet he was quite an expert carpenter, and framed many houses and barns, and built ox-wheels, etc. He died in August, 1807. His widow died 4 March 1825.

Their children were:

1 John, b. 7 May 1764; d. 2 April 1782.

2 Sarah, b. 11 Oct. 1767; m. 1795, Samuel Hanscom.
3 Susannah, b. 17 Jan. 1770; m. 1790, William Clark.
4 Hannah, b. 20 Nov. 1772; d. 6 June 1857; unm.
5 Lydia, b. 20 July 1779; d. 4 April 1832; unm.
6 Mary, b. 1 April 1782; m. Walter Marshall; died 18 March 1871.
7 Levi, b. 27 May 1786; m. Eunice Stillings.
8 Ira, b. 9 Dec. 1788; m. Fanny Langdon.

11-11-5

Samuel Libby, born on the farm that had been his grandfather's, 13 Jan. 1743; married, 1772, Mary Staples.

He was a farmer, and lived always on the farm of his birth. He built the house now standing, about five rods from where the old house stood, in a direction slightly north of east. He died suddenly, 15 Nov. 1813. His widow died 30 Dec. 1833.

They had thirteen children, but all died in infancy except the following.

1 Samuel, b. 2 April 1781; was a farmer, and always lived on the homestead; died 19 July 1852; unmarried.
2 Jane, b. 17 April 1783; m. 7 April 1816, Edward Quincy Oxford. She had two daughters, one of whom married Thomas Adlington, and now occupies the homestead.
3 Mary, b. about 1787; died in childhood.
4 Lydia, b. 26 Dec. 1790; d. 30 April 1868, on the homestead; unmarried. She was the last of the name on the homestead of Matthew Libby, 11.

11-11-6

Seth Libby, born in Kittery, now Eliot, Me., 15 Feb. 1745; married, 1774, Mary Junkins.

He was a farmer. He lived with his father until a short time before his own death, when he moved a small house from the river up to the inland end of his father's farm, and settled there. He died in the summer of 1794. His widow died in March, 1812.

Their children were:

1 Seth, b. 1775; died about 1811, in Portsmouth. He was at work in a brick-yard, and a bank fell onto him. He was unmarried.
2 Thomas, b. 26 Nov. 1776; m. 1st, Sophia (Remmick) Hodgdon; 2d, Sarah Hammond.
3 Mary, b. 1779; m. 8 Aug. 1817, Charles Fernald.
4 Andrew, b. 4 Aug. 1782; m. Patience B. Dorr.
5 Sally, b. 1785; d. 14 June 1847; unmarried.
6 Dennis, b. Aug. 1788; worked as gardener for Portsmouth gentlemen; died 13 April 1861; unmarried.

FIFTH GENERATION.

1-1-2-2

JETHRO LIBBY, born in Scarborough, about 1726; married first, 31 Jan. 1754, MARY LIBBY, 1-1-5-1; second, 5 March 1761, HANNAH (WOODBURY) MOODY, widow of Daniel Moody, and daughter of Israel Woodbury, of Cape Elizabeth.

He was a farmer. Before he was married he bought land in the interior of the town of Scarborough, on which he afterward settled. His house stood about thirty rods southeast of the present residence of Charles Libby, 1-1-2-2-11-3. He died about 1795. His widow died 11 Sept. 1821, aged 85.

Children by first wife:

1 Edmund, b. 1754; served in the Continental army and died on his return home, with some relatives, in Portsmouth, N. H.
2 James, b. 2 Aug. 1757; m. 1st, Betsey Small; 2d, Sarah (Woodbury) Dyer.

By second wife:

3 Benjamin, b. Sept. 1762; m. 1st, Elizabeth Hunnewell, 7-1-5-1; 2d, Hannah Moody.
4 Jethro, b. 1763; m. Lettice Wescott.
5 Hannah, m. 29 June 1794, William Tate of Falmouth.
6 Charles, b. 8 April 1767; m. Mary Libby, 1-4-1-6-2.
7 Mary, b. 8 Feb. 1769; m. James Libby, 1-4-1-6-4.
8 John, b. 17 Dec. 1770; m. Dorcas Roberts.
9 Joanna, m. Nathaniel Babb of Westbrook.
10 Abigail, m. 25 April 1810, John Buggy, or Bugbee, an Irishman.
11 William, b. 7 March 1778; m. Keturah Hanscom, 9-5-6-1-2.

1-1-2-6

MAJ. HATEVIL LIBBY, b. 28 Nov. 1736, in Scarborough; married, 29 June 1756, JANE WATSON, a native of Ireland.

He removed to St. George, (now Warren), shortly before Jan. 1764, and in that month bought a large tract of land on which he afterward settled. He was for many years one of the principal inhabitants of Warren, and possessed in a high degree the confidence of his townsmen. His wife died 26 Sept. 1819, and he 24 Sept. 1820. The main part of his homestead is now occupied by George Spear.

S. O. Sibley

Children, born in Scarborough:

1 Eliakim, b. 1 Jan. 1757; m. Rachel Jameson.
2 John, b. 1758; m. Catherine James.
3 Nathan, b. 6 May 1761; m. Elizabeth Lermond.

Born in Warren:

4 Mary, b. 1764; m. John Payson.
5 Elizabeth, b. 1769; m. Wm. Kirkpatrick.
6 Jane, b. 1771; m. 1824, Henry Wagner.
7 Hatevil, [Capt.], b. 1773; m. Elizabeth Gay. He was a farmer and lived on the west side of George's River. His grand nephew, Wm. K. Cutting, lived with him in his old age and now has the homestead farm. He died 12 Jan. 1849. His widow died 15 April 1861. No children.
8 James, died young.
9 David, b. 1778; m. Susan Gay.
10 Isaac, b. 1780; m. Eleanor Gay.

1-1-3-4

JONATHAN LIBBY, born in Scarborough, 5 Feb. 1735; married HANNAH HUNNEWELL, 7-1-2-2.

He was, like his father, a housewright; but seems to have given his chief attention to farming. He lived where Charles Milliken now lives. He died 19 Aug. 1760. His widow outlived him many years.

Children:

1 Richard Hunnewell, b. 8 Dec. 1756; m. Esther Hanscom, 9-5-6-4.
2 Lydia, b. 4 July 1759; m. 24 Dec. 1776, William Foss.
3 Susannah, b. 24 April 1760; m. 12 April 1781, Ebenezer Carl.

1-1-3-5

JOTHAM LIBBY, born in Scarborough, 5 April 1737; married 29 Oct. 1761, CATHERINE SKILLIN, daughter of Edward and Sarah (Miller) Skillin of Scarborough.

He was a farmer. He lived on part of his father's homestead until about 1788, and then settled in Cape Elizabeth on what is now known as the Palmer place. He died in 1825. It is said that he had seventeen children by his one wife, but the names of only fifteen can be learned. All his sons that grew up followed the sea. Scarcely anything is known of them individually. None except Edward, however, had any children.

Children of Jotham and Catherine Libby:

1 Benjamin, bap. Feb. 1763.
2 Catherine, bap. April 1764; m. Benjamin Means.
3 Rebecca, bap. Dec. 1765; m. 1st, 6 Nov. 1794, William Rice; 2d, Jeremiah Jordan.
4 Elizabeth Lidden, bap. Aug. 1767; m. 5 Nov. 1794, Braddock Palmer.
5 Jotham, m. 1790, Catherine McIntosh of Portland, died of yellow fever.
6 Edward Skillin, bap. Nov. 1771; m. Sarah Dunn.
7 John, bap.
8 Mary, b. 5 June 1775; m. 1798, Abel Chase.
9 Lydia, bap. Oct. 1777; m. 26 May 1796, John Richardson.

10 Jonathan, bap. Jan. 1779; was a sailor.
11 Joseph, bap. Mar. 1782.
12 Susannah, bap. Mar. 1782; died in old age on her father's homestead in Cape Elizabeth; unm.
13 William, killed in boyhood by being run over by a loaded team.
14 Harry.
15 Augusta, bap. Aug. 1787.

1-1-3-8

JOAB LIBBY, born in Scarborough, 13 Sept. 1745; married, 21 Sept. 1769, SUSANNAH LOMBARD of Gorham.

From the time of his marriage he lived in Gorham, and from that place enlisted in the Continental army. His house was near Horsebeef Falls. He died 17 April 1781. His widow married as second husband, 20 Oct. 1784, Jedidiah Lombard.

Children:

1 John, b. 13 July 1770; m. Hannah Gray of Standish. He was a farmer. He died about 1815, leaving no children. His widow married Gabriel Welch of Raymond.
2 Jonathan, b. 9 Oct. 1772; m. 1st, Mary Stevens; 2d, Abigail Jordan.
3 Susannah, b. 3 Jan. 1777; m. Jeremiah Dorsett, 12 Jan. 1797.

1-1-3-9

JOSIAH LIBBY, born in Scarborough, 13 Sept. 1745; married 16 Mar. 1778, SARAH LIBBY, 10-5-4-4.

He was a farmer and lived until old age near the Buggy meeting-house in Scarborough. In 1815, his five oldest sons having already settled in Pownal, he followed them with all the rest of his family except Josiah, and bought the farm now occupied by widow Abigail Tuttle. There he died 15 Jan. 1826. His widow died 24 May 1840.

Children:

1 Alexander, b. 6 Aug. 1778; m. Elizabeth Libby, 1-4-1-6-5.
2 Allison, b. 24 Oct. 1781; m. Lucy and Hannah Libby, 10-2-4-2-9 and 11.
3 Joab, b. 17 April 1783; m. Sarah Jones.
4 Abraham, b. 1 July 1785; m. 1st, Eunice Tyler; 2d, Mary Brown.
5 Sally, b. 6 Sept. 1787; m. 11 May 1825, John G. Crocker.
6 Mary, b. 10 Sept. 1789; m. 4 April 1827, Samuel McIntire.
7 John, b. 7 Nov. 1791; m. 1st, Miriam Libby, 11-7-2-4-3; 2d, Abigail Grace; 3d, Martha Moses.
8 Elizabeth, b. 7 Oct. 1793; d. 8 Dec. 1833; unm.
9 Josiah, b. 10 Dec. 1795; m. 1st, Abigail Moody; 2d, Mary (Palmer) Shackford.
10 Hanson, b. 21 Dec. 1797; m. Lydia Lake.
11 Salome, b. 11 Feb. 1800; m. 27 Oct. 1829, Eaton Nichols.

1-1-5-9

LIEUT. JONATHAN LIBBY, born in Scarborough, 1752; married Sept. 1783, ABIGAIL LIBBY, 10-2-4-7.

He always lived on his father's farm. He was an enterprising man, and increased the size of his farm a great deal by purchase.

He was a lieutenant in the Revolution. The following was found among his papers:

West Point, Nov. 30th, 1779.
A Dream.
Dreamed on the 28th instant, at night, that I was at home, in the West Room, to-bed with my brother Daniel, and thought I saw Death come into the door, in likeness to a Negro Boy—his visage very ghostly and frightful—and approach the bed where we were, with a scythe in his hand. My brother starting out of bed, I thought he struck him with the scythe, and seemed to cut him into two pieces, and I saw no more of him, but awoke, and behold, it was a dream!

JON[A] LIBBY'S DREAM.

It is remarkable that his brother *did* come to an untimely end only a few years later.

He engaged some in ship-building. He was selectman of Scarborough 1799-1804. He died 21 March 1805. His widow died 28 Sept. 1846.

Children:

1 Daniel, b. 3 Nov. 1784; had the homestead; died 6 April 1878; unmarried.
2 Joseph, b. 24 March 1786; a cooper; washed overboard on the way to the West Indies, 14 March 1807.
3 George Washington, b. 28 Feb. 1788; d. 19 Aug. 1791.
4 Elizabeth, b. 19 Dec. 1790; d. in infancy.
5 George, b. 29 Feb. 1792; went to sea in 1810, and never returned.
6 Lavinia, b. 19 April 1794; m. 1818, John Pilsbury.
7 Elizabeth, b. 25 March 1796; d. 15 March 1822; unmarried.
8 John, b. 9 Nov. 1798; m. Sarah Waterhouse.
9 Silas, b. 25 Dec. 1800; followed the sea; was last heard from on a steamer on the Mississippi River. about 1838.
10 Albert, b. 10 Jan. 1802; m. 2 June 1833, Mary, dau. of Jonathan and Martha (Davis) Stevens, of Kittery. He was a carpenter. He died in Kittery, 6 May 1838. His widow married —— Bailey, of Portsmouth, N. H. Children:
 1 Mary Frances, b. 18 Feb. 1834; m. William Tompson, 5-7-14-7-5.
 2 Caroline, b. 13 July 1836; d. 25 Feb. 1837.
 3 Abigail, b. 30 Nov. 1838; d. 6 July 1839.

1-1-6-4.

MAJ. JOSIAH LIBBY, born in Scarborough, 16 Feb. 1746; married first, 28 Feb. 1769, EUNICE LIBBY, 5-7-13; (died 23 March 1776); second, 28 Nov. 1776, ELIZABETH (PARCHER) FOSS.

He received the homestead farm of his uncle-by-marriage, Jos. Fogg, 9-7, for caring for him and his wife. This homestead, increased somewhat by purchase, he always occupied. He was a well-to-do farmer. He served in the Revolution as captain, and was afterward a major in the militia.

His second wife died 21 Jan. 1810, and he married again, 19 June 1810, Mary, widow of John Jones, daughter of Deacon Chase of Saco. She was the mother, by a previous husband, of the first wife of Andrew Libby, 11-7-7-8. She was subject to crazy periods and in one of them cut her throat. She died 16 July 1843. Her husband, Major Libby, had died nineteen years before, 1 Mar. 1824.

His children, by first wife, were:

1 Anna, b. 19 May 1770; m. 26 Dec. 1811, Elias Foss.
2 Rhoda, b. 17 June 1772; m. 2 Mar. 1791, David Tyler.
3 Phineas, b. 18 Mar. 1774; m. 30 Oct. 1795, Mary, dau. of Hannah (Fogg) Meserve, 9-8-6. He was a sailor. He died in the West Indies, 20 Dec. 1801. His widow died in Wales, about 1824. Children:
   1 Cyrus, died in boyhood.
   2 Irene, m. David Owen of Wales, Me.
   3 Mary Ann, posthumous, died aged about 40, in Wales; unm.
4 Joseph, [Major], b. 16 Mar. 1776; m. 1st, 27 Sept. 1798, Elizabeth Libby, 11-7-11-3; (died in Scarborough, 26 Sept. 1843); 2d, 2 Oct. 1844, Abigail (Rice) Shaw of Yarmouth. He was among the first settlers of Wales, and was for many years a prominent farmer and tavern keeper there. After the death of his brother-in-law, George Libby, he returned to Scarborough and took care of his orphaned children until his second marriage, when he removed to Yarmouth. He died there, about 1854, and his widow married —— Cobb. Only child:
   1 Phineas, died in Wales, aged 24; unm.

By Hannah Plaisted, 11-7-3-1, who kept house for him after his first wife's death:

5 Elizabeth, bap. 2 Nov. 1777; m. Joseph Foss. She was of all her father's children, the favorite. 'Twas she he had to live with him, and to her he left the homestead.

By second wife:

6 Cyrus, b. 15 Oct. 1778; m. Lois Libby, 5-7-14-2.
7 Daniel, b. 20 Jan. 1780; m. Rebecca Libby, 10-2-1-5-2.
8 Eunice, b. 1783; d. 3 Dec. 1805; unm.
9 Caroline, m. 18 Oct. 1804, Stephen Harmon.

1-1-6-5

PHINEAS LIBBY, born in Scarborough, 22 July 1749; married 20 Feb. 1772, SARAH LIBBY, 10-2-4-4.

He lived and died on his father's homestead on Oak Hill. His death occurred 17 July 1798. His widow died 27 Oct. 1821.

Children:

1 Elizabeth, b. 29 July 1772; m. Capt. Moses Libby, 5-7-8-2.
2 Sarah, m. Capt. Sewall Libby, 11-7-7-6.
3 Josiah, m. Abigail Thomes,

1-2-1-1

HAM LIBBY, born in Dover, N. H., about 1735; married first, ESTHER DREW; second, Sarah, dau. of Benjamin and Deborah (Stimpson) Wentworth.

He was a farmer, and settled in Nottingham, where he died about 1790. He was a sergeant in the expedition against Crown Point.

Children, all by first wife:

1 James, b. Jan. 1765; m. Nancy Crockett.
2 Elizabeth, m., probably, Moses Wentworth.
3 Esther, m. Samuel Marsh of Northwood.

1-2-1-2

BENJAMIN LIBBY, born in Dover, N. H., about 1737; married ABIGAIL TITCOMB. He was a tanner and farmer in Dover, where he died in the fall of 1821. His wife was living when he made his will, June 1815.

Children:

1 Sarah, m. 16 Sept. 1781, Francis Winkley, jr., of Barrington; died 25 April 1843. They joined the Canterbury Shakers.
2 Anne. m. 16 Sept. 1781, Disco Wentworth.
3 Daniel, b. 1762; m. Polly Hodgdon; died 14 July 1801. His widow married, 12 Dec. 1810, Capt. Benjamin Brown of Moultonborough. Children:
   1 Charlotte, b. 1795; died 30 May 1797.
   2 Charles, died 28 June 1797.
   3 ——, died 3 Oct. 1798.
   4 Daniel, b. Sept. 1801; m. 19 Oct. 1840, Hannah Fields, dau. of Robert and Mary (Fields) Neal of Portsmouth, N. H. He was brought up by his uncle Moses Hodgdon, a lawyer in Dover. At 16 he went to sea and followed that calling until 1851, rising to the captain's position. After retiring he lived at Portsmouth, where he died 28 Aug. 1878, and his widow still lives. No children.
4 Mary, married —— Leighton.
5 Abigail, m. 10 Sept. 1809, William Blake.
6 Betsey, living in 1815.
7 Enoch, m. Martha Parsley of Strafford.

1-2-1-3

CAPT. JAMES LIBBY, born in Dover, N. H., 27 July 1739; married 31 Aug. 1768, LYDIA RUNNALS, widow of Joseph Runnals. He lived in Dover, at what was called Bellamy, or Back River. He was a tanner and farmer. His wife Lydia died 29 March 1787, and he married a second wife, who, it is thought, outlived him.

Children, all by his first wife:

1 Joseph, married Joanna Hall. He was a farmer, in Barrington. He left no children. His wife outlived him.
2 James, died in March, 1791.
3 Joshua, b. 22 May 1773; m. Susannah Kenniston.
4 Martha, m. Joshua Hodgdon of Ossipee, N. H.

1-2-3-1

JOSHUA LIBBY, baptized in Portsmouth, N. H., 28 Sept. 1729; married —— ——. Nothing appears of him but the baptizing of his children, viz.:

1 Hanson, bap. 13 Sept. 1756; probably died young.
2 Luke, bap. 4 Sept. 1758; m. Nancy Crocker.

1-4-1-4

ASA LIBBY, born in 1737, in Scarborough; married, 15 April, 1759, ABIGAIL COOLBROTH, of Scarborough.

He was a farmer. He moved to Falmouth a few years after his marriage, and thence, probably a short time before the Revolution, to Gray. He served in the Continental army eight months. He and John Nash went to Gray about the same time, and both lived with Daniel Libby, 1-5-2-5, until they had built houses and cleared some land. Asa Libby settled about two miles west of Gray Corner. His house stood some distance southerly of the road leading to Windham. There he lived until old age, and then went to live with his son, Asa, in Belgrade. There his wife died, about 1814, and he died 5 Nov. 1828.

Their children were:

1 Arthur, b. 28 Feb. 1760, in Scarborough; m. Mary Allen.
2 Joel, b. 9 Nov. 1762, in Scarborough; married Mehitable Nash.
3 Abigail, m., as second wife, Job Young, of Gray.
4 Betsey, m. Oliver Humphrey of Gray.
5 Asa, m. 1st, Lydia Hayden; 2d, Lucretia (White) Dutton.
6 Sally, m. Samuel, son of Job Young.
7 Shuah, m. Aaron Humphrey, brother of Oliver, above.

1-4-1-6

Ichabod Libby, born in Scarborough, 1742; married 27 Nov. 1764, Mary Fickett.

He was a farmer. He settled in the northern part of his native town, on land now owned by Dennis Green, son of Mary (Libby) Green, 1-4-1-6-4-3. He died 18 Nov. 1828. His wife died 8 July 1813.

Children:

1 Hanson, m. Abigail Myrick.
2 Mary, b. 15 Dec. 1768; m. Charles Libby, 1-1-2-2-6.
3 Dennis, b. 1771; m. Elizabeth McKenney.
4 James, b. 12 May 1773; m. Mary Libby, 1-1-2-2-7.
5 Elizabeth, b. 9 March 1776; m. Alexander Libby, 1-1-3-9-1.

1-4-4-3

Deacon Paul Libby, born in Dover, N. H., 7 Sept. 1736; married first, Mary Tibbetts, daughter of Ensign Edward Tibbetts; second, 2 April 1797, Hannah Tibbetts, daughter of Joseph and Elizabeth (Hussey) Tibbetts.

He always lived on his father's homestead in Rochester. He filled, at various times, the position of selectman of the town, and other minor offices. His death took place 23 May 1812. His widow married Daniel Whitehouse. She died in Newport, Me., 12 July 1848.

Children, by first wife:

1 John, bap. 15 April 1768; died young.

By second wife:

2 Isaac, b. 31 Dec. 1797; married in Boston, Sophia Pierce. He lived in Boston until advanced in years, and then returned to his native town, and bought a small farm, on which he died about ten years later, 23 April 1872. His only child died in infancy.

3 Enoch, b. 29 Dec. 1799; m. Sarah Lord.
4 Paul, b. 18 April 1802; m. Elizabeth Sherburne.
5 John, b. 14 Sept. 1804; m. 12 April 1835, in Orono, Me., Ruth, dau. of Dr. Abner and Dorcas (Godfrey) Knowles of Unity. He left New Hampshire at the age of 23, and went with his brother Enoch onto a large farm, which they had purchased in Newport, Me. After a few years he removed down the Penobscot River to Orono, and went into the lumbering business, which he continued until old age. His wife died 15 April 1868, and he was married again, 6 Dec. 1873, to Lydia C. Heath. He now spends his summers in Orono, and his winters in Brooklyn, N. Y. Children:
  1 Hester L., b. 24 June 1836; m. 14 Sept. 1856, Samuel Libby, 1-4-4-3-3-1.
  2 Ellen, b. 31 Jan. 1842; unm. She is a teacher.
  3 Isabel, b. 28 Nov. 1844; d. 4 Oct. 1845.
6 Samuel, b. 3 Feb. 1807. He removed to Virginia when about 21, and assumed the name of Blake. He died in Berryville, 10 April 1879, leaving three sons and two daughters under that name.

1-4-4-4

Isaac Libby, born in Dover, N. H., 11 Feb. 1738; married Sarah Coleman. He lived in Rochester, whither his father had removed, until 1798 or 9. His farm was that now owned by —— Tibbetts. From Rochester he moved to Farmington, N. H., and thence, almost immediately, to Porter, Me. He was a Free Will Baptist preacher a short time before leaving Rochester, and was afterward a member of the church of Elder John Buzzell, in Parsonsfield, Me. He lost his life on a journey between Porter and Saco. He died in Hollis, but was carried back to Porter and buried. His widow died in 1813.

Children, all born in Rochester:

1 Joseph, died at the age of 27; unm.
2 Hanson, b. 19 Nov. 1774; m. Lydia Wallingford.
3 Keziah, b. 28 Mar. 1776; m. 11 Mar. 1797, Wm. French.
4 Mary, b. 26 May 1779; m. 28 Nov. 1802, Jacob French, a brother of William; died 18 Mar. 1852.
5 Tobias, b. 2 April 1783; m. Abigail Randall.

1-4-5-1

James Libby, born in Portsmouth, N. H., 1747; married, 3 Feb. 1774, Sarah Gibbs. He removed from Portsmouth, probably in 1786, to Wendall, now Goshen, N. H. He was a farmer there and lived to an advanced age.

Children:

1 James, married Polly Sherman. He was a farmer in North Goshen. Children:
  1 Sally, b. 1808; died 4 Aug. 1829.
  2 John, b. 1809; died 13 Feb 1836.
  3 Marion, m. —— Kenniston; went west.
  4 Horace.
  5 Abigail, b. 1818; d. 5 Nov. 1847.
  6 Wealthy, m. S. H. Stowell.
2 Deborah, never married.

1-4-5-3

JOSEPH LIBBY, born in Portsmouth, N. H., about 1762; married first, MARY COLE, daughter of Ebenezer and Mary (Wentworth) Cole; second, MEHITABLE LEAVITT, daughter of Thomas Leavitt of Parsonsfield, Me.

In his younger days he was a school-teacher; after his marriage, a farmer. With his first wife, he lived in Conway, N. H. After his second marriage he lived in Parsonsfield, where he died 7 Feb. 1846. His widow died in Freedom, N. H., 10 April 1857.

Children, by first wife:

1 Polly, m. John Hayes, and went to New York.
2 Margaret, m. 29 Nov. 1810, Jeremiah Leavitt, her step-uncle.
3 Joseph, m. 1st, Josephine Carroll; (died about 1837); 2d. 1840. Julia Wallis. He was a tailor by trade, and carried on his business in Boston. About 1838 he became a broker. He at length became crazy and escaped from an asylum to Paris, France, where he lived until his death, May 1872. His wife followed him to France, and, after his death, returned to Boston, where she now lives. No children.
4 Ebenezer, b. Oct. 1804; m. Rachel Burt.
5 John, died young.

By second wife:

6 Love L., } died in early
7 Sarah A., } womanhood.
8 John, b. 14 April 1820; m. Jane, dau. of Coker and Mary (Cushing) Merrill, of Parsonsfield. He is a farmer in Freedom, N. H. Children, all born in Freedom:
    1 Laura A., b. 8 May, 1848; m. 6 June 1875, Frank C. Tyler.
    2 Sarah J., b. 16 July 1850; unm.
    3 John C., b. 23 July 1854; m. 30 May 1876, in Cambridgeport, Mass., Susie, dau. of Geo. and Martha (Leavitt) Wilkinson. Child:
        1 George E., b. 12 April 1878, in Freedom.
    4 Rose E., b. 12 March 1864.

1-5-2-3

JOSEPH LIBBY, born in Scarborough, 24 March 1732; married first, 7 Jan. 1758, MARY HUSTON; second, 4 April 1782, HANNAH HANSON, of Windham.

He grew up, and was married, in Falmouth. About 1760 he removed to Gorham. He settled first on Queen street, but afterward bought the mill privilege at Horse Beef Falls, and carried on a sawmill. He died 5 Feb. 1801. His second wife outlived him some years.

Children, by first wife; born in Falmouth:

1 Dorcas, m. 23 Nov. 1775, Geo. Waterhouse, 10-2-2-9.

Born in Gorham:

2 Mary, b. 28 March 1761; m. Matthias Murch.
3 John, b. 10 March 1764; m. Phebe Knight.
4 William, b. 28 Oct. 1769; m. Anna (Webb) Boulton.
5 Sarah, m. 16 Dec. 1790, Thomas Blake of Westbrook.
6 Charlotte, b. 25 Sept. 1776; m. 25 Aug. 1795, James Thomas.
7 Joseph, b. 13 June 1780; m. Mercy Whitney.

By second wife:

8 Mary, b. 12 Nov. 1783; m. 11 June 1799, Wm. Frost.

1-5-2-4

CAPT. SAMUEL LIBBY, born in Falmouth, Me., 1 Feb. 1737; married first, Mary Frost; (died 1762, in Gouldsborough); second, JEMIMA LEIGHTON.

With his first wife's family, —— Leighton and family, and John Tracy and family, he left Falmouth and became one of the first settlers of Gouldsborough. He was a farmer and settled on the farm now owned by H. M. Soule and Elisha and James Libby, 1-5-2-4-2-1-2 and 3. During the Revolution he was captain of a company that was formed to guard the coast from Castine to Machias. He died in March, 1825.

Children, all by second wife:

1 Mary, b. 1763, the first female child born in Gouldsborough; died Mar. 1848; unm.
2 Joseph, b. 25 April 1765; m. Bathsheba Gibbs.
3 Abby, married, 1791, Job Gibbs.
4 Betsey, b. 1770; d. 1842; unm.
5 Lydia, b. 1780; m. 7 May 1798, Gowen Wilson.

1-5-2-5

DANIEL LIBBY, born in Falmouth, Me., in the year 1742; married, 1 July 1762, SARAH DOUGHTY of Falmouth, a sister of Capt. James Doughty that afterward settled in Gray.

Daniel Libby was one of the earliest settlers of Gray, removing thither probably in 1764. As his wife used to say, there was at that time "not a piece of mowing-field big enough for her to spread her apron on." For a period their provisions had to be all carried from Falmouth, and he used to earn money by working in Falmouth, until his lands became productive. He bought a great deal of wild land, from which he afterward gave each of his sons a farm. He gave to the town the lot on which are now the cemetery and town-house. His house, where were held the town meetings for some time, was where that of the widow of Edward Maybury now is. In 1778, New Boston, as the place was then called, was incorporated as the town of Gray, and in that year and several following years, Daniel Libby served as selectman. He died after a residence in Gray of more than sixty years, 25 Nov. 1826. His widow died 3 May 1831.

Their children were:

1 William, b. 9 Jan. 1763; m. Jane McCarfrey.
2 Joseph, b. 1764; m. Mary Young.
3 Betsey, m. Ephraim Staples of Gray.
4 Sarah, m. Daniel Green of Portland.
5 Nancy, m. —— Sawyer, and Thomas Dutton.
6 Jonathan, m. Abigail Clark.
7 Daniel, m. Hannah Colley.
8 Dorcas, m. —— Nason, and Stephen Furbish.

9 Clarissa, died in girlhood.
10 Hannah, m. Samuel Nash of Gray.
11 Benjamin, b. April 1778; m. Abigail Green and Mary Lunt.
12 Sophia, } twins, b. } m. William Green.
13 Abia, } Feb. 1781; } died in girlhood.
14 Mary, m. 11 Nov. 1804, Chas. Thaxter of Bangor.
15 Charlotte, m. Moses Harris of Gray.

1-6-2-1

BENJAMIN LIBBY, born in Berwick, Me., about 1735; married, 13 March 1760, ELIZABETH SMITH, daughter of Capt. John Smith of Berwick.

He engaged in the coasting trade. Some years before the Revolution, he settled at Frenchman's Bay, on the coast of what is now Hancock County. It was said by his son Benjamin that he with a neighbor named Clark, built the first wharf on that bay, and the first vessel that sailed from it. During the Revolution he was driven away by the British. He left his property and fled in an open boat some 300 miles along the coast, and landed in safety at York Beach. He afterward settled on a farm in Kittery. He died in the year 1805. His widow died with her son Ichabod, in Tuftonborough, N. H., (where it is thought her husband also died), about 1824.

Children:

1 Hanson, b. 14 Dec. 1760; m. Anna Libby, 1-6-5-11.
2 Thankful, bap. 1763; died young.
3 Anna, bap. 1765; m. Daniel Colby; died about 1794, in Sandwich, N. H.
4 Betsey, bap. 1767; m. Wm. Fullerton of Wolfborough; died 1799. Six children.
5 Experience, bap. 1770; died young.
6 Ichabod, bap. 1771; m. Molly Leavitt.
7 Sarah, bap. 1773; m. Enoch Quimby of Sandwich.
8 Margaret, b. about 1775; m. Amos Quimby.
9 Benjamin, b. 15 March, 1777; m. Susan Demerit.
10 Polly, bap. 1782; m. 5 April 1802, John French.
11 Harriet, m. —— Howe, a preacher it is thought.

1-6-2-4

JOSEPH LIBBY, born in Berwick, Me., about 1744; married, 7 April 1771, LYDIA SHOREY. He lived at first at Pine Hill, in Berwick, and thence moved to Milton, N. H., where he settled on a farm near Milton Mills, now owned by Daniel Guptil. He died 10 March 1817. His widow died in Wakefield 13 June 1839.

Children:

1 Ichabod, m. Mary Keay.
2 Agnes, m. 13 June 1792, Stephen Clark.
3 Lydia, m. 2 Oct. 1794, Wm. Clark of Dixmont, Me.
4 Adah, m. Francis Berry of Milton.
5 Hannah, died in 1824; unm.
6 Elisha, died at the age of about 35; unm. He was mistaken for another man, and murdered on a steamer on the coast of Maine. He was a carpenter.

7 Joseph, b. 1784; m. Hannah Cook.
8 John, b. 1785; m. Sally Langley and Dolly Wiggin.
9 Lucy, m. Enoch Cook of Wakefield.
10 Mark, b. 13 Feb. 1790; m. Nancy Cook.
11 Nathan, b. 18 Mar. 1792; m. Olive Berry.
12 James, b. 1794; d. Feb. 1832; unm. He was a farmer and school-teacher.

1-6-2-7

NATHAN LIBBY, born in Berwick, Me., about 1753; married, 12 Jan. 1778, RUTH SHOREY. He was a farmer and lived on his father's homestead. He died in the summer of 1804 or 5. His widow died about 1835.

Children:

1 Elisha, b. 22 Sept. 1778; d. Feb. 1855; unm. He always lived on his father's homestead.
2 Alice, b. 16 Jan. 1782; m. 26 Dec. 1830, Benj. G. Lord. She had no children, and lived with her brother.

A child of Thomas Lee, brought up in the family:

a Patty (Libby), m. Daniel Abbott. She had a son before her marriage.
1 Isaac (Libby), b. 1819; d. Feb. 1842; unm.

1-6-5-2

DANIEL LIBBY, born in Berwick, 28 Mar. 1746; married 4 Aug. 1774, LUCY CHADBOURNE.

He settled in North Berwick, on a farm now occupied by Mark Wallingford. There he died 23 Oct. 1790. His wife died about the same time.

Children:

1 Abigail, b. 29 Sept. 1775; m. 5 Dec. 1804, Aaron Chick.
2 Lois, b. 20 April 1777; m. 1796, John Guptil.
3 Molly, b. 14 July 1779; m. 1798, Nathaniel Guptil.
4 Samuel, b. 16 May 1781; m. Mary J. Johnson.
5 Jeremiah, b. 28 Mar. 1783; d. young.
6 Sarah, b. 6 July 1785; m. Thomas Chase.
7 Daniel, b. 26 Sept. 1787; died of dropsy, aged about 15.
8 Levi, b. 21 Aug. 1789; m. Lydia A. Chick.

1-6-5-3

LIEUT. JEREMIAH LIBBY, born in Berwick, 28 Dec. 1747; married ELIZABETH GUPTIL.

He was a blacksmith. He lived in Berwick until 1789, and then settled in Lebanon. He was at one time selectman of that town. He died about 1816. His widow died 14 Oct. 1828, in Berwick.

Their children were:

1 Olive, m. 1786, Isaac Stillings.
2 Abigail, m. 17 Dec. 1788, Stephen Shorey.

1-6-5-5

LIEUTENANT JOHN LIBBY, born 20 Nov. 1751, in Berwick; married 20 Dec. 1773, SARAH WOODSUM.

About the time of his marriage, he settled and cleared a farm in what is now the northwest corner of North Berwick. There he spent his life, engaging in milling, as well as farming, and became one of the principal men of that locality. His wife died 1 Oct. 1828. He died 1 Mar. 1837.

His children were:

1 Daniel, b. 21 Jan. 1775; m. Experience Pray.
2 Sally, b. 1 June 1777; m. 30 Nov. 1800, Tilley Abbott.
3 Ebenezer, b. 1 Feb. 1779; m. Hannah Smiley.
4 Alice, b. 2 Dec. 1780; m. Capt. David Libby, 1-6-9-3-1.
5 David, b. 18 Jan. 1783; d. in infancy.
6 Dorcas, b. 29 Aug. 1784; m. 23 June 1801, John Burnham Hanson of Lebanon.
7 John, b. 12 Oct. 1786; m. Abigail Libby, 1-6-9-10-3.
8 Pelatiah, b. 8 Dec. 1788; was a school-teacher; d. Mar. 1811; unm.
9 Ivory, b. 1 Feb. 1793; m. Olive Pray.

1-6-5-9

DEA. BENJAMIN LIBBY, born in Berwick, 18 Jan. 1758; married 15 Sept. 1779, POLLY HEARL.

He was a Revolutionary soldier. He was taken prisoner and confined at Charleston, S. C., and when he was freed, walked all the way home. Soon after his marriage, he settled in Lebanon, and cleared the farm now occupied by George Frank Libby, 1-6-9-3-1-7-1. While in Lebanon he was a deacon of the Baptist church; also in Albion, whither he removed in 1818—in all forty years. He died in Albion, 24 May 1834. His widow died 19 July 1845.

Children:

1 Dorcas, b. 7 April 1780; m. 1802, Jacob Abbott.
2 John, b. 10 Mar. 1782; m. Mary Ann Felker of Embden, Me. He died in Brooks, 8 Feb. 1859. His widow died 17 Feb. 1860. No children.
3 Wentworth, b. 6 May 1784; m. 1st, Eunice Hardison; 2d, Charlotte Parsons.
4 Benjamin, b. 17 Sept. 1786; m. 1810, Betsey Keay. In 1818 he was chosen selectman of Lebanon, and that same year left town. He settled at China Village, Me., where he was for many years a much respected citizen. He was deacon of the Baptist church; postmaster twenty years; a member of the state legislature. He died in April, 1844. His widow died in April, 1864. They had no children.
5 Oliver, b. 23 Dec. 1788; m. 1st, Hannah Delano; 2d, Lydia Littlefield.
6 Lucy, b. 5 Sept. 1791; m. Joseph Hardison.
7 Daniel, b. 7 Dec. 1793; m. 1st, Elizabeth Scores; 2d, Nancy B. Palmer.
8 Polly, b. 31 March 1796; was a school teacher; died in Embden, 1821; unmarried.
9 Nabby, b. 19 July 1798; m. 1818, Daniel Gowen.
10 Isaac, b. 14 Sept. 1803; d. 3 Jan. 1804.

1-6-5-10

SAMUEL LIBBY, born in Berwick, Me., 24 Aug. 1760; married 3 Jan. 1782, BETSEY HARDISON.

He cleared a farm about a mile north of East Lebanon Village, and there lived and died. Though chiefly a farmer, he was also a tanner. His death took place about 1827. His widow died in the fall of 1834.

Children:

1 Polly, m. 29 Dec. 1811, as second wife, Hiram Pray.
2 Nancy, m. Isaac Hanscom of Lebanon.
3 Thomas, died a young man, unmarried, of disease contracted in the war of 1812.
4 Parmelia, m. as first wife, 1809, Hiram Pray.
5 Eliza, d. in girlhood, 1 May 1808, at Nathan Coggswell's in Berwick.
6 Nahum. He was a saddler, and settled in Topsham, Me. He married there Dolly ——, and died 1823, leaving no children. His widow married again and lived in Lewiston.
7 Sally, b. 28 Mar. 1795; m. 28 Nov. 1816, Paul Wentworth.
8 John, m. Polly Hodgdon.
9 Betsey, m. —— Lancaster.
10 William Pepperell, b. 12 Dec. 1803; m. Sarah Drown.
11 Charlotte, m. Hiram Keay.

1-6-5-15

JAMES LIBBY, born 31 Jan. 1774, in Berwick; married, 7 Feb. 1805, SALLY JOHNSON, daughter of Noah and Sarah (Goodwin) Johnson of Kittery.

He had his father's homestead at Blackberry Hill, Berwick, and lived there until 1815, when he moved to Litchfield. In Litchfield he died, 24 Feb. 1861. His wife died 23 Sept. 1860.

Their children were:

1 Daniel, b. 16 Nov. 1805; d. 6 Feb. 1815.
2 Lois, b. 14 July 1807; m. 21 Feb. 1847, William Spear.
3 Samuel W., b. 10 April 1809; m. Lovina Hopkins.
4 Alvah, b. 4 May 1811; m. Hannah Richardson.
5 Oliver, b. 23 June 1813; m. 21 Jan. 1835, Bethiah, dau. of James and —— (Liston) Alexander of Litchfield. He resides in California. No children.

The preceding born in Berwick; the following in Litchfield:

6 Sarah, b. 33 May 1815; m. 16 Nov. 1852, Daniel Bryant.
7 Eliza Prime, b. 14 Sept. 1817; m. 12 April 1838, Isaac Randall.
8 Olive, b. 28 March 1820; m. 28 Jan. 1855, Isaiah Jordan.
9 Susan, b. 20 March; d. 12 May 1822.

1-6-9-3

EBENEZER LIBBY, b. 8 Feb. 1748, in Berwick; married, 16 Dec. 1770, ELIZABETH QUINT of Berwick.

He was a farmer and lived about two and a half miles from South Berwick Village, on the road to Portsmouth, on a farm called Old Fields. 26 Nov. 1776, he went out in an American privateer, probably the Charming Polly; at any rate he was one of the crew of that vessel when she was captured, 16 May 1777. He was carried to England. It appears that he was afterward exchanged, but he never reached home. His fate was never known. His widow married, 27 Oct. 1788, Capt. John Gowell of Berwick.

Children:

1 David, b. 1772; m. Alice Libby. 1-6-5-5-4.
2 Mary, b. 9 July 1775; m. 1796, Alexander Worster.
3 Elizabeth, m. James Bunker of Farmington, N. H.

1-6-9-4

Capt. Charles Libby, born in Berwick, 16 Dec. 1749; married, 16 July 1772, Sarah Pray.

He received by will one-half of his father's homestead, and lived in the old house; but (it is said) in a law suit about some injustice done him when he was an officer in the militia, spent all his property, and had to relinquish the homestead. He moved up to Lebanon in 1791, and very soon pined away and died. He was buried on the farm now occupied by B. L. E. Gowen. He was a Revolutionary soldier. His widow married second, 2 Feb. 1796, John Legro of Lebanon.

Children:

1 Abigail, m. 14 July 1793, her cousin, Benj. Pray.
2 Experience, m. 16 Feb. 1812, Samuel Brock.
3 John, b. 1777; m. 1833, Nancy, dau. of David and —— (Wingate) Farnham; d. 15 March 1848. His widow died 20 July 1867. He was a carpenter, and lived on a small farm near Lebanon Center, now owned by Nathan Jenness. He had no children.
4 Jeremiah, followed the sea; disappeared when a young man; unmarried.
5 Joshua, b. 27 May 1785; m. 1st, Alice Pray; 2d, Sarah Grant.
6 Nathaniel, b. 22 Dec. 1790; m. Tirzah Lord.

1-6-9-8

Benjamin Libby, born in Berwick, Me., 4 Nov. 1756; married, 1781, Mary Hamilton

He was a farmer. He moved to Sanford soon after his marriage and lived on the road between Mount Hope and Springvale. From Sanford he moved to Gardiner where he died of typhoid fever about 1815. His widow removed to Pittsfield and died about 1845.

Children:

1 Jonathan, b. 1782; m. Hannah Knox.
2 Benjamin, m. —— Edgecomb.
3 Solomon, b. 1788; m. Jane McCausland.
4 Abigail, b. 30 Oct. 1790; married John Jones of Gardiner, afterward of Union; died in Union, 2 Mar. 1876. Children:
   1 Benjamin Libby (Jones), b. June 1817; m. Jane M. Edwards.
   2 Lucy Lindley (Jones), b. 5 Aug. 1819; m. 1 Sept. 1867, Thomas A. Davis.
   3 William Henry (Jones), b. 25 May 1821; unm.

4 Aroline Emma (Jones), b. 1 June 1823; m. Andrew Libby, 1-1-2-6-2-3-6.
5 Sarah Emeline (Jones), b. 2 June 1827; d. 21 Sept. 1828.
6 Sarah Abbie (Jones), b. 25 Dec. 1828; m. 6 Sept. 1857, Samuel G. Hills.
7 John Emery (Jones), b. 15 Sept. 1830; unm.
8 Augustus Levi (Jones), b. 30 Nov. 1833; m. Anna M. Hodsdon.
5 Betsey, b. 9 April 1794; m. 1st, William Henry Jewett; 2d, James Hunter; died 16 Oct. 1876.
6 Sarah, died at the same time with her father and of the same fever; unm.
7 ——, son, was a sailor; died of yellow fever.

1-6-9-10

James Libby, born in Berwick, Me., 18 Aug. 1760; married 7 Nov. 1782, Hannah Woodsum. He was a farmer. He moved to Lebanon soon after his marriage and lived there until his death, 22 June 1832. His widow died 15 May 1840.

Children:

1 Betsey, b. 9 Jan. 1785; m. —— Nichols of Ossipee, N. H.; died 13 Sept. 1848.
2 James, b. 8 Dec. 1787; m. Nabby Goodwin and Peggy (Gowell) Chapman.
3 Abigail, b. 1 Jan. 1790; m. John Libby, 1-6-5-5-7.
4 Permitta, b. 3 Feb. 1792; m. 8 Dec. 1814, Edmund Keay; d. 9 April 1850, in Lebanon.
5 Mary, b. 4 Jan. 1794; m. William Forbes; d. 5 July 1869.
6 Jeremiah, b. 14 May 1796; m. Lucy Guptil.
7 Rebecca, b. 24 June 1798; m. 1st, Amos Langley; 2d, Dea. Isaac Brackett; d. 19 July 1848.
8 Jacob, b. 29 Mar. 1800; d. 22 Nov. 1820.
9 Dorcas, b. 26 July 1802; m. 31 Jan. 1828, John Pender.
10 Moses, b. 15 Mar. 1805; m. Hulda Langton.
11 David, b. 30 March 1808; m. Mary Brackett and Roxanna Rogers.

1-6-9-12

Dea. John Libby, born in Berwick, Me., 2 Jan. 1768; married, 27 Feb. 1791, Mary Gowen, daughter of Patrick and Abigail (Woodsum) Gowen of Berwick.

He lost his father at an early age, and served his time at the tanner's trade, at Blackberry Hill, with Patrick Gowen. He afterward married his daughter, and settled on wild land on Mount Hope, Sanford, where he ended his days. His chief occupation was farming, but he also carried on tanning, currying, and shoemaking. He was deacon of the Calvin Baptist church in East Lebanon. His wife died 17 Dec. 1850. He died 25 Nov. 1851.

Their children were:

1 Elias, b. 27 Sept. 1793; m. Mehitable Butler.
2 Draxey, b. 7 March 1795; d. 4 Sept. 1800.
3 Aphia, b. 7 May 1797; d. 19 Sept. 1800.
4 Adah, b. 7 Feb. 1799; m. 25 April 1847, Levi Abbott.
5 Ebenezer, b. 4 April 1801; m. Susan Butler, sister of Mehitable.
6 Aphia, b. 15 March 1803; m. Nehemiah Butler, brother of Susan.

7 John, b. 31 Jan. 1805; m. Olive Littlefield of Sanford. He lives on Spring Street, Gardiner. Children:
  1 Joanna, b. 14 Feb. 1840, in Sanford; m. Elbridge Trafton.
  2 Mary Ellen, b. 25 Feb. 1843, in Avon; unm.
  3 Rosilla, b. 2 Dec. 1845; died aged four years.
  4 Ada E., b. 1 Dec. 1847, in Avon; m. Eugene Danforth.
8 Ivory, b. 1 Jan. 1807; m. Mary Butler, sister of Nehemiah.
9 Charles, b. 9 June 1809; m. Patience H. Plummer.
10 Draxey, b. 11 June 1811; m. 22 Oct. 1835, Mark Evans Marshall.
11 Rhoda, b. 22 July 1813; m. 1st, Wm. Chadbourne; 2d, Nehemiah Butler, her deceased sister's husband.
12 Otis Robinson, b. 8 Sept. 1818; m. Mercy C. Clark.

1-7-6-3

John Libby, born in Portsmouth, N. H., about 1755; married 11 April 1781, in Portsmouth, Hannah Varrill. He was a soldier of the Revolution and was at the battle of Bunker Hill. He afterward lived in Newburyport, Mass., where he died about 1835. It is said he had a second wife but her name is not known.

Children, all by first wife:

1 Hannah, b. 6 Jan. 1786; died about 1838; unm.
2 Deborah, b. 18 July 1789; died about 1849; unm.
3 John, b. 26 Nov. 1791; m. Sophia Sargent of Newburyport. He followed the sea, as mate. He died at Newburyport about 1858, and his widow two years later. No children.
4 Theodore, b. 5 Sept. 1793; m. Deborah Cushing.

5-2-3-1

Samuel Libby, born in Scarborough, 12 April 1768; married 10 June 1794, Lydia Fogg, 9-6-6-3.

He was a forehanded farmer. About the time of his marriage, he settled on the homestead of his great-grandfather, John Jones, and always abode there. He was two years town treasurer; also proprietor's clerk. From about the year 1795 until his death, he kept a record of the deaths in Black Point parish. The record is still continued by his son, and has been of great assistance to the compiler of this work. He died 7 Nov. 1851. His widow died 14 April 1854, aged 89.

Children:

1 Lydia, b. 7 July 1795; m. Joseph Libby, 10-2-1-6-3.
2 Sarah, b. 28 Nov. 1796; m. Jordan Libby, 5-7-14-9.
3 Mary, b. 6 Oct. 1798; m. Shirley Libby, 10-1-6-4-2.
4 Hannah, b. 22 Sept. 1800; vowed she would never marry a Libby; saw all the rest of the family married to persons of their own name, and then, 21 Mar. 1842, m. Solomon Bragdon, a son of Olive (Libby) Bragdon, 10-2-4-5.
5 son, born and died 5 Jan. 1803.
6 Ebenezer, b. 4 June 1804; m. Mary Libby, 10-2-1-1-5-2.

5-2-3-8

Luther Libby, born 1 July 1786, in Scarborough; married 14 Oct. 1821, Lydia McKenney, daughter of Dominicus and Mary

(Hasty) McKenney of Limington. [See McKenney and Hasty, pp. 63 and 55].

He lived and died on the farm and in the house that were his father's. He was forehanded and left a good property. His wife, Lydia, the mother of his children, died 22 Sept. 1843. He married second, 18 Dec. 1846, Abigail, daughter of William Files of Gorham. He died 17 Oct. 1847. She married again, 19 July 1860, Rev. Sargent Shaw, and died in Gorham, June 1880.

Children, all by his first wife:

1 Ebenezer, b. 11 Dec. 1822; d. 17 March 1827.
2 Dominicus, b. 9 Jan. 1826; m. 27 Nov. 1853, Harriet E. Libby, 11-7-1-4-4-8. He lived on his father's homestead until recently, when he sold and bought the farm on Beach Ridge, on which he has since lived. His wife died 1 Aug. 1865. Children:
  1 Lucy Hannah, b. 28 Aug. 1858; d. 17 May 1873.
  2 John Lincoln, b. 11 July 1863.
3 Hannah, b. 15 May 1827; d. 13 May 1838.
4 Ebenezer Peter, b. 1 March 1830; m. 1st, 19 Oct. 1853, Mary F., dau. of Ruth (Libby) Johnson, 11-7-2-6-11; (died 26 Sept. 1861, with her father); 2d, June, 1863, in New Brunswick, Mary Ann, dau. of Walter and Nancy (Linkletter) Glover of Lower Canada. He is a farmer and hunter, and has spent his time between Westbrook, where he owned a farm, Scarborough, and the British Provinces, where he now lives. Children, by first wife:
  1 John S., b. 5 May, 1855; d. 15 Oct. 1863, in Westbrook.
  2 Mary Elizabeth, b. 25 Nov. 1856, in Westbrook; m. 4 May 1876, George B. Jacobs.

  By second wife:

  3 Annie Isabelle, b. 6 Feb. 1865, in Lower Canada.
  4 John, b. 18 Jan. 1867.
  5 Sarah, b. 20 Aug. 1868.
  6 Asa, b. 4 July 1873, in Scarborough.
  7 Abbie, b. 8 July 1875.
  8 Hattie, b. 25 July 1877.
  9 Clara Susan, b. 27 Dec. 1878.
5 Sumner, b. 10 Oct. 1833; m. 21 May 1856, Mary Lancaster Libby, 11-7-2-4-8-6. Previous to his marriage, he exchanged his part of his father's real estate with William Henry Libby, 11-7-7-8-5, for his father's homestead. He built the house now standing. He had naturally great artistic genius, but died young, 10 July 1864, of consumption. His wife died 24 Jan. 1864. Children:
  1 Lydia Estelle, b. 15 Aug. 1857; m. 17 Sept. 1879, Dea. Nelson T. Wright of Lunenburgh, Vt.
  2 Alice Woodbury, b. 1 Oct. 1859; unm.
  3 Edward Augustus, b. 15 Jan. 1862. In Feb. 1881, he went to Rockford, Ill., where he is a collector for a publishing firm.
6 Lewis, b. 26 March, 1839; m. May, 1861, Rachel A., dau. of Jedediah Graffam of Portland. His chief employment was in iron founding. He enlisted in the war; was mustered in in Co. D, 20th Maine, 2 Nov. 1865; died in hospital, 7 July following. His widow married a Chadbourne. Only child:
  1 Edwin, died young.

5-2-7-1

Lemuel Libby, born in Scarborough, 8 Nov. 1770; married, 11 June 1795, Patience Whitmore, daughter of Capt. Benjamin Whitmore of Gorham.

When he was married he bought a farm in Gorham, the same now occupied by —— Meserve, next south of Silas Libby, 10-1-8-1-2-2. There he lived until about 1835, when he accompanied his son to Wayne, where his wife died, 18 Jan. 1845, and thence to Readfield, where he died, 9 Feb. 1858.

Children:

1 Mary, b. 7 June 1796; m. Elder Peter Libby, 11-6-2-1-6.
2 Ebenezer, b. 29 Nov. 1797; m. Emeline Harding.
3 Abigail, b. 25 Aug. 1800; d. 28 July 1838, in Buxton; unm.
4 Lucy, b. 2 Feb. 1803; d. Dec. 1819, in Westbrook; unm.
5 Louisa, b. 12 June 1807; d. 30 Sept. 1821; unm.
6 Elizabeth Hustin, b. 5 July 1809; m. 7 May 1829, Francis Libby Rounds, son of Mehitable (Libby) Rounds, 11-6-2-1-2.
7 Ann, b. 23 Dec. 1811; m. 5 Sept. 1833, Charles Watts.
8 Samuel, b. 11 June 1816; d. 1 Sept. 1821.

5-2-7-5

Nehemiah Libby, born in Scarborough, 14 Feb. 1783; married, 2 Nov. 1814, Parmela Harmon, daughter of Daniel and Abigail (Milliken) Harmon of Scarborough.

He succeeded to his father's homestead. He was out in the war of 1812. He was a number of years selectman of the town. He died 23 Feb. 1841. His widow died 24 Jan. 1865.

Their children were:

1 Mary Ann, b. 17 Sept. 1815; d. 2 May 1817.
2 Mary Ann, b. 7 Feb. 1818; m. Rev. Wm. Smith.
3 Susannah, b. 17 July 1821; kept a boarding-house in Saco, where she died, 27 Aug. 1879; unm.
4 Abigail, b. 17 Oct. 1823; m. Joseph Blanchard.
5 Lucy Elizabeth, b. 18 Feb. 1826; m. Alpheus Fernald.
6 Nehemiah Granville, b. 28 Nov. 1828. He went to California when a young man, and has since lived there. He now lives in Iowa City, Placer Co. He was postmaster awhile and then went into trade. He married a widow about 1861, who died after four years, leaving:
   1 Juliette, b. 1864.
7 Joseph White, b. 10 Oct. 1831; m. 2 May 1858, Maggie B., dau. of Rev. David and Jane (Brackett) Newell of Gorham. He learned the carriage maker's trade, but settled on the homestead farm. He served ten months in Co. C, 12th Maine Vols., thereby destroying his health. In consequence he sold the homestead, and bought into a photograph business in Great Falls, N. H. This was continued three years under the firm name Smith & Libby, and he has since been a carpenter. He lives in Biddeford. Children:
   1 Clarence Granville Blanchard, b. 28 Sept. 1859.
   2 Winifred Josephine, b. 22 Feb. 1865.

5-7-8-1

Abner Libby, born in Scarborough, 27 Dec. 1766; married, 15 Nov. 1789, Anna Harding, born 30 Aug. 1767, daughter of a Cape Cod coaster who settled at Mount Desert.

In his younger days he went several voyages to the West

Moses Libby

AT THE AGE OF 93

Indies. He afterward picked up the blacksmith's trade. In 1792 or 3, he settled at Limington Corner, on the farm now owned by John Libby, 5-7-8-1-2-11. He built a blacksmith shop there, and engaged in blacksmithing many years. He afterward opened a general store, and also kept public house.

He taught the first school in Limington. He was town clerk from 1793 to 1800; selectman 1794 to 1802; town treasurer 1804 to 1809. He was a justice of the peace about forty years, and, there being no lawyer there for many years, did a great deal of business which it now falls to attorneys-at-law to perform. For many years he filled a larger place in the community in which he lived, than probably any other of the townsmen.

He died 5 May 1043, in Scarborough. His widow died 30 Dec. 1857.

Their children were:

1 Elias, b. 12 March 1790, in Scarborough; m. Jane Jewell.
2 Parmenio, b. 22 Nov. 1791, in Scarborough; m. 1st, Eunice Jewell; 2d, Fannie Ward; 3d, Eliza Larrabee.

Born in Limington:

3 Stephen, b. 22 Nov. 1793; m. Sarah Chase.
4 Abner, b. 4 July 1796; m. 1st, Salome Jackson; 2d, Almira Allen.
5 Margaret, b. 19 Sept. 1798; m. 9 July 1816, Benjamin Clark.
6 John, b. 11 Jan. 1803; m. 1st, Margaret Waterhouse; 2d, Martha Williams.
7 Betsey Pettingill, b. 13 Aug. 1805; m. 5 July 1826, Joel Allen.
8 Charlotte Neal, b. 17 Nov. 1807; m. 22 Oct. 1828, Almon L. Sawyer.
9 Isaac Harding, b. 14 Aug. 1813; m. Caroline Waldron.

5-7-8-2

Capt. Moses Libby, born in Scarborough, 27 Mar. 1769; married Elizabeth Libby, 1-1-6-5-1.

He settled on a portion of his father's farm and always lived there. He was selectman 1808-1812, 1819, 1823-1825, 1831, 1835, 1837, 1844-1846. Being a man of good ability, he did a great deal of town business. He died 14 Mar. 1869, aged almost 100 years. His wife died 3 Dec. 1844.

Children:

1 Clarissa, b. 10 July 1791; d. 6 Jan. 1792.
2 Caleb, b. 7 Aug. 1794. He was one of the unhappy crew of the privateer *Dash* which sailed from Portland in the war of 1812 and was never heard from.
3 Olivia, b. 24 Jan. 1797; m. 1st, John H. Gould; 2d, Israel Swett.
4 Clarissa, b. 3 Oct. 1799; m. 28 Sept. 1817, Benjamin Dudley.
5 Isabella, b. 15 Jan. 1803; m. William Dow.
6 Sarah, b. 22 Aug. 1805; m. Thadeus Libby, 10-2-4-3-10.

5-7-8-3

Capt. Stephen Libby, born in Scarborough, 4 Nov. 1771; married 13 Jan. 1798, Agnes Hasty. [See Hasty, p. 55.]

In his younger days he followed the sea, but, soon after his marriage, settled on the farm on Oak Hill, now owned by H. J. Libby, 5-7-8-1-1-1, and became a thrifty farmer. He died 20 Nov. 1859. His wife died 5 Nov. 1858.

Their children were:

1 Harriet, b. 3 July 1800; d. 7 Mar. 1814.
2 Lucinda, b. 30 July 1802; m. 7 June 1821, Jeremiah Hill.
3 Benjamin Franklin, b. 30 May 1804; m. 1831, in Charleston, S. C., Ann Maria, daughter of Capt. —— Clark of that place. Up to the time of his marriage he followed the sea, the latter years as master; but after his marriage he was engaged in navigation and in the management of the Clark plantation. He died of pleurisy in 1846. His widow married again and soon afterward the whole family started on a trip to Europe. The steamer was lost with all on board. The mother's harp, which floated ashore, alone remained to tell the tale. Children:
   1 Martha Agnes, b. 1832.
   2 Ann Maria, born about 1834.
4 Margaret Agnes, b. 6 Nov. 1806; m. 17 July 1832, Harrison Jewell Libby, 5-7-8-1-1-1.
5 Ernestine, b. 9 June 1809; m. 3 May 1831, Charles Austin Lord of Portland, for many years editor of the Christian Mirror.
6 Francis, b. 24 June 1813; d. 23 Dec. 1813.
7 Harriet, b. 28 Dec. 1814; m. Rev. William T. Dickson.
8 Sally Maynard, b. 18 Oct. 1818; lives with her sister Margaret Agnes: unm. She was many years a school mistress.
9 Francis, b. 10 Nov. 1821; m. Sally Hayman Tompson, 5-7-14-7-3.

5-7-8-4

Henry Libby, born 14 April 1774, in Scarborough; married March 1794, Margaret Meserve, daughter of Gideon and Elizabeth Meserve. [See Meserve, page 37.]

Until he was married he followed the sea. He then bought the farm of his wife's father, near Oak Hill. There he resided until February, 1809, when he moved to Limington, and settled on a farm exactly in the center of that town. On this farm, he, and his family after him, lived and died. His death occurred 19 Feb. 1847. His wife died 27 Sept. 1841.

Their children were:

1 Eliza, b. 23 June 1794; m. 10 Aug. 1826, William Chick.
2 Margaret, b. 3 June 1796; m. 20 Nov. 1814, Joseph Tyler.
3 Susannah, b. 3 Sept. 1798; m. 15 June 1823, David Richardson.
4 Henry, b. 29 Dec. 1800; d. 5 Sept. 1828.
5 ——, died in infancy, 30 Oct. 1804.
6 Jane, b. 1 March 1803; died 19 May 1834; unm.
7 Nicholas, b. 25 Oct. 1806; d. 27 March 1828; unm.
8 Agnes H., b. 23 Nov. 1808; m. 24 Sept. 1837, Jacob Sawyer.
9 George Washington, b. 10 Jan. 1811; d. 29 June 1832; unm.
10 Maria, b. 26 Nov. 1813; d. 11 Feb. 1873; unm.
11 Mary Ann, b. 5 June 1817; d. 23 Oct. 1834.

5-7-8-10

John Adams Libby, one of triplets, born in Scarborough, 19 March 1790; married 4 Feb. 1810, Abigail Sawyer, daughter of Eben Sawyer of Limington.

In his youth he followed the sea. About 1814 he moved with his father to Limington, where he settled on a farm. In 1850 he moved to Needham, Mass., where he was a farmer until 1863, when he went to live with his son Stillman, in Somerville, and there died 16 May 1871. His widow died 14 May 1877, aged 90.

Their children were:

1 George Washington, b. 24 Feb. 1811, in Scarborough; m. 3 Jan. 1839, Olive Blake, dau. of Jacob and Elizabeth George (Jones) Hale of Ripley, Me. When about 23 he went to Ripley and engaged in tanning, currying, and manufacturing boots. In that place he was town clerk and a captain in the militia. In 1840 he removed his business to Exeter, and later engaged in the dry-goods trade, in which business he was also after his removal in 1854 to Chelsea, Mass., his present residence. Children:
 1 George Stillman, b. 3 Sept. 1848; d. 2 Sept. 1849.
 2 Abbie M., b. 1 Dec. 1851; unm. She is a school-teacher and music-teacher.

2 John Adams, b. 2 April 1813; m. 1st, Dec. 1837, in Ripley, Me., Julia A., dau. of Josiah and Hannah (Purington) Burleigh of Sandwich, N. H.; (died Nov. 1838); 2d, 9 Jan. 1840, her sister, Caroline W. Burleigh. He learned the shoemaker's trade in Limington, and went with his brother to Ripley where he kept a general store, and engaged also in currying and boot-making. He removed to Dexter about 1846, and went into trade there. From that place he moved, about 1853, to East Cambridge, Mass., and thence, a year later, to Chelsea, where he engaged in the shoe trade. He died there 14 May 1877. His wife died 13 Sept. 1873. Children, all by second wife:
 1 Julia Ann, b. 8 Nov. 1840; m. 11 June 1866, Christopher Sargent.
 2 Helen Amelia, b. 13 April 1843; unm.
 3 Frances Adelia, b. 16 May 1848; m. 20 July 1871, James Gould of Chelsea; d. 26 Dec. 1877.

3 Franklin F., b. 12 Aug. 1817, in Limington; unm. He was at first a mechanic, but has been in the dry-goods business forty years. He lives in Boston.

4 Michael, b. 19 Mar. 1819, twin with the following; married in Thomaston, Me., Rebecca Frances, dau. of Bias and Hannah Copeland of Warren. He was for the most part engaged in trade from the time he left home until 1871, since which date nothing is known of him. His widow lives with Franklin in Boston. Children:
 1 Frank Marion, (dau.), b. about 1855, in Boston.
 2 Louise Geneva, b. 1857; d. May, 1878.
 3 Ella Estelle, b. about 1859.
 4 Marita Malcomb, b. about 1868; d. 30 Jan. 1871.

5 Marshall, b. 19 March 1819, twin with Michael; m. 14 Aug. 1842, Mary E., dau. of Cornelius Simmons of Boston; d. 19 June 1851. His widow married a Parcher. Only child:
 1 Francena E., b. about 1844; m. —— Emery.

6 Ansel N., b. 28 Jan. 1821; m. Mary O., dau. of Isaac Smith of Boston. He lives in Littleton, N. H. Children:
 1 Nellie A., b. June 1861; m. Dec. 1880, Wm. Rhodes.
 2 Isaac Winthrop, b. 1863.
 3 Mary Abbie, b. 1866.
 4 George A., b. 1869.

7 Stillman Higgins, b. 3 April 1826; m. 1st, 14 Sept. 1854, Nancy Jane, dau. of —— and Nancy (Meacham) Wedgel of Boston; (died 23 Dec. 1855); 2d, 1 March 1860, Catherine Baker, dau. of Joseph and Emeline (Jones) Wyeth of Chelsea. He removed to Boston in 1841. He was in the dry goods business 33 years, and has since been in the real estate and insurance business. He resides

in Somerville, where he is a prominent politician. He was president of the Common Council in 1876 and 7, and on the board of Aldermen in 1878 and 9. Children, all by second wife:

1 Emma Warren, b. 22 March 1867; d. 13 Oct. 1869.
2 Amiebell, b. 13 Jan. 1871; d. 16 Sept. 1872.
3 Elmer Roswell, b. 16 Sept. 1875.

8 Moses M., b. 28 Sept. 1829; d. 12 July 1855, in Needham; unm.
9 Abbie M., b. 16 Aug. 1832; m. 26 March 1856, Benj. M. Wedger.

5-7-10-6

ELIZABETH LIBBY, born in Limington, Me., 28 Feb. 1783; married, 3 April 1803, MAJOR MOSES MOODY. They lived in Limington a number of years after their marriage, and soon after leaving that place settled on a farm in Cape Elizabeth, where he died. His widow is still living at the age of almost 99.

Children:

1 Major (Moody), b. 4 Feb. 1804, in Limington; m. Nancy Hunnewell; d. 22 June 1839.
2 Benjamin (Moody), b. 21 Feb. 1806; m. Rhoda Bowie; d. 8 Jan. 1837.
3 Eliza (Moody), b. 23 March 1808; m. David Plummer; d. 28 Jan. 1853.
4 Mary Ann (Moody), b. 31 March 1810; m. Wm. Plummer.
5 Eunice L. (Moody), b. 26 March 1812; m. Abner G. Green.
6 Moses L. (Moody), b 22 Oct. 1814; d. 22 Nov. 1836.
7 Hannah H. (Moody), b. 28 Feb. 1817, in Baldwin; m. 9 June 1839, Moses M. Allen; d. 17 July 1865.
8 John L. (Moody) b. 14 Oct. 1819, in Cape Elizabeth; m. Charlotte Libby, 10-5-3-5-1-4; died 2 Oct. 1848. His widow married Zebulon Tyler Libby, 11-7-2-6-4-3.
9 Sarah Jane (Moody), b. 9 July 1822; d. 14 March 1826.
10 Priscilla (Moody), b. 8 Dec. 1824; m. 28 Jan. 1846, Francis Cash of Cape Elizabeth, a farmer. He died 12 Oct. 1877. Children:

1 Moses Maguire (Cash), b. 18 Oct. 1846.
2 Almira (Cash), b. 5 April 1848; d. 30 Jan. 1849.
3 Leroy M. (Cash), b. 22 Sept. 1850; unm.
4 Annie Plummer (Cash), b. 20 May 1855; unm.

5-7-11-1

JESSE LIBBY, born in Scarborough, about 1771; married, 1794, MARY MYRICK of Hampden.

He was reared in Limington, and went with his father to Hampden. He lived there, a farmer and shoemaker, until after the war of 1812, and moved thence to Boston where he was a deputy sheriff many years. He died Jan. 1830. His widow died June 1850, in the same place.

Children, all born in Hampden:

1 Clara, b. Feb. 1798; m. 1822, Thomas Goodwin of Bedford, Mass. d. Aug. 1843.
2 Oliver, b. 2 July 1800; m. 22 Oct. 1826, Maria J., dau. of William and Hannah (Kidder) Brayer of Boston. A few years of his married life were spent in New Hampshire, but the most in Boston, where he was for some time in the flour business. He died 27 June 1851. His widow died 8 Nov. 1878. Children:

1 Mary A., b. 6 Sept. 1828; m. Robert E. Stearns; d. 25 July 1879.
2 Helen M., b. 18 Aug. 1831; d. 14 July 1841.

3 William, b. 14 Sept. 1832; d. 7 Oct. 1832.
4 Adaline A., b. 26 June 1836; m. Jacob Bacon.
5 Harriet L., b. 12 Nov. 1843; unm.
6 Helen M., b. 6 Oct. 1846.

3 Eliza, b. 21 Aug. 1802; m. 1st, Daniel Edes; 2d, April 1823, Ezra O. Eaton.
4 Hiram, b. Dec. 1804; d. Feb. 1846; unm. He was a mason and builder in Boston.
5 Madison, b. Feb. 1807; d. Aug. 1809.
6 Elvira Jane, b. May 1809; m. 1st, James Creed; 2d, as second wife, Calvin Haskell; d. 3 Sept. 1878.
7 Mary Ann, b. 9 June 1811; m., 1833, Calvin Haskell; d. June 1848, in Watertown, Mass.

5-7-11-2

David Libby, born in Scarborough, 16 Dec. 1772; married, 7 Aug. 1796, Hannah Knight of Buxton.

In his early days he was a carpenter, but later his chief occupation was farming. He followed his father to Hampden, where he lived until 1811. He then moved to that part of Frankfort which is now Winterport and settled in the woods. Ten years later he removed to Carmel and cleared a farm which he gave to his son Thomas Jefferson and lived with him until his death, 19 May 1853. His widow died in Bangor, 25 July 1864.

Children:

1 Lewis, b. 9 Feb. 1797, in Limington; m. Mary A. Tompson.
2 Hannah, b. 21 Dec. 1798, in Buxton; m. Peter M. Clark of Newburgh; d. March 1828.
3 Mary, b. 7 Aug. 1801, in Buxton; m. Jacob Sweetsir of Newburgh; d. 8 July 1876, in Hampden.
4 Thomas Jefferson, b. 12 March 1804, in Phipsburg; m. 1st, June 1835, Mary, dau. of Jacob and Harriet (Mitchell) Sherburne of Atkinson; (died 19 Oct. 1841); 2d. Emily, dau. of Isaac and Margaret (McFarland) Russ of Dexter. He sold the homestead in Carmel and bought into a clothing mill and a sawmill. After a few years they were burnt. He has since been a farmer and carpenter. Children, all born in Carmel; by first wife:
  1 Lewis Jefferson, b. 23 March 1836; m. Margaret Braley; d. about 1861.
  2 Amanda, b. 7 Feb. 1838; m. 26 Oct. 1866, Isaac W. Merryman of Rockland.

  By second wife:

  3 Helen, b. 25 Aug. 1847; unm.
  4 Flora, b. 1 May 1849; m. 1 July 1876, Clement Dickinson of Boston, Mass.
  5 Belle, b. 12 Sept. 1852; m. 12 Sept. 1873, Dexter D. Roberts of Stockton.

  Previous to his marriage he adopted:
  a Crosby (Libby), b. about 1828. He was two years old when adopted, and after three months went back to his mother. He lives in Etna. It is believed that he is married, but has no children.
5 Jane Dolbeer, b. 24 Feb. 1807, in Hampden; m. Samuel Emerson of Carmel.
6 Anna Reed, b. 5 Oct. 1809; m. Richmond Hayward.
7 Julia, b. 7 Nov. 1812, in Frankfort; m. Horatio Beal of Bangor.
8 Lucetta, b. 11 July 1815; m. 1 Jan. 1844, Lyman Tyler.
9 Elvira, b. 1 Aug. 1820; m. Samuel Allen of Carmel.

5-7-11-3

Samuel March Libby, born in Scarborough, 11 March 1775; married Eliza Myrick of Hampden, Me. He grew up in Limington, removed thence with his father to Hampden, whence he emigrated in 1819, and settled at Darbytown, three miles from Richmond, Va.

Children:

1 Luther, b. 21 Aug. 1806; m. Elizabeth Crump.
2 Seth, b. 1809; m. Mary Slade of Richmond. He died after a few years, leaving no children. His widow now lives in Galveston, Texas.
3 Sylvia, b. 23 March 1816; unm. She lives in New Kent Co., Va.
4 Oliver, b. 1819; unm. He has lived in Boston, Mass.

5-7-11-6

Hon. Richard Libby, born in Limington, Me., 29 Oct. 1790; married, 13 Aug. 1813, in Wellfleet, Mass., Hannah Holbrook, dau. of Capt. Jesse and Temperance (Higgins) Holbrook of that place.

He was reared in Hampden, Me., and lived there when the war of 1812 came on. During the war he served as lieutenant of a letter of marque, and was twice taken prisoner. At the close of the war, he settled in Wellfleet, Mass., and for twenty-seven years followed the sea, the most of the time as captain. He was afterward at different times postmaster, lighthouse tender, and deputy collector of customs. In 1848 he removed to Boston, where he lived until 1860, when he went to New York, and thence, in 1866, to East Orange, N. J., where he lived with his son Oliver until his death, which took place 17 March 1876.

In politics he was strongly democratic. While living in Wellfleet he served several years as selectman and was twice representative to the state legislature. He was afterward state senator from Suffolk Co. He was an earnest mason, having joined the order in 1812, and was a member of the Methodist Church.

His wife died on a packet between Wellfleet and Boston, 13 Oct. 1858.

Children:

1 Demorin, b. 7 June 1814, in Hampden, Me.; m. 7 June 1843, Susan L., daughter of Jesse and Dorcas Dean of Hampden. He grew up in Wellfleet, and became at length captain of a Cape Cod fishing vessel. In 1841 he quit the sea and has since kept an oyster-house and restaurant in New York City. He was the first to introduce boiled lobsters by rail and steamboat from Boston, which was in 1844; also the Boston style of opening oysters. Child:
   1 Robert H., b. 12 May 1858, in New York City; unm.
2 Robert H. [Hon.], b. 1 Jan. 1816, in Wellfleet; m. Oct. 1838, Betsey, dau. of Henry and Betsey (Holbrook) Baker of Wellfleet. In 1829 he went to Boston and was in the employ of his uncle, Joseph Holbrook in the oyster business until 1841, when he himself engaged in the same business in New York City. In 1856 he returned to Wellfleet, where he has since lived, for the most part

Richard Libby

engaged in farming. He is a Universalist and was some years trustee of the Rev. Dr. Chapin's church. He was lieutenant and afterward captain in the New York militia. He has been three times selectman of Wellfleet, 14 years a justice of the peace, and twice elected to the Massachusetts Senate. Only child :

1 Emily F., b. 26 Aug. 1845; unm. She is a teacher of music.

3 Richard, b. 29 Oct. 1818; m. 21 April 1841, Lucinda, dau. of Jonathan and Abigail (Lewis) Hickman of Wellfleet. He was in the oyster business in Boston some years and then in the fishing business in Swampscott, whence he removed, in 1858, to New York city, where (except two years spent in Philadelphia, in the wholesale fish business) he has since been engaged in the oyster and restaurant business. He served 14 years in the 71st Reg. National Guard of New York. He is a member of the M. E. Church. Children:

1 Franklin Doane, b. 30 April 1845; d. 18 July 1847.
2 Walter Woodman, b. 4 Mar. 1848; d. 17 Aug. 1848.
3 Mary Washington, b. 11 Feb. 1852; m. 25 Dec. 1867, Frederick L. Latimer. Children:
    1 Gertrude May (Latimer), b. 24 Oct. 1868.
    2 Gracie Estelle (Latimer), b. 28 Mar. 1871.
4 George Washington, b. 12 Nov. 1854; unm. He is with Blake & Co., hardware, Chicago.
5 Edith May, b. 19 Feb. 1861.

4 Jesse H., b. 19 June 1820; m. 22 July 1846, Mary J., dau. of William and Susan (Milliken) Sanders of Boston. In early life he went on mercantile and whaling voyages, and in 1849 went to California. After his return he was connected with various railroads, being at one time Assistant Superintendent of the Hudson River Railroad. In 1857 he and his brother Demorin bought a steam sawmill at Great Bend, Penn., and engaged in lumbering He was afterward engaged in manufacturing soap, sinking oil wells, rectifying spirits, and was three years overseer of the dairy house in Central Park. The latter years of his life were spent in the oyster and restaurant business in New York City. He died on his farm in Pearl River, 8 April 1881. Children:

1 George T., b. 15 Aug. 1847; d. 8 June 1851.
2 Franklin, b. 27 May 1849; d. 7 June 1851.
3 Lillie Lee, b. 16 Aug. 1851; d. 24 July 1854.
4 Nellie, b. 19 Nov. 1858; unm.
5 Jennie Louise, b. 6 Oct. 1861; d. 28 June 1865.
6 Carrie Estelle, b. 26 Sept. 1864.

5 Joseph M., b. 10 Feb. 1822; m. 1 May 1845, Mary M., dau. of Reuben and Miranda (Piper) Walton of Waltham. He served an apprenticeship at shoemaking, and was for many years foreman in a shoe manufactory. In 1865 he engaged, with his brother Oliver, in the oyster and restaurant business in New York, but soon returned to Cambridge to a last manufactory. In 1875 he became manager of a last factory in Marlborough, and the following year established himself in the same business, which he still continues. Children:

1 Charles W., b. 2 Feb. 1846, in Boston; m. 30 Nov. 1876, Laura A., dau. of Geo. and Adaline W. (Fisk) Cobleigh of Boston. He was educated in the public schools of Cambridge, and learned the trade of machinist. He has lived in every part of the Union, for the most part in the employ of the various agencies of the Singer Sewing Machine Co., and now lives in Marlborough, Mass. He served an one-hundred days' enlistment in Co. D, 5th Mass. Inf. Children:
    1 Laura A., b. 8 Oct. 1878, in Cambridgeport.
    2 Ella Maud, b. 16 May 1880, in Marlborough.
2 Mary Augusta, b. 15 April 1849; m. 16 April 1877, Emmons Hanscom of Acton, Mass.

3 Elvira H., b. 27 Aug. 1851; m. 20 Aug. 1873, Charles H. Titus of Natick.
4 Joseph M., b. 28 March 1856; d. 5 Feb. 1857.
6 Paulina D., b. 1 Nov. 1825; m. Barzillai Kemp of Wellfleet.
7 Nancy S., b. 24 Oct. 1827; m. John S. Cary of New York; lives in Newark, N. J.
8 Oliver [Major], b. 27 Dec. 1829; m. 20 June 1853, Sarah J., dau. of Geo. P. and Sarah D. (Prescott) Dudley of Boston. In 1856 he removed from Boston to New York City, where he has since been engaged in the restaurant business. He served nine years in the 71st Regiment New York State Militia, and three years in the same regiment of New York Volunteers. He enlisted as sergeant, and was promoted to the rank of second lieutenant, first lieutenant, captain, and finally, major. His residence was East Orange, N. J., from 1866 until 1878, and is now Wellfleet, Mass. Children:
1 Oliver C., b. 21 April 1861; d. 23 April 1861.
2 Oliver, b. 29 Sept. 1862; d. 19 July 1863.
3 Jennie N., b. 15 April 1864, in New York City.
4 Walter F., b. 26 Feb. 1872, in East Orange.
9 Franklin, b. 12 Nov. 1831; d. 30 June 1841.
10 Benton, b. 29 April 1835; d. 9 Feb. 1852; unm.
11 Ann Jane, b. 9 March 1838; m. Capt. Bethuel P. Nickerson of Chatham.

5-7-12-1

Rufus Libby, born in Scarborough, 4 May 1773; married 25 April 1793, Dorcas Strout, daughter of Elisha and Eunice (Freeman) Strout, of Gorham.

At the time of his marriage he settled on a farm in Limington, near the Limerick line. This was his residence until 1836, when his son Philemon sold the homestead and bought the *Dam* farm in Newfield. There his wife died Dec. 1849. He himself died in Limerick, with his daughter Martha, 5 Dec. 1858.

Their children were:

1 William, b. 12 Aug. 1793; m. Esther Brackett.
2 Philemon, b. 14 Dec. 1796; m. 1st, Eliza Strout; 2d, Sally Libby, 11-2-4-3-3.
3 Aphia, b. 21 June 1799; m. 4 Oct. 1818, Robert Brackett.
4 Rufus, b. 18 April 1802; m. Martha Blake.
5 Nathaniel, b. 6 July 1804; m. Lucinda Berry.
6 Martha, b. 21 Nov. 1809; m. William Libby, 11-2-4-3-7.
7 Eunice, b. 4 Jan. 1813; died unmarried.
8 Solomon, b. 26 Nov. 1815; m. Betsey Fernald.

5-7-12-2

Philemon Libby, born in Scarborough, 7 July 1775; married 1 April 1798, Liberty Norris, daughter of Jonathan and Sally (Barker) Norris of Limerick.

When he was married he settled on Pine Hill, Limington. Thence he moved to Conway, N. H., with his brother James, and worked at milling. He returned after a few years and settled on part of his father's homestead. There he lived until after the death of his sons, and then sold his farm, and ended his days with his daughter Lydia. He died 14 May 1852. His wife died 8 Nov. 1821.

Their children, all born in Limington but Lucy and Lydia, were:

1 Sewall, b. 28 Aug. 1798; d. 29 July 1838; unm.
2 Sophia, b. 10 Nov. 1800; m. Daniel Small.
3 Harriet, died in infancy.
4 Lucy, died in infancy.
5 Lucy, b. 10 July 1809, in Conway; m. 13 Oct. 1829, William P. Leavitt of Exeter, N. H.
6 Lydia, b. 28 Jan. 1811, in Conway; m. 14 Feb. 1836, Thomas H. Hyde of Limington, a native of Long Island.
7 Harriet, b. 12 Sept. 1813; m. 10 Sept. 1836, Israel Boody.
8 son, died in infancy.
9 John, b. 28 Aug. 1819; d. 13 Aug. 1840; unm.

5-7-12-4

James Libby, born in Limington, Me., 11 Jan. 1779; married 17 Oct. 1804, Emma Chase, daughter of Deacon Amos and Emma (Elden) Chase of Limington.

He was a carpenter by trade but his chief occupation was farming. He lived first on part of his father's homestead, then in Conway, N. H., then on his part of the homestead in Limington again; and then, in 1818, sold his farm to McArthur, and bought wild land in Bridgton, in the part called New Limington, and cleared the farm now owned by Orin Bryant, on which he ended his days.

His first wife died 20 June 1828, and he married second, 26 Oct. 1829, Dolly (Brigham) Ball, widow of Rev. Reuben Ball of Bridgton. She died 10 Jan. 1858. He died 2 Mar. 1868, aged 89.

His children, all by first wife, were:

1 Emma, b. 15 Aug. 1805, in Limington; m. 25 Dec. 1829, Marshall Bacon of Bridgton.
2 Nancy, b. 3 Oct. 1806, in Conway; m. 7 Feb. 1828, George Meserve; 2d, Henry Pendexter.
3 Deborah, b. 22 Dec. 1807; m. Cyrus Meserve.
4 Harriet, b. 22 Mar. 1810; m. 8 Nov. 1828, Josiah Bacon.
5 James Elden, b. 23 Oct. 1811; m. Lucinda Hilton.
6 Moses, b. 15 July 1813, in Limington; m. Havilah Flint.
7 Lorana, b. 13 April 1815; m. 10 Oct. 1856, David T. Smith. Children:
   1 Francis M. (Smith), b. 29 May 1858, in South Fork, Iowa.
   2 Viola J. (Smith), b. 5 Nov. 1860.
8 Amos, b. 12 Mar. 1817; m. Jane B. Phinney.
9 Abner, b. 7 Feb. 1819, in Bridgton; m. 1st, Sarah A.; 2d, Harriet A., Wadlin.
10 Oliver, b. 20 Nov. 1820; m. Lavina M. Wheeler.
11 Dennis, b. 28 Aug. 1822; m. Sarah A. Taylor.
12 Lewis Mitchell, b. 18 May 1824; m. Hannah C. Rounds.
13 Samuel Appleton, b. 21 Aug. 1826; m. Angeline P. Riley.
14 Susannah, b. 2 June 1828; m. Frank W. Small.

5-7-12-5

Dea. Abner Libby, born in Limington, 29 May 1781; married 5 Jan. 1804, Olive Gray Chase, daughter of Joseph and Olive (Woodman) Chase of Standish.

He had his father's farm, and occupied it until about 1838,

when he removed to Limerick with his mother and his younger children, and settled on the farm now occupied by the widow of Dea. Simeon Higgins. He died with his son Abner A., at Limerick Village, 21 Mar. 1864. His wife died 30 Jan. 1851. He was many years deacon of the Baptist church.

Children:

1 Martha, b. 30 May 1804; m. William Cobb.
2 Joseph Chase, b. 11 Oct. 1805; m. Lois M. Waterhouse.
3 Olive, b. 12 May 1808; m. 3 Nov. 1828, Eleazer McKenney.
4 Alpheus, b. 7 July 1811; m. Marantha Austin.
5 Sarah C., b. 3 Oct. 1813; m. 8 Sept. 1847, Rev. Alvin Felch.
6 Delia, b. 19 Sept. 1817; m. Rev. John Hubbard.
7 Edmund, b. 7 Oct. 1819; m. 1st, Mary E. Howell; 2d, Abbie C. Lee.
8 Alvin, b. 26 Jan. 1822; d. 6 June 1845; unm.
9 Abner Augustus, b. 27 Jan. 1827; m. 1st, Sarah; 2d, Abby, Gilpatrick.

5-7-14-7

RHODA LIBBY, born in Scarborough, 13 June 1792; married, 23 Sept. 1819, CAPT. WM. TOMPSON. [See Tompson, page 75.] He was a sea-captain, and lived on Oak Hill, in Scarborough. He died 15 Jan. 1849. She died in Portland, 23 June 1876.

Their children were:

1 Mary Lancaster (Tompson), b. 20 Jan. 1822; d. 20 Nov. 1841.
2 Benjamin Larrabee (Tompson), b. 5 May 1824; died at sea, of yellow fever, in 1843.
3 Sally Hayman (Tompson), b. 16 Jan. 1826; married Francis Libby, 5-7-8-3-9.
4 John Adams (Tompson), b. 18 Mar. 1828; m. 2 May 1852, Mary Elizabeth Libby, 11-7-11-8-4. He and his brother William removed to Portland when young men and engaged together in the trucking business, which they continued until the latter's death. He has since carried on the business alone. Children, all born in Portland:
   1 Benjamin Franklin (Tompson), b. 26 Aug. 1853; d. 24 Aug. 1856.
   2 Frederick Augustus (Tompson), b. 10 Aug. 1857; unm. He is an architectural draftsman.
   3 Edward Francis (Tompson), b. 30 July 1860; is a student at Colby University.
   4 Charles Howard (Tompson), b. 27 July 1863; d. 10 Oct. 1864.
5 William (Tompson), b. 8 July 1829; m. 1st, 2 May 1852, Mary Frances Libby, 1-1-5-9-10-1; (died 11 Jan. 1854); 2d, 29 Nov. 1855, Helen B., dau. of Hannah (Libby) Randall, 5-7-14-11. He died 28 May 1870. Children:
   1 Mary Alberta (Tompson), b. 2 April 1857.
   2 William Erastus (Tompson), b. 27 Aug. 1859.
   3 Helen Frances (Tompson), b. 6 July 1862.
   4 Howard Chase (Tompson), b. 31 Oct. 1864.
   5 Jennie Davis (Tompson), b. 17 Sept. 1867.

5-7-14-9

JORDAN LIBBY, born 20 Nov. 1796, in Scarborough; married 22 Sept. 1819, SARAH LIBBY, 5-2-3-1-2.

He moved to Gardiner in 1822, and settled on a farm. On the

same farm he died, 7 Oct. 1877. His wife died 23 April 1863. He was an alderman and on the board of assessors a number of years.

Children:

1 Lydia Ann, b. 30 Aug. 1822; m. her cousin, Eben Libby, 10-2-1-6-3-1.
2 Samuel, b. 4 Oct. 1825; m. 9 Oct. 1856, Fannie P., dau. of Rev. William and Nancy (Melcher) Smith of Gardiner. He was a farmer and merchant. He died at Gardiner, 7 Oct. 1877. His widow died 25 April 1800. Children:
  1 Sarah Jane, b. 3 Sept. 1859.
  2 Charles F., b. 4 May 1862.
  3 Horace M., b. 21 Nov. 1864.
3 Cyrus, b. 29 Aug. 1830; m. 17 April 1855, Miranda, dau. of Humphrey and Sarah (Murray) Harmon of Gardiner. Farmer and merchant. He died 17 May 1870. His widow and children still reside in Gardiner. Children:
  1 Hernaldo F., b. 4 Sept. 1856; m. 27 Jan. 1880, Emma C., dau. of Thomas and Mary J. (Blair) Burnham.
  2 Alphonzo J., b. 20 May 1858.
  3 Elverda B., b. 18 June 1868.
4 Dorville J., b. 20 Dec. 1836; m. 31 May 1860, Mary E., dau. of Rev. Calvin White. He is a farmer, and occupies the homestead. Children:
  1 Angie E., b. 6 Aug. 1861.
  2 Fred D., b. 3 Aug. 1863.
  3 Eugene S., b. 28 April 1865.
  4 Lucy H., b. 4 June 1871.
  5 Wilbur L., b. 20 March 1880.

5-7-14-10

Aaron Libby, born in Scarborough, 10 May 1799; married first, 6 Feb. 1823, Rachel, dau. of Dominicus and Mary (Hasty) McKenney; [see p. 63]; (died 21 Oct. 1823); second, 15 Dec. 1824, Ruth Hazeltine, dau. of Wm. Hazeltine of Buxton.

He was one of the first settlers of Lagrange, removing thither in March 1826. He cleared a good farm, on which he lived until his death, 21 Jan. 1873. He was a member of the Freewill Baptist Church. His wife died 30 June 1861.

Children:

1 William H., b. 10 Jan. 1826, in Scarborough; m. 25 Dec. 1853, Cordelia, dau. of Franklin and Mary (Tilden) Heal of Lagrange. He was a farmer and lived in Lagrange always, except a few years spent in Medford. He died 19 April 1875. His family still lives in Lagrange. Children:
  1 Hattie M., b. 6 Feb. 1856, in Medford; m. 11 March 1875, James Greenleaf.
  2 Ada J., b. 12 Nov. 1858.
  3 Nora E., b. 18 Dec. 1862.
  4 Ida May, } twins, b. 6 Nov. 1867, in Lagrange; } d. 20 Sept. 1869.
  5 Delia M., } d. 24 Sept. 1869.
  6 Blanche A., b. 8 Sept. 1870.
2 Rachel J., b. 5 Dec. 1828; m. 1 Feb. 1848, William H. Carleton. Children:
  1 Willie (Carleton), b. 5 April 1849; d. July 1854.
  2 Jennie (Carleton), b. 10 June 1851.
  3 Hattie (Carleton), b. 12 Dec. 1853.

4 Annie (Carleton), b. 15 Dec. 1856; d. 1872.
5 William H. (Carleton), b. 26 May 1857.
6 Frank (Carleton), b. 19 May 1859.

3 Aaron W., b. 28 Dec. 1830; m. 12 Sept. 1858, Isabel, dau. of Nath'l and Eunice (Boobar) Day of Milo. He was a farmer. After his marriage he lived five years in Lagrange, two years in Milo, and then emigrated to Minneapolis, Minn., where he died 15 Oct. 1868, and his widow still lives. Children:
1 Effie, b. 19 May 1859.
2 Belle, b. 12 Aug. 1861.

4 George A., b. 26 Feb. 1833. He went to Sacramento, Cal., in Feb. 1852, and thence to Boise city, Idaho, in 1859. He was married in 1870, but has not been heard from since 1874.

5 Ruth A., b. 19 Dec. 1835; m. 6 Dec. 1854, Simeon H. Kenney of Lagrange. Children:
1 Ella O. (Kenney), b. 22 Oct. 1856; d. 5 Aug. 1875.
2 May F. (Kenney), b. 7 Sept. 1861.
3 Myra E. (Kenney), b. 7 April 1863.
4 Ira B. (Kenney), b. 12 Feb. 1872.

6 Lydia E., b. 12 Feb. 1839; m. 5 June 1858, in Medford, Me., John Day, 2d. Children:
1 George A. (Day), b. 1 June 1860.
2 Ruth E. (Day), b. 19 Aug. 1863.
3 Eunice B. (Day), b. 3 Sept. 1867.
4 Cora E. (Day), b. 31 Dec. 1873.

7 Sarah J., b. 11 Mar. 1841; m. 18 July 1859, Daniel Hasty. Children:
1 George A. (Hasty), b. 21 April 1860; d. 22 July 1860.
2 Addie S. (Hasty), b. 20 June 1861; m. 10 May 1879, Robert O. Dean.
3 Annie C. (Hasty), b. 16 May 1863; m. 30 May 1880, Orin B. Packard.
4 Fred L. (Hasty), b. 2 Sept. 1865.
5 Seth L. (Hasty), b. 18 Nov. 1867.
6 John (Hasty), b. 12 May 1870.
7 Frank J. (Hasty), b. 5 June 1872.
8 Ida M. (Hasty), b. 9 June 1874.
9 Nellie J. (Hasty), b. 5 May 1877; d. 28 Dec. 1877.
10 Margie J. (Hasty), b. 4 Jan. 1879.

8 Seth H., b. 17 Sept. 1844; d. 1 Oct. 1864, in Portland. He was a private in the 20th Me. Vol., enlisting in June, 1862. He contracted chronic diarrhea, and died on his way home on a furlough.

9 Melvin S., b. 12 June 1847. Served in the navy during the late war. He was married in Haverhill, Mass., and when last heard from lived in Harrisburgh, Mich., and had two children.

10 Susan P., b. 8 Nov. 1848; m. 22 Aug. 1870, Currion Dean. Children:
1 John T. (Dean), b. 11 May 1871, in Medford.
2 Frank (Dean), b. 2 May 1879, in Medford.

5-7-14-13

John Libby, born in Scarborough, 17 Oct. 1807; married, 28 May 1830, Jane Milliken, daughter of Abraham and Polly (Leavitt) Milliken.

He had his father's homestead, and resided thereon until 1863. During this time his chief occupation was farming, but, being a man of much enterprise, he also established a general store at Oak Hill, and engaged in ship-building. In 1863 he removed to Portland, and engaged in the trucking business. His wife died 9 Oct. 1870, and he married second, 15 Mar. 1877, Mrs. Jane (Cane) Fitts.

Children:

1 Mary Jane, b. 7 Feb. 1831; m. 25 July 1852, J. S. Sawyer.
2 Seth, b. 7 July 1833; d. 19 June 1854; unm.
3 Richard Milliken, b. 2 Dec. 1835; m. 23 Nov. 1860, Georgianna Libby, 10-2-4-3-10-4. In 1861 he removed to Portland, and has since carried on the trucking business there. Children:
  1 Alice Lilian, b. 20 Oct. 1861; d. 8 Aug. 1878.
  2 Fred Alonzo, b. 23 Oct. 1863; d. 29 Aug. 1878.
  3 Lizzie Caroline Sawyer, b. 18 April 1873.
  4 Kate Webster, b. 21 June 1874.
  5 Charles Edwin, b. 18 Aug. 1876.
4 Lydia, b. 4 March 1842; m. 10 Jan. 1861, John Trefethern, a son of John Trefethern of Kennebunk. He is a clerk for N. Weston, flour merchant, Portland. Children:
  1 Nellie Frances (Trefethern), b. 20 May 1862; d. 25 July 1862.
  2 George Seth (Trefethern), b. 19 Jan. 1863; d. 10 Jan. 1864.
  3 Charles (Trefethern), b. 30 May; d. 8 Aug., 1865.
  4 Edwin (Trefethern), b. 11 Sept. 1866; d. 9 July 1867.
  5 George Elmer (Trefethern), b. 15 Nov. 1867.
  6 Jennie Mildred (Trefethern), b. 9 May 1872.
  7 Eva May (Trefethern), b. 16 Sept. 1879.
5 Benjamin Tompson, b. 28 May 1846; m. 24 Dec. 1877, Addie, dau. of Fred and Eliza (Graves) Kimber, born in England, 12 Nov. 1851. He has been a farmer in Scarborough, a truckman in Portland, and is now on the police force in Portland. No children.

5-7-15-3

Amos Libby, born in Scarborough, 28 July 1794; married, 25 Jan. 1818, Eunice Skillings, daughter of Simeon and Rebecca (Skillings) Skillings. He lived on his father's homestead, and died there, 5 Sept. 1826. His widow died 30 Sept. 1838.

Children, all born in Scarborough:

1 Eliza, b. 3 June 1818; m. Dexter Libby, 10-5-3-5-9.
2 William, b. 11 Dec. 1820; m. 26 March 1848, Hannah, dau. of William and Margaret (Harmon) Stone of Saco. He was a journeyman carpenter until 1851, and from that time carried on business himself. He died 9 June 1881, in Cape Elizabeth, where he had lived from 1855. His wife died 26 April 1870. Children:
  1 Alberta, b. 9 Dec. 1848; m. 13 May 1869, Uranus Stacey.
  2 Georgianna, b. 18 Jan. 1852; d. Aug. 1852.
  3 Francis Albert, b. 22 Feb. 1854; m. 1 May 1876, Addie J., dau. of Jason M. and Lucy W. (Lewis) Carleton of Deering. He is by trade a carpenter, but lives with his wife's father, and carries on hot-house gardening. Children:
    1 Jason Merrill Carleton, b. 31 Dec. 1876.
    2 Aubrey Frank, b. 6 March 1879.
  4 Burton Hubbard, b. 4 March 1856; is a traveling salesman; unmarried.
  5 Edna Belle, b. 3 Oct. 1861; d. 15 Oct. 1876.
  6 Willis Percy, b. 13 May 1864.
  7 daughter, b. 1 March; died 19 May, 1870.
3 Simeon, b. 20 Aug. 1822; died in infancy.
4 Storer, b. 30 June 1824; m. 1 Sept. 1847, Rebecca, dau. of Jotham and Hannah (Burnham) Steward of Hollis. He learned the carpenter's trade, and carried on his business many years in Portland, where he died 28 May 1874, and his widow still lives. Children:
  1 Aldenezi Ernest Millard, b. 22 May 1850; d. 20 May 1873. He was a druggist's clerk. Never married.

2 Major Edward Sweetsir, b. 4 Feb. 1852; m. 25 June 1878, Minnie May, dau. of Chas. F., and Sophia (Ladd) Harvey of St. Johnsbury, Vt. He is a druggist's clerk. No children.
5 Emily, b. 1 Dec. 1826; d. 12 Nov. 1840.

6-3-2-1

Capt. Reuben Libby, born in Rye, N. H., in 1743; married first, in Wolfborough, Sarah Fullerton; (died 10 Feb. 1801); second, Jan. 1804, Abigail (Pinkham) Smith, dau. of Abijah and Rachel (Stokes) Pinkham of Durham.

At the age of sixteen, he enlisted in the English army, and, it is said, was present at Crown Point when George III. was crowned king of England. After two years he returned home. The township of Wolfborough had then been surveyed, and the proprietors, who lived at Portsmouth, offered a hundred-acre lot each, with choice of lots, to the first two settlers. Reuben Libby and —— Blake accepted the offer about 1762, and went across the lake in a canoe to Wolfborough Neck. The following year they made quite a clearing, and other settlers began to come in. His marriage, about 1766, was the first in town. They were married under an oak tree on the shore of the lake, near where Southbridge Village now is. He settled at first on Wolfborough Neck. He afterward removed to a farm on the main road, but died on the Neck, having moved back onto another farm, 9 March 1827. He was the first militia captain in Wolfborough, first represented the town in the state legislature, and was deputy sheriff more than twenty years. His widow died in Methuen, Mass., Sept. 1852.

Children, by first wife:

1 Sarah, b. 22 March 1768; m. Joseph Cotton; d. 9 Aug. 1805, in Sandwich, N. H.
2 Joseph, b. 9 June 1770; died young.
3 Mary, b. 22 Jan. 1773; m. Shadrach Allard; d. 24 Feb. 1802.
4 Nancy, b. 22 Aug. 1776; m. Samuel Small.
5 Esther, b. 9 May 1778; m. Timothy Young.
6 Reuben Abbot, b. 3 June 1780. He lived in Moultonborough a short time and then emigrated to Maine. He married a Miss Harriman of Malta, now Windsor, in 1808, and both died of spotted fever about 1813, leaving no children.
7 Margaret, b. 9 May 1783; m. Daniel Allard.
8 Olive, b. 18 Jan. 1785; m. James Bartlett.
9 Hannah, b. 15 Feb. 1788; died in Center Harbor, N. H., with Mrs. Bartlett, 18 Aug. 1828; unm.
10 Jeremiah, b. 15 July 1792; m. Esther Smith.

By second wife:

11 Smith, b. 26 July 1805; m. Lucretia Garland.
12 Abigail, b. 18 June 1811; m. Charles Collins.

6-3-2-8

Ephraim Libby, born probably in Portsmouth, N. H., 1755; married, 27 Feb. 1783, Judith Page of Gilmanton, N. H.

He removed to Gilmanton, N. H., shortly before his marriage, and lived there until about 1820, when with his son Moses and sons-in-law Glidden and Page, he removed to Broom, Lower Canada, and settled at Knowlton, on the farm of which a portion is now owned by his grandson, Andrew Libby. He was with Arnold in his march through the woods of Maine, and also under Stark and under Gates; serving nearly all through the war. It seems strange now that he and so many other Americans, after shedding their blood to free this country from British rule, should voluntarily relinquish their freedom by emigration to the Canadas. He died in Broom about 1832. His widow returned to Gilmanton and died with her daughter Olive.

Children, all born in Gilmanton:

1 Judith, b. 5 Oct. 1783; m. Jonathan Glidden.
2 Joseph, b. 3 Mar. 1786; died young.
3 Moses, b. 10 Mar. 1788; m. Hannah Flanders.
4 Mary, b. 15 Sept. 1789; probably died young.
5 Hannah Page, b. 14 June 1791; m. Worster Page.
6 Olive, m. Thomas Flanders.

6-3-2-10

Anthony Libby, born probably in Barrington, N. H., about 1759; married 27 Dec. 1791, Lydia Ayers of Barnstead, where he afterward lived. It is said that he was killed on the Lakes during the war of 1812. His widow became crazy and died a few years later.

Children:

1 John, b. 1792; m. Sally Randall.
2 Olley, m. John Nelson of Concord.
3 Catherine, m. 7 Dec. 1817, Thomas Mace of Greenland.
4 Joseph, m. the widow Eliza Glines of Canterbury. He died in Barnstead. His widow, when last heard from, lived in Manchester. Children:
  1 Ann, died in Manchester.
  2 Harriet, m. —— McIntire of Canterbury.
  3 Betsey.
  4 Abram.

6-3-2-11

Benjamin Libby, born in Barrington, N. H., 12 June 1761; married Sarah Mason, daughter of John Mason of Alton.

He grew up on New Durham Ridge, and settled on his father's homestead there. In the latter part of his life he gave this to his son Asa, and settled on a farm in Alton, where his wife died 19 May 1834, and himself, 26 Aug. 1835. His homestead in Alton went to his daughter Sarah.

Children, all born in New Durham:

1 Joseph, m. Aug. 1805, Lymena Kenniston. He lived at home until his marriage, and a day or two afterward left, and never returned. He followed the sea many years. His widow married —— Phenix.
2 Moses, died in the winter of 1821-2; unm. At the age of 16 he went into a ship-yard, and sailed on the first vessel he ever worked on. He rapidly rose, and soon became master in the West India trade. At the time of his death he was sailing for Alfred Curtis of Boston.

3 David Thurstin, b. 27 Oct. 1790; m. Lucinda Parsons.
4 Asa, b. 21 Feb. 1792; m. Nancy Clough.
5 Betsey, m. 22 Dec. 1817, George Brooks.
6 Daniel, b. 15 Sept. 1796; m. Ada Clough.
7 Sarah, b. 27 March 1798; m. 28 Dec. 1818, John Perkins of Alton; d. 6 April 1879.
8 Mary, m. 17 May 1820, Richard Cooper.
9 Nancy, m. Jonathan Eaton of Alton.
10 Martha, m. Jeremiah M. Rollins of Alton.

6-4-1-2

MESHACH LIBBY, born probably in Rye, N. H., 1745; married DEBORAH ELY.

He is credited with being the first settler of Porter, Me. He lived some years after his marriage in Chichester, a short time in Parsonsfield, Me., and, it is said, was living in Pittsfield, N. H. in 1781, and in that year settled in Porter. For settling in that town before 1 Jan. 1784, he received one of four 100-acre lots reserved for such settlers. In 1792 he sold this to David Moulton, and bought the lot of his brother Stephen. There he lived until his death, March 1829. His wife died in 1795, and he married second, the widow Hannah (Cram) Elkins.

Children:

1 Sarah, b. 1771; m. 23 May 1793, Gideon Mason of Porter.
2 Mary, m. William Hill of Porter.
3 Meshach, m. 6 Sept. 1795, Lydia Heard of Rochester; died about 1860, in Sheffield (?), Vt. He left two sons:
  1 Benjamin.
  2 Elijah.
4 Elsie, m. Edward Hill of Conway, N. H.
5 Elizabeth, died in childhood. She was the first white child born in Porter.
6 Eunice, b. 22 Aug. 1787; m. Jacob Hurd; d. 30 Dec. 1852, in Porter.

6-4-1-5

JONATHAN LIBBY, born in Epsom, N. H., 1751; married HANNAH McCOY, daughter of John and Margery McCoy of Nottingham, N. H. He settled in Porter, Me., with the rest of the family and moved thence to New York State, where he died, in Junius, about 1825. His wife died about 1820.

Children:

1 Levi, m. Hannah Libby, 6-4-1-8-3.
2 William, m. Betsey Prouts. He was a farmer. He formerly lived in North East, Erie Co., Penn., and moved thence about 1855. He is believed to have died in Illinois. Only child:
  1 John. His whereabouts are unknown.
3 Eleanor, m. John Southwick.
4 Phebe, m. ——— Dickerson. One child.
5 David, married in Canada. One child.

6-4-1-6

ENOCH LIBBY, born in Epsom, N. H., about 1755; married

Mary Newbegin, dau. of John and Bethia (Gould) Newbegin of Gorham, Me.

He came to maturity in Chichester, N. H., and moved thence to Parsonsfield, Me., of which place he was one of the original proprietors. He became *non compos mentis*, the result of fits, and in 1795 was placed under guardianship. He died probably in the year 1811. His widow was afterward a nurse in Portland, and died there about 1825.

Children:

1 Jacob, m. 18 May 1806, Eunice Scammon.
2 Isaac, was made the ward of Edmund Coffin of Biddeford, and probably died in youth.

6-4-1-8

Simeon Libby, born probably in Chester, N. H., about 1760; married Hannah Knowles, dau. of Daniel and Mary (Blake) Knowles of Porter, Me.

He removed to Porter with his father, and lived with him until his death. He then sold the homestead and bought another farm in the same town, which he also sold, in 1817, and emigrated to New York State. He died in Bath in 1827. His widow died in Busti, 1845. They were both members of the Baptist church in Porter.

Children, all born in Porter.

1 John, b. 30 Jan. 1792; m. Mary G. Fox.
2 Samuel, b. 1794; m. Sarah, dau. of Jacob Williams of Batavia, N. Y. He afterward married a second wife and was living in California in 1863. No children.
3 Hannah, b. 1796; m. 1st, Levi Libby, 6-4-1-5-1; 2d, Geo. Seavey.
4 Isaac, b. 1798; m. in Bath, N. Y., Margaret Prouty. She died in Chautauqua Co. He married again and lived when last heard from in Lundy's Lane, Erie Co., Penn. No children.
5 Josiah, b. 9 Feb. 1799; m. Mary P. Leavitt.
6 Simeon, b. 1800; m. in Norwich, Vt., Abigail Trask. He settled in Vermont in 1820, and became a successful farmer. He was deacon of the F. W. Baptist church at Brookfield. He died 3 Jan. 1879, in Randolph, leaving a widow but no children.
7 Job, b. 1802; m. 27 June 1822, Ruth P., dau. of John and Deborah (Gilman) Fox of Porter. They died childless.
8 Daniel, b. 1803; m. in Leroy, N. Y., Sarah, dau. of Joseph Farley of Batavia. He died 17 April 1879, in Dansville, leaving his wife, but no children.
9 Abram, b. 11 April 1805; m. 22 Feb. 1849, in Porter, Judith Hurd. He lived in New York state until he was 30 years old, and then moved back to Vermont, and thence to Maine. He now lives in South Hiram. No children.
10 Lemuel Rich, b. 20 June 1807; m. Electra, dau. of Adolphus Bangs of Leroy, N. Y., where they still live. No children.
11 Mary, b. 1810; m. in Bath, Aaron Houghtaling.
12 Julia Ann, b. 1812; m. Jesse W. Downing of Brookfield, Vt.

6-4-1-9

Lieut. Stephen Libby, born probably in Chester, N. H., 26 April 1763; married first, Mary Knowles, daughter of Daniel and Mary (Blake) Knowles; (died Oct. 1816); second, 9 Jan. 1817, NANCY MATTHEWS, daughter of Francis and Lydia (Matthews) Matthews; (died 9 Jan. 1818); third, 17 Mar. 1818, SALLY MATTHEWS, sister of Nancy.

He settled in Porter, Me., with his father, and received his hundred-acre lot from the proprietors. This he sold to his brother Meshach, and bought a large tract of land adjoining and east of his brother's original lot. This farm on which he lived many years now comprises many homesteads. He owned the third sawmill in the town, built near the mill now owned by John Weeks. He died 25 Oct. 1855, aged 92. His widow died 16 Dec. 1866.

Children, by first wife:

1 James, b. 5 June 1784; m. 17 July 1808, Phebe Benson. He removed to New York, and thence to Ohio, where he died. He had five children.
2 Daniel, b. 3 April 1786; m. Mary Rundlet.
3 Josiah, b. 23 Mar.; d. 8 June 1788.
4 Mary, b. 30 July 1789; m. 27 Jan. 1811, Josiah Weeks.
5 Jemima, b. 22 Aug. 1791; m. 21 Oct. 1810, Joshua Weeks of Bartlett, N. H.; died 12 May 1879.
6 Stephen, b. 21 May 1793; m. Dorothy Blake.
7 Sally, b. 20 Jan. 1795; m. 4 Dec. 1817, Jordan Stacy.
8 John, b. 20 Feb. 1797; m. Nancy Libby, 1-4-4-4-2-1.
9 David, b. 16 Jan. 1799; m. Dorothy Brooks.
10 Aphia, b. 6 Dec. 1800; m. 16 Nov. 1820, Ralph King.
11 Olive, b. 5 July 1802; m. 14 May 1820, Wm. Hodsdon.

By second wife:

12 Lydia, b. 23 Dec. 1817; m. 17 Oct. 1847, Wm. Perry.

By third wife:

13 ——, son, died in infancy.
14 Daniel, b. 19 March 1821; m. 29 Oct. 1854, Almira, dau. of Joseph and Emily Howard of Lovell. He lived on the homestead farm now occupied by his widow. He died 12 April 1872, and his widow married Wm. Chapman. Children:
   1 Janette J., b. 19 May 1857; unm.
   2 Charles F., b. 19 March 1859; m. 1 May 1880, Abbie A., dau. of Oren and Abbie Rumery (Doten) Taylor. He is a farmer. Child:
      1 Fred Orin, b. 12 May 1881.
   3 Alonzo S., b. 15 Dec. 1860; unm.
   4 Emma T., b. 26 April 1862; m. April, 1881, in Boston, Mass., Joseph Mitchell.
   5 Hattie E. H., b. 3 Jan. 1865; d. 22 Nov. 1866.
   6 Melvin D., b. 17 Dec. 1869.
15 Albion, b. 9 June 1823; m. Harriet Bragg. Children:
   1 daughter, died very young.
   2 George W., b. 25 Dec. 1854, in Saco; m. Emma J., dau. of Ezra and Emma Thompson of Porter, where he lives. Child:
      1 Nora May.
16 Nancy, b. 28 April 1825; m. 9 Aug. 1851, Ezekiel Jenness.
17 William T., b. 23 Dec. 1827; m. 13 April 1854, Susan, dau. of Dudley J. and Susan R. (Miller) Marston of Lowell, Mass. He has always been a farmer in Porter. Children:
   1 Walter J., b. 7 Jan. 1855; m. 25 Nov. 1878, Arvilla, dau. of John and Melissa (Storer) Walker of Brownfield.
   2 Nancy E., b. 30 Aug. 1860; m. 30 Aug. 1876, Melvin Walker, brother of the last.

3 Georgianna S., b. 23 Feb. 1865.

18 Thomas, b. 23 Dec. 1827; d. 23 March 1828.

19 Gideon, b. 19 June 1830; m. first, 11 March 1854, in Biddeford, Catherine, dau. of James McMann of St. John, N. B.; (died 16 June 1875, in New York City); 2d, 10 Oct. 1876, Mary Jane, dau. of Wm. and Sarah A. (Nute) Love of Dorchester, Mass. He is a clairvoyant physician in New York City. Son:

1 Joseph J., b. 1 Jan. 1855, in London, Canada West.

6-4-4-2

Isaac Libby, born probably in Rye, N. H., 1750; married first, Abigail ——; (died 9 Aug. 1792, in her 38th year); second, Anna Dillingham.

He was a farmer. After his marriage he lived a short time in Chichester, and then settled in Pittsfield, whence, about 1790, he removed to Strafford, Vt. He lived in Strafford until about 1811, when he removed with his son Joseph to Tinmouth, Vt., where he died in April, 1813. His second wife outlived him, and, having no children, returned to her own people.

Children:

1 Betsey, m. Amasa Chamberlain.

2 Anna, m. William Walbridge of Strafford.

3 Simon, b. 31 March 1778; m. Ama Morse.

4 Sally, m. 1st, —— Nelson; 2d, Walter Hayes.

5 Joel, died aged 24; unm. He was a farmer in Strafford.

6 Joseph, b. 2 Nov. 1785; m. Mabel Walbridge.

7 Miriam, died 12 April 1813, in Tinmouth, N. H.; unm.

6-4-4-4

Bennet Libby, born probably in Rye, N. H., Jan. 1754; married Eleanor Haynes of Epsom, born 11 May 1750.

He removed from Epsom, N. H., where he grew up, to Strafford, Vt., about 1793, and after a few years moved back to Canterbury and joined the Shakers in 1803. All his daughters and one son stayed with the Shakers through life. He was at the battle of Bunker Hill, but having adopted the peace principles of the Shakers, never drew the pension to which he was entitled. He died Sept. 1837. His wife died 12 Nov. 1808.

Children:

1 Matthias, b. 13 Aug. 1777; m. Sarah Keys.

2 Isaac, b. 14 Nov. 1779; m. Sally Bayles.

3 Bennet, b. 3 June 1782; m. 18 July 1819, Betsey, dau. of Peter and Phebe (Otis) Blaisdell of Pittsfield, N. H. He was a carpenter. He removed from Canterbury to Pittsfield, where, and in Concord, he lived many years. He at length joined the Shakers, and died with them 8 April 1869. His wife left the society in 1847 and went to Rockland, Mass., where she had relatives. There she lived until her death, 10 May 1869. Children:

1 Lavinia E. A., b. 5 June 1820; m. 1855, John Mackin of Rockland.

2 Olive M., b. 31 Dec. 1821; continues with the Shakers.

3 Mary J., b. 22 Nov. 1823; d. 22 Feb. 1870, in Rockland, Mass.; unm.

4 Hannah, b. 15 April 1785; d. 27 Sept. 1834.

5 Annie, b. 27 May 1788; d. 26 May 1814.
6 Olive, b. 10 Mar. 1791; d. 21 Sept. 1815.
7 Polly, b. 6. July 1793; d. 23 Jan. 1809.
8 John H., b. 1 May 1796; m. Miriam B. Davis.
9 Sarah, b. 23 Nov. 1798; d. 1 Mar. 1822.

6-4-4-6

Job Libby, born probably in Epsom, N. H., 14 Feb. 1759; married 24 Mar. 1785, Rebecca Pearson, a native of Newbury, Mass.

He was reared in Epsom and lived a few years after his marriage on the old turnpike about one-half mile from Epsom Center, near where the clothing-mill afterward was. From Epsom he moved to Strafford, Vt., and thence, with his eldest son, to Enosburgh, where he died 26 Mar. 1836, and his widow, 5 Mar. 1843.

Children:

1 Caleb B., b. 19 Nov. 1785, in Epsom; m. Dorothy Avery.
2 Jonathan Pearson, b. 18 Nov. 1787; m. Theodate Prescott.
3 John Batchelder, b. 8 Feb. 1790; m. Abigail Clark.
4 James, b. 25 May 1792, in Strafford, Vt.; m. Eliza L. Vaughan.
5 Abigail Pearson, b. 14 Oct. 1794; m. John Dunaven.
6 Naomi Locke, b. 14 Feb. 1797; d. 8 April 1799.
7 Alice Pearson, b. 3 Jan. 1805; m. Elijah Lucas.
8 Ruhamah, married Josiah Avery.
9 Nathan, b. 20 Jan. 1809; d. 30 March 1809.

6-4-4-8

Nathan Libby, born in Epsom, N. H., 20 July 1767; married, 6 Jan. 1791, Abigail Fowler, daughter of Symonds and Hannah (Weeks) Fowler of Epsom. He inherited his father's homestead farm and gristmill, and died on the homestead 19 Jan. 1814. His family occupied it until after the death of his widow, 17 Dec. 1843, and it then passed out of the family.

Children, all born in Epsom:

1 Nathan, } twins, born } died 7 April 1792.
2 Abigail, } 11 Mar. 1792; } died 9 April 1792.
3 Lucy, b. 20 July 1793; m. John Sherborne Haynes.
4 Hannah, b. 8 March 1795; d. 13 March 1802.
5 Peggy, b. 9 Aug. 1797; d. 23 March 1802.
6 Nathan, b. 13 May 1803; d. 28 July 1807.
7 Nathan, b. 25 June 1808; m. Savalia Abbot.
8 Benjamin Fowler, b. 31 July 1813; m. Almira A. Rogers.

6-4-4-10

Abraham Libby, born in Epsom, N. H., 15 Aug. 1773; married Abigail (Pearson) McClary, born in Baffield, N. H., 27 July 1772.

He was one of the company known as the "nine partners", which first settled Cassville, in Stanstead, Quebec. The settlement was begun in 1799, and in the next year they moved their families. Abraham Libby settled on the farm now owned by Edw. Hill. He died 10 Jan. 1839. His widow died 5 April 1858.

Children, all born in Stanstead:

1 Nathan, b. 1 June 1801; m. Mehitable Massey.
2 William, b. 26 Feb. 1803; m. Diantha Jane Sinclair.
3 Pearson, b. 24 July 1806; m 14 Mar. 1837, Sophia, daughter of Theophilus and Jane (Sanborn) Cass of Epsom. He lives at Derby Line, Vt. Children.
  1 Oliva, b. 7 April 1845.
  2 William P., b. 5 Aug. 1850; m. 1 July 1878, in Boston, Mass., Clara J. Clark. He lives in Somerville.

6-4-4-12

Joshua Libby, born in Epsom, N. H., 7 Aug. 1778; married, 18 Nov. 1800, Sally Grant, daughter of John Grant of Epsom. He was a farmer. He removed from Epsom to Stanstead, Que., in 1803, and settled eventually at the place now known as Libbytown. He died 26 June 1858, and his widow 20 Dec. 1858. They were both members of the F. W. Baptist Church.

Children:

1 Isaac, b. 5 June 1802; m. Lucy Sherborne.
2 Hannah, b. 5 April 1806; m. Nicholas Carpenter.
3 David C., b. 17 May 1809; m. 14 Mar. 1839, Lucinda, dau. of Cornelius Hyatt. He lives at Derby Line, Vt., and is said to have one daughter.
4 Sarah, b. 1811; m. Benjamin Currier.
5 Charles Grant, b. 27 Jan 1813; m. 1st, 12 Sept. 1840, Relief, dau. of Wm. and Mehitable Dresser; (died 21 July 1855); 2d, Martha J., dau. of Simeon E. and Polly (Orcott) Miner of Burke, Vt. He is by trade a carpenter but carries on a farm and a saw and grist-mill. Children, by first wife:
  1 Osro, b. 4 July 1841; d. 17 Jan. 1861.
  2 Wallace W., b. 22 July 1845; m. 28 Feb. 1878, Julia A. (Sylvester) Jones. He is a farmer.
  3 Lollow L., b. 21 Dec. 1851; m. 24 Dec. 1872, Samuel N. Blair.

By second wife:

  4 Charles W., b. 15 June 1861.
  5 Ulysses G., b. 29 Nov. 1865.
6 Gilman, b. 25 Dec. 1816; m. 1 Sept. 1842, Zelia, dau. of Galen and Lydia (Wilcox) Blodget of Ascot. His life has been divided between farming and milling. He lived in Waterville, Barnston, Rock Island, Forestville, Compton, Wateruille, and finally settled on a farm near Milby. He is a Second Adventist. Children:
  1 Carlos, b. 14 Oct 1843, in Barnston; m 28 April 1864, Abba, dau. of John and Caroline (Kathan) Elliot. He is a teamster in Coaticook. Children:
    1 Carlos Eugene, b. 2 Oct. 1866.
    2 Addie Elizabeth, b. 5 Nov. 1868.
  2 Dilevan Delanson, b. 22 Nov. 1847; d. 26 Nov. 1864.
  3 Orrock C., b. 25 Sept. 1856, in Compton; m. 13 Feb. 1878, Lenza, dau. of Lyman and Sarah (Gurnsey) Aldrich of Ascot. He is a farmer.
7 Olive, b. 9 May 1819; m. 5 Dec. 1843. Sylvanus Griffin.
8 William G., b. 15 Dec. 1820; m. 28 Dec. 1847, Jane, dau. of Lemuel P. and Charlotte (Fletcher) Harvey of Compton. He is a farmer; in religion, Second Adventist. Son:
  1 Locke A., b. 13 June 1853; unm. He is a traveling salesman.

9 James, b. 11 March 1822; m. 1st, 16 Jan. 1846, Harriet, dau. of Wm. and Sophronia (Hubbard) Spencer of Stanstead; (died 5 Dec. 1853, at Derby Line, Vt.); 2d, 6 May 1855, Sarah, dau. of Simeon E. and Polly (Orcott) Miner. He lived at Derby Line ten years, and has since lived at Libbytown in Barnston. He is a farmer, miller, carpenter, and postmaster. Children, by first wife:
1 Chester, b. 11 Aug. 1848; d. 11 Feb. 1852.
2 Hattie, b. 6 Oct. 1853; d. 5 June 1856.

By second wife:

3 Freeman, b. 19 April 1858; m. 25 May 1881, Clara, dau. of Almon and Roanna (Danforth) Searles.
4 Liley, b. 10 July 1860; unm.
5 Lelia, b. 24 Dec. 1863.
6 Homer, b. 7 Nov. 1870.
7 May, b. 2 May 1872.
8 Alzeda, b. 31 Aug. 1875.

6-4-5-6

ABRAHAM LIBBY, born in Rye, N. H., 5 April 1767; married RUTH PALMER of Fayette, Me.

He was reared in Candia, N. H., and emigrated from that place to the interior of Maine. He married in Fayette, and lived there until his death. In Aug. 1800, he was upset in a log canoe on Fayette Pond and, although an expert swimmer, became entangled in the lilies and was drowned. He was a Quaker. His widow married Joshua Perley, in whose family the children were brought up.

They were:

1 James, b. 20 Jan. 1797; m. Mary Mosher.
2 Ruth, married Lorin Adams.

6-4-5-7

ISAAC LIBBY, born in Rye, N. H., 9 Jan. 1771; married ANN SEAVEY of Rye. He was a farmer and always stayed on his father's homestead in Candia. He died 2 Jan. 1835. His widow died 30 Mar. 1837.

Children:

1 Sally, b. 9 Jan. 1794; m. 1st, John Hazeltine; 2d, —— Perry.
2 Mary, b. 17 Dec. 1796; m. Enoch Worthen; d. 14 Mar. 1825.
3 Abigail, b. 25 Mar. 1798; m. Wm. Anderson; d. 13 Mar. 1868.
4 Maria, b. 14 July 1800; d. 21 April 1806.
5 Anna, b. 12 April 1803; d. 14 July 1874; unm.
6 David, b. 11 Nov. 1805; d. 3 Aug. 1839; unm. He was a farmer and died on the homestead.
7 John, b. 17 Mar. 1807; m. Elizabeth Richardson of Chester. He worked in Boston at one time. The latter part of his life was spent in Deerfield, where he died in 1863. His widow died at Brentwood, 1879. No children.
8 James, b. 11 June 1811; m. Betsey Crosby.
9 Gilman, b. 23 June 1814; m. Sallie F., dau. of Benj. and Mary Corning of Manchester. He was a farmer and always lived in Candia. His farm was on High street, so called. He died 29 Jan. 1855, and his widow removed to Manchester. She died 7 Nov. 1872. Only child:
1 Emma A., b. 11 June 1842; m. 5 July 1864, Lyman A. Dickey; died 14 May 1879.

6-4-5-8

JACOB LIBBY, born in Rye, N. H., 20 Mar. 1774; married POLLY KING of Dresden, Me., daughter of —— and Prudence (Umpsted) King.

He was reared in Candia, and went from that place when a young man, to Maine. He was by trade both a cooper and a cordwainer. Upon his marriage he bought a farm in Farmington. He soon sold however, and lived in various towns until shortly before the war of 1812, when he bought a farm in Belmont, and from that town served thirteen months in the army. In 1821 he removed from Belmont to Peru, where his wife died 2 April 1822. He soon after married Mrs. Sophia Rumford, and later moved to Chesterville, where he died Jan. 1836.

Children:

1 Prudence, b. 17 Dec. 1794, in Farmington; m. Wager Hopkins.
2 Arthur King, b. 26 Jan. 1798; m. Betsey, dau. of Jonathan Frohock of Belmont. He lived in Boston for about five years after his marriage, and then became captain of a coaster between Woolwich, Me., and Boston. 13 May 1836, he was knocked overboard by the foreboom of his schooner, and drowned. His widow married Samuel (?) Jordan. He had no children, but adopted:
a Charles (Libby), born about 1822; became a teacher.
3 Ezra, b. 4 March 1800, in Harlem; m. Eliza Brackett of Lincolnville. He followed the sea from eighteen years of age, and was killed by pirates when about 26. Only child:
1 Eliza.
4 Polly, b. 2 Aug. 1802; m. Jesse Coombs.
5 Sarah, b. 16 Aug. 1804, in Palermo; m. Samuel Dexter of Haverhill, Mass.
6 Sophia, b. 2 July 1806; m. Charles Blair of Woolwich.
7 William King, m. Caroline Mains of Woolwich.
8 Roxanna, born in Montville; died May 1877, in Readfield; unm.
9 Bethia, } twins, born 17 Dec. } m. Elisha Harris.
10 Maria, } 1814, in Belmont; } m. John Harris.

6-4-8-2

SAMUEL LIBBY, born in Rye, N. H., July 1757; married, 21 Sept. 1780, MEHITABLE SEAVEY, dau. of Wm. and Ruth (Moses) Seavey of Rye.

He was a cordwainer by trade, but engaged much in fishing and coasting voyages. During the Revolution he served a while in the land forces and was present at Burgoyne's surrender. He also went on four privateering cruises, and was twice captured. After the war he lived on a small place in Rye until 1807, when he removed to Chichester and settled on a farm. About 1834 he sold his farm and went to live with his daughter Sarah in Allenstown, and in 1842 went to Epsom where he ended his days with his daughter Nancy. He died 27 Feb. 1843. His widow died 9 April 1851.

Children, all born in Rye:

1 Aaron Seavey, b. 10 Aug. 1781; d. 26 Mar. 1806, in the West Indies, of yellow fever. He was unmarried.

2 Samuel, b. 14 Mar. 1783; d. 23 Jan. 1857, in Epsom; unm. He was a farmer and always lived with his parents and sisters.
3 Sarah, b. 15 May 1785; m. Webster Salter.
4 William Seavey, b. 26 Feb. 1787; m. 1st, Sarah Farrington; 2d, Elizabeth Winfield.
5 Nancy Griffith, b. 13 July 1789; m. Amos Davis.
6 Hetty, bap. 3 Sept. 1792; died young.
7 Mehitable, b. 1 Feb. 1795; m. Caleb Pearson of Schenectady, N. Y.; died 26 Sept. 1880.
8 Ruth Moses, bap. 4 June 1797; died young.
9 Daniel Rand, b. 28 Feb. 1800; d. 26 Sept. 1804.
10 Richard, b. about 1802; m. Sarah T. Sanborn. He went away soon after his marriage and, except that he went once to the house of his brother in Newburg, N. Y., was never afterward heard from. There was no apparent cause for his leaving and it seemed very strange, as he had always been a very steady young man. His widow lived with his father about eight years and then married Daniel Libby, 6-4-8-4-9.
11 Maria, b. 1804; m. 1st, Amasa Seavey; 2d, Jonathan Brown.

6-4-8-3

Jethro Libby, born in Rye, N. H., 1759; married Abigail Libby, 6-4-4-5.

He went to Epsom, N. H., at an early age and served his time with a Mr. Burbank, from whom he received, on coming of age, one hundred acres of land adjoining the Deerfield line. He settled on that land and lived there until his children were grown up, when he lost his property by misfortune, and was obliged to give up his homestead. Twenty years later it was repurchased by Michael M. Libby, 6-4-8-3-1-2. The remaining years of his life were spent in Allenstown, where his wife died in 1835, and he, March 1843.

Children, all born in Epsom:

1 David, b. 17 Dec. 1779; m. Martha Dolbeer.
2 Levi, b. 1782; m. Abigail Farrington.
3 Richard, b. 1784; m. Esther Langley and Abigail Chase.
4 Sarah, died 30 Sept. 1848; unm.
5 Ebenezer, died Jan. 1852, in Allenstown, N. H.; unm. He lived with his parents until their death, and then lived with his sister Martha.
6 Rachel, b. 1788; m. 1st, John Wells; 2d, William Macrillis; died 10 June 1848.
7 Jesse, b. 1790; m. Rachel Tandy.
8 Ruhamah, married David Tandy; died 23 Nov. 1858.
9 Francis, m. Anna, dau. of John P. Sanborn of Deerfield. She died in Deerfield. He afterward married again in Lisbon, N. H., and after a few years emigrated to Wisconsin. No children.
10 Martha, m. George Carleton of Pembroke; died Jan. 1864, in Allenstown.

6-4-8-4

Richard Libby, born in Rye, N. H., 1762; married 16 Nov. 1788, in Gorham, Me., Sarah Ross of North Yarmouth.

He went with his father from Rye to Gorham, and when he was married settled on the farm now owned by Otis Purington. The building he at first lived in is still standing. He was a cooper by trade, and when he built his house, converted the first building into a cooper shop. He died 7 Sept. 1838. His wife died 19 April 1833. They were both Quakers.

Children:

1 James, married 23 Jan. 1812, Sarah Grant of Saco. He was a farmer in Yarmouth Children:
  1 Susan, b. 2 June 1812; m. William Marston.
  2 Hannah R., b. 22 April 1814; m. James Flanders.
  3 Sarah Ann, b. 20 June 1816; d. Feb. 1817.
  4 Eliza Willard, b. 10 Feb. 1818; lives in Lowell, Mass.; unm.
  5 Mahala Ann, b. 16 Nov. 1820; m. Aaron Grant.
  6 Richard, b. 17 Feb. 1823; died aged 20.
  7 Mary Jane, m. Joseph Grant.
2 Walter, emigrated to New York State.
3 Joel, b. 10 Oct. 1792; m. Joanna Clay and Fanny Silla.
4 Sarah, b. 1794; d. 25 Mar. 1856; unm.
5 Hannah R., b. 1796; d. 25 Mar. 1877. She was never married, but took care of her sister Sarah and brother David, who, as well as Mary, were foolish. When David died, she considered her life-work ended, and lived only three days. After her death the homestead was sold.
6 Reuben, b. 1798; m. 20 Aug. 1822, in North Yarmouth, Olive Marston; died 29 Oct. 1825. His widow married, 8 Oct. 1835, Jacob Tuttle. Children:
  1 John Marston, b. 15 Nov. 1823; d. 22 July 1824.
  2 Reuben, died 1825, aged two months.
7 David, d. 22 Mar. 1877.
8 Ann, m. 18 Sept. 1834, Wm. Roberts.
9 Daniel, b. 1804; m. Sarah T. (Sanborn) Libby, widow of Richard Libby, 6-4-8-2-10; died 10 July 1857. His widow died 27 Nov. 1867.
10 Mary, b. 30 Sept. 1808; d. 6 May 1824.
11 Amos, m. 1 Dec. 1831, Anne T. Roberts. He settled in Illinois, where, it is said, he married again.

6-4-8-5

Reuben Libby, born in Rye, N. H., 1763; married, 11 Sept. 1794, Abigail Irish, daughter of Thomas and Delilah (Skillings) Irish of Gorham.

He was carried by his father to Gorham, Me., where he grew up. He learned the trade of shoemaker, and always worked at it. He lived on what is now part of the farm of Isaac Johnson. He died young, 15 Oct. 1807, and the family was broken up. His widow died with her son Samuel, 14 April 1856.

Children:

1 Jane, m. 15 Jan. 1818, Jacob Irish.
2 Ann, m. Benj. Burnal of Baldwin.
3 Thomas, b. 1798; m. Nancy Hilborn.
4 Samuel, b. 5 Oct. 1799; m. Sally Libby, 10-5-4-1-1-3.
5 Asa, m. 1st, Abigail Douglass; 2d, Mary Kennison.
6 Mary, b. 1805; d. 12 April 1825.
7 Delilah, b. 16 April 1807; m. 27 Nov. 1827, Hanson Newcomb.

6-4-8-9

Isaac Libby, born in Gorham, Me., 27 June 1776; married Rebecca Crockett, daughter of Pelatiah Crockett of Gorham.

He lived in Pownal after marriage, until 1810, when he moved to Albion, and thence, about 1822, to Thorndike, where he lived a long time. His last years were spent in Troy, where he died 28 Feb. 1855. He was a farmer and miller. His wife died in Thorndike, 1822.

Children:

1 Anna, b. 23 Oct. 1799; m. 1st, James Arlin; 2d, Wm. Parker; 3d, Daniel Denico; d. Sept. 1864.
2 Mary, b. 20 June 1801; m. 1st, Ezekiel Wyman; 2d, Amos Potter.
3 Betsey, b. 22 June 1803; m. 1st, Henry Johnson; 2d, Chandler Hopkins.
4 Clement Phinney, b. 8 May 1805; m. Caroline Cottle.
5 Ebenezer, b. 19 Aug. 1808; died aged three years.
6 Charles, b. 2 Jan. 1811; m. 1st, Olive Cottle, sister of his brother's wife; 2d, ——; died in Winona, Minn., 2 Mar. 1866. Children, by first wife:
  1 Osman, died in Knox; unm.
  2 Esther, died in Knox; unm.
  3 Charles N., born in Bucksport.
  4 Levi, born in Newbury.

By second wife:

  5 ——.

6-4-8-12

John Libby, born in Gorham, Me., 22 Jan. 1784; married, Joanna Baker, dau. of Samuel and Deborah (Farnham) Baker of Albion, Me.

He left Gorham, a young man, and settled in Albion, on a farm. He was also a shoemaker. He died very suddenly, in his pasture, 26 April 1822. His widow died 13 April 1869, in Winn. They were members of the Baptist church.

Children, all born in Albion:

1 Harriet B., b. 23 July 1812; m. 23 Nov. 1837, Wm. S. Phillips, now of Winn; died 23 June 1879. Children:
  1 Rufus B. (Phillips), b. 27 Jan. 1839; d. 16 Sept. 1840.
  2 George P. (Phillips), b. 15 March 1841; m. 1st, Cynthia D. Lyons; 2d, Cynthia S. Garey.
  3 Harriet W. (Phillips), b. 4 March 1844; m. Daniel W. Stratton.
  4 Sarah C. (Phillips), b. 23 Jan. 1849; m. Isaac Smart.
  5 Benjamin C. (Phillips), b. 11 Jan. 1854.
2 Olivia B., b. 25 Oct. 1815; m. Isaac W. Blenis.
3 Jane, b. 28 May 1818; m. 28 May 1838, in Vassalborough, Me., Ira R. Hodges. They cleared a farm in Winslow, where they lived until her death, 10 May 1872. Children:
  1 Addie B. (Hodges), b. 4 Nov. 1839; m. 28 Sept. 1866, Philip W. Day.
  2 Julia M. (Hodges), b. 7 April 1842; m. 5 March 1873, Horace M. Priest.
  3 Mary J. (Hodges), b. 6 March 1845; m. 27 Nov. 1867, Homer Proctor.
  4 Augusta H. (Hodges), b. 27 Aug. 1847.

5 Henry A. (Hodges), b. 2 June 1851; m. 31 March 1873, Lucretia L. Herrick, Benton, Me.
6 Annie O. (Hodges), b. 9 June 1853.
7 Flora E. (Hodges), b. 22 June 1856.
8 Abbie E. (Hodges), b. 28 Jan. 1859; m. 16 June 1881, Fred A. Bisco; lives in Leicester, Mass.
9 Ida R. (Hodges), b. 27 Sept. 1861.
4 Julia B., b. 5 Oct. 1820; m. Benj. Cloutman.

6-4-8-13

BENJAMIN LIBBY, born in Gorham, Me., 4 May 1786; married PRISCILLA CLAY, dau. of Thomas and Ruth (Gammon) Clay of Gorham.

He was a farmer and cooper. He served one year in the war of 1812, and after his return settled in Gray. He lived there four years and then settled in Albany, where he lived until his death, 10 Oct. 1868. His wife died 17 Sept. 1854.

Children:

1 Ruth C., b. 31 Oct. 1818, in Gray; m. Walter Libby, 6-4-8-4-3-1.
2 William Clay, b. 5 Mar. 1820; m. 31 Mar. 1843, Jerusha F., dau. of Jacob and Lydia (Shedd) Bancroft of Norway, Me. He had his father's homestead farm, and after his death sold it and moved to South Paris, where he has since lived. Children:
1 Jacob B., b. 29 June 1845; d. 15 May 1854.
2 Isaac A., b. 18 Aug. 1847; d. 20 Sept. 1867.
3 William Henry, b. 7 Nov. 1849; m. 28 Oct. 1876, Mary E., dau. of Robert and Lucy P. (Miner) Wheeler of Rhode Island. He is a locksmith. Child:
1 Ethel B., b. 29 April 1878.
4 Almira A., b. 7 July 1853; m. 1 Jan. 1881, William H. Harding of Andover.
5 Mehitable A., b. 24 April 1858; d. 28 April 1863.
6 Reuben A., b. 3 Oct. 1861; d. 7 May 1863.
7 Lydia E., b. 31 Mar. 1865.
3 Benjamin, b. 1 Mar. 1822; m. 12 Nov. 1851, Dorothy Bancroft, sister of his brother's wife. He lived in Albany twelve years after his marriage and then moved to Earlville, Ill., where he died in less than a year, 7 Dec. 1862, and his wife, 1 Mar. 1863. Children:
1 Edwin, b. 29 May 1850; d. 11 June 1875, in Paw Paw, Ill.; unm.
2 Emma, b. 15 July 1852; unm. She lives in Marlborough, Mass., and is known as Emma Tripp.
3 Edgar L., b. 14 July 1854; unm.
4 Mary M., b. 24 June 1856; m. 21 Sept. 1876, Albro Barber of Port Byron, Ill.
5 Florence A., b. 14 March 1859; unm.
6 Walter A., b. 16 March 1861; is called Cory, the name of the man who brought him up.
4 Joanna Clay, b. 9 May 1826; m. 30 June 1878, Isaiah Dorr of Canton, Me.
5 Reuben, b. 10 Feb. 1828; d. 29 April 1864; unm.

6-6-1-2

JACOB LIBBY, born probably in Epsom, N. H., 1747; married UNITY PARKER of Annapolis, N. S.

He went with his father from Epsom to Machias, Me., and was one of the original proprietors of that township. He served in the

Revolution, under Gen. Obrian of Machias, and after the war became one of the first settlers of St. Stephen, N. B. He was a farmer, and lived at St. Stephen, on the land afterward occupied by his sons James and William. He died in 1805, of small pox, caused by a careless physician throwing virus into his face. His widow died about 1824.

Children; all born in St. Stephen:

1 Jacob, b. 1 Aug. 1785; m. Elizabeth Dowdall.
2 James, b. 5 Nov. 1788; m. Levina Styles.
3 Martha, married in St. Stephen, William Andrews.
4 Abigail, married John Hanson in St. Stephen.
5 Sarah, married Stephen Hanson of St. Stephen.
6 Elizabeth, m. 1st, —— Prescott; 2d, Proctor Felton; d. in Boston, Mass.
7 Mary Simpson, m. Wm. Hanson of St. Stephen.
8 William P., married Lucy Crocker of St. Stephen.
9 Hannah, m. Matthew Burns; d. at Fredericton.
10 Susan, m. Moses Akerly; d. at Fredericton.

6-6-1-5

Eben Libby, born in Epsom, N. H., about 1760; married Lydia Young of Gouldsborough, Me.

He was four years old when his father removed to Machias, and 19 when they settled in St. Stephen, where there were at that time only five families. He became a farmer and took up 200 acres of land in what is now the heart of the town, but afterward exchanged for the land in the country now occupied by his son Stephen. He died Sept. 1818, and his widow, July 1843.

Children:

1 Samuel, b. Feb. 1785; died Feb. 1867; unmarried.
2 Asa, b. 8 Aug. 1786; m. Abigail Cutler Stone.
3 Elizabeth, m. 1st, —— Emerson; 2d, Jellison Hall; died 1879.
4 Lydia, died aged nine years.
5 Mabel, died young.
6 William, died young.
7 Sarah, married Moses Aldrich.
8 Eben, b. 1794; died Feb. 1854; unmarried.
9 Temperance, married William Hamon; is living.
10 Stephen R., b. 12 Jan. 1800; m. Mary Hanson.
11 William, b. 1802; died Sept. 1854; unm.
12 Mary, b. 1810; m. 1st, Capt. David Williams; 2d, Abram Marks.

6-6-10-2

Joseph Libby, born in Rye, N. H., 10 Nov. 1765; married, 12 Feb. 1789, Deborah Rand, daughter of Joseph and Deborah (Seavey) Rand of Rye.

In his early years he was a sailor. Soon after his father left Rye, Joseph removed his residence to New Castle, and about 1799 removed thence to Chester, N. H. In 1805 he went from Chester, and settled in that part of Gilmanton which is now Gilford. There he lived until his death, 21 Oct. 1837. His widow died 17 March 1849, in Holderness.

Children:

1 Mary, b. 28 Sept. 1789, in Rye; m. 1st, Abraham Folsom; 2d, Bradstreet Gilman; died 12 May 1865.
2 Joseph, b. 19 Oct. 1791; m. Mehitable C. Rand.
3 Benjamin, b. 27 July 1796, in New Castle; m. Rueney Robinson.
4 Elias, b. 17 March 1802, in Chester; m. Jemima Rand and Clarissa F. Davis.
5 Sally, b. 30 July 1805, in Gilford; died very young.
6 Abram, b. 17 April 1809; m. Dorcas Hibbard.

6-6-10-5

Capt. Jacob Libby, born in Rye, N. H., 19 Dec. 1770; married, 12 Sept. 1793, Mary Brickett, daughter of Bernard and Mary (Hall) Brickett of Chester, now Auburn, N. H.

He was a carpenter by trade. He left home at an early age, and went to Candia, where, by his industry and good management, he became possessed of a good farm and a handsome property. He held many positions of trust. He died 9 June 1849. His wife died 3 May 1845.

Children, all born in Candia:

1 Josiah B., b. 27 Dec. 1794; m. Sallie Robie.
2 Mary, b. 9 Dec. 1798; m. 20 Nov. 1849, Abram L. Morrison of Tilton, N. H.
3 Barnard, b. 11 July 1801; d. 4 May 1840; unm. He always lived at home.
4 Sarah A., b. 26 Feb. 1804; m. 8 Oct. 1823, Levi Barker, who died in Candia, 20 March 1876. Children:
  1 Abraham L. (Barker), b. 19 Feb. 1824; m. 1st, Mary D. Harrington; 2d, Achsah Hadley.
  2 Mary B. (Barker), b. 1 Oct. 1826; m. 3 May 1849, John H. Smith.
  3 Sarah A. (Barker), b. 8 March 1830; m. 29 April 1848, Gilman C. Lary.
  4 Jacob L. (Barker), b. 15 Aug. 1833; m. 7 July 1859, Miranda L. Barker.
  5 Josiah B. (Barker), b. 12 Sept. 1837; m. 18 April 1863, Anna M. Wason.
  6 Levi (Barker), b. 1 April 1843; m. 9 May 1867, Flora A. Libby, 6-6-10-5-1-1-1.
  7 Martha E. (Barker), b. 8 Oct. 1845; m. 16 Jan. 1867, Harry H. Melendy.
5 Eleanor, b. 13 Jan. 1810; m. Isaiah Fogg.

6-6-10-6

Elias Tarlton Libby, born in Rye, N. H., 6 Sept. 1773; married 7 Aug. 1795, Phebe Dennett, daughter of Ephraim (?) and Jane (Boyd) Dennett of Portsmouth.

He was a tailor by trade, but purchased the Globe Tavern, in Portsmouth Plains, and afterward kept a house of entertainment, and also raised garden stuff for the Portsmouth market. He was U. S. deputy marshal under Gen. McCleary of Epsom. He died 1 Aug. 1835, and his widow 12 July 1856.

Children:

1 Mary Tarlton, b. 6 May 1796; m. 1st, 3 Nov. 1814, Capt. Sam'l Starbird; 2d, Joseph Dennett; d. 23 April 1860.

2 George D., b. 1797. He followed the sea. He married in Liverpool, Eng., the mistress of a boarding-house for American officers, and died in 1837, leaving a son two years old.

6-6-10-7

ABRAHAM LIBBY, born in Rye, N. H., 10 Feb. 1777; married first, 21 Oct. 1800, BETSEY HILL of Candia, N. H.; (died 21 May 1824); second, 12 May 1825, Miss SUSAN MOORE; (died 8 April 1827); third, 22 Jan. 1829, BETSEY WHITTIER; (died 29 May 1857.)

He learned the trade of carpenter in Candia, and upon his marriage, removed to Montville, Me., whence, in 1801, he settled in Belfast, where he was a highly respected citizen until his death, 16 Nov. 1858.

Children, by first wife:

1 Sallie, b. 6 Aug. 1801; died in infancy.
2 David, b. 16 Sept. 1803; m. Mary (Batson) Glosson.
3 Clarissa H., b. 5 Sept. 1805; m. 3 Dec. 1835, Capt. D. D. Pinkham.
4 Susan H., b. 16 April 1807; m. 1st, 7 Dec. 1825, Capt. James W. Brown; (died in Cuba); 2d, 26 Dec. 1830, Samuel S. Burd.
5 John Connor, b. 12 July 1808; m. Angeline E. Steele.
6 Elias L., b. 14 Jan. 1810; m. 30 Dec. 1835, Nancy A. Patterson; was lost with schooner Rodney (of which he was captain) in Barnstable Bay, Mass., 5 Nov. 1840. His widow married, 23 Feb. 1845, Ebenezer Roberts of Hingham, Mass. Children:
   1 Helen Leavitt, b. 17 Oct. 1836; d. 21 May 1843.
   2 Mary Augusta, b. 29 Mar. 1841; m. 16 May 1869, Orren Brewster Sears; died 20 Jan. 1870. She was a member of the Methodist Church.
7 Samuel H., b. 12 June 1812; m. 31 Dec. 1835, Mary Elizabeth, dau. of William and Mary (Davis) Greely of Belfast; started for California 16 Mar. 1848, and has not been heard from since. His widow lives in Rockland. Children:
   1 Henry Oliver, b. 30 Nov. 1837; d. 27 Jan. 1865, at St. Thomas, of yellow fever; unm.
   2 May Ella, b. 6 May 1844; m. 23 Mar. 1870, George Elliot of Thomaston.
   3 Abram, b. 5 June 1847; d. 28 Sept. 1848.
8 Alfred Johnson, b. 28 Sept. 1819; m. 11 April 1848, Elizabeth J., dau. of Capt. Joseph and Hannah (Perry) Mitchell of Kittery, Me. He began the cabinet-maker's trade with his brother John, but was dissatisfied and adopted the calling of house-carpenter, in which he continued until his death, 27 April 1875. His widow lives with her daughter in Chelsea, Mass. Children:
   1 Fred M., b. 17 Jan. 1849, in Roxbury, Mass.; m. 27 Sept. 1881, Josephine Crosby, dau. of John and Mary Ann (Fischer) Schaffner of Fort Dodge, Iowa. He was a clerk in Boston some years, and then went west, locating at Stormville, Miss. He has served there as justice of the peace, levee commissioner, representative to the state legislature, and county treasurer. He is now a successful cotton planter.
   2 Jennie L., b. 17 Jan. 1853, in Belfast; m. 2 Sept. 1875, Frank Charland Pitcher of Belfast, now in business in Boston. Child:
      1 Mabel Storm (Pitcher), b. 8 Oct. 1879.

By third wife:

9 Betsey H., b. 27 Dec. 1830; m. Benj. Clark of Auburn.

6-6-10-9

BENJAMIN LIBBY, born in Rye, N. H., 20 June 1782; married RHODA WILKINSON, daughter of Benning and Deborah (Langley) Wilkinson of Gilford.

He learned the trade of tailor in Portsmouth and afterward lived in Gilford where most of his children were born. He removed to Gilmanton in 1822, and soon after bought a farm, still working at his trade from house to house. In 1833 he sold his homestead. He died in Laconia 4 Sept. 1868. His wife died 10 Feb. 1866.

Children:

1 Elizabeth, b. 4 Aug. 1807, in Gilford; m. 3 April 1843, Ebenezer Varney.
2 Jacob, b. 9 April 1809; m. Harriet Wadleigh.
3 George W., b. 19 May 1811; m. Sally W., dau. of Benjamin and Polly (Chase) Sanborn of Meredith; died 10 May 1833, in Belmont. He was a farmer. His widow married Alvah Graves of Meredith. Only child:
  1 Mary O., b. 18 Dec. 1833; m. Lawrence Dow.
4 Polly, b. 15 April 1813; m. Michael Lovin; d. 18 April 1868, in Gorham, N. H.
5 John G., b. 16 Mar. 1818; m. Eliza, dau. of Samuel and Sarah (Wilkinson) Fogg of New Hampton. He was for many years a railroad conductor, and afterward ran a stationary engine. He lived in Laconia, N. H., many years, and then moved to the vicinity of Boston. He died 28 July 1880; a member of the F. W. Baptist Church. Children:
  1 Martha E., } twins, born } died aged 2 years.
  2 Margaret E., } 18 Aug. 1841; } died aged 19 years.
6 Sarah L., b. 19 May 1822, in Gilmanton; m. Aug. 1848, Geo. W. Rowe; d. 18 Sept. 1864.
7 Benjamin Crockett, b. 15 Jan. 1826; m. 13 May 1848, Juliet Smith, dau. of Nicholas Gilman and Shuah P. (Richardson) Dudley of Gilmanton. He was a farmer in Laconia and Candia until 1857, when he removed to Boston, where he has since been a teamster. Children:
  1 Francis Leroy, b. 22 July 1849, in Laconia; m. 26 Nov. 1872, Margaret, dau. of Henry Hartmeyer of Boston. He is a teamster. Children:
    1 Mary Frances, b. 19 April 1874.
    2 Emma Louisa, b. 11 Aug. 1876.
    3 Jennie Ferson, b. 15 Oct. 1878.
    4 William Henry, b. 26 Feb. 1881.
  2 Emma Augusta, b. 6 Oct. 1850, in Candia; m. 5 June 1869, John H. Morse.
  3 Edward Herman, b. 11 Jan. 1853, in Laconia; unm. He is a dry goods salesman in New York City.
  4 Florence Josephine, b. 18 Jan. 1855; m. 2 Aug. 1873, Chaney R. Emmons.
  5 Jessie Fremont, b. 4 April 1857; m. 28 June 1873, Wm. H. Clifford.
  6 Horace Dudley, b. 7 May 1859, in Boston; unm.
  7 Lewis Benjamin, b. 6 July 1861.
  8 Mabel Jenkins, b. 28 March 1864.
  9 Charles Luville, b. 26 Sept. 1870.

9-5-4-2

REUBEN FOGG, born 9 Dec. 1746, in Scarborough; married, 12

Dec. 1769, Rhoda Moody. He was a farmer, and occupied his father's homestead.

Children:

1 Jacob (Fogg), b. 11 Feb. 1771; m. Sally Libby, 5-2-3-2.
2 Polly (Fogg), b. 27 July 1779; died young.
3 Rhoda (Fogg), b. 20 Nov. 1785; m. 7 July 1805, Capt. Hosea Harford of Portland.
4 Reuben (Fogg), b. 16 July 1788; d. aged 15.
5 Mary (Fogg), b. 2 Sept. 1792; m. 15 Dec. 1815, Capt. Ebenezer Andrews.
6 Sophia (Fogg), b. 1 July 1796; m. John Billings of Saco.

9-6-6-4

Abner Fogg, born in Scarborough, 20 Nov. 1766; married, 26 June 1794, Anna Plummer.

He lived on his father's homestead, a farmer. His death occurred 29 Aug. 1847.

Children:

1 Abner (Fogg), b. 10 Jan. 1796; d. 1 July 1853; unm.
2 Mary (Fogg), b. 13 Nov. 1797; d. 9 Jan. 1845; unm.
3 Catherine (Fogg), b. 28 Sept. 1798; m. Deacon James Small. [See Small, page 32.]
4 Sewall (Fogg), b. 1800; m. 28 Nov. 1827, Eliza Harmon. He occupied the homestead farm. Children, among others:
 1 William (Fogg), occupies part of the homestead farm.
 2 Sarah H. (Fogg), m. Robert Libby, 10-1-6-4-2-3.
 3 John (Fogg), lives on part of the homestead.

9-9-9-6

William Fogg, born in Eliot, Me., 3 Nov. 1790; married, 16 June 1821, Betsey Deed Hill, born 9 Aug. 1790, daughter of Samuel and Rebekah Hill. She died 24 Jan. 1846. He then married, 30 Aug. 1846, Mehitable Plummer Moody, daughter of Bradstreet Moody, Esq., of Sanbornton, N. H.

He resided on part of his father's homestead. He was deeply interested in genealogy, and prepared accounts of nearly all the families that lived in Eliot. He filled repeatedly the highest offices in the gift of his townsmen.

Children, all by his first wife:

1 infant son, born and died 16 May 1822.
2 Ann Rebekah (Fogg), b. 12 Jan. 1824; d. 10 Aug. 1843; unm.
3 John Samuel Hill (Fogg), [M.D.], b. 21 May 1826; married, 11 July 1850, Sarah F. Gordon of South Berwick. She died 21 Mar. 1871. He married second, 2 April 1872, Mary Griselda, dau. of Rev. Joseph H. Clinch. He graduated at Bowdoin College, 1846, and at the Boston Medical School, 1850. He resides in South Boston. Children:
 1 William John Gordon (Fogg), b. 7 Aug. 1851; graduated from Harvard College in 1873, and from the Harvard Medical School in 1876.
 2 Charles Joseph (Fogg), b. 29 Oct. 1853; d. 22 Jan. 1856.
 3 Francis Joseph (Fogg), b. 4 Aug. 1857; d. 10 Mar. 1871.
4 Joseph William (Fogg), b. 18 Feb. 1829; d. 2 Mar. 1829.
5 William Ansyl (Fogg), b. 31 May 1832.

10-1-2-2

Reuben Libby, born in Scarborough, in 1745; married Rebecca Weston, daughter of Josiah and Phebe (Parker) Weston of Falmouth. Rebecca Weston was one of the heroic women who carried ammunition to Machias, during the attack of the English. The distance they carried it was about 16 miles, through unbroken woods, with only spotted trees to guide them.

Reuben Libby was about 18 when his father went with his family to Machias. He grew up there, and when he was married, settled in what is now Jonesborough, and cleared him a farm on the south side of Chandler's River. There he died, July 1833. His wife died July 1819.

Children:

1 Reuben, b. 17 April 1776; m. Martha Farnsworth.
2 Rebecca, b. 22 Dec. 1777; m. July 1823, as second wife, Joseph Whitney. She had no children, and died 25 June 1868.
3 Eunice, b. 19 Dec. 1779; d. 4 Aug. 1782.
4 Josiah, b. 16 Mar. 1781; m. Jane Libby, 10-1-2-3-3.
5 Mary, b. 28 Jan. 1783; m. 5 June 1803, Joseph Whitney; died Oct. 1822. Children:
   1 Ruth R. (Whitney), b. 1805; m. 1st, Charles R. Drisko; 2d, Greenlief Watts.
   2 Rebecca (Whitney), b. 1807; lives in Machias.
   3 John H. (Whitney), b. 1810; m. Clarissa Meserve.
   4 George R. (Whitney), b. 1813; m. Martha Noyes.
   5 Eunice R. (Whitney), b. 1816; m. Sylvanus Jenkins.
   6 Ephraim (Whitney), b. 1819; m. Maria Wakefield.
   7 Mary (Whitney), b. 1822; m. 1st, Ephraim Costhell; 2d, James Lawrence.
6 Joseph, b. 9 Dec. 1784; m. Hannah Farnsworth.
7 Nathan, b. 20 May 1787; m. Sibyl Farnsworth.
8 Hannah, b. 1 April 1789; m. 10 Nov. 1811, Samuel Maddocks; died 1 April 1840. He died 25 July 1842. Children:
   1 Louise (Maddocks), b. 1813; m. Charles Ayers.
   2 Abigail (Maddocks), b. 1816; died 1835.
   3 Reuben L. (Maddocks), m. Louisa More; d. 1843.
   4 Horatio G. N. (Maddocks), b. 1819; d. 1839.
   5 Nathan L. (Maddocks), b. 1820, d. 1842.
   6 Joel (Maddocks), m. Louisa, widow of his brother Reuben.
   7 Amanda (Maddocks), b 1824; d. 1840.
   8 Alpheus S. C. (Maddocks), b. 1826.
   9 Susan F. (Maddocks), b. 1828; m. Thomas Berry.
   10 Hannah (Maddocks), b. 1831.
   11 Almena (Maddocks), b. 1833; m. Albee Shorey.
9 Eunice, b. 25 June 1791; m. 26 April 1812, William Kilton; d. Aug. 1867. He died 12 March 1834. Children:
   1 Louvisa (Kilton), b. 1812; m. Henry Kaler.
   2 Lucinda (Kilton), b. 1814; m. Levi Brigham.
   3 Diadem (Kilton), b. 1817; m. Wm. Foster.
   4 Fannie Weston (Kilton), b. 1820; m. —— Smith.
   5 Amasa D. (Kilton), b. 1822; m. Rebecca Johnson.
   6 Ruth K. (Kilton), b. 1825; m. John Nichols.
   7 Benjamin (Kilton), supposed to have died at sea.
   8 Melinda S. (Kilton), m. —— Dixon.

10-1-2-3

Joseph Libby, born in Scarborough, 1747; married Jane Cole. He was carried to Machias when a boy, and there grew up to manhood. He was one of the company that captured the Margaretta in the first naval engagement of the Revolution. He afterward settled in Harrington. "He farmed it some, and hunted some, and gunned some." He died 15 Nov. 1844, aged 97 years and 8 months. His wife died 28 Nov. 1836.

Children, all born in Harrington:

1 Mary, m. Ephraim White.
2 Rebecca, m. Joseph Larrabee.
3 Jane, b. 30 Dec. 1783 (?); m. Josiah Libby, 10-1-2-2-4.
4 Job, b. 30 Dec. 1783; m. Rebecca Mitchell.
5 Eliza, b. 9 Mar. 1785; m. Ichabod Colson.
6 Hannah, m. Fellows Whitney.
7 Ephraim, b. 26 Jan. 1794; m. Sally McCaslin.
8 Stephen, m. Abigail Webb.
9 Abigail, m. Wm. Crockett, 1821.

10-1-2-4

ELIJAH LIBBY, born in Scarborough, 1748; married, 10 Sept. 1783, MARY DRESSER. She died and he married second, her sister, MINDWELL DRESSER.

It is not certain that he went to Machias with his father; yet it is probable that he did, and that when he arrived at manhood, he returned to the locality of his birth. He settled first on a farm in the upper part of Saco, and for many years tended the Nonesuch gristmill. He afterward settled on a farm in Buxton, and there died, 22 Feb. 1825. His wife died soon after.

Children, all by wife Mary:

1 Elias, b. 22 June 1784; m. Martha Bradbury.
2 Daniel, b. 21 Mar. 1788; m. Mary Libby, 10-1-8-4-3.
3 Richard, b. 1791; m. Lucy Libby, 10-1-6-7-6.
4 Daughter, died in infancy.

10-1-2-6

JOSIAH LIBBY, born in Scarborough, 17 Feb. 1758; married 26 Nov. 1778, SARAH HOLMES, heir and probably daughter of Benjamin Holmes of Machias.

He grew up in Machias and became a farmer. His farm was that afterward occupied by his son Luther. He took part in the capture of the Margaretta and it is said that he fired the first shot. He died 11 April 1828. His wife died 7 Nov. 1824.

Children, all born in Machias, now Machiasport:

1 Elijah, b. 14 Sept. 1779; d. 13 Nov. 1867; unm.
2 Lydia, b. 19 Dec. 1780; m. 12 Oct. 1798, John Seavey; died 15 Dec. 1841.
3 Thomas, b. 24 April, 1782; was drowned. He was married but so far as is known had no children.
4 Susan E., b. 10 June 1784; m. Wm. Meservey; d. 12 May 1874.
5 Hannah, b. 15 July 1784 (?); d. 1861, in St. George.
6 William, b. 9 Sept. 1786; died in infancy.
7 Luther C., b. 4 July 1796; m. Mary McCalab.

10-1-2-7

Nathan Libby, born in Scarborough, 1759; married, 1789, Polly Larrabee, daughter of Isaac and Deborah (Larrabee) Larrabee of Machias. [See p. 41.] He was a farmer in Machias, now Machiasport.

Children, all born there:

1 Hannah, m. John Larrabee.
2 Deborah, m. John Dowling.
3 Philip, m. Betsey Larrabee.
4 Otis, b. 1800; m. Phebe Smith.
5 William, b. May 1802; m. Betsey Smith.
6 Olive, m. Turner Dowling.
7 Sarah, m. Daniel Larrabee.
8 Susan, m. Frank Bryant.

10-1-5-5

David Libby, born in Scarborough, 31 Aug. 1755; married, 23 Jan. 1783, Abigail Fitts, heir and probably daughter of Ebenezer Fitts of Machias, born 31 Oct. 1763.

He settled on Pleasant Point, on the east side of Machias River. The farm is still occupied by his descendants. He died 21 Dec. 1833. His widow died in April, 1841.

Children:

1 Elizabeth, b. 10 Aug. 1783; m. John Burnham.
2 Mary, b. 2 May 1785; m. Wm. Holway.
3 Ebenezer, b. 27 May 1787; m. Parmela Andrews.
4 Mariner, b. 3 Aug. 1789; m. Susannah Burnham.
5 Anna, b. 25 Aug. 1791; m. James Eliot.
6 David, b. 1 Sept. 1793; d. 17 Oct. 1832; unm.
7 Phineas, b. 18 Dec. 1795; m. Nancy Grover.
8 Abigail D., b. 2 Feb. 1798; m. Charles Emerson.
9 George, b. 2 Mar. 1802; lives on the homestead; unm.
10 Susan P., b. 14 May 1805; m. Elisha Hanscom.

10-1-5-6

Obadiah Libby, born in Scarborough, 1757; married 30 Aug. 1785, Mary Hill. He was a farmer in Machias and lived on the farm now occupied by Capt. Stephen Small. He died about 1847. His wife died 28 Nov. 1840.

Children:

1 Timothy, b. 3 April 1786; m. 1811, Mrs. Susan Batman, dau. of John and Jane Mitchell of Harrington. He was a sailor and died 25 Oct. 1873. His wife died 22 Oct. 1847. Children:
    1 Rebecca, b. 15 Oct. 1819; m. —— Larrabee.
    2 Nancy, b. 19 Jan. 1821; m. Horace Foster. Children:
        1 Francis (Foster), b. 1 Aug. 1842; m. Almira Ackley.
        2 Sarah (Foster), b. 6 Nov. 1843; m. —— Rice.
        3 Mary E. (Foster), b. 20 Oct. 1845; m. —— Albee.
        4 Horace (Foster), b. 18 Sept. 1847; d. 28 Feb. 1849.
        5 Susan (Foster), b. 11 Nov. 1849; m. —— Rice.
        6 Lewis (Foster), b. 18 Nov. 1851; m. Nettie A. Smith.
        7 Samuel (Foster), b. 27 Nov. 1853; d. same day.

8 Annie (Foster), b. 27 Sept. 1855; m. —— Flynn.
9 Prose M. (Foster), b. 7 Aug. 1857.
10 Olive (Foster), b. 7 Jan. 1860; m. —— Clark.
3 Mary Jane, b. 25 Dec. 1825; d. 5 Aug. 1829.
2 Enoch, b. 15 Sept. 1788; m. Rebecca Larrabee.
3 Sarah, b. 14 Feb. 1792; m. 10 June 1818, James C. Fletcher.
4 Mary, b. 5 Feb. 1795; m. Moses Pettigrove.
5 Martha, b. 27 Dec. 1799; m. Benj. Rice; d. 19 April 1841.
6 William, b. 6 July 1804; died young.

10-1-5-7

DANIEL LIBBY, born in Scarborough, about 1763; married HANNAH EASTMAN, daughter of —— and Margaret (Bryant) Eastman of Machias, whither he was carried in infancy by his father. He was a farmer, and lived in that part of Machias which is now Machiasport. He died April, 1844, and his widow 22 May 1866.

Children:

1 Esther, b. 28 Dec. 1800; m. Aug. 1820, George Hadley; died 15 Aug. 1859.
2 Lydia, b. 13 Nov. 1802; d. 13 July 1879.
3 Joanna, b. 3 Dec. 1804; m. 1st, 2 April 1831, Nathaniel Holmes; 2d, P. Babb.
4 Daniel, b. 27 July 1807; m. Lucy S. Huntley.
5 Betsey, b. 22 Aug. 1809.
6 Hannah, m. Winkworth S. Allen; died Feb. 1844.
7 William B., [Capt.], b. 19 Oct. 1813; m. 28 Jan. 1847, Margaret, dau. of Wm. M. and Lydia (Holmes) Fletcher of Crawford. His wife died in Machiasport, 23 Sept. 1858, and he in East Machias, 25 Oct. 1868. Children:
  1 Juliette F., b. 3 Dec. 1848; m. Arthur Gadcomb; died 26 Oct. 1875.
  2 Ella B., b. 26 April 1850.
  3 Melville O., b. 14 Dec. 1852.
  4 Corris Ann, b. 2 Oct. 1854; married in Canton, Mass., —— Nelson.
8 Sarah, m. 1st, Benj. Shaw; 2d, Rev. —— Stone.
9 Catherine B., b. July, 1823; m. Winkworth S. Allen.

10-1-6-4

ROBERT LIBBY, born in Scarborough, 1757; married, 9 Sept. 1787, HANNAH PROUT. She died 9 Nov. 1791. He then married, 12 June 1792, REBECCA TRICKEY, 10-8-4-3.

After his first marriage he lived in a part of the house of his father-in-law, on Prout's Neck. He subsequently settled on the farm now occupied by Robert Libby, 10-1-6-4-2-3. He died 29 May 1835. His widow died 15 Oct. 1840.

Children, by first wife:

1 Oliver, b. 6 Mar. 1790; was *non compos mentis;* died 28 Mar. 1834.

By second wife:

2 Shirley, b. 2 April 1794; m. Mary Libby, 5-2-3-1-3.

10-1-6-5

Dea. Isaac Libby, born in Scarborough, 1760; married 11 Dec. 1783, Sarah Waterhouse, daughter of Joseph and Rachel (Norman) Waterhouse. [See page 80.]

He was a farmer. He settled on Standish Neck soon after his marriage, and moved thence to Freedom, in 1800. His homestead in Freedom went to his son Abram, and is now owned by Daniel Webster. He died with Abram, 1 Dec. 1838, and his widow, 15 April 1839. He was many years deacon of the Christian church in Freedom.

Children:

1 Hannah, bap. 20 Nov. 1785, in Scarborough; m. Abel Works of Unity.
2 Isaac, bap. 29 June 1788, in Scarborough; died young.
3 Joseph, b. 31 July 1788, in Standish; m. Lucy H. Grant.
4 David, m. 1st, Mary Fowler; 2d, Abigail Libby, 10-5-4-7-5.
5 Robert, b. 6 Sept. 1790 (?); m. Anna Clark Hasty.
6 Sally, b. 1792; died aged 22.
7 Betsey, b. 1794; died 1865, with Abram's widow; unm.
8 Josiah, died at the age of 14.
9 Isaac, b. 1797; m. Hannah Abbott of Freedom; died 1832. Children:
  1 Moses, died aged 23; unm.
  2 Rebecca, b. 1827; m. —— Warren of Freedom.
10 Abram, b. 2 April 1801; m. 13 Sept. 1840, Jane, dau. of Ephraim and Abigail (Hunnewell) Bragdon of Durham. He was a farmer, and had the homestead in Freedom. He died very suddenly, 13 Dec. 1862. His widow married —— Hussey. Children:
  1, 2 sons, died at birth.

10-1-6-7

Capt. David Libby, born at Blue Point, in Scarborough, 1770; married, 14 Jan. 1790, Elizabeth McKenney, dau. of Samuel and Lydia (Rand) McKenney of Scarborough.

He was carried by his father to Providence, R. I., and either there or elsewhere, was bound out to a carpenter. He, however, ran away to sea, and was ever afterward a mariner, rising to be master. He returned to his native town, where he at length married. About 1791 he was captured at sea by the French, and was five years a prisoner. He afterward followed the sea until 1814, when he settled on a farm in Newry, but being discouraged by a severe frost which cut off his crops, sold, and moved his family to Chebeague Island. He continued to follow the sea until his death, 26 April 1818. His widow moved her family back to Saco. She died with her daughter, in Standish, 20 April 1848.

Children:

1 Hannah, died in infancy, 13 Dec. 1790.
2 Samuel, b. 3 Sept. 1791; m. Sarah S. Ellenwood.
3 Aaron, b. 7 Oct. 1796; m. Emily Woodsum.
4 David, b. 16 Feb. 1798; d. 17 Jan. 1820; unm. He was drowned by the upsetting of a small boat while going ashore on Cape Ann.
5 George, b. 22 May 1800; m. Fanny Prescott.

6 Lucy, b. 29 April 1802; m. Richard Libby, 10-1-2-4-3.
7 Ephraim, b. 2 Mar. 1804; m. Mary Palmer.
8 Lydia, b. 3 April 1806; m. 17 Feb. 1822, Thomas Hodgdon.
9 Abraham. b. 2 Mar. 1808; m. Hannah Hancock.
10 Eliza, b. 13 Jan. 1810; m. 2 Aug. 1829, Wiliam C. Moulton of Saco.

10-1-8-1

CAPT. THOMAS LIBBY, born in the old garrison on Scottow's Hill, Scarborough, 12 Nov. 1754; married 15 Mar. 1781, MARY LIBBY, 10-2-1-4.

He served as sergeant in the Revolution. After he left the army his uncle George Libby gave him a piece of wild land, then in Scarborough, now in Gorham, on condition that he should support him the remainder of his life. He built his house about 20 rods southeast of the present residence of Silas Libby, 10-1-8-1-2-2, and cleared a farm. He was a captain in the militia.

His first wife, his children's mother, died 19 May 1810. His second wife was Phebe (Jordan?) Ward, widow of Wm. Ward; married 13 Oct. 1811, died 26 Mar. 1822, aged 60. 14 Nov. 1822, he married Betsey Brackett, and she died 6 Jan. 1825, aged 46. He then, 6 Sept. 1825, married Mary, daughter of George Waterhouse, 10-2-2-9. He died 26 June 1836. His widow died with her own relatives, 30 Jan. 1869.

Children:

1 Jane, b. 2 April 1782; m. 30 Nov. 1808, Daniel Babb.
2 Benjamin March, b. 14 May 1784; m. Elizabeth Babb.
3 Thomas, b. 9 Feb. 1786; d. 27 Oct. 1797.
4 Samuel Hubbard, b. 29 Sept. 1789; m. Charlotte Tibbetts.
5 Elizabeth, b. 3 July 1791; m. 29 Sept. 1816, George Ward.
6 Mary, b. 29 Oct. 1794; m. 18 Feb. 1821, William Ward.
7 Thomas, b. 15 Aug. 1798; m. 20 Dec. 1821, Martha, dau. of Jesse Ward of Gorham. He was a farmer. He lived after his marriage in Baldwin, Scarborough, and in Biddeford where he died, 3 Dec. 1854. His widow went to Great Falls, N. H., where she is thought to have married again. Children:
   1 Emeline, died in Biddeford aged 16 years.
   2 Lucius, is a farm hand; unm. when last heard from.
   3 Jesse, was drowned, aged about 18 years.
   4 Achsah, m. —— Drew of Great Falls.
   5 Almira G., b. 17 Dec. 1841.
   6 daughter.

10-1-8-2

CAPT. ZEBULON LIBBY, born in Scarborough, about 1757; married, 19 Oct. 1780, LYDIA ANDREWS, daughter of Deacon Amos and Anne (Seavey) Andrews of Scarborough.

A year or two after his marriage, he settled on a portion of his father's large purchase which was then in Scarborough, but is now in Saco. There he always lived. He served three years in the Revolution, and was afterward a captain in the militia. He died 6 Dec. 1836. His widow died 9 Dec. 1838.

Children:

1 Amos, b. 29 Jan. 1781; m. Mercy Black.
2 Mary Ingersoll, b. 11 Mar. 1783; m. Josiah Black.
3 John, b. 20 Dec. 1784; m. Anna Maxwell.
4 Hannah Knight, b. 9 Oct. 1786; m. 2 Mar. 1806, John Carter.
5 Eunice, b. 6 July 1788; m. 21 Dec. 1809, Elijah Buzzell.
6 Anna, b. 24 Feb. 1791; m. 24 Sept. 1815, Robert Carle.
7 Timothy, b. 9 Oct. 1793; m. Mehitable Richards.
8 Lydia, b. 23 Sept. 1795; m. 16 Oct. 1817, Aaron Black.
9 David, b. 15 Sept. 1798; m. Olive Watson.
10 Josiah, b. 10 May 1800; d. 7 Feb. 1801.
11 Clarissa Milliken, b. 25 Feb. 1802; m. 3 Oct. 1822, John Edgecomb.

10-1-8-3

SOLOMON LIBBY, born in Scarborough, 1759; married, 31 Jan. 1782, SARAH SEAVEY, daughter of Thomas Seavey of Scarborough.

He served three years in the Revolution. Upon his marriage he settled on part of his father's purchase, and there lived until his death, a farmer. His house stood where Phineas Libby's carriage-house now is. He died 3 Mar. 1832. His widow died 14 Jan. 1851, aged 88.

Children:

1 Esther, b. 2 Oct. 1783; m. 27 Feb. 1826, John Berry.
2 Olive, b. 24 Aug. 1784; m. 1 Dec. 1803, John Berry, jr.
3 Philip, b. 11 Nov. 1785; m. Christiana Howe.
4 Ebenezer, b. 6 Sept. 1787; m. Sarah Foster.
5 Jane, b. 9 Aug. 1789; m. 1 April 1811, Jonathan Morse.
6 Solomon, b. 9 Aug. 1791; m. Dorcas Foss.
7 Reuben, b. 2 July 1793; m. Rebecca Keene.
8 Hannah, b. 27 Aug. 1795; m. Joseph Gould.
9 Asa, b. 1 Dec. 1797; m. Lucy House.
10 Sarah, b. 22 Sept. 1800; m. 16 Nov. 1826, Daniel Dresser.
11 Josiah, b. 10 Aug. 1802; m. Mary (Haines) Jacobs.
12 Mary, b. 12 Sept. 1804; m. 18 May 1828, Daniel Milliken.
13 Phineas, b. 22 Oct. 1807; m. 1st, Nancy Atkinson; 2d, Sarah M. Fogg.

10-1-8-4

PHILIP LIBBY, born in Scarborough, 16 May 1762; married MARY MCKENNEY. [See McKenney, p. 63.]

He was always a farmer. Soon after his marriage he built a house on a portion of his father's farm, near the house now occupied by Thomas S. Libby, 10-1-8-4-4-4. His death, which occurred 26 Feb. 1810, was recorded as follows: "Philip Libby fell from his horse and broke his neck; was found dead in the road." His widow died 27 July 1854, aged 89.

Children:

1 Eunice, b. 5 Jan. 1789; d. 12 June 1876; unm.
2 George, b. 18 April 1792; m. 1st, Sally Foss; 2d, Eliza Carter.
3 Mary, b. 20 Oct. 1794; m. Daniel Libby, 10-1-2-4-2.
4 Moses, b. 30 Nov. 1796; m. Fannie Seavey.
5 Betsey, b. 28 April 1799; m. 1 Dec. 1824, Eli Edgecomb.
6 Lucy, b. 17 Nov. 1803; d. 28 Aug. 1876; unm.

7 Philip, b. 19 July 1806; m. 23 June 1830, Catherine, dau. of Pelatiah and Sally (Elwell) Harmon. He settled in Hollis, (now Dayton), on the farm now occupied by Samuel Roberts. His wife died 14 June 1869. He died 17 Oct. 1870. Children:

1 Roxanna Foss, b. 22 Nov. 1830, in Saco; m. Sept. 1859, Hezekiah Drew.

2 Mary E., b. 22 Jan. 1833; m. Aug. 1863, Jeremiah Drew.

8 Phebe, b. July, 1810; m. 24 June 1830, David Warren.

10-1-8-5

JOHN LIBBY, born in Scarborough, 24 March 1764; married, 11 Oct. 1787, DRUSILLA GRAFFAM of Scarborough. He lived in Saco until 1816, when he removed to Greene, and settled on the farm which he occupied until his death. He died 8 Feb. 1849. His wife died 1 Aug. 1844.

Children, all born in Saco:

1 Josiah, b. 1788; was killed by a sled, 1 Jan. 1800.
2 Deborah, b. 19 Nov. 1789; m. Simeon Turner of Leeds.
3 Thomas, b. 24 Dec. 1791; m. Joanna Turner.
4 Zebulon, b. 28 June 1794; m. Jane Turner.
5 Nancy, b. 3 Sept. 1796; m. Daniel Blake of Turner.
6 Dorcas, b. 4 Dec. 1798; m. Samuel Maloon.
7 Abigail, b. 19 March 1801; d. 24 March 1841; unm.
8 John, b. 5 July 1804; m. Caroline Hawes.
9 Josiah [Rev.], b. 16 Nov. 1806; m. 3 March 1833, Phebe, dau. of Jacob and Rhoda (Thayer) Leavitt of Minot. He was a farmer and shoemaker. While yet a young man he was ordained a preacher of the F. W. Baptist denomination, and afterward preached in many places. The last years of his life were spent in Biddeford, where he died 8 July 1866, and his widow, 5 June 1880. Children:

1 George Parcher, b. 27 Jan. 1834, in Greene; m. 7 Dec. 1853, Andelusia C. Gould; died 31 Oct. 1855. He was a shoemaker and cotton-mill operative. He had no children, and his widow now lives with a sister in Biddeford.

2 Lovina Leavitt, b. 2 Oct. 1835, in Monmouth; d. 5 Jan. 1842.

3 Elias Graffam, b. 20 June 1837; d. 6 Jan. 1842.

4 Eunice Parcher Monroe, b. 18 Aug. 1839, in Leeds; m. 29 Jan. 1862, Wm. M. Lowell of Biddeford.

5 Lovina Leavitt, b. 18 June 1842, in Greene; died 6 Sept. 1853, in Biddeford.

10 Jane, b. 23 April 1810; m. Lewis Dillingham.

10-2-1-1

JEREMIAH LIBBY, born in Scarborough, 5 Nov. 1746; married 16 Nov. 1770, ANNA LIBBY, 1-1-6-6.

He was a farmer, He lived in Scarborough until after the birth of all his children, and then removed to Buxton and settled on a farm now owned in part by the heirs of Moses K. Wells, and in part by Ivory Libby, 10-2-1-1-9-1. He died 15 Nov. 1816. His widow died in Standish about 1826.

Children:

1 Ruth, b. 18 June 1771; m. 11 Sept. 1797, Benjamin Brown.
2 Josiah, b. 2 Jan. 1774; m. 1st, Sarah, 2d. Ruth, Elden.
3 Abigail Hubbard, b. 17 Dec. 1775; m. 4. Jan. 1798, Ebenezer Burnham.

4 Zachariah, b. 24 Dec. 1777; m. Priscilla Knight.
5 Joel, b. 22 Oct. 1780; m. Hannah Knight.
6 Jane, b. 15 Oct. 1782; m. 7 Sept. 1814, Capt. Increase Robinson of Standish; died 20 Mar. 1819. Previous to her marriage she bore a son:
  1 Phineas, b. 22 Feb. 1806; m. 1st, Susan Hancock; 2d, Clarissa A. Beede.
7 Hulda, b. 15 Mar. 1784; m. 1 April 1804, Isaac Stone.
8 Eunice, b. 2 Nov. 1787; m. 8 Jan. 1818, Jonathan Rumery.
9 Jeremiah, b. 9 June 1791; m. Emma Elden.
10 Lucy, b. 10 June 1795; died at the age of four years.

10-2-1-2

Theophilus Libby, born in Scarborough, 15 April 1749; married Hannah Berry, daughter of Jonathan and Relief (Nason) Berry.

He settled on land given him by his father, then in Scarborough, now in Gorham. He cleared a farm and built his house on the site of the one now occupied by the widow of Levi Libby, 10-2-1-2-3-8. He died 10 Nov. 1822. His wife died about 1803.

Children, all born in Scarborough:

1 Samuel, died at home, a young man.
2 Jonathan, b. Feb. 1774; m. Lydia Larrabee.
3 Ephraim, b. 28 Jan. 1781; m. Ruth Lord.
4 Relief, married Moses Smith.
5 Dorcas, m. 4 Feb. 1802, Samuel Brown.
6 Theophilus, m. Patty Sprague.
7 Elizabeth, b. 1785; m. Josiah Larrabee.
8 Sarah, b. Oct. 1788; m. Elder Seth Norton.
9 Richard H., b. 1796; m. Jane (Clark) Baker.
10 Ruth, b. 1797; died in May 1870; unm. She lived with her brother Richard.

10-2-1-5

Samuel Libby, born in Scarborough, 17 Dec. 1759; married 8 Jan. 1783, Abigail Graffam, daughter of Josiah and Catherine (Whidden) Graffam of Scarborough.

He was a farmer and lived where Enos Hubbard Libby, 10-2-1-5-13-2, now lives. He died very suddenly, of heart trouble, 8 March 1819. He was a Revolutionary soldier, and his widow drew a pension for his services. She died 9 March 1856.

Their children were:

1 Caleb, b. 19 Aug. 1783; d. 24 Oct. 1783.
2 Rebecca, b. 24 July 1784; m. Daniel Libby, 1-1-6-4-7.
3 Caleb, b. 14 Oct. 1786; m. 1st, Sarah Webster; 2d, Abbie Simonton; 3d, Sarah (Daniels) Flood.
4 Samuel, b. 25 Sept. 1788; d. 30 Sept. 1788.
5 Mary, b. 5 Aug. 1789; m. 27 Mar. 1836, Wm. Graffam.
6 Theophilus, b. 1 Mar. 1792; m. 1st, Deborah Webster; 2d, Sally Wood.
7 Catherine, b. 28 Dec. 1793; m. 7 Feb. 1813, Benjamin Moses of Durham.
8 Enos, b. 13 Oct. 1795; m. Lydia Libby, 5-7-15-5.
9 Abigail, b. 15 May 1797; m. 24 June 1832, Moses Whitney of Casco.
10 Samuel, b. 7 Mar. 1799; m. Mary Cleaves.
11 Eliza, b. 11 Jan. 1801; m. 19 Aug. 1821, Chas. Simpson of Kittery.
12 Jairus, b. 31 Mar. 1804; d. 14 Oct. 1805.
13 Jairus, b. 25 Oct. 1806; m. Hannah Stevens.

10-2-1-6

Richard Hubbard Libby, born in Scarborough, 27 Oct. 1763; married, 12 Jan. 1786, Anne Berry, daughter of Jane (Libby) Berry, 1-1-6-2.

He had his father's homestead on Scottow's Hill, and occupied it until he had passed the prime of life. He then sold it to Nathaniel Waterhouse, 10-2-2-12, and removed to Gardiner. He settled on the farm now occupied by Eben Libby, 10-2-1-6-3-1. He died 19 June 1837. His widow died 6 Feb. 1859.

Children:

1 Elizabeth, b. 6 Aug. 1786; m. 3 Dec. 1807, Robert Harmon.
2 Elisha, b. 16 Oct. 1788; m. Mary Edgecomb.
3 Joseph, b. 5 Aug. 1790; m. Lydia Libby, 5-2-3-1-1.
4 Asa, b. 16 May 1793; m. Sarah A. Caldwell.
5 John, b. 25 June 1795; m. Mercy Robinson.
6 Abial, b. 3 April 1798; d. 10 Oct. 1819; unm.
7 Phineas, b. 8 Feb. 1802; d. 6 Dec. 1818.
8 Emily, b. 17 Dec. 1806; d. 28 Nov. 1819.

10-2-2-11

Joseph Waterhouse, born in Scarborough, 12 Feb. 1754; married Lydia Harmon. He was a farmer, and lived at first near Scottow's Hill, but about 1782, removed to Standish Neck. His wife died 28 Mar. 1836, aged 80. He died 2 Aug. 1837. He was a Revolutionary pensioner.

Children:

1 Lydia (Waterhouse), bap. 3 Aug. 1777; m. —— Webb.
2 William Harmon (Waterhouse), m. Sarah B. Smith.
3 Elizabeth (Waterhouse), m. Joseph Nason.
4 Josiah (Waterhouse), m. Rebecca Brown of Windham.
5 Olive (Waterhouse), m. Edward Anderson of Windham.
6 Joseph (Waterhouse), died in Albany, Me.
7 Montgomery (Waterhouse), died 9 Oct. 1825, aged 23; unm.
8 Mary (Waterhouse), m. Wm. Davis of Limington. She was the mother of Hon. Wm. G. Davis of Portland.
9 Abigail (Waterhouse), m. Levi Haskell.
10 Martha (Waterhouse), m. Geo. Anderson of Windham.

10-2-4-2

Lemuel Libby, born about 1749, in Scarborough; married, 11 Nov. 1772, Mehitable Bragdon, daughter of Elisha and Mehitable (Jordan) Bragdon of Scarborough.

He was a farmer. He lived at first on Scottow's Hill, in a house that was afterward moved onto the Broad-turn road, and occupied by Thomas Henderson. He then settled in what is now Gorham, on land that had belonged to the Bragdons. He built a little house near the apple trees now standing away to the eastward of the present house. About 1796 he bought a house of a Mr. Frost, and moved it onto the farm, and lived in that until 1806, when he moved into a new house, built on the newly-completed road. This house was afterward sawed in two parts: the one part now forms the residence of Mrs. Laura McKenney, 10-2-4-2-2-1, and the other forms part of the house of Lewis J. Libby, 10-2-1-2-3-2-1. His wife died 24 May 1817. He died 28 Sept. 1829, aged 80.

Children, born in Scarborough:

1 Solomon, died an infant.
2 Sarah, b. 24 April 1774; died 31 Dec. 1872, in her 99th year. She was never married, but bore to Joseph Deering a child which took the name:
  1 Laura (Libby), b. 5 Sept. 1798; m. Oct. 1842, Jedediah McKenney of Danville.
3 Mehitable, m. 20 Feb. 1800, Timothy Plummer.
4 Elizabeth, m. 21 Dec. 1800, Israel Perry.
5 Solomon, died aged 3 years.
6 child, died in infancy.

Born in Gorham:

7 Lemuel, b. 10 Jan. 1784; m. Narcissa Harmon.
8 Abraham, b. 10 Dec. 1784; m. Phebe Moulton.
9 Lucy, m. Allison Libby, 1-1-3-9-2.
10 Mary, m. Samuel Small, 7 June 1810.
11 Hannah, b. July, 1789; m. Allison Libby, 1-1-3-9-2.
12 Darius, died aged 3 years.
13 Olive, died aged 6 months.
14 Darius, b. July, 1795; m. Phebe Small.
15 Apollos, b. May, 1798; d. Oct. 1801.

10-2-4-3

Dominicus Libby, born in Scarborough, 27 Dec. 1751; married, 4 Dec. 1781, Dorothy Small. [See p. 32.] He was a farmer, and lived where Henry Libby, 10-2-4-3-9-6, now lives. He died 18 Dec. 1822. His widow died 31 Oct. 1846.

Children, all born in Scarborough:

1 Elliot, b. 22 Dec. 1782; m. Nancy Boswell.
2 Samuel, b. 30 Aug. 1784; m. Sarah Beals.
3 Enoch, b. 23 Feb. 1787; m. Elizabeth Welch, Lavinia (Owen) Marshall, and Eliza Waterman.
4 Abigail, b. 24 Dec. 1788; m. 3 Jan. 1808, John Beals.
5 Jacob, b. 7 Aug. 1791; m. 19 Oct. 1820, Phebe, dau. of Dea. Edmund and Phebe (Cushing) Higgins. She died in Portland, 16 Sept. 1824. Jacob was a cooper. He died 15 Mar. 1870. No children.
6 Dominicus, b. 28 Sept. 1793; d. 18 May 1820; unm.
7 Abner, b. 17 Aug. 1797; m. Harriet Newbegin.
8 Cary, b. 9 Nov. 1798; m. ——— ———.
9 Hiram, b. 2 Dec. 1800; m. Mary Waterhouse.
10 Thaddeus, b. 10 Jan. 1803; m. Sarah Libby, 5-7-8-2-6. He was a farmer. In 1834 he moved to Saco, and there died, 22 Feb. 1841. His widow returned to her father, and had the homestead farm on Oak Hill. She died 10 Feb. 1880. Children:
  1 Drusilla, b. 3 June 1828; m. 20 April 1849, Frederick B. Hurlbert.
  2 Clarissa Dudley, b. 7 Sept. 1832; d. 8 Feb. 1845.
  3 Cornelia Caroline, b. 23 Dec. 1834; d. 8 April 1836.
  4 Georgianna, b. 20 Oct. 1836; m. R. M. Libby, 5-7-14-13-3.
  5 Thaddeus Alonzo, b. 14 Aug. 1840; unm.; lives on the homestead of his mother's father.
11 Sarah, b. 20 Dec. 1808; m. 26 June 1842, Josiah Mitchell.

10-2-4-8

Enoch Libby, born in Scarborough, about 1765; married first, 8 Mar. 1798, Rebecca Harmon, daughter of Samuel and Mary (Smith) Harmon; (died 15 Oct. 1816); second, 1 Jan. 1821, Abigail Libby, 10-5-4-1-6. He was a farmer, and lived on the farm now occupied by his oldest son. He died 25 Sept. 1843. His widow died 1872.

Children, by first wife:

1 Lot, b. 8 Dec. 1800; owns and occupies his father's homestead; a bachelor.
2 Rosanna, b. 9 Dec. 1802; m. 14 Oct. 1821, Rev. Stephen Waterhouse.
3 Betsey, b. 22 Mar. 1804; m. 17 Jan. 1822, Josiah Mitchell.
4 Rodney, b. 22 May 1805; m. 1st, Louisa F. Waterhouse, (sister of Stephen, above mentioned); 2d, Hannah Harmon.
5 Miranda, b. 17 Dec. 1807; m. as 2d wife, Rev. Stephen Waterhouse; died 18 Sept. 1881.
6 Leonard, b. 30 Oct. 1810; m. Martha A. Waterhouse.

By second wife:

7 Rebecca, b. 9 May 1823; m. 10 Nov. 1842, Francis S. Frost.
8 Andrew Jackson, b. 26 April 1829; m. 17 Oct. 1851, Charlotte M., dau. of Bradbury and Affie (Bryant) Woodman of Buxton. He was a farmer and lived on part of his father's farm. He died 21 Feb. 1880. Children:
 1, 2, infants, died unnamed.
 3 Ernest Albert, b. 30 Oct. 1864.
 4 William Bradbury, b. 12 May 1866.
 5 Leonard, b. 18 Mar. 1868.
 6 Stephen Waterhouse, b. 15 Feb. 1870.
 7 infant, born and died 11 April 1872.
 8 Frederick Jackson, b. 22 May 1873.

10-2-4-9

Samuel Libby, born in Scarborough, shortly previous to the Revolution; married Eleanor Patrick, daughter of Thomas and Catherine (Fickett) Patrick of Gorham. She died 18 Aug. 1833. He married second, 16 Aug. 1835, Mrs. Mehitable McLellan, daughter of Henry and Mercy Harmon. He always lived on his father's homestead, a farmer. He died 12 June 1854, and his widow married Benjamin Moses of Durham. She died 12 Mar. 1868.

Children, all by his first wife:

1 Patrick, b. 5 May 1811; m. Olive B. Foy.
2 Lorenzo Dow, b. 7 Feb. 1816; m. 1st, Ann Andrews; 2d, Martha Ellen Moore.
3 Samuel Manson, b. 13 Sept. 1829; m. 17 Feb. 1853, Hannah Jane, dau. of Dominicus Fogg, 9-8-1-11. He occupied the homestead farm. Children:
 1 Mary Frances, b. 24 Jan. 1854.
 2 William Loring, b. 27 Oct. 1855.
 3 Charles Sumner, b. 1 Mar. 1859.
 4 Lydia Elenor, b. 6 June 1862.
 5 Frank, b. 4 Jan., d. 18 May, 1864.
 6 Eliza Ella, b. 22 Nov. 1866.

10-4-1-1

JOSEPH LIBBY, born in Kittery, now Eliot, Me., 16 June 1750; married PRISCILLA CARL of Saco.

He was carried to Saco by his father, in infancy, and there grew up, a millwright and housewright, like his father. He however devoted himself more to farming than to mechanical pursuits, and, about 1780, became one of the early settlers of Limington. He cleared a farm close by Maloy Mountain, on which he died 6 Feb. 1835. His wife died 14 Oct. 1828.

Children:

1 Joseph, b. 7 Mar. 1773; m. 1st, Lydia Kennard; 2d, Lois (Pitman) Evans.
2 Benjamin, b. 30 April 1775; m. Margaret McArthur.
3 Sally, b. 4 April 1777; m. Dr. Samuel Thompson, 13 April 1802.
4 Daniel, b. 4 May 1779; m. Dorcas McDonald.
5 Shuah, b. 10 Nov. 1781; m. 25 Dec. 1799, Samuel Manson.
6 Patience, b. 14 Nov. 1783; d. 19 Nov. 1809; unm.
7 Gideon, b. 23 Feb. 1786; died of fever in the West Indies, a young man.
8 Mary, b. 29 Feb. 1788; m. 5 Sept. 1805, Samuel Edgerly.
9 David, b. 13 May 1790; left home a young man, and was never but once heard of afterward.
10 Martha, b. 3 May 1792; d. 8 May 1797.
11 Priscilla, b. 20 May 179 ; m. Simon Willett.
12 Harriet, b. 20 Feb. 1799; m. 1st, 13 May 1822, Aaron Higgins; 2d, John Lane.

10-4-1-6

DAVID LIBBY, born in Saco, Me., 25 March 1765; married, 17 Nov. 1793, ELIZABETH CLEAVES, daughter of Robert Cleaves of Saco, from Beverly, Mass. He was, like his father, an excellent wheelwright, but his chief occupation was farming. Soon after his marriage, he settled on a large farm on the Buxton road, in Saco, and there died 16 May 1811. His widow outlived him fifty years, and died 5 Nov. 1861, aged 91.

Children, all born in Saco:

1 Enoch Staples, b. 26 Aug. 1794; d. 18 Aug. 1795.
2 David, b. 30 Nov. 1796; m. Sally Berry.
3 Sarah, b. 21 March 1799; d. 26 Feb. 1837; unm.
4 Anna, b. 1 March 1801; m. 19 Nov. 1821, Edmund P. Dennett of Buxton; d. 2 Feb. 1842.
5 Joseph, b. 16 March 1803; m. 3 July 1836, Deborah, dau. of Geo. and Deborah (Beals) Chandler of Livermore. She died 27 Sept. 1839, and he married second, her sister Angelina. He is a shoemaker by trade. He lived in Boston eleven years preceding his marriage, and in Livermore, on the farm of his wife's father, seven years following. He has since lived in Saco. Child:
   1 Sarah Ann Elizabeth, b. 16 Aug. 1838; is unmarried.
6 Tristram, b. 4 May 1805; m. Sarah H. Butterfield and Dolly Belknap.
7 Elizabeth, b. 24 July 1807; m. Peter Eaton.
8 Daniel, b. 8 Oct. 1810; m. Dorcas G. Dennett.

10-4-1-8

Daniel Libby, born in Saco, Me., 28 March 1772; married, 1797, Mary Tarbox of Biddeford, born 10 March 1776. He lived on his father's homestead, a farmer and millwright. He died 3 Sept. 1842. His widow died 6 Sept. 1854.

Children, all born in Saco:

1 Shuah, b. 10 April 1798; m. 9 Jan. 1828, George Toppan. They lived on the homestead farm.
2 Martha, b. 22 Nov. 1799; m. John Welch; died 29 April 1832.
3 Joseph, b. 15 Sept. 1801; d. 15 July 1832; unm.
4 Mary, b. 13 May 1803; d. 15 July 1832; unm.
5 Eunice, b. 13 Mar. 1805; d. 6 Jan. 1835; unm.

10-4-3-2

George Libby, born in Kittery, now Eliot, Me., 21 Jan. 1760; married, 19 Nov. 1799, Mary Bartlett, daughter of Nathan Bartlett of Eliot. He always lived on his father's homestead, in the same house in which he was born; a farmer and cobbler. His wife died 28 Nov. 1814. He died 19 Oct. 1838.

Children, all born in Eliot.

1 Theodore, b. 28 Feb. 1800; was a bachelor and always lived on the homestead; died 23 Mar. 1871.
2 Sarah Ann, b. 20 July 1802; m. Dr. Benj. Colby of Saco.
3 Joseph, b. 5 Nov. 1804; d. 8 April 1806.
4 Mary Jane, b. 22 Jan. 1807; m. 16 Sept. 1830, John Moody of Lebanon.
5 Alice, b. 26 April 1809; m. Raymond Brooks of Alfred.
6 Asa, b. 22 Jan. 1813; m. Elizabeth R. Yeaton.

10-4-6-1

Gideon Libby, born in Eliot, (then Kittery), 2 Sept. 1772; married, 18 Jan. 1801, Anna Hammond, dau. of Jonathan and Elizabeth (Remmick) Hammond. About the time of his marriage, he settled on a farm on the "back road" in Eliot, and there lived and died. He always worked considerably as ship-carpenter. He died 6 April 1857. His widow died with her son Isaac, in the next house, 19 April 1857.

Children, all born in Eliot.

1 Simon, b. 10 Feb. 1802; was by trade a cabinet-maker, but followed the sea. He went several whaling voyages. At the time of his death, he was in the U. S. navy. He was lost in attempting to walk from Portsmouth to his home in Eliot during a snow storm, and several days later was found frozen to death in Spruce Creek. He died 26 Dec. 1837; unm.
2 Elizabeth, b. 26 Feb. 1804; m. Daniel Hill.
3 Isaac, b. 29 Dec. 1806; m. 19 June 1834, Sarah E., dau. of John Russell. He was a tanner by trade. At one time he carried on business in Shapleigh, but for the most part worked as journeyman, living in the next house to his father's. He died 12 July 1861. Children:
   1 Sarah Elizabeth, b. 11 Oct. 1835; m. Melville Hanscom.
   2 Olive Jane, b. 1 Dec. 1839; d. 1 Oct. 1840.
4 Jane H., b. 1 Mar. 1810; m. 1836, Daniel Goodwin.

10-4-6-3

Solomon Libby, born in Eliot, Me., 31 July 1777; married 15 Dec. 1806, Elizabeth Hammond, daughter of Jonathan and Elizabeth (Remmick) Hammond. During the few years immediately succeeding his marriage he kept a tavern near Spruce Creek. He then bought the farm now occupied by his son, and there died, 30 Jan. 1844. His widow died in Jacksonville, Fla., on a visit to her daughter, 22 May 1852.

Their children were:

1 Frances, b. 11 Aug. 1807; m. 1 Jan. 1829, Capt. Charles Willey of Portsmouth, N. H.

2 Hammond, b. 30 April 1814; m. 28 June 1838, Ann Maria, dau. of John Fogg, 9-9-9-3. At the age of 19, he began to go on coasting voyages. He continued five years, rising to mate. The three years following he was captain of a steamer on the St. Johns River, Florida. He has since tilled his father's homestead in Eliot. Children:

1 Fanny Yale, b. 20 May 1845; is unmarried.

2 Charles Albert, b. 6 Nov. 1847; obtained the trades of blacksmith and carriage-maker; is in business at Black's Station, Yolo Co., Cal.; unm.

10-5-1-1

Elisha Libby, born in Scarborough, 28 July 1754; married 16 Dec. 1777, Eunice Jones, daughter of Samuel Jones of Scarborough. He was a farmer. In 1782 or 3, he settled in Buxton on the farm now owned by Frank Nichols. There he died in July, 1821, and his widow 5 Sept. 1839.

Their children were:

1 Eunice, m. 12 Jan. 1800, Nathaniel Wilbur.

2 Samuel, b. 18 June 1780; m. Betsey Towle.

3 Phebe, b. 7 Mar. 1784; m. 23 Sept. 1802, Ethan Wilbur.

4 Jane, b. 18 June 1788; m. 14 June 1812, Josiah Edgerly.

5 Daniel, b. 28 Oct. 1790; m. Lydia Spencer.

6 Elisha, b. 11 April 1795; was a bachelor; lived with his brother Benjamin; died 23 Mar. 1868, only a day before his brother. They were both buried in one grave.

7 Benjamin, b. 31 May 1798; m. Clarissa Noble.

10-5-1-2

Moses Libby, born in Scarborough, 13 May 1756; married, 5 April 1781, Anna Libby, 11-7-1-2. He moved to Gray, Me., in March 1782, and settled on wild land, which he had received from his father. He first built a hovel, a log-house, with only one room, about four rods south of the present house, the middle portion of which he afterward built and moved into. He died in the latter part of May, 1804. His widow died Aug. 1827.

Children:

1 Moses, b. 25 Dec. 1781; m. Sally Lawrence.

2 Andrew, b. 20 Nov. 1786; m. Susan H. Small.

3 William, b. 27 Aug. 1791; always lived on the homestead, a bachelor; d. 15 July 1864.
4 Anna, b. 5 July 1795; m. 11 July 1819, Curtis Stiles.

10-5-1-4

BENJAMIN LIBBY, born in Scarborough, 17 Feb. 1760; married, 2 Dec. 1788, PHEBE RACKLIFF, daughter of Benjamin and Sarah (Jordan) Rackliff of Scarborough. He was a farmer. He removed to Gorham shortly after his marriage and settled on the farm now occupied by Martha A. (Libby) Wescott, 10-5-1-4-4-2. He lived in a log-house until about 1811, and then built the one now standing.

Children:

1 Solomon, b. 5 Oct. 1789, in Scarborough; m. Martha Fogg.
2 Anna, b. 27 Sept. 1791; m. 13 July 1815, Luther Flood.
3 Paulina, b. 17 Nov. 1793, in Gorham; m. 5 June 1815, Samuel Woodman of Buxton; d. 8 Feb. 1820.
4 Benjamin, b. 27 Sept. 1795; m. 1st, 1 Mar. 1821, Ann, dau. of Edmund and Hannah (Morton) Wescott; (died after seven weeks); 2d, 8 June 1823, Betsey, dau. of Abigail (Dam) Wescott, 11-7-5-4. He was a farmer and always lived on the homestead. He was out in the war of 1812, and served just long enough to draw a pension. His wife died 16 July 1866, and he married 3d, Nov. 1868, Lavinia (Harris) Tapley of New Gloucester, now living in Brownfield. He died 24 Mar. 1871. Children, all by his second wife:
   1 Martha, b. 8 Mar. 1824; d. 24 April 1824.
   2 Martha A., b. 14 June 1825; m. 21 Mar. 1847, Dr. William Wescott.
   3 Jordan P., b. 19 Feb. 1830; d. 4 Sept. 1846.
   4 Ai S., b. 13 May 1837; d. 8 Mar. 1843.
5 Elisha, b. 30 May 1797; d. 2 Feb. 1798.
6 Jordan, b. 28 Feb. 1799; d. Jan. 1820.
7 Hannah Rackliff, b. 5 Aug. 1801; d. 1 June 1868; unm.
8 Phebe, b. 31 Mar. 1804; m. 1st, 14 June 1827, Joseph F. Hamblin; 2d, Thomas Davis.
9 Martha, b. 3 Nov. 1807; died aged 18.

10-5-1-10

RUFUS LIBBY, born in Scarborough, 23 April 1777; married first, 13 Dec. 1798, CHARLOTTE PLUMMER, daughter of Jesse Plummer; (died 26 Jan. 1825); second, 27 Dec. 1825, Esther Libby, 11-7-11-5; (died 27 Jan. 1841); third, 1841, Mrs. Ann Lord, daughter of Abraham Bickford. Rufus Libby had his father's homestead. He always lived on it, and died 1854. His widow lives in Biddeford.

Children, all by his first wife:

1 Mary, b. 24 June 1799; m. as first wife, Parker Libby, 10-5-3-5-1.
2 Hannah, b. 29 Dec. 1800; m. her deceased sister Mary's husband.
3 Charlotte, b. 10 Dec. 1803; d. 8 Oct. 1827; unm.
4 Lydia, b. 28 Jan. 1805; m. George Libby, 11-7-11-8.
5 Eliza, b. 1 Feb. 1807; d. 14 Oct. 1829; unm.
6 Osgood, b. 18 Sept. 1810; m. Eliza Plummer and Deborah (Roberts) Sawyer.

7 Cornelius, b. 19 July 1813; m. 2 May 1841, in Wales, Me., Lucy Ann, dau. of Rufus Marr, 1-6-3-2-9. He has resided successively in Scarborough, Wales, Farmingdale, Litchfield, and, since 1870, in Wales. He has been employed successively and conjointly as farmer, ship-carpenter, country trader, and house-carpenter. Children, born in Wales:
   1 Hattie L., b. 16 Mar. 1844; m. 3 Dec. 1877, Stanwood Given.
   2 Mary R. E., b. 11 July 1847; d. 18 Aug. 1863, in Wales.
8 Ellen, b. 3 Aug. 1816; d. 27 Nov. 1821.

10-5-2-1

Mark Libby, born in Scarborough, 2 Mar. 1751; married 6 Nov. 1770, Relief Berry of Scarborough. He bought of James Gray of Saco, the farm in Scarborough on which he ever afterward lived. There was a house on the farm when he bought it, but he afterward tore it down and moved the Mitchell house onto the same site. In that he died, 6 Nov. 1840, aged 91. His widow died 12 Jan. 1844, aged 92.

Children, all born in Scarborough:

1 Reuben, b. 13 Sept. 1772; m. Dorothy Libby, 10-5-5-12.
2 Mercy, b. Oct. 1777; d. 24 July 1831; unm.
3 Hannah, bap. 30 Sept. 1779; d. in infancy.
4 Hannah, b. 2 April 1782; m. 1808, William Ingalls.

10-5-2-3

Reuben Libby, born in Scarborough, 3 Mar. 1755; married 15 Nov. 1781, Mercy Marr, 1-5-3-2-3. After his family was mostly grown up he removed to Gardiner and settled on a farm. He died about 1822. His widow died about 1841.

Children:

1 Sally Hanscom, b. 21 Sept. 1783; m. 5 Oct. 1805, Reuben Dyer of Cape Elizabeth.
2 Samuel Marr, b. 23 Dec. 1785; m. Mercy Dyer, and Sarah (Libby) Brown, 11-7-8-3-1.
3 Octavia, b. 28 Jan. 1788; m. 3 July 1805, James Sawyer of Cape Elizabeth.
4 Pemala, b. 11 May 1790; m. Silas Bartlett.
5 Cyprus, b. 27 Feb. 1794; m. Sarah Maxwell.
6 Sewall, b. 4 Dec. 1797; m. Catherine Haley.
7 Abigail, b. 9 Aug. 1799; m. 1st, Josiah Dill; 2d, Reuben Dyer, the same that married her sister.

10-5-2-9

Samuel Small Libby, born in Scarborough, 2 May 1781; married Rebecca (Ross) Borden, widow of Seth Borden, and dau. of Robert and —— (Hewey) Ross of Wales. In 1809 he moved to Wales and settled on the homestead of his wife's father. He always lived there afterward, and died 23 Dec. 1839. His widow died 25 Mar. 1843.

Children:

1 Seth, b. 5 June 1806, in Webster; m. Susan Alexander.
2 Rebecca, b. Jan. 1808, in Webster; m. H. N. Alexander.
3 Samuel King, b. 13 Feb. 1810, in Wales; m. 15 Feb. 1837, Eliza, dau. of Capt. Joseph and Mary (Gray) Jack. He was a farmer in Litchfield, where his widow now lives. He died 20 Mar. 1872. Children:
  1 Joseph E., b. 13 Feb. 1839, in Wales; was lieutenant of Co. B, 15th Maine Vol.; died at Carrolton, La., 6 Sept. 1863; unm.
  2 Mary J., b. 6 Aug. 1844, in Wales; m. 28 Aug. 1864, Wm. H. Bosworth.
  3 Eliza E., b. 2 April 1847, in Wales; d. 19 Nov. 1865.
  4 Samuel E., b. 28 April 1853, in Litchfield; d. 13 April 1859.
4 Hannah, b. 10 June 1812; m. Enos Wilkins of Greene.
5 Jane, b. 12 Oct. 1816; m. Joseph Jack of Litchfield.
6 Mary Elizabeth, b. 16 Sept. 1820; m. Harvey Jack.
7 Josiah, b. 29 Mar. 1822. He removed to Massachusetts, where he married Olive Langley of Charlestown. She died a year later, and he afterward went to California, where he died, 10 Dec. 1869. No children.

10-5-2-11

Rufus King Libby, born in Scarborough, 30 Sept. 1788; married, 17 Nov. 1812, Roxanna Jones, daughter of Phineas and Ruth (Ames) Jones. He always lived on his father's homestead in Webster. His first wife, the mother of his children, died 20 Nov. 1842. 16 June 1843, he married Betsey, daughter of Josiah Jones of Lewiston. He died 7 May 1867.

Children, all born in Webster:

1 Ruth J., b. 21 Jan. 1813; m. 14 Jan. 1837, Phineas Wright.
2 Elizabeth J., b. 2 April 1815; m. 21 Oct. 1838, Samuel Haley.
3 Rufus, b. 30 July 1817; d. 21 Nov. 1843; unm.
4 Phineas J., b. 21 June 1821; m. 22 Sept. 1844, Salenda T., dau. of Dominicus and Lety (Jones) Weymouth, of New Portland. He was at first a farmer; afterward a butcher. He died in Lewiston 10 Nov. 1852. His widow married G. Henry Nevenes. Children:
  1 Georgianna C., b. 13 June 1845; d. 6 Dec. 1854.
  2 Roscoe W., b. 13 April 1847; m. 13 Dec. 1870, Sarah J., dau. of Kingman D. and Jane F. (Adams) Oakes of Dover. He is a painter in Salem, Mass. Children:
    1 Eda May, b. 14 Oct. 1871, in Dover; d. 30 Dec. 1871.
    2 Willie C., b. 10 Feb. 1873, in Dover; d. 20 Oct. 1876.
    3 Harry L., b. 5 July 1876, in Salem.
    4 Edith M., b. 2 March 1878.
    5 Frank W., b. 2 June 1880.
  3 Emma H., b. 6 Dec. 1851; d. 15 Oct. 1853.
  4 Mary E., b. 21 March 1853; m. 13 June 1872, Abram Butts.
5 Elbridge G., b. 16 Jan. 1825; m. 9 Jan. 1850, Martha V., dau. of Nathaniel and Betsey (Witherell) Getchell of Monmouth. He is a farmer. He lived in Wales during the first fifteen years of his married life, and then settled on the homestead in Webster. Children, all born in Wales:
  1 Roxanna E., b. 11 Oct. 1850; m. Henry Annis.
  2 Charles H., b. 12 Sept. 1853; d. 3 Mar. 1854.
  3 Minnie J., b. 19 June 1858; d. 24 Oct. 1869.
6 Samuel M., b. 2 Sept. 1828; m. 10 July 1860, Charlotte M., dau. of Joseph and Polly (Read) Dill of Lewiston, where he now lives, a soap manufacturer. Children, so far as known:

1 Edith G., b. 1866.
2 Frank H., b. 1869.

7 Charles, b. 1830; died the next year.

8 Charles E., b. 7 May 1834; m. 28 May 1859, Elizabeth, dau. of Jonathan and Betsey (Alexander) Colby of Webster. He is a farmer. He lived with his parents until seven years after his marriage, and then settled on the farm in Wales on which he now lives. Child:

1 Irvin R., b. 18 Mar. 1867.

10-5-3-4

JOHN SKILLINGS LIBBY, born in Scarborough, 23 Nov. 1761; married, 15 Feb. 1787, RHODA CUMMINGS of Cape Elizabeth. He was a farmer and lived where now lives John S. Libby, 10-5-3-4-7-2. Samuel Libby records his death: "1807, Dec. 8th. John Libby died in a cave. He has been crazy about nine months." His widow died 28 Aug. 1849, aged 86.

Children, all born in Scarborough:

1 Mark, b. 11 July 1787; d. 22 Oct. 1807. Samuel Libby records: "Mark Libby died in the 21 year of his age. Death occasioned by his horse starting: ran against Theodore Libby's bayonet and ran it into his side: lived nine days after." It was at a militia muster. Theodore Libby referred to, is 11-7-2-7.

2 Lydia, b. 18 Jan. 1789; d. 11 Jan. 1834; unm. She was crazy, and was confined in a small building. After repeated efforts, she one day set fire to this, and died a few days later, from her burns.

3 Eunice, b. 25 Dec. 1791; m. 12 Oct. 1812, Edward Skillings.

4 Eliakim, b. 19 Sept. 1793. He always lived on the homestead, and died 15 Feb. 1857, a bachelor.

5 Thomas, b. 7 Jan. 1795; died in the war of 1812.

6 Nathan, b. 4 Jan. 1797; m. Mary L. Babb.

7 Isaiah, b. 17 May 1799; m. Elmira Skillings and Miriam Butterfield.

8 William, b. about 1803; m. 5 June 1828, Lucy, dau. of Simeon and Rebecca (Skillings) Skillings. He was a sailor, and died 6 June 1845. His widow died 8 Jan. 1871. Children, all born in Scarborough:

1 Sarah Maria, b. 9 May 1828; m. David B. Libby, 10-5-3-4-6-1.

2 William Johnson, b. 22 Aug. 1832; is a farmer in Scarborough; bachelor.

3 Lydia Ellen, b. 9 June 1838; m. Dennis Libby Green, son of Mary (Libby) Green, 1-4-1-6-4-3.

9 Mehitable, b. 25 Dec. 1805; m. Andrew Taylor.

10 John Skillings, b. 15 Oct. 1807; m. Eliza Berry.

10-5-3-5

AMOS LIBBY, born in Scarborough, 1 Dec. 1763; married, 25 Oct. 1792, SARAH HUNNEWELL, 7-1-5-4. He always lived on his father's homestead. His death occurred 14 May 1840. His widow died 18 Jan. 1851.

Children, all born in Scarborough:

1 Parker, b. 12 Aug. 1795; m. 1st, 28 April 1819, Mary Libby, 10-5-1-10-1; (died 8 July 1821); 2d, her sister Hannah, 14 April 1822. He was a farmer, and lived in Cape Elizabeth, where his son Geo. O. afterward lived. Children, all born in Cape Elizabeth, by first wife:

1 Sarah, b. 6 June 1820; m. 8 Feb. 1843, Freeman Scammon of Weld.

By second wife:

2 Rufus, b. 10 Nov. 1823; d. 22 May 1824.
3 Polly, b. 2 April 1824; d. 5 Oct. 1826.
4 Charlotte, b. 7 June 1826; m. 1st, John L. Moody, 5-7-10-6-8; 2d, Zebulon T. Libby, 11-7-2-6-4-3.
5 Mary E., b. 17 March, d. 1 June, 1828.
6 Hannah E., b. 12 May 1829; d. 15 Feb. 1851; unm.
7 infant, born and died 11 April 1831.
8 Lydia, b. 16 April 1832; m. 17 June 1858, Daniel Plummer.
9 Drusilla, b. 6 Sept. 1834; m. 27 Aug. 1865, Horace A. Wright.
10 Lucinda, b. 14 Oct. 1836; d. 15 Nov. 1838.
11 George Osgood, b. 3 Jan. 1839; m. 25 Dec. 1878, Diana R., dau. of Oliver and Sarah A. (Ricker) Boothby of Saco. He was a farmer. He lived on his father's homestead, and died very suddenly, 26 Aug. 1881. No children.
12 Lucy Ellen, b. 27 April 1841; m. 10 Nov. 1868, Ezra R. Wright.
13 Deborah F., b. 15 June 1843; is deaf and dumb; lives at home.

2 Dorcas, b. 21 Feb. 1796; never married; lived with her brother Amos on the homestead until he died, and has since lived with Dexter.
3 Polly, b. Nov. 1797; died 10 April 1799.
4 Elihu, b. 14 May 1800; m. Nancy Dyer.
5 daughter, died in infancy.
6 Enos, b. 8 Sept. 1805; m. Dorcas Stone.
7 Amos, b. 16 Aug. 1807; d. 6 Dec. 1875. He was a bachelor, and always lived on the homestead.
8 Mark, b. 22 June 1810; m. 26 Jan. 1837, Jane Libby, 1-1-3-9-9-1; (died 2 Jan. 1842); 2d, Elizabeth, dau. of Benjamin and Lois (Philips) Hatch of Wells. He settled on a farm near his father's, and has lived there since. Children:
  1 Eliza Jane, b. 30 Jan. 1839; d. 2 Mar 1853.
  2 Julia A., b. 22 July 1841; m. 11 Dec. 1861, John E. Brazier of Portland, fresco-painter. Children:
    1 Charles John (Brazier), b. 27 Nov. 1862.
    2 Grace Isabelle (Brazier), b. 25 Feb. 1866.
  3 Lucinda A., b. 21 Feb. 1843; m. 1 July 1863, Geo. E. Gilman of Scarborough.
  4 Priscilla Florilla, b. 30 Sept. 1845; m. 10 Sept. 1866, David L. Newcomb of Portland, cooper. He is a son of Jesse R. Newcomb of Scarborough. No children.
9 Dexter, b. 5 April 1816; m. 10 June 1840, Eliza Libby, 5-7-15-3-1. He settled on the north part of the homestead of his wife's grandfather Libby, and still lives there. Children:
  1 Emily Jane, b. 29 March 1841; m. 29 March 1866, Edwin Moody; d. 19 June 1871.
  2 Eliza Frances, b. 5 Jan. 1849; is unm.
  3 Amos Fred, b. 15 April 1863.

10-5-4-1

SIMEON LIBBY, born in Scarborough, 3 Sept. 1755; married, first, 22 Dec. 1783, ABIGAIL SMITH of Biddeford; (died 8 May 1802); second, 24 June 1807, MRS. ANN PHINNEY, daughter of Simon Huston.

He served through the Revolutionary war, and for a number of years afterward followed coasting. Shortly after his marriage he removed to Gorham, and settled on the farm now owned by Lewis Libby, 10-5-4-1-8-3. He died 11 March 1830. His widow died 7 Jan. 1849.

Children, by first wife; born in Scarborough:

1 Simeon, b. 11 Jan. 1784; m. Sally Lombard.
2 Joseph Cutts, b. 4 Dec. 1785; m. Betsey and Love Phinney.

Born in Gorham:

3 Rebecca, b. 4 Oct. 1787; m. 26 Dec. 1819, Benjamin Carsley.
4 Olive, b. 10 March 1790; m. Caleb Richardson.
5 Daniel, b. 18 March 1792; m. Martha and Alice Morton.
6 Abigail, b. 28 June 1794; m. Enoch Libby, 10-2-4-8.
7 Samuel, b. 21 April 1797; d. 18 April 1822; unm. He was a school-teacher.
8 Ai, b. 21 Nov. 1799; m. Martha Skillings and Elizabeth Files.

By second wife:

9 Stephen, b. 8 Aug. 1808. He followed the sea from his 16th year. He went on a whaling voyage about 1845, and was never afterward heard from.

10-5-4-2

Allison Libby, born in Scarborough, 6 April 1757; married, 15 Feb. 1781, Sarah Dam, 11-7-5-3.

He served through the Revolution. After the war, he became one of the first settlers of the northern part of Gorham. The removal took place in February. There was no road from Scarborough to Gorham Corner, nor to Saccarappa. His only route was by Stroudwater Village. From Stroudwater he went back to Saccarappa, thence by a logging road into Windham, crossed the river on the ice at Horse-beef falls, and then by another logging road, with all his possessions loaded upon an ox-sled, reached his lonely home.

There he cleared the farm now occupied by Wm. Wescott, and lived until his death, 14 May 1816. His widow married, second, 20 March 1825, Major Daniel Small of Limington, and died in Gorham, 23 Feb. 1849, aged 88.

Children, born in Scarborough:

1 Sarah, b. 14 Sept. 1781; m. Daniel Brown.
2 Olive, b. 5 Mar. 1783; d. June 1786, in Gorham.
3 Ephraim, b. 30 Oct. 1784; m. Mary Blake.

Born in Gorham:

4 Allison, b. 8 Mar. 1787; m. Lois Cross.
5 Thomas, b. 22 Jan. 1789; d. 8 July 1807.
6 Abigail, b. 24 Feb. 1791; m. 28 Feb. 1819, James Thomes of Gorham.
7 Hugh, b. 26 May 1793; m. Theodosia Small.
8 Henry, b. 15 July 1795; m. Dorcas Jordan.
9 Joseph, b. 11 Sept. 1797; m. Eunice Lombard.
10 James, b. 20 Jan. 1800; m. 14 Nov. 1832, Esther P., dau. of Jane (Libby) Irish, 10-5-1-8. Right after his marriage, he settled on the farm now occupied by Jacob Irish. In 1836, he sold that and bought the place on which his children now live. He died 18 Mar. 1864. His widow died 11 April 1876. Children:
   1 Benjamin Irish, b. 12 Nov. 1833; unm.
   2 Elizabeth Ann, b. 28 Sept. 1835; m. 19 Dec. 1857, Lemuel Jordan of Raymond.

3 Sarah Small, b. 7 Jan. 1841; d. 6 Oct. 1875; unm.
4 Ephraim, b. 19 April 1846; is a bachelor.
5 Lauriette, b. 8 Feb., d. 21 Mar., 1850.

11 Bryant, b. 22 Feb. 1802; m. 10 Feb. 1829, in Lagrange, Elizabeth, dau. of John and Elizabeth (Jackson) Waterhouse of Poland. He, with his two younger brothers, settled in what is now Lagrange, Me., and built the third log cabin which was built within the present limits of the town. His two brothers were dissatisfied and returned, but he cleared a farm there and made a permanent settlement. He took an active interest in town matters, and for a number of years filled the positions of selectman and town treasurer. In March 1847, he moved back to Gorham and took his mother to live with him. He lived on a farm now owned by —— Jackson, and died there 23 Feb. 1858. His widow died 22 July 1878, in Saccarappa.

Children, all born in Lagrange:

1 Eliza Jane, b. 28 Oct. 1831; d. 23 Dec. 1831.
2 Mary Abby, b. 21 Oct. 1832; m. 31 May 1856, Eben L. Nason of Westbrook.
3 Sarah S., b. 24 May 1835; m. 2 Oct. 1855, Dwinal Pride of Westbrook.
4 William H., b. 1 Dec. 1836; m. 18 Oct. 1862, Susan A. Ward of Windham. Soon after his father's death, he became a clerk in a hotel in Portland, and at length married the proprietor's daughter. They afterward moved onto a farm in Windham, and there he has since lived. He now carries on a stage business between North Windham and Portland. No children.
5 Bryant, b. 26 Dec. 1846; m. 24 Dec. 1879, Viola, dau. of John and Lucretia (Wood) Newcomb of Harrison. He is a teamster in Bridgton. No children.

12 Lothrop, b. 14 May 1804; m. 21 Sept. 1837, Frances, dau. of Asa and Frances (Jackson) Knight of Westbrook. Previous to his marriage he cleared himself a farm in Lagrange and another in Corinth. Upon his marriage he bought mills in Westbrook. From 1840 he was for 18 years superintendent of the Cumberland and Oxford Canal. Since giving up that position he has been a farmer in what is now Deering. Children, all born in Westbrook, now Deering:

1 Martha Jane, b. 4 July 1838; m. 23 Feb. 1867, Edward D. Starbird of Deering.
2 Leonice, b. 26 Oct. 1840; m. 22 Feb. 1862, Benj. S. Cobb of Deering.
3 Louisa, b. 15 Nov. 1842; m. 11 Sept. 1878, Andrew Fisher of Hyde Park, Mass.
4 Emeline, b. 24 Jan. 1845; m. 22 Aug. 1865, Jesse Gay of Saco.
5 Josephine, b. 23 Nov. 1847; m. 23 Nov. 1865, Charles H. Cobb.
6 Noah, b. 10 Oct. 1850; d. 20 Jan. 1852.

13 Jeremiah Noyes, b. 12 Jan. 1808; m. Lucy Bangs.

10-5-4-3

EDWARD LIBBY, born in Scarborough, 10 Feb. 1859; married 2 Oct. 1791, ELIZABETH LIBBY, 11-7-7-2.

Although but a boy, he was at the battle of Bunker Hill, and served all through the war of the Revolution. After the war he bought land in Gorham, cleared a portion of it, and built a log-house. He then went to Scarborough, married Elizabeth, and took her to her wilderness home. There they lived and died: he, 15 Mar. 1848; she, 27 April 1853.

Children, all born in Gorham:

1 Sewall, b. 10 Jan. 1793; m. Achsah Hall.
2 Dorothy, b. 4 Sept. 1794; m. Thomas Johnson.
3 Sarah, b. 11 June 1796; m. 4 Feb. 1823, John, son of Hannah (Libby) Jones, 10-5-4-9.
4 Gardner, b. 22 Jan. 1798; m. Hannah Moulton.
5 Hannah, b. 18 Jan. 1800; m. 22 Sept. 1823, Reuben Shaw.
6 Marrett, b. 3 May 1802; m. Mary Libby, 1-1-2-2-4-6.
7 Eliza, b. 8 May 1804; m. 1st, 4 Dec. 1822, John Johnson; 2d, Wm. Johnson.
8 Joseph, b. 10 March 1806; m. Mary Allison Libby, 10-5-4-15-2.
9 Alvah, b. 11 Feb. 1808; m. Ann Harmon.
10 Ebenezer How, b. 22 Dec. 1810; m. Catherine R. Irish.
11 Maria G., b. 9 April 1813; d. 10 Oct. 1832.

10-5-4-7

MARK LIBBY, born in Scarborough, 15 Feb. 1765; married, 24 May 1785, ANNA LIBBY, 10-5-1-7.

He was one of the early settlers of Unity. The removal took place when Samuel was an infant. The mother, with him in her arms, accomplished the entire distance on horseback. Their only guides were spotted trees, which enabled them to keep the bridle-path. He built his log cabin on the spot where he ever afterward lived, and, in process of time, cleared a good farm.

He and his wife were members of the Methodist Church. He died 22 June 1838, and she 12 Sept. 1850.

Children:

1 Anna, b. 1787; m. 1806, John McDaniel. He married second, her aunt, Lucy Libby.
2 Rufus, b. 1789; died 1808.
3 Mark, b. 1791; died 1814, in Plattsburgh, N. Y. His death was occasioned by his being prematurely ordered on duty after recovering from the measles. He took cold and died.
4 Samuel Dean, b. 24 March 1793; m. Betsey Libby, 10-1-6-5-4-1.
5 Abigail, b. 4 Sept. 1797; m. David Libby, 10-1-6-5-4.
6 Sally, b. 1 June 1802; unm.; lives on the homestead.
7 Elisha, b. 12 April 1805; m. Sarah Patterson.
8 Allison, b. 12 April 1807; m. Sarah J. Mitchell.
9 Rufus B., b. 6 Nov. 1809; is a bachelor; lives on the homestead.

10-5-4-10

JOSIAH S. LIBBY, born in Scarborough, 21 Oct. 1773; married first, 22 June 1796, SARAH LIBBY, 11-7-11-2; (died 31 Mar. 1798, in Pownal); second, 3 Feb. 1806, LYDIA (HARMON) DAVIS of Durham, widow of Aaron Davis of Portland.

He went to Pownal a young man, built a log hut in the midst of the woods, cleared a little land, and lived there some time alone. Thither, later, he took his wife, and there she died. Left alone with his infant daughter, he returned to Scarborough, and for eight years worked for his father-in-law. He then married again, and went back to his farm in Pownal, and there lived until his death, which occurred 14 Nov. 1841. His widow died Feb. 1870.

Children, by first wife:

1 Sarah, b. 6 Dec. 1797; never married. She always lived in the family of her uncle, George Libby, and became a "second mother" to his orphaned children. She died 22 Jan. 1863.

By second wife:

2 Daniel, b. 25 Dec. 1807; married 5 Jan. 1862, Sarah E. Libby, 10-2-1-2-3-10-1. He always lived on his father's homestead, and died 23 Nov. 1878, leaving a family of small children, who still retain the farm. His wife died 9 July 1875. Children:
  1 Mary Etta, b. 30 Dec. 1862; is a teacher.
  2 Thomas Lester, b. 27 Nov. 1864.
  3 Charlotte Emma, b. 18 Dec. 1866.
  4 Irving Roscoe, b. 14 April 1868.
  5 Howard Josiah, b. 12 Aug. 1871.
  6 Sarah Maud, b. 4 July 1875; d. 8 Sept. 1875.

3 Eliza Ann, b. 26 Mar. 1809; m. Wm. Tufts.

4 Esther, b. 26 Feb. 1811; m. Ephraim White.

5 Harriet, b. 3 Aug. 1813; m. 1st, 27 Sept. 1838, Perez Chapin Brown; 2d, Geo. Chapman.

6 Hiram L., b. 29 Dec. 1815; d. 27 July 1873. He lived always on the homestead, a bachelor.

7 Aaron, b. 29 April 1818; m. 26 Jan. 1845, Mercy Libby, 1-1-3-9-10-2. He settled, and still lives, on part of his father's homestead. Children:
  1 Sarah Frances, b. 24 Oct. 1845; m. Geo. W. Larrabee.
  2 Josiah Hanson, b. 6 Aug. 1847; m. 17 Jan. 1877, Luella A., dau. of Anthony and Lydia (Jordan) Frost of Pownal. He lived at home until his marriage, and then settled on his wife's father's farm. Besides being a farmer, he, and his father also, are makers of hay-poles. Children:
    1 Alice Cecil, b. 21 Dec. 1877.
    2 Ada Rose, b. 3 Oct. 1879.
  3 Ada Antoinette, b. 2 Aug. 1852; d. 23 Sept. 1879; unm.
  4 Willie Tufts, b. 13 April 1859.

8 John Robinson, b. 25 July 1821; d. 28 Feb. 1822.

9 Josiah, b. 4 Sept. 1824; was a carriage-maker; died in Boston of small-pox, 25 Jan. 1846; unm.

10 Lydia, b. 22 May 1827; m. William Brown.

10-5-4-13

MORRIS LIBBY, born in Scarborough, 7 Sept. 1780; married MARY ANN SWAIN, daughter of Eliphalet and Mollie (Shaw) Swain of Wilton.

He was a farmer. After the death of his father he went to live with his sister Charlotte in Jay. He lived in Wilton after his marriage until 1834, when he removed to Avon. In Avon he lived until his death, which took place 18 Jan. 1860. He was a member of the Methodist Church. His wife died in May, 1864.

Children, all born in Wilton:

1 Rufus Winn, b. 21 May 1820; m. 1st, 16 Nov. 1843, Ruth B., dau. of Rev. Henry Cushman; (died 26 Mar. 1847); 2d, 7 Nov. 1849, Betsey, dau. of William and Mary (Dyer) Phillips of Weld. He always lived in Avon, and died there 24 Nov. 1858. He was a farmer and school-teacher: a member of the Methodist Church. His widow married, 28 May 1866, Rodney Stearns of Weld. Children, by first wife:
  1 Augusta, b. 18 Sept. 1844; m. Alexander Flanders.
  2 Helena, b. 18 Feb. 1846; m. Charles Clemons.

By second wife:

3 Charles, b. 21 Dec. 1850; d. 7 Aug. 1852.
4 Sarah Jane. b. 31 Oct 1852; m. 24 June 1871, Benj. Rand; died 1 Feb. 1878. Children:
 1 Henry L. (Rand), b. 2 June 1872.
 2 Jennie B. (Rand), b. 12 July 1875.
5 Florida D., b. 31 Aug. 1854; d. 14 Mar. 1861.
6 Lewis R., b. 4 April 1857; m. Leora, dau. of Thomas and Hannah (Parker) Carleton; died 4 Feb. 1874, having outlived his wife. Child:
 1 Mabel L., b. 19 May 1873; lives with Mrs. Stearns.
7 Clara Maria, b. 28 July 1859; d. 11 Dec. 1879.

2 Mary Ann, b. 27 Aug. 1822; m. Daniel Robinson. Her daughter, Lelia Josephine Robinson, has taken the regular course through the Boston Law School, and has just been refused admission to the bar.
3 Sally Esther Lancaster, b. 16 July 1827; m. Ebenezer Averill Butterfield.

10-5-4-15

Solomon Libby, born in Scarborough, 23 March 1785; married Fanny Sylvester of Freeport, Me. He went to Freeport when he was 21, and went to work in a ship-yard. After his marriage he removed to Brunswick, where he settled on a place now owned by Benjamin Morse. He worked as ship-carpenter in many of the near towns. His wife died in 1843, and he in 1861.

Children, all born in Brunswick:

1 Cyrus T., b. 22 Jan. 1808; m. Rebecca Strout of Cape Elizabeth. He learned the carpenter's trade in Portland, and soon after removed to Illinois, where he went into business. He died about 1870, and his widow two years later. Children:
 1 Rebecca, born in Portland.
 2 Susan, born in Illinois.
2 Mary Allison, b. 8 April 1810; m. Joseph Libby, 10-5-4-3-8.
3 Joseph Varney, b. 15 April 1812; m. 20 Sept. 1836, Mary Ann Libby, 10-5-4-1-2-3. He was a house-carpenter. Soon after his marriage he settled in Gorham, on the place now occupied by his son, Cyrus S. Libby. He died Oct. 1872. His widow still lives in Gorham. Children:
 1 Lizzie Rensselaer, b. 27 Sept. 1838; m. Feb. 1871, Joseph Hine of Schofield, Mich.
 2 Cyrus S., b. 9 Feb. 1841; m. Sept. 1866, Martha, dau. of Wyer and Patience (Ayer) Pike of Cornish. He is a carpenter. Children:
  1 Cora Estelle, b. 8 Dec. 1868.
  2 Lauranda Clements, b. 14 April 1870.
 3 Charles F., b. 27 Jan. 1843; d. 11 Feb. 1844.
 4 Frances Ann, b. 3 Jan. 1845; is unmarried.
 5 Catherine Elder, b. 15 July 1850; d. 27 Sept. 1850.
 6 Randall E., b. 20 July 1852; d. 22 Sept. 1852.
 7 Lulu M., b. 1 March 1856; d. 1 Aug. 1856.
4 Desire L., b. 22 Nov. 1817; m. Lebbeus Ward.
5 Frances Jane, b. 22 Jan. 1820; m. 1st, 4 Jan. 1847, Frederick A. DeCreney; 2d, Isaac Varney.
6 Esther A., b. 21 Aug. 1824; m. Walter Breckinbridge of Arkansas.
7 Solomon, b. Sept. 1826; m. Lucy Scopeland of Brunswick. He learned the carpenter's trade, and was many years in business in Brunswick. About 1860 he removed to Oakland, Cal., where he has since been in business. No children.

10-5-4-16

DEMAS LIBBY, born in Scarborough, 4 May 1787; married, 1 Oct. 1807, MARY BERRY, daughter of Solomon and Hannah (Jones) Berry of Scarborough. He was a farmer, and always lived on his father's homestead. He died 20 April 1872. His wife died 7 Oct. 1856.

Children, all born in Scarborough:

1 Solomon, b. 23 July 1808; m. 18 Sept. 1834, Abigail, dau. of Thomas and Mary (McKenney) Jackson of Cape Elizabeth. Almost immediately after his marriage he settled on the farm in Gorham now occupied by his widow. He died 19 July 1875. Children:
  1 Ellen, b. 24 July 1836; m. 31 Dec. 1863, Daniel Wescott; d. 31 Oct. 1877.
  2 Ivory, b. 21 Sept. 1839; m. 2 Jan. 1868, his cousin, Susan A., dau. of Henry S. and Abigail (Stevens) Jackson. Soon after his marriage, he bought and settled on the farm in South Windham, on which he has since lived. Children:
    1, 2 died in infancy.
    3 Ruth Ella, b. 28 Dec. 1876.
  3 Mary Abigail, b. 16 Oct. 1846; m. 1st, 14 Sept. 1867, William R. Maybury; 2d, her cousin, Henry B. Jackson.
  4 Maranda Jane, b. 17 Aug. 1851; is unm.
2 Ivory, b. 22 April 1810; d. 23 Sept. 1847; unm.
3 Allison, b. 6 May 1813; d. 9 June 1813.
4 Demas, b. 8 July 1815; m. Mehitable Libby, 1-1-3-9-2-6.
5 Lewis, b. 18 Aug. 1820; d. 2 Jan. 1821.

10-5-5-1

ROBERT LIBBY, born in Scarborough, 20 Oct. 1761; married ELIZABETH MARCH, 11-6-1-5.

After his marriage he lived awhile with his uncle Roger Libby, 1-1-2-3. He then settled in Limington and cleared the farm now occupied by Shirley Libby, 10-5-5-10-3. About 1830, he sold this and went to live with his daughters in Sebago, where his wife died, 21 Mar. 1838, and he, 5 Oct. 1847.

Children, born in Scarborough:

1 Annie, b. 9 July 1785; m. Abraham Cousins.
2 Polly, b. 5 May 1788; m. John Libby, 10-5-5-2-1.

Born in Limington:

3 Elizabeth, b. 14 April 1791; m. 31 Oct. 1823, Joseph Blake.
4 Sally, b. 20 Nov. 1793; m. John Pugsley of Sebago.
5 Jane, b. 1 May 1797; m. 13 July 1826, John Meserve of Sebago.
6 Lucy, b. 23 Mar. 1800; m. 6 Oct. 1825, James Brown, son of Ruth (Libby) Brown, 10-2-1-1-1.

10-5-5-2

HARVEY LIBBY, born in Scarborough, 18 Dec. 1763; married, 16 March 1790, SARAH SMALL of Limington.

He served through the Revolution, and afterward settled in Limington, about a mile west of what is now Limington Corner, on the farm now occupied by the widow of his son David S. Libby. There he lived until his death.

His first wife died 1 Nov. 1830, and he married second, Polly, daughter of Simeon Strout of Limington. He died 28 Feb. 1849, and his widow 5 Oct. 1855.

Children, all born in Limington:

1 John, b. 7 Oct. 1790; m. 13 Feb. 1816, Mary Libby, 10-5-5-1-2. Immediately after his marriage, he settled on wild land in Limington, but two or three years later removed to Sebago, and cleared a farm in what is known as New Limington, now owned by Peter Sawyer. In 1833 he moved onto another farm in Sebago, where he died 2 Dec. 1862. His widow died 7 Sept. 1875. Children:
   1 Mary, b. 4 Dec. 1819; m. 17 Aug. 1851, Richard F. Meserve.
   2 James Frazier, b. 29 Dec. 1821; is a bachelor. He learned the shoemaker's trade in Lynn, and was afterward a manufacturer there. In 1861 he returned home to take care of his parents, and has since lived on the homestead farm.
   3 Eliza, b. 21 Sept. 1823; m. 19 Sept. 1850, Wm. H. Allen.

2 Sarah, b. 14 Oct. 1792; m. 21 Jan. 1813, Humphrey Small, a son of Elizabeth (Dam) Small, 11-7-5-2.

3 James Frazier, b. 23 Nov. 1794; was one of the crew of the privateer "Dash," which sailed from Portland in the war of 1812, and was never heard from.

4 Mary, b. 26 Dec. 1796; m. 5 Mar. 1818, Moses Chase.

5 Nathaniel, b. 25 Mar. 1799; m. Elizabeth L. and Catherine Staples.

6 Jacob, b. 20 April 1801; died 28 Mar. 1822, from being crushed by a falling chimney; unm.

7 Anna, b. 17 May 1803; m. 9 Dec. 1824, John M. Staples.

8 Dorothy, b. 20 Aug. 1805; m. 14 April 1825, Abraham Tyler.

9 Elmira, } twins, born } m. Joseph Small.

10 Statira, } 21 Aug. 1807; } m. 25 Nov. 1830, Sewall Thompson.

11 Robert, b. 3 July 1809; d. 14 May 1829.

12 David Small, b. 10 July 1812; m. 28 March 1839, Martha L., dau. of Dorothy (Libby) Small, 5-7-12-9. He was a house-carpenter by trade, but from the time of his marriage was chiefly occupied in farming. He lived on his father's homestead, and died there 20 Nov. 1878. Children:
   1 Frances Woodman, b. 28 Mar. 1840; m. 10 Aug. 1857, Charles M. Bragdon.
   2 Abbie Johnson, b. 18 Feb. 1842; m. 1 Jan. 1873, John M. Purinton.
   3 Celia Louise, b. 22 July 1845; m. 27 April 1867, as second wife, Charles M. Bragdon.
   4 Martha Ellen, b. 13 Sept. 1847; m. 26 May 1877, Solomon Woodberry of Boston, printer. Child:
      1 Ralph Libby (Woodberry), b. 11 Feb. 1880; d. 18 June 1880.
   5 Frank Willard, b. 17 July 1850; m. 26 May 1877, Lizzie S., dau. of Rollins and Almira (Bangs) Philpot of Limerick. Lived at home until 1880, when he moved to Limerick, and became an agent for agricultural implements. No children.
   6 Stephen Millard, b. 25 Sept. 1857; is a clerk in Ipswich, Mass.

13 Stephen Meserve, b. 21 Jan. 1815; m. Lois S. Chase.

10-5-5-9

NATHANIEL LIBBY, born in Scarborough, about 1778; married first, 9 Nov. 1801, LUCY WESTON, daughter of Daniel Weston of Cape Elizabeth; (died 31 Aug. 1806); second, 28 Aug. 1808, LORANA MOSES, daughter of Daniel and Lydia (Coolbroth) Moses. He lived on part of his father's homestead, and died 22 April 1826. His widow died 11 Sept. 1839.

Children, by first wife:

1 Lucy, b. 21 April 1804; m. 27 Jan. 1829, Capt. Freeman Smith of Portland, a son of Capt. Freeman Smith of Wellfleet, Mass. He died 14 Nov. 1878. Children:
  1 Mary Elizabeth (Smith), b. 28 Aug. 1833; m. 29 July 1852, Daniel W. Nash of Portland, a stove dealer. Children:
    1 Ella Frances (Nash), b. 22 May 1853; m. 25 Dec. 1878, Peter S. Nickerson.
    2 Carry Adelaine (Nash), b. 17 April 1856.
    3 Daniel Freeman (Nash), b. 19 Oct. 1858.
  2 Helen Augusta (Smith), b. 29 Oct. 1838; m. 24 Sept. 1864, Frederick Bucknam; d. 12 May 1878. Children:
    1 Frederick William (Bucknam), b. 3 Aug. 1872.
    2 Helen Adelaide (Bucknam), b. 8 Dec. 1876.
2 Joseph Weeks, twin with Lucy, b. 21 April 1804; m. Mary Jordan.

By second wife:

3 Edward, b. 13 March 1809; m. Asenath Sanborn and Harriet F. Smith.
4 Freeman, b. 22 April 1811; m. Soranah Sanborn and Mehitable S. Brackett.
5 Mary, m. 25 Dec. 1837, Stephen Sanborn.
6 David, was a cripple; died 3 Nov. 1839.
7 Sally, b. 27 April 1818; d. 1 Dec. 1840; unm.
8 Ansel, b. 29 Aug. 1821; m. 8 Aug. 1849, Eliza Ann, dau. of Thomas and Sarah (Heseltine) Carter. In his younger days he followed the sea. He afterward settled on a part of the homestead of Capt. Anthony Libby, 1-1-2-7. There he died 24 Mar. 1868, and his widow still lives. Children:
  1 Thomas Jefferson, b. 8 Nov. 1850; d. 3 July 1851.
  2 Thomas Carter, b. 19 Aug. 1853; is unmarried.
  3 Lorana, b. 10 Dec. 1855; m. 1879, Stephen Harmon.
  4 William Smith, b. 7 Oct. 1858; is unmarried.

10-5-5-10

Luke Libby, born in Scarborough, 2 Feb. 1780; married, 19 May 1808, Susannah Matthews, daughter of John and Catherine (Moses) Matthews. He settled on half of his father's homestead, and increased it considerably in size by purchase. His wife died 12 Feb. 1852. He died 23 Mar. 1858.

Children:

1 Julian, b. 24 June 1809; m. 17 April 1834, James R. Milliken.
2 Simon, b. 1 Mar. 1811; m. 1st, 26 Jan. 1837, Annie, dau. of Benjamin and Mary Ballard of Argyle; (died 8 Mar. 1850); 2d, 19 Nov. 1850, Mrs. Sally (Pratt) Ricker of Paris, Me.; (died Dec. 1872); 3d, 19 Oct. 1873, Elsie, dau. of Benjamin and Lydia Stanton of Poland. Seven and one-half years he spent in the woods of Penobscot county. The six years following his marriage he lived in Scarborough, and then settled on the farm in Poland on which he has since lived. He is a member of the F. W. Baptist Church. Children, all by first wife:
  1 Mary Ann, b. 13 May 1840; m. Orlando Keene.
  2 Ellen, b. 21 April 1843; m. 1864, Wm. Waring of Fall River, Mass.; d. 20 July 1874.
  3 Charles Orington, b. Mar. 1846; d. 23 April 1849.
  4 Hannah E., b. 4 May 1848; d. 15 Jan. 1849.
3 Shirley, b. 3 Jan. 1813; m. Mary E. Sinclair.
4 Daniel, b. 13 Oct. 1816; m. Nancy Hasty.

5 Lydia, b. 6 June 1818; m. 13 Dec. 1849, Nathaniel Milliken.
6 Hannah, b. 29 Sept. 1820; m. 16 April 1840, Lorenzo Rice of Saco.
7 Catherine, b. 4 April 1823; m. 1st, 7 Oct. 1845, John Lombard; 2d, Nathan Cram.
8 Susan Frances, b. 12 June 1825; m. 13 Dec. 1849, Wm. M. Boothby.
9 George Prout, b. 4 Feb. 1827; m. 8 Oct. 1854, Mehitable D., dau. of Thomas C. and Mehitable (Moulton) Carter. He lives on his father's homestead, a forehanded farmer. Children:
    1 Susie Caroline, b. 11 Jan. 1856; m. 26 Nov. 1879, Frederick A. Miller.
    2 Charles Edwin, b. 14 Feb. 1858; unm.
    3 Ada Almeda, b. 11 Aug. 1866.

10-5-6-1

Reuben Libby, born in Scarborough, about 1761; married, 6 Feb. 1782, Elizabeth Burnham of Scarborough. He died a few years after his marriage, (before 1789), and his widow went to Danville with the rest of Luke Libby's family. She lived at one time with her husband's brother Humphrey.

Children:

1 Silas, m. Mary Boyd; emigrated to Kentucky.
2 Rhoda (?).

10-5-6-2

Dominicus Libby, born in Scarborough, 13 June 1763; married 4 Jan. 1790, Dorothy McKenney. [See page 63.]

He removed to Danville, now a part of Auburn, with his mother and four younger brothers, and settled on a farm. He died 5 Jan. 1836. His wife died 24 Feb. 1817. All but four of his children lived at home and died unmarried. The homestead finally went to Mrs. Jordan, and is now occupied by James Clark.

Children:

1 Jane, b. 12 Oct. 1790; d. 23 Mar. 1874.
2 Moses, b. 5 Mar. 1792; m. 24 Jan. 1819, Mary Ann, dau. of Stephen and Priscilla (Martin) Larrabee of Danville. He was a farmer in Danville. He and his wife were members of the Methodist Church. His death took place 28 June 1837. His widow is living at the age of 87. Children:
    1 John Nelson, b. 2 March 182 ; unm. He is blind, and has been a farmer and tradesman.
    2 Asenath, b. 16 July 1823; d. 9 Sept. 1844; unm.
    3 Dorothy Jane, b. 19 May 1825; d. 13 Mar. 1843.
    4 Stephen L., b. 3 Dec. 1827; d. 9 May 1831.
    5 Dominicus, b. 5 Dec. 1829; died 3 May 1864, before Richmond, Va. He was a member of the 7th Maine Volunteers, and afterward a veteran in the 23d.
    6 Lorenzo Fletcher, b. 9 July 1831; d. 10 July 1831.
    7 Priscilla Martha, b. 3 June 1833; m. 1st, 13 July 1856, Charles Hearn; (died 5 May 1867); 2d, 15 Sept. 1870, Chas. W. Wallace. No children.
    8 Mary Ann, b. 16 Oct. 1836; d. 23 Dec. 1853.
3 Hannah, b. 11 Aug. 1794; d. 9 June 1844.
4 Luke, b. 24 Jan. 1796; d. 23 Jan. 1813.
5 Polly, b. 14 Oct. 1797; d. 25 June 1835.

6 Dominicus, b. 24 June 1799; d. 14 July 1836.
7 Dorothy, b. 30 June 1801; m. Jonathan Libby, 10-5-6-4-1.
8 William, b. 7 Mar. 1803; m. 26 Nov. 1847, Ann Libby, 10-5-6-5-9; d. 12 April 1850. His widow lives with her sister's husband, Moses Libby. No children.
9 Rufus, } twins, born { d. 9 Feb. 1846.
10 Eunice, } 10 Aug. 1805; { m. 21 Oct. 1840, Wm. M. Jordan; died 1 Dec. 1876. Her husband died 18 Sept. 1872. Children:
  1 Hannah (Jordan), b. 11 Nov. 1841; d. next day.
  2 Rufus L. (Jordan), b. 28 Aug. 1843; d. 6 April 1845.
  3 William A. (Jordan), b. 24 June 1846.

10-5-6-4

Luke Libby, born in Scarborough, 1767; married Betsey Mitchell, daughter of Jonathan and —— (Lovett) Mitchell of Cape Elizabeth. He removed to Pejepscot, (afterward Danville, and now Auburn), and cleared a farm, on which he lived until his death, 13 Oct. 1800. His widow married Thomas Murray, and continued to live on the homestead. She died 15 June 1856.

Children:

1 Jonathan, b. 29 Feb. 1798; m. Mary Jordan.
2 Dorothy, b. Feb. 1800; m. Wm. Jordan.

10-5-6-5

Isaac Libby, born in Scarborough, 1768; married 10 Nov. 1793, Dorothy Meserve. [See page 37.] He settled in Danville, on the farm (now in Auburn) which is at present occupied by Moses H. and Wm. M. Libby, his son Isaac's sons. He died 14 May 1822. His widow died 29 Aug. 1825.

Children:

1 William, b. 20 Jan. 1795; m. Nancy Jordan.
2 Jonah, b. 17 Nov. 1797; m. Hepsibeth Hanscom.
3 Margaret, died aged about ten years.
4 Luke, b. 8 Jan. 1801; m. Mary Larrabee.
5 Isaac, b. 12 Nov. 1801; m. Abigail S. Hanscom.
6 Hannah, b. 12 Feb. 1805; m. 10 Dec. 1828, Charles Jordan.
7 Dorothy, b. 2 Feb. 1807; m. 14 April 1829, Chas. Peoples; d. 21 Jan. 1879.
8 Margaret, b. 28 March 1809; m. Moses Libby, 1-4-1-6-3-8.
9 Ann, b. 7 May 1811; m. William Libby, 10-5-6-2-8.
10 John, b. 23 Aug. 1813; d. 23 Nov. 1836; unm.

10-5-6-7

William Libby, born in Scarborough, 1 Jan. 1772; married, 20 Jan. 1797, Hannah McKenney. [See page 63.]

He settled on a farm in Danville, on which he lived until his death, 1 April 1847. He was a member of the Methodist Church. His widow died 22 Mar. 1866. Except the youngest, their children all lived and died on the homestead farm, unmarried.

They were:

1 Esther, b. 7 May 1798; died 19 Oct. 1869.
2 Lucy, b. 1802; died 22 Mar. 1819.
3 Sarah, b. 1805; d. 8 Feb. 1833.
4 Dorothy, b. 1808; d. 21 July 1835.
5 Gardner, b. 1811; d. 22 Mar. 1836.
6 Philip, b. Mar. 1816; m. Betsey Ann, dau. of Samuel Goss of Danville; d. 11 Jan. 1846. His widow married Isaac Libby, 6-4-1-6-1-1. Only child:
  1 Lucy, died aged 10 years.

10-7-1-2

John Libby, born in Kittery, (now Eliot), Me., 29 Jan. 1760; married, 7 June 1781, Sarah Leathers, daughter of Robert Leathers of Durham, N. H.

He was by trade a blacksmith. He settled in Durham in the spring before his marriage and, except a few years spent in Dover, N. H., lived there until his death. He was shipsmith on board a vessel which was captured by a French privateer in 1798, and for nearly a year lay in a French prison, which so impaired his health that he never recovered. He died 20 June 1812. His widow died 27 July 1850.

Children:

1 Ephraim, b. 6 Dec. 1781; was never married. He was a sailor. He attempted to jump for a wager across a street in Boston, and received injuries which resulted in his death a few months later in Charleston, S. C. He died 1 July 1811.
2 Sarah, b. 1 April 1783; m. Enoch French of Gardiner, Me.
3 Mary, b. 22 Feb. 1785; d. 22 Oct. 1785.
4 Deborah, b. 25 Aug. 1786; m John Parks.
5 John, b. 8 May 1788; m. 21 Aug. 1810, Hannah Wells of Dover. He was a blacksmith in Durham Village, where he died 15 March 1824, and his widow, 24 June 1868. Children:
  1 Harriet C., b. 2 Dec. 1810; m. 21 Aug. 1836, Wm. H. Gage of Walpole, N. H.
  2 Mehitable W., b. 3 July 1814; is unmarried.
  3 Mary B., b. 6 Mar. 1816; m. 6 Oct. 1837. Albert Jackson.
  4 Susan S., b. 4 June 1818; d. 14 Dec. 1847; unm.
  5 John D., b. 22 Feb. 1820; was a mason; died in Boston, 15 Jan. 1853; unm.
6 Robert, b. 6 Feb. 1790; m. Sarah Tyler of Gardiner, Me. He was a sailor, and died in Canton, China, in 1832. Children:
  1 Robert, left Gardiner about 1845.
  2 Sarah.
  3 ——, daughter.
7 Joseph, b. 3 Feb. 1793; m. Louisa Myers.
8 Abigail, b. 26 April 1795; m. 1st, Wm. Brown; 2d, Silas Coolidge of Boston, Mass.
9 George, b. 20 July 1797; m, Abigail Nutter. He was a ship-carpenter, and died at sea, 1837. His widow married Phineas Wentworth and died about 1843. Only child:
  1 daughter, died in infancy.
10 Morrill, b. 19 Sept. 1801; m. Mary Nutter of Portsmouth, He was a carpenter and after his marriage lived in Newmarket, where he died in November, 1830. His widow married Oliver H. Thompson, and died 12 Sept. 1873. Children:

1 Sarah E., b. 2 Jan. 1825; m. Nathaniel Robinson of Boston. Children:
 1 Charles E. (Robinson), b. 18 Dec. 1846.
 2 Frank G. (Robinson), b. 1 Aug. 1848.
2 Louisa, b. 1826; m. Jesse T. Cram; d. 9 Aug. 1873.
11 Jedediah, b. 8 Aug. 1806; never married. He died in Bangor, Me., about 1833, from over-exertion in wrestling.

10-7-1-3

JOEL LIBBY, born in Kittery, now Eliot, Me., 13 May 1762; married first, 20 Dec. 1789, BETTY STAPLES; (died 24 July 1793); second, 15 Dec. 1793, SARAH HANSCOM, daughter of Jonathan Hanscom. He always lived on his father's homestead, and died 20 Oct. 1807. His widow tore down the house which his great-grandfather had built, and erected the one now standing on the same site. She died 27 Jan. 1842.

Children, by first wife:

1 Joel, b. 18 Nov. 1790; d. 21 July 1875. He was a bachelor and always lived on the homestead.
2 Ephraim, b. 8 Nov. 1792; died in infancy.

By second wife:

3 Sarah, b. 18 Dec. 1794; d. 22 April 1823; unm.
4 Betty, b. 18 April 1796; died in infancy.
5 Elsie, b. 14 Nov. 1797; m 8 Oct. 1818, Ebenezer Bartlett.
6 Rachel, b. 10 Dec. 1799; m. 17 Feb. 1827, James Rogers.
7 Abigail Hanscom, b. 17 Dec. 1801; m. 14 Dec. 1828, James L. Paul; died 10 Jan. 1836.
8 Moses, b. 6 Jan. 1805; m. 1st, 24 April 1842, Pisidia, widow of Thomas Leach, dau. of —— Parsons of Kittery; (died 5 Feb. 1845); 2d, 12 Sept. 1847, Martha Ann, dau. of Jonathan and Elizabeth (Place) Godsoe. He has always been a farmer on his father's homestead. Children, by first wife:
 1 Charles William, b. 20 Nov. 1843; is a sailor; unm.
 2 Mary Abby, b. 30 Nov. 1844; d. 27 Sept. 1867; unm.

By second wife:

 3 Frances Ellen, b. 2 Aug. 1848; is unmarried.
 4 Leonard Appleton, b. 29 Oct. 1850; unm. He learned the carpenter's trade in Haverhill, Mass., where he has since worked as journeyman.
 5 Clara Ann, b. 13 April 1853; unm.

10-7-1-4

DAVID LIBBY, born in Kittery, now Eliot, Me., 15 May 1764; married, 15 Nov. 1789, ABIGAIL TOBEY, daughter of Samuel Tobey. He was a shoemaker by trade, but lived on, and tilled, a portion of his father's homestead. For a number of years he was one of the selectmen of Eliot. He died 17 Sept. 1857. His wife died 29 March 1849.

Children, all born in that part of Kittery now Eliot:

1 James, b. 20 Sept. 1790; m. 16 Jan. 1821, Jane Libby, 10-4-6-4. He was a shoemaker, and settled on part of his father's farm. He was drowned in the Piscataqua River in 1827, and, the same year, 16 Dec., his widow married Capt. Caleb Frost. No children.

2 David, b. 26 Oct. 1792; m. Betsey Hanscom.
3 John, b. 20 Dec. 1794; d. 19 Aug. 1803.
4 Mary, b. 17 March 1797; m. 20 May 1817, Deacon Alpheus Hanscom.
5 Oliver, b. 6 Jan. 1799; m. Elizabeth Henderson.
6 Jeremiah, b. 6 April 1801; m. Julia F. Hammond.
7 Abigail, b. 6 July 1803; m. 13 Dec. 1828, James K. Paul.
8 Isaac, b. 6 Aug. 1805; m. 21 Oct. 1840, Mary, dau. of Solomon and Abigail (Lord) Neal of South Berwick. He is a farmer. Since his marriage he has lived on the homestead of his wife's father in South Berwick. Child:
  1 Isaac, b. 12 Aug. 1841, in South Berwick; is a bachelor, and lives at home. He has been one of the selectmen of the town.
9 William, b. 10 March 1808; m. Sally Scammon and Mississippi Cox.

10-7-1-6

Clement Libby, born in Kittery, now Eliot, Me., 4 Sept. 1768; married, 24 Nov. 1791, Phebe Tibbetts, daughter of David and Mary (Tibbetts) Tibbetts of Rochester, N. H.

He settled on the farm in Rochester, N. H., now occupied by Edward Mills, and lived on it until his death. The following he himself recorded: "I came to Rochester to reside October the 2d 1790." "I moved into my own house the 13th of June 1796." "I raised my barn the 8th day of November 1796." He died 31 July 1848, and his widow 14 Sept. 1849.

Children, all born in Rochester:

1 Isaac, b. 7 Nov. 1792; m. 2 June 1832, Dorothy, dau. of Samuel and Sarah (Ham) Allen. He was a trunk-maker, and also cultivated a small piece of land on which he dwelt, now occupied by his widow. He died 19 Oct. 1873. No children.
2 Anna, b. 27 May 1795; d. 20 May 1867; unm.
3 Ezra, b. 15 May 1798; d. 15 July 1814.
4 Jesse, b. 31 Oct. 1800; m. 14 June 1834, Sophia, dau. of William and Tamsen (Baker) Heard. He was a trunk-maker by trade. He lived in Reading, Mass., a short time including the period of his marriage, and then returned to his father's homestead. He died 1 Nov. 1839. His widow married Silas Tibbetts, and then Joshua Hubbard, and now lives at Rochester Village. Child:
  1 Mary Charlotte, b. 24 June 1835; m. Samuel Marston; d. Sept. 1863.
5 Amos, b. 11 May 1803; d. 14 Sept. 1825; unm.
6 Asa, b. 16 April 1806; d. 31 Jan. 1810.
7 Mary, b. 22 April 1811; d. 20 May 1830.

10-7-1-7

Ezra Libby, born in Kittery, now Eliot, Me., 20 Dec. 1770; married first, 7 Jan. 1798, Mary, daughter of Wm. Remmick; (died 29 Nov. 1801); second, 23 Dec. 1802, Elizabeth Tobey, daughter of Anne (Fogg) Tobey, 9-9-4.

In his younger days he was a fisherman. After his first marriage he lived awhile on a farm in Rochester, N. H. Upon his second marriage he settled on the homestead of his wife's father, in Eliot, and there lived until his death, which took place 13 April 1847. His widow died 18 Aug. 1859, in her 91st year.

Children, all by second wife:

1 John, b. 1 Nov. 1803; d. 20 Sept. 1830; unm. He was a cabinet maker.
2 Alexander, b. 3 June 1805; m. 30 Nov. 1837, Deborah, dau. of Samuel and Ursula (Nute) Chick of Eliot. He settled on the portion of his father's farm which his widow now occupies. He died 15 Nov. 1877. Children:
  1 Mary Ann, b. 24 Mar. 1839; m. 28 Nov. 1866, Alvin Dixon.
  2 John Edwin Burr, b. 2 Dec. 1841; m. 26 Jan. 1871, Maria L., dau. of George and Louisa (Spollet) Clement of Merrimack, Mass. He has lived in Merrimack since his 22d year, a carriage-maker. Child:
    1 George Edwin, b. 30 Sept. 1874.
  3 Ursula Amanda, b. 10 April 1848; m. 18 Nov. 1869, Henry Leach.
  4 Helen Arabel, b. 5 Jan. 1853; m. 9 Nov. 1876, Wm. A. Hodgdon.
  5 Lizzie Hammond, b. 9 Feb. 1855; d. 29 Mar. 1855.
  6 Wilmot Clifton, b. 10 Oct. 1857; unm.; is a shoemaker.
3 Anna, b. 24 Sept. 1807; d. 16 Nov. 1869; unm.
4 Mary, } twins, { died aged 3 months.
5 Elizabeth, } twins, { died aged 1 month.
6 Caroline, b. 5 Sept. 1815; unm. She lives on her father's homestead.

11-2-2-1

Matthew Libby, born in Kittery, Me., about 1758; married, 5 April 1781, Lois Hanscom. He grew up and was married in Kittery. He afterward settled in Shapleigh, where he died before July 1796, and where his widow married, 2 June 1802, James Davis.

Children:

1 Lydia, married 24 Dec. 1801, John Dore.
2 John, married Judith Frye.
3 Samuel, b. 1792; m. Olive Kimball.

11-2-3-1

Robert Libby, born in Scarborough, 24 Aug. 1769; married, 31 May 1798, Lydia Bean, daughter of —— and Eliza (Thomas) Bean of Limerick.

The first years of his married life were spent in Limerick. He then returned to Newfield and settled on the farm now owned by Samuel Burbank. He lived there until old age, and then went to live with his daughter in Buxton. There his wife died 26 June 1849, and he, in June, 1864, aged nearly 95.

Children, beside three who died young in Limerick:

1 Sally, b. 7 Oct. 1800; m. Thomas Brooks of Porter.
2 Eliza, b. 26 June 1804; m. as 1st wife, Simeon Clay.
3 Miriam, b. 6 June 1805; m. as 2d wife, Simeon Clay.
4 Charles, b. 7 Oct. 1806; m. 29 Dec. 1834, Sarah, dau. of Richard and Susannah (Mason) Dunnells. He settled on the homestead of William Libby, 11-2-5, and there died 11 Oct. 1846. His widow married, 23 Jan. 1851, Horatio Dunnells and still occupies the homestead. Children:
  1 Susannah Dunnells, b. 27 Mar. 1836; m. 18 Feb. 1872, Daniel Ellis.
  2 Lydia, b. 18 Aug. 1838; unm.

3 Charles Cushing, b. 8 May 1845; m. 7 Feb. 1869, Melissa P., dau. of Eben and Lucinda (Ellis) Trafton. Children, all born in Oxbow, Me.:
  1 William Trafton, b. 30 Jan. 1870.
  2 John Franklin, b. 30 Jan. 1872; d. 1874.
  3 Mary Belle Ella, b. April, 1876.
  4 Isaac Orlando, b. 1879.

5 Lucy, b. 19 Dec. 1808; d. 18 Dec. 1846; unm.
6 Dolly, b. 19 May 1810; d. 10 Nov. 1835; unm.
7 William, b. 26 Dec. 1811; m. Abigail Swett. He was a farmer. He moved from Newfield to Canaan, thence to Brighton, and thence to Iowa, where he died. His widow was living in Charles City in 1872. Children:
  1 Harrison, m. 14 Feb. 1864, Almira S., dau. of Asa and Abigail C. (Curtis) York. They were divorced in 1867, and she married Charles H. Clark of Brighton. Child:
    1 Samuel A., b. 1864; lives with his mother.
  2 Esther, m. John Walker of Canaan; died in 1863.
  3 Miriam.
  4 Nellie, died of diphtheria.
8 David, b. 20 Aug. 1813; m. 1 Dec. 1839, Sally, dau. of Daniel and Nancy (Thompson) Moulton. In his younger days he worked at stone-work, and has worked more or less at that calling ever since; but his chief occupation has been farming. He lived on a farm in Parsonsfield 16 years following his marriage, and has since lived in Newfield Village. They had no children, but adopted a daughter of Taylor and Betsey (Holmes) Eastman of Parsonsfield, and a daughter of Wallace Russell of Biddeford. They took the names:
  a Elizabeth (Libby), b. 8 Jan. 1846; m. James A. Clifford.
  b Mabel Russell (Libby), b. 2 Aug. 1867.
9 Lydia, b. 25 April 1815; d. 1 Dec. 1816.
10 Ann, b. 28 Feb. 1818; m. as 3d wife, Simeon Clay of Buxton, and still lives.

11-2-3-3

ZEBULON LIBBY, born in Scarborough, 29 March 1773; married, 12 Oct. 1806, JEMIMA SMITH, daughter of Thomas Smith of Newfield, Me. He lived on his father's homestead, and died 16 April 1851. His wife died 5 Oct. 1840.

Children, all born in Newfield:

1 Sally, b. 21 June 1807; m. John Lougee.
2 Daniel, b. 11 July 1810; m. Abigail M. Lougee.
3 Wentworth, b. 20 Sept. 1815; m. 1st, Abby Foy; (died 9 Aug. 1849); 2d, Mary B., dau. of Daniel and Sally (Thompson) Moulton of Newfield. He owned mills in Newfield, and carried on lumbering. He died 22 Sept. 1851. His widow died 8 Jan. 1852. Children, by first wife:
  1 Elsie, died in maidenhood, in Dover, N. H., with her mother's relatives.
  2 Harriet P., b. 12 July 1849; d. 20 Oct. 1849.

By second wife:

  3 Wentworth, b. 19 Nov. 1851; d. 27 Feb. 1852.
4 Mary, b. 3 May 1818; m. John Dodge of Boston.
5 Isaac, b. 20 Dec. 1820; m. 5 Aug. 1847, Abigail, dau. of Abigail (Libby) Dorman, 11-2-3-5. Before his marriage he followed the sea. He then settled on the farm in Newfield now owned by C. C. Adams. He had been sun-struck on a whaling voyage, which

caused occasional spells of craziness ever after. In one of these he climbed forty feet into a pine tree, and threw himself off backward onto a ledge. He died the next day, 5 Aug. 1852. His widow married Simon Stone, 11 Dec. 1862. Children:

1 James, b. 10 April 1848; d. 10 July 1855.
2 Ellen Maria, b. 27 Jan. 1850; d. 1 July 1871.
3 Herbert, b. 3 March 1853; d. 5 Aug. 1860.

6 Nancy, b. 23 Dec. 1829; m. 1 Sept. 1850, Chas. D. Staples.

11-2-4-1

ADJT. NATHANIEL LIBBY, born in Kittery, now Eliot, Me., 22 Feb. 1763; married, 20 Nov. 1785, MIRIAM GILPATRICK, daughter of Joseph Gilpatrick of Limerick.

When a young man he taught school in Limerick and there became acquainted with Miriam Gilpatrick. When they were married they received from her father wild land, and there he settled and cleared a farm. He was a Revolutionary soldier, and, during the latter years of his life, drew a pension. He was adjutant of a militia regiment; was a skilled land surveyor, and for many years a justice of the peace.

His wife Miriam, having borne him eleven children, died, in December, 1823, and, 14 Sept. 1824, he married Eleanor, widow of Enoch Staples. She died Nov. 1825, and he then married Mrs. Catherine Milliken of Scarborough. After her death, June, 1839, he married Abigail (Burrows) Guppy of Berwick. She outlived him, and died with her son James Guppy, in Dover, N. H., about 1870. After his third wife's death, he went to live with his daughter Eliza, in Newfield, and there died 24 May 1855.

Children, all born in Limerick:

1 Abigail, b. 15 Mar. 1786; m. June 1809, Edward Mulloy.
2 Eliza, b. 29 Mar. 1788; m. Joshua Small Libby, 11-2-5-4.
3 Haven Gilpatrick, b. 17 July 1791; m. Mary, dau. of Jonathan Smith of Limerick. He was a farmer and lived with his father. He died 8 Aug. 1822. His widow married John Staples, and died 27 May 1830. Child:
    1 Nathaniel, b. 20 Feb. 1816; d. 21 Jan. 1842; unm. He was a blacksmith.
4 Polly Gilpatrick, b. 1 Feb. 1795; d. 3 Nov. 1819; unm.
5 Oliver, b. 9 Oct. 1797; d. 30 Nov. 1819; unm.
6 Salome, b. 3 May 1800; m. Noble Meserve.
7 Sidney Smith, b. 18 Aug. 1802; m. Mary Small.
8 Helena, b. 12 June 1805; m. Joseph Libby, 11-2-4-3-5.
9 Joseph Gilpatrick, b. 29 Sept. 1807; m. Nancy Ann Gilpatrick.
10 Nathaniel, b. July 1811; died at the age of two years.
11 Abigail, b. 29 April 1813; d. 27 Mar. 1850; unm.

11-2-4-3

JOSEPH LIBBY, born in that part of Kittery, Me., which is now Eliot, 13 May 1767; married, 1795, SARAH STAPLES, daughter of Samuel and Sarah (Mendum) Staples of Scarborough.

He was by trade a shoemaker, and worked as journeyman in Portsmouth, N. H. During two years following his father's removal to Limerick, he worked with "old 'Squire Adams" in Kittery. He next lived two years with his father, and then began to work as ship-carpenter. About 1797 he bought wild land in Limerick, and there cleared a farm. He lived on it until 1844, when his son Nathaniel exchanged it for a farm in Chesterville, Me., and took him thither to live. There he died, 15 April 1852. His wife died in Limerick, Jan. 1839.

Children:

1 Joshua Mendum, b. 29 Sept. 1795; m. Betsey, dau. of David and Sarah (Chute) Sawyer of Cornish. He was a farmer in Brownfield, where he died 20 Oct. 1881. He had no children, but adopted Sally, dau. of Asahel and Charity Cole of Cornish. She took the name.
 a Sally C. (Libby), m. Isaac Stewart of Brownfield.
2 William, b. 2 Sept. 1797; died aged two years.
3 Sarah, b. 2 Nov. 1801; m. Philemon Libby, 5-7-12-1-2.
4 Hall Staples, b. 14 Mar. 1803; m. Almeda Hammonds.
5 Joseph, b. 10 Nov. 1806; m. Helena Libby, 11-2-4-1-8.
6 Nathaniel, b. 25 Oct. 1808; m. 26 Nov. 1833, Miriam Gilpatrick Libby, 11-2-5-4-1. In 1856 he sold his farm in Chesterville, and returned to Limerick. He lived about eight years on the farm now owned by Rufus Lane, and then bought the farm which he now occupies. Children:
 1 Sarah Elizabeth, b. 4 July 1835; m. 24 Nov. 1870, Joseph Cressey of Gorham.
 2 Ivory Franklin, b. 23 Jan. 1838; m. 29 Aug. 1877, Mary B., dau. of Josiah and Alvira (Brackett) Marston of Limington. He lives with his father, a carpenter. No children.
 3 Elizabeth, b. 10 July 1842; d. 4 Mar. 1843.
7 William, b. 21 June 1811; m. Martha Libby, 5-7-12-1-6.
8 Lucy, b. 21 Dec. 1813; m. Samuel Staples.
9 Samuel S., b. 12 July 1818; m. Huldah H. Cole.

11-2-4-4

Azariah Libby, born in Kittery, now Eliot, Me., 20 Feb. 1770; married, 1791, Jane Staples, daughter of Benj. Staples of Newfield. He settled on his father's homestead. In the winter of 1820-1 he sold it and bought the farm on which he died, and on which his unmarried children have all lived. His wife died 7 Mar. 1821. He died 8 Feb. 1854.

Children, all born in Limerick:

1 Luke, died at the age of seven years.
2 Jane, } twins, } d. 28 Jan. 1878; unm.
3 Nancy, } born 1796; } m. James Spinney of Eliot.
4 Hannah, } twins, born } m. 9 Mar. 1828, Harvey Newbegin.
5 Sarah, } about 1798; } died in infancy.
6 Lucinda, died in infancy.
7 Olive, b. 1803; d. 2 Aug. 1847; unm.
8 Statira, b. Feb. 1805; d. 18 Sept. 1849; unm.
9 Louisa, b. 7 Oct. 1807; lives at home; unm.
10 Simon, b. 22 Oct. 1809; lives at home; unm.
11 Azariah, b. Nov. 1810; d. 7 Feb. 1831.

11-2-5-1

Benjamin Libby, born 5 May 1781, in Newfield, Me.; married, 19 Dec. 1816, Clarissa Dorman, daughter of Charles and Susan (Boothby) Dorman of Newfield.

He was the second male child born in Newfield. At his marriage he settled on the farm now occupied by his son Sylvanus, and there died, 7 Aug. 1871. His wife died 18 Dec. 1846.

Children, all born in Newfield:

1 Alvan [M.D.], b. 10 May 1818; m. 23 Oct. 1845, Hannah Jeffords, dau. of John and Lydia (Fisk) Bourne of Wells, Me. He graduated from the Dartmouth Medical College in 1842, and soon after began practice in Wells, where he married and continued his practice until his death, 21 June 1874. He was a member of the Maine Medical Association. His widow died 11 July 1880. Children:
   1 Mary Louisa, b. 11 Oct. 1846; d. 22 Nov. 1866.
   2 Clara Anna, b. 13 Sept. 1849; d. 14 Jan. 1877.
   3 Olive Bourne, b. 12 Oct. 1852; d. 20 Jan. 1874.
   } All three graduated at Kent's Hill, and died of consumption; unmarried.
   4 John Gair, b. 7 Dec. 1854; unm. He graduated at Bowdoin College in 1876, and is now principal of the Richmond High School.
   5 Emma Adelaide, b. 19 July 1858.
   6 George Alvan, b. 11 March 1860.

2 Sylvanus, b. 11 June 1820; m. 30 Nov. 1843, Olive, dau. of Joseph and Sarah (Murray) Keen of North Berwick. He has always lived on the homestead farm. Children:
   1 Lovina, b. 29 Sept. 1844; m. 16 May 1867, Nahum Smith.
   2 Clarissa, b. 13 Jan. 1847; m. 18 Sept. 1872, Moses B. Dennett of Pittsfield, N. H.
   3 Emerson Coburn, b. 7 Jan. 1853; m. 10 Aug. 1876, Susan E., dau. of Orin and Joanna (Heath) Edgecomb of Fryeburgh, Me. He lives at home. Children:
      1 Eda Frances, b. 16 Feb. 1877.
      2 Lester Emerson, b. 15 Mar. 1879.

3 Emerson Coburn, b. 23 Mar. 1822; died 20 Sept. 1850; unm.

4 John Anderson, b. 18 Aug. 1827; d. 19 July 1835.

11-2-5-4

JOSHUA SMALL LIBBY, born in Newfield, Me., 9 July 1787; married, 1811, ELIZA LIBBY, 11-2-4-1-2.

He was a carpenter by trade and when he was married built the house in Newfield now occupied by his granddaughter, Sarah E. Cressey. He lived on and cultivated his farm there until old age, but died with his daughter in Limerick, 23 Aug. 1879. His wife died 27 Oct. 1871.

Children, all born in Newfield:

1 Miriam Gilpatrick, b. 21 Jan. 1812; m. Nathaniel Libby, 11-2-4-3-6.

2 William Nason, b. 12 Feb. 1816; m. Mary Drown, dau. of his uncle Edward Libby's wife. He was a farmer in Newfield and died 27 Jan. 1858. His widow married, 7 Dec. 1858, John Young. Child:
   1 Irene, b. 1853; d. 1869.

3 Oliver Cromwell, b. 5 April 1820; m. 17 Nov. 1848, Judith L., dau. of James and Hephzibah (Davis) Watson of Shapleigh. When he was married he settled on part of the homestead of Robert Libby, 11-2-3-1. There he has since lived, a farmer. No children.

4 Haven Gilpatrick, b. 10 June 1824; m. 9 June 1864, Martha B., widow of Nathaniel Crosby, dau. of Nathaniel and Elmira (Garland) Edwards. He is a farmer in Newfield. Child:
   1 Emma Bessie, b. 28 Jan. 1865.

11-6-1-11

COL. JAMES MARCH, born in Scarborough, 9 Feb. 1769; married, 9 July 1800, SALLY JOSE, daughter of John and Abigail (Milliken) Jose of Buxton. He lived at Gorham Corner, and died 29 March 1823. His widow died in Portland 22 Aug. 1863.

Children:

1 Anna (March), b. 16 May 1801, in Scarborough; m. 21 Feb. 1826, Capt. John Farnham of Boston, Mass.
2 Abigail Munson (March), b. 5 July 1803; m. 26 Jan. 1825, Daniel Marrett of Portland, a son of the Rev. Daniel Marrett of Standish; died 15 Mar. 1856. Her husband died 3 Dec. 1875. Children:
  1 Edwin A. (Marrett), b. 12 Mar. 1826; m. 25 April 1850, Mary Louisa, dau. of Samuel and Cynthia (Aldrich) Nelson of Milford, Mass. He is a dry-goods dealer in Portland. No children.
  2 James S. (Marrett), b. 30 May 1827; m. 17 Oct. 1855, Sarah Jane, dau. of Hon. Jason Gorham of Barre, Mass. He is of the firm of Marrett, Bailey & Co., carpet dealers, Portland. Children:
    1 Elizabeth March (Marrett), b. 10 Aug. 1856.
    2 Charles Gorham (Marrett), b. 23 Feb. 1861.
  3 Orlando M. (Marrett), b. 19 May 1829; m. Louisa O., dau. of Dorothy (Libby) Small, 5-7-12-9; died 9 Jan. 1870.
3 Hannah (March), b. 9 Dec. 1805; m. 9 Sept. 1828, Dr. William H. Peabody.
4 Sarah Jose (March), b. 29 Dec. 1807, in Gorham; m. 1st, Col. Samuel L. Valentine; 2d, James Ginn.
5 Mary Maria (March), b. 21 Jan. 1809; m. 5 Sept. 1830, Isaac C. Irish.
6 Lucinda Page (March), b. 6 Oct. 1812; m. 10 April 1837, John C. Proctor of Portland.
7 Emily Porter (March), b. 6 Nov. 1814; m. 2 Sept. 1835, Charles Roby of Gorham.
8 Caroline Elizabeth (March), b. 17 July 1822; m. 27 Dec. 1848, Augustus F. Gerrish of Portland. He is receiving teller of the Casco National Bank. Children:
  1 Caroline Maria (Gerrish), b. 18 Oct. 1849.
  2 Frank Scott (Gerrish), b. 4 Sept. 1853.

11-6-2-1

FRANCIS LIBBY, born in Scarborough, 17 March 1761; married 18 March 1784, LUCY MOULTON, daughter of Jonathan and Sarah (Dow) Moulton of Scarborough.

In December, 1776, he enlisted in the Revolutionary army and served three years. On one occasion he rowed Gen. Washington across the Hudson and back, and received a drink of liquor as a reward for the service.

He lived with his father until April, 1788, and then settled in Buxton on a farm of 100 acres, which he had purchased of Capt. Daniel Eldridge. There was a house on it, and that he occupied until 1800, when he built the one now standing, occupied by Frederick D. Emery. There he lived until his death, 24 Jan. 1847.

The mother of his children died 21 Aug. 1819, and he married second, 23 Sept. 1823, Dorcas, widow of Matthew Higgins, daughter of Lydia (Libby) Plummer, 1-1-5-8. She died 9 Jan. 1851.

Children of Francis Libby:

1 Daniel, b. 15 Sept. 1784; m. Elizabeth Warren.
2 Mehitable, b. 15 Nov. 1785; m. 23 Feb. 1806, Samuel Rounds.
3 Isaac, b. 24 Feb. 1788; m. Susannah Rounds.
4 Ruth, b. 30 June 1790; m. 3 Sept. 1812, Joseph Bradbury.
5 Joseph, b. 13 Dec. 1793; m. Rhoda M. Davis and Lucy Jenkins.
6 Peter [Rev.], b. 11 April 1796; m. 13 Jan. 1822, Mary Libby, 5-2-7-1-1. The year after his marriage he moved to Gorham, and for five years was in trade. He then removed to Scarborough, where he carried on the carpenter's business a number of years. He was also a justice of the peace, and surveyed land a great deal. In 1837 he was ordained an elder of the Freewill Baptist denomination, and subsequently preached in many parts of Maine. In 1870 he bought a farm at Buxton Center, on which he still resides. He had no children, but adopted Anna Libby Woods, a daughter of Joseph and Ann (Woods) Woods, named for her cousin, Anna (Libby) Jordan, 10-2-1-5-6-1. She took the name:
   a Anna (Libby), b. 15 Sept. 1826, in Portland; m. Major Josiah Libby, 10-2-1-1-9-4.
7 Anna, b. 15 Sept. 1798; m. 18 Dec. 1833, Tristram Scammon.
8 Nahum, b. 5 Sept. 1800; m. Sophia Marr.
9 Samuel Sanborn, b. 15 Mar. 1802; m. 1st, 10 Aug. 1825, Eliza, dau. of Allen and Martha (Morris) Davis; (died 23 Nov. 1837); 2d, Catherine, widow of Moses Starbird, dau of Daniel Fogg. (Martha (Morris) Davis was a daughter of Rhoda (Libby) Morris, 1-1-5-6.) His second wife died 23 Jan. 1853, and that same year he went to California. He was heard from the following year, but never afterward. Child, by second wife:
   1 Eliza Davis, m. 12 Jan. 1864, Geo. W. Parker of Bangor.

11-6-2-3

Isaac Libby, born in Scarborough, 13 Aug. 1764; married, 30 Oct. 1792, Abigail Jose, daughter of John and Abigail (Milliken) Jose of Buxton. He lived with his uncle Richard Libby until manhood, and then settled in Buxton, on the farm now occupied by Chas. H. Watts. About 1830 he sold that farm and bought what has since become the Freewill Baptist parsonage. There he died, 6 Jan. 1844, and his widow, 3 Nov. 1854.

Children, all born in Buxton:

1 Abigail, b. 31 July; d. 4 Aug., 1794.
2 Alexander, b. 21 Oct. 1795; m. Nancy Loring.
3 Sophia, b. 2 Jan. 1798; m. 31 Sept. 1821, Moses K. Wells.
4 Sarah Jose, b. 17 Sept. 1799; m. 1st, 27 Oct. 1835, Samuel Watts, jr.; 2d, Peter Paine.
5 Richard Jose, b. 15 Sept. 1801; m. Jane W. Merrill.
6 William Eaton, b. 8 March 1804; d. 30 July 1806.
7 William Eaton, b. 24 April 1806; d. 8 Dec. 1814.
8 Isaac, b. 22 Feb. 1809; m. Miriam Usher, Harriet S. Merritt, and Hannah J. (Tenney) Allen.

11-6-5-4

Richard Libby, born in Scarborough, 8 Jan. 1782; married, 3 July 1819, Elizabeth Mills, daughter of Jacob Mills of Limerick.

He lived on his father's homestead and built the house now standing. He was first selectman of Scarborough in 1828, 1829, and 1830. He died 10 Oct. 1833. His widow married Benjamin Haines of Saco, and died in Newburyport, Mass., 28 Feb. 1879.

Children, all born in Scarborough:

1 Horace, b. 10 May 1820; d. 4 May 1839.
2 Keziah, b. 21 Feb. 1823; m. Benaiah Libby, 11-6-5-5-3.
3 Olivia M., b. 2 Jan. 1826; d. 26 Oct. 1845.
4 Sarah Jane, b. 30 Sept. 1828; m. 17 Nov. 1845, Harris Pearson.
5 Richard, b. 14 Dec. 1830; m. 6 Oct. 1855, Sarah H., dau. of John and Nancy (Lydston) Pearson of Newburyport, Mass. He is a baker, and lives in Madison, N. H. Children, all born in Newburyport:
 1 Carrie Lizzie, b. 2 April 1857; d. 19 March 1863.
 2 Hattie Pearson, b. 14 March 1859.
 3 Lizzie Lydston, b. 30 April 1866.
 4 Edward Wesley, b. 20 Jan. 1870.
 5 Susie Davis, b. 26 May 1875.

11-6-5-5

THOMAS LIBBY, born in Scarborough, 11 Dec. 1784; married, 2 Dec. 1809, MARY PLUMMER, daughter of Ai and Elizabeth (Plummer) Plummer. He settled on Prout's Neck, now known as Libby's Neck. He was a farmer, but in the latter part of his life his place became a summer resort, and he kept boarders. He died 9 April 1871. His wife died 27 April 1841.

Children, all born in Scarborough:

1 Silas Jason, b. 20 Jan. 1811; m. 1st, 1 Nov. 1838, Hannah, dau. of Benjamin and Lydia (McDonald) Haines of Saco; (died 1 Dec. 1843); 2d, 27 Oct. 1851, Phebe Libby, 10-5-2-1-1-3. He built a house near his father's and kept summer boarders, cultivating his farm also. He died 1 Nov. 1878. His widow continues to have summer boarders. Children, by first wife:
 1 Thomas Jason, b. 24 Mar. 1840; m. 4 May 1864, in New Orleans, La., Harriet Ann, dau. of Edw. W. and Harriet A. (Kercheval) Farrah of Keene, N. H. He carries on a large seaside boarding-house close by his father's. Children:
  1 John James Kercheval, b. 10 Feb. 1865, in New Orleans.
  2 Mary Lillian, b. 29 July 1866; d. 16 Aug. 1866.
  3 Isa May, b. 15 July 1867.
  4 Veranus Warren, b. 26 Nov. 1868.
  5 Leonard Wilson, b. 21 Aug. 1871.
  6 Annie Louise, b. 5 Feb. 1874.
  7 Lloyd Lester, b. 15 Sept. 1876.
 2 Hannah Louise, b. 21 Sept. 1843; m. Alonzo Googin.

By second wife:

 3 Annie Maria, b. 20 July 1854; m. 21 Aug. 1876, Ira C. Foss; died 22 Aug. 1876.
2 Mary Jane, b. 3 Aug. 1812; d. 9 July 1851; unm.
3 Benaiah, b. 2 Nov. 1814; m. 27 Mar. 1845, Keziah Libby, 11-6-5-4-2. He built the house now occupied by his daughters, and kept boarders. He died 4 June 1878. His wife died 11 June 1876. Children:
 1 Ella Olivia, b. 8 Nov. 1852; m. —— Lee.
 2 Mary Elizabeth, b. 14 Nov. 1860.

4 Veranus, b. 7 Aug. 1816; m. 27 Aug. 1866, Margaret Jones of Wales, Great Britain; d. 1 May 1868. He always lived at home. No children. His widow returned to her native land.
5 Elizabeth, b. 18 Aug. 1818; m. 31 Aug. 1858, as second wife, James F. Coolbroth.
6 Minerva, b. 29 Aug. 1820; d. 26 Dec. 1879; unm.
7 Margaret, b. 31 July 1822; m. 28 Nov. 1849, Eben Seavey.
8 Ann Maria, b. 9 Sept. 1824; d. 24 June 1853; unm.
9 Elmira, b. 10 Oct. 1826; d. 25 Oct. 1826.
10 Clara Jane, b. 12 May 1828; married George Washington Libby, 11-7-11-8-1.
11 Elmira, b. 14 Oct. 1830; m. 22 Sept. 1853, James F. Coolbroth, died 25 Feb. 1855.
12 Sophronia E., b. 10 Feb. 1833; d. 4 Sept. 1878; unm.

11-6-5-6

PETER LIBBY, born in Scarborough, 5 Dec. 1786; married 13 April 1815, TAMSEN QUINBY, daughter of Nathan Quinby of Westbrook. When a young man he moved to Saccarappa, in Westbrook, and was for a number of years a teamster. During the rest of his life he was a millman. He died 26 Aug. 1876, and his widow, 23 Sept. 1878.

Children, all born in Westbrook:

1 Joseph Partrich, b. 14 Mar. 1816; m. 24 May 1839, Emily, dau. of Jeremiah and Persis (Russell) Virgin of Bethel. He learned the carpenter's trade and was employed in the repair shop of the cotton mills at Saccarappa about 20 years. He then engaged in the manufacture of paper boxes, and continued this business in Portland until his retirement in 1875. Since 1870, he has been deacon of the Congregational Church at Saccarappa. No children.
2 Benjamin Franklin, b. 1 Jan. 1819; m. Sarah Bradbury of Buxton. He became manager of Rope's knife and fork factory, and after a few years, when it was removed from Saccarappa to Meriden, Conn., he went there also. After a few years he left, and a year later became interested in the Meriden Lock Co., of which he has since been agent. Children:
   1 Martha Ellen, b. about 1840; married in New York and soon died.
   2 Frank Mordough, b. about 1842; m. Hennie Adams of New Jersey; died 1878. His widow married again. Child:
      1 Nellie, born about 1873.
3 Hannah, b. 6 March 1821; m. John Russell.
4 Edwin Ruthin, b. 16 April 1831; m. 1st, 14 April 1861, Harriet E., dau. of Thomas and Mary (Burnham) Whitten of Buxton; (died 13 Dec. 1872); 2d, Susan J., dau. of Isaac and Almira (Rowe) Thomes of Baldwin. He has always been a teamster. Children, by first wife:
   1, 2 children, died in infancy.
   3 Mary Adeline, b. 8 July 1865.

By second wife:

   4 Charles Albert, b. 13 Dec. 1873; d. 27 July 1874.
   5 Georgianna, b. 26 Nov. 1874.
   6 Edna Armine, b. 5 July 1876.
   7 Willietta, b. 10 Oct. 1878; d. 27 April 1880.
5 George Albert, } twins, born } d. 29 Sept. 1852, in W. Meriden, Ct.
6 Charles William, } 1 Feb. 1833, } was drowned in Beaver Pond, 10 June 1845.

Zenas Libby

11-6-5-8

Zenas Libby, born in Scarborough, 25 July 1792; married, 31 Oct. 1816, Miriam Fogg, 9-5-4-2-1-2. He removed to Portland when a young man, and was for very many years a surveyor of lumber. He died 7 Nov. 1848, and his widow, 12 Aug. 1876.

Children, all born in Portland:

1 Horatio Thomas, b. 8 Aug. 1818; d. 23 Aug. 1818.
2 Miriam, b. 1 Sept. 1819; d. 11 Sept. 1822.
3 Alma Louise, b. 17 May 1821; m. 29 April 1846, Jacob Thatcher Waterhouse.
4 Miriam J., b. 8 Dec. 1823; m. 9 Dec. 1845, James N. Winslow; died 30 Aug. 1872. He was formerly the Portland agent of the Eastern Express Co., and is now interested in the Portland Stone Ware Co. Children:
 1 Frankie (Winslow), b. 17 Sept. 1846; d. 17 Dec. 1849.
 2 Zenas (Winslow), b. 17 Nov. 1848; d. 17 Jan. 1869.
 3 Grace (Winslow), b. 28 June 1852; m. 19 Nov. 1873, John Lynch, jr. Children:
  1 James Winslow (Lynch), b. 20 Sept. 1874.
  2 Ella Barker (Lynch), b. 6 Mar. 1877.
 4 James Herbert, b. 8 Oct. 1856; m. 8 Dec. 1879, Helen Burnside Knight; lives in Baltimore, Md. Child:
  1 Burnside (Winslow), b. 3 Aug. 1881.
 5 Minnie (Winslow), b. 3 Sept. 1858; d. 9 Mar. 1877.
 6 Florie (Winslow), b. 1 Dec. 1863.
5 Sarah Cordelia, b. 3 Dec. 1826; m. 18 Nov. 1852, William Henry Cushing.
6 *Horatio Thomas*, b. 27 Mar. 1830; m. 27 June 1871, Mary Louise, dau. of Elliot and Mary (Skillings) Wescott of Cape Elizabeth. He was for many years a junk dealer in Portland. In 1880, he removed to the South and engaged in stock-raising. Child:
 1 Ralph Wescott, b. 6 June 1877.
7 Lendall Washington, b. 22 Feb. 1832; d. 18 Mar. 1871; unm.

11-7-1-4

William Libby, born in Scarborough, 16 May 1763; married 29 Sept. 1785, Mary Fogg, 9-6-6-1. He removed to Gorham when a young man and settled on the farm at White Rock now owned by —— Davis. About 1802 he returned to Scarborough and settled on the farm on Beech Ridge, on which he lived until his death. He died 1 Oct. 1838. His widow died 23 Feb. 1840.

Children, all born in Gorham:

1 Lydia, b. 13 June 1787; d. 15 Dec. 1863; unm.
2 William, b. 1 Feb. 1789; m. Apphia Harmon.
3 Mary, b. 20 Oct. 1792; d. 21 March 1873; unm.
4 Luther, b. 16 Jan. 1794; m. Hannah Libby, 1-1-2-2-6-3.
5 Andrew, } twins, born } m. Betsey Berry.
6 Moses, } 29 Mar. 1796; } m. Mary Mitchell.
7 Hannah, b. 8 July 1801; m. 1st, 18 Nov. 1828, Rev. John Purkis of Gray; 2d, Francis Barrows.

11-7-1-8

Andrew Libby, born in Scarborough, 27 May 1771; married Sarah Cummings of Gray. He was a farmer, and owned and occupied four different places in Gray. In his old age he and his wife went to live with his son Elias in Windham, and there they both died, she, 21 Feb., and he, 31 March, 1855.

Children, all born in Gray:

1 Christiana, m. 16 May 1819, John Small.
2 Elias, b. 4 Nov. 1796; m. Elizabeth Hawkes.
3 Ebenezer Cobb, b. 19 Feb. 1800; m. Dorcas Leighton.
4 Joseph, b. 5 March 1801; m. Hannah, dau. of Seth and Abigail (Hawkes) Ramsdell of Gray. He settled on a farm in Poland, near Mechanic Falls, now occupied by his niece, Mrs. Sarah A. Robertson, 11-7-1-8-3-3. His wife died 7 Feb. 1861. He died 19 Jan. 1871. No children.
5 Esther, b. 13 Sept. 1803; m. 11 June 1826, Peter M. Ramsdell.
6 Lucinda, b. 3 Nov. 1805; lives in Portland; unm.
7 Charlotte, b. 6 July 1808; m. John Elliot.
8 Lucy, b. 31 Dec. 1810; m. 1 Oct. 1829, Alvan Skillings.

11-7-1-10

David Libby, born in Scarborough, 18 March 1776; married, Mary Cobb, daughter of Jedediah and Abigail (Jordan) Cobb of Gray. When first married he settled on the farm now owned by Wm. Emery. He afterward moved onto the farm now occupied by his son Almer. He died with his youngest daughter, in Cumberland, 19 July 1864. His wife died in Gray, 18 Feb. 1833.

Children, all born in Gray:

1 Jedediah Cobb, b. 15 Oct. 1796; m. Hannah Prince.
2 William, b. 1800; d. 1821, at sea.
3 Andrew Burns, b. 7 April 1803; m. 8 June 1828, Hulda W., dau. of John and Mary Manchester of Windham. Previous to his marriage he followed the sea three years and worked as farm hand in various states. Shortly after his return to Gray, he settled on the farm on which he has since lived. Children:
  1 Mary, b. 10 June 1834; unm.
  2 Caroline Hunt, b. 7 Feb. 1840; m. 25 Dec. 1871, Cushman Hall.
4 Paulina, b. 1805; m. 22 Feb. 1822, Solomon N. Ramsdell.
5 Almer, b. 4 Jan. 1810; m. 24 April 1831, Rebecca C. Libby, 10-5-1-2-1-2. He lives on his father's homestead. He learned the brick-mason's trade with Benj. Ross of Portland, and has worked as journeyman in various places. Children, all born in Gray:
  1 Sarah Ann, b. 7 May 1832; d. 5 April 1838.
  2 Mary Abby, b. 2 May 1834; m. 1 May 1859, Valentine Cook Hall of Windham.
  3 Charles Henry, b. 11 Dec. 1835; d. 12 July 1860; unm. He was a brick-mason.
  4 Eliza Jane, b. 30 Dec. 1837; m. 4 March 1865, Jos. H. Ramsdell.
  5 Julia Ann, b. 6 Nov. 1839; d. 11 April 1849.
  6 John Stillman, b. 23 March 1841; unm. He has been in California since 1864; is now a farmer in Paicines.
  7 Ellen Frances, b. 22 Nov. 1843; m. Andrew Libby, 11-7-1-8-2-2.
  8 Sumner Holmes, b. 23 Dec. 1846; d. 1 Sept. 1849.
  9 George Warren, b. 18 Nov. 1848; m. 17 March 1875, Evelyn, dau. of Emery and Ann G. (Blake) Allen. He is a brick-mason by trade, but has now settled on the farm of his father-in-law in Gray. Child:
    1 Clarence Allen, b. 21 Jan. 1876.
  10 Sarah Louisa, b. 7 Jan. 1851; unm.
  11 Sumner Holmes, b. 17 Oct. 1852; unm. Lives at home.
6 Eliza, b. Sept. 1812; m. 1st, Nathaniel Small; 2d, Daniel Leighton; 3d, Ephraim Morrison.

11-7-1-11

SIMON LIBBY, born in Scarborough, 19 Dec. 1778; married, 23 Jan. 1800, ELIZABETH SMALL, daughter of Isaac and Susan (Hobbs) Small of Gray. He lived upon and cultivated his father's homestead on Dutton Hill, in Gray. He was a natural mechanic and used to make wheels, plows, etc. He excelled in framing buildings and was known as Master Libby. He died 14 Aug. 1858. His wife died 23 Jan. 1836.

Children, all born in Gray:

1 Isaac, b. 19 Jan. 1801; m. 5 Aug. 1819, Comfort, dau. of James and Mary (Leighton) Weymouth of Gray. He was a farmer, cooper, and small trader in Gray, and was in business as wharf-builder in Portland. He died of consumption at his father's house, 30 July 1833. His wife died 13 March previous. Children:
   1 Julia Ann, m. Nathaniel Rideout of Cumberland.
   2 Lydia Hicks, m. James Harris.
   3 Emily Jane, m. Alfred Hodgdon.
   4 Russell Streeter, died aged 3 or 4 years.
   5 ——, lived only one month.

2 Miriam, b. 15 July 1802; d. 28 June 1869; unm.

3 David, b. 21 April 1804; m. Martha Weymouth.

4 Willard, b. 17 May 1806; m. Huldah K. Stiles.

5 Susan, b. 28 April 1808; d. 21 June 1880; unm.

6 Esther, b. 25 Dec. 1810; d. 3 April 1841; unm.

7 Simon, b. 22 Jan. 1812; m. 3 July 1845, Harriet M., dau. of Adam B. and Jane (Haskell) Pride of Cumberland. He is a farmer. Children:
   1 Byron G., b. 15 Dec. 1847, in Gray; unm. He lives in Auburn; a blacksmith.
   2 Daniel H., b. 2 Sept. 1849, in Gray; unm. He is an iron-molder in Lewiston.
   3 Adam W., b. 7 Dec. 1851, in Cumberland; unm. He is a marble-worker in Auburn.

8 Alfred, b. 4 Oct. 1814; m. 5 Mar. 1845, Mary W., dau. of Nathaniel and Jane (Leighton) Abbott of Gray. He is a farmer and has always occupied his father's homestead. His wife died 21 Feb. 1879. Children:
   1 William Wallace, b. 28 March 1846; m. 13 Jan. 1874, Mary E., dau. of Robert and Lucy G. (Leighton) Leighton of Falmouth. A year before his marriage he bought and settled on the farm which he now occupies in Falmouth. No children.
   2 Silas Haines, b. 4 Feb. 1848; d. 29 Jan. 1873; unm. He was a butcher and marketman.
   3 Edward Hustin, b. 1 March 1850; unm. A farmer.
   4 Betsey Jane, b. 19 Jan. 1852; unm.
   5 Simon, b. 2 Feb. 1854; unm. He is a farmer.
   6 Fanny, b. 30 Jan. 1856; m. 8 Oct. 1879, Rufus Legrow.
   7 Alfred, b. 27 May 1857; d. 14 March 1858.
   8 Esther Ann, b. 15 Dec. 1859; unm.

9 Frances, b. 1 April 1816; m. Alpheus Frank.

10 Mahala, b. 20 July 1818; m. 18 April 1842, Silas Haines.

11 William, b. 11 April 1821; m. 11 June 1854, Adaline B., daughter of Moses and Leonice (Pride) Knights of Gray. When he was married he settled on the farm on which he has ever since resided. Children:
   1 Willard Henry, b. 27 Mar. 1856; unm.
   2 Mahala Haines, b. 1 July 1859; died 2 Jan. 1881; unm.
   A dau. of Mrs. Libby, seven years old when she married Mr. Libby, took the name:
   a Callie A. (Libby), m. 1 Sept. 1866, Edwin L. Field.

11-7-2-4

MATTHIAS LIBBY, born in Scarborough, 5 Jan. 1762; married, 14 July 1785, ESTHER LIBBY, 11-7-8-1.

He settled on part of his father's homestead, and became a well-to-do farmer. He and his wife joined the Congregational Church 2 March 1788. He died early in life, but is remembered as an exemplary christian. Samuel Libby recorded his death: "1807, April 9, fast day, Matthias Libby died. Got a great cold; had the pleurisy fever; affected his vitals; raised a great deal; sick but a short time. He was heard to say he never was sick one day before since his remembrance." Old people used to say that his grandson, Samuel T. Libby, 11-7-2-4-8-4, whose portrait is given further on, bore a remarkable resemblance to him. After his death his family continued on the homestead. 11 July 1816, his widow married, as his second wife, the Rev. Thomas Lancaster. She lived with her son Storer after her husband's death, and died 13 Oct. 1840.

Children, all born in Scarborough:

1 Lydia, b. 2 Aug. 1787; m. 8 March 1812, John Cummings, jr., of Standish; d. 26 Nov. 1819.
2 Hannah, b. 29 April 1790; m. 25 March 1813, Zebulon Berry; died 1 Nov. 1818.
3 Miriam, b. 30 July 1792; m. 8 April 1812, John Libby, 1-1-3-9-7; died 16 Dec. 1818.
4 Esther, b. 25 Dec. 1794; m. 23 May 1819, George Tate.
5 Mary, b. 30 Oct. 1796; m. 7 Aug. 1815, Moses Rice.
6 Edward, b. 9 April 1798; m. Abigail Libby, 1-4-1-6-4-2.
7 Matthias, b. 24 July 1800; d. 3 Jan. 1819, in Pownal; unm. He had gone with his brother Storer into the eastern woods, lumbering. They were both taken with fever. Matthias died with his sister Hannah in Pownal, but Storer reached home, and, after a very severe illness, which destroyed his voice, recovered.
8 Storer, b. 3 Nov. 1802; m. Dorothy Lancaster Tompson.
9 Erving, b. 22 Aug. 1804; d. 6 March 1819.
10 Dorothy, b. 27 July 1806; d. 19 March 1819.

11-7-2-6

CAPT. JOSHUA LIBBY, born in Scarborough, 31 Aug. 1768; married, 16 Feb. 1791, RUTH LIBBY, 11-7-11-1. He was a farmer, and had his father's homestead. He always lived on it, and died 23 Oct. 1834. He was selectman 1822, 1826, and 1827, and town treasurer 1817-1827. His wife died 24 Nov. 1831.

Children, all born in Scarborough:

1 Sherborn, b. 3 Sept. 1791; m. Mary Watson.
2 Joshua, b. 10 July 1793; m. Mary Small.
3 Simon, b. 2 Feb. 1795; m. Phebe Webb.
4 Johnson, b. 4 Feb. 1797; m. Eveline Tyler.
5 Addison, b. 17 Feb. 1799; d. 27 Sept. 1800.
6 Addison, } twins, born } m. Emma Maxcy.
7 Hannah, } 20 April 1801; } m. 23 Jan. 1820, Andrew Taylor of Portland; d. 18 Sept. 1829.

8 Woodbury, b. 25 Dec. 1803; m. 26 June 1828, Abigail Meserve. [See Meserve, page 37.] Two years after his marriage, he moved onto what had been the homestead of his uncle Matthias Libby. There he lived until 1870, when he removed to the homestead of his wife's father. He lived there until his death, 14 Aug. 1879, and there his widow still abides. Children:
 1 Hannah Frances, b. 2 Aug. 1829; m. David D. Clough.
 2 Ruth Ann, b. 2 Dec. 1831; m. 12 Nov. 1854, John W. Bristow.
 3 Lucretia, b. 22 Sept. 1833; m. John Libby, 11-7-1-4-4-5.
 4 Nancy Meserve, b. 8 Feb. 1835; unm.
 5 John Franklin, b. 19 Jan. 1837; d. 26 April 1870; unm. He was a carpenter.
 6 Jefferson Woodbury, b. 2 June 1839; d. 15 Jan. 1868. He was a blacksmith. He served three years in Co. C, 12th Maine.
 7 Edwin Augustus, } twins, b. 21 June 1841; } died 1 Jan. 1870.
 8 Henry Harrison, } were farmers; } died 14 Oct. 1869. He served three years in Co. I, 17th Maine.
9 Frances, b. 27 Oct. 1806; m. 11 Sept. 1834, John N. Jones.
10 Matthias, b. 20 Feb. 1808; m. Lydia Jones.
11 Ruth, b. 10 March 1810; m. 5 June 1828, James Johnson.
12 George, b. 14 Oct. 1812; m. Damaris Small.
13 Esther, b. 20 Aug. 1814; m. 6 Nov. 1834, Horace Meserve.

11-7-2-7

Capt. Theodore Libby, born in Scarborough, 18 July 1773; married, 10 Dec. 1808, Sarah Harmon of Standish. He lived on the farm afterward owned by his sons, and died 5 July 1825, leaving a good property. His widow married, 4 Nov. 1828, Wm. Wescott of North Yarmouth, and died in Scarborough, 12 Feb. 1860.

Children, born in Scarborough:

1 Cyrus, b. 20 Dec. 1809; d. 23 March 1881; unm.
2 Eliza, b. 27 Oct. 1811; m. 12 Dec. 1833, James L. Deering.
3 Hannah, b. 22 Oct. 1814; m. Dennis M. Skillings.
4 Theodore, b. 29 Nov. 1819; d. 28 Jan. 1866; unm.

11-7-2-9

Salome Libby, born in Scarborough, 15 Oct. 1778; married, 11 June 1799, Moses McKenney; died 1 July 1843. He died 24 March 1828. [See page 63.]

Children, born in Scarborough:

1 Mahala (McKenney), b. 1803; d. Nov. 1825; unm.
2 Hannah (McKenney), b. 13 Jan. 1805; m. John Chapman.
3 John (McKenney), b. 26 Feb. 1809; m. Statira Skillings.
4 William (McKenney), b. 27 April 1811; m. Delia Ward.
5 Joshua (McKenney), b. Dec. 1831; m. Elinor, only child of Abigail (Libby) Bugbee, 1-1-2-2-10. He lives in Winn. Children:
 1 John Henry Goddard (McKenney), lives in Winn.
 2 Moses Benjamin Franklin (McKenney), b. 1841; m. 15 Oct. 1870, Frances Alice, dau. of Samuel and Frances (Wilding) Lewis of Manchester, Eng. He is a junk dealer in Portland. Child:
  1 Francis Lewis (McKenney), b. 22 Aug. 1876.
 3 Abbie Libby (McKenney), lives in Winn; unm.
 4 Joshua (McKenney), lives in Winn; unm.
 5 Mary Ellen (McKenney), twin with Joshua; m. Jerome B. Chapman.

11-7-6-A

Francis Libby, born about 1786; married Sally Burnham, daughter of Job and Mary (Obrian) Burnham of Machias.

He was by birth a Getchell. He received the homestead of his foster father, and became a well-to-do farmer. He died 11 Dec. 1846. His wife died 11 July 1842.

Children:

1 Sally, b. 15 Aug. 1806; died 5 March 1847.
2 Joseph, b. 29 Dec. 1807; died 7 Jan. 1838.
3 Eliza, b. 13 Mar. 1809; died 28 Feb. 1839.
4 Charles, b. 29 Dec. 1810; lives in Machiasport.
5 Sophia, b. 6 Oct. 1812.
6 Leonice, b. 13 April 1815; died 6 Sept. 1836.
7 James Monroe, b. 13 July 1818; died 31 Aug. 1819.
8 Leonard, b. 13 July 1820.
9 Mary Ann, b. 28 Sept. 1822; died 17 April 1837.
10 Caroline, b. 27 July 1825; died 13 May 1838.
11 Francis, b. 20 June 1830.
12 Jerome B., b. 13 March 1833; m. 1st, —— Thompson; 2d, 10 May 1874, Etta E. Colbath. He is a mariner, living in Machiasport. Children, by first wife:
  1 Jerome Francis.

By second wife:

  2 Etta May, b. 1875.

11-7-7-3

Daniel Libby, born in Scarborough, 3 April 1772; married Polly Hoyt of Durham. He went east and cleared a farm on the boundary line between Durham and Pownal. His first little two-room house he built on the Durham side of the road that forms the division line, but he afterward built the one now occupied by his son-in-law, Geo. W. Gee, on the Pownal side. He died 8 May, and his wife 22 July, 1848.

Children, born in Durham:

1 Daniel [Rev.], b. 22 Feb. 1804; m. 9 Aug. 1832, Eunice Russell, dau. of Dea. Joseph and Lucy (Sumner) Wheeler of Dixfield. Although blind, he obtained an education, and became a Congregational clergyman. He was the first settled minister at Dixfield, and afterward preached at Minot. He died 4 May 1839. Only child:
  1 Daniel Sumner, b. 16 Jan. 1837, in Minot; unm. He inherits his father's blindness, and lives with his mother in Dixfield. He is a member of the Congregational Church.
2 Hannah, b. 20 April 1806; m. 1 July 1838, as second wife, her cousin, George W. Gee.

Born in Pownal:

3 Hamor, b. 27 Oct. 1810; m. 15 April 1832, George W. Gee.
4 Dorothy, b. 28 Jan. 1813; d. 12 May 1836; unm.

11-7-7-5

WALTER LIBBY, born in Scarborough, 13 Nov. 1776; married, 11 April 1800, ELIZABETH JORDAN, daughter of Benjamin Allen Jordan of Gorham. After his marriage he lived a short time each in Standish and Pownal, and then settled in Durham, on the farm afterward owned by Leonard Parker. In 1845 he sold his farm and went to live with his son Walter in Pownal, and there died, 22 March 1855. His widow died in Durham 23 Feb. 1840.

Children, born in Gorham:

1 Axey, b. April 1801; m., as 1st wife, James Arthur Merrill of Falmouth.

Born in Pownal:

2 Daniel, b. 17 Dec. 1802; m. Sarah Osgood.
3 Esther, m. Joseph Weeks of Durham.
4 Benjamin, b. July 1809; died 2 Nov. 1824.
5 Mary, m. Charles Parker of Durham.
6 Walter, b. 26 Dec. 1812; m. Sarah Davis Thoits.
7 Eliza, m., as second wife, J. A. Merrill.
8 Horace C., b. 7 Dec. 1817; m. 16 Nov. 1840, Harriet Libby, 10-5-4-3-1-2. He is a stone-cutter and worked many years with his brother Daniel. He lived in Durham until 1874, serving in the highest offices in that town, and has since lived with his brother Daniel's son in Massachusetts. No children.

11-7-7-6

CAPT. SEWALL LIBBY, born in Scarborough, 6 March 1779; married, 15 Dec. 1808, SARAH LIBBY, 1-1-6-5-2. He followed the sea from his youth, and became a captain in the West India trade, sailing from Portland. He died in Portland 29 April 1830. His widow died Sept. 1842.

Children, born in Scarborough:

1 Cyrene, b. 27 March 1809; d. 11 July 1859; unm. She was blind many years.
2 Sewall, b. 1 March 1811; died about 1833; unm. At the age of 16, it is said, he went as mate of a brig to the West Indies, and, by the death of the captain, the chief command of the vessel, on the home voyage, fell to him. He filled the position so creditably that he was immediately placed in command of her. He died of small-pox at the age of 26.
3 Cornelius, b. 10 June 1814; never married. He followed the sea, and rose to be mate. He lost his hearing by a blow from a falling spar, and was compelled to relinquish his calling. He then became a house-painter, and removed to California, where he died.
4 Alvin, followed the sea; was last heard from in New York.

11-7-7-8

ANDREW LIBBY, born in Scarborough, 27 Dec. 1783; married first, 11 Oct. 1811, ABIGAIL, daughter of —— and Mary (Chase) Tappan; (died 11 November 1813); second, 20 Aug. 1815,

MARGARET TODD, daughter of Wm. Todd of Freeport. He lived on his father's homestead, and died Feb. 1863. His wife died 22 April 1853.

Children, all born in Scarborough:

1 Tappan, b. 25 Jan. 1817; m. 5 Jan. 1844, Catherine Skillings, dau. of Dea. Wm. and Sarah (Moses) Cummings. He settled on the "carrying-place farm," which his father had owned. He is a farmer and milkman, supplying the Portland market. Children:
  1 Sarah Margaret, b. 3 May 1845; m. 29 July 1874, Levi Morrill of Green Bay, Wis.
  2 Phebe Ann, b. 14 Dec. 1846; d. 13 Aug. 1852.
  3 William Cummings, b. 19 Feb. 1849; d. 17 July 1849.
  4 Esther Rand, b. 15 June 1850; m. 12 July 1875, Dr. Chas. H. Witham.
  5 Mary Jane Cummings, b. 29 Aug. 1853; m. 5 Aug. 1875, Chas. C. Nourse.
  6 Elizabeth Patience, b. 33 Nov. 1855; unm.
  7 Anna Lowell, b. 16 Aug. 1860; d. 3 May 1876.
  8 Hattie Hayes, b. 9 May 1863; d. 21 Sept. 1866.
2 Jane, b. 7 Oct. 1818; m. William W. Haines; d. 2 Oct. 1865.
3 Dorothy Ann, b. 25 July 1822; d. 25 April 1842.
4 Phebe Ann, b. 8 July 1824; m. 1845, John B. Merrill: d. Sept. 1846.
5 William Henry, b. 1 Oct. 1828; m. 21 Aug. 1853, Mary A., daughter of Moses and Esther (Lufkin) Littlefield of Turner. He had his father's homestead, but sold it and removed to Portland, where he has been for many years head clerk in Cobb's bakery. Children, born in Scarborough:
  1 Frederick William, b. 19 July 1854; d. 19 Sept. 1855.
  2 Emma Jennie, b. 3 Aug. 1855; m. 8 Aug. 1872, Geo. L. Day.
  3 Maria Haskell, b. 4 June 1857; m. 5 Dec. 1877, Almon G. Hanscom.
  4 William Frederick, b. 22 Aug. 1859; m. 7 Feb. 1879, Kate L., dau. of Daniel and Bridget (Carter) Cochran. He is a broommaker. Child:
    1 George C., b. 2 Feb. 1880.

Born in Portland:

  5 Walter Frank, } twins, b.
  6 Charles Davis, } 2 June 1863.
  7 Mary Ella, b. 1 April 1865; d. 12 Sept. 1865.
  8 Albert Henry, b. 3 Oct. 1867.
6 Ezra Carter, b. 28 Aug. 1832; m. 19 Nov. 1864, Sarah C., daughter of Ammi and Mary (Lake) Cotton of Brunswick. He lived in Cape Elizabeth and in Westbrook, and is now a farmer in Scarborough. Children:
  1 Walter R. Fluent, b. 10 Sept. 1870, in Westbrook.
  2 William Shailor, b. 28 Feb. 1872, in Westbrook.
  3 ——, b. 24 Jan., d. 3 Feb., 1875, in Westbrook.

11-7-8-2

EDWARD LIBBY, born in Scarborough, 7 Nov. 1770; married, 5 April 1789, JANE LIBBY, 11-7-1-5. He settled near White Rock, in Gorham, and there died, 19 Aug. 1848. His wife died 19 Jan. 1844.

Children:

1 Esther, m. 11 Sept. 1811, Jonathan Files.
2 Joseph, m. Mehitable Moses.

3 Cary, m. Betsey Haskell of New Gloucester.
4 Morris, m. Jane Latham. During her life he lived in Raymond, but after her death, Nov. 1828, he returned to his father's home. About 1847 he bought land in Stoneham, where he died in the spring of 1878. In his old age he married a second wife, who died shortly after he did, childless. Children by his first wife:
   1 Eliab, b. 17 Feb. 1826; m. Sarah Hopkins. He lives in San Francisco, California. One child.
   2 son, died Oct. 1828, aged 10 weeks.
5 Solomon, b. 1798; m. 24 March 1823, Susan, dau. of James and Mary (Roberts) Sturgis. He was a farmer at White Rock, where he died 20 Sept. 1860. His wife died 26 July 1862. Children:
   1 Caroline Sturgis, b. 13 Nov. 1826; m. June 1852, Josiah P. Chadbourne.
   2 Esther Plummer, b. 6 Feb. 1829; m. Wm. H. Murch, 1-5-2-3-2-2-4.
   3 Charlotte, b. 26 July 1831; m. 30 April 1854, Geo. W. Johnson, a son of Lydia (Libby) Johnson, 1-5-2-3-3-2.
6 Andrew, b. 2 April 1800; m. Sophronia Small.
7 Charlotte, died at the age of 18.
8 Edward, b. 8 Aug. 1804; m. Aug. 1841, Christania, dau. of Samuel D. and Mary (Strout) Strout of Raymond. He lived on the homestead until the death of his parents, and soon after settled in Raymond on the farm now owned by Horace Strout, and there died, 13 Jan. 1867. His widow married, 10 Dec. 1876, Henry Spiller, and still lives. Edward Libby had no children, but adopted an infant daughter of Samuel and Betsey (Carpenter) Brown of Poland, which took the name:
   a Ella Brown (Libby), b. 3 April 1865.
9 Mary, m. 23 Feb. 1837, Joseph Leavitt of Newfield.

11-7-8-3

JOSEPH LIBBY, born in Scarborough, 6 March 1772; married ANNA PLUMMER, daughter of Jeremiah and Sarah (Eldrich) Plummer. When his first child was an infant, he removed to Pownal, where he cleared the farm now occupied by the widow of his son Jeremiah. He worked much at teaming, going sometimes as far as Boston. His death occurred 27 Aug. 1832. His widow died 19 April 1857.

Children:

1 Sally, b. 15 Dec. 1795; m. 1st, 8 Aug. 1817, Samuel Brown; 2d, Samuel Marr Libby, 10-5-2-3-2. Previous to her marriage she bore a daughter:
   1 Almira (Libby). She was brought up by her grandparents, and married, 18 May 1842, Isaac S. Brown.
2 Anna, b. 4 Aug. 1797; m. 6 Feb. 1826, Caleb Estes.
3 Mary, b. 22 May 1799; d. 20 March 1821; unm.
4 Lydia, b. 13 March 1801; m. 1st, Wm. Estes; 2d, Timothy Keith.
5 Esther, b. 30 March 1803; m. 11 Feb. 1824, Ebenezer Brown.
6 Miriam, b. 21 March 1805; m. 10 Feb. 1831, Nicholas Tuttle.
7 Olive, b. 27 Sept. 1807; m. 13 Nov. 1836, Elias Knights.
8 Joseph, b. 16 June 1809; m. Julia A. Libby, 11-9-7-7-7.
9 Jane, b. 2 Aug. 1811; d. 9 Dec. 1819.
10 Louisa, b. 1 Jan. 1814; m. 1st, Geo. W. Bryant; 2d, Arnold Z. Tuell.
11 Edward, b. 3 July 1816; d. 23 Nov. 1856; unm. He lived at home; a farmer and harness-maker.
12 Ruth, b. 16 Feb. 1818; m. John H. Tuttle.
13 Jeremiah, b. 9 Nov. 1819; m. 31 Jan. 1850, Elvira, dau. of Charles and Joanna (Tuttle) Wilson of Freeport. He lived on the homestead and died 18 Nov. 1877. Children:

1 Ellery Drew, b. 31 July 1851; m. 27 Nov. 1873, Josephine A., dau. of Capt. Martin and Eliza Ann (Drinkwater) Noyes of Yarmouth. He has been a blacksmith, a harness-maker, a house-painter, a house-carpenter, a photographer, and is now employed in a shoe-factory in Freeport. Child:
1 Sylvanus Martin, b. 3 April 1879, in Pownal.
2 Bertie, b. 25 Jan. 1861; d. 5 Sept. 1861.
3 Elvina Amanda, b. 1 Sept. 1866.
4 Charles Wilson, b. 2 Nov. 1867.
14 Cary, b. 18 Nov. 1821; d. 21 April 1852; unm. He lived at home.

11-7-11-7

Simon Libby, born in Scarborough, 5 Sept. 1785; married, 12 Aug. 1813, Hannah Berry, daughter of Solomon and Hannah (Jones) Berry. He lived at home until after the birth of six of his children, and then left Scarborough and settled on a farm in what was then Monmouth, now Wales. He died there, 26 Dec. 1848. His widow died in Scarborough, 18 March 1868.

Children:

1 Jane, b. 3 Oct. 1813; d. 1 Feb. 1817.
2 George Thompson, b. 1 May 1815; unm. He is a farmer.
3 Jane, b. 1 April 1817; m. 23 May 1842, Major Plummer.
4 Furber, b. 22 July 1819; m. 31 Oct. 1847, Betsey E., dau. of Timothy and Mary (Bran) Staples of Belgrade. He was employed seven years in Hallowell in the oil-cloth business, and then returned to the homestead farm, on which he has since continued. Children:
1 George T., b. 28 Dec. 1849; unm.; is a locomotive engineer.
2 Edwin F., b. 11 April 1852; unm.; is a locomotive fireman.
3 Ella B., b. 2 Jan. 1854; m. April, 1876, Geo. M. Douglas.
4 Willis H., b. 31 July 1855; unm.; is in a machine-shop in Allston, Mass.
5 Lester E., b. 10 April 1858; unm.; is a telegraph operator.
6 Ida L., b. 15 Aug. 1861.
7 Everett L., b. 16 July 1864; d. 31 Dec. 1864.
5 John Robinson, b. 5 Feb. 1822; died 30 Feb. 1868, in Monson. He was a stage driver. Children:
1 Charles, b. about 1845; lives in Boston (?). He was married and lived in Lewiston, where his wife died in 1880, leaving three children.
2 Effie; died unmarried.
6 Esther, b. 7 Feb. 1824; m. Abram Plummer; died 16 March 1879.
7 Simon, b. 30 Oct. 1828; d. 16 March 1829.
8 Hannah, b. 18 March 1830; m. Wm. Dunham.
9 David O., b. 31 March 1832; lives in Greene, Me.

11-7-11-8

George Libby, born in Scarborough, 4 Feb. 1791; married, 3 Oct. 1824, Lydia Libby, 10-5-1-10-4. He always lived on his father's homestead. He and his brother tore down the house which had been their grandfather's and built, on the opposite side of the road, the one now standing. He died 2 Nov. 1840. His wife died 5 Sept. 1839.

Children:

1 George Washington, b. 12 April 1825; m. 23 Sept. 1852, Clara Jane Libby, 11-6-5-5-10. He built a house on part of his father's farm, and there lived until his death, which occurred 21 Feb. 1879. He was deacon of the Congregational Church from 1853 until his death. During the latter years of his life, he was station-master of the Scarborough Beach station of the Boston & Maine Railroad. Children:
 1 George Thomas, b. 25 Sept. 1854; unm.
 2 Clara Jane, b. 13 Oct. 1856; unm.
 3 Minerva Ellen, b. 1 June 1858.
 4 Asa Therburne, b. 13 Oct. 1860; d. 16 Nov. 1862.
 5 Mary Lydia; b. 9 Feb. 1862.
 6 Florence Louise, } twins, b.
 7 Alice Amelia, } 9 Feb. 1864.
 8 Fannie Maria, b. 30 March 1865.
 9 Elizabeth Ann, b. 12 Nov. 1866.
 10 Simon Henry, b. 19 March 1869.
 11 Sarah Almira, b. 15 Sept. 1871.
2 John Adams, b. 28 Aug. 1826; d. 24 July 1832.
3 Benjamin Franklin, b. 21 Nov. 1827; d. 7 Aug. 1832.
4 Mary Elizabeth, b. 22 March 1830; m. John A. Tompson, 5-7-14-7-4.
5 Esther Frances, b. 6 June 1832; d. 27 Aug. 1832.
6 John Adams, b. 4 Dec. 1833; m. Harriet, dau. of John and Sarah Jones (Hustin) Robinson. He lives on the homestead farm. Children:
 1 James Robinson, b. 17 Jan. 1864; d. 11 Sept. 1864.
 2 John Herbert, b. 22 Jan. 1865.
 3 Sarah Louisa, b. 17 April 1866.
 4 Mary Tompson, b. 29 Oct. 1870, in Portland.
 5 Irving Clarence, b. 29 March 1872, in Portland.
 6 Ernest Merrill, b. 22 April 1878; d. 5 July 1879.
7 Simon, b. 31 March 1835; m. 1st, 14 May 1867, Mrs. Louisa R. (Robinson) Moody, a sister of his brother's wife; (died 10 July 1878); 2d, 30 March 1881, Sarah O., widow of Emery Moody, dau. of Charles and Salome (Drew) Bean of Bowdoinham. From 1863 until 1877, he was a truckman in Portland. He then returned to Scarborough and bought from Edward Tompson [see page 75] the Tompson homestead, which had been in that family 150 years. No children.
8 Esther Ellen, b. 2 Nov. 1836; m. 6 Dec. 1855, Milton Higgins.
9 Lydia Frances, b. 18 July 1839; d. 17 Dec. 1862; unm.

11-9-5-3

James Libby, born in Berwick, Me., 18 Aug. 1767; married, 28 June 1798, Polly Ayers, daughter of Elisha and Mary (McLellan) Ayers of Newfield.

He left Berwick, and lived afterward in Newfield and in Limerick. He was at first a country trader, and then a farmer in the latter place, where he died 29 Nov. 1836. His widow died in Burlington 22 Aug. 1858.

Children:

1 Amzi, b. 10 March 1799; m. Mary Chard.
2 Mary, b. about 1801; m. Rev. Daniel Brackett.
3 Asenath, b. about 1803; m. Bray Lunt.
4 Mark L., b. about 1806; m. Cordelia Hastings.
5 Sally, died in infancy.
6 Susan, b. Nov. 1808; m. Dr. Moses Lunt.

7 Sarah D., b. 28 Oct. 1810; lives in Boston; unm.
8 James, died in infancy.
9 Jane D., b. Aug. 1814; m. Jesse R. Warner; died 9 Oct. 1870.
10 Lewis, died in infancy.
11 Nancy A. b. 28 May 1819; died 8 Sept. 1881, in Boston; unm.
12 Hannah T., b. 3 Sept. 1821; died 1844; unm.
13 James Lewis, born about 1823; married a southerner. When last heard from, at the beginning of the late war, he was a dentist in southern Illinois.

11-9-5-5

Dea. Mark Libby, born in Berwick, Me., 28 May 1771; married, 30 June 1808, Olive Lord of Berwick. He lived on his father's homestead and died 1 April 1842. He was a deacon of the Congregational Church. His wife died 15 Oct. 1825.

Children, all born in Berwick:

1 James, b. 30 April 1809; m. 1 July 1832, Elizabeth H., daughter of Daniel and Betsey (Hayes) Quimby. He received from his father the old Fogg homestead. There he lived until his death, 4 Sept. 1878, and his widow still lives. Children:
  1 Mary Elizabeth, b. 7 Feb. 1837; m. 23 May 1863, Enoch George Adams, a graduate of Yale College. He served through the civil war and rose to the rank of brevet-major. They removed to Oregon in 1866 and he is now editor and proprietor of the *Columbian*. He lives in St. Helen. Children:
    1 Blanche Hermine (Adams), b. 22 Oct. 1871.
    2 Bernal Henry (Adams), b. 16 June 1873.
    3 James Birney (Adams), b. 21 Sept. 1876.
  2 Olive Esther, b. 7 Nov. 1840; m. 1 Jan. 1860, Joseph M. R. Adams, brother of Enoch.
2 Nathaniel, b. 4 Oct. 1810; d. 21 May 1841; unm. He was a farmer and lumberman.
3 Olive, b. 22 June 1814; d. 21 May 1841; unm.
4 Elizabeth, b. 11 March 1817; m. 29 Oct. 1846, Capt. John Gowell.
5 Mary, b. 12 Jan. 1819; d. 7 March 1837.
6 Mark, b. 29 Aug. 1822; m. 22 Feb. 1846, Eliza A., dau. of John and Susan (Smith) Chadbourne. (John Chadbourne was a grandson of Elizabeth (Libby) Chadbourne, 1-6-5-4.) He settled on his father's homestead, and followed farming successfully until 1873, when he sold the farm, and built a residence in South Berwick Village, where he has since abode. He was at one time the Democratic candidate for representative to the state legislature. Children:
  1 Mary Emma, b. 9 Sept. 1851; unm.
  2 Mark Addison, b. 20 July 1855; unm.
  3 Susan Olivia, b. 4 May 1857; d. 24 Dec. 1873.
  4 Eliza Annabel, b. 4 July 1859; d. 9 July 1873.
  5 Hattie Eveline, b. 8 April 1861; d. 30 Jan. 1866.
  6 Edwina Frances, b. 7 May 1863; d. 14 Nov. 1871.

11-9-7-2

Stephen Libby, born in Berwick, Me., 12 April 1764; married, 17 April 1790, Sally Butler, daughter of Moses and Mercy (Wentworth) Butler of Sanford. He was brought up in Shapleigh. Soon after his marriage, he settled in Limerick, on the farm now occupied by Walter Pierce. He was a farmer and wheelwright. He died 19 Oct. 1833, and his widow, 15 Dec. 1851.

Children, born in Shapleigh:

1 Nathaniel, b. 10 April 1791; m. Anna Ricker.
2 Nancy Gerrish, b. 22 April 1793; m. John Cook Libby, 11-9-7-3-1.

Born in Sanford:

3 Bridget, b. 7 Dec. 1794; m. 23 March 1819, Nathaniel Ricker.

Born in Limerick:

4 Lovina, b. 29 Dec. 1796; m. 9 Oct. 1833, Paul Hussey.
5 Silea, b. 3 March 1799; m. 1 Jan. 1822, Hiram Joy.
6 Stephen, b. 20 Nov. 1801; m. Nancy Libby, 11-9-7-3-7, and Mary Jane Bradeen.
7 William, b. 21 Sept.; d. 30 Sept., 1802.
8 Cyrus, b. 24 Jan. 1804; m. Drusilla Woodsom.
9 Rook Thurston, b. 27 Jan. 1806; m. Emily Lord and Marion Bradbury.
10 Thomas Butler, b. 9 Dec. 1808; m. Eunice Butler.
11 Alice, b. 22 May 1810; d. 2 Aug. 1850; unm.
12 Mary, b. 4 April 1815; d. 13 Aug. 1832; unm.

11-9-7-3

Samuel Libby, born in Berwick, Me., about 1767; married, 1792, Anna Cook of Shapleigh. He lived in that part of Shapleigh which is now the southwest part of Acton, on the farm now occupied by Reuben Winchell. He died probably in the spring of 1817, and his widow married Love Roberts.

Children, all born in Shapleigh:

1 John Cook, b. 15 Sept. 1793; m. Nancy Gerrish Libby, 11-9-7-2-2.
2 Polly, b. 25 Oct. 1795; m. 6 Nov. 1817, Thomas F. Kinsman.
3 Asa, b. 25 Jan. 1798; m. Abigail Libby, 11-9-7-8-3.
4 Clarissa, b. 11 March 1800; d. 2 July 1864, in Exeter; unm.
5 Samuel, b. 18 June 1806; m. Melinda A. Hussey.
6 Calvin, b. 18 June 1808; m. Nancy C. Mills.
7 Nancy, m. Stephen Libby, 11-9-7-2-6.

11-9-7-7

Zebulon Libby, born in Shapleigh, Me., 15 May 1780; married, Dorcas Holmes, daughter of John and Dorcas (Weymouth) Holmes of Berwick. He was a farmer. He early removed to the interior of Maine. He lived some years in Smithfield, and in 1829 removed to Palmyra. He afterward settled in Pittsfield, on the farm now owned by Alfred Hodgkins, and there died, 7 July 1869. His wife died 11 July 1869, in Palmyra.

Children:

1 John Y., b. 25 Nov. 1802; m. Sarah Merrow.
2 Polly, b. 3 May 1805; m. George Gleason.

3 Peter, b. 24 June 1807; m. Sophia Bickford and Mrs. Priscilla Gordon.
4 Alice, b. 26 Nov. 1809; m. Arthur Bickford.
5 Lovici, b. 4 Feb. 1812; died 5 Oct. 1813.
6 Stephen, b. 3 Dec. 1815; died 11 Dec. 1815.
7 Julia Ann, b. 6 Sept. 1821; m. Joseph Libby, 11-7-8-3-8.

11-9-7-8

PETER LIBBY, born in Shapleigh, Me., 3 July 1781; married, 31 Dec. 1801, SARAH BEAN, daughter of "Bill" Bean of Shapleigh.

In the winter of 1802-3, he moved from Shapleigh to Fairfield, and settled in the wilderness. A few years later he moved to Smithfield, where he became a very successful farmer. He was selectman many years, was a justice of the peace, and represented his town in the state legislature. He died 11 Aug. 1862. His wife died July 1857.

Children, born in Fairfield:

1 William, b. 14 April 1803; died the next month.
2 Asa M., b. 13 June 1804; m. Sarah A. Cook and Joanna B. Powers.
3 Abigail, b. 3 July 1807; m. Asa Libby, 11-9-7-3-3.
4 Hannah, twin with Abigail, b. 5 July 1807; m. 1823, Seth Gage.

Born in Smithfield;

5 Sally, b. 30 Oct. 1809; d. 1818.

11-9-7-10

JOHN LIBBY, born in Shapleigh, Me., 5 Feb. 1790; married, 20 June 1813, BETSEY BEAN, daughter of William and Susan (Gilbert) Bean of Shapleigh. He had his father's homestead in Shapleigh. He was a thrifty farmer, but, becoming surety for some of his neighbors, lost his all. In February, 1833, he removed to what was then Dearborn, afterward Waterville, and now West Waterville. "In all the towns in which he lived, he held places of honor and trust." He died in Waterville 8 May 1871, and his widow 16 Dec. 1872.

Children, all born in Shapleigh:

1 John Mayhew, b. 25 Feb. 1815; m. Louisa F. Witham.
2 Hannah M., b. 15 April 1817; m. Jefferson Hersom.
3 Peter D., b. 30 June 1824; m. Keziah C. Gage.
4 Edward B., b. 7 July 1826; unm. Has always lived on the homestead farm.
5 Betsey A., b. 5 April 1828; m. Crowell Bickford.

11-9-8-7

LEVI LIBBY, born in Berwick, Me., 27 May 1786; married, 12 Feb. 1807, EUNICE STILLINGS of Berwick. 15 Feb. 1808, he moved to Clinton, and ten years later to Benton, where he cleared from the wilderness the farm on which he ended his days, now occupied by his second daughter. He died 30 Oct. 1860, and his widow, 12 April 1867.

Children:

1 Oliver, b. 15 Dec. 1808; m. Hannah Plummer.
2 James, b. 29 July 1811; m. Mary Tyler.
3 Olive, b. 30 Dec. 1812; m. 1830, Ira Plummer.
4 Mary Elizabeth, b. 25 Dec. 1828; m. 9 March 1851, Asaph Willey.
5 Sarah J., b. 8 June 1832; d. 17 Jan. 1858.

11-9-8-8

DEA. IRA LIBBY, born in Berwick, Me., 9 Dec. 1788; married, 26 April 1813, FANNY LANGDON, daughter of Joseph and Sarah (Nowell) Langdon of Lebanon. He always lived on his father's homestead. He was a skillful mechanic and was somewhat noted as a horse and cattle doctor. He was deacon of the F. W. Baptist church in North Berwick. His death occurred 18 Feb. 1840. His widow died in Limerick, 12 Feb. 1871.

Children, all born in Berwick:

1 Sarah Ann, b. 10 Sept. 1815; m. 12 June 1836, Joseph Emery.
2 Susan, b. 26 July 1817; m. 22 Oct. 1837, Jeremiah Emery.
3 Hannah J., b. 14 March 1821; m. 29 March 1845, John Wilkerson.

11-11-6-2

THOMAS LIBBY, born in Kittery, now Eliot, Me., 26 Nov. 1776; married first, 1 Dec. 1814, SOPHIA (REMMICK) HODGDON; (died 31 Dec. 1822); second, 19 Oct. 1823, Sarah, daughter of George and Mary (Weeks) Hammond. He lived on his father's homestead, and died 18 Sept. 1852. His widow died 6 Oct. 1852.

Only child, by first wife:

1 Alvin, b. 27 July 1819; m. 1852, Jane, dau. of Samuel and Catherine (Raynes) Parker of York. He lived on his father's homestead until 1858, when he bought and removed to a farm at Spruce Creek, in Kittery. Four years later he removed to the Cutts farm on which he still lives. Children:
   1 Frank Wilmot, b. 29 Oct. 1853; d. 25 May 1856.
   2 Harriet Edna, b. 4 March 1855; unm.
   3 George Byron, b. 26 Aug. 1857; unm. Except his father, he is the only lineal male descendant of Samuel Libby, 11-11.
   4 Mary Etta, b. 25 Nov. 1860.
   5 Carrie Estella, b. 21 April 1864.
   6 Lucy Jane, b. 12 Sept. 1868.

11-11-6-4

ANDREW LIBBY, born in Kittery, Me., 4 Aug. 1782; married, 15 April 1819, PATIENCE B. DORR, daughter of Joseph and Hannah (Brackett) Dorr of Shapleigh, Me. (Joseph Dorr was a son of Lydia (Libby) Dorr, 11-2-2-1-1.) When a young man, he removed to Wakefield, N. H. here he bought a farm. He lived on that and on another which he afterward bought, until his death, 15 Sept. 1828. His widow removed with her family to Kittery, where she married about 1846, Wm. Manson. She died 13 Nov. 1869.

Children, all born in Wakefield:

1 Seth, b. 10 Jan. 1820; died with his sister, in Kittery, 25 Nov. 1861. He was twice married. His first wife died about three years after their marriage. The second, whose maiden name was Mary Carney, outlived him, and married again in Cambridgeport, Mass. He was by trade a baker, but became a truckman in Boston. Children, by first wife:

1 child, died in infancy.

By second wife:

2 Mary Jane, b. 17 Sept. 1859, in Cambridge.

2 Hannah Brackett, b. 11 Aug. 1821; d. 16 Dec. 1838.

3 Andrew Brackett, b. 6 April 1823; d. 18 Sept. 1828.

4 Daniel Rollins, b. 15 May 1825; d. 15 Sept. 1828.

5 Mary Hutchins Brackett, b. 15 March 1827; d. 16 Sept. 1828.

6 Sarah Elizabeth, b. 18 May 1829; m. 22 Nov. 1849, Joshua Hall Sanborn of Kittery.

James B. Libby

SIXTH GENERATION.

1-1-2-2-2

Dea. James Libby, born in Scarborough, 2 Aug. 1757; married first, Betsey Small, daughter of David Small of Gray; (died 15 Nov. 1796); second, Mrs. Sarah (Woodbury) Dyer.

He was at first a lumberman, and then a farmer. He lived in Gray a short time after his marriage, and then settled in Danville on the farm now owned by —— Sawyer. He served under Lafayette in the storming of Stony Point, and was met by him in Portland, on his visit to America, and recognized. He was deacon of the Baptist church in Danville. His death took place 5 May 1828, and his widow died in Poland 18 April 1841.

Children, all by first wife:

1 Sally, b. 2 Aug. 1780, in Gray; m. 1st, Nathaniel Nason; (died 3 Feb. 1819); 2d, Nathan Haskell; died 2 July 1832.
2 Polly, b. 24 Oct. 1782; m. Joel Kimball.
3 David, b. 3 March 1785; m. Dorcas Nason.
4 Martha, died in childhood.
5 Martha, b. 1 Jan. 1793, in Danville; m. Nathaniel Gates.
6 James, b. 25 Oct. 1796; m. Nancy Fulton.

1-1-2-2-3

Benjamin Libby, born in Scarborough, Sept. 1762; married, first, 4 July 1782, Elizabeth Hunnewell, 7-1-5-1; (died Dec. 1813); second, Hannah Moody, daughter of Scribner Moody of Whitefield.

He served all through the Revolution. After his marriage, he settled on Dutton Hill, in the town of Gray, on the road leading to Windham. Soon after the birth of his eleventh child, he removed further into the wilderness, and settled in Canaan, where he lived until after the death of his first wife. During that time he served as quartermaster in the war of 1812. After his second marriage, he lived in Whitefield, and there died, 2 Aug. 1831. His widow died in Augusta, 25 Nov. 1872.

Children, by first wife, born in Gray:

1 Humphrey, b. 29 Oct. 1783; m. Jan. 1817, Harriet McCausland. He was a farmer in Canaan. He was drowned while driving logs, May 1832. His widow died in Pittsfield, Sept. 1878. Only child:
  1 John. He was in government employ during the late war, and died in New Orleans, La., in the winter of 1865. He left a wife and child in New Hampshire.
2 Sally, b. 24 Sept. 1785; m. 1 Jan. 1802, John Haines.
3 Hannah, b. 21 Dec. 1788; m. 25 Nov. 1815, Moses Woodbury.
4 Thankful, b. 7 March 1790; m. 8 March 1812, Isaiah Woodbury.
5 John, b. 7 July 1791; d. 13 Nov. 1804.
6 Phebe, b. 16 Feb. 1796; d. 12 March 1873, in Canaan; unm.
7 Charles b. 8 Jan. 1798; m. Feb. 1825, Louisa, dau. of Daniel Goodwin of Canaan. In 1845, he removed from Canaan to Vinland, Wis., and became one of the well-to-do inhabitants of that place. His wife died 20 May 1874, and he now lives among his daughters. Children:
  1 Caroline Matilda, b. 13 Dec. 1827; m. 20 May 1848, Hiram P. Burrell.
  2 Frances Adelaide, b. 30 Dec. 1830; m. 1 June 1847, Kingsly Smith.
  3. Ann Louisa, b. 18 Sept. 1834; m. 16 Feb. 1864, William Frasier.
  4 Charles, b. 10 Jan. 1836; d. 19 Nov. 1836.
  5 Olive Smith, b. 31 March 1838; m. 16 Mar. 1861, Wesley Hatch; died 6 March 1873.
  6 Abby Augusta, b. 21 Aug. 1843; m. 16 Jan. 1864, Alvin P. Braley.
8 David, b. 29 Oct. 1799; m. Elizabeth McCausland, a niece of his brother's wife.
9 Joanna, b. 4 Sept. 1802; m. 22 Nov. 1824, Thomas Maxwell.
10 William, b. 16 May 1804; m. Rachel Emery.
11 Ann, b. 15 Aug. 1806; m. Thomas Maxell.

By second wife, born in Whitefield:

12 Mary Elizabeth, b. 1822; m. John Mosman.
13 Benjamin F., b. 29 Dec. 1824; m. 1 Dec. 1852, Esther A., daughter of Everett W. and Margaret (Partridge) Ware of Whitefield. Previous to his marriage he spent two and one-half years in California. He has since been a farmer, and has long lived in Augusta. He is a member of the Methodist Church. Children, all born in Augusta:
  1 James E., b. 5 Oct. 1858.
  2 Everett W., b. 13 July 1861.
  3 Frank H., b. 15 Aug. 1864.
  4 Myra K., b. 11 May 1867.
  5 Winslow, b. 7 April 1870.
  6 Lottie M., b. 26 March 1873.
14 James G., b. 1826; d. July 1876; unm. He was a piledriver, and died in Seattle, Wash.
15 Joseph E., b. 24 Feb. 1831; m. 29 Sept. 1854, in Charlestown, Mass., Emma, dau. of Robert and Rhoda (Wheaton) King of East Machias, Me. He still lives in Charlestown, a teamster. Children:
  1 John M., b. 1857.
  2 Frank, b. 1861.
  3 Emma, b. 1864.
  4 Fred, b. 1867.

1-1-2-2-4

JETHRO LIBBY, born in Scarborough, 1763; married, 1788, LETTICE WESCOTT, daughter of Josiah Wescott. He was a farmer and settled soon after his marriage in Gorham. He afterward carried on a coopering business. He died 9 Feb. 1849. His wife died 3 May 1852.

Children:

1 Hannah Woodbury, b. 1789; m. Wm. Chase; d. 24 Nov. 1843.
2 Elliot, b. 21 Aug. 1792; m. Susan Hall.
3 Parmelia, m. 4 Dec. 1817, Samuel Flood of Gorham.
4 Jethro, b. 19 March 1796; m. Olive Flood.
5 Josiah W., b. 28 April 1798; m. Eliza Hall.
6 Mary, b. 11 Aug. 1800; m. Marrett Libby, 10-5-4-3-6.
7 Benjamin, died aged two years.
8 William, b. 3 Sept. 1804; m. Jane Cannell.
9 James, was lost with the brig Elizabeth Ann, William H. Savage, master, in Boston harbor, 9 March 1836.
10 Alfred, b. 4 Dec. 1811; m. 27 Nov. 1838, Esther Libby, 1-1-2-2-11-4. He lived with his father for the most part until the latter's death, and then exchanged the homestead farm with Joshua L. Brown for a farm and store at Great Falls, Gorham. He has since been engaged in the staging business, as overseer in Corey's chair factory, as lumberman, and other things. Having no children, he adopted:
  a Lizzie Wescott (Libby), b. 30 May 1847; unm. She was a daughter of John and Charity (Humphrey) Wescott.

1-1-2-2-6

Charles Libby, born in Scarborough, 8 April 1767; married 22 Dec. 1791, Mary Libby, 1-4-1-6-2. He was a farmer. His uncle John gave him his farm to support him, and he sold it and bought the Shute farm on Beech Ridge, and there lived until his death, 14 May 1850. His wife died 22 Oct. 1837.

Children, all born in Scarborough:

1 Lettice, b. 18 Nov. 1793; d. 6 May 1873; unm.
2 John, b. 12 Jan. 1795; d. 19 May 1860; unm.
3 Hannah, b. 27 Dec. 1800; m. Luther Libby, 11-7-1-4-4.
4 infant, born and died, 23 Oct. 1802.
5 Mary, b. 14 Sept. 1804; m. 14 March 1825, Wm. Strout.
6 Charles, b. 25 Dec. 1806; d. 5 June 1807.
7 Abigail, b. 25 Dec. 1808; m. Joseph Libby, 1-1-3-9-1-2.
8 William, b. 13 Nov. 1810; m. 1 Dec. 1836, Ann H., dau. of James and Keziah (Berry) Harmon of Buxton. He is a farmer and lives on his father's homestead. He is deaf and dumb. Children:
  1 Mary, b. 25 May 1839; m. Wm. Henry Mitchell.
  2 James William, b. 2 May 1842; m. 9 June 1874, Mary Jane, dau. of Patrick and Eliza Jane (Baird) Lary. He is a farmer and butcher in Gorham. Children:
    1 William Albert, b. 9 June 1875.
    2 Norman Leslie, b. 27 April 1877.
  3 John Augustus, b. 16 May 1849; m. 1 Jan. 1873, Louisa, dau. of James and Irene (Hodgdon) Deering of Gorham. He is a farmer and lives at home. Children:
    1 Selden Clifford, b. 23 July 1873.
    2 Albion Topliff, b. 16 Oct. 1875.
  4 Lettice Ann, b. 14 May 1851; d. 29 April 1858.
  5 Daniel Clarence, b. 5 July 1857; unm.

1-1-2-2-8

JOHN LIBBY, born in Scarborough, 17 Dec. 1770; married, 29 July 1802, DORCAS ROBERTS of Gorham. He removed to Gorham and settled on a farm adjoining that of his brother Jethro, now occupied by the sons of Capt. Caleb Libby. He died 10 March 1826, and his widow, 16 March 1864.

Children, all born in Gorham:

1 Joanna, b. 21 June 1803; m. April 1845, Chas. Quimby.
2 Charles, b. 30 Dec. 1804; m. 28 Nov. 1833, Sophronia, dau. of Ebenezer and Salome (Green) Shaw of Standish. He was a farmer in Gorham for eight years succeeding his marriage, and then removed to Harrison Village, where he followed shook-making, boating on the canal, working in a wire factory, and other occupations, until his death, 28 June 1873. His widow still lives in Harrison Village. Only child:
  1 Roswell, b. 23 July 1835; m. 22 Nov. 1863, Achsah C., dau. of Asa and Olive (Charles) Brickett of Stow. He run a canal boat fourteen years, and, during the rest of his life, was a shookmaker. He served nine months in Co. B, 23d Maine Vol. He died 4 Feb. 1876, and his widow married, 10 July 1880, Joseph S. Walker of Fryeburgh. Only child:
    1 Zoa Mabel, b. 17 Feb. 1868.
3 Lucy Roberts, b. 16 July 1806; m. March 1842, Samuel S. Babb.
4 John, b. 8 Sept. 1808; d. 2 April 1822.
5 Benjamin, b. 15 July 1810; d. 27 July 1810.
6 Caleb [Capt.], b. 25 Aug. 1812; m. 20 Nov. 1845, Betsey, dau. of Lemuel and Sarah (Phinney) Rich of Standish. He always lived on his father's homestead, except seven years during which he carried on the Gorham town-farm. He was a captain in the militia. His death took place 14 Jan. 1876, and his widow died 7 Oct. 1879. Children:
  1 John Woodbury, b. 4 March 1847; unm. He and his brother occupy the homestead farm.
  2 Sarah Rich, b. 1 Nov. 1849; unm.
  3 William Frederick, b. 21 Nov. 1852; m. 25 Nov. 1874, Alta G. (Brimblecom) Libby, widow of Ebenezer Libby, 10-5-4-2-9-7. No children.
7 Woodbury Storer, b. 19 May 1816; m. 10 May 1846, Aphia Thatcher, dau. of John Moody. He was a farmer. He settled in Scarborough soon after his marriage, and there died, 16 April 1879. His wife died 4 Feb. 1853. Children:
  1 Marilla L., b. 3 July 1846, in Gorham; d. 28 May 1853.
  2 Aurelius Francisco Antonio Gotie, b. 16 Aug. 1849, in Waterford: m. 17 Dec. 1875, Georgia Anna, dau. of Nathan Marshall and Bethulah (Tibbetts) Fenderson of Scarborough. He is a joiner and lived until recently on his father's homestead. No children.
8 Elmira, b. 7 Nov. 1821; m. 21 March 1850, Stephen Harris.
9 William Frederick, b. 5 Sept. 1823; was killed by an accident, 25 April 1848, in Bridgton; unm.

1-1-2-2-11

WILLIAM LIBBY, born in Scarborough, 7 March 1778; married, 18 May 1806, KETURAH HANSCOM, 9-5-6-1-2. He was a farmer, and always lived on his father's homestead. He died 5 July 1858. His wife died 27 Jan. 1843.

Children:

1 Hannah, b. 9 Dec. 1808; m. 4 April 1830, John Hunnewell, 7-1-5-3-4; d. 8 Dec. 1867.

2 Elbridge, b. 28 Oct. 1810; m. 1st, 25 April 1838, Ellen P., dau. of Zenas Pratt of Cape Elizabeth; (died 31 Oct. 1840); 2d, 31 Jan. 1844, Mary J., dau. of Richard and Eunice (Trickey) Johnson of Westbrook; (died 22 Feb. 1850); 3d, 26 Oct. 1853, Anna Watson, dau. of John and Sarah (Huston) Robinson. He is a farmer. He owns a part of his father's homestead, but he also owns and resides on the adjoining farm, formerly the homestead of John Buggy. Only child:

1 Ellen Caroline, b. 10 July 1839; d. 7 Nov. 1840.

3 Charles [Dea.], b. 27 July 1812; m. 2 June 1840, Louisa, an adopted dau. of John Robinson. He is a farmer and occupies his father's homestead. He also markets milk in Portland. He is deacon of the Freewill Baptist Church Only child:

1 Julia Catherine, b. 27 March 1843; m. 14 Aug. 1862, James Johnson, son of Ruth (Libby) Johnson, 11-7-2-6-11.

4 Esther, b. 11 Oct. 1814; m. Alfred Libby, 1-1-2-2-4-10.

5 Mary J., b. 23 Aug. 1816; d. 18 Oct. 1851; unm.

6 William [Dea.], b. 16 Aug. 1818; m. 2 Dec. 1847, Arabella R., dau. of Hermann and Nizaula (Hutchinson) Towne of Albany. At the age of 23 he went to Harrison and engaged in trade. His venture was unsuccessful and he was afterward six years a clerk in Francis Blake's variety store there. In 1850 he removed to Portland, and after serving about five years as bookkeeper in a publishing house, bought the book business of Geo. Lord on Exchange street. A year later, he was chosen cashier of the Auburn Bank, Auburn, (since the First National Bank), and removed to that place. He filled that position eighteen years, and during the last six years, has held the same position in the Manufacturer's National Bank, Lewiston. He is a member of the Freewill Baptist church, and has filled the office of deacon in the Casco Street Church, Portland, and in the church in Auburn. No children.

7 John, b. 5 July 1820; d. 16 July 1820.

8 Julia Ann, } twins, b. 8 April 1823; d. 18 Oct. 1840; unm.

9 Catherine, } twins, b. 8 April 1823; m. 1st, 14 Mar. 1850, Elbridge G. Moody; 2d, William Jones.

1-1-2-6-1

Eliakim Libby, born in Scarborough, 1 Jan. 1757; married, Rachel Jameson, daughter of —— and Sarah (McLellan) Jameson of Warren. He grew up in Warren and settled on a farm about two miles west of Warren Village, and there died, 20 Sept. 1833. His widow died 11 Feb. 1843.

Children, all born in Warren:

1 Jane, b. 17 Oct. 1782; m. 9 July 1807, John Rokes; d. 8 Jan. 1875.

2 Mary, b. 21 July 1784; m. 7 Aug. 1806, Abner Farrington; d. 9 Oct. 1841.

3 Samuel, b. 4 Nov. 1786; m. Nancy, dau. of Archibald and Eleanor (Parsons) Crawford of Warren. He was at first a farmer, and then a trader in his native town. Later he kept a country store in St. George, and later still removed to Rockland, where he engaged in the grocery business, and was also concerned in the lime business and in navigation. He was a member of the Baptist Church, and served a number of years in the Rockland City Council. No children.

4 Sarah, b. 29 Sept. 1788; m. 1832, Abraham Norwood.
5 Hatevil, b. 30 April 1791; m. Elizabeth Rivers.
6 Henry, b. 13 Aug. 1794; m. 1819, Rosanna, dau. of Alexander and Elizabeth (Mero) Kellock. Before his marriage he bought land in the upper part of Warren, on which he afterward built, and lived there a number of years. He then took his father's homestead, cleared it from debt, and there lived until his death, 2 Oct. 1829. His widow married, 1831, James Hathorne, and died in Liberty, 9 Dec. 1873. Children:
  1 Mary Jane, b. 18 April 1820; m. 1843, Wm. W. Fogerty.
  2 William Henry, b. 10 Feb. 1822; was drowned 20 Sept. 1837.
  3 Edwin, b. 3 April 1824; d. 13 March 1826.
  4 Elizabeth, b. 22 April 1826; m. 1849, Simon T. Long; d. 11 May 1852.
  5 Amelia H., b. 26 June 1829; d. 14 Jan. 1830.
7 Rufus, b. 19 Aug. 1799; d. 13 June 1800.
8 Edward, b. 13 April 1801; m. Margaret Wallis.

1-1-2-6-2

John Libby, born in Scarborough, 1758; married Catherine James, daughter of Capt. Patrick and Phebe James of Warren. He was a farmer, and cleared the farm now occupied by Mary V. (Libby) Starrett, 1-1-2-6-2-4-1. He lived there always until his death, 26 Dec. 1841. His wife died 22 March 1830.

Children:

1 William, b. 9 Jan. 1782; m. 4 Jan. 1810, Elizabeth, dau. of John and Elizabeth (McNiel) Watts. He was a farmer in Union, where he died 24 April 1843, and his widow, 27 Feb. 1863. Children, all born in Union:
  1 Margaret, b. 29 Aug. 1811; m. 1835, John Lindley; d. Sept. 1879, in Brooklyn, N. Y.
  2 Catherine, b. 25 Dec. 1813; d. 26 Dec. 1833; unm.
  3 Eliza A., b. 29 Oct. 1816; m. Nathan M. Gleason; d. 17 May 1876.
  4 Lucinda C., b. 3 Oct. 1818; m. Dec. 1842, Moses Hawes; d. 20 Dec. 1870.
2 Nancy, m. 1 June 1807, Joseph Copeland; d. 27 Aug. 1843.
3 James, married Sarah Copeland.
4 Alexander, b. 29 Nov. 1789; m. 15 June 1827, Catherine W., dau. of George and Isabel (Watts) Jameson. He lived and died on his father's homestead. The old house, nearly ninety years old, is now occupied by his daughter. He died 13 Aug. 1875. His wife died 17 Jan. 1847. Children:
  1 Mary Vose, b. 15 July 1828; m. 28 June 1879, Gilbert A. Starrett.
  2 Martha Ann, b. 22 April 1830; d. 14 June 1847.
  3 Catherine Louisa, b. 23 July 1832; d. 27 April 1862; unm.
  4 William Jones, b. 28 Feb. 1835; d. 18 April 1838.
5 Margaret, m. Alexander Anderson; d. 18 Sept. 1850.
6 Elizabeth, m. 4 Nov. 1816, Wm. Crane; d. 13 Sept. 1880.

1-1-2-6-3

Nathan Libby, born in Scarborough, 6 May 1761; married Elizabeth Lermond, daughter of Alexander and Mary (Harkness) Lermond of Warren. He grew up in Warren. Shortly after his marriage, he took up a farm in the northwest part of the town. On that farm he lived until his death, which took place 7 March 1837. His widow died 6 July 1844. The homestead is now occupied by the families of his daughters, Esther and Hannah.

His children were:

1 Esther, b. 12 July 1787; m. 5 Nov. 1805, Benj. Kellock; died 8 Mar. 1832.
2 Louis, b. 9 Sept. 1789; d. 16 Sept. 1793.
3 Barbara, b. 20 Jan. 1792; d. 26 Mar. 1794.
4 Oliver, b. 18 Mar. 1794; m. 1st, 5 July 1821, Hannah, dau. of Robert and Lydia Matthews; (died 29 Dec. 1827); 2d, 5 Feb. 1829, Caroline, dau. of Wm. and Mary (Dingley) Jackson. When he was married, he bought a farm in Waldoborough, but when health failed his wife, he returned to his father's. Upon his second marriage, he settled on land which he received from his wife's father, and there lived until old age. He died with one of his daughters, in Warren, 14 July 1875. His widow died 28 Jan. 1878. Children, all born in Warren; by first wife:
   1 Lydia M., b. 1822; d. 4 Aug. 1847; unm.

   By second wife:

   2 Sewall, b. Oct. 1829; d. Oct. 1831.
   3 W. Watson, b. 30 Oct. 1831; d. 2 Feb. 1855; unm.
   4 Hannah, b. 8 Dec. 1833; m. 3 Oct. 1856, Benj. F. Milliken.
   5 Mary C., b. 7 Oct. 1836; unm. She lives in Nashua, N. H.
   6 Esther A., b. 15 July 1838; m. David Clendenin.
   7 Angelica J., b. 2 Nov. 1841; m. 1st, John Kelly; 2d, Henry A. Spaulding.
   8 Melinda F., b. 27 Oct. 1844; m. 2 May 1867, in Pelham, N. H., William H. Moulton.
   9 Nathan, } twins, b. } has been in Insane Asylum 16 yrs.
   10 Nathaniel, } 11 May 1847; } m. 18 July 1874, Harriet A., dau. of Jesse and Harriet N. (Young) Robbins. He was a private in Co. K., 12th Maine. He afterward learned the carpenter's trade in Lawrence, Mass., and the mason's trade in Presque Isle, Me. He died in Lowell, Mass., of consumption, 12 May 1876. His widow lives in Melrose. Only child:
      1 Rosa Y., born in Aug., died in Dec., 1875.
5 George, b. 22 Jan. 1796; d. 20 Aug. 1843; unm. He worked at farming, in his father's sawmill, and on stone-work.
6 Rosanna, b. 22 Feb. 1798; m. 28 March 1822, Alexander Young.
7 Hannah, b. 25 July 1801; m. 13 Jan. 1825, James Stevens; died 9 Sept. 1841.
8 William, b. 7 Oct. 1805; d. 10 Feb. 1830; unm.

1-1-2-6-9

David Libby, born in Warren, Me., 1778; married Susan Gay, daughter of Wellington Gay. He was a farmer, and always lived on his father's homestead. He also engaged to some extent in tanning. He died 8 Jan. 1847. His wife died 22 July 1841.

Children:

1 Mary G., died in Fitchburgh, Mass.; unm.
2 James, born 1807; m. 1830, Margaret P. Morse. He had the homestead farm. He now lives in Fitchburgh. Child:
   1 Sarah L.
3 Edward G., b. 14 Dec. 1819; m. Sarah Woodcock.

1-1-2-6-10

Isaac Libby, born in Warren, Me., 1780; married Eleanor Gay, daughter of Wellington and Susan (Thomas) Gay of Friendship. He always lived in his native town, and died there 28 April 1833. His widow died 13 March 1874.

Children, all born in Warren:

1 Anthony, b. 9 Nov. 1815; m. Louisa Robinson and Mary C. Wyllie.
2 Ebenezer G., b. 1819; m. 1846, Harriet A., dau. of Capt. Wm. and Lucy (Wyllie) Hall. She died 24 Nov. 1852. He removed to California, where he married again, and died in 1874, leaving three children.
3 Ellen G., b. 6 Oct. 1827; m. 13 Nov. 1849, Wm. K. Cutting; d. 24 Sept. 1862.

1-1-3-4-1

Richard Hunnewell Libby, born in Scarborough, 8 Dec. 1756; married Esther Hanscom, 9-5-6-4. He was a farmer, and lived and died on his father's homestead farm. He was a Revolutionary soldier, and afterward a pensioner. He died 27 March 1820. His wife died 1 July 1814.

Children, all born in Scarborough:

1 Rhoda, b. 1 June 1784; m. 28 Jan. 1806, Samuel Haines; d. 13 Sept. 1815.
2 Daniel, b. 1 March 1786; m. Abigail Hanscom.
3 Hannah, b. 19 Aug. 1794; d. 28 Jan. 1814; unm.
4 Susannah, b. 25 Aug. 1797; d. 3 Nov. 1821; unm.
5 Anna, b. 30 March 1799; d. 27 April 1823.
6 Jonathan, b. 31 Aug. 1801; d. 22 April 1824; unm.
7 Lydia, b. 4 Oct. 1803; m. 4 Nov. 1824, Peter Elder of Windham.
8 Abigail, died 16 July 1826; unm.

1-1-3-5-6

Edward Skillin Libby, born in Scarborough, 1771; married, 12 Dec. 1793, Sarah Dunn, daughter of Samuel and —— (Johnson) Dunn of Westbrook.

At the age of 13 he went to sea with James Deering of Portland. He followed the sea ever afterward, but never sailed in any other man's vessel, and rose to be mate. He was in Havana when his youngest child was born, 12 Sept. 1804; sailed two days later, and died of yellow fever ten days out. At the time of his marriage he and his wife's brother, Enoch Dunn, a bachelor, bought a farm in Gray, and there all his children were born. After his death his widow married John Smith. She died at the age of 83.

Children:

1 Samuel, died at the age of 20½ years. He was in the war of 1812.
2 Sarah, died at the age of about 20 years; unm.
3 Silas, b. 12 Sept. 1804; m. in New York City, Mary Elizabeth, dau. of Andrew Cox. He kept a hotel in New York some time. For many years he has been a farmer in Dover, N. H. He and his wife parted, and she married second, Stephen Van Austin of New York. Children:

1 Edward, died aged 4 years, in Gray, Me.
2 Mary, died aged 3 years, in New York.
3 daughter, died aged 18 months.

1-1-3-8-2

JONATHAN LIBBY, born in Gorham, Me., 9 Oct. 1772; married first, MARY STEVENS of Windham; second, ABIGAIL JORDAN, daughter of Isaac Jordan of Raymond. He was always a farmer, The latter portion of his life was spent in Standish, on the farms now owned by Curtis Shaw and Wm. Wescott. He died on that now owned by the latter, in January, 1848. His second wife died about 1845.

Children, by first wife, born in Standish:

1 Joab, born 24 April 1793; married Jane Marwick and Sarah Libby, 10-5-4-2-3-1.
2 Daniel, b. 7 March 1800; m. 4 March 1845, Eunice F., dau. of Elijah and Mary (Thomson) Cook of Casco. He died in Windham, 15 June 1854. His widow married, 25 Jan. 1856, Levi Varney of Winslow, and died there 5 Nov. 1868. Children:
   1 James C., b. 4 Feb. 1847, in Gorham; m. 9 May 1871, Sarah E., dau. of Solomon and Harriet G. (Parsons) Bolster of Easton, Me., where he now lives. Children:
      1 Fred E., b. 12 Feb. 1872, in Fort Fairfield.
      2 Myrtie J., b. 24 July 1874, in Fort Fairfield.
      3 Lyle E., b. 3 Aug. 1877, in Fort Fairfield.
   2 Lavina A., b. 2 April 1851, in Windham; m. 5 Feb. 1871, David Bolster, brother of Sarah.
3 Mary, m. 4 June 1820, Jacob Morton of Standish.
4 Richard, died at the age of four years.

By second wife, born in Gorham:

5 Thomas, died June, 1876, in Casco; unm. His life was spent logging and in sawmills.
6 Susan, m. Bradley Cram of Gorham.
7 Margaret, m. 1st, James Cates; 2d, David Frost.
8 Jane, b. 4 July 1816; m. James Staples.
9 Abigail, } twins, born } m. Chas. Dingley.
10 Ann Rebecca, } 4 June 1823; } m. Andrew R. Gay.

1-1-3-9-1

ALEXANDER LIBBY, born in Scarborough, 6 Aug. 1778; married, 6 Aug. 1800, ELIZABETH LIBBY, 1-4-1-6-5. He and his brother Allison removed to Pownal and settled on adjoining lands. The farm which Alexander cleared is now owned by Wm. Tucker. On it he spent his life, and there died, 1 March 1849. His wife died 18 April 1847. He married second, Harriet Casely, who married, after his death, Benj. Fogg.

Children:

1 Almira, b. 21 May 1802; m. Sewall Brown.
2 Joseph, b. 29 Nov. 1804; m. Abigail Libby, 1-1-2-2-6-7, and Maria Jones.
3 Hannah, b. 30 May 1812; m. Reuben Sawyer.
4 Dennis, b. 21 Jan. 1816; m. Susan Libby, 1-4-1-6-3-10.

1-1-3-9-2

ALLISON LIBBY, born in Scarborough, 24 Oct. 1781; married 30 Aug. 1806, LUCY LIBBY, 10-2-4-2-9. He removed to Pownal and cleared the farm on which he ever afterward lived. He was several years a selectman of that town. His wife died 28 Feb. 1840, and, 14 Oct. 1840, he married her sister Hannah. He died 31 Oct. 1852. His widow died in Yarmouth, about 1865.

Children, all born in Pownal:

1 Fanny, b. 15 Dec. 1806; m. 11 Jan. 1827, Zenas Berry.
2 Emily, b. 31 Aug. 1808; m. 19 Jan. 1832, Richard Knights.
3 Mary Ann, b. 4 Feb. 1810; m. 30 Nov. 1830, Sewall Jones.
4 Darius, b. 4 Jan. 1812; m. 18 Jan. 1838, Lucinda Libby, 1-1-3-9-7-2. He lived on his father's homestead, and died there, 15 Oct. 1863. His widow and third child still occupy the same. Children:
    1 Georgie Anna, b. 23 Jan. 1843; m. 1st, Freeman J. Knight; 2d, Charles H. Moulton; 3d, James S. Thomas.
    2 Edwin, b. 17 July 1844; d. 18 Dec. 1862.
    3 Lendall Augustus, b. 16 Feb. 1847; m. 1 April 1876, Carrie, dau. of Tristram and Mary Ann (Kimball) Woodman of Gorham. He was a private in Co. C, 31st Maine Infantry. Children:
        1 Eva May, b. 31 July 1877.
        2 Jennie, b. 8 May 1880.
    4 Francis Warren, b. 1 Jan. 1851; m. Catherine Haskell. Only child:
        1 James A., born 1874.
5 Lucy, b. 3 March 1814; m. 29 April 1834, as second wife, Zenas Berry of Buxton.
6 Mehitable, b. 23 Jan. 1816; m. Demas Libby, 10-5-4-16-4.

1-1-3-9-3

JOAB LIBBY, born in Scarborough, 17 April 1783; married, 1806, SARAH JONES, daughter of Hannah (Libby) Jones, 10-5-4-9. He followed his older brothers to Pownal and settled on the farm now occupied by Stephen Larrabee. He owned a coaster, and during some portions of the year, used to make voyages to Boston. 7 Oct. 1827, while tacking in Plymouth harbor, just inside Gurnet Light, he was knocked overboard by the boom of his vessel and drowned. His widow married, 24 Jan. 1841, Charles H. Tyler, and died 30 March 1872.

Children, all born in Pownal:

1 Miriam, b. 26 Jan. 1809; d. 26 Nov. 1811.
2 John, b. 7 Sept. 1811; d. June 1829.
3 Cyrus Jones, b. 8 Nov. 1813; m. Delinsa Douglass.
4 Jane, b. 4 Sept. 1815; d. 7 Aug. 1818.
5 Sarah Ann, b. 19 Aug. 1817; m. Levi Libby, 1-1-3-9-9-3.
6 George Washington, b. 23 Nov. 1819; m. Sarah J. Thrasher.
7 William Jones, b. 31 March 1822; m. 29 May 1845, Mary Ann Libby, 1-1-3-9-9-2. He was a sailor and then a farmer. After his marriage he lived in Levant, Cape Elizabeth, and Pownal, in which latter place he died, 26 April 1864. His widow married, 1866, Darius Palmer. Only child:
    1 ——, died at birth.
8 Harriet, b. 29 Aug. 1824; d. 17 Dec. 1832.
9 Miriam Jane, b. 10 Aug. 1827; died in July 1848; unm.

1-1-3-9-4

ABRAHAM LIBBY, born in Scarborough, 1 July 1785; married first, EUNICE TYLER, daughter of Rhoda (Libby) Tyler, 1-1-6-4-2; (died 5 Nov. 1831); second, 8 March 1832, MARY BROWN of Yarmouth. He removed to Pownal before his marriage, and cleared the farm now occupied by Wm. Tufts. He lived there until his death, 12 Oct. 1860. His widow died 6 June 1872.

Children, by first wife:

1 Zebulon, b. 1 Dec. 1813; d. 4 Feb. 1835; unm. He was burnt to death in a logging camp in the eastern woods.
2 David Tyler, b. 31 Oct. 1815; m. Hannah L. True.
3 Phineas, b. 1 May 1817; m. Mary A. Waldron and Nancy A. Noyes.
4 Alfred Cotton, b. 22 Dec. 1818; m. 18 Sept. 1848, Elizabeth Libby, dau. of Almira (Libby) Brown, 1-1-3-9-1-1. He went to sea at 16, and at length rose to be captain. One year after his marriage he quit the sea, and has since been an operative in the Biddeford cotton mills. Children:
   1 Abby Cora, b. 4 May 1851, in Falmouth; d. 21 March 1854.
   2 Charles Alfred, b. 25 March 1854; m. 1st, 29 Jan. 1873, Jennie O., dau. of Calvin and Mary (Lord) Bennett of Alfred; (died 5 Jan. 1877); 2d, 10 April 1878, Emma F., dau. of Shapleigh Smith of Biddeford. She died 14 July 1879. Only child:
      1 Myra Cora, b. 10 Jan. 1874.

Adopted child:

   a Elizabeth Etta (Libby), b. 28 May 1859; m. Aug. 1879, Wm. McCorrison of Saco.

5 Cyrus, b. 23 Oct. 1821; m. 10 Dec. 1848, Julia P., dau. of James and Lydia (Estes) Goddard of Pownal. In 1845 he bought a farm, on which he has ever since resided. He has been a selectman of Pownal several years. No children.
6 Charles, b. 19 Feb. 1823; m. 1st, 10 Aug. 1845, Lucy Ann Doan of Durham; (died 28 March 1850); 2d, 5 Jan. 1851, Hannah E., dau. of Stephen and Sally (Doan) Davis. She died 18 April 1852. He was a wheelwright in North Pownal. During the gold fever he went to California, but died before reaching the diggings, 13 Aug. 1852. Children, by first wife:
   1 Leroy Woodbury, b. 25 Jan. 1847; m. 30 May 1871, Abbie E., dau. of Frederick and Mary (Parcher) Manson of Rockland. He was brought up by his uncle Cyrus. He is a dealer in agricultural implements in Marysville, Kansas. Children, all born there:
      1 Lendal Cyrus, b. 7 May 1872.
      2 Mary Alice, b. 19 March 1874.
      3 Herbert Manson, b. 16 Sept. 1875.
      4 Walter Woodbury, b. 10 Feb. 1877.
      5 Ethel Lucy, b. 29 Nov. 1878.
      6 Edith Estelle, b. 17 May 1880.
   2 Lendall Eugene, b. Dec. 1849; d. 9 May 1850.

By second wife:

   3 Oscar, b. Jan. 1852; d. 3 June 1852.

7 Abraham, b. 29 Sept. 1824; m. 5 April 1849, Lavinia A., daughter of Benjamin M. and Ruth (Ray) Lane of Greene. He served four and one-half years in the late war. He now lives in Auburn. Children:
   1 Lucua A., b. 10 Jan. 1850, in Durham; m. 8 Feb. 1866, George O. Newton.
   2 Eunice T., b. 1 July 1852, in Auburn; m. July 1870, Frank J. Shaw.

3 Inez O., b. 17 April 1855; unm.
4 Llewellyn D., b. 11 Jan. 1857; unm.
5 Charles J., b. 27 Dec. 1858; m. Susan Ella Snow. Child:
1 Charles H., b. 30 May 1877, in Auburn.
6 Elmer E., b. 9 July 1861.
8 Rhoda, b. 30 Jan. 1826; m. 4 May 1848, Richard F. Lombard.
9 True Page, b. 20 Dec. 1827; d. 12 Aug. 1852; unm.
10 Artemisia, b. 8 Sept. 1829; m. 21 Sept. 1848, Seth D. Estes.
11 Eunice, b. 14 Sept. 1831; m. 2 Dec. 1849, Otis C. Jones.

By second wife:

12 George Furguson, b. 14 Dec. 1832; m. 1st, 1 Jan. 1854, Cynthia, dau. of Jacob Cotton; (divorced and married Tristram Harris of Portland, Oregon); 2d, 30 March 1873, Sophia W., dau. of Christopher and Lydia (Pitcher) Miller of Waldoborough. He has worked at shoemaking, harness-making, and carpentering, but chiefly at farming. He has lived in many places in Maine and Massachusetts, and one summer in Michigan. He now lives in Deering, Me. Children, by 1st wife:
1 Anson Ganselo, b. 11 Jan. 1856, in Pownal; unm. He lives in Falmouth, Me.
2 Cincanetta Gertrude, b. 6 Nov. 1857; unm.

By second wife:

3 Lewis Colby, b. 4 Nov. 1873, in Milton, Mass.
4 George Levonzo, b. 31 July 1876, in Falmouth, Me.
5 Elgia Merton, b. 11 April 1879, in Falmouth.
13 Freeman, b. 14 June 1836; m. 24 Sept. 1854, Fannie P., dau. of Jacob and Ruth (Bailey) Cotton. He has been a farmer, carpenter, and photographer. He now lives in Portland. Children, born in Pownal:
1 Leonard Freeman, b. 26 Nov. 1857; m. 29 Oct. 1879, Nellie G., dau. of Levi and Mary (Haskell) McAllister of Franklin. He is a photographer.
2 Christina Lillian, b. 11 May 1860; m. 27 Feb. 1879, Josiah Herbert Stevens.

1-1-3-9-7

JOHN LIBBY, born in Scarborough, 7 Nov. 1791; married first, 8 April 1812, MIRIAM LIBBY, 11-7-2-4-3; (died 16 Dec. 1818); second, April 1820, ABIGAIL GRACE of Scarborough; third, MARTHA MOSES, daughter of Daniel and Lydia (Coolbroth) Moses of Scarborough.

He settled on a farm in Pownal, directly opposite that on which his father afterward lived, and there resided until his second marriage. From that time until his death, he was in the trucking business in Portland. He died in June, 1842. His widow outlived him some years.

Children, by first wife, born in Pownal:

1 Matthias, b. 1813; d. in Portland, Nov. 1862; unm. He went with his father to Portland, and, like him, was a truckman.
2 Lucinda, b. 17 Dec. 1816; was brought up by her mother's mother; m. Darius Libby, 1-1-3-9-2-4.
3 Storer, b. 18 Nov. 1818; m. 1st, 7 April 1846, Nancy B., dau. of Josiah and Sally (Blake) Stevens of Westbrook; (died 18 March 1854); second, 10 Oct. 1861, Mary H., dau. of Stephen and Rebecca (Hamlin) Larry of Gorham. He was brought up by his father's

mother. When he married he bought part of his wife's father's farm, and there lived until 1870. He then sold it to the City of Portland, to be annexed to Evergreen Cemetery, and bought a small place at Morrill's Corner, Deering, where he has since resided. Children, by first wife:

1 Franklin Storer, b. 28 April 1848; unm. He is a streetcar-driver.
2 Oscar Fremont, b. 26 Feb. 1850; d. 10 Aug. 1867.
3 Nancy Buckley, born 15 Dec. 1853; m. Fred Melville Libby, 10-5-4-1-2-7-1.

By second wife:

4 Oscar Fremont, b. 23 July 1868.

By second wife:

4 Harriet, never married. She was a dressmaker in Portland many years. In 1876 she removed to California and there died.
5 John, never married. He was drowned by the upsetting of a small boat at Little Chebeague Island, 11 Aug. 1846.
6 Hannah, died in childhood.

By third wife:

7 Edmund Page, b. 8 March 1830; m. 3 July 1852, Lucy E., dau. of Moses and Anne (Brackett) Winslow of Deering. He was a cooper in Portland. He died on a West India voyage, taken for his health. His widow still lives in Portland. Children:
  1 Augustus Sanborn, b. 19 May 1854; m. 19 Aug. 1875, Florence M., dau. of Thomas R. and Sarah S. (Whitcomb) Lovejoy. He is shipping clerk with Deering, Milliken & Co., Portland. Children:
    1 Florence Lilian, b. 9 March 1878; d. 16 April 1879.
    2 Edna Whitcomb, b. 22 June 1880.
  2 Sarah B., b. 7 Jan. 1856; d. 26 April 1869.
  3 Moses W., b. 21 Oct. 1859; unm.
8 Abigail, b. 25 March 1833; m. David Libby, 10-4-1-6-2-3.

1-1-3-9-9

Josiah Libby, born in Scarborough, 10 Dec. 1795; married first, 28 Oct. 1817, Abigail Moody, daughter of John and Mercy (Foss) Moody; (died 2 Jan. 1842); second, 20 July 1842, Mary (Palmer) Shackford, daughter of Elizabeth Lidden (Libby) Palmer, 1-1-3-5-4. He was a farmer, first in Scarborough and then in Cape Elizabeth, and died in the latter place, 15 May 1847. His widow still survives.

Children, all born in Scarborough; by first wife:

1 Jane, b. 11 Jan. 1818; m. Mark Libby, 10-5-3-5-8.
2 Mary Ann, b. 11 Jan. 1820; m. William Jones Libby, 1-1-3-9-3-7, and Darius Palmer.
3 Levi, b. 11 Nov. 1823; m. 3 July 1842, Sarah Ann Libby, 1-1-3-9-3-5. He is a farmer, and lives on his father's homestead in Cape Elizabeth. Children:
  1 William Jones, b. 24 Oct. 1842; d. 19 July 1858.
  2 Sumner Cummings, b. 18 Nov. 1844; d. 30 Dec. 1864, in Salisbury Prison. He was a private in Co. C, 12th Me. Inf.
  3 Levi, b. 1 Dec. 1846; unm.
  4 Charles Nelson, b. 15 June 1849; d. 27 Oct. 1879; unm.
  5 Mary Ellen, b. 30 May 1852; d. 7 Nov. 1854.
  6 Frederick Elwood, b. 18 Oct. 1855; unm.
  7 Almon Wesley, b. 18 Aug. 1859; unm.
4 Miriam, b. 29 March 1827; m. 1 Sept. 1842, Charles E. Cash.
5 Olive, b. 25 Aug. 1830; d. 2 Sept. 1832.

By second wife:

6 Abbie, b. 1 Jan. 1843; m. 1 Jan. 1863, Geo. Shackford.
7 Joseph, b. 10 May 1846; d. 1848.

1-1-3-9-10

HANSON LIBBY, born in Scarborough, 21 Dec. 1797; married, 9 July 1820, LYDIA LAKE, daughter of Eleazer and Mercy Lake. He went with his father to Pownal. After his marriage, he lived a short time in the then recently vacated house of his brother John, and soon after settled on a part of the farm of his wife's father. There he died, 14 Feb. 1869, and his widow and son still live.

Children:

1 Sarah, b. 7 Sept. 1820; m. Henry Merritt.
2 Mercy, b. 31 Aug. 1821; m. Aaron Libby, 10-5-4-10-7.
3 Mary, died aged 2½ years.
4 Mary, b. 23 Sept. 1826; m. 29 Oct. 1854, Joseph Randall.
5 Hanson, b. 2 Nov. 1829; m. 23 Dec. 1851, Mary Susan, dau. of John and Hannah (Getchell) Sawyer of Durham. He settled on his father's homestead, a few years after his marriage, and still lives there. Children:
  1 Lois Marietta, b. 13 May 1853; unm.
  2 James, b. 25 June 1855; m. Nellie, dau. of Charles and Mary Ann (Rogers) Rice. He is a farmer in Durham. No children.
  3 Albert, b. 21 Oct. 1861.
  4 Henry Scott, b. 29 April 1863.
  5 Frederick, b. 3 Feb. 1865.

1-1-5-9-8

JOHN LIBBY, born in Scarborough, 9 Nov. 1798; married, 26 Nov. 1834, SARAH WATERHOUSE, daughter of John and Mehitable (Harmon) Waterhouse. He is a farmer. He settled at Dunstan Landing, in his native town. In 1860–1, he served as representative to the state legislature.

Children:

1 Elizabeth, b. 2 April 1835; m. 2 May 1845, Albus R. Fickett of Cape Elizabeth.
2 Albert, b. 26 May 1841; m. May, 1875, Catherine, dau. of Cyrus and Elizabeth Ann (Newcomb) Harmon. He was a railroad employee. He died 19 April 1877. Only child:
  1 Ethel Elbertha, b. 4 Jan 1877; d. 23 Oct. 1881.
3 George Henry, b. 1 Feb. 1849; unm.

1-1-6-4-6

CAPT. CYRUS LIBBY, born in Scarborough, 15 Oct. 1778; married, 23 Dec. 1800, LOIS LIBBY, 5-7-14-2.

He went to sea while yet a boy, and rose rapidly to the command of a ship. He was in the East India trade until the war of 1812. In the course of that war he commanded the Juno, a privateer, and the Leo, under a letter of marque. After the war he

Cyrus Libby

was engaged in the European trade, and continued, with some intermissions, until the year before his death. He represented Scarborough in the first legislature of Maine, 1820, and afterward, in 1832. He was four years a selectman of the town. He died 18 Aug. 1838. His widow died in Portland, 22 April 1866.

Children, all born in Scarborough:

1 Phineas, b. 30 Sept. 1801; m. Lucinda Harmon.
2 Cyrus, b. 13 Sept. 1804; unm. He followed the sea from boyhood. He rose to be captain, and sailed to most all the principal ports of the commercial world. He is now a school-teacher in Victoria, Australia.
3 Drusilla, b. 9 March 1809; d. 10 Oct. 1829; unm.
4 Foxwell Cutts, b. 24 Nov. 1811; d. 9 Jan. 1842, in New Orleans; unm.
5 Dorville, b. 7 Feb. 1814; m. Harriet A. Cole, Mary Ellen Whitney, and Vesta Snell.
6 Lydia, b. 13 Jan. 1817; m. 30 Nov. 1838, Phineas Foss, a son of Elizabeth (Libby) Foss, 1-1-6-4-5.
7 Josiah, b. 26 March 1821; m. 8 Oct. 1851, Rachel, dau. of Garry and Ellena (White) Wells of Three Mile Bay, N. Y. He lived at home until the building of the Atlantic and St. Lawrence Railroad was begun, and then became a contractor on that road. He ever afterward followed the same business, in many places. He died in Three Mile Bay, where he had married, 22 March 1854. His widow married Elijah Green. Only child:
   1 Lydia, b. 9 Oct. 1852; m. 8 Oct. 1873, David F. Barber.
8 Elizabeth, b. 26 Jan. 1823; m. 17 Nov. 1848, Samuel Brackett.
9 Susan Caroline, b. 19 Oct. 1825; m. 25 Feb. 1844, Thomas C. Elwell of Buxton.

1-1-6-4-7

Daniel Libby, born in Scarborough, 20 Jan. 1780; married, 31 July 1806, Rebecca Libby, 10-2-1-5-2. He was a farmer. He lived on many farms in Scarborough, and finally, the year before his death, which occurred 24 Nov. 1846, moved into the house in which his widow afterward died, 7 Nov. 1864, and his daughters still live.

Children:

1 Eunice, b. 13 Jan. 1808; unm.
2 Lois, b. 25 Dec. 1810; unm.
3 Caleb, b. 1 March 1812; m. 13 Jan. 1832, Nancy, dau. of Parker and Sally (Clough) Morgan of Eppingham, N. H. He was a farmer. He lived in Eppingham, after his marriage, until 1841. He then moved to Westbrook, and thence, three years later, to Scarborough, where he settled on part of the homestead of his mother's father. His wife died 3 June 1854. 17 Dec. 1863, he married Mrs. Martha Lord, and died 12 Feb. 1865. His widow married, 24 Sept. 1867, Warren Knight. Children:
   1 Edwin Augustus, b. 22 Oct. 1832; m. April, 1858, Eliza Jane Gross of Brunswick. When he was married he moved to Saco where his wife died, 7 Aug. 1859. He then went to Burlington, Mass., and from that place enlisted in a Massachusetts volunteer regiment. He served about a year and died 27 June 1864, in Nashville, Tenn. Only child:
      1 Edwin, born 7 Aug., died 19 Sept., 1859.
   2 Susan Elizabeth, b. 9 Aug. 1834; m. Obadiah Sawyer.
   3 Daniel, b. 20 June 1836; d. 18 Nov. 1864; unm.

4 George Washington, b. 16 July 1838; m. 1st, Mary Welch; 2d, 30 Sept. 1878, Mary J. (Duke) Perkins. He lives at Blue Point, Scarborough. No children.
5 Sarah Jane, b. 31 May 1840; m. 29 Dec. 1863, Stephen G. Ham.
6 Mary Ann, b. 20 March 1842; d. May 1864, in the Insane Asylum, Augusta, Me.
7 Henry, b. 18 Nov. 1845; unm.
8 Joseph Kingsbury, b. 18 July 1848; unm. He left home in October, 1869, and has not since been heard from.

1-1-6-5-3

Josiah Libby, born in Scarborough; married, 21 July 1814, Abigail Thomes. He lived on his father's homestead, and died 29 April 1857. His widow died in Portland, 21 Oct. 1863.

Children:

1 Phineas, b. 11 Nov. 1814; m. 19 Feb. 1854, Susan, dau. of Mary Ann (Moody) Plummer, 5-7-10-6-4. He lived on his father's homestead, and died 5 April 1863. His widow married in Cape Elizabeth, 22 Oct. 1863, James N. Lyons. Children:
  1 Samuel Jones, b. 12 April 1854; m. Sadie Sweeton of Scarborough. No children.
  2 Eliza Plummer, b. 5 Feb. 1856; died aged 14.
  3 William Plummer, b. 9 April 1857; unm.
  4 Alice Alberta, b. 29 Nov. 1859; m. 22 Aug. 1879, Frank B. King.
  5 Ferdinand Phineas, b. 12 Dec. 1861.
2 Mary, b. 2 Dec. 1816; d. 2 Jan. 1822.
3 Miranda, b. 31 Jan. 1821; m. 7 Feb. 1850, Wm. H. Bragdon.
4 Alexine, b. 8 Nov. 1823; m. Ezra Bradbury of Kittery.
5 Isabella Abigail, b. 15 March 1826; m. 15 Sept. 1842, Frederick B. Hurlbert; d. 10 Oct. 1846.
6 ——, died 6 Sept. 1832.

1-2-1-1-1

James Libby, born in Nottingham, N. H., Jan. 1765; married, Nancy Crockett, daughter of David and Sally (Thompson) Crockett of Ossipee, N. H.

He lived on his father's homestead in Nottingham until the winter of 1799-1800. He then sold to Jonathan Cilley, Esq., and removed to Parsonsfield, Me., where he settled on the farm now owned by John and Marston Ames. His house was near the pond. In 1816 he sold this and during the rest of his life rented a farm further north in the same town, where he died, 18 April 1828. His widow died 19 Feb. 1831. They were both buried on the farm now owned by Charles Hobbs.

Children, born in Nottingham:

1 Joseph, b. 19 Nov. 1787; m. Sally Pease.
2 William, m. 16 May 1824, in Westbrook, Me., Mary Tate. He was a farmer and lived on many farms in Westbrook, where he died in March 1854, having outlived his wife about 14 years. No children.
3 Andrew, b. 27 Dec. 1792; m. Elizabeth Lakeman.
4 Ham, b. Nov. 1795; m. Sarah Batchelder.
5 Sally, married Joseph Stevens of Parsonsfield.

Born in Parsonsfield:

6 John, b. 1800; m. Mary Ann Carter.
7 David, died aged seven years.
8 Alvah, b. 6 Nov. 1805; m. Eunice B. Stewart.
9 Martha Crockett, b. 4 April 1809; unm. She has always lived in Parsonsfield.

1-2-1-2-7

Enoch Libby, born in Dover, N. H.; married, 22 July 1821, in Dover, Martha Parsley of Strafford, N. H. They went from Dover to Strafford, and living there a short time, returned to Dover. He died before his wife, whose death took place in 1852.

Children:

1 Benjamin F., is in the post-office at Clinton, N. Y.
2 James W., died soon after they left Strafford.
3 Elizabeth H., b. 1832; lives at Great Falls, N. H.; unm.

1-2-1-3-3

Joshua Libby, born in Dover, N. H., 22 May 1773; married, 1797, Susannah Kenniston, of New Market, N. H.

He learned the shoemaker's trade at first, but the work did not suit him, and his uncle Joseph Libby persuaded him to go onto his farm in Barrington, now Strafford, N. H. He married Susannah Kenniston, who had lived in his uncle's family from girlhood; and lived with his uncle until his death. He was to have had the homestead, but a stronger claim upon it appeared, and he was obliged to move onto a small piece of land which he happened to own. He died in the same town, in the spring of 1834. His widow died in Lawrence, Mass., 10 Dec. 1871.

Children, all born in Barrington, now Strafford:

1 Ira. b. 4 Mar. 1798; m. Betsey Daniels.
2 Joseph, b. 29 Mar. 1800. He went to Virginia when a young man. He wrote home that he had found work for a certain period, and that when his time was out, he would make a visit home. That was the last that was ever heard of him.
3 James. b. July 1802; died about 1826, in New York City; unm.
4 Lydia D., b. 26 June 1804; m. May, 1825, Dea. Ira Caverly; d. Aug. 1839, in Lowell, Mass.
5 Olive O., b. 5 April 1806; m. 1829, Samuel Daniels.
6 Eliza Randall, b. 1808; d. 1811.
7 Susan, b. 14 July 1810; m. 1835, Nathaniel Kimball.
8 Joshua, b. 2 Nov. 1812. He is a farmer in his native town. He has been twice married, but has no children.
9 Eliza, b. 21 May 1815; m. Samuel Cushing of Tamworth, N. H.
10 John Osborn, b. 22 March 1820; m. 22 Oct. 1843, in Lowell, Mass., Jane Gray, dau. of Elisha and Sarah H. (Leonard) Morton of Buckfield, Me. He learned the carpenter's trade in Lowell, and afterward worked as a journeyman in Lowell, Chelsea, and Brookline. In 1854 he went into business himself, in Brookline, and continued it until his death, 13 May 1865. His widow and family still live in Brookline. Children:
    1 Adelaide Augusta, b. 5 Feb. 1845, in Chelsea; m. 13 June 1868, James Sinclair.

2 John Henry, b. 8 Feb. 1847, in Brookline; unm. He is a clerk in the paper and twine business in Boston.
3 Franklin, b. 11 Feb. 1854; unm. He is a clerk in a railway ticket office in Boston.
4 Leonard Morton, b. 27 Dec. 1861. He graduated from the Brookline High School in 1878, and is now in a cutlery store in Boston.

11 Hollis, b. 15 March 1823; d. 18 Jan. 1857, in Lowell, Mass.; unm.

1-2-3-1-2

LUKE LIBBY, born in Portsmouth, N. H., 22 Aug. 1756; married NANCY CROCKER of Exeter, N. H.

He went to Exeter to live when a small boy. He served seven and one-half years in the Revolution, fourteen months of which time he was a prisoner in England. When he was married, he removed to Landaff, N. H., whence in 1800 he removed to Warren, where he was a farmer until old age. He married, as second wife, the widow Goodwin, and died in Piermont, N. H., 8 Jan. 1844.

Children, all by first wife:

1 George, b. 22 Aug. 1792; m. Sally Abbott.
2 Nathaniel P., b. 2 March 1795; m. Nancy Abbott.
3 John W., b. 10 June 1797; m. Betsey Merrill.
4 Stephen, b. 20 Oct. 1799; m. Margaret, dau. of Ichabod and Hannah (Chesley) Watson. He settled in Pittsfield, N. H., soon after his marriage and was twelve years watchman in the mills there. He died in Northfield, Vt., on a visit, 3 Feb. 1849. His wife kept boarders for thirty years, and died 11 Feb. 1861. Children:
    1 Watson P., b. 24 June 1823, in Vermont; d. Oct. 1855, in Illinois; unm.
    2 Lovey W., b. 6 Aug. 1828, in Vermont; m. 1st, Isaac S. Twambly; 2d, Harris W. Niles; d. May, 1870.
    3 Mary J., b. 12 April 1835, in Pittsfield; m. 1st, 14 July 1855, Seth Hayes; 2d, Charles Eastman.
5 Ezra Bartlett, b. 24 Oct. 1801; m. 1st, Mary Gibbin Haman; 2d, Eva K. (Sindier) Cummings.
6 Anna P., b. 26 Feb. 1804; d. 21 Jan. 1816.
7 Jonathan M., b. 8 March 1806; d. 7 Dec. 1815.
8 Obadiah C., b. 15 Dec. 1807; was a laborer; died in Pelham, Mass.

1-4-1-4-1

ARTHUR LIBBY, born in Scarborough, 28 Feb. 1760; married MARY ALLEN, daughter of Isaac and Dolly (Leighton) Allen of Falmouth.

He moved from Gray to Falmouth before his marriage. He lived several years on the farm afterward owned by Hiram Emery. He then sold and settled in Windham, on the farm now occupied by the widow of Samuel Libby, 1-4-1-4-1-3-1. The original house, built in the fall of 1802, is still standing. He died in June, 1835, and his widow in March, 1846.

Children, born in Falmouth:

1 William, b. 6 Dec. 1786; m. Hannah Gould.
2 Abigail, b. 27 July 1789; m. John Cummings.

3 Gideon, b. 2 Dec. 1791; m. Jane Prince.
4 Isaac, b. 1 April 1794; m. Sally Humphrey.
5 Asa, b. 15 June 1797; m. Rachel Coombs.
6 Peter, b. 1 March 1800; m. Ann Knight.

Born in Windham:

7 James, b. 15 June 1803; unm. He has always been a farmer in his native town.
8 Martha, b. 2 June 1805; m. Samuel Frank of Gray.
9 Betsey, b. 24 Dec. 1808; died aged eight years.
10 Lewis, b. 20 Oct. 1811; m. Eliza Knight.

1-4-1-4-2

Joel Libby, born in Scarborough, 9 Nov. 1762; married Mehitable Nash, daughter of John and Elizabeth (Andrews) Nash of Gray. He was a farmer and mechanic, and lived about one mile from his father's on the road from Gray Corner to West Gray. He was stung to death by bees, 5 July 1820. His widow died in Westbrook, 13 Aug. 1843.

Children, all born in Gray:

1 Elinor, b. 15 June 1786; m. 1st, 15 Oct. 1805, Wm. Delano; 2d, Samuel Jones.
2 Anna, b. 2 Feb. 1788; m. Alexander Jellison of York.
3 Andrew, b. 15 April 1790; m. Nancy J. Pulsifer of Sumner.
4 Eunice, b. 28 June 1792; m. 1st, 3 July 1816, James Weymouth; 2d, Wm. Moore.
5 Elijah, b. 20 Aug. 1794; m. Lydia Howe.
6 Ebenezer, b. 2 June 1796; m. Louisa Winslow.
7 Abigail, b. 21 Sept. 1798; m. Isaac Carson.
8 Olive, b. 12 Oct. 1806; m. Geo. W. Burnham.

1-4-1-4-5

Rev. Asa Libby, born in Scarborough; married, first, Lydia Hayden; (died at the birth of her son); second, Lucretia (White) Dutton.

He was a Baptist preacher. He preached many years while living in Gray, and at length became the settled minister in Belgrade, where he died in the spring of 1810. His widow died 8 Aug. 1830.

Children, by first wife:

1 Lydia, died unmarried.
2 Jerusha, m. William Smith of Sidney.
3 John, b. 15 July 1794; m. Polly Mills.

By second wife:

4 Abigail, married George Dunn.
5 Thankful, married Joshua Townsend.

1-4-1-6-1

Hanson Libby, born in Scarborough, about 1766; married, 2 Oct. 1788, Abigail Myrick. He removed to Gorham, and settled at White Rock, on the farm afterward known as the David Swett place. There he died, in the year 1796. His widow married, 16 Jan. 1797, Enos Newcomb. She died 27 Oct. 1834.

Children:

1 Elizabeth Meserve, b. 1789, in Scarborough; m. 25 Nov. 1807, Benj. Irish.
2 Hannah, b. 1790; m. Caleb Smart of Thornton, N. H.
3 Mary, b. 5 Nov. 1791, in Gorham; m. 28 Nov. 1816, Elisha Irish.
4 John Jay, b. 28 May 1793; m. Sally Burbank.
5 Anna Hanson, b. 29 April 1795; d. 26 March 1810.

1-4-1-6-3

Dennis Libby, born in Scarborough, 1771; married, 9 Oct. 1793, Betsey McKenney. [See page 63.] He removed to Danville, then a wilderness, and took up the farm on which his sons Caleb, Dennis, and Moses afterward lived. He and his wife died of measles; he, 21 March, she, 23 March, 1826.

Children, all but the first born in Danville:

1 Abner, b. 1794; d. Sept. 1815; unm.
2 Hanson, b. 1796; m. Polly Martin.
3 Eunice, b. 1797; d. June 1833; unm.
4 Mary, b. June 1799; d. Sept. 1870, in Portland; unm.
5 Lydia, b. 1801; m. Samuel Roberts; d. 3 Sept. 1832.
6 Caleb, b. 10 May 1803; m. Lydia Briggs.
7 Dennis, b. 16 April 1805; m. Sarah R. Warren.
8 Moses, b. 8 Aug. 1807; m. Margaret M. Libby, 10-5-6-5-8.
9 Hannah, b. 1809; m. 3 Sept. 1857, Jacob S. Richardson.
10 Susan, } twins, b. Feb. 1811; m. Dennis Libby, 1-1-3-9-1-4.
11 Betsey, } twins, b. Feb. 1811; m. Joseph Lang of Portland.

1-4-1-6-4.

James Libby, born in Scarborough, 12 May 1773; married, Mary Libby, 1-1-2-2-7. He settled on the homestead farm and lived there until his death, 12 April 1856. His wife died 26 Sept. 1848.

Children:

1 George, b. 1 Nov. 1794; died in the war of 1812; unm.
2 Abigail, b. 13 June 1804; m. Edward Libby, 11-7-2-4-6.
3 Mary, b. 18 Aug. 1808; m. Feb. 1827, Thomas Green.
4 Ichabod, b. 13 Dec. 1811; d. 8 July 1839; unm.

1-4-4-3-3

Enoch Libby, born in Rochester, N. H., 29 Oct. 1799; married, 15 April 1827, Sarah Lord, daughter of David and —— (Manson) Lord of South Berwick, Me. He removed to Newport, Me., then a new territory, and settled on a large tract of land on which he has ever since lived. His wife died 12 April 1879.

Yours truly
Saml. Libbey.

Children, all born in Newport:

1 Samuel, born 1 July 1829; married 14 Sept. 1856, Hester L. Libby. 1-4-4-3-5-1. He prepared for college, but ill health kept him from entering. He then read law three years with ex-Gov. Washburn, then of Orono, but abandoned the law for trade. He has been a successful pharmacist in Orono since 1854. He has been trustee of the Orono Savings bank, trustee of the State Normal Schools, has held commissions as trial justice, notary public, coroner, and filled other positions of trust. He was representative to the legislature in 1860-1, and was Republican candidate for Senator in 1880, but was defeated with the rest of the ticket. Children:
  1 John Charles, b. 24 Aug. 1859.
  2 Carrie E., b. 15 Oct. 1762.

2 Richard Henry, b. 5 Mar. 1831; m. 1st, Aug. 1859, Lydia A., dau. of Zenas and Malinda P. (Gray) Moore of Castine; (died 14 Oct. 1874); 2d, 18 May 1876, Clara M., widow of Ossian Hurd of Harmony, dau. of Jonathan and Elizabeth (Emerson) Davis of Palmyra. He is a farmer, on the homestead. He has always lived in Newport, save two years in Michigan. Only child:
  1 Minnie Geneva, b. 20 Nov. 1860.

3 Charles Francis, b. 6 Mar. 1832; m. 1st, Elizabeth, dau. of Rev. Henry Nason; 2d, 29 Nov. 1862, Albina B., dau. of Mark and Statira (Murphy) Weeks of Lagrange. He is a farmer in his native town. No children.

1-4-4-3-4

Paul Libby, born in Rochester, N. H., 18 April 1802; married, Elizabeth Sherburne, daughter of Joseph and Mary (Alley) Sherburne. He is a farmer, and has always occupied his father's homestead. His wife died 5 Oct. 1869, and he married, 9 Feb. 1873, Mrs. Eliza A. Otis, daughter of Millet and Mary Ann (Blaisdell) Wedgewood.

Children:

1 Nathaniel Sherburne, b. 31 Oct. 1821; m. 19 Nov. 1851, Manella Hibbert, dau. of Samuel and Charlotte (Wilkinson) Fogg of New Hampton, N. H. He lived at home until his marriage, and then removed to Chemung, N. Y., and took a contract of the Erie Railroad. Railroad contracting has since been his business. His residence is Washington, N. J. Children:
  1 Esther Frances, b. 9 April 1853, in Chemung, N. Y.; m. 13 May 1879, Geo. M. D. Dawes. Child:
    1 George Nathaniel (Dawes), b. 6 July 1880.
  2 Frank Wesley, b. 28 March 1858; unm. He is a professor of music.

2 Joseph Tibbetts Sherburne, b. 31 Oct. 1823; m. 4 Oct. 1849, Abby, dau. of Stephen and Susan (Calef) Wingate of Farmington. He served an apprenticeship at the printer's trade, and went into business in Dover. He is now half owner and one of the editors of the *Dover Enquirer* and the *Daily Republican*. He served as lieutenant in the late war. He was clerk of the common council of Dover many years, and is now a member of the New Hampshire Legislature. Children, all born in Dover:
  1 Ella Eudora, b. 20 June 1851; m. 20 June 1870, Charles H. Horton, jr., of Boston.
  2 Marie Abby, b. 5 Sept. 1853; m. 30 Dec. 1879, Charles E. Manock of Dover.
  3 Lizzie Etta, b. 9 Aug. 1857; unm.
  4 Flora Belle, b. 29 May 1866.

3 Lydia Sherburne, b. 11 June 1825; m. 2 Dec. 1850, Alonzo Mitchell.

4 Mary Elizabeth, b. 15 May 1833; m. Thomas F. Snow.

1-4-4-4-2

HANSON LIBBY, born in Rochester, N. H., 19 Nov. 1774; married, 16 May 1794, LYDIA WALLINGFORD of Rochester.

He moved with his father to Porter, Me., and settled on the farm now occupied by Trueworthy C. Libby, his grandson. He was one of the leading men in Porter. Under the plantation organization, he filled the office of treasurer, and after the town was organized, he was town clerk twenty consecutive years. He was also a justice of the peace. His death took place 23 June 1861. His wife died 22 Feb. 1843.

Children:

1 Nancy, b. 1797; m. John Libby, 6-4-1-9-8.
2 Abigail, b. 1803; m. 20 May 1824, Henry Mason; died 3 Feb. 1857.
3 James, b. 1806; d. 1823.

1-4-4-4-5

TOBIAS LIBBY, born in Rochester, N. H., 2 April 1783; married, 29 Sept. 1805, ABIGAIL RANDALL, daughter of Thomas and Mary (Huckins) Randall of Lee, N. H. He went to Porter, Me., with his father, and became a well-to-do farmer. He was twice selectman. His homestead is now occupied by Albert Stanley. He died 30 June 1858. His widow died 19 Feb. 1868.

Children:

1 John Mills, b. 21 Aug. 1806; m. Lovina G. Guptill.
2 Isaac, b. 5 Sept. 1809; m. Roxanna Towle.
3 Nancy, b. 24 July 1811; m. 12 Dec. 1835, John Stanley; d. 13 Aug. 1873.
4 Randall, b. 31 Oct. 1815; m. Sarah Towle.
5 Tobias, b. 27 Jan. 1821; m. Judith F. Towle.
6 Edwin Ruthwin, b. 11 July 1825; m. July 1846, Margaret, dau. of Thomas Rice of Freedom, N. H. He died at home, 18 Sept. 1854. Only child:
   1 Hattie R., b. 15 Feb. 1847; m. George Dow.
7 Abigail, b. 17 June 1829; m. 8 May 1853, Joseph T. Rice of Porter. Children:
   1 Edwin Ruthwin (Rice), b. 21 Aug. 1854; d. 9 July 1873.
   2 Thomas Clinton (Rice), b. 23 Oct. 1856; d. 11 May 1863.
   3 John W. (Rice), b. 22 Sept. 1858; m. 19 July 1879, Sarah Mias. Child:
      1 Edwin L. (Rice), b. 20 Nov. 1879.
   4 Lillie May (Rice), b. 1 Sept. 1865.
   5 Susie L. (Rice), b. 5 Nov. 1867; d. 21 Feb. 1868.
   6 Eva W. (Rice), b. 20 June 1871.

1-4-5-3-4

EBENEZER LIBBY, born probably in Conway, N. H., Oct. 1804; married, 1826, in New York State, RACHEL BURT. He was a mason. He went to New York State at the age of 21, and died in Varysburgh, 2 Feb. 1876. His wife died 28 Feb. 1864.

Children:

1 Edwin, b. 23 Aug. 1827, in Batavia, N. Y.; m. 1847, Melvina Fay of Java, N. Y.; died in 1874, in Tama Co., Iowa. His widow married Stephen Hall and lives in Toledo, Iowa.

2 Joseph, b. 18 Sept. 1829; m. 1st, Elizabeth Warner; (separated after a few years); 2d, 12 Nov. 1854, Phebe M., dau. of Daniel and Cynthia (Tucker) Kimball of Wellsborough, Penn. He worked in the lumber woods of Pennsylvania ten years, was a farmer in Penfield, Ohio, 11 years; is now a farmer in Varysburgh. Children, by first wife:

1 Mary Jane, b. 11 March 1847; m. 12 Dec. 1866, James H. Donaldson, since of South Hartford, N. Y. She was carried to Wisconsin by her mother and there left in a strange family. When she grew older she returned to New York in search of her father's relatives, became acquainted on the route with a man and his wife who persuaded her to go home with them. Father and daughter each supposed the other dead, and it was left for this work to unite them. Children:

1 Rosa A. (Donaldson), b. 15 Sept. 1867.
2 James H. (Donaldson), b. 16 Feb. 1869; d. 19 Sept. 1874.
3 Arthur S. (Donaldson), b. 16 Dec. 1870.
4 Nettie C. (Donaldson), b. 1 Jan. 1872.
5 Norman S. (Donaldson), b. 3 Nov. 1874.
6 Mary Jane (Donaldson), b. 28 Jan. 1876.
7 James H. (Donaldson), b. 30 Mar. 1878.
8 William J. (Donaldson), b. 3 Dec. 1879; d. 1 Sept. 1881.

By second wife:

2 Georgianna, b. 10 Aug. 1862.
3 Emma T., b. 1 May 1871; d. 10 Aug. 1872.
4 Florence, b. 19 Oct. 1874.

3 William, b. 23 Aug. 1831, in Bethany, N. Y.; m. 1st, 22 Oct. 1852, Amy F., dau. of Marshall and Amy (Nichols) Judd of Strafford; (died 14 July 1877); 2d, 22 Sept. 1878, Annie Bryson, of Irish parentage. He is a mason by trade, but since 1873 has been a farmer, in Varysburgh. He is a member of the Freewill Baptist Church. Children:

1 Amy R., b. 22 Oct. 1855, in Varysburgh; d. 11 Oct. 1856.
2 ———, son, b. 11 Sept. 1858; m. 4 April 1877, Adell, dau. of Lot and Mary Shaw of Sheldon; lives in Varysburgh. No children.

4 Alphonzo, b. Oct. 1833, in Batavia; died 16 Oct. 1859; unm.

5 Catherine, b. Nov. 1835; m. Anthony Cronkhite, now of Dunningville, Mich.

6 Ruth, b. 18 Sept. 1839; m. 1st, 1854, Thomas Girard; 2d, 1879, Alexander Topping.

1-5-2-3-2

MARY LIBBY, born in Gorham, Me., 28 March 1761; married, 1 March 1781, MATTHIAS MURCH of Gorham.

Previous to his marriage, he followed the sea, and he went on one three years' voyage after his marriage. He settled at Horse Beef, now called Mallison Falls, and owned the gristmill and sawmill which had belonged to his wife's father. He served three years in the Revolution, and lived to be a pensioner.

Children:

1 William (Murch), died at sea; unm.
2 Matthias (Murch), m. Lydia Shackford. Children:

1 Abial W. (Murch), m. Frances Rand.
2 Lucy S. (Murch), m. Daniel A. Peasley and Oliver A. Gould.
3 Margaret A. (Murch), m. Wm. Smith.
4 William Henry (Murch), m. 17 June 1853, Esther Plummer Libby, 11-7-8-2-5-2. He is a hay-dealer in Portland. Children:
    1 George T. (Murch), b. 27 Dec. 1855; m. 9 June 1878, Lilian, dau. of Peter DeRoshé of Waterville.
    2 Marietta S. (Murch), b. 19 June 1861; unm.

3 Mary (Murch), m. Peter Crockett.
4 Benjamin (Murch), died young.
5 Joseph (Murch), died young.
6 Eastman (Murch), died young.
7 Betsey (Murch), died young.
8 Charlotte (Murch), m. Jacob Quimby.
9 Daniel (Murch), lives in Gorham.
10 Dorcas (Murch), b. 18 Oct. 1819; unm. She lives in Portland.

1-5-2-3-3

John Libby, born in Gorham, Me., 10 March 1764; married, 12 March 1789, Phebe Knight. He was a farmer and always lived near Horse Beef Falls, where his father's mills were. He died 10 March 1826. His widow died about 1842.

Children:

1 Hannah, b. 22 Sept. 1789; m. Harry Stevens.
2 Lydia, b. 11 Aug. 1791; m. Dec. 1815, Benjamin F. Johnson.
3 Statira, b. 2 April 1793; m. 28 Feb. 1822, Joseph Cox.
4 Tyng S., b. 8 Dec. 1797; m. Sarah Crowell.
5 Samuel, b. 23 May 1800; d. 22 Aug. 1874; unm. He spent his life in the mills at Horse Beef.
6 Ebenezer, b. 16 July 1804; d. 20 April 1831; unm. He was a carpenter in Augusta, and in Vassalborough, where he died.
7 Peter, b. 1809; d. 21 Dec. 1830; unm.

1-5-2-3-4

William Libby, born in Gorham, Me., 28 Oct. 1769; married, 8 March 1797, Anna (Webb) Boulton, daughter of Eli and Anna Webb. He left home when his children were all small, and was never heard from afterward. His widow died 28 Dec. 1855, aged 93.

Children:

1 Dorcas, b. 22 Feb. 1798; m. 30 April 1815, James Wescott.
2 Lorana, b. 21 Nov. 1800; m. Samuel Freeman.
3 William B., b. 19 Jan. 1803; m. 2 Aug. 1837, Harriet, daughter of Thomas and Jane (Loring) Beck of Portland. He was a carpenter by trade, and before his marriage worked in the West and South. After his marriage, he lived in Windham, Brownfield, and finally in Biddeford, where he lost his life by falling into the wheelpit of Mill No. 2, Laconia Corp., 5 Jan. 1857. His widow married, 12 March 1861, Thomas Hampson. Children:
    1 ———, died in infancy in Windham.
    2 Lizzie B., b. March 1841, in Windham; m. 26 March 1869, Hartley S. Littlefield.
    3 Mary J., b. 15 March 1845, in Brownfield; m. 2 July 1864, Chas. B. Hight of Dayton.

4 Elizabeth, b. 1 May 1805; d. 22 Nov. 1828; unm.

1-5-2-3-7

JOSEPH LIBBY, born in Gorham, Me., 13 June 1780; married, 24 June 1801, MERCY WHITNEY, daughter of Joseph and Mehitable (Stevens) Whitney of Gorham. He was a house-carpenter. He lived at first on the five-acre lot on which the house of Lewis Brackett now stands, and afterward settled on a farm in North Gorham. He died with his son Daniel, 2 April 1843. His widow died with Edmund in Portland, 22 May 1860.

Children, all born in Gorham:

1 Roxanna, b. 15 Nov. 1802; m. 27 Sept. 1827, Wm. Files.
2 Harriet, b. 10 June 1804; died same year.
3 Stephen, b. 27 May 1807; m. Mary W. Lowe.
4 Ansel, b. 22 Nov. 1809; d. 12 May 1868; unm.
5 Edmund, b. 14 Mar. 1812; m. 29 July 1838, Hannah E., dau. of Wm. and Margaret (Chesley) Elder of Windham. He was a shoemaker by trade. About 1855 he removed to Portland, and engaged in the shoe business with C. J. Walker. He was afterward of the firms of Tyler, Lamb & Co., Libby & Brown, and, finally, Sawyer, Webb & Co. He died 21 Oct. 1872. His widow lives in Brooklyn, N. Y. Children, all born in Gorham:
   1 Elfreda, b. 19 May 1840; m. 1 Oct. 1860, Wm. D. True.
   2 Daniel W., b. 12 Nov. 1841; d. 25 Aug. 1842.
   3 Margaret, b. 25 July 1844; m. 2 Oct. 1873, in Portland, Wm. P. Sturgis, now of Brooklyn.
6 William, b. 7 Nov. 1814; m. 1st, 1838, Elizabeth, dau. of John and Hannah (Bangs) Hamblen; (died 1839); 2d, Feb. 1844, Charlotte, dau. of Lydia (Libby) Johnson, 1-5-2-3-3-2; (died 13 Nov. 1864, in Windham); 3d, 18 Feb. 1868, Jennie P., dau. of Reuben Rideout of Cumberland; (died 12 Dec. 1869, in Chelsea, Mass.) He is a house-carpenter. He removed to Portland, his present residence, in 1864. Children, by 1st wife:
   1 Edgar, died in childhood, in Gorham.

   By second wife:

   2 Elizabeth, b. 15 June 1845, in Gorham; unm.
   3 Lydia, b. 19 Dec. 1848; m. 14 Aug. 1868, Henry R. Nickerson.
   4 Elbridge William, b. 21 Dec. 1853; m. 14 Aug. 1878, Lucy, dau. of John and Caroline (Sharpe) Good of New Brunswick. He is of the firm of Spaulding & Libby, grocers, Portland. No children.
   5 Lelia, b. 27 Feb. 1856, in Windham; d. 17 Nov. 1862.
   6 Mabel, b. 9 Nov. 1858; d. 16 Nov. 1862.
7 Daniel, b. 15 July 1818; m. Dec. 1843, Parmelia, dau. of Henry and Anna (Varney) Moore of Windham. He became a shoemaker, and worked with his brother Edmund, first in Gorham, and then in Portland, until the latter's death. He has always resided on a small farm near Little Falls, Gorham. Children:
   1 Charles J., b. 5 Aug. 1847; m. 28 May 1874, Lizzie J., dau. of Harriet (Libby) Carr, 10-5-4-2-9-6. He lives with his father. No children.
   2 Anna Augusta, b. 11 Aug. 1851; m. Jos. E. Libby, 10-5-4-2-9-10.

1-5-2-4-2

JOSEPH LIBBY, born in Gouldsborough, Me., 25 April 1765; married, 27 Oct. 1799, BATHSHEBA GIBBS, whose mother was by birth a Pope. He was a farmer and lumberman. He settled on land next adjoining his father's farm and lived there until his death, 12 Sept. 1822. His widow died 22 April 1858.

Children:

1 Daniel, b. 13 Jan. 1800; m. Mary Ann Whitaker.
2 Thankful, } twins, born } m. Millins Uram.
3 Lydia, } 17 Dec. 1801; } m. 27 March 1824, Abel Hovey.
4 Joseph, b. 12 Jan. 1805; m. Priscilla Wilson.
5 Belinda, b. 22 Feb. 1807; m. 26 Dec. 1828, Curtis Guptill.
6 Jemima, b. 30 Sept. 1809; m. Elliot Nichols.

1-5-2-5-1

WILLIAM LIBBY, born in Falmouth, Me., 9 Jan. 1763; married JANE MCCAFFREY, a niece of the wife of Joseph Webster of Gray. He cleared the farm now owned by Freeland E. Libby, 1-5-2-5-1-7-3, and always lived there. In addition to his farming he engaged in lumbering, and built saw and grist mills at Dry Mills. He died 4 Sept. 1856, aged 93. His wife died 16 Sept. 1843.

Children:

1 James, b. 2 Sept. 1786; m. Mehitable Low.
2 Sally, b. 12 Aug. 1788; m. April, 1831, John Muchemore.
3 Jane, b. 8 March 1790; m. 14 Dec. 1807, Samuel Clark; died 13 Dec. 1879.
4 Mary, b. 7 Feb. 1792; m. 1st, —— Brayman, a recruiting officer in the war of 1812, who proved to have another wife; 2d, Daniel Harris.
5 Joseph, b. 5 Feb. 1794; m. Mary Simonton.
6 Dorcas, b. 7 April 1796; died a little girl, from a fall from a fence.
7 William, b. 2 Feb. 1798; m. Deborah Brown.
8 Dorcas, b. 11 Sept. 1800; m. 13 Oct. 1857, James Harding of Standish; d. 9 May 1874.
9 Frances, b. 13 Sept. 1802; m. Sumner W. Foss.
10 Charles, b. 29 March 1804; m. Abigail Cummings.
11 Parker Sawyer, b. 13 Nov. 1806; m. Emeline Harris.

1-5-2-5-2

JOSEPH LIBBY, born in Gray, Me., in 1764; married MARY YOUNG, daughter of Nathaniel and Susannah (Lamine) Young. He owned and carried on the farm in Gray now owned by George McConky, but lived at Gray Corner, where he was in trade some years. He died 28 Dec. 1815. His widow died in Portland 28 Sept. 1839.

Children:

1 Lamine, was a cattle drover. He died at Brunswick, a young man; unmarried.
2 Mary Young, m. 13 Oct. 1823, Henry Homer of Portland.
3 Joseph, died in 1839, in New York; unm.
4 Nathaniel, b. 19 Nov. 1800; m. Sophia Churchill.
5 Delaw, b. 21 Oct. 1799 (?); m. Mary E. Emerson,

1-5-2-5-6

JONATHAN LIBBY, born in Gray, Me., about 1769; married ABIGAIL CLARK. Upon his marriage he settled on a farm west of Gray Corner, now owned by Horace O. Stimpson. He afterward moved onto a farm nearer the village, now owned by George Dolly. There he died in the summer of 1836. His widow died in May, 1855.

Children:

1 Jedediah, b. 1793; m. 8 March 1837, Mary Pearce of New Gloucester. He settled on a farm in New Gloucester soon after his marriage, and lived there until his death, in old age. His wife outlived him about eight years. No children.
2 Susan, b. 15 July 1795; m. Ezekiel Jordan.
3 George, b. 30 Jan. 1798; m. Mary Ann Stimpson.
4 Richard, b. Feb. 1801; m. 1831, Mary Harris, dau. of Nathaniel and Joanna (Young) Martin of Newport, Me. He was a farmer. He left Gray a young man and, soon after his marriage, became one of the first settlers of Aroostook Co. He died 27 April 1860. His widow died 16 Sept. 1873. Children:
   1 William H., b. 20 June 1834, in Oldtown; d. 1 May 1835.
   2 Mary E., b. 24 April 1836; d. 21 Oct. 1869, in Boston; unm.
   3 Sarah A., b. 13 Feb. 1838, in Moluncus; d. 22 Sept. 1851.
   4 Daniel W., b. 4 Feb. 1840; unm. He is head filer in a sawmill in Minneapolis, Minn.
   5 Abbie E., b. 5 May 1842; m. Charles P. Kendall, a painter.
   6 Amanda A., b. 15 Oct. 1844; d. 7 Nov. 1847.
   7 Emma L., b. 11 Dec. 1846; m. George M. Estes.
   8 Hattie F., b. 12 May 1850, in Lincoln; unm.
   9 Richard O., b. 30 June 1854, in Mattawamkeag; unm. He is a conductor on the Old Colony Railroad.
5 James, b. 15 April 1802; m. Harriet Hayden.
6 Ebenezer. He followed the sea from youth, and was last heard from as captain of a river steamer.
7 Samuel, b. 11 April 1805; m. 17 Oct. 1831, Abbie F., dau. of John and Mary (Green) Hustin of Portland. He was a farmer in New Gloucester a number of years, and then went to Portland, where he kept first a meat shop, then a grocery, and finally a toy and confectionery store. He died 11 Aug. 1873. Children:
   1 Mary Abigail, b. 12 Oct. 1833; d. 31 Aug. 1834.
   2 Mary Jane, b. 21 Jan. 1836; m. 11 July 1858, Peter W. Plummer.
   3 Sarah Annie, b. 13 Oct. 1838; unm.
8 William, b. 9 Aug. 1809; m. 10 March 1836, Sarah, adopted daughter of Thomas Osgood, and daughter of Wm. and Dorcas (Sawyer) Crane, of Portland. He went to Portland when a young man, and was many years overseer on the Deering farm. He died 2 Aug. 1865. His widow lives with her daughter in Gray. Children:
   1 Lydia Osgood, b. 19 Oct. 1836; m. 23 Feb. 1860, Edward S. Griffin.
   2 Ellen Jane, b. 5 Feb. 1839; m. 9 June 1868, Alonzo D. Page of Gray.
9 Jonathan, b. 31 Jan. 1812; m. Matilda S. Bacon.
10 Sarah, m. Henry R. Robinson of Brewer.
11 Joseph, b. 23 Oct. 1818; m. Nancy Foster.

1-5-2-5-7

CAPT. DANIEL LIBBY, born in Gray, Me., about 1771; married, HANNAH COLLEY, daughter of James and Sylvia (Harris) Colley of Gray. He settled on a farm north of Dry Mills. When the war of 1812 came on, he sold his farm and served through the war as captain. After the war, he settled on a small place south of Dry Mills, and there lived until his death, which took place in the spring of 1844. His widow died in Portland two years later.

Children:

1 Thomas. He served in the war of 1812 as drum-major, and after the war enlisted in the regular army. He was stationed at one time at Houlton, and report came that he was married. His company was ordered off and he was never afterward heard from.
2 Susan, m. 12 Jan. 1825, John Hustin.
3 Sylvia, b. 7 Aug. 1801; m. 4 July 1821, Nathaniel P. Cushman.
4 Sarah, m. Isaac Libby, 6-4-1-6-1-1.
5 Daniel, died on a whaling voyage; unm.
6 Emeline, m. John Mitchell of Yarmouth.
7 Almira, b. 2 Feb. 1819; m. 8 Aug. 1847, James Brown; d. 1 June 1870, in Dorchester, Mass.
8 Mary Ann, m. Edwin Davenport.

1-5-2-5-11

Benjamin Libby, born in Gray, Me., April 1778; married first, 30 Oct. 1800, Abigail Green, daughter of Daniel Green of Portland; (died Dec. 1805); second, Mary Lunt, daughter of Michael and Sarah (Skillings) Lunt of Portland. He lived on a part of his father's farm until Nov. 1836, when he moved onto a garden-spot near the Corner, where he lived until his death, 4 Nov. 1841. His widow died 11 Nov. 1869.

Children, by first wife:

1 Benjamin, b. 5 July 1802; m. Martha Starbird. He was killed in the Mexican war, Sept. 1856. No children. His widow married first, ——— Munroe and then ——— Blount.
2 William, b. 19 Dec. 1805; m. Axcy Gilpatrick. He removed to Weston, Aroostook County, when a young man, married there, and became a farmer. He died 1 July 1838, leaving his wife, but no children.

By second wife:

3 Lemine, b. 25 Aug. 1811; m. 1st, Mary Ann Farrar; 2d, Phebe Yeaton. He was a farmer. He was at work in New Hampshire, married there, and settled in Meredith, now Laconia, where he died 22 March 1870. He served three years against the Rebellion. Children, all by first wife:
   1 Ellen Louisa, m. Edmund Kidder of Wilton.
   2 Mary Jane, died aged 22 years, of consumption.
   3 Ann Elizabeth, m. Page Bruce of Laconia.
   4 Addie, died at the age of seven years.
   5 Sarah, married George Kelly of Meredith.
   6 Charles, lives in California; unm.
   7 Fanny, m. George Ellenwood of Manchester.
   8 Eliza Gertrude, died aged 22.
   9 George, died aged one year.
4 Abigail, b. 14 Aug. 1816; m. 10 Oct. 1847, Isaac S. Lunt, her mother's brother. She lives where her father died.
5 Ellen, b. June, 1818; m. 2 May 1839, John K. Clough of Meredith, N. H.
6 Louisa, b. 7 March 1821; m. Reuben Cobb of Gray.

1-5-2-5-12

Sophia Libby, born in Gray, Me., Feb. 1781; married, 1803, William Green, a brother of her brother Benjamin's wife, born 5 Sept. 1780. He removed from Gray to Portland, where he was a trader many years, and died 13 Oct. 1867. His wife died 1 Jan. 1861.

Children, born in Gray:

1 William (Green), b. 1 Oct. 1803; d. 26 July 1804.
2 Mary T. (Green), b. 19 Nov. 1805; m. Richard Green of Plymouth, Mass.
3 Abiah Libby (Green), b. 14 Aug. 1807; m. Samuel Wyllie; d. 4 Aug. 1879.
4 Caleb, b. 6 May, d. 25 Dec., 1808.
5 Henry W. (Green), b. 12 Nov. 1809; m. Elizabeth ——.
6 William C. (Green), b. 3 April 1811; m. Susan Bickford; d. 3 June 1839. No children. His widow married Daniel F. Knights.
7 George Washington (Green), b. 14 May 1813; married, 21 May 1833, Clarissa L., dau. of Joseph and Abigail (Nash) Hayden of Gray. He is a coal dealer in Portland. Only child:
  1 Joseph William (Green), b. 21 Dec. 1844; m. 25 Dec. 1869, Olive, dau. of Isaac V. and Frances H. (Lawson) Worden of Portland; died 13 May 1880. He was in company with his father. No children.
8 Sophia L. (Green), b. 24 Feb. 1816; m. Daniel Brown; died 29 Mar. 1874. Daniel Brown was a son of George H. Brown of Kennebunk, and became a carpenter in Portland, where he died, 24 Feb. 1878. Children:
  1 Mary Eliza (Brown), m. Wm. Soule of Auburndale, Mass.
  2 Daniel H. (Brown), lives in East Boston, Mass.
  3 —— (Brown), died in infancy.
  4 George Wyllie (Brown), m. 22 April 1879, Lenora Estella, dau. of Amesbury B. and Martha Ann (Coombs) Seavey of Bethel. He is a carpenter in Portland. No children.
9 Charles T. (Green), b. 23 July 1818; died 19 Aug. 1872, in Boston. He was thrice married, but had no children.
10 James Harris (Green), b. 17 April 1821; m. Ellen Abbott; died May, 1867, in Lowell, Mass.
11 Benjamin F. (Green), b. 18 May 1822; m. 1st, 23 Oct. 1845, Mary Ann, dau. of Edward and Mary Finney of Portland; (died 8 Mar. 1862); 2d, 20 Aug. 1863, Dorcas, dau. of Charles and Dorcas (Farren) Pennell of Portland. He is a sea-captain. Children, by first wife:
  1 Sarah W. (Green), b. 29 Dec. 1845; m. William St. John; d. 31 Aug. 1872.
  2 Ellen S. (Green), b. 19 April 1847; m. Frank Newhall of Portland.
  3 Emma A. (Green), b. 15 Aug. 1850; d. 11 April 1870.
  4 Daniel W. (Green), b. 2 March, d. 6 May, 1857.

By second wife:

  5 William F. (Green), b. 11 Oct. 1864.

Born in Portland:

12 Sarah W. (Green), b. 4 April 1825; d. 16 Sept. 1826.
13 Sarah W. (Green), b. 16 July 1826; d. 22 Oct. 1831.

1-6-2-1-1

HANSON LIBBY, born in Berwick, Me., 14 Dec. 1760; married, 10 Dec. 1782, ANNA LIBBY, 1-6-5-11. At the age of 15 he was captured with his father's schooner, and was five years a prisoner at Halifax. He settled in Tuftonborough, N. H., upon his marriage, and lived there, a farmer, until his death, 1 Dec. 1805. His widow died 30 Sept. 1823.

Children, all born in Tuftonborough:

1 Rebecca, b. 23 Sept. 1783; m. Rev. Samuel Knowles; died 12 Sept. 1863, in Ossipee.
2 Daniel, b. 24 Feb. 1785; m. Mary Abbott.
3 Abigail, b. 24 July 1786; d. 14 Dec. 1790.
4 Betsey, b. 24 June 1788; m. David Hull; d. 12 July 1854, in Tuftonborough.
5 Lydia, b. 2 July 1790; m. John White; d. 11 Jan. 1867, in Tuftonborough.
6 Jenny, b. 20 Feb. 1792; m. Robert Sargent.
7 Levi, b. 24 March 1794; m. Mary Canney.
8 Jeremiah, b. 10 Oct. 1796; d. 22 Aug. 1811.

1-6-2-1-6

ICHABOD LIBBY, born, probably in Berwick, Me., Jan. 1770; married POLLY LEAVITT, born 10 March 1772, daughter of Josiah Leavitt of Strafford, N. H. He settled in Tuftonborough, N. H., then a wilderness, and became at length a comfortable farmer. A few years before his death he removed to Wolfborough, and there died, 23 Nov. 1833. He was many years a deputy sheriff. His widow died 4 April 1856.

Children:

1 Josiah L., m. 1816, Mary, dau. of Jonathan and Shuah (Stevens) Morrison of Tuftonborough, where he was a farmer until his death, 7 June 1833. His widow died 30 Oct. 1870. Only child:
  1 Shuah M., b. 18 Dec. 1819; m. 18 April 1843, Otis Evans.
2 Belinda, b. 18 Dec. 1799; m. Capt. Jonathan Morrison; d. 19 May 1846.
3 John Smith, b. 1801; d. aged 2½ years.
4 Dudley Leavitt, b. 23 Oct. 1803; m. 7 Oct. 1827, Sarah Ann, dau. of Samuel and Nancy (Chase) Wiggin of Tuftonborough. He was a farmer, living always in Tuftonborough and Wolfborough, and introduced many improvements. He was a captain in the militia cavalry, and a member of the Congregational Church. His death took place in New York City, 29 Dec. 1856. His widow still lives in Wolfborough. Children:
  1 Anne Mary, b. 26 July 1828, in Tuftonborough; d. 29 Mar. 1829.
  2 Sarah Elizabeth, b. 14 March 1830, in Wolfborough; m. 26 Dec. 1854, Augustine D. Avery of Wolfborough. Children:
    1 Mary Elizabeth (Avery), b. 16 Nov. 1855; d. 20 Oct. 1856.
    2 Dudley Libby (Avery), b. 11 Aug. 1857; d. 24 June 1874.
    3 Samuel Augustine (Avery), b. 5 Mar. 1860; d. 27 Aug. 1861.
    4 Samuel (Avery), b. 14 March 1862.
    5 Belle (Avery), b. 17 March 1866.
  3 Anne Mary, b. 23 Jan. 1832; d. 15 March 1852.
  4 Helen Mariah, b. 3 April 1835, in Tuftonborough; m. 8 Jan. 1857, Joseph L. Avery of Wolfborough. Children:
    1 Joseph William (Avery), b. 14 Aug. 1867; d. 16 Oct. 1867.
    2 Joseph Clifton (Avery), b. 1 June 1874.
  5 Arabella Amanda, b. 23 Nov. 1837; d. 4 April 1863.
  6 Emily Caroline, b. 8 Sept. 1840; d. 8 Oct. 1875.
5 James S., b. 2 Nov. 1805; m. Lydia B. Edmunds and Hannah M. Moore.
6 George W., b. 15 Feb. 1808; m. 1 Jan. 1835, Sarah Elnora, dau. of James and Nancy (Nudd) Young of Wolfborough. He learned the tanner's trade, and after living several years in Tuftonborough, removed to New York, where he was in business some time. He then retired to Newark, N. J., his present residence. He is a Second Adventist. Children:

1 Annette Frances, b. 25 May 1836, in Roxbury, Mass.
2 James Young, b. 26 July 1838, in Tuftonborough; d. 30 Aug. 1843.
3 Susan Ellen, b. 7 May 1845.
4 Sarah Maria, b. 27 Mar. 1849, in Wolfborough; m. 28 Aug. 1867, Louis Burnett Jennings. Child:
  1 Gertrude Libby (Jennings), b. 16 Oct. 1871.
5 George William, b. 14 April 1851, in Moultonborough; lives in Milwaukee, Wis.

7 Mary, } twins, born } m. Wm. P. Colton; d. 1850.
8 Sarah. } 20 Nov. 1810; } m. Eliot Colton.
9 Ira Allen, b. 2 May 1813; m. 25 Mar. 1846, Ann E., dau. of Col. Benj. and Eliza (Russell) Edmunds of Brooklyn, N. Y. He was in the dry goods business in Rochester, N. Y., before his marriage, and afterward moved to New York City, where he was successively a member of the firms of Carleton & Co., and Clark, Libby & Co. He died in Brooklyn, 14 Dec. 1876. Children:
  1 Charles Ira, b. 1 Feb. 1847, in Brooklyn; d. next day.
  2 Catherine Elizabeth, born 6, died 17, Feb. 1848.
  3 Annie Malena, b. 25 May 1851; m. 20 June 1872, Dr. Wm. H. Bates; d. 4 Nov. 1877.
  4 Mary Amanda, b. 2 Feb. 1855, in New York City; m. 14 April 1880, Dr. Bates.
  5 Benjamin Edmunds, b. 26 June; d. 24 July 1863, in Islip, L. I.

10 William P., b. 8 May 1817; m. Mary Louisa Bridge.

1-6-2-1-9

Dr. Benjamin Libby, born at Frenchman's Bay, on the coast of Hancock County, Me., 15 Mar. 1777; married, 5 April 1802, Susan Demerit, daughter of Paul and Betsey (Davis) Demerit of Farmington, N. H. He studied medicine with Dr. Samuel Quimby of Boston, obtained his diploma, and at the age of 23 began practice in Tuftonborough, N. H., and 16 months later removed to Farmington. He lived there 15 years, practicing his profession, and also engaging in trade. He enlisted as private for the invasion of Canada in the war of 1812, but was ordered onto the staff of surgeons. After the war closed he returned home, and at once removed to Goshen Gore, Vt., and settled on 400 acres of land. He practiced there, and in Danville, until his removal to Compton, Que., in 1829. He lived in Compton until his death, 9 Oct. 1858. His widow died 24 Dec. 1861.

Children:

1 Clarissa, b. 1803, in Farmington; died in infancy.
2 John, b. 1805; m. Eliza Stanton of Danville, Vt.
3 Jefferson, b. 1806; died May 1833. He studied medicine, but died before graduation.
4 Christopher Columbus, b. 23 Sept. 1807; m. Calista Hyatt.
5 Elgiva, b. 1809; } live on their father's
6 Clymena, b. 1811; } homestead; unm.
7 Tama, b. 1813, m. 1841, John Saunders.
8 Amarilla, b. 1815, in Goshen Gore, Vt.; m. Ashel Aldrich.
9 William Pitt, b. 14 July 1816; m. Sarah Parker and Elizabeth Sanders.

1-6-2-4-1

Ichabod Libby, born in Berwick, Me., about 1772; married, 29 April 1793, Mary Keay.

He removed from Berwick to Dixmont in 1800, and thence, in 1819, to Ohio. He lived about three years in Euclid, and the rest of his life in Newburgh, about ten miles distant. He was always a farmer. He and his wife were members of the Baptist Church. He died 8 Sept. 1826. His widow died 13 April 1840, in Bedford, Ohio.

Children:

1 George, died aged 14 years.
2 Mary, m. 1833, in Brooklyn, O., James Pettibone.
3 Lydia, m. 1820, David Mansur of Monroe, Me.
4 Rufus, b. 1 Oct. 1801; m. Cassandria Foster.
5 John [Major], b. 28 Jan. 1805; m. Jan. 1854, Mrs. Hannah (Culver) Morse of Bedford. He was a farmer. He rose to the rank of major in the state militia. He died 6 June 1870, in Bedford. Children:
  1 Charles Fremont, } died in
  2 daughter, } infancy.
6 Elisha. He was a railroad contractor in the south, and a merchant at Port Hudson, La. He was one of those killed by the explosion of the steamer *General Brown*, while racing on the Mississippi River, in 1837.
7 Eliza, m. Dec. 1830, in Newburgh, Geo. C. Robinson.
8 George, b. 11 Oct. 1813; m. 1st, 16 Dec. 1845, at Springfield, Penn., Susan L., dau. of Jesse Palmer of Cleveland, O.; (they were divorced through a misunderstanding purposely brought about by others, and she married again, and died in California in 1870); second, 18 May 1848, Mrs. Eliza Axtell, dau. of Silas Pool of Woodstock. She died 25 April 1867. He has been an athletic performer, a musician, and a farmer, and has lived many years in North Ridgeville. Only child, by first wife:
  1 Josephine, b. 10 Sept. 1846; m. Geo. Gore; died 1870.

1-6-2-4-7

Joseph Libby, born in Berwick, Me., in 1784; married, 1807, Hannah Cook, daughter of Ebenezer and Keziah (Davis) Cook of Wakefield, N. H. He was a farmer, and lived first in Milton, and then in Wakefield, where he died 6 Jan. 1866. His wife died in Milton in 1817.

Children:

1 Lucy, b. 1809; m. Asa Miller; d. 1852.
2 George, b. 1811; unm. His home is in Wakefield.
3 Mary J., b. 1813; d. 1814.
4 James L., b. 26 July 1815; m. 10 July 1837, Caroline, dau. of Daniel and Mary (Allen) Page. He is a farmer in Wakefield. Children:
  1 Daniel, b. 28 Aug. 1838; d. 14 May 1856.
  2 Charles Albert, b. 2 June 1840; m. 1st, 31 Dec. 1861, Mary Eliza, dau. of Dr. Sumner and Susan H. (Wentworth) Gilman; (died 6 Oct. 1866); 2d, 29 Oct. 1868, Sarah Kimball, dau. of Reuben and Joanna (Bullard) Nichols of Reading, Mass. He is a contractor and builder in Stoneham, Mass. Children, by first wife:
    1 Daniel Sumner, b. 12 July 1863.

By second wife:

    2 Bessie May, b. 22 Feb. 1874, in Stoneham.
  3 Maie C., b. 25 Jan. 1853; unm.

1-6-2-4-8

JOHN LIBBY, born in Berwick, Me., 1785; married first, 3 Feb. 1803, SALLY LANGLEY, daughter of David and Betsey (Cottle) Langley of Rochester, N. H.; second, DOLLY WIGGIN, daughter of Josiah Wiggin of Ossipee.

He was a carpenter by trade, and lived in Rochester during his first wife's lifetime. Shortly after his second marriage he removed to Wolfborough, where he became a farmer. He died 12 March 1848. His wife Dolly died 20 Dec. 1840.

Children, by first wife:

1 Lydia, b. 22 Aug. 1803; m. 29 Jan. 1824, Wm. P. Mitchell of New Durham, N. H.

By second wife:

2 George W., b. 16 Aug. 1808; m. 12 Feb. 1837, Ruth W., dau. of Lyford and Mercy (Wiggin) Shorey of Wolfborough. Since his marriage he has lived on the farm now occupied by him, about two miles from Wolfborough Bridge. Children:
  1 Mark A., b. 24 Nov. 1838; d. 26 May 1842.
  2 Martin A., b. 30 Nov. 1840; m. 26 Feb. 1870, Martha E., dau. of Morris H. and Catherine (Champion) Leavitt of Effingham. He is a shoemaker and lives with his father. No children.
  3 Mercy M., b. 2 Oct. 1842; m. 6 Jan. 1869, Freeman Wilkins of Hudson, Mass.
  4 James R., b. 28 July 1844; d. 19 Feb. 1847.
  5 Helen M., b. 11 June 1849; m. 21 Dec. 1869, Jasper H. Warren.
  6 Frank G., b. 4 Dec. 1852; d. 20 March 1869.

3 John A., b. 16 June 1811; m. 11 Feb. 1859, Hannah S., dau. of Hiram and Susan (Hill) Ham of Wolfborough. He has always been a farmer in Wolfborough. Children:
  1 Estella F., b. 8 July 1859.
  2 George E., b. 25 Dec. 1861.
  3 Anna V., b. 1 Feb. 1864.
  4 C. Mabel, b. 13 Oct. 1872.

4 Mark, b. 1813; died about 1824.

5 Sarah P., b. April, 1815; m. March, 1848, Joseph Langdon.

1-6-2-4-10

MARK LIBBY, born in Berwick, Me., 13 Feb. 1790; married, Feb. 1808, NANCY COOK, daughter of Ebenezer and Keziah (Davis) Cook of Wakefield, N. H. In 1811 he moved from Wakefield to Bolton, Quebec, and there lived until his death, 9 Jan. 1851. His widow died 16 Aug. 1878.

Children:

1 Lydia, b. 4 June 1809, in Wakefield; m. Daniel Chamberlain and William Giddings; d. 15 May 1880.

2 Harriet. b. 23 Nov. 1811, in Bolton; m. Ephraim Dudley Bailey; d. 17 Dec. 1872.

3 Lucy, b. 9 Sept. 1813; died in childhood.

4 Luther, b. 26 Dec. 1815; m. Anna Knowlton.

5 Samuel Emerson, b. 13 May 1818; m. Mehitable, dau. of Elisha and Martha Smith of Lisbon, Mass. He was a carpenter. He lived a while in Rock Island, Que., and afterward moved to Burlington, Vt. About 1849 he left his family and went to California. He is supposed to be dead. His widow died 13 May 1879, in Elgin, Ill. Children:

1 Martha Maria, b. 12 Dec. 1837; m. 6 Feb. 1855, Charles Warren Higgins.
2 Ellen, b. 16 March 1840; m. Nov. 1863, George B. Farrar; d. 4 Aug. 1870, in Elgin, Ill.
3 Dorcas, b. 26 Dec. 1841; m. July, 1869, John C. Coburn.
4 Flora, b. 17 Nov. 1843; m. 3 Sept. 1864, James Colson.

6 Lee, b. 28 Feb. 1821; m. 15 July 1822, Hannah, dau. of Wm. and Polly (Stocum) Delines of Swantown. He always lived in his native place, and died there 25 April 1879. His wife died 18 Mar. 1849. He was a member of the Second Advent Church. Children:
1 Agnes A., b. 11 Nov. 1844; m. 3 July 1872, Prescott E. Knights.
2 Caroline E., b. 2 March 1847; m. 8 June 1875, Melvin Hoyt.
3 Sophia A., b. 9 Feb. 1849; m. Stillman Knowlton.

7 William Wallace, b. 15 April 1824; m. 1st, 10 May 1854, Mary, dau. of John and Mary (Purdee) Barber; (died 24 Sept. 1868); 2d, Mrs. Anna ——, dau. of Asa P. and Anna (Turner) Blake. He is a carpenter and carriage-maker, but lives on a small farm. He is a member of the Second Advent Church. Children:
1 Martha Medora, b. 16 June 1855.
2 John Hiram, b. 15 Oct. 1856.
3 Lucy Marion, b. 13 July 1859; d. 16 March 1860.
4 William Henry, b. 29 May 1861.
5 Mary Armina, b. 30 Oct. 1863.
6 son, b. 30 March 1868; died aged three weeks.

8 Mark Furber, b. 25 June 1826; m. 9 Jan. 1863, in St. Paul, Minn., Mrs. Harriet Newel Cook, dau. of Abraham and Jane (Sloan) Pettijohn of Sardinia, Ohio. Until about the age of 40, he was a bridge-builder. He then went to Minnesota, where he is now a farmer, in West St. Paul. Children:
1 Ethel Nancy, b. 11 Nov. 1863, in West St. Paul.
2 Carrie Lena, b. 17 March 1865.
3 Frederick Mark, b. 17 July 1867.

9 Dorothy Ann, b. 3 Sept. 1829; m. Jonathan Buswell Drew; d. 14 May 1859.

10 Hiram Cortes, b. 17 Dec. 1831; married in Ontario a daughter of Lieut. Beatee of the English army. He died about 1879, in New London, where his widow lived when last heard from. Children:
1 Charles, b. about 1854.
2 Mary, b. about 1856.

11 Dorinda, b. 23 Dec. 1834; d. 28 Jan. 1863; unm.

1-6-2-4-11

NATHAN LIBBY, born in Berwick, Me., 18 March 1792; married, June 1816, OLIVE BERRY, daughter of Francis and Sally (Grant) Berry of Milton, N. H.

Soon after his marriage he removed to Wakefield, N. H., where he settled on wild land and cleared the farm which he occupied 48 years. He died 13 Aug. 1870, and his widow, 10 Dec. 1871. They were members of the Freewill Baptist Church until 1854, and then became Second Adventists.

Children:

1 Joseph, b. 5 May 1817, in Milton; m. 18 July 1840, Caroline M., dau. of James and Jerusha (Packard) Aldrich of Lebanon, N. H. He early removed to Massachusetts. After the war he went to Old Point Comfort, Va., and established a mercantile business. He afterward left this to his brother and returned to New England, where his occupation is that of hotel keeper. His wife died in Somerville, Mass, 20 Jan. 1881. Children:

1 Adah, b. 28 March 1852, in Charlestown, Mass.; m. July 1879, Clarence Watson.
2 Cary, b. Dec. 1854; d. 1 March 1857.
3 Nathan Herbert, b. 26 Aug. 1862, in Somerville.
4 James A., b. 29 Feb. 1864.
5 Joseph, b. 19 Aug. 1866.

2 Sarah, b. 14 May 1819; m. Satchell Weeks.
3 Francis, b. 1 May 1822, in Wakefield; m. 27 Oct. 1853, in Boston, Clara Hosmer, dau. of Amasa and Sarah (Butler) Wilde of Williamstown. He was a hotel-keeper in the West, and died at Atchison, Kansas, 21 Oct. 1864. Child:
1 Sarah Frances, b. 17 July 1854; lives in Boston with her mother.
4 Lydia, b. 22 June 1824; m. James Shorey of Wakefield.
5 Mark, b. 9 Sept. 1826; d. 15 Sept. 1828.
6 Adah, b. 26 Dec. 1828; died in 1832.
7 James B., b. 26 March 1831; was a printer in Boston, where he died 2 March 1874, and his widow still lives.
8 John Garvin, b. 24 March 1833; m. 9 Nov. 1864, in Marysville, Cal., Margaret M., dau. of James Byrne of Boston, Mass. He is of the firm of Dakin & Libby, commercial soap manufacturers, San Francisco. Children:
1 Olive Kate, b. 23 Aug. 1865, in Virginia City, Nevada.
2 Jennie, b. 5 Feb. 1867, in Grass Valley, Cal.; d. 29 June 1867.
3 John Frank, b. 25 July 1869, in San Francisco.
4 Lillie Maria, b. 2 Feb. 1872.
5 Sarah Elizabeth, b. 8 Jan. 1874.
6 Fred Nathan, b. 7 Aug. 1875.
7 Joseph Harrison, b. 14 May 1877.
9 Horace, b. 30 July 1835; m. 1st, 18 Aug. 1855, Joan Pray, dau. of Daniel and Joan (Pray) Ross of Boston; (died 12 Feb. 1868, in Arlington); 2d, 23 Dec. 1870, Mrs. Ellen A. Lawford, dau. of Robert Condon of Digby, N. S. He is a clerk, living in Boston. Children, by first wife:
1 Georgianna, b. 16 Nov. 1856, in Boston.
2 Mary Joan, b. 7 May 1859.
3 Fred B., b. 17 June 1862.

By second wife:

4 Horace, b. 21 April 1871.
5 Robert Charles Winthrop, b. 6 July 187 .
6 Olive Berry, b. 16 Dec. 187 .
10 Elizabeth, b. 12 May 1837; m. Hiram Jones.
11 Rufus R., b. 15 Sept. 1839; d. 13 Jan. 1857.
12 Harrison, b. 22 Nov. 1841; unm. He was connected with the army in Virginia and North Carolina during the whole war. After the war he went into his brother's general store at Old Point Comfort, near Fortress Monroe, Va., and now succeeds to the business. He is a prominent politician, being on almost all the Republican committees of Virginia. In 1880 he was tendered the nomination to Congress from the second district, but declined on account of business.
13 Washington, twin with last, b. 22 Nov. 1841; m. 27 March 1866, Ellen M., dau. of Dea. John and Margery (Wiggin) Farnham of Wakefield. He is a farmer, living on the homestead. Children:
1 Agnes E., b. 10 Nov. 1867.
2 Nathan J., b. 10 Oct. 1873.
3 Olive M., b. 26 July 1877.
4 Lucy M., b. 3 March 1880.

1-6-5-2-4

SAMUEL LIBBY, born in Berwick, Me., 16 May 1781; married, 25 Oct. 1806, in Newcastle, MARY J. JOHNSON of Kittery. He was some years toll gatherer at Damariscotta Bridge, in Newcastle, and was also a surveyor of wood and bark. He was also a tanner, and later kept a boot and shoe store. He finally moved to Whitefield, where he died, 9 Feb. 1823. His widow died in Damariscotta, 4 Sept. 1861.

Children:

1 Hannah J., b. 8 Dec. 1810; m. 1827, Rufus Flye.
2 Daniel, b. 8 Jan. 1812; d. 18 March 1836. He was a millwright. He went to Stillwater to build a mill, and died there, unm.
3 Samuel, b. 16 Dec. 1812; m. Sarah Bastow of Nobleborough, Me. He was a tailor by trade, and carried on his business successively in Camden, Stillwater, Skowhegan, Rockland, and Nobleborough, and thence removed to Olympia, Washington Territory. He there took up land and cleared a farm. He also engaged in trade and held the office of postmaster. He died 20 April 1870, leaving sons Joseph B. and George B., and perhaps other children.
4 Phebe M., b. 11 June 1816; m. 1st, Washington Flye of Rockland; 2d, Capt. Deak of Bangor; died 1 Mar. 1871.
5 Joseph, b. 27 Sept. 1817; m. Ann E. Hall.
6 Lucy Ann, b. 27 Dec. 1818; m. Robert D. Metcalf.
7 William M., b. 11 Aug. 1820. He was a cabinet-maker. He worked several years in Bangor, and spent two and one-half years in California. He died eight days after his return home, 30 Jan. 1851. Unmarried.
8 Levi, b. 29 Mar. 1822; d. 26 Sept. 1823.

1-6-5-2-8

Levi Stone Libby, born in Berwick, Me., 21 Aug. 1789; married, 22 May 1814, Lydia H. Chick, daughter of Peter and Abigail (Haskell) Chick of Limington.

He learned the blacksmith's trade in Portsmouth, N. H., and afterward worked for one Mayall in Gray, in a carding and fulling mill. Three years later he went into that business himself in Limington, and continued it until 1820, when he settled on a farm in Cornish. From 1844 until 1853, he lived in Hiram, and lived in Standish from that time until his death, 26 April 1867. His widow died in Cornish, 4 Aug. 1870.

Children:

1 Lucy Ann, b. 23 Feb. 1816; m. 1st, 1 June 1836, Daniel Cross; 2d, 12 March 1843, Henry Thompson; 3d, William Chadbourn.
2 Mary Abbie, b. 3 June 1818; m. 8 May 1842, Thomas J. Richardson; d. 22 June 1881.
3 Daniel Jeremy, b. 13 July 1820; m. Mary Chase.
4 Zilpha H., b. 11 April 1822; m. 6 July 1846, Rev. Joseph Smith.
5 William B., b. 29 May 1830; d. 16 Feb. 1833.
6 Louisa B., b. 13 Sept. 1832; m. 12 Oct. 1851, Geo. E. Chadbourn.
7 William Henry Harrison, b. 16 March 1835; m. 18 Nov. 1869, Jennie F., dau. of William and Jane (Campbell) Hudson of Lowell, Mass. He spent 12 years mining on the Pacific coast. In 1863 he returned to Standish. He has since been employed in farming, freighting, butchering, and (now) manufacturing ready-made clothing. He is postmaster at Standish. His only child died in infancy.

1-6-5-5-1

Daniel Libby, born in Berwick, Me., 23 Jan. 1775; married, 1800, Experience Pray, daughter of Stephen and ——— (Guptil) Pray. He lived with his father until 1806, and then settled on land which his father gave him in another place. He lived there until his death, 17 June 1863, aged 88. His wife died 26 Nov. 1843.

Children, all born in Berwick:

1 David, b. Nov. 1800; died aged 6 years.
2 Abraham Pray, b. 26 Jan. 1802; m. Sally Pray.
3 Alice, m. 11 March 1832, Lewis Downs of Lebanon.
4 Catherine, m. Tristram Fall of Berwick.
5 Lucretia, m. 8 May 1831, Moses Pray of Lebanon.
6 Sally, died aged about five years.

1-6-5-5-3

Ebenezer Libby, born in Berwick, Me., 1 Feb. 1779; married, 19 Feb. 1804. Hannah S. Smiley, daughter of Thomas and Ruth (Crosby) Smiley of Winslow, Me.

In the spring of 1800, he went to Winslow, and worked at lumbering, part of the time for Thomas Smiley, and part of the time for himself, until his marriage. He then settled on a farm in Albion. In 1848, he swapped this for another, in the northeast part of the same town, and there died, 2 Sept. 1857. His widow died 31 Aug. 1863.

His was the first barn in Albion raised without liquor, which was in 1835.

His children were:

1 Daniel, b. 25 Mar. 1804; m. 1st, Loney Broad; 2d, Frances A. Smiley.
2 John, b. 17 Sept. 1806; m. Hannah Libby, 1-6-5-9-5-2.
3 Ruth, b. 17 July 1809; m. 1st, John Fall; 2d, Lysander Putnam.
4 Thomas S., b. 18 Feb. 1819; m. Martha Miles.
5 Joseph Lyman, b. 19 July 1821; m. Hester A. Quinn.
6 Joanna, b. 12 Sept. 1823; d. 3 Aug. 1825.
7 Albert T., b. 12 April 1826; m. Martha J. dau. of Thomas and Betsey (Fowler) Bradstreet of Albion; died in Albion, 9 July 1862. His widow died 26 April 1863. Children:
   1 Charles, b. May, 1860; d. 6 Feb. 1862.
   2 Allie T., b. Jan. 1862; d. 28 Dec. 1862.
8 Hannah, b. 6 May 1828; m. S. R. Webb of Albion.
9 Ebenezer, b. 5 June 1830; m. Mary R. Pratt.

1-6-5-5-7

John Libby, born in Berwick, Me., 12 Oct. 1786; married, 23 Feb. 1809, Abigail Libby, 1-6-9-10-3. He was a farmer in North Berwick until 1836, when he removed to Bradford, Me. There he was a farmer, and owned saw and grist mills. He filled, at various times, all the highest town offices. His death took place 17 June 1858. His widow died 9 April 1868.

Children, all born in what is now North Berwick:

1 Sophronia, b. 7 May 1811; d. 7 April 1820.
2 Isaac, b. 8 June 1813; m. Mary Worster.
3 Pattie, b. 15 Sept. 1816; d. 18 June 1819.
4 John, b. 27 Dec. 1827; m. Mary E., dau. of Jacob C. and Sally (Hanson) Tasker. He worked at farming and milling until Nov. 1857, when he went to California, and went the next spring to Frazier's River. After about four years nothing was heard of him until his relatives were informed that he died 26 Feb. 1879, in Lead City, Dakota. Children:
  1 Nora, b. 28 March 1853; unm.
  2 Ivory, b. Dec. 1854; d. 21 Oct. 1861.
  3 Jessie F., b. 4 Feb. 1857; unm.

1-6-5-5-9

Capt. Ivory Libby, born in Berwick, Me., 1 Feb. 1793; married, 26 Nov. 1812, Olive Pray, daughter of Joseph and Dorcas Pray of Lebanon. He was a farmer on his father's homestead in what is now North Berwick, until 1845, when he sold out and, in company with his son Hebron, opened a general store at Great Falls, N. H. Four years later he bought the farm in Lebanon on which he lived until his death, 30 Aug. 1860. He was a captain in the North Berwick militia. His widow died 25 April 1879.

Children, all born in North Berwick:

1 Mary, b. 17 May 1813; m. 28 Aug. 1831, as first wife, Hon. Frederick A. Wood; died 31 Dec. 1851.
2 Caroline, b. 1 Nov. 1814; m. 10 Nov. 1834, Luke Pierce.
3 Dorcas, b. 24 April 1817; m. Charles E. Goodwin; d. 22 Aug. 1856.
4 Hebron, b. 10 Aug. 1819; m. 28 May 1842, Harriet, dau. of Samuel and Elizabeth (Wentworth) Pray of Lebanon. He went to Great Falls in 1839, and removed thence to Lebanon, with his father, in 1849. In 1859 he again removed to Great Falls, and thence, in 1866, to Boston, where he is now a dealer in real estate and mortgages. Children:
  1 Mary Jane, b. 8 May, d. 25 Aug., 1843.
  2 Athelbert E., b. 28 May 1846; d. 31 Dec. 1851.
  3 Samuel P., b. 15 Oct. 1848; m. 1 Nov. 1873, in Boston, Nellie Pratt, dau. of James Cromack.
  4 Wilbur L., b. 12 Feb. 1853; unm. He is a mariner.
  5 Herbert E., b. 10 June 1856; d. 24 May 1866.
  6 Hebron A., b. 7 Jan. 1859; unm.
  7 Forrest L., b. 19 Aug. 1864.
5 Martha, b. 31 March 1821; m. 21 May 1842, Willis N. Butler; d. 27 Nov. 1853.
6 Louisa, b. 2 June 1823; m. James Clark of Lebanon.
7 Harriet, b. 14 May 1825; m. 20 Aug. 1843, John P. Staples.
8 Ruth, b. 16 March 1827; m. 19 Jan. 1853, Hon. F. A. Wood.
9 Sarah, b. 15 Dec. 1829; d. 3 Nov. 1850; unm.
10 Ivory, b. 1 Sept. 1831; m. 29 Nov. 1852, Nancy, daughter of Abraham and Sarah (Goodwin) Hanscom. From 1854 until 1857 he was a miner in California. He served one year in the 8th Maine Reg. Band. On his return home in 1862, he settled on the farm now occupied by his sister Caroline, and bought from his brother Hebron the mills on Little River Falls. In 1870 he exchanged the mill and house for the farm he now occupies. He has been a trial justice since 1871, and has served four years as selectman. Children:

1 Roscoe, b. 1 Oct. 1853; m. 1874, Emma O., dau. of Geo. W. and Mary E. (Atkinson) Goodrich of Berwick. He was two years in the blacksmith business in E. Rochester, N. H., but is now a farmer, living with his father. Children:
  1 Herbert, b. 26 Aug. 1876.
  2 May, b. 16 Dec. 1879.
2 Harvey, b. 11 July 1860; unm.
3 Dana, b. 18 Sept. 1863; d. 28 Aug. 1865.
4 Sarah, b. 16 Aug. 1865.
5 Dana, b. 22 March 1867.
6 Mary, b. 1 Dec. 1868; d. 6 Jan. 1869.
7 Hattie, b. 17 March 1871.
8 Lettie, b. 20 Feb. 1873.

11 Olive, b. 10 Oct. 1833; m. 1 Dec. 1853, Edwin Hanscom.
12 Clara, b. 18 June 1838; m. 9 Oct. 1858, Alpheus S. Hanscom.
13 John, b. 23 Dec. 1839; m. 11 Sept. 1862, Sabina, dau. of Sabina (Libby) Dillingham, 1-6-9-3-1-1. He lives on his father's homestead in Lebanon, a farmer and school-teacher. He was for some years a preacher of the Baptist Church, and is now a deacon of the church in Lebanon. He is president of the York County Young Men's Christian Association. His wife died 24 July 1880. Children:
  1 Carrie, b. 5 May 1864.
  2 Grace, b. 5 June 1866.
  3 Lucy Belle, b. 11 June 1869.
  4 Elsie, b. 26 Sept. 1872.
  5 Irving, b. 16 Aug. 1876.
  6 John Dillingham, b. 28 May 1880.

1-6-5-9-3

WENTWORTH LIBBY, born in Lebanon, Me., 6 May 1784; married first, 4 Dec. 1807, EUNICE HARDISON; (died 15 Aug. 1826); second, 6 Mar. 1827, CHARLOTTE PARSONS. He died 5 Aug. 1862. His widow died 19 June 1864.

Children, by first wife:

1 Rebecca, b. 1 Dec. 1808; d. 16 Jan. 1826.
2 Jane, b. 12 June 1811.
3 Eunice, b. 10 July 1813.
4 Isaac, b. 16 March 1816; d. 12 April, same year.
5 Isaac H., b. 12 Sept. 1817.
6 Mary, b. 14 Feb. 1823.

By second wife:

7 Frances Ann, b. 16 Nov. 1827; m. 15 May 1845, Alvan W. Thurston.
8 Nancy, b. 22 Jan. 1830.
9 Priscilla, b. 1 Nov. 1832.
10 Charlotte, b. 3 May 1834.
11 Daniel, b. 18 March 1836; m. 29 March 1874, Adeline A. Watson; lives in Parkman, Me. Child:
  1 Addie Mary, b. 2 Sept. 1876.
12 Betsey, b. 24 May 1838.
13 John, b. 8 Aug. 1840.
14 Julia A., b. 22 Dec. 1842.
15 Corris Jane, b. 2 March 1846; d. 15 Sept. 1847.

1-6-5-9-5

OLIVER LIBBY, born in Lebanon, Me., 23 December 1788; married first, 16 Sept. 1813, HANNAH DELANO, daughter of Elder

Zebedee Delano; (died 24 Nov. 1815, in Lebanon); second, 1 May 1817, LYDIA LITTLEFIELD, daughter of Ebenezer Littlefield. She died in 1848.

He lived on the homestead farm six years after his marriage, and then removed to Albion, where he lived seven years. He then exchanged farms with his brother John, and lived eight years in Embden. Eight years later he returned to Albion. Late in life he went to New York State, and died in Harrison, 2 Sept. 1859.

Children, by first wife:

1 Nathaniel B., b. 4 Sept. 1814; m. 8 Dec. 1850, Martha, dau. of Moses and Hannah (Hussey) Noble of Berwick. He followed the sea until his marriage, and is now a farmer in Albion. He was living in Great Falls, N. H., when the war broke out, and served three years in the 4th N. H. Vol. Children:
   1 Frederick M., b. 7 Sept. 1853, in Farmington, N. H.; m. 25 Dec. 1879, Jennie Lambert; lives in Lawrence, Mass.
   2 Estelle, b. 27 Jan. 1855, in Lawrence, Mass.; m. 1875, Willard H. Sprague of Columbia, Me.
   3 Charles P., b. 5 Feb. 1858, in Norway, Me.; d. 10 July 1860.
   4 Elfie, b. 12 Jan. 1860, in Norway, Me.
   5 Nettie, b. 9 Mar. 1862; d. 4 Aug. 1863, in Great Falls, N. H.

By second wife:

2 Hannah, b. 26 Dec. 1817; m. John Libby, 1-6-5-5-3-2.
3 Polly, b. 12 April 1820; m. Chas. Stratton of Albion.
4 Betsey, b. 24 Jan. 1822; d. 10 Aug. 1825.
5 Lois, b. 16 Feb. 1824; d. 16 Sept. 1825.
6 Betsey, } twins, b. 17 April } d. 1850; unm.
7 Lois, } 1827, in Embden; } d. 16 May 1827.
8 Julia Ann, b. 1 July 1831; m. John Whitney of Newburgh, Me.; d. 31 July 1859.
9 Laura, b. 27 Nov. 1833, in Albion; died 1852.

1-6-5-9-7

DANIEL LIBBY, born in Lebanon, Me., 7 Dec. 1793; married first, Jan. 1819, in Marblehead, Mass., ELIZABETH SCORES of that place; (died 11 May 1837); second, 3 Oct. 1837, NANCY B. PALMER of Albion.

Upon his marriage he settled on a farm in Albion, Me., and there lived until about 1848. From that time he lived successively in China, Waterville, Albion, and finally in China, where his wife died, 4 Dec. 1872. He then sold his place and boarded with Mrs. Hollis Broad and Willard Lancaster until his death, 28 July 1876.

Children, all by his first wife:

1 Mary Jane, b. 7 Oct. 1821; m. 17 March 1843, Zimri Heywood of Winslow.
2 Albion Chroghan, b. 8 Oct. 1823; m. Roanna Briggs Royal. He was in the Mexican war and was honorably discharged. He never returned home however, but became a stage driver on the overland route to California. When last heard from, about 1871, he was in Los Angeles Co., California. His wife and a daughter are in Cambridge, Mass.

3 Elizabeth, b. 6 May 1825; m. May 1846, Otis Starkey, jr.; died 12 Dec. 1851, in Waterville.
4 Edward Scores, b. 22 April 1827; d. 20 Nov. 1854; unm.
5 Sarah, b. 27 March 1829; d. 19 June 1837.
6 Daniel, b. 25 Jan. 1831; m. 11 Feb. 1855, Caroline Melissa, dau. of Jeremiah and Jane Uran (Hobbs) Wardwell of Winslow. He was a farmer in Winslow 12½ years, and then became a middleman in cattle and other things. Since 1875 he has lived in Waterville. No children.
7 Abigail, b. 18 Aug. 1835; d. 20 May 1837.

1-6-5-10-8

JOHN LIBBY, born in Lebanon, Me., about 1797; married POLLY HODGDON, daughter of Benjamin Hodgdon of Ossipee, N. H. He worked at farming and lumbering. He was killed in a sawmill in the interior of Maine, by a log rolling over him. This was in the fall of 1822, and two weeks later, in September, his wife died in Ossipee of fever.

Only child:

1 Thomas Hodgdon, b. 11 Nov. 1819, in Ossipee; m. 14 April 1843, Mary A., dau. of John and Amy (Lord) Goodwin of Lebanon. He lived with his mother's father until he was fourteen. From that time he worked at many callings, latterly shoemaking, until 1850, when he settled on the farm in Lebanon since occupied by him. He has since been a farmer, shoemaker, and peddler. Children, all born in Lebanon:
   1 John Goodwin, b. 25 Feb. 1844; died unmarried. He was a member of the 17th Maine Vol., and was among the missing of the battle of Chancellorsville, May 1863.
   2 Amanda, b. 20 Jan. 1848; d. 24 Oct. 1867.
   3 Ruth, b. 24 Feb. 1849; d. 15 March 1849.
   4 Charles Henry, b. 15 June; d. 13 Oct., 1852.
   5 Charles Henry, b. 21 Oct. 1855; m. 9 March 1876, Alice J., dau. of Geo. and Emily (Butler) Pray of Sanford. He lives at home, and carries on the homestead farm. His wife died 15 April 1881. Child:
      1 Ernest Pray, b. 26 July 1877.
   6 Willie, b. 15 July, d. 23 Aug., 1857.
   7 Thomas Franklin, b. 17 Jan., d. 29 Aug., 1861.
   8 Jennie Goodwin, b. 19 March, d. 20 Oct., 1863.
   9 John Goodwin, b. 11 Feb. 1866.

1-6-5-10-10

WILLIAM PEPPERELL LIBBY, born in Lebanon, Me., 12 Dec. 1803; married, 30 March 1826, SARAH DROWN, daughter of Dea. Henry and Isabella (Morrison) Drown of Rochester, N. H.

He removed to Chesterville in 1829, and thence to Bond Co., Ill., in 1837. While in Maine he was for the most part a country merchant, but in Illinois he was a farmer until his death, in Elm Point, 4 March 1864. His widow died 13 April following. They were both members of the Presbyterian Church.

Children:

1 Amanda Filzalan, b. 12 Aug. 1826; m. Leander D. Jernigan. Seven children.

2 Malvina Dunnath, b. 1 Oct. 1828; d. 30 March 1841.
3 William Albert, b. 13 Aug. 1832; m. 12 Nov. 1857, Nancy E., dau. of Wm. and Nancy (Finley) Parsley of Elm Point. He was engaged in trade, as clerk and as principal, in Elm Point and in St. Louis, until the war, and since the war has been a farmer in Elm Point. His wife died 9 Dec. 1870. Children:
 1 Harriet M., b. 7 Jan. 1859.
 2 Joel H., b. 27 Nov. 1861.
 3 William P., b. 28 June 1865.
 4 Rose M., b. 15 May 1867.
 5 Nancy D., b. 17 Oct. 1869.
4 Sarah Adeline, b. 12 Jan. 1833; m. Albert H. McLain. Nine children.
5 Henry Washington, b. 9 Oct. 1835; d. 26 Sept. 1845.
6 Ivory Hobbs, b. 16 Aug. 1837; m. 1st, Sarah Shake; (died); 2d, Amanda Jernigan. He is a farmer at Newton, Kans. One child by his first wife, and six by his second.
7 Samuel Harrison, b. 22 Oct. 1840; m. 17 March 1862, Nancy E., dau. of James and Mary M'Cracken of Bethel, Ill. He served three years in the late war, and is now a farmer. Children:
 1 Sallie M., b. 17 Dec. 1864.
 2 James W., b. 5 April 1866.
 3 Ella A., b. 23 Dec. 1868.
 4 Henry P., b. 28 March 1870; d. 2 May 1871.
 5 John A., b. 3 May 1872.
 6 M'Cracken, b. 2 Nov. 1880; d. 25 July 1881.
8 John Barber, b. 22 Oct. 1842; m. Laura A. McLain. He is a farmer at Newton. Five children, one deceased.
9 Edward Payson, b. 20 Dec. 1844; m. Alice Lirnaweaver; lives in Newton, a farmer. No children.

1-6-5-15-3

Samuel Wentworth Libby, born in Berwick, Me., 10 April 1809; married, 5 Dec. 1844, Lovina Hopkins, daughter of Oliver and —— (Prescott) Hopkins of Peru, Me. He was reared in Litchfield. Since 1835 he has been engaged in the manufacture of bricks, in Augusta, Richmond, Bath, Brunswick, and Lewiston, his present residence. He served as selectman in Litchfield, and has been twice a member of the Lewiston City Council. His wife died 1 March 1877.

Children:

1 Samuel Orator, b. 21 March 1847, in Litchfield; m. May 1868, Nancy Jane Knight of Peru. He served 1½ years in the Maine cavalry in the late war. He afterward learned the photographer's art and was in business in Augusta at the time of his death, which took place 21 May 1869. No children. His widow lives in Illinois.
2 Horace, b. 28 Sept. 1848; m. 7 Dec. 1874, Amanda, dau. of John H. and Martha H. (Sleeper) Pettengill of Lewiston, where he resides. Their only child died in infancy.
3 Sherburn, b. 28 May 1852, in Lewiston: d. 20 Aug. 1853.
4 Daniel Oliver, b. 23 July 1854; d. 19 Nov. 1860.
5, 6 twin sons, b. 7 Sept., died in October, 1864.

1-6-5-15-4

Alvah J. Libby, born in Berwick, Me., 4 May 1811; married, 3 May 1846, Hannah Richardson, daughter of Abijah and Elizabeth (Johnson) Richardson of Litchfield. He removed to Bath, where he was in business many years, and died 13 Aug. 1877. His wife died 23 Dec. 1875.

Children:

1 Ella Annette, b. 18 April 1848, in Litchfield; m. 28 Aug. 1876, Geo. E. McIntire, now of Medford, Mass.
2 Irving Alvah, b. 1 March 1853, in Bath; m. 16 April 1873, Charlotte R., dau. of Thomas and Alice (Wylie) Oliver of Phipsburg. He lives in Bath. No children.
3 Clara Adelaide, b. 31 Oct. 1856; m. 1 July 1875, Wm. D. Oliver.

1-6-9-3-1

CAPT. DAVID LIBBY, born in Berwick, Me., 1772; married first, ALICE LIBBY, 1-6-5-5-4; (died about 1807); second, 28 Dec. 1808, ANNE SMITH, daughter of Ichabod and —— (Jones) Smith.

He went to Lebanon a young man, and opened a store on the spot afterward occupied by the Baptist parsonage. After about twelve years he was ruined by a dishonest partner, and afterward gained a livelihood by tending a grist and carding mill, and from the small farm on which he always lived. He was a captain in the militia. He died 5 Dec. 1821. His widow died 14 March 1871, aged 85.

Children, by his first wife:

1 Sabina, b. 29 April 1802; m. 12 Dec. 1824, Paul Dillingham.
2 Fanny, b. 1 Jan. 1804; m. 14 Sept. 1826, Ebenezer Brackett.
3 Clarissa, b. 7 Nov. 1805; m. 29 Nov. 1841, Geo. Littlefield.

By second wife:

4 Ebenezer, b. 29 July 1809; m. 1st, 23 Nov. 1844, Joanna M., dau. of Ebenezer and Betsey (Roberts) Pray; (died 16 Feb. 1847); 2d, 19 Aug. 1850, Lucetta, dau. of Stephen and Elizabeth (Gerrish) Fall of Lebanon. Upon his marriage, he settled on the farm in Lebanon which he has since occupied. Only child, by first wife:
   1 Owen, b. 23 Aug. 1845; m. 29 Dec. 1870, Lucie L., dau. of Isaac and Mehitable (Smith) Guptil of North Berwick. He is a farmer in Lebanon. Children:
      1 Clifton Guptil, b. 10 Nov. 1871, in North Berwick.
      2 Cecil Winthrop, b. 10 Nov. 1873, in North Berwick.
5 Alice, b. 24 April 1811; m. 20 Dec. 1835, Charles Chase.
6 Eliza Ann, b. 23 July 1813; d. 5 Nov. 1832, in Great Falls, N. H.
7 Robert, b. 13 June 1815; m. 4 April 1836, Hannah, dau. of Thomas and Mary (Lord) Murray of Lebanon. He was a shoemaker. When he was married he bought the house and small piece of land now occupied by the widow, Ruth (Libby) Wood, 1-6-5-5-9-8. There he died, 2 Feb. 1856. His widow and son sold, and bought the farm they now occupy. Only child:
   1 George Frank, b. 18 June 1838; m. 25 Nov. 1859, his cousin, Irene L., dau. of Samuel and Jane (Murray) Usher of Biddeford. Children:
      1 Mary Jane, b. 3 Sept. 1860.
      2 Clara, b. 26 Oct. 1862.
      3 Almeda, b. 3 June 1865.
      4 Lizzie, b. 12 Jan. 1869.
      5 Nellie, b. 21 Sept. 1870.
      6 Nettie, b. 13 Jan. 1872.
8 Phebe, b. 30 May 1817; m. Amos Conwell of Iowa.
9 David, b. 1819; never married. He was a farmer. He served through the Mexican war, and died in hospital, at New Orleans, La., Dec. 1848.
10 Isetta, b. 17 Dec. 1821; d. 20 April 1822.

1-6-9-4-5

Joshua Libby, born in Berwick, now South Berwick, Me., 27 May 1785; married first, 1807, Alice Pray, daughter of Thomas Pray of Lebanon; second, 1826, Sarah Grant, daughter of Edw. and Betsey (Leavitt) Grant, also of Lebanon.

In his earlier days he was a carpenter, but after his second marriage, a farmer. He was a justice of the peace and a trial justice. He died 22 Nov. 1858. His widow died in Boston, in 1876.

Children, by first wife:

1 Charles, b. 1809; died from burns, aged about 4.
2 Thomas, b. 1811; d. 1865, at sea; unm. He was always a sailor except five years spent in the regular army.
3 Lucius P., b. 20 July 1815; m. 1st, 10 Mar. 1839, in Missouri, Eleanor Bennings Cousins of New York City; (died of cholera, 1851); 2d, 1 Jan. 1860, Sarah J. Long of Kentucky. He is a carpenter by trade, and lives in Perry, Ill. He served in the Union army through the late war, as master-mechanic in the quartermaster's department. Only child:
 1 Mary Eleanor, b. 7 Dec. 1847, in Perry; m. 14 March 1871, Rev. Charles F. Williams.

By second wife:

4 Edward P., b. 14 May 1827; m. 1st, Nov. 1847, Louisa, dau. of Jacob and Lucy Hersom of Lebanon; (died 1852, in Lebanon); 2d, June, 1853, in Lynn, Mass., Marion D. Mercy of Fairlee, Vt.; (died June, 1880). He is a mason and has built many large buildings, both in the East and West. He now lives in Fairlee. Only child:
 1 Frank M., b. 4 July 1854, in Chelsea, Mass.; unm. He is an express messenger in Colorado.
5 Jeremiah Leavitt, b. 16 April 1829; m. 21 Nov. 1852, Elizabeth E., dau. of John and Deborah I. (Wellman) Hepstenstall of Lynn, Mass. He learned the shoemaker's trade at Great Falls, N. H., and in 1848 went to Lynn, Mass. He worked there at his trade until 1860, when he engaged in the manufacture of soles, which business he still successfully continues. Children:
 1 Charles H., b. 5 July 1854; unm. He graduated from Amherst College in 1880, and is now in the Boston Law School.
 2 Walter M., b. 27 April 1858; unm. He is in company with his father.
 3 Everett E., b. 11 April 1861.
 4 Edith M., b. 19 Nov. 1867.
 5 Sarah L., b. 11 March 1875.
6 Charles H., b. 4 Feb. 1832; m. 12 Nov. 1857, Julia A., dau. of Thomas and Dorcas (Goodwin) Legro of Lebanon. He served as private through the war. He lived for the most part on his father's homestead until 1871, when he removed to Saugus, Mass., and engaged in the leather business in Lynn. Children:
 1 Ellery C., b. 8 March 1859; unm.
 2 Florence L., b. 14 Nov. 1860; unm.
 3 Frederick, b. 22 Nov., d. 27 Nov., 1867.
 4 Fannie B., b. 4 March 1869.
 5 William H., b. 14 Nov. 1872; d. 25 Sept. 1873.
7 Lydia A., b. 16 Dec. 1835; m. 1862, Isaac H. Welton of Boston.
8 Theodosia M., b. 8 June 1838; m. 29 Jan. 1866, Erastus H. Curtis.

1-6-9-4-6

Nathaniel Libby, born in Berwick, Me., 22 Dec. 1790; married, 24 Nov. 1813, Tirzah Lord, daughter of Nathan Lord of Lebanon.

In his early days he followed the sea. When he was married he bought mills in Ossipee, N. H., and lived there about twenty years. He removed thence to Bethlehem, where he was engaged in lumbering many years, and finally settled on a farm. He served as selectman of Bethlehem many years, and also represented the town in the state legislature. He was a member of the Congregational Church. His death took place 18 July 1840. His widow died 24 Oct. 1846.

Children:

1 Mercy L., b. 24 May 1814, in Lebanon; m. 5 April 1836, Benj. Noyes of Haverhill, N. H.; died 15 April 1847.

2 Charles, b. 28 Aug. 1816, in Ossipee; m. Phebe P. Aldrich.

3 Sarah Ann, b. 7 May 1818. She and her sister Hannah, while in Lowell, Mass., were led astray by the Mormons. They both married, in Nauvoo, Ill., 20 Nov. 1845, George Albert Smith, one of the leaders. He was born in Potsdam, N. Y., 26 June 1817, and died in Salt Lake City, 1 Sept. 1875. Beside the two sisters he had three other wives. Sarah died of consumption, 12 June 1851. Her only child was:

1 John Henry (Smith), b. 18 Sept. 1848, near Council Bluffs, Iowa; m. 1st, 20 Oct. 1866, Sarah Farr, born in Salt Lake City 30 Oct. 1849; 2d, 4 April 1877, Josephine Grosbeck, born in Salt Lake City 13 Oct. 1857. Reared a Mormon, his conscience has been educated to think polygamy right, and he has the utmost faith in the sainthood of Joseph Smith and others. He is one of the Twelve Apostles of the Mormon Church, representative to the territorial legislature of Utah, and a member of the Salt Lake City Council. Children, by wife Sarah:

1 John Henry (Smith), b. 28 Feb. 1868; d. 20 Sept. following.
2 George Albert (Smith), b. 4 April 1870.
3 Lorin Farr (Smith), b. 22 April 1872; d. 9 July following.
4 Don Carlos (Smith), b. 18 March 1874.
5 Ezra Chase (Smith), b. 22 Sept. 1876.

By wife Josephine:

6 Sarah Ann (Smith), b. 22 Oct. 1878.

By wife Sarah:

7 Charles Warren (Smith), b. 3 Aug. 1879; d. 7 Dec. 1879.
8 Winslow Farr (Smith), b. 19 Jan. 1881.

By wife Josephine:

9 Nicholas Groes (Smith), b. 20 June 1881.

4 Elizabeth R., b. 19 March 1821; m. 2 July 1840, Samuel Noyes of Haverhill; d. 25 Oct. 1854.

5 Daniel Lord, b. 28 Oct. 1823; m. 1st, 29 May 1855, Mary Caroline, dau. of Nathaniel and Mary (Craigen) Reynolds of Greenfield, N. H.; (died 29 Jan. 1869, in Oshkosh, Wis.); 2d, 11 June 1872, Laura Ann, dau. of Hartson and Rachel (Chandler) Reed of Phillips, Me. Before his marriage he lived about nine years in Lowell, Mass., and five years in California. Immediately after his marriage he removed to Oshkosh, Wis., where he has since lived. He engaged in the manufacture of lumber, and also in the manufacture of sash, doors and blinds, in which latter business he is a partner in the firm of Williamson, Libby & Co. He was one of the organizers of the Union National Bank of Oshkosh in 1871, and has been its president since. He has been twice alderman, and twice county supervisor. Children, by first wife:

1 George Arthur, b. 26 Aug. 1858; d. 11 Dec. 1875.
2 Frank Herman, b. 9 April 1860.
3 Mary Aseneth, b. 18 July 1862.

By second wife:

4 Carrie Rand, b. 13 June 1873.
5 Charles Arthur, b. 9 Feb. 1875.

6 Jeremiah Colby, b. 30 Dec. 1825; m. 3 June 1852, Susan Maria, dau. of Enoch and Susannah (Brown) Kenney of Whitefield. He learned the cabinet-maker's trade, and afterward followed the sea six years. In 1848 he settled in Whitefield and was employed in a sawmill, and thence removed to St. Johnsbury, Vt. Two years he was out in the war, and afterward moved to Coaticook, Que., from which place he moved in 1867 to Whitefield, where he has since resided. Since the war he has been a millwright. Children:

1 Carrie E., b. 12 Oct. 1853; m. 12 May 1875, Albert W. Johnson of Whitefield. Child:
  1 Ellis C. (Johnson), b. 10 Mar. 1878.
2 Katie E., b. 23 Mar. 1866, in Coaticook.
3 Avie G., b. 4 Sept. 1869.

7 Hannah Maria, b. 6 June 1828; m. Geo. A. Smith, as above told. She is still living. Children:

1 Charles Warren (Smith), b. 16 Jan. 1849, near Council Bluffs; m. 5 Oct. 1868, Isabel Martin. He is a farmer in Provo City. Children:
  1 Hannah Isabel (Smith), b. 26 Nov. 1869.
  2 Sophrona Lydia (Smith), b. 8 Feb. 1871.
  3 Lucy Meserve (Smith), b. 20 Sept. 1873; d. 24 March 1880.
  4 Tirzah Libby (Smith), b. 13 March 1876; d. 4 April 1881.
  5 Jessie (Smith), b. 14 May 1878.
  6 Ethel (Smith), b. 12 Jan. 1880.
  7 Zora (Smith), b. 14 Sept. 1881.
2 Sarah Maria (Smith), b. 1 Jan. 1856, in Provo City, Utah; m. 4 July 1879, Byron Oliver Colton. Child:
  1 Stella Smith (Colton), b. 6 June 1880.
3 Eunice Albertine (Smith), b. 6 Mar. 1860; d. 28 Oct. 1863.
4 George Albert (Smith), b. 7 April 1862; d. 28 Oct. 1863.
5 Grace Libby (Smith), b. 14 May 1865.

8 John Quincy Adams, b. 12 Dec. 1830; m. 12 Mar. 1857, Aurelia Chase, daughter of Baker and Sophronia (Abbot) Dodge of Whitefield. He followed the sea three years, and has since been a lumberman. Except two and one-half years from 1849, spent in California, and from 1866 to 1872, spent in Oshkosh, Wis., his residence has been Whitefield. He is now in the lumber business in West Newbury, Vt. He represented Whitefield in the N. H. Legislature in 1874 and 1875. Adopted children:

a Effie Josephine (Libby), (dau. of George and Sarah (Bean) Hodgdon), b. 5 Sept. 1856; m. 1 Jan. 1879, Williard H. Armington.
b Elmer Plumer (Libby), (son of George and Sarah R. Barnard), b. 18 Aug. 1862.

9 George W., b. 6 Nov. 1833; m. 5 Nov. 1859, Ellen A., dau. of William F., and Caroline (Webb) Bell of Whitefield. At fifteen he went to California where he stayed seven years. He has since been a lumber manufacturer in Whitefield. He is now in company with his brother Nathaniel, doing a large business. He has been selectman of the town and twice, 1868 and 1869, representative to the legislature. Children:

1 George W., b. 4 April 1863.
2 Bertha C., b. 29 Sept. 1868.

10 Nathaniel W., b. 22 March 1836, in Bethlehem; m. 29 June 1864, Marinna B., dau. of Wm. R. and Mehitable B. (Cole) Sawyer of Whitefield. He has always been a lumberman, and always, except three years in Oshkosh, lived in Whitefield. Children:

1 Milford F., b. 10 May 1867.
2 Willie H. L., b. 26 July 1871.
3 Martha L. E., b. 9 April 1873.
4 Daniel W., b. 21 July 1875.

11 Henry C., b. 2 Aug. 1839; m. 22 Nov. 1865, Ellen M., dau. of Henry and Evelyn (Farr) Thomas of Littleton, N. H. He lives in Bethlehem, where he owns the Alder Brook mill, formerly owned by his father. Children:

1 Theresa Blanche, b. 7 Sept. 1866, in Whitefield.
2 Herman Thomas, b. 6 July 1868, in Whitefield.
3 Grace Evelyn, b. 13 June 1878, in Whitefield.

1-6-9-8-1

Dea. Jonathan Libby, born either in Berwick or Sanford, Me., 1782; married, 27 Dec. 1808, Hannah Knox of Lebanon.

He was a farmer, and settled in Livermore immediately after his marriage, from which place he moved in 1822 to Corinna. He lived in Corinna, on the farm now owned by Namo Haskell, until old age, but died with his daughter Sarah, in Bangor, 29 July 1856. He was a deacon in the Baptist Church. His wife died about 1851.

Children, all born in Livermore:

1 Benjamin, b. 2 Dec. 1804; m. Susan Knowles and Mary Coffin.

2 Daniel, b. 11 Jan. 1807; m. 1st, 29 March 1832, Florena Blaisdell; (died 11 June 1846, in Orono, Me.); 2d, 18 Oct. 1848, Jane W., dau. of Joseph and Jane (Webster) Mitchell of Freeport. He was successfully engaged in farming, lumbering, and milling, in Orono, about thirty years. In 1866 he removed to a farm in Webster Plantation, and thence, in 1871, to Molunkus, where he ran the Read Hotel until his death, 12 July 1873. Children, by first wife:

1 Augustus, b. 31 Aug. 1833, in Corinna. After an apprenticeship with Samuel Libby, 1-4-4-3-3-1, in the druggist's business, he went into business himself in Biddeford, where he continued until his death, 21 Aug. 1865; unm.
2 daughter, b. 25 May 1846; d. 27 May 1846.

By second wife:

3 Flora M., b. 5 Dec. 1853; m. James B. Libby, 1-5-2-5-6-5-3.

3 Leander S., b. 28 Aug. 1808; m. Hannah P. Crowell.
4 Lydia, b. 1810; m. John Dow; died in 1835.
5 Sarah, b. 1812; m. Col. David Thomas.
6 Abby, b. 1814; m. John Dow, above mentioned.
7 Betsey, b. 1816; m. John March.

1-6-9-8-2

Benjamin Libby, born in Sanford, Me., about 1784; married Abigail Edgecomb of Gardiner. He was at first a mill hand, and afterward bought a farm in Pittsfield, where he died in 1825. His wife died 18 April 1828.

Children, all born in Gardiner:

1 Sarah, b. 25 Dec. 1809; m. Joseph Albee; d. 4 Jan. 1880.
2 Joseph E., b. 13 June 1811; unm. He followed the sea. He served in the war and when last heard from was in Hong Kong.

3 Ebenezer, b. 27 July 1813; d. 16 May 1814.
4 Mary, b. 26 May 1815; m. 2 Dec. 1832, Geo. A. Emery of Vassalborough, now of Lock Haven, Penn. Children:
  1 George M. (Emery), b. 22 Feb. 1834, in Fairfield, Me.
  2 John C. (Emery), b. 18 Aug. 1836; m. Maria L. Clark.
  3 Thankful B. (Emery), b. 16 Oct. 1838; d. 12 Nov. 1838.
  4 Benjamin L. (Emery), b. 2 May 1840; m. Ann C. Freeman.
  5 Orlando H. (Emery), b. 29 June 1842; m. Mary E. Pearsall.
  6 James M. (Emery), b. 1 Jan. 1845; m. Luella Clark.
  7 Silas W. (Emery), b. 1 Sept 1846; d. 7 April 1850.
  8 Joseph L. (Emery), b. 2 March 1848; m. Jennie C. Freeman.
5 Benjamin, b. 3 Aug. 1817; m. 13 Aug. 1845, Lucy A., dau. of Nathaniel and Mary (Snell) Atwood of Fairfield. He was a sailor and lumberman until 1852, when he settled on a farm in Fairfield. He was a lieutenant in the war, and on his return home removed to Nebraska, where he lived until 1875. In that year he was burnt out, and removed to his present farm in Zephyr, Kans. Children:
  1 George E., b. 2 March 1849; d. 21 Dec. 1852.
  2 Georgie E., b. 10 Jan 1853; m. 1 Nov. 1878, in Beloit, Kans., —— Ensworth. Child:
    1 Alice M. (Ensworth), b. 12 Aug. 1879.
  3 Annie L., b. 13 Aug. 1854; m. 12 Oct. 1872, in Pawnee City, Neb., C. H. Curtis. Children:
    1 Maud A. (Curtis), b. 7 Oct. 1873, in Pawnee City, Neb.
    2 Nellie (Curtis), b. 14 Aug. 1875; d. 9 March 1879.
    3 Lucy B. (Curtis), b. 8 Aug. 1879, in Zephyr, Kans.
6 Emily, b. 11 Jan. 1821; m. 1842, in Hartland, Me., John Hanscomb.
7 Hannah, died in childhood.

1-6-9-8-3

SOLOMON LIBBY, born in Sanford, Me., 1788; married JANE McCAUSLAND of Gardiner.

He was many years a farmer in Pittsfield. After his wife's death in 1841, he removed to Pennsylvania and engaged in lumbering. In 1864 he went back to New Hampshire and thence, a year later, removed to Minnesota, where his daughter Juliette then lived. He went away about 1874 and has not since been heard of.

Children, all born in Pittsfield:

1 Sanford, b. 1815; married, in the West Indies, Henrietta Jones of Germany; died in 1879. Children:
  1 Mary.
  2 Fred.
  3 Julia.
2 Mary Jane, m. 1st, Rufus Briggs; 2d, Isaac Tesdell.
3 John S., b. Aug. 1820; m. Oct. 1844, Caroline, daughter of Dr. L. O. and Mary C. (Cook) Wood of Eaton, N. H. He worked before marriage in lumber mills in Pittsfield, and afterward in Bangor. He served about a year in the 1st Me. H. Artillery, and was killed before Petersburgh, 18 June 1864. He was an earnest member of the Methodist Church. Children:
  1 John F., b. 27 March 1847; d. July 1850.
  2 Forrest O., b. 31 March 1854. He was connected with the Hotel Brunswick, in Boston, but has not been heard from lately. He was married in 1878.
  3 Sarah L., b. 22 Aug. 1857; unm. She lives with her mother in Bangor.
4 Albert. He was a lumberman in Pennsylvania. He went west with his father and has not since been heard from. He was unmarried.

5 Solomon, b. about 1822. He also was a lumberman in Pennsylvania, and was drowned at about the age of 22; unm.
6 Eliza A., b. 22 Jan. 1826; m. 22 Nov. 1853, Samuel Gregg.
7 Betsey Hunter, b. 4 Oct. 182 ; m. 1850, in Boston, John Q. Adams. He was a printer and died 2 April 1867. Children:
   1 John Shaw (Adams), b. 9 Feb. 1852.
   2 Victor Hugo (Adams), b. Sept. 1855.
   3 Clara Ellen (Adams), b. 18 June 1861.
   4 George Washington (Adams), b. 17 Nov. 1862.
   5 Edward Everett (Adams), b. 1 May 1865.
   6 Mary Ella (Adams), b. 6 June 1866.
8 Elvira S., b. 1830; m. —— Woodhouse; lives in Pennsylvania.
9 Juliette, m. Moses Maxham; d. 1876, in Albion, Minn.
10 Salome D., b. 4 March 1837; unm. She lives in Melrose, Mass.

1-6-9-10-2

James Libby, born in Lebanon, Me., 8 Dec. 1787; married, 1 Jan. 1811, Abigail Goodwin. He was a farmer, and soon after his marriage removed to Ossipee, N. H., where he died 1 Jan. 1850. His first wife, the mother of all his children, died 19 May 1826, and he married second, Abigail Austin of Somersworth, N. H.; (died after 16 years); third, Mrs. Margaret (Gowell) Chatman.

Children:

1 Almira, b. 16 Jan. 1812; d. 13 Dec. 1849; unm.
2 Peninnah, b. 28 June 1813; d. 27 Sept. 1832.
3 Reuben G., b. 13 June 1815; m. Mrs. Rhoda Luxton, in Quincy, Ill., where he was when last heard from.
4 Hannah, b. 26 March 1817; m. 1st, July 1841, Parkman White; 2d, 3 July 1880, Pepperell Frost of North Hampton, N. H.
5 Phebe, b. 23 Feb. 1819; m. 25 June 1845, Samuel Teele; died 17 June 1880, in Somerville, Mass.
6 Dorcas, b. 24 Dec. 1822; m. 9 June 1850, Charles C. Barton.
7 James C., b. 10 May 1826; m. Susan Briard.

1-6-9-10-6

Jeremiah Libby, born in Lebanon, Me., 14 May 1796; married, 17 Nov. 1822, Lucy Guptil, daughter of John Guptil of Berwick. He lived in his native town many years and then emigrated to Minnesota, where he died in 1867.

Children:

1 Abigail, b. 23 July 1823; d. 5 March 1826.
2 Jacob, b. 24 Feb. 1825; lives in Minnesota. He has a wife and children.
3 Lois, b. 17 March 1827.
4 Olivia, b. 28 Oct. 1829.

And other children, among them sons, but none of the latter had children.

1-6-9-10-10

Moses Libby, born in Lebanon, Me., 15 Mar. 1805; married, 28 Feb. 1828, Huldah Langton, daughter of Timothy Langton of Eliot. He was a blacksmith, and moved about considerably, but finally settled in Boston, where he died 19 June 1848, and his widow, 14 June 1881.

Children:

1 James Langton, b. 27 Oct. 1828, in Chichester, N. H.; m. 28 Sept. 1860, Agnes Snape, dau. of Dorcas (Libby) Pender, 1-6-9-10-9. He was in the express business in Boston and New York until 1862, and from that time until 1865 was engaged in transporting sick and wounded soldiers. In 1865 he settled on the farm he now occupies, in Worcester, Mass. Children:
   1 Charles Elmer, b. 4 Jan. 1862, in New York.
   2 George Arthur, b. 28 Nov. 1863.
   3 Frederick Worcester, b. 8 Feb. 1866, in Worcester.
   4 Edgar Walter, b. 17 June 1867; d. 10 Sept. 1867.
   5 Isabel Worcester, b. 28 Feb. 1869.
   6 Bessie Bell, b. 8 Nov. 1870; d. 29 Nov. 1870.
   7 Herbert Augustus, b. 10 Dec. 1871.
   8 Frank Edward, b. 6 Dec. 1873.
   9 Martha Bertha, b. 24 March 1877.

2 Moses H., b. 30 Nov. 1831; m. Adeline M. ——. He is a real estate agent, auctioneer, and justice of the peace in South Boston. Children:
   1 Thomas H., keeps a grocery store.
   2 Mary A.
   3 George, deceased.
   4 Anna, m. —— White. Two children.
   5 Henry N., works for his brother.
   6 Roland.
   7 Ednah, deceased.

3 Hosea Wait [Dr.], b. 28 June 1834; m. 1st, 2 Nov. 1856, in Marblehead, Ohio, Mrs. Lavina A. Richardson, dau. of Hubbard and Sally Hallister of Perkins; (died 20 Dec. 1859, in Marblehead); 2d, 1 Nov. 1861, in Boston, Mass., Mary A., dau. of John and Mary Robie of Exeter, N. H.; (died 6 May 1866, in Cleveland, Ohio); 3d, 10 Sept. 1868, Violette Gates, dau. of Isaac and Uranah (Gates) Bancroft of Worcester, Mass. He received a common school education, read medicine, attended two courses of lectures, but was too poor to go on and graduate. The result of long studies was the belief that the vegetable kingdom was the only one to take remedial agents from. He went to Sandusky, Ohio, in 1854, and engaged in practice. Being refused advertisement by a paper in Oberlin, Ohio, he started a paper there known as the *Oberlin New Era*, which destroyed the other paper in two years, and is now the only paper published there. He has since published two medical journals. Starting as he did without a diploma, and refusing to accept established theories, he met with opposition on all points; but, by his success, has established a large practice, and is now recognized and consulted by many physicians. He is located in Boston, but has a sub-office in Cleveland, where he was permanently located many years. He has made nearly 34,000 examinations. Only child, by third wife:
   1 Pinnetta Jane, b. 1 Sept. 1869, in Cleveland.

4 Huldah Jane, b. 30 July 1836, in Somersworth, N. H.; m. Daniel J. Joy.

5 Julia Elizabeth, b. 24 Nov. 1838, in Boston; m. Ira Frye.

1-6-9-10-11

David Libby, born in Lebanon, Me., 30 March 1808; married first, Mary Brackett; (born 6 April 1813; died 20 May, 1849, in Acton); second, 1853, Roxanna Rogers, daughter of Nath'l and Susan (Kent) Rogers. He was a farmer and blacksmith. He died in Brownfield, Me., where his widow still lives, 16 Oct. 1862. He was a member of the Baptist Church.

Yours Truly
Dr H. W. L'Hubey

Children, by first wife:

1 James W., b. 2 Aug. 1833; d. 1 Jan. 1853.
2 Naomi B., b. 16 Jan. 1838; d. 4 Aug. 1843.
3 Mary A., b. 8 Jan. 1842; d. 4 March 1842.
4 George E., b. 17 March 1846, in Acton; unm.; is a farm hand.

By second wife:

5 Ella M., b. 6 Aug. 1854, in Dover, N. H.; unm.
6 Lucinda P., b. 19 June 1856, in Brownfield, Me.; unm.
7 Frank A., b. 27 March 1860; lives at home.
8 David D., b. 19 April 1862; is a blacksmith.

1-6-9-12-1

ELIAS LIBBY, born in Sanford, Me., 27 Sept. 1793; married MEHITABLE BUTLER, daughter of Nathaniel and Tabitha (Joy) Butler of Sanford. About the time he was married, he settled on part of his father's farm. He increased it to its present size and lived on it until his death, 12 Dec. 1874. His wife died 15 Sept. 1870. It is now occupied by his four unmarried children.

His children were:

1 Mary, b. 8 Feb. 1819; m. 1840, Benjamin F. Hanson.
2 Tabitha Jane, b. 13 Aug. 1821; unm.
3 Asenath, b. 24 Feb. 1823; unm.
4 Luther Samuel, b. 28 Feb. 1825; m. Roena Libby, 1-6-9-12-5-3.
5 Susan, b. 11 Feb. 1828; unm.
6 Nathaniel Butler, b. 4 Dec. 1831; m. 6 May 1860, Susan Jane Libby, 1-6-9-12-5-7. He learned the blacksmith's trade at Great Falls, N. H., and worked as journeyman there, except one and one-half years spent in Iowa, until 1862, when he went and settled on a farm in Orleans, Iowa. No children.
7 John Howard, b. 8 June 1835; d. 31 March 1836.
8 Elias Howard, b. 26 Oct. 1837; unm.
9 Mehitable Josephine, b. 18 Jan. 1841; m. Wm. Howard Hill of Sanford.

1-6-9-12-5

EBENEZER LIBBY, born in Sanford, Me., 4 April 1801; married, SUSAN BUTLER, sister of his brother's wife. Upon his marriage, he settled on the farm now occupied by his son Moses, and there lived until his death, a farmer and shoemaker. He died 7 Dec. 1843. His widow lives with her daughter Susan, in Iowa.

Children, all born in Sanford:

1 John Butler, b. 10 Nov. 1824; m. 8 Mar. 1851, Ada, dau. of Aphia (Libby) Butler, 1-6-9-12-5. He worked in cotton mills until 1854, when he bought the farm which he has since occupied. He has been selectman. Children, all born in Sanford:
  1 Emma Rosina, b. 11 Mar. 1856; unm.
  2 Eben Herbert, b. 1 June 1860.
  3 Charles Irving, b. 11 Aug. 1862.
  4 John Haven, b. 25 Oct. 1864.
  5 Parepa Rasa, b. 26 Aug. 1867.
  6 Lewis Butler, b. 8 June 1869.
2 Moses Hebron, b. 5 Oct. 1826; m. 5 Feb. 1850, Martha, dau. of Rufus and Miriam (Fernald) Moulton of Sanford. He has always lived on his father's homestead, a farmer. He has been selectman several years. Children:

1 Orville Vinton, b. 21 Mar. 1851; m. 1st, 14 Oct. 1876, Susan A., dau. of Rufus and Almira (Jacobs) Bennett; (died 18 April 1878); 2d, 14 Nov. 1880, Abbie J., dau. of Joseph and Sarah (Hurd) Shaw. Since March 1876 he has been a member of the firm of Nowell & Libby, general merchants, Sanford Corner. No children.
2 Susan Annette, b. 11 Sept. 1852; m. 1877, Chas. A. Bodwell.
3 Martha Francena, b. 26 June 1854; m. Theodore B. Hobbs of Sanford.
4 Moses Hebron, b. 17 April 1858; unm.
5 Ida May, b. 23 July 1861; m. 1 Feb. 1879, Frank H. Gerrish.
6 Loren Wirtie, } twins, born } d. 24 Feb. 1873.
7 Lillian Iona, } 17 Nov. 1867; }
8 Ella Moulton, b. 2 Feb. 1870.
9 Fred Loren, b. 8 April 1875.

3 Roena, b. 23 Jan 1829; m. Luther Samuel Libby, 1-6-9-12-1-4.
4 Ada Ann, b. 28 April 1831; m. 10 Feb. 1863, Wm. F. Johnson.
5 Ivory Ashton, b. 1 Sept. 1833; m. 8 Mar. 1858, Beulah A., dau. of Jotham and Dorinda (Moore) Stevens of Great Falls, N. H. He worked six years shoemaking. In 1856 he settled in Winneshiek Co., Iowa, where he has since lived, and whither his cousins have followed him. He is a well-to-do farmer. Children:

1 Viola I., b. 29 Dec. 1858; m. 2 April 1878, Henry W. Potter; died 3 Mar. 1881.
2 Dora M., b. 3 April 1860; m. 31 Dec. 1879, John Walton.
3 Milton O., b. 28 Dec. 1861.
4 Flora E., b. 25 April 1865.
5 Frank E., b. 17 Mar. 1867.
6 Fred O., b. 2 Feb. 1869; d. 12 Mar. 1874.
7 Ivory H., b. 18 Mar. 1870; d. 6 Oct. 1870.
8 Minnie A., b. 21 June 1874.
9 Walter R., b. 24 Nov. 1876.

6 Eben Howard, b. 12 May 1836; d. 16 Nov. 1855.
7 Susan Jane, b. 5 May 1838; m. Nathaniel Butler Libby, 1-6-9-12-1-6.
8 Tabitha Angeline, b. 5 Aug. 1840; m. Jan. 1867, Oscar C. Cole of Fayette, Iowa.

1-6-9-12-8.

Dea. Ivory Libby, born in Sanford, Me., 1 Jan. 1807; married, 16 Aug. 1829, Mary Butler, sister of his brothers' wives. He lived at home until Jan. 1833, when he moved to Avon, Me. There he bought a farm and lived until March 1854, when he returned, and settled on the farm he now occupies in Berwick. He is deacon of the Baptist church in North Berwick.

Children:

1 Julia Ann, b. 16 Jan. 1830; m. 7 Mar. 1850, Richard M. Ellsworth of Avon. Children:

1 Laura Emma (Ellsworth), b. 15 Nov. 1852.
2 Fred (Ellsworth), b. 6 Sept. 1855.
3 Julia Etta (Ellsworth), b. 5 Feb. 1863.

2 Philander Hartwell, b. 18 Dec. 1831; m. Mary L. Lougee. He is a farmer at Pine Hill, Berwick. He served ten months in the late war. Children:

1 Henry W., b. 16 May 1858; d. 21 Dec. 1879.
2 Elmer E., b. 19 Sept. 1861.
3 Arabell L., b. 17 May 1865.
4 Maud L., b. 8 Aug. 1867.
5 ———, b. 22 April, d. 10 May, 1869.
6 John T., b. 1 Sept. 1875; d. 13 Oct. 1877.

7 Jessie Imer, b. 7 Aug. 1879.
3 Mary Jane, b. 3 Feb. 1834; d. 6 Oct. 1876; unm.
4 Rhoda Angie, b. 24 May 1836; m. 13 Oct. 1864, Daniel H. Toothaker of Phillips, Me. Children:
1 Cora Affie (Toothaker), b. 28 Sept. 1865.
2 Ivory N. (Toothaker), b. 26 May 1867; d. 4 Oct. 1873.
3 Nettie Lulu (Toothaker), b. 10 Feb. 1875.
4 Grace Edna (Toothaker), b. 18 Dec. 1878.
5 Ivory Butler, b. 31 March 1839. He went to California with Philander in 1857. Philander shortly returned home, and Ivory has not been heard from for about 22 years.
6 Gilbert Nathaniel, b. 19 March 1842; m. 11 July 1872, in Prairie du Chien, Wis., Belle McNebo. He removed to Orleans, Iowa, in 1869. He is a farmer. Children:
1 son, died in infancy.
2 Mabel Blanche, b. 9 March 1875.
3 Cora Belle, b. 15 March 1878; d. 14 July 1878.
7 Aphia, b. 19 Feb. 1844; d. 18 Feb. 1870; unm.
8 Moses Albion, b. 5 July 1848; unm. He went to New York when about 21, and has been a baggage-master on the Erie Railroad.

1-6-9-12-9

Charles Libby, born in Sanford, Me., 9 June 1809; married, 28 Aug. 1836, Patience H. Plummer, daughter of John and Phebe (Hobbs) Plummer of Sanford.

When he was married he removed to Phillips, where he had already purchased a farm. He lived there until April, 1867, when he moved back to Great Falls. In 1874 he built a house on Berwick side, which he has since occupied.

Children, all born in Phillips:

1 Phebe Jane, b. 8 June 1837; m. 22 Dec. 1857, Thomas C. Eaton of Strong.
2 Charles Osbourne, b. 15 June 1840; m. 5 March 1871, Mary Overton, dau. of Joseph and Nancy C. (Barrett) Robinson of Roane Co., Tenn., where he has since lived. Children:
1 Charles Yates, b. 29 July 1876.
2 Anna May, b. 22 April 1879.
3 Vesta Annira, (called Edith), b. 12 April 1844; m. 11 April 1876, Herbert F. Oliver of Wakefield, Mass.
4 Patience Samantha, b. 19 May 1848; m. 24 June 1875, Edwin A. Peary of Phillips.
5 Floresta Aletha, b. 9 Aug. 1853; d. 16 June 1865.

1-6-9-12-10

Drancy Libby, born in Sanford, Me., 11 June 1811; married, 22 Oct. 1835, Mark Evans Marshall. He died 21 May 1873. She is still living.

Children:

1 John Edward (Marshall), b. 27 Oct. 1836; m. 1st, 4 March 1863, Lizzie M. Smith; (died 21 April 1865); 2d, 18 Nov. 1869, Mary D. Rand. Children, by first wife:
1 Helen F. (Marshall), b. 4 Dec. 1863; d. 15 Aug. 1864.
2 Eddie (Marshall), b. 16 March; d. 9 April, 1865.
2 Daniel Sharp (Marshall), b. 14 July 1838; d. 4 Aug. 1838.

3 Lucy Annira (Marshall), b. 22 July 1839; unm.
4 Casper E. (Marshall), b. 20 Dec. 1841; m. 10 Nov. 1867, Laura A. Brackett. Child:
  1 Hattie A. (Marshall), b. 14 May 1869.
5 Mary Frances (Marshall), b. 18 June 1844; m. 1878, Lewis C. Flagg.

1-6-9-12-12

OTIS ROBINSON LIBBY, born in Sanford, Me., 8 Sept. 1818; married, 7 March 1846, MERCY C. CLARK, daughter of James and Lydia (Brock) Clark of Berwick. He has always lived on his father's homestead, a farmer and shoemaker.

Children:

1 Oliver Clark, b. 4 Feb. 1847; m. 4 June 1876, in St. Louis, Mo., Annie, daughter of Philip and Joanna (Finaky) Lacy of St. Louis. He lives with his father, a farmer. Children:
  1 George, b. 17 May 1877, in Chelsea, Mass.
  2 Fanny Edith, b. 2 March 1879, in Berwick.
2 Susan Anna, b. 5 June 1848; m. Harrison Webster.
3 Clifford, b. 20 Nov. 1849; unm.
4 John Dana, b. 21 June 1851; unm.
5 Lydia Jane, b. 11 Nov. 1852; m. Thomas H. Knox.
6 Mary Augusta, b. 6 Aug. 1854; m. April 1873, Frank E. Newcomb.
7 George Otis, b. 16 Nov. 1855; unm.
8 James Uriah, b. 2 July 1857; unm.
9 Charles Oscar, b. 12 Dec. 1858; unm.
10 Rosabell, b. 30 May 1860; unm.
11 Clara Eleanor, b. 16 July 1862.
12 Frank Edwin, b. 20 Nov. 1863.
13 ——, b. 16 Aug., d. 21 Aug., 1865.

1-7-6-3-4

CAPT. THEODORE LIBBY, born in Newburyport, Mass., 5 Sept. 1793; married, 24 March 1818, DEBORAH CUSHING of Maine. He was a sea-captain, sailing first from Newburyport and afterward from Portland, Me. He died in Havana, Cuba, about 1842. His widow died in Newburyport, about 1846.

Children, all born in Newburyport:

1 Sarah, died young.
2 William Parker, b. 22 May 1821; died at sea about 1840.
3 Sarah Dodge, b. 1 March 1823; m. Capt. Mark Griffin.
4 John Watson, b. 11 April 1827; m. 1 Dec. 1847, Susan N., dau. of Samuel C. and Miriam (Chase) Hovey of Groveland, Mass. In his earlier days he was a locomotive engineer, living in California. He is now a wood-machinist at Groveland Mills, Groveland, Mass. Children:
  1 William P., b. 20 July 1848, in Groveland; m. 20 July 1868, Asenath P., daughter of Gilman N. and Sophia G. (Hopkinson) Parker. He is a shoemaker in Groveland. Child:
    1 John Cushing, b. 17 Oct. 1879.
  2 Mary Ella, b. 8 Jan. 1851; m. 15 July 1871, Nathaniel Donald of York, Me.
5 Eliza Ann, b. 19 July 1829; m. John A. Banks and Levi Taylor.

Elias Libby

5-2-3-1-6

Ebenezer Libby, born in Scarborough, 4 June 1804; married, 9 Oct. 1831, Mary Libby, 10-2-1-1-5-2. He has always lived on his father's homestead, a well-to-do farmer. He has been chairman of selectmen four years, and town treasurer three years.

Children, all born in Scarborough:

1 ——, born and died 20 Aug. 1832.
2 Maria, b. 10 Sept. 1833; m. 23 Feb. 1865, Ira Witham of Portland; d. Mar. 1881.
3 Samuel, b. 12 Aug. 1835; m. 21 Nov. 1860, Lucy Ann, dau. of Wm. H. Hunnewell, 7-1-5-3-3. He was at one time in trade in Saccarappa, Westbrook, and afterward freight agent of the Portland and Rochester Railroad. Children:
  1 Addie Leone, b. 3 Mar. 1862, in Westbrook.
  2 Ella Lillian, b. 4 Jan. 1864.
  3 William Eben, b. 7, d. 19, May 1866, in Portland.
  4 Forest Elmer, b. 3 Oct. 1867.
  5 Annie Sarah, b. 3 Sept. 1870.
4 Lucy Anna, b. 29 Oct. 1837; unm.
5 Hannah Eliza, b. 13 Oct. 1842; unm.
6 Jane Watson, b. 19 Oct. 1844; m. 21 Feb. 1867, Henry S. Jones.
7, 8 twin daughters, born and died 19 June 1847.
9 Ebenezer Scott, b. 12 Oct. 1848; unm.

5-2-7-1-2

Ebenezer Libby, born in what is now Gorham, then Scarborough, 29 Nov. 1797; married, 3 Nov. 1825, Emeline Harding, daughter of Capt. David and Eunice (Davis) Harding of Gorham.

He drove a bread-cart in Portland six years, and was then in trade in Buxton, at Spruce Swamp, seven years. He then lived a short time in Hartford, and Scarborough, and the next six years lived in Appleton, as agent for a lumbering company. In 1839 he settled on a farm in Wayne, and seventeen years later bought a farm in Readfield, where he lived fifteen years. He died with his daughter in North Livermore, 27 Feb. 18 . His wife died in Readfield, 11 Sept. 1870.

Children:

1 William F. Hart, b. 26 Sept. 1827; m. Rachel Coburn, dau. of Joseph Marcy and Ann (Furbush) Richardson of Greene, where he now lives. Children:
  1 Lucy Maria, b. 3 July 1857; unm.
  2 Abby Ann, b. 7 Nov. 1863; d. 28 Oct. 1879.
2 Edward H., b. 6 Sept. 1830; unm. His chief occupation has been that of clerk.
3 Ann Maria, b. 8 May 1832; m. Charles F. Roberts of Livermore.
4 Emeline, b. Oct. 1839; d. Jan. 1841.

5-7-8-1-1

Rev. Elias Libby, born in Scarborough, 12 Mar. 1790; married, first, 28 Nov. 1809, Jane Jewell; (born 27 Aug. 1789, on Fox Island; died 27 Dec. 1852); second, Hannah McGraw.

He grew up in Limington and gained the blacksmith's trade by working in his father's shop. Shortly after his marriage he removed to Limerick. He was there in business as blacksmith and carriage-maker, and also carried on a large general store.

In 1821 the Freewill Baptists held their first meetings in the central part of Limerick, and Elias Libby soon became the leader of the movement. The next year a church of thirty members was formed, and he, having been ordained a preacher, first took charge of it. He continued to be an active elder of that denomination throughout his life. He was instrumental in establishing a paper called "The Morning Star," which was published by him and others for many years in Limerick, in the interest of the Freewill Baptists, and is still continued at Dover, N. H.

In these various capacities he was one of the leading inhabitants of Limerick throughout a long life, and died there, 2 April 1871.

Children, by first wife:

1 Harrison Jewell, b. 18 June 1811, in Limington; m. Margaret Agnes Libby, 5-7-8-3-4.
2 Francis Orville, b. 20 Sept. 1814, in Limerick; m. Harriet S. Wright.
3 James Brackett, b. 1 Aug. 1816; m. Hannah C. Morrell.
4 Jane T., b. 1 Oct. 1818; m. Hon. Joseph Hobson of Saco.
5 Susan Ann, b. 27 Dec. 1820; m. 16 Sept. 1841, Hon. Moses McDonald.
6 Elizabeth C., b. 18 Dec. 1822; m. Rev. Ebenezer Jordan.
7 Roanna, b. 18 Nov. 1824; died 10 Nov. 1841.
8 Elias Osgood, b. 17 Aug. 1829; m. 15 Oct. 1855, Sarah Long, dau. of James and Mary A. B. (Lillie) Whiting of Boston. He graduated at Bowdoin College in 1851, and entered the Andover Theological Seminary, but ill health compelled him to leave after two years. He then entered the counting-room of his brothers in Portland, but soon after removed to Boston, where he engaged in the book-publishing business, as a member of the firms of J. French & Co., and E. O. Libby & Co. He died in New Orleans, La., 31 Oct. 1860. His family now lives in New York City. Children:
   1 Lillie Whiting, b. 15 Jan. 1857.
   2 Harrison Jewell, b. 1 April 1858.

By second wife:

9 Georgia, m. 15 Feb. 1876, Fred G. Harmon of Standish.

5-7-8-1-2

Dea. Parmenio Libby, born in Scarborough, 22 Nov. 1791; married first, 10 Nov. 1814, Eunice Jewell, a cousin of his brother's wife; (died 16 April 1820); second, 4 Nov. 1822, Fanny Ward, daughter of George Ward of Fryeburgh; (died 12 Sept. 1829); third, 23 Feb. 1831, Eliza Larrabee, daughter of Samuel and Martha (Irish) Larrabee. She died 23 April 1861.

He learned the blacksmith trade with his brother in Limerick, and worked there several years after in company with him. He then settled on the homestead farm at Limington, building himself a shop, and there stayed until his death, 14 Oct. 1875. He was many years deacon of the Congregational Church at Limington Corner.

Children, by first wife:

1 Rosetta Thompson, b. 20 Sept. 1815, in Limerick; m. 3 Sept. 1843, Moses Blake of Limington.
2 Anna, b. 17 May 1817, in Limington; m. Andrew Johnson of Philadelphia, Penn., where she now lives.
3 Eunice Jewell, b. 6 April 1819; d. 24 March 1820.

By second wife:

4 Eunice Jewell, b. 21 Sept. 1823; m. James Myrick.
5 George Ward, b. 30 June 1825; d. 19 June 1826.
6 George Ward, b. 29 Nov. 1826; m. 17 June 1866, Mary, dau. of John and Nancy (Norton) Cole of Limington. He was seven years a miner in California, and seven years in company with his brother Asa in a general store at Limington Corner. Upon his marriage he settled on the farm in Limington, on which he has since lived. Children:
 1 Fanny Ward, b. 15 Nov. 1866.
 2 Edward Norton, b. 17 July 1868.
 3 Nancy Charlotte, b. 16 May 1870.
 4 Eunice, b. 26 May 1872.
 5 Lewis, b. 8 March 1874.
7 Asa Charles, b. 3 Sept. 1829; m. 10 Sept. 1856, Addie L., dau. of Eben Hill of Buxton. He kept a small store at Limington Corner until his marriage, and then, after a year in the West, engaged in the country produce trade, in Portland, with his brother James, to whom he sold out a few years later, and went into business with his brother George at Limington Corner. Since his brother's marriage he has been a dealer in hats, caps, etc. Children:
 1 Annie, born and died in Portland.
 2 Eddie, born and died in Limington.
 3 Charles, born and died in Limington.
 4 William, born and died in Limington.

By third wife:

8 Fanny Ward, b. 29 Nov. 1831; m. 2 July 1854, Sylvester Marr, a grandson of Eunice (Libby) Lord, 1-6-5-14. He is a flour merchant in Portland. Children:
 1 Dennis Elvyn (Marr), b. 22 Sept. 1855; d. 24 Aug. 1859.
 2 Mary Eliza (Marr), b. 31 July 1859.
 3 Frank Sylvester (Marr), b. 20 June 1862; d. 10 Nov. 1864.
 4 Fred Howard (Marr), b. 19 Dec. 1865.
 5 Albert Edward (Marr), b. 14 Mar. 1868; d. 23 April 1869.
9 Martha, b. 9 April 1833; m. 4 Feb. 1855, Joshua S. Boothby.
10 James Irish, b. 15 Sept. 1835; m. 17 Nov. 1859, Mary W., dau. of Wm. and Sarah (Sweetsir) Kilgore of Portland. He is a wholesale dealer in country produce, and manager of the Casco Bay Steamboat Co. He is a member of the Second Congregational Church. Children:
 1 William Kilgore, b. 13 July 1860; d. 25 Aug. 1872.
 2 James Edwin, b. 15 May 1863.
 3 Harry Forester, b. 11 April 1865.
 4 George Franklin, b. 4 March 1868.
 5 Alice Eliza, b. 15 March 1870.
11 John, b. 21 Dec. 1837; m. 17 June 1865, Mary Ellen, dau. of Daniel R. and Nancy (Waterhouse) Bean of Limington. He served two years in Co. E, 10th Maine Vol., and has since lived on the homestead farm. Only child:
 1 Anna Bertha, b. 5 Feb. 1878; d. 29 Jan. 1881.
12 Mary Elizabeth, b. 10 March 1840; d. 3 Sept. 1864; unm.

13 Henry, b. 5 Sept. 1842; m. 18 Feb. 1873, Nellie M., dau. of Walter H. and Sarah B. (Wentworth) Moody of Limington. He is a marketer of country produce, living at Limington Corner. No children.
14 Nancy Yeaton, b. 23 Sept. 1845; m. 15 July 1868, Geo. G. Hackett of Canada.
15 Franklin, b. 16 April 1849; unm. He went to Chicago in 1876, which place he left the next year, and has not since been heard of.
16 Albert Johnson, b. 13 Feb. 1851; m. 23 Dec. 1875, Flora A., dau. of Joseph B. and Mary E. (Sweetsir) Blanchard of Portland. He is a traveling salesman for J. F. Mullen & Co., of Boston. Child:
   1 Gertrude Eliza, b. 12 Dec. 1877, in Portland.

5-7-8-1-3

STEPHEN LIBBY, born in Limington, Me., 22 Nov. 1793; married, 3 Aug. 1814, SARAH CHASE, daughter of Joseph and Olive (Woodman) Chase of Standish.

He learned the blacksmith's trade with his father, and went into business at Limington Corner. He was next in business alone at Dam's Mills, Newfield, and then with his brother Elias at Limerick. He was then in the dry goods business in Portland a short time and afterward was gone to sea two years. After his return he engaged in the carriage-making business in Limerick, and finally became a house-carpenter. He died 7 July 1869. His widow died 18 March 1875.

Children:

1 Mary, b. 4 Dec. 1814, in Limington; unm. She lives at the homestead in Limerick.
2 Caleb, b. 4 Nov. 1816, in Newfield; d. aged 15 months.
3 Olive Ann, b. 20 Oct. 1820; m. 3 Sept. 1848, Galen W. Bowditch; lives at home.
4 Stephen, b. 5 May, 1823; m. 1st, 25 Jan. 1854, Nancy E., dau. of Jones and Sarah (Eaton) Perry; (died Oct. 1865); 2d, 10 Aug. 1870, Shuah A., dau. of Samuel and Susannah (Foss) Sawyer of Limington. He is a house-carpenter. Children, by first wife:
   1 William Jones, b. 7 Mar. 1856, in Somerville, Mass.; d. 15 April 1880; unm.
   2 Albert Stephen, b. 5 Nov. 1858; unm.
   3 Sarah Melissa, b. 7 Sept. 1860, in Charlestown, Mass.; unm.
   4 Emma, b. 13 Oct. 1863; d. 18 Mar. 1864.

By second wife:

   5 Nancy Lee, b. 6 Mar. 1871, in Limerick.
   6 Harry Minott, b. 21 July 1873.
   7 Ralph Sawyer, b. 30 Sept. 1875, in Limington.
   8 Susie May, b. 4 Jan. 1877.
   9 Bessie Olive, b. 21 April 1880, in Limerick.
5 Abner Chase, b. 3 April 1825, in Limington; m. 28 Nov. 1849, Lucy S., dau. of Artemas and Desire H. (Stevens) Felt of Greenwood, where he now lives. He is town clerk. Children:
   1 Lydora F., b. 13 May 1853, in Portland; married 24 Feb. 1870, Thomas B. Swan; d. 27 Sept. 1872, at Mechanic Falls.
   2 Jesse F., b. 12 Feb. 1857, in Greenwood; m. 2 June 1879, Eva M., dau. of Emery G. and Rosetta M. (Merrill) Young of Bethel. He is a senior at Bowdoin College, which he entered in 1876, but left upon his marriage, returning in the fall of 1880. In that year he was greenback candidate for representative to the legislature from the Paris district.

5 Lizzie O., b. 11 Oct. 1862; d. 16 Nov. 1863, in Greenwood.
6 Sarah Elizabeth, b. 27 June 1834, in Limerick; m. Dr. Nathan Wiggin.
7 Frederick William, b. 1 March 1837; m. 9 Jan. 1867, Almira, dau. of David and Jane (Warren) Meserve of Limerick. He is a painter and carpenter in his native village. He has been town clerk five years. Children:
  1 Almira Jane, b. 26 Oct. 1867.
  2 Grace Maud, b. 12 Aug. 1875.

5-7-8-1-4

Abner Libby, born in Limington, Me., 4 July 1796; married first, 6 Nov. 1817, Salome Jackson, daughter of Abner and Margaret (Clark) Jackson of Limerick; (died 4 June 1827); second, 22 Sept. 1828, Almira Allen, daughter of Joseph and —— (Sayward) Allen of Waterborough.

He learned the blacksmith's trade, partly with his father and partly with his brother Elias, and when he was of age, went into partnership with Stephen at Limington Corner. When Stephen went to Newfield, Abner became a partner of Parmenio. He soon after bought out Stephen at Newfield, and three years later removed to Brownfield where he was in business four years. He then bought out Elias at Limerick Corner, and carried on business there until about 1871, when blindness stopped him. He died 12 Feb. 1881. His second wife died 19 Nov. 1862.

Children, by first wife:

1 Jackson Farnham, b. March 1821. He was by trade a carpenter. He went to Georgia with a lumbering company. The last news that came of him, about a year later, was a letter saying he was going to East Florida. Never married.
2 Mary Ann, b. 1823; m. William Plaisted of Biddeford.
3 Alphonzo, unm. He went to Iowa at the age of 20, where he was a harness-maker some time, but has since been engaged in the paper trade.
4 Clement, died aged 15 months, in Brownfield.
5 Salome J. G., b. May 1827; m. 24 May 1849, Frank O. Thomes.

By second wife:

6 Joseph Clement, m. about 1854, Abby Jane Ripley of Exeter, Me. He began in the dry goods business in Biddeford, and afterward removed to St. Louis, Mo., where he was engaged in the same business until the war broke out. He served in the quartermaster's department throughout the war, and still lives in St. Louis. Children:
  1 Henry Augustus, born in Biddeford about 1856.
  2 Clara, b. in Limerick.
  3 Bell, b. in St. Louis.
  and several younger.
7 Angeline Avilda, b. 1830; d. 27 Nov. 1832.
8 Ira Saywood, b. 2 Jan. 1833; m. 24 Nov. 1859, Mary A., dau. of Capt. Benjamin and Mary (Bradbury) Gilpatrick of Biddeford, Me. From 1856 until 1861, he was in trade with his brother Henry. He served eleven months as first lieutenant of Co. H, 16 Me. Vol. After his return he was engaged in trade with his brother Albert until 1872, and has since been engaged in marketing timber. In 1862 and 1876 he was elected to the state legisla-

ture by the Republicans, and in 1879 was Greenback candidate for state senator. He was summoned by Governor Garcelon, but the summons was pronounced by the S. J. Court to be illegal. Children:

1 William Thomes, b. 16 Dec. 1860.
2 Almira Allen, b. 28 Dec. 1863.
3 Vara May, b. 7 Feb. 1871.

9 Henry Osgood, b. about 1836; m. 18 Aug. 1866, Emily Jane True of Limerick. He has been in New York since 1866. Child:
1 Herman True, b. Mar. 1874.

10 Almira Allen, b. about 1838; m. 1st, G. Willard Cobb of Yarmouth; 2d, Robert B. Billings of Gorham.

11 Albert Octavius, b. 11 Mar. 1841; m. 13 July 1873, Berthie Eudora, dau. of Chas. and Lydia P. (Jordan) Chapman of Dexter, Me. He received an academic education, and early engaged in the dry goods business in his native town. He continued this successfully until 1872, when he removed to New York City, and since 1873 has been engaged in manufacturing and importing millinery goods. While in Limerick he was elected by the Republicans to the state legislature. Child:
1 Allan Ogden, b. 21 Jan. 1874, in New York City.

12 Angeline Avilda, b. 1842 or 3; died aged two years.

13 Susan Hannah, b. about 1845; m. Ansel J. Cheney of Sanford.

5-7-8-1-6

REV. JOHN LIBBY, born in Limington, Me., 11 Jan. 1803; married, 7 Aug. 1823, MARGARET WATERHOUSE, daughter of Mary (Libby) Waterhouse, 5-7-8-6.

In his twenty-first year he was converted and joined the Methodist church. For fifteen years he was a preacher of that faith, and at the same time lectured on temperance, throughout the state. During 1838 and 9 he published in Philadelphia, Penn., the "Farmers' Cabinet," and the "Ladies' Garland," and also had a large agricultural warehouse. In 1840 the latter was burned, and he sold out and removed to Iowa City, Iowa, where he became pastor of a Methodist church, and while there changed his views to Universalism.

In 1842 he went to St. Louis, Mo., where, except one year which he spent in Illinois, he lived until his death. In St. Louis he continued his ministerial labors, and also published the "Mississippi Valley Farmer." Later he took a very active part in the cause of prohibition, and published the "Gospel of Temperance," and the "Youth's Temperance Educator." He also became an active Odd Fellow, and twice served as representative to the Grand Lodge of the United States. In these varied capacities, aiming always for the improvement of his fellow-men, he spent the remainder of a useful life. His death took place 18 Aug. 1868.

His wife died 30 Sept. 1853, and he married second, 18 May 1858, Mrs. Martha Williams, daughter of Edmund and Elizabeth Loane of Baltimore, Md. She still lives.

Children:

1 Melville B. C., b. 24 Dec. 1824; m. 29 April 1845, Mary Eliza, dau. of Matthew and Eliza (Cochran) Johnson of St. Louis. He learned the printer's trade in his father's office in Philadelphia,

and after the removal to St. Louis continued to work on his father's paper. In 1846 he took charge of the publishing department of the "St. Louis Union," now the "Globe Democrat," which position he held until 1852. He then, in company with other printers, started the "Morning Signal," but the next year sold out, and engaged in the wholesale paper and twine business, which he still continues as one of the firm of Libby & Williams. He has taken much interest in Odd Fellowship, and has been honored by all means in the power of his lodge.

2 Almon Augustus, b. 13 Feb. 1826; d. 29 Aug. 1828.

3 Elijah C., b. 28 May 1828; died 14 July 1844. He jumped from a height of 30 feet into the Mississippi River, to save a drowning child. He accomplished his purpose, but died soon after of injuries then received.

4 George Gardiner, b. 24 April 1831; d. 19 Feb. 1832.

5-7-8-1-9

Isaac Harding Libby, born in Limington, Me., 14 Aug. 1813; married, 11 Nov. 1833, Caroline M. Waldron, daughter of Aaron C. and Eleanor (Goodwin) Waldron of Limington.

He was a harness-maker. In addition to his trade he kept a tavern. He lived in the house that had been his father's, and died 24 Dec. 1860. His widow still occupies the old house. They were both members of the Congregational Church.

Children, all born in Limington:

1 Almon Augustus, b. 6 Oct. 1833; m. 24 Jan. 1861, Mary M., dau. of Silas Durgin of Limerick; d. 28 July 1863, in Limington. His widow died in Limerick in 1865. Only child:

1 Carrie Bell, b. 24 Oct. 1861.

2 Julia Caroline, b. 18 Sept. 1836; d. 26 Nov. 1842.

3 Charlotte Elizabeth, b. 30 Sept. 1840; d. 16 May 1858.

4 Leonidas, b. 17 June 1842; d. 7 Oct. 1859.

5 Francis Orville, b. 23 May 1846; m. 5 Feb. 1869, Susan, dau. of Arthur and Caroline (Usher) Boothby of Limington; d. 6 Oct. 1869. His widow lives with her parents. Only child:

1 Stella Frances, b. 1869, in Limington.

6 Julia Caroline, b. 16 July 1849; d. 2 April 1852.

7 Ella Ann, b. June, 1852; d. 20 Feb. 1853.

8 Isaac Harding [Rev.], b. 17 May 1855; unm. He was early converted, and determined to enter the ministry. Poor health prevented a liberal education, and in the winter of 1876-7 he began to preach as supply for the Congregational church at North Waterford. 17 May 1878, he was ordained pastor of the Congregational church of Stowe, Me., and Chatham, N. H., and after two years resigned, and accepted his present charge over the Congregational church at Casco, Me.

5-7-8-3-9

Francis Libby, born in Scarborough, 10 Nov. 1821; married, 17 May 1849, Sally Hayman Tompson, 5-7-14-7-3. He lived on the homestead on Oak Hill until 1864. During that time his occupation was for the most part farming, although he was engaged in trade a short time. He served a short time also in Co. C, 12th Me. Vol. In August, 1864, he removed to Portland, where, and in Chelsea, Mass., whither he removed in 1874, he has been engaged in the trucking and express business.

Children:

1 Benjamin Franklin, b. 9 June 1850; m. Hattie, dau. of Samuel and Mary Ann Libby (Redman) Hobbs of Biddeford. He is a clerk on the Portland and Boston steamboat line. Children:
   1 William Tompson, b. 31 Dec. 1872, in Biddeford, Me.
   2 Mabel Catherine, b. 9 Dec. 1874, in Chelsea, Mass.
2 William Dickson, b. 16 Dec. 1851; unm. He is a clerk in Hollidaysburgh, Penn.
3 Stephen Augustus, b. 8 Dec. 1853; unm. He is a telegraph operative.
4 Mary Catherine Tompson, b. 18 Jan. 1856; d. 19 Oct. 1881; unm.
5 Frank E., b. 12 Dec. 1858; died very young.

5-7-11-2-1

Lewis Libby, born in Limington, Me., 9 Feb. 1797; married, 17 Feb. 1822, Mary Ann Tompson, daughter of Joseph and Betsey (Clements) Tompson of Frankfort.

After his marriage he lived about eight years on a farm in Frankfort, (now Winterport); about three years in Hampden; and then settled on the farm in what is now Winterport, on which he ever afterward lived. He died 27 April 1874. His widow and youngest son still live on the homestead.

Children, all born in Frankfort:

1 John Tompson, b. 6 Dec. 1822; d. 7 May 1826.
2 Betsey Clements, b. 12 Jan. 1824; d. 3 May 1826.
3 Joseph T., twin with following, b. 5 Dec. 1825; lives in Waterloo, Iowa. He has a wife and three children.
4 David, twin with last, b. 5 Dec. 1825; m. 1st, 19 Feb. 1853, Mary, dau. of Daniel and Rebecca (Eldredge) Littlefield of Winterport; (died 17 April 1864); 2d, 17 April 1865, Mary A., dau. of Lozier V. and Eliza (Spaulding) Torrey. After he became of age he worked about six years in the mills in Hudson, and then bought the homestead farm of his mother's father, on which he has since lived. Children, by first wife:
   1 Carrie Etta, b. 18 April 1859, in Winterport; m. 28 July 1878, A. W. Hardy.

By second wife:

   2 Mary Eliza, b. 15 Oct. 1868.
   3 Cora Mabel, b. 28 Nov. 1870.
   4 Hattie Matilda, b. 3 June 1873.
5 Mary E., b. 25 Dec. 1827; m. Albert Whitney.
6 Minot C., b. 24 Sept. 1829; m. Jan. 1858, Betsey T., dau. of Prentiss and Wilmot (Fenderson) Clements. From the age of twenty, ten years, he was a peddler, and then bought a farm in Winterport on which he lived until his death. He served eight months in Co. H, 16th Maine Vol. He died 16 Oct. 1864, and his widow married, 30 Sept. 1865, Samuel Littlefield. Children:
   1 George H., b. 20 Jan. 1860; d. 5 Dec. 1868.
   2 Albert W., b. 14 Feb. 1864.
7 John T., b. 6 Aug. 1831; m. 1st, 26 July 1857, Hattie M., dau. of Rev. D. T. and Jane (Chalmers) Clements of Monroe; (died 10 Aug. 1872); 2d, 25 Dec. 1873, Mary A., dau. of Joel T. and Mary A. (Page) Collier of Brooks. He was a farmer until 31 years of age, and then removed to South Boston, Mass., where he has since been a jobber of country produce. Children, by first wife:
   1 Chalmers H., b. 12 Dec. 1858, in Monroe; unm. He is a student at Bates College.

By second wife:

2 Lewis Trew, b. 2 Jan., d. 14 Jan., 1878.

8 Allen D., b. 24 Oct. 1833; m. June 1866, in Minneapolis, Minn., Hannah J., dau. of John and Lydia A. (Foss) Garvey of Houlton, Me. He is now in business in Minneapolis. Children:

1 Byron J., b. 20 March 1867.
2 Lewis, b. 27 April 1868.
3 Viola M., b. 21 April 1871.
4 Stella G., b. 1 Oct. 1875.
5 ———, b. 10 Aug. 1879.

9 Orren Lewis, (known as Lewis), b. 1 April 1837; m. 14 May 1876, in Waterloo, Iowa, Missouri, dau. of John and Barbara (Saylor) Speicher of Black Hawk Co. Up to the time of his marriage he led a roving life, living in many places in Minnesota, Illinois, Ohio, and other states. He first went west in 1858, and has lived there since, except Dec. 1867—May 1870, spent at home. His chief occupation has been teaching school, but he has also been a trader, and is now a hotel keeper. Since his marriage, he has lived in Waterloo, Iowa. Children:

1 John, b. 4 March 1877.
2 Thomas Ray, b. 5 Jan. 1879.

10 Otis J., b. 8 Sept. 1839; m. 21 June 1865, Louisa C., dau. of Alfred J. and Caroline (Davis) Roberts of Brooks. He is a farmer and justice of the peace in his native town. He was in the war. Children:

1 Louis Alfred, b. 20 March 1867; d. 27 March 1874.
2 Ernest, b. 14 March 1877.

11 Charles H., b. 13 Aug. 1842; m. 18 Sept. 1870, Nellie M., dau. of Dea. Daniel and Sarah H. (Hussey) Foster of Fort Fairfield. He is a farmer. No children.

12 Ann T., b. 4 Dec. 1844; m. William H. Jones of Boston.

5-7-11-3-1

Capt. Luther Libby, born in Hampden, Me., 21 Aug. 1806; married, 10 Jan. 1833, Elizabeth Crump, born 28 Aug. 1815, in Richmond, Va.

He went to sea soon after his father settled in Virginia, and followed that calling seventeen years. He then engaged in business as ship chandler and commission merchant and was for many years one of the leading business men of Richmond. His connection with the famous Libby Prison may be well given in the words of his son.

"My father was engaged in the business of ship chandler, grocer, and commission merchant, and had a lease on the building for three years. When the war broke out his business was suspended, as his whole trade was with the North, but he still retained possession of the building, and General Winder, who was in command of Richmond at that time, notified him that he desired the building for a prison and if his goods were not removed within a certain time, he would throw them into the street. Winder took forcible possession of the building, and converted it into a prison. The name was derived from the simple fact of the sign of Libby & Son remaining over the door."

He died 28 Aug. 1871. His wife died 26 July 1865.

Children:

1 James Edward, b. 31 Aug. 1836; d. 13 Oct. following.
2 George W., b. 7 July 1839: m. 29 Oct. 1868, Alice A. Crump, born 15 June 1842, in New Kent Co. He served four years in the Confederate army. He still lives in New Kent Co. Children:
   1 Stanhope, b. 29 July 1869, in New Kent Co.
   2 Luther, b. 8 Sept. 1871, in New Kent Co.
   3 Mary Elizabeth, b. 20 Jan. 1874, in Memphis, Tenn.
   4 George W., b. 18 Sept. 1876, in Richmond.

5-7-12-1-1

William Libby, born in Limington, Me., 12 Aug. 1793; married Esther Brackett, daughter of Joshua and Lydia (Hasty) Brackett.

He lived at home a short time after his marriage, and then settled in "New Limington," in the town of Bridgton, on the farm now occupied by John H. Rose. In 1846, he removed to Newfield to take care of his parents, and in 1858, went thence to Great Falls, N. H., where he died Mar. 1862. He was by trade a shoemaker, and always worked some at it; but while at Great Falls, this formed his sole occupation.

His wife Esther, the mother of his children, died in Bridgton, 7 June 1842. He married as second wife, Martha (Blake) Libby, his brother Rufus' widow.

Children:

1 Dorothy, b. 26 April 1818, in Limington; m. 21 April 1839 Lewis Newcomb of Bridgton.
2 William, b. 18 Sept. 1819, in Bridgton; m. 1st, Joanna, dau. of Moses and Joanna T. (Lane) Sawin of Southborough, Mass.; (died 13 Nov. 1860, in Southborough); 2d, 8 June 1862, Sarah Ann, dau. of Marshall and Sarah (Blood) Temple of Hopkinson. He was a carpenter. He died 14 April 1880, in West Upton, where his widow still lives. Children, by first wife:
   1 Mary J., b. Sept. 1845, in Hopkinson.
   2 Charles W., b. Oct. 1847, in Marlborough; d. Sept. 1849.
   3 William F., b. 7 Dec. 1850, in Southville; m. Julia ——; lives in Marlborough. Children: (?)
      1 William, b. 1871.
      2 John, b. 1877.
      3 Ellen, b. 1879.
      4 Frank, b. 1880.
   4 Sarah C., b. 29 April 1854; d. 14 Mar. 1857.
   5 Alice M., b. 16 Aug. 1856; married in 1874.
   6 Susie, b. 21 Nov. 1858; d. Aug. 1859.

By second wife:

   7 Delosa E., b. 20 Mar. 1862; married 4 July 1880.
   8 Carrie, b. 14 June 1864; died 8 Oct. 1866.
   9 Charles M., b. 29 April 1866.
   10 Amy S., b. 12 Aug. 1871, in Westborough.
   11 Maggie, b. 6 Feb. 1874; d. 6 Mar. 1877.
3 Eliza Ann, b. 5 April 1821; m. 8 Jan. 1843, Edw. White of Harrison.
4 Mary J., b. 18 Aug. 1824; m. Richard Lang of Rye, N. H.
5 Dorcas E., b. Nov. 1825; m. Nahum Record of Great Falls, N. H.
6 Lydia B., b. 17 Dec. 1827; m. 1st, 15 Sept. 1847, Levi H. Hamblen of Boston, Mass.; 2d, 17 Aug. 1854, Francis Winn of Bridgton, Me.

7 Rufus Brackett, b. 11 Dec. 1829; m. Sophronia Wood, dau. of Samuel and Sophronia Wood (Odian) Chadbourn of Great Falls, N. H. He is a carpenter near Boston. Children:
1 Lydia Augusta, b. 3 Feb. 1853, in Boston; m. Chas. H. Fernald.
2 George Royal, b. 7 Aug. 1854, in Boston; d. 27 July 1855, in Great Falls.
3 Charles Benjamin, b. 29 Jan. 1856, in Great Falls; m. Catherine, dau. of Michael W. and Catherine (Callahan) McKeon of Boston, where he is a clerk. Children:
1 Charles E., b. 27 March 1875.
2 Annie A., b. 26 March 1877.
3 George W., b. 11 Aug. 1879.
4 George Albert, b. 6 June 1858, in Bridgton; m. 9 July 1879, Ellen, dau. of Patrick and Mary (Murray) Glenn of Dublin, Ireland. Excepting three years spent as private detective, he has been an expressman. Child:
1 George Chadbourn, b. 9 May 1880, in Dedham.
5 Rufus Brackett, b. 18 July 1860, in Chelsea, Mass.; d. 25 Aug. 1863.
8 Lucinda Brackett, b. 18 March 1833; m. Benjamin Dalton, an Englishman, now of Dover, N. H.
9 James Orin, b. Aug. 1835; m. 31 Dec. 1858, Elizabeth J., dau. of Hugh and Tabitha (Ingalls) Bennett of Bridgton. At 14 he went to Boston, and there learned the carpenter's trade. After living there twelve years he returned to Bridgton, and went into business. He soon after engaged in carriage-making, which he continued until his death, 1881. Children:
1 Frank Orin, b. 26 Feb. 1870.
2 Eva May, b. 23 April 1872.
3 Walter Hugh, b. 19 May 1874; d. 2 Sept. 1876.
4 Kate Lizzie, b. 26 June 1876.
10 Royal, b. March, 1837; m. Jan. 1869, Martha, dau. of Thomas and Harriet (Ingalls) Ridlon of Bridgton. He is a blacksmith by trade. He served three years in a Massachusetts volunteer regiment, and for several years after his marriage followed the sea. Children:
1 George White, b. 21 Feb. 1870, in Bridgton.
2 Benjamin Dalton, b. about 1874.

5-7-12-1-2

Philemon Libby, born in Limington, Me., 14 Dec. 1796; married first, 8 July 1824, Eliza Strout of Limington; (died June, 1826); second, 20 Sept. 1829, Sally Libby, 11-2-4-3-3. He was a farmer. He lived on the homestead in Limington until 1836, when he sold, and bought the *Dam* farm in Newfield, on which he lived until his death, 29 May 1846. His widow died in Portland 25 Sept. 1880.

Children, by first wife:

1 Jacob Cushing, b. 25 Aug. 1825; m. 11 May 1849, Margaret M., dau. of Ithiel and Miranda (Blake) Philbrick of Standish. At the age of 21 he went to Lowell, Mass., and was employed in the cotton mills until a short time before his death, which occurred in Lowell 11 Jan. 1852. His widow returned to Great Falls, N. H., where she married, 27 Nov. 1861, Samuel D. Whitehouse. Children:
1 Novella Adelaide, b. 24 Sept. 1850; m. 7 June 1873, Charles F. Pray of Rollingsford.

2 Ansel Jacob, b. 24 April 1852; m. 5 July 1879, Sarah Ida, dau. of Leonard S. R. and Mary Ann (Davis) Gray of Dover, N. H. At 15 he entered a book store in Great Falls, and two years later went to Boston, where he was in a wall-paper store until 1874. He was afterward clerk a short time in the bookstore of John M. Gatehouse at Dover, and then went to Chicago, where he is now a traveling salesman for John J. McGrath, jobber in paper-hangings. No children:

By second wife:

2 Eliza Ann, b. 18 Dec. 1830; m. Luke L. Newbegin of Portland.
3 Caroline Perry, b. 5 May 1833; m. John I. Durgin of Limerick.
4 Aphia Jane, b. 11 Sept. 1835; m. Edward Dalton, an Englishman.
5 Sarah Dorcas, b. 1 Oct. 1837, in Newfield; m. Appleton N. Burnal.
6 Joshua Mendum, b. 12 Aug. 1840; m. 11 April 1876, Mrs. Hannah Shepard, dau. of Joseph and Rebecca (Langley) Dunnels of Newfield. His boyhood was spent in the mills at Great Falls. From 21 he worked twelve years in Limerick at farming, and since his marriage has lived on his wife's place in Newfield. No children.
7 Mary Ellen, b. 8 Sept. 1844; m. David N. Ward of New York.

5-7-12-1-4

RUFUS LIBBY, born in Limington, Me., 18 April 1802; married, 25 June 1833, MARTHA BLAKE, daughter of Nathaniel and Rebecca (Higgins) Blake of Gorham.

He went to Bridgton at the same time with his brother William, and settled on a farm. In 1840 he removed to Newfield, and thence, five years later, to Great Falls, where the remainder of his life was spent in the cotton mills. He died 29 Dec. 1848. His widow married William Libby, and now lives with her son Charles.

Children:

1 Francis Blake, b. 9 May 1834, in Newfield; m. 27 Nov. 1851, Mary Jane, dau. of Nathan and Hannah (Littlefield) Hanson of Sanford. He worked at first in the cotton mills but soon learned the shoemaker's trade and has since, for the most part, worked in the shoe shops. He and his brother each served two years in Co. A. 1st N. H. Heavy Artillery. Children:
  1 Emma Etta, } twins, b. } d. 22 Feb. 1859.
  2 Frank Eugene, } 12 Jan. 1856; } m. 24 Oct. 1877, Ida L., dau. of Joseph and Mary A. (Seella) Fountain. He has been in the office of the Great Falls Mnfg. Co. since he was 16 years old; first as office boy, and now as asst. paymaster. Children:
    1 Roy Fountain, b. 25 April 1878.
    2 Edward Everett, b. 18 May 1880.
  3 Ida Belle, b. 14 Feb. 1861.
  4 Emma Etta, b. 25 Sept. 1862.
  5 Harry, b. 8 May 1873.
2 Charles Wesley, b. 7 Sept. 1841, in Newfield; m. 13 Oct. 1866, Mary Abby, dau. of John and Clarissa (Gale) Nason of Great Falls. He is a shoemaker. For five years following their return from the war, he and his brother were in business on Main street. They now both work in the shoe manufactory. Child:
  1 Clara Bell, b. 20 May 1869.

5-7-12-1-5

Nathaniel Libby, born in Limington, Me., 6 July 1804; married, 11 Oct. 1827, Lucinda Berry, daughter of John and Jane (Milliken) Berry of Saco.

He learned the carpenter's trade of John Brackett of Limington and worked as journeyman in Saco. The year after his marriage he settled on a farm in West Newfield and employed himself as a cattle drover, marketing in Brighton. In 1846 he removed to Great Falls, N. H., and in 1852 to Portsmouth, and worked at his trade in both places. In July 1855, he emigrated to Rock Co., Wis., and settled in Evansville, where he worked at his trade until his death, 14 Feb. 1881.

Children:

1 Catherine, b. 16 Mar. 1829, in Newfield; m. Oct. 1840, Thomas P. Miles of Limerick.
2 John, b. 16 May 1831; d. 18 Sept. 1847.
3 William, b. 26 Oct. 1834; m. 5 July 1855, Julia Ann Ricker of Great Falls. He learned the carpenter's trade, and in 1853 went to Wisconsin, and has lived in Evansville since that time except four years spent on a farm in Chancellorsville, Va. He is a leading architect and builder. Children:
   1 Frank, b. 23 Nov. 1855; d. 17 May 1856.
   2 Maybelle Inez, b. 18 Dec. 1856; unm.
   3 Irven Aston, b. 7 July 1860, in Great Falls, on a visit of his parents.
   4 William Ernest, b. 3 July 1865.
   5 Henry Elmer, b. 12 July 1872, in Chancellorsville.
   6 Emily Gertrude, b. 25 May 1875.
4 Henry Austin, b. 28 March 1837; m. 1st, 1862, Phebe Rook (died 1867); 2d, 1868 Phebe Ann Cook. He was engaged in the shoe, express, and livery business, in Evansville, where he died 17 Nov. 1870. No children.
5 Harrison, b. 29 March 1839; m. 1st, Nov. 1859, Lettice, dau. of Dea. Argalous and Sarah Ballard, from New York; (died 1861); 2d, 1863, Jennie Dorman. He engaged in the shoe business in Evansville. In 1869 he went into the livery business in Oregon, Wis., and in 1873, in Lena, Ill., where he is now a horse dealer. Children, all by second wife:
   1 Ida Belle, b. 1862, in Evansville.
   2 Frank, b. 1865.
   3 Arthur, b. Sept. 1870.
6 Frances Lavinia, b. 20 Oct. 1841; m. 15 Feb. 1860, Byron Campbell of LaPorte, Ind.
7 Lucinda, b. 16 March 1844; d. 1848.
8 Caleb Ansel, b. 6 Nov. 1846, at Great Falls, N. H.; m. 6 Nov. 1869, in Evansville, Lucilla, dau. of Daniel and Nancy (Cook) Crandall. He is by trade a carpenter. He is the owner of several patents on inventions of his own, and is engaged in the agents' supply business, and in the sale of his patents. He is also editor and proprietor of the Evansville Weekly "Pudding-Stick." Children:
   1 Fred Nelson, b. 30 Dec. 1871, in La Cygne, Kan.
   2 Abnon, } twins, b. 19 Jan. 1874,
   3 Alice, } at Point Pleasant, Iowa.
   4 son, b. 18 Sept. 1881.
9 Nathaniel E., b. 17 Aug. 1850; unm. He learned telegraphy, but gave it up on account of ill health, and has since been engaged as carpenter and school-teacher.

5-7-12-1-8

Solomon Strout Libby, born in Limington, Me., 26 Nov. 1815; married, 15 July 1838, Betsey Fernald, daughter of James and Mehitable (York) Fernald of Newfield.

He learned the trade of blacksmith with Elder Elias Libby, 5-7-8-1-1, and engaged in business in Newfield. He sold out soon after his marriage, and from that time worked as journeyman in many places in Maine, New Hampshire, and Massachusetts, until 1856, when he settled on a farm on Pine Hill, Berwick, and there lived until his death, 28 Jan. 1869. His widow lives in Great Falls, N. H.

Children:

1 Mark Fernald, b. 3 June 1839, in Newfield; d. 15 Aug. 1841.
2 Morrill Woodman, b. 18 July 1840, in Wakefield, N. H.; m. 7 Feb. 1861, Sarah, dau. of Robert and Betsey Hill of New York State. He is a journeyman blacksmith, now living in Manchester, N. H. Children:
    1 Ina Belle, b. 20 Dec. 1861; m. 14 Aug. 1879, Fred Mesgar of New York City.
    2 Hattie Edna, b. 13 May 1863; d. 20 March 1866.
    3 John B., b. 4 July 1864; d. 18 July 1865.
    4 Sadie Estelle, b. 31 Aug. 1865.
    5 Minnie Alfraetta, b. 30 Sept. 1867.
    6 Grace Adella, b. 18 Oct. 1869.
    7 Morrill Firth, b. 26 Oct. 1872.
    8 Myrtie Josephine, b. 10 April 1875.
    9 Louisa May, b. 27 Sept. 1877.
3 Keziah Fernald, b. 3 March 1843, in Great Falls; d. 17 April 1844.
4 Mary Ellen, b. 30 May 1849; d. 18 April 1850.
5 Marvin Wentworth, b. 20 Dec. 1851, in Great Falls; m. 25 Oct. 1870, Lizzie I., dau. of Nathaniel and Adeline (Hersom) Hersom of Lebanon, Me.; (died Nov. 1876); 2d, 15 Oct. 1877, Carrie E., dau. of Samuel and Eliza (Hodgdon) Hersom of Berwick. He learned the machinists trade in Manchester, N. H., and has since worked as journeyman. He lives in Berwick. Children, by first wife:
    1 Carrie Emma, b. 15 Dec. 1873, in Lebanon.

    By second wife:

    2 Jesse Lina, b. 28 Dec. 1879, in Andover, Mass.
6 Amy Maria, b. 8 April 1856, in Berwick; m. 30 Sept. 1872, Geo. F. Young of Lancaster, N. H.

5-7-12-4-5

James Elden Libby, born in Conway, N. H., 23 Oct. 1811; married, 16 Mar. 1838, Lucinda Hilton, daughter of Daniel and Lydia (Allen) Hilton of Denmark. He lived at home until two years after his marriage, and then bought the farm near by, on which he has since lived.

Children:

1 Clarissa Ann, b. 2 April 1839; m. Theodore Frost.
2 Rolinda Fellows, b. 12 July 1841; m. 28 April 1866, Albert Jack.
3 Daniel Hilton, b. 6 Mar. 1848; d. 15 June 1849.

4 Horace Billings, b. 15 May 1851; m. 10 June 1871, Lucy B., widow of Algernon Webb, dau. of John and Mehitable (Barker) Davis of Naples. He worked eight years in a tannery, and then in a woolen mill. Resides in Bridgton. Children:
  1 Norman H., b. 7 Feb. 1873.
  2 Leon Elden, b. 21 Sept. 1876.
5 Ashbel, b. 28 April 1853; m. Hattie Frisbee. He is a teamster in Lower Lake, Cal., whither he removed in 1874. No children.
6 Cora Frantien, b. 15 Jan. 1855.
7 Mary Louisa, b. 1 July 1858.
8 John Pinkham, b. 28 July 1863.

5-7-12-4-6

Moses Libby, born in Limington, Me., 15 July 1813; married, 16 July 1837, Havilah Flint, daughter of James and Lucy (Hale) Flint of Bridgton, Me. He now lives in Waltham, Mass.

Children:

1 Laura Ann, b. 11 June 1840, in Bridgton; d. 9 April 1853.
2 Louisa Havilah, b. 12 Nov. 1849, in Waltham; d. 10 Sept. 1853.
3 James Edwin, b. 14 Nov. 1852, in Waltham; m. 8 Oct. 1874, Noriah Agnes, dau. of James Clare. Children:
  1 Laura Ann, b. 25 Dec. 1875.
  2 Harry Edwin, b. 13 Mar. 1880.
4 Frank Hartwell, b. 23 Mar. 1857; d. 24 Dec. 1860.

5-7-12-4-8

Amos Libby, born in Limington, Me., 12 Mar. 1817; married, 17 April 1842, Jane B. Phinney, daughter of Rev. Joseph and Sally (Whitney) Phinney of Harrison, Me.

He is a carpenter by trade. He has spent his time between Harrison, Me., and Waltham, Mass. His wife died 10 Nov. 1872, and since that time he has lived all the time at Waltham, where he is a foreman in A. T. Stearns' blind factory.

Children:

1 Abby Frances, b. 27 Jan. 1844, in Harrison; m. 8 Feb. 1859, Rev. Chas. W. Foster.
2 Helen Jane, b. 26 Oct. 1849, in Waltham; m. Preston U. Hamlin; d. 30 June 1881, in New York.
3 Andrew Winslow, b. March, 1851, in Harrison; d. March, 1853.
4 Edwin Fremont, b. 19 Feb. 1856; is a sewing-machine agent; lives in Portland; unm.
5 Herbert Filmore, b. 26 May 1858; is a clerk in the office of the Clerk of Courts of Cumberland Co., Me.; resides in Portland; unmarried.

5-7-12-4-9

Abner Libby, born in Bridgton, Me., 7 Feb. 1819; married, first, 14 Feb. 1847, Sarah Abbie Wadlin, daughter of John and Kate (Chadbourne) Wadlin of Belfast, Me. She died 16 Feb. 1849. He married, second, 13 Oct. 1853, her sister Harriet A. Wadlin.

He is a blacksmith. He went to Boston in 1843. He is now in business there, residing in Charlestown.

Children, by first wife:

1 Emma K., b. 14 Feb., d. 20 Feb., 1849, in Boston.

By second wife:

2 Jeannetta E., b. 3 June 1857, in Boston.
3 Loring A., b. 16 Sept. 1859, in Boston.
4 Freddie A., b. 22 Nov. 1864; d. 2 July 1868, in Charlestown.

5-7-12-4-10

Oliver Libby, born in Bridgton, Me., 20 Nov. 1820; married, 20 May 1858, Lavina Margaret Wheeler, daughter of Alanda and Ann (Farmer) Wheeler of Hopkinton, Iowa.

He is a carpenter. Previous to his marriage he worked in nearly all the large cities of the Union. When he was married, he settled in Plattsburgh, Mo., and moved thence, in 1863, onto a farm in Gentry County, near Atlantus, where he still resides. His wife died 16 Jan. 1875.

Children:

1 Dora Ann, b 8 July 1860, in Plattsburgh; m. 18 Sept. 1880, Seth Thomas Goodwin.
2 Emma Jane, b. 22 May 1862, in Plattsburgh; m. 25 July 1880, John Benton Coffey.
3 Alpheus Alanda, b. 10 May, d. 9 Aug., 1866, in Cascade, Iowa.
4 Hattie Eunice, b. 1 Jan. 1868, near Atlantus, Mo.
5 Ida May, b. 4 July 1871, near Atlantus; d. 11 April 1875, in Maryville, Iowa.

5-7-12-4-11

Dennis B. Libby, born in Bridgton, Me., 28 Aug. 1822; married, 7 Nov. 1850, Sarah A. Taylor, daughter of Spencer and Lydia (Swan) Taylor of Ruggles, Ohio.

At the age of twenty he went to Massachusetts, and learned the carpenter's trade. He afterward lived successively in Weston, Waltham, Concord, and Lowell, Mass.; New York; Milwaukee, Cottage Grove (where he was married), and Door Creek, Wis.; Cascade, Iowa; and St. Joseph, Mo. In 1876 he settled permanently at Fairbury, Nebraska.

Children:

1 Ella S., b. 28 Oct. 1851, in Door Creek, Wis.; m. 15 Feb. 1872, John W. Marlow.
2 Clara, b. 17 Sept. 1853, in Cascade, Iowa; d. 9 Oct. 1854.
3 Carrie, b. 2 May 1856, in Cascade; m. 26 July 1875, Lewis W. Culver.
4 Amelia, b. 16 Oct. 1860, in Cascade; d. 23 Nov. 1864.

5-7-12-4-12

Lewis Mitchell Libby, born 18 May 1824, in Bridgton, Me.; married first, 4 Dec. 1850, Hannah C. Rounds, daughter of George and Rebecca (Prentiss) Rounds of Hiram; second, 1 July 1869, Sarah E., widow of Seth L. Chase, daughter of Alexander and Sarah (Evans) McKeen of Lovell, Me.

Except that he served in the war from August, 1862, until its close, he lived at home and carried on the homestead farm, until after his father's death. Upon his second marriage, he moved onto his wife's place, near the village, where he now lives.

Children, all by first wife:

1 James Franklin, b. 20 Sept. 1851; m. 6 Dec. 1874, Abby Frances, dau. of John and Alice (Perry) Cranmore of North Conway, N. H. At the age of 18 he went to Boston. After three years he returned to Bridgton, and two years later went into the clothing business, in which he now is. Children:
  1 John Cranmore, b. 19 April; d. 24 Aug., 1877.
  2 Fred Alton Irving, b. 25 Aug. 1879.
2 Caroline Prentiss, b. 21 Aug. 1853; m. Calvin Randall.
3 Emma Chase, b. 22 Dec. 1856; m. Willis Downs.
4 Rebecca, b. 7 Mar. 1859; d. 14 Dec. 1865.
5 Annie, b. 14, d. 25, Sept. 1866.

5-7-12-4-13

Samuel Appleton Libby, born 21 Aug. 1826, in Bridgton, Me.; married, 13 Oct. 1856, Angeline P. Riley, daughter of David M. and Sarah (Farnham) Riley of Bridgton.

He is a carpenter. In May 1853, he went west, and worked for his brothers Oliver and Dennis, until June 1856, when he returned home, married, and again went to Iowa, where he has since continued.

Children:

1 Wilbur E., b. 13 Aug. 1857, in Cascade, Iowa.
2 Rossie E., b. 27 Nov. 1859, in Sand Spring, Iowa.
3 Florence I., b. 3 Dec. 1861, in Hopkinton, Iowa.
4 Eugene R., b. 4 Jan. 1864.
5 Alvra C., b. 24 July 1866.
6 Mabel F., b. 9 Oct. 1868.
7 Evelyn S., b. 9 Dec. 1870.
8 Annette N., b. 22 Feb. 1873.
9 Melvin A., b. 21 Nov. 1877.

5-7-12-5-2

Joseph Chase Libby, born in Limington, Me., 11 Oct. 1805; married, Lois McLellan Waterhouse, daughter of Joseph and Esther (Fogg) Waterhouse of Westbrook.

After his marriage he lived a few years each in Gardiner and in Thomaston, and in 1839 settled permanently in East Thomaston, now Rockland. He was in business successively as a manufacturer of boots and shoes, a dealer in the same, dealer in stoves and tinware, dealer in lime and groceries, ship-builder, (in company with I. K. Kimball), proprietor of steam manufactory, (burnt in 1855—the largest that ever existed in Rockland), and from 1856 until his death, as a stove and hardware dealer. He was a member of the Rockland City Council in 1871. He died 13 June 1879. His widow died 2 Oct. 1880.

Their children were:

1 Frederick Waterhouse, b. 20 March 1828, in Gardiner; m. 27 Aug. 1849, Adelaide W., dau. of Dr. Zenas and Sophia (Chamberlain) Colby of Rockland. He began life as a ship-carpenter. In 1847 and 8 he was in trade in Rockland, and the next year went to California, where he stayed until 1860. He served a year in the band of the 6th Me. Vol., and has since lived in South America. Child:
  1 Eda Helen, b. 1850; d. 1853.

2 Helen Amanda, b. 3 May 1830; d. 12 Nov. 1854; unm.

3 Edwin [Capt.], b. 28 Feb. 1832, in Thomaston; m. 9 Sept. 1856, Mary F., dau. of Benjamin Cook of Rockland. He was first mate of foreign-going vessels 1849-1854, and captain 1855-1861. In April, 1861, he enlisted in Co. H, 4th Me. Vol., was promoted to adjutant of the regiment the next year, and to captain of Co. D in 1863; was killed during the Battle of the Wilderness, 5 May 1864. Post No. 16, G. A. R., located at Rockland, bears in his honor the name Edwin Libby Post. His widow died in Boston, 1 Dec. 1879. Children:
  1 Mary Helen; lives in Boston; unm.
  2 Edwina; m. —— Sargent of Boston.

4 Arthur [Capt.], b. 29 Dec. 1834; m. 1st, Ellen F., dau. of Andres and Lydia (Butler) Dwinal of Rockland; (died 21 Jan. 1873); 2d, 18 Jan. 1874, Carrie, dau. of Joseph and Eveline (Thorndike) Andrews of Camden. He learned the tin-plate worker's trade and in 1856 engaged with his father in the stove and tinware business under the style of J. C. Libby & Son. The firm was dissolved in 1870, and he soon after started business in the same line in Rockport. He served three years in the 4th Me. Vol., and became captain of Co. A. Children, by first wife:
  1 Ella M., b. 19 Aug. 1855; d. 26 Sept. 1856.
  2 William Arthur, b. 29 Dec. 1857; unm.

5 Lucius Henry, b. 28 May 1838, in Rockland; m. 17 Nov. 1866, Mary Berry, dau. of Hollis M. and Sarah F. (Clough) Kirkpatrick of Camden. He is a tin-plate worker and except two years in business in Vinalhaven, has been connected, first as workman and then as partner, with his father. Only child:
  1 Eda Helen, b. 28 Dec. 1869.

6 Charles Adams, b. 24 Aug. 1842; m. 25 Sept. 1879, Ida, dau. of Walter P. and Mehitable (Marston) Flanders of East Haverhill, N. H. He was at first a clerk for, and then (since 1870) a member of the firm of J. C. Libby & Sons. He served three years in the late war. He was treasurer of Knox County in 1867 and 1868, and a member of the Rockland City Council in 1872.

7 Frank Cobb, b. 15 Dec. 1843; m. 25 April 1868, Hannah, dau. of John and Salina (Butler) O'Neil of Thomaston. He followed the sea until 1867, when he fell from the mast-head of the schooner Ocean Star. He was afterward a member of the firm of J. C. Libby & Sons; later carried on a patent roofing business; and now lives in Colorado, where he owns in gold mines. Children:
  1 James Edwin, b. 10 Oct. 1869.
  2 Charles Pressey, b. 26 Jan. 1871.
  3 Olive Chase, b. 23 Sept. 1875; d. 13 Aug. 1876.

5-7-12-5-4

Alpheus Libby, born in Limington, Me., 7 July 1811; married, Oct. 1839, Marantha Austin, daughter of Nathaniel and Lydia (Hall) Austin of Salem, N. H.

He removed to Thomaston in 1833, and thence, in 1836, to Portland, where he still resides. He was for many years a flour merchant.

His only child is:

1 Delia Hall, b. 18 May 1841; m. 26 Jan. 1865, John G. Stetson.

5-7-12-5-7

EDMUND LIBBY, born in Limington, Me., 7 Oct. 1819; married, first, 25 May 1846, MARY E. HOWELL, daughter of Robert and ——— (Emery) Howell of Portland. She died 21 June 1857. He married second, 11 Sept. 1861, Abbie C., daughter of Capt. John and Abigail (Bickford) Lee of Oxford.

He was in business as grocer, in Portland, from 1841; as baker, in Yarmouth, from 1847, and in Auburn, where he now resides, from 1853. Previous to 1869 he had a bake-shop in Lewiston also, but now confines his business to Auburn.

Children:

1 Robert Howell, b. 16 Aug. 1846, in Portland; m. Dec. 1873, Mary E., dau. of Col. Moses and Sarah E. (Dolbeer) Starbird of Freeman. He is a locomotive engineer; has resided in Greenville, Penn., since 1869. Child:
  1 Edmund Guy, b. Aug. 1878, in Greenville.
2 Fannie A., b. 7 Feb. 1849, in Yarmouth; m. June 1874, S. F. Richards.
3 Charles E., b. 8 Oct. 1853, in Auburn; is in partnership with his father.

5-7-12-5-9

ABNER AUGUSTUS LIBBY, born in Limington, 27 Jan. 1827; married, 25 June 1850, SARAH GILPATRICK, daughter of Joseph H. and Sarah (Burnham) Gilpatrick of Limerick. She died 3 Nov. 1857, and he married, 10 May 1858, her sister, Abby Gilpatrick.

He lived at home until a few years after his marriage, and then bought the house at Limerick Corner, now occupied by his widow, and went into trade. He was a number of years selectman of Limerick. He died 17 Feb. 1866.

Children, by first wife:

1 Olive Gray, b. 13 Dec. 1851.
2 Alvin A., b. 11 March 1853; removed to Bridgeport, Conn., at the age of 17, and has since been a clerk in a clothing store there. Unmarried.
3 Austin, b. 9 May 1855; d. 7 Jan. 1858.

By second wife:

4 Ernest, b. 7 Aug. 1860.

6-3-2-1-10

JEREMIAH LIBBY, born in Wolfborough, N. H., 15 July 1792; married, 25 Sept. 1815, ESTHER SMITH, daughter of Thomas and Mary Ann Smith of Shapleigh, Me.

He was lamed by an accident in infancy, and had always to go with a crutch. In consequence he learned the trade of shoemaker. He lived successively in Brookfield, at Mill Village, on Wolfborough Neck with his father, at Wolfborough Bridge, and finally in Moultonborough. His wife died in Moultonborough, 12 Jan. 1857, and he married the next year Mary Jane, daughter of Dr. Thomas Shannon of that place. He died 29 Aug. 1874. His widow is still living.

Children:

1 Sarah Fullerton, b. 3 July 1816, in Brookfield; m. Wm. Davis.
2 Mary Ann, b. 27 Sept. 1818, in Wolfborough: m. Timothy Brewster.
3 Ivory Chamberlain, b. 1 Oct. 1820; d. in infancy.
4 Olive Margaret, b. 31 Oct. 1821; m. 9 Sept. 1848, Levi Brown.
5 Charles Spring, b. 3 March 1824; m. 1st, Alzira, dau. of Nathaniel and Anna (Wiggin) Caverly of Tuftonborough; (died 15 Nov. 1855, in Boston); 2d, Ellen Budd of Boston. When of age he went to Boston, and was several years in the trucking business, and then became foreman in a refinery of burning fluids. In 1864, on account of ill health, he retired to a farm in Island Pond, Vt., and there died 15 April. His widow married John A. Caldwell of New York City. Children, by first wife:
   1 Laura Alzira, b. 8 April 1846; m. 16 Dec. 1864, Chas. Gilman.
   2 Fanny Caroline, b. 22 June 1849; m. 9 Oct. 1869, Henry S. Gray.

   By second wife:

   3 Etta, lives with her mother.
6 Reuben Abbot, b. 22 June 1826; unm. From 1849 to 1869 he lived in California and Montana. In the latter year he returned to Dover, N. H., and is now day police there.
7 Thomas Smith, b. 14 April 1830; m. Martha, dau. of Ebenezer and Maria Smith of Shapleigh, Me. He became a teamster in Boston. About five years after his marriage he removed to Knox County, Ill., and ten years later to Oberlin, Kansas, where he died Aug. 1878. Children:
   1 Levi, born in Shapleigh.
   2 Thomas, born in Shapleigh.
   and others born in the West.

6-3-2-1-11

CAPT. SMITH LIBBY, born in Wolfborough, N. H., 26 July 1805; married, 12 Oct. 1834, in Exeter, Me., LUCRETIA GARLAND, daughter of Stephen and Dorothy (Trickey) Garland of New Durham, N. H. He early emigrated to the interior of Maine, and has lived in Exeter many years, a farmer. He was representative to the state legislature in 1843, was assistant messenger of the house 1844 and 5, and messenger of the senate 1847 and 8.

Children, all born in Exeter:

1 Edwin, b. 14 Nov. 1835; unm. He was a sailor several years, and served three years in the late war. He now lives in Exeter.
2 Elbridge, b. 30 Jan. 1841; m. 25 Nov. 1874, Elinor, dau. of Stephen and Louisa (Penly) Packard of Monmouth. He is a boot and shoe manufacturer in Foxcroft, Me. Child:
   1 Ethel, b. 9 Sept. 1876, in Exeter.
3 Abbie, b. 2 May 1843; unm.
4 Byron, b. 26 Aug. 1845; m. 30 June 1875, Effie, dau. of Enoch J. and Judith (Caswell) Ames of Exeter. He served nearly five years in Co. H, 15th Me. Vol. He is now a teamster in Boston, Mass. Children:

1 Reginald Byron, b. 15 May 1876, in Boston.
2 Edwin Raynor, b. 17 April 1878, in Boston.
3 Robert Harold, b. 14 April 1880.
5 Reuben, b. 19 Aug. 1848; unm. He is a farmer in Exeter.

6-3-2-8-3

Moses Libby, born in Gilmanton, N. H., 10 March 1788; married Hannah Flanders, daughter of Thomas Flanders of Gilmanton. He removed with his father from Gilmanton to Broom, Lower Canada, about 1820, and there died 23 March 1827. He was a farmer. His widow married Jacob Basford, and died a few years later.

Children:

1 Moses, b. in Gilmanton; m. Elmira, dau. of Moses Davis. He was a carpenter, and owned the farm on which his father died. He died early in life, (aged 37), and his widow married Sewall Lawrence. Children:
  1 Mary Etta, died young.
  2 Cynthia, died young.
  3 Emily.
  4 George Moses, b. 24 May 1847; m. 14 Aug. 1874, in Milford, N. H., Nancy Maria, dau. of John and Melinda (Burroughs) York of Nashua, N. H., in which latter place he now lives. Child:
    1 Bernice Melinda, b. 12 March 1880, in Nashua.
  5 son, died young.
2 Andrew, b. 13 May 1819; m. Nancy Davis, sister of Moses' wife. He was born in Gilmanton, but was reared and has always lived at Broom, a farmer. Children:
  1 Mary S., b. 28 Dec. 1841; d. 23 Oct. 1874; unm.
  2 Eliza A., b. 31 March 1843; unm.
  3 Moses, b. 11 Feb. 1845; unm.; farmer.
  4 Nelson, b. 25 July 1847; m. Eliza, dau. of Andrew Stevens. He is a farmer. Children:
    1 Alice Matilda, b. 10 Sept. 1874.
    2 Nancy Ellen Louisa, b. 5 Sept. 1876.
    3 daughter, b. 8 Sept. 1880.
  5 Charles, b. 18 March 1850; m. Amy Catherine, dau. of Richard and Mary Ann (Doherty) Marsh. He is a mechanic. Children:
    1 Carmy Delbert, b. 18 Dec. 1876.
    2 Andrew Richard, b. 24 May 1880.
  6 Lyman, b. 24 Aug. 1852; unm.; farmer.
  7 Augustus, } twins, born } unm.; farmer.
  8 Augusta, } 17 May 1854; } d. 29 Nov. 1854.
  9 Israel E., b. 23 Jan. 1855; unm.
  10 Howard, b. 3 June 1857; unm.
3 Joseph, born in Knowlton, Broom; m. Cynthia Magowen. He was a farmer in Troy, Vt., when the Civil War broke out. He enlisted and died in the service, leaving a widow, three sons and a daughter, who afterward moved to some American milling town.
4 Elmira, m. Hiram Drew.
5 Hiram, died 1866, with Mrs. Drew. He was a farmer; never married.

6-3-2-10-1

John Libby, born probably in New Durham, N. H., 1792; married, 13 Aug. 1815, Sally Randall, daughter of Richard and Charity (Drew) Randall of Loudon, N. H. He was a farmer in

Barnstead. He died young, of a fever, the result of a severe cold caught while working in his saw-mill, 16 March 1825. His widow married Henry Livingston, and then Nathan Junkins, and died in Tuftonborough, 1878.

Children:

1 Abigail P., b. 7 Jan. 1817; m. John T. May.
2 Richard R., b. 15 Nov. 1819; m. Feb. 1841, in Strafford, where he afterward lived, Mary D., dau. of Samuel and Lydia (Whitehouse) Mills of Dover. He was a brickmaker. He died in New Durham, 16 Aug. 1866. His widow died in Strafford 6 March 1869. Only child:
  1 Hannah S., b. 1 Oct. 1841, in Dover; m. 14 April 1864, John W. Avery of Strafford.
3 Lavinia M. A., b. 16 May 1824; m. Gilman Merrill; lives in Amesbury, Mass. Children:
  1 Ruth (Merrill), b. 1851; m. Fred Morris. Children:
    1 Elmer G. (Morris), b. 15 Feb. 1872.
    2 Frederick A. (Morris), b. 1876.
  2 John F. W. (Merrill), b. 1853; unm.
  3 Ann C. (Merrill), b. 1856; m. B. C. Colby.
  4 Willard G. (Merrill), b. 1859; unm.
  5 Arthur H. (Merrill), b. 1864; d. 1865.
  6 Clarence A. (Merrill), b. 1866.

6-3-2-11-3

Dr. David Thurstin Libby, born in New Durham, N. H., 27 Oct. 1790; married, 11 Oct. 1818, Lucinda Parsons, daughter of Thomas and Lucy (Bradbury) Parsons of Parsonsfield, Me.

David T. Libby began the study of medicine with Dr. Sargent of New Durham, and then went to Effingham, N. H., where he completed his education with a Dr. Clark. He practiced a short time in Parsonsfield, Me., where his wife belonged, and in 1820 established himself at Wolfborough Bridge, where he continued to practice successfully until his death, which occurred 27 Aug. 1834.

On account of the annoyance experienced in being confounded with another Dr. Libby, who resided in a neighboring town, (Dr. Benjamin Libby, 1-6-2-1-9?), he had his name changed to Livy, which name his family retained. His widow died in Meredith, N. H., 30 Aug. 1877.

Their children were:

1 Annette Augusta, b. 9 July 1819; m. 14 Dec. 1837, Hon. Jeremiah Forest Hall, M.D., of Portsmouth, N. H.
2 Harriet Byron, b. 19 April 1821; m. William E. Alexander, a leading merchant of Savannah, Ga.
3 Caroline Elizabeth, b. 20 June 1823; m. Rev. John M. M. Caldwell, now president of the Rome Female College, at Rome, Ga.
4 Julia Amanda, b. 17 Mar. 1825; d. 19 Sept. 1826.
5 Edwin Parsons, b. 22 July 1827; went to sea, and died of fever in the hospital at Calcutta, Aug. 1845.
6 David Henry, b. 3 June 1832; was drowned in the lake, in front of his mother's house, 26 Dec. 1840.
7 Mary Allen, b. 27 Oct. 1834; m. 10 Jan. 1857, Hon. Samuel Winkley Rollins, now Judge of Probate for Belknap County, residing at Meredith, N. H.

6-3-2-11-4

ASA LIBBY, born in New Durham, N. H., 21 Feb. 1792; married, 18 May 1820, NANCY CLOUGH, daughter of Isaac and Sarah (Carr) Clough of Alton. He was a farmer, and always lived on his father's homestead on New Durham Ridge. He died 6 March 1836. His widow still lives.

Children, all born in New Durham:

1 Isaac Carr, b. 7 Nov. 1821; m. 1849, Clara S., dau. of John C. and Abigail (Stevens) Chamberlain. He had his father's homestead, which he sold out of the family in 1854, but still lives on New Durham Ridge. He is a member of the Second Advent Church. Child:
  1 Viola Augusta, b. 5 Aug. 1854; unm.
2 Sarah Mason, b. 1 Dec. 1823; m. 1849, John Davis; died 26 July 1863. Children:
  1 Lydia (Davis), b. 6 Feb. 1854.
  2 Jose (Davis), b 9 June 1859.
3 Hannah Clough, b. 25 June 1825; m. 14 Feb. 1843, Eliphalet H. York of Dover.
4 David Thurston [Rev.], b. 24 Feb. 1828; m. 1849, Elizabeth G., dau. of Joseph B. and Sarah (Holmes) Chamberlain. He is a farmer and shoemaker in New Durham. In 1874 he was ordained a preacher of the Second Advent denomination. Children:
  1 Asa E., b. 8 April 1852; m. 1873, Emma J., dau. of Joseph and Betsey (Scruten) Berry; d. 28 Nov. 1879. He was a clerk in a grocery store in Farmington. His family live with his father. Child:
    1 Ervin A., b. 7 March 1875.
  2 Frank H., b. 8 July 1854; unm. He is a clerk in a shoe store in Boston.
5 Josephine B., b. 1 May 1831; m. Charles H. Willey.
6 George Franklin, b. 23 April 1834; unm. He is a shoecutter and works now in Dover, N. H.

6-3-2-11-6

CAPT. DANIEL LIBBY, born in New Durham, N. H., 15 Sept. 1796; married, 10 March 1817, ADA CLOUGH, daughter of Isaac Smith and Joanna (Carr) Clough of Alton.

Soon after his marriage he removed from Alton to Tuftonborough, where the burden of his life was spent in farming. He died on a small farm in Wolfborough, (where his widow still lives), 3 Aug. 1862. He was a member of the Christian Baptist church, and six years captain in the militia.

Children:

1 John Mason, b. 21 Nov. 1818, in Alton; m. 1st, 1840, Polly H., dau. of Wm. and Dolly (Snell) Wiggin; (died 17 April 1854); 2d, Ann M. (Swett) Horn, dau. of Robert and Polly Swett; (died 22 Mar. 1864); 3d, 1870, Mrs. Susan Pingree, dau. of Isaiah and Sarah (Stevens) McIntire. He followed the sea portions of two years, but has since been a successful farmer in Tuftonborough. Children, by second wife:
  1 Charles, b. 17 Oct. 1855; d. 12 April 1859.
  2 Fred C., b. 3 May 1860; unm. He is a clerk in Boston.
2 Ann Carr, b. 20 May 1820; m. John Fullerton and Nathan Morrison; d. 6 Aug. 1850.

3 Leonora, b. 12 Aug. 1822; d. 4 Mar. 1825.
4 Moses, b. 26 July 1824; m. Vesta R. Wiggin.
5 Sarah M., b. 10 July 1825; d. 29 Mar. 1827.
6 Daniel, b. 9 May 1827, in Tuftonborough; m. 1853, Martha A., dau. of John R. and Abiah (Brewster) Hayes of Wolfborough, where he is now a farmer. Children:
   1 Emma F., b. 1 May 1856; m. David Fullerton.
   2 Edwin D., b. 24 June 1857, in Tuftonborough; unm. He is a shoemaker.
   3 John H., b. 30 Dec. 1860; is a mason.
   4 Harry E., b. 8 June 1876, in Wolfborough.
7 Nancy J., b. 31 Aug. 1829; m. Wm. Thomas; d. 1841.
8 Isaac C., b. 12 March 1831; d. same day.
9 Isaac Smith, b. 12 July 1833; m. 1857, Emily, dau. of Thomas Kenney of Milton, N. H.; died 27 Sept. 1865, in Tuftonborough. He was by trade a shoemaker, but followed farming. His widow married again and lived in Lynn, Mass. Children:
   1 Melvina, } twins.
   2 Alvena, }
10 Elizabeth J., b. 1 Oct. 1835; } died of croup
11 Charles F., b. 1 Nov. 1836; } 10 May 1838.
12 Charles A., b. 19 June 1840; m. 1867, Evelyn E., dau. of Jonathan and Elizabeth C. (Wiggin) Hersey. He is a farmer. In 1869 he moved to Manchester, Iowa. He has been two years class-leader in the Methodist church. He served two years in the late war. Child:
   1 Lizzie A., b. 1870.
13 James W., b. 8 June 1843; d. 27 Aug. 1863, at Point Lookout, Md., after a year's service against the rebellion.

6-4-1-5-1

Levi Libby, born in New Hampshire; married, 13 Mar. 1814, Hannah Libby, 6-4-1-8-3. He grew up in Porter, Me., and went thence to New York State. He died early, and his widow married George Seavey of Genesee Co., N. Y. They joined the Mormons and emigrated to Utah.

Children:

1 Truman, went to Utah with the Seaveys, but was reported to have left them and settled in Nebraska.
2 Isaac, was last heard from in Illinois.
3 Eliza, married Alvin Torry.
4 Jane.
5 James W., b. 27 Feb. 1826, in Bath, N. Y.; m. 12 April 1855, Eliza, dau. of Caleb and Betsey (Irons) Mosher of Bath. He was reared from infancy by his uncle Isaac Libby. He went west in 1845, and worked at the carpenter's trade in Wisconsin and Minnesota until 1852. From that year till 1872 he lived in Elkader, Kans., and has since lived in Volga City. He and his wife are both members of the M. E. Church. He has been fifteen years a justice of the peace. Children:
   1 Anna M., b. 30 Mar. 1856; m. 26 Nov. 1876, Louis M. Goodwin.
   2 Margaret, b. 26 Jan. 1858; d. 25 March 1861.
   3 Frank A., } twins, born } died 10 Jan. 1863.
   4 Fred W., } 22 Aug. 1860; } is a brakeman.
   5 Hattie, b. 18 Feb. 1865.
   6 Lincoln, } twins, born } died 29 June 1870.
   7 Leon, } 14 Feb. 1869; }

6-4-1-6-1

JACOB LIBBY, born probably in Chichester, N. H., about 1780; married, 18 May 1806, in Saco, EUNICE SCAMMON.

He grew up in Parsonsfield, Me., and afterward lived in Saco, where he began to learn the blacksmith's trade. He gave it up, however, and went to sea. He afterward sailed for Capt. John Dix of Portland, and was cast away, and the whole crew lost, 1811. His widow married Capt. Jacob Warren.

Children:

1 Isaac, b. 15 Jan 1807, in Portland; m. 1st, Sarah Libby, 1-5-2-5-7-4; 2d, Betsey Ann (Goss) Libby, widow of Philip Libby, 10-5-6-7-6.
2 Jacob, b. 1810; never married. He learned the machinist trade in Boston, and became engineer of a steamer on the Arkansas River, where he is supposed to have died of yellow fever, a young man.

6-4-1-8-1

JOHN LIBBY, born in Porter, Me., 30 Jan. 1792; married, 6 Aug. 1815, MARY G. FOX, daughter of John and Deborah (Gilman) Fox of Porter.

He lived on a farm in Porter until about 1821, when he emigrated to New York, and settled in the woods near Utica. He stayed there only about a year, because his wife was taken with fever and ague. He started for home, but lived for lengthy periods in various places along the road, and did not reach Maine until about 1834. He bought the Broad farm in Brownfield, and lived there until his death, 10 Oct. 1835. His family afterward lived in Parsonsfield, Porter, Freedom, N. H., Porter, Parsonsfield, and in 1849 moved to Biddeford, where the widow died, 4 Sept. 1865.

Children:

1 Lucinda Fox, b. 15 Jan. 1816; m. Rev. Francis Ayer of Cornish, a Methodist preacher.
2 Deborah Gilman, b. 10 June 1818; m. Samuel Chamberlain of Brownfield.
3 Joseph Maurice, b. 26 Feb. 1821; m. 1st, Eliza J., dau. of Gardner and Relief (Thayer) Penniman of South Braintree, Mass.; (divorced); 2d, ——— ———. He is a carpenter and is in business in Malden. Child, by first wife:
   1 Margaret Ellen, b. 17 May 1846; m. Ebenezer Moulton.
4 John Colby, b. 12 Oct. 1828, in Tamworth, N. H.; m. 1st, 9 Jan. 1862, Sarah Olive, dau. of Jeremiah and Miranda (Burnham) Hill; (died 18 March 1865); 2d, 13 Aug. 1865, Bernice M., dau. of Richard and Miriam (Thurlo) Taylor of Byron, Me. He learned the carpenter's trade with his brother in South Braintree, Mass., and afterward worked as journeyman in Biddeford. In 1858 he engaged in the undertakers business which he continued until 1877, when he removed to the farm in Naples on which he now resides. He is a Second Adventist. Children, all born in Biddeford:
   1 Maurice Colby, b. 13 July 1866.
   2 John Bertie, b. 7 Aug. 1869; d. 8 March 1874.
   3 Olive Bernice, b. 13 Nov. 1874; d. 29 July 1878.
   4 Jesse Clinton, b. 29 Aug. 1877.
   5 Mary Emma, b. 19 Nov. 1879.
5 Mary Asenath, b. 3 May 1834; m. Melville Black.
6 Julia Ann, b. 26 Aug. 1836; m. Rev. Abial W. Sibley.

6-4-1-8-5

Josiah Libby, born in Porter, Me., 9 Feb. 1799; married, 1825, Mary P. Leavitt, daughter of Jonathan and Elizabeth (Hutchins) Leavitt of Conway, N. H.

He was of Brownfield, Me., at the time of his marriage, but soon after bought a farm in South Conway, N. H., on which he lived about twenty-five years. His health failing him, he went to Saratoga Springs, and lived there two years. He never recovered, but spent the rest of his life in alternate visits to his relatives in New York, and his children in Massachusetts. He died with Mrs. Currier, in Lawrence, Oct. 1866. His wife died in Lowell, 29 June 1856.

Children:

1 Leavitt J., b. 21 July 1826, in Brownfield; m. in Philadelphia, Penn., Elizabeth Hyres. He was a hotel-keeper in the West; is supposed to be dead. His widow lives in Philadelphia. Children:
  1 William.
  2 Emma.
2 Oscar F., b. 10 Feb. 1828, in Conway; m. in Lowell, Mass., Lucinda Gilman. He was a railroad contractor and died of cholera, in Illinois. His widow survives. No children.
3 Mary E., b. 19 Jan. 1830; m. 15 May 1848, James M. Currier, who died 21 Jan. 1862. They were the first couple married in Lawrence.
4 Eben L., b. 29 Jan. 1833; lives in South America. He followed the show business, performing remarkable feats of strength.
5 Ellen S., b. 20 March 1834; m. 11 July 1856, Edwin Lyford of Lawrence. No children.
6 Harriet A., b. 16 April 1836; m. Sept. 1855, Stephen Kenney, who died 22 Feb. 1872.
7 Lucy A., b. 11 Sept. 1838; m. 3 July 1857, Joseph Abbott.
8 Francena A., b. 11 July 1840; m. 6 May 1865, R. F. Sargent of Lawrence.
9 Laroy N., b. 29 Sept. 1848; unm. He lives in West Gardiner, Mass., a finisher in a chair factory.

6-4-1-9-2

Daniel Libby, born 3 April 1786, the first male born in Porter, Me.; married, 19 March 1809, Mary Rundlet, daughter of Joshua and Phebe (Chapman) Rundlett of Parsonsfield. He was settled by his father on a lot of wild land near the center of Porter, and began to clear himself a farm: but he was stricken down by fever nine years after his marriage, and died 19 Sept. 1818. His wife remained a widow and brought up her young family without assistance. She died 3 Sept. 1863.

Children:

1 Levi Smith Chapman, b. 23 March 1810; m. Eliza D. Boothby.
2 Mahala, b. 19 Oct. 1811; m. John Pilsbury of Shapleigh; d. Feb. 1837, in Danvers, Mass.
3 Phebe Rundlet, b. 31 Jan. 1813; m. Geo. W. Ward of Wells.
4 Joshua Rundlet, b. 24 March 1815; m. Elzira Boothby.

6-4-1-9-6

STEPHEN LIBBY, born in Porter, Me., 21 May 1793; married, 23 Jan. 1814, DOROTHY BLAKE, daughter of Thomas and Hannah Blake of Meredith, N. H. He settled on land given him by his father. His homestead is now occupied by Henry M. Libby, 6-4-1-9-8-1-2, and Samuel Redlon, jr. His wife died 10 Dec. 1847, and he, 4 Dec. 1868.

Children:

1 Joseph L., b. 15 Oct. 1814; m. 14 Dec. 1843, in Roxbury, Mass., Mary, dau. of Francis and Mary (Marshall) Whitney of Natick, Mass. Upon his marriage he settled on the farm in his native town on which he has since resided. He is a member of the General Baptist church of Brownfield. Children:
 1 Charles F., b. 2 Nov. 1844; d. 11 Feb. 1850.
 2 Mary Jane, b. 6 Dec. 1845; unm.
 3 Joseph M., b. 8 Dec. 1847; unm.
 4 Annah A., b. 19 March 1850; m. 25 Dec. 1877, Wm. Douglass.
 5 Josephine F., b. 11 June 1853; m. 2 May 1872, John D. Varney.
 6 Caroline D., b. 12 Oct. 1855; m. 27 Oct. 1879, George Hunneman; d. 16 Dec. 1879, in Boston.
 7 Rosella, b. 21 April 1857; m. 21 Feb. 1877, Andrew Cole.
2 James. b. Jan. 1817; m. Mary Nute; lives in Wolfborough, N. H. Child (probably):
 1 Lydia C., b. 1840; unm.
3 Daniel, b. Oct. 1819; d. Sept. 1841; unm. He was a member of the M. E. Church.
4 Hannah, b. 2 April 1822; m. 17 July 1842, Daniel E. Smith.
5 Mary, b. 10 June 1824; d. March, 1842.
6 Joel T., b. 13 July 1826; m. 7 May 1848, Ruth L., dau. of Samuel and Mercy (Tibbetts) Billings of Porter. He had his father's homestead, and has since been a farmer in his native town. He has been selectman. Children:
 1 Samuel B., b. 17 Feb. 1849; m. 1st, 24 Feb. 1870, Relief, dau. of Nathaniel and Harriet (French) Rounds; (died 10 May 1872); 2d, Mary, dau. of Madison and Martha (Walker) Linscott of Brownfield. He is a cooper in Freedom, N. H. Children, by first wife:
  1 Relief R., b. 4 May 1872, in Pennsylvania; d. 25 Feb. 1876, in Porter. She caught her clothes on fire and was so burned that she died.

  By second wife:

  2 Delbert, b. 2 March 1875, in Brownfield, Me.
  3 Emma Maud, b. 10 Nov. 1876.
 2 Alphonzo J., b. 26 March 1853; unm. He is in the sewing machine business.
 3 James E., b. 24 Sept. 1857; d. 13 Oct. 1857.
 They adopted, 10 Nov. 1860, a daughter of Charles and Eliza Ann (Abbot) Floyd of Porter. She was called:
 a Marie A. (Libby), b. 20 March 1859; m. 30 April 1876, Moses Fox, jr.
7 Isabella, b. 17 Nov. 1828; m. 14 Dec. 1851, Wm. Brown; died March 1870.
8 Abigail M., b. 10 Dec. 1831; m. 18 Jan. 1853, Thomas T. Billings; d. 16 Jan. 1868.

6-4-1-9-8

JOHN LIBBY, born in Porter, Me., 20 Feb. 1797; married, 17 Nov. 1816, NANCY LIBBY, 1-4-4-4-2-1. He settled on the homestead farm of his wife's father, and lived there until his death, 21 Jan. 1878. His wife died Nov. 1847, and 20 Nov. 1848 he married Mrs. Anna Tibbetts, daughter of Carr Leavitt. She died 30 March 1872.

Children:

1 Trueworthy C., b. 23 April 1817; m. 12 Dec. 1838, Hannah E., dau. of Eunice (Libby) Hurd, 6-4-1-2-6. He lives on the homestead farm, a farmer. Children:

- 1 John T. C., b. 16 Jan. 1841; m., March 1875, Martha A., dau. of James and Abby (Merrill) Moore of Parsonsfield, where he now lives, a school-teacher and farmer. No children.
- 2 Henry M., b. 10 Dec. 1846; m. 30 June 1870, Orra A., dau. of Moses T. and Hannah (Gerry) Smith of Hollis. He is a farmer in Porter. Children:
  - 1 Lizzie J., b. 7 Aug. 1871, in Cornish.
  - 2 Sidney T., b. 26 Feb. 1874, in Porter.
  - 3 Lillia H., b. 18 Sept. 1877.
  - 4 Orra A., b. 21 April 1880.
- 3 Thomas M., b. 19 Nov. 1851; unm.

2 Hanson, b. 15 May 1821; m. 1st, 7 Dec. 1843, Susan, dau. of Samuel and Isabella (French) Tibbetts of Parsonsfield; (died 24 Oct. 1854); 2d, 15 May 1856, Mary A., dau. of Lemuel and Mary (Berry) Sawyer of Porter. He is a farmer in Porter. He is a member and clerk of the G. P. Baptist church. Children, by first wife:

- 1 Lydia A., b. 4 Dec. 1846; m. 7 Dec. 1865, Capt. Joseph O. Gentleman of Eaton, N. H.
- 2 Lavina A., b. 25 Feb. 1848; m. Aug. 1868, Marshall W. Wadsworth of Hiram.
- 3 James H., b. 30 Aug. 1850; d. 12 Sept. 1850.
- 4 Hanson S., b. 9 Feb. 1852; m. 5 Sept. 1880, Carrie E., dau. of Matthew and Clarissa (Ingersoll) Fowler of Skowhegan, Me. He has lived since 1872 in Boston, Mass., where he is a clerk in a wholesale drug store.
- 5 Charles L., b. 6 May 1854; m. 28 Oct. 1877, Martha M., dau. of James M. and Martha (Walker) Linscott of Parsonsfield. He is a farmer in Brownfield: a member of the General Baptist Church. Child:
  - 1 Grace B., b. Oct. 1878, in Brownfield.

By second wife:

- 6 Susie E., b. 17 Feb. 1859; unm.
- 7 Clarence J., b. 3 Feb. 1864.
- 8 daughter, b. 5 March, d. 21 March, 1867.
- 9 Elmer E., b. 21 March 1869.
- 10 Frank C., b. 25 May 1871.

3 Henry M., b. 9 Jan. 1826; m. 1 Jan. 1850, Mary A., dau. of Trueworthy and Abigail (Burley) Chamberlain of Brookfield, N. H. He is a farmer, carriage-maker, and carpenter. He lived in Porter, on the homestead farm, until 1864, and from that time until Nov. 1880, lived in Brookfield. He now lives in Wakefield. While in Porter he was several years town clerk and also a justice of the peace. Children:

- 1 Freeman C., b. 4 Feb. 1851; m. 3 Dec. 1876, Lorea S., dau. of Thomas C. and Margie A. (Fife) Rogers of Lawrence, Mass. He lives in Salem, N. H. Child:
  - 1 Burton W., b. 4 Sept. 1877, in Lawrence.
- 2 Augusta A., b. 24 Oct. 1852; d. 17 Sept. 1863.
- 3 Cora E., b. 16 July 1855; d. 27 Sept. 1863.
- 4 Herbert A., b. 8 May 1859; d. 16 Feb. 1860.
- 5 Matilda C., b 19 Jan. 1862; d. 24 Sept. 1863.
- 6 Tillie A., b. 17 April 1866, in Brookfield, N. H.
- 7 Stella E., b. 26 Aug. 1868; d. 15 Jan. 1870.

6-4-1-9-9

David Libby, born in Porter, Me., 16 Jan. 1799; married first, 29 March 1821, Betsey Towle; second, Dorothy Brooks. He was a farmer, and died in 1840. His widow married, 3 Oct. 1841, Phineas Thompson, and died about 1844, in Parsonsfield.

Children, all by second wife:

1 Susan, unm. She is *non compos mentis*, and is supported by the town of Porter.
2 William, unm. He became crazy, and has not been heard from for many years.
3 Sarah, died aged twenty-three.
4 David W., b. 6 Oct. 1834; m. 1 Jan. 1863, Sarah Jane, dau. of Joseph and Lucinda (Brown) Thompson of Newfield. He was adopted by Alfred Woodman of Woodman's Mills, and bore his name until he was 18 years old. He was chiefly engaged in milling until his marriage, and has since lived on the homestead farm of his wife's father. Since 1870 he has run a general store at Woodman's Mills. He has been selectman of Newfield. Children:
   1 John James, b. 11 Sept. 1863.
   2 Ada, b. 4 Aug. 1865.
   3 Sarah Jane, b. 8 Jan. 1870; d. 14 Dec. 1873.
5 Mary Elizabeth, m. Capt. Robert O'Brine of Walton, N. S.

6-4-4-2-3

Simon Libby, born 31 March 1778, in Pittsfield, N. H., it is said; married 14 Jan. 1802, in Strafford, Vt., Ama Morse, daughter of David and Esther Morse.

He kept a general store at Strafford (where he grew up) for a while, and afterward removed to Epsom, N. H., where he was toll-gatherer at one time, but his chief occupation was teaching school. He died 3 Feb. 1812. His widow married Amos Baker, and died with her eldest daughter, in Easton, N. Y., May, 1863.

Children:

1 Lucinda, b. 19 Nov. 1803, in Strafford, Vt.; m. 1st, Sanford Benson; 2d, Constant Sisson.
2 Joel, b. 9 Sept. 1806; m. 9 Sept. 1838, in Boston, Mass., Julia Ann, dau. of Peter and Hannah Wood of Manchester, N. H. He was brought up by a farmer in Epsom, and when a young man, removed to Boston, where he lived some years. He died in Chelsea, where his widow still lives, 10 Feb. 1879. Children, all born in Boston:
   1 Joel, b. 16 Sept. 1839; d. 13 July 1841.
   2 Amy B., b. 1 July 1842; died 29 June 1874, in Chelsea.
   3 William H., b. 30 July 1844; m. Mary Jane, dau. of Sylvester Hunt.
   4 Charles O., b. 7 Aug. 1850; d. 21 July 1870, in Chelsea.
3 Abigail, b. 22 Nov. 1808; m. Daniel Bassett.

6-4-4-2-6

Capt. Joseph Libby, born in Pittsfield, N. H., 2 Nov. 1785; married, 22 Jan. 1811, in Sharon, Vt., Mabel Walbridge, daughter of John Walbridge. He was at first a farmer, but afterward a carpenter. He died in Danby, Vt., 10 Jan. 1830. He was a captain in the militia. His widow died with her eldest son, in Johnson, Vt., 9 Feb. 1867.

Children, all born in Danby:

1 Isaac Tichenor, b. 9 April 1812; m. Nancy Frisbee.
2 Lovine, b. 29 Aug. 1813; m. Eliza B. Gale and Ann Shekleton.
3 Louisa, b. 25 April 1815; m. 14 Oct. 1831, Orren Spaulding; died 14 Feb. 1856.
4 Angelina, b. 19 Jan. 1817; m. 10 Oct. 1839, Charles K. Hill.
5 Harrison W., b. 24 Jan. 1819; m. 1st, 12 Feb. 1845, in Rutland, Vt., Sophronia Richardson; (died 25 Dec. 1846); 2d, Harriet P. Stacker. He was a tailor. He died 10 June 1848, in Rutland. By his second wife he had a son, born four months after his own death. The mother went with him to Massachusetts and was never heard from.
6 Caroline, b. 20 March 1821; m. 8 Sept. 1840, Albert S. Burditch; d. 26 May 1855, in Granville, N. Y.
7 Lima, b. 1 Nov. 1823, m. 2 Sept. 1851, Joseph B. Foster; d. 4 July 1854.
8 John W., b. 5 June 1826; d. 21 March 1833.

6-4-4-4-1

Matthias Libby, born in Epsom, N. H., 13 Aug. 1777; married, 1800, Sarah Keys, daughter of Peter and Rhoda (Durkee) Keys of Pittsfield, Vt.

In his younger days he taught school. During his married life he lived on a farm in Pittsfield, and there his wife died in the spring of 1821. He became crazy at his wife's death, and for some time peddled dry-goods in New York State. He afterward recovered and lived in Lowell, Mass., as a contractor and jobber. Reason afterward failed him again, and he died in Brattleborough, Vt., Feb. 1857.

Children, all born in Pittsfield:

1 Bennet, m. 1st, Martha J. Huntress; 2d, Agnes Little.
2 Elvira, b. 1808; d. Aug. 1877, in Taunton, Mass.; unm.
3 Rhoda, b. 1811; died in infancy.
4 Haynes M., b. 24 Nov. 1813; m. Lucinda Bisbee.
5 William K., b. 26 Sept. 1815; m. Susannah S. Kimball.
6 John, b. 1817; d. 1828.
7 Justin, b. 1818; d. 1820.

6-4-4-4-2

Isaac Libby, born in Epsom, N. H., 14 Nov. 1779; married, 1800, Sally Bayles of Tunbridge, Vt.

He was a carpenter and millwright, and lived in Strafford, Vt., (where he came to maturity) until after the death of his wife, 17 May 1830. The family was then broken up, and he lived among his children until his death, May, 1847, in Richmond, Vt. He served one year in the war of 1812.

Children, all born in Strafford:

1 Alvin, b. 6 March 1802; m. Juliann Alger.
2 Elinor, b. 13 Nov. 1803; m. Wm. Coburn.

3 Sally, b. 4 Nov. 1805; m. Dec. 1831, Jesse C. Coburn.
4 Isaac Haynes, b. 28 Jan. 1808; m. Nov. 1837, Louisa Hall of Enfield, N. H. He was a carpenter until his marriage, and then removed to Lowell, Mass., where he soon after became a locksmith. His wife died in 1878, and in 1880 he went to live with his sister Esther in Northfield, Vt. He had three children that all died in infancy.
5 John Bayles, b. 10 March 1810; d. Feb. 1821.
6 Lotan, b. 8 April 1812; m. 1st, Luvia Chamberlain; 2d, Sarah Williams; 3d, Adeline C. Burton. He died in Northfield, Vt., May, 1863. His widow and family live in Lowell, Mass. Children, by first wife:
  1 Franklin J.
  2 Charles W.
  3 Luvia A., married Charles E. Howe.

By third wife:

  4 ——, died in infancy.
  5 Fred L.
  6 Celia A.
7 Esther, b. 11 Dec. 1814; m. 22 Nov. 1834, Wm. Allen.
8 Alonzo, b. 22 Feb. 1818; m. 22 April 1849, Lovisa W., dau. of John and Lovisa (True) Ayers of Berlin, Vt. He lived in various places (among others, Stanstead, Que., where he stayed five years) until his marriage, and then bought a farm in Northfield, Vt. In 1854 he removed to the adjoining town of Berlin, where he has since lived. Children:
  1 Alonzo S., b. 9 Sept. 1853, in Northfield, Vt.; unm.
  2 Marcia L., b. 16 Dec. 1857, in Berlin.
9 John Bayles [Rev.], b. 21 July 1820; m. 23 July 1845, Bathsheba, dau. of Joseph and Lydia (Dow) Preston of Strafford. He was brought up by one Jacob Kiblin. When he was of age he became a preacher of the Christian denomination, and remained in the ministry, as pastor of several churches, until his health failed him. His last years were spent on a farm in Newport, N. H., where he died, 24 Feb. 1872, and his widow still lives. Children:
  1 Sarah Maria, b. 14 Jan. 1849, in Richmond, Vt.; m. 25 July 1869, Harvey Ford Deming.
  2 John Preston, b. 2 July 1852, in Hartland, Vt.; unm. He is a farmer in Newport.
  3 Julia Annie, b. 27 Dec. 1854, in Croydon, N. H.; unm.
10 Clarissa, b. 22 Dec. 1822; m. Arnold Evans.
11 Janette, b. 13 Nov. 1828; m. Wm. Coburn.

6-4-4-4-8

JOHN H. LIBBY, born in Strafford, Vt., 1 May 1796; married, 12 March 1820, MIRIAM B. DAVIS, daughter of Ephraim and —— (Yeaton) Davis of Epsom.

He went from Canterbury, where his father was living with the Shakers, to Epsom, when a boy. He was later a watchman in Boston, and a carpenter in Salem and Danvers. After his marriage he lived in Epsom and Pittsfield until 1827, and then went to Lowell, Mass., and later to Norwich, Conn., in both which places he engaged in the manufacture of bobbins for the factories. He died in Concord, N. H., 27 Jan. 1843. His widow died 16 March 1843, with the Shakers.

Children:

1 William G., b. 3 Oct. 1820, in Pittsfield; unm. He followed the sea six and one-half years, and then, in 1843, joined the Shakers at Canterbury.
2 John M., b. 28 Nov. 1821, in Epsom; d. 8 Feb. 1847, in Lowell, Mass. He was a sailor some years, and then married and became a bobbin-maker in Lowell.
3 Eliza Ann, b. 3 Aug. 1823; d. 2 Dec 1856, in Shaker Village.
4 Mary Jane, b. 28 April 1825, in Pittsfield; m. in Stockton, Cal., Wm. Gilbert.
5 Martha Maria, b. 28 Dec. 1827, in Dracut, Mass.; d. 15 Sept. 1828.
6 Sarah D., b. 12 Jan. 1830, in Lowell; unm. She lives with the Shakers in Canterbury.
7 Charles D., b. 2 Nov. 1833; m. Mary Refujio, dau. of Eujenio and Polonia Pice Garcia of Santa Barbara, Cal. He followed the sea, and at the time of his death was in the coasting trade between Santa Barbara and San Francisco. He died 24 Oct. 1878. Children:
   1 Isabelle V., b. 24 April 1862, in Stockton, Cal.
   2 Charles F., b. 5 Dec. 1863, in Santa Barbara.
   3 Mary J., b. 2 July 1865, on Santa Cruz Island.
   4 Isadora, b. 16 April 1867.
   5 Adella, b. 6 Sept. 1870, in Santa Barbara.
   6 Christina, b. 24 Dec. 1871.
   7 Clarence, b. April, 1872.
   8 Eujenio, b. 29 Jan. 1874.
   9 Alice F., b. 26 July 1878; d. 2 March 1880.

6-4-4-6-1

Caleb B. Libby, born in Epsom, N. H., 19 Nov. 1785; married, 1 Dec. 1816, Dorothy Avery, daughter of Jonathan and Martha (Dudley) Avery of Gilmanton, N. H.

He removed to Enosburgh, Vt., before his marriage, and cleared the farm on which he ever afterward lived. He died 10 March 1861. His widow died 11 April 1873. They were both members of the Freewill Baptist church.

Children, all born in Enosburgh:

1 Flavilla L., b. 30 Nov. 1818; m. 18 Dec. 1838, Charles S. Roberts.
2 Nathan, b. 17 Dec. 1820; m. 17 Dec. 1844, Emily, dau. of John and Armida Whitcomb of Enosburgh. He is a farmer. Children:
   1 Sophia W., b. 28 Oct. 1850, in Enosburgh; m. 4 April 1874, Eugene S. Pease of Enosburgh. Child:
      1 Mabel E. (Pease), b. 4 Jan. 1876.
   2 Fred O., b. 29 Nov. 1860, in Enosburgh.
   3 Edson A., b. 28 Aug. 1862, in Enosburgh.
3 Josiah A., b. 7 Nov. 1822; m. 1 Jan. 1849, Susan K., daughter of Hiram and Susannah (King) Smith of Bakersfield. He is a farmer. In 1876 he left Enosburgh and went west. He now lives in Fergus Falls, Minn. Children:
   1 Wilbur J., b. 22 May 1856, in Enosburgh; m. Mary, daughter of Mitchell and Maggie Duclos of Sheldon, Vt. Children:
      1 Herbert J., b. 29 Jan. 1876, in Fergus Falls.
      2 Leon E., b. 4 Jan. 1878.
      3 Maud I., b. 29 Dec. 1880.
   2 Herbert J., b. 21 Oct. 1858, in Bakersfield; d. 8 Dec. 1861.
   3 Hattie L., b. 27 Feb. 1862, in Irasburgh, Vt.
4 Levina A., b. 5 Aug. 1825; m. 2 March 1854, Hiram Ladd.
5 Pearson C., b. 22 Aug. 1827; d. 25 Dec. 1829.

6 Caleb J., b. 4 Nov. 1829; m. 16 June 1852, Emily J., dau. of Clark and Sally (Corse) Barnes of Enosburgh. He is a farmer in East Berkshire. Children:
 1 Emma F., b. 20 July 1853, in Enosburgh; m. 3 July 1873, Geo. W. Simonds; d. 6 June 1874, in Plattsburgh, N. Y.
 2 Sarah J., b. 20 May 1855.
 3 Clark B., b. 3 Jan. 1857; d. 27 Jan. 1862.
 4 Hattie A., b. 5 May 1858, in Derby; d. 25 Dec. 1861.
 5 Flora A., b. 16 July 1860.
 6 Katie B., b. 26 Feb. 1863; d. 9 April 1880.
 7 Frank J., b. 24 May 1865.
 8 Carlos M., b. 26 March 1868; d. 8 July 1870.
 9 Leon G., b. 7 Nov. 1872, in Enosburgh.
 10 Walter E., b. 22 Dec. 1874, in Berkshire.
 11 Myrtie A., b. 6 Jan. 1876.
7 James, b. 27 Feb. 1832; m. 1 Jan. 1856, Susan H., dau. of Harvey D. and Delia (Snell) Hayes of Enosburgh. He is a farmer in Enosburgh. Children:
 1 Fairetta, b. 4 Sept. 1858; d. 2 Jan. 1862.
 2 Fairetta, b. 3 April 1862.
 3 Flora R., b. 31 May 1866; d. 16 July 1866.
 4 Harvey C., b. 2 July 1869.
 5 Alma C., b. 28 May 1875; d. 5 April 1876.

6-4-4-6-2

Jonathan Pearson Libby, born in Epsom, N. H., 18 Nov. 1787; married Theodate Prescott, daughter of Samuel and Mary (Drake) Prescott of Epping.

He lived with his uncle Jonathan Pearson, in Epsom. He learned the trade of carpenter, and also taught school. After his marriage he lived in Pittsfield, where he was a member of the Congregational church, and for many years a justice of the peace. He died 26 Dec. 1847. His wife died 8 Nov. 1846.

Children, all born in Pittsfield:

1 Samuel Prescott, b. 4 May 1817; m. Nancy V. Rand of Deerfield. He lives in Bow. No children.
2 Mary Rebecca, b. 24 Aug. 1818; m. 23 July 1843, James M. Godfrey, now of Epping Corner, N. H.
3 Hannah Tucker, b. 8 Feb. 1820; m. Chas. Baker; d. 13 Feb. 1856, in Epping.
4 Eben Berry, b. 6 March 1822; m. 23 Aug. 1853, Ann E., dau. of Capt. John and Rachel (Low) Houstin of Nashua, N. H.; died in Nashua, 4 Oct. 1856. His widow lives with her son in Derry, N. H. Only child:
 1 Ina Elmore, [Dr.], b. 29 June 1854, in Nashua; m. 9 Dec. 1878, Kate Alice, dau. of Luther and Elizabeth (Smith) Gray of Nashua. He is a physician.
5 Betsey Drake, b. 24 July 1824; d. 29 July 1844.
6 Ruhama Pearson, b. 14 Feb. 1827; d. 6 May 1855; unm.
7 Theodate Ann, b. 19 June 1828; d. 2 Jan. 1852.
8 Susan Berry, b. 20 Dec. 1829; d. 1 Sept. 1846.
9 Sarah Caroline, b. 16 Feb. 1832; d. 7 May 1846.

6-4-4-6-3

Dea. John Batchelder Libby, born in Epsom, N. H., 8 Feb. 1790; married, 10 Feb. 1810, Abigail Clark, daughter of Ebenezer and Hannah (Holt) Clark of Enosburgh, Vt.

He was one of the first settlers of Enosburgh, and cleared the farm now owned by his son Luther and daughter Rebecca. There he lived until his death, 3 July 1843. He was deacon of the Freewill Baptist church. His wife died 14 Feb. 1843.

Children:

1 Rebecca P., b. 17 March 1812; m. 4 March 1846, Lucius Grant of Cambridge, Vt.
2 Simon, b. 11 Aug. 1814; m. 10 Jan. 1838, Caroline, dau. of Thomas and Rhoda (Brown) Potter of Waterville, Vt. He is a farmer. He removed from Enosburgh to Underhill, 1881. Children:
  1 Mary Jane, b. 4 June 1840; m. 20 Jan. 1868, John Stevens.
  2 Eliza, b. 1 April 1851; d. 22 Jan. 1868; unm.
  3 Monroe, b. 18 March 1853; unm.
  4 Alfred, b. 3 Oct. 1855; m. 11 June 1872, Ann, dau. of Almon and Elizabeth (Edwards) Gallup of Cambridge. He is a farmer. No children.
  5 Elvia M., b. 13 May 1862, in Bakersfield; m. 18 May 1875, Irvin Gleason.
3 Fanny M., b. 25 Nov. 1818; m. 24 Nov. 1824, Wm. H. Martin.
4 Hannah M., b. 16 Sept. 1820; d. 4 Jan. 1827.
5 Luther C., b. 24 Aug. 1823; m. 13 March 1849. Emily W., dau. of Lucius and Aurelia (Bennett) Grout of Elmore, Vt. He is a farmer, and occupies part of his father's homestead. He and his wife are members of the Methodist Church. Children:
  1 Melissa A., b. 7 June 1851; m. 19 Sept. 1872, Eugene G. Hall.
  2 John F., b. 13 March 1857; unm. He lives at home.
6 Angeline H., b. 28 Jan. 1830; m. 1 Feb. 1860, Wm. N. McAllister.

6-4-4-6-4

JAMES LIBBY, born in Strafford, Vt., 25 May 1792; married, Dec. 1813, ELIZA L. VAUGHAN, daughter of George and Emily (Wilkinson) Vaughan of Boston, Mass.

He went to Boston when 16 years old, and entered a dry goods store. He afterward went into business himself in Claremont, Vt., but after a few years, on account of the fall in goods resulting from the declaration of peace at the close of the war of 1812, his business proved unsuccessful. He returned to Boston, and while there became a member of the Congregational Church. About 1826 he removed to Albany, N. Y., and thence, a few years later, to Brooklyn. He was in business in both places, and in the latter lived until his death, 23 Nov. 1858. His widow still lives.

Children:

1 Nathaniel Smith, b. 1 Aug. 1816, in Boston. He followed the sea some years, and then settled in New York City, where he is now a carpenter. He has been twice married, but has no children.
2 Eliza Vaughan, b. 12 Nov. 1820, in Charlestown, Mass.; m. 11 Feb. 1846, Thaddeus B. Curtis.
3 James, b. Feb. 1821; m. Dorothea, dau. of Abigail P. (Libby) Dunaven, 6-4-4-6-5. When a boy he went into a ship-chandler's store in New York. After a few years he went to Burlington, Vt., where he was clerk in a store some years, and then went into business himself. He soon after removed to Buffalo, N. Y., where he still lives. He has had the office of city comptroller. He has two daughters and a son, James, a clerk in Buffalo.

4 George, b. 1822; d. 1823.
5 Walter, b. March, 1829, in Albany, N. Y.; d. 7 Dec. 1852; unm. He was an artist of much promise.
6 Emily Rebecca, b. 17 Dec. 1831; m. 4 Jan. 1849, Eben Barrows.
7 Caroline Maria, b. 10 Jan. 1838, in Brooklyn; unm. She lives with her mother.

6-4-4-8-7

NATHAN LIBBY, born in Epsom, N. H., 25 June 1808; married SAVALIA ABBOT, daughter of William and Dorcas (Parker) Abbot of Pembroke, N. H. He was a carpenter and wheelwright. The last twenty years of his life were spent in Philadelphia, Pa., where he followed teaming, and died 19 Oct. 1874. His widow still lives.

Children:

1 Elvira, b. 29 Jan. 1831, in Pembroke; m. 14 July 1853, in Lawrence, Mass., Joseph Clinton Boyden.
2 Charles, b. 5 Oct. 1832; d. 11 Aug. 1836.
3 Herman Osgood, b. 28 Dec. 1834; d. 19 March 1856; unm.
4 Cynthia Ann Osgood, b. 25 Oct. 1836; m. Jan. 1875, Daniel Parnum Thissell of Dracut.
5 Abigail, b. 19 Sept. 1838; m. 26 April 1860, John Stevens of Andover, Mass.
6 Charles, b. 20 March 1841, in Piermont; m. 25 April 1867, in Concord, N. H., Carrie A., dau. of Edw. and Nancy (Smith) Twates of Ottawa, Ont. He served nearly three years in the war. He has now worked for a long time in the Abbot Downing carriage shop in Concord. Children:
   1 Ella Abbie, b. 23 June 1868.
   2 Charles Edward, b. 6 May 1870.
7 Sarah Clay, b. 15 Sept. 1842; m. 20 Sept. 1867, Geo. F. Boyden.
8 Mary Abbot, b. 28 Nov. 1844, in Wentworth; m. 12 Oct. 1868, Stephen P. Richardson.
9 Henry Cutter, b. 16 Aug. 1846; m. 29 April 1879, Mary C., dau. of Amherst and Anne (Chase) Coult of Auburn, N. H. He is a mechanic; a member of the M. E. church.
10 George Nathan, b. 15 Oct. 1848. He is a clerk in a liquor saloon in Boston. He has been married, and it is thought has had children.

6-4-4-8-8

BENJAMIN FOWLER LIBBY, born in Epsom, N. H., 31 July 1813; married, 12 Nov. 1834, ALMIRA A. ROGERS, daughter of John and Polly (Eaton) Rogers of Greenfield, N. H. He learned the shoemaker's trade in Exeter, N. H., and has since confined himself almost exclusively to that calling. After his marriage he lived in Concord, until his removal, in 1859, to Lowell, Mass., his present residence.

Children:

1 Byron, b. 19 Sept. 1835, in Concord; m. Aug. 1857, Harriet, dau. of John and Judith (Johnson) Eaton of Concord. He has always been employed on railways. He has lived since 1861 in Quincy, Ill., and for many years has been superintendent of the stock yards of the C. B. & Q. R. R. In 1878, and twice since, he was elected an alderman of the city. Children:

1 Carrie, b. 9 April 1860, in Hannibal, Mo.; d. 27 June 1862.
2 Jennie, b. 11 Jan. 1862, in Quincy.
3 Carrie, b. 11 Aug. 1863.
4 Charles, b. 2 July 1866.

2 Mary Larkin, b. 24 Jan. 1841, in Epsom: d. 5 Sept. following.
3 Charles Henry, b. 18 Feb. 1843, in Concord: d. 23 Oct. 1864; unm. He had won praise in exhibiting and lecturing upon his brother's panoramas
4 John Fowler, b. 3 April 1846; unm. He is a scenic artist.

6-4-4-10-1

Nathan Libby, born in Stanstead, Que., 1 June 1801; married Mehitable Massey; died 9 June 1839.

Children:

1 Runannah, b. 14 Jan. 1823.
2 Barton, b. 12 Feb. 1825; m. Eliza Wells.
3 Charles, b. 10 Sept. 1827; died 1859.
4 Mary, b. 28 Feb. 1831.
5 Abraham, b. 19 Oct. 1833.
6 Alvah B., b. 19 Aug. 1835; lives in Medford, Minn.
7 John, (Joseph?), b. 4 Aug. 1837.
8 John, (Joseph?), b. 9 Jan. 1839.

6-4-4-10-2

William Libby, born in Stanstead, Que., 26 Feb. 1803; married, 3 March 1831, Diantha Jane Sinclair, daughter of David and Cynthia (Porter) Sinclair of Monmouth, Me.

He was a lumberman until his marriage, and then a farmer in Stanstead fourteen years. He then went to Boston and worked twenty years for the Fitchburgh Railroad as carpenter. He lost his hand in 1863, and since 1868 has been a gate-tender in Charlestown, for the same railroad.

Children:

1 Alfred W., b. 3 Oct. 1832, in Stanstead; m. 5 March 1857, Mary E., dau. of George and Fanny B. Lockwood of Saugus, Mass. He has been employed in a grocery store very many years. Children:
1 Ella F., b. 5 Jan. 1858, in East Saugus; died 17 April 1858.
2 Nellie F., b. 26 March 1860.
3 Annie L., b. 7 July 1862; d. 9 Dec. 1866.
4 Annie J., b. 27 May 1868.

2 Louisa Jane, b. 30 April 1834; m. Alphonzo Stoddard.
3 Royal James, b. 17 May 1836; died 31 May 1866; unm. He served three years in the American war.
4 Elsiemena, b. 29 May 1839; married 25 Dec. 1865, in Charlestown.
5 Lizzie Leola, b. 20 April 1855, in Charlestown; unm.

6-4-4-12-1

Isaac Libby, born in Epsom, N. H., 5 June 1802; married Lucy Sherborne, daughter of Margaret (Libby) Sherborne, 6-4-4-11. Upon his marriage he settled upon the farm in Cassville, Que., on which he ever afterward lived. He was a Freewill Baptist. His wife died 7 Sept. 1858, and he married second, Mrs. Sarah Knight, daughter of Nathaniel and Margaret (Wadley) Batchelder. He died 15 Feb. 1872.

Children:

1 Roxanna, b. 2 Nov. 1826; d. 26 Oct. 1848; unm.
2 Mary, b. 25 Aug. 1828; m. Noah Glidden; d. 7 Aug. 1870.
3 Lewis, b. 13 March 1830; d. 15 Jan. 1851; unm.
4 Emeline, b. 30 Oct. 1831; m. Harmon Phenix.
5 Harvey H., b. 5 June 1834; m. Sarah Ann, dau. of Sherburn and Susan Brown of Brown's Hill, Stanstead. At the age of 22, he, his father, and his uncle Gilman bought what is now known as Libby's Mills—grist and sawmills, blacksmith-shop and dwelling-houses. Hollis and George bought out their uncle Gilman, and later Harvey and Hollis bought out the others. They afterward divided, Harvey taking the sawmill which he since run in connection with farming. He and his wife are members of the Congregational church. Children:
  1 Nellie Frances, b. 7 Sept. 1860, at Libby's Mills.
  2 Erwin F., } twins, born } d. 13 Oct. 1865.
  3 Edwin Harvey, } 18 July 1865; } d. 3 Sept. 1865.
  4 Katie Maria, b. 31 Aug. 1867; d. 16 Aug. 1872.
6 George F., b. 10 Sept. 1835; m. 1st, 25 March 1866, Cordelia A., dau. of David B. and Lydia (Emery) Davis of Stanstead; (died 21 Aug. 1869); 2d, 9 Aug. 1877, Addie E., dau. of Daniel and Adaline E. (Partridge) Ames of Stockton, Me. He was engaged eight years with his brothers in the mills. He afterward began shipping produce to Lowell, Mass., and a few years after his marriage, removed there and became a salesman in the wholesale produce business. In 1875, he went into that business himself. He is a member of the Freewill Baptist church. Children:
  1 Cordelia D., b. 18 Aug. 1869; d. 28 Sept. 1869.
  2 Clarence I., b. 5 June 1878; d. 9 Aug. 1878.
7 Hollis, b. 23 July 1838; m. 1865, Orcelia Knight, daughter of his step-mother, by her first husband, Charles Knight. He owned in Libby's Mills many years and then sold out and became a farmer in Rock Island. Children:
  1 Mellie, b. 1871.
  2 Frank, b. 1874.
8 Lucy Ann, b. 29 Aug. 1840; m. John Sturm.
9 Austin Lyman, b. 9 May 1845; m. 25 Dec. 1873, Clara M., dau. of Horace and Mary J. (Jackson) Place of Hatley. He lives on his father's homestead, a farmer. He is a member of the Congregational church. Children:
  1 Harry Oscar, b. 23 Aug. 1875; d. 20 April 1877.
  2 Guy Place, b. 10 Jan. 1881.

6-4-5-6-1

James Libby, born in Fayette, Me., 20 Jan. 1797; married, 5 Feb. 1824, Mary Mosher, daughter of Brice and Peace (Gifford) Mosher of Wilton.

After he became of age he settled in Dexter, Me., and lived there about eight years, when he was persuaded by his step-father, Joshua Perley, to return to Temple, and live with him. He soon after bought his farm, and after about twenty years removed to Temple Village. He died with his son 12 Dec. 1880. He was a member of the Freewill Baptist church, and was the clerk many years.

Children:

1 James N., b. 24 April 1825, in Dexter, Me.; m. 27 Nov. 1856, Elmira, dau. of Isaac and Hannah (Woods) Russell of Farmington. He has been successively a farmer, shovel-handle maker, a mill-owner, country trader, and at present fruit-grower. Since his marriage he has lived in Temple, Farmington, West Farmington, and is now in Temple. No children.
2 Lewis Mosher, b. 11 March 1827; died 28 June 1879; unm. He lived alone on the homestead farm, and the circumstances of his death caused suspicion of foul play.
3 Mary Emeline, b. 8 Oct. 1834, in Temple; unm. She is in the Insane Asylum.

6-4-5-7-8

James Libby, born in Candia, N. H., 11 June 1811; married, 4 July 1836, Betsey Crosby of Lowell, Mass., born 2 Feb. 1807, daughter of Abraham and Mary (Tibbetts) Crosby.

He served an apprenticeship at the blacksmith's trade in Raymond, N. H., and ever afterward worked at it. He lived in Lowell, and North Chelmsford, Mass., and Brookfield, Vt. His latter years were spent in Lowell in the employ of the Boston and Lowell Railroad. He died 24 Oct. 1852; his widow still lives in Lowell.

Children:

1 Charles Freeman, b. 7 March 1837, in Lowell; m. 15 Nov. 1854, Julia Augusta Tinker, b. 30 July 1835, dau. of Joseph and Abigail (Jordan) Tinker of Ellsworth, Me. He has been engaged in the book business since 1854, in New York, Philadelphia, and Boston. He has been in the latter place since 1864, and is a member of the firm of Sullivan Bros. & Libby, book auctioneers. Children:
  1 Charles Freeman, b. 5 May 1860; is a printer.
  2 Mary Crosby, b. 15 Dec. 1862.
  3 Fred James, b. 28 March 1866.
  4 Sarah Elliot, b. 28 Aug. 1871; d. 11. Feb. 1872.
2 George Francis, b. 4 May 1840, in North Chelmsford; m. 3 June 1863, Rebecca F., dau. of Dr. George and Hannah (Patterson) Pierce of Lowell. The most of his life has been spent in Lowell. He is a member of the firm of H. H. Wilder & Co., stoves and kitchen furnishing goods. Children:
  1 Jennie Gertrude, b. 20 March 1864, in Lowell.
  2 George Crosby, b. 15 Dec. 1867, in Lowell.
3 Betsey Amanda, b. 16 June 1840; d. 21 Feb. 1847.

6-4-5-8-7

William King Libby, born in Palermo, Me., 25 Oct. 1808; married Caroline Mains, daughter of James and Martha (Blair) Mains of Woolwich, Me.

He followed the sea from boyhood, and continued that calling some years after marriage, rising to the master's position. Upon quitting the sea he engaged in pressing, or "screwing" hay. In 1845 he removed his family from Woolwich to Augusta. He began work as ship-carpenter, and being naturally of a mechanical turn, soon became a first-class workman. After about ten years he removed to Hallowell, from which place he enlisted in Co. D, 30th Me. Vol. He died in the hospital in New Orleans, La., 28 June 1864. His widow still lives.

Children:

1 Jacob, b. 6 Oct. 1830, in Woolwich; m. 16 Dec. 1869, in Hallowell, Betsey T., dau. of William S. and Mary A. (Douglass) Gordon of Manchester. He was a riverman many years, and since 1866 has been a member of the lumber firm of Burrill & Libby, Augusta. No children.

2 William Henry, b. 2 March 1832; m. 15 Nov. 1853, Mehitable D., dau. of James and Sarah (Getchell) Tibbetts of Augusta. He came to maturity in Augusta, where he has since lived. Up to 1860 he worked at river-driving and ship-carpentering. In winter he also taught writing-school in many towns in Kennebec County. In the year mentioned he was appointed to a place on the police force, being elected to the city council the same year. From 1861, five years, he was city marshal of Augusta. From 1864 until 1877 he was deputy U. S. marshal for the district of Maine. Since 1865 he has been a coroner of Kennebec County. In 1867 he became a deputy sheriff for his county, and held that position until 1875, when he was elected sheriff, to which office he was elected two terms following. He has also served five years as alderman. Children:
1 Carrie M., b. 2 Oct. 1854; unm.
2 Mary H., b. 14 Nov. 1856; d. 16 July 1862.
3 William H., b. 7 April 1860.
4 Walter F., b. 2 April 1862.
5 Mary A., b. 7 June 1864.
6 Augusta, b. 23 Dec. 1866.
7 Arthur D., b. 15 April 1870.
8 Charles H., b. 19 Dec. 1872.

3 James M., b. 30 Sept. 1833; unm. He followed the sea from 17, and soon after adopted Mobile, Ala., as his home. He served in the Union army in the war.

4 Louisa W., b. 14 Jan. 1836; died 14 July 1879; unm.

5 Jackson M., b. 22 Oct. 1837; m. 28 Jan. 1860, Harriet Frances, dau. of Augustus L. and Mary E. (Owen) Dunn of Augusta. He was formerly connected with the logging business on the Kennebec, but has since been connected with the state house, of which he is now engineer and janitor. He served nearly two years in Co. E, 3d Me. Vol. Children:
1 Frank J., b. 13 Aug. 1863, in Hallowell.
2 Florence G., b. 16 June 1867, in Augusta.
3 Minnie, b. 31 Jan. 1870.
4 Alice May, b. 9 Aug. 1875.

6 Mariah H., b. 13 Sept. 1841; is married in the West.

7 Edwin H., b. 26 July 1843; m. 6 Aug. 1870, Ella E., dau. of Greenlief and Lusanah Lord. He is a teamster in Hallowell. Children:
1 Charles, b. 8 July 1873; died 24 July 1873.
2 Maud, b. 26 July 1875; died 14 Feb. 1876.

8 Joseph Lincoln, b. 22 June 1847; m. Julia E. Nolan of Augusta. He has been turnkey and afterward jailor in the county jail, but now lives in Hallowell. Child:
1 Lottie M., b. Dec. 1879.

9 John H., twin with the last, b. 22 June 1847; m. Jennette Meigs. He is a barber in Hallowell. Child:
1 Harry J., b. 1871.

10 Caroline A., b. 10 June 1852; m. George Coutts; died 2 May 1875.

6-4-8-2-4

William Seavey Libby, born in Rye, N. H., 26 Feb. 1787; married first, 23 Sept. 1809, in Salem, Mass., Sarah Farrington, daughter of Deacon Daniel and Sarah Farrington of Windsor, Vt.; (died 20 June 1826, in Newburgh, N. Y.); second, 25 July 1827, Elizabeth Winfield, daughter of Dr. Richard Winfield of New York City.

In his early years he lived in Salem, Mass., and was a member of the Tabernacle Church there. Soon after his marriage he removed to Newburgh, N. Y., where he was an architect and builder about fifty years. His last years were spent at New Brighton, Staten Island, where he died 28 April 1869. His widow survives.

Children, all born in Newburgh; by first wife:

1 Sarah, b. 14 Oct. 1810; m. Wm. Pembroke; d. 15 July 1880.
2 Mehitable, b. 5 Dec. 1812; d. 17 March 1836; unm.
3 Anne, b. 11 Nov. 1814; m. 5 May 1841, Augustns W. Sexton.
4 Jane, b. 14 Feb. 1817; m. July 1844, Buckley C. Morse.
5 William, b. 7 March 1820; m. Elizabeth Marsh.
6 Rachel Farrington, b. 2 March 1822; d. 13 April 1840.
7 Elizabeth Farrington, b. 17 May 1824; unm.
8 Maria, b. 16 June 1826; d. 11 July 1826.

By second wife:

9 Mary Virginia, b. 9 Sept. 1828; m. Benj. L. Amerman of New York City.

6-4-8-3-1

David Libby, born in Epsom, N. H., 17 Dec. 1779; married, 4 Oct. 1804, Martha Dolbeer, daughter of Nicholas and Mary (Randall) Dolbeer of Epsom, previously of Rye.

Upon his marriage he bought a farm chiefly in Allenstown, but on the Epsom line, and lived there more than 35 years. When his son Michael bought the old homestead in Epsom, he went onto it with him. He died 16 May 1843. His widow died 22 April 1854.

Children, all born in Epsom:

1 John, b. 6 Aug. 1805; died same day.
2 Michael M., b. 30 Nov. 1806; m. 1st, 15 Oct. 1834, Mary, dau. of John and Abigail (Blake) Moulton of Kensington, N. H.; (died 23 July 1854); 2d. 30 May 1855, Mrs. Susan C. Goss, dau. of Samuel and Susannah (Churchill) Badger of Deerfield. He was a farmer. After his marriage he lived a few years in Stratham and Kensington, and then, in 1842, settled on his grandfather's homestead in Epsom. There he died 5 Nov. 1862. He was an earnest christian. His second wife died 11 March 1862, without children. Children, by first wife:
   1 Mary B., b. 6 June 1835, in Stratham; was a teacher eighteen years; m. 11 Feb. 1875, Calvin Dowst.
   2 Martha A., b. 22 Nov. 1837; unm. She and her sister occupy the homestead farm.
   3 Emma A., b. 2 July 1840, in Kensington; d. 2 Oct. 1860.
3 Mary D., b. 4 Oct. 1809; m. 3 May 1832, John Durgin of Barnstead; lives in Exeter, N. H. Children:

1 George Oscar (Durgin). b. 23 March 1834, in Salisbury, Mass.; m. 27 July 1860, Margaret, dau. of John and Kate (Dee) Cheney of Ireland. He is an express messenger, living in Portland. Children:
  1 Warren (Durgin), b. 3 April 1861, in Exeter, N. H.; d. 8 April 1863.
  2 Henry G. (Durgin), b. 29 Aug. 1862.
  3 Carl Oscar (Durgin), b. 19 Jan. 1864.
  4 Mary L. (Durgin), b. 29 Nov. 1865.
  5 Martha L. (Durgin), b. 23 Nov. 1868, in Lewiston, Me.
  6 John (Durgin), b. 23 Nov. 1868.
  7 Percy (Durgin), b. 26 Dec. 1870.
  8 Annie May (Durgin), b. 20 Nov. 1872, in Portland, Me.; d. 7 March 1873.
  9 George Ellery (Durgin), b. 13 May 1875.
2 Lucinda E. (Durgin), m. 1st, Andrew J. Haines; 2d, Fred F. Pike.
3 Daniel V. (Durgin), died in hospital at Baton Rouge, La., June, 1863. He was a private in the 8th N. H. Vol.
4 Mary (Durgin).

4 David, b. 14 Feb. 1813; d. 3 Aug. 1819.
5 Lucinda, b. 15 July 1815; m. 16 Dec. 1842, Daniel F. Wadleigh of Kensington; died 12 Aug. 1873, in Green Ridge, Mo.
6 David, b. 8 Aug. 1819; m. 26 July 1846, Dolly J., dau. of Pelatiah and Sophia (Demerit) Jones of Lee. In his younger days he was employed in stone work. 29 May 1854, in Paradise, Penn., while drilling out an old charge, it exploded, destroying his sight. He has since, as before, lived in Manchester, N. H., employed in the manufacture and sale of brooms, and the sale of washing machines, etc. Children:
  1 ——, born and died 30 Nov. 1847.
  2 Eugene, b. 22 March 1850; d. 20 Aug. 1852.
  3 Eugene G., b. 29 Aug. 1855; m. 2 July 1877, Annie, dau. of Owen and Delia McCloskey of Somerville, Mass. He and Frank are in the tripe and tallow business, in South Hooksett. No children.
  4 Frank H., b. 17 Aug. 1857; m. 31 May 1881. Ida A., dau. of Arah W., and Anna J. (Ward) Prescott of Hooksett.
7 Martha J., b. 6 July 1822; d. 11 July 1840.

6-4-8-3-2

Levi Libby, born in Epsom, N. H., 1782; married Abigail Farrington, of Pittsfield, N. H. He was a farmer in his native town, and died there July, 1821. His widow died 22 Oct. 1855.

Children:

1 Nancy, b. 1813; m. 1st, John Hackett; 2d, Sherburne Haynes; 3d, Joseph Perkins.
2 Abraham Rowell, b. 22 July 1815; m. Elizabeth Jane Hildreth.
3 Moses, b. 25 April 1817; m. Elizabeth G. Parlin.
4 Levi W., b. 1819; died 19 Oct. 1868, in Provincetown. He first married Mary J. Lancaster of Cherryfield, Me., and then a woman from the Provinces. He was in the stage and livery business.

6-4-8-3-3

Richard Libby, born in Epsom, N. H., 1784; married first, Esther Langley, daughter of James and Esther (Shaw) Langley of Deerfield; (died 17 Nov. 1817); second, 19 Nov. 1818, Mrs.

Miriam (Collins) Goodhue; (died 8 Jan. 1824); third, ABIGAIL CHASE, daughter of Moses and Susan (Kelley) Chase of Deerfield.

He owned and occupied several farms in the immediate vicinity of his birthplace, and the last twenty years of his life were spent in Allenstown where he died 11 Feb. 1866. His widow died in Epsom, 23 July 1870.

Children, all born in Epsom, by first wife:

1 Esther, b 27 Nov. 1810; m. John Wiggins of Hooksett.
2 Isaac, b. 24 April 1812; m. Amy ——; lives in Deerfield, N. H. He was many years a milkman in Lowell, Mass., where his wife now lives. No children.
3 True, b. 15 Nov. 1814; died aged seven days.
4 Mirrian, b. 4 May 1816; m. Joseph Glover of Canterbury, N. H.
5 Ruth, b. 8 Nov. 1817; m. Eben Chase of Boscawen.

By third wife:

6 Moses, b. 12 Oct. 1826; m. 12 May 1864, Rosetta, dau. of True and Eliza Langley of Deerfield. He is a farmer and settled on a farm in Epsom, previously occupied by his father. Children:
    1 Etta I., b. 12 March 1865, in Allenstown.
    2 Walter R., b. 14 July 1867.
    3 James T., b. 5 Nov. 1869.
    4 Kidder H., b. 5 Jan. 1872, in Epsom.
    5 John L., b. 12 June 1874.
7 Theodate, b. 1 Jan. 1828; d. 11 July 1861.

6-4-8-3-7

JESSE LIBBY, born in Epsom, N. H., 1790; married, 27 June 1816, RACHEL TANDY of Deerfield. He died in Allenstown, Dec. 1862.

Children:

1 Charles.
2 Jane.
3 William T., b. 30 April 1822; m. Eleanor M. ——.
4 Electra.

6-4-8-4-3

JOEL LIBBY, born in Gorham, Me., 10 Oct. 1792; married first, 21 Dec. 1815, JOANNA CLAY, daughter of Thomas Clay of Gorham; (died 11 March 1817, in Gorham); second, 31 Jan. 1819, FANNY SILLA of Gorham.

He was a carpenter by trade. He owned and lived on, successively, farms in Baldwin, Gorham, and Raymond. He died in the latter town, 22 July 1856. His widow died 24 May 1871.

Children, by first wife:

1 Walter, b. 7 June 1816, in Gorham; m. 2 June 1839, Ruth C. Libby, 6-4-8-13-1. He is a farmer and carpenter in Albany, where he has lived since 1838. Children:
    1 Abigail Ann Priscilla, b. 30 May 1841; m. Sept. 1870, Oakes P. Wilbur.
    2 Benjamin Joel, b. 15 Nov. 1843; d. 8 Dec. 1871; unm. He was a carpenter.

3 Stephen Wentworth, b. 12 Nov. 1845; unm. He is a miller.
4 Thomas Albion, b. 25 March 1850; m. 1 Dec. 1877, Ida, dau. of Wm. Perley and Clara A. (Oliver) Putnam of Bethel. He is a farmer. Children:
  1 Anna, b. 6 June 1878, in Albany.
  2 Fanny, b. 30 Aug. 1880, in Albany.
5 Samuel Wells, b. 10 Sept. 1855; unm. He is a carpenter and mill-hand.

By second wife:

2 Ephraim Silla, b. 2 Jan. 1820, in Baldwin; m. 5 Aug. 1846, Mary Quimby, dau. of Isaac R. and Betsey (Quimby) Warren of Denmark, Me. Since his marriage he has lived for the most part on his farm in Denmark, but is a carpenter by trade, and has worked in many places in this and neighboring states. Children:
  1 Elizabeth Ann, b. 23 Oct. 1849, in Dracut, Mass.; m. 1st, 20 Sept. 1865, Edw. Dresser; (died 15 Nov. 1876); 2d, 2 Jan. 1878, Osborne Foster Richardson. Children:
    1 Mary Pink (Dresser), b. 20 Dec. 1866.
    2 Hattie Drusilla (Dresser), b. 10 May 1868.
    3 Edward Burton (Dresser), b. 24 April 1872.
    4 Perley Foster (Richardson), b. 7 Feb. 1879.
  2 Orren Quimby, b. 23 Sept. 1851, in Dracut; m. 21 Jan. 1874, Mary Abby, dau. of Wm. E. and Betsey B. (Smith) Brown of East Fryeburgh. He is a farmer. Children:
    1 Fannie Etherlyn, b. 22 June 1875.
    2 Dana Quimby, b. 29 March 1880.
3 Levi, b. 9 Dec. 1821; m. 2 Oct. 1859, Esther, dau. of Geo. and Abigail (Estes) Knights of Standish. Before his marriage he was a lumberman. Upon his father's death he bought out the other heirs to the homestead in Raymond, and has since lived on it. Child:
  1 Annie Mildred, b. 10 July 1861.
4 Lot Davis, b. 8 Feb. 1824; m. 14 Oct. 1855, Hannah McLain. He is a farmer and has lived in many places, but is now in Windham. Children:
  1 Lucy, b. 4 June 1857, in Raymond.
  2 Charles, b. 31 Aug. 1868 in Raymond.
5 Joanna, b. 20 June 1826; m. Samuel Gilson.
6 Martha Silla, b. 13 Feb. 1829, in Gorham; m. 1st, 11 Aug. 1850, Nathan Mason; 2d, Benj. Davis.
7 Charles Edwin, b. 18 Oct. 1831; m. 18 Oct. 1859, Rebecca S., dau. of Samuel and Mary Cash of Casco. He has been chiefly employed as farmer, mill-hand, etc. He lives in Gorham. Children:
  1 Mary Jane, b. 26 Oct. 1863, in Raymond.
  2 Lizzie Ellen, b. 2 Oct. 1865.
  3 Sarah Ross Towle, b. 2 May 1869, in Gorham; d. 22 March 1878.
  4 Nellie Mildred, b. 3 July 1877.
8 Tyng, b. 30 May 1835; m. 1st, 26 May 1865, Mary Brazier of Raymond; 2d, 26 April 1876, in Gloucester, Mass., Mrs. Mary E. Barter. He served three years in the war. He now lives in Gloucester. No children.

6-4-8-5-3

Thomas Libby, born in Gorham, Me., 1798; married Nancy Hilborn, dau. of Robert and Betsey (Stockman) Hilborn of Oxford, Me.

He was a cooper and farmer. He settled in Oxford on a farm, and there died, 3 Jan. 1852. His widow occupied the homestead until her death, 25 Aug. 1863.

Children, all born in Oxford:

1 Andrew Jackson, b. 1 Nov. 1828; m. Caroline E. Blake; died 3 June 1863, in Oxford. His wife died 16 May 1863, in Great Falls, N. H. He was at first a farmer, and then in the fancy goods business in Great Falls. No children.
2 Mary Louisa, b. 11 Dec. 1832; married Warren Soule of New York City.
3 William Stockman, b. 17 July 1835; married, at the age of 18, Margaret W., dau. of John and Susan Flye of Hiram. He lives in Faribault, Minn. Children:
   1 Llewla, b. 11 Oct. 1855; was killed by a runaway horse in Great Falls, N. H., 7 Sept. 1860.
   2 Llewellyn Hubert, b. 9 March 1869.
4 Esther Ann, b. 24 Aug. 1838; m. John B. Greene of Lewiston.
5 Harriet Ellen, b. 23 July 1844; lives with Mary; unm.
6 Francis Augustus, b. 28 Dec. 1845; m. 6 Sept. 1864, Julia S., dau. of Wm. and Belinda (Ingalls) Morrison of Sweden, Me. He learned the blacksmith's trade, and worked as journeyman until his marriage. He then served one year in the 30th Me. Vol., and upon his return settled on the farm in Bridgton, which he has since occupied. Children:
   1 George Albert, b. 22 June 1869.
   2 Linda May, b. 28 Oct. 1871.
   3 Warren Soule, b. 2 Jan. 1875.
   4 Myron Leroy, b. 28 July 1878.
7 Sarah Jane, b. 8 Aug. 1848; m. N. John Shannon of Rochester, Minn.
8 Justina Alice, b. 3 Feb. 1850; m. Harry W. Zeller of Waseca, Minn.

6-4-8-5-4

Samuel Libby, born in Gorham, Me., 5 Oct. 1799; married, 21 Oct. 1833, Sally Libby, 10-5-4-1-1-3. He was a farmer. One year after his marriage he settled on the farm which he afterward lived on, now occupied by his widow and son. He died 18 April 1875.

Children:

1 William Henry Peabody, b. 16 May 1834; died 14 April 1840.
2 Phineas Ingalls, b. 23 Aug. 1838; m. 10 Jan. 1860, Eliza Ellen, dau. of Joseph and Eliza (Walker) Ricker of Peru, Me. He is a well-to-do farmer; also a shoemaker. Children:
   1 ——, b. 17 Jan., d. 12 Feb., 1864.
   2 Louella Dockum, b. 14 April 1865.
   3 Mabel Florence, b. 29 Oct. 1867; d. 29 June 1880.
   4 Nellie Adell, b. 31 May 1874; d. 22 July 1880.
3 Albert Francis, b. 20 Oct. 1843; d. 14 Jan. 1845.
4 William F., b. 10 Nov. 1845; d. 9 July 1862.

6-4-8-5-5

Asa Libby, born in Gorham, Me., about 1802; married, first, Abigail Douglass, daughter of John and —— (Gray) Douglass of Denmark, Me.; (died 14 March 1831, in Denmark); second, Mary Kennison, daughter of David and Delilah Kennison of Denmark.

He was a cooper by trade and always worked at it, but living on a farm. He lived in Denmark until 1851, when he settled on a farm in West Bridgton. In 1870, he bought the house in Bridgton Center, now occupied by his children, and there died 25 Nov. 1874. His widow died 11 April 1875.

Children, by first wife:

1 Thomas, b. 27 July 1824, in Denmark; m. 1st, 9 Aug. 1846, in Westbrook, Susan, dau. of Thomas Roberts; (died 1 Feb. 1852); 2d, in Laurelton, Penn., Ann, dau. of William and Eliza (Switzer) Pursley of Laurelton. Since 1852, he has been in Union Co., Penn., most of the time lumbering, but now farming. Children, by first wife:
  1 Ann Maria, b. 2 Aug. 1847, in Cape Elizabeth, Me.; m. L. W. Brown.
  2 Fannie, b. 22 Oct. 1851, in Cape Elizabeth; m. F. O. Bolton.

By second wife, all born in Laurelton:

  3 William, b. 12 Oct. 1858; m. 24 June 1880, Vesta, dau. of Daniel and Elizabeth (Marts) Horner. Child:
    1 James, b. 17 Dec. 1880.
  4 John, b. 16 Feb. 1861.
  5 James, b. 18 Feb. 1862.
  6 Cary, b. 19 Nov. 1864.
  7 Thomas, b. 28 Nov. 1865; d. 12 Sept. 1870.
  8 Asa, b. 19 Nov. 1866.
  9 Samuel, b. 19 Aug. 1867; d. 12 Sept. 1870.
  10 David, b. 1 Jan. 1869.
  11 Mary Ellen, b. 7 Dec. 1875.
  12 Charles, b. 7 Aug. 1878.

2 Asa, b. 5 June 1826; d. 1 May 1827.

3 Asa, b. 25 March 1829; m. 14 Nov. 1855, Harriet O., dau. of William and Dorothy (Cobb) Bragdon of Limington. He is a farmer in Gorham. His wife died 25 March 1879, and he married, 28 Feb. 1880, Augusta Marine. Children:
  1 Charles Llewellyn, b. 15 March 1859, d. 3 Oct. 1863.
  2 Hattie Ella, b. 20 May 1865; d. 29 March 1880.
  3 Charles Frank, b. 5 Sept. 1868; d. 20 March 1871.
  4 William, b. 24 June 1870.
  5 Leslie, b. 24 Sept. 1874; d. 5 April 1880.

4 William Franklin, b. 25 Feb. 1831; d. 10 May 1832.

By second wife:

5 Nathan Granville, b. 9 Nov. 1843; d. 24 Jan. 1862. He was a private in Co. E, 12th Maine.

6 Mary Abbie, b. 1 June 1849; m. July, 1874, Curtis Gray.

7 Jane Delia, b. 30 June 1852; m. 3 Sept. 1878, Frank Ham.

8 Samuel Nelson, b. 9 Sept. 1854; d. 14 May 1872, in Worcester, Mass.

9 Reuben Edward, b. 11 Nov. 1856; unm.

10 Hattie Alice, b. 12 Jan. 1862; unm.

6-4-8-9-4

Clement Phinney Libby, born in Pownal, Me., 8 May 1805; married, 22 Oct. 1829, Caroline Cottle, daughter of Ezra and Anna (Snow) Cottle of Bucksport.

He went from Thorndike to Bucksport in 1827, and was married there two years later. He has since lived in Hampden, Unity, and his present residence, Freedom, a farmer. He is a member of the Methodist church.

Children:

1 Rebecca Ann, b. 2 Nov. 1830; m. 13 Dec. 1854, Daniel Webster.

2 George Henry, b. 2 Aug. 1832; m. 5 July 1853, Sylvia, dau. of Sylvanus and Eleanor (Cottle) Simpson. After his marriage he removed to Winona, Minn., where his wife died, 26 Sept. 1856, and his two children about the same time. He has since been engaged in mining and is now in Colorado.
3 James Alford, b. 15 Aug. 1834; d. 15 April 1864, in Unity; unm. He was a farmer, and spent two years in Minnesota, where he caught the cold which caused his death.
4 Alonzo Emery, b. 15 March 1837; m. 24 Dec. 1862, Adeline, dau. of Lorenzo Dow and Lorana (Rackliff) McGray of Unity; died 21 Aug. 1867. He served two years in Co. A, 4th Me. Vol., and rose to be 1st Lieut. He died of consumption. His widow married, 3 May 1880, Edmund Fuller. Son:
    1 James W., b. 30 Oct. 1866.

6-6-1-2-1

Jacob Libby, born in St. Stephen, N. B., 1 Aug. 1785; married, 11 June 1806, Elizabeth Dowdall, daughter of John Dowdall of Magaguadovic, N. B. He died in his native town, 9 Aug. 1858. His wife died 15 May 1855.

Children, all born in St. Stephen:

1 Jane, b. 14 April 1807; m. Jacob Tuttle.
2 William H., b. 3 Aug. 1808; m. Fanny Cushion, and Piety Barter.
3 Eliza, b. 25 Jan. 1810; m. Andrew P. Bunker.
4 Adeline, b. 9 July 1811; m. Aaron Palmer.
5 Lucinda, b. 3 May 1813; m. Samuel Perkins.
6 Ellis, b. 22 Nov. 1815; m. Abigail K. Tuttle.
7 Rebecca M., b. 19 Nov. 1817; m. Moses Carleton.
8 Hannah M., b. 14 Nov. 1820; m. Allan McDonald.
9 Sarah A., b. 3 March 1823; m. Samuel N. Howe.
10 Levi W., b. 31 Aug. 1825; went to California, and his whereabouts are now unknown.
11 Charles J., b. 14 Dec. 1827; m. Levina Falkonham.
12 Mary T., b. 24 Nov. 1830; m. John Fairfield.
13 Roxanna, b. 17 Nov. 1835.

6-6-1-2-2

James Libby, born in St. Stephen, N. B., 5 Nov. 1788; married, 28 June 1810, Levina Stiles of Dorchester, N. B., born 21 June 1790. He was a farmer and lumberman, and always lived at St. Stephen. After his death his farm was divided. The house lot is now owned by Robert Moore. He was a member of the Methodist church. 16 March 1858, he died, and his widow, 20 Dec. 1860.

Children, all born in St. Stephen:

1 John, died, aged a few weeks.
2 Mary E., b. 14 June 1812; m. William Haley of St. Mary's Bay, N. S.
3 Jacob, b. 2 Sept. 1814; m. 16 Nov. 1845, Phebe Shaw, dau. of Mary S. (Libby) Hanson, 6-6-1-2-7. He engaged in lumbering on the St. Croix River for himself until 1856, and has since been in the employ of Alex Gibson, first at Lephreaux, and then at Marysville, whither he moved his family in 1867. Children, all born in St. Stephen:
    1 Unity, b. 4 Oct. 1846; died 26 March 1847.
    2 Lucilla L., b. 24 Feb. 1848; died 5 July 1849.
    3 Clara A., b. 18 March 1850; unm.

4 Howard A., b. 4 June 1852; unm. Since 1876 he has been a bookkeeper in Eureka, Cal.
5 Georgianna, b. 17 June 1854; unm.
6 Freeman H. T., b. 5 Nov. 1856; unm.
7 Jacob Judd, b. 8 May 1859.
8 Hezekiah McK., b. 13 Aug. 1861; died 25 Feb. 1863.

4 Josiah S., b. 17 Dec. 1816; m. 5 Oct. 1835, Charlotte, dau. of James and Mehitable (Hanson) Hanson. He is a farmer and lumberman. He lived just outside St. Stephen until a few years since, when he removed to his present residence in Calais, Me. No children.
5 Elizabeth D., b. 13 June 1820; unm.
6 Hannah B., b. 3 March 1823; m. 16 Jan. 1841, Elias Foster.
7 Julia C., b. 17 April 1825; m. James Turner of St. Patrick, N. B.
8 William Parker, b. 13 Dec. 1828; unm. He is a farmer in St. Stephen.
9 James, b. 21 Jan. 1831; d. 9 June 1839.
10 Robert Webb, b. 21 May 1833; m. 8 April 1852, Catherine, dau. of Harry and Eliza (Young) Hatch of St. Patrick. He is a farmer and carpenter in St. Stephen. Children:
1 Styles, b. 7 March 1853; d. 1 Jan. 1857.
2 Arthur H., b. 24 Jan. 1857.
3 Christiana, b. 13 Aug. 1859.
4 Lillian M., b. 1 Sept, 1865.
5 Robert A., b. 8 July 1870.

6-6-1-2-8

Capt. William Parker Libby, born in St. Stephen, N. B., 24 Oct. 1798; married 21 Sept. 1828, Lucy F. Crocker, daughter of Robinson and Jane (Marple) Crocker. He was always engaged in the lumber business. He was a member of the Methodist church and a captain in the militia. He died in St. Stephen, 12 Oct. 1857. His widow still lives.

Children, all born in St. Stephen:

1 George Brewer, b. 14 July 1829; died 1860, in Peru; unm.
2 William Robinson, b. 14 April 1831; was drowned in 1861; unm.
3 John Warren, b. 14 April 1833; went to California early, and has not been heard from for some years.
4 Rowland Crocker, b. 15 March 1835; married, in Minnesota, Helen Mudgett. He is in the lumber business in Hastings, Minn. Child:
1 Helen May, b. about 1867.
5 Unity Jane, b. 3 April 1837; d. 22 Aug. 1838.
6 Amanda Jane, b. 3 Oct. 1839; m. Moses Porter Upton.
7 Lucy Maria, b. 10 July 1842; m. 1 Jan. 1856, Albert G. Olney.
8 Timothy C., b. 23 March 1845.

6-6-1-5-2

Asa Libby, born in St. Stephen, N. B., 8 Aug. 1786; married, 6 Dec. 1815, Abigail Cutler Stone, daughter of David and Deborah (Chesley) Stone of Milford, Me.

In his youth he was a ship-carpenter and sailor, and at the age of 24 enlisted in the British army. When the war of 1812 broke out he deserted and went to Maine. He lived in Edingburg from 1815 until 1833, and then in Howland until 1840. During those years he was employed on the river and in the woods. In 1840 he became a farmer in Greenbush, Me., where he died 7 Feb. 1854. During his later years he was an earnest member of the Freewill Baptist church.

Children:

1 Sally A., b. 6 Dec. 1816, in Edingburg; d. 23 Oct. 1835.
2 Mary S., b. 1 Nov. 1818; m. 23 June 1853, in Marysville, Cal., Louis H. Bonestell. She was one of the first teachers in San Francisco.
3 Joseph E., b. 1 May 1820; was drowned 29 April 1842, while river-driving at Passadumkeag Falls.
4 Nancy D., b. 12 Jan. 1823; m. 20 July 1845, Isaac Young; died 10 May 1863.
5 Almira B., b. 29 March 1825; died 4 Oct. 1836.
6 David S., b. 22 Aug. 1828; m. 23 March 1857, Mary A., dau. of Henry and Susan (Low) Young of Greenbush. He is by trade a carpenter, but has been chiefly engaged in lumbering. He was a private in Co. D, 9th Me. Vol. In 1876 he went to San Francisco as clerk for J. G. Hodge & Co., and on the failure of that house in 1878, went to Nevada, and was engaged two years in putting machinery into quartz mills. He now lives in Newport Village in his native county. Children:
  1 Flora, b. 2 July 1858, in Greenbush; m. 13 Sept. 1879, John M. Holbrook.
  2 Alice, b. 23 June 1866.
  3 Charles Truman, b. 2 Nov. 1868.
7 Lydia A., b. 2 Feb. 1831; m. 24 Aug. 1851, James M. White.
8 Emma M., b. 5 Dec. 1833, in Howland; m. Sept. 1867, in San Francisco, John Truman Bonestell, brother of Louis.
9 Sarah E., b. 11 Dec. 1836; unm.
10 Abba M., b. 14 Aug. 1840; m. 15 June 1862, Charles L. Young.

6-6-1-5-10

STEPHEN R. LIBBY, born in St. Stephen, N. B., 12 Jan. 1809; married MARY HANSON. He is a farmer in his native town.

Children, all born in St. Stephen:

1 Asa, b. 11 May 1832; is a farmer. Children:
  1 Stephen R., b. 18 Dec. 1860.
  2 John F., b. 30 May 1862.
  3 Cordelia E., b. 8 March 1864.
  4 Charles C., b. 1 Feb. 1866.
  5 Susannah L., b. 7 Dec. 1869.
  6 Asa L., b. 15 Nov. 1871.
  7 Alford H., b. 25 June 1874.
  8 Nehemiah M., b. 25 Feb. 1876; died 26 Aug. 1878.
  9 David A., b. 29 Nov. 1878; died 4 July 1881.
2 Charles W., b. 29 July 1834; is a farmer. Children:
  1 John H., b. 24 June 1861.
  2 Mary E., b. 11 March 1863.
  3 Charles M., b. 18 Dec. 1865.
  4 Sarah E., b. 7 Feb. 1867.
  5 Addra A., b. 5 March 1869.
  6 Jane A., b. 13 Aug. 1872.
  7 Effie A., b. 4 Sept. 1874.
  8 Florence E., b. 4 Sept. 1876.
3 Jane A., b. 15 Aug. 1836.
4 David W., b. 15 March 1839; is a carpenter in St. Stephen. Children:
  1 William H., b. 22 March 1860.
  2 Mary E., b. 24 Sept. 1862.

Yours Truly D. S. Libbey

3 Schyler F., b. 24 Sept. 1864; died 1 Oct. 1864.
4 Elizabeth A., b. 5 Nov. 1865; died 19 Nov. 1865.
5 Schyler F., b. 18 Dec. 1866.
6 David J., b. 31 March 1869; died 31 March 1869.
7 Sarah A., b. 5 Nov. 1870.
8 David J., b. 5 July 1872.
9 Almer, b. 21 Sept. 1875.

5 Stephen R., b. 19 May 1846; is a carpenter. Children:
1 Ida E., b. 19 May 1865.
2 Susie M., b. 2 March 1867.
3 David S., b. 4 May 1869.
4 George H., b. 24 June 1872.
5 Frederick H., b. 24 Jan. 1875.
6 William T., b. 7 Jan. 1879.

6 James W., b. 25 Dec. 1849; is a farmer. Children:
1 Stephen R., b. 12 Oct. 1872.
2 Henry H., b. 13 Nov. 1874.
3 Willard F., b. 27 March 1876.
4 Clara M., b. 9 Dec. 1880.

7 Mary F., b. 9 Feb. 1852.

6-6-10-2-2

Joseph Libby, born in Rye, N. H., 19 Oct. 1791; married, first, 2 March 1815, Mehitable C. Rand, daughter of Philbrick and Jemima (Bean) Rand of Gilford, N. H.; (died 25 July 1834); second, 26 Nov. 1835, Olive Haines.

He grew up in Gilford, N. H. He was a fisherman seven years, and served one year in the war of 1812. He then settled on half his father's homestead farm, and, except three years spent in Northfield, always lived there. His wife died 19 Dec. 1875, and he, 29 Aug. 1877. He was several years selectman of Gilford, and a member of the Freewill Baptist Church.

Children:

1 Philbrick Rand, b. 10 Feb. 1817; m. 25 Jan. 1844, Arvilla, dau. of Levi and Martha (Hunt) Lovitt. He is a farmer, and occupies his father's homestead. He is a member of the Freewill Baptist Church. Children:
1 Reuben S., b. 29 Aug. 1846; m. 19 March 1872, Alice J., dau. of Geo. W. and Mary H. (Clough) Mason of Gilford. He received an academic education, and graduated from Bryant and Stratton's Commercial College. He lived in Manchester three years following his marriage, and has since lived on the homestead farm. Child:
1 Albert J., b. 27 May 1877, in Gilford.
2 Albert W., b. 13 Jan. 1851; d. 18 May 1856.

2 Vienna G., b. 30 April 1820; m. 12 Oct. 1841, Jeremiah Smith; died 12 Oct. 1858.

6-6-10-2-3

Benjamin T. Libby, born in New Castle, N. H., 27 July 1796; married, 31 Dec. 1818, Ruenna Robinson, dau. of Moses and Mary (Cass) Robinson of Gilford. He died in Gilford, the town in which he was reared, 5 Nov. 1862. His widow died 5 May 1879.

Children, born in Gilford:

1 Mary Ann, b. 2 Feb. 1821; m. 1850, John E. Wiggin; died 18 Aug. 1855.
2 Benjamin F., b. 27 July 1827; m. 1st, 27 Sept. 1846, Eliza A., dau. of Jasper and Abigail (Rowe) Glidden; (died 13 May 1875, in Laconia, N. H.); 2d, June 1871, Hannah, dau. of Jonathan Artig of Jersey City, N. J. He went "railroading" when a boy, and always continued. He was an engineer on the Central Railroad 19 years, three of them as foreman of engineers. He died in Jersey City 17 Aug. 1877. His widow died 25 Jan. 1878. Children, by first wife:
    1 Clara O., b. 11 June 1848; m. 4 March 1869, John Merrill.
    2 George F., b. 20 March 1854; m. 14 Aug. 1875, Katie A., dau. of Patrick and Ellen (Hart) Horrogen of Jersey City, where he now lives. He was for some time a steamship fireman, and is now a locomotive engineer. Children:
        1 Katie A., b. 21 June 1857, in Jersey City.
        2 Benjamin F., b. 6 May 1876; d. 9 May 1876.
        3 George Horace, b. 8 May 1877.
    3 Serepta, died in infancy.

By second wife:

    4 Mary Rueuna, b. 7 June 1872.
    5 Annie, b. 8 July 1874.

6-6-10-2-4

Elias Libby, born in Chester, N. H., 17 March 1802; married first, 10 Feb. 1826, Jemima Rand, daughter of Philbrick and Jemima (Bean) Rand of Gilford; (died 2 June 1834); second, 10 May 1835, Clarissa F. Davis, daughter of Phineas and Betsey (Clark) Davis.

He always lived on the homestead farm in Gilford, N. H., except one year spent in a fish yard in Newcastle. After his father's death the homestead was divided between Elias and Joseph. Elias had the home half and lived and died in the old house. His death took place 12 Jan. 1846. His widow died 27 Oct. 1870.

Children, by first wife:

1 Joseph P., b. 1828; m. Fanny, daughter of Daniel and Annie (Davis) Gove. He was a farmer and carpenter; a member of the Second Advent Church. He died 10 Feb. 1881. His wife died 2 July 1864. No children.
2 Sarah, b. Jan. 1830; m. 13 April 1854, Morrell Weeks; died 15 Aug. 1861.
3 George, b. June, 1833; d. 1843.

By second wife:

4 Mary F., b. 2 Sept. 1836; m. 26 Feb. 1854, Francis L. Gilman.
5 John V., b. 16 March 1841; died in the summer of 1862.
6 Caroline A., b. 3 May 1843; unm.

6-6-10-2-6

Abram Libby, born in Gilford, N. H., 17 April 1809; married first, 16 Feb. 1832, Dorcas Hibbard, daughter of Joshua and Hannah (Tenny) Hibbard; (died 12 April 1856, in Gilford); second, 20 May 1858, Betsey G., daughter of James Hoyt.

He is a farmer. He lived awhile in Plymouth during his first wife's life, and after his second marriage, settled in Belmont, where he now lives.

Children, by first wife:

1 Cyrus, b. 12 Dec. 1836, in Plymouth, N. H.; m. Lizzie, daughter of James Evans of Tamworth. He is a shoemaker by trade, and now lives in the West.
2 Luther L., b. 27 Aug. 1839; d. 13 June 1862, in St. Augustine, Fla., in his country's service.
3 Emily D., b. 5 April 1856, in Gilford; m. Frank Grant.

6-6-10-5-1

Josiah B. Libby, born 27 Dec. 1794, in Candia, N. H.; married, 30 May 1821, Sallie Robie, daughter of Walter and Dorothy (Tilton) Robie of Candia. He was engaged in coopering and farming in his native town until 1824, when he removed to Nashua and engaged in the stone business. He died 31 Oct. 1834. His relict remained a widow, and still lives in Nashua.

Children:

1 Jacob, b. 27 Feb. 1822; m. 9 Jan. 1845, Belinda A., dau. of Eben and Aliva (Fisk) Rideout of Nashua. He was in the boot and shoe business many years, and is now retired. He has served several terms as alderman in the Nashua city government, and as representative to the state legislature; is a member of the First Congregational Church. Only child:
 1 Flora A., b. 7 May 1846; m. Levi Barker, 6-6-10-5-4-6.
2 Edward R., b. 9 Aug. 1823; d. 6 Aug. 1825.
3 Jane F., b. 5 June 1825; m. David B. Fiske. Children:
 1 Willie F. (Fiske), b. 16 June 1855; d. 28 July 1856.
 2 Delia Pierce (Fiske), b. 21 April 1857.
 3 Harry Libby (Fiske), b. 7 Dec. 1862.
 4 Katie F. (Fiske), b. 15 Aug. 1865.
4 Dorothy Anne, b. 21 April 1827; unm.
5 Mary H., b. 29 March 1828; d. 4 Jan. 1830.
6 Thomas F., b. 22 Dec. 1831; d. 8 Aug. 1832.
7 Sarah R., b. 30 June 1832; d. 16 Oct. 1838.

6-6-10-7-2

David Libby, born in Belfast, Me., 16 Sept. 1803; married, 19 Aug. 1824, in Boston, Mary A. (Batson) Glosson, daughter of Samuel Batson of Marblehead, Mass. He was a sea-captain, and died 28 Dec. 1836. His widow married William Holt.

Children:

1 Stephen B., b. 7 July 1825; m. 18 Dec. 1845, Susan W. McKenney. He was lost at sea 2 May 1847, and his widow died in Lincolnville in 1871. Child:
 1 Ellen M., b. 30 Sept. 1846; died 1850.
2 David H., b. 19 Aug. 1827; m. 20 March 1849, Sarah M., dau. of Samuel and Charlotte (Bird) Hook of Belfast. He is a sea-captain. Children:
 1 Nelly M., b. 1 May 1853; died 7 Sept. 1854.
 2 Theresa, b. 23 June 1855.
3 John A., b. 1832; m. Ann J. ——; lives in Belfast, a sailmaker.
4 Mary E., b. 24 Oct. 1833; m. John E. Blake.

6-6-10-7-5

John Connor Libby, born in Belfast, Me., 12 July 1808; married, 28 March 1833, Angeline Ellen Steele, daughter of Andrew and Mary (Scott) Steele of Castine, Me. He is a cabinet-maker by trade, and has lived in Stockton many years.

Children:

1 John Francis, b. 11 May 1834; m. 20 Sept. 1857, Rebecca Jane, dau. of John and Roxanna (Staples) Peabody of Stockton. He was a ship-master. He sailed in the bark Topeka from St. John, N. B., Feb. 1873, and never was heard from. His widow married Samuel Avery. Children:
  1 Mary Angie, b. 2 Jan. 1860.
  2 Roxanna P., b. 7 July 1863; d. 18 Sept. 1864.
  3 Irene P., b. 8 April 1866; d. 16 July 1866.
  4 Frank P., born and died 29 Dec. 1869.
2 George Washington, b. 10 June 1838; m. 10 June 1860, Marietta, dau. of Willard and Jane (Dickey) Mudgett of Stockton. He was a clerk in Boston some years, and in 1863 became a member of the firm of Mudgett & Libby, lumber-dealers and ship-builders, Stockton. In 1872 he removed to Minneapolis, Minn., where he is a contractor and builder. Children:
  1 Minetta B., b. 14 June 1866, in Stockton.
  2 Aurilla M., b. 23 Dec. 1868.
  3 Albert H., b. 11 June 1880, in Minneapolis.
3 Clara P., b. 30 Aug. 1840; d. 2 Nov. 1840.
4 Mary Angeline, b. 11 Dec. 1841; d. 4 July 1846.
5 Elias David, b. 14 June 1844; m. 14 June 1866, Elizabeth G., dau. of Peleg and Catherine (Griffin) Staples of Stockton. He served three years in the 6th Maine Battery, enlisting as private, and mustered out 2d lieut. He was a hardware dealer in Stockton until 1873, when he removed to St. Paul, Minn., where he is engaged in the manufacture of iron cornices, window-caps, etc. Children:
  1 Allen S., b. 15 May 1867.
  2 Faustie H., b. 13 Sept. 1868.
6 William Littlefield, b. 10 Sept. 1846; m. 25 Aug. 1877, Orella H., dau. of James L. and Lydia (Blanchard) Griffin of Stockton. He has followed the sea from childhood, and is now master of the schooner Jennie Beasley of Rockport. Child:
  1 Edward White, b. 28 July 1879, in Stockton.

6-6-10-9-2

Jacob Libby, born in Gilford, N. H., 9 April 1809; married Harriet Wadleigh.

For fifteen years after his marriage he was a stage driver between Concord and Laconia. He was afterward a railroad conductor, and later in the bakery and confectionery business in Lake Village. For three years he represented Center Harbor in the state legislature. He died in Gilford, 8 March 1857. His widow died 23 June 1871, in Laconia.

Children:

1 George Addison, b. 25 Nov. 1836, in Gilmanton, N. H.; m. 30 Nov. 1856, in Madison, Wis., Mary Adeline, dau. of Isaac and Abigail (Seavey) Hadley of Hudson, N. H. At 18 he went to Madison, Wis.; went thence to Palmyra in 1863, and from that place

enlisted in Co. E, 1st Wisconsin Vol. Artillery; since the war has lived in Milwaukee, and in Janesville, Wis., and is now a contractor in the gas and pipe fitting business. Children:

1 Leon Delbert, b. 15 March 1859, in Madison.. Is in company with his father.
2 Abby Harriet, b. 20 April 1862, in Palmyra.
3 Ella May, b. 19 March 1870.
4 George Hiram, b 29 March 1876, in Janesville.

2 Charles A., b. 25 March 1839, in Center Harbor; m. 23 Jan. 1873, in Chicago, Edna M., dau. of George E. Blake of Providence, R. I., where he now lives. He is employed on the P. and Worcester R. R. He served three years in Battery B, R. I. Light Artillery. No children.
3 Martha A., b. 14 May 1841, in Gilford; unm.
4 Frank F., b. 18 Sept. 1846, in Gilford; m. 2 Sept. 1871, Esther, dau. of Daniel and Harriet (Ladd) Sanborn of Sanbornton, N. H. He is a machinist in Jersey City, N. J. He served two years in the 3d Vt. Light Artillery. Children:

1 Eula May, b. 6 Jan. 1874.
2 Morton Jacob, b. 14 Sept. 1876.

9-5-4-2-1

Jacob Fogg, born in Scarborough, 11 Feb. 1771; married, 30 May 1790, Sally Libby, 5-2-3-2. He was a farmer, and lived with his father. He died 20 Feb. 1808. His widow married, 28 Feb. 1810, James Randall.

Children:

1 Polly (Fogg), b. 17 Nov. 1790; m. 7 Jan. 1817, Abraham Osgood of Portland.
2 Miriam (Fogg), b. 7 March 1793; m. Zenas Libby, 11-6-5-8.
3 Sally (Fogg), b. 9 June 1795; m. 22 Sept. 1816, Thomas F. Andrews.
4 Reuben (Fogg), b. 19 Aug. 1797; d. 29 July 1817.
5 Aphia (Fogg), b. 10 Jan. 1800; m. 21 May 1823, Enos H. Dyer of Cape Elizabeth.
6 Benjamin (Fogg), b. 29 May 1802; m. Sarah Ann Tewkesbury.
7 Silas (Fogg). b. 1805; m. Mercy Davis.
8 Jacob (Fogg), b. 18 April 1808; m. 11 March 1829, Artemisia, dau. of Rhoda (Libby) Tyler, 1-1-6-4-2.

10-1-2-2-1

Reuben Libby, born in Jonesborough, Me., 17 April 1776; married, 16 Feb. 1804, Martha Farnsworth, daughter of Isaac and Hannah (Hill) Farnsworth of Jonesborough. He was a farmer in his native town, and died a young man, 11 Dec. 1817. His widow married, 20 June 1827, John Holmes of Machias.

Children, all born in Jonesborough:

1 Oliver, b. 19 Aug. 1804; was killed by a rolling log, a young man.
2 Hiram, b. 9 May 1806; m. 27 Nov. 1827, Keziah, dau. of Asa and Betsey (Weston) Farnsworth of Jonesborough. He removed to Beddington, where he was a farmer and lumberman. He died three years after marriage, 25 June 1830. His widow died in Jonesborough, 2 Nov. 1840. Children:

1 Asa F., b. 9 Sept. 1828, in Beddington; m. 10 July 1858, Nancy V., dau. of Samuel and Esther (Whitney) Watts of Jonesborough. He is a farmer and lumberman in Beddington. He has served as selectman, town clerk, etc.; is a member of the Freewill Baptist Church. Children:

1 Ella A., b. 9 Feb. 1860; d. 13 Aug. 1864.
2 Hiram L., b. 29 March 1862; d. 23 April 1865.
3 Mabel Alice, b. 8 Nov. 1868.
4 Ellery H., b. 19 Oct. 1871.
5 Omah F., b. 4 March 1880.

2 Martha, b. 9 Sept 1830; d. 29 March 1837, in Harrington.

3 Calvin, b. 2 Feb. 1808; m. Priscilla Peoples.
4 Fannie, b 13 Nov. 1809; m. Capt. A. Mitchell.
5 Hannah, b. 20 June 1811; m. Freeman Barry.
6 Deborah, b. 22 March 1813; m. 5 May 1836, Robert Stewart.
7 Ichabod, b. 19 Dec. 1815; d. 8 Dec. 1818.
8 Reuben, b. 1 March 1818; m. 30 April 1850, Louisa, dau. of Mark L. and Mary (Palmer) Cates of Northfield. He is a farmer in Kingston, Minn. Children:

1 Sarah L., b. 19 April 1851, in Deblois; m. 5 Dec. 1869, in Wesley, Me., John A. Guptil.
2 Martha R., b. 22 May 1853; m. 1 April 1877, Geo. W. Cassady.
3 Ella P., b. 6 Jan. 1855; m. 16 Dec. 1871, William W. Guptil.
4 Loren W., b. 25 Nov. 1858, in Northfield; unm.
5 Mary P., b. 26 July 1862.
6 Carrie A., b. 9 June 1865.
7 Helen V., b. 20 Dec. 1868.
8 Eunice L., b. 23 Sept. 1871, in Wesley, Me.
9 Olive W., b. 10 Feb. 1877, in Forest City, Minn.

10-1-2-2-4

Josiah Libby, born 16 March 1781, in Jonesborough, Me.; married, 5 June 1803, Jane Libby, 10-1-2-3-3.

He settled at first on a farm in Jonesborough, and then settled on wild land in Charleston, Me., where he lived until old age. He died in No. 11, R. 1, plantation, Aroostook County, Me. His widow died 11 July 1862, in Atkinson.

Children, born in Jonesborough:

1 Matilda C., b. 3 March 1804.
2 Beriah W., b. 23 Jan. 1806; m. Maria Wharton.
3 Reuben, b. 16 April 1808; d. 25 Nov. 1812.
4 Alfred W., b. 11 April 1810; m. Mary Strout.
5 Daniel M., b. 20 April 1812; m. 6 Nov. 1837, Mary, dau. of William Dunning of Charleston. He was a farmer, and also kept a house of entertainment. He died in Charleston, 15 Oct. 1846. No children.
6 Moses P., b. 9 July 1814; m. Weltha A. Fox.

Born in Charleston:

7 Jane, b. 3 May 1817; d. 23 Aug. 1820.
8 Josiah, b. 9 Dec. 1819; married 25 Feb. 1847, Christiana C. Libby, 10-1-2-3-7-5; settled in Atkinson, Me., where he still resides. No children.
9 Fellows W., b. 24 Sept. 1822; d. 8 Sept. 1826.
10 Hannah W., b. 25 Aug. 1825; m. Amaziah N. McCaslin.

10-1-2-2-6

Joseph Libby, born in Jonesborough, Me., 9 Dec. 1784; married, 22 April 1807, Hannah Farnsworth, daughter of Isaac and Hannah (Hill) Farnsworth of Jonesborough.

He lived on his father's homestead in Jonesborough until 1825, and then settled in Beddington, where he stayed until 1845. From Beddington he moved to Rutland, Wis., but returned two years later and lived in Beddington until his death, 9 Dec. 1853. He was a farmer and lumberman. After his wife's death he married Louisa Clark, now living in Ellsworth.

Children:

1 Otis S., b. 17 Aug. 1808; m. Delaine, dau. of Phineas and Hannah (Booth) Whitten of Steuben; died in Steuben, Sept. 1837. No children.
2 Edmund, b. 2 April 1810; m. Mary Pinio.
3 Irene, b. 9 May 1811; m. James Lovejoy; died Aug. 1846, in Rutland, Wis.
4 Annie, b. 10 March 1813; m. David B. Keith; died March, 1840.
5 Amy, b. 24 July 1817; m. Israel Griffin.
6 Sally B., b. 5 Dec. 1820; d. 13 Aug. 1823.
7 Joshua, b. 7 April 1822; married, 1st, 19 May 1845, Sophia, dau. of Stephen and Cynthia (Parrott) Smith of Columbia; (died 23 March 1850, in Beddington); 2d, 3 Sept. 1850, Susan A., dau. of Jonas and Fannie (Smith) Bowers of Machias. He is a farmer and lumberman. After his marriage he lived successively in Columbia, Deblois, Beddington, and Machias, and in 1871 removed to Minneapolis, Minn., his present residence. Children, by first wife:
   1 Emeline A., b. 20 May 1847, in Columbia; d. 30 July 1860.
   2 Levi W., b. 1 May 1852, in Deblois; d. 16 Sept. 1863.

   By second wife:

   3 Sarah S., b. 30 Nov. 1860, in Beddington; d. 28 Feb. 1864.
   4 Joseph B., b. 13 July 1863, in Machias.
   5 Albert N., b. 24 May 1865.
   6 Lucy C., b. 28 June 1869.
8 Sally B., b. 29 April 1824; m. Jeremiah Griffin.
9 Daniel F., b. 5 Sept. 1826; m. 3 Aug. 1849, Caroline A., dau. of Caleb and Judith (Lynam) Joy of Gouldsborough. He is farmer and lumberman in Deblois. He has served 29 years as town clerk, and 27 years as constable, and as postmaster eight years. Children, all born in Deblois:
   1 Florestine H., b. 16 May 1852; d. 13 May 1852.
   2 Frank A., b. 28 May 1853; m. 3 Nov. 1875, Ellen, dau. of Geo. and Sarah (Woods) Merritt of Deblois. Child:
      1 Harrie, b. 23 Feb. 1879, in Deblois.
   3 Judith Abbie, b. 6 Dec. 1855; unm.
   4 Alma E., b. 3 May 1858; unm.
   5 Howard J., b. 25 June 1860.
   6 M. Ada, b. 25 May 1863.
   7 Selden B., b. 1 Sept. 1865.
10 Richard A., b 20 April 1828; m. 10 Nov. 1860, Annie, dau. of Ezra and Mary (Torrey) Boynton of Deblois. He is a farmer and lumberman. His wife died 18 Oct. 1875. Children:
   1 Carrie E., b. 3 May 1861; d. 17 Sept. 1865.
   2 Kate M., b. 25 March 1863; d. 19 Nov. 1877.
   3 Sherman, b. 18 March 1865.
   4 Minnie, b. 2 June 1868; d. 28 Oct. 1879.
   5 Rosie, b. 21 June 1870.
   6 Sadie, b. 22 June 1872; d. 18 Oct. 1879.
   7 Irene, b. 2 May, d. 15 July, 1875.
11 Almira, b. 9 Oct. 1830; m. Pearson Gould.

10-1-2-2-7

Nathan Libby, born in Jonesborough, Me., 20 May 1787; married, 3 May 1821, Sibyl Farnsworth, daughter of Asa and Betsey (Weston) Farnsworth of Jonesborough.

He was a farmer, and lived and died on his father's homestead. He always kept his farm in good condition, yet paid more attention to lumbering, mill-building, etc. He died 3 Aug. 1842. His widow died 28 Dec. 1880.

Children:

1 George W., b. 3 Nov. 1823; m. 8 Jan. 1865, Elizabeth E., daughter of Phineas and Lydia H. (Tabot) Noyes. He occupies the homestead farm. Children:
  1 Mary Alice, b. 6 May 1866.
  2 Luella J., b. 22 May 1869.
  3 Bessie E., b. 9 Oct. 1871.
2 Betsey W., b. 29 July 1826; unm.
3 Rebecca W., b. 24 Dec. 1828; d. July 1831.
4 Mary E., b. 19 Feb. 1831; m. 5 June 1858, George E. Farnsworth. They live in Caribou. Children:
  1 Wilber Irving (Farnsworth), b. 9 March 1859.
  2 Simon Barry (Farnsworth), b. 13 Nov. 1861.
  3 Lizzie Nash (Farnsworth), b. 7 Jan. 1867.
  4 Ellery Bollman (Farnsworth), b. 5 Sept. 1871.
  5 Omas Libby (Farnsworth), b. 2 May 1875.
5 Lewis H., b. 16 July 1833; m. Oct. 1854, Eliza A. E., dau. of Josiah W. and Sophia W. (Farnsworth) Dorman. He has lived since 1859 in Kingston, Minn. Children:
  1 Willard Nathan, b. Oct. 1855, in Millbridge, Me.; m. Sarah Lloyd. They have one son.
  2 Lyman Pitt, b. Oct. 1869.
  3 Millard A., b. Sept. 1872.
  4 Laura S., b. Sept. 1874.
6 Ellery Bollman, b. 2 July 1837; served one year in the Union army; died in the service, at Fort Sumner, Washington, D. C., 6 Aug. 1863; unm.

10-1-2-3-4

Job Libby, born in Harrington, Me., 30 Dec. 1783; married Rebecca Mitchell. He had a son:

1 Fellows, living in Harrington.

10-1-2-3-7

Ephraim Libby, born in Harrington, Me., 26 Jan. 1794; married Sally McCaslin, born 14 Dec. 1797, daughter of John and Mary (Knowles) McCaslin.

He was a farmer. He had his father's homestead, and lived on it until after his death, and then moved to Charleston and settled. His wife died 11 June 1864. He still survives, at the age of 86.

Children, all born in Harrington:

1 Freeman M., b. 14 Jan. 1823; m. 11 Dec. 1851, Marriam K. Lowell, dau. of Thomas and Lucinda (Corliss) Lowell of Dixmont. He is a farmer and lumberman, residing in Charleston. Children, born in Charleston:

1 Adda E., b. 23 March 1853; m. Alpheus Parker.
2 Ella C., b. 9 Dec. 1855; d. 17 Oct. 1875.
3 Willis E., b. 23 Aug. 1857.
4 Dora L., b. 6 Sept. 1859.
5 John L., b. 14 Oct. 1861.
6 Jane, b. 12 Dec. 1863.
7 Charles H., b. 19 July 1866.
8 Augusta M., b. 6 Dec. 1868.
9 Elmer E., b. 6 Sept. 1870.
10 Arthur L., b. 17 Dec. 1871.
11 Kate May, b. 6 May 1873.
12 Ora Prince, b. 21 Aug. 1876.
13 Melvin F., b. 23 Oct. 1878.

2 Syrene Ann, b. 15 Aug. 1824; d. 8 Dec. 1830.
3 William, b. 23 April 1826; d. 17 May 1826.
4 Joseph F., b. 2 April 1827; m. Emeline Smith. He lives in Charleston and is believed to have the following children:
1 David, b. 1862.
2 Axie, b. 1863.
3 Ai, b. 1867.
4 Henry, b. 1868.
5 Flora, b. 1870.
6 Georgie, b. 1872.
7 Nancy, b. 1873.
8 Mattie, b. 1875.
9 Joy, b. 1877.

5 Christiana C., b. 4 March 1829; m. Josiah Libby, 10-1-2-2-4-8.
6 Melvina C., b. 19 Nov. 1833; m. William H. Sias.
7 Samuel N., b. 21 Jan. 1836; m. 1st, Augusta Wilbur; (died after two years); 2d, Jane Darden. He lives at Windsor Mills, Que.
8 Nancy Almeda, b. 25 April 1839; m. William Foss.

10-1-2-3-8

STEPHEN LIBBY, born in Harrington, Me.; married first, ABIGAIL WEBB; second, ——— ———. He lives in Millbridge, Me.

10-1-2-4-1

ELIAS LIBBY, born in Saco, Me., 22 June 1784; married, 30 May 1810, MARTHA BRADBURY, daughter of Joseph and Patience (Goodwin) Bradbury of Buxton.

He was a farmer. He settled on his father's homestead in Buxton, when he was first married, and, except a brief period in Saco, and a briefer one in Hollis, always lived there afterward. He died 26 Feb. 1872. His wife died 19 April 1871.

Children:

1 Mindwell, b. 26 Oct. 1810; m. 2 Sept. 1832, Isaac York.
2 Mary, b. 27 June 1813; d. 26 April 1834, unm.
3 Jacob Bradbury, b. 2 May 1815; m. Charity York.
4 Elsie, b. 22 Feb. 1817; m. Aaron Foss of Oldtown.
5 Josiah, b. 19 Nov. 1818; went to sea in 1842, and was never afterward heard from.
6 Charles, b. 17 Feb. 1821; m. Eliza A., dau. of George and Julia (Church) Merrill. She died in Feb. 1859. 21 Aug. 1861, he married Eliza Ann, dau. of Samuel and Susan (Woodman) Dyer. When he was first married he settled on a farm in Scarborough, where he has ever since resided. Only child, by first wife:

1 Charles Albion, b. 21 Nov. 1857.
7 Lucy, b. 8 Dec. 1822; m. Bryant Gilman.
8 Elijah, b. 24 Feb. 1825; } bachelors; occupy the
9 Stephen, b. 3 Dec. 1826; } homestead farm.
10 Martha, b. 17 Dec. 1828; m. 7 Sept. 1868, Stillman Rand.

10-1-2-4-2

Daniel Libby, born in Saco, Me., 21 March 1788; married Mary Libby, 10-1-8-4-3.

He was a farmer, and lived where his son Amos now lives. He died 8 Dec. 1857. His widow died 7 June 1874.

Children:

1 Philip, b. 23 Jan. 1817; d. 20 June 1877; unm.
2 Stephen, died in infancy.
3 Amos, b. 11 Aug. 1822; m. 1st, 16 Jan. 1849, Elizabeth, dau. of Asa and Hannah (Milliken) Haines. She died 1 March 1874. He married, 2d, 24 June 1878, Mary, dau. of Samuel and Abigail (Tyler) Rice. When he was married, he settled on a part of the farm of his great-grandfather, Thomas Libby, 10-1-8, and became a cattle drover. By the death of his brother Philip, he came into the whole of his father's homestead, and has since resided on it, confining himself to farming. Only child:
1 Emily Jane, b. 28 Jan. 1850; m. 28 Jan. 1872, Living G. Hill.

10-1-2-4-3

Richard Libby, born in Saco, Me., 1791; married, 19 Sept. 1824, Lucy Libby, 10-1-6-7-6.

He was a farmer. He lived at home until about 1831, and then bought the farm in Standish, now unoccupied, owned by Isaac York. On this farm he died, 30 Aug. 1863. His widow sold the place, and died with her daughter Sarah, 6 May 1874.

Children, born in Buxton:

1 Sarah M., b. 8 May 1825; m. 13 Dec. 1856, John Burnham.
2 Elizabeth, b. 12 Sept. 1828; m. George M. Libby, 11-7-2-4-6-1.

Born in Standish:

3 David Bradbury, b. 12 April 1831; m. 13 Feb. 1856, Lydia A., dau. of Paul and Lydia (Haley) Pendexter of Parsonsfield. At the age of twenty he went into the employ of his uncle Thompson, in Westbrook, at that time a butcher. From his marriage until 1866, he was in business, first as butcher, and then as grocer, in Brunswick. He then became a farmer in Pownal, where he still lives. Children:
1 Matilda, b. 22 Dec. 1856; m. 1 May 1879, Willis M. Lake.
2 Lucy, b. 1 Jan. 1858; d. 17 April 1867.
3 David Ernest, b. 16 Sept. 1859.
4 Arthur Bradbury, b. 16 Jan. 1862; d. 14 Aug. 1862.
5 Carrie Mabel, b. 23 Sept. 1863.
6 Arthur Woodbury, b. 22 Nov. 1868.
7 Lucy May, b. 2 May 1872.
8 Ethel Maud, b. 5 July 1874.
4 Mary, b. 8 Sept. 1835; m. Charles Mitchell.
5 Narcissa, b. 27 Feb. 1839; m. Eli Weeman.

10-1-2-6-7

LUTHER C. LIBBY, born in Machiasport, Me., 4 July 1796; married first, 8 Jan. 1811, MARY MCCALAB, daughter of Moses McCalab of Gouldsborough; (died 10 Nov. 1836); second, SARAH QUIMBY, daughter of John and Sarah Quimby of Vermont; (died 2 Dec. 1843); third, 15 Feb. 1857, Lucy F. Johnson.

The homestead farm of his father fell to him, and he cultivated it until his death, 15 April 1878. He was a member of the Baptist Church.

Children, by first wife:

1 James, b. 8 March 1816; m. Sarah E. Flynn.
2 Abigail, b. 11 Jan. 1818; m. Capt. John Colbath.
3 Josiah, b. 14 June 1821; was drowned 7 July 1846.
4 Lucy F., b. 10 May 1823; m. George Tucker, in Cape Ann, Mass.
5 Luther, b. 11 Sept. 1828; died in Newport, R. I., aged 20.
6 Susan, b. 9 June 1830; m. Stephen Pettigrove.
7 Phebe, b. 10 Dec. 1832; m. Warren Page.
8 Sarah, b. 7 March 1835; m. Capt. Andrew J. Cole.

By second wife:

9 Mary E., b. 16 Dec. 1840; died 7 July 1864.
10 John F., b. 16 Nov. 1842; m. 15 Oct. 1871, Mary E., dau. of Lyman and Clarissa (Colbath) Cole of Harrington. He occupies the homestead. Child:
  1 Aubine, b. 1871.

10-1-2-7-3

PHILIP LIBBY, born in Machiasport, Me.; married BETSEY LARRABEE.

Children:

1 Abraham, died unmarried.
2 Nathan. He had two children:
  1 ——, deceased.
  2 Alice, b. 1865; lives in Machiasport.
3 Harriet, deceased.
4 Lorinda, married —— Robbins of Machiasport.
5 Mary.
6 Clara, deceased.

10-1-2-7-4

OTIS LIBBY, born in Machiasport, Me., 1800; married PHEBE SMITH, daughter of Daniel and Phebe (Larrabee) Smith of Machiasport. He was a farmer, and died in his native place in 1866.

Children:

1 Catharine, married —— Foss.
2 Lucinda, married —— Dowling.
3 Hannah, deceased.
4 Elizabeth, deceased.
5 Sewall, b. 20 May 1835; m. 15 Nov. 1857, Frances A. Mitchell; lives in Machiasport. Children:
  1 Benjamin L., b. 15 Nov. 1858.
  2 Annie M., b. 7 July 1860; m. 31 July 1880, George Wood.
  3 Adavilla A., b. 28 May 1863; m. 30 Aug. 1880, Geo. W. Cobbins.

4 Phebe E., b. 5 Jan. 1865.
5 Arthur W., b. 7 March 1868.
6 George Herbert, b. 30 March 1875.
6 Charles, born 1838.

10-1-2-7-5

William Libby, born in Machiasport, Me., May 1802; married Betsey Smith, sister of his brother's wife. He died in Whitneyville, 12 July 1845, and his widow married William Larrabee of Machiasport.

Children:

1 William, b. 18 Nov. 1822; m. 11 Nov. 1847, Philinda A., dau. of Wm. and Nancy (Lyons) Ramsdell of Lubec. He is a farmer and lumberman in Whitneyville. In the late war he served three years in Co. C, 12th Me. Vol. He is a member of the Congregational Church. Children:
1 Cora, b 29 Aug. 1848; m. 10 Sept. 1870, Chas. E. Lincoln.
2 Julia, b. 4 July 1850; unm.
3 Frank, b. 5 May 1855; unm. He removed to Washington Ter. in 1876, and has since been a lumberman.
4 Hamlin, b. 12 March 1857; died 4 July 1858.
5 Lettie May, b. 26 Feb. 1861.
2 Roxanna, b. 8 June 1824; m. 1 April 1841, Harrison T. Albee of Whitneyville; died 17 Dec. 1852.
3 Nathan, b. 3 Aug. 1826; died in 1850; unm.
4 George Stillman, b. 23 May 1833; died 1850.
5 Horatio Nelson, b. 28 April 1836; died 1843.
6 Philinda, b. 1845; m. 18 May 1869, Alden Smith.

10-1-5-5-3

Ebenezer Libby, born in Machias, now Machiasport, 27 May 1787; married Parmela Andrews, daughter of John and Mary Ann (Cheever) Andrews.

He settled on a farm near by his father's. He was a lieutenant in the revenue cutter at the time of his death, which took place suddenly, 7 Aug. 1831. His widow died 4 Sept. 1867.

Children:

1 Mary Ann C., b. 25 Aug. 1812; m. James Foster.
2 Charles E., b. 15 Oct. 1814; m. Mary (Nason) Libby, widow of Mariner F. Libby, 10-1-5-5-4-1.
3 Henry A., b. 8 Jan. 1817; m. Hannah Foster.
4 Jane M., b. 25 Dec. 1818; d. 1 Jan. 1852; unm.
5 Parmelia A., b. 16 June 1821; m. Albert C. Nash.
6 Clarissa F., b. 13 Nov. 1823; m. John C. Ames.
7 Eben F., b. 28 Nov. 1826; m. 12 Oct. 1852, Rebecca A., daughter of Nelson and Sarah A. Wood of East Machias. He was a carpenter by trade; lived in Lowell, Mass., from 1856 to 1864; in Beacon Falls, Conn., until 1873; then removed to Westfield, Conn., where he died, 27 Aug. 1876, and his family still resides. He served one year in the 33d Mass. Vol. Children:
1 Ella A., b. 15 May 1854; d. 7 May 1870.
2 Laura J., b. 11 Mar. 1857; m. 24 April 1878, Charles B. Canada.
3 Charles E., b. 1 April 1859.
4 Alice G., b. 29 Aug. 1865.
5 Clara S., b. 22 Dec. 1869.

8 Alonzo Bradford, b. 29 Sept. 1829; m. 2 Oct. 1852, Ann Judson, dau. of Rev. Charles and Elizabeth (Foster) Emerson. He was a school-teacher until his marriage; since then a farmer in Machiasport. Children:
1 Lizzie A., b. 24 March 1854.
2 Addie M., b. 3 Nov. 1856.
3 Nellie M., b. 23 Feb. 1859.
4 Annie B., b. 13 May 1861.
5 Mason A., b. 10 March 1869.
6 Charles E., b. 16 July 1873.

10-1-5-5-4

DEA. MARINER LIBBY, born in Machiasport, Me., 3 Aug. 1789; married SUSANNAH BURNHAM, daughter of Job and Mary (Obrian) Burnham of Machias.

He was a farmer and had his father's homestead. He was many years a deacon of the Baptist Church. His wife died 10 Dec 1820. He lived single forty years after her death, and died 15 Sept. 1860.

Children:

1 Mariner F., } twins, b. { m. Mary Nason.
2 Susan B., } 3 Dec. 1820; { m. 16 June 1844, Hiram R. Nason.

10-1-5-5-7

DEACON PHINEAS LIBBY, born in Machiasport, Me., 18 Dec. 1795; married, 19 July 1823, NANCY GROVER, daughter of Ebenezer and Esther (Forster) Grover of Cutler.

He was a farmer and lumber-surveyor. Soon after his marriage, he settled in the "Holmes Bay district" in Cutler, and about 1852 moved thence to Cutler Harbor, where he was postmaster two terms, 1857 to 1865. He served one or more terms in the Maine legislature, and was for many years a deacon of the Baptist Church. He died 26 July 1867. His wife had died twenty-two years previous, 15 Sept. 1845.

Children, born in Machiasport:

1 Orinda, b. 4 April 1825; was her father's housekeeper until his death; now lives in Washington, D. C.
2 A. Judson, b. 26 June 1826; d. 32 Sept. 1845, in Cutler.
3 Phineas B., b. 25 Dec. 1827; died in the spring of 1870, in California.

Born in Cutler:

4 David J., b. 18 April 1830; died in California.
5 Benjamin B., b. 5 April 1832; d. 5 Dec. 1853, in Elizabethtown, Cal.
6 Eben G., b. 16 Jan. 1834; died at sea, 26 Aug. 1856.
7 Boardman, b. 13 April 1836; d. 20 July 1860, in Cutler.
8 Winfield S., b. 8 June 1839; was lost at sea, March 1855.
9 Agenoria H., b. 22 Nov. 1842; m. 17 Sept. 1864, Bernard T. Hanley, Esq.; now living in Washington, D. C. She was the only one of the family that is known to have married.

10-1-5-6-2

Enoch Libby, born in Machias, Me., 15 Sept. 1788; married Rebecca Larrabee, daughter of Rebecca (Libby) Larrabee, 10-1-2-3-2. He lived and died in Machiasport.

Children:

1 Olive A., married Abraham Holmes.
2 William, married —— Huntley. No children.

10-1-5-7-4

Capt. Daniel Libby, born in what is now Machiasport, Me., 27 July 1807; married, 23 Sept. 1842, Lucy S. Huntley, daughter of Isaac S. and Sarah (Munson) Huntley of Wesley. He died in Machiasport, 24 Dec. 1858, and his widow still lives there.

Children:

1 Hannah A., b. 14 March 1844; m. 1 April 1865, James E. Gough.
2 John Leander, b. 8 Dec. 1845; m. 25 Dec. 1878, Mary E., dau. of Issachar and Henrietta (McLellan) Lancaster of Trescott. He is a sea-captain. Child:
 1 Hollis Willard, b. 18 Feb. 1880.
3 Lucy E., b. 10 Dec. 1848; m. 2 Oct. 1878, James A. Lancaster.
4 Sarah E., b. 9 Sept. 1851; m. 23 Aug. 1873, Wm. H. Wier.
5 Emma V., b. 14 Sept. 1853; m. 6 Sept. 1872, Christopher Bancroft.
6 Cora H., b. 19 May 1857; died 3 Nov. 1860.

10-1-6-4-2

Shirley Libby, born in Scarborough, 2 April 1794; married, 1 June 1824, Mary Libby, 5-2-3-1-3. He lived on his father's homestead, a farmer, and died there 8 Feb. 1871. His wife died 16 May 1851.

Children:

1 Louisa, b. 8 Oct. 1826; m. Milton Libby, 10-5-2-1-1-6.
2 Charles Whitman, b. 9 Feb. 1829; m. 17 Nov. 1871, Amanda Simpson, dau. of Moses and Miranda (Carter) Waterhouse; Moses Waterhouse being son of Richard, son of Nathaniel Waterhouse, 10-2-2-12. He is a farmer, and lives with his father-in-law on Scottow's Hill, Scarborough. He has been selectman. No children.
3 Robert, b. 31 July 1833; m. 16 Oct. 1862, Sarah Harmon Fogg, 9-6-6-4-4-2. He lives on the homestead, a farmer. Children:
 1 Allen Edgar, b. 15 July 1864.
 2 William Shirley, b. 1 June 1867.
4 Horatio, b. 7 Jan. 1836; lives on the homestead; unm.

10-1-6-5-3

Joseph Libby, born in Standish, Me., 31 July 1788; married, 1811, Lucy H. Grant, daughter of Benjamin and Susan (Perkins) Grant of Saco, Me., from Ipswich, Mass.

He grew up in Freedom and cleared a farm in the northeast corner of that town. After 13 years he gave his cleared farm to his brother Isaac for wild land in Albion, and lived there 21 years. He then went with his son Robert to Exeter, and there they together cleared a third farm. He died in Albion, Feb. 1864. His widow died 10 April 1877, in Garland.

Children:

1 Harriet, b. 12 June 1812; m. Jan. 1837, Joel Work.
2 Robert, b. 1 Feb. 1814; m. 1st, 15 Nov. 1836, Betsey, dau. of his aunt, Hannah (Libby) Work of Albion; (died 21 Aug. 1844, in Albion); 2d, 25 March 1845, Julia Ann, dau. of John and Lucy (Work) Rogers of Troy; (died 15 Jan. 1855, in Exeter); 3d, 10 Oct. 1856, Catherine H., dau. of James and Content (Morrill) Pilsbury of Garland; (died 3 May 1873, in Exeter). He is a farmer, and has lived in many places, but since 1876 for the most part with his daughter Elizabeth, in Etna. Children, by first wife:
  1 Abel W., b. 14 March 1838, in Albion; m. April 1875, in Exeter, Mary Goudy; died 23 July 1878, in Lead City, Colorado. He was a farmer until going west.
  2 Hillman R., b. 16 Oct. 1839; died 3 Jan. 1847.
  3 Almeda, b. 18 May 1842; died Oct. 1863.
  4 Elizabeth, b. 31 July 1844; m. Oct. 1866, Alvin A. Soule.

By second wife, born in Exeter:

  5 Esther Jane, b. 24 June 1846; died 14 July 1846.
  6 Louisa M., b. 3 Sept. 1847; m. Oct. 1873, Samuel Banton.
  7 Lucy G., b. 14 March 1849; d. 30 April 1856.
  8 John R., b. 15 March 1853; unm.

By third wife:

  9 Hattie, b. 1 June 1857, in Garland; died May, 1868.
  10 Herbert J., b. 25 Oct. 1859, in Exeter; d. 1 April 1877.
  11 Elmer G., b. 14 Feb. 1863.
  12 Mabel Julia, b. 31 July 1865, in Carmel.
  13 Willebe H., b. 3 Dec. 1867.
  14 Charles A., b. 28 Sept. 1870, in Exeter.
3 Sally, b. 16 Dec. 1815; d. 22 Aug. 1870, in Carmel; unm.
4 Mary, b. 29 May 1818; m. Jeremiah Rowe of St. Albans.
5 Joseph, b. 7 Nov. 1820; m. Angeline Casey of Farmington. He removed to Minnesota about 1854, and is supposed to be still living there. Children:
  1 son, } both married.
  2 daughter. }
6 Artemas, b. 8 Jan. 1823; m. Louisa H. Snow.
7 Louisa S., b. 11 Nov. 1825; m. 11 June 1843, B. G. Murch.
8 Elmyra, b. 24 Jan. 1828; m. 24 Jan. 1850, James Pilsbury.
9 Maria, b. July 1830; m. Rufus Downs.

10-1-6-5-4

David Libby, born in Standish, Me., about 1789; married, first, Mary Fowler, of Unity; second, Abigail Libby, 10-5-4-7-5.

Children, by first wife:

1 Betsey, b. 8 March 1812; m. Samuel D. Libby, 10-5-4-7-4.
2 Ann, b. 1814; m. William Davis.

By second wife, among others:

3 ——, married William Paddock of Fairfield.
4 Charles, lives in Bradford.
5 ——, married Alden B. Strout.

10-1-6-5-5

Robert Libby, born in Standish, Me., 6 Sept. 1790; married, 8 Oct. 1815, Anna Clark Hasty. [See page 55.]

He served his time with one of his mother's brothers in Scarborough. After his marriage he lived a while in Buxton; he later removed to Freedom, and died in China, 13 Jan. 1876. His wife died in Freedom, 14 Nov. 1856.

Children, all born in Buxton:

1 Margaret, b. 9 Aug. 1816; m. 9 Nov. 1837, William Colley; died 22 Jan. 1874. Children:
  1 Ann Hasty (Colley), b. 31 Aug. 1838, in Albion; d. 2 Oct. 1846.
  2 Julia Ernestine (Colley), b. 14 April 1845; m. Darius Forbes Gilman.
  3 Josephine Mary (Colley), b. 23 Aug. 1850; m. George Jackson.
  4 William Everett (Colley), b. 2 Feb. 1855.
2 Sarah, b. 30 May 1818; m. 1st, 15 Oct. 1867, Elijah Winslow; (died 31 March 1875); 2d, 17 Oct. 1877, Thomas Blackwell Lincoln.
3 Cyrus, b. 29 Sept. 1823; m. Dec. 1847, Frances Ellen, dau. of Henry and Sarah (Strout) Dyer, of Portland. He was out in the late war, and died on his return home, at the house of Cyrus Libby, 10-1-8-1-2-2, in Gorham, 14 Nov. 1864. His widow married Richard Sanborn of Gorham, and removed to Aroostook County. Children:
  1 Charles Augustus, b. 2 June 1852, in Freedom; died 10 Sept. 1853, in Portland.
  2 Anna Clark, b. 22 Sept. 1855, in Portland; m. —— Hillman.

10-1-6-5-8

Isaac Libby, born in Standish, Me., 21 April 1797; married, 10 Oct. 1826, Hannah Abbott, daughter of Reuben and Mercia (Marr) Abbott. He was a farmer in Freedom, where he died, 10 March 1832. His widow died 7 November 1872.

Children:

1 Rebecca, b. 29 Aug. 1828; m. 25 Dec. 1850, Alfred Warren. Children:
  1 Peace Eleanor (Warren), b. 19 Feb. 1852; m. 14 Feb. 1875, Geo. W. Bridges.
  2 Moses Alfred (Warren), b. 5 Sept. 1857; unm.
2 Moses W., b. 16 Jan. 1830; d. 11 July 1856; unm.

10-1-6-7-2

Samuel Libby, born in Scarborough, 3 Sept. 1791; married Sarah S. Ellenwood, daughter of John and Zeruiah (Abbott) Ellenwood of Bethel. He was of a roving disposition, and lived in many places, working at milling, carpentering, and farming. He died in Bethel, 30 April 1837, and his widow in Portland, 15 March 1858.

Children:

1 Veranus, born in Milan, N. H.; m. Ann Smith of Newry; lives in Chelsea, Mass.
2 Zeruiah, } twins; died in infancy.
3 Elvira, }

4 Jane, born in Gilead; m. Thomas A. Miller.
5 John, } twins; died in infancy.
6 Joanna, }
7 ———, born in Bethel; died aged a few hours.
8 Lucy Thais, m. Cyrus Brock of Lyman.
9 John Ellenwood McKenney, b. 2 Sept. 1830, in Buxton; m. 6 Nov. 1854, Sarah Ann, dau. of Samuel and Dorcas (Burnell) Small of Portland. He learned the carpenter's trade, and has lived for the most part in Saco, working at his trade except a short time spent on a farm in Lyman. Children:
1 George Thomas, b. 8 June 1856, in Portland; m. 28 Nov. 1878, Amanda R., dau. of James and Rebecca Brown of Hollis. He is in a shoe shop in Rochester, N. H. No children.
2 John Atwood, b. 28 Feb. 1858, in Scarborough.
3 Frederick Clifford, b. 11 Feb. 1860, in Saco; d. 24 July 1861.
4 Medora Seavey, b. 4 May 1862.
5 Veranus Alonzo, b. 16 Nov. 1864.
6 Maria Teressa, b. 27 March 1867.
7 Edward Adolphus, b. 22 Dec. 1869; d. 2 Sept. 1873.
8 Emma Louise, b. 12 July 1874.
9 Sadie Edna, b. 10 July 1877, in Lyman.

10-1-6-7-3

Aaron Libby, born in Saco, Me., 7 Oct. 1796; married, 4 April 1824, Emily Woodsum, daughter of Abner and Betsey (Berry) Woodsum of Saco. He was a farmer and millman. Until his marriage he worked at home. He then lived a short time in Hollis, then in Clinton until 1842, and then settled in Detroit, where he died 25 Sept. 1866. His wife died 3 Aug. 1867.

Children:

1 Orin, b. 11 Jan. 1825, in Hollis; m. 1st, 6 Oct. 1850, Abby G., dau. of Zebulon and Sally (Durgin) Blake of Detroit; (died 22 Nov. 1851); 2d, 7 April 1853, Margaret, dau. of Ebenezer and Margaret (Lord) Clement, of Detroit. He is a farmer and lumberman in Detroit. He has served in all the higher town offices. Children, by first wife:
1 Charles H., b. 10 July 1851; m. 15 Oct. 1880, Hattie Hobart, in East Pepperell, Mass., where he is a carpenter.

By second wife:

2 Aaron C., b. 20 Jan. 1855; unm.
3 Orin E., b. 20 Nov. 1859; unm.
4 George H., b. 2 Oct. 1861.
5 Florence A., b. 7 Oct. 1863.
2 Dyer Woodsum, b. 27 Jan. 1827, in Clinton; m. 1st, 27 April 1851, Salome J., dau. of Winthrop and Caroline (Gilman) Gibson of Benton; (died 30 Aug. 1862, in Benton); 2d, 4 July 1863, Mary E., dau. of David and Caroline (Wyman) Simonds of Pittsfield. He was a carpenter until 1868, when he settled on his present farm in Pittsfield. Children, all by second wife:
1 Waldo Emerson, b. 5 Sept. 1864; d. 16 April 1865.
2 Carrie Emily, b. 25 March 1867.
3 Henry Woodsum, b. 30 Nov. 1869; d. 29 Aug. 1874.
4 Leon Leslie, b. 10 Nov. 1872.
3 Simon, b. 6 Jan. 1829; d. 7 May 1830.
4 David Freeman, b. 3 June 1831; m. 16 Nov. 1857, Nancy Marie, dau. of Thomas and Mary A. (Ross) Bowman of Detroit. He is a farmer and lumberman in Detroit. Children:

1 Alice Emma, b. 23 Nov. 1858; is a teacher.
2 Mae. b. 12 Nov. 1860; died 26 May 1881. She was a teacher of much promise.
3 L. Linette. b. 26 Jan. 1863.
4 Everett Ethelbert, b. 6 Oct. 1867.
5 Grace Evangeline, b. 4 Aug. 1869.

5 Lizzie A., b. 3 Nov. 1833; m. 10 Aug. 1856, Hiram W. Blake.
6 George E., b. 20 Feb. 1836; m. 1st, 16 Sept. 1861. Rosilla M., dau. of Elias Humphrey of Pittsfield; (died 11 Feb. 1862); 2d, 24 March 1863, May M., dau. of R. B. and Orilla (Heald) Mills of Palmyra. He was a carpenter and lumberman until his second marriage, when he went to California. In 1866 he returned to Detroit, and became a farmer. He served three years as selectman there. In 1879 he became agent for F. Shaw & Bros. of Boston, and took charge of two of their tanneries, one in Saint Regis Falls, and one in Colton, N. Y., in which latter place he resides. Children, by second wife:
1 George W., b. 3 Feb. 1869.
2 Rosa M.. b. 23 March 1870.

7 Emily J., b. 14 Aug. 1838; m. June 1867, Lindley M. Densmore.

10-1-6-7-5

George Libby, born in Saco, Me., 22 May 1800; married, 5 Feb. 1826, Fanny Prescott, daughter of Stephen and Elizabeth (Hewes) Prescott of Buxton.

He settled at what is now called Libby's Corner, in Deering, near Portland, and was widely known as a trader and tavern-keeper. He also engaged largely in the coopering business. He died 22 Dec. 1878, and his wife 19 April 1879.

Only child:

1 Priscilla, b. 15 Nov. 1826; died 21 June 1848; unm.

He adopted an infant found in the woods near his house, which took the name:

a George (Libby). b. about 8 April 1849; d. 13 June 1852.

He then adopted an infant, son of Margaret McCoy of Halifax, who was called:

b George (Libby), b. 23 Oct. 1852; m. Rosanna H., dau. of Wm. and Fanny (Hodgdon) McNelly of Clinton. (Fanny Hodgdon was a daughter of Lydia (Libby) Hodgdon, 10-1-6-7-8). He inherited his father's property, and still lives at Libby's Corner. Children:
1 Priscilla Gracie, b. 13 July 1876.
2 May Kidder, b. 16 Dec. 1878.

10-1-6-7-7

Ephraim Libby, born in Saco, Me., 2 March 1804; married 26 Oct. 1828, Mary Palmer, daughter of Joses and Mary (Atkinson) Palmer of Hollis.

He worked in the mills at Barr Mills until 1837, and then, after living a year in Westbrook, now Deering, removed to a farm in Clinton, where he lived until his death, 25 April 1867. The mother of his children died 12 Feb. 1861, and he married second, 12 Jan. 1862, in Canaan, Electra Pettigrew.

George Libby

A. A. Libby

Children:

1 Susan, b. 16 Sept. 1830, in Hollis; m. 10 Sept. 1851, Henry McNelly.
2 Statira, born 18 Nov. 1832; m. 15 Nov. 1853, in Clinton, Lauriston Foss; died 6 Feb. 1860.
3 Morris, b. 6 Nov. 1836; d. 8 Aug. 1841.
4 Horace, } twins, born 7 Feb. } d. 18 Jan. 1844.
5 Morris, } 1843, in Benton; } d. 12 Sept. 1843.
6 Ella A., b. 25 Jan. 1846; died 1 March 1847.
7 Ellis P., b. 7 Sept. 1848; m. 20 Dec. 1869, Nellie V., dau. of Rufus and Phebe (McNelly) Joy of Clinton. He is a teamster. He has lived in Wisconsin and Massachusetts, and since 1870 has lived in Clinton, Me. Child:
 1 Nina Mildred, b. 13 Aug. 1880.

10-1-6-7-9

ABRAHAM LIBBY, born in Saco, Me., 2 March 1808; married, HANNAH E. HANCOCK, daughter of John Lane and Hannah (Prescott) Hancock of Buxton.

Upon his marriage he settled on a ten-acre lot near Portland, at what is now called Libby's Corner, and lived there until his death. The house was a very large one, and for some time he made a practice of putting up countrymen and their teams. He soon engaged in coopering, and later added the business of blacksmith and carriage maker. In addition to these he kept a general store. These buildings formed a line all along the road, and in 1844, fire catching in the cooper shop, all were burned. He rebuilt all but the cooperage, and continued in business as blacksmith and carriage maker until his death, 21 May 1855.

Children, all born in Westbrook, now Deering:

1 Arthur Albion, b. 3 Oct. 1831; m. 7 Jan. 1858, Louisa J., dau. of Amos and Mary Fowler (Bradeen) Andrews of Westbrook. At the age of 18 he took charge of his father's grocery store, and a year later became bookkeeper for his uncle John L. Hancock, who was then in the beef packing business in what is now Deering. Upon his uncle's removal to the West, he continued the business for himself, but was not successful, and, following his uncle to Chicago, was for many years foreman for Cragin & Co., of which firm his uncle had become a member. After seven years, he himself, with a small capital, engaged in packing tongues. Later, A. McNeill and his own brother became his partners, and the business was extended. They used the firm name of A. A. Libby & Co. until 1874, when it was changed for the present one of Libby, McNeill & Libby. Adopting strict principles of fair dealing, the firm met with great success. In 1875 they added to their immense business in barreling beef, that of canning cooked corned beef, and in the latter form their production has won such a name that their exports of canned goods equal or exceed those of all other packers in this country. They now employ from 800 to 1400 men, and slaughter daily from 800 to 1200 head of cattle. Children:
 1 Annie Louisa, b. 10 Oct. 1858, in Westbrook; m. 7 Sept. 1880, Wm. F. Burrows of Chicago.
 2 Mabel Valeria, b. 15 March 1860.
 3 Carrie Amanda Malvinda, b. 16 Feb. 1862, in Chicago.
 4 Arthur Albion, b. 6 Oct. 1864.

5 Emma A., b. 24 May 1867.
6 Ethel E., b. 19 May 1870; died 1 April 1872.
7 Perl G., b. 7 Aug. 1875.

2 Malvina Valeria, b. 19 Nov. 1835; d. 19 Sept. 1837.
3 Charles Perly, b. 19 Oct. 1838; m. 26 May 1864, Jennie S., dau. of Elisha and Margaret Maria (Rich) Taylor of Westbrook. Until his marriage he was in the employ of his brother in Maine. After his marriage he was in the employ of Cragin & Co., beef packers, in Chicago, until he was admitted into partnership with his brother. No children.

10-1-8-1-2

BENJAMIN MARCH LIBBY, born in Scarborough, now Gorham, 14 May 1784; married ELIZABETH BABB, daughter of Thomas and Sarah (Moses) Babb.

When he was married he built and settled on the northern part of his father's homestead, but soon after bought his brother Samuel's house, and there lived until his death, 26 June 1836. His widow married second, Nathaniel Meserve of Freedom, N. H., and died 6 Jan. 1861.

Children of B. M. Libby:

1 Eunice, b. 13 Dec. 1809; m. 10 Feb. 1831, Shirley Harmon.
2 Silas, b. 31 Dec. 1811; m. 1st, Olive Moulton; 2d, Sarah Dyer.
3 Amos, b. 17 May 1814; d. 4 Sept. 1815.
4 Moses, b. 6 Sept. 1817; d. 18 Sept. 1821.
5 Arthur, b. 6 Dec. 1819; m. 1st, Miriam A. Mason; 2d, Elizabeth A. Dresser.
6 Rufus, b. 26 July 1823; m. Almira S. Emery.

10-1-8-1-4

SAMUEL HUBBARD LIBBY, born in Scarborough, now Gorham, 29 Sept. 1789; married, 30 Oct. 1814, CHARLOTTE TIBBETTS, daughter of Stephen and Mehitable (Tibbetts) Tibbetts of Standish.

While his father was still living he bought a house from Moses Harmon, and moved it onto his father's farm, where it now stands. He lived there but a short time, and then moved to Effingham, (now Freedom), N. H. He afterward lived in Scarborough, Hiram, and Brownfield, Me., and in about 1834 settled in Denmark, Me., where he died 20 June 1864. His widow married Charles Kimball of Bridgton, and now lives with her daughters in Buxton.

Children:

1 Ivory, b. 8 Oct. 1815, in Scarborough; d. 17 June 1855; unm.
2 Benjamin, b. 4 Oct. 1817; m. Eliza Haddock.
3 Mehitable, b. 25 Sept. 1819; m. 10 Aug. 1845, John Sands Rankins of Buxton.
4 Mary Price, b. 10 May 1822; m. 1 Feb. 1842, Charles Low.
5 Phebe Ann, b. 1 Sept. 1825; m. Daniel McKey.
6 Elizabeth Brackett, b. 16 Feb. 1828; m. 4 July 1849, Francis C. Rankins.
7 Josiah Jose, b. 1 June 1831; d. 22 June 1855; unm.
8 Stephen Tibbetts, b. 24 Sept. 1835, in Brownfield; m. Abby Stone; lives in Denmark, Me., and is thought to have several children.

10-1-8-2-1

AMOS LIBBY, born in his grandfather's house at the "Heath," Saco, 29 Jan. 1781; married, 21 Jan. 1808, MERCY BLACK, daughter of Josiah and Mercy (Cookson) Black of Limington.

He lived on part of his father's farm, and helped tend the None-such mill until after his wife's death, which occurred 20 April 1813. He then enlisted in the American army for one year, and lost his life at Plattsburgh, Canada, 26 Oct. 1813.

Children:

1 Josiah Black, b. 11 Oct. 1808; m. Louisa M., dau. of Job and Jane (Gilford) Bragdon of Hollis. He was brought up by his grandfather Libby. He worked at the carpenter's trade until 1844, and then settled upon wild land in Hollis, and cleared the farm on which he has since resided. Children:
  1 Olive Ann, b. 22 July 1830; m. 1st, 27 Jan. 1848, Ivory Bradbury; 2d. 18 Jan. 1873, John Henry Berry.
  2 Martha Jane, b. 21 Aug. 1833; m. 4 May 1852, Hiram Hooper.
  3 Clara Edgecomb, b. 24 May 1836; m. Hiram Hanson.
  4 George Washington Pike, b. 7 April 1838; d. 22 Oct. 1839.
  5 Sarah Pike, b. 17 Jan. 1842; m. 10 Nov. 1862, Marshall Lowell.
  6 Althea Augusta, b. 19 Oct. 1852; m. 26 Nov. 1873, Leonard Palmer.

2 Lydia Andrews, b. 23 Feb. 1811; m. 3 April 1848, Caleb Jellison of Hollis. She was brought up by her grandmother Black.

10-1-8-2-3

JOHN LIBBY, born in Scarborough, now Saco, 20 Dec. 1784; married, 20 Oct. 1808, ANNA MAXWELL. (Her mother was by birth a Fernald). Anna Libby died 9 March 1838. 9 Dec. 1838, he married HANNAH (RIGGS) BURNAL, widow of David Burnal, and daughter of William T. and Mary (Burnal) Riggs of Bridgton.

In his youth he studied navigation and surveying, with the intention of becoming a mariner. He did not, however, but settled on part of his father's farm, and in 1813 moved thence to Newry, Me. He was a skilled land surveyor, and laid out this town, and many others. In 1836 he left Newry, and after a short residence each, in the towns of Bridgton and Saco, married again, and settled at Gorham Corner, where he died, 23 April 1864, and his widow still lives. He was many years a justice of the peace, and known as Esquire Libby.

Children, by first wife:

1 William, b. 19 Jan., died 21 April, 1809.
2 Joseph Maxwell, b. 17 June 1810; m. Eunice Riggs.
3 John Freeland, b. 29 Aug. 1812; m. Mary Beckford.
4 Amos Andrews, b. 8 Dec. 1817; m. Eunice B. Burnal.
5 Mary Ann, b. 23 July 1820; m. Russell Graves.

By second wife:

6 William H. H., b. 16 Sept. 1840; d. 29 Dec. 1849.

10-1-8-2-7

Timothy Libby, born in Scarborough, now Saco, 9 Oct. 1793; married, 21 June 1826, Mehitable Richards, daughter of Jonathan and Mehitable (Carter) Richards of Saco.

He carried on the homestead farm while his brother David learned the blacksmith's trade. After David returned and set up his shop, he took up the business, and continued it until old age. He has always lived on the homestead farm, except two years in Newry. His wife died 15 Jan. 1817.

Their only child was:

1 Robert Carl, b. 23 June 1828; m. 9 Feb. 1861, Rhoda, dau. of John and Hannah (Buzzell) Welch of Canaan. He spent his life with his father, and died 3 March 1864. His widow married, 8 May 1868, Robert Brown of Lines, N. Y., and still lives with her father-in-law. Robert C. Libby's only child was:
 1 Clarissa Ann, b. 12 March 1862; d. 30 Aug. 1880.

10-1-8-2-9

David Libby, born in Scarborough, now Saco, 15 Sept. 1798; married, 7 Sept. 1823, Olive Watson, daughter of Jonathan and Polly (Deering) Watson of Saco.

He learned the blacksmith trade with Benjamin Chandler, and after working one year in Saco, built a shop on his father's farm, where, with his brother Timothy, he carried on business until 1876, when old age stopped him. Nearly his whole life has been spent on the farm on which he was born. His wife died 5 June 1870.

Children:

1 Mary, b. 7 Jan. 1824; d. 27 Feb. 1826.
2 Sophia Fernald, b. 27 Jan. 1826; m. Charles Stewart.
3 Amos, b. 22 March 1828; m. Mary E. Boulter.
4 John Edgecomb, b. 28 April 1830; m. 26 Sept. 1880, Viola (Carter) Graffam, widow of Geo. Graffam, and dau. of Dennis J. and Lucretia K. (Warren) Carter. He has always lived at home, a farmer.
5 David Watson, b. 28 Aug. 1832; m. 6 Nov. 1853, Lydia, dau. of Daniel and Harriet (Townsend) Townsend of Hollis. He is a blacksmith, doing business in West Buxton, but residing in Hollis. Children:
 1 Hattie Rosilla, b. 5 Feb. 1856.
 2 George, b. 30 Sept. 1860.
6 Eunice Buzzell, b. 14 Jan. 1835; d. 22 Nov. 1856; unm.
7 Mehitable, b. 14 July 1837; d. 7 Aug. 1838.
8 Evens Carl, b. 29 Aug. 1839; m. 1st, 20 Sept. 1862, Anna N., dau. of Nicholas and Olive (Boston) Stiles of Acton; (died 3 June 1874); 2d, 4 July 1875, Esther A., dau. of Humphrey and Mary E. (Cobb) Edwards of Poland. He learned from his father his trade, and was a blacksmith, first as journeyman, and then in business, until 1871, when his health failed. He then removed to Springvale, and learned the shoe-cutter's trade with Butler & Stiles, and continued with them five years, the latter three having charge of the cutting-room. Since 1876 he has been in business as blacksmith, at Springvale. Children, by first wife:
 1 Roland Wilson, b. 19 March 1867.
 2 Edith Sophia, b. 1 Feb. 1869.

By second wife:

8 Arthur Amos, b. 6 June, d. 22 Aug., 1877.
9 George Washington, b. 17 March 1842; d. 12 June 1843.
10 Betsey Oliver, b. 14 Aug. 1846; m. 15 Nov. 1873, John Cobb Burnham of Kittery.

10-1-8-3-3

Philip Libby, born in Saco, Me., 11 Nov. 1785; married, 11 Nov. 1810, Christiana Howe of Greene.

When a young man he removed to Leeds, where he married and lived until 1822, when he moved to Greene. In 1827 he went to Burnham, bought land, and built a log-house—the first house that ever stood where Burnham Village now is. After six years he sold out and bought a farm on Clinton Gore, two miles distant. There he resided until 1862, when he removed to Canaan with his son Philip, and there died, 23 Aug. 1868. He was many years a Methodist class-leader, and selectman of "the Gore." His widow died 14 July 1874, in Canaan.

Children, born in Leeds:

1 Sally, b. 4 March 1811; m. James Ryan.
2 Olive, b. 5 Aug. 1813; m. Joseph Crawford.
3 Philip, b. 10 Feb. 1816; m. April, 1845, Miriam, dau. of Alexander and Sally (Soule) Potter of Clinton. She died 27 Feb. 1850. He was a farmer, and lived with his father on Clinton Gore, until 1862, when they removed to Canaan. He now lives in Fairfield, with his only child:
 1 Christiana, b. 2 April 1846; m. 5 Nov. 1877, Philander B. Bessey.
4 Hartley B., b. 9 Jan. 1822; m. 25 Sept. 1842, Mary J., dau. of Capt. Green and Hannah (True) Bagley. He settled on a farm adjoining his father's in Clinton Gore, and lived there until he bought the old homestead, on which he now resides. Children:
 1 Stephen J., b. 23 April 1844; d. 9 May 1862.
 2 Louville A., b. 18 Feb. 1850; is unmarried.
 3 Hannah M., b. 29 Aug. 1852; d. 22 April 1862.

10-1-8-3-4

Ebenezer Libby, born in Saco, Me., 6 Sept. 1787; married Sarah Foster, daughter of Stephen and —— (Streeter) Foster of Winthrop. He removed to Leeds about the time of his marriage, and lived there, a farmer, until his death, 7 Sept. 1859. His widow died 12 Feb. 1876.

Children:

1 Jane, b. Jan. 1810; m. Geo. R. Stanchfield; died Oct. 1878.
2 Ebenezer Haines, b. 31 Jan. 1812; m. 21 Dec. 1848, Charlotte Caroline, dau. of Aaron and Charlotte (Estey) Hartt of Kingsclear, N. B. He was a lumberman on the St. Croix about fifteen years, and then, upon his marriage, settled on a farm in Kingsclear. He soon after went back to Leeds, and lived on a farm there until 1857. From that year he lived on another farm in Kingsclear, on which he died 25 Dec. 1872. His widow sold the farm and went to Fredericton. Children:

1 Emily Jane, b. 13 Sept. 1849, in Kingsclear; died 8 Dec. 1869.
2 Sarah Albitenah, b. 20 July 1851, in Leeds; unm.
3 Charlotte Ludoska, b. 13 Dec. 1852; d. 20 Dec. 1861.
4 Aaron Haines, b. 3 March 1855; is a teacher.
5 Charles Fremont, b. 3 Jan. 1857; is a farmer in Wisconsin.
6 George Frederick, b. 28 Feb. 1860, in Kingsclear; is a bookbinder in Augusta, Me.
7 Olivia, b. 2 Feb. 1862.
8 Stephen Ulysses, b. 1 July 1864.
9 Henry Artemas, b. 15 Jan. 1866.
10 Caroline Armitta, b. 1 Aug. 1868.

3 Telotsen C., lives in Leeds.

4 Stephen, b. 24 May 1815; m. 28 Sept. 1839, Mary Ann, dau. of Capt. Samuel and Mary (King) Stinchfield of Leeds, where he is a farmer. Children:

1 Eben A., b. 23 Nov. 1840; died 23 May 1863; unm. He was an officer in the 14th Me. Vol.
2 Helen Marr, b. 4 Aug. 1842; m. 15 July 1868, Rev. Aaron Hartt.
3 Charles Frederic, b. 20 Dec. 1843; m. 30 June 1869, Clara H., dau. of Rev. Samuel Hartt of New Brunswick. He is a farmer in Milford, Mass. Children:

1 Caroline S., b. 25 Nov. 1870, in Leeds.
2 Nettie B., b. 20 April 1872.
3 Alice M., b. 1 May 1874; d. 21 Aug. 1875.
4 Addison S., b. 3 Aug. 1875, in Framingham, Mass.
5 Fred E., b. 23 July 1877.
6 Alton, b. 23 Dec. 1878, in Milford; d. 25 Dec. 1878.
7 Mary E., b. 12 Oct. 1879.

4 Henrietta B., b. 10 March 1846; m. 23 Dec. 1866, Salmon C. Brewster.
5 Mary Jane, b. 19 May 1856; m. 25 Dec. 1879, George S. Buck.

5 Aretas Thompson, b. 15 Aug. 1824; m. 15 March 1845, Martha Jane, dau. of Wm. and Patty (Ham) Webber of Wellington, Me. He was chiefly employed in cotton mills, and after his marriage lived seven years in Biddeford. 21 Feb. 1852, he started for California, and has not since been heard from. His widow soon after moved to Sanford, where she now lives. Children:

1 Josephine Adelaide, b. 7 April 1846; d. 9 Sept. 1847.
2 Ellen Bruce, b. 26 July 1848; m. 6 July 1869, John W. Lang.
3 Mary Augusta, b. 23 Feb. 1851; m. 9 June 1870, George W. Butler.

10-1-8-3-6

Solomon Libby, born in Saco, Me., 9 Aug. 1791; married, 5 Nov. 1812, Dorcas Foss, daughter of Peter Foss of Scarborough. He removed to Leeds soon after his marriage, and settled on the farm now occupied by his son Uriah. He also engaged in coopering and shingle-weaving. His death took place 17 Aug. 1863. His wife died 20 Nov. 1856.

Children:

1 Eunice, b. 5 Nov. 1813, in Saco; m. 30 Nov. 1834, Charles Berry; died 6 Feb. 1867, in Turner.
2 Pelatiah F., b. 9 May 1815; m. Betsey Carsur.
3 Uriah, b. 28 April 1817; m. Betsey E. Hallowell.
4 Mary, b. 1 Dec. 1818; m. 17 Sept. 1839, Jason Carsur; died 18 May 1881, in Leeds.
5 Asa, b. 22 Sept. 1820; m. Joan D. Fish.
6 Betsey S., b. 21 Aug. 1824; m. 10 July 1845, Jere Day.
7 Hannah J., b. 25 Oct. 1828; m. 11 May 1849, in Monmouth, Jason Fogg; died in that place 25 June 1853.

10-1-8-3-7.

REUBEN LIBBY, born in Saco, Me., 2 July 1793; married, 1816, REBECCA KEENE, daughter of John and Priscilla (Robinson) Keene of Turner.

About 1814 he left Saco, with his bundle under his arm, and went afoot to Leeds. Two years later he married, and settled in Turner, on a farm, on which he always afterward lived, and died 15 March 1872. His widow died 2 July 1876.

Children, all born in Turner:

1 Priscilla, b. 8 Sept. 1816; m. Axel Oldham.
2 Lucius, b. 22 Nov. 1818; d. 18 Dec. 1839; unm.
3 Reuben, b. 12 Feb. 1821; d. 28 July 1828.
4 Josiah, b. 24 Jan 1823; m. Frances Hussey.
5 Lark, b. 16 March 1825; m. 1st, Christiana J. Philoon; 2d, Harriet A. Bonney.
6 Thomas K., b. 26 May 1828; m. 27 Jan. 1853, Eveline B., dau. of Abraham and Delia (Norris) Gifford. He has always lived on the homestead farm. Only child:
    1 Xallissa M., b. 23 Jan. 1856; m. 1874, Alonzo Edgecomb.
7 Lee, b. 11 July 1831; m. 4 May 1852, Sarah C., dau. of Benjamin and Lydia Richards of Livermore. He is a boot manufacturer in Milford, Mass. Children:
    1 Silas F., b. 19 Feb. 1853, in Livermore; m. 1st, 8 May 1873, Amelia C., dau. of John and Arvilla Dinsmore; (died 17 June 1873, in Putnam, Conn.); 2d, 13 May 1880, Lizzie A., dau. of Wm. B. and Mary M. Vezey of Lynn, Mass. He is a farmer in Milford.
    2 Julia C., b. 22 March 1855, in Abington, Mass.; d. 13 July 1855.
    3 Sarah L., b. 7 Feb. 1857; m. 23 May 1878, James A. Tyler.
    4 Jessie L., b. 25 Oct. 1867, in Mendon, Mass.
8 Phineas, b. 12 April 1834; m. 18 Sept. 1855, Flavilla, dau. of Howard and Diana (Wing) Sylvester of Greene. From 1850 to 1860 he worked at shoemaking in Abington, Mass. He then moved to Virginia, but after six months returned to his native town, where he died 7 May 1861. His widow returned to Abington, and married again. His only child was:
    1 Elsie, b. 1860; lives in Brockton, Mass.; unm.
9 Rebecca, b. 31 Jan. 1837; m. Lewis D. Harford.
10 Xallissa M., b. 27 May 1839; d. 8 May 1841.

10-1-8-3-9

ASA LIBBY, born in Saco, Me., 1 Dec. 1797; married LUCY HOUSE, daughter of Nathaniel P. and Zeriah (Cushman) House of Fayette, Me. He was for the most part a farmer. He moved about considerably, but lived some time at Manchester, N. H., where he died 17 June 1874. He was a member of the Freewill Baptist Church. His wife died in Biddeford 20 Aug. 1847.

Children:

1 Zeriah, b. 24 Feb. 1824, in Chesterville, Me.; m. 21 Sept. 1844, Isaac W. Gould; 2d, 6 April 1862, Cornelius R. VanAelstyn.
2 Asenath C., b. 13 Aug. 1826; m. 19 Jan. 1854, Thomas T. Moore; died 17 Feb. 1875.
3 Mary Jane, b. 20 Aug. 1828; m. Frank Hunt in Biddeford; died 1855.

4 Asa S., b. 16 Aug. 1832; m. 22 Feb. 1852, Eliza A., dau. of James and Anna (Dodge) Buckminster of New Boston, N. H. He is a machinist, and has worked for the most part in Manchester, N. H., and in Lawrence, Mass., where he now lives. Children:
  1 Eliza Annette, b. 31 Aug. 1853, in Manchester; d. 23 Sept. 1857.
  2 James Frederick, b. 3 March 1858; unm.; a photographer in Boston.
  3 Nettie Estelle, b. 23 Sept. 1860.
5 Lucy M., b. 1832; died aged two years.
6 Alvin H., b. 14 April 1834, in Jay, Me.; died in July, 1863, before Fort Wagner; unm. He served five years in the regular army, and went into the war as lieutenant in a N. H. volunteer regiment. At the time of his death he was Asst. Adj. General under Gen. Strong.
7 James A., b. 27 Dec. 1836; went to sea at 16, and has not been heard from since, but he has been reported to be living in South America.
8 Lucy M., b. 20 Nov. 1838; m. 10 Dec. 1864, Willard P. Graves of Alexandria, Va.
9 Isaac W., b. in 1845, in Biddeford; died at the age of five years.

10-1-8-3-11

Josiah Libby, born 10 Aug. 1802, in Saco, Me.; married, 27 Nov. 1827, Mary (Haines) Jacobs, widow of Moses Jacobs, jr., and daughter of Samuel and Lydia (McKenney) Haines.

He was successively a farmer, distiller, farmer, stone-mason, brick manufacturer, and finally, for many years in the last of his life, a stone-mason. He died in Biddeford, 1 Sept. 1868, in the house now occupied by his widow.

Children, all born in Saco:

1 James Curtis, b. 7 Oct. 1828; m. Sarah Chase of Lancaster, N. H. He went west in 1856.
2 Henry Green, b. 1 Jan. 1830; m. 24 Dec. 1852, Laura Washington, dau. of Simeon and Sarah (Packard) Tryon of Pownal. He lived successively in Biddeford, Rockland, Biddeford, Me., and Bridgeport, Conn., where his wife still lives. His present whereabouts are unknown. Children:
  1 Laura M., b. 2 Dec. 1853; d. 13 Nov. 1861.
  2 Henry P., b. 24 March 1855; m. 12 Oct. 1880, Mattie Halloway of South Carolina. He is in trade at Freeport, Long Island, N. Y.
  3 Clara E., b. 18 Nov. 1856; m. 13 Sept. 1876, James H. Trulock.
3 Mary Annah, b. 16 Aug. 1831; d. 18 Sept. 1843.
4 Samuel Haines, b. 2 Feb. 1833; d. 29 Jan. 1834.
5 Maria Jane, b. 3 Dec. 1835; d. 20 April 1852.
6 Philemon Haines, b. 18 Oct. 1837; m. 31 May 1865, Louisa, dau. of Edwin and Sarah (Lockwood) Smith of Bridgport, Conn.; died there 8 June 1871. His widow married, 5 Nov. 1872, Walter G. Tillou of New Haven. No children.
7 Susan Elizabeth, b. 28 March 1840; m. Wm. S. Stevens.
8 Daniel Dresser, b. 25 Feb. 1842; m. 17 Oct. 1870, Bella H., dau. of Abel and Mary (Hodgkins) Dennett of Kennebunk. He is by trade a barber, and has been in business in Biddeford many years. Child:
  1 Orin Cilley, b. 28 Sept. 1875.
9 Josiah Franklin, b. 25 Oct. 1843; d. 25 July 1845.
10 Ellen, b. 10 Aug. 1846; m. Geo. H. Andrews.

10-1-8-3-13

PHINEAS LIBBY, born in Saco, Me., 22 Oct. 1807; married, 15 Sept. 1832, NANCY ATKINSON, daughter of Thomas Atkinson of Buxton. She died 8 April 1835, aged 30. He then married, 15 May 1837, SARAH M. FOGG, daughter of William and Abigail (Milliken) Fogg.

He is a well-to-do farmer and shoemaker, and ever since his marriage has lived on the farm of his birth. His wife died 15 May 1880.

Child, by first wife:

1 Alpheus, b. 31 March 1835; m. 26 Nov. 1862, Olive J., dau. of Silas and Eliza (Coolbroth) Harmon. He lives at home a farmer. No children.

Children, by second wife:

2 William Fogg, b. 11 Feb. 1838; m. 6 May 1864, Nancy Ellen, dau. of Seth and Frances A. (Neal) Gurney of Saco. After a brief high school and academic education, and two years as clerk in dry goods stores in Saco, and Boston, Mass., he became clerk in the grocery store of Porter Ford of Biddeford. In 1872, he, with Jos. Etchells, bought out the business, which has since been continued under the style of Libby and Etchells. Children:
   1 Fred Gurney, b. 11 Jan. 1865; d. 22 Feb. 1881.
   2 Harry Wilson, b. 15 Oct. 1870.
   3 Gracie Louise, b. 4 July 1872.
   4 daughter, born and died 27 Jan. 1874.
   5 Sarah Frances, b. 27 Oct. 1878.
3 Hiram Henry, b. 14 Oct. 1839; graduated at Monmouth Academy; read law one year with Philip Eastman of Saco; graduated from Harvard Law School 1865; began the practice of law in Fond du Lac, Wis., soon after, and there died, 16 April 1872, unmarried.
4 Sarah Dresser, b. 16 Jan. 1842; m. 25 Sept. 1865, Otis Joslyn.
5 Nancy Atkinson, b. 10 June 1843; d. 29 Nov. 1847.
6 Mary Abbie, b. 8 March 1845; m. 20 Dec. 1866, Isaac L. Milliken.
7 Nancy Atkinson, b. 27 Oct. 1849; lives at home; unm.

10-1-8-4-2

GEORGE LIBBY, born in Saco, Me., 18 April 1792; married first, SALLY FOSS; second, 27 Feb. 1837, ELIZA CARTER.

He was a farmer, and lived on his father's homestead. His second wife died 3 June 1852. He died 8 June 1858.

Children, all by first wife:

1 Eunice, b. 8 Dec. 1819; m. Cyrus King of Saco.
2 Moses, b. April 1822; d. 15 Jan. 1870, in Portland; unm.
3 William Henry, b. April 1825; m. Lydia S., dau. of Abraham and Eunice (Seavey) Tyler. He was a farmer, and lived near by his father's. He died 30 Jan. 1862. His widow married, 18 Feb. 1868, George E. Johnson, and still lives on the homestead. Children:
   1 George, b. 18 June 1849; d. 3 Nov. 1851.
   2 Sarah Ann, b. 29 July 1850; d. 25 Oct. 1851.
   3 Georgianna, b. 29 March 1852; m. Albert Robinson.
   4 Sally, b. 19 Nov. 1854; m. 12 March 1873, Robert Graffam.
   5 Eunice Buzzell, b. 16 March 1861.

10-1-8-4-4

MOSES LIBBY, born in Saco, Me., 30 Nov. 1796; married, 1835, FANNIE SEAVEY, daughter of Job and Betsey (Tyler) Seavey.

He settled on part of his father's homestead, and died 29 Jan. 1879. His wife died 29 Oct. 1872.

Their children were:

1 Joseph White, b. 27 Jan. 1836; m. 1 Feb. 1877, Marie Louise, dau. of Leon and Lizzie (Potter) Blouin of New Orleans, La. He left Maine for Louisiana in Jan. 1865, and engaged in cotton culture. Since Jan. 1869, he has been successfully engaged in cultivating sugar cane, and the manufacture of sugar. Child:
   1 Fanny Edith, b. 4 Sept. 1878, in New Orleans.
2 Thomas, b. 22 Nov. 1837; d. 14 Sept. 1842.
3 Phebe, b. 12 June 1841; d. 9 Dec. 1856.
4 Thomas Seavey, b. 20 Oct. 1846; m. 5 Nov. 1865, Emma E., dau. of Joseph and Susan (Ellis) Marston of Canton, Me. He lives on the homestead. Child:
   1 Thomas Franklin, b. 18 July 1866.

10-1-8-5-3

REV. THOMAS LIBBY, born in Saco, Me., 24 Dec. 1791; married, 7 Nov. 1811, JOANNA TURNER. 10 Feb. 1828, at Wilton, Me., he was ordained a preacher of the Freewill Baptist denomination, and continued in that church until his death, which occurred in Mercer Co., Ill., 13 March 1879. His wife died in March, 1853, in the same place.

Their children were:

1 Tabitha, b. 8 March 1813, in Leeds; m. Jefferson Fuller.
2 John, b. 2 Oct. 1814; m. Dorothy D. Dixon.
3 William T., b. 11 Sept. 1816; has not been heard from for 35 years.
4 Nancy, b. 30 Nov. 1819; m. J. D. Dixon.
5 Thomas, b. 10 Oct. 1821; m. Olive Simonds.
6 Joanna, b. 17 May 1824, in Chesterville, Me.; m. Wm. Burns.
7 Emulus S., b. 16 Dec. 1826; died in Joy, Me.
8 Josiah, b 16 Oct. 1827; m. Susannah Pollock.
9 Caroline, b. 16 April 1829; m. Joseph Perse.
10 Drusilla, b. 3 Jan. 1832; m. George Brown.
11 Lovina, b. 21 May 1834, in Jay; m. John Brown.

10-1-8-5-4

ZEBULON LIBBY, born in Saco, Me., 28 June 1794; married JANE TURNER, daughter of William and Joanna Turner of Leeds. He went with the rest of the family to Greene, and moved thence, in 1857, to Lisbon, where he died in 1859.

He had the following children:

1 Simeon T., b. 19 Jan. 1825, in Leeds; m. Harriet L. McKenney.
2 Charles O., b. 1830; lives in Lisbon.
3 Daniel B., b. 1835; lives in Auburn.
4 Levi L., born 1840; m. 2 June 1872, Clara S., dau. of Nathan and Samantha M. (Pearson) Nourse of Arlington, Mass. He is a carpenter in Malden. Child:
   1 Arthur L., b. 14 Jan. 1874, in Malden.

10-1-8-5-8

JOHN LIBBY, born in Saco, Me., 5 July 1804; married, 7 Jan. 1829, CAROLINE HAWES, daughter of Ichabod and Mary (Graves) Hawes of Monmouth, Me. He settled at first on his father's homestead farm in Greene. At the age of 50 he moved to Minot, and thence to New Gloucester, in both which places he worked at shoemaking. He died in Lewiston, 5 April 1879. His wife died in the same place 12 July 1866.

Children, all born in Greene:

1 Elvira D., b. 27 Nov. 1831; m. 1 May 1855, Frederick A. Tinkham, now of Lewiston. Children:
  1 Abbie (Tinkham), b. 8 March 1856.
  2 Charles (Tinkham), b. 16 Nov. 1858; deceased.
  3 Nettie (Tinkham), b. 10 Feb. 1864.
2 Marginna S., b. 3 May 1834; m. 12 Nov. 1866, Thomas Teed; died 12 Nov. 1866 in Lewiston.
3 Seth B., b. 10 Nov. 1836; unm. He is a shoemaker in Lynn, Mass.
4 Melissa A., b. 10 April 1839; m. 1st, 1 Jan. 1862, Wm. H. H. Graham; 2d, Daniel Bowers.
5 Silas C., b. 6 Jan. 1841; m. 19 Oct. 1867, Francilla S., dau. of Jonathan and Sarah (Dill) Wright of Lewiston, where he is now a harness-maker. Children:
  1 Herbert, b. 25 Feb. 1870.
  2 Maud, b. 20 Feb. 1878.
6 Abigail, b. 6 Oct. 1842; died 11 Nov. 1854.
7 Drusilla, b. 3 Aug. 1844; died 2 Oct. 1848.
8 Alfred P., b. 23 July 1846; died 27 Sept. 1848.
9 Alfred P., b. 4 Feb. 1849; unm. He lives in Lewiston.
10 John Thomas, b. 11 July 1851; m. 20 June 1878, Mary Ann, dau. of John Hickey of Biddeford. He is a harness-maker. Child:
  1 Alfred, b. 5 Nov. 1878.

10-2-1-1-2

JOSIAH LIBBY, born in Scarborough, 2 Jan. 1774; married first, 30 Nov. 1797, SALLY ELDEN, daughter of Nathan and Elizabeth (Roberts) Elden of Buxton; (died 5 Dec. 1802); second, her sister, RUTH ELDEN.

He served an apprenticeship at the house-carpenter's trade, with Capt. Burbank of Scarborough. Upon his marriage he settled on a farm in West Buxton, now owned by the heirs of Benjamin Mace, and there lived until about 1835, when he moved to Waterford and bought a farm. Five years later he settled on wild land in Jackson, where he cleared a farm, and died, 15 April 1846. His widow died in Bangor, with her son Wm. E., 15 May 1853.

Children, by first wife:

1 Nancy, b. 10 Sept. 1798; m. 1st, Colman Knight; 2d, Warren Williams.
2 Nathan, b. 1 July 1801; m. Maria Dunnell.

By second wife:

3 Josiah, b. 11 July 1806; m. Almira Williams.
4 William E., b. 4 Feb. 1807; m. Catherine Higgins.

5 Sally, b. 26 Oct. 1810; m. 1 Jan. 1832, Stephen Higgins.
6 Samuel, b. 25 April, d. 14 May, 1813.
7 Ruth, b. 22 Jan., d. 29 March, 1815.
8 Samuel, b. 6 Sept. 1816; d. 29 June 1820.
9 Chase Elden, b. 7 Jan. 1820; m. Mary E. Emerson.
10 Mary, b. 23 Sept. 1823; d. 8 March 1828.
11 Phebe, b. 8 May, d. 1 July, 1828.

10-2-1-1-4

Zachariah Libby, born in Scarborough, 24 Dec. 1777; married, 21 Feb. 1802, Priscilla Knight, daughter of Nathaniel Knight.

He was a blacksmith. He accompanied his father to Buxton, and the year following settled on Bonny Eagle Island, in Phillipsburg, now Hollis. In 1811 he bought the farm now occupied by Elisha Davis, and built the brick house now standing. In 1832 he settled on the farm now occupied by Marshall R. Libby, 10-2-1-1-4-5-6.

The mother of his children died 19 Sept. 1828. He married Lucy Norton, a sister of his son Jeremiah's wife, 12 Feb. 1837, and died 24 Oct. 1839, in Gorham. His death was occasioned by an unexpected explosion while blasting a well at Gorham Corner. His widow married, 30 Nov. 1845, Nathaniel Bacon of Gorham.

Children:

1 Nathaniel, b. 16 Nov. 1802, in Scarborough; m. Sally Davis.

Born in Phillipsburg, now Hollis:

2 Ruth, b. 9 April 1802; d. 9 Aug. 1818.
3 Orin, b. 15 April 1806; m. Mary Miles.
4 Hiram, b. 3 Jan. 1809; d. 19 Oct. 1812.
5 Jeremiah, b. 16 Oct. 1811; m. Ruhamah Norton.
6 Levi, b. 1 Jan. 1818; d. 2 July 1840, on a lumbering expedition in Georgia; unmarried.
7 Gibbens, b. 17 Oct. 1822; m. 2 April 1856, Mrs. Anna McIntosh, dau. of Robert and Sarah (Simpson) Rogers of New Brunswick. He went to Boston at the age of 21, where he followed various vocations, but chiefly that of hotel clerk, and afterward proprietor. He died 22 Aug. 1876. His widow still lives in Boston. Children:
   1 Alice P., b. 15 Feb. 1859; m. 26 Nov. 1879, T. J. Sproul.
   2 Emma F., b. 21 April 1865; died 3 Aug. 1865.

10-2-1-1-5

Joel Libby, born in Scarborough, 22 Oct. 1780; married, 2 April 1804, Hannah Knight, daughter of Nathaniel and Ruth (Elden) Knight of Westbrook.

He was a farmer. He lived at first on Bonny Eagle Island, of which he owned all but ten acres.. 19 Jan. 1826, he moved to Gardiner, and settled on a large farm at Libby Hill, where he died on the 30th of October following. His widow died 1 Aug. 1851.

Children, born in Standish:

1 John, b. 15 Jan. 1805; m. 2 Sept. 1834, Hannah, dau. of Stephen and —— (Whitten) Ryder. He has lived in Gardiner always, except six years in Farmingdale. His wife died 4 Aug. 1880. No children.
2 Mary, b. 5 March 1807; m. Ebenezer Libby, 5-2-3-1-6.
3 Lucy, b. 6 July 1810; m. Shem Weeks.
4 Eliza, b. 7 May 1813; d. 26 June 1816.
5 Joel, b. 9 July 1816; d. 19 Jan. 1825.
6 Hiram, b. 9 Jan. 1820; m. 23 Oct. 1842, Nancy S., dau. of Deacon Michael and Patience (Knox) Hildreth; died in Gardiner, Sept. 1881. Children:
  1 William H., b. 26 March 1846; m. 17 Sept. 1870, Mary M., dau. of Hubbard and Helen M. (Robinson) Goldsmith.
  2 George A., b. 8 April 1850; d. 4 Jan. 1851.
  3 H. Frances, b. 26 Oct. 1862.
7 Joel, b. 26 March 1827, in Gardiner; lives in San Francisco, Cal.; unmarried.

10-2-1-1-9

Jeremiah Libby, born in Scarborough, 9 June 1791; married, 29 Oct. 1815, Emma Elden, daughter of Nathan and Elizabeth (Roberts) Elden of Buxton.

He settled on his father's homestead, a farmer and millman. About 1823 he tore down the old house, and built, on a remote part of his farm, the house now occupied by his oldest son. He died 27 July 1844. His wife died 23 Oct. 1842.

Children, all born in Buxton:

1 Ivory, b. 23 May 1816; m. Eliza Ann Davis.
2 Harriet, b. 28 May 1818; m. 6 Jan. 1843, Samuel Davis.
3 Eunice, b. 26 April 1822; m. 9 Dec. 1845, Reuben Harmon.
4 Major Josiah, b. 17 Oct. 1825; m. 1st, Triphena Moses; 2d, Anna Libby, 11-6-2-1-6-*a*.
5 John, b. 16 Dec. 1827; m. 24 Aug. 1853, Octavia Sawyer. He has lived about thirty years in New Bedford, Mass., where he is a baker. Children:
  1 Dora C., b. 1856.
  2 William, b. 1860.
  3 Mary T., b. 1865.
  4 John H., b. 1867.
6 Nathan, b. 12 July 1829; m. Miriam, dau. of America Bisbee of Norway, Me. He learned the trade of machinist. He lived in Norway until 1864, and then emigrated to Ohio. He soon after became a locomotive engineer, and followed that calling, living for the most part in Pennsylvania, until his death, 1881. His widow now lives in Norway, Me. Children:
  1 George, b. 12 July 1856; unm. He is a locomotive fireman.
  2 Fred W., b. 1858; is a locomotive engineer in New York.
  3 Edith May, b. 1861.
  4 ——, died, aged nine months.
7 Alonzo, b. 24 Dec. 1838; m. 25 May 1875, Medora L., dau. of Isaac and Euphresia (Daniels) Williams of Sonora, Cal. In 1858 he went to New Bedford, Mass., and thence, in 1860, to California. He is proprietor of the *Gold Spring Cottage* ranche, in Jamestown. No children.

10-2-1-2-2

Jonathan Libby, born in Scarborough, Feb. 1774; married, 10 Feb. 1803, Lydia Larrabee, daughter of Nathaniel and Sally (Hunnewell) Larrabee.

He settled on a farm in Durham, and there died, 20 Feb. 1836. His widow died in June, 1867, in New Gloucester.

Children, all born in Durham:

1 Samuel, b. 4 May 1803; m. May, 1833, Fatina, dau. of Elizabeth (Libby) Larrabee, 10-2-1-2-7. He is a farmer in Auburn. Children:
  1 Mary R., b. 4 May 1834; d. Aug. 1834.
  2 Betsey J., b. 15 Jan. 1836; m. 20 Oct. 1861, John W. Wilson.
  3 Eliza A., b. 25 May 1839; m. 1 Jan. 1875, Jeremiah Hanscom.
  4 Lydia F., b. 11 May 1844; m. 1 Jan. 1875, Matthias Ripley.
2 Micah, b. 18 Feb. 1806; m. 15 April 1838, Jane, dau. of Jonathan and Jane (Tarr) Brown of Bowdoin. He was a school-teacher and farmer in Litchfield, where he died, 29 June 1867, and his widow still lives. Only child:
  1 Frances J., b. 28 Aug. 1845; m. 12 Dec. 1880, Abel Purinton, jr.
3 Hannah, b. 8 Jan. 1808; m. March, 1850, Rufus Cobb.
4 Dorcas, b. 25 Dec. 1810; m. Stephen Libby, 10-2-1-2-3-9.
5 Sarah, b. 1 Jan. 1813; lives in Alfred, Me.; unm.
6 Eliza, b. 28 Nov. 1815; m. 6 Dec. 1843, John Mitchell.
7 Adeline, b. 10 June 1818; m. Sept. 1840, Nathaniel Hunnewell.
8 Theophilus, b. 5 Dec. 1822; died in Durham, Oct. 1880; unm.
9 Nathaniel, b. 8 Oct. 1824; m. Oct. 1851, Dorcas, dau. of Moses and Polly (McKenney) Hunnewell; died Nov. 1860, in Danville, now Auburn. His widow lives in North Pownal. They had one child, which died young.

10-2-1-2-3

Ephraim Libby, born in Scarborough, now Gorham, 28 Jan. 1781; married, 25 Nov. 1802, Ruth Lord, daughter of Jacob Lord and Ellen Berry. He always lived on his father's homestead, and died 8 Jan. 1830. His widow died 8 Aug. 1850.

Children:

1 Susan, b. 6 Feb. 1798; m. 2 March 1825, John S. Elwell.
2 Alvan, b. 9 Dec. 1802; m. Mary Babb.
3 Jacob, b. 7 April 1805; m. Mary Babb.
4 Hannah, b. 29 Jan. 1807; d. March 1832; unm.
5 Seth Norton, b. 30 April 1808; d. 1836.
6 Sarah, b. 21 Jan. 1810; d. aged 17.
7 Samuel, b. 1 Dec. 1812; lives in Scarborough; unmarried.
8 Levi, b. 1 Nov. 1814; m. 1 Dec. 1850, Martha, dau. of Daniel and Hannah (Graffam) Babb. He lived on the homestead always after his marriage, and died 1 Aug. 1875. Children:
  1 Seth Norton, b. 4 March 1853.
  2 Walter Edgecomb, b. 25 June 1855; m. 18 April 1877, Nellie, dau. of Oliver and Roxanna (Evans) Fletcher. Child:
    1 Eliza Esther, b. 16 Aug. 1878.
  3 Squire Levi, b. 15 May 1858.
  4 Charlotte, b. 9 July 1861.
  5 Eugene Ernest, b. 1 Sept. 1869.
9 Stephen, b. 26 Nov. 1816; m. 1842, Dorcas Libby, 10-2-1-2-2-4. In 1845 he moved to Litchfield, where he lived 22 years. He then lived four years in Wales, and then, after living seven in Monmouth, moved to Auburn, his present residence. He is a farmer. Children:

1 Wiley E., b. 7 Feb. 1843, in Scarborough; m. 1st, 25 March 1871, Clara L., dau. of Chas. H. and Esther A. (Fabyan) Potter of Monmouth; (died 23 Dec. 1872); 2d, 26 April 1876, Adelia M., dau. of Joel and Lydia N. (Cole) Moore of Gouldsborough, Me., where he is now a farmer. Children, by first wife:
1 Melville G., b. 17 July 1872, in Monmouth.

By second wife:

2 Alice D., b. 12 Aug. 1877, in Auburn.
2 Roscoe, b. 31 Jan. 1845, in Scarborough; m. 26 March 1871, Frances A., dau. of Oren P. and Hasadiah (Jackson) Cole of Greene. He is a farmer with his father. Child:
1 Milton, b. 23 Aug. 1872.
10 Ephraim, b. 12 Nov. 1818; m. Charlotte, dau. of Samuel and Mary (Buxton) Cutter. He went to Pownal at the age of 23. He is a farmer in Richmond. Children:
1 Sarah Elizabeth, b. 5 April 1844; m. Daniel Libby, 10-5-4-10-2.
2 Rachel C., b. 25 March 1848; m. 26 March 1867, Henry C. Brown.
3 Howard, b. 1 April 1851; d. 6 May 1870.
11 William, b. 26 April 1820; m. 25 April 1855, Anna, dau. of Joseph Thompson and Angeline (Carr) Phetteplace of Dawkins Mills, Ohio. In 1854 he removed to Hamden, Ohio, and has since lived in that neighborhood. He and his wife are members of the M. E. Church. Children:
1 Julia, b. 29 Feb. 1856, in Dawkins Mills; m. March 1874, in the same place, John Tucker.
2 Eliza, b. 24 Nov. 1858, in Wilkesville; m. 4 Dec. 1876, Abraham Long.
3 Sarah Elizabeth, b. 23 Sept. 1860; m. 20 Dec. 1879, William Montgomery.
4 Lucy Jane, b. 26 Jan. 1862, in Dawkins Mills; d. 1 Sept. 1865.
5 Peda Nima, b. 29 June 1864; d. 24 Aug. 1865.
6 Mary Angeline, b. 28 July 1866.
7 Howard Joseph, b. 19 June 1868; d. 16 Oct. 1871.
8 Alfred Willis, b. 10 Aug. 1870.
9 Emma Leona, b. 27 Nov. 1873.
10 Charles Elmer, b. 12 Feb. 1876.
11 Ellen, b. 21 May 1878.
12 Squire, b. 5 May 1824; m. 8 April 1849, Jane, dau. of Capt. Joseph and Betsey (Buxton) York. At the time of his marriage he had been working some time for the then widow York, and, after marrying her daughter, continued to live there until a year before his death. He died in Portland, 10 Feb. 1862. His widow lives with her son in St. Louis, Mo. Children:
1 Alfred, b. 15 July 1852; m. 30 Dec. 1874, Maggie B. Cannell of Westbrook; died 30 July 1876, in Deering. He was a teamster. He had no children. His widow married John A. Wilkey of Detroit, Mich.
2 Willis, b. 14 May 1854. He is a shoe-cutter. Unmarried.

10-2-1-2-6

Theophilus Libby, born in Scarborough, about 1783; married Patty Sprague. He died in Princeton, Me.

Children:

1 Henrietta, b. 1816; lives in Princeton; unm.
2 James, a Methodist minister; deceased.
3 Sarah Ann, m. Cyrus Larrabee; lives in Durham.
4 Richard, deceased.
5 Theophilus, deceased.

10-2-1-2-9

Richard H. Libby, born in Scarborough, 1796; married, June 1835, Jane (Clark) Baker, widow of Judah Baker, and daughter of Samuel and Elizabeth (Baker) Clark of Litchfield.

He was a farmer. He visited his sister Norton, at Litchfield, and finally married and settled there. He died 5 April 1876. His wife had died thirty years before—30 Aug. 1845.

Children, all born in Litchfield:

1 Nathaniel J., b. 7 April 1836; m. 6 Jan. 1863, Nancy, dau. of Robie and Margaret (Allen) Lydston of Bowdoin. He is a farmer; resides in Litchfield. Children:
 1 George N., b. 4 July 1864.
 2 Nellie Jane, b. 5 May 1866.
 3 Lewis Osborn, b. 17 June 1867.
 4 Ara Brooks, b. 11 Jan. 1869.
 5 James Lydston, b. 7 Dec. 1871.
 6 Edwin Lamson, b. 22 Oct. 1873.
2 Elizabeth Ann, b. 2 June 1838; m. 8 Nov. 1860, Hon. Edwin D. Lamson of Richmond, Me., born in Boston, Mass., 12 Oct. 1834. He is a druggist. He has been representative to the state legislature, and is now senator from Sagadahoc Co. Children:
 1 Florence E. (Lamson), b. 6 Nov. 1861, in Richmond.
 2 Josie A. (Lamson), b. 20 Jan. 1863, in Richmond.
3 Nancy Jane, b. Jan. 1840; d. June, 1845.
4 Harriet Norton, b. 12 June 1842; m. June, 1865, L. S. Brooks.
5 Clark C., b. Aug. 1843; d. Oct. 1845.

10-2-1-5-3

Caleb Libby, born in Scarborough, 14 Oct. 1786; married, first, 31 Jan. 1811, Sarah Webster, daughter of Ebenezer Webster of Cape Elizabeth; second, 30 Jan. 1817, Abigail Simonton of Durham; third, 1826, Sarah (Daniels) Flood from Exeter, N. H.

He early removed to Portland, where he was for many years a stevedore. He died 31 May 1837. His widow died in La Salle, Ill., 18 Aug. 1854.

Children, all born in Portland; by first wife:

1 Eliza, b. 5 Aug. 1812; d. 7 March 1827.
2 John Webster, b. 15 May 1816; m. Oct. 1840, Jane (Rowe) Bolton, dau. of James and Abbie (Noble) Rowe, adopted daughter of an uncle named Bolton. Mr. Libby was brought up by his grandmother Libby, but early removed to Portland, where he has been many years in business as edge-tool-maker. Children:
 1 George Henry, b. 20 Aug. 1841; m. 1 Jan. 1868, Emma, dau. of James and Charlotte (Allan) Nutter of Trescott. He served two years in the 12th Maine Reg., and lost an arm. He has since been a clerk in the office of the Treasurer of Portland. No children.
 2 Abba Sarah, b. 7 Feb. 1844; m. 13 July 1868, Rev. Chas. V. Hanson.

By second wife:

3 Sarah Webster, b. 3 Dec. 1817; d. 30 July 1838; unm.
4 Sophia Hunt, b. 27 Sept. 1820; m. 27 Aug. 1848, Levi S. Brown.

5 Horatio Nelson, b. 5 Oct. 1823; m. 28 July 1863, Hattie Louise, dau. of Albert and Mary Barnes of Johnson Co., Da. He resides in Marengo, Iowa. Children:
 1 Jesse Mae, b. 7 Nov. 1864.
 2 Nelson Hervey, b. 26 Oct. 1875; d. 5 Nov. 1877.
 3 Walter Ray, b. 7 Feb. 1879.

By third wife:

6 Eliza E., b. 27 April 1827; m. 6 April 1853, Stephen E. Foster.
7 Abigail, b. 22 June 1830; d. 16 April 1831.
8 Caleb Henry, b. 12 Sept. 1834; m. 1st, 13 Sept. 1865, in Brooklyn, Iowa, Jane E., dau. of Henry Newall and Elizabeth Alice (Montgomery) James of Franklin Co., Vt.; (died 23 May 1872); 2d, 10 June 1873, Minerva, dau. of David and Elizabeth (Porter) Shoemaker of Ashland Co., Ohio. He early went west, and has been in business in Brooklyn many years. Child, by first wife:
 1 George Frederick, b. 6 Aug., d. 26 Aug. 1867.

Child, by second wife:

 2 Sarah Elizabeth, b. 4 May 1875.

10-2-1-5-6

THEOPHILUS LIBBY, born in Scarborough, 1 March 1792; married first, 25 Dec. 1812, DEBORAH WEBSTER, daughter of Ebenezer and Anna (Wescott) Webster of Cape Elizabeth; (died 30 Sept. 1825); second, 5 Feb. 1826, SALLY WOOD, daughter of Isaiah and Sally (Taylor) Wood of Standish.

After his marriage he lived in Portland until 1827, in the occupation of stevedore. In the year mentioned he bought a farm in Danville, now part of Auburn, and there lived until his death, which occurred 16 May 1856. His widow died 15 Jan. 1874.

Children, by first wife:

1 Anna, b. 5 Jan. 1814; m. John W. Jordan.
2 Nelson, b. 25 April 1816; d. 15 Aug. 1816.
3 Ebenezer W., b. 22 Sept. 1818; d. 23 Sept. 1818.
4 Charles S., b. 14 Sept. 1820; m. 1st, 9 Oct. 1843, Sarah G. Cushing of North Weymouth, Mass.; (died 4 June 1845); 2d, 27 April 1845, Ann Maria, dau. of Charles and Eliza Stevens of Boston, Mass.; (died 25 April 1853); 3d, 16 Oct. 1857, Eliza S. (Nutting) Libby, widow of his brother Henry I. Libby; (died 13 March 1859); 4th, 6 Nov. 1862, Lizzie Loring; (died 25 April 1864); 5th, 24 Dec. 1870, Nancy T. Manwell, dau of Levi and Clarissa (Foster) Chandler of Winthrop, Me. When he was 21 he went to Massachusetts. He was some years head clerk of the Neponset House. After his third marriage he settled on a farm in New Gloucester, Me., but his wife died soon after, and he returned to Massachusetts. He served from Sept. 1864, until the close of the war, in Co. B, 64th New York Regiment. He died 11 June 1879, in Winthrop, Me., where his widow still lives. Children:
 1 and 2 sons, by first wife; died in infancy.
 3 child, by second wife; died in infancy.
 4 Elizabeth Maria, by third wife, b. 20 Feb., d. 21 May, 1859.
5 Mary W., b. 16 March 1823; d. 16 Sept. 1824.

By second wife:

6 Elizabeth Ilsley, b. 3 Dec. 1826; m. Hiram W. Gould.
7 Jane, b. 10 May 1828; m. 25 Dec. 1855, James Harrison.

8 Henry I., b. 16 May 1830; m. Elizabeth, dau. of John R. and Mary (Stinchfield) Nutting of Danville; d. 4 Jan. 1854. His widow married his brother, Charles S. Libby. Only child:
 1 Charles Hiram, b. 6 July 1852; m. 28 March 1870, Maria S., dau. of Rev. Ira G. and Mary M. (Wagg) Ridlon of Lewiston. He was in early life a peddler, but is now a farmer in Lisbon. Children:
  1 Nettie E., b. 4 March 1871.
  2 Charles Edgar, b. 26 Nov. 1874.
  3 George I., b. 26 April 1876.
  4 Mary Edna, b. 6 Aug. 1879.

9 Ebenezer W., born 11 Feb. 1832; m. 1 Jan. 1856, Judith H. Libby, 10-5-6-5-5-3. He is a farmer in Durham. Children:
 1 Herbert A., b. 24 April 1857.
 2 Marcia E., b. 15 April 1861.
 3 Greenfield T., b. 27 May 1870.
 4 Alice M., b. 17 Dec. 1873; d. 9 March 1874.
 5 Edith F., b. 17 Dec. 1875.
 6 Carrie E., b. 20 Jan. 1878.

10 George, b. 31 Dec. 1833; m. 21 Jan. 1863, Sophronia A., dau. of Benjamin H., and Sarah (Skillings) Henderson of Anson. He was in trade in Lewiston, two years, but the rest of his life (since his marriage) has been spent in farming, in Minot, since 1875. Children:
 1 Alberta L., b. 21 Dec. 1863.
 2 Henry A., b. 15 March 1867.
 3 Sarah W., b. 20 April 1869.
 4 Annie M., b. 27 Sept. 1877.

11 Azariah, b. 28 May 1836; m. 1 Jan. 1859, Ruth Ellen, dau. of Washington and Elizabeth J. (Haskin) Parker of Durham. Except a short period spent in Durham, he has always occupied the homestead farm. Children:
 1 Theophilus, b. 14 May 1859, in Danville.
 2 Warren L., b. 14 April 1862.
 3 Washington E., b. 29 Jan. 1866.
 4 Charlotte E., b. 16 July 1867.
 5 Millard G., b. 27 Aug. 1869, in Auburn.
 6 Emma L., b. 27 Oct. 1871.
 7 William B., b. 14 June 1873.

12 Sarah W., b. 7 Jan. 1839; is unmarried; a short-hand writer in Boston.

10-2-1-5-8

Enos Libby, born 13 Oct. 1795, in Scarborough; married Lydia Libby, 5-7-15-5.

He worked at ship-carpentering in Kittery and in Falmouth. At the time of his death he lived on his father-in-law's farm in Scarborough. The story of his death is a warning one. He was drowned in Mill Creek, 22 Aug. 1833, while in a state of intoxication. His little son, who was with him, was also drowned. After his death, his widow kept a boarding-house in Biddeford, and died 29 Jan. 1869.

Their children were:

1 Samuel, b. 1824; was drowned 22 Aug. 1833.

2 Gardner, b. 10 July 1831; m. 7 Feb. 1860 Henrietta A., dau. of Josiah and Nancy (Smith) Spofford of Portland. He learned the painter's trade. For twenty-three years he had charge of the painting department of the Laconia repair-shop. He is now in business as painter and dealer in painters' supplies. Child:

1 Emily Gertrude, b. 25 July 1862.

3 George Washington, b. 1829; d. 22 Oct. 1857; unmarried. Always after his father's death, he lived with Daniel Larrabee, in Scarborough.

4 Abbie, b. 1833; m. 1st, 5 July 1852, Joseph B. Walker; 2d, Frank Stetson.

10-2-1-5-10

SAMUEL LIBBY, born in Scarborough, 7 March 1799; married, 1822, MARY CLEAVES, daughter of Margaret Cleaves, who was a daughter of Israel Cleaves of Hollis. Upon his marriage he settled on the homestead of his wife's grandfather, and always lived there afterward. He died 3 June 1875. His wife died 31 July 1822.

Their children were:

1 Israel, b. 12 Oct. 1822; m. Dec. 1846, Mary, dau. of Alexander and Margaret (Gray) Grant of Lyman. He has always been a farmer, except six years, including the time of his marriage, during which he was in trade at Goodwin's Mills. He lives on the homestead. Child:

1 Joshua, b. 22 March 1848; m. 1st, Hattie, dau. of Hiram and Lucinda (Jellison) Dillow of Dayton; (they were divorced, and she married, Nov. 1877, Henry Emmons of Lyman); 2d, Emma, widow of John Temple, and dau. of Wm. Goodwin of Lyman. He is a horse-car conductor in Boston. Children, by first wife:

1 Charles, } twins, born } d. 7 Jan 1875.
2 Frank R., } 6 Sept. 1870; } lives with his mother.

2 Miranda, b. 14 Feb. 1824; m. Ward S. Knapp.

3 Mary Elizabeth, b. Feb. 1826; m. James H. Moore of Brunswick, Me.

4 Samuel, b. 27 April 1833; lives at home; unm.

5 Louisa Maria, b. 9 May 1843; m. Wm. W. Drew.

10-2-1-5-13

JAIRUS LIBBY, born in Scarborough, 25 Oct. 1806; married, 1 Dec. 1831, HANNAH STEVENS, daughter of Eliab and Rebecca (Pendexter) Stevens of Limington. He always lived on his father's homestead, and died there 19 Aug. 1863. His widow still survives.

Their children were:

1 Abigail Ann, b. 10 Sept. 1832; m. 26 June 1852, James W. Tucker.

2 Enos Hubbard, b. 21 Dec. 1833; m. Emeline Libby, 10-2-4-9-2-2. He lives on his father's homestead. Children:

1 Annie Andrews, b. 10 Dec. 1860.
2 Abbie Tucker, b. 16 May 1862.
3 Stevens, b. 2 April 1864.
4 George Henry, b. 5 May 1866.
5 Charles Hubbard, b. 2 Feb. 1868.
6 Justice Lewis, } twins, born }
7 Eugene Miller, } 16 Oct. 1869; } d. 28 Sept. 1870.
8 Eugene Miller, b. 11 Nov. 1873.
9 John Edward, b. 4 Dec. 1874.
10 Mabel Julia, b. 10 June 1877.

3 Eliab Stevens, b. 22 Oct. 1835; d. 30 May 1845.

10-2-1-6-2

Elisha Libby, born in Scarborough, 16 Oct. 1788; married 28 Dec. 1815, Mary Edgecomb, daughter of Thomas Edgecomb of Parsonsfield.

He learned the trade of ship-carpenter at Stroudwater Village, and also worked as house-carpenter; but his chief occupation was farming. He settled in Gardiner on the farm now owned by Eliakim Norton, and died 24 April 1878. He had a second wife, the widow Harmon of Scarborough, and married third, Mrs. Abigail Whitney, now living in West Gardiner.

Children, all by first wife:

1 Stillman B., b. 17 Dec. 1816, in Parsonsfield; m. 3 Nov. 1846, Lydia S. dau. of Lemuel and Betsey (Holbrook) Standish of Bath. He is a farmer in Gardiner. Child:
 1 Florence E., b. 21 Oct. 1855.
2 Hannah E., b. 11 July 1818; m. 1 Oct. 1839, Hiram Hildreth.
3 James E., b. 9 Dec. 1820, in Gardiner; d. 26 May 1830.
4 Elizabeth A., b. 22 Dec. 1825; m. 18 April 1849, Joseph Sippers.

10-2-1-6-3

Joseph Libby, born in Scarborough, 5 Aug. 1790; married, 24 Aug. 1818, Lydia Libby, 5-2-3-1-1. He removed to Gardiner in Feb. 1819, and has ever since lived on the farm then purchased. His wife died 5 Nov. 1877. He still survives, at the age of 90.

Children, all born in Gardiner:

1 Eben, b. 4 June 1819; m. 4 Sept. 1845, Lydia Ann Libby, 5-7-14-9-1. He has always lived on his father's homestead; has been alderman, and member of the city council several times. Children:
 1 Emma M., b. 4 Dec. 1847; d. 4 Feb. 1868; unm.
 2 Lorenzo, b. 3 Sept. 1851; d. 22 Nov. 1851.
 3 Mary J., b. 25 May 1853; d. 16 Aug. 1855.
 4 Henrietta, b. 6 April 1856. She has eleven descents from John Libby, the emigrant; is descended from five of his children; and is of the seventh, eighth and ninth generations.
 5 Everett D., b. 28 Jan. 1858; d. 10 Oct. 1863.
 6 Sarah Ann, } twins, b. 29 June;
 7 Amanda S., } died 24th and 25th of Aug., 1859.
2 Abial, [M.D.], b. 1 Oct. 1822; m. 1st, 14 Dec. 1851, Harriet Louisa, dau. of Samuel Ford and Elizabeth (Hathorn) Blair of Richmond; (died 28 Oct. 1862); 2d, 27 July 1865, Susan, widow of Capt. Joseph S. Hathorn, and dau. of James and Lucy (Hildreth) Lennan of Richmond. He was educated at the Gardiner Lyceum, Monmouth Academy, and Maine Medical School, graduating from the latter in 1846. He subsequently attended a course of lectures at the Jefferson Medical College, Philadelphia. In 1849 he began practice in Richmond, Me., where he has since continued. 6 Aug. 1861, he was commissioned assistant surgeon of the 4th Reg. Maine Vol., and the following March was promoted to surgeon, but resigned on account of his wife's sickness. Children, by first wife:
 1 Harriet Elizabeth, b. 9 April 1854; graduated at Kent's Hill, Me., 1873, and spent three years in Paris, studying French.
 2 Martha Carlton, b. 26 Dec. 1856; d. 21 July 1857.
 3 Joseph Blair, b. 1 Aug. 1859; d. 16 July 1860.
 4 Georgianna Knox, b. 6 Sept. 1861; d. 11 Aug. 1862.

By second wife:

5 Alice M., b. 30 April 1867.
6 Fannie Lucille, b. 21 March 1872.
7 Frederick Joseph, b. 24 Nov. 1874.

3 Mariam, b. 24 Dec. 1824; d. 6 Oct. 1826.

10-2-1-6-4

Asa Libby, born in Scarborough, 16 May 1793; married, 20 Dec. 1820, in St. Davids, N. B., Sarah A. (Caldwell) Gray, daughter of John C. and Amelia (Hitchings) Caldwell of Schoharie, N. Y.

He served in the war of 1812, and for his service received a land grant. In 1817 he went east, and settled at St. Davids, N. B., where he married and lived until 1830. He was engaged in lumbering. In 1830 he removed to the wilderness of what is now Alexander, Me., and there lived until his death, 17 May 1872. At various times he filled the offices of county commissioner and justice of the peace, and the highest town offices. He was a member of the Methodist Church. His widow died 13 Feb. 1879.

Children:

1 Richard Hubbard, b. 10 March 1821; m. 1st, 20 Nov. 1847, Sarah B., dau. of John and Abbie (Robinson) Stanchfield of Robbinston; (died 20 Nov. 1856); 2d, in Wausau, Wis., Nellie M. Briggs. He settled first in Alexander, lived then at Milltown, where his wife died, and then went west. He now lives in Fairfax, Kan. Children:
   1 Edgar, b. 9 March 1862.
   2 Fred, b. April 1867.

2 Oliver H., b. 28 Dec. 1823; m. 1 Dec. 1858, Helen A., dau. of Isaiah T. Foster of Cooper, Me. He lives on the homestead farm in Alexander. He is one of the selectmen. His wife died 13 June 1866. Children:
   1 George W., b. 8 Oct. 1859.
   2 Carrie H., b. 23 April 1862.

3 Ann B., twin with the last; b. 28 Dec. 1823; m. 12 Jan. 1852, Francis McKusick; died 31 Jan. 1875, in St. Cloud, Minn.

4 Asa, b. 4 Jan. 1826; m. 12 Jan. 1852, Olive, dau. of Abial and Eunice (Townsend) Abbott of Alexander. He went to Minnesota in 1858, and is now living in St. Cloud.

5 Alice B., b. 16 July 1827; m. 12 Jan. 1852, Hampden Cottle; died 26 Feb. 1855, in Alexander.

6 Abner Winslow, b. 26 April 1829; m. 15 June 1857, Ursula, dau. of John K. and Elizabeth (Gooch) Damon of Alexander. He removed to Minnesota in 1858, and died in Watab, 23 March 1869.

7 Amelia F., } twins, born } died 29 May 1840.

8 Amanda T., } 19 Feb. 1834; } m. 7 Sept. 1855, Charles Stanchfield; died 21 April 1865, in Alexander.

10-2-1-6-5

Col. John Libby, born in Scarborough, 25 June 1795; married Mercy Robinson, daughter of Stephen Robinson of Gardiner.

He was by trade a shoemaker, but always resided upon, and cultivated, a farm. He was a colonel in the state militia. He died 29 Sept. 1858. His widow died 12 Oct. 1871.

Children, all born in Gardiner:

1 Asa, b. 15 Dec. 1820; m. 1st, 1 Jan. 1851, Mary E., dau. of Daniel Hildreth of Gardiner; (died 3 Aug. 1851); 2d, Oct. 1856, Mary E. Sweetland. He is a teamster in Salem, Mass. Only child:
  1 George W., b. 23 Dec. 1857, in Gardiner.

2 Phineas, b. 26 March 1824; m. 27 Dec. 1855, Caroline Frances, dau. of Melgar and Susan Waterman of New Orleans, La. She died 1 June 1880, in Lewiston. He is a bookbinder; has lived in different places in Massachusetts and in Maine, and is now at Lewiston. Children:
  1 William Everett, b. 20 Aug. 1857, in Roxbury, Mass.
  2 Lucy Ella, b. 3 Jan. 1861, d. 13 April 1865, in Roxbury.
  3 Susie Jane, b. 29 March 1866, in Boston, Mass.
  4 Charles Melgar, b. 3 Aug. 1867, in Augusta, Me.
  5 Anna Waterman, b. 9 Nov. 1871, in Augusta; d. 9 Jan. 1880, in Lewiston.
  6 Henry Phineas, b. 20 July 1875, in Augusta; d. 3 Jan. 1880, in Lewiston.

3 Stephen Robinson, b. 14 Dec. 1828; m. 14 April 1861, in Morrison, Ill., Lydia Plummer, dau. of Joseph and Elizabeth (Robinson) Roberts. He received an academic education. He taught school and worked at farming until 1854, when he removed to Whiteside County, Ill., where he has followed the same callings. Children:
  1 Mary Addie, b. 6 June 1862.
  2 Howard Xanthus, b. 7 Nov. 1865.
  3 Helen Maria, b. 15 March 1868; d. 30 Nov. 1869.
  4 Mildred Anna, b. 26 June 1871.
  5 John Herschel, b. 13 Aug. 1876.

4 Richard H., b. 18 Nov. 1830; m. Susan Capen. He lives in the West; has one son.

5 Mercy A., b. 12 Aug. 1832; is unmarried; a milliner.

6 Hannah E., b. 11 Aug. 1834; d. 27 Jan. 1853.

7 John Wesley, b. 5 Feb. 1836; lives in West Gardiner, a farmer; unmarried.

8 Lydia M., b. 12 April 1838; m. John Mercer.

9 Joseph Benjamin, b. 22 May 1841; is a carriage maker in Gardiner; unmarried.

10 Mary E., b. 1 May 1846; is forewoman in a shoe factory in Lynn, Mass.; unmarried.

10-2-2-11-2

William Harmon Waterhouse, born in Scarborough, 14 Oct. 1779; married, 31 Jan. 1802, Sarah B. Smith, daughter of Capt. Ephraim and Elizabeth (Harding) Smith of Gorham. He was a farmer, and lived where John A. Bodge now lives, in North Gorham. His wife died 10 Oct. 1845. He died 4 Nov. 1867.

Children, all born in Gorham:

1 Thomas S. (Waterhouse), b. 5 April 1803; lives in Gorham.

2 Daniel (Waterhouse), b. 27 Sept. 1805; d. 31 Aug. 1807.

3 Freeman (Waterhouse), b. 25 July 1807; d. 9 Oct. 1809.

4 Levi H. (Waterhouse), b. 30 Sept. 1809; lives in St. John, N. B.

5 Samuel S. (Waterhouse), b. 21 July 1811; m. 1st, 3 June 1838, Ann, dau. of Wm. and Eunice (Nason) Bolton; (died 24 Oct. 1859); 2d, 22 Nov. 1861, Eleanor, widow of George Small of Raymond, by birth a Patten of Richmond, Me.; (d. May 1872); 3d, 1874, Priscilla Frances (Libby) Ward, 10-5-4-3-6-2. He was at first a painter, and then a cotton-mill operative. Since 1848 he has been a farmer, owning the farm that had belonged to his grandfather Smith. He has been four years selectman of Gorham. Children, by first wife:

1 Julia Adeline (Waterhouse), b. 21 Aug. 1840; m. Joel Wilson; died 28 Nov. 1874.
2 Elbridge H. (Waterhouse), b. 24 Nov. 1842; d. 17 June 1862.
3 Melvin C. (Waterhouse), b. 20 Aug. 1846; d. 19 Dec. 1864.
4 Charles M. (Waterhouse), b. 19 Aug. 1849; m. Emma, dau. of Stephen and Emeline (Jordan) Wescott.
5 Mary Etta (Waterhouse), b. 19 June 1854; m. 27 Nov. 1878, Howard Small of Gorham.

By second wife:

6 Hattie E. (Waterhouse), b. 3 Jan. 1865; d. 11 Aug. 1867.

6 Gardner (Waterhouse), b. 22 Jan. 1814; lives in Standish.
7 Sumner (Waterhouse), b. 31 Oct. 1816; d 13 Aug. 1868.
8 Elizabeth Jane (Waterhouse), b. 29 May 1818; died 18 Dec. 1853, in Portland; unmarried.
9 Prentiss M. (Waterhouse), b. 8 Sept. 1820; m. 1st, 13 Sept. 1846, Sarah Rounds of Buxton; (died 8 Dec. 1866); 2d, 30 June 1869, Sarah Libby, 10-5-4-2-9-3. He was by trade a machinist, but spent the latter years of his life on a small farm in Gorham, where he died 9 April 1871. Children, all by first wife:
1 Mary M. (Waterhouse), b. 20 June 1847; m. James Henry Libby, 10-5-4-1-1-6-4.
2 Annie A. (Waterhouse), b. 11 Jan. 1850; m. Charles Cloudman.
3 Albert E. (Waterhouse), b. 4 Nov. 1853.
4 Freddie P. (Waterhouse), b. 5 Feb. 1858; d. 29 Sept. 1860.

10-2-4-2-7

Lemuel Libby, born in Scarborough, now Gorham, 10 Jan. 1784; married, Oct. 1814, Narcissa Harmon, daughter of Isaac and Sarah (Milliken) Harmon of Scarborough. He was a farmer and carpenter. Except about thirteen years spent at Black Point, with the widow of Capt. Anthony Libby, 1-1-2-7, his life was spent for the most part on his father's homestead, and he died there 7 Dec. 1854. His widow died in Auburn, with her son Abram, about 1870.

Children:

1 Harriet Berry, b. 2 June 1815; m. 11 March 1844, Zebulon B. Deering.
2 Isaac, b. 15 Feb. 1817; m. 1st, 31 Oct. 1847, Elizabeth P., dau. of Charles and Eliza (Emerson) Morris of Scarborough; 2d, 9 May 1857, Mahala A., dau. of Hannah (McKenney) Chapman, 11-7-2-9-2. He is of the firm of Hanson & Libby, carriage and wheel wrights, Portland. Children, by first wife:
1 Georgianna Morris, b. 16 Nov. 1849, in Scarborough; m. 1 Jan. 1867, Isaac Dunham of Brooklyn, N. Y.
2 Charles James Morris, b. 24 April 1851; unm. He works in a kerosene oil factory, in Brooklyn.

By second wife:

3 Frances Elizabeth, b. 10 April 1861, in Patten, Me.
4 Frederick Herbert, b. 14 March 1863, in Westbrook.

3 Abram, b. Oct. 1821; m. Hannah Linscott of Buxton. He is a farmer. He had the homestead, and occupied it until about 1860, when he removed to his present farm in Auburn. Children:
1 Julia, b. 2 Nov. 1849; m. Horace Ross of Yarmouth.
2 Amanda Olive, b. 28 July 1851; unm.
3 George A., b. 16 June 1853; unm.
4 Joseph B., b. 8 May 1856; unm.

5 Charles L., } twins, born
6 William B., } 16 May 1859.
7 Frank E., b. 1863.
8 Everett E., b. 1865.

10-2-4-2-8

ABRAHAM LIBBY, born in Scarborough, 10 Dec. 1784; married, 24 March 1814, PHEBE MOULTON, daughter of Charles Pine and Olive (Fabyan) Moulton of Scarborough.

In his younger days he was a cooper. He afterward settled on a farm in Wilton, from which town he removed, in 1840, to Hancock County, Ill., where he lived until his death, 4 June 1848. He was a member of the M. E. Church, and was a local preacher. His wife died 14 Aug. 1841.

Children:

1 Charles Moulton, b. 19 Jan. 1815, in Brownfield; m. 24 July 1843, Pluma. dau. of Richard Andrews of Hancock County, Ill. He was a farmer in McDonough County, Ill., where he died 11 March 1874, and his widow still lives. Children:
1 Warren, b. 14 Oct. 1845; unm.; is a farmer in Smith Co., Kans.
2 Lavinia, b. 24 Dec. 1847; m. Robert Chapin.
3 Franklin, b. 27 June 1853; died 5 Aug. 1863.
4 Seth, b. 21 April 1855; unm.; lives at home.
2 Mehitable, b. 22 June 1817, in Gorham; d. 18 June 1835.
3 Olive Moulton, b. 21 April 1820, in Wilton; m. 21 April 1842, John W. Farrell, who died 19 Sept. 1852.
4 Cyrus Fenderson, b. 3 Nov. 1823; m. 10 April 1855, Rhoda E., dau. of Anson and Caroline (Perkins) Hobart. Previous to his marriage he worked three years in the lead mines in Wisconsin. Upon his marriage he emigrated to Oregon. He built the first dwelling-house in Silverton, where he has lived most of the time since, and has been engaged as saddler, farmer, and (now) in the livery business. Children:
1 Marion F., b. 27 April 1854; unm.
2 Minerva M., b. 3 May 1858; m. 2 Dec. 1873, W. G. Daws.
3 Daniel T., b. 6 Dec. 1860.
4 Louisa C., b. 13 Aug. 1862; d. 4 Oct. 1879.
5 Eleanor A., b. 25 April 1864.
6 Jasper F., b. 5 March 1866, in Portland.
7 Warren G., b. 22 April 1868, in Silverton.
8 Effie L., b. 7 Aug. 1870.
9 Charles F., b. 25 May 1872.
10 Lora May, b. 9 Aug. 1878.
5 Eleanor, b. 11 March 1827; died 18 June 1830.
6 Phebe Ann, b. 24 Oct. 1831; m. 24 March 1861, Velzer Shaw of Scandia, Kans. Children:
1 Eva G. (Shaw), b. 22 Jan. 1863, in Berlin, Ill.
2 Amos Dewitt (Shaw), b. 26 Nov. 1865, in Rock Island, Ill.
3 Orris Eugene (Shaw), b. 6 May 1868, in Poweshiek Co., Iowa.
4 Marcus Zenephon (Shaw), b. 18 April 1870.
5 Charles Moulton (Shaw), b. 3 Oct. 1872, in Marshall Co., Kan.
6 Ella Olive (Shaw), b. 17 June 1877, in Republic Co., Kan.

10-2-4-2-14

DARIUS LIBBY, born in Scarborough, now Gorham, July, 1795; married PHEBE SMALL, daughter of Reuben and Sally (Patch) Small of Limington. He was a farmer. He lived successively in

Gorham, Westbrook, Portland, Gorham, on Hoop Island, Buxton, and finally Gorham, where he died in July, 1873.

Children:

1 Irene B., b. 7 Nov. 1829; m. Wm. Metcalf of Gorham.
2 Oliver Francis, b. 26 Aug. 1831; m. 1st, 16 Nov. 1853, Mariam P. Metcalf; (died 28 Dec. 1854); 2d, Sarah A. Haines. He lived, when last heard from, in Prairie Village, Ill. Children; by first wife:
  1 son, died very young.

By second wife:

  2 Elma, b. 1861.
  3 Elinor, b. 1862.
  4 Edward, b. 1864.
  5 Frank, b. 1873.
  6 Paul, b. 1875.
3 Charles H., b. 3 Aug. 1863; m. Cordelia E. Jones of Illinois. He was living in Oregon, and is supposed to have lost his life in an Indian raid, during the Rebellion. Children:
  1, 2 died young.
  3 Samuel.
  4 Frank.
  5 Edwin.
4 Sarah P., b. 28 Dec. 1836; m. Capt. Charles H. Doughty.
5 Edward A., b. 30 July 1839; m. Emily Elizabeth, dau. of Moses and Olive (Hersom) Foye of Berwick. He lives in Rochester, N. H. Children:
  1 Hermon E., b. 20 Jan. 1861.
  2 Frank L., b. 20 Jan. 1864.
  3 Linnwood E., b. 31 May 1867.
  4 John W., b. 23 Sept. 1869.
  5 Delmah C., b. 8 Dec. 1873.
  6 Emily E., b. 2 May 1878.
  7 Beulah L., b. 13 March 1881.
6 Mary Ann, b. 15 Sept. 1842; m. Andrew Doughty of Chebeague Island.
7 Phebe J., b. 1 Aug. 1844; m. 10 Dec. 1865, William Cole, jr.

10-2-4-3-1

Elliot Libby, born in Scarborough, 22 Dec. 1782; married, 21 Dec. 1806, in Portland, Nancy Boswell of Conway, N. H., born 3 June 1784. He early removed to Portland, where he was for many years a hardware dealer. He died 10 April 1825. His widow died 30 May 1840.

Children, all but Converse born in Portland:

1 Lucretia, b. 14 Sept. 1807; m. 7 Oct. 1829, Nehemiah P. Cram.
2 Lucy Ann, b. 27 April 1809; m. Dec. 1832, Alfred Randall.
3 Elliot, b. 6 Dec. 1811; d. 28 Sept. 1854, in Monterey, Cal.; unm.
4 Converse, b. 30 June 1814, in Gorham; m. 8 Feb. 1838, Nancy, dau. of John and Anne (Larrabee) Meserve. He was a farmer. He led a somewhat roving life, but settled, finally, in Buxton, where he died 1 May 1876, and his widow still lives. Children:
  1 Ann, b. 27 March 1840, in Brunswick; m. Samuel A. Hill of Buxton.
  2 Helen Maria, b. 4 July 1844, in Durham; m. 7 Jan. 1872, Mark Hill of Buxton.

3 Lucy Randall, b. 15 Aug. 1846, in Scarborough; lives with her mother; unmarried.
4 Mary Johnson, b. 20 Aug. 1850; m. 1st, 2 June 1872, Wm. H. Norton; 2d, 15 June 1876, Daniel Wentworth.
5 Frederick, b. 24 Oct. 1818; d. 5 Nov. 1856, in East Saginaw, Mich.; unmarried.
6 Henry, b. 12 July 1820; d. 29 Aug. 1821.
7 Charlotte Paine, b. 6 Aug. 1822; m. John H. Butler, Esq., of Boston, Mass.
8 Henry, b. Feb. 1825; d. Sept. 1825.

10-2-4-3-2

Samuel Libby, born in Scarborough, 30 Aug. 1784; married, 23 Feb. 1808, Sarah Beals, daughter of Isaiah and Agnes (Skillings) Beals of Scarborough.

He and his brother Enoch left home when of age, and bought wild timber lands on the bank of the Kennebec River, in what is now Richmond, of a man named Foxcroft. After living on it awhile, and making improvements, it came to light that Foxcroft had not owned the land, and they were compelled to give it up to the rightful owner. Having exhausted their savings in the purchase and improvement of these lands, in losing them they became homeless.

Samuel afterward lived in Wales, in Starks, in Industry, in Farmington, and finally bought a farm in Strong, on Taylor Hill, where he died 3 April 1853. His wife had died in the same place, 24 Jan. 1848.

Children, born in Wales:

1 Harriet, b. 25 March 1810; m. —— Taylor of Strong; d. 31 July 1849.
2 Washington, b. 17 March 1812; is a bachelor. He went to Boston at the age of 17; was five years in the Quincy market; lived ten years in Alton, Ill., returning to Boston in 1847, and joining his brother, Isaiah B., in the flour and grain business—W. & I. B. Libby; he continued the business with his brother, and after his death, until 1868, when he sold out, and went to Chicago "to nominate Gen. Grant"; he bought out the St. James hotel there, and kept it until the great fire in 1871; has since been a capitalist, residing in Chicago.
3 Isaiah B., born 5 Sept. 1813; m. 29 Dec. 1836, in Boston, Mrs. Lucy Mary Kinsell, dau. of Nathaniel and Lucy (Fowle) Stone of Roxbury; died 28 Jan. 1858. His widow is still living. Children:
 1 Isaiah Franklin, b. 28 Oct. 1838; m. Mary Carter of Waltham. He was many years in business in his father's store, as a member of the firm of Eustis & Libby, but is now a bookkeeper in Chicago. Children:
  1 Frederic C., b. 7 Dec. 1861, in Chelsea, Mass.
  2 Gertrude, b. 7 June 1869, in Newton, Mass.
 2 Eliza J., b. 2 May 1841; died 19 Jan. 1845.
 3 George W., b. 2 Aug. 1847; m. Addie, dau. of John Hinckley of Boston. He is a bookkeeper, living in Charlestown, Mass. Children:
  1 Ella F., b. 28 Jan. 1873.
  2 Grace, b. 3 July 1879.
 4 Ella Florence, b. 3 March 1849; m. Melbourne S. Halladay.
4 Dominicus, b. 5 Sept. 1813; died in Boston, 25 Oct. 1835.

5 Francis, b. 1 July 1816; m. 28 Nov. 1848, Jane L., dau. of Charles and Abby (Hogaborn) Brown of Ottawa, Ill. In 1840 he removed to Alton, Ill., taking with him a Pitts' threshing-machine, the first thresher and cleaner in Illinois. In 1842 he and his brother Washington established a manufactory at Alton, where the machines are still made. He afterward bought a farm of 1800 acres in La Salle County, and lived there until his death, in Ottawa, 4 July 1864. Children, all born in Ottawa:
- 1 Frank, b. 1849; died in infancy.
- 2 Elnora, b. 8 Sept. 1850; m. 26 Dec. 1871, Will C. Griffith of Taylorville, Ill., now of Indianapolis. Children:
  - 1 Frank (Griffith), b. 15 Oct. 1873, in Taylorville.
  - 2 Harry L. (Griffith), b. 8 March 1875.
  - 3 ——— (Griffith), b. 18 June 1881.
- 3 Lucy A., b. 28 Jan. 1852; m. 15 Oct. 1873, Warren C. Riale, of the firm of Riale Bros., grocers, Ottawa. Child:
  - 1 Florence E. (Riale), b. 16 Oct. 1878.
- 4 Maria, b. 1854; died in infancy.
- 5 Amanda, b. 1856; died in infancy.
- 6 Josephine, b. 11 Feb. 1858; m. 11 Sept. 1877, Frank A. Kendall, of the firm of Booth & Kendall, hardware dealers. Child:
  - 1 Grace Ella (Kendall), b. 8 May 1881.
- 7 Wallace, b. 27 March 1860.
- 8 Howard, b. 7 June 1863.

6 Jane S., b. 2 July 1818; m. James Elliot.

7 Samuel, b. 12 May 1819, in Starks; m. 10 July 1842, Jerusha, dau. of George and Ann B. (Butterfield) Morton of New Vineyard. He supported his parents, and had the homestead farm. In 1864 he sold, and moved to New Vineyard, where he died the same year, 14 Sept. He was a member of the Methodist Church. His widow married Jousha Sprague. Children:
- 1 Ann Butterfield, b. 23 June 1843; m. 17 Nov. 1866, Hiram A. Wright.
- 2 Sarah Beals, b. 4 Aug. 1847; m. 6 Aug. 1865, Elbridge M. Vaughan.

8 Lucy Ann, b. 2 July 1826, in Industry; married Tallman Libby, 10-2-4-3-3-5.

10-2-4-3-3

Capt. Enoch Libby, born in Scarborough, 23 Feb. 1787; married, first, Elizabeth Welch, daughter of William and Mary (Smith) Welch of Richmond; (died 1 Sept. 1842); second, Lavinia (Owen) Marshall of Vassalborough; (died 3 Jan. 1851); third, Eliza Waterman, daughter of Dr. Waterman of Litchfield.

He went from Scarborough to Richmond with his brother Samuel. He lived there until his death. He was a well-to-do farmer, captain in the militia, selectman, etc. He died 11 March 1863. His widow died in Gardiner, Nov. 1868.

Children, by first wife:

1 William, b. 13 Dec. 1812; m. Martha T. Smith.

2 Enoch, b. 15 Nov. 1815; m. 1st, 5 May 1845, in Shiloh, Ill., Matilda, dau. of Wm. Cooper; (died 21 June 1866); 2d, Mrs. Hannah K. Plummer, dau. of Stephen Osgood. He left home at the age of 25, and went to Illinois. In 1846 he returned, and went into the grocery business in Augusta, with his brother Bradbury, (firm name, B. Libby & Co.), where he still continues. Children:
- 1 Theodore A., b. 7 Feb. 1846; d. 13 Jan. 1873, in Augusta; unmarried.

2 Charles A., b. 22 Nov. 1848; d. 29 Aug. 1863.
3 Jennie, b. 12 April 1853; m. June 1871, Stephen P. Eaton.
4 George C., b. 22 Jan. 1865.

3 Bradbury, b. 15 April 1819; m. Nancy B., dau. of Geo. Weeks of Sidney. He early removed to Augusta, where he was in the grocery business until his death, which occurred 5 May 1879. Only child:
1 Mary C., b. 9 Oct. 1851; lives in Augusta, with her mother; unmarried.

4 Mary A., b. 20 Jan. 1822; m. Lawrence J. Joice.

5 Tallman, b. 20 June 1824; m. 28 March 1851, Lucy Ann Libby, 10-2-4-3-2-8. He is a farmer. He lived with his father until 1856, and then removed to his present abode, South Ottawa, Ill. Children:
1 Edward W., b. 5 Jan. 1852; m. 8 Jan. 1874, Loretta, dau. of John T. and Harriet (Homan) Miller. Children:
1 Elbridge Tallman, b. 24 Jan. 1877.
2 Burton Hard, b. 3 June 1878.
3 Lou M., b. 10 Aug. 1879.
2 Isaiah B., b. 17 Jan. 1856, in Richmond; unm.

6 Eliot, b. 14 July 1827; m. 10 March 1853, Arabella H., dau. of Daniel and Mary (Tarbox) Webber of Richmond. He learned the carpenter's trade in Portland, and was afterward in business there, with various partners, at first as builder, and then as sash and blind manufacturer. In 1854 he settled on the homestead in Richmond, and continued there twelve years, after which he moved to Gardiner, where he has since been in business as builder. Children:
1 Walter E., b. 16 May 1856; d. 12 March 1880.
2 Mary A., b. 1 June 1863.

7 Martha J., b. 20 March 1829; m. John T. Robinson.
8 Elizabeth, b. 19 May 1832; m. Samuel W. Jack.
9 Abigail, b. 17 Jan. 1836; m. Melvin Dinslow.

By third wife:

10 Franklin W., b. 10 April 1853; lives in Strawn, Ill.

10-2-4-3-7

Abner Libby, born in Scarborough, 17 Aug. 1797; married 23 Sept. 1830, Harriet Newbegin, daughter of Solomon and Nancy (Hanscom) Newbegin of Westbrook.

He was a farmer. He lived in Saccarappa, Westbrook, from the age of 21 until his marriage; then three years in Otisfield; then in Harrison until shortly before his death, which took place in Paris, Me., (where his widow still lives), 16 June 1866. He served several terms as representative to the state legislature and as selectman.

Children:

1 Sarah J., b. 21 Sept. 1831, in Otisfield; d. 22 Oct. 1845.

2 Plummer A., b. 21 Sept. 1838; m. 25 Dec. 1864, Melinda M., dau. of Moses and Sally (Brackett) Fogg of Harrison. He is a farmer. In 1864 he went to Illinois, where, except one year spent at home, he has since lived in Union since 1874. Children:
1 Stella Lillian, b. 12 May 1866, in Rutland, Ill.
2 Annie May, b. 1 May 1876, in Union.
3 Frank Leslie, b. 31 Oct. 1877, in Union.

3 Harriet E., b. 24 Nov. 1841, in Harrison; m. 4 Nov. 1860, Swasey G. Burnell, now of Paris.

4 Georgianna, b. 9 Jan. 1848; died aged 18 months.
5 Franklin P., b. 24 July 1852; m. 5 Aug. 1879, Clara B., daughter of Joseph and Mary (Richardson) Parker of Norway, Me. He is a tinner.

10-2-4-3-8

Cary Libby, born in Scarborough, 9 Nov. 1798; married, in Lynn, Mass., Martha Goss of Marblehead, Mass. He lived in Lynn until his death.

He had children:

1 Lucy, died unmarried.
2 George Elliot, b. 1836; m. Olive A. ———. He is a heeler by trade, but is now on the police force. Child:
  1 Cary, b. 1871.

10-2-4-3-9

Hiram Libby, born in Scarborough, 2 Dec. 1800; married, 12 Jan. 1822, Mary Waterhouse, daughter of Abigail (Libby) Waterhouse, 5-2-7-4. He was a farmer, and lived on the farm of his birth. He died 3 Sept. 1875. His widow died in the fall of 1880.

His children were:

1 Abba Celia, b. 25 Feb. 1824; m. 29 Nov. 1846, Ammon Low.
2 Dominicus, b. 11 July 1827; m. Tabitha, dau. of John and Ann (Babb) Harmon. He lives on part of his father's homestead. Child:
  1 Charles Elson, b. 16 Dec. 1855; m. 18 June 1878, Susie F., dau. of Nathan L. and Mary Ann (Knights) Huston of Falmouth. Child:
    1 Ella Pearl, b. 7 Jan. 1879.
3 Dorothy Ann, b. 6 March 1829; m. 21 Dec. 1848, Franklin Torrey.
4 Eunice Colby, b. 4 Dec. 1834; m. Sumner Libby, 10-5-5-9-3-2.
5 Emily, } twins, born } d. 1880; unm.
6 Henry, } 25 Sept. 1837; } lives on the homestead; unmarried.

10-2-4-8-4

Rodney Libby, born in Scarborough, 22 May 1805; married, 24 May 1829, Louisa F. Waterhouse, daughter of Mary (Libby) Waterhouse, 5-7-8-6. She died 21 Dec. 1849. 18 June 1851, he married Mrs. Hannah Doliff, daughter of Dummer and Hannah (McDaniel) Harmon. He was a farmer, and lived near by his father's homestead. He died 24 Jan. 1878. His widow died 10 July, following.

Children, all by first wife:

1 Mary Elizabeth, b. 20 Dec. 1829; d. 20 Dec. 1851; unm.
2 Rose Ann, b. 9 Oct. 1832; is unm.
3 Margaret W., b. 18 June 1835; m. 29 Jan. 1860, John H. Berry.
4 Leander Valentine, b. 14 Aug. 1837; m. 25 May 1861, Alice A., dau. of Simeon H., and Alice (Pinkham) Pitts of Hollis. He learned the blacksmith's trade in Portland with Benjamin Stevens. He is now one of the firm of Hearn & Libby, blacksmiths, Saco, Me. No children.

5 Harriet Ann, b. 16 Aug. 1839; m. 31 Dec. 1859, Charles H. Towle.
6 Miranda W., b. 14 Feb. 1841; m. 17 April 1873, James Frederic Chapman.
7 Frank Enoch, b. 26 June 1843; m. 22 Nov. 1868, Hannah F. ———. He went to Dennison, Iowa, soon after his marriage, and lived there until 1874. He then returned to Maine. In 1879 he again went west, and now lives in Colorada Springs, Col. Children:
 1 Charles Francis, b. 24 May 1870.
 2 Alfred Guy, b. 24 March 1872.
8 Charles Elijah, b. 17 Oct. 1844; m. 13 Sept. 1876, Ella A., dau. of Geo. and Livia (Stevens) Slemmons of Westbrook. He occupies the homestead farm. Child:
 1 Lucian Percy, b. 17 April 1877.

10-2-4-8-6

Leonard Libby, born in Scarborough, 30 Oct. 1810; married, 27 Nov. 1839, Martha Ann Waterhouse, daughter of Nathaniel and Grace (Hewes) Waterhouse. (Nathaniel Waterhouse was a son of Nathaniel Waterhouse, 10-2-2-12.)

Upon his marriage he settled on the homestead of David Libby, 10-1. He lived there, a farmer, until his death, which occurred 15 Jan. 1881. His widow and son Roswell still occupy the homestead.

Children:

1 Roswell, b. 2 Nov. 1843; m. 23 June 1870, Martha A., dau. of Eben S. and Abigail (Whitmore) Fifield of Deer Island. He is a can-maker, and has always been in the employ of the packing companies of Portland, but has resided with his father in Scarborough. Children:
 1 Alice Lenora, b. 13 Aug. 1871.
 2 Florence Augusta, b. 9 May 1873.
 3 Hattie Estelle, b. 23 Sept. 1876.
2 Amerretta, b. 21 Sept. 1846; d. 10 Aug. 1849.
3 Lot, b. 23 Sept. 1851; m. Anne Burnell. He lives in Gorham, a can-maker. No children.

10-2-4-9-1

Patrick Libby, born in Scarborough, 5 May 1811; married, 25 April 1839, Olive B. Foy, daughter of Nathaniel and Lydia (Chute) Foy of Leeds, Me. He is a farmer, and has always lived on a farm near his father's. His wife died 7 Dec. 1880.

Children, all born in Scarborough:

1 Mary Ellen, b. 3 June 1840; m. 23 July 1855, Simeon Skillin.
2 Greenleaf, b. 2 Jan. 1844; d. 5 Nov. 1844.
3 Roscoe Green, b. 8 Oct. 1848; m. 29 April 1878, Nellie May, dau. of James M. and Susan F. (Parker) Small of Deering, born 11 Feb. 1863. He is a farmer; lives with his father. Child:
 1 Emeretta May, b. 6 July 1879.
4 Albert Stevens, b. 23 Jan. 1851; m. Cora I. Carr; lives in Sandown, N. H. Child:
 1 Edwin A., b. May 1880.

10-2-4-9-2

LORENZO DOW LIBBY, born in Scarborough, 7 Feb. 1816; married, first, 13 Aug. 1835, ANN ANDREWS, daughter of Isaac and Elizabeth (Warren) Andrews of Scarborough; (died 29 Sept. 1849); second, 20 March 1857, MARTHA ELLEN MOORE, daughter of Wm. Edward and Agnes (Mackey) Moore of Portland. He lived in Scarborough, a farmer, until 1849, and has since been a mover and raiser of buildings, in Portland.

Children, by first wife, born in Scarborough:

1 Sumner, b. 10 Jan. 1836; m. 27 Aug. 1860, Mary E., dau. of Elliot F., and Mary Ann (Frye) Clark of Portland. He is senior member of the firm of Libby & Dimmock, blacksmiths and horse-shoers, Portland. Children:
  1 Fred Mariner, b. 31 March 1861; d. 19 Oct. 1862.
  2 Fred Barker, b. 31 March 1863.
2 Emeline, b. 18 April 1839; m. Enos Hubbard Libby, 10-2-1-5-13-2.
3 Samuel, b. 19 Oct. 1842; lives in Scarborough; unm.
4 George Washington, b. 29 Aug. 1844; m. 1 Aug. 1868, Annie G., dau. of Nathaniel S. and Louisa (Frank) Lawrence of Gray. He is a journeyman horse-shoer, and resides in Deering. No children.

By second wife; born in Portland:

5 Warren Andrews, b. 29 June 1858.
6 Charles Albert, b. 17 Feb. 1860.
7 Nellie Ashton, b. 9 Dec. 1862.
8 Edward Everett, b. 30 March 1865.
9 Myra Bell, b. 30 Oct. 1868.
10 Mary Elizabeth, b. 1 Nov. 1872.

10-4-1-1-1

JOSEPH LIBBY, born 7 March 1773, in Saco, Me.; married, first, 30 Nov. 1797, LYDIA KENNARD of Limington; second, LOIS (PITMAN) EVANS of Dover, N. H.

He lived in Limington until after the death of his first wife, and then moved to Portland, where he married again. In Portland, he worked as ship-carpenter. He died in June, 1836. His widow died Sept. 1853, in Boston, Mass.

Children, by first wife, born in Limington:

1 Martha, b. 13 March 1800; m. Levi Barker of Lovell, Me.
2 William. When last heard from he was a bachelor.
3 Elizabeth, b. 26 Oct. 180 ; died in Bartlett, N. H.
4 Joseph, b. 29 Oct. 1809; m. Thankful Willey.

By second wife, born in Portland:

5 Charles Henry Smith, b. June, 1823; followed the sea; was mate; died in Boston, Sept. 1873; unmarried.
6 Harriet Higgins, b. Aug. 1825; m. 24 Feb. 1850, Wm. Dyer Mariner of Portland, a son of James Mariner of Cape Elizabeth. Children:
  1 Edwin Herbert (Mariner), b. 23 Dec. 1850; m. 3 Feb. 1874, Ada O., dau. of Wm. B. and Mary G. (Bridgham) Bennett of Cape Elizabeth. He is a letter-carrier in the Portland post-office. Children:

1 Hattie W. (Mariner), b. 6 Sept. 1874.
2 Herbert G. (Mariner), b. 22 Feb. 1876.
3 Harrison E. (Mariner), b. 16 Feb. 1878.

2 Frank Hermon (Mariner), b. 22 Aug. 1853; is a bricklayer; unmarried.

3 Lucy Ella (Mariner), b. 29 July 1859; d. 26 Aug. 1862.

4 Fred Everett (Mariner), b. 26 Oct. 1869.

7 Benjamin, b. Aug. 1827; was a seaman; died in Boston, Mass , Jan. 1852; unmarried.

10-4-1-1-2

Benjamin Libby, born in Saco, Me., 30 April 1775; married first, 25 Dec. 1797, Margaret McArthur, the first female child born in Limington, daughter of John and Mary (Miller) McArthur.

He settled on his father's homestead. He was justice of the peace, selectman, etc. His first wife died 30 June 1814, leaving a young family, and he married second, Patience, daughter of Daniel Ridlon of Hollis. He died Feb. 1866. His wife died the next year.

Children, all born in Limington:

1 Ferdinand, b. 28 Nov. 1798; d. young.

2 Harrison, b. 29 Aug. 1802; d. young.

3 Benjamin Carl, b. 24 April 1804; m. 24 May 1827, Irene Meads, dau. of Francis and Mary (Crouch) Meads. He was a farmer and justice of the peace. He died 6 Aug. 1871. His widow died 4 Sept. 1876. Children:

1 Margaret Anna, b. 17 Dec. 1827; m. 26 Dec. 1855, Byron Woodman Watson of Warner, N. H.

2 Maria Meads, b. 22 Nov. 1829; lives in Haverhill, Mass.; unm.

3 Priscilla Moody, b. 3 July 1832; d. 28 Jan. 1846.

4 Benjamin Franklin, b. 12 April 1834; d. 28 Sept. 1864.

5 Pamela Foss, b. 31 Dec. 1835; m. 12 Oct. 1869, in Cleveland, Ohio, Theodore Weld Otis.

6 Elbridge Ogden Hoffman, b. 6 Jan. 1838; d. 10 Nov. 1878, in California.

7 Mary Ellen, b. 8 Dec. 18 ; is a teacher in Cleveland, Ohio.

8 Kate Julia, b. 25 Dec. 1843; lives in Portland; unm.

9 Harriet Isabelle, b. 8 Oct. 1846; lives in Cleveland, Ohio, a teacher.

4 Eleanor, b. 13 Sept. 1806; d. 1813.

5 Pamelia, b 6 Dec. 1808; m. 24 March 1827, Elder Nahum Foss; d. 19 Dec. 1872, in Topeka, Kan.

6 Margaret, b. 6 May 1813; m. 21 July 1842, Alvah Leavitt.

10-4-1-1-4

Daniel Libby, born in Saco, Me., 4 May 1779; married, 29 Nov. 1804, Dorcas McDonald, daughter of Abner and Mary (Wiswall) McDonald. He early settled on a farm in Limington, on which he lived, died, and was buried. He died about 1861. His widow died later with her daughter Green in Portland.

Children, all born in Limington:

1 Abner, left home at the age of 27, and was never afterward heard from. Was not married.

2 David, b. 2 June 1807; m. Charlotte Stevens.

3 Ferdinand, b. 10 June 1809; m. Jane Smith.
4 Sally, died at the age of 5 years.
5 Mary M., m. 21 Feb. 1841, Robert Mitchell.
6 Gideon, m. 20 March 1837, Lydia T., dau. of James and Ruth (Roberts) Horn of Somersworth, N. H. He was a shoemaker by trade. In November, 1847, for reasons unknown to the compiler, he deserted his wife with six children under nine years of age. 7 Jan. 1848, he wrote to her from Providence, R. I., but she has not heard from him since. She and her family live in Portland. Children:
  1 James, b. 24 Dec. 1838, in West Milan, N. H.
  2 Harrison Daniel, b. 26 Feb. 1840, in Limington, Me.
  3 Frank Gideon, b. 17 Oct. 1841, in Great Falls, N. H.; d. in Camp Fort Tyler, Texas, 10 May 1864.
  4 Lydia Ann, b. 20 March 1843, in Lowell, Mass.; d. 7 May 1846, in Limington.
  5 Arthur, b. 20 Nov. 1844, in Cambridgeport, Mass.
  6 Justin, b. 29 March 1846, in Limington.
  7 Mary Elizabeth, b. 7 April 1847, in Limington; m. 5 June 1868, Hiram C. Ayers of Portland. He died in Cleveland, Ohio, 17 Jan. 1873. Child:
    1 Ella Augusta(Ayers), b. 26 Oct. 1868.
7 Jane, m. 19 Dec. 1842, George Green of Portland.
8 Arthur, d. in Limington, aged 22.
9 Caroline, m. Thomas Bowditch of Troy, N. Y.
10 Ansel Lewis, m. Leonice Allen.

10-4-1-6-2

David Libby, born in Saco, Me., 30 Nov. 1796; married, 5 Oct. 1823, Sally Berry, daughter of John and Jane (Milliken) Berry of Saco. He lived on his father's farm, and sold off the most of it in small pieces. He died 13 April 1871. After his death his widow sold what remained, and bought the house she now occupies in the village.

Children, all born in Saco:

1 Martha Jane, b. 27 Dec. 1825; m. 12 Nov. 1856, Samuel M. Harmon of Buxton.
2 Sarah Elizabeth, b. 7 Jan. 1828; is in the Insane Asylum at Augusta. She was never married.
3 David, b. 14 Feb. 1830; m. 4 April 1852, Abigail Libby, 1-1-3-9-7-8. He was for many years in business in Portland, as blacksmith. He now lives in Thomasville, Ga. His wife died 27 Aug. 1880. Children:
  1 Frank, b. 6 Jan. 1853; m. 13 June 1878, in Portland, Mrs. Almira Hull. She died in Dublin, Ga., 4 July 1881. Child:
    1 daughter, b. 1881.
  2 Ellen, b. 2 March 1855; d. 21 Aug. 1873.
  3 Emma, b. 29 June 1863; d. 29 March 1872.
  4 Sadie, b. 2 June 1870.
4 Caroline, b. 23 July 1832; m. 25 July 1857, Otis R. Hamilton of Lynn, Mass.
5 Joseph Franklin, b. 13 Dec. 1834; d. 23 June 1853.
6 Gideon, [Rev.], b. 13 March 1837; m. 9 April 1871, in Sterling, Ill., Maria, dau. of T. Quigley of Janesville, Ohio. He was prepared for college at the Saco high school, and graduated at Bowdoin in 1863. He graduated at the Garrett Biblical Institute in 1867, and became a clergyman of the Methodist Episcopal Church. From that time, except one year that he was teacher of mathematics in the Rock River Seminary, he preached in Illinois. He died in Kings, Ill., 6 Sept. 1879. His widow now lives in Sterling. Children:

1 Cora May, b. 6 Sept. 1872, in Alden, Ill.
2 Eddie LeRoy, b. 24 Dec. 1873; d. 28 Aug. 1874, in Dunlieth.
3 Frank, b. 14 Sept. 1876, in Channahon.
4 Grace Lorena, b. 22 Dec. 1879.

7 William Henry Harrison, b. 29 Jan. 1840; m. 5 Aug. 1861, in Cambridgeport, Mass., Emma A., dau. of Jeremiah and Susan L. (Keyes) Crosby of Orland, Me. He is a carpenter by trade. He worked in Massachusetts a short time before the war, and enlisted in the 17th Mass. Infantry. After his discharge he worked in the navy yards at Charlestown, Mass., and Kittery, Me. In 1865 he moved to Louisville, Ky., and in 1873 settled on a quarter-section in Reno, Rice Co., Kans., where he has since been a farmer. Children:

1 Irene M., b. 12 Aug. 1863, in Chelsea, Mass.
2 William G., b. 25 April, d. 7 Oct., 1867, in Louisville.
3 Emma C., b. 3 June, d. 2 Aug., 1869, in Louisville.
4 Helen C., b. 29 Nov. 1870; d. 2 May 1871, in Louisville.
5 Mary E., b. 28 Oct. 1872; d. 23 Jan. 1873, in Louisville.
6 Walter G., b. 17 Oct. 1874, in Rice Co., Kan.
7 Edna C., b. 13 Nov. 1878, in Rice Co., Kan.

10-4-1-6-6

Tristram Libby, born in Saco, Me., 4 May 1805, married first, 16 June 1830, Sarah H. Butterfield of Boston; (died 11 Aug. 1831); second, 30 July 1833, Dorothy Belknap, daughter of John and Ruth (Fay) Belknap of Westborough, Mass. He is a cabinet-maker by trade, and worked in Boston on piano-fortes from 1828 to 1845. He then settled on a farm in Livermore, Me., and lived on it until 1875, when he bought the farm he now lives on in Canton, Me. His wife died in Canton, 13 Oct. 1878.

Children, by first wife:

1 Charles McIntire, b. 26 June, d. 24 Aug., 1831.

By second wife:

2 Sarah L., b. 24 May 1834; m. 20 Jan. 1853, John S. Whitney.
3 Ann E., b. 10 April 1836; m. 1st, 21 Jan. 1858, Eliphalet C. Morse; 2d, 27 Sept. 1871, Asa H. Gould.
4 Maria R., b. 8 Jan. 1838; m. 2 Oct. 1867, Alderman Baker.
5 William, b. 11 April 1839; m. 8 Oct. 1874, Caroline F., dau. of Theodore H. and Joan S. (Fosdick) Lunt of Reading, Mass. He enlisted for three years in Co. C, 20th Me. Infantry, and was permanently disabled at Petersburgh, Va. Unfitted for a life of bodily labor, he took a preparatory course at Hebron, and subsequently graduated from Colby and Newton institutions. He is now the settled pastor of the Baptist Church in North Sutton, N. H. Children:
   1 Wilfred Hale, b. 31 Dec. 1877.
   2 Percival Tristram, b. 15 April 1880.
6 Mary A., b. 24 March 1841; m. 2 May 1867, Albion W. Bryant of Andover, Me.
7 Shuah A., b. 8 Sept. 1843; m. 19 May 1869, Charles J. W. Robinson of Island Falls, Vt.
8 Eleanor S., b. 6 Feb. 1847; m. 21 Jan. 1873, Everett J. Mann of Natick, Mass.
9 Florilla, b. 4 May 1849; d. 3 April 1866.
10 Adelia C., b. 9 May 1851; d. 12 Feb. 1868.

10-4-1-6-8

Daniel Libby, born 8 Oct. 1810, in Saco, Me.; married, 5 Sept. 1829, Dorcas G. Dennett, daughter of John and Elizabeth (Gould) Dennett of Buxton. He was a cooper by trade, and afterward took up carpentering. He was in business in Buxton until 1844, except brief periods that he was in Boston and Westborough, Mass. From 1844 his life was spent in Saco, in Biddeford, (where he was in trade), and in Boston, in business as carpenter and as grocer. He died in Biddeford, 20 Jan. 1852. His widow died in Saco, 24 Jan. 1881.

Children:

1 Frederick Fogg, b. 11 July 1830; m. Hannah A. Hutchins of Kennebunk. He worked at carpentering, and as an operative in the cotton mills. He died 2 Aug. 1859. His widow married John Brackett of Buxton, and died in Biddeford about 1865. Children:
   1 Emma Frances, b. 23 Dec. 1851; m. Frank Hoppins.
   2 George Winfield, b. 13 March 1853: is a journeyman carpenter.
   3 Albert William, b. 17 Aug. 1855; went to sea in boyhood, and has not been heard from for many years.
   4 Hosea Austin, b. 7 Jan. 1857; d. 2 Sept. 1858.

2 Darius G., b. 11 July 1834; m. 17 Nov. 1860, Mary E., dau. of Elijah and Sarah (Huntress) Hamlin of Brownfield. He is a carpenter by trade, but has also been in the second-hand furniture business. He resides in Saco. Children:
   1 Rosilla Ellen, b. 23 Sept. 1861.
   2 Howard Hamlin, b. 31 Dec. 1863.
   3 Edward Ellsworth, b. 28 Feb. 1865.
   4 Elvira Jane, b. 17 Sept. 1869.
   5 Frank Haines, b. 13 Sept. 1873.

3 Jason Hovey, b. 5 Sept. 1838; m. 1 Jan. 1857, Sylvia M., dau. of John Darling of Auburn, Me. After his marriage he lived in Auburn, with his father-in-law. He partially learned the shoemaker's trade, and was a clerk in a grocery store. About 1868 he moved back to Biddeford, and was a barber until his last sickness. He died 7 Aug. 1879, having outlived his wife, (she died 18 July 1877), and his five children. They were:
   1 Charles Orlando, b. 4 Jan. 1863; d. 9 Jan. 1865.
   2 child, died in infancy.
   3 child, died in infancy.
   4 Lili Josephine, b. 8 Oct. 1873; d. 12 Feb. 1876.
   5 Jason Eugene, b. 2 Oct. 1875; d. 11 Aug. 1877.

4 Elizabeth Adeline, b. 24 Sept. 1840; m. 13 Dec. 1866, Charles H. Smith of Buxton.

5 Charles Orlando, b. 8 March 1843; m. 3 Jan. 1866, in Darlington, S. C., Mrs. Mary Jane Dubose, dau. of Wiley J and E. A. K. (Fulwood) Floyd of that place. He served four years (in two enlistments) in the Maine Infantry. He was discharged in Charleston, S. C., and immediately settled in Darlington, where except three years, (1868-1870), during which he was chief marshal, he has since been a merchant. No children.

6 Alice Ann, b. 27 April 1847; m. 1st, Bernice R. Bean of Buxton; 2d, Michael McGawley of Lewiston.

7 Frances Anna, b. 24 Aug. 1850; d. 16 Jan. 1876; unm.

10-4-3-2-6

Asa Libby, born in Eliot, Me., 22 Jan. 1813; married, 28 Nov. 1833, Elizabeth R. Yeaton, daughter of Barnabas and Philadelphia (Jinkins) Yeaton of Newcastle, N. H. He served a seven years' apprenticeship with Samuel M. Dockum of Portsmouth, N. H., in the cabinet maker's trade, and worked as journeyman in Portsmouth until 1850. In that year he started business in South Berwick, Me., and the next year removed his business to Boston, Mass., where he continued it until his death. He was killed by the bursting of a cannon in a 4th of July celebration in Boston, 1857. His widow still lives where she has lived most of the time since her marriage, on the homestead farm in Eliot.

Children:

1 Mary Ann, b. 16 April 1834, in Newcastle; m. 22 Aug. 1858, Thomas J. Burt of Buxton.
2 Orlando, b. 28 Nov. 1835; learned the cabinet maker's trade with S. M. Dockum, and worked for his father in Boston. He enlisted in Co. D, 5th Reg. N. H. Vol., and, after three months' service, returned home to die. He died in Eliot, 1 July 1862, unmarried.
3 George Wallace, b. 19 March 1837, in Portsmouth, N. H.; married, 26 Nov. 1866, Fanny C., dau. of Henry and Adeline (Yeaton) Tarlton of Newcastle. He is by trade a cabinet maker, but works at carpentering in Dorchester, Mass. He served as musician in the 13th Reg. N. H. Vol. Children:
   1 Addie, b. 19 July 1868, in Newcastle.
   2 Emma, b. 18 July 1870, in Dorchester.

Born in Eliot:

4 Joseph Winslow, b. 6 Nov. 1838; m. 24 April 1862, Lucy Ann, dau. of Alexander and Mary (Taylor) Pettigrew of Kittery. He is a farmer. He lived on part of his father's homestead farm until about 1872, and then bought the farm near by, which he now lives on. Children:
   1 Alfred Woodbury, b. 10 March 1863.
   2 Cora Estelle, b. 6 Nov. 1865.
   3 Flora Belle, b. 4 Aug. 1868.
   4 Nellie May, b. 18 June 1871.
5 Henry Harrison, b. 8 Aug. 1840; m. 17 Jan. 1864, Addie, dau. of *John and Betsey (Lear) Wight of* Newcastle, N. H. He learned the cabinet maker's trade with his father, but, after his father's death, worked in a molding manufactory. He died in South Boston, Mass., 17 Jan. 1864. His widow lives with her mother in Newcastle. Only child:
   1 Orlando, b. 28 Oct. 1869, in South Boston.
6 Alfred Appleton, b. 28 March 1842; he was a journeyman carpenter. He served in the war as principal musician of the 5th N. H. Regimental band. He died in Eliot, 22 April 1877; unm.
7 Ellen Flora, b. 25 Dec. 1843; m. Isaac Austin Packard.
8 Frank Folsom, b. 18 Jan. 1846; was a carpenter; died 14 Jan. 1871, in Lynn; unm.
9 Kate Elizabeth, b. 29 Feb. 1848; m. Washington A. Elwell of South Berwick.
10 Alice Jane, b. 16 April 1850; died same day.

10-5-1-1-2

Samuel Libby, born in Scarborough, 18 June 1780; married, 26 Jan. 1809, Betsey Towle, daughter of Phineas and Sarah (Leavitt) Towle of Buxton. He grew up in Buxton, and settled on half his father's homestead farm. 27 Feb. 1847, his wife died, and himself 4 March 1849.

Their children were:

1 James, b. Oct. 1809; m. Sarah Berry of Limington. About 1838 he went to Lowell, Mass., (where he married), to work in the powder mills. About 1848 he settled on a farm in Stow, Mass., and lived there until about 1875, when, his wife having died, he sold his farm. It was reported that he had removed to Nova Scotia. Children:
  1, 2 died in infancy.
  3 Josephine, married —— Baker.
2 Phineas, b. 22 Oct. 1811; m. Mary Hanson.
3 Eunice, b. 4 Nov. 1813; m. John Alexander of Biddeford.
4 Harriet, b. 22 Jan. 1816; m. 29 Jan. 1843, as second wife, John Alexander.
5 Elisha, b. 20 June 1818; m. Elizabeth B. Wilson.
6 Olive, b. 28 Dec. 1820; died aged nineteen.
7 Sarah Towle, b. 14 March 1825; m. 21 Feb. 1847, Stillman Hanson.
8 Joseph Gardner, b. 19 May 1827; m. 18 Nov. 1854, Ellen H., dau. of Nathaniel and Lucy (Thurston) Googin of Saco. Since 1852 he has been employed in the cotton mills in Biddeford. Children:
  1 Christie Belle, b. 24 Oct. 1868; d. 17 April 1874.
  2 Harry Remington, b. 19 June 1872; died 22 April 1874.
  A daughter of Jeremiah Blaisdell of Lebanon, whom they took to live with them in 1876, bears the name:
  a Hattie Parmelia (Libby), b. 1 July 1867.

10-5-1-1-5

Daniel Libby, born in Buxton, Me., 28 Oct. 1790; married Lydia Spencer, daughter of William Spencer of Baldwin. He removed to Baldwin, married, and settled on the farm now occupied by Hiram Spencer. There he died, 15 Dec. 1855, and his widow, 21 Aug. 1858.

Children, all born in Baldwin:

1 Dearborn Blake, b. 8 Sept. 1822. He always lived on the homestead. He married Kate ——, and died 25 April 1867. His widow married Geo. H. Noble, and went west, with her children. They were:
  1 Eliza Jane, born about 1866.
  2 Dearborn Walter, born about 1867.
2 Sarah, b. 28 April 1826; m. 28 June 1848, John C. Hill.
3 Eliza Jane, b. 16 Aug. 1830; d. 29 Aug. 1863; unm.
4 Olive Maria, b. 12 Sept. 1838; m. Chas. R. Noble.

10-5-1-1-7

Benjamin Libby, born in Buxton, Me., 31 May 1798; married, 16 Aug. 1836, Clarissa Noble, daughter of George and Sarah (Spencer) Noble of Baldwin. He lived on part of his father's homestead, a farmer, and died 24 March 1868. His widow lives with her son George.

Children, all born in Buxton:

1 Stephen Hanson, b. 5 June 1837; m. Jan. 1861, Adeline, dau. of Ira and Eliza (Wallace) Wallace of Westbrook. He lives in Saccarappa, a mill-hand. His wife died 15 June 1878. Children:
  1 Clara Ellen, b. 3 Nov. 1861; d. 13 Jan. 1862.
  2 Ada Lilla, b. 19 Feb. 1863; m. 13 May 1879, Charles H. Strout of Westbrook.

3 Stephen Ira, b. 16 May 1865.
4 Elisha, b. 10 Jan. 1867.

2 Albert, b. 4 June 1839; m. 13 Feb. 1863, Mary Ellen, dau. of Daniel and Martha (Noble) Edgerly of Parsonsfield. After his marriage, he owned and occupied a farm in Buxton three years, and one in Cornish five years. Since Oct. 1871 he has been a hostler in Saccarappa. Children:

1 Clara Emma, b. 7 June 1864.
2 Frank Arthur, b. 1 Dec. 1866.
3 Bertie Leroy, b. 29 April 1879.

3 son, b. 5, d. 6, Jan. 1845.

4 George, b. 31 Nov. 1847; m. 8 Dec. 1878, Rose, dau. of Thomas and Margaret (Burns) McGuire of Calais, Me. He lives in Saccarappa, a day laborer. No children.

10-5-1-2-1

Moses Libby, born in Scarborough, 25 Dec. 1781; married, 28 May 1809, Sally Lawrence, daughter of Ephraim and Sally (Sartelle) Lawrence of Gray. He was carried to Gray when three or four months old. He was a farmer, and had his father's homestead, which he increased in size from 50 to 170 acres. He died 26 Sept. 1850. His widow died 2 April 1864.

Children, all born in Gray:

1 Mary, b. 10 Sept. 1809; d. 5 March 1849; unm.

2 Rebecca Cobb, b. 20 May 1812; m. Almer Libby, 11-7-1-10-5.

3 David Lawrence, b. 16 Aug. 1814; m. 10 May 1843, Elizabeth Ann Jordan, born 10 June 1815, dau. of Israel and Hannah (Deake) Jordan of Gray. He started life for himself at the age of 21, and soon earned enough to buy the farm now occupied by Noah Ricker. He let this until his marriage, and then settled on it himself. Twelve years later he bought out the other heirs of his father's homestead, and has since lived there. No children.

4 Louisa, b. 13 Oct. 1816; m. 4 Dec. 1844, Joseph Mountfort of Gray.

5 Charles Welch, b. 7 Feb. 1819; m. Mary Jane Mayberry.

6 Ephraim, b. 30 Aug. 1821; lost his mind by fits; always lived on the homestead, and died 28 Oct. 1878.

7 Asa B., b. 31 July 1824; m. 1st, 19 May 1850, Mary Susan, dau. of Thomas and Nancy (Clark) Webster of Gray; (died 22 April 1862, in Hammond, Wis.); 2d, 18 June 1863, in Hammond, Julia W. Barrows of Worcester, Mass. She died at River Falls, Wis., 1872. He removed to Wisconsin soon after his first marriage. He lived for some time in Hammond, St. Croix Co., and while there filled the positions of justice of the peace, county supervisor, and chairman of the board of supervisors of the town. He now resides in New Richmond. Children, by first wife:

1 Martin N., b. 8 May 1851; d. 16 May 1851.

By second wife, born in Hammond:

2 Orrin G., b. 9 June 1864.
3 William S., b. 24 Jan. 1866.
4 Mabel G., b. 28 March 1868.
5 Lottie L., b. 13 March 1870.

8 Warren, b. 27 May 1827; m. 23 Nov. 1864, Mary Matilda, dau. of Abdel George and Maria (Paullin) Kiler of Yellow Springs, Ohio. After becoming of age, he studied at Whitestown, N. Y., Oberlin, O., and Antioch, and became a teacher. He served three years as volunteer in a Wisconsin regiment, and ruined his health in the service. He afterward lived in Wisconsin, Missouri, and Ohio, and since 1879, at Colorado Springs, Col., where his health

has improved, and he is occupied as newspaper agent and dealer in 5 and 10 cent goods. He had no children, but in 1876 adopted from the Mount Auburn orphan asylum at Cincinnati, O., a child:

a Annie Maria Legge, b. 28 Oct. 1870, on Guernsey Island, Eng.

9 Nathaniel S., b. 14 Jan. 1830; m. 18 April 1852, Sarah L. Freeman of Gray. He lived at home, carrying on the homestead after his father's death, until 1856. He then went west, and has cleared farms successively in Roscoe, Minn., Hammond, Wis., and in Linneus, Linn Co., Mo., where he has lived since 1866. He and his wife are members of the Congregational Church. Children:

1 Oscar F., b. in Gray, 9 Dec. 1852; is practicing law in Laclede, Mo.; unm.
2 Mary Louisa, b. in Gray, 19 April 1855; m. 26 March 1877, Joseph B. Chittom; died 17 Sept. 1881.
3 Walter, b. 31 Aug. 1858, in Roscoe, Minn.
4 Ernest L., b. 9 July 1860, in Roscoe,
5 Lucy T., b. 11 Feb. 1863, in Hammond, Wis.
6 Sarah T., b. 18 May 1866, in Hammond.
7 Lucius F., b. 10 March 1869, in Hammond.
8 Lottie L., b. 6 June 1870, in Linn Co., Mo.
9 Nathaniel, b. 13 June 1874, in Linn Co.
10 Gracie G., b. 28 June 1879.

10 Lyman Moses, b. 22 Aug. 1833; m. 15 Dec. 1875, Carrie Arnquist of Star Prairie, Wis. In 1852, he apprenticed himself to Matthias Libby, 11-7-2-6-10, in Portland, for the carpenter's trade. He did not complete it, however, but went to Waltham, Mass., and was two years in a furniture store. In 1855, he settled in what is now the town of Hammond, St. Croix Co., Wis., and became a builder. After the war he was employed in Missouri, rebuilding county buildings which had been destroyed during the war. In 1872, he returned to Wisconsin, and settled in New London, where he owns and runs the "Excelsior" steam planing mill, and carries on a general commission and lumber trade. Children:

1 Agnes Bell, b. 19 Nov. 1876, in New Richmond.
2 Lyman, b. 14 Aug. 1878, in New Richmond.

10-5-1-2-2

Capt. Andrew Libby, born in Gray, Me., 20 Nov. 1786; married, 13 July 1809, Susan H. Small, born 9 Feb. 1787, daughter of Isaac and Susan (Hobbs) Small of Gray.

He settled at first on Dutton Hill, but in 1817 settled on the farm now occupied by his son-in-law Whitney. There he lived and died. He was a captain in the militia, and was a number of years selectman of Gray. His wife died 2 Dec. 1852. He died 28 May 1872.

Children, all born in Gray:

1 Ann, b. 9 Nov. 1809; m. 22 Sept. 1835, Seth Leavitt. Previous to her marriage, she bore a son who took the name:

1 Jedediah (Libby), b. 16 Jan. 1834; was brought up by his grandfather Libby, and is now a farmer in Gray. He married, 27 Jan. 1869, Hetta, dau. of Samuel B. and Almira (Hayes) Parsons of Gray. Children:

1 Nettie Weston, b. 2 Feb. 1871.
2 Harry Lee, b. 18 Oct. 1875.

2 Lewis, b. 12 Oct. 1811; m. Harriet, dau. of Lemuel Jackson of Paris, Me. He settled on the farm in Gray now occupied by John Hunt. In 1852 he went to California, mining, but soon became a contractor for paving streets in San Francisco. In 1854, he returned to his native town, and died a week later, 4 Sept. 1854. His widow died 10 July 1873. Children:

1 Hiram Francis, born about 1837; d. 12 Nov. 1856.
2 Jackson, b. May, d. 15 Aug., 1841.
3, 4, 5 children; died in infancy.

3 Emeline H., b. 9 Aug. 1814; m. Winslow Hicks.
4 Aphia S., b. 12 Sept. 1816; m. Silas Leighton.
5 Matilda Cobb, b. 6 Jan. 1819; d. 12 Oct. 1858; unm.
6 William Andrew, b. 6 June 1821; m. 23 July 1848, Sophia B., dau. of Matthew and Fannie (Delano) Stetson of New Bedford, Mass. She now lives in Fairhaven, Mass. Children:
1 Fannie S., b. 26 June 1851, in Fairhaven; m. 17 Nov. 1870, Wm. F. Alden.
2 Mary H., b. 9 Feb. 1854; died 22 Jan, 1863.
3 William A., b. 1 July 1856.
4 Susie E., b. 28 Aug. 1858.
5 Lester L., b. 20 Aug. 1860, in Ottowa, Ill.; died 20 April 1872.
6 Almer, b. 2 March 1862.
7 Della M., b. 3 April 1865.

7 Susan S., b. 14 Oct. 1823; m. 24 Feb. 1850, Solomon Conant of Westbrook.
8 Sophia, b. 12 May 1826; d. 23 Nov. 1855.
9 Maria Frances, b. 20 Jan. 1830; m. 30 Oct. 1850, Alfred S. Whitney of Gray.

10-5-1-4-1

SOLOMON LIBBY, born in Scarborough, 5 Oct. 1789; married, 3 March 1818, MARTHA FOGG, daughter of George Fogg of Buxton. He was a farmer. Two years after his marriage he removed to what was then Harrison, now Naples, and settled on the farm occupied now by his children. He died 24 Aug. 1863. His wife died 26 Aug. 1859.

Their children were:

1 George Warren, b. 21 March 1819; m. 2 Feb. 1869, Mrs. Amanda Moody, dau. of Joseph and Lydia (Walker) Bennett. He has always lived at home, a farmer. His wife died 10 March 1876. No children.
2 Dorcas Ann, b. 21 Aug. 1820; m. John Lamb of Naples.
3 Jordan, b. 13 Feb. 1822; died 25 June 1832.
4 Hezekiah, b. 19 Oct. 1824; m. 4 Aug. 1856, Laura Nelson, dau. of Ziba and Almira (Forbes) Thayer of Paris, Me. From the age of 19, he was eight years a clerk in Harrison and Paris. He then removed to Portland, and was two years a clerk with H. J. Libby & Co. From Portland he removed to Boston, where he was nine years a salesman, and then became a member of the dry goods house of Anderson, Heath & Co. He stayed with them until a few months after the great fire of 1872. In 1877 the firm of Libby & Clark was formed, in which he continued until his death, which occurred very suddenly, 17 Oct. 1881. Children:
1 Georgie Anna, b. 19 June 1857, in Paris; unm.
2 Ella Josephine, b. 4 April 1859, in Boston.
3 Alice May, b. 20 Dec. 1864.

5 Caroline, b. 5 Feb. 1827; died 16 July 1832.
6 Martha Frances, b. 25 June 1829; m. March 1853, Merrill T. Files of Gorham.
7 Jordan Rackleff, b. 23 April 1832; m. 11 Feb. 1862, Mary Ann, dau. of Wm. and Sophia (Gammon) Wetherbee of Naples. He lives on part of the homestead, a farmer. No children.
8 Carrie, b. 18 Feb. 1836; lives at home; unm.

10-5-1-10-6

OSGOOD LIBBY, born in Scarborough, 18 Sept. 1810; married first, 4 May 1834, ELIZA PLUMMER, daughter of Moses and Margaret (Simonton) Plummer of Raymond; (died 29 May 1838); second, 14 March 1841, Deborah (Roberts) Sawyer, born 18 Aug. 1813, daughter of Reuben and Rebecca (Majory) Roberts of Casco. He has always been a farmer on his father's homestead.

Children, all born in Scarborough; by first wife:

1 Rufus, b. 12 July 1835; d. 6 July 1836.
2 Eliza Ellen, b. 28 Sept. 1837; d. 9 April 1838.

By second wife:

3 Franklin Sawyer, b. 5 Feb. 1842; m. 20 Oct. 1868, Annie G., dau. of Charles F. and Emeline (Richards) Dow of Cape Elizabeth. He served nine months in Co. H, 25th Maine Vol. He is a blacksmith by trade, but has been a butcher since 1870. He lives in Cape Elizabeth. Children:
  1 Lottie May, b. 7 April 1870, in Scarborough.
  2 Charles Franklin, b. 29 March 1877, in Scarborough.
4 Dennis Jinkins Sawyer, b. 13 May 1845; m. 27 Dec. 1870, Sarah Jane, widow of Frederick W. Nichols, and dau. of Sylvanus and Annie D. (Golder) Ling. He is a farmer, and lives on a part of his father's farm. Only child:
  1 Edward Elmer, b. 26 Jan. 1879.
5 Eliza Plummer, b. 13 May 1845; d. 30 Jan. 1851.
6 John Osgood, b. 27 Jan. 1849; d. 3 Feb. 1851.
7 Charlotte Eliza, b. 29 May 1853; d. 15 Feb. 1866.
8 Henry Rufus, b. 7 Sept. 1855; m. 19 Feb. 1876, Mary Catherine Libby, 11-7-2-6-2-5-1. He lives with his father. Children:
  1 John Osgood, b. 22 April 1877.
  2 Carrie Ella, b. 22 Sept. 1878.

10-5-2-1-1

CAPT. REUBEN LIBBY, born in Scarborough, 13 Sept. 1772; married DOROTHY LIBBY, 10-5-5-12. He always lived on his father's homestead. He was a militia captain. His death occurred 10 Sept. 1877. His wife died 6 March 1874.

Children, all born in Scarborough:

1 Bradford, b. 5 Sept. 1812; m. 1844, Caroline, dau. of Caroline (Libby) Harmon, 1-1-6-4-9. About 1850 he moved to Portland, where he worked as ship-carpenter. He died there, 17 Oct. 1864. His widow died in Foxborough, Mass., 9 Feb. 1874. Children, all born in Portland:
  1 Milton, b. 12 Dec. 1850; m. 17 Oct. 1874, Harriet Susan Libby, 10-5-5-9-3-9. He is an Eastern Railroad employee, residing in Portland. No children.
  2 Cordelia, died 10 July 1853.
  3 Angelia, b. 23 April 1853; d. 23 Aug. 1876, in Scarborough; unm.
  4 Marietta, b. 23 Feb. 1855; is unmarried.
2 Arexine, b. 10 July 1814; lives at home; unm.
3 Phebe, b. 23 March 1816; m. Silas J. Libby, 11-6-5-5-1.
4 Harretta, b. 9 July 1818; unm.; is a milliner in Portland.
5 Stillman, b. 10 Sept. 1820; d. 26 Oct. 1864. He was a bachelor, and lived at home.

6 Milton, b. 12 March 1823; married 10 June 1872, Louisa Libby, 10-1-6-4-2-1. He removed to Portland, where he was for a long time a truckman, and is now an employee of the W. U. Telegraph Co. Children:
   1 Mary Louise, b. 7 Jan. 1853; is unmarried.
   2 Charles Frank Milton, b. 1 Aug. 1865; d. 5 Dec. 1869.
   He also adopted a son of Thomas Gould of Portland, and gave him the name:
   a Frank Everett Robert (Libby), b. 4 June 1872.
7 Lucy Ann, b. 30 Jan. 1825; m. Augustus Bean of Tuftonborough, N. H.
8 Mary Frances, b. 19 June 1828; is unmarried.
9 Benjamin Franklin, b. 28 Dec. 1831; lives at home, a bachelor.

10-5-2-3-2

Samuel Marr Libby, born in Scarborough, 23 Dec. 1785; married first, Mercy Dyer, daughter of David and Hannah (Higgins) Dyer of Cape Elizabeth; (died 9 Dec. 1831); second, Sarah (Libby) Brown, 11-7-8-3-1.

He went with his father to Gardiner, and settled on a farm. He had at times worked as ship-carpenter, and occasionally after his removal to Gardiner, went down to Portland to work; but his chief occupation was farming. After living in Gardiner a few years, he sold his farm to his brother Sewall, and bought another in Litchfield. After his first wife's death, he bought a farm in Lewiston, and there died 8 June 1858. His wife died 26 Oct. 1854.

Children, by first wife, born in Scarborough:

1 Hiram, b. 9 Dec. 1810; m., 1838, Elizabeth L., dau. of Simeon and Mary (Stevens) Lawrence of Gardiner; (died 9 April 1861); second, 1 July 1863, Lucy Jane, widow of Charles Buzzell, dau. of John and Sarah (Harmon) Robinson of Portland. He went from Gardiner to Boston in 1845, and thence to Cape Elizabeth, in 1850, where he has since been a farmer. Children:
   1 Emma, b. 15 May 1839; m. 1st, 31 July 1862, Geo. S. Dyer; 2d, 14 June 1876, Wm. E. Keith.
   2 Charles, b. 12 Jan. 1846; d. 22 Aug. 1847.
2 Catherine, died in Scarborough, 8 Nov. 1812, an infant.

Born in Gardiner:

3 Arthur, b. 30 Oct. 1814; m. 14 Oct. 1850, Prudence Emerson, dau. of Nathaniel and Elizabeth (Emerson) Montgomery of Boothbay, Me. He was a sailor 16 years, and then settled in Boston, Mass., where he still resides, a carpenter. Only child:
   1 Sarah Emily, b. 4 July 1854; is unm.
4 Lovinda, b. 25 Sept. 1819; m. 1 Jan. 1839, Jos. L. Small.
5 Benjamin, died at the age of 8 years.
6 Sylvanus, died at the age of 2 years.
7 Sylvanus Dyer, m. 2 Oct. 1851, in San Francisco, Cal., Sarah A., dau. of Josiah and Sarah (Jordan) Dunn of Dixfield, Me. He settled in Port Gamble, Wash., in 1858, and still lives there. No children.
8 Mercy Jane, died 29 May 1858; unm.
9 Gardner, died aged two years.
10, 11 infants, born and died in Litchfield.

By second wife, born in Lewiston :

12 Joseph, b. 15 Aug. 1835; m. 30 June 1860, Abbie C., dau. of John and Caroline (Smith) Small of Bowdoin. He was a carpenter by trade, and was at work in Boston when the war broke out. He enlisted in Co. K, 19th Mass. Vol., and served until the close of the war. After the war he resided in Boston until May, 1867, when he removed to New York, and thence, in 1869, removed to Calfornia. He died 6 Feb. 1880, in Oakland, where his widow still lives. Children:

1 Charles Cyrus, b. 16 June 1861, in Bowdoin; d. 9 March 1862.
2 George Elmer, b. 1 Dec. 1865, in Cape Elizabeth, Me.
3 Edith Carrie, b. 5 Aug. 1869; died 9 May 1877.

13 Sarah, b. 7 Dec. 1837; m. Moses Briggs.

10-5-2-3-5

Cyprus Libby, born in Scarborough, 27 Feb. 1794; married, 5 Feb. 1826, Sarah Maxwell, daughter of William and Ruth (Davenport) Maxwell of Cape Elizabeth. He was a farmer. He removed with his father to Gardiner, and lived there until his death, 19 Feb. 1847. His widow still lives.

Children :

1 William M., b. 28 May 1816; m. Olive Pease of Anson, Me. He lived in Gardiner a short time after his marriage, and then went to Milford, Mass., where he was a truckman. His wife died in Milford, and he then went to Boston, and shortly after to Minnesota. From that state he started across the country for Pike's Hill. He was never afterward heard from, and is supposed to have been killed. Children:

1 Abbie, married in Massachusetts.
2 Frances, is married.
3 Charles, died at about the age of fifteen.
4 Maria, is married.

2 Sewall, b. 16 Nov. 1817; lives in Gardiner.

3 Catherine Fogg, b. 9 Feb. 1820; m. Ebenezer Sawyer of Cape Elizabeth.

4 Shirley, b. 4 May 1822; m. 25 Nov. 1845, Mary A., dau. of Elizabeth (Libby) Harmon, 10-2-1-6-1; (died 4 March 1853); 2d, 27 Nov. 1867, Abiah E., dau. of Lemuel and Eliza J. (Wolcot) Redding of Vermont. He is a farmer. In 1865 he removed from Gardiner to Belchertown, Mass., where he has since lived. Children, by first wife:

1 Clarence E., b. 3 June 1847; m. 27 Nov. 1871, Susie F., dau. of Andrew and Ann Magrath of Calais, Me. He was employed seven years in the Boston market, and for eight years has been a policeman. Adopted child:

a Clarence (Libby), b. 8 June 1871, in Calais.

2 Henry H., b. 7 May 1852; unm. He is in the cattle business in Nebraska.

By second wife:

3 Gertrude A., b. 30 June 1871, in Belchertown.

5 Reuben, b. 25 March 1824; married 31 Dec. 1854, Nancy M., dau. of James and Martha C. (Beecher) Stoddard of Gardiner. He learned the mason's trade, and in 1857 removed to Minnesota. In the latter part of his life he was in the flour and feed business. He died in Winona, of consumption, 10 June 1881. Children:

1 George F. P., b. 24 March 1856, in Gardiner.
2 Frederic S., b. 4 Oct. 1858, in St. Peter, Minn.

3 Minnie M., b. 25 Sept. 1861; died 22 Oct. 1862.
4 Capitoba B., b. 26 May 1864, in Winona; died 22 Sept. 1864.
5 Mary F., b. 24 Aug. 1866.
6 Reuben W., b. 12 March 1870; died 27 July 1873.
7 Sarah M., b. 7 July 1872; died 24 May 1874.
8 Henry W., b. 10 Feb. 187 .
9 Rubie M., b. 11 Aug. 187 ; died 14 March 187 .

6 Rufus Marr, b. 26 Aug. 1826; married in Boston, Sophronia A., dau. of Ebenezer and Louisa (Pease) Pratt of Anson, Me. He was a house-carpenter. When a young man he removed to Boston, where his widow now lives. He died in Cape Elizabeth, Me., 17 Feb. 1879. Children:
1 Reuben Wallace, died in infancy.
2 Clarendon Lynn, died in infancy.
3 Adell Louisa, b. 11 Aug. 1857; m. Chas. E. Collins of Anson, Me.
4 Harry Lee, b. 6 Aug. 1857; is an ornamental painter.
5 Charles Franklin, died aged four years.
6 Ernest Bertrand, died aged five months.
7 Jessie Bird, b. 23 Nov. 1864.
8 Millian Durant, b. 8 Aug. 1866.
9 Thursa Estella, b. 9 Feb. 1868; died in October following.

7 Ruth M., b. 16 Dec. 1828; m. Jonathan Norris of East Livermore.
8 George F., b. 30 May 1830; died in 1831.
9 Mary P., b. 28 April 1833; unm.; lives in Lewiston.
10 Woodbury J., b. 5 Oct. 1836; m. 5 July 1869, Isabella Jane, dau. of Sylvanus and Isabella (Glendenning) Hussey of Mapleton, Minn. He learned the mason's trade in Boston, but has been a farmer since 1865. Children:
1 Mary Lelah, b. 17 May 1870, in Mapleton; d. 2 March, 1872.
2 Gertrude M., b. 29 Dec. 1873, in Mapleton.
3 Catherine B., b. 5 June 1879, in Mapleton.

11 Sarah E., } twins, born } died aged 22.
12 Lucy A., } 22 July 1840; } died in infancy.

10-5-2-3-6

SEWALL LIBBY, born in Scarborough, 4 Dec. 1797; married, 20 Oct. 1821, CATHERINE HALEY, daughter of Joshua and Ann (Dill) Haley of Lisbon. He went with his father to Gardiner, where he settled on his father's homestead, and lived until his death, 11 March 1874. His wife died 17 Aug. 1871.

Children, all born in Gardiner:

1 Alvin B., b. 2 Sept. 1822; m. 27 April 1851, in Boston, Mrs. Hannah Fickett, dau. of Adams and Hannah (Champney) Foster. He is by trade a carpenter. Since 1844 has lived for the most part in Boston. Since 1871 he has been engaged in the manufacture and sale of artists' woodwork. No children.
2 Joshua, b. 10 March 1824; d. 7 June 1832.
3 Dexter, b. 27 Sept. 1826; m. 27 Sept. 1855, Susan S., dau. of Eliakim and Susan (Shaw) Norton of Gardiner. He and Dennis spent three years from 1851 in California. After his return he was in the hardware business in Gardiner until his death, 29 Oct. 1865. His widow married, 3 Jan. 1869, Orrison Dill. Children:
1 Cora E., b. 8 Sept. 1856; d. 7 June 1863.
2 Clara E., b. 27 Nov. 1857; d. 11 Sept. 1858.
3 Frankie, b. 3 Oct. 1859; d. 13 March 1862.
4 Freddie, b. 18 April 1862; d. 23 June 1863.
5 George Dexter, b. 15 Aug. 1864.

4 Dennis M., b. 4 Dec. 1829; m. 1st, 22 Sept. 1859, Patience, dau. of Michael and Patience (Knox) Hildreth of Gardiner; (d. 29 Jan. 1865); 2d, Ann O. Adly; (d. 30 Nov. 1868). He was in the stone business in Gardiner, and died there 8 Oct. 1871. Children, by first wife:
1 Patience Nettie, b. 6 Jan. 1865; d. 22 Sept. 1865.

By second wife:

2 Napoleon Howard, b. 9 Nov. 1868.
5 Cordelia, b. 10 Dec. 1831; d. 29 Nov. 1873.
6 Eunice H., b. 23 Jan. 1836; m. 23 Feb. 1863, Enos Edgecomb.
7 Mercy A., b. 27 May 1838; m. 11 Feb. 1862, Moses Mansland.

10-5-2-9-1

SETH LIBBY, born in Webster, Me., 5 June 1806; married, 17 Sept. 1835, SUSAN ALEXANDER, daughter of Thomas and Betsey (Dixon) Alexander. He settled at first on a small farm in Webster, but after his father's death he took the homestead in Wales, where he has since lived.

Children, born in Webster:

1 William Alexander, b. 22 June 1836; m. 1st, 11 Dec. 1866, in Boston, Mass., Emma A., dau. of Luke Bicknell; (d. 20 April 1867); 2d, 30 Dec. 1869, Frances J., dau. of Elizabeth (Libby) Haley, 10-5-2-11-2. He learned the mason's trade in Boston, and is now in business in Lewiston. Child:
1 Josiah Milton, b. 28 Aug. 1871, in Lewiston.
2 Rebecca Laura, b. 29 April 1838; m. Edwin Lyman.

Born in Wales:

3 Llewellyn Small, b. 11 Sept. 1842; m. 7 July 1866, Maria T., dau. of Wm. Jordan. He served two years in the late war, and now lives with his father, a farmer. No children.
4 George Henry, b. 24 Aug. 1844; m. 25 Aug. 1868, Anita Crosas, dau. of Oliver O. and Sarah B. (Osgood) Carlton of East Boston. He is by trade a ship and house-joiner, and has lived in East Boston since 1865. Child:
1 Herbert Alphonzo, b. 23 Jan. 1869, in East Boston.
5 Josiah Nelson, b. 28 April 1849; d. 2 Dec. 1873, in East Boston.

10-5-3-4-6

NATHAN LIBBY, born in Scarborough, 4 Jan. 1797; married, 11 Oct. 1821, MARY LEDOIT BABB, daughter of Peter and Lucy (Bailey) Babb of Westbrook. At the age of 19 he went to Saccarappa, Westbrook, and went to work for a stone-mason. Soon after he went into business himself, and continued it until about five years before his death. The remainder of his life he worked in the Cumberland paper-mills. He died 12 Nov. 1855. His widow died 8 Sept. 1876, with her daughter, in Meriden, Conn.

Children, all born in Westbrook:

1 David Bailey, b. 11 June 1823; married 1846, Sarah Maria Libby, 10-5-3-4-8-1. He is a stone-mason at Saccarappa. Children:
1 Aphia Maria, b. 15 Dec. 1846, in Scarborough; m. 31 Aug. 1875, Oliver P. McCarty.

2 Lucy Jane, b. 22 Dec. 1848, in Westbrook; is unm.
3 Mary Etta, b. 30 April 1850, in Westbrook; m. 17 Nov. 1866, Charles Fickett.
4 Angier Haskell, b. 7 July 1853, in Westbrook; lives at home; unmarried.
5 Susie Ellen, b. 22 July 1858, in Westbrook; m. 30 May 1880, Alden P. Mason.

2 Rhoda Ann, b. June, 1825; caught her clothes afire and was burned to death, May, 1828.
3 Mary Elizabeth, b. April, 1827; died aged one year.
4 Cyrus Edwin, b. 3 May 1828; m. 1st, 1852, Ann J., dau. of James and Betsey (Jordan) Cobb of Westbrook; (died 1 March 1864); 2d, May 1872, Sarah D. Gaskill of Norwich, Conn. He is a house-carpenter. He lived in the vicinity of Westbrook until about 1869, when he removed to Meriden, Conn. Children, all by first wife:
1 Martha E., b. 27 Feb. 1853, in Cape Elizabeth; m. Isaac C. Libby, 1-6-5-2-8-3-2.
2 Fred E., b. 22 Sept. 1858, in Westbrook; died 22 Sept. 1881; unm.
3 Annie C., b. 30 Aug. 1861; died 3 May 1863.
5, 6 died in infancy.
7 Mary Eliza, b. 3 May 1834; m. 19 Feb. 1852, Israel Augustus Redman of Ellsworth.
8 Rebecca Jane, b. 1 May 1837; m. 7 Sept. 1856, Jabez Mariner of Cape Elizabeth. Children:
1 James Elmer (Mariner), b. 14 May 1861.
2 Mary Wolcott (Mariner), b. 9 Dec. 1866.
9 Harriet Babb, b. 3 Sept. 1839; m. Charles Wolcott of Wethersfield, Conn.
10 Affa Maria, b. 12 Sept. 1841; died Sept. 1847.
11 Lucy, died aged 6 months.
12 Ella Frances, b. 20 Feb. 1846; m. Charles Lewis of Meriden, Conn.

10-5-3-4-7

ISAIAH LIBBY, born in Scarborough, 17 May 1799; married, first, 27 Jan. 1825, ELMIRA SKILLINGS, daughter of Simeon and Rebecca (Skillings) Skillings; (died about 1834); second, 25 Dec. 1840, MIRIAM BUTTERFIELD, daughter of Wm. and Susannah (Boothby) Butterfield of Standish. Shortly after his marriage, he began to work in Portland, and after his first wife's death he removed thither. He was successively a truckman, confectioner, and grocer. He died 25 May 1872. His widow still lives in Portland.

Children, by first wife, born in Scarborough:

1 Lucy Ann, b. 17 Jan. 1825; m. 15 May 1866, Granville M. Bradbury.
2 John Skillings, b. 5 July 1828; m. 16 Nov. 1857, Mary Frances, dau. of Ezekiel and Betsey (Harmon) Prout of Scarborough. He lived with his grandmother Libby and uncle Eliakim, and had the homestead farm in Scarborough. Children:
1 Clarence Eugene, b. 2 Aug. 1860.
2 Mary Ellen, b. 14 Feb. 1863.
3 Oscar Franklin, b. 12 Oct. 1871.
3 Statira, b. 21 Oct. 1831; died aged two years.

By second wife, born in Portland:

4 Susan Frances, b. 15 March 1843; m. 3 Aug. 1864, William G. Patch of Portland.

5 Samuel Butterfield, b. 31 March 1845; m. 7 May 1862, at the age of 17, Albertina V., dau. of —— and —— (Roberts) Olds of Portland. She was untrue to him, and he left her, and went into the war. He served until the close. She bore several children during the period that she was his wife, of whom the author knows nothing. He married second, his cousin Olive, dau. of Wm. and Mary (Mussey) Butterfield of Standish. He lives in Cape Elizabeth, and has for some years been employed in supplying traders with fancy goods from a cart. Children, by second wife:
1 Geneva, b. 14 May 1871.
2 Minnie Eva, b. 23 May 1877.
3 Georgia Ellen, b. 5 Oct. 1878.

6 Abbie Jane, b. 9 March 1847; m. 1 May 1865, Lewis Pray of Portland, a carriage manufacturer. He is a son of Ira Pray of Sandwich, N. H. No children.

10-5-3-4-10

John Skillings Libby, born in Scarborough, 15 Oct. 1807; married, 4 July 1829, Eliza Berry, daughter of James and Betsey (Harmon) Berry of Buxton. He early removed to Portland, and was for many years a barber there. He died 13 Jan. 1877, in Wakefield, Mass. In his latter years he became an active temperance worker, and was buried by a lodge which he formed in Massachusetts. His widow lives with her son Hosea I.

Children, all born in Portland:

1 James Berry Insley, b. 11 Dec. 1832; m. 27 Aug. 1857, Lucinda E., dau. of Benjamin and Sophronia (Caldwell) Hutchins of Dixfield. He is an hostler in Portland. Children:
1 James Benjamin, b. 11 Jan. 1858.
2 Eliza Elenette, b. 9 March 1865.
3 Hosea Decatur, b. 17 Sept. 1867.
4 Frederick Charles, b. 17 Aug. 1870.

2 Hosea Insley, b. 6 April 1834; is a bachelor; a plasterer and stucco-worker in Portland.

3 John Franklin, b. 18 Oct. 1835; went out in the Mechanic Blues, Co. B, 1st Maine Vol.; served three months, and died shortly after his return home, 27 May 1862. He was not married.

4 Charles Henry, born and died Oct. 1837.

5 Elizabeth Ellen, b. 2 Oct. 1838; m. 4 Jan. 1860, Joseph B. Parsons of Portland, a son of S. N. Parsons of Cape Elizabeth. Children:
1 Mary Ella (Parsons), b. 2 Oct. 1860; d. 3 Jan 1862.
2 Charlotte R. (Parsons), b. 2 Nov. 1861.
3 Albert Dow (Parsons), b. 30 April 1864.
4 Samuel N. (Parsons), b. 27 July 1866; d. 13 June 1868.
5 Charles Henry Dow (Parsons), b. 27 Feb. 1871.
6 Josephine Beals (Parsons), b. 27 May 1873.

6 Mary Frances, b. 18 May 1841; d. 27 May 1850.

7 Ann Maria, b. 12 Sept. 1842; is unmarried.

8 Alice Henrietta, b. 28 June 1848; m. Robert Chase.

10-5-3-5-4

Elihu Libby, born in Scarborough, 14 May 1800; married, 25 Dec. 1827, Nancy Dyer, daughter of Samuel and Mary (Young) Dyer of Cape Elizabeth. He settled on part of his father's homestead, and there died, 29 Nov. 1856. His widow and family still occupy the farm.

Children, all born in Scarborough:

1 Samuel Francis, b. 6 Dec. 1828; m. 6 Dec. 1857, Octavia, dau. of Benjamin and Content (Elliot) Bailey of Deering. He was a farmer and teamster. He settled on the homestead farm of his father-in-law. There he died, 5 Aug. 1876, and his widow still lives. Only child:
  1 Frank, b. 29 Dec. 1859; calls himself Benjamin Franklin. He is a market-gardener.
2 Mary Elizabeth, b. 13 Nov. 1830; m. 27 Dec. 1857, Richard G. Rice.
3 Sarah, b. 29 Nov. 1832; is unmarried.
4 Amos, b. 14 Nov. 1834; m. 16 Oct. 1859, Lucy Ellen, dau. of Otis and Rhoda (Babb) Trickey of Westbrook. He learned the carpenter's trade in Portland, and subsequently became a truckman. In Sept. 1862, he enlisted in the army, and died at Arlington Heights, 26 Nov. 1862. His widow and family live on her grandfather's homestead. Children:
  1 Otis Elwood, b. 6 Feb. 1861, in Portland.
  2 Mabel Almora, b. 8 April 1863, in Deering.
5 Susan Bailey, b. 26 May 1837; d. 9 Aug. 1862; unm.
6 Dorcas Esther, b. 11 Dec. 1838; d. 12 Nov. 1872; unm.
7 James Lewis, b. 13 Dec. 1840; d. 1 Nov. 1861; unm.
8 William Dyer, b. 9 April 1844; m. 24 Sept. 1868, Lucy Maria Larrabee, 11-7-2-6-4-2-2. He lives with his father-in-law, on a farm, and also carries on his business as carriage maker. Children, all born in Scarborough:
  1 John Marshall, b. 24 Sept. 1869.
  2 Carrie Wilmena, b. 13 Sept. 1871.
  3 Barak Littlefield, b. 22 June 1874.
  4 William Martin, b. 20 Oct. 1876.
  5 Theresa May, b. 12 May 1879.
9 Nancy Caroline, b. 17 Sept. 1845; d. 24 Dec. 1869; unm.
10 Alvin Bacon Rand, b. 6 March 1848; lives at home; unmarried.

10-5-3-5-6

Enos Libby, born in Scarborough, 8 Sept. 1805; married, 20 Sept. 1831, Dorcas Stone, daughter of Daniel and Susan (Crockett) Stone of Limington. He settled on a farm in Scarborough, near the Cape Elizabeth line, and still lives there.

Children, all born in Scarborough:

1 Augusta Lowell, b. 7 Dec. 1834; m. 14 June 1864, Ansel A. Thurston of Scarborough.
2 Asbury, b. 5 March 1836; m. 10 Jan. 1872, Olive A., dau. of John and Olive (Swett) Moody. He is in company with his brother William Henry, in the ice business, making their ice on their own farm, and marketing it in Portland. Child:
  1 Olive Bertha, b. 15 Sept. 1877.
3 William Henry, b. 13 July 1838; m. 4 April 1865, his cousin, Susan E., dau. of Nathaniel and Sally (Stone) Hill of Buxton, widow of Henry Hoaghland. He was successively a truckman and carpenter in Portland, and is now in the ice business. His residence is Cape Elizabeth. Child:
  1 Cora Martha, b. 4 Nov. 1869, in Cape Elizabeth.
4 Sarah Ann, b. 24 June 1840; m. Geo. B. Thurston.
5 Ellen Caroline, b. 1 Sept. 1842; m. Elbridge G. Johnson.
6 Freedom, b. 30 Oct. 1844; m. 28 June 1870, Ruth, dau. of Ruth (Libby) Johnson, 11-7-2-6-11. He is a blacksmith by trade, and is in business close by his father's home. Children:
  1 Charles Johnson, b. 28 March 1871.
  2 Ella May, b. 9 Sept. 1879.

10-5-4-1-1

Simeon Libby, born in Scarborough, 11 Jan. 1784; married Sally Lombard, daughter of Richard and Lydia (Bangs) Lombard.

Soon after his marriage he removed to Otisfield, and cleared a farm, whereon he lived until 1832. He then took his family back to Gorham to live with his brother-in-law, Simon Lombard, a bachelor, and he worked as carpenter in Bangor. After a few years he returned to Gorham, and settled on the farm now occupied by Charles Martin Libby, 10-5-4-1-1-6-6. His wife died 18 July, and he, 14 Dec., 1870.

Children, all born in Otisfield:

1 Abigail, b. 26 Nov. 1810; m. —— Carsley.
2 Simon, b. 21 June 1812; m. Rebecca A. Morse.
3 Sally, b. 26 Aug. 1814; m. Samuel Libby, 6-4-8-5-4.
4 John, b. 26 Nov. 1816; d. 3 Dec. 1817.
5 Solomon Lombard, b. 27 Oct. 1818; m. Mary A. Bangs.
6 Samuel, b. 22 Aug. 1820; m. Rosalia B. Lombard and Damaris Stone.
7 Joseph, b. Oct. 1822; d. 3 Aug. 1825.
8 Benjamin Franklin, b. 6 Oct. 1824; m. Lavinia P. Whitney.
9 Henry True, b. 9 Oct. 1826; m. 28 Oct. 1851, Sarah Cobb of Standish. He enlisted as private in the 1st Maine Reg. of Cavalry, and was afterward promoted to supernumerary second lieutenant. In 1863 he was master mechanic on Fort McClary, Kittery Point. His occupation before the war was that of millwright, and since the war he has been engaged in setting up stationary engines and boilers. His wife died June 1872, in Standish, and he now lives in Washburn, Aroostook County. Children:
 1 Edwin T., b. Oct. 1854, in Portland; m. 2 Sept. 1874, Sarah F. Hill of Parsonsfield. He is by trade a blacksmith, and was some time in business at Lake Sebago.
 2 Rosalia B., b. Feb. 1858, in Portland; m. 1880, in Hiram.
 3 Henrietta, b. March 1861, in Windham; d. Oct. 1872, in Standish.
 4 Wenzel C., b. Oct. 1865, in Portland.
 5 J. Bertwell, b. Oct. 1870, in Standish.
10 Betsey Cobb, b. 14 Nov. 1828; m. Wilder Mack Libby, 10-5-4-1-8-2.
11 Edwin E., b. 6 April 1831; m. 21 May 1854, Lydia G., dau. of James and Lucy (Lombard) Nason of Windham. He has been a journeyman carpenter. He now resides in North Windham. Children:
 1 James Edwin, b. 2 Nov. 1855, in Portland; m. 16 Jan. 1877, Lila M., dau. of Stephen B. and Mary E. (Porter) Smith of Portland. He is a stair-builder in Portland. Child:
  1 Edwin Stephen, b. 18 Feb. 1879.
 2 George Albion, b. 6 Sept. 1857, in Windham. He is a music teacher. Unmarried.
 3 William Francis, b. 26 Nov. 1865, in Gorham.
 4 Albert Edward, b. 2 Aug. 1871, in Gorham.

10-5-4-1-2

Joseph Cutts Libby, born 4 Dec. 1785, in Scarborough; married, 15 Feb. 1809, Betsey Phinney, daughter of Stephen and Anna (Hastin) Phinney. She died 7 March 1824, and in October, 1826, he married her sister Love Phinney. He lived at first on the farm now owned by Randall Elder, and afterward on that now owned by his son, Daniel Cutts Libby. He died 6 Sept. 1835. His widow died 22 May 1851.

Children, all born in Gorham:

1 David P., b. 9 Jan. 1810; m. Ann L. Hodges.
2 Mary Ann, b. 21 April 1811; d. 24 Aug., following.
3 Mary Ann, b. 16 June 1812; m. Joseph Varney Libby, 10-5-4-15-3.
4 Stephen, } twins, born } died same day.
5 Simeon, } 16 June 1814; } died 21 Aug. same year.
6 Elizabeth, b. 8 June, d. 5 Oct., 1815.
7 Daniel Cutts, b. 22 Oct. 1817; m. 19 March 1851, Ruth Woodman, dau. of Daniel and Octavia (Woodman) Mosher. He settled on his father's homestead farm, and has ever since resided thereon. Children:
  1 Fred Melville, b. 20 April 1852; m. 2 May 1872, Nancy Buckley Libby, 1-1-3-9-7-3-3. He lives at home.
  2 Ida Octavia, b. 16 Dec. 1853; m. 7 Jan. 1875, Albert M. Hamblen.
  3 Andrew Clinton Mosher, b. 12 Aug. 1855; d. 6 June 1863.
  4 Ella Winona, b. 22 Jan. 1857.
  5 Mary Alice, b. 6 June 1860.
  6 Andrew Clinton, b. 28 April 1863.

10-5-4-1-5

Daniel Libby, born in Gorham, Me., 18 March 1792; married first, 22 Jan. 1818, Martha Morton; (died 31 Dec. 1821); second, 19 May 1822, her sister, Alice Morton. He lived on the farm now occupied by Daniel Johnson. He was of a mechanical turn, and used to make carts, wheels, plows, etc. He died 11 May 1826. His widow married second, 29 Sept. 1828, Henry W. Elwell, and third, —— Bourne. She died 6 April 1874, in East Bridgewater, Mass.

Children, by first wife:

1 Albert Harding, b. 20 Dec. 1819; m. 12 Aug. 1845, Eliza Ann, dau. of Samuel and Elizabeth (Murch) Woodward of Gorham. He learned the blacksmith trade, and excels in his art. He was a number of years foreman of the smith shop of the Portland Company, Portland, Me., and since 1859 has been foreman in the smith shop in Dunkirk, N. Y., which was formerly that of the Erie R. R. Co., and now run by H. G. Brooks & Co. Children:
  1 Josephine A., b. Sept. 1847; m. 18 Oct. 1877, Francis Suke.
  2 Clara Isabel, b. 14 June 1854; m. 25 Dec. 1877, Arthur S. Scott.
  3 Frank Loring, b. 10 April 1856; is a blacksmith; unm.

By second wife:

2 Daniel F., b. 24 Aug. 1823; m. Roxanna L. Jones.
3 Samuel S., b. 22 Jan. 1825; m. 3 July 1856, Patience E., dau of David and Eliza (Bowie) Farr of Portland. Except two West India voyages, and one half-day in the powder-mills at Gorham, (during which half-day—the first of an intended permanent service—it strangely happened that three mills and a canal-boat were blown up, he being one of only seven who escaped alive), he was, until 1876, a steel-worker in the Portland Company's works. He is now a farmer in Durham. Children:
  1 Eugene S., b. 19 Nov. 1860.
  2 Samuel W., b. 9 Jan. 1864.

3 Alice E., b. 29 Dec. 1866.
4 Milton J., died young.
5 Hannah B., b. 22 April 1871.
6 Bertie V., b. 30 June 1874.
7 John B., b. 10 Sept. 1876.

4 Martha, married Alden Reed.

10-5-4-1-8

Ai Libby, born in Gorham, Me., 21 Nov. 1799; married, first, 1 Dec. 1824, Martha Skillings, daughter of Benjamin and Ann (Hamblen) Skillings; (died 11 Oct. 1831); second, 3 March 1833, Elizabeth Files, daughter of Joseph and Ann (Haskell) Files. He lived on his father's homestead, and died there 22 June 1837. 3 March 1854, his widow married Samuel Johnson.

Children, by first wife:

1 Wilder Mack, b. 3 March 1825; d. 21 Sept. 1826.

2 Wilder Mack, b. 15 Feb. 1827; m. 2 April 1850, Betsey Cobb Libby, 10-5-4-1-1-10. He lived at home four years after his marriage, and then bought the farm on which he has since resided. He has been sexton of the Methodist church more than twenty years. Children:
   1 Olive Adelaide, b. 8 Sept. 1852; m. 25 Aug. 1870, James L. Haines.
   2 Emma Eudora, b. 22 July 1855; m. 30 Nov. 1873, Cortez F. Berry.
   3 Albert Francis, b. 21 Dec. 1858; unm. He is a blacksmith, and carries on his business close by his father's.
   4 Gertrude Lillian, b. 19 March 1865.
   5 Alice Inez, b. 22 June 1869.

3 Lewis, b. 10 Jan. 1829; is a bachelor. He lives on the homestead farm. He has been three years selectman, and two years collector, of Gorham.

4 Franklin Skillings, b. 12 June 1831; m. 1 Jan. 1854, Abby P., dau. of Stephen and Lydia (Parker) Heald of Lovell, Me. He was a blacksmith. He was in the employment of the Portland Company, — the last five years of his life as foreman. His widow and only surviving son live in Gorham. Children:
   1 Ai Henry, b. 25 July 1855; d. 25 Oct. 1856.
   2 Lewis F., b. 21 Sept. 1857; m. 8 Aug. 1879, Lillie Plummer of Gorham. He is a farmer. Child:
      1 Frank S., b. 26 Sept. 1880.
   3 Charles Johnson, b. 12 April, d. 3 May, 1859.
   4 Howard, b. 12 Sept., d. 24 Nov., 1860.

Children of Ai Libby, by second wife:

5 Martha, b. 20 Sept. 1834; m. 2 Jan. 1854, Charles Johnson.

6 Rose Ann, b. 6 April 1836; m. 23 April 1855, Matthew Johnson.

10-5-4-2-3

Ephraim Libby, born in Scarborough, 30 Oct. 1784; married, 26 Jan. 1807, Mary Blake, daughter of John and Deborah (Tuckerman) Blake of Gorham. He owned and lived on, at different periods of his life, three farms in Gorham, and one in Naples. At the time of his death he was living with his son Andrew, but he died in Gorham on a visit to his son Allison, 6 Oct. 1866. His wife died 18 April 1866.

Children, all born in Gorham:

1 Sally, b. 22 Oct. 1808; m. Capt. Joab Libby, 1-1-3-8-2-1.
2 Deborah, b. 5 March 1810; m. 1 Jan. 1828, Jacob Dingley.
3 Eliza, b. 18 Feb. 1812; d. 20 Aug. 1813.
4 Abigail, b. 12 May 1814; m. Samuel Pearce of New Gloucester.
5 Allison, b. 7 Feb. 1817; m. 4 June 1848, his cousin, Mary P., dau. of Peter and Thankful (Blake) White of Sebago. He is a farmer, and, except four years in Harrison, has always lived in Gorham. Children, all born in Gorham:
  1 Abby Jane, b. 18 Feb. 1849.
  2 Charles Edward, b. 20 July 1852; unm. He is an employee in the paper mills in Pepperell, Mass.
  3 Harland L. Page, b. 2 Feb. 1856; unm. He is a farmer and school-teacher.
  4 Samuel Lenwood Dingley, b. 25 March 1865.
6 Andrew, b. 9 Aug. 1819; m. 27 Dec. 1843, Mary Ann, dau. of Samuel and Margaret (Jordan) Dingley of Casco. Seven years preceding his marriage he lived at Edes' Falls, (then in Otisfield, now in Naples), four of which years he was in the employ of Wilkinson Edes. He then removed to Raymond, and went into the lumber business. In 1860 he bought and moved onto the place he now occupies in Casco, and has since been a farmer. He is also a member of the firm of Libby, Gould & Strout, sugar shook and stave manufacturers. He was three years one of the selectmen of Raymond, and the same number in Casco. Children:
  1 Margaret Ellen, b. 6 June 1846; m. 11 March 1849, Isaiah B. Gould of Raymond.
  2 Harriet Elizabeth, b. 9 July 1850; is unmarried.
7 Hugh, b. 21 Dec. 1822; d. 5 Jan. 1823.

10-5-4-2-4

Allison Libby, born in Gorham, Me., 8 March 1787; married Lois Cross, daughter of Dea. Thomas and Lucy (Hovey) Cross of Gorham.

He settled in Harrison soon after his marriage, and cleared a farm in the north part of the town, and thereon resided until 1831. He then bought the farm now occupied by his son. The latter years of his life were of a roving description. He died with his sister Abigail, in Harrison, 10 Aug. 1869. His wife died 25 Feb. 1860.

Children, all but the first born in Harrison:

1 James P., d. 21 Nov. 1812, aged a few weeks.
2 Harriet Cross, b. 23 May 1814; m. 1st, Eben Richardson; 2d, Jonathan Seavey.
3 Leonard Cross, b. 12 June 1817; m. 24 Oct. 1847, Abigail B., dau. of Joshua and Joanna (Rose) Trafton. He is a farmer, and has lived nearly all his life on the farm he now occupies in Harrison. Children:
  1 Charles Badger, b. 11 Oct. 1848; d. 3 Nov. 1851.
  2 Ellen Preble, b. 10 July 1850; unm.
  3 Herbert Appleton, b. 8 Aug. 1853; unm.; lives at home.
4 Caroline, b. 27 May 1819; m. 1st., Nathaniel Harmon; 2d, Daniel Richardson.
5 Louisa, b. 15 Dec. 1820; m. Daniel Richardson, the same that married Caroline.
6 Ann, b. 15 July 1822; m. John Goddard.
7 Mary Gage, b. 12 Aug. 1827; m. Major Plaisted, 11-7-3-6-6.

10-5-4-2-7

Hugh Libby, born in Gorham, Me., 26 May 1793; married, 23 March 1826, his cousin, Theodosia Small, daughter of Elizabeth (Dam) Small, 11-7-5-2. He was a farmer, and owned and occupied several farms. He was for many years sexton of the Congregational church. He died with his son John Francis, 8 July 1872. His wife died 10 April 1850.

Children:

1 infant, born and died 11 June 1827.
2 Elizabeth, b. 23 June 1828; d. 10 Feb. 1829.
3 William Henry, b. 28 Feb. 1830; m. 28 Jan. 1868, in San Francisco, Cal., Catherine, dau. of John and Mary (Lions) Norton of Roxbury, Mass. He went to California in 1853. He is now in the express business in San Francisco. Children:
  1 William Henry, b. 25 Dec. 1868.
  2 John Thomas, b. 22 March 1870.
  3 Catherine Frances, b. 9 Jan. 1872.
  4 Charles Watson, b. 6 March 1874.
  5 Alice Elizabeth, b. 5 Nov. 1876.
  6 Albert Small, b. 25 July 1879.
4 Elizabeth Dam, b. 1 Jan. 1832; m. John Watson of St. Paul, Minn.
5 John Francis, b. 17 May 1834; married 27 Nov. 1862, Zilpha Libby, 10-5-4-2-13-1. He was in California from 1856, three years, and has since resided in his native town. He is a house-painter, but lives on a farm. Child:
  1 Lee Allen, b. 21 Dec. 1864.
6 Thomas Roby, b. 17 Dec. 1839; m. 3 March 1861, Abby, dau. of Leander and Eliza Ann (Rumery) York of Hollis. He is a saw-mill hand, and lives in Hollis, on Bonny Eagle Island. Children:
  1 William Eugene, b. 21 March 1862.
  2 George Edwin, b. 4 Dec. 1865.
  3 Elizabeth Etta, b. 24 Jan. 1869.
  4 Bertie Lee, b. 16 June 1876.

10-5-4-2-8

Henry Libby, born in Gorham, Me., 15 July 1795; married, 5 Dec. 1822, Dorcas Jordan, daughter of Hezekiah and Eunice (Davis) Jordan of Raymond.

He lived in Raymond always after his marriage, except a period of five years which he spent in Gorham. He was a carpenter by trade, and always worked at coopering; but lived on a farm. He owned and occupied several farms in Raymond; the last was that now owned by his son-in-law, Sewall Welch. There he died 29 Dec. 1849. His wife died 5 April 1845.

Children, all born in Raymond but 4 and 5:

1 Abigail, b. 29 July 1825; m. 12 May 1850, Sewall Welch.
2 Mary Ann, died at the age of 3 weeks.
3 Susan, b. 1830; d. 21 Feb. 1849.
4 Harriet Eliza, b. 12 June 1832; m. 13 May 1849, Hezekiah Elkins.
5 Dorcas, b. 2 Oct. 1834; m. 11 July 1861, Charles B. Fogg.
6 Thomas, b. 29 July 1837; d. 16 March 1853.
7 Margaret, b. 31 Jan. 1840; m. John Tinney.
8 William Henry, b. 2 July 1842; m. 9 Jan. 1878, Callie, dau. of Geo. and Sarah (Staples) Watkins of Casco. He is a farmer. Children:
  1 Cora Ella, b. 30 Oct. 1878, in Casco.
  2 daughter, b. 10 Aug. 1880, in Casco.
9 Angeline, b. 20 Feb. 1845; d. June 1850.

10-5-4-2-9

JOSEPH LIBBY, born in Gorham, Me., 11 Sept. 1797; married, 5 Oct. 1823, EUNICE LOMBARD, daughter of Ebenezer and Jane (Freeman) Lombard.

He learned the cooper's trade in Raymond, and worked there some years; but returned to Gorham shortly after his marriage. He settled finally on a part of his wife's father's farm, and there died, 4 July 1873, and his widow, 18 Oct. 1880.

Children, all born in Gorham but the first:

1 Simon, b. 14 Aug. 1824, in Raymond; d. 27 Oct. 1825.
2 Simon, b. 28 Feb. 1826; lived at home, a bachelor; d. 1881.
3 Sarah, b. 31 Aug. 1827; m. Prentiss N. Waterhouse, 10-2-2-11-2-9.
4 Mary, b. 2 May 1829; m. Benjamin Graffam.
5 James N., b. 22 March 1831; m. 24 Nov. 1856, Harriet, dau. of Abraham Foster, of Portland. He is a carpenter. He lived in Portland until 1867, when he removed to California. He now lives in San Mateo. Adopted child:
   a Mildred M. (Libby), b. 18 June 1861.
6 Harriet, b. 18 Jan. 1833; m. Richard E. Carr.
7 Ebenezer, b. 10 Aug. 1835; m. Alta G., dau. of Ebenezer G. and Altazerah (Goodwin) Brimblecom of Lynn, Mass. He was a shoemaker by trade, and the working portion of his life was spent in Lynn. He returned to Gorham about 1861, and died 17 May 1865. His widow married William Frederick Libby, 1-1-2-2-8-6-3. Child:
   1 Evelyn Estelle, b. 29 June 1858; d. 28 Sept. 1859.
8 Eliza Ann, b. 10 Aug. 1837; d. 12 Aug. 1842.
9 Jane F., b. 11 May, 1841; m. 9 April 1859, James E. Freeman.
10 Joseph E., b. 14 Feb. 1844; m. 7 May 1871, Anna Augusta Libby, 1-5-2-3-7-7-2. He is a carpenter by trade, and is employed in the carpenter shop of the powder mills of South Windham. He lives on part of his father's homestead. Children:
   1 George Nelson, b. 26 Feb. 1872.
   2 Mabel, b. 10 March 1874.

10-5-4-2-13

JEREMIAH NOYES LIBBY, born in Gorham, Me., 12 Jan. 1808; married, 13 April 1834, LUCY BANGS, daughter of Joseph and Mary (Bangs) Bangs.

He cleared him a farm in Lagrange, but after three years sold it, and returning to Gorham settled on his father's homestead. In 1850, he sold the homestead, and, after carrying on the town farm two years, bought the farm he has since occupied. His first wife died, 15 April 1862, and he married second, 9 Feb. 1869, Mary Ann, daughter of Diamond and Mary (Welch) Kennard of Brownfield.

Children, all born in Gorham:

1 Zilpha, b. 7 March 1835; m. John Francis Libby, 10-5-4-2-7-5.
2 Royal Thomas, b. 26 May, d. 25 July, 1836.
3 Albion K. Parris, b. 19 Sept. 1837; m. 31 Aug. 1864, Caroline M., dau. of Delilah (Libby) Newcomb, 6-4-8-5-7. He lives on half his father's homestead. Children:
   1 Lucy Ann, b. 21 Nov. 1867.
   2 Elmer Hanson, b. 14 Nov. 1874.
4 Ann Maria, b. 20 March 1840; d. 24 Sept. 1856.

5 Mary B., } twins, born } d. 18 July 1844.
6 Daniel Small, } 14 July 1844; } d. 21 Sept. 1851.
7 Jordan, b. 13 June 1847; m. 10 Aug. 1874, Violet A., dau. of Charles and Helen (Berry) Parker of Buxton. He is employed in Hinkley's tannery. Children:
  1 Alge Parker, b. 18 Nov. 1878.
  2 Arthur La Forest, b. 28 May 1880.

10-5-4-3-1

SEWALL LIBBY, born in Gorham, Me., 10 Jan. 1793; married, 18 May 1817, ACHSAH HALL, daughter of Abraham and Elizabeth (Sanford) Hall.

He early settled in Durham, where he became a well-to-do farmer. He also had a saw-mill and grist-mill. He resided on his farm there until late in life, when he sold, and removed to Pownal, where he died 3 June 1868, and his widow 3 Feb. 1869. He served as selectman while in Durham, and as representative to the state legislature.

Children, all born in Durham:

1 Elvira H., b. 28 Nov. 1817; m. 28 Nov. 1841, Ansel Wescott of Gorham, now of Pownal. Children:
  1 Harriet C. (Wescott), b. 18 Oct. 1843, in Gorham; died 13 Aug. 1861.
  2 Achsah A. (Wescott), b. 26 Feb. 1846; m. 22 Aug. 1866, Gilman Parker of Durham, a farmer. Children:
    1 Hattie W. (Parker), b 20 March 1868.
    2 Edgar (Parker), b. 3 Dec. 1869.
    3 Elbridge G. (Parker), b. 20 Nov. 1871.
  3 Mary F. (Wescott), b. 20 June 1847; m. 31 Nov. 1868, George H. Marston of Durham. Children:
    1 Georgia E. (Marston), b. 20 Sept. 1870.
    2 Lewis A. W. (Marston), b. 11 Oct. 1876.
  4 Lewis A. (Wescott), b. 18 April 1851; died 14 Oct. 1875, in San Francisco, Cal.; unm. He learned the trade of carpenter in Boston, and removed to San Francisco in 1874.
2 Harriet, b. 15 June 1819; m. Horace C. Libby, 11-7-7-5-8.
3 Elbridge G., b. 21 May 1821; m. 11 April 1842, Caroline C., dau. of Jeremiah and Mary (Smith) Walker of Yarmouth. He was by trade a veneer-sawyer, and was in business in Yarmouth, and later in Boston. Of late he has been a millwright. Since 1844, except a few years spent in Kansas, Charlestown, and Boston, he has lived in Medford. Child:
  1 Carrie A., b. 27 Nov. 1862, in Charlestown.
4 Alvah, b. 22 Feb. 1823; m. 1st, 2 Oct. 1849, Charlotte S. Hutchinson; (died 17 Aug. 1861); 2d, 20 June 1863, Mrs. Martha E. Richards, dau. of David and Sarah L. (Scovill) Bonner of Boston. He has been a millwright, a dry goods dealer, and a farmer in Illinois. He has lived for the most part in Charlestown and Somerville, Mass., and now lives in North Adams. Children, by first wife:
  1 Warren A., b. 22 Dec. 1850; is a farmer in Morrison, Ill.
  2 James Melvin, b. 15 June 1854; is a bridge-builder in the west.
  3 Etta, b. 8 March 1856; m. Herbert S. Ford of Charlestown.
5 Albion K. P., b. 10 June 1825; m. Maria, dau. of Esther (Libby) Weeks, 11-7-7-5-3. He has been a veneer-sawyer, and later a miller. He lives in Medford, Mass. Children:
  1 Adelaide, b. 6 Dec. 1850; unm.
  2 Clara Bell, b. 10 Dec. 1856; died 12 Nov. 1861.

3 George H., b. 26 April 1859; d. 12 Sept. following.
4 Bertha M., b. 5 Dec. 1861.
5 Effie L., b. 9 Dec. 1865.
6 James H., b. 13 Oct. 1827; died 3 Aug. 1851, in Medford; unm.
7 Melvin, b. 31 July 1839; d. 8 Sept. 1852, in Medford; unm. He and James both learned the veneerer's trade with Elbridge, and were both members of the Methodist Church.

10-5-4-3-4

GARDNER LIBBY, born in Gorham, Me., 22 Jan. 1798; married, 11 Oct. 1821, HANNAH MOULTON, daughter of Abigail (Plaisted) Moulton, 11-7-3-10. Shortly after his marriage he bought and settled on the farm in Standish, now occupied by his son, Daniel I. Libby. There he died, 6 June 1876, and there his widow still lives.

Children, all born in Standish:

1 Miranda, b. 22 Dec. 1821; m. 25 Nov. 1841, Col. Luke Rich.
2 Fanny, b. 25 June 1823; m. 2 Dec. 1846, Joshua H. Littlefield.
3 Peter Moulton, b. 29 March 1825; m. Tabitha D., dau. of Joseph and Hannah (Davis) Martin of Naples. He was a carpenter, and lived on the small piece of land near Lake Sebago, now occupied by his widow. He died 21 Jan. 1872. Children:
1 Rensselaer, b. 6 June 1853; d. 27 June 1878.
2 Ida Louisa, b. 2 Jan. 1859; is unmarried.
4 Anson, b. 12 April 1827; d. 27 July 1830.
5 Abigail, b. 25 March 1829; d. 1 Oct. 1836.
6 Daniel Irish, born 4 Dec. 1831; m. 8 June 1856, Priscilla A., dau. of Richard and Adeline (Lane) Hill of Buxton. He was a teamster in Buxton until 1860, and has since carried on the homestead in Standish. He has no children of his own, but has adopted a son of George H. and Emily (Lord) Stover of Denmark. He bears the name:
a Delbert Austin (Libby), b. 22 May 1875.
7 Maria, b. 1 Jan. 1835; d. 7 Oct. 1836.
8 Ervin, b. 19 Nov. 1837; m. 18 Sept. 1859, Diantha Martin, sister of Peter's wife. He has been successively a farmer, blacksmith, and hotel-keeper. He is now proprietor of the Ervin House, Sebago Lake. No children, but adopted a daughter of Zachariah and Elvira (Blake) Gilman. She now bears the name:
a Nellie H. (Libby), b. 21 Aug. 1864.
9 Mary Elizabeth, b. 22 Aug. 1840; d. 21 Jan. 1860.
10 Levi Davis, b 14 Dec. 1844; m. 1st, 1 May 1866, Thankful E., dau. of Alfred and Rebecca (Hamlin) Chase of Raymond; (died 9 Jan. 1867); 2d, 19 April 1874, Sarah E., widow of Ethan Wilbur, dau. of James and Sarah A. (Beal) Adams of Freeport. He is a carpenter by trade, and is employed in the repair department of the Portland and Ogdensburgh R. R. Children, all by second wife, all born in Standish:
1 Daniel Francis, b. 19 Dec. 1874.
2 James Gardner, b. 26 June 1876.
3 Eva Mabel, b. 15 Oct. 1878.
11 Rensselaer, b. 8 Dec. 1848; d. 10 July 1852.

10-5-4-3-6

MARRETT LIBBY, born in Gorham, Me., 3 May 1802; married, 6 Feb. 1828, MARY LIBBY, 1-1-2-2-4-6.

Five years succeeding his marriage, he lived in Durham, and then settled on the farm in North Gorham, whereon he has since lived. His wife died 7 Nov. 1879.

Children, born in Durham:

1 Edward, b. 7 May 1829; m. 7 Feb. 1862, Sarah Emery, dau. of Asa and Mary (Sylvester) Mitchell of Raymond. He lives with his father. He had been accustomed to work at carpentering, but the loss of an eye by an accident, Aug. 1874, compelled him to give up that calling. He is now a farmer. Children:
  1 Sumner Sherman, b. 7 Feb. 1863.
  2 George Herbert, b. 29 Oct. 1864.
  3 Howard Wilbur, b. 30 Oct. 1866.
  4 Cora May, b. 25 Nov. 1868; d. 6 May 1870.
  5 Albert Warren, b. 20 May 1875; d. 12 July 1880.
2 Priscilla Frances, b. 15 March 1833; m. 1st, 10 Oct. 1854, Daniel D. Ward; 2d, 7 May 1874, Samuel S. Waterhouse, 10-2-2-11-2-5. Child:
  1 Clarence Elwood (Ward), b. 22 July 1855; m. 3 April 1878, Ada B., dau. of John F. and Mary Ann (Thomas) Smith.
3 Eliza Johnson, b. 21 March 1836; m. 1 May 1867, James H. Baker of Portland.
4 John Johnson, b. 20 Dec. 1841; d. 14 May 1842.
5 Clara Arvilda, b. 27 April 1843; m. 28 March 1866, Charles I. McLellan.

10-5-4-3-8

Joseph Libby, born in Gorham, Me., 10 March 1806; married, 22 Nov. 1832, Mary Allison Libby, 10-5-4-15-2. He went to Brunswick at the age of 24, soon married, and shortly afterward settled on the farm which he still occupies. His wife died 24 Sept. 1864.

Children, all born in Brunswick:

1 George Albion, b. 30 Sept. 1833; d. 15 Jan. 1866; unm. He was a house-painter.
2 Ebenezer How, b. 15 April 1835; unm. He is a carpenter by trade, and is now a contractor and builder in Oakland, Cal.
3 Ai Johnson, b. 21 March 1837; m. 31 May 1860, Martha E., dau. of John and Ann Maria (Marsh) Brown of Brunswick. He is a carpenter by trade, and since 1865 has been in business in Brunswick. He served 9 months in Co. D, 25th Maine Vol. Child:
  1 Frank Herbert, b. 2 Nov. 1861.
4 William Harvey, b. 5 Oct. 1838; d. 24 April 1846.
5 Mary Frances, b. 1 March 1841; m. 1st, 8 Sept. 1859, Daniel Gee; 2d, Wm. F. York, ———
6 Betsey Ellen, b. 28 Sept. 1842; d. 3 July 1858.
7 Lyman Rawson, b. 23 Dec. 1845; d. 11 Feb. 1846.
8 Adraanah, b. 23 Dec. 1847; m. 5 May 1872, Charles H. Eaton of Brunswick.
9 infant, b. Sept. 1850; died same year.
10 infant, b. Sept. 1853; d. same year.

10-5-4-3-9

Alvah Libby, born in Gorham, Me., 11 Feb. 1808; married, 18 June 1831, Ann Harmon, daughter of Rufus and Eunice (Sawyer) Harmon of Gorham. Shortly after his marriage, he settled on the farm in Gorham on which he has since lived.

Children, all born in Gorham:

1 Julia Ann, b. 25 Aug. 1833; m. 11 Nov. 1854, Rev. Sargent S. Gray.
2 Almon Lewis, b. 18 June 1835; lives at home; a bachelor.
3 Frances Helen, b. 24 Sept. 1838; m. 1st, 7 Feb. 1867, Harmon Fogg; 2d, 12 March 1876, Lewis Douglass.
4 Ransom Dunn, b. 27 March 1840; d. 29 April 1864; unm.
5 Livonia Etta, b. 1 July 1844; m. 1878, Sewall H. Douglass.
6 Horace Harding, b. 28 July 1849; m. Adell, dau. of Joseph and Eliza (Barnes) Sawyer of Cornish. He learned the carpenter's trade in Nashua, N. H., and is now a journeyman. Child:
  1 Jessie Winona, b. 11 Dec. 1878, in Gorham.
7 Lizzie Lewis, b. 25 Aug. 1856; m. May, 1880, Bion McKenney of Gorham.

10-5-4-3-10

Ebenezer How Libby, born in Gorham, Me., 22 Dec. 1810; married Catherine R. Irish, daughter of Daniel and Abigail F. (Rounds) Irish of Gorham. He died with his father, 15 Feb. 1833. His widow married, 14 Dec. 1836, Joseph Sanborn of Standish, and is still living with her son.

Ebenezer How Libby's only child:

1 Ebenezer Sewall, (he has had his name changed to Sewall Ebenezer), b. 22 Dec. 1832; m. 23 June 1855, Mary Augusta, dau. of Moses and Susan (Hopkinson) Sanborn of Standish. He is a farmer, and occupies the farm which was his step-father's. Children:
  1 Catherine Belle, born 24 Aug. 1856; m. Charles Justin Libby, 10-2-1-1-4-1-9.
  2 Susan Freeman, b. 16 Oct. 1863.
  3 Emma Deborah, b. 19 Dec. 1866; d. 22 June 1875.
  4 Clifford Sewall, b. 24 July 1875.

10-5-4-7-4

Samuel Dean Libby, born in Scarborough, 24 March 1793; married Betsey Libby, 10-1-6-5-4-1. He was a farmer, and lived in Unity. He died 15 April 1866. His family removed to Oakfield, and there his widow died, 30 May 1881.

Children, all born in Unity:

1 Sarah, b. 5 Jan. 1830; unmarried; lives in China, Me.
2 Mary, b. 3 March 1832; m. 15 Sept. 1869, Wm. Luce.
3 Nelson G., b. 24 Dec. 1834; m. 16 April 1861, Louisa, dau. of Samuel and Thirza (Spaulding) Hines of Albion. A year after his marriage, he removed to Aroostook County, where he has since lived, in Maysville and Washburn. Children:
  1 Flora, born 30 Jan. 1862; m. 27 April 1880, her uncle, John F. Bell.
  2 Olive A., b. 4 Feb. 1864.
  3 Charles J., b. 3 Oct. 1866.
  4 Maud J., b. 1 May 1869.
  5 Samuel, b. 11 Dec. 1871.
  6 Betsey, b. 28 Feb. 1874.
  7 Guy Y., b. 15 April 1878.
4 Elisha, b. 13 Dec. 1836; d. 27 June 1863, in New Orleans, La.
5 Gilbert, b. 14 May 1839; m. 23 March 1868, Sarah, dau. of Warren and Abigail (Joy) Goodrich of Burnham, Me. He lives in Oakfield. Child:

1 Fred E., b. 23 June 1873, in Burnham.
6 Benjamin F., b. 15 July 1844; is a bachelor.
7 Samuel C., b. 15 Jan. 1846; is a bachelor.
8 Mark A., b. 20 Feb. 1849; is a bachelor.
9 Marcia E., b. 4 Dec. 1851; m. 13 Oct. 1865, John Freeman Bell; d. 17 Feb. 1879. Children:
1 Frank E. (Bell), b. 13 June 1868.
2 Vinnie E. (Bell), b. 14 May 1870.
3 Nellie M. (Bell), b. 6 July 1873.
4 Albert C. (Bell), b. 15 Jan. 1875.

10-5-4-7-7

ELISHA LIBBY, born in Unity, Me., 12 April 1805; married SARAH PATTERSON of Troy; died Dec. 1868, in Albion.

Children, among others:

1 Nathan P., living in Unity.
2 Ellison L., living in Benton.

10-5-4-7-8

ALLISON LIBBY, born in Unity, Me., 12 April 1807; married, 10 Jan. 1833, SARAH J. MITCHELL, daughter of James and Sally (Rackliff) Mitchell of Unity. He started life in Unity, and after living there fifteen years, sold his farm, and bought that in Albion on which he has since resided.

Children, born in Unity:

1 Dorothy B., b. 27 Jan. 1835; m. 27 Aug. 1858, Thomas Deerow of Freedom.
2 Benjamin R., b. 7 March 1836; m. 6 June 1869, Lucy A., dau of Geo. and Mary (Jones) Goodhue of Albion. He lives with his father, a farmer. Child:
1 Cora B., b. 9 May 1870, in Albion.

10-5-4-16-4

DEMAS LIBBY, born in Scarborough, 8 July 1815; married, 31 May 1837, MEHITABLE LIBBY, 1-1-3-9-2-6. He is a farmer on his father's homestead.

Children, all born in Scarborough:

1 Ai, b. 27 Nov. 1837; m. Emeline, widow of David Fogg, and dau. of Dennis and Margaret (Harmon) Skillings. He left home when 21, and lived near by for a number of years. He was afterward a butcher in several places until 1871. He then removed to Boston, where he has been chiefly employed as mason. Only child:
1 Margaret Helen, b. 5 Nov. 1863, in Scarborough.
2 Allison, b. 16 Sept. 1839; m. 22 Nov. 1866, Annie E. Bearce. He was last heard from in Rhode Island, in 1872.
3 Lucy A., b. 17 Oct. 1841; m. 1 Jan. 1866, Lewis Berry.
4 Alonzo, b. 18 Oct. 1843; d. 25 Sept. 1847.
5 Olive M., b. 18 Oct. 1845; d. 20 Sept. 1847.
6 Alonzo D., b. 8 Jan. 1848; enlisted in 2d Maine Cavalry in Dec. 1863; d. in Florida, 31 Aug. 1864.

7 Alden Keen, b. 4 Jan. 1851; m. 3 July 1876, Catherine, widow of Charles Fisherman, dau. of Solomon and Rebecca (Graffam) Berry. He lives on and cultivates a part of his father's homestead. He is also a carpenter and butcher. Child:
  1 Florence Mabel, b. 12 Oct. 1876.
8 Llewellyn, b. 14 Nov. 1852; d. 13 Oct. 1857.
9 Solomon, b. 16 May 1855; is unmarried.
10 Frank Llewellyn, b. 13 Oct. 1857; m. 8 Sept. 1880, Georgie A., dau. of Sewall and Dorcas (Moody) Fogg of Gorham.

10-5-5-2-5

Capt. Nathaniel Libby, born in Limington, Me., 25 March 1799; married, first, 5 May 1825, Elizabeth L. Staples, daughter of Hiram and Catherine (McArthur) Staples; (died 22 June 1832); second, 9 Jan. 1833, Catherine Staples, sister of his first wife. He lived on his father's homestead and died there, 16 June 1834. His widow married, 21 March 1838, Benjamin Moody.

Children, by first wife:

1 Ann Maria, b. 6 Nov. 1825; m. 6 Nov. 1844, Simeon P. Meeds.
2 Nathaniel, b. 7 March 1830; d. 4 Jan. 1855.

By second wife:

3 Hiram Staples, b. 13 Sept. 1834; m. 7 Dec. 1864, in Portland, Jennie Estella, adopted dau. of Oren Moody. He is by trade a carpenter. He has lived in all parts of the United States, and been variously occupied, but is now in the cattle business, living in Cowley City, Kans. No children. Adopted child:
  a Ella Clay (Libby).

10-5-5-2-13

Dr. Stephen Meserve Libby, born in Limington, Me., 21 Jan. 1815; married, 21 Nov. 1838, Lois S. Chase, dau. of Eleazer and Sarah (Davis) Chase of Buxton. He was a dentist by profession, and during the latter years of his life practiced in Limerick, where he died, 3 Feb. 1855. His widow married, 1 Oct. 1864, Capt. Aaron N. Bradbury.

Children:

1 Stephen Ruthven, b. 16 Dec. 1840; m. 23 Jan. 1861, Mary W., dau. of William and Joanna (Brooks) Swasey of Limerick. He is a bookkeeper in Providence, R. I. Children:
  1 Stephen William, b. 14 July 1861.
  2 Caroline Swasey, b. 18 March 1863.
  3 George Ruthven, b. 7 Dec. 1866.
2 Harvey, b. 12 Feb. 1843; d. July, 1859.
3 Robert Elmer, b. 13 Aug. 1844; lives in Chicago, Ill.; unm.
4 Abbie Chase, b. 7 July 1846; m. Edwin Scammon.
5 Albion Chase, b. 15 Oct. 1848; } live in Osage,
6 John Herbert, b. 26 July 1853; } Iowa; unm.

10-5-5-9-2

Joseph Weeks Libby, born in Scarborough, 21 April 1804; married, 18 March 1831, Mary Jordan, daughter of Nathaniel and Catherine Jordan of Dexter, Me. In 1828 he walked to Dexter, and there bought wild land. He cleared a large farm on which he always lived, and there died, 8 Sept. 1872. His wife died 3 April 1869.

Children, born in Dexter:

1 Edward Freeman, b. 3 April 1832; m. 14 Jan. 1862, Mary Luce, dau. of Timothy and Thankful (Merry) Daggett of Parkman. He has always lived on the homestead farm, a man of feeble health. No children.

2 Ansel Joseph, b. 24 Aug. 1834; m. 1 Nov. 1856, Sarah Maria, dau. of Isaac and Lydia (Jackson) Cobb of Sangerville. He was two years engaged in the hardware business in Dexter, and then began the study of medicine. He received the degree of M.D. from the Maine Medical School in 1860, and began practice at once in Canaan. In Sept. 1862, he entered the army as asst. surgeon of the 24th Maine Vol., and died on Long Island, 28 Dec. following. His widow married, 11 April 1866, Jonathan Nowell of North Vassalborough. Only child:
  1 Freeman Ansel, b. 3 Jan. 1859; graduated from Dartmouth Medical College in 1880, winning the third prize.

10-5-5-9-3

Edward Libby, born in Scarborough, 13 March 1809; married first, 19 June 1832, Asenath Sanborn, daughter of Benjamin and Mercy (Irish) Sanborn of Gorham; (died 21 May 1853); second, 13 Aug. 1853, Harriet F. Smith, daughter of Elliot and Roxanna (Adams) Smith of Baldwin. He has owned and occupied a number of farms in Scarborough, and now lives on what was formerly known as the Hasty place.

Children, by first wife:

1 Sophronia, b. 16 April 1834; d. 19 March 1848.

2 Sumner, b. 1 July 1836; married 28 Nov. 1860, Eunice Colby Libby, 10-2-4-3-9-4. In 1864 he removed to Portland, and thence, in 1867, to Cape Elizabeth, where he was a country trader. He died 13 April 1875. His widow died in the winter of 1880-1. Children:
  1 Elmer Ellsworth, b. 22 June 1862.
  2 Albertus Emery, b. 7 July 1868.

3 Henry Augustus, b. 16 Sept. 1840; lives at home; unm.

4 Georgianna Melissa, b. 29 Sept. 1844; m. 12 May 1867, Joseph Edwin Baker of Portland.

5 Roscoe, b. 2 May 1848; m. 2 Oct. 1869, Nora R., widow of Stephen Libby, 10-5-5-9-4-4. He is a painter in Portland. Children:
  1 Lizzie Asenath, b. 13 May 1871.
  2 Sumner Henry, b. 23 June 1876.
  3 Walter Edward, b. 16 April 1879.

6 Helen Theresa, b. 6 Nov. 1850; m. 12 June 1875, Thomas Dyer.

7 James Moses, b. 4 March, died 22 March, 1853.

By second wife:

8 Stedson, b. 10 Dec. 1855; d. 25 Oct. 1856.

9 Harriet Susan, b. 1 March 1857; m. Milton Libby, 10-5-2-1-1-1-1.

10 Edward Stedson, b. 19 May 1859; unm.

10-5-5-9-4

Freeman Libby, born in Scarborough, 22 April 1811; married first, 4 Dec. 1834, Sorana Sanborn, daughter of Benjamin and

Mercy (Irish) Sanborn of Gorham; (died 10 Nov. 1839); second, 25 July 1840, MEHITABLE SMITH BRACKETT, daughter of Benjamin and Dorcas (Irish) Brackett of Limington. He settled on a farm near his father's homestead.

Children, by first wife:

1 Frances Ann, b. 15 March 1836; d. April 1839.
2 Francis Edwin, b. 28 May 1839; m. 20 Oct. 1862, Julia A. W., dau. of Benjamin F. and Sarah (Barnes) Bryant of Biddeford. He learned the tinsmith's trade in Portland, and afterward worked as journeyman. In 1866 he went into the stove and tinware business in Saco, which he still continues successfully, having removed, in 1875, across the Saco River to Biddeford. Children:
  1 Francis Arnold, b. 12 Dec. 1863; d. same day.
  2 Lunette Frances, b. 2 May 1866.

By second wife:

3 Sarah Jane, b. 10 Jan. 1843; m. 19 Oct. 1863, Jordan D. Johnson.
4 Stephen, b. 15 Nov. 1844; m. 5 Jan. 1867, Nora R., dau. of Jason and Caroline (Hall) Huckins of Boston, Mass.; died 16 Aug. 1868. No children. His widow married Roscoe Libby, 10-5-5-9-3-5.
5 Louisa Josephine, b. 5 Jan. 1851; m. 29 April 1869, Joseph H. Perry.

10-5-5-10-3

SHIRLEY LIBBY, born in Scarborough, 3 Jan. 1813; married, 18 April 1839, MARY E. SINCLAIR of Waterborough. At the age of 25 he went to Limington, and bought the homestead farm of his uncle Robert Libby, and has ever since lived thereon. His wife, Mary E., the mother of his children, died 17 Oct. 1869, and he married, 1 April 1870, Eliza J., widow of Lauren Butterfield, daughter of Simon and Hannah Harriman of Exeter.

Children, all born in Limington:

1 Lucy Ellen, b. 19 Jan. 1840; m. 13 May 1865, James F. Small of Scarborough.
2 Mary Susan, b. 26 Dec. 1841; m. 1 Aug. 1869, Silas Hubbard.
3 Lewis Sinclair, b. 5 Dec. 1848; was a private in the 30th Maine Reg. He was last heard from in New Orleans, La.
4 George Franklin, b. 5 Dec. 1848; m. 17 May 1876, Clara Elizabeth, dau. of Alfred B. and Mary A. (Swett) Marston of Falmouth. He is a farmer. Since his marriage he has lived for the most part with his wife's parents. Children:
  1 Mabel Lenwood, b. 30 May 1877, in Limington.
  2 Bertha May, b. 11 Oct. 1879, in Falmouth.
5 Charles A., born 15 Aug. 1851; m. 16 Dec. 1874, Maria H., dau. of Capt. James N. and Susan (Parker) Small of Deering. He received the degree of M.D. from the N. Y. Homeopathic Medical College, and has since practiced his profession in Arlington, Mass. No children.
6 Eunice M., b. 20 April 1856; lives in Arlington; unm.
7 Lizzie A., b. 19 Jan. 1860.

10-5-5-10-4

DANIEL LIBBY, born in Scarborough, 13 Oct. 1816; married first, 6 April 1841, NANCY HASTY, daughter of Robert Hasty of Scarborough; (died 16 May 1851); second, 5 Oct. 1853, Sarah

A. Winslow of Portland; (died 1855); third, 1862, Maria, daughter of Charles Palmer of Chicago.

He went to Portland a young man and worked for a butcher. After his first wife's death he removed to Westbrook, now Deering, and went into business himself. In 1855 he went to Chicago, where he stayed until 1873. He died with his son, Daniel F. Libby, Dec. 1874.

Children, all by first wife, born in Portland:

1 Daniel Franklin, b. 15 March 1842; m. 29 March 1865, Hannah F., dau. of Lewis and Sally (Wilds) Davis of Biddeford; (died Sept. 1868); 2d, 7 Dec. 1871, her sister, Octavia Davis. The latter died 9 June 1879. He went west in 1861, and learned the cooper's trade in Chicago. He is now a grocer near Oak Ridge, in Biddeford. Children:
   1 Bertha Fonly, b. 28 Nov. 1867; d. 4 Feb. 1870.
   2 Maurice Frank, b. 20 April 1872.
   3 Perley Clinton, b. 12 July 1873.
   4 Harry Appleton, b. 26 Aug. 1876.

2 Charles Albert, b. 10 Dec. 1844; m. 31 Dec. 1873, Amanda F., dau. of Oliver and Sarah (Haley) Dow of Lyman. He is an hostler in Biddeford.

3 Roscoe Gilman, b. 16 Nov. 1846; d. 10 Feb. 1861.

4 Angelina Elizabeth, b. 23 June 1849; m. 26 Oct. 1872, Lewis A. Davis of Biddeford.

5 George Curtis, b. 2 May 1851; is a farmer in California; unmarried.

10-5-6-1-1

Silas* Libby, born probably in Scarborough; married, Oct. 1818, Mary Boyd, born 26 June 1803, in Bracken County, Ky.

He was brought up by his grandmother in Danville, and became a ship-carpenter. He removed to Kentucky about 1817, and, upon his marriage, settled on a farm of 200 acres in Campbell County. He lived there until his death, 24 Oct. 1852. His widow survives.

Children, all born in Campbell County:

1 Elizabeth, b. 22 April 1818; m. Lorenzo Simonds.

2 Mary, b. 16 July 1820; m. Thomas Harburt.

3 Reuben, b. 23 March 1824; m. Oct. 1847, in Brown Co., Ohio, Mary Ann Bench. He was thrown from a horse and so injured that he died in a few days, 14 July 1858. His widow married his brother Edward. His children were:
   1 Maria Prudence, b. 20 Dec. 1848; m. 13 Sept. 1866, John Turner Hopkins, formerly a schoolteacher and farmer, but now a general merchant at Shelbina, Mo. Children:
      1 Elmore Eugene (Hopkins), b. 31 July 1867.
      2 Hugh Eslaman (Hopkins), b. 5 April 1869; d. 4 Dec. 1871.
      3 Clara Manet (Hopkins), b. 3 March 1871; d. 28 March 1872.
      4 Mary Elsie (Hopkins), b. 6 Aug. 1873.
      5 John Paul (Hopkins), b. 5 May 1876.
      6 Lulu Pearl (Hopkins), b. 26 Nov. 1878.
      7 Prudie (Hopkins), b. 19 Oct., d. 14 Dec., 1880.
   2 Auren, b. 29 Jan. 1851; d. 9 June 1867.

*There is a mist about Silas Libby's birth, which the compiler has been unable to scatter. One account says he was not of lawful birth. There are reasons for supposing that he was a son of Eunice Libby 10-5-6-3.

3 William, b. 14 March 1853; unm.
4 Missouri, b. 12 June 1855; m. 27 Oct. 1881, John E. Duncan.
5 Charles Reuben, b. 23 Sept. 1857; m. 9 March 1877, Emma Jane Crocker. He is a farmer. Child:
1 Lucy, b. 31 July 1879, in Marion Co., Mo.
4 Sintha, b. Oct. 1826; m. Alford Rich; died 1867.
5 William, b. 18 July 1828; lives in Kentucky. He is married, and has children.
6 Amen, b. 9 June 1832; died in 1847.
7 Lavinia, b. 27 Aug. 1835; m. 1857, Jesse Barker.
8 Edward, b. 8 Jan. 1837; m. March 1859, his brother Reuben's widow. He is a farmer. He lived in Hancock Co., Ill., from 1864 until 1871, and has since lived in Marion Co., Mo. Children:
1 Silas, b. 6 Jan. 1860; died in the same month.
2 Jasper Newton, b. 9 Jan. 1861; m. June 1879, Mary Hillhouse. He is a farmer, and a member of the Christian Church. Child:
1 Martha Alice, b. June 1880.
3 John Calvin, b. 10 July 1863; is a blacksmith.
4 George Washington, b. 22 Feb. 1866.
5 Melvin Cornelius, b. 9 June 1869.
9 Jonathan, b. 1 Nov. 1840; m. 1868, Lavinia Jenks; died 1876, in Campbell Co. No children.
10 George, b. 22 Aug. 1843; m. —— Paul, and has children.
11 Thomas, b. 1845; died 1846.

10-5-6-4-1

Jonathan Libby, born in Danville, now part of Auburn, Me., 29 Feb. 1798; married first, Mary Jordan, daughter of William Jordan of Lisbon; (died 9 Sept. 1850); second, Dorothy Libby, 10-5-6-2-7.

He was a sailor and fisherman some time, but settled on one-half his father's homestead, and was for the most part a farmer. Several years he served as selectman, and he was a member of the Methodist Church. He died 11 Nov. 1866. His widow died 9 Sept. 1876.

Children, all by his first wife:

1 Elizabeth A., b. 13 Nov. 1825; m. Lemuel Turner.
2 William T., b. 8 Aug. 1828; m. July 1851, Elizabeth, dau. of Charles and Betsey Harriman of Chatham, N. H. When 22 he went to Boston, and was engaged there as clerk and salesman in several dry goods and clothing stores, until his health failed in 1868, and he then returned to his father's homestead in Auburn. While in Boston he became a member of the Baptist Church, and is now deacon of the church in Auburn. Children:
1 Eva W., b. 21 Aug. 1860.
2 Gertrude A., b. 19 Oct. 1864.
3 Justin F., b. 4 Nov. 1867.
3 Mary J., b. 6 March 1833; m. John Stevens of Bridgton.
4 Louisiana, b. 10 Aug. 1835; m. James Wagg of Danville.

10-5-6-5-1

William Libby, born in Danville, now Auburn, Me., 20 Jan. 1795; married Nancy Jordan, daughter of John and Margaret (Peoples) Jordan of Danville. He was a farmer in Danville, and died there 18 Nov. 1836. His widow died 6 May 1843.

Children:

1 Isaac, b. 1823; m. Susan Tarbox.
2 Hannah, m. Joseph Jordan.
3 Margaret, deceased.
4 Elizabeth, m. William Curtis of Wisconsin.

10-5-6-5-2

JONAH LIBBY, born in Danville, now Auburn, Me., 27 Nov. 1797; married, Feb. 1828, HEPSIBETH HANSCOM, daughter of Moses and Mary (McGraw) Hanscom of Danville. He was a farmer, and always lived in his native town. He died 2 June 1863, and his widow 31 March 1864.

Children:

1 Jonah [Captain], b. 22 Aug. 1830; m. 1st, 22 June 1854, Carry Reed; (died 8 Dec. 1856); 2d, 31 Dec. 1864, Maria P., dau. of Robert Wescott. He spent 20 years as clerk and in business in dry goods. Upon his father's death he returned to the homestead farm, and continued there until his death, 31 March 1878. He served three years in the war, rising to be a captain. Only child:
   1 Walter A., b. 2 Aug. 1856; unm.
2 Sarah H., b. 6 April 1834; m. 8 Oct. 1861, John L. Emery; d. 28 Jan. 1881, in Eliot. Me.
3 Dorothy M., b. 25 June 1836; m. 22 Nov. 1864, William P. Waterhouse.
4 George J., b. 30 July 1837; m. 13 March 1868, Mrs. Mary N. Graffam, dau. of James Verrill of New Gloucester. He is a farmer in South Auburn. Children:
   1 Cora, b. 4 May 1870.
   2 Blanche E., b. 23 Dec. 1877; died 28 April 1880.
5 Mary S., b. 17 Dec. 1839; m. 1 Jan. 1869, Solomon Larrabee.

10-5-6-5-4

LUKE LIBBY, born in Danville, now Auburn, Me., 8 Jan. 1801; married, 14 Nov. 1830, MARY LARRABEE, daughter of Isaac Larrabee of Scarborough. He is a farmer in Minot. His wife died 23 Feb. 1876.

Children:

1 Eunice J., b. 14 Feb. 1833; died in April 1863.
2 Hannah L., b. 12 Feb. 1835; m. 1861, Cephas P. Thompson.
3 Isaac L., b. 29 June 1837; m. 1863, Nellie Faard; died in Minot, Feb. 1868. His widow died the next August, in Naples.
4 John W., b. 18 Aug. 1839; m. 1863, Adelia A. Burgess; died in Minot, Feb. 1867. He was a carpenter.
5 Woodbury P., b. 17 Oct. 1840; m. 1863, Mary J., dau. of Collins and Eliza Strout of Raymond, Me. He is a farmer in Minot. Children:
   1 Collins A., b. 1865.
   2 Charles F., b. 1868.
   3 William W., b. 1870.
   4 Eugenia J., b. 1872.
   5 Geneva M., b. 1875.
   6 Arthur E., b. 1877.
   7 Lunitta, b. Jan. 1880.
6 Mary F., b. 21 April 1843; died young.
7 Artemisia, b. 12 Aug. 1845; died young.

8 Luke F., b. 18 May 1847; m. Oct. 1873, Lovina, dau. of Rev. Nathaniel and Hannah (Woodward) Bard of Lisbon. He is a shoemaker.
9 George, b. 20 July 1848; died young.
10 George L., b. 18 March 1852; m. 27 Aug. 1873, Jennie M. Bard, sister of Luke's wife. She died 24 Feb. 1880. He is a shoemaker in Lewiston. Children:
  1 Carrie J., b. 11 June 1874, in Auburn.
  2 Florence M., b. 11 Sept. 1876, in Lisbon.
  3 Joshua A., b. 6 Feb. 1879; d. 17 April 1880.

10-5-6-5-5

Isaac Libby, born in Danville, now Auburn, Me., 12 Nov. 1801; married, Abigail S. Hanscom, daughter of Moses and Mary (McGraw) Hanscom, of Lisbon. He was a farmer and settled on his father's homestead, where he lived until his death, 12 Jan. 1863. He was a member of the Baptist Church. His widow died 26 Feb. 1879.

Children:

1 daughter, born and died 16 Jan. 1830.
2 Orin S., b. 5 Dec. 1831; m. 25 Feb. 1861, Amanda M., dau. of Thomas and Mary (Fickett) Murray, of Portland. He is a farmer in Auburn. Children:
  1 Sumner E., b. 30 April 1862, in Danville.
  2 Evelina E., b. 27 Nov. 1866, in Auburn.
3 Judith H., b. 16 June 1833; m. Eben W. Libby, 10-2-1-5-6-9.
4 William M., b. 18 July 1835; unm. He lives at home.
5 Mary A., b. 10 April 1837; m. Henry Sawyer of New Gloucester.
6 Calvin S., b. 22 June 1840; m. 24 Aug. 1864, Lydia S., dau. of James and Mary C. (Roberts) Mitchell of Palmyra. He lives in Auburn, a farmer. Children:
  1 Lillian A., b. 4 Oct. 1866.
  2 Hamlin J., b. 10 Sept. 1868; d. 24 Sept. 1871.
  3 Mellen, b. 30 Sept. 1870; d. 1 Oct. 1870.
  4 daughter, born and died 18 March 1872.
  5 Mabel A., b. 6 Dec. 1875.
  6 Manley H., b. 9 May 1877; d. 16 July 1880.
7 Greenfield T., b. 7 May 1843; d. 9 Aug. 1862, at Cedar Mountain. He was in the 10th Maine Vol.
8 Moses H., b. 26 Oct. 1844; m. 14 Sept. 1867, Mary E., dau. of Asa and Jane (Skedds) Scott of Oldtown. He lives on the homestead farm. Children:
  1 son, born and died 16 Aug. 1868.
  2 Lester E., b. 16 Sept. 1869.
  3 Jennie E., b. 24 June 1871.
  4 Anson L., b. 16 Nov. 1879.

10-7-1-2-7

Joseph Libby, born in Dover, N. H., 3 Feb. 1793; married, 14 May 1822, Louisa Myers, daughter of John Myers of Leesburgh, Va.

He grew up in Durham, N. H., whither his father removed, and served his time at the carpenter's trade with Jacob Odell. After becoming of age he worked about a year as ship-carpenter on Lake Ontario, and at Baltimore, Md., and then settled in Georgetown, D. C. He was in business as house-carpenter there

Joseph Libby

until 1829, and then became a lumber merchant, and built up a very large and profitable business.

In boyhood he joined the Freewill Baptist Church at Durham, and in Georgetown was a member of the Methodist Church. He died 24 Aug. 1866. His widow died 24 May 1873.

Children, all born in Georgetown:

1 Sarah Ann, b. 1 March 1823; d. 10 Feb. 1824.
2 Joseph, b. 19 July 1824; m. 18 Dec. 1860, Mary R., dau. of Jeremiah Orme. Except two years spent in California, his residence has always been Georgetown, where he and his brother John E., under the firm name of Jos. and J. E. Libby, successfully continue their father's business. Mary R. Libby died 2 Aug. 1876. Children:
 1 Robert Moorman, b. 20 Sept. 1861.
 2 Mary Rebecca Louisa, b. 24 July 1863.
 3 Eleanor Hyde, b. 31 May 1865.
 4 Marcia Malvina, b. 19 Oct. 1866.
 5 Joseph, b. 18 Oct. 1868; d. 21 Aug. 1874.
 6 Charlotte May, b. 6 Sept. 1871; d. 25 June 1872.
 7 Louisa, b. 21 March 1874.
3 Charlotte Myers, b. 20 April 1826; m. 22 June 1843, James King. They removed from Georgetown to San Francisco, Cal., 1851, and there he was assassinated in 1854. In 1872, she married Gen. A. M. Winn. Children:
 1 Charles James (King), b. 1844; lives in San Francisco.
 2 Joseph Libby (King), b. 1845; lives in San Francisco.
 3 William J. (King), b. 1847; d. in San Francisco in 1870, leaving a wife and children.
 4 Annie (King), b. 1849; m. E. Dutton of San Francisco.
 5 Euphemia B. (King), b. 1852; m. Russell Wilson.
 6 George W. R. (King), b 1854; lives in the Sandwich Islands.
4 Catherine Malvina, b. 16 March 1828; m. 14 May 1850, Rev. B. F. Bittinger; d. 23 April 1859. Only child:
 1 Charles J. (Bittinger), d. in August 1879, leaving a wife and two children.
5 Anne Maria, b. 24 Oct. 1829; m. 9 Jan. 1851, Robert B. Moorman of Virginia. Living children:
 1 Martha J. (Moorman), b. 1852; m. —— Buford.
 2 Louisa (Moorman), b. about 1854; m. —— Luck.
 3 John B. (Moorman), b. 1865.
 4 Robert (Moorman), b. about 1871.
6 Louisa Matilda, b. 18 Oct. 1831; d. 12 May 1834.
7 Martha, b. 17 Feb. 1834; m. 29 March 1855, Benj. Miller of Winchester, Va., now of Georgetown. Children:
 1 Benjamin (Miller), b. 1 Feb. 1856.
 2 Frank Libby (Miller), b. 9 Aug. 1857.
 3 Louisa Libby (Miller), b. 3 July 1859.
 4 Henrietta Catherine (Miller), b. 8 April 1861.
 5 Martha (Miller), b. 18 Oct. 1863.
8 Romania, b. 23 March 1836; d. 2 Aug. 1840.
9 John Edward, b. 22 Nov. 1837; m. 7 April 1863, Emily F. Orme, sister of his brother's wife. Children:
 1 Lydia Hyde, b. 11 Feb. 1864; died next day.
 2 Francis Benjamin, b. 7 Aug. 1865.
 3 Clara Orme, b. 21 June 1868.
 4 Helen Johnston, b. 29 Aug. 1870.
 5 John Edward, b. 19 Dec. 1872.
10 Sarah Henrietta, b. 21 Nov. 1839; d. 26 Aug. 1841.
11 Clara Elizabeth, b. 15 Jan. 1842; m. 1st, 18 May 1864, George W. Orme; (died Dec. 1872); 2d, Dr. J. F. Hartigan of Washington. Children:

1 Clara Louisa (Orme), b. 21 Oct. 1865.
2 George William (Orme), b. 10 Jan. 1871.
12 Mary Louisa, b. 7 Dec. 1843; married 1872, Walter O. Alexander of Washington. Children:
1 Mary Louisa (Alexander), b. 7 Nov. 1873.
2 Arthur (Alexander), b. 18 May 1876.
13 Frank, b. 20 Jan. 1847; m. 22 March 1876, Emma M., dau. of Rev. T. J. Valiant. He graduated from Yale College in 1867, and went into business in Washington. He is of the firm of Willett & Libby, lumber merchants. Children:
1 Clara, b. 16 April, died 19 April, 1877.
2 Ethel, b. 5 June 1878.
3 Florence May, b. 15 June 1880.

10-7-1-4-2

Dea. David Libby, born in Kittery, now Eliot, Me., 26 Oct. 1792; married, 10 July 1817, Betsey Hanscom, daughter of Daniel and Lydia Hanscom of Eliot.

He was a tanner. Soon after his marriage, he removed to Portsmouth, N. H., where he was in business many years. In Nov. 1815, he united with the North Church, (Congregational), at Portsmouth, and was afterward its deacon thirty-five years. He died 12 May 1875. His wife's death took place 16 Aug. 1864.

Their children were:

1 Mary Ann, b. Sept. 1818, in Eliot; died 14 Sept. 1820.
2 Mary Elizabeth, b. Jan. 1823; died 24 Jan. 1827.
3 William Langdon, b. 29 July 1826, in Portsmouth; m. 1st, 7 April 1853, Julia Amanda, dau. of William N. and Sarah B. (Hatch) Miller of Newton Center, Mass.; (died 13 July 1879); 2d, 16 Feb. 1881, Mrs. Sarah C. Hatch, dau. of Hiram and Sarah S. (Patten) Sands of Chelsea, Mass. He went to Boston in 1846, and was in the employ of Homer & Caswell, crockery dealers, until 1850, and then with Jarvis & Commerais, glass manufacturers, until they closed their business in 1861, from which time he carried it on himself until 1871, when he changed to the New England Glass Works, at East Cambridge. Children:
1 Edward Drummond, b. 17 April 1854, in Chelsea; unm. He is in company with his father.
2 Alice Langdon, b. 10 May 1858, in Chelsea.
3 Sarah Miller, b. 17 July 1862, in Newton Center.
4 Henry, [Capt.], b. 27 April 1829; m. 1st., 13 Aug. 1850, in Saco, Me., Jane Urena Milliken; (died 27 Nov. 1855, in Chelsea, Mass.); 2d, 30 June 1858, Anna Nelson, dau. of John Nelson and Mary Ann (Mathes) Handy of Portsmouth. He followed the sea from the age of 15, and became an eminent ship-master. He was in the East India trade until the close of the late war, and then in the grain trade between San Francisco and Europe all the time except four years, in which he was in the glass business with his brother, until 1879. In that year he took command of a bark sailing for Japan, and died of malarial fever, off Singapore, 22 Jan. 1880. Children, by first wife:
1 Charles Henry, b. 15 July 1855, on St. Helena; d. 3 Oct. 1855.

By second wife:

2 Mary Anna, b. 8 Aug. 1860; died 26 June 1866.
3 Henry McIntire, b. 4 June 1865, in Calcutta.
4 Anna Nelson, b. 7 Sept. 1872.
5 Eliza Lincoln, b. 16 Feb. 1832; m. 1 Nov. 1854, Harry Green Tanton of Portsmouth,

6 Israel Putnam, b. 14 June 1834; m. 1st. 20 Nov. 1860, Sarah Caroline, dau. of Edward and Sarah (Bacon) Flint of Bedford, Mass.; (died Aug. 1867, in Bedford); 2d, 5 Jan. 1870, Sarah Jane, dau. of Ephraim and Abby (Webber) Chapman of Pittston. He has been in the jewelry business since 1855. He lived in Washington, D. C., until 1880, and then removed to Sioux City, Iowa. Children:
  1 Frank Putnam, b. 20 Nov. 1865; lives in Bedford.
  2 ———, died in infancy.
  3 Thaddeus Hildreth, b. 1 July 1874.

10-7-1-4-5

OLIVER LIBBY, born in Kittery, now Eliot, Me., 6 Jan. 1799; married, 2 Nov. 1823, ELIZABETH HENDERSON, daughter of Thomas and Elizabeth (Hoyt) Henderson of Dover, N. H. He was a shoemaker. In 1840, he moved to Dover, where he was in the shoe business fifteen years. About 1856, he removed to Minnesota, and engaged in the lumber business. He has not been heard from since 1862. His widow died 5 June 1871, in Dover.

Children:

1 William Henry, b. Oct. 1826; m. Hannah Manning of Newmarket, N. H.; d. in Haverhill, Mass., 6 Nov. 1876. He lived in Eliot some years, and served as town clerk. His widow died in Dover, 11 July 1868. Children:
  1 Octavus, b. 1850, in Dover; is a clerk in a hotel in New York City.
  2 Elizabeth Florence, b. Aug. 1853; d. 13 Nov. 1862.
  3 William Oliver, died in infancy, 28 July 1861.

2 Thomas, b. 15 Jan. 1830; m. 8 Jan. 1855, Abby A., dau. of John B. and Annah Drew of Spafford. He is a leather dealer in Haverhill, Mass. Children:
  1 Frank Herbert, b. 19 March 1855; unm.
  2 Isadore Blanche, b. 18 Dec. 1856; m. 8 Aug. 1881, W. Scott Peabody.
  3 Annah Elizabeth, b. 20 July 1859; died 10 May 1862.

3 Alvin R., married, 1852, Octavia L., dau. of Henry A. Frost of Dover. He left Dover, N. H., in 1865, and was in the clothing business in Vineland, N. J., four years, and has since been in the stove and hardware business in Bound Brook. Children:
  1 Charles H., b. 15 June 1852, in Danvers, Mass.; unm. He is a clerk in New York.
  2 George Wilbur, b. 4 July 1873, in Bound Brook.

4 Charles Edwin, b. 15 April 1842; m. 1 Sept. 1871, Ellen Pike, dau. of Abel and Mary E. (Pike) Barnard of Calais, Me. He went to Calais in 1870, and thence, shortly after, to Salina, Kan., where he has since lived. He was a photographer some years, and is now engaged in the sale of musical instruments. Child:
  1 Mary Elizabeth, b. 16 July 1872, in Calais.

10-7-1-4-6

JEREMIAH LIBBY, born in Kittery, now Eliot, Me., 6 April 1801; married, 1834, JULIA F. HAMMOND, daughter of John and Mary (Fernald) Hammond. He received from his father the homestead farm of Azariah Libby, 11-2-4, and there lived and died. He served several terms as selectman of the town, and was postmaster sixteen years.

The mother of his children died 29 July 1863, and he married, second, the widow of James Scott of South Berwick. He died 7 March 1872. His widow died about 1877 in South Berwick.

Children, all born in Eliot:

1 Charles Edwin, b. Aug. 1836; d. 2 Jan. 1839.
2 Howard, b. Oct. 1837; d. 20 Dec. 1845.
3 Albert W., b. 2 Jan. 1840; m. 6 Aug. 1863, Mary Ellen, dau. of Rev. Otis and Sarah (Preston) Holmes. In 1865 he went to New York where he became bookkeeper for Henry A. Taylor, an importer and jobber of silks, etc. Three years later he bought him out and has since, with various partners, continued the business. The firm is now Libby & Ryker. Children:
  1 Albert Holmes, b. 25 Nov. 1868; d. 25 Aug. 1869.
  2 Julia Grace, b. 26 Jan. 1871.
  3 Howard Preston, b. 31 Dec. 1875.
4 Mary Ellen, b. March, 1842; d. 19 Feb. 1850.

10-7-1-4-9

William Libby, born in Kittery, now Eliot, Me., 10 March 1808; married, first, 3 Dec. 1835, Sally Scammon, daughter of Samuel and Sarah (Foss) Scammon of Saco; (died 12 Nov. 1846, in Ellison, Ill.); second, 16 June 1847, Mississippi Cox, daughter of Matthew and Henrietta (Briggs) Cox of Ellison.

He served his time at the tanner's and currier's trades, and carried on business several years. In 1844 he went west, and after engaging three years in the hotel business in Warren County, Ill., settled on a farm in Bureau County. Nine years later he sold this to advantage and immediately removed to the farm in Featherstone, Minn., on which he lived until his death, 21 July 1878. In his youth he joined the Congregational Church, and in Red Wing was a member of the Presbyterian Church. He was a justice of the peace in Red Wing many years.

Children, by first wife, born in Cornville, Me.:

1 William, b. 7 April 1838; d. 20 March 1845, in Monmouth, Ill.
2 Mary Elizabeth, b. 13 Dec. 1839; m. 9 Sept. 1857, James A. Jones.
3 Almira Scammon, b. 12 Feb. 1841; m. 7 June 1878, Henry Thomas Bevans.
4 Sarah, born 22 Oct. 1846, in Ellison, Ill.; m. 10 April 1867, Dewitt Clinton Smith.

By second wife; born in Lamoille, Ill.:

5 Howard, b. 31 March 1848; m. 9 Oct. 1872, Fanelia B., dau. of Samuel W. and Joanna B. (Lewis) Whitenack of Monmouth, Ill. He received a liberal education. In 1871 he went to Montgomery County, Kansas, where he opened up a farm of 400 acres. In 1874 he moved back to Minnesota where he now resides. Children:
  1 Joanna M., b. 6 Sept. 1873, in Parker, Kans.
  2 Lyda May, b. 29 Aug. 1875, in Featherstone, Minn.
  3 Sarah Gertrude, b. 18 May 1877, in the same place.
  4 Charles Howard, b. 5 June 1881, in the same place.
6 John Milton, b. 8 May 1854, in Clarion, Ill.; m. 21 May 1873, Frances E. Evans. He is a music teacher and salesman of musical instruments. Children:
  1 Mary Emma, b. 11 March 1874, in Featherstone.
  2 Fannie Belle, b. 3 March 1877, in Featherstone.

11-2-2-1-2

JOHN LIBBY, born probably in Kittery, Me., about 1784; married, 1805, JUDITH FRYE. He grew up in Shapleigh, and became a farmer. He lived in Newfield some years following his marriage and then moved east, and settled in Wellington, where he died.

Children:

1 Samuel, b. 30 July 1806; m. 1st, Rebecca Knowles; 2d, Ann Elizabeth (Libby) Rose, 11-9-7-3-6-2.
2 Thomas, b. 8 Jan. 1808; m. Christiana, dau. of John and Dorcas (Moody) Boston, of Wellington, where he was a farmer. They separated and he went west, married again, and had two daughters.
3 Lydia, married James Staples; had the homestead.
4 James, married Mary A. Boston.
5 Judith, married Daniel Davis of Wellington.
6 Morris, died about 1850, in Boston, a painter; unm.
7 John F., born 24 Nov. 1818; m. 8 Aug. 1841, Elizabeth B., dau. of Nathaniel and Nancy (Rose) Thurston of Bangor. He learned the painter's trade in Bangor, where he ever afterward lived. Besides being a painter, he was at various times a grocer, and a policeman. His death took place 4 Aug. 1857. Children:
   1 Helen Augusta, b. 26 May 1842; m. 6 June 1859, Samuel Gibson of Bangor.
   2 Charles Henry, b. 25 Jan. 1844; unm. He served three years in the late war.
   3 Elizabeth Frances, b. 26 May 1849; m. 5 Aug. 1874, Charles Sargent of Bangor.
8 David, b. 1820; lives in Wellington.
9 daughter, died young.
10 Cynthia, married John Webb of Troy.
11 Eleanor, married John Connor.

11-2-2-1-3

SAMUEL LIBBY, born in Shapleigh, Me., 1792; married OLIVE KIMBALL. He enlisted from Shapleigh in the war of 1812, and served 18 months. He afterward settled in Athens, and later lived at Wellington. His death took place 29 Sept. 1864. His wife died about 1831.

Children:

1 Lois, b. 1817; m. Rev. Asa Huff.
2 Benjamin D., b. 1820, in Athens; m. Sophia Frye.
3 Cyrus, b. 11 Nov. 1825, in Wellington; m. 16 Feb. 1846, Eleanor, dau. of James and Olive (Staples) Huff of Wellington. He was a farmer six years, and then opened a general store in Wellington. He then sold out and bought in Levant, where he now lives. He has sold his store to a son-in-law. Children:
   1 Emily J., b. 14 June 1848; m. 6 May 1865, Sumner F. Dyer.
   2 Benjamin F., b. 25 Jan. 1850; d. 5 Feb. 1852.
   3 Loantha D., b. 27 June 1851; m. 10 April 1874, E. A. Bean, M.D.
   4 Charles E., b. 14 May 1853; d. 20 Oct. 1872.
   5 Angelia A., b. 18 July 1855; d. 9 Nov. 1872.
   6 Julitt, b. 6 Dec. 1857; m. 6 Dec. 1879, Lewis H. Waugh.
   7 Leonora, b. 10 March 1860; m. 13 Aug. 1878, Orin F. Dore.
   8 Bertha F., b. 11 Feb. 1868.
   9 Daisy L., b. 4 April 1872.

4 George, b. 23 March 1831, in Orneville; m. 22 May 1858, Hattie N., dau. of John and Alice S. (Hutchings) Thurston of Harmony. By trade he was a cooper, but afterward became a trader. He was a member of the Christian Church. His death took place 10 July 1864, in Wellington, and his widow married, 15 Aug. 1867, Benjamin R. Huff, who died 12 Jan. 1878. Children:
 1 John Samuel, b. 28 Aug. 1859; unm.; lives in Harmony.
 2 Eleanor L., b. 23 Sept. 1861; m. Frederick J. Tibbetts.

11-2-3-3-2

Daniel Libby, born in Newfield, Me., 11 July 1810; married, 27 Nov. 1833, Abigail M. Lougee, daughter of John and Nancy (Parsons) Lougee of Parsonsfield. He lived on his father's homestead and died there, 24 Sept. 1857. His widow lives with her daughter, Mrs. Aldrich, in Salem, Mass.

Children, all born in Newfield:

1 Elizabeth, b. 3 Sept. 1834; d. 13 Sept. 1853.
2 John M., b. 1 Sept. 1835; m. 2 April 1858, Harriet, daughter of Nathaniel and Asenath (Kennison) Greenlaw of Eaton, N. H. He is a teacher in Portland, Oregon. Child:
 1 Elizabeth E., b. 7 May 1860.
3 Sarah L., born 11 March 1837; m. 18 Dec. 1855, Moses Aldrich of Salem, Mass. Child:
 1 William W. (Aldrich), b. 5 Feb. 1860.
4 Helen M., b. 27 Feb. 1839; m. William Francis. Children:
 1 Elnore W. (Francis), b. 30 Dec. 1862.
 2 Willie (Francis), b. 23 July 1867; d. 3 Oct. 1868.
 3 Lillian H. (Francis), b. 26 July 1869.
 4 Lena R. (Francis), b. 13 July 1872.
5 Charles L., b. 26 Jan. 1841; served 1½ years in the 6th Maine regiment, and died at Burkittsville, Md., 7 Nov. 1862.
6 Mary A., b. 22 June 1843; m. 2 June 1870, Col. James May. Child:
 1 Daniel L. (May), b. 4 Nov. 1872.
7 Augustus B., b. 15 Jan. 1846; m. 15 Feb. 1876, Cora, dau. of James M. and Charlotte (Crocker) Holbrook of Milford, Mass. He is a powder manufacturer in Maynard, Mass. Child:
 1 Mabel E., b. 5 Feb. 1877, in Maynard.
8 Abbie J., b. 11 Dec. 1847; d. 5 Sept. 1865.
9 Estelle M., b. 19 April 1851; m. 21 Nov. 1876, Geo. Otis Thompson.

11-2-4-1-7

Sidney Smith Libby, born in Limerick, Me., 18 Aug. 1802; married first, 19 March 1829, Mary Small, daughter of Daniel Small of Scarborough. She died in Limerick, 23 Oct. 1839. He afterward married again in Quincy, Mass., and a third time in Vermont. He was a farmer, and died in the fall of 1872 in Bennington, Vt., where his widow and son Samuel lived when last heard from.

Children, by first wife:

1 Loring Small, b. 4 Feb. 1830, in Limerick; m. 15 May 1853, Shuah S., dau. of Nathan and Anna (Goodwin) Ferguson of Eliot, Me. He is by trade a blacksmith. From a year after his marriage until 1867, he lived in Newfield, and then in Ossipee, N. H., until his removal, in 1878, to Salem, Mass., where he is a grocer. While in Ossipee he served as deputy sheriff, and as selectman. He was a member of the Freewill Baptist Church in Parsonsfield until 1878, when he joined the Methodist Church in Salem. Children:

1 Annie Eldora, b. 21 May 1857, in Newfield.
2 Mary Etta, b. 9 June 1859; m. 12 May 1878, Frank Wilbur Abbott.

2 Jeremiah. He was a laborer in Dover and Portsmouth, N. H., and in Beverly, Mass., in which latter place he died, 30 Dec. 1879. Children:
1 Frank W., b. 1859.
2 Lilla A., b. 1861.
3 Winna F., b. 1864.
4 Hattie M., b. 1868.

By second wife:

3 Samuel, lived, when last heard from, in Bennington, Vt.

11-2-4-1-9

Joseph Gilpatrick Libby, born in Limerick, Me., 29 Sept. 1807; married, 4 April 1833, Nancy Ann Gilpatrick, daughter of John and Dolly (Chellis) Gilpatrick of Newfield. He lived with his father until 1843. He lived afterward one year in Newfield, about ten years on the farm in Limerick now owned by the widow of Enoch Durgin, and then settled on the farm near Limerick Village, which his widow still occupies. He died 28 Jan. 1878. He was a musician in the militia.

Children, all but Alvah born in Limerick:

1 Benjamin Franklin, b. 22 Oct. 1833; m. 1st, 11 Nov. 1865, Sarah L., dau. of Isaac and Sarah L. (Hodgdon) Carpenter of Newfield; (died 24 May 1867); 2d, 18 June 1870, Almeda, dau. of Edmund and Fanny (Skillings) Webber of Waterborough. He served three years against the Rebellion, enlisting as bugler of Co. C, 1st Reg. Cavalry, and being detailed to the 1st brigade band, under Gen. Kilpatrick. Since 1867 he has been a painter and paper-hanger in Dover, N. H. No children.
2 John Henry, b. 9 Jan. 1836; m. Augusta Stubbs of Bangor; lives in Boston.
3 James M., b. 26 Nov. 1838; d. 1 Jan. 1863; unm. He was a private in Co. E, 5th Maine Vol.
4 Miriam Gilpatrick, b. 20 Feb. 1842; m. Frank Marr.
5 Alvah Melloy, b. 30 Aug. 1844; m. Josie Davis of Auburn Bay, N. H.; d. 30 April 1877. He was a painter. He served three years in Co. E, 1st Maine Cavalry. Child:
   1 Vivian, b. 20 March 1874.
6 Salome, b. 1 April 1846; m. George Foss.
7 Luther Simmes, b. 8 Feb. 1848; m. 16 April 1874, Mary, dau. of John and Mary (Follett) Ladd of Winthrop, Me. He is a farmer in Limerick. Children:
   1 Arthur Latham, b. 5 July 1875.
   2 Clarence Leonard, b. 9 Sept. 1878.
   3 Marian, b. 1 May 1880.
8 Hannah, b. 20 Sept. 1851; d. 20 Oct. 1851.
9 George Washington, b. 20 Sept. 1855; unm. He lives with his mother.

11-2-4-3-4

Hall Staples Libby, born 14 March 1803, in Limerick, Me.; married, 9 Aug. 1825, Almeda Hammonds, daughter of Samuel and Olive (McDonald) Hammonds of Cornish. He was a farmer. He lived on a number of farms in the towns of Limerick, Denmark, Newfield, and Brownfield, but finally settled on a farm in Limerick, now owned by his son, Hall J. Libby. His wife died 4 March, and he, 29 May, 1875.

Children:

1 George Spinney, b. 17 Oct. 1826; m. 22 Jan. 1852, Susan E., dau. of David H. and Ruth H. (Eastman) Cole of Naples. He worked in the cotton mills at Great Falls, N. H., seven years, and in the woolen mills in his native town thirteen years. He has since been a farmer in Norway, Me. Children:
 1 Herbert C., b. 26 Nov. 1853; d. 7 Dec. 1856.
 2 Frank, b. 16 April 1856; m. 8 Nov. 1879, Ada A., daughter of George W. and Phebe (Greene) Russell of Norway.
 3 Edward E., b. 10 May 1858.
 4 Eugene C., b. 28 Feb. 1860.
 5 Nellie A., b. 8 March 1861; d. 8 Aug. 1866.
 6 Merton, b. 16 Feb. 1863.
 7 Mary E., b. 30 Oct. 1865.

2 Royal Hammonds, b. 20 Feb. 1829; m. 17 Dec. 1860, Lucinda S. daughter of Abner M. and Olive T. (Lewis) Richardson of Limington. He was a stage-driver, ice-man, and carpenter, in Massachusetts, and in 1872 returned to Limerick where he has been a farmer and carpenter. Children:
 1 Laura Sabine, b. 20 Oct. 1861, in Charlestown, Mass.
 2 Royal Victor, b. 13 Aug. 1864, in Limerick, Me.

3 Olive Elizabeth, b. 7 June 1831; is unmarried.

4 Hall Jackson, born 9 July 1833; m. 24 March 1860, Mary Caroline, dau. of Deacon S. S. and Sarah (Watson) Hasty of Limerick; (died 3 April 1869); 2d, 4 Nov. 1871, Mary L., dau. of Deacon J. and Ruth S. (Pierce) Bickford of Buxton. At the age of 19 he went to Massachusetts, and ever since, except one year in the 47th Mass. Vol., has been employed in the ice business. Since 1874, he has been foreman for the Boston Ice Co., at North Chelmsford. Children:
 1 George B., b. 19 July, d. 10 Sept., 1862.
 2 Samuel Hammonds, b. 20 Nov. 1864.
 3 Carrie Mabel, b. 8 Dec. 1872; d. 7 May 1873.
 4 Leon Bickford, b. 1 June 1874; d. 19 Sept. 1874.
 5 Harry Chester, b. 28 Nov. 1875.

5 Sarah Hammonds, b. 19 Feb. 1837; m. 17 June 1864, Leander B. Staples.

6 Samuel Hammonds, b. 16 March 1840; d. 28 July 1871; unm.

7 Charles Freeman, b. 11 Jan. 1843; unm. He is an operative in woolen mills.

8 Elijah Tibbetts, b. 18 Nov. 1846; m. 14 April 1870, Ida A., dau. of Charles and Lydia A. (Day) Eastman of Limerick. A rheumatic fever at the age of 14 caused the loss of the use of his legs, and in consequence he learned the watchmaker's trade. He is now in business in Milton Mills, N. H. Child:
 1 Aubery DeVere, b. 15 May 1872 in North Berwick.

11-2-4-3-5

Joseph Libby, born in Limerick, Me., 10 Nov. 1806; married Helena Libby, 11-2-4-1-8. He was a farmer, and lived on the farm now occupied by his son, Oliver Libby. He died Feb. 1851. His wife died March 1850.

Children:

1 Mary, b. 1833; m. 3 April 1860, John F. Keay.

2 Oliver, b. 12 Sept. 1836; m. 31 Dec. 1861, Malinda Virginia, dau. of Jonathan and Sophia (Heald) Warren of Limerick. He has always lived on the homestead, except six years, 1871-1876, during which he was employed in the ice business in Cambridge, Mass. Children:
  1 Arvilla May, b. 4 May 1862.
  2 Harrison, b. 26 June 1867.
  3 Oscar Clinton, b. 23 July 1869.
3 Benjamin, died aged six years.
4 Catherine, died aged four years.
5 Alvarado, b. 1844; d. 2 June 1862, at Ship Island. He was a private in Co. E, 12th Maine.

11-2-4-3-7

William Libby, born in Limerick, Me., 21 June 1811; married, 28 Nov. 1830, Martha Libby, 5-7-12-1-6. Soon after his marriage he settled on the farm now occupied by Lewis Colby's widow. He was a farmer, but in his latter years, on account of lameness, followed peddling. He died 9 Dec. 1855. His widow died 13 May 1862.

Children, all born in Limerick:

1 Rufus, b. 1 Jan. 1831; m. 6 April 1861, Joanna, dau. of Jeremiah and Elizabeth (Tibbetts) Lord of Berwick. He is a laborer in Berwick. Children:
  1 William, b. 6 March 1863.
  2 George Elmer, b. 23 March 1865.
  3 Addie May, b. 25 Nov. 1866.
  4 Charles Edwin, b. 9 Jan. 1869.
  5 Ella Frances, b. 10 Feb. 1871.
  6 Frank Ellsworth, b. 13 Sept. 1873.
  7 Elizabeth Jane, b. 1 Nov. 1876.
2 Joseph, b. 26 May 1833; m. 2 Aug. 1855, Nancy, dau. of Ezra and Ruth (Pendexter) Miles of Limerick. He is a carpenter by trade, and, since about 1870, has had charge of the repair shop of the Great Falls Manufacturing Co. No children.
3 Charles Gardner, b. 1 April 1836; m. 9 Sept. 1858, Jane H., dau. of Jonathan and Sophia (Heald) Warren. He lived at home until after his mother's death, and still lives in Limerick. He served nine months in the 27th Maine. Children:
  1 Hattie Stearns, b. 12 Aug. 1860; m. 19 Sept. 1880, Lewis A. Welch.
  2 Martha Angeel, b. 23 March 1863.
4 Azariah, b. 28 Nov. 1839; d. 28 Dec. 1840.
5 Aaron, b. 21 June 1841; m. 27 Nov. 1872, Laura B., dau. of Luther and Thirsa (Tibbetts) Tibbetts of Amesbury, Mass. He has taken the homestead farm of Azariah Libby, 11-2-4-4, with Simon and Louisa to support. No children.
6 Emily F., b. 21 Nov. 1844; d. 7 Aug. 1846.
7 Philemon, b. 6 April 1847; lives in Somersville, Mass.; unm.
8 Statira Louisa, b. 4 Feb. 1850; m. 4 Dec. 1867, as first wife, Charles H. Palmer of Hollis; d. May 1870.
9 Lucy Emily, b. 29 Oct. 1852; m. as 2d wife, C. H. Palmer.
10 Phebe Lavinia, b. Oct. 1855; d. Jan. 1856.

11-2-4-3-9

Samuel S. Libby, born in Limerick, Me., 12 July 1818; married, 29 Jan. 1843, Huldah H. Cole, daughter of Caleb and Mary

(Readell) Cole of Limerick. He has been a farmer in Limerick and Limington, and now in Denmark, Me.

Children, all born in Limerick:

1 Isaiah C., b. 4 Jan. 1844; m. 1 May 1866, Hannah H., dau. of Benjamin and Almira (Norton) Marr of Limington. He is in the employ of the Boston Ice Co., in East Cambridge, Mass. Children:
  1 J. Herbert, b. 14 Feb. 1867, in Denmark.
  2 Winnifred M., b. 29 Oct. 1875, in Denmark.
2 Ellen E., b. 27 April 1849; m. 29 Oct. 1879, George Hanson.
3 Mary E., b. 11 Jan. 1853; m. 3 July 1869, Frank C. Jewett; died 3 June 1871.

11-6-2-1-1

Daniel Libby, born in Scarborough, 15 Sept. 1784; married, 6 Aug. 1810, Elizabeth Warren, daughter of James and Martha (McLellan) Warren of Gorham. In his early days he was a schoolteacher. Soon after his marriage he settled on a farm in Gorham, and there continued until his death, which occurred 17 May 1839. His widow died 13 March 1878.

Their only child was:

1 Charles Oliver, b. 14 May 1811; m. Hannah McDougall.

11-6-2-1-3

Isaac Libby, born in Scarborough, 24 Feb. 1788; married, 25 March 1809, Susan Rounds, daughter of Joseph Rounds of Buxton. He served a three years' apprenticeship with Alexander McLellan at the blacksmith's trade. Soon after his marriage he opened a blacksmith shop at Gorham Corner. There he died, 24 June 1851. His widow died in Portland, 29 April 1871.

Children, all born in Gorham:

1 Lucy Ann Moulton, b. 18 Sept. 1809; m. 27 Oct. 1836, Joseph T. Hoole of Chicago, Ill.
2 Harriet Rounds, b. 8 Sept. 1812; d. 29 July 1841; unm.
3 Abigail G., b. 13 April 1815; m. 15 Oct. 1840, Albert S. Cobb.
4 Susan, b 23 Oct. 1817; d. 14 Jan. 1839; unm.
5 Olive Gage, b. 7 March 1820; m. 1st, Mulbury Merrill; 2d, Gilbert Bradbury of Buxton.
6 Adaline, b. 28 Aug. 1822; m. 17 Feb. 1847, Samuel Thompson of Lowell, Mass.
7 Rhoda Davis, b. 9 April 1826; m. 22 Jan. 1848, Manthano Pickering of Portland.
8 Joseph Francis, b. 30 Jan. 1829; m. 1st, 25 July 1850, Eliza J., dau. of John and Jane (Knights) Brazier; (died 29 Aug. 1859); 2d, 11 July 1863, Sabra Ann, dau. of Abraham and Mary (Hatch) Preble of Whitefield. He removed to Portland, and went into the livery business, in which he still continues. Children, all born in Portland, by first wife:
  1 Charles Frank, b. 21 Feb. 1851; m. 4 Nov. 1873, Abbie, dau. of Joshua W. and Sophia A. (Dresser) Sawyer of Portland. He is a bookkeeper in Boston, residing in Chelsea. Children:
    1 Ella Louise, b. 21 Aug. 1874; d. 6 March 1879.
    2 Maud Isabel, b. 19 Aug. 1876.
    3 Frank Joshua, b. 22 Oct. 1878.

Joseph Libbey

2 Mary Ella, b. 14 Jan. 1854; m. 1 Jan. 1873, Arthur W. Booker, a son of Daniel Booker of Lisbon. He is bookkeeper for the W. U. Telegraph Co. in Portland. Children:
  1 Frank Wilder (Booker), b. 30 July 1873.
  2 son, b. 3 Aug., died 22 Aug., 1875.
  3 Annie Jeanette (Booker), b. 23 Jan. 1877.
  4 Arthur Buzzell (Booker), b. 19 Oct. 1879.
3 Abba Eliza, b. 6 May 1859; unm.

By second wife:

4 Annie Frank, b. 29 Aug. 1864.

11-6-2-1-5

Deacon Joseph Libby, born in Buxton, Me., 13 Dec. 1793; married, 30 Oct. 1822, Rhoda Morris Davis, a sister of his brother Samuel's wife; (died 8 Aug. 1824); second, 7 Sept. 1826, Lucy Jenkins, daughter of Southworth and Huldah (Wright) Jenkins of Barre, Mass. She died 24 July 1869.

He learned the trade of blacksmith with his brother Isaac, but after working about two years, was so injured by a fall from a horse that he was obliged to quit. He then determined on an education, and worked his way through Bowdoin College, graduating in 1821. He became principal of the Portland High School, and filled the position nearly thirty years. He then went into the hay business, and continued it until his death, 27 Aug. 1871. He was a deacon of the Third Parish (Congregational) Church, and one of the trustees of Bowdoin College.

Children, by first wife:

1 Francis Allan, b. 3 Oct. 1823; d. 14 Aug. 1848; unm. He graduated from Bowdoin College in 1843, and began the study of law. He did not like it, however, and became train agent for an express company between Portland and Boston. He was killed by an accident on the cars, in Kennebunk, Me.

By second wife:

2 Wealthy Ann Jenkins, b. 5 Dec. 1827; d. 9 Dec. 1831.
3 Joseph Edwards Dwight, b. 12 Feb. 1830; d. 2 May 1873, in the Insane Asylum at Augusta; unm.
4 Wealthy Ann Daggett, b. 23 Nov. 1831; d. 4 May 1832.
5 Lucy Ellen Moulton, b. 2 May 1833; m. 29 Sept. 1859, Rev. John H. Windsor.
6 Mary Elizabeth, born 23 Jan. 1836; m. 1 Jan. 1863, Alexander Y. Thompson.
7 Rhoda Louisa, b. 4 April 1838; m. 5 Nov. 1862, Wm. L. Alden of Portland, a flour merchant. Children:
  1 Joseph Libby (Alden), b. 15 Aug. 1865; d. 4 Sept. 1866.
  2 John (Alden), b. 16 Oct. 1870.

11-6-2-1-8

Nahum Libby, born in Buxton, Me., 5 Sept. 1800; married, 2 March 1823, Sophia McLellan Marr, daughter of Dennis and Sarah (Morris) Marr. Sarah Morris was a daughter of Rhoda (Libby) Morris, 1-1-5-6. He learned the mason's trade with David Patrick of Gorham, and soon after removed to Portland, where he has since done business as mason. He has also been assistant street commissioner. His wife died 27 Oct. 1876.

Children:

1 Charles Morris, b. 17 Feb. 1824; m. 28 Oct. 1852, Annie M., dau. of Joseph and Sarah (Goodwin) Osborn of Northfield, Vt. After a changeable life he is now janitor of Fluent block, in Portland. Children:
  1 Frances Ann, b. 2 June 1854, in Fitchburgh, Mass.; m. 18 Jan. 1872, Asa Gorham Crosby.
  2 Alice Jose, b. 7 April 1859, in Keene, N. H.; unm.
2 Caroline Elizabeth, b. 8 Nov. 1832; m. 6 Jan. 1875, Joseph Ring.
3 William Henry Harrison, born and died 4 April 1841.

11-6-2-3-2

Alexander Libby, born in Buxton, Me., 21 Oct. 1795; married, 2 Nov. 1819, Nancy Loring, daughter of Ignatius and Abby (Soule) Loring of Gorham.

He lived on a farm in Buxton eight years following his marriage, and then removed to a farm in Hartford, and thence, twelve years later, to a farm in Sumner. He lived on his farm in Sumner eight years, and then, his health failing him, bought a hotel in Woodstock, where he died three years later, 1 March 1851. He was active in town matters, and served one term in the state legislature. After his death his widow removed to Lowell, Mass., with her sons, and there died 19 Feb. 1856.

Children, born in Buxton:

1 William E., b. 18 Nov. 1818; m. Martha K. Adams.
2 Mary, b. 13 Jan. 1821; m. 30 Nov. 1841, Wm. Churchill.
3 Alexander, b. 15 Dec. 1822; m. Angie Bent, in Paris, Me.; died 21 July 1846. No children. His widow married Charles (?) Pinney in Lowell.
4 Frederick, b. 12 Oct. 1825; m. Mary Bent; d. 4 Oct. 1855. No children. His widow married Albert Felton of Paris, Me.

Born in Hartford:

5 Isaac L., b. 12 Sept. 1827; m. Hattie Nute. He is a policeman in Lowell, Mass.
6 Albert E., b. 24 Aug. 1833; m. 1866, Hattie Noyes. He is also a policeman in Lowell. Children: (?)
  1 Mary J., b. 1868.
  2 Mabel, b. 1873.
7 Almon, b. 24 Nov. 1834; m. June, 1869, Mary Morrill; d. 19 Feb. 1875, in Wilmington, Mass. No children.
8 child, twin with Almon, born same day; died in infancy.

11-6-2-3-5

Richard Jose Libby, born in Buxton, Me., 15 Sept. 1801; married, 20 Dec. 1835, Jane W. Merrill, daughter of James and Susannah (Whitney) Merrill of Buxton. He settled on the small farm to which his father moved about 1830, and lived there until 1856, increasing it by purchase during the time to a large farm. In 1856 he bought the farm on which his widow and sons now live, and there died, 22 Feb. 1870.

Children, both born in Buxton:

1 George Humphrey, b. 8 Sept. 1836; m. 23 Sept. 1866, Nancy M., dau. of Peter and Eliza (Sands) Emery. He is a farmer. He served two and a half years in two enlistments in the late war. Children:
  1 Ira Frazier, b. 18 Oct. 1867.
  2 Eliza Sands, b. 1 Feb. 1872.
2 William Eaton, b. 1 Oct. 1838; unm. He is an invalid, and lives with his brother.

11-6-2-3-8

REV. ISAAC LIBBY, born in Buxton, Me., 22 Feb. 1809; married first, 4 June 1837, Miriam Usher of Limerick; (died 16 Nov. 1840, in Lewiston); second, 5 June 1842, HARRIET S. MERRITT of Brunswick; (died 18 Nov. 1846); third, 4 Sept. 1848, HANNAH J. (TENNEY) ALLEN, widow of Joseph W. Allen, daughter of John and Sally (Stinchfield) Tenney of Raymond.

He early felt himself called to preach the Gospel of Christ, and with this purpose, by his own exertions, obtained an education. He became a Freewill Baptist clergyman, and preached in many places in Maine. He was chiefly instrumental in forming the church in Lewiston Falls, and was for a number of years its pastor. He died in Lewiston, 18 Oct. 1866. His widow married, 14 Feb. 1870, William Young of Auburn.

Children, by second wife:

1 Helen Maria, b. 1 April 1843, in Cape Elizabeth; m. 26 Sept. 1863, Fenelon B. Rice.
2 Malcom H., b. 20 Aug. 1844, in Lewiston; d. 14 Jan. 1847, in Farmington.

By third wife:

3, 4 twin daughters, b. 11 Nov. 1849, in New Gloucester; d. 1 Dec. 1849.
5 Eugene Harvey, b. 26 Sept. 1851, in Lewiston; m. 20 Oct. 1872, Eva Florence, dau. of Orville W. and Sarah Helen (Parker) DeGolyer of Addison, Mich. He took a commercial course at Hillsdale College, Michigan, and during three years following his marriage, was a farmer near Hastings, Neb. Since 1876, he has lived in Auburn, Me. Children:
  1 Helen Anna, b. 7 Dec. 1873.
  2 Nellie Maud, b. 15 July 1877.
6 Julius Augustus, b. 12 May 1854, in Sabattus Village; was drowned with his younger brother by the upsetting of a boat on Lake Auburn, 24 July 1869.
7 Cecil Burgess, b. 10 Dec. 1855, in Lewiston; d. 24 July 1869.

11-7-1-4-2

WILLIAM LIBBY, born in Gorham, Me., 1 Feb. 1789; married, 27 Jan. 1814, APPHIA HARMON. He was a farmer and carpenter. He lived in Buxton, then in Bridgton, and finally in Sweden. He died in Buxton, 26 May 1865. His wife died in Sweden 14 April 1863.

Their children were:

7302. 1 Calvin E., b. 2 Nov. 1814; m. 1st, 18 May 1843, in Poland, Eliza A., dau. of Rev. John Purkis; (died 3 Sept. 1845); 2d, 21 June 1846, in Great Falls, N. H., Sarah L., dau. of Cutting Moulton. He was a school-teacher and physician until his first wife's death, and has since been a mechanic. He lives in Richmond, Me. Children by first wife:

1 Edwin A., b. 20 June 1844, in Bethel; m. 1st, 1867, Sarah Jordan of Poland; (died about 1869); 2d, Abbie Langley of Epping, N. H.; 3d, June, 1878, in Gardiner, Alma Baker. He was a drum major in the late war; is now superintendent of a shoe factory at Richmond. Child:

1 ——, son, born 1880.

2 Amy B., b. 5 June 1845; m. Samuel Garland.

By second wife:

3 A. Judson, b. 27 April 1850, in South Berwick; unm. He served a short enlistment in the late war.

4 Abbie P., b. 18 Oct. 1852, in Parsonsfield, Me.; m. June, 1870, in Lynn, Mass., Eben R. Richardson.

5 Jessie B., b. 27 Dec. 1856; died 14 Dec. 1872, in Lynn.

7303. 2 Mary F., b. 30 Oct. 1816; m. William P. Stevens of Gorham.

7304. 3 Rebecca H., b. 17 Jan., 1819; m. John Clark of Lowell.

7305. 4 Eunice D., b. 18 Feb. 1821; m. Daniel B. Sanders of Albany.

7306. 5 William F., b. 22 Aug. 1823; m. Lucy Maxwell of Biddeford. He has lived in Lowell, Mass., from about 18 years of age, and has been at different times overseer in the cotton mills and machine shops. Children:

1 Harriet E., b. 1849; unm; is a saleswoman.

2 Mary Helen, b. 1855; unm.

7307. 6 Julia A., b. 8 Feb. 1827; m. Freeman C. Deering of Saco.

7308. 7 Harriet M., b. 15 June 1829, in Bridgton; m. 5 Oct. 1851, Eben N. Perry of Cape Elizabeth, a native of Porter. He is of the firm of Perry & Flint, wholesale produce dealers, Portland. He was enrolling officer for Cape Elizabeth and Scarborough during three years of the war, and has since, at different times, held the offices of collector and of treasurer, in Cape Elizabeth, deputy sheriff of Cumberland County, sheriff of the same, (1869-1872), and trial justice. Children:

1 Luella M. (Perry), b. 3 Oct. 1852, in Saco; died Jan. 1854.

2 Florence M. (Perry), b. 21 Jan. 1857, in Lewiston.

3 Herbert B. (Perry), b. 5 Sept. 1865, in Cape Elizabeth.

7309. 8 Alonzo H., b. 11 July 1833, in Sweden; m. 1st, Nov. 1855, Ellen J., dau. of —— and Hannah (Parker) Sweetsir of Lowell; 2d, 22 Oct. 1868, Mrs. Abbie A. Brewer, dau. of James and Abigail (Fairfield) Brackett of Weston, Me. He early went to Lowell to work in the mills. From his marriage until 1861 he lived in Virginia, in the employ of an uncle of his wife, who was agent for a New York land and coal company. He was afterward engaged in setting up looms in Biddeford and Lewiston. After his second marriage he removed to Portland, where he was a deputy sheriff two years, and then two years crier of the superior court, holding at the same time the position of agent for the society for the prevention of cruelty to animals. Since 1874 he has had charge of the company boarding-house at Cumberland Mills. Children, both by his first wife:

1 Charles May, b. 27 Feb. 1857, in Lowell; unm. He is a clerk in a wholesale drug store in Boston.

2 John C. Fremont, b. 13 March 1861, in Cabell Co., W. Va.; is a student in Oberlin College, Ohio.

7310. 9 Dorcas Anna, b. 8 Mar. 1838; m. 2 Jan. 1867, Daniel Brooks, a native of Buxton, now clerk in the law office of Hon. Wm. L. Putnam, Portland. No children.

7311. 10 Clara, b. 8 Jan. 1845; m. John H. Nichols of Lynn.

11-7-1-4-4

Luther Libby, born in Gorham, Me., 16 Jan. 1794; married Hannah Libby, 1-1-2-2-6-3. When he was married he settled on the farm in South Gorham, on which he has since resided. He is a shoemaker by trade, but has given his chief attention to farming. His wife Hannah, died 2 Sept. 1841, and he married second, 22 Jan. 1843, Sarah P., daughter of Samuel Files. She died 24 Aug. 1878.

Children, all by first wife:

1 Charles, b. 5 Sept. 1817; d. 5 Nov. 1826.
2 Martha, b. 24 May 1820; d. 21 Aug. 1826.
3 William Henry, b. 28 Jan. 1822; d. 22 Sept. 1826.
4 Lucy Ann, b. 27 Feb. 1824; m. 28 Nov. 1847, David Webster Babb of Westbrook.
5 John, b. 23 Dec. 1825; m. 13 Nov. 1853, Lucretia Libby, 11-7-2-6-8-3. He took his grandfather's homestead on Beech Ridge, and cared for his grandparents. He was several years collector of Scarborough. He died 25 Sept. 1879, and his family still occupies the homestead. Children:
   1 Charles Franklin, b. 3 Oct. 1855; m. 15 Oct. 1879, Jennie, dau. of Wm. and Lucinda (Wescott) Riggs of Gorham, Me. No children.
   2 Hattie Meserve, known as Hattie May, b. 4 April 1857; d. 29 July 1881; unm.
   3 Martha Coleman, b. 29 Dec. 1860; d. 22 Jan. 1871.
   4 Abbie Ella, b. 24 Nov. 1864.
6 Charles, died very young.
7 Mary F., b. 14 Dec. 1829; m. 21 Nov. 1848, John Brown of Westbrook.
8 Harriet E., b. 17 Nov. 1831; m. Dominicus Libby, 5-2-3-8-2.
9 Francis Beverly, b. 4 July 1834; m. 1st, 21 Sept. 1861, Mary E. Tounge of Dayton; (died 30 Jan. 1871); 2d, 17 Dec. 1874, Mrs. Mary E. Howe, dau. of James Pennell of Westbrook; (died 6 Sept. 1877); 3d; 27 June 1881, Anna S., dau. of James and Jane (Haskell) Pennell, a half-sister of his second wife. He served three years as corporal in the 9th Maine Vol., and 14 months afterward as clerk in the commissary department. He settled in Portland in 1871, where he was turnkey of the county jail in 1871-2, and a deputy sheriff of Cumberland County from 1873 to 1881. He is now proprieter of a boot and shoe store. Children, by the first wife:
   1 Edgar Fernald, b. 8 Aug. 1865.
   2 Mary Eliza, b. 1 May 1867; d. 1 Jan. 1868.
10 Hannah Catherine, b. 7 Oct. 1836; m. 19 Oct. 1855, Joseph P. Files.
11 Martha C., b. 22 June 1840; d. 1 Aug. 1860.

11-7-1-4-5

Rev. Andrew Libby, born in Gorham, Me., 29 March 1796; married, 11 Sept. 1817, Betsey Berry, daughter of Solomon and Hannah (Jones) Berry of Scarborough.

After his marriage he settled in Standish. In 1824, he removed to Bridgton, and thence, in 1833, to Sweden, where he has since resided. About 1826 he became a member of the Freewill Baptist Church in Sweden, and was afterward an ordained preacher.

The mother of his children died 9 March 1859, and he married second, 29 Nov. 1860, Mrs. Sobrina Wormwood, daughter of Peter and Betsey (Farington) Dresser of Fryeburgh. She died 3 July 1878.

Children, born in Standish:

1 Hannah, b. 23 Feb. 1817; m. John Bennett.
2 Esther, b. 9 Nov. 1820; m. John Hazen of Bridgton.
3 Lydia, b. 17 Aug. 1823; m. 28 Nov. 1847, William H. Burnham of Portland. Children:
  1 Lizzie Jane (Burnham), b. 6 March 1849; unm.
  2 Laura Statira (Burnham), b. 8 Nov. 1850; unm.

Born in Bridgton:

4 Samuel B., b. 11 Sept. 1827; m. 1st, 26 Dec. 1849, Nancy L., dau. of George and —— (Brooks) Abbott of Waterborough; (she and her husband separated, and she afterward married —— Ward of Rockland, and then —— Whitney of Buxton); 2d, 11 Sept. 1854, Clarissa A., dau. of Frederick and Clarissa (Brown) Denning of Oxford. He drove a team two years; worked at York's Hotel in Saco six years; followed the sea two years; was a clerk in the store of J. G. Deering of Saco thirteen years; and then settled in Oxford, where he has since been a farmer. Children, by first wife:
  1 Lydia Anna, b. 11 June 1850; m. 8 June 1867, Ephraim G. Webster of Cape Elizabeth.
  2 Emma Maria, b. 4 Sept. 1852; unm. She was reared in the family of a Mr. Green, in Saco, whose name she bears.

  By second wife:

  3 Ida M., b. 22 Dec. 1857; m. 18 Feb. 1879, Geo. E. Sawyer of Poland. Child:
    1 Lynwood G. (Sawyer), b. 8 Oct. 1879.
  4 William, b. 27 Dec. 1866, in Oxford.
5 Andrew, b. 31 May 1830; m. 1st, 4 April 1859, Christiana C., dau. of Moses D. and Rebecca L. (Dearborn) Smart of Fryeburgh; (died 28 Oct. 1862); 2d, 3 Oct. 1863, her sister, Kate D. Smart. He is a farmer and carpenter, and lives on his father's homestead in Sweden. He served about a year in the union army in the late war, as artificer. Child:
  1 Charles S., b. 3 Nov. 1866, in Sweden.
6 Mary Elizabeth, b. 21 Oct. 1832; unm.
7 Ann Maria, b. 31 Oct. 1835; m. Joseph Gilman.
8 Aaron, b. 29 Jan. 1837; m. 10 July 1859, Lucetta L. Smart, sister of his brother's wives. He lives on his father's homestead. Children:
  1 May E., b. 31 Dec. 1863; d. 17 July 1875.
  2 Ellsworth L., b. 13 May 1865.
  3 Freddie H., b. 22 March 1872; d. 7 March 1877.
  4 Wilber E., b. 22 May 1876.
  5 Freddie, } twins, b. { d. 15 Feb. 1879.
  6 Ernest, } 19 Sept. 1878; { d. 13 Nov. 1879.

11-7-1-4-6

Moses Libby, born in Gorham, Me., 29 March 1796; married, 17 April 1822, Mary Mitchell, daughter of Richard and Lydia (Remmick) Mitchell of Scarborough. (Richard Mitchell was a son of Keziah (Libby) Mitchell, 11-6-3.)

He learned the shoemaker's trade of his brother, Luther Libby, and worked at it in Scarborough. In 1825 he removed to Bridgton and settled on the farm now occupied by his widow. There he died, 17 March 1878.

Children, all but the eldest born in Bridgton:

1 Catherine Remmick, b. 30 April 1823, in Scarborough; m. 29 Dec. 1844, Jos. K. Bemis.

2 William Mitchell, b. 6 Aug. 1825; m. 17 Oct. 1854, Susan M., dau. of Charles William and Dorcas (Harmon) Waterhouse of Sweden. He lives on the homestead, a farmer. Children:
  1 Ella Maria, b. 23 Aug. 1855; m. 27 Dec. 1874, Geo. H. Brown.
  2 Charles William, b. 23 March 1859.
  3 Carrie Etta, b. 10 Nov. 1867.

3 Moses Fogg, b. 23 Sept. 1828; m. 24 Aug. 1851, Esther B., dau. of Henry G. and Abigail P. (Merrill) Kimball of Lovell. He lives in West Bethel. Children:
  1 Mary Emma, } twins, b. 10 April 1852; d. 22 Jan. 1869.
  2 Abbie Ella, } d. 24 April 1852.
  3 Abbie Ella, b. 5 Sept. 1857.
  4 Frank Melvin, b. 18 June 1859; d. 14 April 1862.
  5 Hattie Stover, b. 12 April 1861; d. 8 March 1864.
  6 Maggie Leonice, b. 8 Aug. 1871.

4 Mary Jane, b. 18 March 1831; m. James Neal.

5 John Purkis, b. 10 May 1833; d. 19 Feb. 1838.

6 Richard, b. 31 May 1835; m. 29 April 1858, Maria G., dau. of Joseph and Mary (Pattee) Hastings of Sweden. He learned the carpenter's trade. Directly after his marriage he became one of the first settlers of what is now Easton, Aroostook County, and there settled on a farm. He soon left it, however, and worked at his trade. From 1871 to 1874 he was foreman of a sawmill in Mapleton. He is now settled in Presque Isle. Children:
  1 Horace C., b. 22 June 1859, in Letter C, R. 1.
  2 Perley S., b. 15 Dec. 1861, in Fremont Plantation.
  3 Edward E., b. 2 March 1864, in Maysville.
  4 daughter, died at birth, 10 March 1867, in Easton.
  5 Hadley F., b. 21 March 1872, in Mapleton.

7 John Purkis, b. 20 Dec. 1839; m. 1st, Sept. 1861, Mary, dau. of Wm. and Susan (Gilson) Kimball; (died 26 Dec. 1864); 2d, March, 1868, Martha, dau. of Edward and Lydia (Pierce) Simpson of Easton, Me. At 19 he emigrated to Aroostook Co., Me., and from that place served an enlistment in the 8th Me. He has since been a farmer in Easton. Children, by first wife:
  1 John William, b. 1 July 1864, in Easton.

By second wife:

  2 Mary Mariah, b. 3 Sept. 1868.
  3 Addie Estelle, b. 1 Sept. 1872.
  4 Guy Pitcher, b. 30 Aug. 1874.
  5 Ray Stevens, b. 4 Nov. 1879.

8 Eliza, b. 9 Dec. 1840; m. 7 Aug. 1859, Chas. Nevers.

9 Lucy Ann, b. 30 Sept. 1842; m. George Haskell.

10 Lydia, b. 9 Oct. 1844; d. 9 Sept. 1845.

11-7-1-8-2

Elias Libby, born in Gray, Me., 4 Nov. 1796; married, 8 April 1821, Elizabeth Hawkes of Windham. He removed to Windham a young man, and, a year after his marriage, settled on the farm on which he ended his life. He lived some time in what is now the porch, (a little house which he hauled from a neighboring farm), and afterward built on the brick house now standing.

Children, all born in Windham:

1 Ebenezer H., b. 9 May 1822; m. Marietta P., dau. of John Messer. He graduated at the college in Waterville in 1851, and became a Freewill Baptist clergyman. He preached in many places, but

ended his days on a farm in Windham. He died 18 Sept. 1868, and his widow 16 July 1876. Children:

1 Edwin M., b. 25 Aug. 1853, in Wayne; d. 2 March 1874.
2 Elmira Adelpha, b. 26 Feb. 1855, in Wayne; d. 17 March 1879.
3 Sumner Fremont, b. 10 Jan. 1857, in Wayne; d. 23 Oct. 1859.
4 Anna B., b. 9 April 1859, in Wayne; d. 23 June 1865.
5 Lizzie Etta, b. 15 May 1861, in Turner; m. 31 Jan. 1881, Samuel H. Town.
6 Fred Elias, b. 2 Sept. 1864, in Oxford.
7 Althea Mertis, b. 10 April 1867, in Windham.

2 Andrew, b. 22 Feb. 1824; m. 7 May 1850, Martha A., dau. of James and Martha (McLellan) Harding of Standish. Before his marriage he bought a farm in South Windham, now owned by Edwin Hunnewell, and there lived until 1853, when he settled on Standish Neck, on the farm on which his son, Willie M. Libby, now lives. He died 9 Nov. 1878. He was an enterprising farmer, and was many years agent for the Farmers' Insurance Co. of Gorham. His wife died 17 March 1876, and he married second, 22 Feb. 1877, Ellen F. Libby, 11-7-1-10-5-7. She now lives with her father. Children:

1 Willie Marrett, b. 21 Feb. 1851, in Windham; m. 16 Jan. 1878, Martha J., dau. of Joseph and Sarah (Towle) Wilson of Parsonsfield. He was educated at the Westbrook Academy, and now carries on the farm that was his father's. Children:
   1 Wilbert Andrew, b. 20 Feb. 1879.
   2 Katie M., b. 10 Nov. 1880.
2 Ida Marilla, b. 3 July 1853; d. 5 June 1862.
3 Martha Harding, b. 6 Aug. 1856, in Standish; d. 24 June 1862.
4 George Wesley Harding, b. 1 May 1861; is a student at Colby University.
5 Charles Sager, b. 13 Aug. 1866.

3 Elihu, b. 30 Jan. 1826; m. 30 Sept. 1855, Elizabeth M., dau. of John and Huldah (Maxwell) Elliot of Windham. He is a farmer in Gorham, N. H. Children:

1 Walter C., b. 21 Oct. 1856, in Windham.
2 Alma B., b. 30 Aug. 1859, in Windham.
3 Charles C., b. 1 July 1861, in Gorham, N. H.
4 Eugene W., b. 5 Oct. 1868, in Gorham, N. H.

4 Sarah P., b. 20 July 1828; m. 1st, 6 May 1849, Thomas Ingersoll; 2d, 22 March 1859, Clinton T. McIntire of Portland. Only child:

1 Charles Frederick (Ingersoll), b. 3 Sept. 1850; d. 3 Oct. 1872; unm.

5 Albert Mitchell, b. 27 Aug. 1830; m. 7 March 1864, Ellen M., dau. of Zachariah and Ruth (Washburn) Field of Cumberland. He has been a farmer in Windham, and recently in Standish. Children, all born in Windham:

1 Ida Violet, b. 30 Jan. 1865.
2 Willis Elmer, b. 11 Oct. 1867.
3 James Alfred, b. 18 Nov. 1869.
4 Emma Adelia, b. 28 June 1872.
5 Nelson Elroy, b. 27 Aug. 1875.
6 Charles Frederick, b. 28 Jan. 1878.
7 Georgie May, b. 20 March 1880.

6 Lydia L., b. 13 March 1833; m. 3 May 1853, John M. Elliot.

7 Daniel C., b. 6 March 1835; m. 8 Dec. 1859, Almeda Gould of Leeds. He followed the sea from the age of 15, and continued until the war broke out. In 1862, he removed to California, where he has since lived, for the most part in San Francisco, where he is now a policeman. No children.

8 Rebecca H., b. 28 March 1837; d. 26 May 1837.

9 Hannah A., b. 29 March 1838; m. 14 April 1863, Charles A. Haskell. They occupy the homestead farm.

11-7-1-8-3

EBENEZER COBB LIBBY, born in Gray, Me., 19 February 1800; married, first, DORCAS LEIGHTON; (died 24 Nov. 1832); second, 31 Oct. 1853, Hannah Elliot; (died 9 Feb. 1849); third, 20 May 1849, Mary Shaw of Standish.

He settled on one of the farms in Gray on which his father had lived, and there remained until a few years before his death, when he removed to Standish. He died with his son in Falmouth, 4 Oct. 1872. His widow still survives.

Children, all by first wife:

1 Wilson, b. 19 May 1829; m. 1st, 25 April 1852, Mary Ann, dau. of Ithiel and Susan (Shaw) Blake; (died 15 Aug. 1867); 2d, 23 Dec. 1869, Hattie A., dau. of Luther Edwards of Casco; (died 4 Sept. 1874); 3d, 8 Oct. 1878, Mrs. Caroline E. (Whiting) Ramsdell of Falmouth. He lived with his father on the homestead in Gray until 1865, when he bought the farm in Falmouth, on which his son Wilson now lives. Since his third marriage he has lived on his wife's homestead at Falmouth Foreside. Children, by the first wife:
   1 Charles Eben, b. 19 Feb. 1853; d. 28 Sept. 1866; unm.
   2 Orlando Shaw, b. 26 July 1854; unm. He is a farmer.
   3 Elmedah Blake, b. 22 March 1856; unm.
   4 Wilson Woodbury, b. 27 May 1858; m. 25 Dec. 1879, Elizabeth Mary, dau. of Daniel S. and Almira (Clough) Merrill of Cumberland. Child:
      1 Herman Wilson, b. 8 July 1880.
   5 Orin Marquis, b. 4 Dec. 1859; unm.
   6 Susan Blake, b. 24 July 1863.
   7 Sarah Ann, b. 8 Oct. 1865.

   By second wife:

   8 Edwin Raymond, b. 1 Dec. 1873; d. 4 Sept. 1874.
2 Florinda, b. 1830; d. 6 Feb. 1849.
3 Sarah Ann, b. 15 Nov. 1832; m. 11 Aug. 1855, Alexander Robertson of Poland.

11-7-1-10-1

JEDEDIAH COBB LIBBY, born in Gray, Me., 15 Oct. 1796; married, 5 Sept. 1816, HANNAH PRINCE, daughter of Sylvanus and Sally (Boston) Prince of Cumberland. From his boyhood until 1835, he followed the sea, and has since been a farmer. He lived until 1862 on the farm now owned by Joseph H. Ramsdell. He has since lived in a number of places, but is now at Gray Corner.

Children, all born in Gray:

1 Matilda Cobb, b. 3 July 1817; m. Seth Ramsdell.
2 Clarissa Ann, b. 21 March 1819; m. 2 July 1843, Elias S. Foster.
3 William Reed, b. 7 Jan. 1821; enlisted in the U. S. navy at the age of 19, and was never afterward heard from.
4 George Washington, b. 18 Jan. 1825; m. 22 March 1871, in Lowell, Mass., Silvia Matilda, dau. of William and Jael (Prince) Willard of Waterford, Me. He learned the carpenter's trade in Waterford, and soon after removed to Massachusetts, where he worked at his trade some years, and, since 1864, has been employed in the manufacture of musical instruments. His present residence is Bedford. Children:

1 son, b. 11, died 15, Nov. 1855, in Monroe, Mich.
2 Clarence Jenness, b. 10 May 1859; unm. He is a clerk in the coal business; a member of the Congregational Church.

5 Betsey Reed, b. 8 Feb. 1827; m. George Thurston.

6 Augustus Franklin, b. 8 Oct. 1829; m. 15 Sept. 1855, in Lowell, Mass., Ann, dau. of Johnson and Phebe (Atwood) Robinson of Johnson, Vt. He learned the carpenter's trade in Portland, and, after working as journeyman some time, in 1857 went into business at Gray Corner. Children:
1 Ida Florence, b. 16 March 1859.
2 Arte Eliza, b. 4 Jan. 1862.

7 Charles Edward, b. 2 April 1832; m. 3 Aug. 1858, Elizabeth, dau. of Wm. and Elizabeth (Millian) Crocker of Nova Scotia. He is a carpenter and builder at Gray Corner. Children:
1 Jessie, b. 5 Sept. 1860; d. Feb. 1862.
2 Isabel Frances, b. 4 Jan. 1862.
3 Hattie Elizabeth, b. 3 Aug. 1864.
4 Fred Walter, b. 1 March 1867.

8 Henry Sylvanus, b. 31 July 1834; m. 17 Nov. 1860, Phebe E., dau. of John and Esther (Wilcox) Moshier of Kempt, Nova Scotia. He followed the sea from his ninth year until 1868, and then confined himself to harbor service. Since 1876 he has been 1st assistant light-house tender at the Cape Lights. Children:
1 Amy Belle, b. 7 April 1863.
2 Harry Elmer, b. 22 Oct. 1865.
3 Laura Frances, b. 18 Jan. 1868.
4 Charles Blanchard, d. 5 Nov. 1871, aged 5 months.

9 Albion Wesley, b. 5 Oct. 1838; m. 5 Aug. 1860, Sarah Harmon; d. Sept. 1865, in Brunswick, Ga. He was a private in the 30th Maine Reg. Issue:
1 child, died at the age of two years.

10 Jedediah Clinton, b. 16 July 1841; d. 21 March 1855.

11-7-1-11-3

David Libby, born 21 April 1804, in Gray, Me.; married Martha Waymouth, daughter of James and Mary (Leighton) Waymouth. He was by trade a carpenter, but settled on a farm near by his father's homestead. He died 1 July 1881. His wife died 22 July 1855.

Children, all born in Gray:

1 Mary Elizabeth, b. 1 March 1827; unm.

2 James Richmond, b. 4 Oct. 1829; d. 25 Oct. 1851; unm.

3 Isaac, b. 22 Nov. 1831; m. 1 Dec. 1856, Mary F., dau. of Ephraim and Fanny (Small) Lawrence of Gray. He learned the carpenter's trade with his father, and since his marriage has been in business himself. Children, all born in Gray:
1 Elsie Janet, b. 11 Dec. 1859.
2 Gertrude Alice, b. 15 Aug. 1861.
3 Alice Amanda, b. 6 Feb. 1864.
4 Walter Henry, b. 19 Sept. 1871.

4 Martha Frances, b. 20 May 1834; m. Clinton W. Staples.

5 Alfred, b. 25 Sept. 1836; d. 7 Feb. 1851.

6 John Henry, b. 6 May 1839; m. 1 May 1871, Fanny T., dau. of Jacob and Emily G. (Nash) Stiles. Soon after his marriage, he bought the farm in Gray on which he has since resided. Children:
1 Maud Ella, b. 20 Aug. 1872, in Cape Elizabeth.
2 child, born 4 Sept. 1880.

7 Bradford, b. 5 July 1842; m. 18 Feb. 1864, Mary E., dau. of William and Susan (Gooding) Anderson of Yarmouth. He is a farmer, and, except the two years following his marriage, has always lived on the homestead in Gray. Children:

1 George Willis, b. 22 July 1865, in Yarmouth.
2 Jennie Eva, b. 14 Sept. 1869.
3 Herbert William, b. 18 Nov. 1874.
4 Minnie Belle, b. 3 June 1878.
5 Charles F., b. 3 June 1880.

8 Susan Jane, b. 24 Nov. 1845; m. John B. Nash.
9 Charles Dana, b. 3 Nov. 1848; unm. He is a carpenter.
10 George, b. 18 March 1851; m. 10 March 1879, Emma, dau. of Jacob and Emily (Nash) Stiles of Gray. He has settled on the farm which was his wife's father's. No children.

11-7-1-11-4

Willard Libby, born in Gray, Me., 17 May 1806; married, 8 Aug. 1829, Huldah K. Stiles, daughter of Stephen and Rachel (Howe) Stiles of Bridgton. Soon after his marriage he settled in Danville, since annexed to Auburn, and has since resided there.

Children, born in Gray:

1 Stephen Addison, b. 18 Oct. 1830; m. 28 Dec. 1858, Elizabeth E., dau. of Jacob and Emily (Nash) Stiles of Gray. He was a locomotive engineer many years. In 1867 he bought the farm in Gray, on which he has since resided. Children:
  1 Mabel Edith, b. 22 Jan. 1868.
  2 Herbert Chester, b. 24 Dec. 1869.

2 Simon, b. 11 Aug. 1832; m. 7 April 1859, Frances A., dau. of L. and Polly (Woodson) Caswell of Harrison. He was an engineer on the Grand Trunk Railway, but afterward settled on a farm in Aroostook County, near Presque Isle. He died 23 Oct. 1861. His widow married George Oakes, and lives in New Haven, Conn. Children:
  1 Willard A., b. 13 Dec. 1859; unm. He is a machinist in New Haven.
  2 Charles L., b. 8 Nov. 1861; unm. He lives in Auburn.

Born in Danville:

3 Willard W., b. 21 Oct. 1834; d. 17 Dec. 1837.
4 Betsey J., b. 21 Nov. 1836; d. 24 June 1843.

11-7-2-4-6

Edward Libby, born in Scarborough, 9 April 1798; married, 6 April 1823, Abigail Libby, 1-4-1-6-4-2. He lived on his father's homestead five years after his marriage, and then it passed into the hands of his uncle Theodore. He then moved on to a smaller place near by, and there lived until 1851. In that year he removed to Pownal and bought the Jones tavern, and six years later bought the farm on which he died, on which his widow still lives. His death occurred 27 Sept. 1868.

Only child:

1 George Matthias, b. 10 Sept. 1823; m. Elizabeth Libby, 10-1-2-4-3-2. He has always lived with his parents, and now carries on the homestead farm in Pownal. Children, all but the oldest born in Pownal:
  1 Alfaretta, b. 21 April 1850, in Standish; m. Nathaniel Wilber of Pownal. She was a graduate of the state normal school, and a very successful teacher.

2 Miltimore Watts, b. 29 Sept. 1851; m. 28 March 1878, Lida, dau. of Peter and Mary Frame of Winchester, Ill. In 1871 he went to Jacksonville, Ill., where he learned the mason's trade, and has lived most of the time since. In December 1880 he went into business as butcher. Child:
 1 Everett C., b. 15 March 1879.
3 Mary Eveline, b. 20 Sept. 1853; unm. She was a teacher, and then learned the dressmaker's trade.
4 James Willard, b. 15 Dec. 1856; m. 1st, 12 Feb. 1876, Elizabeth M., dau. of Abraham and Maria (Elsie) Foster of Portland; (divorced); 2d, 27 March 1881, Nellie M., dau. of Thomas and Margaret (Droney) Kenney of Cumberland. He is in the wholesale produce business in Portland. No children.
5 Charles Edgar Bean, b. 8 Sept. 1861; is a student in Bowdoin College.
6 Fannie Orabell, b. 24 March 1864.
7 George Hobart, b. 14 Nov. 1866.

11-7-2-4-8

Storer Libby, born in Scarborough, 3 Nov. 1802; married, 19 Aug. 1821, Dorothy Lancaster Tompson. [See page 75.]

After his mother's marriage to Parson Lancaster, he worked out farming in different places. He worked one year with his brother-in-law Berry, in Pownal, and one year with his brother-in-law Rice, then of Gorham. He worked two years for his father-in-law, and, in 1821, married his granddaughter. Two years after his marriage he removed to Pownal, and bought and cultivated a small place, occupying his spare time by butchering and marketing. In 1829 he returned to Scarborough, to again take charge of Parson Lancaster's farm, and on his death, two years later, bought out the other heirs. Thus the Lancaster place, on which his wife's grandfather had lived during a pastorate of more than fifty years, came into his hands, and on it he lived until his death, 7 March 1873. His widow still occupies his homestead.

He was bred a Democrat, and voted with that party until the rise of the Republican party, when he stopped voting entirely. His sentiments were those of the Republicans. Brought up in the days of New England rum, he was always a practicer of total abstinence. Though not a church-member, his household was filled with religious influences; the daily Bible reading was as regular as breakfast. His whole character may be seen in the epithet by which he was known at a period when nicknames were given to many in his locality — most of them derived from unfavorable peculiarities. His was "Old Silver Piece."

Children:

1 son, died at the age of ten days, in Scarborough.
2 Thomas Lancaster, b. 20 May 1824, in Pownal; m. Mary E. Batchelder.
3 Elizabeth Ann Tompson, b. 16 June 1826; m. 15 Sept. 1856, George W. Odell of Greenland, N. H., a son of Dr. Odell of the same place. Children:
 1 George Edward (Odell), b. 6 Sept. 1857; unm.
 2 William Allen (Odell), b. 20 April 1859.
 3 Joseph Warren (Odell), b. 21 Sept. 1862; d. 14 Nov. 1864.

Samuel T Libby

FROM A DAGUERREOTYPE

4 Samuel Tompson (Odell), b. 24 May 1864.
5 Dorothy Lancaster (Odell), b. 8 May 1866; d. 10 June 1877.

4 Samuel Tompson, b. 12 Oct. 1828; m. 1 June 1856, Hannah Elizabeth, dau. of Daniel and Jane (Hildebrant) Pruden of Mendham, N. J. He early became a member of the Congregational Church. In 1852, under the auspices of the American Board of Missions, he went to Pine Ridge, Indian Territory, as steward of a girl's boarding school there. Two and one-half years later he returned home, but immediately went back and took charge of the girl's school at the Wheelock missionary station. There he married one of the teachers and passed the rest of his life. Beside being steward, and having the chief care of the temporal affairs of the station, he was also superintendent of the Sabbath-school, leader of the prayer-meetings, and gradually became accustomed to conducting the church services. He at length became one of the elders of the church, (Presbyterian). At the time of the war he was unable to return north, and was obliged to serve as commissary in the Choctaw army. He died from the effects of a sunstroke received while in the army, 18 Oct. 1866. Two years later his widow and children returned east, and since 1872 the former has been mistress of a boarding-house in Orange, N. J. Children:

1 Fannie Edwards, b. 8 March 1857; unm.
2 Mary Elizabeth, b. 24 Sept. 1858; d. 3 July 1860.
3 Daniel Pruden, b. 18 April 1860.
4 Samuel Byington, b. 20 Feb. 1863.
5 Cornelia, b. 22 Aug. 1866.

5 Matthias*, b. 29 April 1831, in Scarborough; m. 24 Dec. 1859, Eliza Gookin Thornton, born in Biddeford, 9 June 1835, daughter of James Brown and Eliza (Gookin) Thornton of Scarborough. Upon reaching his majority, he went to Portland and bound himself for one year to Simeon Higgins, to learn the carpenter's trade. In 1856, after working as journeyman for Mr. Higgins three and one-half years, he went into business himself, in company with Samuel F. Tibbetts. In this connection, and also in his business alone, after the dissolution of the partnership in 1858, he was very successful; but the depression of the value of real estate in which he had invested gave rise to embarrassments which contracted his business, and from which he has not yet (1881) recovered. His wife died 24 July 1877. Children, born in Portland:

1 Charles Thornton, b. 28 Sept. 1861. In his ninth year, having received his primary instruction from his mother, he entered the public school. He was advanced by the usual routine, taking the classical course through the High School, until his graduation, July 1879, when he received one of the "Brown" silver medals for scholarship. In September following he passed his examination for admission to Harvard College. How the preparation of this volume has delayed his entrance three years may be seen in the preface. 3 July 1881 he was admitted into the Second Congregational Church of Portland—Rev. Charles A. Dickinson, pastor.
2 Cornelia Maynard, b. 8 Sept. 1866; known almost exclusively by the name Picco; a contraction of pickaninny, a term applied to her by her nurse before she was named.

6 Mary Lancaster, b. 11 Aug. 1833; m. Sumner Libby, 5-2-3-8-5.

7 Edward Augustus, b. 2 Jan. 1836; unm. He has been a country trader at Oak Hill, (Scarborough), East Deering, and other places, and was in the trucking business in Portland a number of years. He is a member of the Congregational Church in Scarborough, and was for many years superintendent of its Sabbath-school. He is now a farmer in Greenland, N. H.

8 Sarah Tompson, b. 15 Sept. 1838; unm.; lives with her mother.

*See portrait opposite page 545.

9 Esther Lancaster, b. 5 March 1841; m. 28 Jan. 1869, Rev. Leonard W. Harris.
10 Cornelia Maynard, b. 26 July 1843; d. 10 June 1863.
11 William Storer, b. 5 Feb. 1847; d. 25 May 1863.
12 John Tompson, b. 3 Aug. 1849; d. 9 Jan. 1868.

11-7-2-6-1

SHERBORN LIBBY, born 3 Sept. 1791, in Scarborough; married, 4 Dec. 1817, MARY WATSON, daughter of Mary (Hasty) Watson. [See page 55.] He took up wild land in Richmond, and cleared the farm on which he ever afterward lived. He died 13 Jan. 1868. His widow still survives.

Children, born in Richmond:

1 John Watson, b. 16 April 1819; m. 20 April 1848, Elizabeth M. Libby, 11-7-2-6-2-1. He occupies the homestead farm. He has been selectman of Richmond eight years. Children:
  1 Mary Eva, b. 3 May 1853; m. Oct. 1876, J. B. Hathorn.
  2 Charles, b. 10 May 1856; d. Oct. 1857.
  3 Charles S., b. 26 Jan. 1858.
2 Hannah, b. 12 Dec. 1821; m. 20 Oct. 1853, Benjamin Flanders.
3 Mary Jane, b. 12 March 1826; m. 15 Sept. 1856, John R. Weston.

11-7-2-6-2

JOSHUA LIBBY, born in Scarborough, 10 July 1793; married, 1816, MARY SMALL. [See Small, page 32.] He lived on his father's homestead—a well-to-do farmer. He died 5 March 1848. His widow died 15 Nov. 1849.

Children, all born in Scarborough:

1 Elizabeth M., b. 25 Oct. 1816; m. John Watson Libby, 11-7-2-6-1-1.
2 Johnson, b. 20 Feb. 1819; d. 24 Oct. 1823.
3 James Small, b. 19 July 1820; m. 24 Nov. 1846, Jane R., dau. of Joseph and Elizabeth (Jordon) Wescott of Cape Elizabeth. He early became a contractor for work involving the employment of laborers. He gradually adopted wharf-building as a specialty, and has for many years done a heavy business in that line. He lived on a part of the homestead until 1870, when he removed his residence to Portland. 1858-9, he represented Scarborough and North Yarmouth in the state legislature. Children:
  1 Ella Wescott, b. 18 Oct. 1847; unm.
  2 Mary Abbie, b. 22 May 1850; unm.
  3 Josephine Wescott, b. 18 May 1854; unm.
4 Benjamin, b. 18 Nov. 1821; m. 17 April 1850, Mary Ann, dau. of John Mills and Louise (Worcester) Parker of Scarborough. He learned the carpenter's trade of Edward and Joseph Chenery of Westbrook, and soon after went into business in Portland, where he has since continued. Children:
  1 Charles Edwin, b. 30 Jan. 1851; unm. He is in company with his brother-in-law in the fruit business,—Chaffin & Libby.
  2 Mary Louise, b. 14 Sept. 1852; m. 9 May 1877, Charles R. Chaffin.
5 Johnson, b. 4 July 1824; m. 1st, Catherine M., dau. of Hon. Randall and Charlotte (Wescott) Skillings of Cape Elizabeth; (d. 18 Dec. 1853); 2d, 24 Jan. 1855, Lydia M., dau. of Charles and Hannah (Meserve) Moulton. (Hannah (Meserve) Moulton is a daughter of Hannah (Libby) Meserve, 11-7-2-8.) He lives on part of his father's homestead. He has been town treasurer three years, and chairman of selectmen twelve years. Children, by first wife:
  1 Mary Catherine, b. 28 Nov. 1853; married Henry Rufus Libby, 10-5-1-10-6-8.

James S. Libby

By second wife:

2 Edna Estelle, b. 1 May 1856; unm.
3 Eugene Homer, b. 14 Oct. 1858.
4 Moulton C., b. 15 July 1860.
5 Alice, b. 16 April; d. 23 April, 1863.

6 Sarah Maria, b. 6 Dec. 1825; m. 13 Feb. 1851, Joshua Hanscom.
7 Emily Frances, b. 15 Sept. 1827; d. 10 May 1830.
8 Washington, b. 10 March 1829; m. 22 Feb. 1854, Mary A., dau. of James and Abbie B. (Merryman) Dunning of Harpswell. He learned the carpenter's trade with his uncle Matthias, and almost at once went into business in Portland. Children, all born in Portland:

1 Abbie Helen, b. 4 Feb. 1855; d. 26 Jan. 1872.
2 Maria Frances, b. 17 March 1857; d. 28 Oct. 1869.
3 Eliza May, b. 17 Nov. 1860; d. 25 Oct. 1878.
4 Joshua Clement, b. 14 Aug. 1862.
5 Hattie Bishop, b. 18 Aug. 1865.
6 George Washington, b. 2 April 1867; d. 6 Jan. 1871.
7 George Washington, b. 20 Oct. 1870.

9 Joshua, b. 6 Feb. 1832; m. 2 Nov. 1859, Helen Marr, dau. of Capt. David and Lavinia (Reed) Stearns of Richmond, Me. He went to Richmond a young man, and became a clerk in a general store there. He soon after went into his business himself, and continued successfully until his health failed him, when he sold out and removed to Portland, where he died 8 April 1872, and his widow still lives. Children:

1 Helen May, b. 3 Sept. 1861.
2 Lavinia, b. 24 Nov. 1864; d. 7 Oct. 1868.

10 Mary Frances, b. 15 July 1833; m. Hiram Dunning.
11 Reuben Crosby, b. 8 Jan. 1836; married, 1859, Hannah Maria, dau. of Radcliffe and Nancy (Moorehouse) Royston of Mineral Point, Wis. He learned the carpenter's trade with his brother Washington, and immediately went west, where his sister Sarah was living. He has worked as journeyman carpenter, and as miner, but is now a salesman in an agricultural warehouse at Mineral Point, Wis. Children:

1 Thomas Walter, b. 23 July 1860.
2 Ellacitta, b. 6 Aug. 1869.
3 Annie May, b. 11 Dec. 1872.
4 Radcliffe Royston, b. 13 July 1877.
5 Violet Maud, b. 4 Sept. 1880.

11-7-2-6-3

Simon Libby, born in Scarborough, 2 Feb. 1795; married, 24 Nov. 1814, Phebe Webb, daughter of John and Sarah (Leighton) Webb of Westbrook.

He was by trade a tanner and currier, and soon after his marriage settled in Portland. In 1819 he removed to Richmond, onto a farm of eighty-one acres, and there abode until his death. In connection with his farm, he carried on brick-making, and sometimes worked at his trade. He died 5 Aug. 1843. His widow died 29 April 1881.

Children, born in Westbrook:

1 Ruth, b. 12 March 1815; d. Aug. 1816, in Portland.

Born in Portland:

2 John Webb, b. 14 Nov. 1816; m. 25 Jan. 1840, Betsey Bates, dau. of Parker and Ruth (Bates) Dingley of Bowdoinham. He took the

homestead farm. He also, until 1855, carried on brick-making, but since that date has followed farming only. He is a member of the Freewill Baptist Church, and was for six years superintendent of the Sabbath-school. His wife died 18 April 1881. Children:

1 Henry Marshall, b. 21 April 1850; m. 16 Dec. 1875, Mary Jane, dau. of Hetherton and Hannah A. (Walker) Earle of Litchfield. He has been a boarding-house keeper in Litchfield, and now in Richmond. No children.

2 Fred Joshua, b. 31 Jan. 1853; m. 11 June 1881, Hannah Elizabeth, dau. of Joseph and Esther Ann (Curtis) Bailey of Bowdoinham.

3 Maria Frances, b. 17 Nov. 1855; unm.

4 John Fuller, b. 3 Feb. 1863; is a student at Bowdoin College.

3 Joshua Brackett, b. 23 Aug. 1818; m. 1st, 4 July 1854, Sarah E., dau. of Capt. David and Lavinia (Reed) Stearns; (died 4 Oct. 1855); 2d, 14 Oct. 1860, Eliza Newell, dau. of William and Zeluma (Bates) White of Bowdoinham. He began to follow the sea at the age of 25, and soon rose to be captain. He crossed the Atlantic 42 times, and was never shipwrecked. In 1870 he retired and settled at Richmond. Children, born in Bowdoinham:

1 Sarah Eliza, b. 13 Aug. 1865.

2 Frank Joshua, b. 2 June 1870.

Born in Richmond:

4 Ruth Ann, b. 6 March 1820; m. 1 April 1838, Aaron Buker.

5 Sarah Webb, b. 23 Feb. 1822; unm.

6 Eliza Baker, b. 6 July 1823; d. 31 July 1838.

7 Simon Henry, b. 2 Feb. 1825; m. 12 Dec. 1860, Clara E., dau. of Capt. Nathaniel and Sarah (Thompson) Merrill of Falmouth. He learned the carpenter's trade with his uncle Matthias in Portland, and has since carried on business there and in Deering. Child:

1 Harry Merrill, b. 5 Nov. 1867, in Portland.

8 Phebe Emma, b. 27 Aug. 1826; m. 23 Oct. 1853, William Kilby.

9 Eunice Martha, } twins, born { m. 19 Sept. 1849, William Dingley.

10 Bethany Frances, } 10 June 1830; { m. 29 June 1863, Edward Norton.

11 William Addison, b. 19 July 1833; unm. He is a carpenter in Portland.

12 Deborah Ellen, b. 12 Jan. 1836; d. 2 March 1855; unm.

11-7-2-6-4

Johnson Libby, born in Scarborough, 4 Feb. 1797; married, 30 Sept. 1821, Eveline Tyler, daughter of Lucy (Trickey) Tyler, 10-8-4-6. When he was married he bought land, and built the house now occupied by his widow. Lameness unfitted him for manual labor, and he kept a country store. He died 5 Feb. 1845.

Children, all born in Scarborough:

1 Eliza Ann, b. 15 Feb. 1822; m. Thomas Skillings.

2 Lucy, b. 30 May 1823; m. 9 Dec. 1841, John S. Larrabee, a grandson of Philip Larrabee. [See page 41.] Children:

1 Philip Johnson (Larrabee), b. 12 April 1844; m. 1 Jan. 1872, Sarah L., dau. of Joseph D. and Mercy (McKenney) Ballard of Buxton. He graduated from Tufts College in 1867; is a lawyer in Portland. Child:

1 Philip Francis (Larrabee), b. 29 Oct. 1872.

2 Lucy Maria (Larrabee), b. 26 Dec. 1846; m. William Dyer Libby, 10-5-3-5-4-8.

3 Zebulon Tyler, b. 23 Jan. 1825; m. 18 April 1850, Charlotte (Libby) Moody, 10-5-3-5-1-4, widow of John L. Moody, 5-7-10-6-8. He

settled on his father's homestead, bought adjoining land, and became a farmer. He died 19 Sept. 1864, and his family still occupies the homestead. Children:

1 Annie Maria, b. 14 Nov. 1851; m. Horace A. Wright.

2 Charles Zebulon, b. 5 May 1855; m. 28 June 1878, Abbie J., dau. of Caleb Moulton. Child:

1 Laura Ethel, b. 27 Feb. 1879.

3 Phebe Ellen, b. 1 March 1850; d. 22 July 1868.

4 George Osgood, b. 1 Oct. 1857; unm.

4 Horace B., b. 19 Oct 1827; m. 1st, Mary Townsend, adopted daughter of Capt. Samuel Stanford of Portland; (died after ten years); 2d, Louisa R. Lamphere of Boston; (divorced after about one year); 3d, Mary Elizabeth —— of Randolph, Mass.; (died after about six years); 4th, about 1876, Mrs. Mary Eliza (Speare) Stetson of Randolph. He learned the trade of carpenter with his uncle Matthias in Portland, and engaged in business there. He was afterward in business in Boston, and soon after his third marriage removed to his present residence in Randolph. Only child, by third wife:

1 Frank, b. Sept. 1867.

5 Addison, b. 8 Aug. 1830; m. 1st, 11 Nov. 1855, Elizabeth Kilborn of Cape Elizabeth; (died July 1856); 2d, 26 Jan. 1862, Marcia, dau. of David and Margaret (Davis) Lawrence of Yarmouth. He is a carpenter in Portland. Children, by first wife:

1 daughter, died Aug. 1856, at the age of six weeks.

By second wife:

2 Lizzie Gertrude, b. 14 March 1865; d. 3 July 1865.

3 Herbert Lawrence, b. 29 Sept. 1866; d. 4 Oct. 1867.

4 Hattie Frances, b. 22 March 1868.

5 Grace Edwin, b. 26 Sept. 1870.

6 Hattie Lawrence, b. 28 Nov. 1871.

6 John Tyler, b. 29 April 1832; m. 17 Feb. 1856, Ellen C., dau. of Rushworth and Mary (Harmon) Rich of Portland. He is a contractor and builder in Portland. Children:

1 Henry Sylvester, b. 12 Nov. 1856; unm.

2 Fred Willistine, b. 12 Oct. 1859; d. 7 Oct. 1861.

3 Herbert Johnson, b. 3 Jan., d. 30 July, 1869.

4 Mary Ellis, b. 9 Dec. 1865.

7 Granville, b. 21 May 1834; m. 24 April 1855, Amanda M., dau. of Samuel and Sarah (Howard) Richards of Portland. He served an apprenticeship with his brother Horace, at the carpenter's trade. For twenty years he has been in the employ of the Kerosene Oil Company in Cape Elizabeth. His wife died 5 July 1876. He married second, 28 Aug. 1881, M. Annette, dau. of Stephen and Almira (Day) Cartland of Deering. Children:

1 Frank Russell, b. 5 Jan. 1856; d. 18 Feb. 1859.

2 Amanda, b. 17 July 1860; d. 12 Aug. 1861.

3 Granville Linwood, b. 20 Sept. 1862.

4 Lawrence Richards, b. 30 Dec. 1865.

5 Maurice, b. 10 Nov. 1873; died on the same day.

8 Charles S., b. 17 July 1836; m. 19 Nov. 1862, Georgiana, dau. of Nathaniel and Eunice (Bond) Hasty of Portland. He learned the painter's trade in Portland. In 1864 he settled on a small farm in Cape Elizabeth, but still carries on his business in Portland. Children:

1 Frank Wilber, b. 15 March 1863.

2 Charles Bacon, b. 29 April 1866.

3 Maud Marion, b. 31 March 1874.

9 Phebe H., b. 23 Aug. 1838; d. 25 March 1853.

11-7-2-6-6

ADDISON LIBBY, born in Scarborough, 20 April 1801; married EMMA MAXCY of Deer Island. He was by trade a blacksmith, and lived some years in Portland. Then he settled in Camden, where he lived until his death, 4 July 1870. His widow still lives.

Their children were:

1 John Q. A., b. 20 May 1825, in Warren; m. Sarah A., dau. of Oliver Edwards; lives in Camden. He served three years in the war.
2 Harriet A., b. 21 March 1827, in Portland.
3 Josiah A., b. 20 Dec. 1829; died 25 Nov. 1861, in Camden.
4 Ruth G., b. 11 March 1831; died 20 Aug. 1833.
5 Addison, b. 20 Dec. 1833; d. 18 July 1838, in Portland.
6 Addison, b. 11 March 1835; married in Islesborough, Eliza Pendleton; died in Islesborough, 15 Nov. 1863.
7 Frank G., b. 17 July 1837; m. 22 Oct. 1861, Laura A., dau. of Ephraim and Jane (Thayer) Coombs of Islesborough, where he has since lived. He is a sailor. Children:
   1 Herbert P., b. 22 Sept. 1864; died 15 Nov. 1879.
   2 Maud M., b. 29 Aug. 1868.
   3 Willie F., b. 19 April 1871.
8 Melvin, b. 17 April 1839; lives in Camden.
9 Susan H., b. 15 Sept. 1842; died 15 Sept 1872.
10 Sarah A., b. 28 March 1844.
11 Findly B., b. 3 April 1845; m. Harriet, dau. of Oliver Edwards; lives in Camden. He served three years in the war.

11-7-2-6-10

MATTHIAS LIBBY, born in Scarborough, 20 Feb. 1808; married, 9 June 1833, LYDIA JONES, daughter of John and Lydia (Wescott) Jones of Scarborough. He was by trade a carpenter. He removed to Portland soon after his marriage, and was for many years a successful contractor and builder. His death took place 4 Aug. 1859; his widow survives.

Children, born in Scarborough:

1 Susan Jones, b. 3 Feb. 1834; d. 10 Dec. 1867, at Augusta; unm.

Born in Portland:

2 Orlando, b. 24 Jan. 1836; m. 20 Feb. 1861, Frances Augusta, dau. of Isaac and Ann (Estes) Randall of Deering. He was a carpenter. He was killed by a fall from a church in Portland, 10 Dec. 1866. Child:
   1 Orlando, b. 20 May 1867.
3 Frederics Matthias, b. 27 Sept. 1843; m. 2 Dec. 1874, Mrs. Mary J. Perkins, dau. of James and Mary Ann (Witham) Neal of Bangor. He is in the First National Bank of Portland as general bookkeeper. No children.

11-7-2-6-12

GEORGE LIBBY, born in Scarborough, 14 Oct. 1812; married, 14 March 1832, DAMARIS SMALL, daughter of David and Elizabeth (Jordan) Small of Scarborough. [See page 32.] After his marriage he lived at home three years, and then on the Jewett place three years. In 1839 he bought the farm in Falmouth on which he has since abode. His wife died 16 Jan. 1879.

Children:

1 David Franklin, b. 29 May 1833; m. 20 Nov. 1856, Abbie E., dau. of Greenleaf and Annie (Batson) Wiggin of Portland. He learned the carpenter's trade, but became a hackman in Portland. Children, born in Portland:
  1 Carrie Emma, b. 23 Dec. 1859; unm.
  2 George Franklin, b. 21 July 1863; d. 13 March 1872.
  3 Willie Ring, b. 23 Aug. 1866.
2 Elizabeth Small, b. 23 Feb. 1835; m. 3 Jan. 1864, Sewall B. Bailey.
3 Emily Frances, b. 21 Dec. 1836; m. Wm. H. Allen.
4 Darius Small, b. 16 Jan. 1840, in Falmouth; d. 6 May 1864; unm. He enlisted in Aug. 1862, in Co. H, 17th regiment of Maine volunteers. He was among the missing on the second day of the Seven Days battle.
5 James Harrison, b. 11 April 1841; m. Ella Holbrook of Charlestown, Mass., where he has since lived. He is of the firm of Fessenden & Libby, masons, Boston. His wife died in the fall of 1878. Only child:
  1 George Harrison, b. 5 April 1874.
6 George Henry, b. 4 Dec. 1843; d. 16 March 1862; unm. He was a private in Co. C, 12th Maine, and died on Ship Island.
7 Mary, b. 13 Nov. 1845; m. 12 July 1868, Granville C. Horr.
8 Catherine, b. 26 March 1847; m. Gilford R. Morrill.
9 Emma Etta, b. 6 Oct. 1848; d. 9 Dec. 1854.
10 Reuben Small, b. 11 Dec. 1850; d. 4. Dec. 1852.
11 Reuben Small, b. 12 Nov. 1852; unm. He is a journeyman mason.
12 Wilborn, b. 4 Aug. 1854; } live at home—farmers; unmarried.
13 Albert, b. 20 Nov. 1856; }

11-7-7-5-2

Daniel Libby, born in Pownal, Me., 7 Dec. 1802; married, 4 Dec. 1828, Sarah Osgood, daughter of Joseph and Hannah (Gerrish) Osgood of Durham. He was by trade a stone-cutter and mason. He worked on the State House at Augusta, and afterward owned a stone quarry in Sullivan. Later he removed to East Cambridge, Mass., where he was in the same business until his death, 5 Aug. 1840. His widow died in Boston, 20 Oct. 1874.

Their children were:

1 Elizabeth, b. 22 Dec. 1829, in Augusta; m. 1856, S. R. Wetherbee.
2 Osgood Franklin, b. 9 Sept. 1833; died 25 May 1837.
3 Frederick, b. 4 Oct. 1835; died 23 Nov. 1835.
4 Franklin O., b. 15 April 1839; unm. He went to California to engage in gold mining. Upon the breaking out of the war he was one of the California hundred that joined the 2d Massachusetts cavalry. He lived in Boston after the war, and in 1869 removed to Idaho, where he is supposed to have been killed by the Indians, as he has not been heard from since 1870.
5 Elbridge Osgood, b. 5 Sept. 1842; d. 18 July 1843.
6 Adelaide E., b. 28 Oct. 1844, in Durham; m. 1st, —— Webb; 2d, John M. Kilgore; lives in Lowell, Mass.
7 Joseph Osgood, b. 7 June 1846, in East Cambridge; d. 17 Aug. 1846.
8 Daniel LeRoy, [Rev.], b. 10 Dec. 1849; m. 4 July 1871, Minnie R., dau. of Capt. Charles and Matilda (Merryman) Ward of Freeport, Me. He was brought up by his uncle Horace in Durham. He

graduated at Kent's Hill, and later took a course at the St. Lawrence University and Theological School. He was six years pastor of a church in Hammond, St. Lawrence Co., N. Y., four years of a church in Provincetown, Mass., and is now pastor of the First Universalist Church in Medford, Mass. Children:

1 Marion Rosamond, b. 31 Dec. 1872.
2 Horace Victor, b. 20 Feb. 1875.

11-7-7-5-6

WALTER LIBBY, born in Pownal, Me., 26 Dec. 1812; married, 8 Oct. 1835, SARAH DAVIS THOITS, daughter of Simeon and Rebecca (Grant) Thoits of Pownal.

He was a fisherman until he reached his majority, and has since been engaged in farming and stone-work. He lived ten years on a farm in Pownal, five years on a farm in Freeport, and has been since 1875 a farmer in Yarmouth.

Children:

1 Greenleaf Rogers, b. 14 July 1836, in Augusta; m. 2 June 1866, Sarah, dau. of Benjamin P. and Lucy (Tyler) Roberts of Durham. He served four and a half years in Co. K, 12th Maine Vol., and has since been in the livery business in Yarmouth. Children:
 1 George Frank, b. 15 March 1867, in Freeport.
 2 Addie May, b. 10 Nov. 1870, in Yarmouth.
 3 Ernest Clifton, b. 2 May 1879.
2 Frances Ellen, b. 14 June 1838; m. Samuel True of Yarmouth.
3 Sarah Augusta, b. 18 Dec. 1840, in Durham; m. William C. Sweetsir.
4 Eliza Merrill, b. 7 Oct. 1846; m. in Boston, Ernest ——, a southerner. She left her father's home, and has not been heard from since 1873.

11-7-8-2-2

JOSEPH LIBBY, born about 1793; married, 22 May 1823, MEHITABLE MOSES, daughter of Josiah and Elizabeth (Harmon) Moses of Standish.

He was reared in Gorham, and when a young man removed to Raymond, where he cleared a farm. About 1833 he sold this and moved onto the homestead of his wife's father, on Standish Neck, and there abode until his death, 7 Feb. 1861. His wife died 9 May 1861.

Children:

1 Marshall, b. 19 April 1824; m. 18 Nov. 1849, Eliza A., dau. of David and Hannah (Milliken) Sawyer. His occupations have been various. He is now employed in the pulp factory at Great Falls, Gorham. Only child:
 1 Frederick Augustus, b. 3 Feb. 1851; m. 11 June 1871, Sarah A., dau. of F. F. and Eliza J. (Bailey) Knight of Naples. Children:
  1 Herbert Jackson, b. 10 Jan. 1875; d. 19 Jan. 1875.
  2 Bertie Augustus, b. 15 Aug. 1876.
  3 Arthur Jackson, b. 29 April 1879.
2 Sarah Ann, b. Jan. 1826; m. William Smith.
3 William, b. 20 April 1828; m. 22 Dec. 1850, Lydia Ann, dau. of Wm. and Anna (Young) Clay. He has always lived on his father's homestead, a farmer. Children:

1 Addie Alberta, b. 28 Feb. 1853.
2 George Perley, b. 27 Sept. 1857; d. 25 March 1878.
3 William Clarence, b. 11 Nov 1859; d. 9 May 1860.
4 Ella Medora, b. 6 July 1866.

4 Jane, m. 14 Dec. 1854, Benj. Wardsworth Merrill.
5 Mary Adeline, m. Wm. S. Hanscom of Standish.
6 Martha Ellen, died 4 Feb. 1840, aged 6 weeks.

11-7-8-2-3

Cary Libby, born in Gorham, Me., about 1795; married, first, Betsey Haskell, daughter of Job and Judith Haskell of New Gloucester; (died 30 Nov. 1836, in Gorham); second, 27 Aug. 1842, Mrs. Elizabeth Chase. He was for the most part a farmer. After his first wife's death he lived in Saco, where he died about 1854.

His children, all by his first wife, were:

1 Mary Jane, b. 17 Nov. 1822, in New Gloucester; m. 24 March 1842, Lothrop L. Crockett of Naples.
2 Louisa, b. 15 Jan. 1825, in Windham; m. Alvah Weed of Baldwin.
3 Adeline, b. in Gorham; m. 16 June 1853, Josiah S. Chase.
4 Addison C., born 1832, in Windham; m. Margaret ——. He has lived many years in Somerville, Mass., and has been engaged in peddling paper, etc. Children: (?)
  1 George, b. 1864.
  2 Fred, b. 1867.
  3 William, b. 1869.
  4 Emeline, b. 1872.
  5 Ella. b. 1876.
5 Harriet, born at the Forks of the Kennebec River; m. 22 June 1861, John A. Haskell; died 1876.

11-7-8-2-6

Andrew Libby, born in Gorham, Me., 2 April 1800; married, 6 Jan. 1830, Sophronia Small, daughter of Dorothy (Libby) Small, 5-7-12-9. He was engaged at different times as farmer, schoolteacher, and trader, and died early, 7 May 1848. His widow removed with her family to Saccarappa, Westbrook, and died in that town, 12 Oct. 1868.

Their children, all born in Gorham, were:

1 Melissa, b. 21 May 1832; m. 8 Dec. 1850. Orin Babb.
2 Sophronia, b. 6 June 1834; died 2 Nov. 1836.
3 Sophronia L., b. 2 June 1836; m. 21 Nov. 1855, George E. Cole.
4 Alonzo, b. 31 July 1838; died 12 April 1840.
5 Alonzo, b. 6 Feb. 1841; m. 19 June 1864. Alice Anna, dau. of Levi F. and Mary Ann (Grant) Boothby of Buxton. He grew up with his uncle. David S. Libby, 10-5-5-2-12, and attended the Limington Academy. Later he learned the shoemaker's trade at Gorham, and afterward worked in wire and paper mills. He was a member of Co. I, 1st Me. Vol., three months men, and served his enlistment. In 1865 he went to Davenport, Iowa, and was engaged six months in the grocery business. Upon his return to Saccarappa he bought out his brother-in-law, Orin Babb, in the milk business. This business he has greatly increased, and is also an extensive farmer. He has won many prizes on his thorough-bred cattle, and is an officer in several agricultural and breeders' associations. In 1874, 1876, and 1877, he was first selectmen of Westbrook. Children:

1 Fred Bartlett, b. 18 July 1865, in Buxton; d. 18 June 1867.
2 Alice Josephine, b. 7 May 1868, in Saccarappa, Westbrook.
3 George Johnson, b. 23 May 1872.

6 Henrietta, b. 3 April 1843; m. 5 Jan. 1864, Bryce M. Edwards.
7 Laura Frances, b. 9 April 1845; m. 31 Dec. 1874, Alonzo F. Cook.
8 Marianna, b. 24 Aug. 1849; m. 18 Dec. 1873, Frederick Walker.

11-7-8-3-8

JOSEPH LIBBY, born in Pownal, Me., 16 June 1809; married, 14 April 1839, JULIA A. LIBBY, 11-9-7-7-7. In April, 1834, he removed to Palmyra, where he took up a piece of land, and lived there until about 1846, when he moved to his present residence in St. Albans.

Children, born in Palmyra:

1 Edward, b. 15 May 1840; m. 18 June 1871, Narcissa Alvena, dau. of Daniel and Ruth (Boynton) Sampson. He is a farmer and lumberman in St. Albans. Child:
 1 Mabel E., b. 24 May 1876, in St. Albans.
2 John H., b. 23 April 1843; d. 4 Oct. 1856.
3 Joseph Frank, b. 20 Oct. 1845; m. 27 Aug. 1870, Ellen, dau. of Josiah and Hannah (Winslow) Magoon of Fairfield. He is a carriage maker and blacksmith in Fairfield. His wife died 26 Feb. 1877. Children:
 1 Lilly F., b. 9 June 1871; d. 3 Jan. 1874.
 2 Mary L., b. 3 Aug. 1872.
 3 Julia E., b. 2 Feb. 1875.

Children, born in St. Albans:

4 Flora A., b. 19 April 1848; m. 8 Feb. 1868, Richard C. Parkman. Children:
 1 Nora J. (Parkman), b. 3 Jan. 1869.
 2 Ernest L. (Parkman), b. 11 Oct. 1875.
 3 Horace J. (Parkman), b. 2 April 1878.
 4 ——— (Parkman), b. 17 Nov. 1880.
5 Betsey E., b. 29 Nov. 1850; m. 17 Nov. 1873, Albion B. Parkman of St. Albans. Children:
 1 George E. (Parkman), b. 21 March 1877.
 2 Frank L. (Parkman), b. 28 June 1879.
6 Albion K., b. 17 July 1853; m. 4 Sept. 1879, Estella M., dau. of Bela and Louisa (Turner) Lancaster. He is a blacksmith at Caribou. No children.
7 Preston W., b 14 March 1856; m. 9 Jan. 1877, Violetta E. Knight. He lives with his father. Children:
 1 Clarence E., b. 9 Nov. 1877.
 2 Edna, b. 20 April 1880.
8 Alice S., b. 8 March 1858; unm.
9 John H., b. 8 Oct. 1861.
10 George, b. 7 Jan. 1864; d. 29 May 1869.

11-9-5-3-1

AMZI LIBBY, born in Limerick, Me., 10 March 1799; married, 30 Oct. 1825, in Portland, MARY CHARD, daughter of David and Anna (Warner) Chard of Annisquam, Mass.

For a number of years, including the period of his marriage, he was a grocer in Portland. He afterward returned to Limerick, and removed thence in 1834 to Burlington, Me. There he cleared himself a farm and lived until his death. Roads were built through his land, making him the possessor of all the land round the cross-roads, known as Libby's Corners. During his residence in Burlington he was occupied as hotel keeper, postmaster, surveyor, and justice of the peace; he was also at one time a representative to the state legislature, and was county commissioner several years. His death took place 14 Jan. 1860. A few years before he had become a member of the Congregational Church. His widow now lives in the West.

Children:

1 Harriet C., b. 23 March 1826, in Portland; m. 23 March 1847, Henry H. Page.
2 William, b. 28 Feb. 1828, in Limerick; died 23 Aug. 1830.
3 Elizabeth C., b. 9 April 1830; m. 5 Aug. 1857, Chas. O. Bradbury.
4 Annie C., b. 10 May 1833; m. 2 Dec. 1858, George H. Warren.
5 Charles R., b. 5 July 1836, in Burlington; m. 20 March 1860, Mary C., dau. of Isaac and Eliza (Page) Hanson of New London, Wis. He lived on the homestead farm and served as postmaster. After six years he sold and went west. He was engaged in lumbering several years, and since 1872 has been postmaster of New London. Children:
  1 George D., b. 13 Nov. 1873.
  2 Robbie, b. 11 April 1878.
6 Henry A., b. 28 Feb. 1839; m. Mary Frances, dau. of Andrew and Jane (Bradberry) Woodman of Burlington. He served three years in the 14th New York Vol. After the war he lived four years in Burlington, and then removed to New London, Wis., where he is now a dealer in real estate. His wife died 1 May 1870. Child:
  1 Edith, b. 17 May 1865.
7 Mary E., b. 2 April 1841.
8 John P., b. 8 Sept. 1844; m. 16 Nov. 1877, in St. Paul, Minn., Lizzie Gates. He removed to St. Paul in 1865, and has since been bookkeeper for a lumber company. No children.

11-9-5-3-4

Mark L. Libby, born in Limerick, Me., June 1807; married, June 1831, Cordelia Hastings, daughter of Samuel and Rebecca (Lambert) Hastings of Boston. He was a carpenter in Portland, Me., some years, and afterward removed to Foxcroft, where his wife died, 12 Feb. 1881. He has been for some years a dentist in San Francisco, Cal.

Children, all born in Portland:

1 Delia A., born 1 Jan. 1835; m. 24 Jan. 1856, John G. Mayo, jr., of Foxcroft. Children:
  1 Mary C. (Mayo), b. 30 Aug. 1857.
  2 Francis C. (Mayo), b. 14 Feb. 1859; d. 9 Dec. 1862.
  3 Walter J. (Mayo), b. 18 April 1873.
  4 Annie M. (Mayo), b. 2 April 1876.
2 Frances E., b. 25 April 1838; unm.
3 Susan E., b. 7 Feb. 1842; m. May, 1865, Wm. H. Martin. Child:
  1 George H. (Martin), b. 23 July 1866.
4 Mary C., b. 15 March 1846; d. 24 April 1846.

11-9-7-2-1

Nathaniel Libby, born in Shapleigh, Me., 19 April 1791; married, 14 Sept. 1815, Anna Ricker, daughter of Elizabeth

(Libby) Ricker, 11-9-5-4. He was brought up in Limerick, and lived there until the fall of 1826, when he bought a farm in Lyman, after living on which a number of years, he bought another in the north part of the same town, on which he abode until his death, 24 June 1857. His wife died 30 July 1849.

Children:

1 David, b. 6 Jan. 1816; m. 1845, in Boston, Sarah, dau. of William and Lois (Littlefield) Butler of Sanford, Me. He lived with his father until about 1839, when he went to Massachusetts. In 1852 he returned to Maine, and again took up farming. He died in Kennebunkport, 25 April 1857. Children:
  1 Helen, deceased.
  2 Ansel. When last heard from he and his mother were living in Dedham, Mass.

2 Aaron Ricker, b. 5 Feb. 1818; m. Rosina, dau. of David and Sally (Sawyer) Jaqueth of Jaffrey, N. H. In Lyman he was deacon of the Baptist Church and lieutenant in the militia. In 1852 he removed to Kennebunkport, and there bought a farm on which he lived until his death, 21 May 1876. His widow died 13 Sept. 1880. Children:
  1 Lewis Nathaniel, born 23 Jan. 1846; m. 8 May 1870, Aurianna, dau. of Rev. Wm. A. Sargent of Vineland, N. J.; d. 24 Nov. 1870, in Kennebunkport. He spent his life between Jaffrey, N. H., and Vineland, N. J., where lived his uncle, Samuel Jaqueth. He died of consumption. His widow returned to her father, and married, about 1876, —— George. Lewis' only child:
    1 Lewis Wayland, born after his father's death.
  2 Charles Chester, b. 10 April 1849; unm.
  3 Edmund Dornam, born 1 Nov. 1851; unm. He graduated from Dartmouth College in 1879, and is now studying civil engineering in Hanover, N. H.
  4 Willie Howard, b. 15 Jan. 1855; unm.
  5 Lizzie Anna, b. 7 Aug. 1857; m. Oct. 1876, Daniel Cleaves.

3 Lovina, b. 28 March 1820; m. 24 Jan. 1843, B. F. Baker of Brookline, Mass.

4 Stephen, born 1 Nov. 1825; d. 8 Oct. 1866, in Brookline; unm. He lived with his father until his majority. The rest of his life was passed in the neighborhood of Boston, Mass., at first at the carpenter's trade, and later as conductor on the horse railroad between Brookline and Boston.

5 Nathaniel Lewis, b. 1 Nov. 1825; d. 13 Oct. 1832.

6 Elizabeth Ann, b. 17 Nov. 1829; unm. She lives with her sister in Brookline, Mass.

11-9-7-2-6

Stephen Libby, born in Limerick, Me., 20 Nov. 1801; married first, Nancy Libby, 11-9-7-3-7; (died about 1831); second, 29 Feb. 1836, Mary Jane Bradeen, daughter of Jos. and Dorothy (Wilson) Bradeen of Waterborough.

He was a cabinet maker and a carpenter, but his chief occupation was milling. He, with his brother, R. Thurston Libby, owned the "Scratch Mill" in Limerick, and also erected a new mill near by. When his brother moved away, he bought him out. He lived there, on one or the other side of the Little Ossipee, until 1855, when he removed to Minnesota, onto a farm. In the Indian troubles in 1862, he returned to Limerick, bringing all his family but William Wallace and Charles, who went into the Indian army. He died with the former, who had returned and settled on a farm in Waterborough, 19 Dec. 1868. His widow still lives, in Waterborough.

Children, all by his second wife:

1 William Wallace, b. 30 Nov. 1836; m. 17 May 1868, Abbie F., dau. of Samuel and Sally (Goodwin) Lougee of Parsonsfield. He sold his farm in Waterborough in 1873, and was engaged in milling at Chadbourne's mills, in the same town, until 1879. He is now a farmer in Saco. Children:
 1 Louis Clifford, b. 10 March 1869, in Waterborough.
 2 Gertrude Clare, b. 24 May 1874, in Waterborough.
 3 Alma Inez, b. 12 Jan. 1877; d. 6 Nov. 1879.
2 Rosalthea, b. 31 March 1839; m. Silas C. Robbins of Phillips, Me.
3 Charles Loring [Rev.], b. 21 Jan. 1844; m. 27 July 1867, in Anoka, Minn., Emma A., daughter of Samuel and Cordelia (Hill) Richardson of Limington, Me. He was engaged in adventure, lumbering, and carpentering until 1872, when he became a preacher in the M. E. Church. The next year he joined the Minnesota conference of that church, and in 1879, on account of his health, changed to the Colorado conference, in which he still is. He resides in Denver, Col. Children:
 1 Nellie J., b. 3 Oct. 1868, in Grow, Minn.
 2 Fred L., b. 26 Aug. 1870, in Anoka, Minn.
 3 Harry P., b. 20 Sept. 1872, in Anoka.
 4 Rolla, b. 12 April 1876, in Atwater, Minn.
4 Mary Alice, b. 14 June 1850; m. James Everett Chandler of Biddeford.

11-9-7-2-8

Cyrus Libby, born in Limerick, Me., 24 Jan. 1804; married, 4 Nov. 1824, Drusilla Woodsom, daughter of William and Theodosia (Thompson) Woodsom of Waterborough. Upon his marriage he settled on part of his father's homestead. In 1852 he removed to Waterborough and bought the farm on which his son Cyrus now lives. Seventeen years later he moved back to Limerick onto the farm now occupied by his widow and son Isaac, and there died, 13 June 1872.

Children, all born in Limerick:

1 Silea, b. 11 April 1825; d. 31 Aug. 1828.
2 Melissa, b. 3 March 1827; d. 28 Sept. 1841.
3 Cyrus, b. 1 Jan. 1830; m. 13 Feb. 1859, Lavinia L., dau. of Obed and Sarah W. (Locke) Varney of Rochester, N. H. After his marriage he lived one year at home; then six years in another house on the same farm; and then, in 1866, bought the homestead and has since occupied it. Children:
 1 Charles Edward, b. 13 Feb 1861.
 2 Sarah Winslow, b. 4 April 1863.
 3 Lavinia Emma, b. 30 June 1866.
 4 Cyrus Osgood, b. 27 April 1871.
4 Sarah E., b. 5 Dec. 1831; m. 10 Oct. 1852, Charles A. Whipp.
5 Catherine M., b. 5 Oct. 1833; m. 31 May 1854, Isaac T. Storer.
6 William, died in early childhood.
7 Stephen, died in early childhood.
8 Susan, b. 29 Dec. 1838; m. 1st, Mark Thwing; 2d, George Gayman of Dedham, Mass.

9 Stephen, b. 19 Dec. 1839; m. 27 Aug. 1872, Abby O., dau. of George and Sally (Moulton) Moore of Newfield. He is a farmer. No children.
10 William Osborn, b. 29 Oct. 1841; m. ——— McKusick. He is a sergeant in the Boston police. No children.
11 Lauren Colby, b. 17 Oct. 1844; lives in South Boston, a teamster.

11-9-7-2-9

Rook Thurston Libby, born in Limerick, Me., 27 Jan. 1806; married first, 28 Dec. 1831, Emily Lord, daughter of John and Abra (Chadwick) Lord of Somersworth, N. H.; (died 25 June 1851, in Saco); second, Marion Bradbury, daughter of Jacob and ——— (Locke) Bradbury of Hollis, Me.; (died Oct. 1861, in Auburn, Me.); third, Martha J. Wyman.

He learned the trade of millwright at Great Falls, N. H., and soon after, with his brother Stephen, built a saw and grist-mill on the Little Ossipee River. He stayed there about ten years, and then, after working awhile in Saco, built a grist-mill in Hollis, which he ran about eight years. He then moved to Saco, and about twelve years later moved to Auburn, and for a number of years had charge of the woodwork in the Bates corporation in Lewiston. He died in Auburn, 18 Feb. 1871.

Children, by first wife:

1 Mary, b. 27 Oct. 1832; d. 12 June 1855; unm.
2 Ivory Emerson, b. 7 Sept. 1834; m. 3 Nov. 1859, Lucinda, dau. of James and Nancy (Stevens) Leavitt of Waterborough; d. Nov. 1866, of consumption. He had two children who died in infancy.
3 Lucinda, b. 13 Feb. 1836; d. 17 May 1862; unm.
4 Emily J., b. 21 Nov. 1837; m. Frank Simmons, the sculptor; died 18 Sept. 1871, in Rome, Italy.
5 George, b. 16 Jan. 1840; d. in infancy.
6 Martha, b. 25 Feb. 1842; died in infancy.
7 George, b. 25 Jan. 1845; d. 2 Sept. 1846.
8 Charles H., b. 1 Nov. 1846; d. 9 Jan. 1858.
9 Harriet A., b. 26 March 1849; d. 12 June 1861.

By second wife:

10 Elsie Etta, b. 10 March 1852; m. 2 March 1874, James Hamilton of Harrison.
11 Ida M., b. 1857; d. 4 June 1864.
12 Jennie T., died 28 Dec. 1861.

11-9-7-2-10

Thomas Butler Libby, born in Limerick, Me., 9 Dec. 1808; married, 20 March 1834, his cousin, Eunice Butler, daughter of Wm. and Lois (Littlefield) Butler of Sanford. He settled on his father's homestead and there died, 8 June 1842. His widow married, 4 Feb. 1844, Walter H. Pierce, of Limerick, and still occupies the homestead farm.

Children, born in Limerick:

1 Almeda Jane, b. 9 Dec. 1834; m. 10 Jan. 1859, Wm. Albert Lang of Limerick.

2 Lois B., b. 25 Feb. 1836; m. 15 May 1857, Elisha Wadleigh of Parsonsfield.
3 Martin Van Buren, b. 20 June 1837. 1 Jan. 1855, having followed the sea two years, he left home for another voyage, and was never afterward heard from.
4 Stephen Frank, (known as Frank S.), b. 26 March 1840; m. 16 June 1863, Sarah J., dau. of John and Nancy (Davis) Fisk of Waterborough, widow of Daniel C. Warren of the same place. He was a truckman in Boston six years. Since his marriage he has lived on the farm that was Warren's, in Waterborough. Children:
  1 Ellsworth Lincoln, b. 12 June 1865.
  2 Edward Everett, b. 27 July 1867.
  3 Warren Sumner, b. 11 June 1871.
5 Butler, b. 6 Feb. 1842; m. 19 Dec. 1863, Sarah E., dau. of John and Sarah Ann (Harper) Brooks of Limerick. At the age of 17 he went to Boston, where he was successively a clerk in a restaurant, truckman, (employe and proprietor), clerk in a wholesale dry goods house; and, in 1869-70, proprietor of a variety store in East Cambridge. Out of that time he served about three years in the 11th Mass. Light Artillery. In 1870 he moved his family to Waterborough, Me., and became a salesman for the Cleveland Lightning-rod Co. He continued in their employ six years with marked success, and then went into business himself as the Cable Lightning-rod Co. He has been Republican candidate for representative from Waterborough in the state legislature. Children:
  1 John Hervey Burnside, b. 15 Sept. 1864, in Limerick.
  2 Lillian M., b. 20 March 1867, in East Cambridge.

11-9-7-3-1

Capt. John Cook Libby, born in Shapleigh, Me., 15 Sept. 1793; married, 27 Feb. 1817, Nancy Gerrish Libby, 11-9-7-2-2. He lived on his father's homestead, in what is now Acton, until his removal to Limerick, where he settled on the farm now owned by his son Asa. He was a very ingenious man, bricklayer, shoemaker, wheelwright, carriage maker, etc.; but his chief livelihood was farming. Before leaving Shapleigh, he was captain of a cavalry company in the militia, and during the last years of his life, was a justice of the peace.

Children, born in Shapleigh:

1 Sally, b. 16 Feb. 1818; m. 25 Dec. 1849, James Johnston.
2 Asa, b. 19 Aug. 1820; m. 29 June 1852, Lydia, dau. of George S. and Olive (Knight) Lord of Limington. He is a farmer and mason, and has always lived on his father's homestead in Limerick. Children:
  1 Charles Herbert, b. 27 June 1853; m. 14 Sept. 1878, Annie M., dau. of Wm. Johnson of Parsonsfield. He was a schoolteacher and mason until his 21st year, when he became a clerk in his uncle's drug store in Saco. In 1879 he removed to Denver, Col. Child:
    1 Josephine H., b. 21 March 1880, in Denver.
  2 Emma Jane, b. 22 Feb. 1855; m. 2 Oct. 1877, Geo. E. Tuxbury of Saco.
  3 Mary Abbie, b. 26 Feb. 1857; unm.
  4 John Wilbur, b. 9 Aug. 1859; unm.
  5 Nancy Alice, b. 5 March 1861.
  6 Albert Ellsworth, b. 20 Feb. 1863.
  7 Eugene Asa, b. 26 July 1867.
  8 Annie Celia, b. 30 Jan. 1870.

3 Stephen Cook, [M.D.], b. 1 April 1822; m. 27 June 1852, Sarah A., dau. of James and Nancy (Davis) Frost of Limington. He graduated from the Worcester Medical College, Massachusetts, and went into the employ of Dr. Nathaniel Brooks of Saco. About five years later he bought out his apothecary store, and went into practice himself. Both his business and his practice he continues successfully to the present day. He has served in both branches of the city government, and in 1874 was Republican candidate for mayor. He is clerk and one of the deacons of the Baptist Church. Children:
  1 Edwin Jackson, b. 10 July 1856; d. 10 Aug. 1856.
  2 Carrie Emma, b. 28 Sept. 1857; d. 20 Jan. 1878.
  3 Frank Howard, b. 4 Nov. 1862.
  4 Ella Frost, b. 30 Sept. 1866.

4 John, b. 6 Feb. 1826; m. Hannah Edgerly of Exeter; d. 30 July 1860, in Saco. He was a machinist by trade, but his health failed him soon after he completed it. His widow was a tailoress in Bangor, and died about 1874. No children.

Born in Limerick:

5 Samuel Jackson, b. 17 June 1830; d. July 1854; unm. He was a schoolteacher, a daguerreotyper, and at one time an assistant officer in the Boston House of Correction.

6 Ann, b. 16 July 1831; m. Alfred Mitchell of Lewiston.

7 Silea, b. 1 Feb. 1835; m. 23 Dec. 1855, Charles F. Barker.

11-9-7-3-3

Asa Libby, born in Shapleigh, now Acton, Me., 25 Jan. 1798; married, 27 Dec. 1827, Abigail Libby, 11-9-7-8-3.

In 1825, he settled in East Pond Plantation, now Smithfield, and became one of the leading inhabitants of that town, serving many years as selectman. He and his wife were both members of the Freewill Baptist Church. She died 29 Dec. 1852, and he married, 16 May 1856, Paulina (Dore) Thompson. He died 16 Nov. 1869. His widow died 10 April 1881.

Children, all by first wife:

1 Sarah, b. 11 Feb. 1829; died 2 Jan. 1847; unm.

2 Hannah G., b. 8 Nov. 1833; m. 6 Nov. 1851, Asa Horn. They occupy the homestead farm.

3 Seth G., b. 24 April 1835; m. 1st, about 1860, Emma N. Merrow; 2d, about 1866, Angie N. Hussey. He was a farmer. About 1872 he removed to West Waterville, where he lived until his death, 20 Nov. 1880, and where his family still lives. Children, by first wife:
  1 daughter, died at the age of two years.

  By second wife:

  2 Ida Mabel, b. 1 Nov. 1868.
  3 Frank R., b. 29 Sept. 1874.

11-9-7-3-5

Samuel Libby, born in Shapleigh, Me., 18 June 1806; married, 3 Aug. 1829, Melinda A. Hussey, daughter of Peter and Lydia (Hussey) Hussey of Somersworth, N. H. He was a carpenter by trade, and, in his young days was in the furniture business in Waterville. In Exeter he lived on a farm, and owned mills with his brother Calvin. In 1855 he bought mills in Dexter, and about 1870 removed his residence thither, and settled on the farm now occupied by his widow and son Samuel. He died 29 March 1874.

Children, born in West Waterville:

1 Alonzo Clark, b. 10 June 1832; m. 1st, 10 May 1857, Emily, dau. of Samuel and Charity (Burton) Hooper; (died 23 Sept. 1870); 2d, 13 March 1871, her sister, Lenora C. Hooper. He and his brother Edwin own and run saw and grist-mills in Dexter. Children, by first wife:
 1 Charles F., b. 10 Sept. 1857; d. 9 May 1858.
 2 Charles F., b. 17 April 1859; unm. He is a weaver in Lawrence, Mass.

By second wife:

 3 Ernest Linwood, b. 24 May 1874.
 4 Effie Mabel, b. 3 June 1879.

2 Samuel H., b. 27 May 1834; unm. He is a farmer.

Born in Exeter:

3 Charles Hurd, b. 18 Feb. 1836; m. 12 Dec. 1863, Almira B. Hooper, sister of his brother's wives. He was chiefly occupied in milling until 1867, when he went onto the homestead of his wife's father in Sangerville, and there died, 7 July 1871. His widow married, 29 July 1875, Jefferson H. Wood and lives in Saco. Child:
 1 Rosa Estelle, b. 16 Jan. 1865, in Dexter.

4 Melissa D., b. 22 March 1838; m. John Martin, jr.

5 Clara Augusta, b. 4 Nov. 1840; m. Albert L. H. Libby, 11-9-7-8-2-3.

6 Edwin Greenwood, b. 29 June 1844; m. 15 Jan. 1870, Kate, dau. of Levi C. and Lucy (Potter) Morgan. Child:
 1 Artie Estella, b. 25 Jan. 1873.

7 Ellen Frances, b. 24 July 1848; m. 29 Oct. 1870, Chas. G. Crowell.

11-9-7-3-6

Calvin Libby, born in Shapleigh, Me., 13 June 1808; married, 4 May 1831, Nancy C. Mills, of Dover, N. H. He was by trade a house-carpenter, but engaged also in farming and milling. He was a member of the Freewill Baptist Church. He settled in Exeter, Me., where he died, 12 Dec. 1861, and his widow still lives.

Children:

1 George F., b. 16 March 1832; m. 1st, 27 May 1862, Flavilla, dau. of Joshua and Cynthia Bates of Fairfield; (died 21 April 1863); 2d, 20 June 1864, Laura M. F., dau. of Daniel and Betsey Clark of Anson; (died 31 March 1880); 3d, 15 Sept. 1880, Lissie S., dau. of Abram and Abigail Kneeland of Winterport. He is a farmer and millman in Exeter.

2 Ann Elizabeth, b. 18 May 1835; married 1st, ——Rose; 2d, Samuel Libby, 11-2-2-1-2-1.

3 John C., b. 31 Oct. 1837; died 14 June 1864, in the army. He was a farmer and millman.

4 Mary A., b. 2 July 1841.

5 Asa M., b. 24 Nov. 1845; is a farmer and shoemaker.

6 Emma C., b. 26 July 1853; d. 5 Dec. 1880, in Auburn.

11-9-7-7-1

JOHN Y. LIBBY, born, probably in Shapleigh, Me., 25 Nov. 1802; married SARAH MERROW of Shapleigh. He went east and died in Pittsfield, where he had lived some time, 8 June 1881. His wife died 6 Oct. 1872.

Children:

1 Jane, b. in West Waterville; died 21 Nov. 1839.
2 Lovina, died at the age of 16.
3 Eveline, married Lebbeus Burse of Pittsfield.
4 Madison, b. 23 Sept. 1829; m. Eliza A., dau. of Nicholas and Elizabeth (Chambers) Dodge of Bradford. He enlisted in Baker's D. C. Cavalry, Co. I, and was afterward transferred to the 1st Maine Cavalry. He was killed in the raid on the Welden railroad, 27 Oct. 1864. His widow married, 8 Sept. 1868, John A. Snell of China. Children:
   1 Augustine B., born 5 Dec. 1855, in Pittsfield; m. 7 Dec. 1879, Carrie E., dau. of Amasa S. and Mahala (Newcomb) Gerrish of Burnham, Me. He is a bookkeeper.
   2 Edward M., b. 23 Dec. 1858; unm.
   3 Lida M., b. 5 Nov. 1863.
5 James Wesley, b. 1832; married, in Clinton, Me., Mary Jane Hunter, and settled in that place. Children: (?)
   1 Charles, b. 1870.
   2 Levis, b. 1873.
6 Ira M., b. 25 Aug. 1834; m. 2 June 1867, Lucy S., dau. of Adoniram and Sybil (Runnells) Millett of Burnham. He is a mechanic, living in Pittsfield Village. Children:
   1 Herbert A., b. 1 July 1868.
   2 Arthur L., b. 15 March 1870.
   3 Carrie M., b. 25 May 1872; d. 24 Aug. 1872.
   4 A. Roy, b. 17 Sept. 1874.
7 Alonzo, b. 17 Oct. 1835, in Palmyra; m. 30 Dec. 1865, Martha, dau. of Sullivan and Jane (Adams) Collamore of Pittsfield. Children:
   1 Nancy C., b. 8 April 1867, in Pittsfield.
   2 Amy D., b. 11 Aug. 1869.
   3 Elsia J., b. 11 March 1872.
   4 Earl H., b. 23 Feb. 1874.
   5 Grace V., b. 10 Nov. 1875.
   6 Bessie M., b. 8 June 1878.
8 Melissa, b. 27 Dec. 1837; m. Lewis B. Curtis.
9 George W., b. 20 Feb. 1840; m. Roseltha, dau. of Elbridge Patten; died 16 Oct. 1875.
10 Seth, b. 25 March 1842; m. in Lewiston, Annie M. Waite; lives in Melrose, Mass.
11 Delphina, b. 28 Nov. 1844; died 4 May 1845.
12 Josiah W., b. 9 April 1846; m. 6 March 1877, Emma J., dau. of Oliver C. and Mary A. (Emery) Baker of Palmyra. No children.

11-9-7-7-3

PETER LIBBY, born probably in Shapleigh, Me., 24 June 1807; married, first, SOPHIA BICKFORD, daughter of Arthur Bickford of Waterville; (died 1843, in Palmyra); second, Mrs. Priscilla Gordon. He was a farmer, and lived for the most part in Pittsfield, where he died, Aug. 1880.

Children, all born in Pittsfield, all by first wife:

1 Mahala C., b. 28 Aug. 1828; m. Samuel Ells.

2 Climma B., b. 24 Feb. 1830; m. Nathan W. McCausland.
3 Horatio B., born 2 Jan. 1833; married, in Pennsylvania, Annie C. Emigh; lives in Pittsfield. No children.
4 Stephen, b. 5 Aug. 1878; m. 26 Jan. 1858, Mary A. (Libby) Avery, 1-1-2-2-3-8-5; died about 1866, in Detroit, Me., where his family now lives. His widow married, 26 Oct. 1868, Thomas Rollins. Children:
  1 Mahala A., b. 18 July 1858; died 6 June 1864.
  2 Lanson A., b. 12 Feb. 1860; died 1 Aug. 1880.
  3 Lizzie A., b. 18 March 1862.
  4 Stephen A., b. 6 April 1864.
5 Lanson, b. 4 April 1841; m. 4 March 1861, Anna T., dau. of John T. and Mary (Pratt) Ham of Palmyra. Children.
  1 Warren Chester, b. 17 June 1862.
  2 Sophia, b. 17 July 1864.
  3 Annie M., b. 2 Sept. 1866.
  4 William R., b. 8 July 1868.
  5 Josie B., died 5 Sept. 1875.
  6 Georgie B., died 28 Aug. 1876.
  7 Josie Bertha, b. 2 Oct. 1879.
  8 Fred E., b. 26 July 1881.

11-9-7-8-2

Asa M. Libby, born in Fairfield, Me., 13 Jan. 1804; married first, Sarah Ann Cook, daughter of James Cook of Tamworth, N. H.; (died 12 Nov. 1840, in Pittsfield, Me.); second, 23 March 1843, Joanna B. Powers, daughter of Rev. Francis and Joanna (Brown) Powers of Norridgewock.

In his younger days he taught school, began a college course, and then studied medicine. Shortly before his marriage he settled on a farm in West Waterville. He engaged also in manufacturing chairs. From 1835 until 1847 he engaged in milling in Pittsfield and Hermon. He was then a farmer in Smithfield, in Avon, and finally, from 1857, in West Waterville. There he died, 9 Aug. 1879, and his widow still lives.

Children, by his first wife:

1 William V. T., born 12 May 1833, in West Waterville; m. 29 March 1856, Annie W., dau. of John T. and Bethiah (Witham) Parker, of Farmington. Up to the time of his marriage, he was engaged in lumbering. He then went into the meat and grocery business in West Farmington, where he has since continued. Children:
  1 Elwin H., b. 6 June 1864.
  2 Mittie D., b. 15 June 1866.
  3 Bertie A., b. 8 Feb. 1877.
2 Sophia Maria, b. 7 Oct. 1836; d. 5 Oct. 1838, in Pittsfield.
3 Albert L. H., b. 25 Aug. 1839, in Pittsfield; m. 12 Jan. 1862, Clara Augusta, 11-9-7-3-5-5. He followed farming and lumbering in Avon, Exeter, and Dexter, until 1873. 29 April 1861, he enlisted in the U. S. service, the first volunteer from Exeter, and served until December following, when he was discharged on account of sickness. Since 1873 he has been traveling agent for a sewing-machine company. Children:
  1 Dora A., b. 9 Jan. 1863, in Exeter.
  2 Grace L., b. 20 March 1865, in Dexter.
  3 Charles A., b. 12 July 1867, in Exeter.
  4 Harry W., b. 28 March 1875, in Exeter.

By second wife:

4 Sarah Ann, b. 20 Oct. 1844, in Hermon; m. 11 May 1875, Evanda H. Wood of Winslow.

5 Truman D., b. 22 Oct. 1848, in Smithfield; unm. He has been a telegrapher, and is now a manufacturer of clothing in Lewiston.

6 Winfield Scott, b. 27 Aug. 1851, in Avon; m. 23 May 1877, Annie E., dau. of Capt. Elijah M. and Amantha (Sanborn) Shaw of Lisbon. He had been some time in a law office, and was preparing for college, when, in 1871, he was offered the opportunity to learn telegraphy, which he accepted. Since 1875 he has been manager of the W. U. telegraph office at Lewiston. Children:
   1 Truman H., b. 29 April 1878; d. 28 May 1878.
   2 Gertrude B., b. 16 June 1879.

11-9-7-10-1

John Mayhew Libby, born in Shapleigh, Me., 25 Feb. 1815; married Louisa F. Witham, daughter of Dea. Samuel and Ruth (Merrow) Witham. In 1853 he bought the Railroad House in what is now West Waterville, and kept it as a hotel until 1864. He has also been engaged in farming, lumbering, and butchering. In 1863 he was representative to the legislature, and he has served as selectman in both Waterville and West Waterville. He was three years a trustee of the West Waterville savings bank.

Children, born in Dearborn:

1 Andrew John, b. 7 Nov. 1834; m. 7 Nov. 1856, Abbie W., dau. of David P. and Martha (Bowman) Morrison of Sidney. He is a farmer and cattle-dealer. In company with his sons he owns and runs a grocery store. He has been president of the North Kennebec agricultural society, and is one of the directors of the West Waterville National Bank. Children:
   1 Morrison, b. 5 July 1859; unm.
   2 Andrew D., b. 15 Aug. 1860; unm.
   3 Gertie A., b. 26 March 1863.
   4 John B., b. 8 July 1868.

2 John Fairfield, b. 6 Oct. 1838; d. 20 Aug. 1869; unm. He prepared for college, but feeble health prevented his entering. He was afterward employed by the Dunn Edge Tool Co., first as clerk, and then as traveling agent. In 1867 he became a member of the firm of Tilton, Libby & Hitchcock, doing a heavy business in agricultural tools, etc., in Chicago, Ill.

11-9-7-10-3

Peter D. Libby, born in Shapleigh, Me., 30 June 1824; married, 24 Jan. 1848, Keziah C. Gage. He has always been a farmer, and lived on the homestead in West Waterville.

Children:

1 Marilla G., b. 26 May 1848.
2 Chloe P., b. 6 Feb. 1850.
3 John C., b. 26 Aug. 1852; died 27 Jan. 1880.
4 Reuben G., b. 26 Oct. 1854; m. Kate J. ——. Child:
   1 Willie, b. 1880.
5 Mayhew P., b. 18 May 1857.
6 Everett E., b. 5 Aug. 1859.

U. S. Libbey

11-9-8-7-1

Oliver Libby, born in Clinton, Me., 15 Dec. 1808; married, 8 Aug. 1830, Hannah Plummer, daughter of Aaron and Mary (Ballard) Plummer of Albion. He settled in Unity Plantation, and cleared the farm on which he has since abode.

Children, all born in Unity Plantation:

1 Amasa, b. 14 March 1832; m. 10 June 1858, Hannah, dau. of William and Jane (Plummer) Grant of Province, N. B.; d. 9 Oct. 1870, in Houlton. He removed to Houlton in 1861, and settled on the farm still occupied by his family. Children:
  1 Lizzie J., b. 10 Feb. 1859, in Benton.
  2 Edwin A., b. 11 Aug. 1863, in Houlton.
  3 Mary E., b. 15 July 1866, in Houlton.
2 Daniel C., b. 17 Dec. 1835; m. 15 Sept. 1861, Sarah E., dau. of Stephen and Rachel (Catlin) Perkins. He lives with his father. Children:
  1 Stephen P., b. 10 Oct. 1862.
  2 Katie M., b. 1 July 1865.
  3 Charles O., b. 24 March 1868.
  4 George R., b. 20 June 1870.
3 Charles A., b. 15 May 1838; m. 4 July 1860, Elizabeth Burton of Pittsfield. He was a farmer in Pittsfield. He was drowned in Augusta, 17 July 1863, — the result of an unlucky step. His widow married Calvin Jacobs. Children:
  1 Bertha M., b. 12 May 1862; m. 19 June 1879, George Flagg, jr.; died 9 April 1881.
  2 Charles A., b. 10 July 1864.
4 Mary P., b. 13 May 1842; m. 8 July 1865, Erastus Grant.
5 Lizzie, b. 1 May 1847; d. 15 July 1862.
6 Ira P., b. 28 April 1852; m. 30 Jan. 1879, Ida P., dau. of James and Rachel (Kincaid) Rideout. He is a farmer in Unity Plantation. No children.

11-9-8-7-2

James Libby, born in Clinton, Me., 29 July 1811; married Mary Tyler of Windsor. He removed from Windsor about 1869, to his present residence in Patten, Me.

He has the following children:

1 Elias T., b. 1842; lives in Patten.
2 James O., b. 1845; m. Mary J. ——; lives in Patten. Child:
  1 Annie L., b. 1873.
3 Hanscom L., b. 1849; lives in Patten.
4 daughter; is in the Insane Asylum.

SEVENTH GENERATION.

1-1-2-2-2-3

Dea. David Libby, born in Gray, Me., 3 March 1785; married Dorcas Nason, daughter of Isaac and —— (Wilson) Nason of Minot.

He lived in Minot after his marriage until 1817, when he settled in Poland. He lived on a farm but was always engaged more or less in lumbering. He was deacon of the F. W. Baptist Church. His death took place 19 Sept. 1839, and his widow died 24 Nov. 1845.

Children:

1 Simon, b. 11 July 1804, in Minot; d. 6 May 1813.
2 Huldah, b. 25 June 1806; d. 6 Aug. 1839; unm.
3 Susan, b. 1 Dec. 1808; m. Nathaniel Rounds; d. 12 Jan. 1855.
4 Isaac, b. 2 July 1811; d. 28 Nov. 1835; unm.
5 Alvah, b. 23 Feb. 1814; d. 19 March 1839; unm.
6 Almon [Rev.], b. 23 Feb. 1814; m. 19 Jan. 1843, Hannah N., dau. of Levi and Jane (Emery) Hall of Gorham. He was educated at Parsonsfield academy, and was afterward pastor of the F. W. Baptist churches in Kittery, Limerick, Brunswick, Georgetown, Cape Elizabeth, and Bowdoinham. Since 1871 he has lived in Lewiston. Children:
   1 Jane H., born 11 Feb. 1845, in Cape Elizabeth; m. 29 Jan. 1872, Capt. Franklin White of Bowdoinham.
   2 Susan A., b. 11 Oct. 1846, in Kittery; d. 6 Nov. 1847.
   3 Almon C., b. 24 Dec. 1848, in Brunswick; unm. He graduated at Bates College in 1873, and is now a civil engineer in Buena Vista, Col.
   4 Annie M., b. 25 Feb. 1851; is a teacher.
   5 Charles Sumner, b. 2 Nov. 1854; unm. He graduated at Bates College in 1876, and is now a lawyer in Buena Vista.
   6 Willie F., b. 6 Aug., died 25 Dec., 1859, in Georgetown.
7 Simon, born 15 Jan. 1820, in Poland; m. 1st, 15 June 1844, Louisa, dau. of John and —— (Ryerson) Cole of Poland; (died 29 July 1850); 2d, 23 March 1853, Mrs. Elva S. York, dau. of Sprague and Susan (Stevens) Keene of Poland. He is a farmer in his native town. He has been three years selectman, and many years justice of the peace. Children, both by his first wife:
   1 Jesse M., b. 28 March 1846, in Danville; m. 27 Dec. 1871, Kittie E., dau. of Luther and Mary L. (White) Perkins of Poland. He graduated at Bates College in 1871, and after serving one year as principal of the Boynton High School at Eastport began the study of law with Strout & Holmes of Portland.

He was admitted to the bar of Androscoggin County in 1875, and is now practicing at Mechanic Falls. In 1877-8 he represented Poland and Minot in the state legislature. No children.

2 Abbie L., b. 3 June 1850, in New Gloucester; d. 25 Sept. 1865.

8 David [Rev.], b. 2 June 1822; m. 1st, 12 April 1848, Mary C., dau. of Isaac and Susan (Morse) Smith of Lisbon; (died 20 Sept. 1867); 2d, 5 May 1868, Mrs. Maria C. Perley, dau. of David and Betsey (Smith) Vining of Lewiston. He became a member of the Freewill Baptist Church in 1835, and a preacher in 1845; has been pastor of the church in Harrison three years, and in Harpswell two years; for the most part has lived and preached in South Lewiston. Children: by first wife:

1 Mary E., b. 11 April 1851; m. 24 June 1880, Marshall P. White.

2 Isaac S., b. 14 July 1853; d. 9 Sept. 1873.

By second wife:

3 Willis A., b. 3 Dec. 1870.

9 Jesse M., b. 2 Oct. 1824; d. 24 Oct. 1845.

1-1-2-2-2-6

Rev. James Libby, born in Danville, now Auburn, Me., 25 Oct. 1796; married, 1 April 1819, Nancy Fulton, daughter of Robert and Rebecca (Coombs) Fulton of Lisbon.

He lived with his father, and had the homestead farm. He became a Freewill Baptist clergyman, and in 1831 sold the homestead, and removed to Poland, where he was pastor of the Freewill Baptist Church thirty years. Although 85 years old, he still preaches occasionally, and frequently conducts funeral services. His wife died 14 Jan. 1871.

Children:

1 Betsey S., b. 7 Sept. 1821, in Danville; m. 3 May 1840, James H. Fernald.

2 William F., b. 24 April 1823; m. 12 May 1844, Mary A., dau. of Walter and Mercy (Haines) Johnson of New Gloucester. He was by trade a carpenter. He early showed some talent as a writer, and published for awhile in Boston a magazine called "The Youth's Cabinet." In 1846 he sailed from New Bedford as carpenter on board a whaler, and died in July 1847, in Hobart Town, Australia. His widow married David Blake of New Gloucester. Children:

1 Ella, b. 30 Jan. 1845; m. W. Frank Cook; d. Jan. 1867.

2 Clara, b. 2 Nov. 1846; m. Watson Pinkham of Casco.

3 Henrietta D., b. 20 May 1826; m. 10 Jan. 1870, Ervin Smith.

4 Mary B., b. 20 Nov. 1829; m. 2 July 1846, Daniel Hutchinson.

5 James Albert, [Rev.], b. 3 July 1832, in Poland; married 1st, 28 Feb. 1859, Lizzie H., dau. of John and Hannah (Maxwell) Magquire; (died 26 March 1866); 2d, 18 Jan. 1869, Angie, dau. of Henry and Olive (Woodard) Davis of Lisbon; (died 8 Nov. 1877); 3d, 31 March 1879, Mary A., dau. of Rev. Hubbard and Ann (Noyes) Chandler of Poland. He received an academic education, and in 1859 was ordained a preacher of the Second Advent denomination. He has since devoted himself for the most part to evangelical labors; has also written for the press, both in prose and verse. Children, by second wife:

1 Albert Evelith, b. 11 Nov. 1870, in Poland.

2 Olive May, b. 13 May 1877, in Lynn, Mass.

6 Moses M., b. 3 Jan. 1835; d. 3 Dec. 1835.

7 Moses M., b. 23 March 1837; m. May 1870, Zuriel, dau. of Joseph and Laura Towle of Porter. He is a shoemaker in Lynn, Mass. No children.
8 John L., b. 10 Jan. 1840; m. 1860, Sarah W., dau. of Joshua and Sarah (White) Purington of Lisbon; lives in Auburn. Children:
  1 Edward L., b. 20 Feb. 1863.
  2 Ferdinand J., b. 11 March 1865.
  3 Charles H., b. 6 Feb. 1867.
9 Charles S., b. 25 Nov. 1843; d. 4 Jan. 1866, in Poland; unm. He served nine months in Co. G, 23d Maine Vol.

1-1-2-2-3-8

David Libby, born in Gray, Me., 29 Oct. 1799; married, 13 July 1826, Elizabeth McCausland, daughter of Thomas and Sarah (Demon) McCausland of Gardiner.

In his younger days he was a lumberman on the Penobscot. In 1835 he removed from Hartland to Bangor. He was a truckman there eleven years, and, after living a year in Boston, Mass., became a stevedore in the former city. He afterward worked on stone, and was in trade two years. He now lives with his son. His wife died 9 March 1862, in Detroit, Me.

Children:

1 Sarah, b. 30 June 1827; m. Frank Burronghskill.
2 Phebe, b. 8 March 1829; unm. "She has not been heard from for a long time, and it is unknown whether she is living or not."
3 Benjamin, b. 15 Aug. 1830; m. 2 Dec. 1855, Eunice, dau. of John and Nancy (Carr) Berry, of Pittsfield. He followed the sea five years, and then learned the tanner's trade in Detroit. He has followed that occupation since, and has been foreman in a large number of tanneries; his family residing for the most part on a farm in Detroit. In April, 1881, he removed to New Limerick, where he is now foreman of C. & W. J. Shaw's tannery. Children:
  1 Annie F., b. 20 Oct. 1856; m. 16 June 1877, Frank Smith.
  2 Flora A., b. 25 Sept. 1858.
  3 Nellie A., b. 4 Jan. 1860.
  4 Georgia B., b. 5 Nov. 1864.
  5 Eva R., b. 3 July 1871.
  6 Walter B., b. 23 Jan. 1875.
4 Helen D., b. 16 April 1832; m. James Taylor.
5 Mary A., b. 14 April 1839; m. 1st, 19 Feb. 1854, John C. Avery; 2d, Stephen Libby, 11-9-7-7-3-4; 3d, Thomas Rollins.
6 Emma J., b. 23 March 1842; m. Sept. 1858, Alfred Pusher.
7 Caroline, b. 3 Jan. 1849; m. 7 July 1871, Albert Wooster.

1-1-2-2-3-10

William Libby, born in Gray, Me., 16 May 1804; married, 4 April 1833, Rachel Emery, daughter of Benjamin and —— (Whitten) Emery of Skowhegan, Me. He was a farmer in Canaan until 1845, and then went west with his brother Charles, and settled in Vinland, where he died 30 April 1873, and his widow 11 June 1874. He was a member of the Freewill Baptist Church.

Children, all born in Canaan:

1 Benjamin E., b. 22 March 1834; m. 28 March 1863, Rebecca, dau. of Hiram and Mary (Delameta) Mirack. He lives in Royalton, Wis. Only child:
  1 Edwin, b. 26 March 1864, in Vinland.
2 Orra, b. 19 Dec. 1835; m. 4 June 1856, Manthano Kimball.
3 Edwin, b. 15 May 1838; d. 4 Jan. 1865, in Vinland; unm.
4 John F., b. 22 Dec. 1842; m. Nov. 1874, Mary Ann, dau. of John and Catherine (Thompson) Furness of Vinland. He lives on his father's homestead. Children:
  1 Charles Delbert, b. 28 Sept 1875.
  2 Carrie Rachel, b. 17 April 1877.
  3 William Furness, b. 22 Jan. 1879.
5 Esther, b. 20 April 1844; m. 10 Dec. 1865, William Courtney; d. 4 Nov. 1875.

1-1-2-2-4-2

Elliot Libby, born in Gorham, Me., 21 Aug. 1792; married, 13 April 1822, Susan Hall, daughter of Timothy and Abigail (Austin) Hall of Falmouth. He died early, after a roving life, occupied in lumbering and farming, 1 Nov. 1845, in Harrison. His widow married, 20 Nov. 1852, Richard Jackson, and third, —— Perham. She now lives with her son Timothy.

Children:

1 Abby H., b. 30 Sept. 1823, in Derby, Vt.; m. 5 Feb. 1843, in Boston, Mass., Joel Jennison.
2 Rebecca, b. 16 Oct. 1825, in Portland, Me.; m. 4 Dec. 1845, in Boston, Joseph L. Lang.
3 Susan J., b. 8 Jan. 1828, in Westbrook, Me.; m. 28 April 1850, in Waterford, Elliot Chase.
4 James Q., b. 13 Dec. 1829; m. 2 Nov. 1858, Malvina A., dau. of Ezekiel W. and Nancy (Kilgore) Dustan of Waterford; died in Waterford, 26 Oct. 1866. His widow now lives in Cambridgeport, Mass. Child:
  1 Lyman Henry, b. 5 Sept. 1860.
5 Timothy H., b. 3 March 1832, in Standish; m. 22 April 1860, Marcia S., dau. of Zebulon and Maria (Cushman) Preble of Bowdoinham. He is in the trucking business in Boston. No children.
6 Hiram L., b. 27 Nov. 1834, in Naples; m. 1 May 1862, Margaret A., dau. of Sumner and Sally (Arthurton) Kimball of Waterford. He is a carriage smith by trade, and is now in business in Norway. Child:
  1 Minnie F., b. 29 July 1863, in Waterford.
7 Maria H., b. 12 Oct. 1840, in Albany; was struck by a locomotive, 16 Nov. 1880, and instantly killed; unm.
8 Ulvilda E., b. 4 March 1845, in Harrison; m. 24 Jan. 1867, in Boston, Thomas C. Byram.

1-1-2-2-4-4

Capt. Jethro Libby, born in Gorham, Me., 19 March 1796; married, 26 Dec. 1819, Olive Flood, daughter of Morris and Lydia (Roberts) Flood of Gorham. He helped build the Cumberland and Oxford Canal, and was afterward employed on it until his death, which took place in Harrison, 26 Aug. 1840. His widow died in Harrison, 14 Feb. 1872.

Their children were:

1 Elliot, b. 23 Sept. 1820, in Gorham; m. 18 Nov. 1840, Frances Jane, dau. of Henry and Paulina (Tuttle) Tuttle of Portland. His life was mostly spent on the canal, in shook manufacturing, and in lumbering. In 1864 he and others went south to engage in cotton culture, and he died of yellow fever, 4 Nov. 1864, in New Burne, N. C. His family still lives in Harrison. Children:
 1 Henrietta, b. 8 Feb. 1844; died 13 Sept. 1845.
 2 Julietta, b. 16 Sept. 1846; m. 10 Dec. 1870, Charles A. Lang.
 3 Ella Isabel, b. 3 Feb. 1858; m. Wm. A. Wheeler of Lynn, Mass.
 4 Arthur Willis, b. 23 Nov. 1859; unm.
2 Lydia Ann, b. 20 July 1822, in Raymond; m. 25 Oct. 1840, Geo. W. Walker.
3 Mary Jane, b. 19 Nov. 1824; d. 14 June 1846; unm.
4 Eliza Flood, b. 17 Nov. 1826; m. Thomas Francis of New Market, N. H.
5 Juliett, b. 16 May 1830; m. Albion Kimball of Harrison.
6 Albert, b. 27 April 1832, in Naples; died 19 June 1846.
7 Lucinda, b. 13 June 1834; died 19 Dec. 1843.
8 Philena, b. 19 Oct. 1835; m. 9 May 1854, Charles A. Case.
9 Jethro, b. 29 Oct. 1837; died 22 Nov. 1840.
10 Alfred, b. 11 May 1839; m. 10 Aug. 1865, Rosina, dau. of John and Olive (Plummer) Fields of Bridgton. He has for the most part been employed on the canal, and as cooper. He served nine months in Co. B, 23d Maine Vol. No children.

1-1-2-2-4-5

Josiah W. Libby, born in Gorham, Me., 28 April 1798; married, 10 June 1821, Eliza Hall, daughter of Robert and Anne (Hall) Hall of Falmouth. He learned the cooper's trade in his father's cooper-shop. After his marriage he lived in Falmouth, Bradford, Bangor, Charleston, Carthage, Norway, Bridgton, and Saco. His widow still lives.

Children:

1 Robert M., m. Cordelia Newman of Carthage. He has been a horse dealer in Boston. No children.
2 Eliza Ann, unm.; is a milliner in Boston.
3 Parmelia W., m. 5 Sept. 1854, Dr. Charles B. Stover of Newburyport, Mass.
4 Louisa, m. James Thorborn of New York City.
5 Rachel Josephine, m. Seth T. Dame of Boston.
6 John, died young.
7 Mary, died 19 May 1876, in Boston; unm.
8 Freeman, m. Mrs. Rebecca Harmon of Saco; lives in Missouri.
9 Hannah, m. 1st, George Ricker; 2d. Geo. G. Bailey.
10 Fanny O., married Henry P. Bohart of Braman Hill, Kansas.

1-1-2-2-4-8

William Libby, born in Gorham, Me., 3 Sept. 1804; married Jane Cannell, daughter of Philip and Rebecca (Greene) Cannell of Standish. He was variously occupied as sailor, canal-boatman, teamster, clerk, etc., until about the year 1840, when he settled on the farm in Standish on which he lived until his death, 28 March 1881.

His wife died 2 May 1872, and he married second, 30 Dec. 1872, Mrs. Maria P. Wood, daughter of William B. and Betsey (Palmer) Lillis of Dorchester, N. H.

Children, all by his first wife:

1 Maria, b. 19 Nov. 1832, in Standish; m. 31 Aug. 1857, John M. Hall of Auburn.
2 Nelson Purse, b. 31 Oct. 1834, in Naples; m. 15 Oct. 1862, Mary J., daughter of Frederick P. and Angeline (Lewis) Case of Swansea, Mass. He worked chiefly at carpentering until 1870, and then settled on the homestead farm. He served one year in Co. C, 12th R. I. Vol. His wife died 28 March 1877. Children:
  1 William Frederick, b. 13 May 1864, in Bristol, R. I.
  2 Clara Elliot, b. 7 Sept. 1866, in Dighton, Mass.
  3 Joseph Lewis, b. 7 Dec. 1868, in Dighton.
  4 Charles Morrison, b. 10 Dec. 1870, in Standish.
3 Clara Melinda, b. 18 June 1841; m. Edw. F. Elliot; d. 31 May 1866.
4 Almira Morrison, b. 16 Nov. 1845; m. as second wife, Edward F. Elliot of Rumford

1-1-2-6-1-5

Hatevil Libby, born in Warren, Me., 30 April 1791; married, 8 Feb. 1816, Elizabeth Rivers of Cushing, Me. He remained with his parents until 1824. The next seven years he lived on the farm which had been his brother Henry's, and then bought a farm on George's River, and there lived until his death, 8 Oct. 1849. His widow died 26 Dec. 1851.

Children:

1 Rachel, b. 30 Oct. 1816; m. 21 March 1838, Myrick Stetson.
2 Rufus [Dea.], b. 22 Sept. 1818; m. 27 Feb. 1839, Barbara L., dau. of Esther (Libby) Kellock, 1-1-2-6-3-1. He lived with his parents until their decease, and then bought a farm about a mile distant. In 1861 he bought an adjoining farm, and there died, 11 Aug. 1873. He was a deacon of the Baptist church. Children:
  1 Benjamin, b. 20 April 1841; m. 5 March 1862, Mary A., dau. of Thomas and Lucy T. (Thomas) Skinner. He served in the late war, first as private in Co. B, 24th Maine, and then as assistant under Surgeon Harlow. He is now a butcher, in Warren. Children:
    1 Eliza K., b. 8 April 1863.
    2 Charles B., b. 19 Feb. 1866.
    3 Julia L., b. 9 May 1870.
    4 Rufus V., b. 8 April 1876.
  2 Granger H., b. 27 Dec. 1844; m. 22 Sept. 1872, Ida E., dau. of Prentiss and Sarah A. (Allen) Leland of Sherborn, Mass. He served nearly three years in Co. C, 1st Maine Cavalry. He afterward lived two years in Baltimore, Md., and is now a hat maker in Milford, Mass. His wife died 5 Jan. 1873, only three months after marriage.
  3 George E., b. 18 July 1849; m. 10 Oct. 1880, Julia A., daughter of Peter and Caroline (Morey) Powers of Jefferson. He is a carpenter in Warren.
  4 Alton V., b. 27 Sept. 1853; d. 10 Oct. 1864.
  5 John K., b. 14 June 1857; m. 10 May 1881, Cora E., dau. of Wm. Fish of Appleton, Me. He lives in Iowa.
  6 Hattie M., } twins, b. 29 Nov. 1860; { d. 12 June 1861.
  7 Mary M., } { d. 25 June 1861.
3 Mary Ann, b. 27 Jan. 1821; m. Miles Hemenway.

4 Hannah, b. 9 Jan. 1823; m. 13 Sept. 1843, Wm. B. Stetson; d. 22 May 1867.
5 Edward, b. 9 March 1825; d. 26 March 1826.

1-1-2-6-1-8

EDWARD LIBBY, born in Warren, Me., 13 April 1801; married, 18 June 1833, MARGARET WALLIS, daughter of Charles and Eleanor (Cushman) Wallis of Waldoborough. He served seven years in the U. S. army. After his marriage, he settled on his father's homestead and lived there until his death, 19 Feb. 1841. His widow still lives.

Children, all born in Warren:

1 Allen, b. 15 May 1834; m. 25 Nov. 1868, in Providence, R. I., Agnes, dau. of Jenkin and Janette S. (McDougall) Pearson. He is a machinist. He served nine months in the 5th Mass. Inf., and three years in the U. S. signal service. Since his marriage, he has lived in Providence. Children:
  1 Charles Edward, b. 15 Oct. 1871.
  2 Cora Frances, b. 22 April 1875.
  3 Bertha Louisa, b. 1 July 1877.
2 Sarah F., b. 6 Jan. 1836; m. 6 June 1867, George A. Lownsberry of Concord, Mass.
3 Joseph W., b. 21 Dec. 1837; d. 8 Nov. 1864, in Washington; unm. He followed the sea until the war broke out and then enlisted in the 20th Maine Infantry. He died in the service, of wounds received before Petersburgh.
4 Seth, } twins, b. 10 April 1840, { d. 8 Nov. 1840.
5 Mehitable, } twins, b. 10 April 1840, { d. 21 Oct. 1840.

1-1-2-6-2-3

JAMES LIBBY, born in Warren, Me., about 1786; married, 25 Oct. 1810, SARAH COPELAND, daughter of Joseph and Sarah (Meloney) Copeland. He was a farmer in Warren. He died 7 May 1829. His wife died 17 Jan. 1827.

Children:

1 John, b. 25 July 1812; m. 29 Dec. 1839, Frances, dau. of John and Margaret (Boyd) Pierce of Prospect. He is a farmer and blacksmith at North Prospect. Children, all born in Prospect:
  1 John F., b. 11 Dec. 1840; m. 11 April 1863, Mary E. C., dau. of Capt. Nathan and Sarah (Crocker) Harding. He is a general merchant in Prospect. He is also assistant postmaster. He has been first selectman since 1877, and has been town treasurer six years. Children:
    1 Sanford, b. 23 July 1865.
    2 Grace M., b. 28 Sept. 1868.
    3 Harvey H., b. 6 May 1870.
    4 John N., b. 5 Dec. 1879.
  2 Georgia, b. 24 Dec. 1846; d. 30 May 1869; unm.
  3 Oria, b. 3 Feb. 1848; unm.
2 Sanford, b. 1814; m. Aug. 1838, Eliza J., dau. of Samuel and Anna (Farrington) Dilloway. He removed to Camden, where he was a ship-carpenter and builder, and died 26 Oct. 1878. His widow died 26 Sept. 1879. Children:
  1 Sarah Josephine, b. 21 Dec. 1838; d. 2 Oct. 1864; unm.
  2 Frances E., b. 15 Jan. 1843; d. 11 March 1857.

3 Alice A., b. 28 Sept. 1845; d. 14 April 1857.

3 Patrick, b. 1816; d. 1849, in Mobile, Ala.; unm.

4 Alexander, b. 10 Oct. 1818; m. Oct. 1841, Margaret W., dau. of Robert and Margaret (Winchenbach) Jordan of Augusta. During the early part of his life he was a ship-carpenter, and worked in the South as well as in the North. He also engaged in getting out ship-timber from the woods in Virginia. During the war he bought a farm in Smithfield, Va., and has lived there ever since, with the exception of three years spent in a planing mill in Boston, Mass. He is a member of the Baptist Church. Children:
- 1 Eliza H. V., b. 16 Aug. 1842; d. 1 Aug. 1868; unm.
- 2 William B., b. 12 Sept. 1853; d. 1 Dec. 1860.
- 3 James A., b. 9 Jan. 1857; m. 18 Dec. 1879, Rosa V., dau. of Charles C. and Bettie (Bain) Grice of Portsmouth, Va. Only child:
  - 1 Margare. b. 14 Nov. 1880; d. 14 April 1881.
- 4 Virginia F., b. 14 April 1859; d. 23 Sept. 1860.
- 5 Frank S., b. 27 March 1864.

5 Nancy C., b. Jan. 1820; m. 1st, Erastus Jameson; 2d, 12 Dec. 1847, Albert Johnson.

6 Andrew, b. June 1822; m. 7 June 1846, Aroline Emma Jones. 1-6-9-8-4-4. He was a shoemaker in Union. He was postmaster and town clerk from 1851 until his death, 13 July 1857. His widow died 4 Oct. 1860. Only child:
- 1 Martha I., b. 6 June 1847; d. 26 June 1859.

7 Margaret, b. Aug. 1824; m. 25 Dec. 1851, John L. Crane.

1-1-2-6-9-3

EDWARD G. LIBBY, born in Warren, Me., 14 Dec. 1819; married, 1844, SARAH WOODCOCK, daughter of Nathan and Margaret (Waring) Woodcock. He is a farmer in his native town.

Children:

1 Susan M., b. 22 July 1845; m. 31 Jan. 1870, Capt. Otis D. Averill of St. George. Children:
- 1 Allen B. (Averill), b. 22 Nov. 1870.
- 2 Percy E. (Averill), b. 8 May 1876.
- 3 Irene Adella (Averill), b. 4 Dec. 1878.
- 4 Susie (Averill), b. 23 March 1881.

2 James C., b. 28 Feb. 1847; m. 28 Sept. 1871, Nellie N. Goodenow. He is a joiner in Warren, and lives on part of the original Libby homestead there. Child:
- 1 Clarence Otis, b. Oct. 1872.

3 Mary Emma, b. 3 April 1849; d. 24 Dec. 1858.

4 Joseph G., b. 6 Oct. 1851; d. 20 Oct. 1854.

5 William Vesper. b. 23 March 1854; m. 26 Nov. 1879, Ida M. Thomas of Thomaston. He is a joiner, and lives in Warren. Child:
- 1 Eva G., b. 22 Nov. 1880.

6 Clementine C., born 24 April 1856; m. 1 Jan. 1881, Forrest E. Lermond.

1-1-2-6-10-1

ANTHONY LIBBY, born in Warren, Me., 9 Nov. 1815; married first, 20 June 1835, LOUISA ROBINSON, daughter of Moses and Priscilla Robinson of Cushing; (died Sept. 1849); second, MARY C. WYLLIE, daughter of Robert and Mary (Anderson) Wyllie of Warren; (died 12 April 1859). He lives in Warren.

Children, by his first wife:

1 Isaac, b. 22 Oct. 1835; m. 27 Oct. 1865, Emily F., dau. of Thomas and Rachel (Vinal) Burton of Cushing. He is a farmer in Warren. Children:
  1 Henry J., b. 1 May 1867.
  2 Lois R., b. 12 Sept. 1870; died 15 July 1873.
  3 Oliver B., b. 8 April 1875.
  4 Hattie M., b. 24 Feb. 1877.
  5 Hiram B., b. 12 Aug. 1880.
2 Ira, b. 22 Sept. 1837; m. June, 1861, Keziah, dau. of Cornelius and Julia (Counce) Hyler of Cushing. He is a ship-carpenter in Warren. Children:
  1 Alice J., b. 29 April 1862.
  2 Emma B., b. 19 Feb. 1865; died 18 July 1875.
  3 Erdine, b. 11 March 1872.
  4 Ballard H., b. 18 May 1875.
  5 Fannie I., b. 18 May 1877.
3 William, b. 11 Aug. 1839; m. Deborah Fifield of Deer Island. He is a sailor. Children:
  1 Julia A., b. 12 March 1872.
  2 Arthur W., b. 7 April 1874.
4 Charles L., b. 4 Sept. 1841; m. 8 May 1866, Mary E., dau. of Alex and Elizabeth (Robinson) Hoffres of Cushing. He is a ship-carpenter in Warren. Children:
  1 Cora A., b. 23 June 1866.
  2 Jeremiah H., b. 13 June 1868.
  3 Otis A., b. 1 Jan. 1871.
  4 Edith A., b. 15 June 1873.
  5 Ada S., b. 30 March 1877.
5 Thomas G., b. 3 Aug. 1844; m. 1st, Jane A., dau. of Lawrence and Mary Hyler of Cushing; 2d, Jennie F. Ginn. He is a sailor. Children, by first wife:
  1 Enoch.

By second wife:

  2 Annie Bell, b. 27 March 1873.
  3 Iola Louisa, b. 3 June 1875.
  4 Lottie May, b. 14 Dec. 1877.
  5 Lizzie M., b. 14 June 1879.
6 Ann E., b. 18 Dec. 1846; m. Mark D. Jameson of Cushing.
7 Sarah L., b. 28 July 1849; married in Fitchburgh, Mass.

By second wife:

8 George A., b. 19 Jan. 1853; died 13 May 1874.
9 Mary E., b. 8 Feb. 1855; m. Granville Lord.

1-1-3-4-1-2

Daniel Libby, born in Scarborough, 1 March 1786; married, 29 Nov. 1815, Abigail Hanscom, daughter of Daniel and Mary (Dam) Hanscom, 9-5-6-3 and 11-7-5-7. He lived on his father's homestead, and died there 7 Sept. 1820. His widow died 16 July 1826. Their children went to live with their mother's relatives in Limington.

Children:

1 Hannah, b. 4 July 1816; d. 2 Oct. 1858, in Limington; unm.
2 Freedom, b. 28 July 1819; m. 10 Dec. 1846, Mary A., dau. of John and Mary (Bryant) Babb of Limington. He has always lived in Limington, a shoemaker by trade, but chiefly engaged in farming. Since 1855, he has owned and occupied his grandfather Hanscom's homestead. His wife died 16 March 1854. Children:

1 Edwin Hanscom, b. 10 Dec. 1848; d. 3 Oct. 1871; unm.
2 Frank, b. 29 July 1852; m. Nov. 1873, Sarah, dau. of Andrew and Emily (Tallyrand) Baker. He lives with his father. His wife died 23 Aug. 1879. Child:
  1 Gertrude, b. 25 Dec. 1878.

1-1-3-8-2-1

Capt. Joab Libby, born in Standish, Me., 24 April 1793; married first, Jane Marwick, daughter of Hugh Marwick of Portland; (died 21 Jan. 1827); second, 8 Aug. 1827, Sarah Libby, 10-5-4-2-3-1.

He served one year in the war of 1812. He afterward worked in a sawmill in Raymond Village. About 1826 he went into partnership with John S. Stackpole, in the blacksmith business at Raymond Village, and continued it about eight years. Having learned the trade in that time, he removed to Naples, and set up a shop which he run alone many years. Later, he bought land, and became a farmer. He is a pensioner of the war of 1812.

Children, by first wife:

1 Mary Jane, b. 3 Feb. 1819; m. Geo. McLellan and Jason Plummer.
2 Caroline S., b. 11 Oct. 1821; m. 19 April 1846, as his first wife, Jason Plummer.
3 Charles Atwood, b. 16 Jan. 1826; d. 10 June 1827.

By second wife:

4 Charles Albert, b. 26 Sept. 1828; d. 1 June 1830.
5 Albert Marwick, b. 20 Jan. 1831; d. 21 June 1837.
6 Julia Adeline, b. 8 Nov. 1832; m. 7 May 1854, Franklin Blake.
7 Francis Radox, b. 21 May 1838; m. 22 Oct. 1863, Lois F., daughter of Nathaniel Cook of Brownfield. He served nine months in the 25th Maine. He now lives in Albany, N. H. Children, all born in Brownfield, Me.:
  1 Erving Roscoe, b. 25 Nov. 1864.
  2 Emma Lena, b. 5 April 1869.
  3 Mary Jane, b. 28 May 1871; d. 15 Feb. 1875.
  4 Howard Raymond, b. 22 Feb. 1877; d. 6 Nov. 1878.
8 Allison, b. 21 Sept. 1840; m. 15 Jan. 1867, Eliza J., dau. of Edward Henry and Sarah Ann (Hill) Morse of Norway. He is a farmer and lives with his father. Children, all born in Naples:
  1 Hattie May, b. 9 May 1872.
  2 Jason Plummer, b. 6 July 1873.
  3 Florence Mabel, b. 10 Feb. 1876.
  4 George Albert, b. 12 March 1878.
  5 Freddie, b. 5 May 1880.

1-1-3-9-1-2

Joseph Libby, born 29 Nov. 1804; married first, 23 Oct. 1828, Abigail Libby, 1-1-2-2-6-7; (died 23 April 1831); second, 22 Dec. 1831, Maria Jones, daughter of Hannah (Libby) Jones, 10-5-4-9.

When he was first married he bought a farm in Pownal, near his father's, and there lived until two years after his second marriage, when he removed to Palmyra. There he lived until his death, 13 July 1841. The following January his widow sold the farm, and returned to Pownal. Four years later she removed to Biddeford. 18 Aug. 1845, she married Zenas Berry of Buxton, and is now a widow in Saco.

Children, by first wife:

1 infant, died a few days before its mother.

By second wife:

2 Mary Abby, b. 12 Jan. 1833; m. Sumner Bragdon. Children:
  1 Charles Sumner (Bragdon), b. 27 May 1864.
  2 Lizzie Anna (Bragdon), b. 17 Dec. 1865; d. 31 Dec. 1875.
  3 Ernest Gay (Bragdon), b. 25 March 1873.
3 Joseph Henry, b. 15 May 1836; m. 27 Sept. 1859, Betsey, dau. of Stephen and Isabel (Huff) Otis of Norridgewock. His life has been spent in the cotton mills in Biddeford. He has been an overseer since 1865. Children:
  1 James Leon, b. 9 May 1860; unm. He is of the firm of Hall & Libby, grocers, Saco.
  2 Maria Isabel, b. 23 Nov. 1862.
4 John Fairfield, b. 5 May 1838; d. 15 Dec. 1862, in Georgetown, D. C.; unm. He was a private in Co. B, 5th Maine Infantry.
5 Hannah Elizabeth, b. 8 April 1840; m. Joseph Bishop Severance of Biddeford.

1-1-3-9-1-4

Dennis Libby, born in Pownal, Me., 21 Jan. 1816; married, 16 Dec. 1838, Susan Libby, 1-4-1-6-3-10. He was a farmer in his native town, where he died 24 March 1860. He and his wife were members of the M. E. Church. She died in Charlestown, Mass., 8 May 1875.

Children, all born in Pownal:

1 Almira, b. 24 July 1839; d. 14 April 1841.
2 Delia I., b. 21 March 1842.
3 Appleton A., b. 17 Aug. 1845; d. 8 May 1869, in Augusta; unm. He enlisted in Co. H, 32d Maine, and died in camp.
4 Addie M., b. 18 Feb. 1850; m. 4 May 1869, Estus A. Morrill of Charlestown, Mass. Children:
  1 Maud L. (Morrill), b. 7 Oct. 1870; d. 28 Nov. 1872.
  2 Vernon H. (Morrill), b. 4 Jan. 1873.
  3 Ethel M. (Morrill), b. 8 Sept. 1875.
  4 Charles Sumner (Morrill), b. 28 April 1880.
5 Ella E., b. 21 April, died 8 July, 1854.

1-1-3-9-3-3

Cyrus Jones Libby, born in Pownal, Me., 8 Nov. 1813; married, June 1835, Delinsa Douglass, daughter of Israel and Patience (Sylvester) Douglass of Hallowell.

He lived in Pownal, Hallowell, St. Albans, Hermon, and in Dec. 1846, settled on the farm he has since occupied, in Carmel. In his younger days, he followed the sea, and he served through the Aroostook war.

Children:

1 Lovina C., b. 13 Feb. 1836, in Pownal; m. 14 May 1853, John Bean.

2 Allen Cobb, b. 20 Jan., died 15 Sept., 1838.
3 Tryphena, b. 13 July 1839; m. 14 Sept. 1861, Hartwell McLaughlin.
4 Lorenzo Dow, b. 29 Jan. 1842; m. 29 Jan. 1868, Elizabeth M., dau. of William and Mary (Freathy) Willey. He served four years in the late war; now lives in Oldtown. Children: (?)
 1 Bertrand W., born 1871.
 2 Mary H., born 1875.
 3 Eveline, born 1879.
5 Celestia B., b. 18 May 1844; m. 3 Feb. 1864, James Roundy.
6 Adelaide, b. 29 Aug. 1846; m. 10 Feb. 1870, Amos Roundy.
7 Eben Burton, born 22 Nov. 1848; m 26 April 1878, Geneva, dau. of Ammi and Maria (Preble) McLaughlin of Levant. He is a farmer in Carmel. Only child:
 1 Mabel, b. 4 June 1878.
8 Cyrus G., b. 7 Feb. 1851; m. 6 Sept. 1878, Lizzie G., dau. of Benj. and Susan (Shaw) Lathers of Hermon. He is a farmer in Hermon. Child:
 1 Cecil M., b. 15 April 1879.
9 Josephine, b. 19 April 1853; d. 30 Aug. 1864.
10 Elwell, b. 28 Feb. 1855; d. 20 Aug. 1864.
11 Lewis, b. 24 June 1856; d. 19 Nov. 1857.
12 Sophronia, b. 25 Sept. 1858; m. 7 Nov. 1880, Tyler D. Strout.
13 Mary F., b. 20 June 1860; d. 11 Nov. 1860.

1-1-3-9-3-6

George Washington Libby, born in Pownal, Me., 23 Nov. 1819; married, Dec. 1841, Sarah J. Thrasher, daughter of Ebenezer and Lydia (Edwards) Thrasher of Cape Elizabeth.

He was a clerk in a grocery store in Portland until 1841, and then crossed over and established himself in business in Cape Elizabeth, near Fort Preble. From 1845 until 1849, he followed the sea for the most part, and from the latter year until 1853, lived in California. Since his return he has lived in Cape Elizabeth, and has been chiefly occupied as trader, mason, and carpenter. He has been twice a selectman of Cape Elizabeth. His wife died 28 Feb. 1880.

Children, all born in Cape Elizabeth:

1 James Sargent, b. 9 Nov. 1842; married, in Chicago, Ill., Frances ———. He served a while in the army in the late war, and then entered the navy. After the war he followed the sea until 1871, and has been, since 1872, a policeman in Chicago. Child:
 1 son, born about 1878.
2 George Melville Dallas, b. 9 Feb. 1844; m. Ella ———. He learned the trade of printer with B. Thurston & Co., in Portland. In 1868 he removed to Chicago, where he is now a member of the firm of Tiffany & Co., book and job printers.
3 Sarah Lucretia, b. 16 June 1846; died in 1849.
4 Benjamin Thrasher, b. March, 1850; m. Mary E., dau. of Harrison Sawyer. He is a journeyman printer in Chicago. Children:
 1 son.
 2 Frank.
 3 daughter; died Feb. 1880.
 4 daughter.
5 Mary Emeline, b. 16 June 1854; is a compositor.
6 Frank Eugene; died in Feb. 1857, aged 7 months.
7 Harry Frank, b. 26 June 1863.

1-1-3-9-4-2

DAVID TYLER LIBBY, born in Pownal, Me., 31 Oct. 1815; married, 14 July 1839, HANNAH L. TRUE, daughter of Bela and Mary (Mitchell) True of Pownal. He is a farmer. He lived in Pownal until 1872. He served that town as selectman, and represented it in the state legislature in 1858 and 1859. In 1872, he removed to Auburn, where he still resides. He has for some time been deacon of the Freewill Baptist Church in Pownal.

Children:

1 Drusilla, b 9 Feb. 1840; m. 30 Oct. 1859, Wm. E. Keith.
2 Lewis Fenwick, b. 17 July 1842; m. 22 Oct. 1865, Parthenia F., dau. of Rev. D. C. and Jane (Metcalf) Burr. He was a private in the 10th Maine Vol. He is now a contractor and builder in Auburn. No children.
3 Charles Henry, b. 19 Feb. 1845; m. 16 Oct. 1866, Eliza, dau. of Alvin and Harriet (Jones) Austin; d. 25 Aug. 1868, in Muskegon, Mich. His widow married Robert Molean of Lynn, Mass. Only child:
  1 daughter, born and died, Nov. 1867.
4 Frederick Elwood, b. 28 Jan. 1847; m. 1 May 1870, Cornelia S., dau. of Frank and Cornelia (Smith) Cross. For eight years he has been a contractor and builder in Muskegon, Mich. Child:
  1 Maud Ellen, b. 7 Oct. 1874, in Muskegon.
5 Mary Ada, b. 1 Nov. 1848; m. 31 Dec. 1871, Edwin W. Paine.
6 Edwin Stanley, b. 6 Jan. 1851; m. 26 June 1875, Emma F., dau. of Phineas and Mary Ellen (Wentworth) Spoffard of Webster. He is a carpenter in Webster. Child:
  1 Harry Stanley, b. 27 Aug. 1877, in Webster.
7 Hannah Frances, b. 30 Dec. 1852; m. 30 June 1872, George A. Davis.
8 Florence Percy, b. 21 July 1855; m. 21 May 1876, Amasa W. Mason.
9 Martha York, b. 6 Feb. 1857; m. 15 Feb. 1880, John C. Cushing.
10 David Thaxter, b. 10 March 1859; unm.
11 Alice Cora, b. 18 Sept. 1862.

1-1-3-9-4-3

REV. PHINEAS LIBBY, born in Pownal, Me., 1 May 1817; married first, 31 March 1844, MARY ASHLEY WALDRON, daughter of David and Mary (Blake) Waldron of Portland; (died 8 Nov. 1846, in Windham); second, 27 May 1847, NANCY ANN NOYES, daughter of Edward W. and Frances (Chute) Noyes of Windham.

In 1839 he began preaching; in 1841 he received a local preacher's license; in 1853 he joined the Methodist Conference at Biddeford. He continued in the conference, preaching in Newfield, Cape Elizabeth, Fayette, and other places, until 1867, when he withdrew. In 1863 and 1864 he represented Fayette in the state legislature. He is now a joiner and painter in Paris, Me.

Children, by first wife:

1 Frances Ellen, b. 29 Aug., d. 14 Dec., 1845, in Portland.

By second wife:

2 George Edward, } twins, b. 29 July 1848, in Falmouth; d. 1 Oct. 1850.
3 Benjamin Franklin, } twins, b. 29 July 1848, in Falmouth; was drowned in Cape Elizabeth 17 Sept. 1855.
4 Elizabeth Ellen, b. 3 March 1850, in Cumberland; m. 30 Sept. 1877, Columbus Richardson.

5 Ella Ashley, b. 14 Feb. 1852, in Cumberland; m. 12 Feb. 1868, Samuel Ray.
6 Sarah Mitchell, b. 14 May 1854, in Newfield; m. 27 Aug. 1870, Virgil D. Rawson.
7 Alvra Hatch, b. 1 July 1856, in Cape Elizabeth; m. 18 May 1877, Julia Adelaide, dau. of Jeremiah and Adelia (Rich) Kimball. Children:
  1 Elsie Maud, b. 25 May 1878, in Norway.
  2 Harry Clinton, b. 1 Jan. 1881, in Paris.
8 Franklin Raymond, b. 17 June 1858, in Raymond; unm.
9 Charles, b. 15, d. 18, April, 1860, in Industry.
10 Fannie Meade, b. 15 May 1863, in Fayette.
11 Frederick Hamlin, b. 16 Sept. 1867, in Paris.

1-1-6-4-6-1

Phineas Libby, born in Scarborough, 30 Sept. 1801; married, 16 May 1824, Lucinda Harmon, daughter of Zachariah and Elizabeth (Milliken) Harmon.

After his marriage he worked one year on the farm of his wife's father; four years in Lagrange, where he took up land and cleared a farm; two years on his father's farm; eleven years in Portland, nine as truckman and two as stevedore; a few years in the employ of the Saco Water Power Co., as foreman of the outdoor laborers; and then removed to Saco, where he bought the small place he now occupies, and has since carried on market gardening. He was a deputy sheriff of York County, 1853-1861, and fourteen years a constable of Saco.

Children:

1 Cyrus, b. 20 Oct. 1824, in Scarborough; m. 5 May 1850, Sophia Libby, 1-2-1-1-1-6-2. He is a shoemaker by trade, but in 1855 bought the farm he now occupies, and has since been a farmer. Children, all born in Saco:
  1 Alvinza, b. 23 April 1851; m. 5 Dec. 1877, Eva A., dau. of Jackson and Susan (Clay) Came of Saco. He is a carriage maker in Biddeford. No children.
  2 Forest, b. 2 Feb. 1853; d. 18 Feb. 1856.
  3 Adin, b. 11 Feb. 1855; m. 23 May 1879, Clara E., dau. of John and Sarah (Joy) Foot of Biddeford. He is a molder. Child:
    1 Mabel, b. 4 March 1880, in Biddeford.
  4 Mary Emmagene, b. 30 Oct. 1856; unm.
  5 Forestine, b. 26 Oct. 1859; m. 23 March 1878, Edwin T. Phillips.
  6 Cora Ella, b. 31 Aug. 1861.
  7 Roland, b 9 Sept. 1863.
  8 Granville, b. 1 Feb. 1866.
  9 Rosina, } twins, b.
  10 Fostina, } 18 May 1858.
2 Lorinda, b. 3 June 1820, in Lagrange; d. 18 Jan. 1843, in Saco; unm.
3 Drusilla, b. 17 Nov. 1827; m. 17 May 1862, James Peacock.
4 Lucinda, b. 12 Oct. 1829, in Scarborough; died in Saco, 8 Sept. 1879; unm.
5 Granville, b. 2 Sept. 1831, in Scarborough; died in Saco, 28 Aug. 1860; unm. He was a machinist.
6 Foxwell Cutts, b. 29 July 1833, in Portland; m. 29 June 1856, Lovinia W., dau. of John and Sarah (McLucas) Nason of Waterborough. He is a journeyman tailor and has worked in many cities. Until 1870 he kept his family in Limerick, Me. At that time his house was burnt and he went west. He now lives in Chicago. Child:

1 La Forest Ellsworth, born in Waterborough, Me.

7 Elizabeth Ellen, b. 29 July 1835; m. 5 June 1876, Josiah M. Smith of Gardiner.

8 Dorville, b. 17 Aug. 1837; m. 2 July 1866, in Pittsburgh, Penn., Josephine, dau. of Philip and Mary (Hill) Sheplar. He graduated at Bowdoin College in 1862. He was then principal of the Saco High School six months, principal of the First Ward schools in Pittsburgh, Penn., six months; Provisional Professor of Mathematics at the Western University of Pennsylvania two years; and principal of the Washington schools in St. Louis, Mo., two years. In 1868, he removed to San Francisco, Cal., and was three years in the book and stationery business (Libby & Swett). He then entered his present position in the firm of A. L. Bancroft & Co., publishers and booksellers. Only child:

1 Dorville, b. 24 June 1872, in San Francisco.

9 Aurelius, b. 26 July 1839; d. 29 Oct. 1843.

10 Ernestine, b. 11 Nov. 1841, in Biddeford; d. 7 March 1842.

11 Lorinda Ernestine, } twins, b. 2 April } m. Chas. M. Milliken.

12 Aurelius Eugene, } 1846, in Saco; } m. 18 Nov. 1868, Martha Ann, dau. of John L. and Martha (Hanson) Moulton of Buxton. He served three years in Co. E, 1st Maine Cavalry. He afterward learned the machinist trade, but became a clerk for Alfred Pierce, baker. Since his enrollment as a soldier, he has been known as Eugene A. Libby. Only child:

1 Frank, b. 11 Dec. 1877; was choked to death in swallowing, 17 July 1879.

13 Augusta Melverdia, b. 16 Oct. 1847; m. 2 June 1868, Gardner P. Waterhouse.

1-1-6-4-6-5

Dorville Libby, born in Scarborough, 7 Feb. 1814; married first, 1 May 1841, Harriet A. Cole, daughter of Josiah and Hannah (Greely) Cole of Paris, Me.; (died 17 Aug. 1864); second, 27 April 1865, Mary Ellen Whitney, daughter of Abel and —— (Cole) Whitney of Standish; (died 23 May 1868); third, 4 March 1869, Vesta, daughter of Eleazer and Martha (Drake) Snell of Turner.

He began to go to sea when nine years old. He became captain in 1837, and, until 1847, sailed in the West India trade. In 1845 and 1846 he represented Cape Elizabeth and Scarborough in the state legislature. In 1847 he quitted the sea, and soon after became yard master in Portland, of the Atlantic and St. Lawrence Railroad. Afterward, for eighteen years, he was Inspector and Boarding officer of the U. S. customs district of Portland and Falmouth. He is now in the trucking business.

Children; by first wife:

1 John Watson, b. 25 Dec. 1842; d. 3 Feb. 1853.

2 Mary Harriet, born 5 Nov. 1845; m. 25 March 1868, Charles Rich of Portland, a broker. No children.

3 Edwin Coolbroth, b. 25 May 1848; m. 25 Nov. 1873, Annie (Eldridge) Kimball, adopted daughter of William E. Kimball of Portland. For several years he followed the sea. He is now a clerk with Russell, Lewis & Co., lumber merchants. Children:

1 Mary Rich, b. 6 Jan. 1875, in Deering.
2 Edwin Foss, b. 31 Oct. 1876, in Portland.
3 Carle Washburne, b. 11 Oct. 1878, in Portland.

4 Julia, b. 9 Nov. 1849; d. 5 Jan. 1852.

Dorville Libby

5 Susan Jane, born 4 Feb. 1852; m. 21 April 1875, Benjamin Morse Mitchell. No children.
6 Josiah Cole, b. 2 Sept. 1853; d. 28 April, 1862.
7 Julia A., b. 25 March 1856; m. 3 Nov. 1875, Edward H. Chase. He is a fish inspector in Portland. Children:
  1 Grace Mildred (Chase), b. 30 Oct. 1876.
  2 Edward Irving (Chase), b. 24 June 1878.
  3 Lawrence Libby (Chase), b. 4 Oct. 1879.
8 Anna Watson, b. 21 Nov. 1858, in Portland; d. 10 Dec. 1870.
9 Lizzie, b. 18 Nov. 1860; d. 16 May 1862.
10 Dorville, b. 15 June 1863.
11 Charles Henry, b. 16 Aug., died 16 Sept., 1864.

By second wife:

12 Edna Warren, b. 18 March 1866; d. 19 March 1867.

1-2-1-1-1-1

Joseph Libby, born in Nottingham, N. H., 19 Nov. 1787; married, 3 Jan. 1814, Sally Pease, daughter of Asa and Sally (Parsons) Pease of Cornish, Me.

He was carried by his father to Parsonsfield, Me., and there grew up. He afterward moved to Westbrook, Me., and thence, in the fall of 1832, started for New York with an emigrant wagon. He settled on a farm in Olcott, Niagara County, and there died 17 Jan. 1873. His wife had died 25 Dec. 1853.

Their children were:

1 Martha, b. 18 Sept. 1814; m. Abner Crossman.
2 William, b. 3 July 1816; d. aged 6 years.
3 Mary J., b. 29 Aug. 1821; m. Thomas Brockway. No children.
4 William, b. 16 June, d. 18 Aug., 1825.
5 Ann Maria, b. 1 Dec. 1827; m. 19 Sept. 1855, Charles McClew. Children:
  1 Eugene J. (McClew).
  2 Agnes (McClew).
  3 Charles Herbert (McClew).
6 Thomas Lewis, b. 26 Oct. 1829; m. 10 Dec. 1868, Maggie Coulter of Newfane. He became a sailor. When the Rebellion broke out, he was in the British service, but joined the U. S. navy soon after, and served three years. After his marriage, he settled in Saginaw, Mich., where he entered the police force, and is now (1881) city marshal. Children:
  1 Edwina C., b. 26 Sept 1870.
  2 Emma J., b. 4 May 1873; d. 2 Oct. 1874.
  3 Albert L., b. 18 July 1875.
  4 Vern Edwin, b. 3 Dec. 1878.
7 Lydia Pease, b. 10 Aug. 1832; m. 11 Nov. 1855, Lafayette W. Wisner.
8 Sarah, b. 14 April 1833; m. George Clement.

1-2-1-1-1-3

Andrew Libby, born in Nottingham, N. H., 27 Dec. 1792; married, 4 Oct. 1817, in Boston, Mass., Elizabeth Lakeman, daughter of Nathaniel and Elizabeth (Smith) Lakeman of Ipswich, Mass.

He left his home in Parsonsfield at the age of nineteen, and worked on a farm in Westbrook, and, later, in Portsmouth, N. H.

About 1814 he went to Boston, where he lived six years. He then returned to Portland, where he spent the rest of his life in countless occupations, among which may be mentioned those of butcher, toll-gatherer, etc. He died 11 Sept. 1864. His widow still lives.

Children, born in Boston:

1 William Henry, b. 9 March 1819; m. 26 Nov. 1846, in Thompson, Conn., Deborah C., dau. of Welcome and Deborah (Crocker) Pincin of Bridgewater, Mass. He is a painter and paper-hanger. Most of his life has been spent in Deering, Me., where he now lives. Children:
  1 George Washington, b. 4 May 1848; unm.
  2 Luella Amanda, b. 7 April 1852; d. 7 April 1877; unm.

Born in Portland:

2 Eliza Ann, b. 12 July 1822; m. 7 Dec. 1843, Seth H. Brackett.
3 Caroline Mary, b. 19 Dec. 1824; m. 2 March 1847, Ebenezer Trask of Beverly, Mass.
4 George Washington, b. 1 Feb. 1826; was drowned in the Canal Basin, in Portland, 23 June 1838.
5 Nancy Baker, b. 2 Jan. 1832; m. 15 June 1858, Josiah Sterling.
6 Charles Henry, b. 27 Oct. 1835; m. 29 Feb. 1864, Esther J., dau. of Edw. and Mary (Tarr) Tuttle. He learned the painter's trade, but became an oiler on ocean steamers. He was lost in the burning of the steamer Atlantic, off Wood Island. He was one of seven who got onto a spar. Five had fallen of and found watery graves before his hold was loosed. One only was saved. The widow married, 19 Jan. 1868, Wm. Fisher. Child:
  1 Mary Elizabeth, b. 7 Dec. 1864.

1-2-1-1-1-4

HAM LIBBY, born in Nottingham, N. H., Nov. 1795; married, Sept. 1819, SARAH BATCHELDER, daughter of Benjamin and —— (Brown) Batchelder of Parsonsfield, Me.

After his marriage he lived on the farm of his father-in-law until 1833. In that year he moved to Effingham, N. H., and lived there until 1846. After two years spent in Parsonsfield, he removed to Wakefield, N. H., where his wife died, 22 June 1856. In 1857, he married Miss Mary A. Fogg of Ossipee, N. H., and lived in that place until her death, in 1865, and then went to live with his son, in Wolfborough, N. H., where he died, 16 March 1866.

Children, born in Parsonsfield:

1 Hannah Batchelder, born 20 June 1820; m. 2 Feb. 1846, Paul Wentworth.
2 John B., born 12 June 1822; m. 3 April 1853, Hannah, dau. of Jonathan and Mary (Osgood) Tyler of Bradford, Mass. Before his marriage, he lived in Haverhill, Brookline, and Boston, Mass. From the time of his marriage until his death, 23 May 1865, he was a market gardener in Bradford. Child:
  1 Jennie, b. 26 March 1862.
3 Nancy Y., b. 21 April 1824; m. 1st, Lewis Wingate; (died 16 Oct. 1848); 2d, H. A. F. Colcord; died 16 June 1855.
4 James H., b. 21 June 1827; d. 14 Oct. 1851; unm.

5 Alvah S. [Capt.], b. 5 Dec. 1830; m. 17 Oct. 1850, Abbie E., dau. of Otis R. and Sarah (Oliver) Pray of Macadavie, N. B. He left home in 1846, and lived in Haverhill, Brookline, and Boston, Mass., until his marriage. From 1850 to 1858, he lived in Wakefield and Ossipee, N. H., and then settled in Wolfborough, where he is now of the firm, Libby, Varney & Co., manufacturers of boxes and box-shook. In 1862, he enlisted in the 16th N. H. Vol., and rose to the position of Captain of Co. G, 1st N. H. H. Artillery (147 men, 4 lieutenants). He served in the N. H. legislature in 1872 and 1873, and has filled various town offices. He is a member of the Freewill Baptist Church. Children:
1 Sarah Ellen Rand, b. 28 July 1852; m. 28 Jan. 1878, Everett Charles Randall. Two children.
2 Edward Judson, b. 5 April 1856; m. 27 Nov. 1880, Bessie, dau. of John C. Drew.
3 Fred Sumner, b. 16 Nov. 1865.

6 Ira, b. 7 Jan. 1833; m. Nancy Y., dau. of John and Mary (Young) Matthews of Wakefield. He lived in Belmont, Mass., from his marriage until 1865, in Bradford, farming, the next ten years, in Wolfborough, milling, two years, and in 1877 removed to Reno, Nevada. Children:
1 Charles, b. 1866; d. 1873.
2 son, b. 1878.

Born in Effingham:

7 Edward J., b. 10 Nov. 1835; d. 10 Nov. 1854.
8 Mary C., b. 21 Oct. 1838; m., 1857, Job Mathes.
9 Louisa, b. 22 Feb. 1843; m. 17 June 1865, Gilbert S. Fowler of Haverhill, Mass.

1-2-1-1-1-6

John Libby, born in Parsonsfield, Me., 1800; married, 25 Sept. 1825, Mary Ann Carter, daughter of —— and Elizabeth (Young) Carter of Wakefield, N. H.

When he was married he removed to Saco and bought a sawmill near the site of the Laconia mills. When those mills were built he sold, and from that time until his death worked as journeyman carpenter. He died 12 June 1872. His wife died 30 July 1871.

Children, born in Saco:

1 Elizabeth Ann, b. 25 May 1826; m. 24 Aug. 1845, Joshua Eaton of Kennebunkport.
2 Sophia, b. 30 June 1828; m. Cyrus Libby, 1-1-6-4-6-1-1.

Born in Biddeford:

3 James, b. 16 Oct. 1830; d. 26 Aug. 1833.
4 Abbie Tuck, b. 1 April 1833; unm.
5 Mary Ann, b. 15 Sept. 1836; m. 20 July 1862, Gilman R. Brackett of Portland.
6 John, b. 24 July 1839; unm. He was a private in Co. I, 17th Maine, and died of wounds received at Fredericksburgh.
7 George Washington, b. 13 June 1842; m. 15 Dec. 1864, Sabra S., dau. of David G. and Mary J. (Storer) Littlefield of Wells. He has always worked in cotton mills, and is now an overseer in the Pepperell mills. He enlisted in Co. I, 17th Maine Vol., but was discharged after a few months for disability. Children:
1 Howard Carter, b. 2 June 1866, in Wells.
2 Hermon Aliston, b. 28 Aug. 1869, in Biddeford.

1-2-1-1-1-8

ALVAH LIBBY, born in Parsonsfield, Me., 6 Nov. 1805; married, 11 Aug. 1826, in Portland, EUNICE B. STEWART, daughter of Jotham and Hannah (Burnham) Stewart of Scarborough.

He left home at the age of eighteen, and went to Portland. He learned the mason's trade with James Crockett, and immediately went into business himself. He continued in the masonry business until 1840, when he engaged in the stove business. This he continued until 1870. In 1871 he retired to Deering, where he died, 9 Nov. 1879, and his widow still lives.

He was for eighteen years one of the overseers of the poor, and was several times a member of the city council. He was chairman of the building committee of the Mechanics' building, Portland.

Children, all born in Portland:

1 Ellen Frances, b. 5 July 1827; m. 18 Oct. 1848, Benj. B. Miller.

2 Mary Elizabeth, b. 29 July 1829; m. 21 Feb. 1850, Capt. John Dexter Carlisle. No children.

3 James Edward, b. 13 May 1832. He went to sea before he was sixteen. He died on a voyage made with his brother-in-law, as second mate, 1 March 1853.

4 Major Sweetsir, b. 16 Sept. 1835; m. 1st, 13 Oct. 1856, Louisa, dau. of William Sheafe of Portland; (died 21 April 1860); 2d, 12 Nov. 1862, Mary A., daughter of Capt. Stephen and Mary (Ingraham) Knight of Portland; (died 10 Jan. 1865); 3d, 7 Oct. 1870, Hannah Elizabeth Haines of Biddeford. He graduated at the High school and became his father's partner in the stove business, in which he is now engaged in Mount Vernon, Ill. Children, by first wife:

   1 James E., b. 10 Sept., died 30 Oct., 1859.

   By second wife:

   2 Walter Converse, b. 18 Sept. 1863; was reared by his father's mother.

   By third wife:

   3 Harry Alvah, b. 12 Jan. 1872.
   4 Lucy Sweetsir, b. 18 Dec. 1872; died June 1874.
   5 May Bell, b. May 1874.
   6 Guy Preston, b. 22 April 1877.
   7 Emma Irvine, b. Oct. 1879.

5 Miles Thomas Stewart, b. 11 Nov. 1837; m. 24 Oct. 1867, Nellie W., dau. of Capt. William and Margaret Adie of Portland. He graduated at the Portland High School, and was a clerk with Hardy & Knight, wholesale woolen merchants, until 1865, and since that time has been with his brother-in-law, Kilborn. His wife died 4 Aug. 1875. Only child:

   1 Herbert French, b. 12 Feb. 1875.

6 Albion Henry, } twins, b. 7 May 1840; } d. 25 Sept. 1841.
7 Alvah Augustus, }

8 Lucietta Sweetsir, b. 26 July 1842; m. 4 Oct. 1864, William Thomes Kilborn of Portland, one of the largest carpet dealers in the state. Children:

   1 Carrie Harward (Kilborn), b. 21 Aug. 1865.
   2 William Senter (Kilborn), } twins, b. 1 Sept. 1867; } d. 19 Sept. 1868.
   3 Alvah Stewart (Kilborn), }
   4 Philip Carlisle (Kilborn), b. 7 April 1869.
   5 James Edward (Kilborn), b. 13 Aug. 1871.
   6 Gertrude Libby (Kilborn), b. 21 Sept. 1873.
   7 Joseph Walker (Kilborn), b. 26 Nov. 1875.

Ahab Libby

8 William S. (Kilborn), b. 19 Sept. 1879.
9 Eunice Augusta, } twins, b. } unm.
10 Alvah Augustus, } 19 Nov. 1846; } m. 29 Jan. 1873, Mary Ellen, dau. of Capt. Joseph and Mary G. (Mosher) Alexander of Billerica, Mass. He served one year in Co. D, 1st Maine Battalion. He was clerk with Wm. T. Kilborn until 1872, and then removed to Boston, where he has been in the same business. Child:
1 Joseph Harolde, b. 21 March 1877, in Billerica.
11 Albion Henry, b. 16 Sept. 1849; m. 16 Sept. 1872, Nellie Clark, dau. Benjamin and Catherine (Clark) Rolfe of Portland. He graduated from the Portland High School and was for three years a clerk with Locke, Meserve & Co., wholesale dry goods. He then went into the carpet store of his brother-in-law, and, soon after, removed to Boston, where he followed the same business. Child:
1 Maud Elinor, b. 22 July 1873, in Somerville, Mass.

1-2-1-3-3-1

IRA LIBBY, born in Barrington, now Strafford, N. H., 4 March 1798; married BETSEY DANIELS, daughter of Joseph and Mehitable (Daniels) Daniels of Strafford. He was a farmer in Strafford until 1836, when he removed to Dover. His death took place 4 April 1844. He was drowned in a pond, formed by heavy rains, where the City Hall of Dover now stands. His widow died 4 Nov. 1869.

Children, born in Strafford:

1 Nancy, b. 15 July 1822; m. 20 April 1846, Joseph D. Hall.
2 Lydia Lovett, b. 28 Jan. 1824; m. 26 July 1847, Micajah Gilman.
3 Eliza, b. 13 Jan. 1826; m. 7 Dec. 1846, George W. Stevens.
4 Martha Susan, b. 24 Jan. 1828; m. Joseph O. Caswell.
5 Adline, b. 27 Sept. 1830; unm.
6 James Hodgdon, b. 4 Oct. 1833; m. Ann Augusta, dau. of Tobias and Hannah (Temple) Hall of Barrington. He was by trade a house-painter. His wife died in Portsmouth, 16 June 1866, and he then returned to Dover, where he became a partner of H. W. Twambly, a dealer in sporting articles. He died 12 July 1874. He served three years in Co. H, 7th N. H. Vol. Children:
1 Edgar A., b. 31 Jan. 1858; d. 27 Sept. 1863.
2 Floretta E., b. Jan. 1862; d. 4 Nov. 1863.
7 Ira, b. 5 Dec. 1835; m. 1st, Sarah Elizabeth Smith; (died 16 Aug. 1859, in Exeter, N. H.); 2d, 24 Aug. 1862, Mary Elizabeth, dau. of William and Mary N. (Brown) Cunningham of Belfast, Me. Since 1860, he has been in the employ of Wm. Russell & Son, paper manufacturers, the greater part of the time as foreman. Children, by first wife:
1 Frank Oliver, b. 4 Jan. 1855, in Dover, N. H.; unm.
2 Isabelle Florence, b. 7 May 1857, in Dover, N. H.; unm.
3 Sarah Elizabeth, b. 14 Aug. 1859, in Exeter, N. H.; died aged two weeks.

By second wife; born in Belfast:

4 Arthur Russell, b. 22 Dec. 1863; d. 24 Nov. 1864.
5 Albert Henry, b. 2 June 1866.
6 Willie Cunningham, b. 18 March 1867.

Born in Dover:

8 John Eri, b. 26 May 1838; d. 31 Dec. 1841.
9 Ann Janette, b. 4 Jan. 1841; m. 17 Jan. 1862, Henry W. Twambly of Dover.

10 John Eri, b. 4 Nov. 1843; m. 19 June 1872, Adline Goudy of Lynn, Mass. His wife died 12 June 1876, and he is now with H. W. Twambly, in Dover. Child:
   1 Cora Augusta, b. 6 June 1873, in Lynn.

1-2-3-1-2-1

GEORGE LIBBY, born in Landaff, N. H., 22 Aug. 1792; married SALLY ABBOTT, daughter of John and Phebe (Wells) Abbott.

He was a blacksmith by trade, but also carried on farming. He always lived in Warren, the town in which he was brought up, except a brief period, about 1847, which he spent in southern Illinois, and a year following, in Piermont, N. H. He repeatedly served as moderator and selectman in Warren, and was a justice of the peace. He died 8 Jan. 1879. His wife died 16 May 1872. They were both members of the M. E. Church.

Children, all born in Warren:

1 Hazen, b. 10 June 1815; m. 1st, 26 Nov. 1835, Mehitable S., dau. of Timothy and Ruth (Smith) Clifford; (died 27 Feb. 1849); 2d, 29 Oct. 1850, Augusta M., dau. of Aiden and Shuah (Philbrick) Ingraham of Haverhill, N. H. He learned the blacksmith's trade with his father, and was engaged successively in Wentworth, Warren, Rumney, Plymouth, Concord, and Lyman. About 1876 he gave up his trade for farming, and is now a country merchant. Children, by first wife, born in Wentworth:
   1 George William, b. 17 May 1836; m. 15 Aug. 1865, Amanda J. Libby, 1-2-3-1-2-1-2-1. He is a blacksmith and machinist. He now lives in North Haverhill, Mass. No children.
   2 Martin V. B., b. 1 July 1837; m. 9 Nov. 1859, Mary Louisa, dau. of Henry and Belinda (Clark) Blaisdell of Lake Village, N. H. He is a horseshoer in Lowell, Mass. In his younger days he worked in many places, but at length entered the employ of Stevens & Currier, in Lowell. After working for them nine years, he went into business for himself. He was working in Lawrence, Mass., when the Pemberton Mill fell, and was one of the three that entered the basement to release those that were living. He was a private in Co. C, 6th Mass. Inf., and took part in its memorable passage through Baltimore. Children:
      1 Fred Valmore, b. 22 June 1862, in Lowell.
      2 Ernest Linwood, b. 15 May 1868, in Lowell.
   3 Lottie, b. 2 Sept. 1838; m. Alpha Clement.
   4 Lucusta, b. 10 June 1840; m. Joseph C. Boynton.

Born in Warren:

   5 Ruth R., } twins, born } d. 24 May 1842.
   6 Sally C., } 28 Dec. 1841; } m. Henry N. Merrill.
   7 Lucaby Ophelia, b. 7 Feb. 1843; m. 1st, Otis F. Philbrick; 2d, her uncle, Walter Libby.
   8 Elphameo Mascleno, b. 29 March 1847; had his name changed to Albert Clifford. He married, 24 Nov. 1870, Josephine, dau. of David O. and Louisa (Hamilton) Bancroft of East Windsor, Conn. He served nine months against the Rebellion, and has since been a farmer in Connecticut. Children:
      1 Walter B. (Clifford), b. 7 May 1875.
      2 Edith D. (Clifford), b. 25 May 1876.
   9 Pheolu, b. 22 Feb. 1849; m. 4 July 1871, Ella, dau. of Nathan and Oxirene (Noyes) Hewett of Rutland, Vt. He is a blacksmith in Chittenden, Vt. Child:
      1 Clurana, b. 25 May 1876; d. 13 March 1879.

By second wife:

10 Hettie M., b. 12 Nov. 1852; d. 9 April 1861.
11 Harry W., b. 8 Aug. 1856; m. 3 April 1878, Eva J., dau. of Philip T. and Roxanna (Caldwell) Ingram of Topsham, Vt. He is a blacksmith in Oxford, N. H.
12 Hazen Selden, b. 28 Jan. 1858; d. 10 Aug. 1861.

2 Anna, b. 3 Nov. 1816; m. Geo. W. Tennant.
3 John Abbott, b. 12 Nov. 1822; m. 25 July 1842, Angeline, dau. of Joseph and Rachel (Abbott) Prescott of Bath, N. H. He learned the blacksmith's trade with his father. For six years, following his marriage, he was a farmer in Vermont. He then started the blacksmith business in Piermont, N. H., and has since continued there. Children:

1 William Abbott, b. 14 Sept. 1843, in Warren; m. 9 Aug. 1864, Lucy A., dau. of Elbridge G. and Harriet (Bradbury) Stone of Hanover, N. H. He is a blacksmith in Bradford, Vt. Children:

1 Lettie Stone, b. 1 March 1867.
2 Elbridge Gerry, b. 12 July 1868.
3 John Edward, b. 12 Dec. 1871.

2 Emily Alice, b. 8 Aug. 1845, in Newbury, Vt.; m. 5 Jan. 1865, Edward Underhill.
3 Caroline Ellen, b. 9 Nov. 1847, in Bradford, Vt.; m. 9 Nov. 1865, Israel N. Webster.
4 John Erving, b. 2 July 1850, in Piermont; m. 18 Nov. 1869, Luna A., dau. of Luther W. and Julia A. (Chase) Mead. He is in the blacksmith business in company with his eldest brother, and is also in the livery business in the same place. Child:

1 Alice May, b. 25 April 1880.

5 Mary Naomi, b. 30 March 1854; d. 6 April 1856.
6 Elmer Prescott, b. 11 April 1861.

4 Walter, born 29 July 1826; m. 1st, 20 July 1847, Sarah Jane, dau. of Geo. and —— (Merrill) Bixby; (died 12 Feb. 1860); 2d, his brother Hazen's daughter Lucaby. He is a blacksmith and farmer, occupying his father's homestead in Warren. Children, all by his first wife:

1 Amanda Jane, born 16 April 1849; m. George W. Libby, her cousin.
2 Elizabeth Ann, b. 27 Oct. 1855; m. Charles E. Batchelder; died after seven months, in May, 1870.
3 Sarah Luella, b. 28 Sept. 1857; m. Benjamin F. Page of Stratford.
4 Walter Scott, b. 25 Jan. 1859; died aged three years.

5 Mary, b. 26 Oct. 1830; m. John Ames.

1-2-3-1-2-2

Nathaniel P. Libby, born in Landaff, N. H., 2 March 1795; married Nancy Abbott. He grew up in Warren, N. H., and is now a farmer there.

He has a son:

1 Ezra, born 1827; lives in Warren.

1-2-3-1-2-3

John W. Libby, born in Landaff, N. H., 19 June 1797; married Betsey Merrill. He was reared in Warren, and has always been a farmer there. His wife died 8 April 1879.

Children, all born in Warren:

1 Samuel Merrill, born 8 Sept. 1827; m. 17 June 1855, Ann, dau. of Henry and Hannah (Whiteman) Albert of Eaton, N. H. He was engaged in milling and farming until 1870, and has since been employed by the B. L. & M. R. R. as bridge carpenter. Children:
  1 Abbie A., b. 9 July 1857, in Warren, N. H.
  2 Lena G., b. 4 Sept. 1876, in Wentworth, N. H.
2 Ezra Bartlett, married Maria, dau. of Benjamin Page of Warren. He is a farmer and hunter, and lives on the homestead on which he first settled, in Warren. No children.
3 Mary Merrill, died unmarried.
4 Robert Merrill, married Elizabeth Page, a sister of Maria. He is a farmer, occupying his father's homestead. Child:
  1 Ralph, b. 12 Oct. 1869.
5 Hannah Merrill, married Nicholas Whiteman.
6 Benjamin Merrill, b. 10 Oct. 1835; married Sarah A. Eastman. He has been engaged in farming and milling. He now lives in Wentworth, and is one of the selectmen of that town. Children:
  1 Fred E., b. 28 Nov. 1865, in Warren.
  2 Walter S., b. 11 June 1868, in Warren.
7 George Washington, married Emerenzo French of Haverhill, N. H. He has been for the most part a farmer, and now lives in Wentworth. Children: (among others?):
  1 ——, married Edwin Sherwell of Gilford, N. H.
  2 Sadie,
  3 Belle, } died in three weeks, in 1877, of diphtheria.
  4 Elmer,
  5 son, b. 30 Sept. 1881.
8 Judith Merrill, married William Alvah Foster of Wentworth.

1-2-3-1-2-5

EZRA BARTLETT LIBBY, born in Warren, N. H., 24 Oct. 1801; married first, 23 Aug. 1831, MARY GIBBIN HAMAN, daughter of Joseph and Sarah Haman of Compton; (died 23 Oct. 1849); second, 30 Sept. 1852, MRS. EVA K. CUMMINGS, daughter of Francis and Betsey Sindier. He is a shoemaker and farmer in his native town.

Children, all born in Warren, by first wife:

1 Mary Jane, b. 25 June 1832; died 22 Aug. 1834.
2 Joseph Haman, b. 31 July 1834; died 17 Aug. 1834.
3 Mary Jane, b. 25 June 1835; died 7 Sept. 1837.
4 Ezra Walton, b. 27 Sept. 1837; m. 25 May 1865, Ann Elizabeth, dau. of Robert Henry and Christiana Arabella (Conway) Stowe of Prince George County, Va. He served three years in the 12th N. H. Vol. Since the war he has been for the most part employed in hotels, but for the last two years has been a watchman in the U. S. treasury dept. at Washington. Children:
  1 Gertrude Bell, b. 10 Feb. 1871, in Manchester, N. H.
  2 Ann Elizabeth, b. 9 Oct. 1872; died 22 Jan. 1873.
  3 Eddie Walter, b. 5 Sept. 1874.
  4 Hartley Dame, b. 7 Oct. 1878, in the District of Columbia.
5 Nancy Judson, b. 3 Dec. 1839; died in Boston, 3 Jan. 1875; unm.
6 Sarah Jane, b. 4 Feb. 1844; m. Harry Chamberlain.
7 Russell, b. 27 Oct. 1846; died 15 Jan. 1849.

By second wife:

8 Russell, b. 4 Feb. 1854.

9 Albion Wilbur, b. 4 May 1857; m. 6 Sept. 1876, Rachel, dau. of David and Sally Steward of Camden, Me. He is a farmer in Warren. Children:
   1 L. G., b. 17 Jan. 1878.
   2 Silas M., b. 23 Jan. 1880; died 12 March 1880.

1-4-1-4-1-1

William Libby, born in Falmouth, Me., 6 Dec. 1786; married, 14 Nov. 1809, Hannah Gould, daughter of Moses Gould of New Portland.

For some years after his marriage, he divided his time between Windham and Gray. In 1820, he moved from Gray to Windham, and settled on the farm afterward occupied by his son Arthur. In 1832, he removed to Falmouth, onto the farm that his son Edward now occupies. He died with his son Fernald, who was then living in the last mentioned town, 10 March 1861. His widow died in Portland, 14 Dec. 1864.

Children:

1 Abigail, b. 1 June 1810; m. Joseph Knight.
2 Arthur, b. 12 Jan. 1812; m. 28 Feb. 1836, Nancy Ann, dau. of Samuel and Mary (Leighton) Cobb. At the time of his marriage, he settled on the farm now occupied by his widow, and there lived until his death, 22 June 1880. Children:
   1 Sarah Ann, b. 9 Nov. 1837; m. Daniel Libby, 1-4-1-4-1-4-11.
   2 Frances Maria, born 27 Jan. 1840; m. 9 March 1858, Royal W. Wentworth.
   3 Phebe Louisa, b. 6 Jan. 1842; m. 9 Jan. 1863, Thomas Fields.
   4 Mary Elizabeth, b. 26 Dec. 1843; m. 3 Sept. 1863, Charles H. Leighton.
   5 Cynthia Jane, b. 7 Feb. 1846; d. 1873: unm.
   6 Mahala Wilson, b. 14 Nov. 1849; m. 23 Nov. 1872, Charles W. Wentworth.
   7 Lucy Ellen, b. 8 Nov. 1852; unm.
   8 Sophronia, b. 10 Feb. 1857; d. 28 Aug. 1859.
   9 William Edward, b. 4 July 1859; unm.
3 William, b. 13 Oct. 1813; never married. He lived in Falmouth on the farm now occupied by his brother Edward, until one year before his death, when he went to Portland. He died there 27 Dec. 1858.
4 Elizabeth, b. 4 Oct. 1815; d. 19 Nov. 1831.
5 Moses Gould, b. 27 July 1817; m. May, 1848, Eunice M., daughter of Rea and Harriet (Field) Elder. In his younger days he worked in stone quarries. Soon after his marriage he bought a farm above Windham Center, and lived there until 1871, when he settled on the farm he now occupies. Children:
   1 Preston Day, b. 7 Nov. 1848; m. 18 Nov. 1874, Clara R., dau. of Joseph and Lydia D. (Binford) Wescott. Children:
      1 Fred Stephen, b. 27 Sept. 1875, in Windham.
      2 Mabel Elizabeth, b. 21 Oct. 1877, in Windham.
   2 Charles Granville, b. 26 Dec. 1849; m. 26 Nov. 1878, Nancy A., dau. of Smith and Sarah Adams (Skillings) Hadlock of Peak's Island, Portland. Son:
      1 Melville Everett, b. 6 Nov. 1879, in Portland.
   3 Jason Hanson, b. 28 Aug. 1852; d. 5 March 1872.
   4 Angeline Smith, b. 3 May 1854; unm.
   5 Marcia Ellen, b. 18 May 1856; d. 6 March 1872.
   6 Elverton Crosman, b. 15 Jan. 1858; unm.
   7 George Dana, b. 23 May 1860.
   8 Herbert Clarkson, b. 9 Aug. 1862.

9 Cyrus Almon, b. 5 May 1865.
10 Frederick S., b. 1 Aug. 1867; d. 8 March 1872.
6 Asa, b. 9 Oct. 1819; m. 18 Nov. 1844, Martha Libby, 1-4-1-4-1-3-4. He is a farmer. He has lived in many places in his native locality. He now lives in Windham. Children:
1 Newell, b. 6 April 1844, in Windham; d. 12 Oct. 1849.
2 Salome Ann, b. 10 Dec. 1845, in Limington; d. 26 June 1854.
3 Sylvanus Prince, b. 28 Feb. 1848, in Falmouth; d. 10 Sept. 1857.
4 Alfred Allen, b. 10 Sept. 1850, in Limington; unm. He is a carpenter in Portland.
5 Edward, b. 2 April 1853, in Windham; m. 24 March 1877, Eunice, dau. of Sarah Jane (Libby) Black, 1-4-1-4-1-3-5. He is a farmer and peddler in Cumberland. Child:
1 Oscar Alfred, b. 1 Nov. 1879, in Falmouth.
6 Salome Ann, b. 9 Sept. 1855; m. Bela L. Black.
7 Martha Ellen, b. 24 Nov. 1858; d. 28 March 1859.
8 Martha Ellen, b. 21 June 1861, in New Gloucester; m. 3 July 1880, Clarence E. Lowell.
7 Mary Jane, b. 27 Jan. 1822; m. 9 Nov. 1845, Moses Elliot.
8 Salome, b. 16 March 1824; m. 12 June 1847, Alfred R. Allen of Gray. He was killed by an explosion in the powder mills in Windham, 6 May 1856. Only child:
1 William Alfred (Allen), b. 8 May 1849, in Falmouth; m. 15 Aug. 1867, Kate W., dau. of John and Kate (McDonald) Carle of Eastport. He is a stair-builder. He has worked as journeyman, but is now in business in Portland. Children:
1 Anna Bell (Allen), b. 26 Dec. 1868, in Portland.
2 William Fernald (Allen), b. 30 Nov. 1870, in Marblehead, Mass.
3 Emma Ada Rogers (Allen), b. 30 April 1872, in Boston.
4 Nellie (Allen), b. 1 July, d. Sept., 1874, in Portland.
5 George Bartlett (Allen), b. Sept. 1875.
6 Harry Frederick (Allen), b. Oct. 1876.
7 Benjamin Franklin (Allen), b. 8 Nov. 1877.
8 Eva May (Allen), b. 4 Nov. 1879; d. 13 Feb. 1880.
9 Lucy Ann, b. 6 April 1826; m. Zacheus O. Lambert.
10 Edward Gould, b. 2 Aug. 1828; m. 1st, 10 Nov. 1854, Mary Elizabeth, dau. of John and Frances (Cash) Williams of Portland; (died Feb. 1862, in Portland); 2d, 25 June 1863, Sarah J., dau. of Neal and Margaret (McLellan) McDonald of Nova Scotia. When twenty-three, he went to Portland and learned the blacksmith trade with the Portland Co. Except two years spent in Dunkirk, N. Y., he was in the employ of that company until 1873, when he settled on the farm he now occupies. Children:
1 Clara Ella, b. 12 Feb. 1865, in Portland.
2 Louisa Isabel, b. 6 Jan. 1867, in Dunkirk, N. Y.
3 Mary Elizabeth, b. 1 Feb. 1869, in Portland.
11 Hannah, b. 31 Jan. 1831; m. 1st, 8 Nov. 1852, Alexander Bartlett; 2d, 8 Nov. 1862, James Burns.
12 Joseph Gould, b. 22 Feb. 1835; m. 7 Jan. 1854, Helen M., dau. of Charles and Judith (Wallace) Tukey of Portland. He learned the carpenter's trade in Portland, and was afterward in business in Chelsea, Mass., and later in Portland. He lived a number of years on a farm in New Gloucester. In 1878 he settled on the farm he now occupies, in Falmouth. He is a member of the Methodist Church, and superintendent of the sabbath-school. Children:
1 Maria Josephine, b. 4 May 1855; m. 30 Aug. 1871, Willis E. Chase.
2 Charles Gardner, b. 4 July 1858; m. 1st, 24 Sept. 1877, Alice M., dau. of Seth Snow; (died Jan. 1879); 2d, 9 Nov. 1879, Emily F., dau. of Chas. H. and Miranda (Nutting) Blanchard. He is a carpenter, and lives in Falmouth, near his father. Child:

1 Charles Herbert, b. 26 April 1878, in Portland.
3 Joseph Gould, b. 14 April 1861, in South Malden, Mass.
4 Edward Francis, b. 8 Aug. 1863; d. 17 June 1865.
5 Anna Kimball, b. 10 April 1865; d. 21 April 1866.
6 Anna Kimball, b. 9 July 1867, in Portland.
7 Edward Francis, b. 10 March 1870, in New Gloucester.
8 Helen Maria, b. 22 March 1872.
9 William Arthur, b. 31 March 1874, in Portland.

13 Fernald, b. 20 Jan. 1838; m. 12 Jan. 1865, Lucy E., dau. of Eliza Ann (Libby) Skillings, 11-7-2-6-4-1. He is a carpenter in Dover, N. H. Children:
1 Ella Gertrude, b. 29 May 1866, in Portland.
2 Cora Eliza, b. 12 Oct. 1868, in Portland.
3 Edward Thomas, b. 29 June 1872; d. 4 Feb. 1876.

1-4-1-4-1-3

Gideon Libby, born in Falmouth, Me., 2 Dec. 1791; married, 21 Jan. 1813, Jane Prince, daughter of Sylvanus and Sarah (Boston) Prince of North Yarmouth. He was a farmer. He owned and occupied a number of farms in Windham and Gray, and spent his latter days in Windham, where he died, 12 Aug. 1870. His widow died in Falmouth, 21 May 1877.

Children:

1 Samuel, b. 21 Nov. 1813; m. 1838, Keziah, dau. of James and Sarah (Pride) Stuart. He settled on his grandfather's homestead, and lived there until his death, 19 April 1866. Children:
1 Sarah Jane, b. 9 Sept. 1839; m. 9 June 1860, Oliver Hanson.
2 Ann Maria, b. 18 Sept. 1842; d. 29 Jan. 1844.
3 Ann Maria, b. 18 Feb. 1844; d. 7 May 1863.
4 Patia McIntosh, b. 19 March 1849; d. 10 Jan. 1866.
5 Frances Ellen, b. 3 Sept. 1851; m. 17 Feb. 1872, Major H. Merrill.
6 Charles Addison, born 31 July 1855; d. 6 Sept. 1870. He was struck by cars in driving a hayrack across a track in Westbrook.
7 James William, b. 14 Jan. 1857; unm.

2 James, b. 19 Nov. 1815; m. 16 June 1837, Mary Libby, 1-4-1-4-1-4-1. He is a farmer at Windham Center. Children:
1 Samuel, born 2 March 1838; m. 6 March 1862, Mary Elizabeth, dau. of Samuel and Betsey (Johnson) Leighton. He is a farmer, and has lived on many farms in Windham, Falmouth, Westbrook, and where he now lives, Cumberland. Child:
1 Louisa Mary, b. 23 Jan. 1863, in Cumberland.
2 Elias Humphrey, born 27 Jan. 1840. He was of Co. H, 17th Maine, and died at Fredericksburgh.
3 Richard Lamb, b. 16 Feb. 1842; m. 25 Oct. 1868, his cousin Anna, dau. of Hulda (Libby) Black. He lived on various farms in Windham and Falmouth until 1875, when he bought the farm he now occupies, in Gorham. He served three years in the 17th Maine. Children:
1 Alton Brackett, b. 8 Oct. 1869, in Windham.
2 Harland Carter, b. 11 Oct. 1872, in Windham.
3 Walter, b. 19 Nov. 1875, in Gorham.
4 Richard Everett, b. 24 March 1878.
5 ——, b. 18 Aug. 1880.
4 Henry Lewis, b. 8 Nov. 1844; unm. He lives in Boston, Mass.
5 Laura Etta, b. 19 May 1847; m. 27 June 1864, Uriah Cobb.
6 Hannah Elizabeth, b. 14 Jan. 1850; m. 25 May 1867, Isaac Cobb.
7 Elnora, b. 28 Sept. 1852; d. 17 April 1878; unm.

8 James Dow, b. 8 Feb. 1855; d. 22 April 1864.
9 Charles Clarence, b. 24 April 1857; m. 4 Oct. 1879, Sarah, dau. of Orin and Sarah (Allen) Moses of Standish. Child:
1 Fanny Beatrice, b. 6 May 1880, in Windham.

3 Hulda, b. 1 Sept. 1818; m. 21 April 1844, Charles Black.
4 Martha, b. 21 Jan. 1821; m. 5 Nov. 1843, Asa Libby, 1-4-1-4-1-1-6.
5 Sarah Jane, b. 6 June 1823; m. 5 Nov. 1843, Joab Black.
6 Peter, b. 14 March 1826; m. 22 Jan. 1852, Lucy A., dau. of Richard and Lucy M. (Webber) Webber of Great Chebeague Island, Casco Bay. He is a farmer in his native town. Children:
1 Charles, b. 23 June 1853; d. 23 Oct. 1853.
2 Marcena Boody, b. 24 Sept. 1854; m. 29 March 1874, Amos L. Field.
3 Millard Filmore, b. 26 Dec.; d. 27 Dec., 1855.
4 Edwin Harmon, b. 11 Nov. 1857; unm.
5 Emma Elvira, b. 3 March 1860; unm.
6 William Fremont, b. 26 Jan. 1862.
7 Delia Ann, b. 13 Jan. 1864.
8 Samuel Prince, b. 9 July 1866.
9 Freeland Staples, b. 24 Oct. 1868.

7 Bela Prince, b. 25 March 1829; m. 6 May 1853, Mary S., dau. of Rea and Harriet (Fields) Elder. He served nine months in Co. F, 25th Maine. He lived in various places in the vicinity of Windham until 1870, when he bought the farm on which he has since lived. Children:
1 Lucius Prince, b. 3 April 1854; unm.
2 Marshall, b. 19 July 1857; unm.
3 Sumner, b. 1 April 1860.

8 Gideon, b. 30 Dec. 1831; m. 25 Dec. 1854, Betsey Elder, sister of his brother's wife. He lived with his father until one year before his death, which took place 5 Oct. 1870. His family soon after settled on the place he now occupies. Children:
1 Harriet Ellen, b. 28 Oct. 1855; unm.
2 Orren Wilson, b. 9 Aug. 1858; unm.
3 Flora Belle, b. 23 Feb. 1865.

1-4-1-4-1-4

Isaac Libby, born in Falmouth, Me., 1 April 1794; married, 16 March 1817, Sally Humphrey, daughter of Betsey (Libby) Humphrey, 1-4-1-4-4. After his marriage he lived three years in Gray, four years in Westbrook, and then settled on the farm in Windham which he has since occupied. His wife died 29 May 1858.

Children:

1 Mary, married James Libby, 1-4-1-4-1-3-2.
2 Betsey, b. 1821; m. 25 Nov. 1849, Charles Deering.
3 Catherine, m. John Cobb of Windham.
4 Lucinda, m. 18 Nov. 1848, Samuel Cobb.
5 Elbridge, b. 14 Jan. 1827; d. June 1827.
6 Asenath H., b. March 1828; m. 7 Aug. 1853, Wm. F. Sawyer.
7 Susan, born Oct. 1832; m. 28 Nov. 1852, Joseph West.
8 Isaac, b. 13 Feb. 1834; m. 2 Jan. 1859, Mary A., dau. of James and Huldah (Cobb) Elliott. When he was married, he bought a farm in the east part of Windham, and there lived until 1874, when he bought his present homestead. Children:
1 Flora Ella, b. 4 Aug. 1859; d. 17 Oct. 1860.
2 Thomas Orin, b. 15 Feb. 1862.
3 Uriah Cobb, b. 18 March 1864.
4 Abram Ingersoll, b. 20 Jan. 1867.
5 Ethel Linda, b. 21 Feb. 1877.

9 Joseph, b. 12 May 1838; m. 4 July 1862, Eliza, dau. of Michael and Jane Cash of Portland. He served nine months in Co. F, 25th Maine Vol. He carries on his father's homestead. Children:
 1 Frank Fessenden, b. 5 March 1863.
 2 Ella May, b. 14 Nov. 1872.
10 Caroline, died in infancy.
11 Daniel, married, 24 Nov. 1867, Sarah Ann Libby, 1-4-1-4-1-1-2-1. He lives at Cumberland Mills, Westbrook.

1-4-1-4-1-5

Asa Libby, born in Falmouth, Me., 15 June 1797; married Rachel Coombs. He removed east and lived in many towns. His death occurred in Bradford, 1 Jan. 1874, and his widow died in the same place, 15 Sept. 1878.

Their children were:

1 Mary E., b. 28 Nov. 1818, in Holden; m. James Savage.
2 Asa, born in Anson; m. Deborah Carleton. She died in New York; it is not known whether or not he is living.
3 Arthur, b. 12 May 1822; m. 16 Sept. 1845, Cynthia Ann, dau. of Zenas and Sarah Littlefield (Spencer) Drinkwater of Orneville. He settled in Bangor soon after his marriage, and became a lumber surveyor. His death took place 19 Feb. 1880. He was a member of the Freewill Baptist Church. Children:
 1 Almeda Elizabeth, b. 3 Jan. 1848, in Orneville; m. Richard S. Davis. Child:
  1 Charles Franklin (Davis), b. 8 Feb. 1871.
 2 George Henry, b. 17 March 1852, in Bangor; m. Emma M., dau. of Luke W. and Abbie M. (Dudley) Page of Orono. Child:
  1 Flora May, b. 27 April 1880.
 3 Charles William, b. 13 Aug. 1854; m. Ada Delphine, dau. of Aaron D. and Mary (Colbath) Watson of Bangor. Child:
  1 Arthur Aaron, b. 27 Feb. 1877; died 8 Oct. 1878.
 4 Arthur Franklin, b. 30 Dec. 1856; m. Mary Ann, dau. of James and Sarah Jane (Tate) Sullivan of Bangor. Children:
  1 Frank Allen, b. 31 Dec. 1876.
  2 George Edward, b. 23 Aug. 1878.
  3 Arthur, b. 17 Aug. 1880.
 5 Zenas Allen, b. 21 May 1859.
 6 Seth Drinkwater, b. 23 Dec. 1860.
 7 Flora May, b. 21 Dec. 1862; d. 31 July 1867.
 8 Cynthia Ann, b. 22 Aug. 1866.
4 Rachel, died in Bradford, unmarried.
5 Raymon, b. 31 July 1827; m. 14 Oct. 1847, Eliza A., dau. of Joseph and Eliza (Wolse) Hall of Orneville. He has lived in Bradford ever since his marriage. Children:
 1 Sarah E., b. 23 Sept. 1848; m. 7 Feb. 1874, Seth L. King.
 2 Charles O., b. 5 Nov. 1832; d. 5 May 1853.
 3 Abbie J., b. 11 Feb. 1854; d. 11 March 1854.
 4 Arasina H., b. 14 Jan. 1856.
 5 Ida M., b. 20 Dec. 1859; m. 7 Oct. 1876, Manley G. Brackett. Child:
  1 Elwood M. (Brackett), b. 18 June 1879.
 6 Addie A., b. 11 Jan. 1861.
 7 Daniel H., b. 28 June 1873.
6 Almeda, married in Orneville, John Moses.
7 Adeline, b. 1 Aug. 1831; m. 22 Oct. 1851, George W. Wentworth; died Feb. 1857.
8 Merrit, b. 29 Nov. 1833; whereabouts unknown.
9 James, b. 12 Sept. 1836; died 4 July 1838.
10 Abby R., b. 29 April 1839; m. William C. Davis.

1-4-1-4-1-6

Peter Libby, born in Falmouth, Me., 1 March 1800; married, 18 June 1826, Ann Knight, daughter of Elijah and Elizabeth (Hustin) Knight. A year before his marriage, he bought the place which his widow occupies, and there lived until his death, 25 May 1867.

Children:

1 Lewis, b. 28 Jan., d. 11 Dec., 1827.
2 Lorenzo Dow, b. 29 Sept. 1829; m. 23 Feb. 1852, Elmira M., dau. of George and Elizabeth (Haines) Field. He lived on part of his father's homestead until 1862, and then bought the farm he now occupies. Children:
  1 Charles Thomas, b. 28 April 1852.
  2 Lizzie Ann, b. 16 Dec. 1853; m. Frank L. Rounds.
  3 Harris Burnham, b. 14 Nov. 1856; d. 14 Nov. 1867.
  4 Aretas Pratt, b. 11 June 1860; unm.
  5 Cora Zelora, b. 9 July 1861; d. 1 Dec. 1864.
  6 Abby Helen, born 17 Dec. 1863; m. 28 July 1879, Edward Manchester.
  7 Christania Rowe, b. 8 March 1866.
  8 Hattie Manchester, b. 29 April 1867.
  9 George Bowers, b. 11 Feb. 1869.
  10 Sadie Morrill, b. 7 Sept. 1872.
  11 Eben Herbert, b. 14 Aug. 1874; d. 14 Sept. 1875.
3 Lewis, b. 12 April 1831; d. 6 Sept. 1840.
4 Minerva Ann, b. 27 Nov. 1833; m. 25 Dec. 1851, Jonah Austin.
5 Daniel Knight, b. 16 Nov. 1835; d. 18 June 1838.
6 ——, } twins, b. } d. 7 March 1837.
7 ——, } 2 March 1837; } d. 13 March 1837.
8 Mary Elizabeth, b. 14 Feb. 1838; unm.
9 Margaret, b. 9 March 1840; unm.
10 Lewis, b. 6 July 1843; d. 9 Oct. 1843.
11 Charles Addison, b. 12 March 1846; d. 27 March 1849.
12 Thomas Merrill, b. 6 Dec. 1847; d. 9 July 1851.

1-4-1-4-1-10

Lewis Libby, born 20 Oct. 1811, in Windham, Me.; married, 12 Nov. 1833, Eliza Knight, sister of his brother's wife. He lived in many places in Windham, and followed many callings, until 1866, when he bought the farm he now occupies, and has since confined himself to farming.

Children:

1 Elbridge, b. 21 April 1834; m. 1st, 10 Jan. 1861, Laura Ellen, dau. of Hiram and Susan (Green) Varney; (died Sept. 1861); 2d, 20 March 1864, Olive A., dau. of Silas and Eliza Ann (Dolly) Lamb. He served through the war in Co. K, 9th Maine. Children, by first wife:
  1 Laura Jane, b. 9 June 1861; lives with her father's parents.

  By second wife:

  2 Silas, b. about 1867.
  3 William, b. about 1872.
2 Elizabeth Maxwell, b. 12 May 1835; m. 10 Sept. 1854, John Reed Rogers.
3 Arthur, b. 6 Feb. 1837; d. 7 June 1837.
4 ——, born and died 7 April 1838.

5 Arthur, b. 1 May 1839; d. 28 Feb. 1865; unm. He went out in Co. D, 3d Vermont Vol. He served out his enlistment, but died of chronic diarrhea, soon after his return home.
6 Stephen Huston, b. 27 May 1841. He was of Co. K, 9th Maine, and was killed at Fort Sumter, July 1863.
7 Margaret Knight, b. 18 Dec. 1843; m. James H. Allen.
8 Daniel Knight, b. 14 Aug. 1845; d. 7 April 1846.
9 Martha Ellen, b. 21 June 1848; m. Melville C. Irish.
10 Lewis, b. 28 Oct. 1850; m. 5 Jan. 1878, Harriet J., dau. of Peter and Lucy A. (Page) Whitney. He is a farmer and teamster. No children.
11 Catherine, b. 10 June 1854; m. 1st, 11 Nov. 1871, Charles M. Manchester; 2d, Rensselaer C. Kilborn.

1-4-1-4-2-3

Andrew Libby, born in Gray, Me., 15 April 1790; married Nancy Pulsifer, daughter of Ephraim and Betsey (Gilbert) Pulsifer of Gloucester, Mass. He served a seven years' apprenticeship at the carpenter's trade, and that was ever after his chief occupation, although while in Poland he lived on a farm. He lived in Poland after his marriage until 1850, and then removed to Auburn, where he lived until his death, 30 Aug. 1874. His widow survives.

Children:

1 Julia A., b. 16 Aug. 1820; m. John C. Moore of Greene.
2 Nancy, b. 4 Nov. 1821; died in 1824.
3 Gilman Gilbert, b. 12 Dec. 1822; m. 1st, Dec. 1844, Margaret, dau. of Edward and Rebecca (Whitman) Lothrop of Buckfield; 2d, his cousin Martha, dau. of Ephraim and Lucy (Davis) Pulsifer of Poland. He is a shoemaker. He lived in Auburn until 1879, and then removed to Boston. Children, by first wife:
  1 Nancy Jane, b. 10 May 1846; d. 17 Dec. 1863.
  2 Carroll Wesley, b. 6 Sept. 1848; m. 1st, 17 Oct. 1869, Alice B., dau. of George G. and Betsey B. (Bonney) Chaffin of Sumner, Me.; 2d, Almie L., dau. of Francis L. and Lucinda E. (Walling) Hyde of Randolph, Vt. He was engaged as shoemaker, spool-maker, horse-car driver, and nursery salesman until his second marriage, and then settled on a farm in Sumner. Child:
    1 Lydia Jane, b. 25 Dec. 1870; d. 25 June 1876.

  By second wife:

  3 Annie, died very young.
  4 Nellie Gilbert, b. 1862.
  5 Mattie, b. 1868.
4 Clara B., b. 27 Sept. 1824; m. 27 April 1853, Joseph Small.
5 Rachel Pulsifer, b. 1 Jan. 1827; d. 21 April 1872; unm.
6 Sophia M., b. 8 Feb. 1828; m. 1st, Wm. B. Patterson of Dover, N. H.; 2d, —— Gillis of Halifax, N. S.
7 Eunice, b. 9 Sept. 1829; m. Charles Johnson of Dover.

1-4-1-4-2-5

Elijah Libby, born in Gray, Me., 20 Aug. 1794; married, 25 Oct. 1821, in Greenwood, Lydia Howe, daughter of Isaac and Rachel (Merrill) Howe of Ipswich, Mass. He was in the war of 1812. Soon after the close of the war he settled in Greenwood, where he married, and ever afterward resided. He was, like his father, a farmer and mechanic. He was a member of the Methodist Church, and at one time held a commission as a justice of the peace. His wife died 16 June 1871. He died 29 Oct. 1880.

Children:

1 Henry. b. 16 June 1822; m. 1st, Olive, daughter of Eunice (Libby) Waymouth, 1-4-1-4-2-4; (died 4 May 1864); 2d, Ann P. (Jordan) Swift of Greenwood. He lived in Molunkus and Mattawamkeag until 1863, and has since lived in Greenwood. He has been employed in shingle-making, spool-making, etc. Children, all by his first wife:
  1 James, m. S. J. Morgan of Bethel. He served an enlistment in the 16th Me. Vol., and is now a spool-maker at Locke's Mills, Greenwood. He has two children.
  2 Richard, enlisted in the 16th Me. Vol., 2 Sept. 1864, and died of measles, 29 Jan. 1865.
  3 Eunice, unmarried.
  4 Lydia, married George Johnson of Boston.
  5 Danville, born about 1857.
  6 Olive, b. 23 April 1864; died in August following.

2 David N., born 15 Nov. 1823; m. Sarah T., dau. of Joseph Moody; died 30 Dec. 1853, in Canton, Me. He was an overseer on the railroad. Children:
  1 Ellen.
  2 Winfield Scott, b. Jan. 1852; died 7 Dec. 1853.

3 Danville J., b. 6 Sept. 1826; m. 12 Dec. 1852, Esther Chase, dau. of Edmund and Mary Ann (Chase) Bowker of Woodstock. He learned the carpenter's trade, but has been, since 1854, a farmer in Woodstock, Me., of which town he has four times served as selectman. Children:
  1 George E., b. 16 Sept. 1853, in Paris, Me.; d. 13 April 1854.
  2 Herbert J., b. 3 April 1856; unm.
  3 Mary L., } twins, b. }
  4 Marion, } 12 April 1860; } d. 5 Sept. 1860.

4 Andrew J., b. 1 Sept. 1828; m. Joanna C., dau. of Samuel Rand of Lisbon. He is a carriage-maker in Lewiston. No children.

5 Joseph W., b. 29 Oct. 1830; m. 1st, Mary Gilchrist; 2d, Susan Barker; died in March 1858, in Greenwood. He was a carpenter. Children:
  1 Jennie, by first wife; lived, when last heard from, in Ryegate, Vt.
  2 Lydia V., by second wife; lived, when last heard from, with her mother in Massachusetts.

6 Louisa B., b. 26 May 1835; m. —— Cameron; died in Cleveland, O.

7 Lydia J., married, in Greenwood, Edward Hand.

8 George W., died 4 Feb. 1862, in Greenwood; unm. He was a member of Co. I, 17th Maine.

9 Elijah, b. 10 May 1839; m. 18 Oct. 1865, Mrs. Maria M. Howe, dau. of John and Hannah (Bartlett) Morgan of Greenwood. He is a carpenter, living in Greenwood. He was a member of the 10th Me. Vol. Children:
  1 Georgie Etta, b. 14 July 1866, in Greenwood.
  2 Laura Bell, b. 13 Jan. 1868, in Bethel.
  3 Albert Ellsworth, b. 2 Nov. 1869, in Greenwood; d. 4 May 1871.
  4 Louis Napoleon, b. 16 Jan. 1871.
  5 Ernest Eugene, b. 9 Oct. 1875, in Bethel.
  6 Olla May, b. 16 June 1875, in Greenwood.
  7 Dellie Ellsworth, b. 5 Feb. 1876.
  8 Addie Medora, b. 17 April 1879.
  9 David D., b. 8 Nov. 1880.

10 Charlotte, died at the age of 18 years.

11 Mary S., died at the age of three years.

12 Aurelia S., m. Orrin Bisbee; died Nov. 1864.

1-4-1-4-2-6

Ebenezer Libby, born in Gray, Me., 2 June 1796; married first, 30 Nov. 1820, Sarah S. Nason of Freeport; second, 16 Nov. 1824, Louisa Winslow, daughter of John and Sally (Baker) Winslow of Mercer.

At the time of his first marriage he lived in North Yarmouth. From his second marriage until 1845, he lived in Mercer, and then went west. He died in Forestville, Iowa, 24 Nov. 1865. He was a member of the Baptist Church. His wife died 25 April 1863.

Children, all by his second wife:

1 Sally S., b. 23 Oct. 1826; m. Daniel Briggs.
2 Olive J., b. 14 Jan. 1828; m. James Condill.
3 Lorenzo D. [Rev.], b. 15 May 1830; m. 25 Feb. 1855, Lydia R., dau. of Russell and Hannah (Barker) Coburn of Parkman. He is a blacksmith in Brighton, where he is also postmaster. He was a preacher of the Calvin Baptist order from 1867 to 1875, and since 1877 has been a Christian Baptist preacher. He served two years in the 2d Maine Cavalry. Children:
 1 Everett R., b. 1 Dec. 1857, in Mount Vernon; unm.
 2 Anna M., b. 10 May 1863, in New Sharon; unm.
4 Cyrus D., b. 14 May 1832; m. Elmira Banester. He was a farmer. He died 12 Jan. 1860, in Forestville. He was a member of the Baptist Church. Child:
 1 Louisa, b. 6 Feb. 1857.
5 Ebenezer, b. 15 March 1834; d. 11 Aug. 1863, in Natchez, Miss.; unm. He was a private in Co. E, 3d Iowa Vol. He was a member of the Baptist Church.
6 Louisa, b. 7 April 1837; m. 1st, 7 Feb. 1867, Louis Shackley; (divorced in 1868); 2d, 11 March 1873, Peter H. Sweeney. He died 16 Nov. 1878. During the war she was a nurse in the Union hospitals.
7 Hiram S., b. 15 Nov. 1839; m. Alice Roberts. He was a member of Co. B. 21st Iowa Vol. In 1866 he removed to Minnesota, where he was engaged in thrashing. About 1878 he removed to Bozeman, Mont., and started a sawmill. Children:
 1 Charles, b. 15 March 1868.
 2 Alice, b. 10 June 1873.
8 Julia A., b. 14 March 1841; m. 1st, 10 Nov. 1862, Henry Small; 2d, 4 Nov. 1866, Benjamin Fish.
9 Lorinda, b. 23 June 1851; m. Henry Steele; died in Manchester, Iowa, 10 May 1881.

1-4-1-4-5-3

John Libby, born in Gray, Me., 15 July 1794; married Polly Mills, daughter of William and Mary (Trefethen) Mills. He was a farmer in Belgrade until two years before his death, when he went to live with his son in Pittsfield, and there died, 28 June 1878. His wife died 26 Jan. 1876.

Children:

1 Eliza T., b. 1 Nov. 1819; m. H. M. Sawtelle.
2 Asa D., b. 10 June 1821; m. Clementine A. Stickney of Augusta. He is a horse dealer, now, or lately, living in Orono. Daughter:
 1 Clara A., b. 1861.
3 John H., b. 6 Nov. 1823; unm. He lived in Belgrade until 1873, and has since lived in Augusta.

4 Henry Augustus, b. 10 Feb. 1826; m. 2 Oct. 1853, Augusta J., dau. of John and Miriam B. (Kimball) Farnham of Pittsfield. From 1847 to 1854, he was a stage driver. He has since been, consecutively, in the livery business in Hampden, a hotel keeper in Cherryfield, a farmer in Pittsfield, and since 1868, a trader in the last mentioned town. Only child:
  1 Henry F., b. 2 Dec. 1862, in Pittsfield. He is in the drug business in Pittsfield.

5 Milton E., b. 12 Nov. 1829; m. 14 Oct. 1860, Abbie A., dau. of Asa and Mary (Dunn) Joy of Bath. He died 2 Feb. 1876, in Augusta, where his widow still lives. Children:
  1 Florence Gertrude, b. 17 July 1861.
  2 Edward Everett, b. 9 Aug. 1862.
  3 Horace Milton, b. 24 Jan. 1871.

6 Marcellus N., b. 20 Feb. 1833; m. Theresa M., dau. of David and Elizabeth (Getchell) Austin of Canterbury, Conn. He is a wood-turner in Weld, Me. Children:
  1 Grace A., b. 21 May 1866, in Farmington.
  2 Blanch G., b. 17 Aug. 1872, in Belgrade.

7 Barzilla M., b. 25 Oct. 1838; m. 2 Jan. 1870, Mary, dau. of F. L. and Sibyl F. (McKay) Jackson of Bangor. He died in Boston, Mass., 10 Jan. 1876. Child:
  1 Alice May, b. 15 Dec. 1871, in Bangor.

1-4-1-6-1-4

John Jay Libby, born in Gorham, Me., 28 May 1793; married, 1817, Sally Burbank, daughter of Ebenezer and Lucy (Robbins) Burbank of Campton, N. H. His minority was spent chiefly in Gorham and Cape Elizabeth. On becoming of age, he went to Thornton, N. H., where his sister was living. He lived in Thornton, Sandwich, and Campton until 1831, when he settled on a farm in Columbia, where he died, 15 Jan. 1856. His widow died 8 Sept. 1862.

Children:

1 Lucy Robbins, b. 2 March 1819, in Thornton; m. 10 Sept. 1845, her cousin, Benj. Irish.

2 Judith B., b. 16 July 1820; m. 9 Nov. 1837, Jonathan Dowling of Lowell, Mass.

3 Naomi, b. 11 May 1823; m. 4 Jan. 1843, Gideon Matthews.

4 Elizabeth, b. 12 July 1825, in Sandwich; m. 1 March 1845, Geo. H. Haines.

5 John Hanson, b. 23 Nov. 1827; m. 22 Sept. 1850, Catherine B., dau. of Samuel and Cynthia (Chandler) Titus of Columbia. He lived on his father's homestead in Columbia, except two years preceding his father's death, until 1866. He has since lived on the homestead farm of his wife's father. He is also engaged in the manufacture of potato starch. He has been selectman of Columbia several years. Child:
  1 Mary Ellen, b. 16 March 1861, in Columbia.

6 Lois Ann, b. 4 April 1830, in Campton; m. 4 April 1851, Jeremiah Swett.

7 William Burbank, b. 9 June 1835, in Columbia; m. 24 April 1860, Mary Jane, dau. of Caleb and Esther (Irish) Skillings of Gorham, Me. He is a farmer in Gorham. No children.

1-4-1-6-3-2

Hanson Libby, born in Danville, now Auburn, Me., 1796; married Polly Martin, daughter of John and Lydia (McKen-

Yours Truly.
Chas. E. Libby.

ney) Martin of Auburn. Soon after his marriage, he took up a farm in Monmouth, near Leeds Junction. There he lived until his last sickness, and then moved back to his native town, and there died, 26 July 1830. His widow returned after his death, and died 10 Aug. 1838.

Children:

1 Abner, b. 4 Sept. 1819. He had his name changed from Abner Libby to Irville Leslie. He is a Second Advent preacher in Newton Lower Falls, Mass.

2 Sewall Martin, b. 23 Sept. 1821; m. 1 July 1855, Mary B., dau. of Almira (Libby) Brown, 1-1-3-9-1-1. He is a shoemaker by trade. He lived for the most part in Wales and Pownal until 1865, when he removed to Saco, and opened a boarding-house, which he still continues. Children:
   1 Ida Cora, b. 28 Dec. 1856; d. 5 May 1873.
   2 Alfreda Brown, b. 17 Jan. 1860; unm.
   3 Irva Isabella, b 2 Jan. 1863.
   4 Alice May, b. 23 April 1865.

3 Eunice L., b. 15 March 1824; unm. She lives in Saco.

4 Dennis, b. 7 Jan. 1826; unm. He is a sailor.

5 Hanson, b. 1 May 182 ; lives in Franklin, Mass. He has had his name changed to Hanson L. Leslie.

1-4-1-6-3-6

CALEB LIBBY, born in Danville, Me., 10 May 1803; married LYDIA BRIGGS, daughter of Ezra and Betsey (Fickett) Briggs of Weymouth, Mass. He always lived on his father's homestead. He was an active member, and an officer of the M. E. Church. He died 17 April 1867. His wife died 19 April 1858.

Children, born in Danville, now Auburn:

1 Dennis Alvra, b. 12 Dec. 1838; m. 1st, 28 April 1867, Dolorous Frances, dau. of Lemuel and Mary (Prince) Rice of Durham; (died Feb. 1875, in Auburn); 2d, 25 Dec. 1876, Hannah G., dau. of Thomas and Lois (Goodrich) Butler of New Portland. He lived on the homestead farm all but the last eight years of his life; those were spent in one of the shoe factories in Auburn, his residence being for the most part in Lewiston, where he died, 18 Sept. 1880. He was a member of the M. E. Church. Children, all by his first wife:
   1 John Lemuel, b. 2 April 1868, in Durham.
   2 Edgar Harry, b. 2 Feb. 1870, in Durham.
   3 Maud, b. Feb., d. Aug., 1875, in Auburn.

2 Charles Ezra [Rev.], b. 14 Dec. 1844; m. 29 June 1867, Sarah Helen, dau. of Clement Jordan and Elizabeth Basto (Prince) Haskins of Durham. He was educated at the Edward Little Institute and Bangor Theological Seminary. In 1871, having already preached as supply several years, he joined the East Maine Conference of the M. E. Church, and has since served the following churches: Gilford, Lincoln, Brewer, Thomaston, Pittston, Rockport, and Camden, and is now pastor of the M. E. Church at Belfast. Children:
   1 Helen Chestina, b. 10 May 1868, in Auburn.
   2 Ruby Page, b. 1 Dec. 1873, in Brewer.
   3 May Lillian Blanche, b. 12 Dec. 1875, in Thomaston.

3 Caleb Cummings [M.D.], b. 25 March 1847; unm. He studied medicine with Drs. C. S. Chase of Thomaston and S. Whittimore of Gardiner, and attended the Bowdoin and Dartmouth Medical Schools. Since June, 1878, he has been practicing in East Pittston.

1-4-1-6-3-7

Dennis Libby, born in Danville, Me., 16 April 1805; married, 11 Sept. 1841, Sarah R. Warren, daughter of Rufus and Hannah (Harmon) Warren of Durham. He was a farmer and shoemaker, and always lived in his native town. He was a member of the Methodist Church and class-leader during about twenty years preceding his death, which took place 11 Feb. 1851.

Children:

1 Gershom Cox, b. 14 July 1842; m. 28 May 1865, Sarah R., dau. of David and Olive (Griffin) Grose of Auburn. He is a farmer in Auburn. He was a member of the 23d Maine Vol. Children:
 1 Emma Maria, b. 22 Feb. 1866.
 2 Alcena Menetta, b. 10 Oct. 1867.
 3 Frederic Gershom, b 22 Nov. 1878.
2 Hannah Maria, b. 7 Sept. 1845; m. 21 Sept. 1865, Wm. Jordan.
3 Sarah Louisa, b. 14 May 1850; d. 28 Jan. 1851.

1-4-1-6-3-8

Moses Libby, born in Danville, Me., 8 Aug. 1807; married, 26 Oct. 1837, Margaret M. Libby, 10-5-6-5-8. He has always lived on his father's homestead in what was formerly Danville, now Auburn. He is a Methodist and has been classleader many years. His wife died 4 Nov. 1863.

Children:

1 Luella, b. 2 Sept. 1838; d. 28 Jan. 1850.
2 Nellie L., b. 28 April 1842; m. 31 May 1875, Stephen B. Winchester.
3 Moses Leroy, b. 20 July 1854; m. 17 May 1879, Emma E., dau. of Charles and Sarah A. (Hartshorn) Jenness of Swanville, Me. He lives with his father. No children.

1-4-4-4-5-1

John Mills Libby, born in Freedom, N. H., 21 Aug. 1806; married first, 1 Dec. 1832, Lovina G. Guptill, daughter of James and Alice (True) Guptill; (died 13 Feb. 1847); second, 12 Jan. 1852, Susan, daughter of John and Abigail (Huckings) Mills of Freedom, N. H. He was a farmer, and lived where John Stanley now lives. He was a member of the Freewill Baptist Church. He filled the office of town clerk several years. He died 29 March 1865, and his widow married James Stanley. She died Aug. 1870.

Children, all by his first wife:

1 Mary Guptill, b. 12 Aug. 1834; m. 3 April 1863, Cyrus Lora Durgin of Brownfield. Children:
 1 John Albert (Durgin), b. 13 June 1864.
 2 Daniel Bean (Durgin), b. 21 Nov. 1865.
 3 Philip Sheridan (Durgin), b. 17 Aug. 1868.
2 Randall [Captain], b. 25 March 1836; m. Emma, dau. of Henry and Anna (Leavitt) Tibbetts. He was a school teacher and farmer. He was several years town clerk. 26 Sept. 1861, he enlisted as a soldier, and afterward became Captain of Co. A, 11th Maine. He contracted pulmonary consumption in the service, was discharged for disability 24 March 1863, and died in his native town, 8 May 1871. His wife died 16 March 1870, in Skowhegan. No children.

3 James Wallingford, b. 7 May 1838; m. March, 1864, Mary T., dau. of Daniel and Maria (Tibbetts) Towle. He was a farmer, and occupied the homestead. He died 11 Feb. 1877. His widow married —— Hewes of Boston. Children:
1 Nelson T., b. April, 1865.
2 Emma T., b. June, 1870.
3 West D., } twins, born
4 Jennie B., } May, 1872.

1-4-4-4-5-2

Isaac Libby, born in Porter, Me., 5 Sept. 1809; married, 8 April 1833, Roxanna Towle, daughter of David and Sarah (Mardin) Towle. When he married, he settled on the farm now owned by Wm. Sawyer. That place he sold in 1853, and, after living nine months in Porter Village, bought the farm in North Parsonsfield on which he and his son have since lived. He was several years a selectman of Porter.

Children:

1 Sarah Abigail, b. 17 Oct. 1834; m. 3 July 1854, Abner Gibbs.
2 Nehemiah Towle, b. 20 Sept. 1837; m. 21 Feb. 1860, Reliance B., dau. of Thomas and Mary (Banks) Churchill. He has been selectman of Parsonsfield. Children:
1 Emma, b. 2 Nov. 1862.
2 Walter Day, b. 8 Nov. 1864.

1-4-4-4-5-4

Randall Libby, born in Porter, Me., 31 Oct. 1815; married, 3 Sept. 1837, Sarah Towle, daughter of Daniel and Betsey (Mason) Towle.

After his marriage he was a farmer in Freedom, N. H., eight years, and in his native town fourteen years. He then bought mills in South Hiram and run them seven years. He was next in trade in Charlestown, Mass., a short time, and then opened a general store at South Hiram, which he continued until his death, 5 June 1880.

Children:

1 James Monroe, b. 6 March 1838; m. 1st, 26 Nov. 1863, Lizzie A., dau. of John and Eliza Nason; (died 29 Jan. 1870, in Hiram); 2d, 2 April 1871, Nancy Jane, dau. of Daniel and Betty (Smith) Gray of Hiram. He was engaged in farming, in the Great Falls, N. H., factories, and in the Pennsylvania lumber woods, until 1859. He then drove an ice-cart in Boston until 1867; was in trade with his father until 1871; has since been a teamster in Boston. He is of the firm of Morton & Libby. Children:
1 Fred Seymour, b. 15 Aug. 1868.
2 Lizzie W., b. 8 Jan. 1873; d. 8 Aug. 1878.
2 Tobias, b. 27 Oct. 1839; m. 1st, 14 Feb. 1863, Susan, dau. of Abraham Roberts; (died 10 Jan. 1865, in Parsonsfield); 2d, Georgietta Delovin, dau. of Benjamin L. and Sobrina (Bither) Bean of Searsport. He is of the firm of Tobias Libby & Co., teamsters, 56 Fulton and 60 Purchase streets, Boston. His residence is in East Cambridge. Only child:
1 Horace, b. 14 Oct. 1864, in Charlestown, Mass.; d. July, 1865, in Hiram, Me.

3 Isaac, b. 15 July 1841; m. 11 Oct. 1864, Dorcas P., dau. of John and Anna (Matthews) Kezar of Parsonsfield, Me. He lives in East Weymouth, Mass., an expressman. He is a Second Adventist. Children:
  1 Horace R., b. 7 Sept. 1865, in Boston.
  2 John R., b. 20 Dec. 1867; d. 23 May 1880.
4 Abbie, b. 5 Sept. 1843; m. 1 July 1860, Isaac L. French.
5 Mary J., b. 9 Jan. 1844; m. Aaron H. Mason; d. 5 Sept. 1866.
6 Wyman, b. 27 Jan. 1846; m. 29 Nov. 1866, Lucretia H., dau. of Isaac and Susan (Gould) Stanley of Porter. He removed to Boston in February, 1864, and entered the trucking business, in which he has since continued. Children:
  1 Frank W., b. 4 Aug. 1869, in Charlestown.
  2 Clarence W., b. 25 Jan. 1876, in Charlestown.
7 Francis L., b. 9 March 1851; m. 6 Sept. 1870, Adeline, dau. of Jacob and Betsey (Thompson) Stanley of Porter. Since leaving home, in 1869, he has been a teamster. He now lives in Charlestown, Mass. Children:
  1 Jennie, b. 9 Dec. 1871, in Porter.
  2 Guy, b. 31 Aug. 1877, in Porter.
8 Edwin R., b. 27 April 1859; m. 8 March 1879, Hattie A., dau. of Jeremiah and Eliza (Day) Davis of Parsonsfield. He continues his father's business at South Hiram. Child:
  1 Eva E., b. 18 April 1880.

1-4-4-4-5-5

Capt. Tobias Libby, born in Porter, Me., 27 Jan. 1821; married, 27 Jan. 1845, Judith F. Towle, daughter of Nehemiah F. and Sally (French) Towle of Porter.

He was a farmer in Porter until 1859, when he bought lumber mills at South Hiram. After running them about six years, his health began to fail, and he went into trade at Kezar Falls, Parsonsfield, and there continued until his death, 31 Oct. 1868. He was a member of the Freewill Baptist Church. While in Porter, he was a captain in the militia, and filled the offices of selectman and town treasurer. His widow married, 10 Feb. 1870, Wm. T. Taylor.

Children:

1 Evelyn M., b. 27 Jan. 1847; m. 11 Dec. 1867, Chas. F. Wadsworth; died 22 Oct. 1872.
2 Jacob A., b. 15 Dec. 1852; m. 8 April 1875, Lorette, dau. of Justin and Laura (Hatch) Butterfield of Baldwin. He was a clerk in Boston several years, and is now a clothing manufacturer at Kezar Falls. Children:
  1 Gertrude E., b. 21 Feb. 1876, in Porter.
  2 Ethel E., b. 20 Feb., d. 12 June, 1878.

1-5-2-3-3-4

Tyng S. Libby, born in Gorham, Me., 8 Dec. 1797; married, 11 March 1824, in Vassalborough, Me., Sarah Crowell, daughter of Elkanah and Bethiah (Hallett) Crowell of Yarmouth, Me.

He removed to Vassalborough in 1822, and worked as carpenter until 1835, when he engaged in lumbering. Two years later, 5 June 1837, he was crushed to death by rolling logs. The charge of his family was assumed by a bachelor uncle of his wife. She still lives.

Children, all born in Vassalborough:

1 Sarah E., b. 20 Dec. 1824; m. 17 Sept. 1846, Henry M. Sawtelle.
2 Frances M., b. 30 Sept. 1826; m. 29 April 1849, Newell B. Reed.
3 Franklin, b. 30 Sept. 1826; m. Dec. 1847, Ellen M., dau. of Jonathan and Melinda (Perkins) Sturgis of Vassalborough. 1852-1854 he was in California, mining. He then became a farmer, and after living in Pittsfield, Me. until 1859, emigrated to Princeton, Minn., where he has since been a farmer. He has served as county commissioner, and many lesser offices. Children:
  1 Llewellyn Smith, b. 16 June 1850, in Vassalborough; m. 2 Nov. 1872, Etta M., dau. of Milton and Hannah (Jacqueth) Smith of Princeton. He is a farmer and lumberman.
  2 Alice May, b. 27 Jan. 1852, in Augusta; m. March 1871, —— Bulis; died 19 June 1881. Child:
    1 Bertha (Bulis), b. 27 Feb. 1872.
  3 Walter H., b. 4 June 1855, in Vassalborough; m. 5 Oct. 1878, Abbie W., dau. of Isaiah D. and Ellen (Fennemore) Gilman of Princeton. He is a lumberman. Child:
    1 I. D., b 11 July 1879.
  4 Fred, } twins, born
  5 Frank, } 14 May 1861.
  6 Edward S., b. 9 Aug. 1863.
4 William Tyng, b. 16 July 1828; m. Nov. 1853, Hannah M., dau. of Enoch and Sarah S. (Reed) Brown of Vassalborough. Four years from 1849 he spent in California. He was then a farmer in Maine until, in 1861, he removed to Idaho Territory. He engaged there at first in quartz mining, and afterward in building and overseeing flour mills. In 1876, he removed his business to Walla Walla, Washington. Children, all born in Vassalborough:
  1 Felicia H., b. 9 Sept. 1854; m. 20 Oct. 1878, Frederick W. Lee.
  2 Eddie S., b. 19 Oct. 1856; died 17 Jan. 1863.
  3 Mark D., b. 27 Feb. 1858; unm.; graduated from the Maine State College in 1879; is a civil engineer in Kansas.
  4 Tyng S., b. 23 Aug. 1859; lives in Kansas.
  5 William B., b. 31 July 1862.
  6 Eugenia M., b. 28 Jan. 1873.
5 Isaiah C., b. 3 March 1832; m. 1st, June, 1852, Elizabeth, daughter of Israel and Deborah (Stevens) Davis of Montville; (died Jan. 1853, in Montville); 2d, Dec. 1856, Helen R., dau. of James and Emeline (Stevens) Atkinson of Montville; died 6 Jan. 1863, in Freedom. He was a farmer. His widow died in March, 1863. Children:
  1 Ida M., b. Dec. 1858, in Vassalborough; died May, 1861.
  2 Everett, b. Feb. 1860; died Nov. 1861.
6 Evelyn S., b. 9 Oct. 1837; m. 15 Jan. 1857, Chester W. Webber.

1-5-2-3-7-3

Stephen Libby, born in Gorham, Me., 27 May 1807; married, 13 Dec. 1831, Mary W. Lowe, daughter of Nicholas and Lovey (Leighton) Lowe of Gray. He was a shoemaker, but always lived on a farm. About a year before his marriage, he bought of Joseph Haskell the farm on which he ever afterward lived. His wife died 23 March 1881, and he, 3 July 1881.

Children, all born in Gorham:

1 Juliette E., b. 9 Aug. 1832; unm.
2 Adrianna, b. 23 Nov. 1833; m. 14 Sept. 1851, Daniel C. Mellows of Farmington, N. H.
3 Tyng Wilson, b. 17 April 1835; m. 25 Nov. 1862, Kate, widow of Solomon Brackett, dau. of Robert and Mehitable (Sawyer) Mc-

serve of Gorham. He is a farmer. He lived four and one-half years with his wife's father and then bought the farm he has since occupied. No children.

4 Harriet Angeline. b. 29 Sept. 1837; m. 5 March 1868, Charles L. McAllister of Portland.

5 Winfield Scott, b. 3 Oct. 1841; m. 29 April 1877, Izora, dau. of Edwin and Laurietta (Anderson) Hamblen. He is a farmer on his father's homestead. Child:
   1 Edwin Winfield, b. 6 Feb. 1880.

1-5-2-4-2-1

Daniel Libby, born in Gouldsborough, Me., 13 Jan. 1800; married, 8 July 1829, Mary Ann Whitaker, daughter of George and Lucy (Wilson) Whitaker. He followed his father's calling of farmer and lumberman, and has always lived on the homestead farm.

Children:

1 Samuel W., born 30 April 1830; m. 30 Oct. 1859, Emeline, dau. of George and Lydia (Moore) Nason of Millbridge. He has been a general merchant in Gouldsborough since 1854. He is deacon of the Baptist church, and has filled repeatedly the highest town offices. Children:
   1 Frank S., b. 17 Sept. 1864.
   2 Daniel, b. 14 Dec. 1870.

2 Elisha W., b. 12 Feb. 1832; } bachelors; farmers and
3 James A., b. 21 Feb. 1834; } lumbermen; live at home.
4 Lucy A., b. 4 Jan. 1836; unm.
5 R. Amanda, b. 10 Feb. 1839; d. 16 Dec. 1869; unm.
6 Dora E., b. 4 Nov. 1841; m. 18 July 1875, Capt. Jesse Perry.

1-5-2-4-2-4

Joseph Libby, born in Gouldsborough, Me., 12 Jan. 1805; married, 1830, Priscilla Wilson, daughter of Mark and Sarah (Small) Wilson of Steuben.

He removed to Cherryfield when he was married, and was engaged there in farming and lumbering until 1850, when he went west. In May 1850, he landed at the then village of St. Anthony, now Minneapolis, Minn. For five years he was engaged in lumbering on the Rum River, a tributary of the Mississippi. He cut and rafted down the timber that built the second saw-mill, in 1851. In the fall of 1855, he built the first flat boat that ascended the Mississippi above the falls, and polled it four hundred miles to Pokegoma Falls. He has ever since been engaged in lumbering on the Mississippi.

Children:

1 Sarah L., born 2 March 1831; m. Aug. 1852, C. P. Lull; d. 12 Jan. 1853.
2 Lydia H., b. 16 June 1833; d. 2 May 1854; unm.
3 Edward G., b. 5 April 1836; m. July, 1857, Martha E., dau. of Louis and Abigail (Watts) Wakefield of Cherryfield, Me. He is a farmer in Minneapolis. Children:
   1 Kitty, b. 20 Feb. 1859; unm.
   2 Harlan, b. 17 April 1863.
   3 Mattie Louisa, b. 14 Oct. 1868.

4 Mark W., } twins, b. } unm. He is a lumberman.
5 Mary H., } 26 Oct. 1838; } unm.
6 Laura A., b. 9 May 1841; m. Jan. 1870. Theodore Brown.
7 Sophia A., b. 3 May 1845; m. Sept. 1871, Milton Beven of St. Paul.
8 William H., b. 22 July 1848; m. April, 1876, Eliza, dau. of Samuel How, formerly of Calais. Me. He is a farmer. No children.
9 Joseph Eugene, b. 3 Dec. 1850; unm. He is a lumberman.

1-5-2-5-1-1

JAMES LIBBY, born in Gray, Me., 2 Sept. 1786; married, 22 Nov. 1815, MEHITABLE LOW, daughter of Thomas and —— (Brackett) Low of Lyman. Upon his marriage, he received from his father a farm on which he settled and ever afterward lived, a farmer and lumberman. His wife died 30 April 1833, and he married second, 12 May 1841, Rachel, daughter of Jeremiah and Betsey (Jinks) Twitchell of Gray. After her death, which took place 19 Nov. 1842, he married, 6 Aug. 1843, Betsey H., daughter of Stephen and Sarah (Simonton) Thayer of Gray. He died 12 Sept. 1858.

Children, all by his first wife:

1 Lucy, b. 6 Jan. 1817; m. Elijah Hustin of Gray.
2 Caroline, b. 23 May 1819; d. 14 Oct. 1842; unm.
3 Thomas Low, b. 28 May 1821; d. Oct. 1822.
4 Thomas Low, b. 28 May 1823; m. 1st, 1 Feb. 1855, Sarah M. W., dau. of Capt. Bradford and Lavinia (Low) Oakes of Kennebunk; (died 29 Oct. 1857); 2d, 9 Sept. 1866, Amanda A., dau. of Arthur M., and Catherine L. (Fogg) Higgins of Bangor. From 1852 until his marriage, he worked with his brother in Boston, in the paving business, and during the next three years was himself in business in Portland. Since that time he has lived in his native town and engaged in farming, shipping hay, and manufacturing shook. Children, by first wife:
    1 Florence, b. 10 June 1857; died in Sept. following.

    By second wife:

    2 Katie Higgins, b. 10 April 1868.
    3 Wilbert Thomas, b. 28 Oct. 1870.
5 Moses Harris, b. 5 June 1825; m. 1st, Dec. 1848, Clymena, dau. of John and Charlotte (Latham) Small of Casco; (died in Portland, 12 Sept. 1859); 2d, 18 Feb. 1869, Martha, dau. of Warren and Louisa (Prescott) Ware of Saco. In 1847 he went to Boston and learned the paving business, in which he has ever since been engaged except two years, during which he was superintendent of streets in Roxbury. He has been a partner in the firms of Gore, Rose & Co., Gore, Libby & Co., and (at present) John Turner & Co. Children:
    1 James Osgood, b. 25 Aug. 1849, in Gray; m. 28 Nov. 1872, Emma Frances, dau. of Solomon and Ann E. (Hochlander) Thomas of Boston. He is an expressman. Children:
        1 Francis James, b. 14 Jan. 1875.
        2 Sarah Jane, b. 26 Nov. 1879.
    2 Albert Atherton, b. 29 Nov. 1853, in Roxbury; m. 29 Dec. 1875, Isabella Frances, dau. of Abidan and Frances (Gouch) Tarbox. He is of the firm of Kidney and Libby, pavers and railroad contractors. Child:
        1 William Harding, b. 12 Oct. 1876.
    3 Moses Edwin, b. 21 July 1856, in Gray; m. 1 Jan. 1879, Edith Frances, dau. of William and R. H. (Hadley) Howe of Cambridge. He is a clerk. Child:

1 Edith Clymena, b. 5 March 1880.
4 Walter Lincoln, b. 6 Dec. 1858; unm. He is in the express business.
6 Mehitable Thayer, b. 21 June 1827: m. 8 Jan. 1854, Wm. M. Dow.
7 Sarah Jane, b. 17 April 1829; d. 1870, in Boston; unm.
8 Elizabeth Brown, b. 23 April 1831; m. 6 Sept. 1854, Frederick A. Hutchinson of Portland.
9, 10 twins, b. 3 April 1833; died same month.

1-5-2-5-1-5

JOSEPH LIBBY, born in Gray, Me., 5 Feb. 1794; married, 23 Sept. 1823, MARY SIMONTON, daughter of —— and —— (Alden) Simonton of Bristol. He bought and settled on the farm at Dry Mills, in Gray, now occupied by his son, and engaged quite extensively in lumbering and milling. He rebuilt both the saw and grist mills which had been his father's. He died 29 April 1866. His wife died 9 July 1865.

Children:

1 Mary Jane, b. 19 July 1824; d. 7 Oct. 1825.
2 Augustus Hannibal, b. 20 Nov. 1826; d. 25 June 1852.
3 Charles Edward, b. 21 Dec. 1828; m. 15 Oct. 1848, Martha A., dau. of Samuel J. and Ann (Emerson) Foster. He owns and carries on the mills that were his father's, and has also purchased the Webster mills. He has been postmaster at Dry Mills since 1863. He has been three years selectman, and has been the Republican candidate for representative to the legislature. Children:
  1 Edward Francis, b. 19 Feb. 1849; m. 29 Nov. 1871, Emily Augusta, dau. of John and Ann (Hodgdon) Foster. He is employed in his father's mills. Children:
    1 Mary Lizzie, b. 28 Dec. 1873; d. 23 Oct. 1875.
    2 Annie Augusta, b. 9 Aug. 1877.
  3 Augustus Herbert, b. 12 Aug. 1855; d. 9 Sept. 1856.
  4 Frederick Emerson, b. 22 Jan. 1858; d. 10 March 1858.
  5 Wilfred Demel, b. 10 March 1862; d. 17 Jan. 1864.
  6 Jennie Evelyn, b. 16 April 1863.
4 Jacob Clark, b. 6 March 1831; d. 4 March 1836.
5 Caroline Elizabeth, b. 9 July 1833; d. 30 April 1853.
6 Joseph, b. 5 Aug. 1839; d. 26 Aug. 1839.

1-5-2-5-1-7

WILLIAM LIBBY, born in Gray, Me., 2 Feb. 1798; married first, Patience H., widow of James Staples, daughter of Stephen and Mary (Clark) Hall of Windham; (died 17 Dec. 1832); second, 1837, DEBORAH BROWN, daughter of Samuel and Sarah (Hodgkins) Brown of Lovell. He lived on his father's homestead and confined himself strictly to farming. He died 30 July, and his wife 11 Sept. 1873.

Children, by first wife:

1 son, b. Oct. 1832, died aged eight months.

By second wife:

2 Abby Patience, b. 7 Nov. 1838; unm. She lives in Portland.
3 Freeland Elvin, b. 28 April 1840; m. 9 Sept. 1867, Nellie E., dau. of Capt. William and Lucinda (Town) Daniels of Boston. He was in the milk business in Boston, and afterward worked as paver, until 1875, when he returned to his father's homestead in Gray. No children.

4 Ellen Dorcas, b. 23 Jan. 1842; m. 24 June 1866, Benjamin F. Skillin of Gray.
5 Wealthy Maria, b. 18 June 1844; m. 24 June 1867, Geo. D. Clark.
6 Sarah Elizabeth, b. 5 Sept. 1846; m. 8 July 1869, Isaac Granville Waters of Boston.
7 James Parker, b. 6 Jan. 1848; m. 10 March 1878, Janette F., dau. of Stephen and Lois (Pennell) Small of Gray. He learned the blacksmith trade with his brother-in-law Skillin, and worked at it until his marriage, when he settled on the farm which had been his wife's father's. Child:
   1 Stephen William, b. 24 June 1879.
8 Frederick William, b. 30 March 1856; m. June 1880, Rachel, dau. of Ai and Miriam (Foster) Fogg of Gray. He is by trade a painter, and works for his brother-in-law Waters, in the picture-molding business.

1-5-2-5-1-10

Deacon Charles Libby, born in Gray, Me., 29 March 1804; married, 25 Dec. 1833, Abigail Cummings, daughter of Daniel and Hannah (Briggs) Cummings of Gray. After his marriage he kept a hotel at Gray Corner a short time, and then settled on the farm now occupied by Matthew Morrill. There he lived until his death, 13 Feb. 1865. His widow still lives at Gray Corner.

Children:

1 Eleanor Frances, b. 27 Oct. 1834; d. 15 Feb. 1853; unm.
2 Hannah Jane, b. 25 Sept. 1839; d. 22 May 1860; unm.
3 Caroline Emma, b. 3 Dec. 1846; married 27 June 1877, Charles H. Doughty.

1-5-2-5-1-11

Parker Sawyer Libby, born in Gray, Me., 13 Nov. 1806; married, 16 March 1831, Emeline Harris, daughter of Charlotte (Libby) Harris, 1-5-2-5-15.

He was in trade successively at Gray Corner, Fore street in Portland, Gray Corner, North Gray, and Saccarappa. During five years following March, 1847, he was in California. After his return, he was in the grocery business in Portland until about 1860, when he bought the farm in Gray now occupied by his widow and son, Sumner. There he died, 7 April 1871.

Children:

1 Charlotte Harris, b. 29 Jan., d. 19 Nov., 1832.
2 Rotheus Parker, b. 29 March 1833; m. 14 Oct. 1859, Ellen A., dau. of John S. and Harriet (Lyford) Edgerly. He learned the hair-dresser's trade in Portsmouth, N. H., and afterward carried on business in Saco. In April 1869, he left home for Montreal, intending to go into business, and nothing was afterward heard from him. His disappearance was inexplicable. His widow married, 25 Dec. 1875, Wm. H. Friend of Boston. Children:
   1 Annie Gertrude, b. 9 Dec. 1860.
   2 Frank Parker, b. 12 Aug., d. 14 Sept., 1862.
   3 Ernest Parker, b. 11 July 1864.
3 Sumner Freeland, b. 1 July 1838; unm. He is a journeyman mason.
4 John Muchemore, b. 6 Sept. 1842; m. 22 March 1872, Victoria S., dau. of James Foss of Bradley. He worked as clerk in Portland, Gray, and Biddeford until his enlistment in Co. H, 20th Maine,

in which he served three years. During the winter of 1866 and 1867, the first after his return from the war, he served as representative to the state legislature, and during the three years following had charge of a department in the State Reform School. He has since been a trader at Dry Mills and Gray Corner, and is now a clothing manufacturer in the latter place. Child:

1 Carrie Augusta, b. 27 Nov. 1874.

5 Henry Clay, b. 2 April 1844; d. 6 Jan. 1865; unm. He served nearly three years in the 5th Maine Reg. of Infantry.

1-5-2-5-2-4

NATHANIEL LIBBY, born in Gray, Me., 19 Nov. 1800; married, 2 Dec. 1819, SOPHIA CHURCHILL, daughter of Joseph and Alice (Drake) Churchill of Middleborough, Mass. He was a farmer in Greenwood, of which place he was one of the earliest settlers. He died with his son in Paris, 28 Nov. 1873. His widow still lives.

Children:

1 Alice Jane, b. 15 Feb. 1823; m. 3 July 1841, Albert Winslow; d. 20 Sept. 1855.

2 Joseph Lamoine, b. 31 April 1827; m. 4 Nov. 1857, Evelyn L., dau. of Josiah A. and Miriam (Rich) Stuart of Harrison. He is a farmer in South Paris. Children:
  1 Anne Lucretia, b. 13 July 1865.
  2 Willard Lamoine, b. 12 Dec. 1868.
  3 Mary Pearl, b. 9 Dec. 1871.

3 Sarah Sophia, b. 20 Sept. 1832; m. 2 Sept. 1853, Stetson S. Gordon.

4 Nathaniel William, b. 24 June 1834; m. Effie A. Nelson of Cynthiana, Ky. He was an engineer on the Union Pacific Railroad. He was killed by the falling of a bridge under his train, at Wyandotte, Kansas, 14 July 1869. Children:
  1 Robert Edward, b. about 1862.
  2 Claudia, b. about 1864.
  3 Thomas, b. about 1866.

1-5-2-5-2-5

DELAW LIBBY, born in Gray, Me., 21 Oct. (1799?); married, in Calais, Me., MARY E. EMERSON, daughter of Joseph and Lydia (Hall) Emerson of St. Stephen, N. B.

He lived some time in Bangor, engaged in the livery business, and engaging largely in lumbering. He afterward removed to Lowell, Mass., and engaged in the real estate business, and later engaged in the same business in Virginia. He at length returned to Boston, where he died, 7 Sept. 1859. His widow still lives in Calais.

Children:

1 Charles Wheeler, b. 21 Oct. 1826; m. 4 June 1859, Sarah Elizabeth, dau. of James Edward and Catherine C. (Crocker) Stokes of Boston. He lived some years at Calais, and since 1859 has been in the carriage business in Cambridge and Boston. Children:
  1 Kate Amelia, b. 3 Sept. 1861, in Charlestown.
  2 Charles Frederic, b. 12 July 1864, in Cambridgeport.
  3 George Henry, b. 16 July 1870.

2 Joseph, was purser on the Valparaiso, and was lost at sea.

3 Mary Elizabeth, m. 1st, —— Hull; 2d, William H. Hanley.

4 Frank Hall, lives in Chicago, Ill.

5 Augustus F., lives in Brazil, South America.

1-5-2-5-6-2

SUSAN LIBBY, born in Gray, Me., 15 July 1795; married, 15 June 1817, EZEKIEL JORDAN of Cape Elizabeth. He learned the shoemaker's trade in Portland, and went to Gray and set up a shop. Three years after his marriage, he moved back to Portland, and soon after to Cape Elizabeth, where he died 6 Nov. 1842. His widow married, 1 Jan. 1850, William Stanford, who died 14 Jan. 1876. She still survives.

Her children were:

1 Woodbury (Jordan), born 26 April 1818, in Gray; lives in Chelsea, Mass.
2 Mary S. (Jordan), b. 21 March 1820; m. Walter Skillings.
3 Phebe Ann (Jordan), b. 21 April 1822; m. 22 June 1844, Francis Skillings of Cape Elizabeth. He was a bridge and wharf builder in Portland. He was drowned off from Vaughan's Bridge, 21 Jan. 1871. Children:
  1 George (Skillings), b. 3 May 1846, in Cambridge, Mass.; lives in Portland; unmarried.
  2 Hattie E. (Skillings), b. 27 Oct. 1847; m. 21 Dec. 1868, John W. Thomas of San Francisco. No children.
  3 Franklin (Skillings), b. 7 Sept. 1850; m. Julia Crowley; lives in Portland.
  4 Almeda (Skillings), b. 25 April 1852; m. Edwin Hayes; died 26 May 1877.
  5 Ella M. (Skillings), b. 3 April 1853; m. 11 July 1875, George Whidden.
  6 Edwin L. (Skillings), b. 25 March 1855; lives in Kansas City, Missouri; unm.
  7 Susan J. (Skillings), b. 24 May 1857; died 14 Oct. 1878.
  8 Woodbury J. (Skillings), b. 25 July 1859.
  9 Mary J. (Skillings), b. 14 Aug. 1862.
4 George (Jordan), b. 8 Aug. 1823; died in San Francisco, 1876; unm.
5 Betsey (Jordan), b. 11 Oct. 1825; m. Theodore Low.
6 Frank (Jordan), b. 15 Dec. 1827; lives in Chelsea, Mass.
7 Susan Jane (Jordan), b. 16 Jan. 1830; m. as second wife, Theodore Low of Cape Elizabeth.
8 William B. (Jordan), b. 26 April 1835; lives in Cape Elizabeth.
9 Sarah Lavinia (Jordan), b. 7 March 1840; m. 28 Nov. 1867, Charles G. Fickett of Cape Elizabeth, a cooper. Child:
  1 Eva May (Fickett), b. 23 April 1879.

1-5-2-5-6-3

GEORGE LIBBY, born in Gray, Me., 30 Jan. 1798; married, 24 April 1827, MARY ANN STIMPSON, daughter of John and Ann (Simonton) Stimpson of Gray. When a young man he was a trader, but has ever since been a farmer. He has served three terms as collector. His wife died 8 Aug. 1877.

Only child:

1 Woodbury Stimpson, b. 4 Sept. 1828; m. 23 May 1869, Delinda Dustin, dau. of John and Ann (Hodgkins) Foster of Gray. He is a farmer and teacher. Children:
  1 George Woodbury, b. 23 July 1870.
  2 Eleanor Jacobs, b. 26 Jan. 1873.
  3 Lester Smith, b. 9 Aug. 1875.

4 Elizabeth Stanwood, b. 9 May 1879.
5 Foster Hodgkins Stimpson,* b. 10 June 1880.

1-5-2-5-6-5

James Libby, born in Gray, Me., 15 April 1802; married, 10 July 1836, in Corinna, Harriet Hayden, daughter of Enoch and Relief (Adams) Hayden of Corinna.

He left Gray at the age of twenty-eight, and went to Oldtown, where he and his brother Richard were in the milling business six years. He then removed to Molunkus, where he engaged in lumbering. His death took place 15 April 1874. His widow is living.

Children:

1 George H., b. 16 June 1837, in Oldtown; m. 13 Oct. 1860, Martha L., dau. of Warren and Maria (Jackman) Coombs of Mattawamkeag. He and his brother Joseph engaged in hotel keeping in 1861, and were together in the Lincoln House, and in a boarding-house in Kingman, five years. They afterward moved to Mattawamkeag and engaged in lumbering. George's wife died 28 July 1876, and he went to California, where he is now on a dairy farm. Children:
  1 Bertha E., b. 5 Oct. 1862, in Molunkus; died 11 Aug. 1867.
  2 George W., b. 25 Jan. 1869, in Lincoln.
  3 Martha M., b. 17 Dec. 1875, in Mattawamkeag.

2 Joseph W., b. 15 Feb. 1841, in Molunkus; m. 25 July 1866, Georgie, dau. of Daniel Campbell of Greenbush. He went from Mattawamkeag to Elk River, Minn., and engaged in the stage and livery business. His wife died there 3 Sept. 1880.

3 James B., b. 2 Sept. 1843; m. 25 April 1874, Flora M. Libby, 1-6-9-8-1-2-3. He is a farmer in Molunkus; is deacon of the Methodist church, and has held the office of town treasurer for several years. Children:
  1 Fred Harold, b. 2 April 1876.
  2 James H., b. 16 July 1880; died 8 Sept. 1881.

4 Francis E., b. 15 Sept. 1850; m. 26 Feb. 1879, Lizzie, dau. of James and Jane (Jameson) Huntress of Lincoln. He is also a farmer in Molunkus. Child:
  1 Hattie J., b. 17 Sept. 1880, in Lincoln.

5 Irene P., b. 22 June 1853; died 4 June 1854.

1-5-2-5-6-9

Jonathan Libby, born in Gray, Me., 31 Jan. 1812; married, 27 Dec. 1838, Matilda S. Bacon, daughter of Samuel and Ruth (Durgin) Bacon.

He learned the cooper's trade in North Yarmouth with Samuel Bacon, who afterward became his father-in-law, and worked at

---

*He was named by the compiler. It will be seen that his name, Foster Hodgkins Stimpson Libby, includes the surnames of his four grandparents; first the mother's name, then her mother's name, then the paternal grandmother's name, and then the surname. The plan, fully carried out, would demand that all this family should be distinguished from other families of Libbys by these three middle names, and that the different members of the family be distinguished from each other by christian names prefixed. Thus this family might have been: George F. H. S. Libby, Eleanor F. H. S. Libby, Lester F. H. S. Libby, and Elizabeth F. H. S. Libby. Such a method of naming, could it once become general, would make the genealogist's task an easy and sure one. Succeeding generations would thus preserve their pedigrees in their names. Some such method is more necessary for purposes of distinction to-day than was the optional use of middle names a half-century ago.

his trade until 1847. He then moved to Durham, and engaged in business himself in company with E. Dow, whom he bought out soon after and has since continued the business alone. He was a member of the state legislature in 1869. His wife died 17 Dec. 1876.

Children, all born in North Yarmouth:

1 Adelia S., b. 6 March 1839; m. 24 Nov. 1862, Nathaniel I. Jordan.
2 George B., b. 8 March 1841; m. 1868, Julia A., dau. of Oliver Dow of Buxton. He taught school several terms and then became a clerk in a store in Lewiston. After a short time he went to Portland and became traveling salesman for a fancy goods firm. Later he traveled for a Boston firm in the same line, and now for a New York party. His wife died Jan. 1873. His only child died in infancy.
3 Samuel B., b. 29 Jan. 1843; m. 30 Nov. 1871, Cornelia W., dau. of Henry W. and Eliza A. (Eveleth) Paine of Durham. He served an enlistment in the war, and afterward worked at his trade of cooper in various places in the south and west. Since 1868, he has lived with his father, a farmer and cooper. Children:
  1 Etta M., b. 22 Feb. 1874.
  2 Willard T., b. 4 April 1876.
  3 Gertrude E., b. 7 Aug. 1879.
4 Fannie M., b. April 1845; m. June 1867, Andrew G. Fitz.

1-5-2-5-6-11

Joseph Libby, born in Gray, Me., 23 Oct. 1818; married, 1842, Nancy Foster, daughter of William and Lucy (Spencer) Foster of Argyle.

He went to Oldtown a young man and engaged in lumbering. He soon removed to Molunkus, where he has since been a farmer and lumberman. He has served two terms in the state legislature.

Children, all born in Molunkus:

1 William H., b. 3 March 1844; m. 1 Jan. 1870, Maria A., dau. of Oliver Blackwell of Patten. He was eight years a clerk in Molunkus, and has been since 1878 a general merchant at Mattawamkeag.
2 Charles O., b. 28 April 1845; m. 1868, Josephine R., dau. of Humphrey and Susan (Hayden) Chadbourne of Macwahoc. He is a general merchant of Macwahoc; postmaster and justice of the peace. Children:
  1 Gertrude W., b. 13 May 1871, in Macwahoc.
  2 Harry W., b. 27 Dec. 1873.
  3 Susie M., b. 20 March 1876.
  4 Freeland H., b. 26 July 1878.
  5 Jennie K., b. 26 Dec. 1880; died 6 Sept. 1881.
3 Oscar H., b. 22 June 1851; unm.; is a clerk with William.
4 Jennie K., b. 15 Nov. 1852; m. Geo. Metcalf; died 29 Dec. 1880.
5 Ada G., b. 13 Oct. 1857; m. 1879, Melville Bowley.

1-6-2-1-1-2

Daniel Libby, born in Tuftonborough, N. H., 28 Feb. 1785; married, 28 Nov. 1807, Mary Abbott, daughter of Elisha and Mary (Nutter) Abbott of Tuftonborough.

He was a farmer and cooper. In April 1822 he removed to Sandwich, and there lived until his death, 20 Aug. 1869. He and his wife were both members of the Freewill Baptist Church.

Their children were:

1 Hanson, b. 10 Aug. 1808; m. 3 Dec. 1835, Sally M., dau. of Moses and Lydia (Thrasher) Severance of Sandwich. He grew up in Sandwich, and has always lived there, as farmer. He and his wife are members of the Freewill Baptist Church. No children.
2 Elisha, b. 24 Dec. 1809; m. 26 Nov. 1834, Mary J., dau. of John and Elizabeth (Webster) Quimby; died 6 Oct. 1842, in Sandwich. He was a farmer. Children:
  1 George, deceased.
  2 Jeanette, deceased.
3 Mary, b. 16 Feb. 1812; died in infancy.
4 Jane, b. 7 Oct. 1814; died 26 March 1880.
5 Mary A., b. 10 April 1817; m. 22 Feb. 1838, in Lynn, Mass., James M. Allen; died 18 May 1845, in Danvers, Mass.
6 Louisa, b. 26 Sept. 1818; died in infancy.
7 Lydia R., b. 14 April 1820; m. 6 Jan. 1842, in Lynn, Samuel W. Knowles; died 2 Nov. 1853, in Danvers, Mass.
8 Joanna M., b. 28 June 1822, in Sandwich; m. 5 April 1854, Samuel W. Knowles, her deceased sister's husband.
9 John W., b. 23 Oct. 1827; m. 24 Feb. 1853, in Salem, Mass., Mary E., dau. of Eben and Ruth R. (Webb) Greenlaw of Bristol, Me. He learned the trade of shoemaker, and worked at his trade and at farming, until 1858, when he went onto the night watch in Salem, Mass., where he has ever since been connected with the police,—during the last seven years as truant officer.
10 Sarah E., b. 19 Oct. 1830; died 29 March 1856.

1-6-2-1-1-7

Lieut. Levi Libby, born in Tuftonborough, N. H., 24 March 1794; married, 29 Nov. 1821, Mary Canney, daughter of William and Betsey (White) Canney of Tuftonborough.

Early left an orphan, he lived during his minority with Moses Wiggin of Wolfborough, and John Canney of Tuftonborough. Previous to his marriage, he bought a farm in Tuftonborough, and on it resided until his death, 21 Dec. 1877. His wife died 2 July 1862. They were members of the M. E. Church.

Their children were:

1 William K., b. 21 Nov. 1822; m. Betsey N., dau. of Charles and Charlotte (Nutter) Colbath of Farmington; lives in Tuftonborough. Children:
  1 Levi W., b. 5 July 1849; m. Laura A. Staples; lives in Tuftonborough. Child (?)
    1 Addie, born 1877.
  2 Pluma E., b. 25 July 1852; unm.
2 Edmond C., b. 31 Oct. 1827; died 12 Dec. 1849; unm. He was a successful teacher of common schools.
3 Daniel, b. 18 Nov. 1830; m. 11 Oct. 1857, Ann E., dau. of Ira and Betsey W. (Thompson) Canney of Tuftonborough; is a farmer and shoemaker in his native town. He served three years in the 5th N. H. Vol.; is a member of the M. E. Church. Children:
  1 Freeman C., born 14 April 1858; unm.; is a member of the M. E. Church, and is preparing for the ministry.
  2 Edmond C., b. 27 June 1860; d. 25 May 1861.
  3 Nettie C., b. 8 July 1869.
  4 Florence M., b. 1 Sept. 1874.

James S. Libby

1-6-2-1-6-5

JAMES S. LIBBY, born in Tuftonborough, N. H., 2 Nov. 1805; married first, Sept. 1826, LYDIA BOYNTON EDMUNDS, daughter of Joseph and Lydia (Boynton) Edmunds of Haverhill, N. H.; (died 2 May 1845); second, 7 May 1846, HANNAH MARIE MOORE, daughter of Jonathan and Annie (Taylor) Moore of Sanbornton, N. H.; (died 29 April 1871, in North Salem, N. Y.).

James S. Libby learned the hatter's trade with Col. Benj. Edmunds of Plymouth, N. H., whose sister he married, and soon after removed to Shipton, Que., where he engaged in business, and was at one time clerk of courts. After three years he removed to New York City and soon became partner of Jonathan Lovejoy, in Lovejoy's Hotel, famous as the pioneer of hotels on the European plan. He was afterward, for twenty years, sole proprietor of that hotel. He played a prominent part in establishing the first horse railroad, (the Sixth Avenue), and was two terms president of the company. He was a prominent Democrat, and was two terms an alderman, and later was candidate for the office of mayor of New York City, in opposition to Fernando Wood. He continued to reside in New York until his retirement to a country seat in Salem.

Children; by first wife:

1 Joseph Edmonds, b. 10 Oct. 1827, in Plymouth; m. 14 June 1850, Eliza Ann, dau. of Isaac Van Schaack of New York. He was formerly in the hardware business, and has been for some years a farmer in Minnesota. Son:
  1 George Washington, b. 22 Feb. 1853, in New York.
2 Helen M., b. 3 Feb. 1833, in Canada; m. 24 June 1850, Hency Comely Fling of Philadelphia.
3 Charles W., b. 8 Sept. 1837, in New York; died 9 Sept. 1838.
4 James S., b. March, 1842; died in October following.
5 James L., born 17 Feb. 1845; m. 14 Oct. 1868, Jessie A. M., dau. of Daniel and Eliza Burtnett of New York. He was educated in the New York University, and has been in business sixteen years. He is now of the firm of Libby & Spier, manufacturers of linen shirts, collars, and cuffs. Children:
  1 Harry M., b. 14 Oct. 1870.
  2 Jessie B., b. 4 April 1875.

By second wife:

6 Louise, b. 11 March 1847; unm.
7 Charles Allen, b. 14 Sept. 1849, in New Hampshire; m. 7 May 1878, Ella Virginia, dau. of Willis and Mary T. (Willis) Tomkins of Philadelphia, Penn. He was educated at St. John College, and is now manager of his brother's Chicago house. Children:
  1 Lilian Louise, b. 11 July 1879, in Brooklyn, N. Y.
  2 Anna H. L., b. 19 Nov. 1880, in Chicago.
8 Hannah M., b. 8 Dec. 1851; died 26 April 1853.
9 Charlotte M., b. 6 Nov. 1854; died 13 Jan. 1857.

1-6-2-1-6-10

WILLIAM P. LIBBY, born in Tuftonborough, N. H., 8 May 1817; married MARY LOUISA BRIDGE, daughter of Matthew and Mary (Flagg) Bridge of Dover, N. H.

He was four years a clerk in the store of Ira Christie in Dover, and later three years in the counting-room of the Cocheco Manufacturing Co. When twenty-one years of age he left Dover and went to New York, and was clerk for two years in the wholesale house of F. T. Peet & Co. He then removed to Whitehall, N. Y., and engaged in business, but, after a few years, returned to New York and became identified with various business interests, establishing his residence in Brooklyn, where he was for some time a member of the board of education. He is now president and treasurer of the South Brooklyn Saw Mill Co. For several years he has been a member of the South Congregational Church.

His children are:

1 Marie Louise, b. 8 Aug. 1842; m. 2 Dec. 1863, Charles T. Catlin.
2 William H., b. 4 Aug. 1845; m. 10 Feb. 1868, Mollie C., dau. of Perrin Burdick of New York. He was for some years a successful merchant in New York, and is now for the second time visiting the principal cities of the East Indies, China, and Japan, representing a large commercial interest. His wife died 13 Dec. 1877. Children:
  1 William H., b. 18 Dec. 1868; died 6 June 1870.
  2 Paul, b. 7 March 1871.
  3 Maud, b. 19 May 1872.
3 Marion, b. 16 March 1857; unm.

1-6-2-1-9-2

JOHN D. LIBBY, born in Farmington, N. H., 1805; married ELIZA STANTON, daughter of Erastus and Betsey (Shepherd) Stanton of Danville, Vt. He went with his father to Compton, Que., and became a farmer. His death took place 12 April 1842. He was a member of the Freewill Baptist Church. His widow died in Danville, 9 Oct. 1872.

Their children were:

1 Clara C., b. 13 Feb. 1828; m. June 1857, Hiram Ward; died 6 Feb. 1858.
2 Erastus Stanton, b. 3 Jan. 1830; m. 12 Nov. 1871, in Carson, Neva., Jane, dau. of Hermon and Jane (Feder) Shirley of Waukesha, Wis. He lived nineteen years on the Pacific coast; is now in Janesville, Wis. Children:
  1 Mabel E., b. 19 Nov. 1872, in Janesville.
  2 William S., b. 6 Oct. 1874.
  3 Clara M., b. 8 May 1880, in Plymouth.
3 William H., b. June 1833; when last heard from, was in Silver City, Idaho.
4 Mary E., b. 12 Jan. 1835; m. 10 March 1865, Hon. J. A. Blount of Janesville, Wis.; died 16 May 1881.
5 Martha A., b. 15 July 1837; m. 11 Jan. 1852, Harlow Foss. Children:
  1 Avis C. (Foss), b. 19 Dec. 1863, in Barton, Vt.; d. 3 May 1871.
  2 Eva E. (Foss), b. 11 Sept. 1866, in Irasburgh, Vt.
  3 Ellen D. (Foss), b. 29 Sept. 1873, in Irasburgh.
  4 Isadore D. (Foss), b. 17 March 1876.
  5 Seldon H. (Foss), b. 28 Nov. 1877.
6 Carrie L., b. 16 Oct. 1839; m. Sept. 1868, Fred Benoit.

1-6-2-1-9-4

Christopher Columbus Libby, born in Farmington, N. H., 23 Sept. 1807; married, 11 Oct. 1838, Calista Hyatt, daughter of Abraham and Thankful (Cartwright) Hyatt of Ascot, Quebec. He is a farmer. In his younger days he bought and partially cleared a piece of land in Compton, Que., whither he had gone with his father, but upon his marriage he settled on the homestead of his wife's father, and has since continued there.

Children, all born in Ascot:

1 Benjamin Franklin, b. 23 Aug. 1839; lives in Lawrence, Mass. He has been three times married, but has no children.
2 Alice Clarinda, b. 27 March 1842; died 23 April 1860; unm.
3 Victoria Calista, b. 9 April 1844; m. 14 Jan. 1867, John McDougall of Stanstead.
4 Christopher Eugene, b. 17 July 1849; died 18 Aug. 1852.
5 Clarence Eugene, b. 31 July 1853; d. 6 May 1860.
6 Edwin Lorenzo, b. 31 May 1856; m. 6 June 1877, Emma Sabrina, daughter of Franklin and Sabrina (Hurlbutt) Richardson of Biddeford, Me. Children:
  1 Alice Eborn, b. 19 Dec. 1879.
  2 Christopher Edwin, b. 29 April 1881.
7 Olive Aveline, b. 29 July 1858; d. 29 May 1860.

1-6-2-1-9-9

William Pitt Libby, born in Goshen Gore, Vt., 14 July 1816; married first, 1840, Sarah Parker, daughter of Thomas and Sarah (Justin) Parker of Compton; (died in January, 1842); second, Dec. 1844, Elizabeth Sanders, daughter of John and Betsey (Webb) Sanders of Compton. He grew up in Compton, Que., and had his father's homestead farm. His death took place 8 June 1874. His widow died 3 Feb. 1879.

Children, by first wife:

1 Mary Ann, b. 20 Aug. 1841; m. May 1863, Alvah Carr.

By second wife:

2 Charles Henry, b. 9 Sept., died 28 Sept., 1845.
3 Mark Demerit, b 24 Dec. 1846; m. 14 Oct. 1873, Celena, daughter of Robert and Ann (Rowell) Smith of Eaton. He lives on the homestead, a farmer. No children.
4 Clara Jane, b. 6 Aug. 1848; m. 16 Oct. 1877, David T. Wetherell.
5 Selah Pomroy, b. 26 April 1850; d. 25 May 1868.
6 Laura Elizabeth, b. 9 March 1852; m. 31 Oct. 1869, Henry Lane.
7 Frances Marilla, b. 5 March 1854; m. 31 Oct. 1871, John Berry; d. 15 Oct. 1871, in Strafford, N. H.
8 John Wesley, b. 20 Jan. 1856; m. 14 Feb. 1880, in Compton, Jane Brown; died 16 June 1881. He was a farmer. No children.
9 William Henry, b. 8 July 1858.
10 Benjamin Franklin, b. 9 April 1860.
11 Charles Frederick, b. 26 Sept. 1861.
12 George Leslie, b. 15 Feb. 1863; d. 28 Jan. 1879.
13 Helen Grace, b. 27 March 1865; d. 25 Jan. 1879.
14 Cora Lee, b. 14 March 1868.

1-6-2-4-1-4

RUFUS LIBBY, born in Dixmont, Me., 1 Oct. 1801; married, 25 Dec. 1831, CASSANDRIA FOSTER, daughter of Richard Foster of Jackson, Ohio. He was a farmer in Bedford, Ohio, where he died 17 Oct. 1869. His widow still lives.

Children, all born in Bedford:

1 Dyantha, b. 25 June 1834; d. Sept. 1839.
2 Rachel, b. 19 Jan. 1836; m. 23 Oct. 1875, Thomas W. White.
3 Ellsworth W. [Capt.], b. 4 March 1838; m. 21 Oct. 1874, Rebecca Ann, dau. of J. Foster of Wilson. He is a farmer. He served four years in the 33d Ohio Reg., and rose to be captain. Children:
  1 Rufus R., b. 8 Oct. 1876, in Bedford.
  2 Annie V., b. 12 March 1879, in Bedford.
4 Edwin Sullivan, b. 11 March 1840; m. 21 Dec. 1870, Lottie E., dau. of William and Eliza (Dunham) Wheeler. He served eighteen months in the 67th Ohio Vol. He is a farmer. Children:
  1 Vernon W., b. 18 Nov. 1872, in Bedford.
  2 Lucy Bell, b. 28 Jan. 1878, in Bedford.
5 Iantha A., b. 9 Oct. 1842; m. 8 March 1866, Dwight N. Hamlin.
6 Casandria S., b. 15 Sept. 1844; unm.
7 Silistria R., b. 6 March 1847; m. 20 Jan. 1867, Jonas H. Harroff.
8 Mary M., b. 8 Oct. 1854; m. 21 Oct. 1878, William T. Hughes of Georgetown, Col.

1-6-2-4-10-4

CAPT. LUTHER LIBBY, born in Bolton, Quebec, 26 Dec. 1815; married, 9 Oct. 1835, ANNA KNOWLTON, daughter of Lyman and Sophia (Whitcomb) Knowlton of South Stukely.

He cleared a large farm in the back part of his native town, and always afterward lived there. He built a sawmill on the outlet of a pond since known as Libby Pond, and engaged in the manufacture of potash. He was a captain in the militia. He died 20 Oct. 1880. His wife died 25 Sept. 1864.

Children, all born in Bolton:

1 Lucy Maria, b. 12 Jan. 1837; d. 12 Sept. 1859.
2 David George, b. 3 Dec. 1838; d. 13 Jan. 1840.
3 David, b. 24 April 1840; d. 19 March 1863; unm.
4 Mark, b. 25 Aug. 1842; m. 8 Oct. 1868, Hester Ann, dau. of Isaac and Caroline (Elmer) Lawrence of South Stukely. He is a mill owner and mechanic in Shefford, Quebec. Children:
  1 Elwood Homer, b. 2 Oct. 1869; d. 28 March 1871.
  2 Lucy Ardenne, b. 24 Nov. 1870.
  3 Ruth Evelyn, b. 20 Jan. 1872, in South Stukely.
  4 Selwyn James, b. 6 Nov. 1873, in Shefford.
  5 Malcolm Mark, b. 29 June 1878.
  6 Annie Louisa, b. 26 Nov. 1880.
5 Harriet Sophia, b. 14 May 1844; d. 11 Aug. 1861.
6 Leander, b. 11 Aug. 1846; unm. He is a carpenter.
7 Elizabeth Ann, b. 31 May 1848; m. Sept. 1867, Daniel Connolly.
8 Almira Alvira, b. 24 March 1850; m. 25 Jan. 1879, Manvis R. Drew; d. 25 May 1880.
9 Lyman Miles, b. 8 Sept. 1852; m. 12 May 1879, Sally Sophia, dau. of Sherborn and Nancy (Currier) Blake. He is a farmer, and lives on part of his father's homestead. Child:
  1 Mabel Marian, b. 13 May 1879.

1-6-5-2-4-5

JOSEPH LIBBY, born in Newcastle, Me., 27 Sept. 1817; married, 20 Nov. 1842, ANN ELIZABETH HALL, daughter of Daniel and Mary (Ganthner) Hall of Nobleborough.

He lived in many places until 1840, when he engaged in the livery business in Brewer, where he has since continued. He has also been engaged in the boot and shoe business, in the grocery business, and as undertaker.

Children, all born in Brewer:

1 William Allen, b. 12 Nov. 1843; m. 16 Oct. 1864, Leontine Letetia, dau. of Ira and Mary Jane (Dorr) Wardwell of Penobscot. He is in the coffin business in Bangor. He served two years in the 22d Maine Vol. Children:
  1 Dana W., b. 2 Dec. 1869, in Brewer.
  2 Albert Dudley, b. 2 Aug. 1872, in Brewer.
2 Ann Lavinia, b. 28 April 1846; d. 26 July 1846.
3 Joseph Nelson, b. 13 July 1847; unm. He is a painter. He served two years in the 31st Maine Vol.
4 Samuel, b. 23 Aug. 1851; d. 9 Sept. 1851.
5 Charles Henry, b. 22 Jan. 1854; d. 25 Aug. 1854.
6 Rufus Adelbert, b. 1 Nov. 1856; unm.
7 Mary Elizabeth, b. 7 Aug., d. 2 Sept., 1858.
8 Dana Lincoln, b. 9 March, d. 3 Nov., 1861.
9 Bessie Leone, b. 5 April 1864.
10 Grace Amelia, b. 13 Jan. 1868.

1-6-5-2-8-3

DANIEL JEREMY LIBBY, born in Cornish, Me., 13 July 1820; married, 8 Oct. 1848, MARY CHASE, daughter of Gideon and Salome (Lombard) Chase of Standish. He is a farmer in Searsport, Me.

Children:

1 George Willard [M.D.], b. 29 Jan. 1850, in Hiram, Me.; m. 31 May 1877, Jacova D., dau. of Gabriel A. and Sarah Pribble of Augusta, Ky. He graduated from Kents Hill Seminary in June 1872; began the study of medicine under Dr. Wm. B. Cobb of Standish, attended the Harvard Medical College a short time; was afterward house pupil at the Maine General Hospital, and graduated from the Medical Department of Bowdoin College in 1876. He has since been practicing in Searsport. Children:
  1 Elva Estelle, b. 5 April 1878.
  2 George Willard, b. 13 Sept. 1880.
2 Isaac Chase, b. 1 March 1852, in Cornish; m. 25 July 1877, Martha E. Libby, 10-5-3-4-6-4-1. He received from Wesleyan University the degree of B.A. in 1875, and M.A. in 1878. He was in the High School in Middletown, Conn., four years, and is now Principal of the Great Falls, N. H., High School. Children:
  1 Mary Ledoit, } twins, born
  2 Ruth Ronald, } 19 June 1879.
3 Elva Estelle, b. 27 March 1855, in Standish; m. 8 June 1875, Samuel B. Locke of West Paris, Me. Child:
  1 Linnie Ellen (Locke), b. 2 March 1876, in Paris.

1-6-5-5-1-2

ABRAHAM PRAY LIBBY, born in Berwick, now North Berwick, Me., 26 Jan. 1802; married, 30 June 1825, his cousin, SALLY

Pray, daughter of Archelaus and Sally (Fernald) Pray of Parsonsfield. He lived on his father's homestead, and beside farming, engaged in shoemaking and blacksmithing. After the death of his wife, which took place 12 Sept. 1876, he sold his farm and went to live with his son at Berwick Village. He died there 17 June 1881. He was a member of the Baptist Church, and was at one time the Democratic candidate for representative to the state legislature, but was defeated with his party.

Children, all born in North Berwick:

1 George Hurd, b. 30 Sept. 1826; d. 30 Dec. 1848; unm.
2 Ann Maria, b. 28 July 1828; m. Joseph Dunham of Boston.
3 William Fernald, b. 22 Sept. 1830; m. 14 May 1856, Hannah G., dau. of Caleb and Sylvina (Thurrell) Gray of Wells. He was a farmer and butcher, living with his father until 1869, when he opened a meat market at Great Falls, Berwick side, where he still is. Children:
  1 George Arthur, b. 9 April 1857; d. 20 Dec. 1874.
  2 Albert Francis, b. 28 Oct. 1859; unm.
  3 William Henry, b. 26 Feb. 1864.
  4 Ellen Augusta, b. 14 Jan. 1866.
  5 Freddie Ellsworth, b. 13 Sept. 1868.
4 Sarah Elizabeth, b. 2 July 1836; d. 28 Jan. 1856.

1-6-5-5-3-1

Daniel Libby, born in Albion, Me., 25 March 1804; married first, 26 Nov. 1829, Loney Broad, daughter of Josiah and Elizabeth (Woodcock) Broad of Albion. She died 25 Dec. 1853, in Bradford. As second wife he married, 11 Dec. 1854, Frances A. Smiley, daughter of Thomas and Mary D. (Reed) Smiley of Winslow.

He lived in Albion until he was twenty-eight years old — three years in trade. In 1833 he removed to Houlton, thence to Fort Fairfield in 1842, then to Bradford in 1848, and in 1853 was chosen representative from that class to the state legislature. In 1858 he moved to Limestone where he now resides. He has represented that district twice in the legislature. He resides on a farm, but has many years been postmaster, has held various town offices, and is a justice of the peace.

Children, by first wife:

1 Maria L., b. 5 Nov. 1830, in Albion; m. 8 Oct. 1848, Mark Trafton. Children:
  1 Charles W. (Trafton), b. 7 Sept. 1849; m. Laura A. Flint.
  2 Martha A. (Trafton), b. 15 March 1852; m. Jesse F. Hacker.
  3 Alice Loney (Trafton), b. 9 Feb. 1855; m. J. C. Lunt.
  4 Lizzie Ella (Trafton), b. 21 Nov. 1856.
2 Elizabeth H., b. 9 Feb. 1832, in Albion; m. 5 Nov. 1856, Ephraim Noble Osborne of Winslow. Children:
  1 Cora Cecilia (Osborne), b. 31 Oct. 1857, at Fort Fairfield.
  2 John Emett (Osborne), b. 15 July 1859, at Limestone.
  3 Anna Mary (Osborne), b. 12 April 1861, at Limestone.
  4 Frank Otts (Osborne), b. 9 Dec. 1862, at Limestone.
  5 Fred Willis (Osborne), b. 15 Oct. 1864, at Limestone.
  6 Charles Smith (Osborne), b. 11 Jan. 1867, at Fort Fairfield.

7 Celia Broad (Osborne), b. 16 March 1870, at Fort Fairfield.
8 George Sumner (Osborne), b. 24 Aug. 1872, at Fort Fairfield.

3 Preble D., b. 12 Feb. 1834, in Houlton; d. 5 May 1855, in Bradford.

4 Celia B., b. 26 March 1836, in Houlton; m. 4 March 1866, Henry Cook; d. 9 Dec. 1869. Children:
1 Annett B (Cook), b. 7 Dec. 1866.
2 Fred W. (Cook), b. 26 April 1868.

5 Melissa, b. 5 May 1838, in Houlton; d. 27 July 1841.

6 Chandler A., b. 26 Jan. 1840, in Houlton; m. 1 Jan. 1866, Nancy S., dau. of Stevens and Sophia (Chadborne) Smith of Gorham, Me. He enlisted in 10th Maine Vol., 1861, was promoted to lieutenant and served until 1863. He keeps a livery stable and public house at Fort Fairfield. Children:
1 Loney S., b. 10 March 1868; d. 13 July 1869.
2 Harry S., b. 22 April 1870.
3 Burt P., b. 23 April 1874.
4 Helen L., b. 7 March 1878.

7 Almeda F., b. 13 April 1843, at Fort Fairfield; m. Oct. 1868, Jesse F. Hacker; d. 15 May 1874.

8 Amos B., b. 4 March 1846; m. 26 Feb. 1873, Sarah J., daughter of Elbridge W. and Mary (Johnson) Waite of Fort Fairfield. He is a merchant at Fort Fairfield. Children:
1 Mary Lona, b. 1 Dec. 1873; d. 2 Feb. 1877.
2 Jesse Hacker, b. 24 Nov. 1875.
3 Elbridge Waite, b. 28 Aug. 1877.
4 Violet Almeda, b. 20 Dec. 1879.

By second wife:

9 Ida M., b. 24 Dec. 1855, in Bradford.
10 Charles P., b. 23 Feb. 1858, in Bradford.
11 Clara E., b. 17 March 1860, in Limestone.
12 Eben T., b. 14 Feb. 1862, in Limestone.

1-6-5-5-3-2

John Libby, born in Albion, 17 Sept. 1806; married, 26 Nov. 1835, Hannah Libby, 1-6-5-9-5-2.

He was a farmer and lumberman. Immediately after his marriage he moved to Houlton, where he lived until March 1849, when he moved back to Albion, and after seven years settled in China, Me. In March 1865, he sold his farm there and bought the Capt. John Winslow farm, in Albion, where he now resides.

Children, born in Houlton:

1 Harriet N., b. 24 Sept. 1836; m. Sept. 1856, Ebenezer Prime.

2 Augustus, b. 16 Oct. 1838; m. Georgie A., dau. of John and Hannah (Noyes) Murphy of China, Me. He is a farmer and lumberman; resides in Albion. He served in the 6th Maine Reg. Vol., Co. I. Children:
1 Nattie, b. 21 Feb.; d. 21 Aug., 1868.
2 Nettie, b. 4 May 1869; d. 4 Aug. 1870.
3 Wallace E., b. 29 Jan. 1872.
4 Charles B., b. 26 May 1874.
5 Llewellyn, b. 26 March 1876.
6 Dellie H., b. 28 June 1878.

3 Llewellyn, b. 16 Jan. 1841; m. 13 Aug. 1866, Angie, dau. of Daniel S. and Mary (Rollins) Drake of Albion. He served in Co. G, 24th Maine Vol., and as veteran in Co. D, 9th Maine. He is a merchant at Albion; has been deputy sheriff of Kennebec county, and postmaster at Albion. Children:

1 Albanah H., b. 29 April 1868.
2 Laroy W., b. 14 April 1872.

4 Albanah H., born 18 Sept. 1843; enlisted as veteran in Co. D, 9th Maine Regiment; was taken prisoner at Deep Bottom; died in Salisbury prison, 25 Oct. 1864.
5 Myra E., b. 3 June 1846; m. June, 1861, A. K. P. Strout.
6 Mary Abba, b. 30 March 1849; m. 7 Oct. 1866, Edward P. Taylor.
7 Waldron P., b. 22 Sept. 1851, in Albion; m. 24 Dec. 1874, Hattie J., dau. of Luther and Rebecca (Cameron) Shorey. He is a farmer, in Albion. Child:
   1 Carrie May, b. 13 Nov. 1875.

1-6-5-5-3-4

Thomas S. Libby, born in Albion, 18 Feb. 1819; married, 27 May 1841, Martha Miles, daughter of Abner and Patience (Hunnewell) Miles of Embden.

He was a carriage maker by trade, and settled in Lincoln. He lived on a farm there, and carried on his business, until August, 1861, when he was mustered into the 7th Reg. Maine Vol., Co. C. He died in the service, 4 March 1864, in Philadelphia. His widow still occupies the homestead.

Children, born in Lincoln:

1 Mindia Y., b. 12 April 1842; m. 13 Dec. 1864, Charles Scammon.
2 Ursula A., b. 11 Aug. 1843; m. 12 Jan. 1864, Wm. Gordon.
3 Amasa P., b. 12 Oct. 1845; m. 16 Feb. 1871, Sarah, dau. of Jeremy and Deborah (Wheeler) Nelson of Lincoln. He did service in putting down the Rebellion; is now engaged in traffic in his native town. Children:
   1 Daisy, b. 16 July 1873.
   2 Martha, b. 16 Feb. 1878; d. 14 March 1879.
4 Thomas G., b. 24 March 1848; m. 1 Jan. 1869, Maggie E., dau. of Edwin and Rebecca C. Lane of Vinalhaven. In June 1862, he enlisted as a soldier, and served until April 1865, when he was discharged on account of a wound. He returned home and engaged in carriage painting, and later in house painting. Shortly after his marriage, he went into partnership with his father-in-law, in a general store, where he still continues. Children:
   1 Thomas Edwin, b. 22 Oct. 1869.
   2 Charles Scammon, b. 23 Feb. 1871.
   3 Laroy Lane, b. 28 Aug. 1874; d. 2 Nov. 1878.
   4 Clyde Ethelyn, b. 13 March 1878.
5 Eben T., b. 6 Sept. 1850; d. 24 May 1871, in California; unm.
6 Very E., b. 25 Jan. 1852; m. 31 Oct. 1874, Lucy, dau. of John and Barbara A. (Thayer) Smith of North Haven. He learned the stone-cutter's trade at Vinal Haven, and is now in business at Lincoln. Children:
   1 Eben L., b. 28 Aug. 1875.
   2 Emma F., b. 30 July 1877.
7 Alvin B., b. 6 July 1855; lives in California; unm.
8 Arthur L., b. 25 March 1857; lives in California; unm.
9 Orlando, b. 3 April 1859; lives in California; unm.
10 Frank, b. 7 May 1862.

1-6-5-5-3-5

Joseph Lyman Libby, born in Albion, 19 July 1821; married, 26 Nov. 1843, Hester A. Quinn, daughter of Samuel and Teresa (Gilman) Quinn of Albion.

He has always lived in his native town, a farmer and "natural" blacksmith. He has been twice selectman.

Children:

1 Olive A., b. 15 Sept. 1844; m. 22 Dec. 1866, Ralph L. Baker.
2 Clara, b. 18 Nov. 1848; m. 24 Aug. 1873, George W. Baker.
3 Preble, b. 22 June 1855; m. 6 June 1875, Matilda A., dau. of Daniel H. and Mary A. (Clifford) Blake of Freedom. Children:
  1 Hollis L., b. 14 Feb. 1876.
  2 Gertie M., b. 26 Sept. 1878.

1-6-5-5-3-9

Ebenezer Libby, born in Albion, Me., 5 June 1830; married Mary R. Pratt, daughter of Vinson and Mary (Reed) Pratt of Albion.

He worked at shoemaking until about the time of his marriage, and then became a farmer in Albion, where he still lives.

Children:

1 Cordelia P., b. 14 June 1857; d. 8 Sept. 1863.
2 Myra N., b. 25 Dec. 1867.
3 Cordelia P., b. 16 May 1872.

1-6-5-5-7-2

Isaac Libby, born in what is now North Berwick, Me., 8 June 1813; married, 12 March 1837, Mary Worster, daughter of Mary (Libby) Worster, 1-6-9-3-2. He has always lived on a farm, engaging in milling and lumbering, and for some years has been in partnership with H. D. Barton in a general store. He has served his town in its principal offices, and has been a justice of the peace. In 1867 he was representative to the state legislature.

Children:

1 Daniel, b. 27 Sept. 1839; m. 24 Sept. 1860, Augusta M., dau. of Wm. and Olive S. (Moulton) Randall. He enlisted in Dec. 1863, in the 2d Maine Cavalry, and was killed in Blakely, Ala., by the explosion of a torpedo buried in the road by the enemy, 2 April 1865. His widow married, 16 Dec. 1868, Eros F. L. Bourveau, a French Canadian. Children:
  1 Ady Esther, b. 31 Aug. 1861; d. 17 Oct. 1862.
  2 Herbert J., b. 12 Aug. 1863; d. 7 Aug. 1865.
2 Elizabeth, b. 27 Jan. 1841; m. 1st, 1 May 1859, Octavius W. Severance; 2d, 28 Nov. 1867, Asa W. Severance.
3 Hebron, b. 17 April 1845; m. 1 May 1867, Alsada T., dau. of Elbridge G. and Theresa T. (Stimson) Rose. He died of consumption, 23 Feb. 1868. His widow married, 12 May 1869, Daniel H. Williams.

1-6-9-4-6-2

Charles Libby, born in Ossipee, N. H., 28 Aug. 1816; married, 12 April 1842, Phebe Parker Aldrich, daughter of Meriel and Lydia (Ball) Aldrich of Lisbon, N. H. His early days were spent in his father's mills. Since his marriage he has lived in

Whitefield. During the first eight years he engaged in teaming between Whitefield and Portland. He has since been in the lumber business. He has served several terms as selectman. In religion, he is a Second Adventist.

Children, all born in Whitefield:

1 Henry W., b. 15 Feb. 1843; m. 1st, 11 Feb. 1863, Ermina F., dau. of Oliver and Sarah Kenney of Barford, Que.; (died 14 Jan. 1864); 2d, 30 March 1865, Sarah Drown; (divorced 15 Nov. 1869); 3d, 2 Sept. 1874, Sarah K., dau. of David and Sarah Ann King of Burke, Vt. He is in the lumber business in Burke, Vt. He was in the 5th N. H. Vol., and was wounded. Children:
  1 Charles H. W., b. 20 Dec. 1863, in Barford.

By third wife:

  2 Eugene, b. 20 Nov. 1877.
  3 Clayton, b. 10 Jan. 1881.

2 Albert M., b. 31 March 1845; m. 1 Jan. 1866, Mariah S., dau. of Daniel and Betsey (French) Parker of Lisbon. He is a painter and lumberman. Children, all born in Whitefield:
  1 Walter H., b. 12 July 1866.
  2 Flora B., b. 14 Jan. 1868.
  3 Hattie A., b. 24 Sept. 1870.
  4 Mertie M., b. 4 March 1871.
  5 Ala P., b. 13 Feb. 1875.
  6 Phebe E., b. 2 July 1877.

3 Lorinda O., b. 11 Sept. 1847; m. 20 March 1867, Albert W. Lane.
4 Sarah M., b. 7 Dec. 1851; d. 7 Feb. 1852.
5 Charles W., b. 28 Sept. 1854; unm. He works with his father.
6 Eugene A., b. 18 Nov. 1864; d. 28 May 1867.

1-6-9-8-1-1

Benjamin Libby, born in Livermore, Me., 2 Dec. 1804; married first, April 1827, Susan Knowles, daughter of John and Susan (Canada) Knowles; (died 28 Aug. 1832); second, 10 March 1839, Mary Coffin, daughter of Tristram T. and Joanna (Moulton) Coffin of Standish.

He was a farmer. He removed with his father to Corinna, and in 1825 settled on the farm in that town, on which he lived until his death, 10 June 1881.

Children, by his first wife:

1 Henry, b. 28 July 1828; married, in Pennsylvania, Synthia Love. He left home when twenty-one, and has been engaged in lumbering, for the most part in Saginaw Valley, Mich. Children:
  1 Willie H., born 1858, in Wisconsin; is married. Child:
    1 Ellen Elizabeth, b. Dec. 1880, in Saginaw, Mich.
  2 Charles, born in Saginaw, 1861; died March, 1880.

2 Samuel, b. 28 Aug. 1830; m. 9 April 1858, Charlotte, dau. of Braddock and Hannah (Emerson) Crowell; is a farmer in his native town. He worked a while in the mills in Massachusetts, lived three years in Houlton, Me., and served three years in the 11th Me. Vol. Children:
  1 Lenora H., b. Jan. 1861, in Houlton; m. Frank Ames. Child:
    1 Charles Frank (Ames), b. 16 March 1880.
  2 Grace A., b. 30 March 1863, in Dexter.
  3 Corris M., b. 26 March 1868, in Corinna.

By second wife:

3 Caroline, b. 10 May 1839; died 14 Sept. 1842.
4 Clement C., b. 11 Oct. 1844; married, in Mount Morris, Mich., Deborah Estelle, dau. of John and Catherine (Melick) Allen of New Jersey. He was a private in the 11th Me. Vol., and, after his discharge, went to Kansas. After a year he went to Michigan, and was there employed in the lumber business. Upon his marriage he returned home, and lived afterward with his father. He is a sheep and cattle broker. Children:
  1 Forest Leroy, b. 15 Aug. 1874.
  2 Arthur Stephen, b. 9 March 1878.

1-6-9-8-1-3

LEANDER S. LIBBY, born in Livermore, Me., 28 Aug. 1808; married, 8 June 1829, HANNAH P. CROWELL, daughter of Ziza and Temperance Crowell of Corinna. He was carried by his father to Corinna, grew up there, and became a farmer, which vocation he has ever since followed, in the same town. His wife died 30 June 1855, and he married second, 12 Oct. 1856, Rhoda N., daughter of John and Hannah (Norton) Patterson of Bangor.

Children, all by first wife:

1 Syprah, b. 7 Jan. 1831; m. 1st, 7 Jan. 1852, George Osborn; (died in 1863, in the army); 2d, 10 Nov. 1872, G. M. Archer, M.D., who died 21 April 1880.
2 Jonathan, b. 25 Jan. 1832; m. 1 June 1857, Melissa, dau. of Benjamin F. and Aurelia (Lyford) Waymouth of Corinna. He was a private in Co. D, 9th Maine Vol.; is now a farmer in Corinna. Children:
  1 Viola C., b. 5 May 1858; m. William Lander.
  2 George S., b. 10 Feb. 1859.
  3 Emma E., b. 29 July 1862.
  4 Clara M., b. 5 Sept. 1863.
  5 Jennie M., b. 1 June 1865.
  6 Abbie D., b. 5 Sept. 1869.
3 Asa S., b. 15 Dec. 1834; m. 12 Sept. 1855, in Lowell, Mass., Sarah, dau. of Levi and Mehitable (Perkins) Martin. After his marriage he removed to Earlville, Ill., where he followed teaming. His wife died there, 8 March 1872, and he became a farmer in Wall Lake, Iowa. Children:
  1 Clara A., b. 31 Jan. 1861, in Earlville.
  2 Hattie F., b. 10 Aug. 1864.
  3 Freddie W., b. 13 Feb. 1866.
  4 Gertie M., b. 15 May 1868.
  5 Walter B., b. 19 Oct. 1871.
4 Isaac S., b. 4 May 1837; m. 15 March 1857, in Lowell, Mass., Ann, dau. of Dr. Putnam Smith of Brighton, Me. He enlisted from Michigan in the late war, and was shot in the battle of Atlanta, Georgia. He was a lieutenant. His widow married his brother. Daughter:
  1 Ada A., b. 1858.
5 Nelson F., b. 3 Nov. 1839; m. 20 June 1867, his brother Isaac's widow; lives in Chelmsford, Mass. He was out in Co. C, 2d Me. Vol. Daughter:
  1 Blanche, b. 1870.
6 Benson, b. 23 April 1842; died 2 Jan. 1843.
7 Leander M., b. 4 Jan. 1844; was shot before Richmond, 1 Oct. 1864. He was of Co. D, 20th Maine Vol.
8 Hannah F., b. 15 June 1847; m. 20 Oct. 1869, Sullivan White.

9 Abby D., b. 23 Dec. 1850; m. 5 Dec. 1875, Sidney E. Johnson, who died 16 Feb. 1881, in Haverhill, Mass.

10 Isaiah B., b. 3 Jan. 1853; is in a shoeshop in Haverhill, Mass. He has been reported to be married.

1-6-9-10-2-3

Reuben G. Libby, born in Ossipee, N. H., 13 June 1815; married first, in Quincy, Ill., Mrs. Rhoda Luxton; second, about 1860, Martha Gray.

He was a prominent man in Quincy for some years, filling the office of city alderman several terms. The actions of his first wife, who deserted him, and joined the Mormons, so broke down his spirits, that he gave up his business and retired to a farm, on which he lived the rest of his days, taking apparently no interest in the world. He died in March 1879. His second wife died in 1873.

Children, all by his second wife:

1 Francis, b. 15 Oct. 1862.
2 John, b. March 1865.
3 Henry, b. 4 July 1869.

1-6-9-10-2-7

James C. Libby, born in Ossipee, N. H., 10 May 1826; married, 28 Dec. 1848, Susan Briard of Tuftonborough. After three years he went to Boston to work, and never returned to his wife, but married another there. He died in North Hampton, N. H., 3 June 1871.

Only child, by his first wife:

1 Frank, b. 9 Oct. 1849; married, in Weymouth, Mass., 19 April 1873, Frances C. Goodman. He has lived for the most part in Tuftonborough, N. H. Children:
  1 Arthur B., b. 9 May 1874.
  2 Norman E., b. 3 July 1876.
  3 Fred G., b. 25 Aug. 1878.

1-6-9-12-1-4

Luther Samuel Libby, born in Sanford, Me., 28 Feb. 1825; married, 3 April 1852, Roena Libby, 1-6-9-12-5-3.

He learned the trade of blacksmith at Great Falls, N. H., where he worked about fifteen years. In 1857 he went west and settled on a farm in Orleans, Iowa, where he has since lived.

Children:

1 Luther Oscar, b. 22 April 1853, in Berwick; m. 2 April 1876, Kate Isabelle, dau. of Robert and Helen (Conger) Elliott of Oak Dale, Iowa. When he became of age, he opened a general store in Chester, Iowa, where he continued until June 1881, when he removed his stock of goods to Forestburgh, Dak. Children:
  1 Kate Estelle, b. 3 Sept. 1877, in Chester.
  2 Myra Erma, b. 19 Jan. 1880, in Chester.

2 Gusta Roena, b. 9 March 1855, in Berwick; m. 17 Oct. 1876, Charles E. Teetshorn. Child:
  1 Eben Clement (Teetshorn), b. 9 Sept. 1878, in Lincoln, Iowa.

3 Cora Vesta, b. 22 Aug. 1863, in Orleans.

H J Libbey

5-7-8-1-1-1

HARRISON JEWELL LIBBY, born in Limington, Me., 18 June 1811; married, 17 July 1832, MARGARET AGNES LIBBY, 5-7-8-3-4.

When about eighteen years old he entered his father's store as clerk, but soon after engaged in business on his own account. In 1835 he removed to Portland and went into the dry goods business, in partnership with John Williams of Boston, under the firm name of H. J. Libby & Co. That firm continued about two years. He afterward associated his two brothers, Francis and James with him in business under the same firm name as before. That firm continued unchanged until the death of Francis in 1873. It has been very largely identified with the cotton and woolen manufacturers of Maine, and still does business in Portland and New York.

Mr. Libby is President of the First National Bank in Portland, and is a director in many business corporations. He is a member of the State Street Congregational Church, and is connected with many of the charitable institutions of Portland.

Children:

1 Harriet Anna, b. 3 March 1834, in Limerick.
2 Ernestine Lord, b. 19 July 1835, in Limerick.
3 Margaretta Agnes, b. 19 Aug. 1837, in Portland.
4 Ellen Harrison, b. 11 Dec. 1840, in Portland.
5 Julia Austin, b. 29 Sept. 1843; m. 14 June 1871, William Trickey Holt, a grandson of David Trickey, 10-8-6-4. He graduated at the Harvard Law School, and became a member of the New York bar; is now in the ranch and stock business in Colorado. His wife died 28 Dec. 1878, at Colorado Springs. Children:
   1 Eleanor Libby (Holt), b. 4 March 1874, in Denver, Col.
   2 Harrison Jewell (Holt), b. 6 Sept. 1875, in Portland.
   3 Julia Agnes (Holt), b. 11 Nov. 1877, in Colorado Springs; died 14 June 1880, in Portland.
   4 William Trickey (Holt), b. 20 Dec. 1878, in Colorado Springs.

5-7-8-1-1-2

FRANCIS ORVILLE LIBBY,* born in Limerick, Me., 20 Sept. 1814; married, 26 Nov. 1839, HARRIET S. WRIGHT, daughter of Christopher and Abigail (Baker) Wright of Portland.

He learned the printer's trade in the office of the "Morning Star," in which his father was chiefly interested, but soon gave it up for mercantile business. He removed to Portland in 1835, and after carrying on business a few years in his own name, became associated with his brother. He was a member of the firm of H. J. Libby & Co. until his death, which took place 12 March 1873. His widow lives in New York City.

Children, all born in Portland:

1 Henry Harrison, b. 5 Sept. 1841; m. 22 June 1865, Mary, dau. of Maj. John M. and Mary G. (Hough) Milliken of Hamilton, Ohio. He spent about two years in travel in Europe, and it was there that he became acquainted with Miss Milliken. He was super-

*See portrait opposite page 96.

intendent of the Royal River Manufacturing Co. one and one-half years, and afterward lived some years in Ohio, on a farm. His wife dying, 17 Oct. 1870, and his only child a few days later, he returned to Portland, and there died 21 June 1874. Child:

1 Harriet S., b. 7 July 1866, in Portland; died 22 Oct. 1870.

2 Frank Willard, b. 20 April 1843; m. 13 June 1866, Mary Stewart, dau. of Edwin and Mary (Carter) Churchill of Portland. He spent a year in Bowdoin College, a year in a law office, and a year in Europe. He then engaged in the insurance business, and has been since 1866 a member of the firm of Dow, Coffin & Libby. No children.

3 Georgianna Howard, b. 12 Jan. 1845; unm.

4 Frederick Augustus, b. 28 March 1847; m. 14 April 1880, Jeannie, dau. of Henry and Sarah (Hopkins) McElderry of Baltimore, Md. After his graduation from the High School he spent a short time in the South, and has since been in the employ of H. J. Libby & Co., one year in New York, and since in Portland.

5 Julia Payson, born 3 Dec. 1849; m. 22 Oct. 1875, Lieut. Rollin A. Ives, late deceased. He was of the 5th U. S. Artillery, and held the position of Assistant Professor of Law, at West Point.

5-7-8-1-1-3

James Brackett Libby,* born in Limerick, Me., 1 Aug. 1816; married Hannah Catherine Morrill, born 12 Aug. 1819, in Kennebunk, daughter of Moses and Mary (Wise) Morrill.

He was a clerk in his father's store from the age of sixteen, and afterward carried on business in Limerick himself until 1846, when he removed to Portland and became a member of the firm of H. J. Libby & Co. For many years he was in charge of the branch house in New York, where, since 1862, most of the business of the firm has been done. He is president of the Harper Manufacturing Co., a director in the International Steamship Co., and is identified with other business corporations. He is a member of the High Street Congregational Church in Portland. His wife died 2 May 1879.

Children, all born in Limerick:

1 Mary Catherine, b. 1 June 1840; m. 5 June 1866, Clarence Hamilton Corning of Albany, N. Y., an iron merchant. He died 12 July 1879. Child:

1 Howard (Corning), b. 28 June 1867, in Portland.

2 Augustus Frost, b. 16 Nov. 1841; m. 18 Dec. 1866, Harriet M., dau. of Augustus C. and Maria T. (Curtis) Robbins of Brunswick. He was fitted for college at the Portland High School, and graduated from Bowdoin in 1864. In 1868 he entered the employ of the firm of H. J. Libby & Co., in New York, and has been a member of the firm since 1873. He is a member of the Congregational Church. Children:

1 Gertrude Morrill, born 3 Nov. 1868, in New York; d. 10 April 1872.

2 James Robbins, b. 1 April 1870, in Brooklyn; d. 14 April 1872.

3 Walter Gillette, b. 26 March 1874, in Brooklyn.

4 Marcia Curtis, b. 26 Feb. 1878, in Summit, N. J.

3 Charles Freeman,† b. 31 Jan. 1844; m. 9 Dec. 1869, Alice Williams, dau. of Hon. Bion and Alice H. (Williams) Bradbury of Portland. He was fitted for college in the Portland High School, and grad-

*See portrait opposite page 204.
†See portrait opposite page 54.

uated from Bowdoin in the same year with his brother. He studied law in the office of Fessenden & Butler in Portland, and in the Columbia Law School in New York, and was admitted to the bar in 1866. The next two years were spent in study and travel in Europe, and on his return to Portland he began the practice of law with Hon. Joseph W. Symonds, under the firm name of Symonds & Libby. That firm was dissolved in 1872 by the appointment of Judge Symonds to the bench of the superior court, and in 1873 the firm of Butler & Libby was formed, with Moses M. Butler as the senior partner, which firm continued until the latter's death in 1879. He was city solicitor in 1871 and 1872. and was attorney for the state for Cumberland County from his election in Sept. 1872 until his resignation in 1878. He has been for several years a member of the school committee of Portland, and is a trustee of the Maine Agricultural Society. Only child:

1 Alice Granger, b. 9 July 1871, in Portland; d. 17 Aug. 1877, in North Conway, N. H.

6-3-2-11-6-4

Moses Libby, born 26 July 1824, in Alton, N. H.; married Vesta R. Wiggin, daughter of William and Dolly (Snell) Wiggin of Tuftonborough.

He was brought up in Tuftonborough, and resided there until 1870, when he moved to Iowa. Here he was a class-leader of the Methodist church. In 1878 he returned to Tuftonborough, where he has since resided, a well-to-do farmer.

Children, all born in Tuftonborough:

1 Asa H., b. 14 July 1848; studied bookkeeping at Vassar College, N. Y., and was employed in that pursuit in Boston, Mass., where he died 20 March 1871; unmarried.

2 Henry Forest, b. 7 April 1850; m. 5 May 1875, Hattie E., daughter of Woodbury L. and Caroline (Allen) Horne of Wolfborough, N. H. At the age of twenty he began the study of dentistry, at first under a private teacher, and then completed his education in the Harvard Dental School. He located in Boston, and has a good practice. During the early part of his practice, he gave considerable attention to sculpture, and carved several groups, which were exhibited and won favorable notice from the Boston press; but as his practice increased, he abandoned the art. His only child is:

1 Arthur Allen, b. in Boston, 10 Oct. 1876.

3 Elizabeth C., b. 18 Aug. 1854; died same day.

4 Willie S., b. 23 Oct. 1856; died same day.

5 George A., b. 11 Oct. 1858; went to Boston at the age of sixteen, where he has since been a clerk in the hardware line.

6-4-1-6-1-1

Isaac Libby, born in Portland, Me., 15 Jan. 1807; married first, 2 Feb. 1827, Sarah Libby, 1-5-2-5-7-4; (died in Gray, 23 Oct. 1848); second, Betsey Ann (Goss) Libby, widow of Philip Libby, 10-5-6-7-6; (died 19 April 1860); third, Mrs. Melissa Stevens of Woodstock, Me.

He learned the trade of blacksmith with Jonathan Knights of Portland. He carried on the blacksmith business in Gray until his first wife's death, and then six years in Paris, Me. He then moved to his present residence, Gorham, N. H., where he has been for the most part employed in the machine shop.

Children, by first wife:

1 Jacob Warren, b. 7 Aug. 1827, in Portland; m. 1st, 18 Dec. 1850, Sophronia A. Bonney; (divorced and married Nathan Weston); 2d. 2 Sept. 1856, Caroline M., dau. of Richard and Temperance (Hamblen) Lombard of Gorham. He learned the trade of harness maker in Portland, and worked as journeyman in many places. He is now in business in Saccarappa, Westbrook, where he has always kept his family. Children, all by his second wife:
 1 Clarinda, b. 8 Sept. 1858; m. 29 Sept. 1875, Frank A. Rounds.
 2 Charles Warren, b. 8 Oct. 1860.
 3 Edwin Dana, b. 13 March 1862.
 4 Franklin Seward, b. 18 May 1865; was drowned by the upsetting of a boat, 13 May 1877.
 5 Freddy, b. 29 March 1867.
 6 Lewis, b. 8 April 1870.
 7 George, b. 1 Dec. 1873.
 8 Willie Barber, b. 29 June 1876; died 23 Sept. 1877.

2 Ann Maria, b. 10 July 1829; m. Benj. Benson of Gorham.

3 Susan Tucker, b. 23 Aug. 1831; m. Orin Dunlap of Portland.

4 Isaac Henry, b. 13 Dec. 1833, in Gray; m. 16 Dec. 1855, Margaret, dau. of Martha (Libby) Frank, 1-4-1-4-1-8. He learned the trade of harness maker in Portland, and worked as journeyman in many places. From 1861 he was himself in business in Poland and in Gray, until 1879, when he gave up his shop at Gray Corner to his eldest son, and engaged in the confectioner's business. Children:
 1 Fanny, b. 2 June 1856; died Aug. 1859.
 2 James Edwin, b. 21 Jan. 1858; unm.
 3 Fanny H., b. 8 Sept. 1860; m. 8 Sept. 1878, Llewellyn D. Cummings of Gray.
 4 Fred Eugene, b. 22 Aug. 1862.
 5 Nellie M., b. 15 Aug. 1864.
 6 Samuel Frank, b. 27 April 1867.
 7 Herbert Milton, b. 7 June 1869.
 8 Julietta, b. 29 April 1872.
 9 Isaac Newman, b. 8 May 1874.

5 Charles Franklin, b. 4 April 1836; m. 26 June 1856, Laura J., dau. of Ira and Sally (Warren) Chandler of Lovell, Me. He learned the saddler's trade, and soon after his marriage set up shop in Limerick, where he has since continued. He has also done business as a barber. Children:
 1 Frank Ira, b. 1 Aug. 1857, in Limerick; died 22 Oct. 1858.
 2 Charles Henry, b. 12 May 1859; unm. He is a cook.
 3 Sarah Chandler, b. 25 June 1861.
 4 Mary Dorr, b. 18 Feb. 1866.
 5 Celestia Ann, b. 25 Feb. 1869.
 6 George Chandler, b. 28 Dec. 1870.

6 George Knox, b. 15 Aug. 1838; unm. He left home when about 21, and has not since been heard from.

7 Daniel Beursted, b. 3 Feb. 1841; is a telegraph operator in San Francisco, Cal. He has been twice married, both times in California. His only child, by his second wife, died young.

8 Francis, b. 27 Feb. 1843; unm. He served two years in the war, and then lived in Boston until his removal, about 1876, to San Francisco.

9 Edwin D., b. 23 Nov. 1845; married, about 1873, Sarah E. Stevens, his step-mother's daughter. He also served two years in the war, and then settled in Boston. Upon his marriage he removed to Chicago, Ill., and has not since been heard from.

By second wife:

10 Sarah A., b. 25 Sept. 1852; m. Dr. Orin Stevens of Oxford.
11 Emma, b. 6 July 1854; m. —— Chase.
12 James B., b. 23 Oct. 1856; unm. He lives in Dakota.
13 Walter C., b. 9 Aug. 1859; died very young.

6-4-1-9-2-1

LEVI LIBBY, born in Parsonsfield, Me., 23 March 1810; married, 23 March 1834, ELIZA DYER BOOTHBY, daughter of Thomas and Sally (Dyer) Boothby of Limington. He has always lived on the spot settled by his father, a well-to-do farmer. He is a christian of the Freewill Baptist faith.

Children:

1 Julia Ann, b. 3 April 1835; m. 13 Jan. 1866, Wm. Franklin York of Standish.
2 Warren, b. 1 Nov. 1836; m. 24 Nov. 1859, Mary, dau. of John and Amy (Lord) Huntress of Hiram. He was a schoolteacher in his young days, and has since been a farmer, occupying the homestead. He is a member of the Freewill Baptist Church, and has filled repeatedly the highest town offices. Child:
  1 Hattie Estelle, b. 3 June 1864.
3 Mary, b. 18 Jan. 1839; d. 27 April 1840.
4 Mary Jane, b. 13 Oct. 1841; d. 27 Feb. 1868; unm.
5 Elzira Boothby, b. 25 Dec. 1843; m. 17 Oct. 1861, Lorenzo Dow Cook.
6 Almeda Bragdon, b. 31 March 1847; m. 4 Dec. 1869, Levi Harmon, jr.; d. 24 Nov. 1877, in Hollis.
7 Thomas Boothby, b. 5 Nov. 1849; m. 6 Aug. 1870, Ruth, dau. of Abial Hall and Rebecca (Gray) Downs of Porter. The first year of his married life was spent in cotton mills in Massachusetts, and in Saco, Me. He has since been a farmer, and now owns the farm on which his uncle Joshua lived until his removal to Standish. Children:
  1 Tobias, b. 23 Nov. 1873, in Porter.
  2 Orison G., b. 11 May 1876.
  3 Almeda, b. 6 Dec. 1879.
8 Roscoe, b. 22 Nov. 1853; m. 1st, 25 Dec. 1873, Esther Jane, dau. of John and Mary Ann (Hubbard) Sargent of Effingham, N. H.; (died 20 Jan. 1875, in Effingham); 2d, 1 July 1876, Hannah Jane, dau. of Joshua and Dorothy (Cooper) Titcomb of Effingham. He is a farmer in Porter. Child:
  1 Joshua Titcomb.

6-4-1-9-2-4

JOSHUA RUNDLET LIBBY, born in Porter, Me., 24 March 1815; married, 23 April 1839, ELZIRA BOOTHBY, daughter of Thomas and Sally (Dyer) Boothby of Limington.

He was a farmer and shoemaker in Porter until about 1855, when he settled on the farm in Standish now occupied by his widow and sons. He died 16 Aug. 1878.

Children, all born in Porter:

1 Mahala Pilsbury, b. 14 June 1840; m. 1st, 25 Oct. 1861, George W. York; 2d, William Melville Berry.
2 Levi Woodbury, b. 11 Aug. 1842; m. 11 Feb. 1872, Lucy F., dau. of Mindwell (Libby) York, 10-1-2-4-1-1. He was a carpenter in

Dorchester, Mass., one year, and has since lived on the homestead farm. He and his brother carry on business as carriage makers. Children:

1 Edgar Lewis, b. 27 March, died 29 June, 1873.
2 Alteen, (daughter), b. 16 Nov. 1875.
3 Ada Estelle, b. 20 Aug. 1878.

3 Frances Ellen, b. 11 Sept. 1844; m. 1 March 1873, Geo. W. Hasty.
4 Lewis Boothby, b. 16 Sept. 1848; m. 24 Jan. 1873, Frances Isabelle, dau. of Isabella (Libby) Brown, 6-4-1-9-6-7. Children:

1 Nellie Maud, b. 10 Feb. 1875.
2 Eva May, b. 20 Aug. 1876.

6-4-4-2-6-1

Isaac Tichenor Libby, born in Danby, Vt., 9 April 1812; married, 15 Sept. 1833, Nancy Frisbee, daughter of James and Lucy (Perry) Frisbee. He was a carpenter until 1866, and then settled on the farm in Johnson, Vt., which he has since occupied. He is a member of the Congregational Church. His wife died 7 April 1863, in Fairfax, and he married second, 21 Nov. 1864, Mrs. Hannah Maxfield, daughter of Martin and Phebe Prindle.

Children:

1 Margaret, b. 21 Oct. 1835; m. 4 May 1857, in Elm Point, Ill., Robert C. Paisley.
2 Edwin R., b. 27 Nov. 1837; d. 3 March 1870, in Elm Point; unm. He was a farmer.
3 Julia A., b. 28 Feb. 1840; unm. Lives in Elm Point.
4 Emmet L., b. 20 Aug. 1842; m. 14 Nov. 1867, Eliza, daughter of Charles and Miranda Parsons. He was one year in the 1st Vt. Cavalry. He is now a carpenter in Johnson. Children:

1 Vernon, b. 20 Sept. 1871.
2 Thomas, b. 3 July 1877.
3 Ada, b. 15 April 1881.

5 Lucy E., b. 23 Dec. 1846; d. 13 Nov. 1865.
6 Mattie F., b. 17 Oct. 1849; m. 22 May 1879, Darwin D. Witherell.
7 Fred Eugene, b. 19 April 1853; unm. He is a barber in Geneva, Wis.

6-4-4-2-6-2

Lovine Libby, born in Danby, Vt., 29 Aug. 1813; married first, 13 Oct. 1836, Elizabeth Gale, daughter of John B. and Julia (Gould) Gale of Millbury, Mass.; (died 12 May 1855); second, 22 Jan. 1859, Ann Shekleton, daughter of Thomas and Anne (Wilson) Shekleton of Frolagh, Ireland; (died 27 Dec. 1865); third, Drusilla (Peasley) Cummings, daughter of John and Ruth (Estey) Peasley of Solon, Me.

After reaching his majority he traveled a while with a circus, and then went to work at shoemaking in Millbury, Mass. He afterward moved to Worcester, and was employed in the machine shop. After his first wife's death he became a truckman. He has been a member of the Methodist Church.

Children, by his first wife:

1 Carrie E., married Spencer Chamberlain of Chicago, Ill.
2 Leander W., b. 1844; lives in Fitchburgh, Mass.

3 George H., b. 15 May 1846; m. 18 Feb. 1871, in St. Louis, Fannie E. Ramsey, born 6 May 1845, in Madison County, Ky. He served in the 25th Mass. Vol. during the war, and after his discharge went west, at first to Chicago, and then to St. Louis, in both of which places he was employed in the shoe shops. He afterward became an actor, and now has charge of a gang of convicts in the state penitentiary. Child:
  1 Claudia Delia, b. 12 Dec. 1871, in St. Louis.
4 Herbert Alonzo, b. 16 Dec. 1851, in Rutland, Mass.; m. 1 Aug. 1875, Margaret Ann, dau. of John and Mary Ann (Bonner) Laverty of Worcester, where he is now a paper-hanger. He was out in the war as drummer, and has since been drummer in the Worcester brass band. Children:
  1 Frederick Joseph, b. 4 Oct. 1876: died 9 Aug. 1877.
  2 Gertrude Fannie, b. 10 Aug. 1878.
  3 John Randolph, b. 28 Sept. 1879.
5 Frank, b. Feb. 1855; died July 1855.

By second wife:

6 Albert W., b. 14 Sept. 1860; unm. He is a wire maker.

6-4-4-4-1-1

Bennet Libby, born in Pittsfield, Vt., about 1803; married first, 13 June 1825, Martha J. Huntress; (divorced, and married Hubbard Lovering, and died in Oakdale, Neb., 16 July 1879); second, 1835, in Allegheny, Penn., Agnes Little. After his second marriage he lived in Pennsylvania. He died in Rochester, 19 Dec. 1856. His widow is living in Washington, D. C.

Children, by first wife:

1 Susan E., b. 24 April 1826, in Dover, N. H.; m. Aug. 1847, Orvill Lovering, now of Oakdale, Neb.
2 Eliza B., b. in Pelham, N. H.; d. in Colebrook, N. H., Dec. 1848.
3 Edwin R., b. 17 June 1831, in Pittsfield, N. H.; m. 1 July 1858, in Kenosha, Wis., Adelaide, dau. of Jeremiah and Betsey (Kent) Lovering. He grew up in Lowell, Mass.; now lives in Lyons, Neb. Children:
  1 Helen B., b. 23 April 1859, in West Point, Wis.
  2 Alice E., b. 15 Oct. 1861.
  3 Alma O., b. 17 July 1864.
  4 Isadore L., b. 21 Feb. 1871, in Lyons, Neb.
  5 Francis Eddie, b. 22 Jan. 1874.

By second wife:

4 William Bennet, a dentist in Washington, D. C.
5 Edgar, a dentist in Pittsburgh, Penn.
6 Addison, a dentist in East Liverpool, Ohio.
7 daughter.

6-4-4-4-1-4

Haynes M. Libby, born in Pittsfield, Vt., 24 Nov. 1813; married, Nov. 1835, Lucinda Bisbee, daughter of Noah and Lucinda (Tarbox) Bisbee, of Lynn, Mass.

At the age of 15 he went to Lynn, and learned the shoemaker's trade. Since his marriage he has followed his calling in Lynn, except our years, during the late war, spent in a box factory.

Children, all born in Lynn:

10098 1 Haynes L., b. 30 July 1836; m. 25 Nov. 1856, Angelina, dau. of Isaac and Julia A. (Walker) Woodbury of Lynn. He served nearly three years in the late war. He is a shoemaker. Children:
1 Charles L., b. 13 March 1856; died in infancy.
2 Charles L., b. 13 June 1857; d. 26 Aug. 1871.
3 Edwin W., b. 29 Oct. 1860; m. Ella F., dau. of Gilbert D. and Mary M. (Edminster) Allen of Lynn. Child:
1 Ida M., b. 17 March 1881.
4 Freddy, b. 2 Aug. 1864; died in infancy.
5 William E., b. 1 June 1866.
6 Etta F., b. 16 May 1872.

10099 2 Justin P., b. 6 Oct. 1840; m. Mary J., dau. of Wm. and Mary J. (Hall) Scarborough of Lynn. He is a shoemaker by trade, and he worked at his trade until 1879, when he went into the manufacture of stains and bottom-finish for shoes. He served in the war. Children:
1 Sarah E., b. 3 Feb. 1863.
2 Lucy A., b. 7 April 1865.
3 Isaac A. C., b. 10 Oct. 1867; died 22 July 1873.
4 Alice A., b. 10 June 1869.
5 Addie E., b. 6 Oct. 1871; d. 9 Dec. 1875.
6 Fred C., b. 3 Oct. 1873.
7 Bertie S., b. 6 March, d. 8 Aug., 1875.
8 Hattie L., b. 7 June, d. 15 Sept., 1878.
9 Luvie H., b. 24 Nov. 1880.

10100 3 William, b. 30 Oct. 1842; m. 11 May 1862, Martha A., dau. of John and Hannah (Parrott) Clark of Lynn; died 30 Oct. 1864, in Washington, D. C., after about two months' service in Co. L, 4th Mass. Heavy Artillery, the same in which his brother served. Only child:
1 Willie A., b. 11 Dec. 1862; d. 30 Aug. 1864.

10101 4 Charles C., b. 8 June 1853; d. 19 Sept. 1855.

6-4-4-4-1-5

5007 10102 William K. Libby, born in Pittsfield, Vt., 26 Sept. 1815; married, 7 Nov. 1839, Susannah S. Kimball, daughter of Ira and Humility (Green) Kimball of Ontario, Canada.

His early days were spent in many wanderings. From the time of his marriage he was a farmer and lumberman. He died 12 Feb. 1881, in Ossian, N. Y., where he had lived from 1847. He was a member of the M. E. Church.

Children:

10103 1 John K., b. 23 Sept. 1840, in Portageville, N. Y.; unm. He lives in Ossian.

10104 2 William H., b. 17 Jan. 1845, in Castile; d. 12 Feb. 1865, at Fort McGruder, Va. He was a private in Co. D., 16th New York Artillery, and was shot while on picket duty.

10105 3 Susan A., twin with last, b. 17 Jan. 1845; m. 21 Sept. 1868, Wellington A. Glenn. Children:
1 Addie L. (Glenn), b. 2 March 1872, in Washington, D. C.
2 William E. (Glenn), b. 28 Aug. 1875.
3 Dallas (Glenn), b. 5 Dec. 1877.

10106 4 Ira K. [Rev.], b. 21 May 1852, in Ossian; m. 1 Jan. 1874, Mary E., dau. of David A. and Sarah (Ely) Wallace of Perry. He taught school until 1879, when he joined the Genesee Conference of the M. E. Church, and has since been stationed in Fremont. Children:

1 William A., b. 30 May 1875; d. 18 March 1876, in Perry.
2 Ransom I., b. 30 May 1878, in Perry.
5 Mary Elvira, b. 22 Sept. 1855; is a teacher.
6 David H., } twins, b. } unm.
7 Darius M., } 5 Sept. 1859; } died 14 Sept. 1865.

6-4-4-4-2-1

ALVIN LIBBY, born in Strafford, Vt., 6 March 1802; married JULIANN ALGER of Strafford. He lived in Strafford until 1832, and then moved to Waltham, Que., where he engaged in farming and lumbering and lived until his death, 9 Nov. 1853. His wife died 18 April 1847.

Children, born in Strafford:

1 William Demon, b. 24 June 1824; m. 20 Oct. 1845, Catherine, dau. of Peter Obadiah and Helen (Leroy) Winters. He remained in Canada until 1866, when he removed to Chicago, Ill., and thence the following year to Marquette. Mich., where he has since lived. His chief occupation has been that of carpenter and millwright, but he is now farming. Children:
 1 Julia, b. 23 March 1847, in Pembroke, Ont.; m. 1st, 27 July 1872, John L. Kerr; 2d, 21 May 1881, Samuel Burt.
 2 William A., b. 6 Dec. 1848; died 19 Dec. 1848.
 3 Alger J., b. 6 April 1851; m. 27 July 1878, Elizabeth, dau. of James and Elizabeth (Davis) Williams. He is a carpenter in Marquette. Children:
  1 Maud Ethel, b. 1879.
  2 Chester Alger, b. 1881.
 4 Carrie L., b. 1 Aug. 1853; m. 1st, 30 April 1874, John Albert French; 2d, William W. Richardson.
 5 Demmon A., b. 7 Sept. 1857; d. 16 Feb. 1870.
 6 Maggie A., b. 12 Dec. 1859; unm. Sheis a teacher.
 7 Kitty H., b. 9 July 1861; is a teacher.
 8 Annie P., b. 19 March 1864.
 9 Rosa A., b. 5 March 1868, in Marquette.
 10 Peter W., b. 4 March 1875; d. 30 March 1875.
2 Jarred Alger, b. 8 March 1827; d. 9 May 1857; unm.
3 Roswell, b. 24 Nov. 1829; d. 2 Dec. 1829.
4 Phebe Lavinia, b. 16 Jan. 1832; m. 20 Sept. 1854, John Wilson.

Born in Waltham, Quebec.

5 Luvia Elizabeth, b. 18 July 1834; m. John J. Cameron.
6 Alvin Alonzo, b. 12 April 1837; m. 1st, 15 March 1862, Almira, dau. of Joel and Mary (Rogers) Wilson; (died 13 Nov. 1871); 2d, 16 March 1875, Mary Louisa, dau. of Sampson and Elizabeth (Johns) Wills of Liverpool, Eng. Children:
 1 Abigail, b. 20 Jan. 1866, in Waltham.
 2 Demon Albert, b. 9 Sept. 1869.
 3 Alvin Alonzo, b. 6 Nov. 1871.
 4 Florence Sarah, b. 25 Sept. 1876.
 5 Annie Louise, b. 23 Aug. 1879, in Pembroke.
7 Juliann, b. 29 Oct. 1839; d. 13 Jan. 1847.
8 Jonathan Albert, b. 26 Feb. 1842; m. 2 June 1867, Isabella, dau. of Robert and Margra (Southerland) Nelson. He lived a short time in Chicago, Ill, and in Wisconsin. He has been a carpenter, but is now turnkey of the jail in Pembroke. Children:
 1 Ira Alvin, b. 6 Oct. 1867; lived only seven days.
 2 Matilda Louisa, b. 4 Feb. 1869.
 3 Eliza Almira, b. 4 March 1872.
 4 Jessie Gray, b. 9 July 1874.

5 James Albert Gordon, b. 23 Oct. 1876.
6 Ira Robert Alger, b. 11 June 1879.
9 Esther Jane, b. 18 March 1844; m. Robert Wilson.

6-4-8-2-4-5

William Libby, born in Newburgh, N. Y., 7 March 1820; married, 8 July 1850, at Fausse Point, La., Elizabeth Marsh, daughter of Jonas and Elizabeth (Morse) Marsh.

When a boy he attended the Newburgh Academy, and was prepared for college at the classical school of the Rev. Joel Phinney. He proposed entering Union College, but was prevented by want of means.

In 1836 he became a clerk in a dry goods jobbing house in New York, and occupied that position, with W. & J. Van Buskirk, Clark & Myers, and Hunt Brothers, until 1850, in which year was formed the firm of Hastings, Libby & Forby. In 1853 Mr. Libby retired from that firm and joined Arnold Graef in the foreign commission woolen business under the firm name of William Libby & Graef in New York and Philadelphia, and Arnold Graef & Libby, in Dresden and Aix-la-Chapelle. That firm dissolved in 1858, and the next year he became associated with A. T. Stewart in the dry goods business. Upon Mr. Stewart's death in 1876 he was his surviving partner, and one of his executors.

He is a director of the National Bank of Commerce, a member of the Executive Committee of the New York Historical Society, a trustee of the Princeton Theological Seminary, and of the College of New Jersey, and is connected with many of the charitable institutions of New York City. Since 1840 he has been a member of the Presbyterian Church.

His children are:

1 William, b. 27 March 1855, in Jersey City, N. J.; m. 7 Dec. 1880, Mary Elizabeth, dau. of Prof. Wm. Henry and Elizabeth (Hayes) Green of Princeton, N. J. In 1877 he graduated from Princeton College, from which he received the degree of Sc. D. two years later. He then pursued his studies abroad, and in 1880 was appointed assistant to Prof. Arnold Guyot of Princeton, in the department of Physical Geography. In November, 1881, he was made an assistant professor in Natural Science in the College of New Jersey.
2 Jonas Marsh, b. 8 April 1857, in Ridgewood, N. J. He graduated at Princeton in 1877, and is now editor of the Princeton Review.
3 Frederick Abbay, b. 10 Feb. 1860, in Jersey City; is a student in Princeton College.

6-4-8-3-2-2

Abraham Rowell Libby, born in Epsom, N. H., 22 July 1815; married Elizabeth Jane Hildreth of Lowell, Mass. He is a blacksmith in Lawrence, Mass. His wife died 29 Oct. 1879.

Children:

1 Abraham Alonzo, b. 14 Feb. 1839; m. 1st, 1868, Sarah A., adopted daughter of John B. Stevens of Charlestown; 2d, 1 May 1878,

Frances Elmira, dau. of Michael T. Delano of Nova Scotia. He is an engineer, and now runs a stationary engine in Boston. Child, by first wife:
- 1 George Washington, died aged two years.

2 Melissa, married, in Lawrence, Charles Paul.
3 George Washington, b. 16 Nov. 1843; is a machinist in Lawrence.
4 Nellie, died in 1862; unmarried.
5 Eugene K., b. 7 Feb. 1852; is a locksmith in Lawrence.
6 Emma.

6-4-8-3-2-3

Moses Libby, born in Epsom, N. H., 25 April 1817; married, 16 Nov. 1843, in Lowell, Mass., Elizabeth G. Parlin, daughter of Abel and Lydia (Goodrich) Parlin of Bingham, Me. Left an orphan, he was brought up by —— Emery. From his majority until his marriage he lived in Lowell, and from that time until 1867 in Epping, N. H., where he owned a saw and grist mill. He then moved to Nottingham and settled on a farm, and there died 18 Dec. 1874.

Children, all born in Epping:

1 Marianna, b. 18 Nov. 1845; d. 21 Oct. 1862.
2 Medora, b. 1 Aug. 1849; d. 24 Jan. 1853.
3 George W., b. 1 Oct. 1853; m. 25 Dec. 1879, L. Ada, dau. of George W. and Mary A. (Colby) Eastman of Derry, N. H. He received an academic education, and took a course at a Bryant & Stratton business college. He has been for the most part engaged in teaching; has held the office of superintendent of schools, has represented Nottingham in the state legislature, and is now one of the auditors of Rockingham County. Child:
- 1 George E., b. 17 Nov. 1881.

4 Sarah M., b. 15 Oct. 1855; m. 29 Nov. 1877, Frank Haley of Lee, N. H. Child:
- 1 Herman Parkman (Haley), b. 8 June 1881.

6-4-8-3-7-3

William T. Libby, born in Epsom, N. H., 30 April 1822; married Eleanor M. ———, born 8 Jan. 1821. He lives in Contoocook, N. H.

Children:

1 William H., b. 19 March 1843; m. Ellen ——, b. 2 July 1851. Children:
- 1 Mary E., b. 13 May 1870.
- 2 Sarah, b. 2 April 1871.
- 3 William, b. 2 Oct. 1872.
- 4 John, b. 2 Dec. 1874.

2 George A., b. 30 Jan. 1845; m. Estella A. ——, born 31 Aug. 1853. Children:
- 1 Freddie O., b. 3 July 1871.
- 2 Stella G. A., b. 29 March 1874.
- 3 Emma H., b. 16 April 1877.
- 4 Mertie May, b. 8 Feb. 1880.

3 Frank D., b. 8 Aug. 1847.
4 Andrew J., b. 15 June 1849; m. Susan M. ——, born 8 Aug. 1850. Children:
- 1 Lillian Isabell, b. 26 March 1872.

2 Ervin Roger, b. 24 Feb. 1875.
3 Albert Robson, b. 21 Sept. 1878.
4 Sarah Elizabeth, b. 13 March 1881.

5 Filmore M., b. 8 Feb. 1851; m. Sarah E. ——, born 22 Aug. 1852. Children:
1 Herbert W., b. 13 June 1869.
2 Eddie A., b. 20 Feb. 1874.
3 Harry W., b. 9 Dec. 1877.
4 Edith May, b. 1 May 1880.

6 Ellen J., b. 5 May 1853.
7 Joseph G., b. 1 Nov. 1855.
8 Emma B., b. 9 Oct. 1857.
9 Clara, b. 20 Feb. 1859.
10 Augusta, b. 13 May 1861.
11 Ida, b. 9 Sept. 1863.
12 Sarah, b. 22 June 1865.

6-6-1-2-1-2

William H. Libby, born in St. Stephen, N. B., 3 Aug. 1808; married first, Frances Cushing; second, Piety Barter, a native of London, Eng. His chief occupation was lumbering. He was a member of the M. E. Church. His death took place in Nov., 1866. His widow survives.

Children, by his first wife:

1 Emma E., b. 6 Sept. 1843; m. Charles Bridges.
2 James L., b. 22 Dec. 1844, in Calais, Me.; m. 23 Aug. 1873, Margaretta, dau. of John and Lavinia (Cronk) Falkonham of St. Martins, N. B. He is a lumberman. Children:
1 Mary Emma, b. 18 Dec. 1875.
2 Fanny Etha, b. 18 Jan. 1877.
3 Ezra Wentworth, b. 9 Oct. 1878.

By second wife:

3 Henry L., b. 5 Jan. 1852, in St. Stephen; is a farmer.
4 Fannie E., b. 1 Sept. 1855.

6-6-1-2-1-6

Ellis Libby, born in St. Stephen, N. B., 22 Nov. 1815; married, 17 April 1841, Abigail Kendall Tuttle, daughter of Reuben and Mary (Kendall) Tuttle of Fairfield, Me.

He was in the lumbering business until 1859, and then became a farmer. He was afterward twelve years sheriff of Charlotte County, and overseer of the poor for about the same time. In religion he is a Methodist.

Children:

1 Mary Viola, b. 27 March 1842, in Milltown, Me.; d. 18 April 1842.
2 Dallas Hill, b. 17 June 1844, in Calais, Me.; died 7 March 1862, in Baton Rouge, La.
3 Viola Carleton, b. 22 July 1846, in Brownville, Me.; married, in Lowell, Mass., Albert J. Bixbee of St. David, N. B.
4 Reuben Elmer, b. 4 March 1849, in St. Stephen; m. 8 Jan. 1873, Elizabeth C., dau. of James McGuire of St. David. He left home and went to the States when 18, and has been employed in lumbering, cartridge manufacturing, and as sewing-machine canvasser; is now manager of the "Singer" office in Concord, N. H. Child:

1 Harry James, b. 7 Dec. 1873, in St. Stephen.

5 Wentworth Roscoe, b. 4 May 1852; m. 11 June 1880, Helen M., dau. of George and Charlotte (Connick) Moore of St. David, N. B. He went to Lowell, Mass., in 1872, and learned the cabinet maker's trade. He worked at it until 1878, then became a sewing-machine agent at Lewiston, Me., and is now in the clothing business in Manchester, N. H., in company with his younger brother.

6 Frank Van, b. 9 May 1855; unm.

6-6-1-2-1-11

Charles J. Libby, born in St. Stephen, N. B., 19 Dec. 1827; married Levina Falkonham, daughter of John and Levina (Cronk) Falkonham of St. Martins, N. B. He has been a farmer and lumberman, but is now at work on the first cotton mill now building in New Brunswick. He is a member of the Methodist Church.

Children, all born in St. Stephen:

1 Ella M., b. 30 Oct. 1855; died 21 May 1868.
2 Roxanna M., b. 9 Dec. 1857; died 21 June 1863.
3 Charles W., b. 4 April 1861; died 22 Dec. 1831.
4 Georgiana, b. 4 April 1863; died 26 May 1864.
5 F. W., b. 22 May 1866.
6 George W., b. 26 March 1863.
7 Nettie L., b. 6 March 1872.
8 Edgar H., b. 29 April 1875.
9 Ellis L., b. 19 July 1878.

10-1-2-2-1-3

Calvin Libby, born in Jonesborough, Me., 2 Feb. 1808; married Priscilla Peoples; lives in Minneapolis, Minn.

Child:

1 Francis Aubine, b. 18 Oct. 1844, in Machias.

10-1-2-2-4-2

Beriah W. Libby, born in Jonesborough, Me., 23 Jan. 1806; married Maria Wharton of Friendship. Upon his marriage he settled on land adjoining his father's farm, and always lived there, a farmer and lumberman. He died 11 Sept. 1875. His wife died 6 July 1864, and he married second, Mrs. Mary Holmes. She outlived him and has married again.

Children, all born in Charleston:

1 Leander, b. 4 Jan. 1833; m. 24 Nov. 1860, Mary Jane, dau. of John and Tryphosa (Stewart) Whiting of Garland; died 15 June 1876. He settled on a farm in Garland, which his widow still lives on. She married second, Warren Stocker. Child:
  1 Willard, b. 1861.

2 Caroline A., b. 28 Oct. 1835; m. 11 June 1856, Samuel Stinson.

3 Weston, b. 6 Nov. 1838; m. March 1863, Mrs. Lavina Norcross, dau. of John and Ann (Carey) Pitton of Dover. He is a farmer. His wife died June 1879, and he then spent a year in the west, but has now returned to his farm in Garland. Child:
  1 Maria, born 1865.

4 Sarah F., b. 4 Sept. 1841; m. 5 April 1869, Silas F. Patterson.
5 Willard, b. 12 April 1843; d. 3 Aug. 1844.
6 Elsira D., b. 9 July 1846; m. April 1870, Albert A. Bennett.
7 Willard B., b. 14 Aug. 1849; m. Georgia Patterson of Hampden, Me. He and Lealmon removed, soon after their mother's death, to Chippewa Falls, Wis., where they still stay. Child:
  1 Harry Weston, b. about 1877.
8 Maria, b. 15 March, d. 25 March, 1852.
9 Clara M., b. 7 April 1853; m. 1 Feb. 1873, Nelson M. Morrow, of Vassalborough.
10 Lealmon R., b. 10 Jan. 1856; m. 10 May 1876, in Woodstock, N. Y., Lizzie Davis.

10-1-2-2-4-4

Capt. Alfred W. Libby, born in Jonesborough, Me., 11 April 1810; married, 21 July 1833, Mary Strout, daughter of James and Sarah (Johnson) Strout of Bradford.

He has always been a farmer, and lives on the farm in Charleston, on which he settled when he was married. He was a captain in the militia, and is a member of the Baptist Church.

Children, all born in Charleston:

1 Sarah J., b. 5 June 1834; m. 15 Nov. 1857, Charles H. Blan.
2 Oliver S., b. 18 Jan. 1836; m. 31 Aug. 1862, Maria S., dau. of Stephen and Betsey (Wheeler) Haynes of Dexter. He is a farmer in Charleston. Child (?):
  1 Fred, b. 1866.
3 Mary, b. 6 March 1837; m. 23 May 1855, James M. Burke.
4 Emily A., b. 11 Nov. 1839; m. 16 Feb. 1873, Nelson C. Hatch.
5 Alfred W., b. 26 April 1842; m. 8 May 1870, Mary A., dau. of Joel Richardson of Cornish; is a farmer in Charleston. Child (?):
  1 Ralph, b. 1874.
6 Urania N., b. 18 Sept. 1844; m. 29 Jan. 1865, Franklin Lancy.
7 James S., b. 25 May 1847; m. 8 Dec. 1879, Cora N., dau. of Samuel Miller of Charleston, where he is a farmer.
8 Amaziah M., b. 18 July 1849; unm. He is a farmer, living in Wheatland, Dakota.
9 Josiah, b. 25 Sept. 1851; m. 8 March 1873, Flora S., dau. of Hezekiah and Hannah (Roberts) Eaton of Charleston. He is a farmer in Wheatland.

10-1-2-2-4-6

Moses P. Libby, born in Jonesborough, Me., 9 July 1814; married, 19 June 1845, Weltha A. Fox, daughter of Edward and Jane (Carson) Fox of Dover, Me.

He grew up in Charleston, and had his father's homestead. Except two years spent in California, he resided in that town until 1859, and then removed to No. 11, R. 1, Aroostook Co., where he died 18 June 1868, and his widow still resides. He was a deacon of the Amity (No. 11) Church.

Children, born in Charleston:

1 Jennie C., b. 29 May 1846; m. 30 Jan. 1864, Joshua J. Seamans.
2 Abbie F., b. 28 Aug. 1847; m. 5 July 1867, James Seamans.
3 Daniel M., b. 16 June 1850; m. 16 Sept. 1871, Manetta E., dau. of William and Margaret (Ryan) Smith. He resides in No. 11, R. 1, a farmer. Has been twice one of the plantation assessors, and is a deacon of the Baptist Church. Children:

1 Clarence D., b. 13 Feb. 1872.
2 Addie M., b. 2 Aug. 1873.
3 Plummer M., b. 29 July 1875.
4 William S., b. 12 Oct. 1880.

4 Hannah W., b. 17 Sept. 1855; m. 29 Nov. 1874, John M. Tracy.
5 Nellie R., b. 29 Sept. 1856; m. 2 Aug. 1878, Nelson R. Williams.
6 Lewis P., b. 17 Sept. 1862, in No. 11, R. 1.

10-1-2-2-6-2

Edmund Libby, born in Jonesborough, Me., 2 April 1810; married, 8 Sept. 1836, Mary Pineo, daughter of Timothy and Susie (Noyes) Pineo of Jonesborough. He was a farmer and lumberman. He lived in Beddington until 1845, when he moved to Deblois, where he died 2 May 1871.

Children:

1 Langdon T., b. 1 June 1837; m. 17 June 1860, Adaline, dau. of Ezra and Mary (Torrey) Boynton. He is a farmer and lumberman in Deblois. He served about a year in the late war. Children:
  1 George Eeddie, b. 4 April 1861; d. 25 March 1863.
  2 Willie Wentworth, b. 20 Aug. 1863; d. 3 Sept. 1865.
  3 Lillian B., b. 15 April 1869.

2 Mary Ada, b. 24 May 1845; d. 9 Sept. 1860.

3 George Raymond, b. 7 Sept. 1848; m. 15 Dec. 1871, Lucy E., dau. of William and Catherine (Puffer) Smith of Columbia. Children:
  1 Walter E., b. 14 Sept. 1872, in Deblois.
  2 George E., b. 15 Feb. 1881, in Deblois.

4 Horace E., b. 10 April 1850; m. 3 April 1875, Sarah E., dau. of Jeremiah and Angeline (Leighton) Gould of Minneapolis, Minn. He is a farmer in Kingston, Minn. Children:
  1 Arthur Leroy, b. 18 Feb. 1876, in Minneapolis.
  2 Cecil Ervin, b 27 July 1879.
  3 Horace Elvertin, b. 26 Dec. 1880, in Kingston.

5 Everette W., b. 28 Aug. 1855; d. 26 Aug. 1858.

10-1-2-4-1-3

Jacob Bradbury Libby, born in Buxton, Me., 2 May 1815; married, 31 July 1837, Charity York, daughter of Isaac and Mary (Maro) York of Standish.

After his marriage, he lived on a great number of farms round about his native town, and at length bought that now occupied by Ivory Berry. There he died, 1 March 1862, and his widow, 16 Oct. 1872.

Children:

1 Mary Frances, born 1 Dec. 1837, in Standish; m. 20 June 1856, William D. Marr.

2 Arvilla, b. 5 Jan. 1839, in Scarborough; d. 19 March 1839.

3 Susan Hamlet, b. 2 Nov. 1840, in Buxton; m. 16 Aug. 1865, Samuel Hanson.

4 Phebe Jane, b. 8 Dec. 1842, in Buxton; adopted the name Maud P.; m. under that name, 29 Aug. 1870, Wm. K. Stevens; died soon after. He is a clerk in a wholesale drug store in Portland. One child:
  1 Maud Lillie (Stevens), died before her mother.

5 Wilson, b. 11 Jan., d 22 Oct., 1844, in Standish.

10778 6 Jason Whitman, b. 14 Jan. 1847, in Buxton; m. 8 June 1874, Anna, dau. of William and Elizabeth (Bugbee) Cleland of Robbinston, Me. He is a painter; resides in Biddeford. Children:
- 1 Statira Bullar, b. 2 July 1875.
- 2 Carleton Walter, b. 11 Oct. 1876.

10779 7 Helen Josephine, b. 30 May 1850, in Saco; d. 28 March 1856, in Biddeford.
10780 8 Jacob Milton, b. 1 Jan. 1852; d. 13 Oct. 1853, in Saco.
10781 9 Vesta Etta, b. 26 May 1854, in Saco; m. Charles Harmon.
10782 10 Arthur Guy Carleton, b. 23 April 1858, in Buxton.

10-1-5-5-3-2

Capt. Charles E. Libby, born in Machiasport, Me., 15 Oct. 1814; married, 11 Nov. 1860, Mary C. (Nason) Libby, widow of Mariner F. Libby, 10-1-5-5-4-1, daughter of Thomas J. and Lois P. (Hanscom) Nason.

He was for many years a master mariner. Since his marriage he has resided on the homestead of his grandfather, previously occupied by Mariner F. Libby. He was representative to the state legislature in 1858.

Children:

1 Eben B., b. 16 Aug. 1861.
2 Lois Ann, b. 18 March 1864.

10-1-5-5-3-3

Henry Allen Libby, born in Machiasport, Me., 8 Jan. 1817; married, 20 Sept. 1852, Hannah Foster, daughter of Nathan and Polly (Mayhew) Foster of Machiasport. He is a farmer, and occupies his father's homestead.

Children:

1 Leon A., born 10 June 1853; married 6 Aug. 1874, Lucy E. Libby, 10-1-5-5-4-1-5. He is a seaman. Children:
- 1 Leon Leroy, b. 20 March 1877.
- 2 Henry Henderson, b. 20 Dec. 1879.

2 Albert N., b. 12 May 1856; m. 19 Sept. 1880, Rose E., dau. of Wm. Bridges of Sedgwick.
3 Sarah P., b. 14 Dec. 1858; died 17 Aug. 1868.
4 Mary A., b. 12 March 1861; m. 12 Sept. 1879, Benjamin C. Huntly.
5 George M., b. 29 April 1863.
6 Sadie A., b. 8 July 1865; died 18 Sept. 1876.

10-1-5-5-4-1

10824 Mariner F. Libby, born in Machias, in that part now called Machiasport, 3 Dec. 1820; married 11 May 1843, Mary Cary Nason, daughter of Thomas J. and Lois P. (Hanscom) Nason of Crawford.

He was a farmer, and always lived on the homestead farm. He died 18 May 1859. His widow married second, 11 Nov. 1860, Capt. Charles Libby, 10-1-5-5-3-2.

Very Truly Yours.

Artemas Libbey.

Children:

1 Francis B., b. 23 Aug. 1845; d. 21 Nov. 1856.
2 George T., b. 8 Feb. 1847; m. 26 Aug. 1877, Carrie Amelia Huntley, daughter of Elisha and Hannah (Wright) Huntley of Cutler. He is a sea-captain, and resides at Machiasport. His only child is:
  1 Alice E., b. 14 June 1877, in Cutler.
3 Walter W., b. 7 Sept. 1848; m. 20 Aug. 1869, Temperance A., dau. of William and Jane E. (Crocker) Richards of Machiasport. She died 15 Dec. 1879, and 19 Sept. 1880, he married the widow Mary J. Graves, dau. of Jotham and Mary (Spencer) Munson of Wesley, Me. He is, like his older brother, a sea-captain. His residence is at Machiasport. His children are:
  1 Minnie T., b. 2 Nov. 1871.
  2 T. Benton, b. 19 Jan. 1873.
  3 Bertha M., b. 9 June 1875.
  4 Susan E., b. 26 March 1877.
  5 Emily E., b. 26 June 1879.
4 Emily N., b. 10 Nov. 1851; m. Frank E. Holmes.
5 Lucy E., b. 29 Oct. 1853; m. Leon A. Libby, 10-1-5-5-3-3-1.
6 Mariner S., b. 4 Aug. 1855; m. 8 Nov. 1879, Lura L. Berry, dau. of Susan (Maddocks) Berry of Marshfield. He is a carpenter, and resides in Minneapolis, Minn.
7 Frank B., b. 14 Nov. 1857.

10-1-6-5-3-6

Hon. Artemas Libby, born in Freedom, Me., 8 Jan. 1823; married, 27 Oct. 1847, Louisa H. Snow, daughter of Myrick and Sarah (Martin) Snow of Winterport.

In the year 1840 he became acquainted with Samuel S. Warren, then practicing law in Albion. A son of Mr. Warren was then studying and reciting to his father, and the latter persuaded Artemas, who was about two years older than his own son, to enter his office and study and recite with him. In the next winter he taught a town school, and then returned to Mr. Warren's office, and began in the summer to read law, keeping up his other studies. He continued to study and read law there, except a few months in the winter occupied in teaching, until the summer of 1844, when Mr. Warren removed to Massachusetts. He then entered the office of Z. Washburn of China, and read law with him the rest of the season. In that fall, 1844, at the age of twenty-one, he was admitted to the bar, and soon after opened an office in Albion. He continued there until his removal in 1848 to Augusta, where he has since resided.

In 1852 he was elected representative to the state legislature from Albion and the towns classed with it. In 1856 he was a member of the executive council of Gov. Samuel Wells. In January, 1875, he was appointed by Gov. Dingley a member of the Constitutional Commission, and on the twenty-fourth of April following, was appointed by the same a justice of the Supreme Judicial Court, which position he still fills. In politics he has always been a Democrat.

His children were:

1 Emma L., b. 12 Feb. 1850, in Albion; m. 5 June 1878, Emmons R. Ellis of Cambridge, Mass.

2 Albert, b. 18 Feb. 1852; died in April following.
3 Arthur, b. 2 Feb. 1854; unm.
4 George W., b. 15 Feb. 1864, in Augusta.

10-1-8-1-2-2

Silas Libby, born in Scarborough, now Gorham, 31 Dec. 1811; married first, Olive Moulton, daughter of Joshua and Lydia (Stone) Moulton; (died 8 April 1841); second, Sarah Dyer, daughter of Henry and Sarah (Sawyer) Dyer of Portland. She died 7 March 1868. He has always been a farmer on his father's homestead in South Gorham.

Children, by first wife:

1 Olive M., b. 7 April 1841; m. Francis Asbury Libby, 10-2-1-2-3-2-2.

By second wife:

2 Sarah Frances, b. 26 Oct. 1846; is unmarried.
3 Benjamin F., died at the age of six months.
4 Henry Dyer, b. 29 June 1851; m. 31 Dec. 1878, Mary, dau. of Lydia Ellen (Libby) Green, 10-5-3-4-8-3. He is a farmer. Child:
 1 William Henry, b. 22 April 1880, in Deering.
5 Eunice H., b. 3 May 1856.
6 Cora E., b. 1 March 1859.
7 Charles H., b. 20 Dec. 1864.

10-1-8-1-2-5

Deacon Arthur Libby, born in what is now Gorham, 6 Dec. 1819; married, 17 June 1846, Miriam A. Mason, daughter of —— and Sophia (Means) Mason of Westbrook. She died 22 July 1854. 2 Dec. 1858, he married Elizabeth A. Dresser, daughter of Robert and Sophia (Rose) Dresser of Portland.

He resides in Portland, where he has been many years a furniture dealer. During the Rebellion, he was in the U. S. service as engineer of the *De Soto*. He is deacon of the St. Lawrence Street Congregational Church.

Children, by first wife:

1 Woodbury Storer, b. 20 March 1847, in Roxbury, Mass.; d. 9 July 1865.
2 Warren Thompson, b. Dec. 1848; resides in San Francisco, Cal.; unmarried.
3 Arthur Clinton, b. 8 Oct. 1850; m. 1 Nov. 1877, Lydia Jane, dau. of David and Pamelia (Dearborn) McKenney of Baldwin. Child:
 1 Arthur Warren, b. 4 March 1879.
4 Mary Emma, b. 17 March 1852; is unmarried.
5 Manetta Elizabeth, b. 11 Oct. 1855; is unmarried.

By second wife:

6 Robert Dresser, b. 6 March 1860; m. 20 Oct. 1879, Maidi L., dau. of James and Catherine (Chute) Hanson of Harrison.
7 Rufus Cutler, b. 3 Oct. 1862.

10-1-8-1-2-6

Rufus Libby, born in Scarborough, now Gorham, 26 July 1823; married Almira S. Emery, daughter of Josiah and Jane (Flood) Emery of Buxton.

He is a carpenter, and resides at Bar Mills, Buxton. His wife died 13 Sept. 1871.

Children, all born in Buxton:

1 Althea Maretta, b. 7 May 1849; m. Clair M. Davis.
2 Elizabeth Jane, b. 24 Dec. 1850; m. 8 Nov. 1871, Samuel Edgerly.
3 Frederick Emery, b. 29 Aug. 1852; m. 31 Dec. 1873, Lillian, dau. of Charles and Eliza T. (Milliken) Elwell. He is a carpenter. Children:
   1 infant, b. 10, d. 20, Jan. 1875.
   2 Evelyn, b. 17 July 1876.
   3 Charles Albert, b. 8 Jan. 1879.
4 Julia Ann, b. 25 Sept. 1854; m. John O. Harris.
5 Josiah Emery, b. 1 Feb. 1858.
6 Arthur Benjamin, b. 21 Oct. 1861.
7 George W., b. 18 Dec. 1863; d. 30 Jan. 1864.
8 Sarah Ellen, b. Nov. 1864.
9 Daniel C., b. March 1867; d. 30 Aug. 1870.
10 Edward Berry, } twins, born 28 Nov. 1870.
11 Martha Permelia, }

10-1-8-1-4-2

BENJAMIN LIBBY, born in Freedom, N. H., 4 Oct. 1817; married, May 1847, in Nassau Co., Fla., ELIZA HADDOCK, daughter of Joseph and Elizabeth (Higginbotham) Haddock. He went south a young man, married in Nassau Co., Fla., and has since been a farmer there.

Children:

1 Martha M., b. 12 Jan. 1848, in Camden Co., Ga.; m. 5 Jan. 1871, Donald T. Haddock.
2 George W., b. 27 June 1849, in Nassau Co.; m. 3 July 1868, Virginia, dau. of Zach and Theresa (Colson) Haddock.
3 Thomas H., b. 5 Dec. 1851; died 10 Oct. 1873.
4 Sophronia A., b. 11 Sept. 1854; m. 10 Jan. 1871, David C. Wildes.

10-1-8-2-3-2

JOSEPH MAXWELL LIBBY, born in Scarborough, now Saco, 17 June 1810; married, 17 Oct. 1833, EUNICE RIGGS, daughter of Wm. T. and Mary (Burnall) Riggs of Bridgton.

He learned the blacksmith's trade with his uncles, Timothy and David Libby. From the time of his marriage until 1857, he resided in Bridgton, and then moved to Chest Springs, Penn., where he built the first frame house, and three years later went twelve miles northwest, and cleared up the farm he now occupies, in Carrolltown, Penn.

Children:

1 Margaret R., b. 30 Sept. 1834; d. 15 April 1838.
2 Adolphus D., b. 22 Nov. 1836; m. 10 Aug. 1856, Ellen S., dau. of Jonas and Susan (Richardson) Brown of Denmark, Me. He served one and one-half years against the Rebellion. He is a farmer.
3 Owen B., b. 15 Dec. 1838; d. 9 Aug. 1857.
4 George W. A., b. 11 April 1840; d. 16 July 1842.

5 David, b. 14 March 1842; m. 7 Jan. 1872, Lizzie A., dau. of John and Mary (Mariner) Riffle of Loretto, Pa. He served about two years in the late war. He is a farmer. One child:
  1 William Adolphus, b. 13 Feb. 1873.
6 Georgianna, b. 28 July 1845; d. 14 May 1849.
7 Maria, b. 30 Sept. 1850; d. 18 Feb. 1877; unm.

10-1-8-2-3-3

John Freeland Libby, born in Scarborough, now Saco, 29 Aug. 1812; married, 12 July 1840, Mary Beckford, daughter of Pinson and Polly (Butler) Beckford of Salem, Mass.

He was in the war against the Seminoles. He afterward drove the stage between Salem and Boston, before the railroad was built. His death occurred 8 Dec. 1872, in Salem, where his widow still resides.

Son of Mary (Beckford) Libby, by a previous husband:

a Henry, born 26 Jan. 1838; took the name Libby; m. 17 May 1864, Ann, dau. of Robert and Margaret Moore of Nova Scotia. He is a morocco dresser; resides in Salem. Children:
  1 Mamie, b. 1 May 1866; d. 25 Dec. 1866.
  2 Bessie M., b. 25 Dec. 1876.
  3 Andrew A., b. 11 Oct. 1878.

Children of John F. and Mary Libby:

1 Jefferson P., b. 16 Sept. 1843; d. 29 Feb. 1844.
2 Perses P., b. 16 Oct. 1845; d. 10 Sept. 1866; unm.
3 Freeland, b. 3 Feb. 1847; m. 12 Sept. 1870, Isabella M., dau. of John E., and Mary Ann (Jenkins) Lank of London, Eng. He lives in Salem, a currier. Children:
  1 Alice, b. 4 Dec. 1871.
  2 John E., b. 12 Sept. 1873.
  3 Hattie, died in infancy, 7 April 1876.
4 Harriet, b. 14 July 1850; m. 26 Aug. 1871, Austin Christian.
5 Mary Ann, b. 5 May 1853; d. 24 Oct. 1866.

10-1-8-2-3-4

Amos Andrews Libby, born 8 Dec. 1817, in Newry, Me.; married, 28 Nov. 1839, Eunice B. Burnal, daughter of David and Hannah (Riggs) Burnal of Gorham.

At the age of seventeen he left home and went to Bridgton, where, with the exception of ten years in Lovell, he has lived ever since. He was at first a shook-maker, but for nearly thirty years has been a wood-turner, and has acquired considerable celebrity in his calling.

Children:

1 Samuel Hazen, b. 1 Feb. 1841, in Lovell; m. 26 Sept. 1865, Harriet F., dau. of Henry Burns of Portland. He has been employed in Brown's bedstead factory since he was eleven years old. For many years he has had charge of the important department of setting up the bedsteads. No children.
2 Martha Ann, b. 28 Nov. 1842, in Gorham; d. 18 June 1849.
3 Clara Edgecomb, b. 17 April 1845, in Lovell; is in the millinery business in Harrison; unmarried.

Born in Bridgton:

4 Emeline Burnham, born 21 Jan. 1848; m. 8 March 1873, Edward Tompson of Standish.
5 Margaret Riggs, b. 11 April 1850; is unmarried.
6 Jennie Elizabeth, b. 19 March 1852; is unmarried.
7 George Clinton, b. 3 July 1855; d. 23 Jan. 1858.

10-1-8-2-9-3

AMOS LIBBY, born 22 March 1828, in Saco, Me.; married, 14 Aug. 1850, in Buxton, MARY E. BOULTER, daughter of William and Mary (Berry) Boulter. He was a blacksmith at West Buxton, where he died of pneumonia, 30 April 1876. His widow married John Gray of South Berwick.

Children, born in Buxton:

1 Mary Olive, b. 20 Jan. 1852; m. James Towle.
2 Charles Henry, b. 18 Oct. 1855; m. Nellie M., dau. of James and Jane (Hill) Luke of Sebec, Me. He has lived in Boston, Mass., in Odell, Ill., and in Warren, Me. He is now a spinner in Sebec, Me. Children:
  1 Mary Ellen, b. 11 March 1879, in Odell, Ill.
  2 Alice, b. 5 Feb. 1881, in Sebec, Me.

10-1-8-3-6-2

PELATIAH F. LIBBY, born in Saco, Me., 9 May 1815; married first, 17 June 1838, BETSEY CARSUR, daughter of Eleazer and Hannah (Stinchfield) Carsur of Leeds; (died 15 July 1872); second, 5 May 1874, Mrs. Mary A. Knowlton, a sister of his first wife. He is a farmer in Leeds, occupying the farm on which he settled in 1838.

Children, all born in Leeds:

1 James W. [Capt.], b. 28 Feb. 1840; m. 1st, 21 June 1864, Octavia J., dau. of Amos and Mary J. (Curtis) Berry of Monmouth; (died 1 April 1871, in Greene); 2d, 27 Sept. 1871, Rosa V., dau. of William V. and Roxannah (Richards) Burnham of Saco. He had attended three terms at the Monmouth Academy, when the breaking out of the war changed his intention of educating himself, and he at once enlisted. He served through the war, and was mustered out captain of Co. K, 14th Maine Vol. He was a farmer in Greene until his first wife's death, then worked five years in the Ames Shovel factory, in Easton, Mass., and has been since 1876 a farmer in Hartford, Me., of which town he is now one of the selectmen. Children, by first wife:
  1 Ida, b. 29 May 1867, in Greene.
  2 Bertha, b. 22 May 1869; died 30 Dec. 1870.

  By second wife:

  3 Edwin W., b. 13 Dec. 1872, in Easton, Mass.
  4 Bessie, b. 6 Aug. 1874.
  5 William L., b. 24 Sept. 1878, in Hartford.
2 Thomas F., b. 28 Nov. 1841; m. 7 March 1868, Mrs. Abbie A. (Kent) Cummings. He is now a farmer in Franklin Plantation. No children.

33

3 Asa L., b. 6 Nov. 1843; m. 1st, 20 Feb. 1865, Adaline, dau. of Benjamin and Salome M. (Dill) Skillings of Leeds; (died 20 May 1878); 2d, 13 July 1879, Annie A., dau of Isaiah and Hannah (Ross) Johnson of Jefferson. He is a clerk in the leading grocery store in Hallowell; a member of the M. E. Church. Children, all by his first wife:
  1 Lewis E., b. 5 Oct. 1865, in Leeds.
  2 Willis B., b. 7 Oct. 1867; died 18 May 1878.
  3 Erwin, b. 1 May 1869, in Greene.
  4 Mary E., b. 31 June 1875, in Hallowell; died 17 May 1878.
4 Samuel Pelatiah, b. 13 Dec. 1845; m. 30 May 1874, Emma L., dau. of Charles Morris of Wayne, where he is now a farmer and mechanic. Children:
  1 Horace J., b. 17 Sept. 1875.
  2 Mabel C., b. 3 April 1879.
  3 ———, b. 1 April 1881.
5 Nancy J., b. 3 July 1849; m. 15 June 1876, George Caswell.
6 Isaac C., b. 4 Dec. 1852; m. 11 Feb. 1875, Albina, dau. of his aunt Hannah J. (Libby) Fogg. He is a farmer in Leeds. Children:
  1 Edna, b. 11 May 1878, in Leeds.
  2 Elmer A., b. 30 Oct. 1880, in Franklin Plantation.

10-1-8-3-6-5

Asa Libby, born in Leeds, Me., 22 Sept. 1820; married, 18 Nov. 1845, Joan D. Fish, daughter of Jira and Joan (Irish) Fish of Leeds.

Except eight years spent in lumbering, he has been a farmer. He lived in Leeds 1845-1854, in Dexter and Cambridge 1855-1869, and then returned to Leeds, where he has since lived.

His children were:

1 Lorin Francis, b. 18 Jan. 1847; m. 4 June 1867, Flora A., dau. of Daniel and Rosilla (Gilbert) Drake of Parkman. He was a farmer until 1878, when he removed to Massachusetts, and has since been employed in a freight house. Children:
  1 Cora Bell, b. 19 Nov. 1868.
  2 Charles Elmer, b. 19 Jan. 1872; died aged five weeks.
  3 Lula Lyden, b. 30 Dec. 1872.
  4 Lorin Percival, b. 11 April 1877.
2 Charles Winslow, b. 30 Sept. 1849; m. 4 Dec. 1869, Phebe, dau. of Nehemiah and Polly (Drake) Leavitt of Cambridge; died 3 Aug. 1870. He was a farmer. No children. His widow married Preston Dagget.
3 Eliza Ella, b. 30 April 1856, in Dexter; m. 29 April 1870, in Monmouth, Will B. Borneman.
4 Elmer Ardell, b. 18 March 1865, in Cambridge; died 4 Oct. 1871.

10-1-8-3-7-4

Josiah Libby, born in Turner, Me., 24 Jan. 1823; married, 13 April 1843, Frances Hussey, daughter of James and Abigail (Elwell) Hussey of Buckfield, Me.

He has always been a farmer in Turner, except three years, during which he was out in the 8th Maine Vol., and four years, 1871-1875, when he was in the meat business in Milford, Mass. Since his wife's death, which occurred 25 April 1879, he has been a clerk in his son's store.

Children :

1 Lucius, b. 13 Nov. 1843; m. 3 July 1868, Elizabeth A., dau. of Thomas and Mary A. (Spear) Leuss of New York. He served one year in the Union army, 1865-1866, and then went to Wisconsin, where he married, and lived until 1878. He now resides in Turner. Children:
  1 Thomas J., b. 3 April 1869.
  2 Edward L., b. 18 Feb. 1873; d. 3 May 1873.
  3 Edward W., b. 31 July 1875; d. 20 Sept. 1877.
  4 Mertie F., b. 8 Sept. 1876.
  5 Charles A., b. 23 Feb. 1880.
2 James H., b. 10 April 1845; m. Orra A., daughter of Wm. P. and Augusta (Rose) Millett. Has always been a farmer in Turner. Children:
  1 Isabella B., b. 18 Nov. 1866; d. 1 Dec. 1874.
  2 James H., b. 6 May 1868.
  3 Frank H., b. 1 Sept. 1869.
  4 Alton, b. 20 Nov. 1871.
  5 Francis, b. 10 April 1873.
  6 Eva M., b. 3 Sept. 1874; d. 3 June 1875.
  7 Adron L., b. 3 May 1877.
  8 Grace E., b. 1 Oct. 1879.
3 Josiah, b. 11 March 1847; m. 4 July 1866, Bell Blackitt of Detroit, Mich. He left Turner in 1864; resided in Detroit until 1865, when his wife died; and has since lived in Montana. He has had four children—two died young, and two now living aged respectively twelve and six years.
4 Charles A., b. 16 Oct. 1849; m. 11 Oct. 1868, Lucy M., daughter of Jeremiah and Ursula Brown of East Livermore. He is proprietor of a country store at North Turner. Children:
  1 Edward P., b. 28 May 1870.
  2 Henry W., b. 7 Feb. 1874.
5 Henry C., b. 16 Feb. 1851; d. 4 March 1852.

10-1-8-3-7-5

Lark Libby, born in Turner, Me., 16 March 1825; married first, 16 May 1847, Christiana J. Philoon, daughter of James and Christiana (Burrell) Philoon; (divorced 1861); second, 1 Nov. 1862, Harriet A. Bonney, daughter of Isaac and Elsie J. (Newell) Bonney. He was a blacksmith in Turner until 1870; a farmer in Peru, Me., until 18 Dec. 1880, when his farm buildings were all burnt; now a blacksmith at Turner again.

Children, by first wife:

1 Georgie A., b. 26 Aug. 1848; d. 26 May 1853.
2 George H., b. 21 Jan. 1854; m. 16 Feb. 1879, Rosanna E., dau. of Ezekiel and Ruth Polon. He resides in Peru—a blacksmith. Child:
  1 Roscoe H., b. 22 Feb. 1880.

By second wife:

3 Georgie A., b. 23 June 1863.

10-1-8-5-3-8

Josiah Libby, born in Chesterville, Me., 16 Oct. 1827; married, 27 May 1872, in Mercer County, Ill., Susannah Pollock, daughter of Robert Pollock.

He is a farmer. He was carried by his father to Mercer Co., Ill., in 1842, and lived there until his removal, in 1864, to his present residence in Benton Co., Iowa. He and his sons have bought, with the intention of settling on it, a farm of 640 acres in O'Brien County, Iowa. He has been a justice of the peace.

Children:

1 William T., b. 15 May 1853; m. 16 Nov. 1876, Eva L., dau. of William Cullum. Child:
  1 Glen Earl, b. 19 July 1877.
2 Joannah C., b. 15 Dec. 1854.
3 Martin H., b. 15 Jan. 1856; m. 30 Nov. 1876, Mary B. Cullum, sister of Eva. Child:
  1 Vernia Mearl, b. 16 Nov. 1879.
4 Charles E., b. 16 Nov. 1858.
5 Mary E., b. 18 Oct. 1860; m. 7 March 1878, John Bailey. Son:
  1 Harry C. (Bailey), b. 5 Oct. 1879.
6 T. S., b. 5 Jan. 1865.

10-1-8-5-4-1

Simeon T. Libby, born in Leeds, Me., 19 Jan. 1825; married first, 16 April 1848, Harriet L. McKenney, daughter of William and Lydia McKenney; (died 11 Jan. 1865, in Lewiston); second, June 1874, Mary A. Carney. He lives in Lewiston.

Children, all by his first wife:

1 Aleander B., b. 16 April 1849, in Lewiston; m. Abbie J. Pilsbury of Vassalborough.
2 Charles O., born 8 Jan. 1851, in Danville; m. Franconia Smith of Greene, where he now lives. Child: (?)
  1 Charles, b. 1873.
3 William B., born 9 Oct. 1853, in Lewiston; died in Wethersfield, Conn.
4 Frank A., b. 12 May 1855.
5 Rosanna L. J., b. 24 Sept. 1857, in Webster; m. 24 July 1875, John C. McPherson of Pictou, N. S.
6 Jacob A., b. 22 Sept. 1860, in Lewiston.
7 Pedora A., born and died 8 June 1862.
8 Joel O., b. 10 Jan. 1865.

10-2-1-1-2-2

Nathan Libby, born in Buxton, Me., 1 July 1801; married, 23 Feb. 1826, Maria Dunnell, daughter of Samuel and Achsah (Hill) Dunnell of Buxton.

He is by trade a shoemaker. He bought farms in several towns in Maine and New Hampshire, living on them and working at his trade. In 1862 he had been living in Buxton about eight years, and went thence to Blooming Grove, Wis. He now lives with his son George, in Lehigh, Iowa.

His children were:

1 Samuel Dunnell, b. 26 Nov. 1827, in Buxton; m. 25 Dec. 1861, in Madison, Wis., Mary Eliza, dau. of John and Sally L. (Grimes) Hall of Hardwick, Vt. He went west in 1850, and in the following year, bought the farm, near Madison, on which he has since lived. He is a member of the M. E. Church. Children:

1 Charles Irving, b. 23 Nov. 1862, in Blooming Grove, Wis.
2 John L., b. 29 Oct. 1864.
3 Edward, b. 9 March 1867.
4 Benjamin, b 9 Sept. 1874.

2 Nathan, b. 19 June 1831, in Tamworth, N. H.; m. 27 Nov. 1856, in Lawrence, Mass., Susan M., dau. of Ivory and Susannah (Rowe) Tarbox of Washburn, Me. He learned the trade of mason, and has been employed as journeyman, and also as builder, in many places. He has lived, since his marriage, in Maine, Massachusetts, Wisconsin, Kansas, Arkansas, and Florida. He is now engaged in the culture of oranges in Limona, in the latter state. Children:
1 Fred W., b. 3 Dec. 1867, in Blooming Grove, Wis.
2 Flora M., b. 5 Aug. 1870, in the same place.

3 George Dana B., b. 15 May 1833; m. 4 Jan. 1866, in Sun Prairie, Wis., Henrietta Bradshaw; is a carpenter. Children:
1 Arthur, b. 1866.
2 Elden, b. 1872.
3 Sarah, b. 1878.

4 Anna Maria, b. 16 Aug. 1835; m. 9 Aug. 1866, in Madison, Wis., Hon. J. G. Knapp; died 10 July 1875.

5 Mark D., b. 27 May 1838, in Buxton; m. 14 Dec. 1859, Mary Jane, daughter of S. and Ann M. (Temick) Gray of Clay Co., Iowa. In 1855 he went to Wisconsin. He enlisted in Sept., 1861, in the 11th Wisconsin Vol., and served through the war. He is by trade a harness-maker, and since the war has divided his time between his trade and farming, living in Wisconsin, Iowa, and Kansas. He is a member of the Methodist Church. Children:
1 George, b. 5 Jan. 1861, in Cottage Inn, Wis.
2 Annie M., b. 4 Dec. 1866.
3 Nathan S., b. 8 Nov. 1869, in Clay Co., Iowa.
4 Bertie, b. 5 Dec. 1872; died 26 June 1873.
5 Lois M., b. 17 Dec. 1874.

6 Achsah D., b. 5 Dec. 1841, in Anson, Me.; m. 24 Nov. 1869, Henry Bradshaw; died 3 Feb. 1878.

7 Sarah E., b. 17 Aug. 1844; m. 27 May 1872, Emery T. Seymour, who died in Iowa City, Iowa, 2 Oct. 1878.

8 Charles H., b. 15 Oct. 1847; died 14 Oct. 1848.

9 Sylvia M., b. 12 Jan. 1850; m. 8 Feb. 1872, Samuel Simons.

10-2-1-1-2-3

JOSIAH LIBBY, born in Buxton, Me., 11 July 1806; married, 11 July 1832, ALMIRA WILLIAMS, daughter of William and Lucy (Weaver) Williams of Fultonville, N. Y.; died 3 Oct. 1836, in West Sparta. He was a carpenter, and went to New York state when quite young. His widow married Jacob Stover, and died 25 Dec. 1870.

Children:

1 William H., b. 8 April 1833, in Fultonville; unm. He was in the dry goods and grocery business, in company with his step-father, until the death of the latter in 1859, and in 1860 bought out a drug store in Dansville. After giving up that business in 1866, he spent four years in Chicago. He is now a tobacconist in Byersville, N. Y.

2 Sarah Ann, b. 2 Nov. 1834; died 27 Oct. 1868; unm.

3 George W., b. 25 Aug. 1836; m. 5 June 1866, Amanda Blank. He carries on a wagon and blacksmith shop in Byersville, N. Y. He served in the war; is a member of the M. E. Church. Child:
1 Fannie E., b. 4 Sept. 1867, in Byersville.

10-2-1-1-2-4

WILLIAM E. LIBBY, born in Buxton, Me., 4 Feb. 1807; married, 27 Sept. 1832, CATHERINE HIGGINS, daughter of Ephraim and Rebecca (Higgins) Higgins of Standish.

He was a farmer in Jackson from his marriage until about 1850, and then removed to Bangor, where he was successively engaged in the livery, trucking, and butcher business. In 1861 he moved from Jackson to Wisconsin, and thence, in 1865, to Iowa City, Iowa, in both which places he kept hotels. In 1868 he removed to San Luis Rey, Cal., where both he and his sons took up government lands. There his wife died, 10 Jan. 1879, and he, 15 Jan. 1881.

Children, all born in Jackson:

1 Rebecca A., b. 2 Nov. 1835; m. 3 Jan. 1853, David R. Foss.
2 Susan M., b. 1838: died young.
3 Benjamin F., b. 1840; died young.
4 Susan M., b. 1 July 1842; m. 1st, 1865, in Madison, Wis., —— Halverson; 2d, 1869, in Iowa City, Iowa, —— Seymour; died 24 March 1870.
5 Benjamin F., b. 7 April 1846; m. 8 Jan. 1874, Margaret, dau. of Charles W. and Sarah J. (Stiles) Stone of San Diego Co., Cal. He was a schoolteacher some years, and is now a general merchant. Children:
 1 Grace, b. 23 Feb. 1875.
 2 Emma, b. 8 Nov. 1876.
 3 Catherine, b. 7 April 1878.
 4 Ann, b. 8 Dec. 1879.
6 William H., b. 6 Dec. 1848; m. 4 Feb. 1875, Mary E., dau. of James M. and Mary (Black) Griffin; is a farmer in San Luis Rey. Children:
 1 Ella, b. 22 Nov. 1875.
 2 Gertrude, b. 6 Sept. 1877.
 3 Robert, b. 23 Feb. 1879.
 4 Harry, b. 8 Jan. 1881.

10-2-1-1-2-9

CHASE ELDEN LIBBY, born in Buxton, Me., 7 Jan. 1820; married, 6 Oct. 1844, MARY E. EMERSON, daughter of Carter and Betsey (Steward) Emerson.

He lived successively in Jackson, Detroit, Bangor, and finally, in Jackson, where he died 19 Dec. 1862. He was, and his wife is, a member of the Freewill Baptist Church. He was for several years one of the selectmen of Jackson.

Children, all born in Jackson:

1 Elma R., b. 1 May 1849; m. 21 Dec. 1867, Ephraim L. Dodge.
2 George A., b. 28 Oct. 1851; m. 13 Oct. 1875, Abbie M. Page. March 1874 he graduated from Dartmouth Medical College, and since March 1875, has practiced medicine in Brooks. No children.
3 Coleman E., b. 24 June 1857; is a farmer and teacher; a member of the Freewill Baptist Church at Pittsfield.
4 Cora E., twin with Coleman E., b. 24 June 1857.

10-2-1-1-4-1

Nathaniel Libby, born in Scarborough, 16 Nov. 1802; married, 28 Nov. 1830, Sally Davis, daughter of Noah and Sally (Larrabee) Davis of Standish.

He was a farmer. After his marriage, he lived two years with his father, four years with his wife's mother, and then settled on the farm near by, where he died, 13 Oct. 1872, and his widow still lives.

Children:

1 Priscilla, b. 9 Sept. 1831; d. 13 Feb. 1833.
2 Charles, b. 26 Nov. 1833; d. 6 Feb. 1852.
3 Henry, b. 7 Jan. 1835; went out in Co. A, 5th Reg. Maine Vol.; served one and one-half years; died at home 27 Feb. 1863, ten days after his return. He was never married.
4 Sarah Ann, b. 24 June 1839; m. 1st, Alfred Thomes; 2d, Samuel Sawyer of Limington.
5 William Davis, born 26 June 1841; m. Lucretia, dau. of Isaac and Hannah (Whitney) Johnson. He is a clothing manufacturer; resides on the homestead. No children. He served four years in Co. K. 12th Maine.
6, 7 Two children, died in infancy.
8 Ruth Arabella, b. 23 Jan. 1849; m. John W. Sanborn.
9 Charles Justin, b. 12 Aug. 1853; m. 28 Dec. 1876, Catherine Belle Libby, 10-5-4-3-10-1-1. He lives at Sebago Lake, Standish, a coat-manufacturer. One child:
  1 Myrta Emma, b. 27 April 1878.

10-2-1-1-4-3

Orin Libby, born in Hollis, Me., 15 April 1806; married Mary Miles, daughter of Francis Miles of Newport, Me.

He learned the tailor's trade at Gardiner, and, after some years, started a shop in Newport, Me., where he died 28 Feb. 1869, and his widow, 26 Oct. 1880.

Children, born in Newport:

1 Francis M., b. 20 May 1836; was drowned in Newport Pond, 4 May 1855.
2 Anson O., b. 19 Feb. 1838; m. 29 July 1865, Rhoda W., dau. of John and Blooma (Chase) Noble of Fairfield. Since his majority he has been a painter. He now has charge of the painting department of the Maine Central R. R. works at Waterville. Children, born in Waterville:
  1 George P., b. 6 May 1867.
  2 Annie L., b. 20 Nov. 1871.
3 Araminta C., b. 3 April 1840; m. 23 Nov. 1863, Joseph Luce.
4 Hollis G., b. 16 Oct. 1842; died at Washington, D. C., of wounds received at the second battle of Bull Run, 17 Sept. 1862.
5 Hiram P., b. 3 Feb. 1847; fell from a bridge in Newport, and was drowned, 15 June 1853.

10-2-1-1-4-5

Jeremiah Libby, born in Hollis, Me., 16 Oct. 1811; married, 30 May 1835, Ruhamah Norton, daughter of Joseph and Nancy (Whitmore) Norton of Standish.

He learned the blacksmith's trade, and went into business with his father. He has continued the business until the present time. In 1858 he built a carriage-shop, and carried on business in that line, employing journeymen to do the wood-work.

Children, all born in Standish:

1 Horace, b. 11 March 1836; m. 27 Aug. 1859, Sarah F., dau. of James and Susan Jane (Jones) Whitney. He learned the blacksmith's trade with his father, and has since worked at that following, in business and as a journeyman, in many places. He has for some years had charge of a blacksmith shop in Biddeford, belonging to Hon. Joseph Hobson, who married Jane T. Libby, 5-7-8-1-1-4. Only child:
  1 Fanny Fern, b. 24 March 1864, in Standish.

2 James, b. 29 Oct. 1837; m. 11 June 1864, his cousin, Mary A., dau. of Dr. James and Lydia (Rackley) Norton of Baldwin. He is a lineman, in the employ of the Western Union Telegraph Co. Has resided in Portland since 1873. Children:
  1 John Howard, b. 15 April 1867; d. 7 June 1868.
  2 Annie Caroline, b. 11 Nov. 1869.
  3 Eugene, b. 25 Dec. 1873.
  4 Amy, b. 13 May 1875.
  5 Edwin James, b. 24 Nov. 1878.

3 Zachariah, b. 26 March 1840; lives at home; unmarried.

4 Levi, b. 4 Nov. 1841; lives at home; unmarried.

5 Franklin, b. 21 March 1843; m. 18 Jan. 1868, Jennie L., dau. of Johnson and Eunice (Weston) Frost of Norway, Me. He is a carriage maker by trade, and does business in the shop his father built. Children:
  1 George Franklin, b. 26 Feb. 1869.
  2 Elsie A., b. 27 Dec. 1870.
  3 Almon Guy, b. 15 Feb. 1875.
  4 Edwin James, b. 16 April 1880.

6 Marshall R., b. 17 Feb. 1847; m. 5 Oct. 1876, Ella, dau. of Bartholomew and Mary (Sanborn) Thorn of Baldwin; lives on his grandfather's homestead. No children. They adopted a child:
  a Lucy Emma (Libby), born in Portland, 26 Nov. 1879.

7 Joseph N., b. 19 July 1849; d. 21 Feb. 1850.

8 Joseph N., b. 27 Dec. 1850; m. 1 Jan. 1872, Nancy F., dau. of Joseph and Lydia (McCorrison) Rumery. He lives in Portland, a carriage painter. No children.

10-2-1-1-6-1

Phineas Libby, born in Buxton, Me., 22 Feb. 1806; married first, 21 Nov. 1824, Susan Hancock, daughter of John and Hannah (Prescott) Hancock of Buxton; second, 18 Nov. 1849, Clarissa A. Beede, daughter of William and Mary (Banks) Beede of Levant.

He grew up with his grandmother Libby, and learned the shoemaker's trade with his uncle Stone. After his marriage he lived successively in Standish, Gardiner, and Carthage. His wife became crazy, and his scanty earnings were unable to support his large family. A portion of his family went onto the town, a portion was cared for by relatives, and he went alone into the newly-settled portion of Penobscot County. His first wife died with her daughter Joanna, 15 Aug. 1879. He now lives with his second wife, on a farm in Woodville Plantation.

Children, by first wife:

1 Jane, b. 1 June 1825; lives in Carthage; unm.
2 Joanna, b. 20 July 1827; m. 25 Nov. 1852, Coleman Brown, a son of Lucy (Libby) Brown, 10-5-5-1-6.
3 Ruth, b. 8 June 1829; m. Samuel Packard.
4 Lucy, b. 5 Dec. 1832; d. 16 March 1852; unm.
5 Abram, b. 17 March 1835; married, 13 Dec. 1863, Lovinia, dau. of James and Nancy (Beatham) Pond of Chester, Me. His early life was checkered. He served during a portion of the war in the 17th U. S. infantry, and was wounded at Gettysburgh. Since the close of the war he has resided on a farm in Chester. Children:
    1 Estella, b. 22 June 1865.
    2 Mabel, b. 25 Dec. 1867.
    3 John Hancock, b. 15 Dec. 1869.
    4 Arthur A., b. 2 March 1872.
    5 Lora, b. 14 Nov. 1874.
    6 Lucy, b. 15 Aug. 1876; d. 20 June 1878.
    7 George W., b. 20 Sept. 1879.
6 Lizzie, b. 2 March 1837; m. Dr. Daniel H. Owen.
7 Anne, b. 15 April 1839; m. Ripley Coolridge.
8 Susan, b. 25 June 1841; m. Marshall Whitney.

By second wife:

9 Hartwell P., b. 6 July 1851; m. 25 Nov. 1875, Carrie, daughter of Elbridge and Diantha (Towle) Crockett. She died 22 Jan. 1877. He is a farmer, and lives with his father. Child:
    1 Arthur, b. 1876.
10 Willie, b. 14 Oct. 1860; d. 17 May 1862.
11 Clara E., b. 1 Aug. 1862; m. 25 Nov. 1875, William L. Hughes.
12 Herbert J., b. 18 Jan. 1864.

10-2-1-1-9-1

Ivory Libby, born in Buxton, Me., 23 May 1816; married, 16 Aug. 1843, Eliza Ann Davis, daughter of Noah and Sally (Larrabee) Davis of Standish.

He has always resided on his father's place—a farmer and teamster.

Children, all born in Buxton:

1 Joseph Ralph, b. 20 March 1845; m. 24 Nov. 1870, Louisa H., dau. of Eben I. and Mary (Thaxter) Larrabee of Limington. He went to Boston in Feb. 1863, where he became a clerk, and afterward traveling salesman in the dry-goods line. He followed the latter calling, (except one year from Aug. 1868, during which he was in business in Portland), until 1871. In January 1871, with H. D. and A. S. Mann, he started business in St. Louis, Mo. He sold out the same year at a large premium, and bought the business (dry goods and carpets) of F. A. Day of Biddeford, Me., where he has since done a large business. In 1877, he was a member of the Common Council of Biddeford, and in 1880 he was delegate from his district to the Republican National Convention which nominated James A. Garfield for President. He is a vice-president of the state organization of the Y. M. C. A. of Maine. Children:
    1 Edith Emma, b. 24 Jan. 1872.
    2 Royal Sumner, b. 26 Nov. 1873; d. 12 May 1874.
    3 Mary Louisa, b. 25 Nov. 1874.
    4 Annie Bell, b. 3 May 1877; d. 5 Sept. 1877.
    5 Alice Helena, b. 14 May 1879.

6 Ralph Garfield, b. 5 July 1881.
2 Cyrus, b. 15 Oct. 1848; m. 7 Jan. 1871, Lizzie H., dau. of William and Hannah (Stone) Perry of Biddeford. At the age of 17 he became a clerk in the dry goods store of F. O. Day, in Biddeford, and except that he was in business in Hollis in 1874, and in Bridgton in 1875 and 1876, has been in the same store ever since—the last years for his brother. Children:
1 Herbert Ivory, b. 11 March 1872.
2 Ires Augusta, b. 20 Dec. 1876; d. 24 March 1877.
3 Martha Ann, b. 15 April 1850; m. 29 Nov. 1866, Wm. M. Davis.
4 Emma, b. 10 April 1856; is unmarried.

10-2-1-1-9-4

MAJOR JOSIAH LIBBY, born in Buxton, Me., 17 Oct. 1825; married first, TRIPHENA MOSES, daughter of Cyrus and Eunice (Underwood) Moses; (died 19 Dec. 1862); second, 2 Oct. 1870, Anna (Wood) Libby, 11-6-2-1-6-*a*.

At his marriage he settled on a farm in Standish. 18 Aug. 1862 he enlisted to serve against the Rebellion. 2 March 1863, he deserted, and resided in Canada until 1869. He now lives on his wife's father's farm.

Children, by first wife, born in Standish:

1 Alphonzo, b. 25 Dec. 1850; m. 20 Nov. 1877, Annie J. Watson of Deering. He is a blacksmith; has been in business at Libby's Corner, (in Deering), and at Saugus, Mass. Child:
1 Clara Fondella, b. May, 1879, in Saugus.
2 Nettie, b. 27 Sept. 1852; is a tailoress; unm.
3 Mary Elvah, b. 15 Nov. 1854; m. 9 Aug. 1879, Geo. H. Doughty.
4 Clarence, b. 29 July 1856.
5 Willie D., b. 28 July 1860.

By second wife, no children, but has adopted Mattie, daughter of Bailey and —— (Smith) Goodwin. She bears the name:

a Mattie Goodwin (Libby), b. 24 Jan. 1874.

10-2-1-2-3-2

ALVAN LIBBY, born in Scarborough, 9 Dec. 1802; married, 6 April 1831, MARY BABB, daughter of John and Abigail (Milliken) Babb. He was a farmer and lived always in the immediate vicinity of his birthplace. He died 11 Feb. 1855. His widow married Ishmael Harmon of Buxton.

Children:

1 Lewis J., born 21 May 1833; m. 16 Feb. 1869, Lydia, dau. of William and Sarah (Gordon) Roberts of Lyman. He is a mason by trade. Since his marriage he has lived on part of the homestead of Lemuel Libby, 10-2-4-2. Children:
1 Alvan, b. 9 April 1863.
2 Lucy Ellen, b. 14 July 1864.
3 William Roberts, b. 9 Nov. 1865.
4 Florence Etta, b. 26 Nov. 1870.
5 Clara McLellan, b. 22 March 1872.
6 Mary Curtis, b. 25 Jan. 1874.
7 Sarah Elizabeth, b. 1 Oct. 1876.
8 Lester Harmon, b. 18 June 1878.

2 Francis Asbury, b. 10 March 1838; m. 1st, 18 June 1862, Olive M. Libby, 10-1-8-1-2-2-1; 2d, 7 May 1878, Ellen E., widow of Archie Kennedy, dau. of Charles and Eunice (Griffin) Pettingill of Portland. He worked at ship-carpentering until his marriage, and then settled on the farm in Buxton, on which he still lives. Children, all by his first wife:
  1 Harriet Louisa, b. 25 Sept. 1863.
  2 Ivory Foss, b. 15 June 1869.
  3 Alice Mabel, b. 15 Jan. 1871.
  4 Everett, b. 7 April 1873.
  5 Olive, b. 18 April 1877; died after six weeks.

10-2-1-2-3-3

JACOB LIBBY, born in Scarborough, 7 April 1805; married, 4 March 1830, MARY BABB, daughter of Jane (Libby) Babb, 10-1-8-1-1. He was a farmer, and, after his marriage, lived successively on the farms now owned by Joseph Harmon, and by Joseph Meserve. His wife died 28 Oct. 1872. In 1875 he removed to Thomaston, and there died, 16 Dec. 1876.

Children:

1 daughter, b. 30 March 1831; d. one month later.
2 Daniel, b. 12 July 1833; d. 7 Feb. 1834.
3 Asenath Jane, b. 22 June 1836; m. William Elwell.
4 John Milton Pierce, b. 2 June 1837; m. 25 Dec. 1860, Mary, widow of Rufus Adams, daughter of Stephen and Rebecca (Adams) Thompson of Harrison. He was a house-carpenter and farmer. He died 31 Oct. 1872, in Gorham, where his widow still lives. Children:
  1 Fred Williams, b. 8 Oct. 1861.
  2 Jennie Melvina, b. 24 May 1863.
  3 Georgianna, b. 9 Sept. 1865.
5 Melvin C. G., b. 1 Feb. 1841; m. 6 Feb. 1868, Sarah M., dau. of Charles and Mary A. (Dyer) Tillson. He is a farmer in Thomaston. His wife died 17 June 1880. Children:
  1 Ada Carey, b. 11 Sept. 1869, in Gorham.
  2 Charles H., b. 19 June 1873, in Gorham.
  3 Mary Katie, b. 11 Aug. 1877, in Thomaston.
6 Daniel Babb, b. 25 May 1847; m. 2 March 1872, Adda M. Starbird of Buxton. She died 17 Jan. 1876. Child:
  1 George L., b. 28 June 1875.

10-2-4-3-3-1

CAPT. WILLIAM LIBBY, born in Richmond, Me., 13 March 1812; married, 9 Sept. 1837, MARTHA T. SMITH, daughter of Ebenezer and Jenette (Sillmore) Smith of Woolwich, Me. He lived at home until he was twenty-two, and then moved to Gardiner, where he was forty years in the lumbering business. He died 5 Oct. 1881, from a fall.

Children, all born in Gardiner:

1 Horatio Smith, b. 30 Sept. 1839; m. 1 June 1870, Frances, dau. of Charles W. and Frances (Huckins) Ayres of Boston. He served three years in 1st Maine Vol. Cavalry—enlisting as sergeant, and being promoted to 1st lieutenant. He has been for many years cashier of the Eastern Express Company's office in Boston. Children:

1 Horatio Ayres, b. 19 March 1876.
2 William Parker, b 23 Dec. 1877.
3 Maguerite, b. 16 Feb. 1880.
2 William B., b. 7 March 1841; d. 28 Aug. 1843.
3 William, b. 18 Feb. 1843; m. 16 Oct. 1868, in Ottowa, Ill., Ellen F., dau. of George N. Kimball. He served two enlistments in the late war—one in the 11th Maine Band, and one in the 29th Maine Band. He is now a farmer in Illinois. Children:
1 George, b. 1870.
2 Harry, b. 1873.
4 Ellen E., b. 7 Aug. 1846; m. 22 Nov. 1866, George B. Safford.
5 Jennie D., b. 7 Sept. 1848; m. 6 Nov. 1879, Augustus Cutts.

10-4-1-1-1-4

JOSEPH LIBBY, born in Limington, Me., 29 Oct. 1809; married THANKFUL WILLEY, daughter of Jonathan and Sally (Rogers) Willey. He settled in Jackson, N. H., where he spent his working life—a farmer. He now lives with his oldest daughter, in Bartlett.

Children, all born in Jackson:

1 Jonathan W., b. 25 Jan. 1831; m. 22 Feb. 1864, Hannah E., dau. of John and Eliza (Stoker) Allen of Bartlett. He lives in Jackson—a farmer. Children:
1 Anas L., b. 29 Dec. 1864.
2 Hetty E., b. 17 May 1867.
3 George W., b. 6 March 1869.
4 Willard H., b. 2 Nov. 1870.
2 Martha, b. 25 July 1834; m. Stephen M. Fall.
3 Harriet H., b. 4 Sept. 1840; m. Isaac Nute.
4 Jacob M., b. 15 May 1843; died in the war, 23 May 1864.
5 William H. H., b. 22 Sept. 1848; m. Josephine, dau. of Larking A. Ross of Bridgton, Me.; died 19 Sept. 1876, in Conway, N. H. No children.

10-4-1-1-4-2

DAVID LIBBY, born in Limington, Me., 2 June 1807; married, 3 June 1827, CHARLOTTE STEVENS, daughter of Daniel and Patience (Stone) Stevens of Limerick. After living in Limerick the few years following his marriage, he went east, and settled at the foot of Bald Mountain. He engaged in getting-out ship timber, which he disposed of at Bangor—twelve miles distant. He afterward became a farmer and still later a cooper. He at present lives with his son David in Greenbush, Me. His wife died 24 Dec. 1874.

Children:

1 Eunice, b. 5 Dec. 1827, in Limerick; m. John Buckley.
2 William Swasey, b. 11 Aug. 1829; m. 12 Aug. 1854, Patience, dau. of Daniel and Patience (Stevens) Miller of Limington. He was a lumberman on the Penobscot River until his 23d year, and then moved to Saco. He almost immediately removed thence to Bridgton, where he has since continued—working in the lumber mills, in the tannery, and the last seven years as currier. No children.
3 David, b. 22 March 1832, in Eddington; m. 17 April 1857, Martha A., daughter of Abram and Martha (Nason) Shaw of Sebago. He is a cooper in Greenbush. Children:

1 Isabelle, b. 27 Dec. 1858, in Sebago; m. 1876, Benjamin Twaddle of Fort Fairfield.
2 Hattie M., b. 15 July 1861, in Levant.
3 Ansil, b. 26 April 1863, in Levant.
4 Arthur, b. 30 March 1867, in Greenbush.
5 Eunice, b. 20 Aug. 1871, in Greenbush.
6 Lottie A., b. 21 Jan. 1876, in Greenbush.

4 Charlotte, b. 6 April 1834; m. Sabine Jordan.
5 Hall J., b. 6 June 1836, in Oldtown; m. Sarah Weymouth; lives in East Cambridge, Mass.
6 Harriet, b. 4 March 1839, in Eddington; is unmarried.
7 Isabelle, b. 11 May 1842; died, 1846, in Eddington.

10-4-1-1-4-3

Ferdinand Libby, born in Limington, Me., 10 June 1809; married first, Jane Smith, daughter of Jonathan Smith of Limerick; (died April, 1864); second, 1 March 1865, Mrs. Sarah Curtis of Biddeford. He was a cooper by trade, and worked in different places in Maine and New Hampshire, but always preserved his residence in Limington, except one year that he lived in Portland. He died at Augusta, of general paralysis, 17 Dec. 1873. His wife had died in the same place a few weeks before.

Children, all by first wife, all born in Limington:

1 John Card, b. 14 April 1828; m. 9 June 1859, Abby B., dau. of Timothy and Abigail (Leaver) Sedgley of Lyman. He was brought up by Deacon Edward Card of Lyman. He is a cooper by trade, and has always lived in Lyman. No children.
2 Henry N., b. 31 Jan. 1830; d. 18 Dec. 1848.
3 Mary Ann, b. 5 Jan., d. 15 Jan., 1832.
4 Frederick H., b. 16 April 1833; d. 20 Jan. 1849.
5 Harriet N., b. 7 Aug. 1835; m. 1st, Albion Ridlon; 2d, Nathan Lane of Buxton.
6 Mary Jane, b. 31 Jan. 1838; m. 10 Aug. 1857, Wm. Spencer.
7 Robert M., b. 26 Jan. 1841; served a three-months enlistment in 1st N. H. Vol., and died in Concord, a few days after his discharge.
8 Arthur, b. 7 March 1843; m. 29 Nov. 1867, Susan, dau. of Ivory and Betsey (Maddox) Clark of Hollis. He served three enlistments against the Rebellion. He is a machinist by trade, and has been employed in Buxton and in Saco. Children:
   1 Rosa Belle, b. 10 Nov. 1870.
   2 Hattie Gertrude, b. 10 Dec. 1875.
9 Dorcas S., b. 14 Jan. 1845; m. —— Randall of Limerick.
10 Frances Ellen, b. 2 June 1847; m. 11 April 1870, Josiah G. Mason.
11 Clinton Green, b. 2 Sept. 1849; m. 17 July 1873, Ann Augusta, dau. of Joseph and Hannah (Mace) Merrill of Great Falls, N. H. Learned the carriage maker's trade with Chas. H. Cutler of Limington. At the age of 21 he went to Lewiston, and worked as journeyman until 1877, and has since lived in Greene. Children:
   1 Fannie Dora, b. 4 Aug. 1875, in Lewiston.
   2 John Arthur, b. 1 Sept. 1879, in Greene.

10-4-1-1-4-10

Ansel Lewis Libby, born in Limington, Me.; married, 14 Aug. 1845, Leonice Allen, daughter of Daniel and Betsey (Leighton) Allen of Gray. He moved to Windham soon after his marriage, and then to Gorham. Soon after the birth of his youngest child, he moved to Lynn, Mass., where he was a foreman in one of the largest shoe manufactories. In 1869 he went west on account of his health, and was foreman in shoe manufactories in Chicago, Detroit, and Portsmouth, Ohio. He died in the latter place Sept. 1870. His widow lives in Lynn, Mass.

Children, born in Windham:

1 Eugene M., b. 10 June 1847; m. 10 June 1875, Ellen Frances, dau. of Enos H. and Martha (Hussey) Sawyer. He was a private in Co. B, 4th Mass. Heavy Artillery. He is now a shoecutter in Lynn. Only child:
  1 Arthur R., b. 10 Sept., d. 28 Nov., 1876.
2 Hortense R., b. 25 Feb. 1850; m. 29 Dec. 1869, Geo. Fuller.
3 Wilbur Chester, b. 26 Aug. 1852, in Gorham; m. 16 April 1879, Euphemia F., widow of John Buchanan, and dau. of Jacob and Flora Gouldrup of Tryon, P. E. I. He lives in Lynn, a shoecutter. No children.

10-5-1-1-2-2

Phineas Libby, born in Buxton, Me., 22 Oct. 1811; married, 1832, Mary Hanson, daughter of Joseph and Joanna (Sawyer) Hanson of Buxton. Upon his marriage he bought a farm near Buxton Center, and lived on it until 1839, when he removed to Bridgton, and settled on the farm now occupied by his son Samuel. He died 13 Sept. 1860. His widow lives with her son Jabez.

Children:

1 Joseph, b. 18 Oct. 1832; m. 23 Nov. 1864, Mary Jane, dau. of James and Jane (Sands) Morrison. Upon his marriage he settled on a farm in West Bridgton. In 1872 he sold and bought the house at Bridgton Center, now occupied by his widow. His death took place 9 Nov. 1874. Child:
  1 Emma Rosilla, b. 9 Dec. 1872, in Bridgton.
2 George Henry, b. 30 April 1835; m. 11 Jan. 1864, his cousin Mary Ann, dau. of Josiah and Verane (Hanson) Harmon of Bridgton. Upon his marriage he engaged in farming. His wife died 28 Oct. 1870, and he has since lived with his brother Jabez.
3 Jabez, b. 22 April 1837; unm. He is a farmer. About 1870 he bought the farm he now occupies, in West Bridgton.
4 Samuel, b. 8 Aug. 1839, in Buxton; m. 14 Feb. 1865, Julia M., dau. of James T. and Mary J. (Adams) Sawyer of Sweden. He is a farmer, occupying the homestead. Children:
  1 Nellie Augusta, b. 10 July 1869.
  2 James Phineas, b. 19 March 1871.
5 James Oliver, b. 11 March 1842; m. Mary Jane Thurston; is a farmer in Conway, N. H. No children.
6 Aaron, b. 31 July 1844; m. 1880, Almira Allen of Harrison; is a farmer in Waterford, Me.
7 John Alexander, b. 11 May 1847; lives in Bethel; unm.
8 Mary Eliza, b. 18 Sept. 1849; m. 5 May 1877, Preble Marean of Standish.
9 Charles Roscoe, b. 8 Aug. 1851; lives at Mechanic Falls; unm.
10 Anna, b. 9 May 1856; m. 1879, John Frank Davis.

10-5-1-1-2-5

Elisha Libby, born in Buxton, Me., 20 June 1818; married, 12 June 1842, Elizabeth B. Wilson, daughter of George and Hannah (Averill) Wilson of Kennebunk.

At the age of sixteen he went to learn the carpenter's trade with Stephen Hanson of Buxton. After four years he went to Saco, and entered the repair shop of the York Manufacturing Company. After ten years he removed to Biddeford, and entered the employ of the Water Power Company, who were then building the Pepperell mills. He still continues with that company. He has served in both branches of the Biddeford City Council.

Children:

1 Franklin Howard, b. 9 April 1843, in Saco; m. 17 April 1868, Sarah D., dau. of Delia (Libby) Hubbard, 5-7-12-5-6. He followed the sea from the age of fourteen, and rose to be master. He quit the sea in 1871, and since 1873 has had charge of the Oakland Beach Hotel, Warwick, R. I. Child:
 1 Arthur Franklin, b. 28 June 1870, in Warwick.
2 Olive, b. 15 May 1845, in Buxton; unm.
3 Edward Hartley, b. 22 Dec. 1851, in Biddeford; m. 1876, Lucy Ellen Moulton of Palmer, Mass. He learned the carpenter's trade with his father. Since 1873 he has been in the employ of the Thorndike Manufacturing Co. in Palmer. Children:
 1 Annie Norton, b. 20 Oct. 1876.
 2 Frank Hartley, b. 14 Aug. 1878.

10-5-1-2-1-5

Charles Welch Libby, born in Gray, Me., 7 Feb. 1819; married, 8 July 1847, Mary Jane Mayberry, daughter of Ezekiel and Betsey (Elder) Mayberry of Windham.

He was a schoolteacher and farmer until 1846, when he went to Boon Co., Ill., and purchased land. He went back to Maine the following summer, married, and returned to Illinois. He lived there ten years. During the time he became a member of the Wesleyan Methodist Church. He also filled, from time to time, the offices of commissioner, supervisor, and superintendent of public instruction for the county, and a number of town offices. In 1856 his health failed and he removed to Goodhue Co., Minn. In Feb. 1858, Minnesota was admitted as a State, and that fall he was elected one of the four representatives at large for Goodhue Co., to the legislature. He continued in Roscoe eleven years, and, during the time, filled important offices in the town and county, and became a member of the M. E. Church. In 1865, he sold his farm and bought another in St. Croix Co., Wis.; and in 1868 sold again, and settled in Bourbon Co., Kans. He served two terms (1869 and 1870) in the lower branch of the Kansas legislature, serving the latter year as chairman of the committee on retrenchment and reform, and filling the second place on the committee of ways and means. The following year, he was appointed state railroad assessor for the sixth judicial district. His farm of 220 acres is about three miles north of the village of Xenia.

Children:

1 Sarah Elizabeth, b. 15 July 1848, in Boone Co., Ill.; m. 29 Dec. 1867, Josiah Lothrop.

2 Louisa F., b. 4 Aug., d. 8 Sept., 1850.
3 Charles Franklin, b. 17 Oct. 1851; m. 16 Aug. 1874, Mary Ann, dau. of Amaziah and Caroline (Hudson) Williams of Xenia. He has one child:
  1 Musetta Grace, b. 20 June 1875.
4 Low Frances, b. 24 Jan. 1854; m. 6 Oct. 1878, Robert E. Matthews.
5 Ivenora, b. 1 Dec. 1856, in Roscoe, Minn.
6 Warren Edward, b. 2 Aug. 1861, in Roscoe.
7 Edgar Josiah, b. 6 Nov. 1867, in St. Croix Co., Wis.

10-5-4-1-1-2

Simon Libby, born in Otisfield, Me., 21 June 1812; married, 20 July 1834, Rebecca A. Morse, daughter of John Morse of Gray; died in Cape Elizabeth, Sept. 1864. His widow died in Scarborough, with her son, 16 Dec. 1872.

Children:

1 Harriet Frances, b. 7 July 1835, in Gray; m. Frank Dennett.
2 Josephine, b. 7 March 1837; m. 3 July 1856, Henry Babb.
3 Appleton, b. 22 May 1840, in Gorham; d. 15 March 1842.
4 Roscoe, b. 27 Dec. 1842; m. 22 March 1866, Abbie E., dau. of Rebecca (Libby) Frost, 10-2-4-8-7. He served one year in the 12th Me. Vol., and three years in the 1st U. S. Heavy Artillery. After the war, he was a blacksmith in Gorham, living in Scarborough, where he died very suddenly, 25 June 1880. Children:
  1 Katie Frost, b. 11 Nov. 1871.
  2 Georgie H., b. 16 March 1876.
5 Lestinia, b. 11 Sept. 1846; m. Seth S. Willard.
6 Fransilia, b. 26 March 1847; m. Samuel Grover of New Haven, Ind.
7 Simeon A., b. 2 June 1854; lives in Kansas; unm.

10-5-4-1-1-5

Solomon Lombard Libby, born in Otisfield, Me., 27 Oct. 1818; married, 21 May 1843, Mary Ann Bangs, daughter of James and Mary (Lakeman) Bangs of Gorham.

He is a skillful mechanic. He writes: "Built Cumberland Paper Mills; was superintendent of the construction of Forts Preble and Scammel, Portland Harbor; master mason on Portland Custom House; in 1868, cut a channel for Presumpscot River through a great land slide that filled the valley below Cumberland Mills, in *six days*—a job for which New York engineers wanted *six months'* time and $15,000." His residence was in the vicinity of Portland until 1869, when he removed to Ashland, Mass., where he now resides on a farm. He is a member of the M. E. Church.

Children:

1 Elenette Montaigue, b. 3 Sept. 1845, in Gorham; d. 4 Sept. 1878, at Augusta; unmarried.
2 Elizabeth Abby, b. 12 Dec. 1847, in Westbrook (Saccarappa); m. 3 July 1872, Edgar O. Tillotson.
3 Adelaide Maria, b. 20 April 1850; d. 27 Sept. 1851.
4 Edgar Howard, b. 3 March 1852; lives in Chicago, Ill.; unmarried. He gained an education by his own efforts, and graduated at Amherst College in 1874. In June 1875 he started the "Scientific Farmer." In May 1878 he became managing editor of the "Amer-

ican Agriculturist." During the following year he visited Europe on a tour of agricultural observation, and made a similar tour of the western states. He has since been engaged in general agricultural journalism; is a contributor to "Scribner's Monthly," "The Nation," "Christian Union," and various agricultural papers.

5 Mary Ida, b. 17 Jan. 1854; is a teacher.

10-5-4-1-1-6

SAMUEL LIBBY, born in Otisfield, Me., 22 Aug. 1820; married, 7 Dec. 1843, ROSALIA B. LOMBARD, daughter of Simon and Jane (Norton) Lombard of Gorham. She died 30 May 1858, and 11 Sept. 1859, he married Damaris W., daughter of Archelaus and Betsey (Emery) Stone of Gorham. He lived on his father's homestead in Gorham, and there died, 20 Sept. 1878.

Children, all by first wife:

1 Sarah Jane, b. 20 April 1845; m. J. A. Smith.
2 Ephraim Alphonzo, b. 1 Nov. 1846; m. 24 Dec. 1870, Victoria, dau. of William and Thomisina (Connell) Hill of Biddeford. He served nine months in Co. F, 25th Maine Vol., and subsequently spent one and a half years in the West. Since his marriage he has been successively engaged as tailor, carpenter, and employee in the cotton mills at Biddeford. Children:
  1 Haydn Samuel, b. 20 Oct. 1871.
  2 Thomisina, b. 12 Sept. 1878.
  3 son, b. 3 Sept. 1880.
3 Louisa R., b. 19 Feb. 1848; d. 4 April 1849.
4 James Henry, b. 8 Aug. 1850; m. 26 Nov. 1868, Melvina M. Waterhouse, 10-2-2-11-2-9-1. He has followed successively milling and farming in Wisconsin, and coat-making and tin-peddling in Maine. He is now a farmer in Mapleton, Me. Children, all born in Gorham:
  1 Walter Prentiss, b. 21 April 1872.
  2 Jesse Clifford, b. 12 March 1874; d. 11 Aug. 1877.
  3 Arthur La Forest, b. 18 Aug. 1876.
  4 Ernest Morse, b. 31 Jan. 1879.
5 Ida L., b. 19 June 1855; d. 1 Oct. 1855.
6 Charles Martin, b. 18 Jan. 1857; m. 15 June 1879, Clara May, dau. of Mark and Susan (Burnett) Cloudman. He lives on his father's homestead. No children.

10-5-4-1-1-8

BENJAMIN FRANKLIN LIBBY, born in Otisfield, Me., 6 Oct. 1824; married, 1 Jan. 1849, LAVINIA P. WHITNEY, daughter of Samuel and Dorcas (Wescott) Whitney of Farmington, Me. He learned the carpenter's trade with his brother Solomon L., and has followed that calling since. He has lived in many places. His present residence is Cape Elizabeth.

Children, born in Gorham:

1 Frank Montraville, b. 11 April 1850; m. 1 Jan. 1871, Dora, dau. of Gideon and Mary Jane (Cobb) Burbank of Cape Elizabeth. He is a stair-builder and wood-turner. He lives in Dover, N. H. Children:
  1 Montraville Leroy, b. 15 Sept. 1872; d. 15 Oct. 1872.

2 Mildred A., b. 29 Nov. 1874.
3 Maud L., b. 19 Feb. 1877.
4 Margie B., b. 29 April 1881.
2 William Leroy, b. 11 Oct. 1852; m. 22 May 1872, Maria, widow of Charles Wm. Parsons, dau. of —— and Hannah (Talbot) Roberts. He is a carpenter at Old Orchard Beach, Saco. Child:
1 Frank H., b. 20 Jan. 1873.

10-5-4-1-2-1

David P. Libby, born in Gorham, Me., 9 Jan. 1810; married, in Roxbury, Mass., Ann L. Hodges of Sandwich, N. H. He led a roving life, but ended his days in his native town. He died 6 March 1864. His widow died 27 Jan. 1870.

Children:

1 William Francis, b. 12 Sept. 1839, in Malden, (now Melrose), Mass.: m. 1 March 1868, Ellen C., dau. of Ira S. and Sarah E. (Le Suer) Hayman of Robinston, Me. He served nearly four years against the Rebellion. Subsequently he worked at tanning in Gorham and lumbering in Pennsylvania, and is now a paver in Boston, Mass. Children:
1 Alice Gertrude, b. 15 Dec. 1868, in Gorham, Me.
2 Charles Ira, b. 20 Sept. 1870, in Gorham.
3 Laura Ella, b. 7 March 1872, in Gorham.
4 Annie Maria, b. 2 March 1874, in Kersey, Penn.
5 Harry Francis, b. 10 March 1876, in Boston, Mass.
6 Edith May, b. 27 May 1878, in Boston.
7 William Percy, b. 7 Sept. 1880, in Boston.
2 Mary Elizabeth, b. 9 Jan. 1843; m. 1st, 17 Aug. 1862, Benj. F. Metcalf; 2d, Wm. H. Bartol.
3 Stephen Phinney, b. 1 Feb. 1845; m. 5 Nov. 1868, Clara E., dau. of Oliver and Mary (Bean) Hanson of Gorham. He works in Hinkley's tannery at Gorham Corner. Children:
1 Fannie Emma, b. 4 April 1870.
2 Clara Eva, b. 4 Sept. 1872.
3 Mary Ann, b. 4 April 1874.
4 Susan Kennie, b. 4 Sept. 1876.
5 Stephen Henry, b. 5 Jan. 1879.
4 Ai, b. 1 June 1850, in Byron, Me.; m. 1st. 27 Feb. 1868, Mary E., dau. of Richard and Temperance (Weeks) Lombard; (died 17 Dec. 1869); 2d, Lavinia, dau. of Eben Spencer of Buxton; (died 8 June 1877). He was a currier in Hinkley's tannery, and in September, 1879, enlisted in the U. S. army. Children; by first wife:
1 Charles, lives with his uncle, John Murray, in Portland.

By second wife:

2 Sarah, lives in Boston, Mass.
5 Ella Jane, b. 28 July 1852, in Byron; m. Madison J. Hayman of Cambridgeport, Mass.
6 Cynthia Belinda, b. 16 May 1856; d. 6 May 1875.
7 Walter Mandell, born 17 Jan. 1859, in Gorham; m. 8 April 1880, Adele, dau. of Wm. and Callie (Bennett) Freeman of Deering. He is employed in Hinkley's tannery also. Child:
1 ——, b. 19 July 1880, in Gorham.

10-5-4-1-5-2

Daniel F. Libby, born in Gorham, Me., 24 Aug. 1823; married, 7 Dec. 1843, Roxanna L. Jones, daughter of Sarah (Libby)

Jones, 10-5-4-3-3. He is a blacksmith. He worked many years for the Portland Co. From 1863 to 1865 he lived in Bridgewater, Mass., and since that time has carried on his business at White Rock, Gorham.

Children:

1 Sarah Frances, b. 27 Oct. 1844; m. Adoniram Soule.
2 Ellen Maria, b. 29 Dec. 1845; d. 18 May 1861.
3 Julia Evelina, b. 13 Nov. 1847; m. 10 July 1867, Albert Wallace of Portland.
4 Albert Francis, b. 1 Dec. 1849; m. 21 Oct. 1872, Martha Jane, dau. of John B. and Mary B. (Folsom) Johnson of Rye, N. H. He is a lather by trade, and has worked in many places. He resides in Rye. Child:
  1 Lillian Bertha, b. 15 July 1873, in Lowell, Mass.
5 Samuel Willis, b. 22 June 1852; m. Mary Leland of Boston, of English parentage. He lives in Webster, Mass. Child:
  1 Mary R., b. 1874.
6 Edward LaForest, b. 16 July 1854; m. Hattie, dau. of John Crockett of Portland. He lives in Durham. Children:
  1 Ernest LaForest, b. 1876.
  2 Bertha May.
  3 John Francis, died in the winter of 1880-1.
7 Clara Leona, b. 15 Aug. 1858; m. 23 Dec. 1880, Henry L. Merrill.
8 Rosa Belle, b. 22 July 1864.
9 Lillian May, b. 24 May 1867; d. 1 June 1871.

11-2-2-1-2-1

Samuel Libby, born in Newfield, Me., 30 July 1806; married first, Rebecca Knowles, daughter of John and Olive (Lord) Knowles of Wellington; (died 28 Nov. 1866); second, 1868, Ann Elizabeth (Libby) Rose, 11-9-7-3-6-2. He is a farmer in Levant.

Children, by his first wife:

1 Alvah, b. 10 June 1828; m. Lydia Ann, dau. of Eleazer and Lydia (Cook) Gould of Kenduskeag. He has been engaged in lumbering in Aroostook Co., trucking in Bangor, and (now) farming in Levant. Children:
  1 Newell P., b. 11 June 1861, in Glenburn.
  2 Elijah Wilber, b. 4 Feb. 1866, in Bangor.
  3 Abbie A., b. 18 Feb. 1868; died 18 May 1870.
  4 Nellie M., b. 16 Feb. 1870.
  5 Perley M., b. 7 Jan. 1872, in Hermon.
  6 Elizabeth J., b. 19 April 1875, in Stetson; d. 23 Oct. 1878.
  7 Alvah M., b. 2 Aug. 1878, in Levant.
2 Matthew, b. 1829; died in 1831.
3 Rebecca, b. 25 Aug. 1831; m. Ruel Phillips of Glenburn.
4 Samuel M., b. 23 Oct. 1833; m. Nancy Gould, a sister of Alvah's wife. He is a butcher, marketing in Bangor.
5 Daniel, b. 1 March 1835; m. Rebecca Drew; is a farmer in Glenburn.
6 John, b. 13 May 1838; lives in Hermon; unm.
7 Mary Ann, b. 15 July 1841; m. Rufus Johnson.
8 Judith, b. 14 June 1845; unm.

By second wife:

9 Villa A., b. 30 June 1869.

11-2-2-1-2-4

JAMES LIBBY, born in Newfield, Me., 1812; married, 1831, MARY A. BOSTON, daughter of John and Dorcas (Moody) Boston of Wellington. He is a farmer. He moved from Exeter to Troy, his present residence, in the spring of 1847. He settled on a farm there, and also engaged extensively in the manufacture of soap.

Children:

1 Benaiah, b. 1833, in Wellington; died in 1834.
2 Joseph, b. 1835, in Exeter; died in 1843.
3 Isaac C., b. 2 June 1837; m. 29 Nov. 1859, Helen M., dau. of Charles and Mary E. (Whitney) Green of Troy. He has been chiefly occupied as drover. He removed to Burnham about 1874, and was afterward postmaster there. Children:
  1 Arthur Preston, b. 5 June 1861, in Troy.
  2 Charles Everett, b. 13 April 1863.
  3 Isaac Howard, b. 27 Oct. 1865.
  4 Ernest Leonal, b. 4 Oct. 1867.
  5 Frank LeRoy, b. 27 May 1871.
  6 Pearl Ashton, b. 14 April 1873.
  7 Helen Green, b. 25 April 1875.
  8 Herbert Carlyle, b. 28 Dec. 1878.
4 Frank D., b. 15 July 1841; m. 23 Feb. 1862, in Detroit, Me., Amy A., dau. of Theodore and Levina (Basford) Harding; is a farmer in Burnham. Children:
  1 Mary A., b. 26 Dec. 1863; died 20 March 1867.
  2 Aubine H., b. 20 Oct. 1873.
5 Agnes, b. 1843; died 1844.
6 Freddie, b. 1845; died 1845.
7 James, b. 30 Aug. 1846; m. 3 June 1873, Nellie F., dau. of J. F. and Almira (Drake) Tinkham of Albion. He attended the Hampden Academy, Maine Central Institute, and Maine State Institute (now Bates College). He read law one year with E. K. Boyle, late of Belfast, and then with Harris M. Plaisted, now governor of the state. In 1872 he was admitted to the bar, and has since practiced in Unity. Children:
  1 Myra P., b. 17 June 1874, in Unity.
  2 Mary A., b. 30 Aug. 1880, in Unity.
8 Jennie C., b. 1848; m. 1869, Melvin Batchelder.
9 Mary A., b. 1851; died 1852.
10 Angie E., b. 1853; m. 1881, R. M. Rogers.
11 William P., b. 1856; m. 1880, Florence M., dau. of Peter and Sylvania (Whiten) Barrows of Burnham; lives at home.

11-2-2-1-3-2

BENJAMIN D. LIBBY, born in Athens, Me., 1820; married, 11 May 1843, SOPHIA FRYE, daughter of James and Mary (Wheeler) Frye of Wellington. He has always been a farmer, and has lived most of the time in Wellington. He was out in the war, and was disabled; has since been constable and collector of the town of Wellington.

Children:

1 Helen L., b. 1844; m. 15 Aug. 1866, D. P. Weeks.
2 Brice H., b. 1846; m. Sarah Dodson. He is a farmer, and lives on the homestead. Children:

1 Ellen J., b. 1870.
2 Cora, b. 1875.
3 Frank. b. 1877.
3 Johnson F., b. 1849; m. 28 May 1870, Mattie A. ——; lives in Wellington. Children:
1 Adah, died April 1879.
2 Martha May.
3 Anna.
4 Alvarado F., b. 1851; m. Oct. 1877, Lizzie M. ——; is a general merchant in Wellington. Child:
1 Willie W., b. 1879.
5 Mary O., b. 1853, in Brighton; m. in Wellington, Feb. 1873.
6 Maranda, b. 1855; m. Sept. 1874, in Cambridge.
7 Clarinda W., b. 1859; m. 13 Dec. 1877, in Wellington.

11-6-2-1-1-1

Rev. Charles Oliver Libby, born in Gorham, Me., 14 May 1811; married, 21 May 1834, Hannah McDougall, daughter of David McDougall of Gorham.

He received an academic education and was subsequently occupied as farmer and teacher in his native town until the year 1844, and during that time was three times chosen selectman. In 1844 he was ordained a Freewill Baptist preacher and was afterward engaged in the ministry in his native state and in New Hampshire. He was president of the Freewill Baptist Foreign Mission Society in 1858, 1859 and 1860. In 1862 he was chosen corresponding secretary of the same society, and in 1867, treasurer, both which positions he filled until the year of death. He died in Dover, N. H., where he had lived from 1868, 21 Dec. 1876. His widow still survives.

Children, all born in Gorham:

1 Oliver, b. 7 June 1835; unm. He graduated from Bowdoin College in 1859, and immediately removed to Wisconsin, where, and in Illinois, he was for some time a teacher. He is now in the real estate and insurance business in Green Bay, Wis.
2 Martha Warren, b. 23 March 1837; m. 31 July 1859, Roscoe G. Smith, then the principal of the seminary in New Hampton, N. H. He died 31 Dec. 1860. No children.
3 Mary Elizabeth, b. 8 April 1839; d. 8 June 1841.
4 Phebe Paine, b. 16 March 1841; m. J. F. McIntire of Boston, who died in Sept. 1877. In Sept. 1880 she married J. J. Dearborn of South Deerfield, N. H.
5 Susan, b. 4 Sept. 1843; m. 31 Oct. 1870, T. M. L. Thompson of Contai, India; died in Contai 24 June 1878.
6 Emily Garland, b. 25 Nov. 1844; m. Woodbury J. Dudley.
7 Mary Elizabeth, b. 26 Jan. 1846; unm. Lives in Dover.
8 Alice Ilsley, b. 4 May 1848; m. R. C. Goodwin of Kittery, Me.
9 Curtis Stanwood, b. 6 Nov. 1850; d. 11 Dec. 1850.

11-6-2-3-2-1

William E. Libby, born in Buxton, Me., 18 Nov. 1818; married, 30 Aug. 1846, Martha K. Adams, daughter of Stephen and Lydia K. (Knight) Adams of Buxton. He was a carpenter, and ever after his marriage, except ten years spent in Paris, Me., resided in Lowell, Mass., where he died 29 May 1879, and his widow still lives.

Children, born in Lowell:

1 Alexander Hamilton, b. 3 July 1847; m. 1st, 30 April 1866, Sarah, dau. of John and Betsey Midgly of Lowell; (divorced); 2d, Amelia F., dau. of John H. and Ellen (Decker) Peters of Worcester, Mass.; (divorced in 1874); 3d, 1876, Mrs. Sarah M. Pattee, dau. of Walter M. and Almira (Davenport) Allen of North Cambridge, Mass. He is by trade a hairdresser, and now follows that calling in Keene, N. H. He served two years in the 2d Mass. Heavy Artillery, being promoted to sergeant. He has been winner of 80 out of 109 pedestrian and other athletic contests; was some time teacher of gymnastics at the Mount Vernon (Ill.) military school, and trainer of O'Leary in his 500-mile walk against Weston in 1875. Children, by second wife only:
  1 Viola L., b. 1869; d. 3 April 1873.
  2 Florence A., b. 2 May 1871.

Born in Paris, Me.:

2 Oliver A., b. 28 Oct. 1849; m. 20 Oct. 1870, Charlotte Philena, dau. of Asa and Eliza (McCorristine) Parker of Carlisle, Mass. He is by trade a printer, and does business in Lowell. Children:
  1 Marshall Parker, } twins, born 17 Aug. 1871,
  2 Margaret Augusta, } in Brattleborough, Vt.
  3 Oliver Carleton, b. 18 Nov. 1872, in the same place.
  4 Charlotte Agnes, b. 18 Nov. 1874, in the same place.
  5 Edward Clifton, b. 18 Dec. 1876, in Springfield, Vt.
3 Mary E., b. 23 Aug. 1851; m. 23 Dec. 1871, Chas. H. Thissell.
4 Lydia A., b. 17 March 1853; d. 19 Jan. 1870.
5 Martha F., b. 18 March, d. 30 April, 1855.
6 Nancy L., b. 18 March 1856; m. 19 Dec. 1878, Daniel Wilson.
7 William B., b. 16 Nov. 1857; m. 3 Oct. 1876, Mabel, dau. of Wm. R. and Harriet A. (Jackman) Dunham of Springfield, Vt. He is a printer, residing in Charlestown, Mass. Child:
  1 Edna Mabel, b. 17 Jan. 1879.

Born in Lowell:

8 Maria H., b. 10 Aug. 1861.
9 Frederic A., b. 17 May 1863; d. 21 Jan. 1864.
10 Martha J., b. 11 May 1865.
11 Wallace N., b. 2 July 1868.

11-7-2-4-8-2

Captain Thomas Lancaster Libby, born in Pownal, Me., 26 May 1824; married, 20 Jan. 1847, Mary Elizabeth Batchelder of Portland, a daughter of Mrs. Richard Pease, by a former husband.

He grew up in Scarborough. When eighteen years old, he went on a European voyage with his uncle, Captain William Hasty. That voyage lasted two years. He then went as mate of a coaster, under his uncle William Tompson, and soon after, his uncle obtaining command of a larger vessel, he became master of the coaster. At the age of twenty-three he commanded a vessel in the West India trade, and from that time until his death was a successful ship-master, sailing from Portland. He died in Cuba, 10 July 1873. His wife died in Portland, 15 Oct. 1871.

Children, all born in Portland:

1 Richard Henry, b. 7 Nov. 1848; d. 1 Sept. 1851.
2 Thomas Lancaster, b. 6 Dec. 1850; d. 7 Sept. 1851.
3 Thomas Henry, (known as Thomas Lancaster), b. 7 Sept. 1852; m. 2 Sept. 1878, Cora, dau. of James and Sarah (Haskins) Jordan of Freeport. His chief occupation has been that of dry goods clerk. He lives in Portland. No children.
4 Woodbury Storer, b. 19 Feb. 1855; d. 7 May 1880; unm. He followed the sea from boyhood, and rose to be mate.
5 Fernandes Sabalious, b. 6 May 1857; m. 1st, in Lynn, Mass., Ida E., dau. of John M. and Elizabeth (Litch) Ryder of Annapolis, Nova Scotia; (died Oct. 1878); 2d, 1879, Mary Ellen, dau. of Patrick and Honora (Griffin) Dow of Lynn. He went from Scarborough to Lynn, Mass., in 1873, and was there an expressman, and then an employee in the shoe shops. In 1881 he removed to Saco, Me. Children; by first wife:
   1 Walter Howard, b. June, 1877; lives with his grandparents, in Annapolis.

   By second wife:

   2 Thomas Lancaster, b. 4 Feb., d. 18 June, 1880.
6 Minnie Rebecca, b. 16 March 1859; m. 28 March 1877, Ira Putnam Woodbury of Portland. Child:
   1 Alice Osgood (Woodbury), b. 6 March 1878.
7 Walter Howard, b. 6 Oct. 1860; d. 30 July 1876, in Greenland, N. H.
8 George B. McLellan, (known as George Batchelder), born 6 April 1862; m. 19 Oct. 1880, Alice Abby, dau. of Elizabeth (Libby) Brackett, 1-1-6-4-6-8. Immediately after his marriage, he removed from Scarborough to Jefferson, Iowa, where his father-in-law lives.
9 Elizabeth Baker, b. 6 Feb. 1870.

FIVE FAMILIES WHOSE PEDIGREES ARE LOST.

FIRST.

There were baptized in the South Church, in Portsmouth, N. H., 30 July 1758, "John and Sarah, children of widow Libby." Of them, one:

John, born about 1752; m. 1st, 24 March 1781, Polly Dame; (buried 23 July 1785); 2d, 6 Nov. 1785, Mrs. Deliverance Steward, widow of James Steward who was killed in the Revolution, and daughter of —— Lear of Newcastle. He was a shoemaker and died in Portsmouth, Sept. 1788. His widow died 9 Jan. 1795. Children, by first wife:

1 ——, buried 31 March 1785.

By second wife:

2 Mary. She was brought up by an aunt named Jackson. She married 28 March 1808, Owen Davis of Portsmouth, and has descendants there.

SECOND.

JOHN LIBBY, a sailor in Portsmouth, N. H., died there 27 Oct. 1821, aged fifty years. It was probably he that married, in Portsmouth, 9 Nov. 1794, Comfort Putnam. He had sons:

1 John; } sailors; are supposed to have been never married. William was boatswain of a British East Indiaman.
2 William; }

THIRD.

NATHANIEL LIBBY (or *Lebby*, as he and his descendants have spelled their name) went from Portsmouth to Charleston, South Carolina, about 1763, and continued there until his death. He was of the company that met under the "Liberty Tree" in 1766, after the repeal of the stamp act, and pledged themselves to resist British rule. Johnson's "Traditions of the Revolution," published in 1851, mentions him as "a zealous patriot of great respectability." He became a mast and spar hewer while in Portsmouth, and engaged in business in Charleston as boat builder. His death occurred about 1805. His wife was a sister of Robert Howard of Charleston. He left six children, of whom two daughters, though married, left no male issue, and the others were as follows:

1 Nathaniel, left no sons.
2 Robert, had one son:
  1 Robert, b. 1805, a practicing physician in Charleston, having charge of the quarantine. He has two sons, both physicians.

3 William, had sons:
  1 Thomas, died without issue.
  2 William, b. 1813; is engaged in the rice milling business in Charleston. He has one son, Thomas, an accountant.
  3 Nathaniel, died without issue.
4 Anna, married Robert Aldrich. Children:
  1 Thomas (Aldrich), a physician in Charleston.
  2 Alfred P. (Aldrich), a lawyer and a judge of the Circuit Court of South Carolina.
  3 Demas (Aldrich), a Lutheran minister in Virginia.
  4 James (Aldrich), a lawyer, now deceased.
  5 Henry (Aldrich), was lost in the Mexican war.

FOURTH.

Daniel Wiggin Libby, born, it is said, in Rochester, N. H., about 1788; went to Augusta, Me., at the age of eighteen; then to Wayne; thence to Leeds; thence to Carthage. He once told a neighbor that he had two brothers, but his descendants never heard him speak of his relatives. He has a son Edwin living in Carthage, and a grandson John F., living in the same place, now representative to the state legislature.

FIFTH.

George W. Libby, born, according to his enlistment papers, in the town of Strafford, N. H., about 1830. He wandered about in boyhood, living with those who would keep him. He finally married in East Lempster, N. H., and from that place enlisted in the 10th N. H. Vol., and died at Washington. He left a widow and four children, and they know nothing of his relatives except that he had a brother Freeman, and a sister; and that in visiting them, soon after his marriage, he went through Portland.

LATE IMMIGRATIONS.

Jacob George Lewis Libby, a native of London, England, emigrated to Boston, Mass., and married there Sarah (Clark) Thompson; forsook her about 1810, and was never afterward heard of. She died 25 Nov. 1848.

Children:

1 Jacob George Lewis, born 22 April 1797; m. 2 July 1820, Elizabeth, dau. of Capt. Supply and Elizabeth (Brown) Simonds of Boston. He graduated from one of the public schools of Boston, receiving a "Franklin" medal, and became a jeweler. He was at one time a member of the Boston City Council. His wife died 10 Aug. 1844, and himself, 4 March 1846. Children:
 1 Sarah Elizabeth, b. 3 Aug. 1824; m. 16 July 1844, William Henry Gray of Boston, from London.
 2 Edward Watson, b. 20 Jan. 1827; m. 4 Oct. 1848, Amelia Anna, dau. of Stephen and Paulina (Webb) Huckins of Eppingham, N. H. He was an engraver, and died 22 July 1873. Children:
  1 Edward Lewis, born 28 July 1849, in Chelsea; m. 11 Nov. 1876, in Philadelphia, Penn., Mrs. Emily C. Foye, dau. of Richard C. and Emerline (Needham) Mason of Baltimore. He is a jeweler in Boston. Child:
   1 Edward Lewis, b. 18 March 1878, in Philadelphia.
  2 William Gray, b. 29 Oct. 1854; unm.
  3 Walter Bailey, b. 26 Oct. 1866, in Boston.
 3 Louisa Gardiner, b. 22 July 1829; died 15 Feb. 1832.
 4 Louisa Maria, b. 12 June 1835; unm.
2 Sarah Clark, b. 31 Dec. 1798; died in July, 1816.

Simon R. Libby, now living in Bridgeport, Conn., was born in Veryan Green, Cornwall, England. His grandfather was a miller in Roseland, Cornwall, and his father, Simon R. Libby, was some time a schoolteacher, and then entered the office of the "Royal Cornwall Gazette" as cashier, which position he held until shortly before his death, which took place in 1877. Beside Simon, above mentioned, Simon R. Libby had a son Charles, now living in London, and three other sons who emigrated to America at about the same time as Simon, but have not been heard from for many years.

Simon R. Libby served a five years' apprenticeship at the blacksmith's trade, and in 1851 emigrated to America. He has since lived in Connecticut, for the most part in Bridgeport, where he married, 9 Feb. 1856, Catherine A., daughter of Daniel and Ann

(Hughes) McHugh of Tumery, Ireland. He is now in business as blacksmith, and has held the offices of justice of the peace, alderman, etc.

Children:

1 Charles H. b. 25 Oct. 1856, in Stratford, Conn.; unm. He is in the "Standard" office.
2 Mary E., b. 25 Oct. 1856, twin with the above.
3 Simon R., b. 19 Nov. 1857; unm.
4 Catherine A., b. 22 Jan. 1859; died 10 March 1860.
5 Emma A., b. 9 June 1867.

Josiah A. Libby, now living in Noank, Conn., was born in Mavagissey, Cornwall, England. His grandfather, John Libby, was a blacksmith, and had sons John and Robert, both blacksmiths. John had children:

1 Samuel, deceased.
2 John. in the employ of his brother Josiah.
3 Ann Eliza, deceased.
4 Josiah A., mentioned above; is a shipsmith.

Horatio Nelson Libby, now living in Elk Creek, Neb., says that his grandfather, William Libby, emigrated from Plymouth Dock, Devonshire Co., Eng., in 1800, and died about 1816; and that his father, whose name was also William, left Plymouth Dock for America in that year. He died in Quebec, while on his way to visit England, about 1855. He left six sons and three daughters, of whom the above is next to the youngest.

Walter S. Libby, now living in Hodgdon, Me., says that his grandfather, William Libby, and his father, John Libby, both lived in England, and that he has five brothers now in the Provinces.

Philip Libby, born in Mount Prospect, Ireland, about 1813, a son of Philip Libby, came to Boston, Mass., a young man; married in 1849, Catherine, daughter of Martin and Julia (Cox) Monahan of Ireland; died in Boston in 1870.

Children:

1 Mary Josephine, b. 1851; married Charles Sanders of New York.
2 Abbie T. Gertrude, b. 1854.
3 Kate. b. 1856.
4 Julia Gertrude, b. 1859.

Thomas Libby, brother of the last, came to Boston about 1848. His wife was Ann, daughter of Patrick and Catherine (McKue) Gibney of Mount Prospect, and died in May 1877.

Children:

1 Mary. born in Mount Prospect; m. John Mitchell.
2, 3 died in infancy.
4 Julia, born in 1849, in Boston; m. Peter Riley.
5 Catherine, b. 1852; unm.

Fred Libby, living in Milwaukee, Wis., says that his father and grandfather both came from the kingdom of Hanover, Germany.

Cornelius B. Libby, living in Walkerton, Indiana, says that his grandfather, George "Libey," lived in Cumberland County, Penn., and had sons William, (his father), John, and Jacob.

Andrew Libby, (properly Labbé), living in Brunswick, Me., is a French Canadian, born at St. John, about fifty miles below Quebec. He married Minnie Baker, and had children:

1 Andrew, m. Ellen Gammish; lives in Brunswick. Child:
  1 Emma.
2 Joseph, died aged four months.
3 Joseph, m. Delia Landree; lives in Brunswick. Children: Edward, and three others.
4 Mary, married Joseph Foster of Bath, Me.
5 Hannah, married Alphonzo Tettro.
6 Catherine, married Joseph Collin of Brunswick.
7 Fred, married Philemon Lenm; lives in Brunswick. Child:
  1 Fred.
8 Ellen, unmarried.
9 Minnie.
10 Alphonzo.

Augustus Libby, a French Canadian, born near Quebec; is a son of Charles, and a grandson of Peter. He lives in Saccarappa, Westbrook, Me. His wife was Mary Mason. Children:

1 Freddie, b. 1875.
2 Mary Jane, b. 1876.
3 Mary Ceno, b. 1880.

Joseph Libby, born in St. Joseph, Canada; was a French Canadian. He died in 1861. Children:

1 Joseph, died aged three years.
2 Levi, b. 1849; was a blacksmith; unheard of for many years.
3 Mary, b. 1851.
4 Carrieloine, b. 1854; died in 1876.
5 Maurice, b. 1855; lives in Fall River, Mass.
6 Cyrus, born in Farmington, Me., 1857; lives in Fall River.
7 Joseph, died in 1860, aged six months.

Lewis Libby, born in Stanfold, Que., 1 Dec. 1843, a son of Francis Libby, a French Canadian. He lives in Fitzwilliam, N. H.

Children:

1 Agnes, b. 7 Oct. 1868, in St. Mousette.
2 Henry, b. 1 March 1869, in Fitzwilliam.
3 Luis, b. 15 May 1871.
4 Joseph, b. 6 Oct. 1872; died, 1874.
5 Frank, b. 6 April 1873; d. 1874.
6 Marie Nelle, b. 29 June 1876.
7 Frank, b. 6 April 1878.
8 John, b. 16 April 1880.
9 Cilana, b. 18 June 1881.

UNCONNECTED RECORDS OF MARRIAGE.

1716, Sept. 9, Portsmouth, N. H., Samuel Brown and Bethiah Libby.
1718, Oct. 23, Portsmouth, N. H., Jonathan Barlow and Elizabeth Libby.
1721, July 9, Portsmouth, N. H., John Peacock and Mary Libby.
1726, Dec. 1, Portsmouth, N. H., John Briard and Agnes Libby.
1728, Dec. 2, Newington, N. H., William Berry and Mary Libby.
1729, Dec. 28, Scarborough, Me., Joseph Berry and Lydia Libby.
1732-3, Jan. 5, Portsmouth, N. H., Jeffrey Wells and Mehitable Libby.
1735, Jan. 30, Portsmouth, N. H., Benjamin Welch and Hannah Libby.
1764, Sept. 20, Cape Elizabeth, Me., Jethro Starbird and Hanny Libby.
1775, Sept. 21, Scarborough, Me., John Durrell and Dorothy Libby.
1777, June 28, Portsmouth, N. H., John Sharples and Mary Libby.
1783, Dec. 7, Berwick, Me., Samuel Hodgdon and Anna Libby.
1790, Jan. 10, Machias, Me., Foster Howard and Mary Libby.
1790, Sept., Scarborough, Me., Capt. Jonathan Andrews and Hannah Libby.
1794, Aug. 20, Scarborough, Me., John Libby and Keziah Warren.
1799, April 30, Buxton, Me., Nathaniel Foss and Keziah Libby.
1803, Dec. 22, Falmouth, Me., Daniel Hart and Sukie Libby.
1806, Jan. 9, Providence, R. I., Samuel Webb and Rebecca Libby.
1809, Dec. 3, Falmouth, Me., Joseph Redman and Sally Libby.
1818, Nov. 25, Dover, N. H., Francis Hanson and Phebe Libby.
1819, Feb. 22, Portland, Me., Samuel Libby and Mary H. Fisher.
1821, Aug. 17, Portland, Me., Eli Leavitt and Mary H. Libby.
1842, Sept. 15, Scarborough, Me., Wm. L. Brown and Sarah L. Libby.
1847, Dec. 9, Cape Elizabeth, Me., George Pride and Lavinia P. Libby.
1851, Dec. 11, Cape Elizabeth, Me., Ezekiel Jordan and Ruth Libby.
1853, Oct. 22, Portland, Me., Benjamin Carter and Lydia T. Libby.
1853, Nov. 12, Saco, Me., Joseph Eaton and Ann Libby.
1861, Feb. 7, Westbrook, Me., Ira T. Libby and Sarah E. Lowell.
1866, May 5, Bridgton, Me., John H. Libby and Almira D. Cotton.
1866, Nov. 29, Portland, Me., Calvin H. Mitchell and Caroline M. Libby.
1868, July 31, Portland, Me., Geo. T. Morris and Mary E. Libby.
1869, April 17, Saco, Me., Joseph Libby and Znar Bella.
1869, Oct. 25, Gray, Me., Solomon B. Foster and Christina Libby.
1873, Sept. 14, Portland, Me., Frank W. Wiswall and Sarah T. Libby.
1873, Dec. 4, Portland, Me., George W. Libby and Annie Donelly.
1874, Dec. 5, Portland, Me., Daniel W. Bussell and Louisa M. Libby.

ADDITIONS AND CORRECTIONS.

Page 48, line 26. For "Enock," read "Enoch."
Page 49, line 37. For "Morrill," read "Morrell."
Page 59, line 16. For "Hannah Tibbetts and Mary Tibbetts," read "Mary Tibbetts and Hannah Tibbetts."
Page 69, line 14. For "Meshack," read "Meshach."
Page 99, line 49. } The sentences, "She was subject to crazy periods,
Page 100, line 11. } and in one of them cut her throat. She died 16 July 1843," should refer to the first wife of the *junior* Maj. Josiah Libby. The widow of the senior Maj. Josiah Libby died a natural death.
Page 108, line 9. For "21," and "23."
Page 140. Nathan Libby, 10-1-2-7, died in 1833, and his widow in 1849.
Page 149. Rebecca Libby, 10-1-5-6-1-1, married Stephen Larrabee.
Page 151. Betsey Libby, 10-1-6-5-7, died 9 March 1864.
Page 157, line 42. Cary Libby married Martha Goss of Marblehead.
Page 174, William Smith Libby, died 10 Nov. 1881.
Page 177, line 10. Lucy Libby was born 10 May 1844; died 31 Aug. 1859.
Page 195, line 12. For "17 Dec.," read "7 Dec."
Page 255, line 46. For "Rasa," read "Rosa."
Page 260, line 20. For "Morrell," read "Morrill."
Page 266, line 24. Joseph T. Libby married Hannah J., dau. of Joseph Lovett of Hudson, and had children, Ida and Hannah.
Pages 293 and 294. Capt. Byron Libby, 6-4-4-8-8-1, married, 12 Sept. 1857, Harriet Ann Eaton. He was some years captain of a ferry-boat at Quincy, and is now superintendent of the stock yards of several railroads centering there. He has served two years as alderman. The names of his children are Jeannie Eaton, Carrie Ann, and Charles Henry.
Page 304, line 21. For "Cushion," read "Cushing."
Page 304, line 29. Levi W. Libby followed lumbering until 1849, when he went from St. Stephen to Milwaukee, Wis. He went thence by the overland route to Oregon, and thence to San Francisco, where he was for two years in business as photographer. For five years following he was engaged in mining, and, as he has not since been heard from, is supposed to have died.
Page 304, line 32. Roxanna, married E. Smith and lives in Waltham, Mass.
Page 315. In the place of what is said of Stephen Libby, 10-1-2-3-8, supply:

Stephen J. Libby, born in Machias, Me., 13 March 1798; married first, 15 Oct. 1825, Abigail Webb, daughter of Howard and Sarah (Thorndike) Webb of Harrington; (died 10 May 1852, in Columbia); second, 16 Dec. 1854, Sarah, daughter of John and Dorcas (Cole) Nichols of Harrington; (died 26 June 1856); third, 28 July 1856, Rebecca Smith, daughter of Eben and Dorcas (Cole) Jordan. He lives in Millbridge, Me.

Children:

1 Samuel, b. 19 Nov. 1828; went to sea when 21 years old, and has not been heard from since.
2 Warren, b. 6 Dec. 1830; died 23 March 1851.
3 Asa, b. 1 Jan. 1832; died in 1862, in Augusta. He was an enlisted soldier.
4 Stinson, b. 15 Aug. 1834; died 13 Jan. 1853.
5 Stephen E., b. 2 June 1836; died 29 June 1836.
6 William H., b. 5 Feb. 1838; died 27 Feb. 1843.

Page 317, line 10. James Libby was drowned at sea, 20 March 1873.

Page 329. Ebenezer Libby, 10-1-8-3-4, was married 28 June 1809.

Page 330, line 12. T. C. Libby is a Calvin Baptist, living in Leeds. He not only has not furnished his own records, but has refused to allow his own brother to copy early family records in his possession.

Page 330. Uriah Libby, 10-1-8-3-6-3, lives in Leeds.

Page 334. John Libby, 10-1-8-5-3-2, lives in Rock Island County, Ill., and Thomas Libby, 10-1-8-5-3-5, lives in Atwater, Minn.

Page 334, line 32. For "Joy," read "Jay."

Page 352. Franklin W. Libby, 10, born 19 April 1853; married 7 Feb. 1878, Hattie F., dau. of Samuel G. and Martha A. (Hancock) Nutting of Litchfield, Me. Children:

1 Jessie M., b. 2 Nov. 1878, in Chatsworth, Ill.
2 Alice E., b. 12 Feb. 1881, in Chatsworth, Ill.

Page 412, line 28. For "on," read "after."

LATER.

Page 78, line 6. For "Piner," read "Pineo."

Page 100, line 11. For "Joseph," read "Josiah."

Page 132. James Libby settled in Washington Co., Ohio, where his wife died 12 June 1858; and himself 11 May 1860. Children:

1 Blake, b. 4 Aug. 1810; married —— Brown.
2 Andrew, is married and lives in Warren Co., Ohio.
3 Balaay (?) S., married William Darson.
4 Jason, served in the late war.
5 Eunice, married James McGregg.
6 Virgil, died in the late war.
7 Eliza Jane, b. 8 June 1823; m. 28 Sept. 1843, Henry W. Myres; d. 20 July 1881. Children:
    1 William L. (Myres), b. 26 April 1845; m. 10 July 1867, Eliza Ann McMann, born 16 Feb. 1846.
    2 Mary J. (Myres), b. 10 July 1848; d. 1 July 1852.
    3 Ellen A. (Myres), } twins, } died 16 April 1863.
    4 Libby Jane (Myres), } b. 1851; }
    5 Martha S. (Myres), b. 29 April 1855; d. 26 April 1881.
    6 Phebe B. (Myres), b. 5 Sept. 1857.
    7 Stephen O. (Myres), b. 22 June 1860; d. 28 July 1862.
    8 James S. (Myres), b. 1 May 1864; d. 16 Aug. 1871.

Page 133, line 25. For "Tinmouth, N. H.," read "Tinmouth, Vt."

Page 142, line 22. For "Newbury," read "Newburgh."

Page 148. According to a later list, Josiah Libby, 10-1-2-6, had beside the children named, the following: Josiah, Joseph, John, Abigail and Sally. Josiah married Susan, daughter of John and Jane Mitchell, and died early. His widow married Jesse Bateman, and then Timothy Libby, 10-1-5-6-1. Her children by Josiah Libby were, David, born 26 May 1809; lost away at sea; and John, born in 1812; married Louisa ——; lives in Harrington. John and Louisa have a son John Benson Libby, now living in Millbridge, Me.

Page 160, line 18. Dorcas Libby died 24 Jan. 1882.

Page 168. Lothrop Libby died 21 Jan. 1882.

Page 210, line 45. Margaret, "5," and Elizabeth, "6," were *children* of John, not grandchildren, as the misplacement indicates.

Page 290. William G. Libby died 25 Dec. 1881. The "Shaker Manifesto" for February devotes a page to his memory, speaking very highly of the strength and beauty of his character. He was an elder during most of the time of his connection with the society.

Page 302, line 13. For "Llewellyn," read "Llewllyn."

Page 308, line 17. Katie A. is not the daughter of George F. Libby, but his wife.

Page 349, line 16. For "1863," read "1833."

Page 363, line 31. For "New London," read "New Richmond."

Page 380, line 5. For "1839," read "1829."

Page 391. Benjamin Miller died 7 Jan. 1882.

Page 394, line 11. Mr. Ryker is the only partner A. W. Libby has had.

Page 412, line 14. For "Bowdoin," read "Bates."

Page 419. James H. Libby married, 5 April 1873, Ella Isadore, dau. of Samuel Holbrook. She died 19 Oct. 1878.

Page 449, line 4. For "Edward H. Chase," read "Edward A. Chase."

Page 450, line 12. George W. Libby married Annie, dau. of James and Mary (Rafferty) Donelly. This marriage will be seen in the list of unplaced marriages on page 541. The compiler was informed by the family that G. W. was unmarried, and it was not until his wife's divorce in Jan. 1882, that the compiler learned the contrary. Children:

1 George, died at the age of two months.
2 Frank George, b. 15 Sept. 1875.

Page 509, line 39. For "1848," read "1858."

Page 512. Harriet F., wife of S. H. Libby, died 25 Dec. 1881.

Page 535. George B. and Alice A. Libby have a son:

1 Walker Brackett Libby Batchelder, b. 18 Nov. 1881. [For reasons for so naming, see foot-note on page 478.]

Matthias Libby

INDEX

OF

CHRISTIAN NAMES OF LIBBYS.

The first column gives the year, or the approximate year, of birth. The second gives the baptismal name. The third gives the place of death, or the place of residence at the time of death, or the place of residence when last heard from; or, of a married female, the surname of her husband. The fourth column gives the page on which found.

A

1850 A. Judson Richmond, Me. 404
1874 A. Roy Pittsfield, Me. 430
1745 Aaron Limington, Me. 43
1796 “ Detroit, Me. 151
1799 “ Lagrange, Me. 67
1818 “ Pownal, Me. 170
1837 “ Sweden, Me. 406
1841 “ Limerick, Me. 399
1844 “ Waterford, Me. 526
1855 “ C. Detroit, Me 323
1855 “ Haines Fredericton, N. B. 330
1818 “ Ricker Kennebunkport, Me. 424
1781 “ Seavey Rye, N. H. 137
1830 “ W. Minneapolis, Minn. 126
1824 Abba Celia Lowe 353
1840 “ M. Young 306
1844 “ Sarah Hanson 340
1814 Abbie Dow 251
1833 “ Stetson 343
1840 “ Mass 367
1843 “ Shackford 218
1843 “ Exeter, Me. 278
1843 “ French 470
1857 “ A. Wentworth, N. H. 456
1850 “ D. Johnson 492
1869 “ D. Corinna, Me. 491
1842 “ E. Kendall 231
1857 “ Ella Bethel, Me. 407
1864 “ Ella Scarboro, Me. 405
1849 “ F. Seamans 506
1823 “ H. Jennison 437
1842 “ Johnson Purinton 173
1847 “ Jane Pray 371
1832 “ M. Wedger 118
1851 “ M. Chelsea. Mass. 117
1852 “ P. Richardson 404
1854 “ T. G. Boston, Mass. 539
1833 “ Tuck Portland, Me. 451
1862 “ Tucker Scarboro, Me. 343
1767 Abby Gibbs 105
1848 “ Augusta Braley 206
1859 “ Eliza Portland, Me. 401
1844 “ Frances Foster 273
1862 “ Harriet Janesville, Wis. 311
1863 “ Helen Manchester 462
1849 “ Jane Gorham, Me. 376
1838 “ Patience Portland, Me. 474
1839 “ R. Davis 461
1838 Abel W. Lead City, Col. 321
1822 Abial Richmond, Me. 344
1705 Abigail Hill 38
1707 “ Nason 32
1729 Abigail Wiswall 60
1730 “ Pike 40
1733 “ Graffam 48
1734 “ Douglass 55
1738 “ Jackson 52
1739 “ Haskell 55
1741 “ Allison 49
1745 “ Warren 42
1745 “ Stone 61
1753 “ Quint 61
1756 “ Libby 69
1762 “ Libby 80
1763 “ Morrison 72
1763 “ Stevens 82
1764 “ Young 102
1766 “ Blake 101
1768 “ Webster 72
1770 “ Shorey 107
1773 “ Pray 110
1774 “ Allen 70
1774 “ Bugbee 96
1775 “ Chick 107
1776 “ Limerick, Me. 86
1778 “ Dorman 85
1778 “ Thurston 94
1779 “ Waterhouse 65
1783 “ Hanscom 93
1786 “ Mulloy 182
1788 “ Beals 157
1789 “ Cummings 222
1790 “ Libby 111
1791 “ Jones 110
1791 “ Thomes 167
1792 “ Hanson 142
1794 “ Libby 167
1795 “ Coolidge 177
1797 “ Whitney 155
1797 “ Libby 169
1798 “ Anderson 136
1798 “ Carson 223
1798 “ Dunn 223
1799 “ Dill 163
1800 “ Buxton, Me. 114
1800 “ Crockett 148
1801 “ Greene, Me. 154
1803 “ Paul 179
1803 “ Mason 226
1804 “ Libby 224
1807 “ Libby 202
1808 “ Libby 207
1806 “ Bassett 287
1810 “ Carsley 373
1810 “ Knight 457
1811 “ Collins 128

B

C

1852 Caroline A. Coutts 297
1868 " A[illegible] Fredericton, N. B. 330
1855 " D. Hunnewell 285
1847 " E. Hoyt 238
1523 " Elizabet Caldwell 280
1832 " " Ring 402
1847 " Ellen Webster 455
1846 " Emma Doughty 475
1840 " Hunt Hall 190
1846 " M. Mitchell 541
1838 " Maria Brooklyn, N. Y. 293
1824 " Mary Trask 450
1827 " Matilda Burrell 206
1833 " Perry Durgin 270
1853 " Prentiss Randall [illegible]
1821 " S. Plummer 4[illegible]
1870 " S. Milford, Mass. 330
1826 " Sturgis Chadbourne 197
1863 " Swascy Providence, R. I. 384
1836 Carrie Naples, Me. 364
1856 " Culver 274
1864 " Lebanon, Me. 243
1862 " A. Medford, Mass. 379
1865 " A. Kingston, Minn. 312
1862 " A. M. Chicago, Ill. 325
1860 " Ann Quincy, Ill. 294
1874 " Augusta Gray, Me. 476
1861 " Bell Limington, Me. 265
1840 " E. Chamberlain 498
1853 " E. Johnson 250
1862 " E. Orono, Me. 225
1878 " E. Durham, Me. 312
1878 " Ella Scarboro, Me. 365
1867 " Emily Pittsfield, Me. 323
1859 " Emma Portland, Me. 419
1873 " Emma Berwick, Me. 272
1864 " Estella Kittery, Me. 203
1864 " Estelle Pearl River, N. Y. 121
1859 " Etta Hardy 266
1862 " H. Alexander, Me. 345
1874 " J. Lewiston, Me. 390
1853 " L. Richardson 501
1865 " Lena W. St. Paul 238
1854 " M. Augusta, Me. 297
1863 " Mabel Pownal, Me 316
1875 " May Albion, Me. 488
1877 " Rachel Vinland, Wis. 437
1873 " Rand Oshkosh, Wis. 250
1871 " Wilmena Scarboro, Me. 372
1848 Carroll Wesley Sumner, Me. 463
1795 Cary Saco, Me. 197
1798 " Lynn, Mass. 157
1821 " Pownal, Me. 198
1864 " Laurelton, Penn. 303
1871 " Lynn, Mass. 353
1844 Cassandria S. Bedford, Ohio 484
1743 Catherine Fogg 56
1764 " Means 97
1793 " Moses 155
1796 " Mace 129
1806 " Fall 241
1823 " Cram 175
1823 " Jones 209
1823 " Cobb 460
1827 " Foss 317
1829 " Miles 271
1835 " Cronkhite 227
1847 " Morrell 419
1852 " Boston, Mass. 539
1854 " Kilborn 463
1855 " Collin 540
1878 " Sandiego Co., Cal. 518
1823 " B. Allen 151
1879 " B. Mapleton, Minn. 368
1856 " Belle Libby 382
1820 " Fogg Sawyer 367
1872 " Frances San Francisco, Cal. 377
1832 " Louisa Warren, Me. 210
1833 " M. Storer 425
1828 " Malvina Bittinger 391
1823 Catherine Remmick Bemis 406
1855 Cecil Burgess Auburn, Me. 403
1879 " Ervin Kingston, Minn. 507
1879 " M. Hermon, Me. 445
1873 " Winthrop Lebanon, Me. 247
1869 Celestia Ann Limerick, Me. 496
1811 " B. Roundy 445
1854 Celia A. Lowell, Mass. 289
1836 " B. Cook 487
1845 " Louise Bragdon 173
1858 Chalmers H. Boston, Mass. 266
1840 Chandler A. Fort Fairfield, Me. 487
1721 Charles Berwick, Me. 39
1749 " Lebanon, Me. 61
1767 " Scarboro, Me. 96
1798 " Wisconsin 206
1804 " Harrison, Me. 208
1804 " Gray, Me. 230
1806 " Newfield, Me. 180
1809 " Berwick, Me. 112
1810 " Machiasport, Me. 194
1811 " Winona, Minn. 140
1812 " Scarboro, Me. 209
1816 " Whitefield, N. H. 249
1818 " Allenstown, N. H. 300
1821 " Scarboro, Me. 315
1822 " Woolwich, Me. 137
1823 " California 215
1825 " London, Eng. 538
1827 " Stanstead, Que. 294
1836 " Bradford, Me. 321
1838 " Machiasport, Me. 318
1841 " Concord, N. H. 293
1845 " Boston, Mass. 198
1845 " California 232
1850 " Broom, Que. 279
1854 " New London, Ont. 238
1860 " Charlestown, Mass. 68
1868 " Windham, Me. 301
1863 " Bozeman, Mont. 465
1869 " Portland, Me. 530
1870 " Clinton, Me. 430
1873 " Greene, Me. 516
1878 " Laurelton, Penn. 303
1838 " A. Augusta, Me. 433
1839 " A. Providence, R. I. 311
1840 " A. Manchester, Iowa 282
1849 " A. Turner, Me. 515
1851 " A. Arlington, Mass. 386
1864 " A. Pittsfield, Me. 433
1867 " A. Exeter, Me. 431
1870 " A. Etna, Me. 321
1880 " A. Turner, Me. 515
1842 " Adams Rockland, Me. 276
1855 " Addison Westbrook, Me. 459
1840 " Albert Stoneham, Mass 236
1844 " " Biddeford, Me. 387
1847 " " Black's Station, Cal. 161
1860 " " Portland, Me. 355
1879 " " Buxton, Me. 511
1857 " Albion Scarboro, Me. 316
1854 " Alfred Saco, Me. 215
1849 " Allen Chicago, Ill. 481
1875 " Arthur Oshkosh, Wis. 250
1866 " B. Warren, Me. 439
1874 " B. Albion, Me. 487
1866 " Bacon Cape Elizabeth, Me. 417
1856 " Benjamin Boston, Mass. 269
1861 " C. Gorham, N. H. 408
1866 " C. St. Stephen, N. B. 306
1849 " Chester Kennebunkport, Me. 424
1857 " Clarence Windham, Me. 460
1845 " Cushing Oxbow, Me. 181
1833 " D. Santa Barbara, Cal. 290
1848 " Dana Gray, Me. 411
1863 " Davis Portland, Me. 196
1875 " Delbert Vinland, Wis. 437
1814 " E. Machiasport, Me. 318
1834 " E. Wales, Me. 165
1853 " E. Auburn, Me. 277

E

F

H

I

J

K

L

M

N

O

P

S

1828 Sophia M. Gillis 463
1850 " W. Pease 290
1858 Sophronia Strout 445
1854 " A. Wildes 511
1833 " E. Scarboro, Me. 188
1836 " L. Cole 421
1824 Squire Portland, Me. 339
1858 " Levi Gorham, Me. 338
1860 Stanhope New Kent Co., Va. 268
1793 Statira Cox 228
1805 " Limerick, Me. 183
1806 " Skillings 68
1807 " Thompson 173
1832 " Foss 325
1875 " Bullar Biddeford, Me. 508
1850 " Louisa Palmer 399
1869 Stella Frances Limington, Me. 265
1875 " G. Minneapolis, Minn. 267
1874 " G. A. Contoocook, N. H. 503
1866 " Lillian Illinois 352
1736 Stephen Berwick, Me. 53
1741 " Shapleigh, Me. 53
1743 " Limington, Me. 43
1763 " Porter, Me. 69
1764 " Limerick, Me. 94
1771 " Scarboro, Me. 65
1783 " Newfield, Me. 86
1793 " Limerick, Me. 115
1793 " Porter, Me. 132
1799 " Pittsfield, N. H. 222
1801 " Waterborongh, Me. 201
1807 " Gorham, Me. 220
1808 " Gorham, Me. 167
1815 " Leeds, Me. 330
1816 " Auburn, Me. 338
1823 " Limerick, Me. 262
1825 " Brookline, Mass. 424
1826 " Buxton, Me. 316
1839 " Limerick, Me. 426
1844 " Scarboro, Me. 386
1878 " Detroit, Me. 431
1804 " A. Detroit, Me. 431
1830 " Addison Gray, Me. 411
1853 " Augustus Chelsea, Mass. 265
1825 " B. Belfast, Me. 309
1822 " Cook Saco, Me. 428
1840 " Frank Waterboro, Me. 427
1837 " Hanson Westbrook, Me. 361
1879 " Henry Gorham, Me. 530
1841 " Huston Windham, Me. 463
1865 " Ira Westbrook, Me. 362
1798 " J. Millbridge, Me. 148
1815 " Meserve Limerick, Me. 173
1857 " Millard Ipswich, Mass. 173
1862 " P. Unity Pl., Me. 433
1845 " Phinney Gorham, Me. 530
1800 " R. St. Stephen, N. B. 142
1846 " R. St. Stephen, N. B. 307
1860 " R. St. Stephen, N. B. 306
1828 " Robinson Morrison, Ill. 346
1840 " Ruthven Providence, R. I. 384
1835 " Tibbetts Denmark, Me. 326
1864 " Ulysses Fredericton, N. B. 330
1870 " Waterhouse Scarboro, Me. 158
1845 " Wentworth Albany, Me. 301
1861 " William Providence, R. I. 384
1879 " " Gray, Me. 475
1864 Stevens Scarboro, Me. 343
1820 Stillman Scarboro, Me. 365
1816 " B Gardiner, Me. 344
1826 " Higgins Somerville, Mass. 117
1802 Storer Scarboro, Me. 192
1818 " Deering, Me. 216
1824 " Portland, Me. 127
1783 Sukie Hart 541
1833 Sumner Scarboro, Me. 113
1836 " Deering, Me. 355
1836 " Cape Elizabeth, Me. 385
1860 " Windham, Me. 460
1844 " Cummings C. Elizabeth, Me. 217
1862 Sumner E. Auburn, Me. 390
1838 " Freeland Gray, Me. 475
1876 " Henry Portland, Me. 385
1852 " Holmes Gray, Me. 190
1863 " Sherman Gorham, Me. 381
1795 Susan Jordan 231
1798 " Elwell 338
1799 " Hustin 232
1808 " Bryant 149
1802 " Akerly 142
1808 " Gray, Me. 191
1808 " Lunt 199
1808 " Rounds 434
1810 " Kimball 221
1811 " Libby 224
1812 " Marston 139
1812 " Cram 213
1817 " Emery 203
1817 " Gorham, Me. 400
1825 " Porter, Me. 287
1828 " Sanford, Me. 255
1830 " Pettigrove 317
1830 " McNelly 325
1832 " West 460
1838 " Gayman 425
1840 " Illinois 171
1841 " Whitney 521
1843 " Thompson 538
1845 " A. Glenn 500
1848 " Anna Webster 258
1852 " Annette Bodwell 256
1820 " B. Nason 319
1837 " Bailey Scarboro, Me. 372
1803 " Blake Falmouth, Me. 409
1825 " Caroline Elwell 219
1784 " E. Meservey 148
1826 " E. Lovering 499
1842 " E. Martin 423
1877 " E. Machiasport, Me. 509
1834 " Elizabeth Sawyer 219
1840 " " Stevens 332
1845 " Ellen Newark, N. J. 235
1825 " Frances Boothby 175
1843 " " Patch 370
1863 " Freeman Standish, Me. 382
1807 " H. Burd 144
1842 " H. Camden, Me. 418
1840 " Hamlet Hanson 507
1845 " Hannah Cheney 264
1828 " J. Chase 437
1820 " Jane McDonald 260
1838 " " Libby 256
1845 " " Nash 411
1852 " " Mitchell 449
1834 " Jones Augusta, Me. 418
1876 " Kennie Gorham, Me. 530
1842 " M. Seymour 518
1845 " M. Averill 441
1805 " P. Hanscom 149
1848 " P. Dean 126
1818 " S. Durham, N. H. 177
1823 " S. Conant 364
1831 " Tucker Dunlap 496
1731 Susannah Scarboro, Me. 51
1733 " Berwick, Me. 52
1747 " Scarboro, Me. 28
1747 " Berwick, Me. 53
1760 " Carl 97
1861 " Cass 69
1770 " Clark 95
1774 " Berwick, Me. 94
1777 " Dorsett 98
1782 " Cape Elizabeth, Me. 98
1784 " Larrabee 67
1798 " Richardson 116
1821 " Saco, Me. 114
1828 " Small 123
1863 " Dunnels Ellis 180
1869 " L. St. Stephen, N. B. 306
1856 Susie Caroline Miller 175

T

U

V

W

INDEX OF SURNAMES.

It should be borne in mind that the same name may occur more than once on a single page; also, that the same name may occur in the index with two or more different spellings.

When it is wished to find the records of a special intermarriage, if the surname be a common one, the preceding index should be used.

A

B

C

D

H

I

J

K

N

O

P

Q

R

S

Y

Z

INDEX OF PLACES.

The main index, in capital letters, includes the states, territories, and provinces, of North America, the countries of Europe, the four other continents, and certain islands. The sub-indexes contain counties, cities, towns, villages, etc., and, in the case of said four continents, countries.

D

E

F

G

H

I

J

K

L

MAINE—*Continued.*

GENERAL INDEX.

In this index it has been purposed to spell each person's name as spelled by himself. When it is not known how any person spelled his name, (1) if all his near relatives used one spelling, the same is given to him; (2) if two or more ways occur among his near relatives, the most probable way is given, with an interrogation mark affixed.

A

B

D

E

F

G

H

I

J

Justices of the Peace.

K

Killed.

L

M

S

T

U

V

W

Records of the Offspring of

....

Number ....

FULL NAME.	DATE OF BIRTH.	PLACE OF BIRTH.

Anna Hatch dau of Capt John Hatch
married Deacon Samuel Small
she was born Apr 17. 1700
md 12 Jan 1716-17
a reason for this early marriage
is to be found in the fact that her father
died about the time of her birth
and her only brother died in aug 1711
leaving her without a home
no doubt she was welcomed to her new
home by the parents of her husband
children born in Kittery Maine
Samuel b 26 May 1718
Anna - Joshua and Elizabeth
The others born in Scarboro
Sarah - Benjamin - James - Mary
Libby record P. 32

Samuel Small
bap 9. Mar 1915
end 29 Mar 1918 S G
Sealed 18 July 1918 M J

Anna Hatch
bap 18 April 1916
end 19 Feb 1918
sealed 18 July 1918 M J

Ruth A Hatch

7121 Benj F Libby	22 Oct 1833	17 Feb 1934
		20 Dec 1934
Almira Weller	1840	14 Feb 1940
		10 Oct 1940 S 24 May 1941

DATE OF DEATH.	PLACE OF DEATH.	DATE OF MARRIAGE.

7020

Wm Langdon Libby b 29 July 1826 N H
bap 19 Sept 1927 end 5 Nov 1925

Julia Amanda Miller b abt 1830
bap 11 May 1927 end 8 Jan 1937
sealed 22 March 1946

6705 Ben Dam Libby b 14 Dec 1840 Standish Main
bap 2 Dec 1944
E 14 Feb 1946 Jan 194

Josephine E Clark abt 1818 or 1840
bap 2 Dec 1944
E 4 Jan 1946 S 10 Jan 1946

6705 Nelson B Libby b 24 Dec 1834 Limerick Maine
bap 19 Apr 1938
E 5 Jan 1938

Emma Ham B 1836
bap 2 Dec 1944
E 18 Dec 1946 S 10 Jan 1946
7 children

6833 Stephen M Libby b 12 Dec 1840 Limerick Maine
bap 21 Jan 1944
E 19 Jan 1944

Mary W Sidney abt 1844
bap 4 Sept 1945
E 18 Sept 1945 S 10 Jan 1946

6852 Joseph E Baker
b abt 1840 Portland Main
bap 2 Dec 1946
E 26 Jan 1943

Georgianna W Libby b 28 Sept 1846
bap 2 Dec 1946
E 17 Feb 1943 S 17 Dec 1940

7074 Cyrus Libby b 11 Nov 1825 Wellington Maine
bap 28 Jan 1926
E 12 Nov 1925

Eleanor Huff b 1829
bap 18 Apr 1945
E 18 Sept 1945 S 10 Jan 1946

F	NAME OF SPOUSE.	DATE OF BIRTH.	PLACE OF BIRTH.

P 400

Am 7215 Joseph Francis Libby
md 11 July 1860
Sabra Ann Dribble
bap 5 Dec 1936
end 31 Mar 1939
sealed 16 Jan 1943

7137 Royal Hammonds Libby P 398
md 17 Dec 1850
Lucinda S Richardson
bap 28 Nov 1936
end 7 Dec 1936
sealed 16 Jan 1941

James King b abt 1822 bap end
md 22 June 1843
Charlotte Myers Libby bap 20 Sept 1927 end 22 Dec 1929 sealed
ch Charles James
Joseph C
William J
Anna

7061 James Staples b 1806
Lydia Libby
bap 11 May 1845 end 18 Sep 1840 bap 20 May 1919 end 24 Jan 1924 sealed 24 May 1946

6107 Joseph Jordan b 1821
7121 Hannah Libby 1821
bap 16 May 1940 end 18 Sep 1940 bap 13 April 1925 end 24 Aug 1925 sealed 10 Jan 1945

6991 George W Dunn 1834
bap 11 May 1940 end 18 Sep 1940 sealed

Clara E Libby 15 Jan 1842
bap 19 July 1943 end 21 Dec 1943 sealed 24 May 1945

Date of Death.	Place of Death.	Remarks.
7040 James A Jones 1835		bap 11 May 1943
		end 18 Apr 1946
Mary E. Libby		end 20 May 1940
		end 30 Nov 1940
		sealed 10 Jan 1947
6902 John L Emery 1830		bap 20 May 1919
		end 24 Jan 1941
Sarah M Libby. 6 Apr 1834		bap 11 May 1945
		end 18 Apr 1946
		sealed 10 Jan 1947
6713 William P Walker 1832		bap 11 May 1845 - Daniels
		end 18 Apr 1941
Dorothy M Libby		
25 June 1856		bap 3 Feb 1937
		end 2 Apr 1937
		seal 18 Dec 1945 SLT
Solomon Larrabee 1836		B 11 May 1945
6715		E 18 Apr 1941
Mary B Libby 17 Dec 1839		B 20 May 1940
		E 30 Nov 1940
		S 18 Dec 1945
6717 Cephas P Thompson 1831		B
		E
Hannah L Libby 12 Feb 1833		B 15 June 1935
		E 7 Mar 1936
		S
7067 Daniel Davis 1810		B 11 May 1945
		E 18 Feb 1944
Judith Libby 1814		B 20 Mar 1919
		E 24 Jan 1924
		S 14 Jan 1947
7068 John Webb 1822		B
		E
Cynthia Libby 1824		B 1 March 1924
		E 6 Mar 1924
		S
6952 Lyman Turner 1821		B 11 May 1945
		E 18 Dec 1944
Elizabeth Libby 13 Nov 1825		B 13 Apr 1925
		E 4 Apr 1925
		S 4 Jan 1947
6956 James Wass 1831		B 11 May 1845
		E 18 Sep 1944
Lovina Libby 19 Aug 1830		B 13 Feb 1937
		E 2 Apr 1937
		S 18 Oct 1945 SLT

Full Name.	Date of Birth.	Place of Birth.
6959 William Lewis	1824	B E
Elizabeth Libby	1830	B 9 Sept 1930 E 6 Oct 1931 S
6963 Henry Sawyer	1833	B 11 May 1945 E 13 Sep 1946
Mary A Libby	10 April 1837	B 23 Dec 1937 E 2 Mar 1939 S 24 May 1946
6789 Robert B Norman	1825	B E
Anna Maria Libby		B 5 March 1929 E 27 March 1929 S
6988 Rev B. F. Billings	1824	B E
Catherine M Libby	16 March 1828	B 20 May 1919 E 24 Jan 1926 S
7022 Henry Green Taylor	1828	B E
Eliza G Lincoln Libby	16 Feb 1832	B 1 Sept 1934 E 15 Oct 1934 S 18 Sep 1935
6956 John Stevens	1829	B 11 May 1945 E 18 Sep 1945
Mary J Libby	6 March 1833	B 16 Sept 1933 E 23 Oct 1933 S 24 May 1945
Benjamin Hilton	1830	B E
Martha Libby	17 Feb 1834	B 22 Sept 1934 E 26 Sept 1934 S
7069 John Cornish	1822	B E
Eleanor Libby	1826	B 7 Oct 1931 E 9 Oct 1931
6960 Orin S Libby	1831	14 June 1932 28 Mar 1933
Amanda M Oakley	1830	2 Dec 1944 2 Jan 1948 9 Apr 1948

DATE OF DEATH.	PLACE OF DEATH.	DATE OF MARRIAGE.	S.
		19 Sept 1927	
Wm H Libby	1826	8 Nov 1926	
Julia A Miller		11 May 1937 8 June 1937 S	
7247 Geo H Libby	1830	B 9 Sept 1930 E 28 Apr 1932	
Nancy M Emery	1843	B 7 Aug 1939 E 1 Feb 1940 S	5 E D
Charles H Libby	1886	B 13 Feb 1937 E 12 May 1937 S	
James F Wasson	1882	15 May 1937 12 May 1938	
Jane H Wasson	1840	B 31 May 1940 E 11 July 1940 S	
6764 Calvin S Libby	1840	B 26 May 1940 E 28 June 1940	8 1
Lydia B Mitchell			
7118		B 10 June 1919 E 8 Oct 1926	
Jeremiah Libby	1832		
Mary J Libby	1836	20 Jan 1945	
		20 Apr 1945	
Joseph Libby			
Mary R Orne	1828	2 Dec 1944 27 Dec 1944	5 6 E D

6714 Ai Johnson Libby. Brunswick Maine
b 21 March 1837
E 23 Dec 1937
E 7 Jan 1938
Martha E. Brown
abt 1841
b 14 Feb 1846
E 11 July 1941
S 10 Jan 1946

6745 Benjamin R Libby b 2 March 1836
b 13 Feb 1937
E 7 Oct 1937
Lucy A Burnham b abt 1840
bap 14 Feb 1943

Fu	Name of Spouse.	Date of Birth.	Place of Birth.
6981 Eliza	4934 Reuben Libby	23 Mar 1824 b 16 Jun 1919 E 4 May 1926	
6965	Mary Ann Bence	ab 1828 c 2 Dec 1944 8 Dec 1944	Eng(?) 22 Jun 1945
Ma	7145 Oliver Libby	12 Sept 1836 23 Dec 1937 14 Sept 1939	Limerick(?)
6787 Robt	Malinda V Warren	ab 1840 2 Dec 1944 13 Dec 1944	Eng(?) 22 [illegible]
Anna	6936 Jonathan Libby	1 Mar 1840 16 Jun 1919 4 May 1926	Kennebec(?)
6988 R Catherine	Hanna Jenks	ab 1844 2 Dec 1944 12 Dec 1940	Eng(?) 22 Jun 1945
7022 Eliza	6701 Daniel Irish Libby	4 Dec 1831 14 Jun 1932 27 May 1933	Standish
6956 Mary	Priscilla A Hull	ab 1835 2 Dec 1944 13 Dec 1944	Buxton S 22 Jun 1945
6911 Mary	6744 Thomas Deering(?)	ab 1831 2 Dec 1944 13 Dec 1944	Freedom(?)
	Dorothy B Libby	27 Jan 1835 13 Jun 1933 9 Mar 1934	Wells(?) S 22 Jun 1945
7069 Q Eliza	7206 Charles Oliver Libby	4 May 1811 Gorham Mass b 16 Jun 1919 E 8 Oct 1926	
6960 Anna	Hannah McDougall	b ab 1816 E 18 Apr 1945 S 14 Aug 1945	S. 21 Nov 1945

Date of Death.	Place of Death.	Remarks.

6996

Walter O Alexander
b abt 1839. Washington D.C.
b 2 Dec 1842
E 23 Jan 1946

Mary Louise Libby
b 7 Dec 1843 Ewington, Or
b 2 Dec 1844
E 18 Jan 1946 Sealed 15 Oct 1943 SEO

7237

Alexander Libby Buckham, Mass
b 15 Dec 1822
bd 28 Aug 1923
E 12 Oct 1926

Angie Bent Paris Mass
b abt 1826
b 18 Apr 1945
E 18 Sep 1945 Sealed 15 Oct 1946 S.I.

6843 Ansel Joseph Libby Dexter. Mass
b 24 Aug 1880
b 12 June 1919
E 24 May 1926

Sarah Maria Cobb Sangerville, Mass
b abt 1838
b 18 Apr 1945
E 18 Sep 1945 Sealed Oct 15 1946 SEO

George Spenny Libby Limerick Mass
b 17 Oct 1826
b 25 Sept 1928
E 16 Nov 1928

Susan E Cole abt 1832 Naples, Mass
b 18 Apr 1945
E 18 Sep 1945 S 15 Oct 1945. SEO
2nd Wife - Melva A. S 15 Oct 1945

FULL NAME.	DATE OF BIRTH.	PLACE OF BIRTH.
12036 Simeon B Rice	ab 1839 bap 23 Jan 1945 E. 14 Aug 1945	Cape Elizabeth Main
Susan Maria Libby	b 1 April 1843 b 14 Sep 1946 E 18 Dec 1946	C. Elis S 18 Oct 1945
1891 Daniel Franklin Libby	b 15 Mar 1842 b 2 Dec 1944 E 8 Dec 1944	Portland. Main
Oclana Dam	ab 1848 b 2 Dec 1944 E 16 Mar 1945	S 8 Jan 1846
6850 Sumner Libby	b 1 July 1836 b 16 June 1919 E 4 May 1926	Scarboro Main
Eunice Colby Libby	b 4 Dec 1844 b 13 June 1935 E 9 Mar 1936	S 18 June 1937
Daniel D Ward	abt 1827 b 2 Dec 1944 E 12 Jan 1946	Campbell co Ky
6281 Smith Libby	abt 1826 b 10 Apr 1926 E 20 Aug 1921	S 17 Dec 1940
6708 Priscilla J Libby	13 March 1833 b 16 Sep 1933 E 23 Oct 1937	S 17 Dec 1940
6920 Woodbury P Libby	b 17 Oct 1840 b 21 June 1948 E 18 Jan 1944	Minot Main
Mary J Stuart	ab 1844 b 23 Jan 1945 4 June 1945	S 18 Dec 1945
6284 Wm T. Libby	9 Aug 1828 b 28 Sep 1928 [illegible] 1928	Danville Main
Elizabeth Harriman	b 1832 b 28 Jan 1946 E 25 May 1945	S 10 Dec 1946

Date of Death.	Place of Death.	Date of Marriage.
7757 Loring Small Libby b 4 Feb 1880	b 2 Dec 1944 E 7 Feb 1945	Limerick, Maine
Susan B Ferguson	ab 1837 b 2 Dec 1944 E 16 Jan 1945	S. 18 Dec 1945
7226 Charles Morris Libby	b 17 Feb 1844 b 1 July 1922 E 23 Nov 1923	Portland, Maine
Annie M Osborn	ab 1828 b 18 Sep 1945 E 18 Sep 1945	S 21 Nov 1945
7913 John Edward Libby b 22 Nov 1837	lap 23 Dec 1937 18 Sep 1939	Georgetown Do
Emily F Orme	ab 188 b 4 Sept 1945 18 Sept 1945	S 21 Nov 1945
7122 John Henry Libby	b 9 Jan 1886 lap 15 Feb 1937 E 7 Oct 1937	
Agnes Stubbs	ab 1850 lap 4 Sep 1945 18 Sep 1945	Sealed 21 Nov 1945
7092 John M Libby b 1 Sep 1881	lap 16 Feb 1937 E 7 Oct 1937	
Harriet Greeness	ab 1839 lap 14 Sept 1945 18 Sept 1941	S 21 Nov 1945 Limerick Maine
7150 Joseph Libby	b 26 May 1883 lap 30 Oct 1933 E 4 Jan 1934	
Nancy Miles	ab 1837 lap 2 Dec 1944	

	NAME OF SPOUSE.	DATE OF BIRTH.	PLACE OF BIRTH.
1203 Jinet			
Hure	6911 Capt. Jonah Libby	b 22 Aug 1839 Cap 16 June 1919 E 4 May 1926	Danville Main
	Carry Rue	ab 1884 Cap 4 Sept 1945 E 14 Sept 1945	S 21 Nov 1946
1891 Dan	6917. John W Libby	b 18 Aug 1839 Cap 16 June 1919 E 4 May 1926	Minot. Main
Oc	Adilia A Burgess	Cap 4 Sept 1943 E 18 Sept 1945	D 21 Nov 1943
6850	7289 Isaac L Libby	b 12 Sept 1827 Cap 19 Sept 1927 E 16 Nov 1928	Hartford Main
Emm	Hallie Nule	abt 1881 Cap 4 Sept 1945 E 18 Sept 1945	S 21 Nov 1945
Dar	6918 Isaac L Libby	b 29 June 1837 Cap 16 June 1919 E 4 May 1926	Minot. Main
6231	Nellie Faaid	b 1841 Cap 14 Sept 1945 E 18 Sept 1945	6 21 Nov 1943
6701	6906 Isaac Libby	b 1823 Cap 1 July 1925 E 13 Nov 1925	Danville. Main
6920	Susan Tailor	abt 1827 Cap 4 Sep 1945 E 18 Sept 1945	S 21 Nov 1940
Man	7060 Thomas Libby	b 8 Jan 1808 Cap 25 Aug 1923 E 12 Oct 1926	Newfield Main
6914	Christiana Bosla	b 1812 Cap 4 Sep 1945 E 18 Sep 1941	S 21 Nov 1940
Eli	7022. Harry J Jenkin	ab 1843 b 11 May 1945 E 18 Sep [illegible]	

DATE OF DEATH.	PLACE OF DEATH.	REMARKS.

6725 Sewall B Douglas b abt 1840 Gorham Maine
app 2 Dec 1944
E 30 Jan 1945

Lucinda E Libby 1 July 1842
app 2 Dec 1944
E 12 Jan 1945 S 18 Dec 1948

6464 Lemon S Libby b 22 June 1840 Danville Maine
app 27 May 1940
E 18 June 1940

Lydia S. Mitchell b 1844
app 14 Feb 1948
E 24 Sept 1948 S 18 Dec 1948

6863 Jordan W Johnson abt 1837 Scarboro. Maine
app 2 Dec 1944
E 18 Feb 1947

Sarah Jane Libby b 10 Jan 1843
app 18 July 1849
E 22 Dec 1947 S 18 Dec 1948

6881 James F Small b 1836 Scarboro Maine
app 2 Dec 1944
E 28 Jan 1948

Lucy Ellen Libby b 19 Jan 1848
app 20 May 1940
E 30 Nov 1940 S 17 Dec 1948

6721 Sargent B Gray Gorham Maine
b 1829
app 2 Dec 1944
E 1 Feb 1945

Julia Ann Libby b 25 Aug 1833
app 7 Feb 1934
E 14 Feb 1934 S 17 Dec 1948

6723 Hannon Fogg abt 1826 Gorham Maine
app 2 Dec 1944
E 31 Jan 1945

Frances H Libby b 29 Sept 1832
app 23 May 1931
E 27 June 1931 S 17 Dec 1948

7096 James May b 1839 Newfield Maine
app 2 Dec 1944
E 17 Jan 1945

Mary A Libby b 22 June 1842

FULL NAME.	DATE OF BIRTH.	PLACE OF BIRTH.
7124 Frank Man	abt 1833 cap 2 Dec 1844 E 27 Feb 1846	Plymouth Mass
Miriam G Libby	b 20 Feb 1842 cap 2 Dec 1844 E 15 Dec 1844	S 17 Dec 1846
6782 William Lewis	abt 1828 cap 2 Dec 1844 E 19 Jan 1846	Unity Maine
Mary Libby	b 3 March 1832 cap 10 Sept 1832 E 3 Nov 1832	S 18 Dec 1845
6882 Silas Hubbard	b 1837 cap 2 Dec 1844 E 9 Feb 1846	Remington Mass
Mary Susan Libby	b 24 Dec 1841 cap 2 Dec 1844 E 17 Jan 1846	S 18 Dec 1840
6934 Jesse Barker	abt 1831 cap 2 Dec 1844 E 19 Jan 1846	Campbell Co Ky
Hannah Libby	27 Aug 1836 cap 15 Feb 1837 E 2 Apr 1837	S 17 Dec 1840
6786 Joseph Libby	b 19 July 1824 cap 1 July 1921 E 13 Nov 1921	Georgetown DC
Mary H Orme	b 1828 cap 2 Dec 1844 E 13 Nov 1845	S 10 Jan 1845
7020 Isaac P Libby	b 14 June 1834 cap 1 Aug 1934 E 13 Oct 1934	Portsmouth NH
Sarah J Chapman	abt 1840 cap 4 Sept 1843 E 18 Sep 1845	S 7 Jan 1846
Sarah E Flint	abt 1832 cap 10 Oct 1831 E 16 Nov 1831	S 10 Jan 1846
6844 Edward F Libby	b 3 Apr 1832 cap 17 Dec 1833 E 27 Jan 1933	Webster Mass
Mary L Bagley	b 18 [illegible] 1845	

DATE OF DEATH.	PLACE OF DEATH.	DATE OF MARRIAGE.
6913 Hiram Staples Libby	b 13 Sep 1834	
	bap 19 Apr 1930	
	d 8 Jun 1935	
Jennie E. Moody	ab 1837	
	bap 4 Sep 1945	
	e 18 Jan 1945	s 10 Jan 1943
6736 Gilbert Libby	b 14 May 1889	
	bap 10 Aug 1939	
	e 19 June 1945	
Sarah Goodwin	ab 1843	
	bap 4 Sep 1945	
	e 18 Apr 1945	s 10 Jan 1943
7236 Frederick Libby	b 12 Oct 1825	Buxton, Maine
	bap 16 June 1919	
	e 7 Oct 1936	
Mary Burnb	ab 1829	
	bap 18 Apr 1943	
	e 12 Sep 1941	s 10 Jan 1943
6703 Edwin Libby	b 14 Nov 1887	
	bap 23 Dec 1937	
	e 28 Aug 1939	
Dianthe Marlin	b 1840	
	bap 18 April 1940	
	e 18 Sep 1945	s 10 Jan 1940
7059 Samuel Libby	b 30 July	Scarfield, Maine
	bap 25 Aug 1920	
	e 8 Dec 1921	
Rebecca Knowles	ab 1810	
	bap 4 Sep 1945	
	e 18 Sep 1941	s 21 Nov 1947
Ann Eliz Libby		
7235 William E Libby	b 15 Nov 1818	Buxton, Maine
	bap 16 June 1919	
	e 11 Dec 1925	
Martha K Adams	b ab 1822	
	b 23 Jan 1943	
	e 21 June 1943	s 21 Nov 1940
6991 Benjamin Mellen		
	d 1830	Winchester Va
	bap 11 May 1943	
	e 18 Sep 1945	
Martha Libby	bu 17 Feb 1834	

FUI	NAME OF SPOUSE.	DATE OF BIRTH.	PLACE OF BIRTH.
7124 F	7041 Henry J Bevans	apr 1837	Cornville, Mas
	" " "	bap 2 Dec 1944 E 26 Jan 1945	
M	Almira O Libby	b 12 Feb 1847 bap 21 June 1941 E 10 June 1942	E 17 Dec 1945
6782	6909. William Curtis	abt 1826	Cornville Maine
Mc		B 11 May 1943 E 18 Sep 1945	
	Elizabeth Libby	9 Sept 1920 b Oct 1931	E 21 Nov 1946
6880	7023 Israel P Libby	14 June 1830 b 1 Sep 1934 E 15 Oct 1934	Portsmouth NH
M	Sarah J Chapman	B 4 Sep 1946 E 18 Sep 1946	E 10 Jan 1946
	6538 Amos A Thurston	ab 1830 B 15 apr 1945 E 18 Sep 1945	
6934	Augusta E Libby	7 Dec 1884 13 June 1935 11 Mar 1939	S 21 Nov 1946
Ha			
	7069 John Connor	ab 1822 11 May 1943 18 Sep 1945	Newfield, Maine
6786	Eleanor Libby	ab 1826 7 Oct 1931 9 Oct 1931	S 21 Nov 1946
M			
	[illegible] F Libby 6891		
7020	Hannah F Davis	ab 1846 bap 12 Dec 1944 18 Mar 1946	Portland, Maine 16 Jan 1946
S	Ella Emily Libby	28 Nov 1867 a 4 Feb 1876	SLD 16 Jan 1946
	6982 Francis E Libby	b 28 May 1837 b 10 Aug 1939 E 12 June 1940	
	Julia A W Bryant	b 1843 b 18 apr 1940 E 19 apr 1940	
6844	Frances A Libby	12 Dec 1863	b 24 Jan 1946 SLP 16 Jan 1946
Ma		a	

DATE OF DEATH.	PLACE OF DEATH.	REMARKS.
7228 John K [illegible]	abt 1829	[illegible], Mass
	b 19 Feb 1946	
	[illegible] 14 Aug 1946	S 21 Oct 1947 68
Lucy Ellen [illegible]	2 May 1833	
	16 Sep 1933	
	23 Oct 1933	
5226 Thomas [illegible]	b 18 Jan 1830	[illegible] N.H.
	9 Sep 1930 - 24 Jun 1932	
Amy A [illegible]	1836	
	[illegible] Sep 45 - 18 Sep 45	S 16 Jan 1946
Frank H [illegible]	19 Mar 1858	
[illegible]	18 Dec 1858	
Annie E	30 Aug 57 - 17 Mar 62	S [illegible] 15 Jan 1945
6696 Peter M [illegible]	b 29 March 25	
	[illegible] 16 June 1919	
	[illegible] 11 Feb 1926	
Tabitha W Martin	abt 1829	
	[illegible] Dec 1944	
	[illegible] 2 Jan 1941	S 16 Jan 1946
[illegible]	[illegible] 1843	
	[illegible] Dec 1944	
	[illegible] 16 Jan 1941	S [illegible] 16 Jan 1946
7021 Henry [illegible]	b 17 Apr 1828	
	[illegible] 16 June 1919	
	[illegible] 2 Dec 1926	
Jane W [illegible]	1853	
	[illegible] 4 Sep 1945	
	[illegible] 18 Aug 1945	
Anna N [illegible]	[illegible] 1905	
	[illegible] 14 Sep 1945	
	[illegible] 18 Sep 1945	S 16 Jan 1946
[illegible] Edward H [illegible]	15 July 1855	
	[illegible] 1911	S [illegible] 16 Jan 1946
[illegible]		
7139 Harry [illegible]	9 July 1833	
	[illegible] 20 Aug 1933	
	[illegible] Jan 1934	
Mary [illegible]	[illegible] 1887	
	[illegible] 24 Aug 1945	S 16 Jan 1946
	[illegible] 18 Aug 1941	
Mary [illegible] Bickford	[illegible] 4 Sep 1945	S 16 Jan 1946
	[illegible]	

6

Gertrude E. Libby
now
Mrs Claus Anderson

Blackfoot, Idaho

R. F. D. 2

1929. Ebenezer B Libby - 22 Dec 1832 Gorham. Mass
30 Mar 1933
8 Jan 1934

Mary a Sanborn 1836
2 Dec 1944

4 ch. Emma D [illegible] 18 Dec 1944 B 16 Jan 1946
b 1866 d 22 Jun 1875 - B L P " "

7212 Mulbury Merrill ca 1816

Olive Gage Libby b 7 March 1820
[illegible] 1 March 1924
B 23 May 1924

Thomas Harlburt b 1816 [illegible] 2 Dec 1944
E 9 apr 1945

1930 Mary Libby 13 apr 1920
9 ap 1933 sealed 24 May 1945

Lucas Berry 1837 2 Dec 1944
18 Jan 1946

7291 Lucy a Libby 12 Oct 1841 19 July 1943 S 24 May 1946
2 Dec 1943

M. B Moorman 1826 1 May 1943
18 Aug 1943

6989 Anna M Libby 24 Oct 1829 [illegible] Mar 1929 S [illegible] May 1946
29 Mar 1929

7140 Leander B Staples
1836 [illegible] 22 Oct 1934
21 Feb 1935

Sarah H Libby 16 March 1840
[illegible] 2 Sept 1937
8 May 1938 S 9 Dec 1941

REMARKS.

Daniel Lee b ab 1837 ma 8 Sep 1859
B 14 Feb 1948 S 28 Oct 1949 to 6216
E 30 Mar 1949

Rev B F Billings ma [illegible] May 1850
Bd 17 May 1948
E 30 Mar 1948
S 31 Oct 1948 to 6948

[illegible] B F Phelps
ma 12 Nov 1873 Sarah [illegible] Cooper
B 14 Feb 1948
E 10 Jun 1948
S 28 Oct 1948 [illegible]

7066 [illegible] ma
John Wells
B 17 May 1948
E 30 May 1948 S 18 March 1950

THE
LIBBY FAMILY
IN
AMERICA
1602-1881

CPSIA information can be obtained
at www.ICGtesting.com
Printed in the USA
LVHW081312031122
732266LV00004B/194

9 781340 845513